HENRY JAMES

HENRY JAMES

LITERARY CRITICISM

French Writers
Other European Writers
The Prefaces to the New York Edition

THE LIBRARY OF AMERICA

Volume arrangement, notes, and chronology Copyright © 1984 by
Literary Classics of the United States, Inc., New York, N.Y.

Distributed to the trade in the United States
and Canada by the Viking Press.

Published outside North America by the Press Syndicate
of the University of Cambridge,
The Pitt Building, Trumpington Street, Cambridge CB2IRP, England
ISBN O 521 30099 I

Library of Congress Catalog Card Number: 84–11241
For Cataloging in Publication Data, see end of volume.
ISBN 0–940450–23–2

First Printing

Manufactured in the United States of America

LEON EDEL,
WITH THE ASSISTANCE OF MARK WILSON,
WROTE THE NOTES AND SELECTED
THE TEXTS FOR THIS VOLUME

Grateful acknowledgement is made to the National Endowment for the Humanities and the Ford Foundation for their generous financial support of this series.

Contents

Each section has its own table of contents.

FRENCH WRITERS

Contents

3

André-Marie and Jean-Jacques Ampère

THE TWO AMPÈRES

WE HAVE BEFORE US three volumes[1] which we have read with extraordinary pleasure. They are the records of the lives of a father and a son; they contain a complete family history. In 1831 Alexis de Tocqueville made in this country that tour which was to be the prelude to the publication of his "Democracy," the most serious book written on America up to that moment by a foreigner. De Tocqueville and Jean-Jacques Ampère were united by a passionate friendship (an *amitié-passion* Sainte-Beuve calls it), and the latter, twenty years afterward, in 1851, followed in the footsteps of the author of the "Democracy," and made a rapid journey from Canada to Mexico. He, too, of course wrote a book, and his "Promenade en Amérique" is a very genial and kindly composition. We bestow at present a very much less irritable attention upon the impressions of the foreign promenader than at the very distant date of M. Ampère's tour. We ourselves should say, indeed, that the European optimist on our shores would at present find it convenient, as a general thing, to keep watch upon his enthusiasm. But M. Ampère's amiable book was certainly disinterested; it was the expression of an eminently appreciative and sociable mind, and we make no exaggerated claim for it in saying that it introduces the author agreeably to American readers. They may be advised, after a glance at it, to pass on to the volumes whose titles are here transcribed and which embody a mass of literary matter now more entertaining to people in general than the author's formal compositions. Jean-Jacques Ampère was an accomplished scholar and a very clever man; but he seems to us a rather striking illustration of the common axiom that between two stools one falls to the ground. He was at once a man of books and a man of the world; an ardent savant and an indefatigable traveller. "He could read," says Sainte-Beuve, "a hieroglyphic phrase on the sarcophagus of a Pharaoh; it befell him one

---

[1] "Journal et Correspondance de André-Marie Ampère." Publiés par Mme. H. C. Paris, Hetzel, 1875. "André-Marie Ampère et Jean-Jacques Ampère. Souvenirs et Correspondance." Recueillis par Mme. H. C. Paris, Hetzel, 1875.

evening before going to sleep to read a Chinese book among
the ruins of Ephesus. We must agree that these are high dilet-
tantisms of the mind, such as are within the reach of a very
select few." He wrote so much, on questions of learning, that
you wonder he should ever have found a moment to leave his
study; and he travelled so much, moved so much in the
world, formed so many personal and social ties, had such a
genius for conversation, for society, and for friendship, that
you wonder he found time to open a book or mend his pen.
The verdict of competent criticism has been that Jean-Jacques
Ampère sacrificed erudition to observation and observation to
erudition; that he lacked exactness as a savant and that he
lacked vividness as a tourist. Scholars find his "Histoire Romaine à Rome" superficial, and, for what it attempts to be,
the profane find it dry. "In the middle of June," he writes in
1862, "I went with Hébert to Subiaco, a wild spot to which
the artist-poet loved to go in search of models. It was during
this little journey, on the road to Tivoli, while the horses were
resting, that I read to Hébert the first lines of 'L'Histoire Romaine à Rome,' and he then told me frankly that my picture
of the Roman Campagna left him cold." Ampère endeavoured to infuse a little more colour into his sketch; but the
opinion of the artist-poet Hébert has, we imagine, remained
that of the general reader, while it is probable, on the other
hand, that the author's lighter touches have done little to mitigate the severity of such an authority as Professor Mommsen
when, for instance, he finds his *confrère* exclaiming with emotion, "I believe in Romulus!" Sainte-Beuve applies to Ampère's style a judgment which he had heard passed upon
another writer whose literary manner was too undemonstra-
tive. "He is like a man who has made a drawing in black-lead.
When he has done he thinks it still too sharp, and he passes
his coat-cuff over it." But if Ampère as a historian falls short
of being a first-rate authority (as a philologist we believe he
is considered much sounder), and if, as a describer, he is less
brilliant and incisive than some men of greater genius and
(possibly) scantier conscience, he recovers his advantages in
his letters, in the things that reveal the man himself. Then we
see how intelligent, how accomplished, how sympathetic,
how indefatigable he was. His letters are always entertaining

and in the highest degree natural. But what completes their charm here is their graceful and harmonious setting—the fact that they are offered us in alternation with a hundred other memorials of a singularly pleasing and interesting circle. We gather from the whole collection the complete picture of a society—a society which by this time has pretty well passed away and can know no more changes. It is motionless in its place; it is sitting for its likeness. Best of all, the picture has one episode as charming as any that was ever imagined by an idyllic poet. André-Marie Ampère, the father of Jean-Jacques, was an eminent man of science; he was the first French mathematician of his time and the inventor of the electric telegraph in so far as the following statement, made in the presence of the French Academy of Sciences, entitled him to the name. "As many magnetized needles as letters of the alphabet, put into movement by conductors communicating with the electric battery by means of a key-board which might be lowered at will, would make possible a telegraphic correspondence that would traverse all distances and be more prompt to transmit thought than either writing or speech." Why this idea was merely enunciated, and never applied, we are unable to say; if it had been at that early day put into practice, André-Marie Ampère would now enjoy a renown that would render these few words of introduction quite superfluous. Invented in time to be used at the battle of Waterloo, the electric telegraph might have given a very different turn to the affairs of mankind. But this contingency having failed, we are reduced to considering the elder Ampère in the comparatively humble light of the extremely diffident lover of Mademoiselle Julie Carron. He was the most candid and artless of men, and the history of his courtship is one of the prettiest love-stories we know.

Jean-Jacques Ampère, as has been said, had a genius for friendship. He never married, but in the course of his life he had two extremely characteristic affections for women. The object of one was Madame Récamier, whose acquaintance he made in his twentieth year (in 1820) and to whom he remained devoted until her death, in 1849. The object of the second was a certain Madame L——, with whom he became intimate in 1853, in Rome. This lady was a young widow, in feeble health, obliged to spend her winters in the South, where she was accompanied by her parents and her little girl. Ampère had spent much of his life in Rome, and it was about this time that he entered upon that long sojourn of which the principal aim was the composition of a history of the Latin State in relation to the present local aspects, and which terminated only with his death. Madame L—— died in Rome in 1859, in a temper of mind which, as Ampère said, made him "touch with his finger the immortality of the soul." His friendship with her parents was intimate, and his affection for her little girl almost paternal. Ampère died at Pau, in March, 1864, leaving a will by which he bequeathed all his literary remains to M. and Madame Cheuvreux, and his private papers (those especially relating to his father) to their young granddaughter. It is in this way that the volumes before us have come to be put forth by Madame Cheuvreux, for the benefit at once of Mademoiselle L—— and of the public at large. We do not know what this young lady has thought of this mass of literature, but the public has given it a very cordial welcome. Madame Cheuvreux is a most graceful and intelligent commentator, and her publication has rapidly passed through several editions.

It is unjust to say that we have here simply the history of a father and a son. The Ampère stock was apparently an excellent one, and the reader is interested in taking it a degree farther back. The father of André-Marie Ampère was a retired merchant at Lyons when the French revolution broke out. Lyons in 1793 revolted from its Terrorist government and was besieged by the National Convention. The victory of the Convention was of course a harvest for the guillotine, and Jean-Jacques Ampère the elder was one of the most admirable of its victims. In prison, before his death, he wrote his wife a letter, which we regret not having space to quote; it gives one a better opinion of human nature. "Do not speak to Josephine," he says at the end, "of her father's misfortune; take good care that she does not know it; as for my son, there is nothing I do not expect from him. So long as you possess them and they possess you, embrace each other in memory of me. I leave my heart to all of you." For so pure an old stoic as this to say on the edge of the scaffold that there was noth-

ing he did not expect from his only son, left the sole support
of two desolate women—this was a great deal. André was at
first stupefied with sorrow, but in time he justified his father's
confidence. It seems most singular that in this blood-
drenched soil an episode so tender, so redolent of youthful
freshness, as the story embodied in the earliest of these letters
should so speedily have bloomed—that, with the hideous
shadow of the scaffold still upon him, André Ampère should
make so artless, so ingenuous, so innocently awkward a figure. His "adorable *bonhomie*"—that is the quality the editor
chiefly insists upon, and it certainly must have been of the
purest strain not to have been embittered by the contact of
wholesale massacre. It was indeed most genuine, and the
young man's notes and letters are full of it. The story is a very
simple one: he encountered Julie Carron, he fell in love with
her, he was put upon probation, he married her, she bore him
a child, she died. The charm is in the way the tale is told—
by himself, by the young girl, and by her sister (the latter an
admirably graphic letter-writer).

At twenty-three André Ampère, stuffed with algebra and
trigonometry, felt in his own small way the lassitude, the
nameless yearnings of Faust. He had given the measure of his
scientific genius and his universal curiosity. We have his own
word for it that by the time he was eighteen he knew as much
mathematics as he ever knew; he had also pushed far into
chemistry and he had cultivated the muse. He had begun various tragedies and he had placed upon the stocks an epic
poem with Columbus for hero and the "Americid" for title.
Many years afterwards his son found among his papers an
ancient yellow scrap, on which the following lines were written: "Having reached the age at which the laws rendered me
my own master, my heart sighed in secret at my still being
so. Free and insensible up to that time, it wearied of its idleness. Brought up in almost complete solitude, study and reading, which had long been my dearest delights, suffered me to
fall into an apathy that I had never felt, and the cry of nature
diffused through my soul a vague, insupportable unrest. One
day as I was walking after sunset beside a lonely brook
. . . . ." And here the fragment ends. What did he see beside the brook? Julie Carron, perhaps. If this is so, it was on

a Sunday in April, 1796, that he took that momentous stroll. He kept a record of his meetings with the young girl, and either then or later he superscribed it in large letters—AMO-RUM. It is filled with small entries like this, which mean little to us now, but which meant much to the poor trembling, hoping, fearing young mathematician:—"*26th September*. I found *her* in the garden, without daring to speak to her.—*3d October*. I went there. I slipped in a few words more to the mother.—*6th October*. I found myself alone with her, without daring to speak to her; they gave me the first *bouts-rimés*.—*10th October*. I filled them out, and slipped them adroitly into her hand.—*13th October*. I had carried back the seventh volume of Sévigné; I forgot the eighth and my umbrella.—*2d November*. I went to get my umbrella.—*7th November*. I didn't speak that day, on account of the death of M. Montpetit.—*9th November*. I spoke again; Julie told me not to come so often.—*12th November*. Mme. Carron was out; I said a few words to Julie, who regularly blew me up and went off. Elise told me to spend the winter without speaking again.—*16th November*. . . . Julie brought me with grace the 'Lettres Provinciales.'—*9th December*. She opened the door for me in her night-cap and spoke to me a moment, *tête-à-tête*, in the kitchen." He stands there before us like an effigy of bashfulness, tongue-tied, with his heart in his throat, a book under his arm and the simple good faith of unspotted youth upon his brow. Mademoiselle Julie was a trifle difficult, as the phrase is; she had already had an excellent offer of marriage, but she had declined it because she thought nothing could make up to her for leaving her parents and her sister. These were plain people, with little money, but what one may call an excellent family tone. They lived in the country, close to Lyons. They thought well of André, but they thought also that there was no hurry, especially as he had as yet no avocation, and it was their idea to keep him at arm's length, though certainly not to let him go. Elise Carron was Julie's elder, and a girl who seems to have combined an excellent heart with the keenest, frankest wit, and with a singular homely felicity of style. She is shrewd, impulsive, positive, humorous, and we should like to quote all her letters. During a part of the winter which followed the entries we have just transcribed Julie Carron was absent from home, and Elise makes it her duty to entertain poor Ampère and to report his condition to his mistress. She has a great kindness for him and, though she wishes to amuse her sister, she stops short of tempting her to laugh cruelly. "Poor A—— is certainly frozen in some corner, or else he is thawing near you, for I have seen him neither through hole nor through window. . . . Will he come to-morrow? I look always from my place and I see nothing. If he comes and mamma goes out, he will call me to an account; I have prepared a thousand little answers— always the same; I wish I knew some that would content him without bringing things on too fast, for he interests me by his frankness and his softness, and especially by his tears, which come out without his meaning it. Not the slightest affectation, none of those high-strung phrases which are the language of so many others. Arrange it as you will, but let *me* love him a little before you love him; he is so good! . . . Mamma insists that Providence will arrange everything; but I say that we must help Providence." Elise's next letter is in its natural vividness almost a little genre picture. "At last he came yesterday, trembling with cold, and still more with the fear that mamma would be displeased at his having been to see you, or rather to get letters for us. But this is how the thing happened: I see that you want details. You must know that mamma now sits in your place, because she has closed up the door, which used to freeze the room, and in consequence we don't see a bit too well, especially when the snow has been piled up. In short, he comes in and doesn't see the little Pelagot who was behind the nose of the stove. As soon as Claudine went out he said: 'Madame, I saw mademoiselle your daughter.' I stopped him short off, making more and more signs; and he, thinking to plaster it up, replied, 'Claudine is gone out; no one can hear us, I will speak lower.' The child opened her eyes as wide as she was able; when I saw that signs didn't help me I spoke to the wench about her work, about her stocking that was not coming on. He was petrified and wanted to patch it up again, but the piece wouldn't fit the hole." At last the little Pelagot goes out with her dilatory stocking, and Elise has a long talk with Ampère, which she relates, *verbatim*, to her sister:—"He perceived the first that

it was beginning to be late—which he forgets so easily when
you are here. He went off and left me quite amazed at his hat
in lacquered cloth, at his fashionable breeches and his little
air, which, I assure you, will change again." "Guess, dear
Julie," she writes later, "at what we pass our time. We make
verses, we scratch them out, and then begin again." And she
goes on to narrate that M. Ampère has been with them and
has filled them with the sacred fire. She must close, for she
has to help her mamma to begin a play, a drama, perhaps a
tragedy! It sounds very odd, hearing of those two little rustic
bourgeoises sitting down among their pots and pans, at their
snow-darkened windows, to literary compositions of this heroic magnitude, and there certainly can be no better illustration of the literary passion of the last century, or of the
universal culture of what was called sensibility.

  But the spring came, Julie was at home again, and in
André's diary the idyllic strain is more emphasized:—"*24th
March*. Mlle. Bœuf came while I was reading the tragedy of
Louis XVI.; we went into the orchard. Elise sat upon the
bench; Julie upon a chair which I brought to her, and I at her
feet; *she* chose my purse to her own taste.—*26th April*. I
went to carry back La Rochefoucauld; I found no one but
Mme. Carron, and asked her leave to bring mamma. I received only a vague answer, but it was satisfactory enough.
Julie, Elise, my aunt, and my cousin came to lunch; I served
the white wine and drank in a glass which *she* had rinsed." A
couple of months later he prefixes to an entry a date in large
capitals. The record deserved the honour, for it has a charming quaintness.—"MONDAY, 3D JULY. They came at last to
see us, at three-quarters past three. [His poor mother had
called, and the Carron ladies were returning her visit.] We
went into the alley, where I climbed into the great cherry-
trees and threw cherries to Julie. Elise, my sister, all of them,
came afterward. I gave up my place to François, who lowered
branches to us, from which we picked ourselves, to Julie's
great entertainment. She sat on a plank on the ground with
my sister and Elise, and I sat on the grass beside her. I ate
some cherries which had been on her knees. We all four went
into the great garden, where she accepted a lily from my
hand, and then we went to see the brook. I gave her my hand

to climb the little wall, and both hands to get over it again; I remained by her side on the edge of the brook, far from Elise and my sister. We went with them in the evening as far as the windmill, where I sat down near her again, while we all four observed the sunset, which gilded her clothes with a charming light. She carried away a second lily which I gave her in passing." André Ampère was a man of genius and destined to be recognised as one; but he was a profoundly simple soul, and his *naïveté* seems to have been unfathomable. It would be impossible to enumerate with a homelier verity the enormous trifles on which young love feeds. André wrote verses; we know not what they were; certainly there is as little attempt here as possible at elegance of form; the poetry is all in the spirit. There, however, it is deep. The little narrative we have just quoted might have been scratched with a clasp-knife on the windmill tower; but the passion it commemorates is of classic purity. Extremes meet; the whole man is in it; it is the passion of Petrarch for Laura, of Dante for Beatrice, of Romeo for Juliet. Extremes meet, we say; and so it seems to us that this artless fragment is, by a happy chance, as graphic, as pictorial, as if a consummate artist had retouched it.

By the time the autumn had come round again Julie knew her mind. When a certain M. Vial comes in and urges André, if his family does nothing for him, to go and seek his fortune in Paris, she pushes him out by the shoulders, and tells him they have no need of his advice. The day apparently has come for Julie to feel the flutters of the heart; we have had no intimation until now that her pretty person (the editor is happily able to establish that it was pretty) was not even a trifle impertinently self-possessed.—"*26th October*. I carried there a little basket of chestnuts. . . . Mme. Carron told me to go into the orchard where *they* were. I found only Julie, who seemed as much embarrassed as I; she called Périsse, but I slipped in some words which had relation to my sentiments. . . . I wanted to go back a moment to the orchard, where she had gone to dry some linen, but she avoided me with even more earnestness than the first time. In the evening she told me to read 'Adèle,' and this led to our talking again upon the passions." He adds a few days later: "We went into the orchard, where I helped to take up the washing; in sport,

after some jest of Elise, Julie gave me a charming blow, with
her fist, on the arm. We supped on chestnuts and we came
home very late." Upon this the editor comments very happily:
"The orchard, the linen-drying, the reading of 'Adèle,' which
provokes a conversation on the passions, André's basket of
chestnuts, the charming blow with the fist that he gets in
play, the frugal supper—is not the picture quite of another
age? Only sixty-and-something years separate us from the moment when André wrote his journal, and yet we are far from
that innocent idyll. Ah, messieurs the realists, you have made
us grow old fast!"

At last, in the spring of 1799, poor André's probation terminates and Julie bestows her hand upon him. We have some
of his letters after the betrothal, in which he addresses his
affianced ceremoniously as "Mademoiselle." There is something very agreeable in this observance of high courtesy in
circumstances amid which it might have been expected to be
a trifle relaxed. Mademoiselle Carron was a poor girl; she
helped in the family washing. But she conversed upon the
passions and she was familiar with a superior standard of
manners. The young couple were married in the month of
August of the same year, and André's friend M. Ballanche
read a long prose rhapsody, by way of an epithalamium, at
the simple wedding-feast. André Ampère obtained some pupils in mathematics at Lyons, and his wife spent much of the
first year of her marriage with her mother in the country. She
was at times, however, with her mother-in-law Madame Ampère, at the latter's modest dwelling at Polémieux, near
Lyons. While she is away her sister Elise writes to her with
inimitable vigour. Elise really makes the dead things of the
past live again. The Carron ladies were hesitating as to where
they should spend the winter. In their actual quarters, the
elder daughter writes, "Mamma finds a great many diversions,
and her health is better. Our good neighbours tell us that if
we were to remain they wouldn't think of carting themselves
over to Charelet, where nevertheless they have already hired
lodgings and laid in a stock of wood, which they would
quickly sell again. In short, they press us, offer us so heartily
all the little distractions that they might share with us. Mme.
Darsay makes much of her books and newspapers; her daugh-

ter puts forward all the people whom she would catch up in one way or another. She says to me: 'We will amuse our mothers, we will both make little caps for the poor, and fritters and tarts; we will pray God, we will write, and then time passes so fast, so fast.' She makes a hotch-potch of all this, and then kisses me with such friendliness, and shows as much enthusiasm as if I were a being capable of inspiring it. Formerly I shouldn't have been surprised at such greetings; I used with these ladies to put in my little word in the talk; I was gay; we were something for them, because they didn't see many people. But at present it is the reverse." I continue to quote Élise Carron for her extreme reality: "There are moments when we must not think of calculating—very true. But there is a time for everything. *A propos* of calculations, I have reason to thank myself for the one which made me decide not to buy a grey dress. What should I have done with it? I should have spoiled it nicely if I had wished to put it on on Sundays on our pretty roads and among the peasant-women at mass, who mount atop of you and surround you with goloshes and muddy sabots. Mme. Mayeuvre herself wouldn't have been so fine as I, and yet she always comes to church in a carriage, but in such simple gowns that I shouldn't have dared to wear mine. I never saw her so much dressed as last evening at the Darsay ladies'. She had been making visits in the afternoon, and had exchanged her little dyed morning dress for a very pretty blue calico, with white sleeves and a hood like ours. Mme. Courageau is also very simple, and if on Sundays I only put on a muslin apron over my old petticoat in green cloth (I wear it with my black spencer) they already cry out that I am dressed up. Yet, since the cold weather, it is only what I wear every day. All this, my sister, may very well not interest you. So much the worse! I *must* write to you and talk to you as if you were here. Haven't I told you that my scribblings don't oblige you to write a line? I send them to you for nothing, and out of it all you can take your choice; you can fish out some things you may be glad to know, as, for example, about our health." In December, 1801, André Ampère obtained the post of Professor of Mathematics at the central school of the department of the Ain, the seat of which was at Bourg. Julie, who had a baby several months old and whose health had begun visibly to decline, remained, for economy and comfort, with her mother. The most charming part of this volume is perhaps the series of letters that passed, during this separation, between the ailing, caressing, chiding, solicitous, practical young wife, and the tender, adoring young husband, whose inadvertences and small extravagances and want of worldly wisdom are the themes of many a conjugal admonition. Poor Ampère was for ever staining his clothes with chemicals; he had his coats and breeches doled out to him like a boy at school. He begins his career at Bourg by deciding not to lodge at the inn, on account of the bad company that frequents it, and then makes himself the joke of the town by going to live with a certain M. Beauregard, whose wife was notoriously disreputable. "I think you very pastoral," Julie writes, "to go reading my letters in the fields; I'm afraid that you scatter them along the road, and that the first people who pass pick them up. If I knew you were more careful, how many pretty things I would confide to you! You would know that I love you, that I have a great desire to see you again, that every evening I have a thousand things to say to you that don't come out, save in sighs; you would know, in short, that when one has gone so far as to take a husband one loves him too much to be separated from him, and that your absence vexes me." Her injunctions about his taking care of her letters seem to have little effect; for shortly after this André writes to her gleefully of another "pastoral" day: "How sweet your letters are to read! One must have your soul to write things which go so straight to the heart—without trying to, it would seem. I remained till two o'clock sitting under a tree, a pretty meadow on the right, the river, with some amiable ducks floating on it, on the left and in front of me; behind was the hospital building. You will understand that I had taken the precaution of saying to Mme. Beauregard, when I left my letter to go on this tramp, that I shouldn't dine at home. She thinks I am dining in town; but as I had made a good breakfast, I only feel the better for dining upon love. At two o'clock I felt so calm, and my mind so at ease, in place of the weariness that oppressed me this morning, that I wanted to walk about and botanize. I went up along the river in the meadows, and arrived within twenty steps of a charming wood that I had seen in the distance at a half hour from the town, and had desired to go through. When I reached it the river, by suddenly coming between us, destroyed every hope of going further, so I had to give it up, and I came home by the road from Bourg to Cezeyriat—a superb avenue of Lombardy poplars."

This gentle strain is intermingled with sadder notes—allusions to the extreme scarcity of money with the young couple and to Julie's constantly failing health. She had an incurable malady and her days were numbered. But in the midst of her troubles she is tenderly vigilant and practical. "Be careful to close your bureau, your room, and my letters, or I shall not dare to write to you. I know nothing of M. Roux. Don't you open yourself too much to M. Clerc? He's a very new acquaintance; suppose he were to take your ideas for himself. Send me your cloth trousers, so that the rats don't eat them." "I don't burn my things," he answers, "and do my chemistry only in my breeches, my grey coat, and my green velvet waistcoat. . . . I beg you to send my new trousers, so that I may appear before MM. Delambre and Villars. I don't know what I shall do; my nice breeches smell still of turpentine. . . . You'll be afraid of my spoiling my nice trousers, but I promise you to return them as clean as I get them." Julie too visibly declines, and the downright Elise, writing to André, breaks out into an almost passionate appeal. "What a happiness if among all the plants whose properties you know there were one that could put all in order again in her nature! What is the use of science if there is none that can restore health to Julie? Make inquiries, talk to the learned, to the ignorant! Simple people often have remedies as simple as themselves—light which God gives them for their preservation. . . . . Ah, why, why did I push self-sacrifice so far as to advise Julie to marry? I admired myself then as I shed my tears; they were for me the triumph of reason; whereas it was to feeling alone that I ought to have listened!" Julie sank rapidly, and died in the summer of 1803.

We have many of André Ampère's letters after the death of his wife, but as he grows older, they naturally lose much of their quaintness and freshness. He becomes absorbed in scientific research and embarks upon metaphysics, and it is with

a certain sadness we learn that the image of Julie Carron fades
from his mind sufficiently to enable him, in 1807, to marry a
second time. There is a note from his sister-in-law Elise upon
this occasion, in which, beneath the expression of an affectionate sympathy with his desire to make himself happy again,
we detect a certain proud disappointment in his not finding
the memory of her sister a sufficient source of happiness.
There is some poetic justice in his second marriage proving a
miserable delusion; he was obliged to separate from his wife
after a few months. He had gone up to Paris after Julie's death
and become instructor in the Polytechnic School, and from
this time opportunity, prosperity, and fame began to wait
upon him. He was a signal example of the almost infantile
simplicity, the incorruptible moral purity, that so often are
associated with great attainments in science, and the history
of his courtship was worth sketching because it shows this
temperament in its flower.

After the death of Jean-Jacques Ampère's young mother,
the interest of these volumes is transferred to her son. The
boy grew up among all-favouring influences, surrounded by
doting grandmothers and aunts, in an atmosphere of learning
and morality. As he is revealed in his own early letters and
those of his friends (there are many of these) he is quite the
type of the ingenuous and intelligent youth who feels, in an
easy, general way, that he is heir of all the ages. More than
anything else Jean-Jacques Ampère is sympathetic; he is ver-
satile, spontaneous, emotional; in 1820 the days of "sensibility" were hardly yet over and the accomplished young man
possessed this treasure. The world was all before him where
to choose. His father, when he had resigned himself to his
not being a mathematician, wished him of all things to write
a tragedy; for, next after algebra and chemistry, verses were
what the elder Ampère most prized. Jean-Jacques, nothing
loth, looked about for a subject, and meanwhile he fell in love
with Madame Récamier. His devotion to this illustrious lady
was the great fact of thirty years of his life, and it is possible,
in the letters before us and in those of the lady herself, published with a commentary by her niece, who was so many
years at her side, to trace even in detail the history of the
affair. It is difficult at this time of day to know just how to

speak of Madame Récamier, and it is a tolerably plausible view of the case to say that there is no need of speaking at all. History has rendered her enthusiastic justice, and in her present reputation there is perhaps something a trifle forced and factitious. She was very beautiful, very charming, and very much at the service of her friends—these are her claims to renown. To people of taste and fancy at the present day, however much they may regret not having known her, she can be little more than a rose-coloured shadow. To hear her surviving friends say to each other with a glance of intelligence, "Ah, *there* was a woman!" simply makes us uncomfortably jealous; we feel like exclaiming, with a certain asperity, that there are as good fish in the sea as ever were caught. To know her by literature is, moreover, not really to know her. We cannot see her beauty, we cannot hear the gracious inflections of her voice, we cannot appeal to her for sympathy; we can only read her letters, and her letters are not remarkable. They have no especial wit or grace; they have only great good sense and, in certain express directions, an immense friendliness. Her history certainly is a remarkable one. Born in the middle class, she married into the middle class and lost early in life the wealth that her marriage conferred upon her. She was never perceived to push or strive; no effort, no eagerness, were ever observable in her career, and yet for fifty years she was literally a social sovereign. She distributed bliss and bale; she made and unmade felicity. She might have unmade it, that is, but fortunately she was incorruptibly kind; her instincts were constructive, not destructive. In 1829, for instance, Prosper Mérimée, then a young man upon the threshold of life, had a fancy to adopt a diplomatic career, and, as a first step, to be appointed secretary of legation in London. The simplest way to compass his desire seems to him to be to apply through a friend to Madame Récamier. Madame Récamier can apply to the ambassador with the certainty of not meeting a refusal. The striking thing is that it is a question not at all of her doing what she can and taking what comes, but of her simply uttering her gentle fiat. Of course her remarkable influence was not simply an accident; she had exquisite gifts, and circumstances favoured her; but it seems rather a mistake to attempt to make a

woman whose action in the world was altogether personal
and destined to expire with her person an object of lasting
interest. None of the various ministers of her renown—not
even the possessor of the infallible memory of Sainte-Beuve—
has to our knowledge repeated any definite utterance of the
"incomparable Juliette" which seems at all noticeable. To
write about her is like attempting to describe a perfume, and
her clever niece, Madame Lenormant, in the volumes she has
devoted to her memory, has perhaps run the risk of making
her the least bit of a bore.

But of course she appeals to our imagination, and if we are
well-disposed that way she may live yet a while by her picturesqueness. Seated every evening in her little economical secular cell at the convent of the Abbaye-au-Bois, or, of a summer
morning, under the trees at the Vallée-aux-Loups, the natural
accessories in her portrait are the figures of the people who
formed the best society in Continental Europe. In her relations with Jean-Jacques Ampère she is perhaps especially picturesque, for they contain just that element of potential
oddity which is considered essential to picturesqueness. Madame Récamier was forty-three years of age when young Ampère was presented to her, he himself being just twenty; she
was exactly of the age which, had she lived, his mother would
have reached. Jean-Jacques then and there fell in love with
her. It was one evening in her little drawing-room, which was
full of great people. She was, as Madame Cheuvreux says
(seeming in feminine fashion to have exactly divined it) "sitting, almost reclining, half hidden in a cloud of muslin, on a
sofa of sky-blue damask of the old 'Empire' form, with the
neck of a gilt swan for its arm." It is not necessary to accuse
Madame Récamier of inordinate coquetry—a charge which,
although we are bound to believe that she enjoyed her sway,
there is no other evidence to support—to explain the fact that
two years later, when she was forty-five, his passion was still
burning. Might she have quenched it? These are of course
mysteries; but it is our duty to suppose that what she did was
wisely done. The event, in fact, proved it. She was an expert
in these matters and she had learned the prudence of sacrificing a part to save the whole. Ampère's flame flickered down
in time to the steady glow of friendship; and if Madame Ré-

camier knew when the golden age ended and the silver began
it is very likely that, under her exquisite direction, the young
man himself never did. But there was certainly a prepossessing boldness in a young fellow of two-and-twenty writing in
this fashion to an extremely distinguished woman of middle
age: "Oh, tell me with truth that there *are* moments in which
it seems that your soul is touched by my fate and takes an
interest in my future; sometimes I have even thought that the
sentiment so pure and tender with which you inspire me was
not without a certain charm for yourself. But I am so afraid
of being in error! Day by day my life centres itself in this
affection. How cruel would it be to take the expression of
your compassion for that of your interest! It is now especially,
while I am away from you, that I am agitated by these fears.
A few words, I entreat you, by way of consolation; but in
heaven's name take care that in order to calm me you don't
let yourself go beyond that which you really feel. What have
I done, indeed, that you should love me? Ah, I have loved
you with all my soul, without deceiving myself about our situation, without entertaining for an instant the thought of disturbing the tranquillity of your existence. I have given myself
up to a hopeless sentiment, which has filled all my heart. I
cannot live either without you or for you; I see all that is
impossible in my fate, and yet how can I renounce that which
is my only joy?" Madame Récamier quietly devised a *modus
vivendi* for her ardent young friend, and he adopted it so successfully that three years later, she being at Rome and in the
first glow of a friendship with Madame Swetchine, the famous ultramontane pietist, he found it natural to write to her,
in allusion to this lady: "In good faith, madame, is it not true
that my place is taken in your heart? I have no right to complain of it; it is not your fault if I have not that sort of religious and romantic imagination which it would be so natural
to have. But I have it less than ever; the desire to please you
made me force my nature; solitude and the law that punishes
sacrilege have sent me back to it. . . . Madame Swetchine is
worth much more to your imagination than I. Bring me back
some friendship; it is all that I deserve and all that I exact of
you." It seems an anomaly that five months after this Ampère,
taking fire at a few words uttered on a certain evening by

Madame Récamier, should be writing to her to ask almost passionately whether their union is after all impossible. M. Récamier is still living, but there had apparently been some allusion to a divorce. Ampère demands an assurance that if, on being at liberty, she should decide to marry, she will bear him in mind. He wishes to feel that there is no one else between them. The thing seems to be less a serious proposal than a sudden, rather fantastic desire on his part to fill out a certain intellectual ideal of the situation. In the way of ideals that of the reader, at this point, is that there should be a record that Madame Récamier, forty-eight years old, and with a husband in excellent health, was annoyed at having this marrying mood attributed to her.

In the autumn of 1823 she had gone to Italy with a little retinue of friends, of whom Ampère was not the least assiduous. She passed the winter in Rome, and the young man, remaining near her, formed, with the stimulus of her sympathy, that attachment for the Eternal City which was to increase from year to year and be the motive of his principal literary work. To be with Madame Récamier was to be socially on a very agreeable footing, for wherever she established herself she was speedily surrounded by brilliant people. This winter and the following summer, which the party spent at Naples, must have been for young Ampère a supremely happy season. To enjoy in Rome the society of the woman whom one considers the embodiment of everything admirable, to have that delightful city offer at every turn its happy opportunities and suggestions—this is to an appreciative spirit a particular refinement of bliss. Madame Récamier remained a second winter in Italy, and Ampère came home at the summons of his father, who appears at this time to have "worried" greatly, in vulgar phrase, about the young man's future, and who was especially impatient to see his tragedies coming forward at the Théâtre Français. During his son's absence in Rome the elder Ampère constantly writes to him on this question, and reports upon the MS. readings that have been given in his own circle—one, for instance, of all places in the world, at the Veterinary School—and upon the corrections and alterations that have been proposed. André Ampère, as he grew older, developed some rather uncomfortable eccentricities; he was in his private life and conversation the most unpractical and ill-regulated of men; and this persistent desire to make a third-rate playwright of a young man really gifted in other directions seems to indicate no little inconsequence of mind. Jean-Jacques's pieces were accepted, or half accepted, at the great theatre, but they were never played, and they are sleeping at this day in its dustiest pigeon-holes. He had indeed a passion for writing verses, and produced, first and last, a prodigious quantity of indifferent rhyme. Often, after having hammered all day at recondite philology, he would sit up half the night scribbling at the dictation of a rather drowsy muse. He wrote in general, thanks to his roving habits, which made odd scraps and snatches of time of value, at all sorts of hours and in all sorts of places. He would begin a chapter of his "Histoire Romaine" on the edge of a table at a café in the Corso; in one of his later letters he speaks of having written a comedy in a railway carriage.

The editor of these volumes gives a great number of his letters to Mme. Récamier, both during the year that followed his separation from her at Naples and at later periods. "It rains," he writes to her from Rome on his way northward; "I am writing this in a dark room, looking out on a dismal little street. At Naples, at least, when it rains, you have before your eyes a great expanse. Instead of the sea and the island of Capri I see an ugly white wall, four feet off. I should have found a certain consolation in going to sit in the Villa Pamfili, on that rock on the edge of the lake where we read about the gardens of Armida and found them again, or on the grass, near Santa Croce in Gerusalemme, where we went on Easter day, or in wandering in Saint Peter's, in the Coliseum, or on the edge of the Tiber." There is little we could quote from these letters, however, even if we had space; they are charming, they speak equally well for the writer and for the sweet sagacity of the woman who inspired them, they denote a delightful relation, but they lack salient points, and in their quality of love-letters they are liable sometimes to weary the cold-hearted third person. Here, nevertheless, is a noteworthy paragraph: "You like me to tell you of my work—to describe my studies as a school-boy does to his mamma. Well, then, this is what seems to me at this moment the most delightful thing in the world, and an infallible means of arriving at almost universal knowledge. It's very simple. It is to note in every book I read the very important points, to concentrate all my attention upon these and to try to completely forget all the rest—and to join to this another observance, namely, that of reading on every subject and in every language only the best that there is. In this way, it seems to me, without uselessly overloading one's mind, one can acquire a deal of very positive and very various knowledge." This was written in 1825, and it may at that moment have been true; it doubtless, indeed, will always have a certain measure of truth. But the march of mind has been so rapid these last fifty years that it is to be feared that no particular method of study, however ingenious, will carry one very far on the way to "universal knowledge." To read even the best only, nowadays, is a task beyond the compass of individuals. But in one way or another Ampère was bent upon superior science, and in pursuit of it he went in the autumn of 1826 to Germany, and spent the winter at Bonn, under the inspiration of Niebuhr and Wilhelm von Schlegel. Madame de Staël had discovered Germany, earlier in the century, for the French at large—Ampère discovered it afresh for the younger generation. Schlegel was an old adorer of Madame Récamier, and a word from her ensured her young friend a prompt and impressive greeting. "At our first interview," Ampère writes, "I admit I was rather disconcerted by his affectation of fine manners and of the French tone; he seemed to avoid speaking of literature, as if it were pedantry. This was not in my account, but I was not discouraged; I let him play the fine gentleman, and now that he has fairly set himself up before me as a man of the world, that I have seen his yellow livery and his order of Sweden, he begins to talk of Sanscrit and the Middle Ages. By a happy chance he is going to begin a course on the German language and literature. What a master of German! This attraction, and that of a magnificent country, will keep me here some time. The mountains which edge the Rhine before reaching this place," he adds—and the writer of these lines has made the same observation—"recall in a striking manner the horizon of Rome." From Niebuhr he got what he could. "I have done very well," he says, "to take no great trouble to learn the old history of Rome; I should have to begin it afresh." For the rest of Ampère's life, it was always a feather in his cap that on leaving Bonn he paid a visit to Weimar and spent three weeks with Goethe. He must himself have recalled this episode complacently, for the great man had made much of him and of the intelligent articles which Ampère had written about his works in the "Globe" newspaper, the organ of serious young France at that time. Wherever he went Madame Récamier's recommendation was of service to him; she had *ci-devant* admirers stationed here and there on purpose, as it were. In Berlin it was the Prince Augustus of Prussia—he who in 1811 had very seriously wished to marry her. Here, in conclusion, are Ampère's impressions of the German mind: "Up to this time Germany inspires me with the greatest respect for its superior men, but with little interest in the common life. Their true superiority resides in imagination and learning; the men who are without these two gifts, who make neither systems nor poems, appear to me plain good people, with little cleverness or sensibility; you need to make an effort of will to talk with them. But a German in whom learning has not extinguished imagination, in whom imagination does not lead learning astray, if good luck wills it that he have lived in Italy to thaw out his senses, and that he have gained experience of practical life by affairs—that man is a man such as one can find only in Germany. There is such a one here—Niebuhr, of whom you must not speak in your letter to Schlegel."

On leaving Germany Ampère went to Sweden and Norway, and for the rest of his life he usually spent half the year in foreign lands. To travel was a passion with him, and though he had little money and was famous for his awkward management of his personal affairs, he appears to have been able to satisfy every impulse of his restlessness. His father's house was not a comfortable home, not because André Ampère was not an extremely affectionate parent, but because extreme naïveté, when the character has taken a melancholy turn, is not always identical with geniality. Jean-Jacques once posted back to Paris from a distance in response to an urgent summons from his sire. The two sat down to dinner, and in a moment—"It's very odd," cried the elder, "but I should have thought that it would give me more pleasure to see you!" This was the lover of Julie Carron at fifty. From the third of these volumes we have left ourselves space to quote nothing. We can only recommend the whole work to curious readers. The letters contained in the third volume are more and more the record of a busy life. Ampère was professor at the Collège de France, member of the Academy of Inscriptions and the Académie Française, and a frequent contributor to the "Revue des Deux Mondes." He was no politician, but he was a consistent anti-imperialist. The letters which Madame Cheuvreux has gathered together throw light here and there on many agreeable and interesting figures—the most pleasing, perhaps, being that very superior man and, in temperament and turn of mind, half Anglican Frenchman, Alexis de Tocqueville. But the whole society represented here—the cultivated liberal France of before the Empire—of outside the Empire—makes, intellectually and morally, a very honourable show. We said just now that it seemed to be sitting for its likeness; we only meant that the portrait was not blurred. We see it at all its hours and in all its moods, and we may believe that, taken by surprise, observed unawares, no group of people could on the whole have supported publicity more gracefully than the two Ampères and their many friends.

Galaxy, November 1875
Reprinted in *French Poets and Novelists*, 1878

Honoré de Balzac

HONORÉ DE BALZAC

T HE FRENCH IN GENERAL do their duty by their great men; they render them a liberal tribute of criticism, commentary, annotation, biographical analysis. They do not, indeed, make them the subject of "memoirs" in the English sense; there are few French examples of that class of literature to which Boswell's "Johnson" and Lockhart's "Scott" belong. But there usually clusters about the image of a conspicuous writer an infinite number of *travaux*, as the French say, of every degree of importance. Many of these are very solid and serious; their authors are generally to be charged with attaching too absolute a value to their heroes. The departed genius is patiently weighed and measured; his works are minutely analysed; the various episodes of his life are made the object of exhaustive research; his letters are published, and his whole personality, physical, moral, intellectual, passes solemnly into literature. He is always in order as a "subject"; it is admitted that the last word can never be said about him. From this usual fate of eminent Frenchmen, one of the greatest has been strikingly exempted. Honoré de Balzac is weighted neither with the honours nor with the taxes of an accumulated commentary. The critic who proposes to study him, and who looks for extrinsic assistance in his task, perceives such aid to be very meagre. Balzac has been discussed with first-rate ability only by one writer. M. Taine's essay, incomplete as it is, may be said at any rate to be essentially worthy of its subject. Sainte-Beuve wrote upon Balzac two or three times, but always with striking and inexplicable inadequacy. There is a long article on the author of the "Comédie Humaine" by Théophile Gautier, which is admirably picturesque but not at all critical. M. Edmond Schérer, a writer upon whom an ample fold of Sainte-Beuve's mantle has fallen, lately published a few pages which are suggestive, but in which he affirms that Balzac is neither an artist, a master, nor a writer. The great novelist's countrymen, in a word, have taken him less seriously than was to be expected. If we desire biographical details we are reduced to consulting the very flimsy gossip of

M. Léon Gozlan. Balzac has indeed what is called his *légende*, but it has been chiefly in the keeping of the mere tattlers of literature. The critic is forced to look for the man almost exclusively in his works; and it must be confessed that in the case of a writer so voluminous as Balzac such a field is ample. We should rather rejoice than regret that there are not more pages to turn. Balzac's complete works occupy twenty-three huge octavo volumes in the stately but inconvenient "édition définitive," lately published. There is a prospect of his letters being given to the world in a complementary volume.

I.

HONORÉ DE BALZAC was born at Tours in 1799; he died at Paris in 1850. Most first-rate men at fifty-one have still a good deal of work in them, and there is no reason to believe that, enormous as had been the demands he made upon it, Balzac's productive force was fully spent. His prefaces are filled with confident promises to publish novels that never appeared. Nevertheless it is impossible altogether to regret that Balzac died with work still in him. He had written enough; he had written too much. His novels, in spite of their extraordinary closeness of tissue, all betray the want of leisure in the author. It is true that shortly before his death he had encountered a change of fortune; he had married a rich woman and he was in a position to drive his pen no faster than his fancy prompted. It is interesting to wonder whether Balzac at leisure—Balzac with that great money-question which was at once the supreme inspiration and the æsthetic alloy of his life, placed on a relatively ideal basis—would have done anything essentially finer than "Les Parents Pauvres" or "Le Père Goriot." We can hardly help doubting it. M. Taine, looking as usual for formulas and labels, says that the most complete description of Balzac is that he was a man of business—a man of business in debt. The formula here is on the whole satisfactory; it expresses not only what he was by circumstances, but what he was by inclination. We cannot say how much Balzac liked being in debt, but we are very sure he liked, for itself, the process of manufacture and sale, and that even when all his debts had been paid he would have continued to keep his shop.

Before he was thirty years old he had published, under a variety of pseudonyms, some twenty long novels, veritable Grub Street productions, written in sordid Paris attics, in poverty, in perfect obscurity. Several of these "œuvres de jeunesse" have lately been republished, but the best of them are unreadable. No writer ever served a harder apprenticeship to his art, or lingered more hopelessly at the base of the ladder of fame. This early incompetence seems at first an anomaly, but it is only partially an anomaly. That so vigorous a genius should have learned his trade so largely by experiment and so little by divination; that in order to discover what he could do he should have had to make specific trial of each of the things he could not do—this is something which needs explanation. The explanation is found, it seems to us, simply in the folly of his attempting, at that age, to produce such novels as he aspired to produce. It was not that he could not use his wings; it was simply that his wings had not grown. The wings of great poets generally sprout very early; the wings of great artists in prose, great explorers of the sources of prose, begin to spread themselves only after the man is tolerably formed. Good observers, we believe, will confess to a general mistrust of novels written before thirty. Byron, Shelley, Keats, Lamartine, Victor Hugo, Alfred de Musset, were hardly in their twenties before they struck their fully resonant notes. Walter Scott, Thackeray, George Eliot, Madame Sand, waited till they were at least turned thirty, and then without prelude, or with brief prelude, produced a novel that was a masterpiece. If it was well for them to wait, it would have been infinitely better for Balzac. Balzac was to be preëminently a social novelist; his strength was to lie in representing the innumerable actual facts of the French civilization of his day—things only to be learned by patient experience. Balzac's inspiration, his stock, his *fonds*, was outside of him, in the complex French world of the nineteenth century. If, instead of committing to paper impossible imaginary tales, he could have stood for a while in some other relation to the society about him than that of a scribbler, it would have been a very great gain. The great general defect of his manner, as we shall see, is the absence of fresh air, of the trace of disinterested observation; he had from his earliest years, to carry out our

metaphor, an eye to the shop. In every great artist who possesses taste there is a little—a very little—of the amateur; but
in Balzac there is absolutely nothing of the amateur, and
nothing is less to be depended upon than Balzac's taste. But
he was forced to write; his family wished to make a lawyer of
him, and he preferred to be a romancer. He mastered enough
law to be able to incorporate the mysteries of legal procedure
in the "Comédie Humaine," and then embarked upon the
most prolific literary career, perhaps, that the world has seen.
His family cut down his supplies and tried to starve him out;
but he held firm, and in 1830 made his first step into success.
Meanwhile he had engaged in several commercial ventures,
each one of which failed, leaving him a ponderous legacy of
debt. To the end of his life he was haunted with undischarged
obligations and was constantly trying new speculations and
investments. It is true, we believe, that he amused himself
with representing this pecuniary incubus as far more mysteriously and heroically huge than it was. His incessant labour
brought him a remuneration which at this day and in this
country would be considered contemptible. M. Gozlan affirms that his annual income, in his successful years, rarely
exceeded 12,000 francs. This appears incredible until we find
the editor of the "Revue de Paris" crying out against his demand of 3,000 francs for the MS. of "Eugénie Grandet."
There is something pitiful in the contrast between this meagre
personal budget and his lifelong visions of wealth and of the
ways of amassing wealth, his jovial, sensual, colossal enjoyment of luxury, and the great monetary architecture as it were
of the "Comédie Humaine." Money is the most general element of Balzac's novels; other things come and go, but
money is always there. His great ambition and his great pretension as a social chronicler was to be complete, and he was
more complete in this direction than in any other. He rarely
introduces a person without telling us in detail how his property is invested, and the fluctuations of his *rentes* impartially
divide the writer's attention with the emotions of his heart.
Balzac never mentions an object without telling us what it
cost, and on every occasion he mentions an enormous number of objects. His women, too, talk about money quite as
much as his men, and not only his ignoble and mercenary

women (of whom there are so many) but his charming women, his heroines, his great ladies. Madame de Mortsauf is intended as a perfect example of feminine elevation, and yet Madame de Mortsauf has the whole of her husband's agricultural economy at her fingers' ends; she strikes us at moments as an attorney in petticoats. Each particular episode of the "Comédie Humaine" has its own hero and heroine, but the great general protagonist is the twenty-franc piece.

One thing at any rate Balzac achieved during these early years of effort and obscurity; he had laid the foundations of that intimate knowledge of Paris which was to serve as the basis—the vast mosaic pavement—of the "Comédie Humaine." Paris became his world, his universe; his passion for the great city deserves to rank in literature beside Dr. Johnson's affection for London. Wherever in his novels Paris is not directly presented she is even more vividly implied; the great negative to this brilliant positive, that *vie de province* of which he produced such elaborate pictures, is always observed from the standpoint of the Boulevard. If Balzac had represented any other country than France, if his imagination had ever left a footprint in England or Germany, it is a matter of course for those who know him that his fathomless Parisian cockneyism would have had on these occasions a still sharper emphasis. But there is nothing to prove that he in the least "realized," as we say, the existence of England and Germany. That he had of course a complete theory of the British constitution and the German intellect makes little difference; for Balzac's theories were often in direct proportion to his ignorance. He never perceived with any especial directness that the civilized world was made up of something else than Paris and the provinces; and as he is said to have been able to persuade himself, by repeating it a few times, that he had done various things which he had not done—made a present of a white horse, for instance, to his publisher—so he would have had only to say often enough to himself that England was a mythic country to believe imperturbably that there was in fact, three hundred miles away, no magnificent far-spreading London to invalidate his constant assumption that Paris is the pivot of human history. Never was a great genius more essentially local. Shakespeare, Scott, Goethe, savour of their native soil; but they have a glance that has only to fix itself a moment to call up easily other horizons. Balzac's power of creation gains perhaps in intensity what it loses in reach; it is certain at any rate that his conception of the stage on which the "Comédie Humaine" is perpetually being acted is surrounded by a Chinese wall. Never was an imagination more in sympathy with the French theory of centralization.

When his letters are published it will be interesting to learn from them, in so far as we may, how his life was spent during these first ten years of his manhood. He began very early to write about countesses and duchesses; and even after he had become famous, the manner in which he usually portrays the denizens of the Faubourg St. Germain obliges us to believe that the place they occupy in his books is larger than any that they occupied in his experience. Did he go into society? did he observe manners from a standpoint that commanded the field? It was not till he became famous that he began to use the aristocratic prefix; in his earlier years he was plain M. Balzac. I believe it is more than suspected that the pedigree represented by this *de* was as fabulous (and quite as ingenious) as any that he invented for his heroes. Balzac was profoundly and essentially *roturier*; we shall see that the intrinsic evidence of his plebeian origin is abundant. He may very well, like his own Eugène de Rastignac, have lived at a Maison Vauquer; but did he, like Rastignac, call upon a Madame de Beauséant and see her receive him as a kinsman? We said just now that we had to look for Balzac almost altogether in his books; and yet his books are singularly void of personal revelations. They tell us a vast deal about his mind, but they suggest to us very little about his life. It is hard to imagine a writer less autobiographic. This is certainly a proof of the immense sweep of his genius—of the incomparable vividness of his imagination. The things he invented were as real to him as the things he knew, and his actual experience is overlaid with a thousand thicknesses, as it were, of imaginary experience. The person is irrecoverably lost in the artist. There is sufficient evidence, however, that the person led a rather hungry and predatory life during these early years, and that he was more familiar with what went on in the streets than with what occurred in the *salons*. Whatever he encountered, however, he observed.

In one of his tales he describes a young man who follows people in the street to overhear what they say. This at least is autobiographic, and the young man is Honoré de Balzac, "devoured by his genius and by the consciousness of his genius," as M. Taine says—with all the unwritten "Comédie Humaine" within him. "In listening to these people I could espouse their life. I felt their rags upon my back; I walked with my feet in their tattered shoes; their desires, their wants—everything passed into my soul, and my soul passed into theirs; it was the dream of a waking man." This glimpse of Balzac laying up data is especially interesting because it is singularly rare. It must be that for years he spent many an hour in silent, instinctive contemplation, for his novels imply a period of preparatory research, of social botanizing, geologizing, palæontologizing, just as Humboldt's "Cosmos" implies a large amount of travel. It happens that most of the anecdotes about Balzac pertain to his productive period, and present him to us in his white friar's dress, getting out of bed at midnight to work, in a darkened room, three weeks at a sitting. The open-air Balzac, as we may call it, has been little commemorated. White Dominican robes, darkened rooms, deep potations of coffee, form the staple of M. Gozlan's reminiscences. Every man works as he can and as he must; and if, in order to write the "Parents Pauvres," Balzac had had to dress himself in a bearskin, we trust he would not have hesitated. But it is nevertheless true that between the lines of the "Comédie Humaine" the reader too often catches a glimpse of the Dominican robe and the darkened room, and longs for an open window and a costume somewhat less capricious. A realistic novelist, he remembers, is not an astrologer or an alchemist.

In 1830 Balzac published the "Peau de Chagrin"—the first work of the series on which his reputation rests. After this, for twenty years, he produced without cessation. The quantity of his work, when we consider the quality, seems truly amazing. There are writers in the same line who have published an absolutely greater number of volumes. Alexandre Dumas, Madame Sand, Anthony Trollope, have all been immensely prolific; but they all weave a loose web, as it were, and Balzac weaves a dense one. The tissue of his tales is

always extraordinarily firm and hard; it may not at every point
be cloth of gold, but it has always a metallic rigidity. It has
been worked over a dozen times, and the work can never be
said to belong to light literature. You have only to turn the
pages of a volume of Balzac to see that, whatever may be the
purity of the current, it at least never runs thin. There is none
of that wholesale dialogue, chopped into fragments, which
Alexandre Dumas manufactures by the yard, and which bears
the same relation to real narrative architecture as a chain of
stepping-stones tossed across a stream does to a granite
bridge. Balzac is always definite; you can say Yes or No to
him as you go on; the story bristles with references that must
be verified, and if sometimes it taxes the attention more than
is thought becoming in a novel, we must admit that, being as
hard reading in the way of entertainment as Hallam or Guizot, it may also have been very hard writing. This it is that
makes Balzac's fertility so amazing—the fact that, whether we
relish its results or not, we at least perceive that the process is
not superficial. His great time was from 1830 to 1840; it was
during these ten years that he published his most perfect
works. "Eugénie Grandet," "La Recherche de l'Absolu," "Le
Père Goriot," "Un Ménage de Garçon," "Le Cabinet des Antiques," belong to the earlier period. "Béatrix," "Modeste Mignon," "Une Ténébreuse Affaire," "Les Illusions Perdues,"
the "Mémoires de deux Jeunes Mariées," "La Muse du Dé-
partement," "Le Député d'Arcis," belong to the latter. Balzac
is never simple, and in a sense which it will be interesting to
attempt to explain, he is always corrupt; but "La Recherche
de Absolu" and "Le Père Goriot"—we will not mention "Eugénie Grandet," which was so praised for its innocence that
the author found himself detesting it—have a certain relative
simplicity and purity; whereas in the "Jeunes Mariées," "Béatrix," and "Modeste Mignon," we are up to our necks in sophistication. If, however, the works of the first half of Balzac's
eminent period are, generally speaking, superior to those of
the second half, it must be added that there are two or three
incongruous transpositions. "Le Lys dans la Vallée," published in 1835, is bad enough to be coupled with "Béatrix";
and "Les Parents Pauvres" and "Les Paysans," finished shortly
before the author's death, are in many respects his most pow-

erful achievements. Most of Balzac's shorter tales are antecedent to 1840, and his readers know how many masterpieces the
list contains. "Le Colonel Chabert" and "L'Interdiction" are
found in it, as well as "La Femme Abandonnée," "La Grenadière" and "Le Message," and the admirable little stories
grouped together (in the common duodecimo edition) with
"Les Marana." The duration of Balzac's works will certainly
not be in proportion to their length. "Le Curé de Tours," for
all its brevity, will be read when "Le Député d'Arcis" lies unopened; and more than one literary adventurer will turn, out-
wearied, from "La Peau de Chagrin" and find consolation in
"Un Début dans la Vie."

We know not how early Balzac formed the plan of the "Comédie Humaine"; but the general preface, in which he explains the unity of his work and sets forth that each of his
tales is a block in a single immense edifice and that this edifice
aims to be a complete portrait of the civilization of his time—
this remarkable manifesto dates from 1842. (If we call it remarkable, it is not that we understand it; though so much as
we have just expressed may easily be gathered from it. From
the moment that Balzac attempts to philosophize, readers in
the least sensible of the difference between words and things
must part company with him.) He complains, very properly,
that the official historians have given us no information about
manners that is worth speaking of; that this omission is unpardonable; and that future ages will care much more for the
testimony of the novel, properly executed, than for that of the
writers who "set in order facts which are about the same in
all nations, look up the spirit of laws which have fallen into
disuse, elaborate theories which lead nations astray, or, like
certain metaphysicians, endeavour to explain what is." Inspired by this conviction, Balzac proposed to himself to illustrate by a tale or a group of tales every phase of French life
and manners during the first half of the nineteenth century.
To be colossally and exhaustively complete—complete not
only in the generals but in the particulars—to touch upon
every salient point, to illuminate every typical feature, to reproduce every sentiment, every idea, every person, every
place, every object, that has played a part, however minute,
however obscure, in the life of the French people—nothing

less than this was his programme. The undertaking was enormous, but it will not seem at first that Balzac underestimated
the needful equipment. He was conscious of the necessary
talent and he deemed it possible to acquire the necessary
knowledge. This knowledge was almost encyclopædic, and
yet, after the vividness of his imagination, Balzac's strongest
side is his grasp of actual facts. Behind our contemporary civilization is an immense and complicated machinery—the machinery of government, of police, of the arts, the professions,
the trades. Among these things Balzac moved easily and joyously; they form the rough skeleton of his great edifice. There
is not a little pedantry in his pretension to universal and infallible accuracy; but his accuracy, so far as we can measure it,
is extraordinary, and in dealing with Balzac we must, in every
direction, make our account with pedantry. He made his
cadres, as the French say; he laid out his field in a number of
broad divisions; he subdivided these, and then he filled up his
moulds, pressing the contents down and packing it tight. You
may read the categories on the back of the cover of the little
common edition. There are the "Scènes de la Vie Privée"—
"de la Vie de Province"—"de la Vie Parisienne"—"de la Vie
Politique"—"de la Vie Militaire"—"de la Vie de Campagne";
and in a complementary way there are the "Études Philosophiques"—(this portentous category contains the picturesque
"Recherche de l'Absolu")—and the "Études Analytiques."
Then, in the way of subdivisions, there are "Les Célibataires,"
"Les Parisiens en Province," "Les Rivalités," "Les Illusions
Perdues," the "Splendeurs et Misères des Courtisanes," the
"Parents Pauvres," the "Envers de l'Histoire Contemporaine."
This goodly nomenclature had a retroactive effect; the idea of
the "Comédie Humaine," having developed itself when the
author was midway in his career, a number of its component
parts are what we may call accomplices after the fact. They
are pieces that dovetail into the vast mosaic as they best can.
But even if the occasional disparities were more striking they
would signify little, for what is most interesting in Balzac is
not the achievement but the attempt. The attempt was, as he
himself has happily expressed it, to "faire concurrence à l'état
civil"—to start an opposition, as we should say in America,
to the civil registers. He created a complete social system—

an hierarchy of ranks and professions which should correspond with that of which the officers of the census have cognizance. Everything is there, as we find it in his pages—the
king (in "Le Député d'Arcis" Louis XVIII. is introduced and
makes witticisms quite *inédits*) the administration, the church,
the army, the judicature, the aristocracy, the bourgeoisie, the
prolétariat, the peasantry, the artists, the journalists, the men
of letters, the actors, the children (a little girl is the heroine
of "Pierrette," and an urchin the hero of "Un Début dans la
Vie") the shopkeepers of every degree, the criminals, the
thousand irregular and unclassified members of society. All
this in Balzac's hands becomes an organic whole; it moves
together; it has a pervasive life; the blood circulates through
it; its parts are connected by sinuous arteries. We have seen
in English literature, in two cases, a limited attempt to create
a permanent stock, a standing fund, of characters. Thackeray
has led a few of his admirable figures from one novel to another, and Mr. Trollope has deepened illusion for us by his
repeated evocations of Bishop Proudie and Archdeacon Grant-
ley. But these things are faint shadows of Balzac's extravagant
thoroughness—his fantastic cohesiveness. A French brain
alone could have persisted in making a system of all this. Balzac's "Comédie Humaine" is on the imaginative line very
much what Comte's "Positive Philosophy" is on the scientific.
These great enterprises are equally characteristic of the French
passion for completeness, for symmetry, for making a system
as neat as an epigram—of its intolerance of the indefinite, the
unformulated. The French mind likes better to squeeze things
into a formula that mutilates them, if need be, than to leave
them in the frigid vague. The farther limit of its power of
arrangement (so beautiful as it generally is) is the limit of the
knowable. Consequently we often see in the visions and systems of Frenchmen what may be called a conventional infinite. The civilization of the nineteenth century is of course
not infinite, but to us of English speech, as we survey it, it
appears so multitudinous, so complex, so far-spreading, so
suggestive, so portentous—it has such misty edges and far
reverberations—that the imagination, oppressed and overwhelmed, shrinks from any attempt to grasp it as a whole.
The French imagination, in the person of Balzac, easily dom-

inates it, as he would say, and, without admitting that the
problem is any the less vast, regards it as practically soluble.
He would be an incautious spirit who should propose hereupon to decide whether the French imagination or the English is the more potent. The one sees a vast number of
obstacles and the other a vast number of remedies—the one
beholds a great many shadows and the other a great many
lights. If the human comedy, as Balzac pours it, condensed
and solidified, out of his mould, is a very reduced copy of its
original, we may nevertheless admit that the mould is of enormous dimensions. "Very good," the English imagination says;
"call it large, but don't call it universal." The impartial critic
may assent; but he privately remembers that it was in the convenient faculty of persuading himself that he could do everything that Balzac found the inspiration to do so much.

In addition to possessing an immense knowledge of his
field, he was conscious that he needed a philosophy—a system of opinions. On this side too he equipped himself; so far
as quantity goes no man was ever better provided with opinions. Balzac has an opinion on everything in heaven and on
earth, and a complete, consistent theory of the universe,
which was always ready for service. "The signs of a superior
mind," says M. Taine, in speaking of him, "are *vues d'ensemble*—general views"; and judged by its wealth in this direction Balzac's should be the greatest mind the world has seen.
We can think of no other mind that has stood ready to deliver
itself on quite so many subjects. We doubt whether, on the
whole, Aristotle had so many *vues d'ensemble* as Balzac. In
Plato, in Bacon, in Shakespeare, in Goethe, in Hegel, there
are shameful intermissions and lapses, ugly blank spots, un-
graceful liabilities to be taken by surprise. But Balzac, as the
showman of the human comedy, had measured his responsibilities unerringly and concluded that he must not only know
what everything is, but what everything should be. He is thus
par excellence the philosophic novelist; his pages bristle with
axioms, moral, political, ethical, æsthetical; his narrative
groans beneath the weight of metaphysical and scientific
digression. The value of his philosophy and his science is a
question to be properly treated apart; we mean simply to indicate that, formally, in this direction he is as complete as in

the others. In the front rank, of course, stand his political and religious opinions. These are anchored to "the two eternal truths—the monarchy and the Catholic Church." Balzac is, in other words, an elaborate conservative—a Tory of the deepest dye. How well, as a picturesque romancer, he knew what he was about in adopting this profession of faith will be plain to the most superficial reader. His philosophy, his morality, his religious opinions have a certain picturesque correspondence with his political views. Speaking generally, it may be said that he had little belief in virtue and still less admiration for it. He is so large and various that you find all kinds of contradictory things in him; he has that sign of the few supreme geniuses that, if you look long enough he offers you a specimen of every possible mode of feeling. He has represented virtue, innocence and purity in the most vivid forms. César Birotteau, Eugénie Grandet, Mlle. Cormon, Mme. Graslin, Mme. Claës, Mme. de Mortsauf, Popinot, Genestas, the Cousin Pons, Schmucke, Chesnel, Joseph Bridau, Mme. Hulot—these and many others are not only admirably good people, but they are admirably successful figures. They live and move, they produce an illusion, for all their goodness, quite as much as their baser companions—Mme. Vauquer, Mme. Marneffe, Vautrin, Philippe Bridau, Mme. de Rochefide. Balzac had evidently an immense kindliness, a salubrious good nature which enabled him to feel the charm of all artless and helpless manifestations of life. That robustness of temperament and those high animal spirits which carried him into such fantastic explorations of man's carnal nature as the "Physiologie du Mariage" and the "Contes Drôlatiques"—that lusty natural humour which was not humour in our English sense, but a relish, sentimentally more dry but intellectually more keen, of all grotesqueness and quaintness and uncleanness, and which, when it felt itself flagging, had still the vigour to keep itself up a while as what the French call the "humoristic"—to emulate Rabelais, to torture words, to string together names, to be pedantically jovial and archaically hilarious—all this helped Balzac to appreciate the simple and the primitive with an intensity subordinate only to his enjoyment of corruption and sophistication. We do wrong indeed to say subordinate; Balzac was here as strong and as frank as he was anywhere. We are almost inclined to say that his profoundly simple people are his best—that in proportion to the labour expended upon them they are most lifelike. Such a figure as "big Nanon," the great, strapping, devoted maid-servant in "Eugénie Grandet," may stand as an example. (Balzac is full, by the way, of good servants; from Silvie and Christophe in "Le Père Goriot" to Chesnel the notary, whose absolutely canine fidelity deprives him even of the independence of a domestic, in "Le Cabinet des Antiques.") What he represents best is extremely simple virtue, and vice simple or complex, as you please. In superior virtue, intellectual virtue, he fails; when his superior people begin to reason they are lost—they become prigs and hypocrites, or worse. Madame de Mortsauf, who is intended to be at once the purest and cleverest of his good women, is a kind of fantastic monster; she is perhaps only equalled by the exemplary Madame de l'Estorade, who (in "Le Député d'Arcis") writes to a lady with whom she is but scantily acquainted a series of *pros* and *cons* on the question whether "it will be given" (as she phrases it) to a certain gentleman to make her "manquer à ses devoirs." This gentleman has snatched her little girl from under a horse's hoofs, and for a while afterward has greatly annoyed her by his importunate presence on her walks and drives. She immediately assumes that he has an eye to her "devoirs." Suddenly, however, he disappears, and it occurs to her that he is "sacrificing his fancy to the fear of spoiling his fine action." At this attractive thought her "devoirs" begin to totter, and she ingenuously exclaims, "But on this footing he would really be a man to reckon with, and, my dear M. de l'Estorade, you would have decidedly to look out!" And yet Madame de l'Estorade is given us as a model of the all-gracious wife and mother; she figures in the "Deux Jeunes Mariées" as the foil of the luxurious, passionate and pedantic Louise de Chaulieu—the young lady who, on issuing from the convent where she has got her education, writes to her friend that she is the possessor of a "virginité savante."

There are two writers in Balzac—the spontaneous one and the reflective one—the former of which is much the more delightful, while the latter is the more extraordinary. It was the reflective observer that aimed at colossal completeness and equipped himself with a universal philosophy: and it was of this one we spoke when we said just now that Balzac had little belief in virtue. Balzac's beliefs, it must be confessed, are delicate ground; from certain points of view, perhaps, the less said about them the better. His sincere, personal beliefs may be reduced to a very compact formula; he believed that it was possible to write magnificent novels, and that he was the man to do it. He believed, otherwise stated, that human life was infinitely dramatic and picturesque, and that he possessed an incomparable analytic perception of the fact. His other convictions were all derived from this and humbly danced attendance upon it; for if being a man of genius means being identical with one's productive faculty, never was there such a genius as Balzac's. A monarchical society is unquestionably more picturesque, more available for the novelist than any other, as the others have as yet exhibited themselves; and therefore Balzac was with glee, with gusto, with imagination, a monarchist. Of what is to be properly called religious feeling we do not remember a suggestion in all his many pages; on the other hand, the reader constantly encounters the handsomest compliments to the Catholic Church as a social *régime*. A hierarchy is as much more picturesque than a "congregational society" as a mountain is than a plain. Bishops, abbés, priests, Jesuits, are invaluable figures in fiction, and the morality of the Catholic Church allows of an infinite *chiaroscuro*. In "La Fille aux Yeux d'Or" there is a portrait of a priest who becomes preceptor to the youthful hero. "This priest, vicious but politic, sceptical but learned, perfidious but amiable, feeble in aspect, but as strong in body as in head, was so truly useful to his pupil, so complaisant to his vices, so good a calculator of every sort of force, so deep when it was necessary to play some human trick, so young at table, at the gaming house, at—I don't know where—that the only thing the grateful Henry de Marsay could feel soft-hearted over in 1814 was the portrait of his dear bishop—the single object of personal property he was able to inherit from this prelate, an admirable type of the men whose genius will save the Catholic Apostolic and Roman Church." It is hardly an exaggeration to say that we here come as near as we do at any point to Balzac's religious feeling. The reader will see that it is simply a lively assent to that great worldly force of the Catholic Church, the art of using all sorts of servants and all sorts of means. Balzac was willing to accept any morality that was curious and unexpected, and he found himself as a matter of course more in sympathy with a theory of conduct which takes account of circumstances and recognises the merits of duplicity, than with the comparatively colourless idea that virtue is nothing if not uncompromising. Like all persons who have looked a great deal at human life, he had been greatly struck with most people's selfishness, and this quality seemed to him the most general in mankind. Selfishness may go to dangerous lengths, but Balzac believed that it may somehow be regulated and even chastened by a strong throne and a brilliant court, with MM. de Rastignac and de Trailles as supports of the one and Mesdames de Maufrigneuse and d'Espard as ornaments of the other, and by a clever and impressive Church, with plenty of bishops of the pattern of the one from whose history a leaf has just been given. If we add to this that he had a great fancy for "electricity" and animal magnetism, we have touched upon the most salient points of Balzac's philosophy. This makes, it is true, rather a bald statement of a matter which at times seems much more considerable; but it may be maintained that an exact analysis of his heterogeneous opinions will leave no more palpable deposit. His imagination was so fertile, the movement of his mind so constant, his curiosity and ingenuity so unlimited, the energy of his phrase so striking, he raises such a cloud of dust about him as he goes, that the reader to whom he is new has a sense of his opening up gulfs and vistas of thought and pouring forth flashes and volleys of wisdom. But from the moment he ceases to be a simple dramatist Balzac is an arrant charlatan. It is probable that no equally vigorous mind was ever at pains to concoct such elaborate messes of folly. They spread themselves over page after page, in a close, dense verbal tissue, which the reader scans in vain for some little flower of available truth. It all rings false—it is all mere flatulent pretension. It may be said that from the moment he attempts to deal with an abstraction the presumption is always dead against him. About what the discriminating reader thus brutally dubs his charlatanism, as about everything else in Balzac, there would be very much more to say than this small compass admits of. (Let not the discriminating reader, by the way, repent of his brutality; Balzac himself was brutal, and must be handled with his own weapons. It would be absurd to write of him in semi-tones and innuendoes; he never used them himself.) The chief point is that he himself was his most perfect dupe; he believed in his own magnificent rubbish, and if he made it up, as the phrase is, as he went along, his credulity kept pace with his invention. This was, briefly speaking, because he was morally and intellectually so superficial. He paid himself, as the French say, with shallower conceits than ever before passed muster with a strong man. The moral, the intellectual atmosphere of his genius is extraordinarily gross and turbid; it is no wonder that the flower of truth does not bloom in it, nor any natural flower whatever. The difference in this respect between Balzac and the other great novelists is extremely striking. When we approach Thackeray and George Eliot, George Sand and Turgénieff, it is into the conscience and the mind that we enter, and we think of these writers primarily as great consciences and great minds. When we approach Balzac we seem to enter into a great temperament—a prodigious nature. He strikes us half the time as an extraordinary physical phenomenon. His robust imagination seems a sort of physical faculty and impresses us more with its sensible mass and quantity than with its lightness or fineness.

This brings us back to what was said just now touching his disbelief in virtue and his homage to the selfish passions. He had no natural sense of morality, and this we cannot help thinking a serious fault in a novelist. Be the morality false or true, the writer's deference to it greets us as a kind of essential perfume. We find such a perfume in Shakespeare; we find it, in spite of his so-called cynicism, in Thackeray; we find it, potently, in George Eliot, in George Sand, in Turgénieff. They care for moral questions; they are haunted by a moral ideal. This southern slope of the mind, as we may call it, was very barren in Balzac, and it is partly possible to account for its barrenness. Large as Balzac is, he is all of one piece and he hangs perfectly together. He pays for his merits and he sanctifies his defects. He had a sense of this present terrestrial life which has never been surpassed, and which in his genius overshadowed everything else. There are many men who are not especially occupied with the idea of another world, but we believe there has never been a man so completely detached from it as Balzac. This world of our senses, of our purse, of our name, of our *blason* (or the absence of it)—this palpable world of houses and clothes, of seven per cents and multiform human faces, pressed upon his imagination with an unprecedented urgency. It certainly is real enough to most of us, but to Balzac it was ideally real—charmingly, absorbingly, absolutely real. There is nothing in all imaginative literature that in the least resembles his mighty passion for *things*—for material objects, for furniture, upholstery, bricks and mortar. The world that contained these things filled his consciousness, and *being*, at its intensest, meant simply being thoroughly at home among them. Balzac possessed indeed a lively interest in the supernatural: "La Peau de Chagrin," "Louis Lambert," "Séraphita," are a powerful expression of it. But it was a matter of adventurous fancy, like the same quality in Edgar Poe; it was perfectly cold, and had nothing to do with his moral life. To get on in this world, to succeed, to live greatly in all one's senses, to have plenty of *things*—this was Balzac's infinite; it was here that his heart expanded. It was natural, therefore, that the life of mankind should seem to him above all an eager striving along this line—a multitudinous greed for personal enjoyment. The master-passion among these passions—the passion of the miser—he has depicted as no one else has begun to do. Wherever we look, in the "Comédie Humaine," we see a miser, and he—or she—is sure to be a marvel of portraiture. In the struggle and the scramble it is not the sweetest qualities that come uppermost, and Balzac, watching the spectacle, takes little account of these. It is strength and cunning that are most visible—the power to climb the ladder, to wriggle to the top of the heap, to clutch the money-bag. In human nature, viewed in relation to this end, it is force only that is desirable, and a feeling is fine only in so far as it is a profitable practical force. Strength of purpose seems the supremely admirable thing, and the spectator lingers over all eminent exhibitions of it. It may show itself in two great ways—in vehemence and in astuteness, in eagerness and in patience. Balzac has a vast relish for both, but on the whole he prefers the latter form as being the more dramatic. It admits of duplicity, and there are few human accomplishments that Balzac professes so explicit a respect for as this. He scatters it freely among his dear "gens d'église," and his women are all compounded of it. If he had been asked what was, for human purposes, the faculty he valued most highly, he would have said the power of dissimulation. He regards it as a sign of all superior people, and he says somewhere that nothing forms the character so finely as having had to exercise it in one's youth, in the bosom of one's family. In this attitude of Balzac's there is an element of affectation and of pedantry; he praises duplicity because it is original and audacious to do so. But he praises it also because it has for him the highest recommendation that anything can have—it is picturesque. Duplicity is more picturesque than honesty— just as the line of beauty is the curve and not the straight line. In place of a moral judgment of conduct, accordingly, Balzac usually gives us an æsthetic judgment. A magnificent action with him is not an action which is remarkable for its high motive, but an action with a great force of will or of desire behind it, which throws it into striking and monumental relief. It may be a magnificent sacrifice, a magnificent devotion, a magnificent act of faith; but the presumption is that it will be a magnificent lie, a magnificent murder, or a magnificent adultery.

II.

THIS overmastering sense of the present world was of course a superb foundation for the work of a realistic romancer, and it did so much for Balzac that one is puzzled to know where to begin to enumerate the things he owed to it. It gave him in the first place his background—his *mise en scène*. This part of his story had with Balzac an importance— his rendering of it a solidity—which it had never enjoyed before, and which the most vigorous talents in the school of which Balzac was founder have never been able to restore to it. The place in which an event occurred was in his view of equal moment with the event itself; it was part of the action;

it was not a thing to take or to leave, or to be vaguely and
gracefully indicated; it imposed itself; it had a part to play; it
needed to be made as definite as anything else. There is accordingly a very much greater amount of description in Balzac than in any other writer, and the description is mainly of
towns, houses and rooms. Descriptions of scenery, properly
so called, are rare, though when they occur they are often
admirable. Almost all of his tales "de la vie de province" are
laid in different towns, and a more or less minute portrait of
the town is always attempted. How far in these cases Balzac's
general pretension to be exact and complete was sustained we
are unable to say; we know not what the natives of Limoges,
of Saumur, of Angoulême, of Alençon, of Issoudun, of Guérande, thought of his presentation of these localities; but if
the picture is not veracious, it is at least always definite and
masterly. And Balzac did what he could, we believe, to be
exact; he often made a romancer's pilgrimage to a town that
he wished to introduce into a story. Here he picked out a
certain number of houses to his purpose, lodged the persons
of his drama in them, and reproduced them even to their local
odours. Many readers find all this very wearisome, and it is
certain that it offers one a liberal chance to be bored. We, for
our part, have always found Balzac's houses and rooms extremely interesting; we often prefer his places to his people.
He was a profound connoisseur in these matters; he had a
passion for bric-à-brac, and his tables and chairs are always in
character. It must be admitted that in this matter as in every
other he had his right and his wrong, and that in his enumerations of inanimate objects he often sins by extravagance. He
has his necessary houses and his superfluous houses: often
when in a story the action is running thin he stops up your
mouth against complaint, as it were, by a choking dose of
brick and mortar. The power of his memory, his representative vision, as regards these things is something amazing; the
reader never ceases to wonder at the promptness with which
he can "get up" a furnished house—at the immense supply of
this material that he carries about in his mind. He expends it
with a royal liberality; where another writer makes an allusion
Balzac gives you a Dutch picture. In "Le Cabinet des Antiques," on the verge of its close, Madame Camusot makes a

momentary appearance. She has only twenty lines to speak, but immediately we are confronted with her domicile. "Leaning against the next house, so as to present its front to the court, it had on each floor but one window on the street. The court, confined in its width by two walls ornamented by rosebushes and privet, had at its bottom, opposite the house, a shed supported upon two brick arches. A little half-door admitted you into this dusky house, made duskier still by a great walnut-tree planted in the middle of the court." We are told furthermore about the dining-room and the kitchen, about the staircase and the rooms on the first floor. We learn that the second floor was an attic, and that it had one room for the cook and another for the femme de chambre, who kept the children with her. We are informed that the woodwork, painted a dirty grey, was of the most melancholy aspect, and that Madame Camusot's bedroom had a carpet and blue and white ornaments. All this is entirely out of the current of the story, which pretends to be short and simple, and which is ostensibly hurrying towards its dénoûment. Some readers will always remember the two brick arches of Madame Camusot's shed, the dirty grey of her walls and the blue and white upholstery of her room; others will say that they care nothing about them, and these are not to be gainsaid.

Three or four descriptions of this kind stand out in the reader's memory. One is the picture of the dark and chill abode in which poor Eugénie Grandet blooms and fades; another is the elaborate and elegant portrait of the beautiful old house at Douai, half Flemish, half Spanish, in which the delusions of Balthazar Claes bring his family to ruin; the best of all is the magnificent account of the "pension bourgeoise des deux sexes et autres," kept by Madame Vauquer, *née* de Conflans, preceded by a glass door armed with a shrill alarm-bell, through which you see an arcade in green marble painted on a wall and a statue of Cupid with the varnish coming off in scales. In this musty and mouldy little boarding-house the Père Goriot is the senior resident. Certain students in law and medicine, from the Quartier Latin, hard by, subscribe to the dinner, where Maman Vauquer glares at them when she watches them cut their slice from the loaf. When the Père Goriot dies horribly, at the end of the tragedy, the kindest thing said of him, as the other boarders unfold their much-crumpled napkins, is, "Well, he won't sit and sniff his bread any more!" and the speaker imitates the old man's favourite gesture. The portrait of the Maison Vauquer and its inmates is one of the most portentous settings of the scene in all the literature of fiction. In this case there is nothing superfluous; there is a profound correspondence between the background and the action. It is a pity not to be able to quote the whole description, or even that of the greasy, dusky dining-room in which so much of the story goes forward. "This apartment is in all its lustre at the moment when, toward seven o'clock in the morning, Madame Vauquer's cat precedes his mistress, jumping on the side-boards, smelling at the milk contained in several basins covered with plates, and giving forth his matutinal purr. Presently the widow appears, decked out in her tulle cap, under which hangs a crooked band of false hair; as she walks she drags along her wrinkled slippers. Her little plump elderly face, from the middle of which protrudes a nose like a parrot's beak; her little fat dimpled hands, her whole person, rounded like a church-rat, the waist of her gown, too tight for its contents, which flaps over it, are all in harmony with this room, where misfortune seems to ooze, where speculation lurks in corners, and of which Madame Vauquer inhales the warm, fetid air without being nauseated. Her countenance, fresh as a first autumn frost, her wrinkled eyes, whose expression passes from the smile prescribed to *danseuses* to the acrid scowl of the discounter—her whole person, in short, is an explanation of the boarding-house, as the boarding-house is an implication of her person. . . . Her worsted petticoat, which falls below her outer skirt, made of an old dress, and with the wadding coming out of the slits in the stuff, which is full of them, resumes the parlour, the dining-room, the yard, announces the kitchen, and gives a presentiment of the boarders." But we must pause, for we are passing from the portraiture of places to that of people.

This latter is Balzac's strongest gift, and it is so strong that it easily distances all competition. Two other writers in this line have gone very far, but they suffer by comparison with him. Dickens often sets a figure before us with extraordinary vividness; but the outline is fantastic and arbitrary; we but half believe in it, and feel as if we were expected but half to believe in it. It is like a silhouette in cut paper, in which the artist has allowed great license to his scissors. If Balzac had a rival, the most dangerous rival would be Turgénieff. With the Russian novelist the person represented is equally definite—or meant to be equally definite; and the author's perception of idiosyncrasies is sometimes even more subtle. With Turgénieff as with Balzac the whole person springs into being at once; the character is never left shivering for its fleshly envelope, its face, its figure, its gestures, its tone, its costume, its name, its bundle of antecedents. But behind Balzac's figures we feel a certain heroic pressure that drives them home to our credence—a contagious illusion on the author's own part. The imagination that produced them is working at a greater heat; they seem to proceed from a sort of creative infinite and they help each other to be believed in. It is pictorially a larger, sturdier, more systematic style of portraiture than Turgénieff's. This is altogether the most valuable element in Balzac's novels; it is hard to see how the power of physical evocation can go farther. In future years, if people find his tales, as a whole, too rugged and too charmless, let them take one up occasionally and, turning the leaves, read simply the portraits. In Balzac every one who is introduced is minutely described; if the individual is to say but three words he has the honours of a complete portrait. Portraits shape themselves under his pen as if in obedience to an irresistible force; while the effort with most writers is to collect the material—to secure the model—the effort with Balzac is to disintegrate his visions, to accept only one candidate in the dozen. And it is not only that his figures are so definite, but that they are so plausible, so real, so characteristic, so recognisable. The fertility of his imagination in this respect was something marvellous. When we think of the many hundred complete human creatures (he calls the number at least two thousand) whom he set in motion, with their sharp differences, their histories, their money-matters, their allotted place in his great machine, we give up the attempt to gauge such a lusty energy of fancy. In reading over Balzac, we have marked a great many portraits for quotation, but it is hard to know what to choose or where to begin. The appreciative reader may safely begin at hazard. He

opens the little tale of "L'Interdiction," and finds the physiognomy of the excellent Judge Popinot thus depicted: "If nature, therefore, had endowed M. Popinot with an exterior but
scantily agreeable, the magistracy had not embellished him.
His frame was full of angular lines. His big knees, his large
feet, his broad hands, contrasted with a sacerdotal face, which
resembled vaguely the head of a calf, soft to insipidity, feebly
lighted by two lateral eyes, altogether bloodless, divided by a
straight flat nose, surmounted by a forehead without protu-
berance, decorated by two huge ears, which bent awkwardly
forward. His hair, thin in quantity and quality, exposed his
skull in several irregular furrows. A single feature recommended this countenance to the student of physiognomy. The
man had a mouth on whose lips a divine goodness hovered.
These were good big red lips, sinuous, moving, with a thousand folds, through which nature had never expressed any but
high feelings—lips which spoke to the heart," &c.

That is certainly admirable for energy and vividness—
closeness to the individual. But, after all, Popinot plays a part;
he appears in several tales; he is the type of the upright judge,
and there is a fitness in his figure being strongly lighted. Here
is Madame de Kergarouet, who merely crosses the stage in
"Béatrix," who rises in answer to a momentary need, and yet
who is as ripe and complete, as thoroughly seen, felt and understood, as if she had been soaked, as it were, for years in
the author's consciousness: "As for the Vicomtesse de Kergarouet, she was the perfect *provinciale*. Tall, dry, faded, full
of hidden pretensions which showed themselves after they
had been wounded; talking much and, by dint of talking,
catching a few ideas, as one cannons at billiards, and which
gave her a reputation for cleverness; trying to humiliate the
Parisians by the pretended *bonhomie* of departmental wisdom,
and by a make-believe happiness which she was always putting forward; stooping to get herself picked up and furious at
being left on her knees; fishing for compliments, and not always taking them; dressing herself at once strikingly and carelessly; taking the want of affability for impertinence, and
thinking to embarrass people greatly by paying them no attention; refusing what she wanted in order to have it offered
to her twice, and to seem to be urged beyond resistance; oc-

cupied with the things that people have ceased to talk about
and greatly astonished at not being in the current of fashion;
finally, keeping quiet with difficulty an hour without bringing
up Nantes, and the tigers of Nantes, and the affairs of the
high society of Nantes, and complaining of Nantes, and criticising Nantes, and making a personal application of the
phrases extracted from the people whose attention wandered,
and who agreed with her to get rid of her. Her manners, her
language, her ideas, had all more or less rubbed off on her
four daughters." Here also, to prove that Balzac's best portraits are not always his harshest, is an admirably friendly portrait of an old rustic gentlewoman, taken from the same
novel: "Mademoiselle Zephirine, deprived of her sight, was
ignorant of the changes which her eighty years had made in
her physiognomy. Her pale, hollow face, which the immobility of her white, sightless eyes caused to look like that of a
dead person, which three or four protruding teeth rendered
almost threatening, in which the deep orbit of the eyes was
circled with red tones, in which a few signs of virility, already
white, cropped up about the mouth and chin—this cold,
calm face was framed in a little nun-like cap of brown calico,
pricked like a counterpane, garnished with a cambric frill, and
tied under the chin by two strings which were always a trifle
rusty. She wore a short gown of coarse cloth, over a petticoat
of *piqué*, a real mattress which contained forty-franc pieces—
as also a pair of pockets sewed to a belt which she put on and
took off morning and night like a garment. Her body was
fastened into the common jacket of Brittany, in stuff matching with that of her skirt, ornamented with a little collar of a
thousand folds, the washing of which was the subject of the
only dispute she ever had with her sister-in-law—she herself
wishing to change it but once a week. From the great wadded
sleeves of this jacket issued two desiccated but nervous arms,
at the end of which moved two hands of a ruddy hue, which
made her arms appear as white as the wood of the poplar.
Her hands, with the fingers hooked and contracted by knit-
ting, were like a stocking-loom for ever wound up; the phenomenon would have been to see them stop. From time to
time she took a long knitting-needle that was planted in her
bosom, and thrust it in between her cap and her head, while

she rummaged in her white hair. A stranger would have laughed at the carelessness with which she stuck the needle back again, without the least fear of wounding herself. She was as straight as a belfry. This columnar rectitude might have passed for one of those egotisms practised by old people, which prove that pride is a passion necessary to life. Her smile was gay."

One of the most striking examples of Balzac's energy and facility of conception and execution in this line is the great gallery of portraits of the people who come to the party given by Madame de Bargeton, in "Les Illusions Perdues." These people are all mere supernumeraries; they appear but on this occasion, and having been marshalled forth in their living grotesqueness, they stand there simply to deepen the local colour about the central figure of Madame de Bargeton. When it lets itself loose among the strange social types that vegetate in silent corners of provincial towns, and of which an old and complex civilization, passing from phase to phase, leaves everywhere so thick a deposit, Balzac's imagination expands and revels and rejoices in its strength. In these cases it is sometimes kindly and tender and sympathetic; but as a general thing it is merciless in its irony and contempt. There is almost always, to us English readers, something cruel and wounding in French irony—something almost sanguinary in French caricature. To be ridiculous is made to appear like a crime and to deprive the unhappy victim of any right that an acute observer is bound to respect. The Dodson family, in George Eliot's "Mill on the Floss"—the illustrious stock from which Mrs. Glegg and Mrs. Pullet issue—are apparently a scantily mitigated mixture of the ridiculous and the disagreeable; and yet every reader of that admirable novel will remember how humanly, how generously these ladies are exhibited, and how in the author's treatment of them the highest sense of their absurdities never leads her to grudge them a particle of their freedom. In a single word, the picture is not invidious. Balzac, on the other hand, in corresponding pictures—pictures of small middle-class ignorance, narrowness, penury, poverty, dreariness, ugliness physical and mental—is always invidious. He grudges and hates and despises. These sentiments certainly often give a masterly force to his touch; but they deepen that sense, which he can so ill afford to have deepened, of the meagreness of his philosophy. It is very true that the "vie de province" of the "Comédie Humaine" is a terribly dreary and sordid affair; but, making every concession to the ignorant and self-complacent stupidity of the small French bourgeoisie during the Restoration and the reign of Louis Philippe, it is impossible to believe that a chronicler with a scent a little less rabidly suspicious of Philistinism would not have shown us this field in a somewhat rosier light. Like all French artists and men of letters, Balzac hated the bourgeoisie with an immitigable hatred, and more than most of his class he hated the provincial. All the reasons for this general attitude it would take us too far to seek; two of them, we think, are near the surface. Balzac and his comrades hate the bourgeois, in the first place, because the bourgeois hates them, and in the second place, because they are almost always fugitives from the bourgeoisie. They have escaped with their lives, and once in the opposite camp they turn and shake their fists and hurl defiance. Provincial life, as Balzac represents it, is a tissue of sordid economies and ignoble jealousies and fatuous tittle-tattle, in cold, musty, unlovely houses, in towns where the grass grows in the streets, where the passage of a stranger brings grotesquely eager faces to the window, where one or two impotently pretentious salons, night after night, exhibit a collection of human fossils. Here and there a brighter thread runs through the dusky web—we remember Véronique Tascheron, Eugénie Grandet, Marguerite Claës, Ursule Mirouët, David and Eve Séchard. White has a high picturesque value when properly distributed, and Balzac's innocent people, who are always more or less tragical dupes and victims, serve admirably to deepen the general effect of dreariness, stinginess and ferocious venality. With what a grasp of the baser social realities, with what energy and pathos and pictorial irony he has moulded these miseries and vices into living figures, it would be interesting to be able to exhibit in detail. It is grim economy that is always in the foreground—it is the clutch of the five franc piece that is the essence of every gesture. It is the miser Grandet, doling out the sugar lump by lump for the coffee of the household; it is that hideous she-wolf of thrift, Silvie Rogron, pinching and persecuting and starving little Pierrette Lorrain; it is the heirs male and female of Doctor Mirouët flocking to the reading of his will like vultures and hyenas.

Balzac's figures, as a general thing, are better than the use he makes of them; his touch, so unerring in portraiture and description, often goes wofully astray in narrative, in the conduct of a tale. Of all the great novelists, he is the weakest in talk; his conversations, if they are at all prolonged, become unnatural, impossible. One of his pupils, as they say in French, Charles de Bernard (who had, however, taken most justly the measure of his own talent, and never indiscreetly challenged comparison with the master)—this charming writer, with but a tenth of Balzac's weight and genius, very decidedly excels him in making his figures converse. It is not meant by this, however, that the story in Balzac is not generally powerfully conceived and full of dramatic stuff. Afraid of nothing as he was, he attacked all the deepest things in life and laid his hand upon every human passion. He has even—to be complete—described one or two passions that are usually deemed unmentionable. He always deals with a strong feeling in preference to a superficial one, and his great glory is that he pretended to take cognizance of man's moral nature to its deepest, most unillumined and, as the French say, most *scabreux* depths—that he maintained that for a writer who proposes seriously to illustrate the human soul there is absolutely no forbidden ground. He has never, that we remember, described what we call in English a flirtation, but he has described ardent love in a thousand forms (sometimes very well, sometimes horribly ill), with its clustering attributes of sensuality and jealousy, exaltation and despair, good and evil. It is hard to think of a virtue or a vice of which he has not given some eminent embodiment. The subject, in other words, is always solid and interesting; through his innumerable fallacies of form and style, of taste and art, that is always valuable. Some of his novels rise much above the others in this dignity and pregnancy of theme; M. Taine, in his essay, enumerates the most striking cases, and his sonorous echo of Balzac's tragic note is a tribute to our author's power. Balzac's masterpiece, to our own sense, if we must choose, is "Le Père Goriot." In this tale there is most of his characteristic felicity and least of his characteristic infelicity. Shakespeare had been before him, but there is excellent reason to believe that beyond knowing that "King Lear" was the history of a doting old man, buffeted and betrayed by cruel daughters, Balzac had not placed himself in a position to be accused of plagiarism. He had certainly not read the play in English, and nothing is more possible than that he had not read it in such French translations as existed in 1835. It would please him to have his reader believe that he has read everything in the world; but there are limits to the reader's good nature. "Le Père Goriot" holds so much, and in proportion to what it holds is, in comparison with its companions, so simple and compact, that it easily ranks among the few greatest novels we possess. Nowhere else is there such a picture of distracted paternal love, and of the battle between the voice of nature and the constant threat of society that you shall be left to rot by the roadside if you drop out of the ranks. In every novel of Balzac's, on the artistic line, there are the great intentions that fructify and the great intentions that fail. In "Le Père Goriot" the latter element, though perceptible, comes nearest to escaping notice. Balzac has painted a great number of "careers"; they begin in one story and are unfolded in a dozen others. He has a host of young men whom he takes up on the threshold of life, entangles conspicuously in the events of their time, makes the pivots of contemporaneous history. Some of them are soldiers, some men of letters, some artists; those he handles with most complacency are young men predestined by high birth to politics. These latter are, as a class, Balzac's most conspicuous failures, but they are also his most heroic attempts. The reader will remember De Marsay, De Trailles, Rastignac, the two Vandenesses, D'Esgrignon, Baudenord, Des Lupeaulx, Tillet, Blondet, Bridau, Nathan, Bixiou, Rubempré, Lousteau, D'Arthez. The man whose career is most distinctly traced is perhaps Eugène de Rastignac, whose first steps in life we witness in "Le Père Goriot." The picture is to some extent injured by Balzac's incurable fatuity and snobbishness; but the situation of the young man, well born, clever, and proud, who comes up to Paris, equipped by his family's savings, to seek his fortune and find it at any cost, and who moves from the edge of one social abyss to the edge of another (finding abysses in every shaded place he looks into) until at last his nerves are steeled, his head steadied, his conscience eased in cynicism and his pockets filled—all this bears a deep imaginative stamp. The *donnée* of "Le Père Goriot" is typical; the shabby Maison Vauquer, becoming the stage of vast dramas, is a sort of concentrated focus of human life, with sensitive nerves radiating out into the infinite. Then there is Madame d'Espard's attempt to prove that her excellent husband is insane and to have him sequestrated; and the Countess Ferraud, who repudiates her husband, when he reappears, crippled and penniless, after having been counted among the slain at the battle of Eylau; and Philippe Bridau, who bullies, sponges, swindles, bleeds his family to death to pay for his iniquities; Madame Marneffe, who drags an honourable family into desolation and ruin by the rapacity of her licentiousness, and the Baron Hulot d'Ervy, who sees his wife and children beggared and disgraced, and yet cannot give up Madame Marneffe; Victurnien d'Esgrignon, who comes up from Alençon to see the world, and sees it with a vengeance, so that he has to forge a note to pay for his curiosity, and his doting family have to beggar themselves to pay for his note; Madame de La Baudraye, who leaves her husband, burns her ships, and comes to live in Paris with an ignoble journalist, partly for the love of letters and partly for the love of the journalist himself; Lucien de Rubempré, who tries to be a great poet, and to give an airing, in the highest places, to the poetic temperament, and who, after irrecordable alternations of delight and of misery, hangs himself in a debtors' prison; Marguerite Claës, who finds her father turning monomaniac and melting down her patrimony, and her motherless brother's and sister's, in the crucible of alchemy, and who fights for years a hand-to-hand duel with him, at great cost to her natural tenderness and her reputation; Madame de Mortsauf, who, after years of mysterious anguish, dies broken hearted, between a brutal husband and a passionate lover, without ever having said a word to offend the one or, as she regards it, to encourage the other; poor Cousin Pons, the kindly virtuoso, who has made with years of patient labour a precious collection of pictures, and who is plundered, bullied, and morally murdered by rapacious relatives, and left without a penny to bury him.

It is the opinion of many of Balzac's admirers, and it was the general verdict of his day, that in all this the greatest triumphs are the characters of women. Every French critic tells us that his immense success came to him through women—that they constituted his first, his last, his fondest public. "Who rendered more deliciously than he," asks Sainte-Beuve, "the duchesses and viscountesses of the end of the Restoration—those women of thirty who, already on the stage, awaited their painter with a vague anxiety, so that when he and they stood face to face there was a sort of electric movement of recognition?" Balzac is supposed to have understood the feminine organism as no one had done before him—to have had the feminine heart, the feminine temperament, feminine nerves, at his fingers' ends—to have turned the feminine puppet, as it were, completely inside out. He has placed an immense number of women on the stage, and even those critics who are least satisfied with his most elaborate female portraits must at least admit that he has paid the originals the compliment to hold that they play an immense part in the world. It may be said, indeed, that women are the keystone of the "Comédie Humaine." If the men were taken out, there would be great gaps and fissures; if the women were taken out, the whole fabric would collapse. Balzac's superior handling of women seems to us to be both a truth and a fallacy; but his strength and weakness so intermingle and overlap that it is hard to keep a separate account with each.

His reader very soon perceives, to begin with, that he does not take that view of the sex that would commend him to the "female sympathizers" of the day. There is not a line in him that would not be received with hisses at any convention for giving women the suffrage, for introducing them into Harvard College, or for trimming the exuberances of their apparel. His restrictive remarks would be considered odious; his flattering remarks would be considered infamous. He takes the old-fashioned view—he recognises none but the old-fashioned categories. Woman is the female of man and in all respects his subordinate; she is pretty and ugly, virtuous and vicious, stupid and cunning. There is the great *métier de femme*—the most difficult perhaps in the world, so that to see it thoroughly mastered is peculiarly exhilarating. The *métier de femme* includes a great many branches, but they may be all summed up in the art of titillating in one way or another the senses of man. Woman has a "mission" certainly, and this is it. Man's capacity for entertainment fortunately is large, and he may be gratified along a far-stretching line; so that woman in this way has a very long rope and no reason to complain of want of liberty. Balzac's conception of what a woman may be and do is very comprehensive; there is no limit to her cleverness, her energy, her courage, her devotion; or, on the other hand, to her vices, her falsity, her meanness, her cruelty, her rapacity. But the great sign of Balzac's women is that in all these things the sexual quality is inordinately emphasized and the conscience on the whole inordinately sacrificed to it. It is an idea familiar to all novelists—it is indeed half their stock in trade—that women in good and in evil act almost exclusively from personal motives. Men do so often, the romancer says; women do so always. Balzac carries this idea infinitely farther than any other novelist, and imparts to the personal motive a peculiar narrowness and tenacity. It suggests the agility and the undulations, the claws and the venom, of the cat and the serpent. That perfectly immoral view of what people do, which we spoke of as one of his great characteristics, is supremely conspicuous in Balzac's dealings with his heroines. "Leur gros libertin de père," M. Taine calls him in relation to certain of them; and the phrase really applies to him in relation to all, even the purest and most elevated. It is their personal, physical quality that he relishes—their attitudes, their picturesqueness, the sense that they give him of playing always, sooner or later, into the hands of man—*gros libertin* that he naturally and inevitably is. He has drawn a great many women's figures that are nobly pure in intention; he has even attempted three or four absolute saints. But purity in Balzac's hands is apt to play us the strangest tricks. Madame Graslin is a saint who has been privy to the murder of her lover and who allows an innocent man to suffer the penalty of the law; Madame Hulot is a saint who at fifty (being very well preserved) offers herself to a man she loathes in order to procure money for her daughter's marriage portion; Madame de Mortsauf is a saint familiar with the most cynical views of life (*vide* her letter of advice to Félix de Vandenesse on his entering upon his career, in which the tone is that of a politician and shrewd man of the world) who drives about with her lover late at night, kissing his head and otherwise fondling him. Balzac's women—and indeed his characters in general—are best divided into the rich and the poor, the Parisians and the rustics. His most ambitious female portraits are in the former class—his most agreeable, and on the whole his most successful, in the latter. Here the women, young and old, are more or less grotesque, but the absence of the desire to assimilate them to the type of the indescribable monster whom Balzac enshrines in the most sacred altitudes of his imagination as the Parisienne, has allowed them to be more human and more consonant to what we, at least, of the Anglo-Saxon race, consider the comfortable social qualities in the gentler sex. Madame Bridau, Madame Grandet, Mademoiselle Cormon, Madame Séchard—these, in Balzac, are the most natural figures of good women. His imagination has easily comprehended them; they are homely and pious and *naïves*, and their horizon is bounded by the walls of their quiet houses. It is when Balzac enters the field of the great ladies and the courtesans that he is supposed to have won his greatest triumphs, the triumphs that placed all the women on his side and made them confess that they had found their prophet and their master. To this view of the matter the writer of these lines is far from assenting. He finds it impossible to understand that the painter of Louise de Chaulieu and Madame d'Espard, of Madame de La Baudraye and Madame de Bargeton, of Lady Dudley and Madame de Maufrigneuse, should not have made all the clever women of his time his enemies.

It is not however, certainly, that here his energy, his force of colour, his unapproached power of what the French call in analytic portrayal "rummaging"—to *fouiller*—are not at their highest. Never is he more himself than among his coquettes and courtesans, among Madame Schontz and Josépha, Madame Marneffe and Madame de Rochefide. "Balzac loves his Valérie," says M. Taine, speaking of his attitude toward the horrible Madame Marneffe, the depths of whose depravity he is so actively sounding; and paradoxical as it sounds it is perfectly true. She is, according to Balzac's theory of the matter, a consummate Parisienne, and the depravity of a Parisienne is to his sense a more remunerative spectacle than the virtue of any *provinciale*, whether her province be Normandy or Gascony, England or Germany. Never does he so let himself go as in these cases—never does his imagination work so at a heat. Feminine nerves, feminine furbelows, feminine luxury and subtlety, intoxicate and inspire him; he revels among his innumerable heroines like Mahomet in his paradise of houris. In saying just now that women could not complain of Balzac's restrictions upon their liberty, we had in mind especially the liberty of telling lies. This exquisite and elaborate mendacity he considers the great characteristic of the finished woman of the world, of Mesdames d'Espard, de Sérisy, de Langeais, de Maufrigneuse. The ladies just enumerated have all a great many lovers, a great many intrigues, a great many jealousies, a terrible entanglement of life behind the scenes. They are described as irresistibly charming, as *grandes dames* in the supreme sense of the word; clever, cold, self-possessed, ineffably elegant, holding salons, influencing politics and letting nothing interfere with their ambition, their coquetry, their need for money. Above all they are at swords' points with each other; society for them is a deadly battle for lovers, disguised in a tissue of caresses. To our own sense this whole series of figures is fit only to have a line drawn through it as a laborious and extravagant failure—a failure on which treasures of ingenuity have been expended, but which is perhaps on that account only the more provocative of smiles. These ladies altogether miss the mark; they are vitiated by that familiar foible which Thackeray commemorated in so many inimitable pages. Allusion was made in the earlier part of these remarks to Balzac's strong plebeian strain. It is no reproach to him; if he was of the "people," he was magnificently so; and if the people never produced anything less solid and sturdy it would need to fear no invidious comparisons. But there is something ineffably snobbish in his tone when he deals with the aristocracy, and in the tone which those members of it who circulate through his pages take from him. They are so conscious, so fatuous, so *poseurs*, so perpetually alluding to their grandeurs and their quarterings, so determined to be impertinent, so afraid they shall not be impertinent enough, so addicted to reminding you that they are not bourgeois, that they do not pay their debts or practise the vulgar virtues, that they really seem at times to be the creatures of the dreams of an ambitious hairdresser who should have been plying his curling-irons all day and reading fashionable novels all the evening. The refinement of purpose in Balzac, in everything that relates to the emphasis of the aristocratic tone, is often extraordinary; and to see such heroic ingenuity so squandered and dissipated gives us an alarming sense of what a man of genius may sometimes do in the way of not seeing himself as others see him. Madame d'Espard, when she has decided to "take up" her provincial *cousine*, Madame de Bargeton, conveys her one night to the opera. Lucien de Rubempré comes into the box and, by his provincial dandyism and ingenuous indiscretions, attracts some attention. A rival who is acquainted with the skeleton in his closet goes and tells Madame d'Espard's friends and enemies that he is not properly a De Rubempré (this being only his mother's name), and that his father was M. Chardon, a country apothecary. Then the traitor comes and announces this fact to Madame d'Espard and intimates that her neighbours know it. This great lady hereupon finds the situation intolerable, and informs her companion that it will never do to be seen at the opera with the son of an apothecary. The ladies, accordingly, beat a precipitate retreat, leaving Lucien the master of the field. The caste of Vere de Vere in this case certainly quite forgot its repose. But its conduct is quite of a piece with that of the young men of high fashion who, after Madame de Bargeton has been a fortnight in Paris (having come very ill-dressed from Angoulême) are seen to compliment her on the "metamorphosis of her appearance." What is one to say about Madame de Rochefide, a person of the highest condition, who has by way of decoration of her drawing-room a series of ten water-colour pictures representing the different bedrooms she has successively slept in? What Balzac says is that this performance "gave the measure of a superior impertinence"; and he evidently thinks that he has bestowed the crowning touch upon a very crushing physiognomy. What is here indicated of Balzac's great ladies is equally true of his young dandies and lions—his De Marsays and De Trailles. The truly initiated reader of the "Comédie Humaine" will always feel that he can afford to skip the page when he sees the name of De Marsay. Balzac's dandies are tremendous fellows from a picturesque point of view; the account of De Marsay in "La Fille aux Yeux d'Or" is an example of the "sumptuous" gone mad. Balzac leaves nothing vague in the destinies he shapes for these transcendant fops. Rastignac is prime minister of France, and yet Rastignac in his impecunious youth has been on those terms with Madame de Nucingen which characterized the relations of Tom Jones with Lady Bellaston. Fielding was careful not to make his hero a rival of Sir Robert Walpole. Balzac's young *gentils-hommes*, as possible historical figures, are completely out of the question. They represent, perhaps, more than anything else, the author's extraordinary union of vigour and shallowness. In this, however, they have much in common with several other classes of characters that we lack space to consider. There are the young girls (chiefly of the upper class) like Modeste Mignon and Louise de Chaulieu; there are the women of literary talent, like Mademoiselle des Touches and Madame de La Baudraye; there are the journalists, like Lousteau and Emile Blondet. In all these cases Balzac "rummages" with extraordinary ardour; but his faults of taste reach their maximum and offer us an incredible imbroglio of the superb and the ignoble. Mademoiselle de Chaulieu talks about her arms, her bosom, her hips, in a way to make a trooper blush. Lousteau, when a lady says a clever thing, tells her he will steal it from her for his newspaper and get two dollars. As regards Rubempré and Canalis, we have specimens of their poetry, but we have on the whole more information about their coats and trousers, their gloves and shirts and cosmetics.

In all this it may seem that there has been more talk about faults than about merits, and that if it is claimed that Balzac did a great work we should have plucked more flowers and fewer thistles. But the greatest thing in Balzac cannot be exhibited by specimens. It is Balzac himself—it is the whole attempt—it is the method. This last is his unsurpassed, his incomparable merit. That huge, all-compassing, all-desiring, all-devouring love of reality which was the source of so many of his fallacies and stains, of so much dead-weight in his work, was also the foundation of his extraordinary power. The real, for his imagination, had an authority that it has never had for any other. When he looks for it in the things in which we all feel it, he finds it with a marvellous certainty of eye, and proves himself the great novelist that he pretends to be. When he tries to make it prevail everywhere, explain everything and serve as a full measure of our imagination— then he becomes simply the greatest of dupes. He is an extraordinary tissue of contradictions. He is at once one of the most corrupt of writers and one of the most naïf, the most mechanical and pedantic, and the fullest of *bonhomie* and natural impulse. He is one of the finest of artists and one of the coarsest. Viewed in one way, his novels are ponderous, shapeless, overloaded; his touch is graceless, violent, barbarous. Viewed in another, his tales have more colour, more composition, more grasp of the reader's attention than any others. Balzac's style would demand a chapter apart. It is the least simple style, probably, that ever was written; it bristles, it cracks, it swells and swaggers; but it is a perfect expression of the man's genius. Like his genius, it contains a certain quantity of everything, from immaculate gold to flagrant dross. He was a very bad writer, and yet unquestionably he was a very great writer. We may say briefly, that in so far as his method was an instinct it was successful, and that in so far as it was a theory it was a failure. But both in instinct and in theory he had the aid of an immense force of conviction. His imagination warmed to its work so intensely that there was nothing his volition could not impose upon it. Hallucination settled upon him, and he believed anything that was necessary in the circumstances. This accounts for all his grotesque philosophies, his heroic attempts to furnish specimens of things of which he was profoundly ignorant. He believed that he was about as creative as the Deity, and that if mankind and human history were swept away the "Comédie Humaine" would be a perfectly adequate substitute for them. M. Taine says of him very happily that, after Shakespeare, he is our great magazine of documents on human nature. When Shakespeare is suggested we feel rather his differences from Shakespeare—feel how Shakespeare's characters stand out in the open air of the universe, while Balzac's are enclosed in a peculiar artificial atmosphere, musty in quality and limited in amount, which persuades itself with a sublime sincerity that it is a very sufficient infinite. But it is very true that Balzac may, like Shakespeare, be treated as a final authority upon human nature; and it is very probable that as time goes on he will be resorted to much less for entertainment, and more for instruction. He has against him that he lacks that slight but needful thing— charm. To feel how much he lacked it, you must read his prefaces, with their vanity, avidity, and garrulity, their gross revelation of his processes, of his squabbles with his publishers, their culinary atmosphere. But our last word about him is that he had incomparable power.

Galaxy, December 1875
Reprinted in *French Poets and Novelists*, 1878

Correspondance de H. de Balzac, 1819–1850, Paris: Calmann Lévy, 1876.

THE FIRST FEELING of the reader of the two volumes which have lately been published under the foregoing title is that he has almost done wrong to read them. He reproaches himself with having taken a shabby advantage of a person who is unable to defend himself. He feels as one who has broken open a cabinet or rummaged an old desk. The contents of Balzac's letters are so private, so personal, so exclusively his own affairs and those of no one else, that the generous critic constantly lays them down with a sort of dismay and asks himself in virtue of what peculiar privilege or what newly discovered principle it is that he is thus burying his nose in them. Of course he presently reflects that he has not broken open a cabinet nor violated a desk, but that these repositories have been very freely and confidently emptied into his lap. The two stout volumes of the "Correspondance de H. de Balzac, 1819–1850," lately put forth, are remarkable, like many other French books of the same sort, for the almost complete absence of editorial explanation or introduction. They have no visible sponsor, only a few insignificant lines of preface and the scantiest possible supply of notes. Such as the book is, in spite of its abruptness, we are thankful for it; in spite, too, of our bad conscience. What we mean by our bad conscience is the feeling with which we see the last remnant of charm, of the graceful and the agreeable, removed from Balzac's literary physiognomy. His works had not left much of this favouring shadow, but the present publication has let in the garish light of full publicity. The grossly, inveterately professional character of all his activity, the absence of leisure, of contemplation, of disinterested experience, the urgency of his consuming money-hunger—all this is rudely exposed. It is always a question whether we have a right to investigate a man's life for the sake of anything but his official utterances— his results. The picture of Balzac's career which is given in these letters is a record of little else but painful processes, unrelieved by reflections or speculations, by any moral or intellectual emanation. To prevent misconception, however, we hasten to add that they tell no disagreeable secrets; they contain nothing for the lovers of scandal. Balzac was a very honest man, but he was a man almost tragically uncomfortable, and the unsightly underside of his discomfort stares us full in the face. Still, if his personal portrait is without ideal beauty, it is by no means without a certain brightness, or at least a certain richness, of colouring. Huge literary ogre as he was, he was morally nothing of a monster. His heart was capacious, and his affections vigorous; he was powerful, coarse and kind.

The first letter in the series is addressed to his elder sister, Laure, who afterward became Madame de Surville, and who, after her illustrious brother's death, published in a small volume some agreeable reminiscences of him. For this lady he had, especially in his early years, a passionate affection. He had in 1819 come up to Paris from Touraine, in which province his family lived, to seek his fortune as a man of letters. The episode is a strange and gloomy one. His vocation for literature had not been favourably viewed at home, where money was scanty; but the parental consent, or rather the parental tolerance, was at last obtained for his experiment. The future author of the "Père Goriot" was at this time but twenty years of age, and in the way of symptoms of genius had nothing but a very robust self-confidence to show. His family, who had to contribute to his support while his masterpieces were a-making, appear to have regretted the absence of farther guarantees. He came to Paris, however, and lodged in a garret, where the allowance made him by his father kept him neither from shivering nor from nearly starving. The situation had been arranged in a way very characteristic of French manners. The fact that Honoré had gone to Paris was kept a secret from the friends of the family, who were told that he was on a visit to a cousin in the South. He was on probation, and if he failed to acquire literary renown his excursion should be hushed up. This pious fraud did not contribute to the comfort of the young scribbler, who was afraid to venture abroad by day lest he should be seen by an acquaintance of the family. Balzac must have been at this time miserably poor. If he goes to the theatre, he has to pay for the pleasure by fasting. He wishes to see Talma (having, to go to the play, to keep up the fiction of his being in the South, in a latticed box). "I shall end by giving in. . . . My stomach already trembles." Meanwhile he was planning a tragedy of "Cromwell," which came to nothing, and writing the "Héritière de Birague," his first novel, which he sold for one hundred and sixty dollars. Through these early letters, in spite of his chilly circumstances, there flows a current of youthful ardour, gaiety, and assurance. Some passages in his letters to his sister are a sort of explosion of animal spirits: "Ah, my sister, what torments it gives us—the love of glory! Long live grocers! they sell all day, count their gains in the evening, take their pleasure from time to time at some frightful melodrama—and behold them happy! Yes, but they pass their time between cheese and soap. Long live rather men of letters! Yes, but these are all beggars in pocket, and rich only in conceit. Well, let us leave them all alone, and long live every one!"

Elsewhere he scribbles: "Farewell, *soror*! I hope to have a letter *sororis*, to answer *sorori*, then to see *sororem*," &c. Later, after his sister is married, he addresses her as *"the box that contains everything pleasing; the elixir of virtue, grace, and beauty; the jewel, the phenomenon of Normandy; the pearl of Bayeux, the fairy of St. Lawrence, the virgin of the Rue Teinture, the guardian angel of Caen, the goddess of enchantments, the treasure of friendship."*

We shall continue to quote, without the fear of our examples exceeding, in the long run, our commentary. "Find me some widow, a rich heiress," he writes to his sister at Bayeux, whither her husband had taken her to live. "You know what I mean. Only brag about me. Twenty-two years old, a good fellow, good manners, a bright eye, fire, the best dough for a husband that heaven has ever kneaded. I will give you five per cent. on the dowry." "Since yesterday," he writes in another letter, "I have given up dowagers and have come down to widows of thirty. Send all you find to Lord Rhoone [this remarkable improvisation was one of his early *noms de plume*]; that's enough—he is known at the city limits. Take notice. They are to be sent prepaid, without crack or repair, and they are to be rich and amiable. Beauty isn't required. The varnish goes and the bottom of the pot remains!"

Like many other young men of ability, Balzac felt the little rubs—or the great ones—of family life. His mother figures largely in these volumes (she survived her glorious son), and from the scattered reflection of her idiosyncrasies the attentive reader constructs a sufficiently vivid portrait. She was the old middle-class Frenchwoman whom he has so often seen—devoted, active, meddlesome, parsimonious, exacting veneration and expending zeal. Honoré tells his sister that "the other day, coming back from Paris much bothered, it never occurred to me to thank *maman* for a black coat which she had had made for me; at my age one isn't particularly sensitive to such a present. Nevertheless, it would not have cost me much to seem touched by the attention, especially as it was a sacrifice. But I forgot it. *Maman* began to pout, and you know what her aspect and her face amount to at those moments. I fell from the clouds, and racked my brain to know what I had done. Happily Laurence [his younger sister] came and notified me, and two or three words as fine as amber mended *maman's* countenance. The thing is nothing—a mere drop of water; but it's to give you an example of our manners. Ah, we are a jolly set of originals in our holy family. What a pity I can't put us into novels!"

His father wished to find him an opening in some profession, and the thought of being made a notary was a bugbear to the young man: "Think of me as dead if they cap me with that extinguisher." And yet, in the next sentence he breaks out into a cry of desolate disgust at the aridity of his actual circumstances: "They call this mechanical rotation living—this perpetual return of the same things. If there were only something to throw some charm or other over my cold existence! I have none of the flowers of life, and yet I am in the season in which they bloom. What will be the use of fortune and pleasures when my youth has departed? What need of the garments of an actor if one no longer plays a part? An old man is a man who has dined and who watches others eat; and I, young as I am—my plate is empty, and I am hungry. Laure, Laure, my two only and immense desires, *to be famous and to be loved*—will they ever be satisfied?"

These occasional bursts of confidence in his early letters to his sister are (with the exception of certain excellent pages addressed in the last years of his life to the lady he eventually married) Balzac's most delicate, most emotional utterances. There is a touch of the ideal in them. Later one wonders where he keeps his ideal. He has one of course, artistically, but it never peeps out. He gives up talking sentiment and he never discusses "subjects"; he only talks business. Meanwhile, however, at this period business was increasing with him. He agrees to write three novels for eight hundred and twenty dollars. Here begins the inextricable mystery of Balzac's literary promises, pledges, projects, contracts. His letters form a swarming register of schemes and bargains through which he passes like a hero of the circus, riding half a dozen piebald coursers at once. We confess that in this matter we have been able to keep no sort of account; the wonder is that Balzac should have accomplished the feat himself. After the first year or two of his career we never see him working upon a single tale; his productions dovetail and overlap, dance attendance upon each other in the most bewildering fashion. As soon as one novel is fairly on the stocks he plunges into another, and while he is rummaging in this with one hand he stretches out an heroic arm and breaks ground in a third. His plans are always vastly in advance of his performance; his pages swarm with titles of books that were never to be written. The title circulates with such an assurance that we are amazed to find, fifty pages later, that there is no more of it than of the cherubic heads. With this, Balzac was constantly paid in advance by his publishers—paid for works not begun, or barely begun; and the money was as constantly spent before the equivalent had been delivered. Meanwhile more money was needed, and new novels were laid out to obtain it; but prior promises had first to be kept. Keeping them, under these circumstances, was not an exhilarating process; and readers familiar with Balzac will reflect with wonder that these were yet the circumstances in which some of his best tales were written. They were written, as it were, in the fading light, by a man who saw night coming on and yet could not afford to buy candles. He could only hurry. But Balzac's way of hurrying was all his own; it was a sternly methodical haste and might have been mistaken, in a more lightly-weighted genius, for elaborate trifling. The close texture of his work never relaxed; he went on doggedly and insistently, pressing it down and packing it together, multiplying erasures, alterations, repetitions, transforming proof-sheets, quarrelling with editors, enclosing subject within subject, accumulating notes upon notes.

The letters make a jump from 1822 to 1827, during which interval he had established, with borrowed capital, a printing house, and seen his enterprise completely fail. This failure saddled him with a mountain of debt which pressed upon him crushingly for years, and of which he rid himself only toward the close of his life. Balzac's debts are another labyrinth in which we do not profess to hold a clue. There is scarcely a page of these volumes in which they are not alluded to, but the reader never quite understands why they should bloom so perennially. The liabilities incurred by the collapse of the printing-scheme can hardly have been so vast as not to have been for the most part cancelled by ten years of heroic work. Balzac appears not to have been extravagant; he had neither wife nor children (unlike many of his comrades, he had no known illegitimate offspring), and when he admits us to a glimpse of his domestic economy we usually find it to be of a very meagre pattern. He writes to his sister in 1827 that he has not the means either to pay the postage of letters or to use omnibuses, and that he goes out as little as possible, so as not to wear out his clothes. In 1829, however, we find him in correspondence with a duchess, Madame d'Abrantès, the widow of Junot, Napoleon's rough marshal, and author of those voluminous memoirs upon the imperial court which it was the fashion to read in the early part of the century. The Duchesse d'Abrantès wrote bad novels, like Balzac himself at this period, and the two became good friends.

The year 1830 was the turning-point in Balzac's career. Renown, to which he had begun to lay siege in Paris in 1820, now at last began to show symptoms of self-surrender. Yet one of the strongest expressions of discontent and despair in the pages before us belongs to this brighter moment. It is also one of the finest passages: "Sacredieu, my good friend, I believe that literature, in the day we live in, is no better than the trade of a woman of the town, who prostitutes herself for a dollar. It leads to nothing. I have an itch to go off and wander and explore, make of my life a drama, risk my life; for, as for a few miserable years more or less! . . . Oh, when one looks at these great skies of a beautiful night, one is ready to unbutton——." But the modesty of the English tongue forbids us to translate the rest of the phrase. Dean Swift might have related how Balzac aspired to express his contempt for all the royalties of the earth. Now that he is in the country, he goes on, "I have been seeing real splendours, such as fine sound fruit and gilded insects; I have been quite turning philosopher, and if I happen to tread upon an anthill, I say, like that immortal Bonaparte, 'These creatures or men: what is it to Saturn, or Venus, or the North Star?' And then my philosopher comes down to scribble 'items' for a newspaper. *Proh pudor!* And so it seems to me that the ocean, a brig, and an English vessel to sink, if you must sink yourself to do it, are rather better than a writing-desk, a pen, and the Rue St. Denis."

But Balzac was fastened to the writing-desk. In 1831 he tells one of his correspondents that he is working fifteen or sixteen hours a day. Later, in 1837, he describes himself repeatedly as working eighteen hours out of the twenty-four. In the midst of all this (it seems singular) he found time for visions of public life, of political distinction. In a letter written in 1830 he gives a succinct statement of his political views, from which we learn that he approved of the French monarchy possessing a constitution, and of instruction being diffused among the lower orders. But he desired that the people should be kept "under the most powerful yoke possible," so that in spite of their instruction they should not become disorderly. It is fortunate, probably, both for Balzac and for France, that his political rôle was limited to the production of a certain number of forgotten editorials in newspapers; but we may be sure that his dreams of statesmanship were brilliant and audacious. Balzac indulged in no dreams that were not.

Some of his best letters are addressed to Madame Zulma Carraud, a lady whose acquaintance he had made through his sister Laure, of whom she was an intimate friend, and whose friendship (exerted almost wholly through letters, as she always lived in the country) appears to have been one of the brightest and most salutary influences of his life. He writes to her thus in 1832:—"There are vocations which we must obey, and something irresistible draws me on to glory and power. It is not a happy life. There is within me the worship of woman (*le culte de la femme*) and a need of love which has never been fully satisfied. Despairing of ever being loved and understood by such a woman as I have dreamed of, having met her only under one form, that of the heart, I throw myself into the tempestuous sphere of political passions and into the stormy and desiccating atmosphere of literary glory. I shall fail perhaps on both sides; but, believe me, if I have wished to live the life of the age itself, instead of running my course in happy obscurity, it is just because the pure happiness of mediocrity has failed me. When one has a fortune to make, it is better to make it great and illustrious; because, pain for pain, it is better to suffer in a high sphere than in a low one, and I prefer dagger-blows to pin-pricks." All this, though written at thirty years of age, is rather juvenile; there was to be much less of the "tempest" in Balzac's life than is here foreshadowed. He was tossed and shaken a great deal, as we all are, by the waves of the time, but he was too stoutly anchored at his work to feel the winds.

In 1832 "Louis Lambert" followed the "Peau de Chagrin,"

the first in the long list of his masterpieces. He describes "Louis Lambert" as "a work in which I have striven to rival Goethe and Byron, Faust and Manfred. I don't know whether I shall succeed, but the fourth volume of the 'Philosophical Tales' must be a last reply to my enemies and give the presentiment of an incontestable superiority. You must therefore forgive the poor artist his fatigue [he is writing to his sister] his discouragements, and especially his momentary detachment from any sort of interest that does not belong to his subject. 'Louis Lambert' has cost me so much work! To write this book I have had to read so many books! Some day or other, perhaps, it will throw science into new paths. If I had made it a purely learned work, it would have attracted the attention of thinkers, who now will not drop their eyes upon it. But if chance puts it into their hands, perhaps they will speak of it!" In this passage there is an immense deal of Balzac—of the great artist who was so capable at times of self-deceptive charlatanism. "Louis Lambert," as a whole, is now quite unreadable; it contains some admirable descriptions, but the "scientific" portion is mere fantastic verbiage. There is something extremely characteristic in the way Balzac speaks of its having been optional with him to make it a "purely learned" work. His pretentiousness was simply colossal, and there is nothing surprising in his wearing even the mask *en famille* (the letter we have just quoted from is, as we have said, to his sister); he wore it during his solitary fifteen-hours sessions in his study. But the same letter contains another passage, of a very different sort, which is in its way as characteristic:—"Yes, you are right. My progress is real, and my infernal courage will be rewarded. Persuade my mother of this too, dear sister; tell her to give me her patience in charity; her devotion will be laid up in her favour. One day, I hope, a little glory will pay her for everything. Poor mother, that imagination of hers which she has given me throws her for ever from north to south and from south to north. Such journeys tire us; I know it myself! Tell my mother that I love her as when I was a child. As I write you these lines my tears start—tears of tenderness and despair; for I feel the future and I need this devoted mother on the day of triumph! When shall I reach it? Take good care of our mother, Laure, for the present and the future. . . . Some day, when my works are unfolded, you will see that it must have taken many hours to think and write so many things; and then you will absolve me of everything that has displeased you, and you will excuse, not the selfishness of the man (the man has none), but the selfishness of the worker."

Nothing can be more touching than that; Balzac's natural affections were as robust as his genius and his physical nature. The impression of the reader of his letters quite confirms his assurance that the man proper had no selfishness. Only we are constantly reminded that the man had almost wholly resolved himself into the worker, and we remember a statement of Sainte-Beuve's, in one of his malignant foot-notes, to the effect that Balzac was "the grossest, greediest example of literary vanity that he had ever known"— *l'amour-propre littéraire le plus avide et le plus grossier que j'aie connu*. When we think of what Sainte-Beuve must have known in this line these few words acquire a portentous weight.

By this time (1832) Balzac was, in French phrase, thoroughly *lancé*. He was doing, among other things, some of his most brilliant work, certain of the "Contes Drôlatiques." These were written, as he tells his mother, for relaxation, as a rest from harder labour. One would have said that no work could have been much harder than concocting the marvellously successful imitation of mediæval French in which these tales are written. He had, however, other diversions as well. In the autumn of 1832 he was at Aix-les-Bains with the Duchesse de Castries, a great lady and one of his kindest friends. He has been accused of drawing portraits of great ladies without knowledge of originals; but Madame de Castries was an inexhaustible fund of instruction upon this subject. Three or four years later, speaking of the story of the "Duchesse de Laugeais" to one of his correspondents, another *femme du monde*, he tells her that as a *femme du monde* she is not to pretend to find flaws in the picture, a high authority having read the proofs for the express purpose of removing them. The authority is evidently the Duchesse de Castries.

Balzac writes to Madame Carraud from Aix: "At Lyons I corrected 'Lambert' again. I licked my cub, like a she-bear. . . . On the whole, I am satisfied; it is a work of profound melancholy and of science. Truly, I deserve to have a mistress, and my sorrow at not having one increases daily; for love is my life and my essence. . . . I have a simple little room," he goes on, "from which I see the whole valley. I rise pitilessly at five o'clock in the morning and work before my window until half-past five in the evening. My breakfast comes from the club—an egg. Madame de Castries has good coffee made for me. At six o'clock we dine together and I pass the evening with her. She is the finest type (*le type le plus fin*) of woman; Madame de Beauséant [from "Le Père Goriot"] improved; only, are not all these pretty manners acquired at the expense of the soul?"

During his stay at Aix he met an excellent opportunity to go to Italy; the Duc de Fitz-James, who was travelling southward, invited him to become a member of his party. He discusses the economical problem (in writing to his mother) with his usual intensity, and throws what will seem to the modern traveller the light of enchantment upon that golden age of cheapness. Occupying the fourth place in the carriage of the Duchesse de Castries, his quarter of the total travelling expenses from Geneva to Rome (carriage, beds, food, &c.) was to be fifty dollars! But he was ultimately prevented from joining the party. He went to Italy some years later.

He mentions, in 1833, that the chapter entitled "Juana," in the superb tale of "Les Marana," as also the story of "La Grenadière," was written in a single night. He gives at the same period this account of his habits of work: "I must tell you that I am up to my neck in excessive work. My life is mechanically arranged. I go to bed at six or seven in the evening, with the chickens; I wake up at one in the morning and work till eight; then I take something light, a cup of pure coffee, and get into the shafts of my cab until four; I receive, I take a bath, or I go out, and after dinner I go to bed. I must lead this life for some months longer, in order not to be overwhelmed by my obligations. The profit comes slowly; my debts are inexorable and fixed. Now, it is certain that I will make a great fortune; but I must wait for it, and work for three years. I must go over things, correct them again, put everything *à l'état monumental*; thankless work not counted, without immediate profit." He speaks of working at this amazing rate for three years longer; in reality he worked for fifteen. But two years after the declaration we have just quoted it seemed to him that he should break down: "My poor sister, I am draining the cup to the dregs. It is in vain that I work my fourteen hours a day; I cannot do enough. While I write this to you I find myself so weary that I have just sent Auguste to take back my word from certain engagements that I had formed. I am so weak that I have advanced my dinner-hour in order to go to bed earlier; and I go nowhere." The next year he writes to his mother, who had apparently complained of his silence: "My good mother, do me the charity to let me carry my burden without suspecting my heart. A letter, for me, you see, is not only money, but an hour of sleep and a drop of blood."

We spoke just now of Balzac's sentimental consolations; but it appears that at times he was more acutely conscious of what he missed than of what he enjoyed. "As for the soul," he writes to Madame Carraud in 1833, "I am profoundly sad. My work alone sustains me in life. Is there then to be no woman for me in this world? My physical melancholy and ennui last longer and grow more frequent. To fall from this crushing labour to nothing—not to have near me that soft, caressing mind of woman, for whom I have done so much!" He had, however, a devoted feminine friend, to whom none of the letters in these volumes are addressed, but who is several times alluded to. This lady, Madame de Berny, died in 1836, and Balzac speaks of her ever afterward with extraordinary tenderness and veneration. But if there had been a passion between them it was only a passionate friendship. "Ah, my dear mother," he writes on New Year's day, 1836, "I am harrowed with grief. Madame de Berny is dying; it is impossible to doubt it. No one but God and myself knows what my despair is. And I must work—work while I weep!" He writes of Madame de Berny at the time of her death as follows. The letter is addressed to a lady with whom he was in correspondence more or less sentimental, but whom he never saw: "The person whom I have lost was more than a mother, more than a friend, more than any creature can be for another. The term *divinity* only can explain her. She had sustained me by word, by act, by devotion, during my worst weather. If I live, it is by her; she was everything for me. Although for two years illness and time had separated us, we were visible at a distance for each other. She reacted upon me; she was a moral sun. Madame de Mortsauf, in the 'Lys dans la Vallée,' is a pale expression of this person's slightest qualities." Three years afterward he writes to his sister: "I am alone against all my troubles, and formerly, to help me to resist them, I had with me the sweetest and bravest person in the world; a woman who every day is born again in my heart, and whose divine qualities make the friendships that are compared with hers seem pale. I have now no adviser in my literary difficulties; I have no guide but the fatal thought, 'What would she say if she were living?'" And he goes on to enumerate some of his actual and potential friends. He tells his sister that she herself might have been for him a close intellectual comrade if her duties of wife and mother had not given her too many other things to think about. The same is true of Madame Carraud: "Never has a more extraordinary mind been more smothered: she will die in her corner unknown! George Sand," he continues, "would speedily be my friend; she has no pettiness whatever in her soul—none of the low jealousies that obscure so many contemporary talents. Dumas resembles her in this; but she has not the critical sense. Madame Hanska is all this; but I cannot weigh upon her destiny." Madame Hanska was the Polish lady whom he ultimately married and of whom we shall speak. Meanwhile, for a couple of years (1836 and 1837), he carried on an exchange of opinions, of the order that the French call *intimes*, with the unseen correspondent to whom we have alluded, and who figures in these volumes as "Louise." The letters, however, are not love-letters; Balzac, indeed, seems chiefly occupied in calming the ardour of the lady, who was evidently a woman of social distinction. "Don't have any friendship for me," he writes; "I need too much. Like all people who struggle, suffer, and work, I am exacting, mistrustful, wilful, capricious. . . . If I had been a woman, I should have loved nothing so much as some soul buried like a well in the desert—discovered only when you place yourself directly under the star which indicates it to the thirsty Arab."

His first letter to Madame Hanska here given bears the date

of 1835; but we are informed in a note that he had at that moment been for some time in correspondence with her. The correspondence had begun, if we are not mistaken, on Madame Hanska's side, before they met; she had written to him as a literary admirer. She was a Polish lady of great fortune, with an invalid husband. After her husband's death, projects of marriage defined themselves more vividly, but practical considerations kept them for a long time in the background. Balzac had first to pay off his debts, and Madame Hanska, as a Polish subject of the Czar Nicholas, was not in a position to marry from one day to another. The growth of their intimacy is, however, amply reflected in these volumes, and the dénoûment presents itself with a certain dramatic force. Balzac's letters to his future wife, as to every one else, deal almost exclusively with his financial situation. He discusses the details of this matter with all his correspondents, who apparently have—or are expected to have—his monetary entanglements at their fingers' ends. It is a constant enumeration of novels and tales begun or delivered, revised or bargained for. The tone is always profoundly sombre and bitter. The reader's general impression is that of lugubrious egotism. It is the rarest thing in the world that there is an allusion to anything but Balzac's own affairs, and the most sordid details of his own affairs. Hardly an echo of the life of his time, of the world he lived in, finds its way into his letters; there are no anecdotes, no impressions, no opinions, no descriptions, no allusions to things heard, people seen, emotions felt—other emotions, at least, than those of the exhausted or the exultant worker. The reason of all this is of course very obvious. A man could not be such a worker as Balzac and be much else besides. The note of animal spirits which we observed in his early letters is sounded much less frequently as time goes on; although the extraordinary robustness and exuberance of his temperament plays richly into his books. The "Contes Drôlatiques" are full of it and his conversation was also full of it. But the letters constantly show us a man with the edge of his spontaneity gone—a man groaning and sighing as from Promethean lungs, complaining of his tasks, denouncing his enemies, in complete ill humour, generally, with life. Of any expression of enjoyment of the world, of the beauties of

nature, art, literature, history, human character, these pages
are singularly destitute. And yet we know that such enjoyment
—instinctive, unreasoning, essential—is half the inspiration of
the poet. The truth is that Balzac was as little as possible of a
poet; he often speaks of himself as one, but he deserved the
name as little as his own Canalis or his own Rubempré. He
was neither a poet nor a moralist, though the latter title in
France is often bestowed upon him—a fact which strikingly
helps to illustrate the Gallic lightness of soil in the moral region. Balzac was the hardest and deepest of *prosateurs*; the
earth-scented facts of life, which the poet puts under his feet,
he had put above his head. Obviously there went on within
him a large and constant intellectual unfolding. His mind
must have had a history of its own—a history of which it
would be very interesting to have an occasional glimpse. But
the history is not related here, even in glimpses. His books
are full of ideas; his letters have almost none. It is probably
not unfair to argue from this fact that there were few ideas
that he greatly cared for. Making all allowance for the pressure and tyranny of circumstances, we may believe that if he
had greatly cared to *se recueillir*, as the French say—greatly
cared, in the Miltonic phrase, "to interpose a little ease"—he
would sometimes have found an opportunity for it. Perpetual
work, when it is joyous and salubrious, is a very fine thing;
but perpetual work, when it is executed with the temper
which more than half the time appears to have been Balzac's,
has in it something almost debasing. We constantly feel that
his work would have been greatly better if the Muse of "business" had been elbowed away by her larger-browed sister.
Balzac himself, doubtless, often felt in the same way; but, on
the whole, "business" was what he most cared for. The "Comédie Humaine" represents an immense amount of joy, of
spontaneity, of irrepressible artistic life. Here and there in the
letters this occasionally breaks out in accents of mingled exultation and despair. "Never," he writes in 1836, "has the tor-
rent which bears me along been more rapid; never has a work
more majestically terrible imposed itself upon the human
brain. I go to my work as the gamester to the gaming-table;
I am sleeping now only five hours and working eighteen; I
shall arrive dead. . . . Write to me; be generous; take noth-

ing in bad part, for you don't know how, at moments, I deplore this life of fire. But how can I jump out of the chariot?" We have already had occasion in these pages to say that his great characteristic, far from being a passion for ideas, was a passion for *things*. We said just now that his books are full of ideas; but we must add that his letters make us feel that these ideas are themselves in a certain sense "things." They are pigments, properties, frippery; they are always concrete and available. Balzac cared for them only if they would fit into his inkstand.

He never jumped out of his chariot; but as the years went on he was able at times to let the reins hang more loosely. There is no evidence that he made the great fortune he had looked forward to; but he must have made a great deal of money. In the beginning his work was very poorly paid, but after his reputation was solidly established he received large sums. It is true that they were swallowed up in great part by his "debts"—that dusky, vaguely outlined, insatiable maw which we see grimacing for ever behind him, like the face on a fountain which should find itself receiving a stream instead of giving it out. But he travelled (working all the while en route). He went to Italy, to Germany, to Russia; he built houses, he bought pictures and pottery. One of his journeys illustrates his singular mixture of economic and romantic impulses. He made a breathless pilgrimage to the island of Sardinia to examine the scoriæ of certain silver mines, anciently worked by the Romans, in which he had heard that the metal was still to be found. The enterprise was fantastic and impracticable; but he pushed his excursion through night and day, as he had written the "Père Goriot." In his relative prosperity, when once it was established, there are strange lapses and stumbling-places. After he had built and was living in his somewhat fantastical villa of Les Jardies at Sèvres, close to Paris, he invites a friend to stay with him on these terms: "I can take you to board at forty sous a day, and for thirty-five francs you will have fire-wood enough for a month." In his jokes he is apt to betray the same preoccupation. Inviting Charles de Bernard and his wife to come to Les Jardies to help him to arrange his books, he adds that they will have fifty sous a day and their wine. He is constantly talking of his

expenses, of what he spends in cab-hire and postage. His letters to the Countess Hanska are filled with these details. "Yesterday I was running about all day; twenty-five francs for
carriages!" The man of business is never absent. For the first
representations of his plays he arranges his audiences with an
eye to effect, like an *impresario* or an agent. In the boxes, for
"Vautrin," "I insist upon there being handsome women." Presenting a copy of the "Comédie Humaine" to the Austrian
ambassador, he accompanies it with a letter calling attention,
in the most elaborate manner, to the typographical beauty
and the cheapness of the work; the letter reads like a prospec-
tus or an advertisement.

In 1840 (he was forty years old) he thought seriously of
marriage—with this remark as the preface to the announcement: "*Je ne veux plus avoir de cœur!* . . . If you meet a young
girl of twenty-two," he goes on, " with a fortune of 200,000
francs, or even of 100,000, provided it can be used in business, you will think of me. I want a woman who shall be able
to be what the events of my life may demand of her—the
wife of an ambassador or a housewife at Les Jardies. But
don't speak of this; it's a secret. She must be an ambitious,
clever girl." This project, however, was not carried out; Balzac had no time to marry. But his friendship with Madame
Hanska became more and more absorbing, and though their
project of marriage, which was executed in 1850, was kept a
profound secret until after the ceremony, it is apparent that
they had had it a long time in their thoughts.

For this lady Balzac's esteem and admiration seem to have
been unbounded; and his letters to her, which in the second
volume are very numerous, contain many noble and delicate
passages. "You know too well," he says to her somewhere,
with a happy choice of words—for his diction was here and
there as felicitous as it was generally intolerable—"*Vous savez
trop bien que tout ce qui n'est pas vous n'est que surface, sottise et
vains palliatifs de l'absence.*" "You must be proud of your children," he writes to his sister from Poland: "such daughters
are the recompense of your life. You must not be unjust to
destiny; you may now accept many misfortunes. It is like myself with Madame Hanska. The gift of her affection explains
all my troubles, my weariness and my toil; I was paying to

evil, in advance, the price of such a treasure. As Napoleon said, we pay for everything here below; nothing is stolen. It seems to me that I have paid very little. Twenty-five years of toil and struggle are nothing as the purchase-money of an attachment so splendid, so radiant, so complete."

Madame Hanska appears to have come rarely to Paris, and, when she came, to have shrouded her visits in mystery; but Balzac arranged several meetings with her abroad and visited her at St. Petersburg and on her Polish estates. He was devotedly fond of her children, and the tranquil, opulent family life to which she introduced him appears to have been one of the greatest pleasures he had known. In several passages which, for Balzac, may be called graceful and playful, he expresses his homesickness for her chairs and tables, her books, the sight of her dresses. Here is something, in one of his letters to her, that is worth quoting: "In short, this is the game that I play; four men will have had, in this century, an immense influence—Napoleon, Cuvier, O'Connell. I should like to be the fourth. The first lived on the blood of Europe; *il s'est inoculé des armées*; the second espoused the globe; the third became the incarnation of a people; I—I shall have carried a whole society in my head. But there will have been in me a much greater and much happier being than the writer— and that is your slave. My feeling is finer, grander, more complete, than all the satisfactions of vanity or of glory. Without this plenitude of the heart I should never have accomplished the tenth part of my work; I should not have had this ferocious courage." During a few days spent at Berlin, on his way back from St. Petersburg, he gives his impressions of the "capital of Brandenburg" in a tone which almost seems to denote a prevision of the style of allusion to this locality and its inhabitants which was to become fashionable among his countrymen thirty years later. Balzac detested Prussia and the Prussians. "It is owing to this charlatanism [the spacious distribution of the streets, &c.] that Berlin has a more populous look than Petersburg; I would have said 'more animated' look if I had been speaking of another people; but the Prussian, with his brutal heaviness, will never be able to do anything but crush. To produce the movement of a great European capital you must have less beer and bad tobacco and more of the French or Italian spirit; or else you must have the great industrial and commercial ideas which have produced the gigantic development of London; but Berlin and its inhabitants will never be anything but an ugly little city, inhabited by an ugly big people."

"I have seen Tieck *en famille*," he says in another letter. "He seemed pleased with my homage. He had an old countess, his contemporary in spectacles, almost an octogenarian—a mummy with a green eye-shade, whom I supposed to be a domestic divinity. . . . I am at home again; it is half-past six in the evening, and I have eaten nothing since this morning. Berlin is the city of ennui; I should die here in a week. Poor Humboldt is dying of it; he drags with him everywhere his nostalgia for Paris."

Balzac passed the winter of 1848–'49 and several months more at Vierzschovnia, the Polish estate of Madame Hanska and her children. His health had been gravely impaired, and the doctors had absolutely forbidden him to work. His inexhaustible and indefatigable brain had at last succumbed to fatigue. But the prize was gained; his debts were paid; he was looking forward to owning at last the money that he made. He could afford—relatively speaking at least—to rest. His fame had been solidly built up; the public recognised his greatness. Already, in 1846, he had written:—"You will learn with pleasure, I am sure, that there is an immense reaction in my favour. At last I have conquered! Once more my protecting star has watched over me. . . . At this moment the public and the papers turn toward me favourably; more than that, there is a sort of acclamation, a general consecration. . . . It is a great year for me, dear Countess."

To be ill and kept from work was, for Balzac, to be a chained Prometheus; but there was much during these last months to alleviate his impatience. His letters at this period are easier, less painfully preoccupied than at any other; and he found in Poland better medical advice than he deemed obtainable in Paris. He was preparing a house in Paris to receive him as a married man—preparing it apparently with great splendour. At Les Jardies the pictures and divans and tapestries had mostly been nominal—had been present only in grand names, chalked grotesquely upon the empty walls. But during the last years of his life Balzac appears to have been a great collector. He bought many pictures and other objects of value; in particular there figures in these letters a certain set of Florentine furniture which he was willing to sell again, but to sell only to a royal purchaser. The King of Holland appears to have been in treaty for it. Readers of the "Comédie Humaine" have no need to be reminded of the author's passion for furniture; nowhere else are there such loving or such invidious descriptions of it. "Decidedly," he writes once to Madame Hanska, "I will send to Tours for the Louis XVI. secretary and bureau; the room will then be complete. It's a matter of a thousand francs; but for a thousand francs what can one get in modern furniture? *Des platitudes bourgeoises, des misères sans valeur et sans goût.*"

Old Madame de Balzac was her son's factotum and universal agent. His letters from Vierzschovnia are filled with prescriptions of activity for his mother, accompanied always with the urgent reminder that she is to use cabs *ad libitum*. He goes into the minutest details (she was overlooking the preparation of his house in the Rue Fortunée, which must have been converted into a very picturesque residence):—"The carpet in the dining-room must certainly be readjusted. Try and make M. Henry send his carpet-layer. I owe that man a good *pour-boire*: he laid all the carpets, and I once was rough with him. You must tell him that in September he can come and get his present. I want particularly to give it to him myself."

His mother occasionally annoyed him by unreasonable exactions and untimely interferences. There is an episode of a letter which she writes to him at Vierzschovnia, and which, coming to Madame Hanska's knowledge, endangers his prospect of marriage. He complains bitterly to his sister that his mother cannot get it out of her head that he is still fifteen years old. But there is something very touching in his constant tenderness toward her—as well as something very characteristically French—very characteristic of the French sentiment of family consistency and solidarity—in the way in which, by constantly counting upon her practical aptitude and zeal, he makes her a fellow-worker toward the great total of his fame and fortune. At fifty years of age, at the climax of his distinction, announcing to her his brilliant marriage, he signs himself *Ton fils soumis*. To his old friend Madame Carraud he speaks thus of this same event: "The dénoûment of that great and beautiful drama of the heart which has lasted these sixteen years. . . . Three days ago I married the only woman I have loved, whom I love more than ever, and whom I shall love until death. I believe that this union is the recompense that God has held in reserve for me through so many adversities, years of work, difficulties suffered and surmounted. I had neither a happy youth nor a flowering spring; I shall have the most brilliant summer, the sweetest of all autumns." It had been, as Balzac says, a drama of the heart, and the dénoûment was of the heart alone. Madame Hanska, on her marriage, made over her large fortune to her children.

Balzac had at last found rest and happiness, but his enjoyment of these blessings was brief. The energy that he had expended to gain them left nothing behind it. His terrible industry had blasted the soil it passed over; he had sacrificed to his work the very things he worked for. One cannot do what Balzac did and live. He was enfeebled, exhausted, broken. He died in Paris three months after his marriage. The reader feels that premature death is the logical, the harmonious, completion of such a career. The strongest man has but a certain fixed quantity of life to expend, and we may expect that if he works habitually fifteen hours a day, he will spend it while, arithmetically speaking, he is yet young.

We have been struck in reading these letters with the strong analogy between Balzac's career and that of the great English writer whose history was some time since so expansively written by Mr. Forster. Dickens and Balzac have much in common; as individuals they strongly resemble each other; their differences are chiefly differences of race. Each was a man of affairs, an active, practical man, with a temperament of almost phenomenal vigour and a prodigious quantity of life to expend. Each had a character and a will—what is nowadays called a personality—that imposed themselves irresistibly; each had a boundless self-confidence and a magnificent egotism. Each had always a hundred irons on the fire; each was resolutely determined to make money, and made it in large quantities. In intensity of imaginative power, the power of evoking visible objects and figures, seeing them themselves with the force of hallucination and making others see them all but just as vividly, they were almost equal. Here there is little to choose between them; they have had no rivals but each other and Shakespeare. But they most of all resemble each other in the fact that they treated their extraordinary imaginative force as a matter of business; that they worked it as a gold-mine, violently and brutally; overworked and ravaged it. They succumbed to the task that they had laid upon themselves and they are as similar in their deaths as in their lives. Of course, if Dickens is an English Balzac, he is a very English Balzac. His fortune was the easier of the two and his prizes were greater than the other's. His brilliant, opulent English prosperity, centered in a home and diffused through a progeny, is in strong contrast with the almost scholastic penury and obscurity of much of Balzac's career. But the analogy is still very striking.

In speaking of Balzac elsewhere in these pages we insisted upon the fact that he lacked charm; but we said that our last word upon him should be that he had incomparable power. His letters only confirm these impressions, and above all they deepen our sense of his strength. They contain little that is delicate and not a great deal that is positively agreeable; but they express an energy before which we stand lost in wonder, in an admiration that almost amounts to awe. The fact that his omnivorous observation of the great human spectacle has no echo in his letters only makes us feel how concentrated and how intense was the labour that went on in his closet. Certainly no solider intellectual work has ever been achieved by man. And in spite of the massive egotism, the personal absoluteness, to which these pages testify, they leave us with a downright kindness for the author. He was coarse, but he was tender; he was corrupt, in a way, but he was immensely natural. If he was ungracefully eager and voracious, awkwardly blind to all things that did not contribute to his personal plan, at least his egotism was exerted in a great cause.

The "Comédie Humaine" has a thousand faults, but it is a monumental excuse.

Galaxy, February 1877
Reprinted under the title "Balzac's Letters" in
French Poets and Novelists, 1878

HONORÉ DE BALZAC, 1902

I

STRONGER THAN EVER, even than under the spell of first acquaintance and of the early time, is the sense—thanks to a renewal of intimacy and, I am tempted to say, of loyalty—that Balzac stands signally apart, that he is the first and foremost member of his craft, and that above all the Balzac-lover is in no position till he has cleared the ground by saying so. The Balzac-lover alone, for that matter, is worthy to have his word on so happy an occasion as this[1] about the author of "La Comédie Humaine," and it is indeed not easy to see how the amount of attention so inevitably induced could at the worst have failed to find itself turning to an act of homage. I have been deeply affected, to be frank, by the mere refreshment of memory, which has brought in its train moreover consequences critical and sentimental too numerous to figure here in their completeness. The authors and the books that have, as we say, done something for us, become part of the answer to our curiosity when our curiosity had the freshness of youth, these particular agents exist for us, with the lapse of time, as the substance itself of knowledge: they have been intellectually so swallowed, digested and assimilated that we take their general use and suggestion for granted, cease to be aware of them because they have passed out of sight. But they have passed out of sight simply by having passed into our lives. They have become a part of our personal history, a part of ourselves, very often, so far as we may have succeeded in best expressing ourselves. Endless, however, are the uses of great persons and great things, and it may easily happen in these cases that the connection, even as an "excitement"—the

---

[1] The appearance of a translation of the "Deux Jeunes Mariées" in A Century of French Romance.

form mainly of the connections of youth—is never really broken. We have largely been living on our benefactor—which is the highest acknowledgment one can make; only, thanks to a blest law that operates in the long run to rekindle excitement, we are accessible to the sense of having neglected him. Even when we may not constantly have read him over the neglect is quite an illusion, but the illusion perhaps prepares us for the finest emotion we are to have owed to the acquaintance. Without having abandoned or denied our author we yet come expressly back to him, and if not quite in tatters and in penitence like the Prodigal Son, with something at all events of the tenderness with which we revert to the parental threshold and hearthstone, if not, more fortunately, to the parental presence. The beauty of this adventure, that of seeing the dust blown off a relation that had been put away as on a shelf, almost out of reach, at the back of one's mind, consists in finding the precious object not only fresh and intact, but with its firm lacquer still further figured, gilded and enriched. It is all overscored with traces and impressions—vivid, definite, almost as valuable as itself—of the recognitions and agitations it originally produced in us. Our old—that is our young—feelings are very nearly what page after page most gives us. The case has become a case of authority *plus* association. If Balzac in himself is indubitably wanting in the sufficiently common felicity we know as charm, it is this association that may on occasion contribute the grace.

The impression then, confirmed and brightened, is of the mass and weight of the figure and of the extent of ground it occupies; a tract on which we might all of us together quite pitch our little tents, open our little booths, deal in our little wares, and not materially either diminish the area or impede the circulation of the occupant. I seem to see him in such an image moving about as Gulliver among the pigmies, and not less good-natured than Gulliver for the exercise of any function, without exception, that can illustrate his larger life. The first and the last word about the author of "Les Contes Drolatiques" is that of all novelists he is the most serious—by which I am far from meaning that in the human comedy as he shows it the comic is an absent quantity. His sense of the comic was on the scale of his extraordinary senses in general,

though his expression of it suffers perhaps exceptionally from
that odd want of elbow-room—the penalty somehow of his
close-packed, pressed-down contents—which reminds us of
some designedly beautiful thing but half-disengaged from the
clay or the marble. It is the scheme and the scope that are
supreme in him, applying this moreover not to mere great
intention, but to the concrete form, the proved case, in which
we possess them. We most of us aspire to achieve at the best
but a patch here and there, to pluck a sprig or a single branch,
to break ground in a corner of the great garden of life. Balzac's plan was simply to do everything that could be done.
He proposed to himself to "turn over" the great garden from
north to south and from east to west; a task—immense, heroic, to this day immeasurable—that he bequeathed us the
partial performance of, a prodigious ragged clod, in the
twenty monstrous years representing his productive career,
years of concentration and sacrifice the vision of which still
makes us ache. He had indeed a striking good fortune, the
only one he was to enjoy as an harrassed and exasperated
worker: the great garden of life presented itself to him absolutely and exactly in the guise of the great garden of France, a
subject vast and comprehensive enough, yet with definite edges
and corners. This identity of his universal with his local and
national vision is the particular thing we should doubtless call
his greatest strength were we preparing agreeably to speak of
it also as his visible weakness. Of Balzac's weaknesses, however, it takes some assurance to talk; there is always plenty of
time for them; they are the last signs we know him by—such
things truly as in other painters of manners often come under
the head of mere exuberance of energy. So little in short do they
earn the invidious name even when we feel them as defects.

What he did above all was to read the universe, as hard and
as loud as he could, *into* the France of his time; his own eyes
regarding his work as at once the drama of man and a mirror
of the mass of social phenomena the most rounded and registered, most organised and administered, and thereby most
exposed to systematic observation and portrayal, that the
world had seen. There are happily other interesting societies,
but these are for schemes of such an order comparatively
loose and incoherent, with more extent and perhaps more va-

riety, but with less of the great enclosed and exhibited quality, less neatness and sharpness of arrangement, fewer categories, subdivisions, juxtapositions. Balzac's France was both inspiring enough for an immense prose epic and reducible enough for a report or a chart. To allow his achievement all its dignity we should doubtless say also treatable enough for a history, since it was as a patient historian, a Benedictine of the actual, the living painter of his living time, that he regarded himself and handled his material. All painters of manners and fashions, if we will, are historians, even when they least don the uniform: Fielding, Dickens, Thackeray, George Eliot, Hawthorne among ourselves. But the great difference between the great Frenchman and the eminent others is that, with an imagination of the highest power, an unequalled intensity of vision, he saw his subject in the light of science as well, in the light of the bearing of all its parts on each other, and under pressure of a passion for exactitude, an appetite, the appetite of an ogre, for *all* the kinds of facts. We find I think in the union here suggested something like the truth about his genius, the nearest approach to a final account of him. Of imagination on one side all compact, he was on the other an insatiable reporter of the immediate, the material, the current combination, and perpetually moved by the historian's impulse to fix, preserve and explain them. One asks one's self as one reads him what concern the poet has with so much arithmetic and so much criticism, so many statistics and documents, what concern the critic and the economist have with so many passions, characters and adventures. The contradiction is always before us; it springs from the inordinate scale of the author's two faces; it explains more than anything else his eccentricities and difficulties. It accounts for his want of grace, his want of the lightness associated with an amusing literary form, his bristling surface, his closeness of texture, so rough with richness, yet so productive of the effect we have in mind when we speak of not being able to see the wood for the trees.

A thorough-paced votary, for that matter, can easily afford to declare at once that this confounding duality of character does more things still, or does at least the most important of all—introduces us without mercy (mercy for ourselves I

mean) to the oddest truth we could have dreamed of meeting
in such a connection. It was certainly *a priori* not to be expected we should feel it of him, but our hero is after all not
in his magnificence totally an artist: which would be the
strangest thing possible, one must hasten to add, were not
the smallness of the practical difference so made even
stranger. His endowment and his effect are each so great that
the anomaly makes at the most a difference only by adding to
his interest for the critic. The critic worth his salt is indiscreetly curious and wants ever to know how and why—
whereby Balzac is thus a still rarer case for him, suggesting
that exceptional curiosity may have exceptional rewards. The
question of what makes the artist on a great scale is interesting enough; but we feel it in Balzac's company to be nothing
to the question of what on an equal scale frustrates him. The
scattered pieces, the *disjecta membra* of the character are here
so numerous and so splendid that they prove misleading; we
pile them together, and the heap assuredly is monumental; it
forms an overtopping figure. The genius this figure stands
for, none the less, is really such a lesson to the artist as perfection itself would be powerless to give; it carries him so
much further into the special mystery. Where it carries him,
at the same time, I must not in this scant space attempt to
say—which would be a loss of the fine thread of my argument. I stick to our point in putting it, more concisely, that
the artist of the Comédie Humaine is half smothered by the
historian. Yet it belongs as well to the matter also to meet the
question of whether the historian himself may not be an artist—in which case Balzac's catastrophe would seem to lose its
excuse. The answer of course is that the reporter, however
philosophic, has one law, and the originator, however substantially fed, has another; so that the two laws can with no
sort of harmony or congruity make, for the finer sense, a
common household. Balzac's catastrophe—so to name it
once again—was in this perpetual conflict and final impossibility, an impossibility that explains his defeat on the classic
side and extends so far at times as to make us think of his
work as, from the point of view of beauty, a tragic waste of
effort.

What it would come to, we judge, is that the irreconcil-

ability of the two kinds of law is, more simply expressed, but
the irreconcilability of two different ways of composing one's
effect. The principle of composition that his free imagination
would have, or certainly might have, handsomely imposed on
him is perpetually dislocated by the quite opposite principle
of the earnest seeker, the inquirer to a useful end, in whom
nothing is free but a born antipathy to his yoke-fellow. Such
a production as "Le Curé de Village," the wonderful story of
Madame Graslin, so nearly a masterpiece yet so ultimately not
one, would be, in this connection, could I take due space for
it, a perfect illustration. If, as I say, Madame Graslin's creator
was confined by his doom to patches and pieces, no piece is
finer than the first half of the book in question, the half in
which the picture is determined by his unequalled power of
putting people on their feet, planting them before us in their
habit as they lived—a faculty nourished by observation as
much as one will, but with the inner vision all the while wide-
awake, the vision for which ideas are as living as facts and
assume an equal intensity. This intensity, greatest indeed in
the facts, has in Balzac a force all its own, to which none
other in any novelist I know can be likened. His touch communicates on the spot to the object, the creature evoked, the
hardness and permanence that certain substances, some sorts
of stone, acquire by exposure to the air. The hardening medium, for the image soaked in it, is the air of his mind. It
would take but little more to make the peopled world of fiction as we know it elsewhere affect us by contrast as a world
of rather gray pulp. This mixture of the solid and the vivid is
Balzac at his best, and it prevails without a break, without a
note not admirably true, in "Le Curé de Village"—since I
have named that instance—up to the point at which Madame
Graslin moves out from Limoges to Montégnac in her ardent
passion of penitence, her determination to expiate her strange
and undiscovered association with a dark misdeed by living
and working for others. Her drama is a particularly inward
one, interesting, and in the highest degree, so long as she
herself, her nature, her behaviour, her personal history and
the relations in which they place her, control the picture and
feed our illusion. The firmness with which the author makes
them play this part, the whole constitution of the scene and

of its developments from the moment we cross the threshold
of her dusky stuffy old-time birth-house, is a rare delight,
producing in the reader that sense of local and material immersion which is one of Balzac's supreme secrets. What characteristically befalls, however, is that the spell accompanies us
but part of the way—only until, at a given moment, his attention ruthlessly transfers itself from inside to outside, from
the centre of his subject to its circumference.

   This is Balzac caught in the very fact of his monstrous duality, caught in his most complete self-expression. He is clearly
quite unwitting that in handing over his *data* to his twin-
brother the impassioned economist and surveyor, the insatiate
general inquirer and reporter, he is in any sort betraying our
confidence, for his good conscience at such times, the spirit
of edification in him, is a lesson even to the best of us, his
rich robust temperament nowhere more striking, no more
marked anywhere the great push of the shoulder with which
he makes his theme move, overcharged though it may be like
a carrier's van. It is not therefore assuredly that he loses either
sincerity or power in putting before us to the last detail such
a matter as, in this case, his heroine's management of her
property, her tenantry, her economic opportunities and visions, for these are cases in which he never shrinks nor re-
lents, in which positively he stiffens and terribly towers—to
remind us again of M. Taine's simplifying word about his
being an artist doubled with a man of business. Balzac was
indeed doubled if ever a writer was, and to that extent that
we almost as often, while we read, feel ourselves thinking of
him as a man of business doubled with an artist. Whichever
way we turn it the oddity never fails, nor the wonder of the
ease with which either character bears the burden of the
other. I use the word burden because, as the fusion is never
complete—witness in the book before us the fatal break of
"tone," the one unpardonable sin for the novelist—we are
beset by the conviction that but for this strangest of dooms
one or other of the two partners might, to our relief and to
his own, have been disembarrassed. The disembarrassment,
for each, by a more insidious fusion, would probably have
conduced to the mastership of interest proceeding from form,
or at all events to the search for it, that Balzac fails to

embody. Perhaps the possibility of an artist constructed on such strong lines is one of those fine things that are not of this world, a mere dream of the fond critical spirit. Let these speculations and condonations at least pass as the amusement, as a result of the high spirits—if high spirits be the word— of the reader feeling himself again in touch. It was not of our author's difficulties—that is of his difficulty, the great one— that I proposed to speak, but of his immense clear action. Even that is not truly an impression of ease, and it is strange and striking that we are in fact so attached by his want of the unity that keeps surfaces smooth and dangers down as scarce to feel sure at any moment that we shall not come back to it with most curiosity. We are never so curious about successes as about interesting failures. The more reason therefore to speak promptly, and once for all, of the scale on which, in its own quarter of his genius, success worked itself out for him.

It is to that I *should* come back— to the infinite reach in him of the painter and the poet. We can never know what might have become of him with less importunity in his con- sciousness of the machinery of life, of its furniture and fit- tings, of all that, right and left, he causes to assail us, sometimes almost to suffocation, under the general rubric of *things*. Things, in this sense with him, are at once our delight and our despair; we pass from being inordinately beguiled and convinced by them to feeling that his universe fairly smells too much of them, that the larger ether, the diviner air, is in peril of finding among them scarce room to circulate. His landscapes, his "local colour"—thick in his pages at a time when it was to be found in his pages almost alone—his towns, his streets, his houses, his Saumurs, Angoulêmes, Guérandes, his great prose Turner-views of the land of the Loire, his rooms, shops, interiors, details of domesticity and traffic, are a short list of the terms into which he saw the real as clamouring to be rendered and into which he rendered it with unequalled authority. It would be doubtless more to the point to make our profit of this consummation than to try to reconstruct a Balzac planted more in the open. We hardly, as the case stands, know most whether to admire in such an example as the short tale of "La Grenadière" the exquisite feeling for "natural objects" with which it overflows like a brimming wine-cup, the energy of perception and description which so multiplies them for beauty's sake and for the love of their beauty, or the general wealth of genius that can calculate, or at least count, so little and spend so joyously. The tale practically exists for the sake of the enchanting aspects involved—those of the embowered white house that nestles on its terraced hill above the great French river, and we can think, frankly, of no one else with an equal amount of business on his hands who would either have so put himself out for aspects or made them almost by themselves a living subject. A born son of Touraine, it must be said, he pictures his province, on every pretext and occasion, with filial passion and extraordinary breadth. The prime aspect in his scene all the while, it must be added, is the money aspect. The general money question so loads him up and weighs him down that he moves through the human comedy, from beginning to end, very much in the fashion of a camel, the ship of the desert, surmounted with a cargo. "Things" for him are francs and centimes more than any others, and I give up as inscrutable, unfathomable, the nature, the peculiar avidity of his interest in them. It makes us wonder again and again what then is the use on Balzac's scale of the divine faculty. The imagination, as we all know, may be employed up to a certain point in inventing uses for money; but its office beyond that point is surely to make us forget that anything so odious exists. This is what Balzac never forgot; his universe goes on expressing itself for him, to its furthest reaches, on its finest sides, in the terms of the market. To say these things, however, is after all to come out where we want, to suggest his extraordinary scale and his terrible completeness. I am not sure that he does not see character too, see passion, motive, personality, as quite in the order of the "things" we have spoken of. He makes them no less concrete and palpable, handles them no less directly and freely. It is the whole business in fine—that grand total to which he proposed to himself to do high justice—that gives him his place apart, makes him, among the novelists, the largest, weightiest presence. There are some of his obsessions—that of the material, that of the financial, that of the "social," that of the technical, political, civil—for which I feel myself unable to judge him, judgment

losing itself unexpectedly in a particular shade of pity. The
way to judge him is to try to walk all round him—on which
we see how remarkably far we have to go. He is the only
member of his order really monumental, the sturdiest-seated
mass that rises in our path.

II

We recognise none the less that the finest consequence of
these re-established relations is linked with just that appearance in him, that obsession of the actual under so many
heads, that makes us look at him, as we would at some rare
animal in captivity, between the bars of a cage. It amounts to
a sort of suffered doom, since to be solicited by the world
from all quarters at once, what is that for the spirit but a
denial of escape? We feel his doom to be his want of a private
door, and that he felt it, though more obscurely, himself.
When we speak of his want of charm therefore we perhaps so
surrender the question as but to show our own poverty. If
charm, to cut it short, is what he lacks, how comes it that he
so touches and holds us that—above all if we be actual or
possible fellow-workers—we are uncomfortably conscious of
the disloyalty of almost any shade of surrender? We are
lodged perhaps by our excited sensibility in a dilemma of
which one of the horns is a compassion that savours of patronage; but we must resign ourselves to that by reflecting
that our partiality at least takes nothing away from him. It
leaves him solidly where he is and only brings us near, brings
us to a view of *all* his formidable parts and properties. The
conception of the Comédie Humaine represents them all, and
represents them mostly in their felicity and their triumph—
or at least the execution does: in spite of which we irresistibly
find ourselves thinking of him, in reperusals, as most essentially the victim of a cruel joke. The joke is one of the jokes
of fate, the fate that rode him for twenty years at so terrible
a pace and with the whip so constantly applied. To have
wanted to do so much, to have thought it possible, to have
faced and in a manner resisted the effort, to have felt life poisoned and consumed by such a bravery of self-committal—
these things form for us in him a face of trouble that, oddly

enough, is not appreciably lighted by the fact of his success. It was the having wanted to do so much that was the trap, whatever possibilities of glory might accompany the good faith with which he fell into it. What accompanies *us* as we frequent him is a sense of the deepening ache of that good faith with the increase of his working consciousness, the merciless development of his huge subject and of the rigour of all the conditions. We see the whole thing quite as if Destiny had said to him: "You want to 'do' France, presumptuous, magnificent, miserable man—the France of revolutions, revivals, restorations, of Bonapartes, Bourbons, republics, of war and peace, of blood and romanticism, of violent change and intimate continuity, the France of the first half of your century? Very well; you most distinctly *shall*, and you shall particularly let me hear, even if the great groan of your labour do fill at moments the temple of letters, how you like the job." We must of course not appear to deny the existence of a robust joy in him, the joy of power and creation, the joy of the observer and the dreamer who finds a use for his observations and his dreams as fast as they come. The "Contes Drolatiques" would by themselves sufficiently contradict us, and the savour of the "Contes Drolatiques" is not confined to these productions. His work at large tastes of the same kind of humour, and we feel him again and again, like any other great healthy producer of these matters, beguiled and carried along. He would have been, I dare say, the last not to insist that the artist has pleasures forever indescribable; he lived in short in his human comedy with the largest life we can attribute to the largest capacity. There are particular parts of his subject from which, with our sense of his enjoyment of them, we have to check the impulse to call him away—frequently as I confess in this relation that impulse arises.

The relation is with the special element of his spectacle from which he never fully detaches himself, the element, to express it succinctly, of the "old families" and the great ladies. Balzac frankly revelled in his conception of an aristocracy—a conception that never succeeded in becoming his happiest; whether, objectively, thanks to the facts supplied him by the society he studied, or through one of the strangest deviations of taste that the literary critic is in an important connection

likely to encounter. Nothing would in fact be more interesting than to attempt a general measure of the part played in
the total comedy, to his imagination, by the old families; and
one or two contributions to such an attempt I must not fail
presently to make. I glance at them here, however, the delec-
table class, but as most representing on the author's part free
and amused creation; by which too I am far from hinting that
the amusement is at all at their expense. It is in their great
ladies that the old families most shine out for him, images of
strange colour and form, but "felt" as we say, to their finger-
tips, and extraordinarily interesting as a mark of the high predominance—predominance of character, of cleverness, of
will, of general "personality"—that almost every scene of the
Comedy attributes to women. It attributes to them in fact a
recognised, an uncontested supremacy; it is through them
that the hierarchy of old families most expresses itself; and it
is as surrounded by them even as some magnificent indulgent
pasha by his overflowing seraglio that Balzac sits most at his
ease. All of which reaffirms—if it be needed—that his inspiration, and the sense of it, were even greater than his task.
And yet such betrayals of spontaneity in him make for an old
friend at the end of the chapter no great difference in respect
to the pathos—since it amounts to that—of his genius-rid-
den aspect. It comes to us as we go back to him that his spirit
had fairly made of itself a cage in which he was to turn round
and round, always unwinding his reel, much in the manner
of a criminal condemned to hard labour for life. The cage is
simply the complicated but dreadfully definite French world
that built itself so solidly in and roofed itself so impenetrably
over him.

It is not that, caught there with him though we be, we
ourselves prematurely seek an issue: we throw ourselves back,
on the contrary, for the particular sense of it, into his ancient
superseded comparatively *rococo* and quite patriarchal
France—patriarchal in spite of social and political convulsions; into his old-time antediluvian Paris, all picturesque and
all workable, full, to the fancy, of an amenity that has passed
away; into his intensely differentiated sphere of *la province*,
evoked in each sharpest or faintest note of its difference, described systematically as narrow and flat, and yet attaching us

if only by the contagion of the author's overflowing sensibility. He feels in his vast exhibition many things, but there is nothing he feels with the communicable shocks and vibrations, the sustained fury of perception—not always a fierceness of judgment, which is another matter—that *la province* excites in him. Half our interest in him springs still from our own sense that, for all the convulsions, the revolutions and experiments that have come and gone, the order he describes is the old order that our sense of the past perversely recurs to as to something happy we have irretrievably missed. His pages bristle with the revelation of the lingering earlier world, the world in which places and people still had their queerness, their strong marks, their sharp type, and in which, as before the platitude that was to come, the observer with an appetite for the salient could by way of precaution fill his lungs. Balzac's appetite for the salient was voracious, yet he came, as it were, in time, in spite of his so often speaking as if what he sees about him is but the last desolation of the modern. His conservatism, the most entire, consistent and convinced that ever was—yet even at that much inclined to whistling in the dark as if to the tune of "Oh how mediæval I *am*!"—was doubtless the best point of view from which he could rake his field. But if what he sniffed from afar in that position was the extremity of change, we in turn feel both subject and painter drenched with the smell of the past. It is preserved in his work as nowhere else—not vague nor faint nor delicate, but as strong to-day as when first distilled.

It may seem odd to find a conscious melancholy in the fact that a great worker succeeded in clasping his opportunity in such an embrace, this being exactly our usual measure of the felicity of great workers. I speak, I hasten to reassert, all in the name of sympathy—without which it would have been detestable to speak at all; and the sentiment puts its hand instinctively on the thing that makes it least futile. This particular thing then is not in the least Balzac's own hold of his terrible mass of matter; it is absolutely the convolutions of the serpent he had with a magnificent courage invited to wind itself round him. We must use the common image—he had created his Frankenstein monster. It is the fellow-craftsman who can most feel for him—it being apparently possible to read him from another point of view without getting really into his presence. We undergo with him from book to book, from picture to picture, the convolutions of the serpent, we especially whose refined performances are given, as we know, but with the small common or garden snake. I stick to this to justify my image just above of his having been "caged" by the intensity with which he saw his general matter as a whole. To see it always as a whole is our wise, our virtuous effort, the very condition, as we keep in mind, of superior art. Balzac was in this connection then wise and virtuous to the most exemplary degree; so that he doubtless ought logically but to prompt to complacent reflections. No painter ever saw his general matter nearly so much as a whole. Why is it then that we hover about him, if we are real Balzacians, not with cheerful chatter, but with a consideration deeper in its reach than any mere moralising? The reason is largely that if you wish with absolute immaculate virtue to look at your matter as a whole and yet remain a theme for cheerful chatter, you must be careful to take some quantity that will not hug you to death. Balzac's active intention was, to vary our simile, a beast with a hundred claws, and the spectacle is in the hugging process of which, as energy against energy, the beast was capable. Its victim died of the process at fifty, and if what we see in the long gallery in which it is mirrored is not the defeat, but the admirable resistance, we none the less never lose the sense that the fighter is shut up with his fate. He has locked himself in—it is doubtless his own fault—and thrown the key away. Most of all perhaps the impression comes—the impression of the adventurer committed and anxious, but with no retreat—from the so formidably concrete nature of his plastic stuff. When we work in the open, as it were, our material is not classed and catalogued, so that we have at hand a hundred ways of being loose, superficial, disingenuous, and yet passing, to our no small profit, for remarkable. Balzac had no "open"; he held that the great central normal fruitful country of his birth and race, overarched with its infinite social complexity, yielded a sufficiency of earth and sea and sky. We seem to see as his catastrophe that the sky, all the same, came down on him. He couldn't keep it up—in more senses than one. These are perhaps fine fancies for a critic to weave about a literary figure of whom he has undertaken to give a plain account; but I leave them so on the plea that there are relations in which, for the Balzacian, criticism simply drops out. That is not a liberty, I admit, ever to be much encouraged; critics in fact are the only people who have a right occasionally to take it. There is no such plain account of the Comédie Humaine as that it makes us fold up our yard-measure and put away our note-book quite as we do with some extraordinary character, some mysterious and various stranger, who brings with him his own standards and his own air. There is a kind of eminent presence that abashes even the interviewer, moves him to respect and wonder, makes him, for consideration itself, not insist. This takes of course a personage sole of his kind. But such a personage precisely is Balzac.

III

By all of which have I none the less felt it but too clear that I must not pretend in this place to take apart the pieces of his immense complicated work, to number them or group them or dispose them about. The most we can do is to pick one up here and there and wonder, as we weigh it in our hand, at its close compact substance. That is all even M. Taine could do in the longest and most penetrating study of which our author has been the subject. Every piece we handle is so full of stuff, condensed like the edibles provided for campaigns and explorations, positively so charged with distilled life, that we find ourselves dropping it, in certain states of sensibility, as we drop an object unguardedly touched that startles us by being animate. We seem really scarce to want anything to *be* so animate. It would verily take Balzac to detail Balzac, and he has had in fact Balzacians nearly enough affiliated to affront the task with courage. The "Répertoire de la Comédie Humaine" of MM. Anatole Cerfberr and Jules Christophe is a closely-printed octavo of 550 pages which constitutes in relation to his characters great and small an impeccable biographical dictionary. His votaries and expositors are so numerous that the Balzac library of comment and research must be, of its type, one of the most copious. M. de Loven-

joul has laboured all round the subject; his "Histoire des
Œuvres" alone is another crowded octavo of 400 pages; in
connection with which I must mention Miss Wormeley, the
devoted American translator, interpreter, worshipper, who in
the course of her own studies has so often found occasion to
differ from M. de Lovenjoul on matters of fact and questions
of date and of appreciation. Miss Wormeley, M. Paul Bourget
and many others are examples of the passionate piety that our
author can inspire. As I turn over the encyclopedia of his
characters I note that whereas such works usually commemorate but the ostensibly eminent of a race and time, every creature so much as named in the fictive swarm is in this case
preserved to fame: so close is the implication that to have
been named by such a dispenser of life and privilege is to be,
as we say it of baronets and peers, created. He infinitely divided moreover, as we know, he subdivided, altered and multiplied his heads and categories—his "Vie Parisienne," his
"Vie de Province," his "Vie Politique," his "Parents Pauvres,"
his "Études Philosophiques," his "Splendeurs et Misères des
Courtisanes," his "Envers de l'Histoire Contemporaine" and
all the rest; so that nominal reference to them becomes the
more difficult. Yet without prejudice either to the energy of
conception with which he mapped out his theme as with
chalk on a huge blackboard, or to the prodigious patience
with which he executed his plan, practically filling in with a
wealth of illustration, from sources that to this day we fail to
make out, every compartment of his table, M. de Lovenjoul
draws up the list, year by year, from 1822 to 1848, of his mass
of work, giving us thus the measure of the tension represented for him by almost any twelvemonth. It is wholly unequalled, considering the quality of Balzac's show, by any
other eminent abundance.

I must be pardoned for coming back to it, for seeming unable to leave it; it enshrouds so interesting a mystery. How
was so solidly systematic a literary attack on life to be con-
joined with whatever workable minimum of needful intermission, of free observation, of personal experience? Some small
possibility of personal experience and disinterested life must,
at the worst, from deep within or far without, feed and fortify
the strained productive machine. These things were luxuries

that Balzac appears really never to have tasted on any appreciable scale. His published letters—the driest and most
starved of those of any man of equal distinction—are with
the exception of those to Madame de Hanska, whom he married shortly before his death, almost exclusively the audible
wail of a galley-slave chained to the oar. M. Zola, in our time,
among the novelists, has sacrificed to the huge plan in something of the same manner, yet with goodly modern differences that leave him a comparatively simple instance. His
work assuredly has been more nearly dried up by the sacrifice
than ever Balzac's was—so miraculously, given the conditions, was Balzac's to escape the anticlimax. Method and system, in the chronicle of the tribe of Rougon-Macquart, an
economy in itself certainly of the rarest and most interesting,
have spread so from centre to circumference that they have
ended by being almost the only thing we feel. And then M.
Zola has survived and triumphed in his lifetime, has continued and lasted, has piled up and, if the remark be not frivolous, enjoyed in all its *agréments* the reward for which Balzac
toiled and sweated in vain. On top of which he will have had
also his literary great-grandfather's heroic example to start
from and profit by, the positive heritage of a *fils de famille* to
enjoy, spend, save, waste. Balzac had frankly no heritage at all
but his stiff subject, and by way of model not even in any
direct or immediate manner that of the inner light and kindly
admonition of his genius. Nothing adds more to the strangeness of his general performance than his having failed so long
to find his inner light, groped for it almost ten years, missed
it again and again, moved straight away from it, turned his
back on it, lived in fine round about it, in a darkness still
scarce penetrable, a darkness into which we peep only half to
make out the dreary little waste of his numerous *œuvres de
jeunesse*. To M. Zola was vouchsafed the good fortune of settling down to the Rougon-Macquart with the happiest
promptitude; it was as if time for one look about him—and
I say it without disparagement to the reach of his look—had
sufficiently served his purpose. Balzac moreover might have
written five hundred novels without our feeling in him the
faintest hint of the breath of doom, if he had only been comfortably capable of conceiving the short cut of the fashion

practised by others under his eyes. As Alexandre Dumas and George Sand, illustrious contemporaries, cultivated a personal life and a disinterested consciousness by the bushel, having, for their easier duration, not too consistently known, as the true painter knows it, the obsession of the thing to be done, so Balzac was condemned by his constitution itself, by his inveterately seeing this "thing to be done" as part and parcel, as of the very essence, of his enterprise. The latter existed for him, as the process worked and hallucination settled, in the form, and the form only, of the thing done, and not in any hocus-pocus about doing. There was no kindly convenient escape for him by the little swinging back-door of the thing *not* done. He desired—no man more—to get out of his obsession, but only at the other end, that is by boring through it. "How then, thus deprived of the outer air almost as much as if he were gouging a passage for a railway through an Alp, *did* he live?" is the question that haunts us—with the consequence for the most part of promptly meeting its fairly tragic answer. He did *not* live—save in his imagination, or by other aid than he could find there; his imagination was all his experience; he had provably no time for the real thing. This brings us to the rich if simple truth that his imagination alone did the business, carried through both the conception and the execution—as large an effort and as proportionate a success, in all but the vulgar sense, as the faculty when equally handicapped was ever concerned in. Handicapped I say because this interesting fact about him, with the claim it makes, rests on the ground, the high distinction, that more than all the rest of us put together he went in, as we say, for detail, circumstance and specification, proposed to himself *all* the connections of every part of his matter and the full total of the parts. The whole thing, it is impossible not to keep repeating, was what he deemed treatable. One really knows in all imaginative literature no undertaking to compare with it for courage, good faith and sublimity. There, once more, was the necessity that rode him and that places him apart in our homage. It is no light thing to have been condemned to become provably sublime. And looking through, or trying to, at what is beneath and behind, we are left benevolently uncertain if the predominant quantity be audacity or innocence.

It is of course inevitable at this point to seem to hear the colder critic promptly take us up. He undertook the whole thing—oh exactly, the ponderous person! But *did* he "do" the whole thing, if you please, any more than sundry others of fewer pretensions? The retort to this it can only be a positive joy to make, so high a note instantly sounds as an effect of the inquiry. Nothing is more interesting and amusing than to find one's self recognising both that Balzac's pretensions were immense, portentous, and that yet, taking him—and taking *them*—altogether, they but minister in the long run to our fondness. They affect us not only as the endearing eccentricities of a person we greatly admire, but fairly as the very condition of his having become such a person. We take them thus in the first place for the very terms of his plan, and in the second for a part of that high robustness and that general richness of nature which made him in face of such a project believe in himself. One would really scarce have liked to see such a job as La Comédie Humaine tackled without swagger. To think of the thing really as practicable *was* swagger, and of the very rarest order. So to think assuredly implied pretensions, pretensions that risked showing as monstrous should the enterprise fail to succeed. It is for the colder critic to take the trouble to make out that of the two parties to it the body of pretension remains greater than the success. One may put it moreover at the worst for him, may recognise that it is in the matter of opinion still more than in the matter of knowledge that Balzac offers himself as universally competent. He has flights of judgment—on subjects the most special as well as the most general—that are vertiginous and on his alighting from which we greet him with a special indulgence. We can easily imagine him to respond, confessing humorously—if he had only time—to such a benevolent understanding smile as would fain hold our own eyes a moment. Then it is that he would most show us his scheme and his necessities and how in operation they all hang together. *Naturally* everything about everything, though how he had time to learn it is the last thing he has time to tell us; which matters the less, moreover, as it is not over the question of his knowledge that we sociably invite him, as it were (and remembering the two augurs behind the altar) to wink at us for a sign. His convictions it is that are his great pardonable "swagger"; to them in particular I refer as his general operative condition, the constituted terms of his experiment, and not less as his consolation, his support, his amusement by the way. They embrace everything in the world—that is in his world of the so particoloured France of his age: religion, morals, politics, economics, physics, esthetics, letters, art, science, sociology, every question of faith, every branch of research. They represent thus his equipment of ideas, those ideas of which it will never do for a man who aspires to constitute a State to be deprived. He must take them with him as an ambassador extraordinary takes with him secretaries, uniforms, stars and garters, a gilded coach and a high assurance. Balzac's opinions are his gilded coach, in which he is more amused than anything else to feel himself riding, but which is indispensably concerned in getting him over the ground. What more inevitable than that they should be intensely Catholic, intensely monarchical, intensely saturated with the real genius—as between 1830 and 1848 he believed it to be—of the French character and French institutions?

Nothing is happier for us than that he should have enjoyed his outlook before the first half of the century closed. He could then still treat his subject as comparatively homogeneous. Any country could have a Revolution—every country *had* had one. A Restoration was merely what a revolution involved, and the Empire had been for the French but a revolutionary incident, in addition to being by good luck for the novelist an immensely pictorial one. He was free therefore to arrange the background of the comedy in the manner that seemed to him best to suit anything so great; in the manner at the same time prescribed according to his contention by the noblest traditions. The church, the throne, the noblesse, the bourgeoisie, the people, the peasantry, all in their order and each solidly kept in it, these were precious things, things his superabundant insistence on the price of which is what I refer to as his exuberance of opinion. It was a luxury, for more reasons than one, though one, presently to be mentioned, handsomely predominates. The meaning of that exchange of intelligences in the rear of the oracle which I have figured for him with the perceptive friend bears simply on his pleading guilty to the purport of the friend's discrimination. The point the latter makes with him—a beautiful cordial critical point—is that he truly cares for nothing in the world, thank goodness, so much as for the passions and embroilments of men and women, the free play of character and the sharp revelation of type, all the real stuff of drama and the natural food of novelists. Religion, morals, politics, economics, esthetics would be thus, as systematic matter, very well in their place, but quite secondary and subservient. Balzac's attitude is again and again that he cares for the adventures and emotions because, as his last word, he cares for the good and the greatness of the State—which is where his swagger, with a whole society on his hands, comes in. What we on our side in a thousand places gratefully feel is that he cares for his monarchical and hierarchical and ecclesiastical society because it rounds itself for his mind into the most congruous and capacious theatre for the repertory of his innumerable comedians. It has above all, for a painter abhorrent of the superficial, the inestimable benefit of the accumulated, of strong marks and fine shades, contrasts and complications. There had certainly been since 1789 dispersals and confusions enough, but the thick tradition, no more at the most than half smothered, lay under them all. So the whole of his faith and no small part of his working omniscience were neither more nor less than that historic sense which I have spoken of as the spur of his invention and which he possessed as no other novelist has done. We immediately feel that to name it in connection with him is to answer every question he suggests and to account for each of his idiosyncrasies in turn. The novel, the tale, however brief, the passage, the sentence by itself, the situation, the person, the place, the motive exposed, the speech reported—these things were in his view history, with the absoluteness and the dignity of history. This is the source both of his weight and of his wealth. What is the historic sense after all but animated, but impassioned knowledge seeking to enlarge itself? I have said that his imagination did the whole thing, no other explanation—no reckoning of the possibilities of personal saturation—meeting the mysteries of the case. Therefore his imagination achieved the miracle of absolutely resolving itself into multifarious knowledge. Since his-

tory proceeds by documents he constructed, as he needed
them, the documents too—fictive sources that imitated the
actual to the life. It was of course a terrible business, but at
least in the light of it his claims to creatorship are justified—
which is what was to be shown.

IV

It is very well even in the sketchiest attempt at a portrait of
his genius to try to take particulars in their order: one peeps
over the shoulder of another at the moment we get a feature
into focus. The loud appeal not to be left out prevails among
them all, and certainly with the excuse that each as we fix it
seems to fall most into the picture. I have so indulged myself
as to his general air that I find a whole list of vivid contributive marks almost left on my hands. Such a list, in any study
of Balzac, is delightful for intimate edification as well as for
the fine humour of the thing; we proceed from one of the
items of his breathing physiognomy to the other with quite
the same sense of life, the same active curiosity, with which
we push our way through the thick undergrowth of one of
the novels. The difficulty is really that the special point for
which we at the moment observe him melts into all the other
points, is swallowed up before our eyes in the formidable
mass. The French apply the happiest term to certain characters when they speak of them as *entiers*, and if the word had
been invented for Balzac it could scarce better have expressed
him. He is "entire" as was never a man of his craft; he moves
always in his mass; wherever we find him we find him in
force; whatever touch he applies he applies it with his whole
apparatus. He is like an army gathered to besiege a cottage
equally with a city, and living voraciously in either case on all
the country about. It may well be, at any rate, that this infatuation with the idea of the social, the practical primacy of
"the sex" is the article at the top of one's list; there could
certainly be no better occasion than this of a rich reissue of
the "Deux Jeunes Mariées" for placing it there at a venture.
Here indeed precisely we get a sharp example of the way in
which, as I have just said, a capital illustration of one of his
sides becomes, just as we take it up, a capital illustration of

another. The correspondence of Louise de Chaulieu and Renée de Maucombe is in fact one of those cases that light up
with a great golden glow all his parts at once. We needn't
mean by this that such parts are themselves absolutely all
golden—given the amount of tinsel for instance in his view,
supereminent, transcendent here, of the old families and the
great ladies. What we do convey, however, is that his creative
temperament finds in such *data* as these one of its best occasions for shining out. Again we fondly recognise his splendid,
his attaching swagger—that of a "bounder" of genius and of
feeling; again we see how, with opportunity, its elements may
vibrate into a perfect ecstasy of creation.

Why shouldn't a man swagger, he treats us to the diversion
of asking ourselves, who has created from top to toe the most
brilliant, the most historic, the most insolent, above all the
most detailed and discriminated of aristocracies? Balzac carried the uppermost class of his comedy, from the princes,
dukes, and unspeakable duchesses down to his poor barons
de province, about in his pocket as he might have carried a
tolerably befingered pack of cards, to deal them about with a
flourish of the highest authority whenever there was the
chance of a game. He knew them up and down and in and
out, their arms, infallibly supplied, their quarterings, pedi-
grees, services, intermarriages, relationships, ramifications and
other enthralling attributes. This indeed is comparatively simple learning; the real wonder is rather when we linger on the
ground of the patrician consciousness itself, the innermost,
the esoteric, the spirit, temper, tone—tone above all—of the
titled and the proud. The questions multiply for every scene
of the comedy; there is no one who makes us walk in such a
cloud of them. The clouds elsewhere, in comparison, are at
best of questions not worth asking. *Was* the patrician consciousness that figured as our author's model so splendidly
fatuous as he—almost without irony, often in fact with a certain poetic sympathy—everywhere represents it? His imagination lives in it, breathes its scented air, swallows this
element with the smack of the lips of the connoisseur; but I
feel that we never know, even to the end, whether he be here
directly historic or only quite misguidedly romantic. The romantic side of him has the extent of all the others; it repre-

sents in the oddest manner his escape from the walled and roofed structure into which he had built himself—his longing for the vaguely-felt outside and as much as might be of the rest of the globe. But it is characteristic of him that the most he could do for this relief was to bring the fantastic into the circle and fit it somehow to his conditions. Was his tone for the duchess, the marquise but the imported fantastic, one of those smashes of the window-pane of the real that reactions sometimes produce even in the stubborn? or are we to take it as observed, as really reported, as, for all its difference from our notion of the natural—and, quite as much, of the artificial—in another and happier strain of manners, substantially true? The whole episode, in "Les Illusions Perdues," of Madame de Bargeton's "chucking" Lucien de Rubempré, on reaching Paris with him, under pressure of Madame d'Espard's shockability as to his coat and trousers and other such matters, is either a magnificent lurid document or the baseless fabric of a vision. The great wonder is that, as I rejoice to put it, we can never really discover which, and that we feel as we read that we can't, and that we suffer at the hands of no other author this particular helplessness of immersion. It is *done*— we are always thrown back on that; we can't get out of it; all we can do is to say that the true itself can't be more than done and that if the false in this way equals it we must give up looking for the difference. Alone among novelists Balzac has the secret of an insistence that somehow makes the difference nought. He warms his facts into life—as witness the certainty that the episode I just cited has absolutely as much of that property as if perfect matching had been achieved. If the great ladies in question *didn't* behave, wouldn't, couldn't have behaved, like a pair of nervous snobs, why so much the worse, we say to ourselves, for the great ladies in question. We *know* them so—they owe their being to our so seeing them; whereas we never can tell ourselves how we should otherwise have known them or what quantity of being they would on a different footing have been able to put forth.

The case is the same with Louise de Chaulieu, who besides coming out of her convent school, as a quite young thing, with an amount of sophistication that would have chilled the heart of a horse-dealer, exhales—and to her familiar friend, a

young person of a supposedly equal breeding—an extravagance of complacency in her "social position" that makes us
rub our eyes. Whereupon after a little the same phenomenon
occurs; we swallow her bragging, against our better reason,
or at any rate against our startled sense, under coercion of the
total intensity. We do more than this, we cease to care for the
question, which loses itself in the hot fusion of the whole
picture. He has "gone for" his subject, in the vulgar phrase,
with an avidity that makes the attack of his most eminent
rivals affect us as the intercourse between introduced indiffer-
ences at a dull evening party. He squeezes it till it cries out,
we hardly know whether for pleasure or pain. In the case before us for example—without wandering from book to book,
impossible here, I make the most of the ground already broken—he has seen at once that the state of marriage itself,
sounded to its depths, is, in the connection, his real theme.
He sees it of course in the conditions that exist for him, but
he weighs it to the last ounce, feels it in all its dimensions, as
well as in all his own, and would scorn to take refuge in any
engaging side-issue. He gets, for further intensity, into the
very skin of his *jeunes mariées*—into each alternately, as they
are different enough; so that, to repeat again, any other mode
of representing women, or of representing anybody, becomes,
in juxtaposition, a thing so void of the active contortions of
truth as to be comparatively wooden. He bears children with
Madame de l'Estorade, knows intimately how she suffers for
them, and not less intimately how her correspondent suffers,
as well as enjoys, without them. Big as he is he makes himself
small to be handled by her with young maternal passion and
positively to handle her in turn with infantile innocence.
These things are the very flourishes, the little technical amuse-
ments of his penetrating power. But it is doubtless in his
hand for such a matter as the jealous passion of Louise de
Chaulieu, the free play of her intelligence and the almost
beautiful good faith of her egotism, that he is most individual. It is one of the neatest examples of his extraordinary leading gift, his art—which is really moreover not an art—of
working the exhibition of a given character up to intensity. I
say it is not an art because it acts for us rather as a hunger on
the part of his nature to take on in all freedom another

nature—take it by a direct process of the senses. Art is for the mass of us who have only the process of art, comparatively so stiff. The thing amounts with him to a kind of shameless personal, physical, not merely intellectual, duality—the very spirit and secret of transmigration.

The Two Young Brides, a critical introduction.
London: William Heinemann, 1902
Reprinted in *Notes on Novelists*, 1914

THE LESSON OF BALZAC[1]

I HAVE FOUND it necessary, at the eleventh hour, to sacrifice to the terrible question of time a very beautiful and majestic approach that I had prepared to the subject on which I have the honor of addressing you. I recognize it as impossible to ask you to linger with me on that pillared portico—paved with marble, I beg you to believe, and overtwined with charming flowers. I must invite you to pass straight into the house and bear with me there as if I had already succeeded in beginning to interest you. Let us assume, therefore, that we have exchanged some ideas on the question of the beneficent play of criticism, and that I have even ingeniously struck it off that criticism is the only gate of appreciation, just as appreciation is, in regard to a work of art, the only gate of enjoyment. You may wonder perhaps why I speak as if we were possessed, in our conditions, of a literary court of appeal, and I hasten to say that the appeal I think of is precisely from the general judgment, and not to it; is to the particular judgment altogether: by which I mean to that quantity of opinion, very small at all times, but at all times infinitely precious, that is capable of giving some intelligible account of itself. Where, among us, at this time of day, this element of the lucid report of impressions received, of estimates formed, of intentions understood, of values attached, is exactly to be looked for—

[1]Delivered for the first time before the Contemporary Club of Philadelphia, January 12, 1905, and repeated on various occasions elsewhere. Several passages omitted in delivery—one of considerable length—have been restored.

that is another branch of the question, to which I am afraid I should have to devote quite another discourse. I do not propose for a moment to invite you to blink the fact that our huge Anglo-Saxon array of producers and readers—and especially our vast cis-Atlantic multitude—presents production uncontrolled, production untouched by criticism, unguided, unlighted, uninstructed, unashamed, on a scale that is really a new thing in the world. It is all the complete reversal of any proportion, between the elements, that was ever seen before. It is the biggest flock straying without shepherds, making its music without a sight of the classic crook, beribboned or other, without a sound of the sheepdog's bark—wholesome note, once in a way—that has ever found room for pasture. The very opposite has happened from what might have been expected to happen. The shepherds have diminished as the flock has increased—quite as if number and quantity had got beyond them, or even as if their charge had turned, by some uncanny process, to a pack of ravening wolves. Let us none the less assume that we may still find two or three of the fraternity hiding under a hedge or astride of some upper limb of a tree; let us even assume that if we set rightly, if we set tactfully about it, we may establish again some friendly connection with them.

Putting, on this basis, then, all our heads together, we may become aware of an intelligent gratitude, deep within our breasts, to any author who consents to fit with a certain fulness of presence and squareness of solidity into one of the conscious categories of our attention. There are literary figures in plenty that scarce fill out even the smaller of these critical receptacles; there are others, on the contrary, that almost strain the larger to breaking. It is to these latter that interested contemplation most fondly attaches itself—to that degree, really, that there seems, on any good occasion, more and more about them to be said. They have the great sign that their immediate presence causes our ideas, whether about life in general or about the art they have exemplified in particular, to revive and breathe again, to multiply, more or less to swarm. I must profess that no Novelist—since we are by common consent confining our attention to that great Company—no Novelist, to my sense, so rewards consideration as he or she (and I emphasize the liberality of my "she") who offers the critical spirit this opportunity for a certain intensity of educative practice. The lesson of Balzac, whom we thus march straight up to, is that he offers it as no other members of the company can pretend to do.

For there are members of the company who scarce produce the effect in question at all. Take, to begin with, close at Balzac's side, his illustrious contemporary Madame George Sand, so suggestive, so affirmative, so instructive, as a dealer with life, as an eloquent exponent of her own, as what we call to-day a Personality equipped and armed, but of an artistic complexion so comparatively smooth and simple, so happily harmonious, that her work, taken together, presents about as few pegs for analysis to hang upon as if it were a large, polished, gilded Easter egg, the pride of a sweet-shop if not the treasure of a museum. Let me add, further—so far as it is a question of the nameable sisterhood too—that Jane Austen, with all her light felicity, leaves us hardly more curious of her process, or of the experience in her that fed it, than the brown thrush who tells his story from the garden bough; and this, I freely confess, in spite of her being one of those of the shelved and safe, for all time, of whom I should have liked to begin by talking; one of those in whose favor discrimination has long since practically operated. She is in fact a signal instance of the way it does, with all its embarrassments, at last infallibly operate. A sharp short cut, one of the sharpest and shortest achieved, in this field, by the general judgment, came out, betimes, straight at her feet. Practically overlooked for thirty or forty years after her death, she perhaps really stands there for us as the prettiest possible example of that rectification of estimate, brought about by some slow clearance of stupidity, the half-century or so is capable of working round to. This tide has risen high on the opposite shore, the shore of appreciation—risen rather higher, I think, than the high-water mark, the highest, of her intrinsic merit and interest; though I grant indeed—as a point to be made—that we are dealing here in some degree with the tides so freely driven up, beyond their mere logical reach, by the stiff breeze of the commercial, in other words of the special bookselling spirit; an eager, active, interfering force which has a great many confusions of apparent value, a great many wild and wandering estimates, to answer for. For these distinctively mechanical and overdone reactions, of course, the critical spirit, even in its most relaxed mood, is not responsible. Responsible, rather, is the body of publishers, editors, illustrators, producers of the pleasant twaddle of magazines; who have found their "dear," our dear, everybody's dear, Jane so infinitely to their material purpose, so amenable to pretty reproduction in every variety of what is called tasteful, and in what seemingly proves to be saleable, form.

I do not, naturally, mean that she would be saleable if we had not more or less—beginning with Macaulay, her first slightly ponderous amoroso—lost our hearts to her; but I cannot help seeing her, a good deal, as in the same lucky box as the Brontés—lucky for the ultimate guerdon; a case of popularity (that in especial of the Yorkshire sisters), a beguiled infatuation, a sentimentalized vision, determined largely by the accidents and circumstances originally surrounding the manifestation of the genius—only with the reasons for the sentiment, in this latter connection, turned the other way. The key to Jane Austen's fortune with posterity has been in part the extraordinary grace of her facility, in fact of her unconsciousness: as if, at the most, for difficulty, for embarrassment, she sometimes, over her work-basket, her tapestry flowers, in the spare, cool drawing-room of other days, fell a-musing, lapsed too metaphorically, as one may say, into wool-gathering, and her dropped stitches, of these pardonable, of these precious moments, were afterwards picked up as little touches of human truth, little glimpses of steady vision, little master-strokes of imagination. The romantic tradition of the Brontés, with posterity, has been still more essentially helped, I think, by a force independent of any one of their applied faculties—by the attendant image of their dreary, their tragic history, their loneliness and poverty of life. That picture has been made to hang before us as insistently as the vividest page of "Jane Eyre" or of "Wuthering Heights." If these things were "stories," as we say, and stories of a lively interest, the medium from which they sprang was above all in itself a story, such a story as has fairly elbowed out the rights of appreciation, as has come at last to impose itself as an expression of the power concerned. The personal position of the three sisters, of the two in particular, had been marked, in short, with so sharp an accent that this accent has become for us the very tone of their united production. It covers and supplants their matter, their spirit, their style, their talent, their taste; it embodies, really, the most complete intellectual muddle, if the term be not extravagant, ever achieved, on a literary question, by our wonderful public. The question has scarce indeed been accepted as belonging to literature at all. Literature is an objective, a projected result; it is life that is the unconscious, the agitated, the struggling, floundering cause. But the fashion has been, in looking at the Brontés, so to confound the cause with the result that we cease to know, in the presence of such ecstasies, what we have hold of or what we are talking about. They represent, the ecstasies, the highwater mark of sentimental judgment.

These are but glimmering lanterns, however, you will say, to hang in the great dusky and deserted avenue that leads up to the seated statue of Balzac; and you are so far right, I am bound to admit, as that I place them there, no doubt, in a great measure, just to render the darkness visible. We do, collectively, with all our dimness of view, arrive at rough discriminations, and by one of the roughest of these the author of the "Comédie Humaine" has in a manner profited; we have for many a year taken his greatness for granted; but in the graceless and nerveless fashion of those who edge away from a classic or a bore. "Oh, yes, he is as 'great' as you like—so let us not talk of him!" My purpose has been to "talk" of him, and I find this form of greeting, therefore, and still more this form of parting, not at all adequate; failing as I do to point my moral unless I show that a really paying acquaintance with a writer can never take place if our recognition remains perfunctory. Our indolence and our ignorance may prefer the empty form; but the penalty and the humiliation come for us with the perception that when the consecration really takes place we have been excluded, so to speak, from the fun. I see no better proof that the great interesting art of which Balzac remains the greatest master is practically, round about us, a bankrupt and discredited art (discredited, of course I mean, for any directed and motived attention), than this very fact that we are so ready to beg off from knowing anything about him. Perfunctory rites, even, at present, are seldom rendered; and, amid the flood of verbiage for which the thousand new novels of the season find themselves a pretext in the newspapers, the name of the man who is really the father of us all, as we stand, is scarcely more mentioned than if he were not of the family.

I may at once intimate that the family strikes me as likely to recover its wasted heritage, and pull itself together for another chance, on condition only of shutting itself up, for an hour of wholesome heart-searching, with the image of its founder. He labors, I know, under the drawback of not being presentable as a classic—which is precisely why there would have seemed to be the less furtherance for regarding him as a bore. His situation in this respect is all his own: it was not given him to flower, for our convenience, into a single supreme felicity. His "successes" hang so together that analysis is almost baffled by his consistency, by his density. Even "Eugénie Grandet" is not a supreme felicity in the sense that this particular bloom is detachable from the cluster. The cluster is too thick, the stem too tough; before we know it, when we begin to pull, we have the whole branch about our heads—or it would indeed be more just to say we have the whole tree, if not the whole forest. It tells against a great worker, for free reference, that we must take his work in the mass; for, unfortunately, the circumstance that nothing of it surpassingly stands forth to represent the rest, to symbolize the whole, suggests a striking resemblance to work of other sorts. Of the mediocrities, and the bunglers too is it true that *they* do not supremely flower—as well as, further, of certain happy geniuses who have flowed in an uncontrolled, an undirected, above all in an unfiltered, current.

But the difference is that, for the most part, these loose and easy producers, the great resounding improvisatori, have not, in general, ended by imposing themselves; when we deal with them conclusively and, as I have said, for clearance of the slate, we deal with them by simplification, by elimination: which may very well be the revenge that time takes upon them to make up for the amount of space they happened immediately to occupy. They are still there, evidently; but they are there under this condition, which enters into account, at every instant, in any pious inquiry about them, and which is attached, intimately, to the appearance they finally wear for us, that the looseness and ease showing as their main sign in the time of their freshness is now a quality still more striking and often still more disconcerting. The weak sides in an artist are weakened with time, and the strong sides strengthened; so that it is never amiss, for duration, to have as many strong sides as possible. It is the only way we have yet made out—even in this age of superlative study of the cheap and easy—not to have so many weak ones as will eventually betray us. Balzac stands almost alone as an extemporizer achieving closeness and weight, and whom closeness and weight have preserved. My reason for speaking of him as an extemporizer I shall presently mention; but let me meanwhile frankly say that I speak of him, and can only speak, as a man of his own craft, an emulous fellow-worker, who has learned from him more of the lessons of the engaging mystery of fiction than from any one else, and who is conscious of so large a debt to repay that it has had positively to be discharged in instalments, as if one could never have at once all the required cash in hand.

When I am tempted, on occasion, to ask myself why we should, after all, so much as talk about the Novel, the wanton fable, against which, in so many ways, so showy an indictment may be drawn, I seem to see that the simplest plea is not to be sought in any attempted philosophy, in any abstract reason for our perversity or our levity. The real gloss upon these things is reflected from some great practitioner, some concrete instance of the art, some ample cloak under which we may gratefully crawl. It comes back, of course, to the example and the analogy of the Poet—with the abatement, however, that the Poet is most the Poet when he is preponderantly lyrical, when he speaks, laughing or crying, most directly from his individual heart, which throbs under the impressions of life. It is not the *image* of life that he thus expresses, so much as life itself, in its sources—so much as his own intimate, essential states and feelings. By the time he has begun to collect anecdotes, to tell stories, to represent scenes, to concern himself, that is, with the states and feelings of others, he is well on the way not to be the Poet pure and simple. The lyrical element, all the same, abides in him, and it is by this element that he is connected with what is most splendid in his expression. The lyrical instinct and tradition are immense in Shakespeare; which is why, great story-teller, great dramatist and painter, great lover, in short, of the image of life though he was, we need not press the case of his example. The lyrical element is not great, is in fact not present at all, in Balzac, in Scott (the Scott of the voluminous prose), nor in Thackeray, nor in Dickens—which is precisely why they are so essentially novelists, so almost exclusively lovers of the image of life. It *is* great, or it is at all events largely present, in such a writer as George Sand—which is doubtless why we take her for a novelist in a much looser sense than the others we have named. It is considerable in that bright particular genius of our own day, George Meredith, who so strikes us as hitching winged horses to the chariot of his prose—steeds who prance and dance and caracole, who strain the traces, attempt to quit the ground, and yearn for the upper air. Balzac, with huge feet fairly ploughing the sand of our desert, is on the other hand the very type and model of the projector and creator; so that when I think, either with envy or with terror, of the nature and the effort of the Novelist, I think of something that reaches its highest expression in him. That is why those of us who, as fellow-craftsmen, have once caught a glimpse of this value in him, can never quite rest from hanging about him; that is why he seems to have all that the others have to tell us, with more, besides, that is all his own. He lived and breathed in his medium, and the fact that he was able to achieve in it, as man and as artist, so crowded a career, remains for us one of the most puzzling problems—I scarce know whether to say of literature or of life. He is himself a figure more extraordinary than any he drew, and the fascination may still be endless of all the questions he puts to us and of the answers for which we feel ourselves helpless.

He died, as we sufficiently remember, at fifty—worn out with work and thought and passion; the passion, I mean, that he had put into his mighty plan and that had ridden him like an infliction of the gods. He began, a friendless and penniless young provincial, to write early, and to write very badly, and it was not till well toward his thirtieth year, with the conception of the "Comédie Humaine," as we all again remember, that he found his right ground, found his feet and his voice. This huge distributed, divided and sub-divided picture of the life of France in his time, a picture bristling with imagination and information, with fancies and facts and figures, a world of special and general insight, a rank tropical forest of detail and specification, but with the strong breath of genius forever circulating through it and shaking the treetops to a mighty murmur, got itself hung before us in the space of twenty short years. The achievement remains one of the most inscrutable, one of the unfathomable, final facts in the history of art, and if, as I have said, the author himself has his own surpassing objectivity, it is just because of this challenge his figure constitutes for any other painter of life, inflamed with ingenuity, who should feel the temptation to represent or explain him. How represent, how explain him, as a concrete active energy? How depict him, we ask ourselves, *at* his huge conceived and accepted task, how reconcile such dissemination with such intensity, the collection and possession of so vast a number of facts with so rich a presentation of each? The elements of the world he set up before us, with all its insistent particulars, these elements were not, for him, a direct revelation—of so large a part of life is it true that we can know it only by living, and that living is the process that, in our mortal span, makes the largest demand on our time. How could a man have lived at large so much if, in the service of art, he had so much abstracted and condensed himself? How could he have so much abstracted and condensed himself if, in the service of life, he had felt and fought and acted, had labored and suffered, so much as a private in the ranks? The wealth and strength of his temperament indeed partly answer the question and partly obscure it. He could so extend his existence partly because he vibrated to so many kinds of contact and curiosity. To vibrate intellectually was his motive, but it magnified, all the while, it multiplied his experience. He could live at large, in short, because he was always living in the particular necessary, the particular intended connection— was always astride of his imagination, always charging, with his heavy, his heroic lance in rest, at every object that sprang up in his path. But as he was at the same time always fencing himself in against the personal adventure, the personal experience, in order to preserve himself for converting it into history, how did experience, in the immediate sense, still get itself saved?—or, to put it as simply as possible, where, with so strenuous a conception of the use of material, was material itself so strenuously quarried? Out of what mines, by what innumerable tortuous channels, in what endless winding procession of laden chariots and tugging teams and marching elephants, did the immense consignments required for his work reach him?

The point at which the emulous admirer, however diminished by comparison, may most closely approach him is, it seems to me, through the low portal of envy, so irresistibly do we lose ourselves in the vision of the quantity of life with which his imagination communicated. Quantity and intensity are at once and together his sign; the truth being that his energy did not press hard in some places only to press lightly in others, did not lay it on thick here or there to lay it on thin elsewhere, did not seek the appearance of extent and number by faintness of evocation, by shallow soundings, or by the mere sketchiness of suggestion that dispenses, for reference and verification, with the book, the total collection of human documents, with what we call "chapter and verse." He never throws dust in our eyes, save only the fine gold-dust through the haze of which his own romantic vision operates; never does it, I mean, when he is pretending not to do it, pretending to give us the full statement of his case, to deal with the facts of the spectacle surrounding him. Then he goes in, as we say, for a portentous clearness, a reproduction of the real on the scale of the real—with a definiteness actually proportionate; though a clearness that in truth sometimes fails (like the sight of the forest of the adage, which fails for the presence of the trees), through the positive monstrosity of his effort. He sees and presents too many facts—facts of history, of property, of genealogy, of topography, of sociology, and has too many ideas and images about them; their value is thus threatened with submersion by the flood of general reference in which they float, by their quantity of indicated relation to other facts, which break against them like waves of a high tide. He may thus at times become obscure from his very habit of striking too many matches; or we may at least say of him, out of our wondering loyalty, that the light he produces is, beyond that of any other corner of the great planted garden of romance, thick and rich and heavy—interesting, so to speak, on its own account.

There would be much to say, I think, had we only a little more time, on this question of the projected light of the individual strong temperament in fiction—the color of the air with which this, that or the other painter of life (as we call them all), more or less unconsciously suffuses his picture. I say unconsciously because I speak here of an effect of atmosphere largely, if not wholly, distinct from the effect sought on behalf of the special subject to be treated; something that proceeds from the contemplative mind itself, the very complexion of the mirror in which the material is reflected. This is of the nature of the man himself—an emanation of his spirit, temper, history; it springs from his very presence, his spiritual presence, in his work, and is, in so far, not a matter of calculation and artistry. All a matter of his own, in a word, for each seer of visions, the particular tone of the medium in which each vision, each clustered group of persons and places and objects, is bathed. Just how, accordingly, does the light of the world, the projected, painted, peopled, poetized, realized world, the furnished and fitted world into which we are beguiled for the holiday excursions, cheap trips or dear, of the eternally amusable, eternally dupeable voyaging mind— just how does this strike us as different in Fielding and in Richardson, in Scott and in Dumas, in Dickens and in Thackeray, in Hawthorne and in Meredith, in George Eliot and in George Sand, in Jane Austen and in Charlotte Brontë? Do we not feel the general landscape evoked by each of the more or less magical wands to which I have given name, not to open itself under the same sun that hangs over the neighboring scene, not to receive the solar rays at the same angle, not to exhibit its shadows with the same intensity or the same sharpness; not, in short, to seem to belong to the same time of day or same state of the weather? Why is it that the life that overflows in Dickens seems to me always to go on in the morning, or in the very earliest hours of the afternoon at most, and in a vast apartment that appears to have windows, large, uncurtained and rather unwashed windows, on all sides at once? Why is it that in George Eliot the sun sinks forever to the west, and the shadows are long, and the afternoon wanes, and the trees vaguely rustle, and the color of the day is much inclined to yellow? Why is it that in Charlotte Brontë we move through an endless autumn? Why is it that in Jane Austen we sit quite resigned in an arrested spring? Why does Hawthorne give us the afternoon hour later than any one else?—oh, late, late, quite uncannily late, and as if it were always winter outside? But I am wasting the very minutes I pretended, at the start, to cherish, and am only sustained through my levity by seeing you watch for the time of day or season of the year or state of the weather that I shall fasten upon the complicated clock-face of Thackeray. I do, I think, see his light also—see it very much as the light (a different thing from the mere dull dusk) of rainy days in "residential" streets; but we are not, after all, talking of him, and, though Balzac's waiting power has proved itself, this half-century, immense, I must not too much presume upon it.

The question of the color of Balzac's air and the time of *his* day would indeed here easily solicit our ingenuity—were I at liberty to say more than one thing about it. It is rich and thick, the mixture of sun and shade diffused through the "Comédie Humaine"—a mixture richer and thicker, and representing an absolutely greater quantity of "atmosphere," than we shall find prevailing within the compass of any other suspended frame. That is how we see him, living in his garden, and it is by reason of the restless energy with which he circulated there that I hold his fortune and his privilege, in spite of the burden of his toil and the brevity of his immediate reward, to have been before any others enviable. It is strange enough, but what most abides with us, as we follow his steps, is a sense of the intellectual luxury he enjoyed. To focus him at all, for a single occasion, we have to simplify, and this wealth of his vicarious experience forms the side, moreover, on which he is most attaching for those who take an interest in the real play of the imagination. From the moment our imagination plays at all, of course, and from the moment we try to catch and preserve the pictures it throws off, from that moment we too, in our comparatively feeble way, live vicariously—succeed in opening a series of dusky passages in which, with a more or less childlike ingenuity, we can romp to and fro. Our passages are mainly short and dark, however; we soon come to the end of them—dead walls, without resonance, in presence of which the candle goes out and the game stops, and we have only to retrace our steps. Balzac's luxury, as I call it, was in the extraordinary number and length of his radiating and ramifying corridors—the labyrinth in which he finally lost himself. What it comes back to, in other words, is the intensity with which we live—and his intensity is recorded for us on every page of his work.

It is a question, you see, of *penetrating* into a subject; his corridors always went further and further and further; which is but another way of expressing his inordinate passion for detail. It matters nothing—nothing for my present contention—that this extravagance is also his great fault; in spite, too, of its all being detail vivified and related, characteristic and constructive, essentially prescribed by the terms of his plan. The relations of parts to each other are at moments multiplied almost to madness—which is at the same time just why they give us the measure of his hallucination, make up the greatness of his intellectual adventure. His plan was to handle, primarily, not a world of ideas, animated by figures representing these ideas; but the packed and constituted, the palpable, proveable world before him, by the study of which ideas would inevitably find themselves thrown up. If the happy fate is accordingly to *partake* of life, actively, assertively, not passively, narrowly, in mere sensibility and sufferance, the happiness has been greatest when the faculty employed has been largest. We employ different faculties— some of us only our arms and our legs and our stomach; Balzac employed most what he possessed in largest quantity. This is where his work ceases in a manner to mystify us—this is where we make out how he did quarry his material: it is the sole solution to an otherwise baffling problem. He collected his experience within himself: no other economy explains his achievement; this thrift alone, remarkable yet thinkable, embodies the necessary miracle. His system of cellular confinement, in the interest of the miracle, was positively that of a Benedictine monk leading his life within the four walls of his convent and bent, the year round, over the smooth parchment on which, with wondrous illumination and enhancement of gold and crimson and blue, he inscribes the glories of the faith and the legends of the saints. Balzac's view of himself was indeed in a manner the monkish one; he was most at ease, while he wrought, in the white gown and cowl—an image of him that the friendly art of his time has handed down to us. Only, as happened, his subject of illumination was the legends not merely of the saints, but of the much more numerous uncanonized strugglers and sinners, an acquaintance with whose attributes was not all to be gathered in the place of piety itself; not even from the faintest ink of old records, the mild lips of old brothers, or the painted glass of church windows.

This is where envy does follow him, for to have so many other human cases, so many other personal predicaments to get into, up to one's chin, is verily to be able to get out of one's own box. And it was up to his chin, constantly, that he sank in his illusion—not, as the weak and timid in this line do, only up to his ankles or his knees. The figures he sees begin immediately to bristle with all their characteristics. Every mark and sign, outward and inward, that they possess; every virtue and every vice, every strength and every weakness, every passion and every habit, the sound of their voices, the expression of their eyes, the tricks of feature and limb, the buttons on their clothes, the food on their plates, the money in their pockets, the furniture in their houses, the secrets in their breasts, are all things that interest, that concern, that command him, and that have, for the picture, significance, relation and value. It is a prodigious multiplication of values, and thereby a prodigious entertainment of the vision—on the condition the vision can bear it. Bearing it—that is *our* bearing it—is a serious matter; for the appeal is truly to that faculty of attention out of which we are educating ourselves as hard as we possibly can; educating ourselves with such complacency, with such boisterous high spirits, that we may already be said to have practically lost it—with the consequence that any work of art or of criticism making a demand on it is by that fact essentially discredited. It takes attention not only to thread the labyrinth of the "Comédie Humaine," but to keep our author himself in view, in the relations in which we thus image him. But if we can muster it, as I say, in sufficient quantity, we thus walk with him in the great glazed gallery of his thought; the long, lighted and pictured ambulatory where the endless series of windows, on one side, hangs over his revolutionized, ravaged, yet partly restored and reinstated garden of France, and where, on the other, the figures and the portraits we fancy stepping down to meet him climb back into their frames, larger and smaller, and take up position and expression as he desired they shall look out and compose.

We have lately had a literary case of the same general family as the case of Balzac, and in presence of which some of the same speculations come up: I had occasion, not long since, after the death of Émile Zola, to attempt an appreciation of *his* extraordinary performance—his series of the "Rougon-Macquart" constituting in fact, in the library of the fiction that can hope in some degree to live, a monument to the idea of plenitude, of comprehension and variety, second only to the "Comédie Humaine." The question presented itself, in respect to Zola's ability and Zola's career, with a different proportion and value, I quite recognize, and wearing a much less distinguished face; but it was there to be met, none the less, on the very threshold, and all the more because this was just where he himself had placed it. His idea had been, from the first, in a word, to lose no time—as if one could have experience, even the mere amount requisite for showing others as having it, *without* losing time!—and yet the degree in which he too, so handicapped, has achieved valid expression is such as still to stagger us. He had had inordinately to simplify—had had to leave out the life of the soul, practically, and confine himself to the life of the instincts, of the more immediate passions, such as can be easily and promptly caught in the fact. He had had, in a word, to confine himself almost entirely to the impulses and agitations that men and women are possessed by in common, and to take them as exhibited in mass and number, so that, being writ larger, they might likewise be more easily read. He met and solved, in this manner, his difficulty—the difficulty of knowing, and of showing, of life, only what his "notes" would account for. But it is in the *waste*, I think, much rather—the waste of time, of passion, of curiosity, of contact—that true initiation resides; so that the most wonderful adventures of the artist's spirit are those, immensely quickening for his "authority," that are yet not reducible to his notes. It is exactly here that we get the difference between such a solid, square, symmetrical structure as "Les Rougon-Macquart," vitiated, in a high degree, by its mechanical side, and the monument left by Balzac—without the example of which, I surmise, Zola's work would not have existed. The mystic process of the crucible, the transformation of the material under æsthetic heat, is, in the "Comédie Humaine," thanks to an intenser and more submissive fusion, completer, and also finer; for if the commoner and more wayside passions and conditions are, in the various episodes there, at no time gathered into so large and so thick an illustrative bunch, yet on the other hand they are shown much more freely at play in the individual case—and the individual case it is that permits of supreme fineness. It is hard to say where Zola is fine; whereas it is often, for pages together, hard to say where Balzac is, even under the weight of his too ponderous personality, not. The most fundamental and general sign of the novel, from one desperate experiment to another, is its being everywhere an effort at *representation*—this is the beginning and the end of it: wherefore it was that one could say at last, with account taken of everything, that Zola's performance, on his immense scale, was an extraordinary show of representation imitated. The imitation in places—notably and admirably, for instance, in "L'Assommoir"—breaks through into something that we take for reality; but, for the most part, the separating rift, the determining difference, holds its course straight, prevents the attempted process from becoming the sound, straight, whole thing that is given us by those who have really *bought* their information. This is where Balzac remains unshaken—in our feeling that, with all his faults of pedantry, ponderosity, pretentiousness, bad taste and charmless form, his spirit has somehow paid for its knowledge. His subject is again and again the complicated human creature or human condition; and it is with these complications as if he knew them, as Shakespeare knew them,

by his charged consciousness, by the history of his soul and
the direct exposure of his sensibility. This source of supply he
found, forever—and one may indeed say he mostly left—sitting at his fireside; where it constituted the company with
which I see him shut up and his practical intimacy with
which, during such orgies and debauches of intellectual passion, might earn itself that name of high personal good fortune that I have applied.

Let me say, definitely, that I hold several of his faults to be
grave, and that if there were any question of time for it I
should like to speak of them; but let me add, as promptly,
that they are faults, on the whole, of execution, flaws in the
casting, accidents of the process: they never come back to that
fault in the artist, in the novelist, that amounts most completely to a failure of dignity, the absence of saturation with
his idea. When saturation fails no other presence really avails;
as when, on the other hand, it operates, no failure of method
fatally interferes. There is never in Balzac that damning interference which consists of the painter's not seeing, not possessing, his image; not having fixed his creature and his
creature's conditions. "Balzac aime sa Valérie," says Taine, in
his great essay—so much the finest thing ever written on our
author—speaking of the way in which the awful little Madame Marneffe of "Les Parents Pauvres" is drawn, and of the
long rope, for her acting herself out, that her creator's participation in her reality assures her. He has been contrasting
her, as it happens, with Thackeray's Becky Sharp or rather
with Thackeray's attitude toward Becky, and the marked jealousy of her freedom that Thackeray exhibits from the first. I
remember reading at the time of the publication of Taine's
study—though it was long, long ago—a phrase in an English
review of the volume which seemed to my limited perception,
even in extreme youth, to deserve the highest prize ever bestowed on critical stupidity undisguised. If Balzac loved his
Valérie, said this commentator, that only showed Balzac's extraordinary taste; the truth being really, throughout, that it
was just through this love of each seized identity, and of the
sharpest and liveliest identities most, that Madame Marneffe's
creator was able to marshal his array at all. The love, as we
call it, the joy in their communicated and exhibited move-

ment, in their standing on their feet and going of themselves and acting out their characters, was what rendered possible the saturation I speak of; what supplied him, through the inevitable gaps of his preparation and the crevices of his prison, his long prison of labor, a short cut to the knowledge he required. It was by loving them—as the terms of his subject and the nuggets of his mine—that he knew them; it was not by knowing them that he loved.

He at all events robustly loved the sense of another explored, assumed, assimilated identity—enjoyed it as the hand enjoys the glove when the glove ideally fits. My image indeed is loose; for what he liked was absolutely to get into the constituted consciousness, into all the clothes, gloves and whatever else, into the very skin and bones, of the habited, featured, colored, articulated form of life that he desired to present. How do we know given persons, for any purpose of demonstration, unless we know their situation for themselves, unless we see it from their point of vision, that is from their point of pressing consciousness or sensation?—without our allowing for which there is no appreciation. Balzac loved his Valérie then as Thackeray did not love his Becky, or his Blanche Amory in "Pendennis." But his prompting was not to expose her; it could only be, on the contrary—intensely aware as he was of all the lengths she might go, and paternally, maternally alarmed about them—to cover her up and protect her, in the interest of her special genius and freedom. All his impulse was to *la faire valoir*, to give her all her value, just as Thackeray's attitude was the opposite one, a desire positively to expose and desecrate poor Becky—to follow her up, catch her in the act and bring her to shame: though with a mitigation, an admiration, an inconsequence, now and then wrested from him by an instinct finer, in his mind, than the so-called "moral" eagerness. The English writer wants to make sure, first of all, of your moral judgment; the French is willing, while it waits a little, to risk, for the sake of his subject and its interest, your spiritual salvation. Madame Marneffe, detrimental, fatal as she is, is "exposed," so far as anything in life, or in art, may be, by the working-out of the situation and the subject themselves; so that when they have done what they would, what they logically had to, with her, we are ready to take it from them. We do not feel, very irritatedly, very lecturedly, in other words with superfluous edification, that she has been sacrificed. Who can say, on the contrary, that Blanche Amory, in "Pendennis," with the author's lash about her little bare white back from the first—who can feel that she has *not* been sacrificed, or that her little bareness and whiteness, and all the rest of her, have been, by such a process, presented as they had a right to demand?

It all comes back, in fine, to that respect for the liberty of the subject which I should be willing to name as *the* great sign of the painter of the first order. Such a witness to the human comedy fairly holds his breath for fear of arresting or diverting that natural license; the witness who begins to breathe so uneasily in presence of it that his respiration not only warns off the little prowling or playing creature he is supposed to be studying, but drowns, for our ears, the ingenuous sounds of the animal, as well as the general, truthful hum of the human scene at large—this demonstrator has no sufficient warrant for his task. And if such an induction as this is largely the moral of our renewed glance at Balzac, there is a lesson, of a more essential sort, I think, folded still deeper within—the lesson that there is no convincing art that is not ruinously expensive. I am unwilling to say, in the presence of such of his successors as George Eliot and Tolstoi and Zola (to name, for convenience, only three of them), that he was the last of the novelists to do the thing handsomely; but I will say that we get the impression at least of his having had more to spend. Many of those who have followed him affect us as doing it, in the vulgar phrase, "on the cheap;" by reason mainly, no doubt, of their having been, all helplessly, foredoomed to cheapness. Nothing counts, of course, in art, but the excellent; nothing exists, however briefly, for estimation, for appreciation, but the superlative—always in its kind; and who shall declare that the severe economy of the vast majority of those apparently emulous of the attempt to "render" the human subject and the human scene proceeds from anything worse than the consciousness of a limited capital? This flourishing frugality operates happily, no doubt—given all the circumstances—for the novelist; but it has had terrible results for the novel, so far as the novel is a form with which criti-

cism may be moved to concern itself. Its misfortune, its discredit, what I have called its bankrupt state among us, is the
not unnatural consequence of its having ceased, for the most
part, to be artistically interesting. It has become an object of
easy manufacture, showing on every side the stamp of the
machine; it has become the article of commerce, produced in
quantity, and as we so see it we inevitably turn from it, under
the rare visitations of the critical impulse, to compare it with
those more precious products of the same general nature that
we used to think of as belonging to the class of the hand-
made.

The lesson of Balzac, under this comparison, is extremely
various, and I should prepare myself much too large a task
were I to attempt a list of the separate truths he brings home.
I have to choose among them, and I choose the most important; the three or four that more or less include the others. In
reading him over, in opening him almost anywhere to-day,
what immediately strikes us is the part assigned by him, in
any picture, to the *conditions* of the creatures with whom he
is concerned. Contrasted with him other prose painters of life
scarce seem to see the conditions at all. He clearly held pretended portrayal as nothing, as less than nothing, as a most
vain thing, unless it should be, in spirit and intention, the art
of complete representation. "Complete" is of course a great
word, and there is no art at all, we are often reminded, that
is not on too many sides an abject compromise. The element
of compromise is always there; it is of the essence; we live
with it, and it may serve to keep us humble. The formula of
the whole matter is sufficiently expressed perhaps in a reply I
found myself once making to an inspired but discouraged
friend, a fellow-craftsman who had declared in his despair
that there was no use trying, that it was a form, the novel,
absolutely too difficult. "Too difficult indeed; yet there is one
way to master it—which is to pretend consistently that it is
n't." We are all of us, all the while, pretending—as consistently as we can—that it is n't, and Balzac's great glory is that
he pretended hardest. He never had to pretend so hard as
when he addressed himself to that evocation of the medium,
that distillation of the natural and social air, of which I speak,
the things that most require on the part of the painter prelim-

inary possession—so definitely require it that, terrified at the requisition when conscious of it, many a painter prefers to beg the whole question. He has thus, this ingenious person, to invent some *other* way of making his characters interesting—some other way, that is, than the arduous way, demanding so much consideration, of presenting them to us. They are interesting, in fact, as subjects of fate, the figures round whom a situation closes, in proportion as, sharing their existence, we feel where fate comes in and just how it gets at them. In the void they are not interesting—and Balzac, like Nature herself, abhorred a vacuum. Their situation takes hold of us because it is theirs, not because it is somebody's, any one's, that of creatures unidentified. Therefore it is not superfluous that their identity shall first be established for us, and their adventures, in that measure, have a relation to it, and therewith an appreciability. There is no such thing in the world as an adventure pure and simple; there is only mine and yours, and his and hers—it being the greatest adventure of all, I verily think, just to *be* you or I, just to be he or she. To Balzac's imagination that was indeed in itself an immense adventure—and nothing appealed to him more than to show *how* we all are, and how we are placed and built-in for being so. What befalls us is but another name for the way our circumstances press upon us—so that an account of what befalls us is an account of our circumstances.

Add to this, then, that the fusion of all the elements of the picture, under his hand, is complete—of what people are with what they do, of what they do with what they are, of the action with the agents, of the medium with the action, of all the parts of the drama with each other. Such a production as "Le Père Goriot" for example, or as "Eugénie Grandet," or as "Le Curé de Village," has, in respect to this fusion, a kind of inscrutable perfection. The situation sits shrouded in its circumstances, and then, by its inner expansive force, emerges from them, the action marches, to the rich rustle of this great tragic and ironic train, the embroidered heroic mantle, with an art of keeping together that makes of "Le Père Goriot" in especial a supreme case of composition, a model of that high virtue that we know as economy of effect, economy of line and touch. An inveterate sense of proportion was not, in general, Balzac's distinguishing mark; but with great talents one has great surprises, and the effect of this large handling of the conditions was more often than not to make the work, whatever it might be, appear admirably composed. Of all the costly charms of a "story" this interest derived from composition is the costliest—and there is perhaps no better proof of our present penury than the fact that, in general, when one makes a plea for it, the plea might seemingly (for all it is understood!) be for trigonometry or osteology. "Composition?—what may that happen to *be*, and, whatever it is, what has it to do with the matter?" I shall take for granted here that every one perfectly knows, for without that assumption I shall not be able to wind up, as I must immediately do. The presence of the conditions, when really presented, when made vivid, provides for the action—which is, from step to step, constantly implied in them; whereas the process of suspending the action in the void and dressing it there with the tinkling bells of what is called dialogue only makes no provision at all for the other interest. There are two elements of the art of the novelist which, as they present, I think, the greatest difficulty, tend thereby most to fascinate us: in the first place that mystery of the foreshortened procession of facts and figures, of appearances of whatever sort, which is in some lights but another name for the picture governed by the principle of composition, and which has at any rate as little as possible in common with the method now usual among us, the juxtaposition of items emulating the column of numbers of a schoolboy's sum in addition. It is the art of the brush, I know, as opposed to the art of the slate-pencil; but to the art of the brush the novel must return, I hold, to recover whatever may be still recoverable of its sacrificed honor.

The second difficulty that I commend for its fascination, at all events, the most attaching when met and the most rewarding when triumphantly met—though I hasten to add that it also strikes me as not only the least "met," in general, but the least suspected—this second difficulty is that of representing, to put it simply, the lapse of time, the duration of the subject: representing it, that is, more subtly than by a blank space, or a row of stars, on the historic page. With the blank space and the row of stars Balzac's genius had no affinity, and he is therefore as unlike as possible those narrators—so numerous, all round us, it would appear, to-day in especial—the succession of whose steps and stages, the development of whose action, in the given case, affects us as occupying but a week or two. No one begins, to my sense, to handle the time-element and produce the time-effect with the authority of Balzac in his amplest sweeps—by which I am far from meaning in his longest passages. That study of the foreshortened image, of the neglect of which I suggest the ill consequence, is precisely the enemy of the tiresome procession of would-be narrative items, seen all in profile, like the rail-heads of a fence; a substitute for the baser device of accounting for the time-quantity by mere quantity of statement. Quality and manner of statement account for it in a finer way—always assuming, as I say, that unless it is accounted for nothing else really is. The fashion of our day is to account for it almost exclusively by an inordinate abuse of the colloquial resource, of the report, from page to page, from chapter to chapter, from beginning to end, of the talk, between the persons involved, in which situation and action may be conceived as registered. Talk between persons is perhaps, of all the parts of the novelist's plan, the part that Balzac most scrupulously weighed and measured and kept in its place; judging it, I think—though he perhaps even had an undue suspicion of its possible cheapness, as feeling it the thing that can least afford to be cheap—a precious and supreme resource, the very flower of illustration of the subject and thereby not to be inconsiderately discounted. It was his view, discernibly, that the flower must keep its bloom, or in other words not be too much handled, in order to have a fragrance when nothing but its fragrance will serve.

It was his view indeed positively that there is a *law* in these things, and that, admirable for illustration, functional for illustration, dialogue has its function perverted, and therewith its life destroyed, when forced, all clumsily, into the constructive office. It is in the drama, of course, that it is constructive; but the drama lives by a law so different, verily, that everything that is right for it seems wrong for the prose picture, and everything that is right for the prose picture addressed directly, in turn, to the betrayal of the "play." These are questions, however, that bore deep—if I have successfully braved the danger that they absolutely do bore; so that I must content myself, as a glance at this point, with the claim for the author of "Le Père Goriot" that colloquial illustration, in his work, suffers less, on the whole, than in any other I know, from its attendant, its besetting and haunting penalty of springing, unless watched, a leak in its effect. It is as if the master of the ship were keeping his eye on the pump; the pump, I mean, of relief and alternation, the pump that keeps the vessel free of too much water. We must always remember that, save in the cases where "dialogue" is organic, is the very law of the game—in which case, as I say, the game is another business altogether—it is essentially the fluid element: as, for instance (to cite, conveniently, Balzac's most eminent prose contemporary), was strikingly its character in the elder Dumas; just as its character in the younger, the dramatist, illustrates supremely what I call the other game. The current, in old Dumas, the large, loose, facile flood of talked movement, talked interest, as much as you will, is, in virtue of this fluidity, a current indeed, with so little of wrought texture that we float and splash in it; feeling it thus resemble much more some capacious tepid tank than the figured tapestry, all over-scored with objects in fine perspective, which symbolizes to me (if one may have a symbol) the last word of the achieved fable. Such a tapestry, with its wealth of expression of its subject, with its myriad ordered stitches, its harmonies of tone and felicities of taste, is a work, above all, of closeness—and therefore the more pertinent image here as it is in the name of closeness that I am inviting you to let Balzac once more appeal to you.

It will strike you perhaps that I speak as if we all, as if you all, without exception were novelists, haunting the back shop, the laboratory, or, more nobly expressed, the inner shrine of the temple; but such assumptions, in this age of print—if I may not say this age of poetry—are perhaps never too wide of the mark, and I have at any rate taken your interest sufficiently for granted to ask you to close up with me for an hour at the feet of the master of us all. Many of us may stray, but he always remains—he is fixed by virtue of his weight. Do not look too knowing at that—as a hint that you were already conscious he is heavy, and that if this is what I have mainly to suggest my lesson might have been spared. He is, I grant, too heavy to be moved; many of us may stray and straggle, as I say—since we have not his inaptitude largely to circulate. There is none the less such an odd condition as circulating without motion, and I am not so sure that even in our own way we do move. We do not, at any rate, get away from him; he is behind us, at the worst, when he is not before, and I feel that any course about the country we explore is ever best held by keeping him, through the trees of the forest, in sight. So far as we do move, we move round him; every road comes back to him; he sits there, in spite of us, so massively, for orientation. "Heavy" therefore if we like, but heavy because weighted with his fortune; the extraordinary fortune that has survived all the extravagance of his career, his twenty years of royal intellectual spending, and that has done so by reason of the rare value of the original property—the high, prime genius so tied-up from him that that was safe. And "that," through all that has come and gone, has steadily, has enormously appreciated. Let us then also, if we see him, in the sacred grove, as our towering idol, see him as gilded thick, with so much gold—plated and burnished and bright, in the manner of towering idols. It is for the lighter and looser and poorer among us to be gilded thin!

Atlantic Monthly, August 1905
Reprinted in *The Question of Our Speech.*
The Lesson of Balzac. Two Lectures. 1905

Balzac. Par Émile Faguet, de l'Académie Française. Les Grands Ecrivains Français. Paris: Hachette, 1913.

IT IS A PLEASURE to meet M. Émile Faguet on the same ground of mastered critical method and in the same air of cool deliberation and conclusion that so favoured his excellent study of Flaubert in the rich series to which the present volume belongs. It was worth while waiting these many years for a Balzac to get it at last from a hand of so firm a grip, if not quite of the very finest manipulative instinct. It can scarce ever be said of M. Faguet that he tends to play with a subject, at least a literary one; but nobody is better for circling his theme in sound and easy pedestrian fashion, for taking up each of its aspects in order, for a sense, above all, of the order in which they *should* be taken, and for then, after doing them successively justice, reaching the point from which they appear to melt together. He thus gives us one of those literary portraits the tradition of which, so far at least as they are the fruit of method, has continued scantily to flourish among ourselves. We cannot help thinking indeed that an ideally authoritative portrait of Balzac would be the work of some pondering painter able to measure the great man's bequest a little more from within or by a coincidence of special faculty, or that in other words the particular initiation and fellow-feeling of some like—that is not too unlike—imaginative projector as well are rather wanted here to warm and colour the critical truth to the right glow of appreciation. Which comes to saying, we quite acknowledge, that a "tribute" to Balzac, of however embracing an intention, may still strike us as partly unachieved if we fail to catch yearning and shining through it, like a motive in a musical mixture or a thread of gold in a piece of close weaving, the all but overriding sympathy of novelist with novelist. M. Faguet's intelligence at any rate sweeps his ground clear of the anecdotal, the question-begging reference to odds and ends of the personal and superficial, in a single short chapter, and, having got so promptly over this second line of defence, attacks at once the issue of his author's general ideas—matters apt to be, in any group of contributors to a "series" of our own, exactly what the contributor most shirks considering.

It is true that few writers, and especially few novelists, bring up that question with anything like the gross assurance and systematic confidence of Balzac, who clearly took for involved in his plan of a complete picture of the manners and aspects of his country and his period that he should have his confident "say" about as many things as possible, and who, throughout his immense work, appears never for an instant or in any connection to flinch from that complacency. Here it is easy to await him, waylay him and catch him in the act, with the consequence, for the most part, of our having to

recognise almost with compassion the disparity between the
author of "La Cousine Bette" exercising his genius, as Matthew Arnold said of Ruskin, in making a like distinction, and
the same writer taking on a character not in the least really
rooted in that soil. The fact none the less that his generalising
remains throughout so markedly inferior to his particularis-
ing—which latter element and very essence of the novelist's
art it was his greatness to carry further and apply more consistently than any member of the craft, without exception, has
felt the impulse, to say nothing of finding the way, to do—
by no means wholly destroys the interest of the habit itself or
relieves us of a due attention to it; so characteristic and significant, so suggestive even of his special force, though in a
manner indirect, are the very folds and redundancies of this
philosopher's robe that flaps about his feet and drags along
the ground like an assumed official train. The interest here—
where it is exactly that a whole face of his undertaking would
be most illumined for the fellow-artist we imagine trying to
exhibit him—depends much less on what his reflection and
opinion, his irrepressible *obiter dicta* and monstrous *suffisances*
of judgment may be, than on the part played in his scheme
by his holding himself ready at every turn and at such short
notice to judge. For this latter fact probably lights up more
than any other his conception of the range of the novel, the
fashion after which, in his hands, it had been felt as an all-
inclusive form, a form without rift or leak, a tight mould,
literally, into which everything relevant to a consideration of
the society surrounding him—and the less relevant unfortunately, as well as the more—might be poured in a stream of
increasing consistency, the underlapping subject stretched, all
so formidably, to its own constituted edge and the compound
appointed to reproduce, as in finest and subtlest relief, its
every minutest feature, overlying and corresponding with it
all round to the loss of no fraction of an inch.

It is thus the painter's aspiring and rejoicing consciousness
of the great square swarming picture, the picture of France
from side to side and from top to bottom, which he proposes
to copy—unless we see the collective quantity rather as the
vast primary model or sitter that he is unprecedentedly to
portray, it is this that, rendering him enviable in proportion

to his audacity and his presumption, gives a dignity to everything that makes the consciousness whole. The result is a state
of possession of his material unlike that of any other teller of
tales whatever about a circumjacent world, and the process of
his gain of which opens up well-nigh the first of those more
or less baffling questions, parts indeed of the great question
of the economic rule, the practical secret, of his activity, that
beset us as soon as we study him. To fit what he was and
what he did, that is the measure of how he used himself and
how he used every one and everything else, into his after all
so brief career (for twenty years cover the really productive
term of it) is for ourselves, we confess, to renounce any other
solution than that of his having proceeded by a sense for
facts, the multitudinous facts of the scene about him, that
somehow involved a preliminary, a pre-experiential inspiration, a straightness of intuition truly impossible to give an
account of and the like of which had never before been
shown. He had not to learn things in order to know them;
and even though he multiplied himself in more ways than we
can reckon up, going hither and thither geographically, leading his life with violence, as it were, though always with intention, and wasting almost nothing that had ever touched
him, the natural man, the baptised and registered Honoré, let
loose with harsh promptitude upon a world formed from the
first moment to excite his voracity, can only have been *all* the
exploiting agent, the pushing inquirer, the infallible appraiser,
the subject of an *arrière-pensée* as merciless, in spite of being
otherwise genial, as the black care riding behind the horseman. There was thus left over for him less of mere human
looseness, of mere emotion, of mere naturalness, or of any
curiosity whatever, that didn't "pay"—and the extent to
which he liked things to pay, to see them, think of them, and
describe them as prodigiously paying, is not to be expressed—than probably marks any recorded relation between
author and subject as we know each of these terms.

So it comes that his mastership of whatever given identity
might be in question, and much more of the general identity
of his rounded (for the artistic vision), his compact and containing France, the fixed, felt frame to him of the vividest
items and richest characteristics of human life, can really not

be thought of as a matter of degrees of confidence, as acquired or built up or cumbered with verifying fears. He *was* the given identity and, on the faintest shade of a hint about it caught up, became one with it and lived it—this in the only way in which he could live, anywhere or at any time: which was by losing himself in its relation to his need or to what we call his voracity. Just so his mind, his power of apprehension, worked *naturally* in the interest of a society disclosed to that appetite; on the mere approach to the display he inhaled information, he recognised himself as what he might best be known for, an historian unprecedented, an historian documented as none had not only ever been, but had ever dreamed of being—and even if the method of his documentation can leave us for the most part but wondering. The method of his use of it, or of a portion of it, we more or less analyse and measure; but the wealth of his provision or outfit itself, the crammed store of his categories and *cadres*, leaves us the more stupefied as we feel it to have been honestly come by. All this is what it is impossible not to regard as in itself a fundamental felicity such as no *confrère* had known; so far, indeed, as Balzac suffered *confrères* or as the very nature of his faculty could be thought of for them. M. Brunetière's monograph of some years ago, which is but a couple of degrees less weighty, to our sense, than this of M. Faguet before us, justly notes that, whatever other felicity may have graced the exercise of such a genius, for instance, as that rare contemporary George Sand, she was reduced well-nigh altogether to drawing upon resources and enjoying advantages comparatively vague and unassured. She had of course in a manner her special resource and particular advantage, which consisted, so to speak, in a finer feeling about what she did possess and could treat of with authority, and particularly in a finer command of the terms of expression, than any involved in Balzac's "happier" example. But her almost fatal weakness as a novelist—an exponent of the art who has waned exactly as, for our general long-drawn appreciation, Balzac has waxed—comes from her having had to throw herself upon ground that no order governed, no frame, as we have said, enclosed, and no safety attended; safety of the sort, we mean, the safety of the constitutive, illustrative fact among facts, which we find in her rival as a warm socialised air, an element supremely assimilable.

It may freely be pronounced interesting that whereas, in her instinct for her highest security, she threw herself upon the consideration of love as the *type* attraction or most representable thing in the human scene, so, assuredly, no student of that field has, in proportion to the thoroughness of his study, felt he could afford to subordinate or almost even to neglect it to anything like the tune in which we see it put and kept in its place through the parts of the Comédie Humaine that most count. If this passion but too often exhales a tepid breath in much other fiction—much other of ours at least—that is apt to come decidedly less from the writer's sense of proportion than from his failure of art, or in other words of intensity. It is rarely absent by intention or by intelligence, it is pretty well always there as the theoretic principal thing—any difference from writer to writer being mostly in the power to put the principal thing effectively forward. It figures as a pressing, an indispensable even if a perfunctory motive, for example, in every situation devised by Walter Scott; the case being simply that if it doesn't in fact attractively occupy the foreground this is because his hand has had so native, so much greater, an ease for other parts of the picture. What makes Balzac so pre-eminent and exemplary that he was to leave the novel a far other and a vastly more capacious and significant affair than he found it, is his having felt his fellow-creatures (almost altogether for him his contemporaries) as quite failing of reality, as swimming in the vague and the void and the abstract, unless their social conditions, to the last particular, their generative and contributive circumstances, of every discernible sort, enter for all these are " worth" into his representative attempt. This great compound of the total looked into and starting up in its element, as it always does, to meet the eye of genius and patience half way, bristled for him with all its branching connections, those thanks to which any figure could *be* a figure but by showing for endlessly entangled in them.

So it was then that his huge felicity, to re-emphasise our term, was in his state of circulating where recognitions and identifications didn't so much await as rejoicingly assault him, having never yet in all the world, grudged or at the best sus-

pected feeders as they were at the board where sentiment occupied the head, felt themselves so finely important or subject
to such a worried intention. They hung over a scene as to
which it was one of the forces of his inspiration that history
had lately been there at work, with incomparable energy and
inimitable art, to pile one upon another, not to say squeeze
and dovetail violently into each other, after such a fashion as
might defy competition anywhere, her successive deposits and
layers of form and order, her restless determinations of appearance—so like those of the different "states" of an engraver's impression; all to an effect which *should* have constituted,
as by a miracle of coincidence it did, the paradise of an extraordinary observer. Balzac lived accordingly, extraordinary
since he was, in an earthly heaven so near perfect for his kind
of vision that he could have come at no moment more conceivably blest to him. The later part of the eighteenth century,
with the Revolution, the Empire and the Restoration, had
inimitably conspired together to scatter abroad their separate
marks and stigmas, their separate trails of character and phys-
iognomic hits—for which advantage he might have arrived
too late, as his hapless successors, even his more or less direct
imitators, visibly have done. The fatal fusions and uniformi-
ties inflicted on our newer generations, the running together
of all the differences of form and tone, the ruinous liquefying
wash of the great industrial brush over the old conditions of
contrast and colour, doubtless still have left the painter of
manners much to do, but have ground him down to the sad
fact that his ideals of differentiation, those inherent oppositions from type to type, in which drama most naturally resides, have well-nigh perished. They pant for life in a hostile
air; and we may surely say that their last successful struggle,
their last bright resistance to eclipse among ourselves, was in
their feverish dance to the great fiddling of Dickens. Dickens
made them dance, we seem to see, caper and kick their heels,
wave their arms, and above all agitate their features, for the
simple reason that he couldn't make them stand or sit *at once*
quietly and expressively, couldn't make them look straight out
as for themselves—quite in fact as though his not daring to,
not feeling he could afford to, in a changing hour when ambiguities and the wavering line, droll and "dodgy" dazzle-

ments and the possibly undetected factitious alone, might be trusted to keep him right with an incredibly uncritical public, a public blind to the difference between a shade and a patch.

Balzac on the other hand, born as we have seen to confidence, the tonic air of his paradise, might make character, in the sense in which we use it, that of the element exposable to the closest verification, sit or stand for its "likeness" as still as ever it would. It is true that he could, as he often did, resort to fond extravagance, since he was apt at his worst to plunge into agitation for mere agitation's sake—which is a course that, by any turn, may cast the plunger on the barrenest strand. But he is at his best when the conditions, the whole complex of subdivisible form and pressure, are virtually themselves the situation, the action and the interest, or in other words when these things exhaust themselves, as it were, in expressing the persons we are concerned with, agents and victims alike, and when by such vivified figures, whether victims or agents, they are themselves completely expressed. The three distinguished critics who have best studied him, Taine, Brunetière and now (as well as before this) M. Faguet—the first the most eloquent but the loosest, and the last the closest even if the dryest—are in agreement indeed as to the vast quantity of waste in him, inevitably judging the romanticist as whom he so frequently, speculatively, desperately paraded altogether inferior to the realist whose function he could still repeatedly and richly and for his greater glory exercise. This estimate of his particularly greater glory is of a truth not wholly shared by M. Taine; but the three are virtually at one, where we of course join them, or rather go further than they, as to the enviability, so again to call it (and by which we mean the matchless freedom of play), of his harvesting sense when he gave himself up in fullest measure to his apprehension of the dense wholeness of reality. It was this that led him on and kept him true to that happily largest side of his labour by which he must massively live; just as it is this, the breath of his real geniality, when every abatement is made, that stirs to loyalty those who under his example also take his direction and find their joy in watching him thoroughly at work. We see then how, when social character and evolved type are the prize to be grasped, the facts of observation and certification, unrestingly social and historic too, that form and fondle and retouch it, never relaxing their action, are so easily and blessedly absolute to him that this is what we mean by their virtue.

When there were enough of these quantities and qualities flowering into the definite and the absolute for him to feed on, feed if not to satiety at least to the largest loosening of his intellectual belt, there were so many that we may even fall in with most of M. Faguet's discriminations and reserves about him and yet find his edifice rest on proportioned foundations. For it is his assimilation of things and things, of his store of them and of the right ones, the right for representation, that leaves his general image, even with great chunks of surface surgically, that is critically, removed, still coherent and erect. There are moments when M. Faguet—most surgical he!—seems to threaten to remove so much that we ask ourselves in wonder what may be left; but no removal matters while the principle of observation animating the mass is left unattacked. Our present critic for instance is "down"—very understandingly down as seems to us—on some of the sides of his author's rich temperamental vulgarity; which is accompanied on those sides by want of taste, want of wit, want of style, want of knowledge of ever so many parts of the general subject, too precipitately proposed, and want of fineness of feeling about ever so many others. We agree with him freely enough, subject always to this reserve already glanced at, that a novelist of a high esthetic sensibility must always find more in any other novelist worth considering seriously at all than he can perhaps hope to impart even to the most intelligent of critics pure and simple his subtle reasons for. This said, we lose ourselves, to admiration, in such a matter for example as the tight hug of the mere material, the supremely important if such ever was, represented by the appeal to us on behalf of the money-matters of César Birotteau.

This illustration gains logically, much more than loses, from the rank predominance of the money-question, the money-vision, throughout all Balzac. There are lights in which it can scarce not appear to us that his own interest is greater, his possibilities of attention truer, in these pressing particulars than in all other questions put together; there could be no better sign of the appreciation of "things," exactly, than so never relaxed a grasp of the part played in the world by just these. Things for things, the franc, the shilling, the dollar, are the very most underlying and conditioning, even dramatically, even poetically, that call upon him; and we have everywhere to recognise how little he feels himself to be telling us of this, that and the other person unless he has first given us full information, with every detail, either as to their private means, their income, investments, savings, losses, the state in fine of their pockets, or as to their immediate place of habitation, their home, their outermost shell, with its windows and doors, its outside appearance and inside plan, its rooms and furniture and arrangements, its altogether intimate facts, down to its very smell. This prompt and earnest evocation of the shell and its lining is but another way of testifying with due emphasis to economic conditions. The most personal shell of all, the significant dress of the individual, whether man or woman, is subject to as sharp and as deep a notation—it being no small part of his wealth of luck that the age of dress differentiated and specialised from class to class and character to character, not least moreover among men, could still give him opportunities of choice, still help him to define and intensify, or peculiarly to *place* his apparitions. The old world in which costume had, to the last refinement of variety, a social meaning happily lingered on for him; and nothing is more interesting, nothing goes further in this sense of the way the social concrete could minister to him, than the fact that "César Birotteau," to instance that masterpiece again, besides being a money-drama of the closest texture, the very epic of retail bankruptcy, is at the same time the all-vividest exhibition of the habited and figured, the representatively stamped and countenanced, buttoned and buckled state of the persons moving through it. No livelier example therefore can we name of the triumphant way in which any given, or as we should rather say taken, total of conditions works out under our author's hand for accentuation of type. The story of poor Birotteau is just in this supreme degree a hard total, even if every one's money-relation does loom larger, for his or her case, than anything else.

The main thing doubtless to agree with M. Faguet about,

however, is the wonder of the rate at which this genius for an infatuated grasp of the environment could multiply the creatures swarming, and swarming at their best to perfection, in that jungle of elements. A jungle certainly the environment, the rank many-coloured picture of France, would have been had it not really created in our observer the joy, thanks to his need of a clear and marked order, of its becoming so arrangeable. Nothing could interest us more than to note with our critic that such multiplications—taken after all at such a rush—have to be paid for by a sort of limitation of quality in each, the quality that, beyond a certain point and after a certain allowance, ever looks askance at any approach to what it may be figured as taking for *insolence* of quantity. Some inquiry into the general mystery of such laws of payment would beckon us on had we the space—whereby we might glance a little at the wondrous why and wherefore of the sacrifice foredoomed, the loss, greater or less, of those ideals now compromised by the tarnished names of refinement and distinction, yet which we are none the less, at our decentest, still ashamed too entirely to turn our backs on, in the presence of energies that, shaking the air by their embrace of the common, tend to dispossess the rare of a certified place in it. Delightful to the critical mind to estimate the point at which, in the picture of life, a sense for the element of the rare ceases to consort with a sense, necessarily large and lusty, for the varieties of the real that super-abound. Reducible perhaps to some exquisite measure is this point of fatal divergence. It declared itself, the divergence, in the heart of Balzac's genius; for nothing about him is less to be gainsaid than that on the other or further side of a certain line of rareness drawn his authority, so splendid on the hither or familiar side, is sadly liable to lapse. It fails to take in whatever fine truth experience may have vouchsafed to us about the highest kinds of temper, the inward life of the mind, the *cultivated* consciousness. His truest and vividest people are those whom the conditions in which they are so palpably embedded have simplified not less than emphasised; simplified mostly to singleness of motive and passion and interest, to quite measurably finite existence; whereas his ostensibly higher spirits, types necessarily least observed and most independently thought out, in the interest of their humanity, as we would fain ourselves think them, are his falsest and weakest and show most where his imagination and his efficient sympathy break down.

To say so much as this is doubtless to provoke the question of where and how then, under so many other restrictions, he is so great—which question is answered simply by our claim for his unsurpassed mastery of the "middling" sort, so much the most numerous in the world, the middling sort pressed upon by the vast variety of their dangers. These it is in their multitude whom he makes individually living, each with a clustered bunch of concomitants, as no one, to our mind, has equalled him in doing—above all with the amount of repetition of the feat considered. Finer images than the middling, but so much fewer, other creative talents have thrown off; swarms of the common, on the other hand, have obeyed with an even greater air of multitude perhaps than in Balzac's pages the big brandished enumerative wand—only with a signal forfeiture in this case of that gift of the sharply separate, the really rounded, personality which he untiringly conferred. Émile Zola, by so far the strongest example of his influence, mustered groups and crowds beyond even the master's own compass; but as throughout Zola we live and move for the most part but in crowds (he thinking his best but in terms of crowdedness), so in Balzac, where he rises highest, we deal, whether or no more for our sense of ugliness than of beauty, but with memorable person after person. He thought, on his side—when he thought at least to good purpose—in terms the most expressively personal, in such as could even eventuate in monsters and forms of evil the most finished we know; so that if he too has left us a multitude of which we may say that it stands alone for solidity, it nevertheless exists by addition and extension, not by a chemical shaking-together, a cheapening or diminishing fusion.

It is not that the series of the Rougon-Macquart has not several distinct men and women to show—though they occur, as a fact, almost in "L'Assommoir" alone; it is not either that Zola did not on occasion try for the cultivated consciousness, a thing of course, so far as ever achieved anywhere, necessarily separate and distinguished; it is that he tried, on such ground, with a futility only a shade less marked than Balzac's, and perhaps would have tried with equal disaster had he happened to try oftener. If we find in his pages no such spreading waste as Balzac's general picture of the classes "enjoying every advantage," that is of the socially highest—to the elder writer's success in depicting particularly the female members of which Sainte-Beuve, and Brunetière in his footsteps, have rendered such strange and stupefying homage—the reason may very well be that such groups could not in the nature of the case figure to him after the fashion in which he liked groups to figure, as merely herded and compressed. To Balzac they were groups in which individualisation might be raised to its very finest; and it is by this possibility in them that we watch him and his fertile vulgarity, his peccant taste, so fallible for delicacies, so unerring for simplicities, above all doubtless the homeliest, strongest and grimmest, wofully led astray. But it is fairly almost a pleasure to our admiration, before him, to see what we have permitted ourselves to call the "chunks" of excision carted off to the disengagement of the values that still live. The wondrous thing is that they live best where his grand vulgarity—since we are not afraid of the word—serves him rather than betrays; which it *has* to do, we make out, over the greater part of the field of any observer for whom man is on the whole cruelly, crushingly, deformedly conditioned. We grant *that* as to Balzac's view, and yet feel the view to have been at the same time incomparably active and productively genial; which are by themselves somehow qualities and reactions that redress the tragedy and the doom. The vulgarity was at any rate a force that simply got nearer than any other could have done to the whole detail, the whole intimate and evidenced story, of submission and perversion, and as such it could but prove itself immensely human. It is on all this considered ground that he has for so many years stood firm and that we feel him by reason of it and in spite of them, in spite of all that has come and gone, not to have yielded, have "given," an inch.

The Times Literary Supplement, June 19, 1913
Living Age, August 13, 1913
Reprinted under the title "Honoré de Balzac, 1913"
in *Notes on Novelists*, 1914

Charles Baudelaire

As a brief discussion was lately carried on[1] touching the merits of the writer whose name we have prefixed to these lines, it may not be amiss to introduce him to some of those readers who must have observed the contest with little more than a vague sense of the strangeness of its subject. Charles Baudelaire is not a novelty in literature; his principal work[2] dates from 1857, and his career terminated a few years later. But his admirers have made a classic of him and elevated him to the rank of one of those subjects which are always in order. Even if we differ with them on this point, such attention as Baudelaire demands will not lead us very much astray. He is not, in quantity (whatever he may have been in quality), a formidable writer; having died young, he was not prolific, and the most noticeable of his original productions are contained in two small volumes.

His celebrity began with the publication of "Les Fleurs du Mal," a collection of verses of which some had already appeared in periodicals. The "Revue des Deux Mondes" had taken the responsibility of introducing a few of them to the world—or rather, though it held them at the baptismal font of public opinion, it had declined to stand godfather. An accompanying note in the "Revue" disclaimed all editorial approval of their morality. This of course procured them a good many readers; and when, on its appearance, the volume we have mentioned was overhauled by the police a still greater number of persons desired to possess it. Yet in spite of the service rendered him by the censorship, Baudelaire has never become in any degree popular; the lapse of twenty years has seen but five editions of "Les Fleurs du Mal." The foremost feeling of the reader of the present day will be one of surprise, and even amusement, at Baudelaire's audacities having provoked this degree of scandal. The world has travelled fast

[1] There had been an exchange of letters on the subject in an American journal.

[2] "Les Fleurs du Mal." Par Charles Baudelaire. Précédé d'une Notice par Théophile Gautier. Paris: Michel Lévy.

since then, and the French censorship must have been, in the year 1857, in a very prudish mood. There is little in "Les Fleurs du Mal" to make the reader of either French or English prose and verse of the present day even open his eyes. We have passed through the fiery furnace and profited by experience. We are happier than Racine's heroine, who had not

> Su se faire un front qui ne rougit jamais.

Baudelaire's verses do not strike us as being dictated by a spirit of bravado—though we have heard that, in talk, it was his habit, to an even tiresome degree, to cultivate the quietly outrageous—to pile up monstrosities and blasphemies without winking and with the air of uttering proper commonplaces.

"Les Fleurs du Mal" is evidently a sincere book—so far as anything for a man of Baudelaire's temper and culture could be sincere. Sincerity seems to us to belong to a range of qualities with which Baudelaire and his friends were but scantily concerned. His great quality was an inordinate cultivation of the sense of the picturesque, and his care was for how things looked, and whether some kind of imaginative amusement was not to be got out of them, much more than for what they meant and whither they led and what was their use in human life at large. The later editions of "Les Fleurs du Mal" (with some of the interdicted pieces still omitted and others, we believe, restored) contain a long preface by Théophile Gautier, which throws a curious side-light upon what the Spiritualist newspapers would call Baudelaire's "mentality." Of course Baudelaire is not to be held accountable for what Gautier says of him, but we cannot help judging a man in some degree by the company he keeps. To admire Gautier is certainly excellent taste, but to be admired by Gautier we cannot but regard as rather compromising. He gives a magnificently picturesque account of the author of "Les Fleurs du Mal," in which, indeed, the question of pure exactitude is evidently so very subordinate that it seems grossly ill-natured for us to appeal to such a standard. While we are reading him, however, we find ourselves wishing that Baudelaire's analogy with the author himself were either greater or less. Gautier

was perfectly sincere, because he dealt only with the picturesque and pretended to care only for appearances. But Baudelaire (who, to our mind, was an altogether inferior genius
to Gautier) applied the same process of interpretation to
things as regards which it was altogether inadequate; so that
one is constantly tempted to suppose he cares more for his
process—for making grotesquely-pictorial verse—than for
the things themselves. On the whole, as we have said, this
inference would be unfair. Baudelaire had a certain groping
sense of the moral complexities of life, and if the best that he
succeeds in doing is to drag them down into the very turbid
element in which he himself plashes and flounders, and there
present them to us much besmirched and bespattered, this
was not a want of goodwill in him, but rather a dulness and
permanent immaturity of vision. For American readers, furthermore, Baudelaire is compromised by his having made
himself the apostle of our own Edgar Poe. He translated, very
carefully and exactly, all of Poe's prose writings, and, we believe, some of his very valueless verses. With all due respect
to the very original genius of the author of the "Tales of Mystery," it seems to us that to take him with more than a certain
degree of seriousness is to lack seriousness one's self. An enthusiasm for Poe is the mark of a decidedly primitive stage of
reflection. Baudelaire thought him a profound philosopher,
the neglect of whose golden utterances stamped his native
land with infamy. Nevertheless, Poe was vastly the greater
charlatan of the two, as well as the greater genius.

"Les Fleurs du Mal" was a very happy title for Baudelaire's
verses, but it is not altogether a just one. Scattered flowers
incontestably do bloom in the quaking swamps of evil, and
the poet who does not mind encountering bad odours in his
pursuit of sweet ones is quite at liberty to go in search of
them. But Baudelaire has, as a general thing, not plucked the
flowers—he has plucked the evil-smelling weeds (we take it
that he did not use the word flowers in a purely ironical
sense) and he has often taken up mere cupfuls of mud and
bog-water. He had said to himself that it was a great shame
that the realm of evil and unclean things should be fenced off
from the domain of poetry; that it was full of subjects, of
chances and effects; that it had its light and shade, its logic

and its mystery; and that there was the making of some capital verses in it. So he leaped the barrier and was soon immersed in it up to his neck. Baudelaire's imagination was of a melancholy and sinister kind, and, to a considerable extent, this plunging into darkness and dirt was doubtless very spontaneous and disinterested. But he strikes us on the whole as passionless, and this, in view of the unquestionable pluck and acuteness of his fancy, is a great pity. He knew evil not by experience, not as something within himself, but by contemplation and curiosity, as something outside of himself, by which his own intellectual agility was not in the least discomposed, rather, indeed (as we say his fancy was of a dusky cast) agreeably flattered and stimulated. In the former case, Baudelaire, with his other gifts, might have been a great poet. But, as it is, evil for him begins outside and not inside, and consists primarily of a great deal of lurid landscape and unclean furniture. This is an almost ludicrously puerile view of the matter. Evil is represented as an affair of blood and carrion and physical sickness—there must be stinking corpses and starving prostitutes and empty laudanum bottles in order that the poet shall be effectively inspired.

A good way to embrace Baudelaire at a glance is to say that he was, in his treatment of evil, exactly what Hawthorne was not—Hawthorne, who felt the thing at its source, deep in the human consciousness. Baudelaire's infinitely slighter volume of genius apart, he was a sort of Hawthorne reversed. It is the absence of this metaphysical quality in his treatment of his favourite subjects (Poe was his metaphysician, and his devotion sustained him through a translation of "Eureka!") that exposes him to that class of accusations of which M. Edmond Schérer's accusation of feeding upon *pourriture* is an example; and, in fact, in his pages we never know with what we are dealing. We encounter an inextricable confusion of sad emotions and vile things, and we are at a loss to know whether the subject pretends to appeal to our conscience or— we were going to say—to our olfactories. "Le Mal?" we exclaim; "you do yourself too much honour. This is not Evil; it is not the wrong; it is simply the nasty!" Our impatience is of the same order as that which we should feel if a poet, pretending to pluck "the flowers of good," should come and present us, as specimens, a rhapsody on plumcake and *eau du Cologne*. Independently of the question of his subjects, the charm of Baudelaire's verse is often of a very high order. He belongs to the class of geniuses in whom we ourselves find but a limited pleasure—the laborious, deliberate, economical writers, those who fumble a long time in their pockets before they bring out their hand with a coin in the palm. But the coin, when Baudelaire at last produced it, was often of a high value. He had an extraordinary verbal instinct and an exquisite felicity of epithet. We cannot help wondering, however, at Gautier's extreme admiration for his endowment in this direction; it is the admiration of the writer who gushes for the writer who trickles. In one point Baudelaire is extremely remarkable—in his talent for suggesting associations. His epithets seem to have come out of old cupboards and pockets; they have a kind of magical mustiness. Moreover, his natural sense of the superficial picturesqueness of the miserable and the unclean was extremely acute; there may be a difference of opinion as to the advantage of possessing such a sense; but whatever it is worth Baudelaire had it in a high degree. One of his poems—"To a Red-haired Beggar Girl"—is a masterpiece in the way of graceful expression of this high relish of what is shameful:—

> Pour moi, poëte chétif,
> Ton jeune corps maladif,
> Plein de taches de rousseur,
> A sa douceur.

Baudelaire repudiated with indignation the charge that he was what is called a realist, and he was doubtless right in doing so. He had too much fancy to adhere strictly to the real; he always embroiders and elaborates—endeavours to impart that touch of strangeness and mystery which is the very *raison d'être* of poetry. Baudelaire was a poet, and for a poet to be a realist is of course nonsense. The idea that Baudelaire imported into his theme was, as a general thing, an intensification of its repulsiveness, but it was at any rate ingenious. When he makes an invocation to "la Débauche aux bras immondes" one may be sure he means more by it than is evident to the vulgar—he means, that is, an intenser perversity. Occasionally he treats agreeable subjects, and his least sympathetic critics must make a point of admitting that his most successful poem is also his most wholesome and most touching; we allude to "Les Petites Vieilles"—a really masterly production. But if it represents the author's maximum, it is a note that he very rarely struck.

Baudelaire, of course, is a capital text for a discussion of the question as to the importance of the morality—or of the subject-matter in general—of a work of art; for he offers a rare combination of technical zeal and patience and of vicious sentiment. But even if we had space to enter upon such a discussion, we should spare our words; for argument on this point wears to our sense a really ridiculous aspect. To deny the relevancy of subject-matter and the importance of the moral quality of a work of art strikes us as, in two words, ineffably puerile. We do not know what the great moralists would say about the matter—they would probably treat it very good-humouredly; but that is not the question. There is very little doubt what the great artists would say. These geniuses feel that the whole thinking man is one, and that to count out the moral element in one's appreciation of an artistic total is exactly as sane as it would be (if the total were a poem) to eliminate all the words in three syllables, or to consider only such portions of it as had been written by candlelight. The crudity of sentiment of the advocates of "art for art" is often a striking example of the fact that a great deal of what is called culture may fail to dissipate a well-seated provincialism of spirit. They talk of morality as Miss Edgeworth's infantine heroes and heroines talk of "physic"—they allude to its being put into and kept out of a work of art, put into and kept out of one's appreciation of the same, as if it were a coloured fluid kept in a big-labelled bottle in some mysterious intellectual closet. It is in reality simply a part of the essential richness of inspiration—it has nothing to do with the artistic process and it has everything to do with the artistic effect. The more a work of art feels it at its source, the richer it is; the less it feels it, the poorer it is. People of a large taste prefer rich works to poor ones and they are not inclined to assent to the assumption that the process is the whole work. We are safe in believing that all this is comfortably clear to most of those who have, in any degree, been initiated into art by production. For them the subject is as much a part of their work as their hunger is a part of their dinner. Baudelaire was not so far from being of this way of thinking as some of his admirers would persuade us; yet we may say on the whole that he was the victim of a grotesque illusion. He tried to make fine verses on ignoble subjects, and in our opinion he signally failed. He gives, as a poet, a perpetual impression of discomfort and pain. He went in search of corruption, and the ill-conditioned jade proved a thankless muse. The thinking reader, feeling himself, as a critic, all one, as we have said, finds the beauty perverted by the ugliness. What the poet wished, doubtless, was to seem to be always in the poetic attitude; what the reader sees is a gentleman in a painful-looking posture, staring very hard at a mass of things from which, more intelligently, we avert our heads.

Nation, April 27, 1876
Reprinted in *French Poets and Novelists*, 1878

Charles de Bernard and Gustave Flaubert

THE MINOR FRENCH NOVELISTS

SAINTE-BEUVE, whose literary judgments are always worth noting, whether they strike us as correct or not, has somewhere a happy sentence about Charles de Bernard— about "that ease and irresponsible grace which was the gift of this first of Balzac's pupils—of him who might have been superior to the master if a pupil ever was so, and especially if he had done more—if, in short, he had lived." I call these words happy in spite of their slight fundamental unsoundness. Charles de Bernard was only in a very imperfect sense a pupil of Balzac. His style has as little as possible in common with that of his great contemporary, and he is guilty of no visible attempt to tread in his footsteps. The two writers belong to two very distinct categories—Balzac to the type of mind that takes things hard and Charles de Bernard to the type of mind that takes things easy. The author of "Gerfaut" was Balzac's protégé rather than his pupil, and though we have Sainte-Beuve's affirmation that Balzac's literary vanity was the "most gross and rapacious" he had ever known, it does not appear that he took umbrage at his "pupil's" ripening talent. How many budding reputations Balzac may have endeavored to drive to the wall, we are of course unable to say; but there are at least two recorded cases of his extending to unfriended genius an open hand. When Stendhal, who for a long time was at once the most powerful and the most obscure of romancers, published his "Chartreuse de Parme," Balzac greeted the book in a long, florid, redundant review, with a series of the handsomest compliments that one literary man ever paid to another. And his admiration was perfectly sincere; the artist was captivated by the artist. In a similar fashion, in 1834, when Charles de Bernard, after coming up to Paris from his native Besançon, to seek his literary fortune, and quite failing to find it, had returned to his provincial nest in some discouragement, Balzac, struck with the promise of a volume of verse which had been the principal result of his excursion, sought him out, urged him to try again, and gave him some fraternal literary advice. He "started" him, as the phrase is. It is true that he started him left foot foremost, and his advice has a singular sound. He recommended him to try his hand at historical novels—something in the line of Walter Scott. Fortunately Charles de Bernard had taken his own measure. He began to write tales, but they were anything but historical. They were short stories of the day, in the lightest style of improvisation. "Gerfaut," his first regular novel, and on the whole his best, alone reveals some traces of Balzac's advice. There is an old castle, and a good deal of killing, a secret closet in the wall, and a very good portrait of a feudal nobleman born too late.

Charles de Bernard has at the present day hardly more than an historical value, and his novels are not to be recommended to people who have anything of especial importance at hand to read. But in speaking of the secondary French novelists it is but fair to allow him a comfortable niche, for if he is not especially worth looking up, he at least leaves you a very friendly feeling for him if he comes in your way. He is old-fashioned, exploded, ineffectively realistic; his cleverness is not the cleverness of the present hour; his art and his artifice seem a trifle primitive and meagre; and yet for all that he is more enjoyable than many of his highly perfected modern successors. If the prime purpose of a novel is to give us pleasure, Charles de Bernard is a better novelist than Gustave Flaubert. "Gerfaut" and "Les Ailes d'Icare" proceed doubtless from a very much less powerful and original mind than "Madame Bovary"; but they are at any rate works of entertainment, of amenity. "Realism," as we understand it now, has been invented since this writer's day, and however much one may admire and applaud it, we cannot but feel that it was a good fortune for a charming story-teller to have come a little before it. And since Balzac has been mentioned, it may really be said that when it comes to being agreeable Charles de Bernard need not shrink from comparison with even so imposing a name. He is slight and loose in tissue, pale in coloring; in a word, a second-rate genius. Balzac is a genius of all time; he towers and overshadows; and yet if half a dozen volumes of each writer were standing on your shelf, and you felt an impulse to taste of the sweets of fiction, you were wiser to take down Charles de Bernard than Balzac. The writer of these lines feels for the author of "Gerfaut" that particular kindness which many people who relish the beautiful qualities of the French mind in their purity entertain for the talents which flourished and fell before the second empire set its seal upon things. It is not taking the matter too tragically to say that Charles de Bernard just escaped. Certainly many of the brilliant writers of the same generation have lived through the empire and held their own against it. To George Sand and Victor Hugo the empire could give nothing, and it could take nothing away from them. But Charles de Bernard was not of that calibre; he ranks, in the degree of his talent, with the Feydeaus, the Octave Feuillets, the Edmond Abouts of literature. Readers who appreciate shades of difference, and who, while they admire the extreme cleverness of these writers, find something that defies personal sympathy in their tone, will discover a great deal to relish in Charles de Bernard. Whether he too would have been corrupted, and his easy, natural manner would have learned the perversities and sophistries of the "decadence," is more than I can say. At any rate, fortune was kind to him; she never gave him a chance. She broke him smoothly off, and in compensation for the brevity of his career she made him a type of some of the agreeable things that were about to pass away. He may represent, to an imaginative critic, the old French cleverness as distinguished from the new. The lightness, the case, the gayety, the urbanity, the good taste, the good spirits, the discretion—of all those charming things that have traditionally marked the cultivated French character at its best Charles de Bernard is an excellent illustration. And he exhibits them in no antique, angular form; he is modern; he is of his time; and they have had a chance to blossom and expand to the height of the modern tone. But he seems to me the last of the light writers in whom these gifts are fresh and free. In the later generation the tone undergoes an indefinable transformation. The cleverness is greater than ever, but the charm is gone; the music is elaborate, but the instrument is cracked. The note grows strident, the sweet savor turns acrid. The gayety becomes forced and hard and the urbanity ironical; the lightness turns to levity. Charles de Bernard answers to one's notion of the Frenchman of an earlier date, who was before all things good company—

who had in a supreme degree the sociable virtues. Thackeray, in his "Paris Sketch-Book," devotes a chapter to him (he was then a contemporary), and gives an abstract of one of his novels. He evidently relished this urbane quality in him, and I remember even to have seen it somewhere affirmed that he had taken him for his model, and declared that it was the height of his own ambition to do for English society what Charles de Bernard had done for French. This last strikes me as a rather apocryphal tale; Charles de Bernard was a satirist, but his satire is to that of "Vanity Fair" what lemonade is to prime Burgundy. In Thackeray there are, morally, many Charles de Bernards. It is as against Eugène Sue and George Sand (whom he seems rather unphilosophically to lump together) that he praises the author of "Les Ailes d'Icare," and he especially commends his gentlemanly tone. The "gentlemanly tone," with its merits and limitations, is an incontestable characteristic of our author. It may be said that in a thoroughly agreeable style good breeding is never an aggressive quality, and that a gentleman who keeps reminding you that he is a gentleman is a very ambiguous personage. But Charles de Bernard is gentlemanly by juxtaposition, as it were. He quietly goes his way, and it is only when you compare his gait with his neighbors' that you see how very well he holds himself. The truth is, that many of his companions in this matter swagger most damnably; and here again, curiously (to return to Balzac), is another point at which the small man is superior to the great. The tone of good breeding Balzac never in any degree possessed; the greatest genius in his line conceivable, he was most absolutely and positively not a gentleman. He sweats blood and water to appear one, but his effort only serves to betray more vividly his magnificent *bourgeois* temperament. M. de Pontmartin, the author of the biographical sketch prefixed to the collected edition of Charles de Bernard's novels, has some rather felicitous remarks upon the difference, in this respect, between his hero and the latter's rivals. "Eugène Sue and Alexandre Dumas, who have had their phase of rubbing shoulders (or of trying to) with the aristocracy, their repeated attempts at flattery and advances to what the hair-dressers and the milliners call the '*monde élégant,*' have never been able to produce anything but caricatures when they endeavored to represent it. Its doors were open to them; they found a passport in the irresistible although imprudent curiosity of its members; the models were there in position, before their eyes; they were dying with the desire to persuade their readers that they lived the same life and breathed the same air; that they were not naturalized, but indigenous. No expenditure of dazzling description, bespangled with armorial mottoes and shields; no female portraits *à la* Lawrence, smothered in silk, and lace, and velvet; no inventories of coach-makers and architects, tailors and jewellers—nothing of all this was spared. But, alas, it might have been; the struggle was vain! The false note sounded in the finest place—the long ear peeped out of the thickest of the lion's skin." This is very well—though it is painful to have to record that M. de Pontmartin too, who understands the matter so well, has been accused of snobbery by no less acute a literary detective than Sainte-Beuve. But Charles de Bernard, though he often wrote of the *monde élégant*, was emphatically not a snob. The point of view of the man who is conscious of good blood in his veins was the one he instinctively took; but in dealing with the people and things that usually excite the snobbish passion, he is always perfectly simple. He is never pretentious; he is easy, natural, and impartially civil.

His literary career was very short; his novels were all published between 1838 and 1847—a period of nine years. His life was uneventful; it was altogether in his works. The author of the short memoir I have mentioned notes the singular fact that although his novels are essentially what are called novels of manners, he led a secluded life and went very little into the world. Gayety and hilarity abound in his tales, and yet M. de Pontmartin intimates that the man himself was rather sombre. "He had long had the good taste to prefer domestic life to the *vie de salon*, and in the evening he liked much better to remain with his wife and children than to go into the world in pursuit of models and originals. And nevertheless, muffled in from the outer world, inaccessible or deaf to its sounds, solitary, almost misanthropic, he seems to have listened at doors or painted from nature. He guessed what he did not see; he heard what he did not listen to!" He had this mark of a man of genius—he divined. His literary personality was apparently quite distinct from his private one, and this, taken in connection with the extreme facility and neatness of his style, entitles him in a measure to be called a man of genius. His inspiration was his own, and he was an excellent writer. If his inspiration was his own, however, it must be added that it was never of a very high order. The most general praise one can give his novels is that they are extremely amusing. The humor is neither broad nor coarse; it is always discriminating, and it is often delicate; but it is humor of the second-rate sort. It is not rich nor suggestive; your entertainment begins and ends with your laugh. Many of his tales are very short, so that half a dozen go into a volume. These are always highly readable, and if you begin one you will be sure to finish it. The best of his novels, "Les Ailes d'Icare," "Un Homme Sérieux," "Le Gentilhomme Campagnard," are no less clever; and yet it may be that here and there an even well-disposed reader will lay them down at the end of a hundred pages. For a serious writer, he will say, you are really too light; it is all too smooth and shallow, too much arranged. Once at least, however, in "Gerfaut," Charles de Bernard seems to have felt the impulse to grasp a subject nearer its roots. In spite of a number of signs of immaturity, this is his solidest and most effective work. His tales are usually comedies; this is a tragedy. The reader cares little for his hero, who is a gentleman of a type excessively familiar in French literature—a distinguished man of letters, of restless imagination, who comes down to the Château de Bergenheim for the express purpose of seducing its pretty mistress, and who, when installed among its comforts, and smothered in hospitality by the husband, proceeds in the most scientific manner to bombard the affections of the wife. Nor are we much more interested in Mme. de Bergenheim herself, who surrenders after a barely nominal siege, and without having at all convinced us that her affections are worth possessing. But the book, in spite of a diffuseness of which afterward the author was rarely guilty, is written with infinite spirit and point, and some of the subordinate figures are forcibly and wittily sketched. Nothing could be lighter and more picturesquely humorous than the portrait of Marillac, the irrepressible Bohemian and *fidus Achates* of "Gerfaut."

"Talent apart, Marillac was an artist tooth and nail—an artist from the point, or rather from the plateau of his great crop of hair to the tips of his boots, which he would have liked to pull out to the mediæval longitude; for he excelled especially in dressing for his profession, and possessed the longest moustaches of literature. If he had no great amount of art in his brain, he had at least its name perpetually in his mouth. Art!—to pronounce the word he rounded his lips like M. Jourdain saying O! Farces or pictures, poetry or music, he did a bit of everything, like a horse who is warranted good either for the shafts or the saddle. When he came out of the musical shafts he bravely got into the literary harness, which he considered his veritable vocation and his principal glory. He signed his name 'Marillac, man of letters.' Nevertheless, in spite of a profound disdain for the *bourgeois*, whom he always spoke of as a grocer, and for the French Academy, to which he had taken an oath never to belong, one could accuse him of no serious defects. One could forgive him being an artist before everything, in spite of everything, an artist—damnation!" A still better image is that of Christian de Bergenheim, the husband of the decidedly inexpensive heroine. It reads, for definiteness and vigor, like a page torn from Balzac. "He was one of those men whom Napoleon had in some sort brought to life again—the type which had been gradually dying out since the feudal ages; a man of action exclusively, spending nothing superfluous in imagination or sensibility, and, on momentous occasions, never letting his soul travel further than the swing of his sabre. The complete absence of that sense which most people call morbid irritability and others poetry had caused the springs of his character to keep their native hardness and stiffness. His soul lacked wings to leave the world of the real; but this incapacity had its compensation. It was impossible to apply a more vigorous arm than his to anything that came under the head of material resistance. He lived neither yesterday nor to-morrow; he lived to-day. Of small account before or after, he displayed at the critical moment an energy the more powerful that no waste, no leakage of untimely emotion, had diminished its force. The few ideas contained in his brain had become clear, hard, and impenetrable, like diamonds. By the inner light of these

fixed stars he walked in all things, as one walks in the sunshine, his head erect, straight before him, ready to crush with
his foot all obstacles and interruptions." A few passages of
that sort, scattered through his novels, mark Charles de Bernard's maximum as an analyst. But if this is the maximum,
the average is very high. He has described all sorts of social
types, narrated all kinds of intrigues, always ingeniously, vividly, and with a natural epicurean irony. Considering that I
do not recommend the reader who is unacquainted with him
to make any great point of retracing his steps along the
crowded highway of what we nowadays call culture, to bend
over our author where *his* march stopped and left him, it may
seem that I am lingering too long upon Charles de Bernard.
But there is another word to say, and it is an interesting one.
Charles de Bernard's talent is great—very great, greater than
the impression it leaves; and the reason why this clever man
remains so persistently second-rate is, to my sense, because he
had no morality. By this I of course do not mean that he did
not choose to write didactic tales, winding up with a goodly
lecture, and a distribution of prizes and punishments. I mean
that he had no moral emotion, no preference, no instincts—
no moral imagination, in a word. His morality was altogether
traditional, and such as it was it seems to have held him in a
very loose grasp. It was not the current social notion of right
and wrong, of honor and dishonor, that he embodied, but
something even less consistent. What we find in him is not
the average morality, but a morality decidedly below the average. He doesn't care, he doesn't feel, and his indifference is
not philosophic. He has no heat of his own, save that of the
raconteur; his laugh is always good-natured, but always cold.
He describes all sorts of mean and ignoble things, without in
the least gauging their quality. He belongs to the intellectual
family—and very large it is in France—of the amusing author of "Gil Blas." All its members know how to write, and
how, up to a certain point, to observe; but their observation
has no reflex action, as it were, and they remain extremely
clever and extremely dry. Yet for all this the author of these
lines is conscious of a tender regard for Charles de Bernard
which he would be sorry not to confess to, in conclusion. He
remembers often turning over, as a child, an old back-parlor

volume of the "keepsake" genus, bound in tarnished watered silk, as such volumes were apt to be. It was called, if memory serves him, the "Idler in France," and it was written—if written is the word—by the Countess of Blessington. With the text he was too timorous to grapple; but the volume was embellished with beautiful steel plates, depicting the delights of the French capital. There was the good old crooked, dirty, picturesque Paris of Charles X. and Louis Philippe—the Paris ignorant of Louis Napoleon and Baron Haussmann, the new Boulevards and the "American quarter." There were pictures of the old Boulevards and the Palais Royal, the staircase at the Opera, the table d'hôte at the Hôtel des Princes, a *salon* in the Chaussée d'Antin. The gentlemen all wore high rolling coat-collars and straps to their trousers; the ladies wore large-brimmed bonnets and cross-laced slippers. The Paris of these antediluvian Parisians seemed to my fancy a paradise; and I suppose that a part of my lurking tenderness for Charles de Bernard rests upon the fact that it appears to live again in his pages.

II.

BUT since those days the novel has flourished more and more, and if all that is needful to make us like a certain order of things is to see it vividly and picturesquely portrayed, we should long since have been won over to an æsthetic *tendresse* for the empire. The empire has had its novelists by the dozen; emulation, competition, and the extraordinary favor which this branch of literature has come to enjoy, have rendered them incomparably skilful and audacious. For entertainment of a high flavor we have only to choose at hazard. If at the same time, however, we are modestly inclined to edification, there must be a certain logic in our choice. The array is somewhat embarrassing; to the term "minor novelists" a formidable host responds. Octave Feuillet, Gustave Flaubert, Ernest Feydeau, Edmond About, MM. de Goncourt, Gustave Droz, the younger Dumas, Victor Cherbuliez, Erckmann-Chatrian—these are some of the names that immediately present themselves. All these names, with one exception (that of Alexandre Dumas), represent a constellation of romances more or less brilliant; and in their intervals glitters here and there a single star—some very clever tale by an author who has tried or succeeded but once. A couple of examples of this latter class are the exquisite "Dominique" of Eugène Fromentin and the crude and vulgar, but powerful and touching "Divorce" of Mme. André Léo. When we cannot look at everything, we must look at what is most characteristic. The most characteristic work in this line, in France, of the last five and twenty years, is the realistic, descriptive novel which sprang out of Balzac, began in its effort at intensity of illusion where Balzac left off, and which, whether or no it has surpassed him, has at least exceeded him. Everything in France proceeds by "schools," and there is no artist so bungling that he will not find another to call him "dear master." Gustave Flaubert is of the school of Balzac; the brothers De Goncourt and Emile Zola are of the school of Flaubert. This last writer is altogether the most characteristic and powerful representative of what has lately been most original in the evolution of the French imagination, and he has for ourselves the further merit that he must always be strange and curious. English literature has certainly been doing some very odd things of late, and striving hard to prove that she could be everything that individual writers chose to make her. But at the best we are all flies in amber, and however furiously we may buzz and rattle, the amber sticks to our wings. It is not in the temper of English vision to see things as M. Flaubert sees them, and it is not in the genius of the English language to present them as he presents them. With all respect to "Madame Bovary," "Madame Bovary" is fortunately an inimitable work.

"Madame Bovary" was M. Flaubert's first novel, and it has remained altogether his best. He has produced little, and his works bear the marks of the most careful preparation. His second performance was "Salammbô," an archæological novel of the highest pretensions. Salammbô is a Carthaginian princess, the elder sister of Hannibal. After this came, at a long interval, "L'Education Sentimentale," a tale of the present day, and lastly appeared "La Tentation de St. Antoine"— archæology again, but in the shape of something that was neither novel nor drama; a sort of free imitation of the mediæval "mystery." "Madame Bovary" was a great success—

a success of merit, and, as they say in France, a success of scandal; but the public verdict has not been flattering to its companions. The mass of the public find them dull, and wonder how a writer can expend such an immensity of talent in making himself unreadable; to a discriminating taste, however, M. Flaubert can write nothing that does not repay attention.

The "scandal" in relation to "Madame Bovary" was that the book was judicially impeached and prosecuted for immorality. The defence was eloquent, and the writer was acquitted, and the later editions of the book contain, in an appendix, a full report of the trial. It is a work upon which it is possible to be very paradoxical, or rather in relation to which sincere opinion may easily have the air of paradox. It is a book adapted for the reverse of what is called family reading, and yet I remember thinking, the first time I read it, in the heat of my admiration for its power, that it would make the most useful of Sunday-school tracts. In Taine's elaborate satire, "The Opinions of M. Graindorge," there is a report of a conversation at a dinner party between an English spinster of didactic habits and a decidedly audacious Frenchman. He begs to recommend to her a work which he has lately been reading and which cannot fail to win the approval of all persons interested in the propagation of virtue. The lady lends a sympathetic ear, and he gives a rapid sketch of the tale—the history of a wicked woman who goes from one abomination to another, until at last the judgment of heaven descends upon her, and, blighted and blasted, she perishes miserably. The lady grasps her pencil and note-book and begs for the name of the edifying volume, and the gentleman leans across the dinner table and answers with a smile—" 'Madame Bovary; or, The Consequences of Misconduct.' " This is a very pretty epigram, but it is more than an epigram. It may be very seriously maintained that M. Flaubert's masterpiece is the pearl of "Sunday reading." Practically M. Flaubert is a potent moralist; whether, when he wrote his book, he was so theoretically is a matter best known to himself. Every out-and-out realist who provokes curious meditation may claim that he is a moralist, for that, after all, is the most that the moralists can do for us. They sow the seeds of virtue; they

can hardly pretend to raise the crop. Excellence in this matter
consists in the tale and the moral hanging well together, and
this they are certainly more likely to do when there has been
a definite intention—that intention of which artists who cultivate "art for art" are usually so extremely mistrustful; exhibiting thereby, surely, a most injurious disbelief in the
illimitable alchemy of art. We may say on the whole doubtless
that the highly didactic character of "Madame Bovary" is an
accident, inasmuch as the works that have followed it, both
from its author's and from other hands, have been things to
read much less for meditation's than for sensation's sake. M.
Flaubert's theory as a novelist, briefly expressed, is to begin
on the outside. Human life, he says, is before all things a
spectacle, a thing to be looked at, seen, apprehended, enjoyed
with the eyes. What our eyes show us is all that we are sure
of; so with this we will, at any rate, begin. As this is infinitely
curious and entertaining, if we know how to look at it, and
as such looking consumes a great deal of time and space, it is
very possible that with this also we may end. We admit nevertheless that there is something else, beneath and behind,
that belongs to the realm of vagueness and uncertainty, and
into this we must occasionally dip. It crops up sometimes irrepressibly, and of course we don't positively count it out. On
the whole, we will leave it to take care of itself, and let it
come off as it may. If we propose to represent the pictorial
side of life, of course we must do it thoroughly well—we
must be complete. There must be no botching, no bungling,
no scamping; it must be a very serious matter. We will "render" things—anything, everything, from a chimney-pot to
the shoulders of a duchess—as painters render them. We believe there is a certain particular phrase, better than any other,
for everything in the world, and the thoroughly accomplished
writer ends by finding it. We care only for what *is*—we know
nothing about what ought to be. Human life is interesting,
because we are in it and of it; all kinds of curious things are
taking place in it (we don't analyze the curious—for artists it
is an ultimate fact); we select as many of them as possible.
Some of the most curious are the most disagreeable, but the
chance for "rendering" in the disagreeable is as great as anywhere else (some people think even greater), and moreover

the disagreeable is extremely characteristic. The real is the most satisfactory thing in the world, and if once we fairly get into it, nothing shall frighten us back.

Some such words as these may stand as a rough sketch of the sort of intellectual conviction under which "Madame Bovary" was written. The theory in this case at least was applied with brilliant success; it produced a masterpiece. Realism seems to me with "Madame Bovary" to have said its last word. I doubt whether the same process will ever produce anything better. In M. Flaubert's own hands it has distinctly failed to do so. "L'Education Sentimentale" is in comparison mechanical and inanimate. The great good fortune of "Madame Bovary" is that here the theory seems to have been invented after the fact. The author began to describe because he had laid up a great fund of disinterested observations; he had been looking at things for years, for his own edification, in that particular way. The imitative talents in the same line, those whose highest ambition is to "do" their Balzac or their Flaubert, give us the sense of looking at the world only with the most mercenary motives—of going about to stare at things only for the sake of their forthcoming novel. M. Flaubert knew what he was describing—knew it extraordinarily well. One can hardly congratulate him on his knowledge; anything drearier, more sordid, more vulgar, and sterile, and desolate than the greater part of the subject-matter of the book it would be impossible to conceive. "Mœurs de Province," the sub-title runs, and the work is the most striking possible example of that remarkable passion which possesses most Frenchmen of talent for making out their provincial life to be the most hideous thing on earth. Emma Bovary is the daughter of a small farmer, who has been able to send her to boarding-school, and to give her something of an "elegant" education. She is pretty and graceful, and she marries a small country doctor—the kindest, simplest, and stupidest of husbands. He takes her to live in a squalid little country town, called Yonville-l'Abbaye, near Rouen; she is luxurious and sentimental; she wastes away with *ennui*, and loneliness, and hatred of her narrow lot and absent opportunities, and on the very first chance she takes a lover. With him she is happy for a few months, and then he deserts her brutally and cynically.

She falls violently ill, and comes near dying; then she gets well, and takes another lover of a different kind. All the world—the very little world of Yonville-l'Abbaye—sees and knows and gossips; her husband alone neither sees nor suspects. Meanwhile she has been spending money remorselessly and insanely; she has made promissory notes, and she is smothered in debt. She has undermined the ground beneath her husband's feet; her second lover leaves her; she is ruined, dishonored, utterly at bay. She goes back as a beggar to her first lover, and he refuses to give her a sou. She tries to sell herself and fails; then, in impatience and desperation, she collapses. She takes poison and dies horribly, and the bailiffs come down on her husband, who is still heroically ignorant. At last he learns, and it is too much for him; he loses all courage, and dies one day on his garden bench, leaving twelve francs fifty centimes to his little girl, who is sent to get her living in a cotton mill. The tale is a tragedy, unillumined and unredeemed, and it might seem, on this rapid and imperfect showing, to be rather a vulgar tragedy. Women who get into trouble with the extreme facility of Mme. Bovary, and by the same method, are unfortunately not rare, and the better opinion seems to be that they deserve but a limited degree of sympathy. The history of M. Flaubert's heroine is nevertheless full of substance and meaning. In spite of the elaborate system of portraiture to which she is subjected, in spite of being minutely described in all her attitudes and all her moods, from the hem of her garment to the texture of her finger-nails, she remains a living creature, and as a living creature she interests us. The only thing that poor Charles Bovary, after her death, can find to say to her lovers is, "It's the fault of fatality." And in fact, as we enter into the situation, it is. M. Flaubert gives his readers the impression of having known few kinds of women, but he has evidently known intimately this particular kind. We see the process of her history; we see how it marches from step to step to its horrible termination, and we do not perceive how it could well have done otherwise. It is a case of the passion for luxury, for elegance, for the world's most agreeable and comfortable things, of an intense and complex imagination, corrupt almost in the germ, and finding corruption, and feeding on it, in the most unlikely and unfavoring places—it is a case of all this being pressed back upon itself with a force which makes an explosion inevitable. Mme. Bovary has an insatiable hunger for pleasure, and she lives amid dreariness; she is ignorant, vain, naturally depraved; of the things she dreams about not an intimation ever reaches her; so she makes her *trouée*, as the French say, bores her opening, scrapes and scratches her way out into the light where she can. The reader may protest against a heroine who is "naturally depraved." You are welcome, he may say, to make of a heroine what you please, to carry her where you please; but in mercy don't set us down to a young lady of whom, on the first page, there is nothing better to be said than that. But all this is a question of degree. Mme. Bovary is typical, like all powerfully conceived figures in fiction. There are a great many potential Mme. Bovarys, a great many young women, vain, ignorant, leading dreary, vulgar, intolerable lives, and possessed of irritable nerves and of a high natural appreciation of luxury, of admiration, of agreeable sensations, of what they consider the natural rights of pretty women, who are more or less launched upon the rapid slope which she descended to the bottom. The gentleman who recommended her history to the English lady at M. Taine's dinner party would say that her history was in intention a solemn warning to such young women not to allow themselves to think too much about the things they cannot have. Does M. Flaubert in this case complete his intention? does he suggest an alternative—a remedy? plenty of plain sewing, serious reading, general housework? M. Flaubert keeps well out of the province of remedies; he simply relates his facts, in all their elaborate horror. The accumulation of detail is so immense, the vividness of portraiture of people, of things, of places, of times and hours, is so poignant and convincing, that one is dragged into the very current and tissue of the story; the reader seems to have lived in it all, more than in any novel I can recall. At the end the intensity of illusion becomes horrible; overwhelmed with disgust and pity, the reader closes the book.

Besides being the history of the most miserable of women, "Madame Bovary" is also an elaborate picture of small *bourgeois* rural life. Anything, in this direction, more remorseless and complete it would be hard to conceive. Into all that makes life ignoble, and vulgar, and sterile M. Flaubert has entered with an extraordinary penetration. The dulness and flatness of it all suffocate us; the pettiness and ugliness sicken us. Every one in the book is either stupid or mean, but against the shabby-colored background two figures stand out in salient relief. One is Charles Bovary, the husband of the heroine; the other is M. Homais, the village apothecary. Bovary is introduced to us in his childhood, at school, and we see him afterward at college and during his first marriage—a union with a widow of meagre charms, twenty years older than himself. He is the only good person of the book, but he is stupidly, helplessly good. At school "he had for correspondent a wholesale hardware merchant of the Rue Ganterie, who used to fetch him away once a month, on a Sunday, send him to walk in the harbor and look at the boats, and then bring him back to college by seven o'clock, before supper. Every Thursday evening he wrote a long letter to his mother, with red ink and three wafers; then he went over his copy books, or else read an old volume of 'Anacharsis' which was knocking about the class room. In our walks he used to talk with the servant, who was from the country like himself." Charles Bovary is one of the persons whose merits and defects and whole earthly fortune are summed up in those only two words we can say about them, "poor fellow." In Homais, the apothecary, M. Flaubert has really added to our knowledge of human nature—at least as human nature is modified by French social conditions. To American readers, fortunately, this figure represents nothing familiar; we do not as yet possess any such mellow perfection of charlatanism. The apothecary is that unwholesome compound, a Philistine radical—a *père de famille*, a free-thinker, a rapacious shopkeeper, a stern moralist, an ardent democrat, and an abject snob. He is a complete creation; he is taken, as the French say, *sur le vif*, and his talk, his accent, his pompous vocabulary, his attitudes, his vanities, his windy vacuity, are inimitably rendered. Except her two lovers, M. Homais is Mme. Bovary's sole male acquaintance, and her only social recreation is to spend the evening with his wife and her own husband in his book-shop. Her life has known, in this line, but two other events. Once

she has been at a ball at the house of a neighboring nobleman, for whom her husband had lanced an abscess in his
cheek, and who sends the invitation as part payment—a fatal
ball, which has opened her eyes to her own deprivations and
intolerably quickened her desires; and once she has been to
the theatre at Rouen. Both of these episodes are admirably
put before us, and they play a substantial part in the tale. The
book is full of expressive episodes; the most successful in its
hideous relief and reality is the long account of the operation
performed by Charles Bovary upon the club-foot of the ostler
at the inn, an operation superfluous, ridiculous, abjectly un-
skilful and clumsy, and which results in the amputation of the
poor fellow's whole leg after he has lain groaning under the
reader's eyes and nose for a dozen pages, amid the flies and
dirt, the brooms and pails, the comings and goings of his
squalid corner of the tavern. The reader asks himself the
meaning of this elaborate presentation of the most repulsive
of incidents, and feels inclined at first to charge it to a sort of
artistic bravado on the author's part—a desire to complete
his theory of realism by applying his resources to the simply
disgusting. But he presently sees that the whole episode has a
kind of metaphysical value. It completes the general picture;
it characterizes the daily life of a community in which such
incidents assumed the importance of leading events, and it
gives the final touch to our sense of poor Charles Bovary's
bungling mediocrity. Everything in the book is ugly: turning
over its pages, my eyes fall upon only this one little passage
in which an agreeable "effect" is rendered. It treats of Bovary's visits to Emma, at her father's farm, before their marriage, and is a happy instance of the way in which this
author's style arrests itself at every step in a picture. "Once,
when it was thawing, the bark of the trees was reeking in the
yard, the snow was melting on the roofs of the outbuildings.
She was upon the threshold; she went in and fetched her umbrella and opened it. The umbrella, of dove-colored silk, with
the sun coming through it, lighted up her white complexion
with changing reflections. Beneath it she smiled in the soft
warmth, and he heard the water-drops fall one by one upon
the stretched silk." To many people "Madame Bovary" will
always be a hard book to read and an impossible one to en-

joy. They will complain of the abuse of description, of the want of spontaneity, of the hideousness of the subject, of the dryness, and coldness, and cynicism of the tone. Others will continue to think it a great performance. They will admit that it is not a sentimental novel, but claim that it may be regarded as a philosophical one, and insist that the descriptions are extraordinary, and that beneath them there is always an idea which holds them up and carries them along. I cannot but think, however, that he is a very resolute partisan who would venture to make this same plea on behalf of "L'Education Sentimentale." Here the form and method are the same as in "Madame Bovary"; the studied skill, the science, the accumulation of material, are even more striking; but the book is in a single word a *dead* one. "Madame Bovary" was relatively spontaneous and sincere; but to read its successor is, to the finer sense, like masticating ashes and sawdust. "L'Education Sentimentale" is elaborately and massively dreary. That a novel should have a charm seems to me the most rudimentary of principles, and there is no more charm in this laborious monument to a treacherous ideal than there is perfume in a gravel-heap. To nothing that such a writer as Gustave Flaubert accomplishes—a writer so armed at all points, so informed, so ingenious, so serious as an artist—can one be positively indifferent; but to think of the talent, the knowledge, the experience, the observation that lie buried, without hope of resurrection, in the pages of "L'Education Sentimentale," is to pass a most comfortless half hour. That imagination, invention, taste, and science should concentrate themselves, for human entertainment, upon such a result, strikes me as the most unfathomable of anomalies. One feels behind all M. Flaubert's writing a large intellectual machinery. He is a scholar, a man of erudition. Of all this "Salammbô" is a most accomplished example. "Salammbô" is not easy reading, nor is it in the least agreeable; but it displays in the highest degree what is called the historical imagination. There are passages in it in which the literary expression of that refined, and subtilized, and erudite sense of the picturesque which recent years have brought to such a development seems to have reached its highest level. The "Tentation de Saint Antoine" is, to my sense, to "Salammbô" what "L'Edu-

cation Sentimentale" is to "Madame Bovary"—what the
shadow is to the substance. M. Flaubert seems to have had in
him the material of but two spontaneous works. The successor, in each case, has been an echo, a reverberation.

III.

A CRITIC has not spoken fully of Gustave Flaubert unless
he has spoken also of MM. de Goncourt. These gentlemen,
brothers, collaborators, and extremely clever writers, have certainly plenty of talent of their own, but it may fairly be suspected that without Flaubert's example they would not have
used their talent in just the way they have done. If we have
nothing in English like M. Flaubert, we are still further from
having anything like Edmond and Jules de Goncourt. Their
works have all been published under their associated names
and produced by their united hands, according to a system
best known to themselves. Everything they have written exhibits a perfect superficial unity. Jules de Goncourt, the younger brother, lately died; and since then the survivor has
published nothing. MM. de Goncourt have written four or
five novels, but it was not as novelists that they began their
career. Their first labors were historical, and they produced a
series of volumes at once solid and entertaining upon the
French society of the last century and the early years of the
present one. These volumes are a magazine of curious facts,
and indicate a high relish for psychological research. In addition MM. de Goncourt are art students, and have published
several elaborate monographs on painters. It has been very
well said of them that the eighteenth century is their remotest
antiquity; that for them the historical imagination ends there,
after a long revel in sights of its goal. If time with these writers terminates at about 1730, space comes to a stop at the
limits of Paris. They are the most Parisian thing I know.
Other writers—Balzac, Sainte-Beuve, Edmond About—are
intensely French; MM. de Goncourt are essentially Parisian.
Their culture, their imagination, their inspiration, are all Parisian; a culture sensibly limited, but very exquisite of its kind;
an imagination in the highest degree ingenious and, as the
French say, *raffiné*—fed upon made dishes. Their inspiration

is altogether artistic, and they are artists of the most consistent kind. Their writing novels strikes me as having been a
very deliberate matter. Finding themselves in possession of a
singularly perfect intellectual instrument—men of the study
and of the drawing-room, with their measured and polished
literary style, their acute observation of material things, their
subtle Parisian imagination, their ingrained familiarity with
questions of taste—they decided that in the novel of the most
consummately modern type they could manifest themselves
most completely. They inevitably went into "realism," but
realism for them has been altogether a question of taste—a
studio question, as it were. They also find the disagreeable
particularly characteristic, and there is something ineffably
odd in seeing these elegant erudites bring their highly complex and artificial method—the fruit of culture, and leisure,
and luxury—to bear upon the crudities and maladies of life,
and pick out choice morsels of available misery upon their
gold pen-points. "Germinie Lacerteux" is the history of an
hysterical servant girl. "Manette Salomon" introduces us to a
depraved Jewess who follows the trade of model in painters'
studios, and who entangles, bewitches, and ruins a young artist of high promise. "Sœur Philomène" is the story of a sister
of charity in a hospital, who falls in love with one of the
house surgeons; while he, having to perform an operation
upon a woman of the town whom he has once loved, and
who has been stabbed by a subsequent lover—an operation
which proves fatal to the patient—drowns his remorse in absinthe, becomes an incurable drunkard, and finally, in self-
loathing, deliberately infects himself, during a dissection, with
some poisonous matter, and dies in horrible tortures. With
MM. de Goncourt the whole thing is a spectacle, a shaded
picture, and the artist's mission is to reproduce its parts in a
series of little miniatures of the highest possible finish. A
novel, for them, is a succession of minute paintings on ivory,
strung together like pearls on a necklace. Their first tale, indeed—"Renée Mauperin," which is also their most agreeable—has more of the old-fashioned narrative quality. I use
"agreeable" here in a purely relative sense. The book is an
attempt to portray the young girl "of the period" in France—
but the young girl of the period at her best, the young girl

whose instincts are pure and elevated. It proposes to show us what "l'éducation garçonnière et artistique" of the day makes of such a character. It does this in a very pretty fashion. I remember no French novel in which the consequences of allowing a young girl a moderate amount of liberty are more gracefully and naturally presented. But it is the people and the doings with which the charming Renée is associated that make us open our eyes. She belongs to an honorable *bourgeois* family who have made a handsome fortune in trade, and she has a brother who is a rising young politician and endowed with irreproachable manners and a profound ambition. The brother, to push his fortunes, determines to make a rich marriage, and selects for this purpose the pretty Mlle. Bourjot, sole heiress of numberless millions. This young lady's family insist upon his changing his name to something noble; so he obtains governmental permission to call himself Mauperin de Villacourt—the name of a small estate belonging to his father. This is not at all to the taste of Renée, who thinks the proceeding snobbish and ignoble, and who, learning that a member of the old race of Villacourt still exists, denuded of everything but the family pride, sends him a copy of the newspaper in which her brother has given legal notice of his intention, in the hope that he will put in a protest. Meanwhile she learns, through Mlle. Bourjot herself, that young Mauperin has long been carrying on an intrigue with her mamma—a lady old enough, in vulgar phrase, to know better. To marry Henri Mauperin under these circumstances is naturally disagreeable to Mlle. Bourjot; but the mamma and the intended at last agree to bring their relations to a close; the daughter appears to be duly informed of their decision; she is reassured and satisfied, and things for a while go forward very comfortably. At last the necessary year has elapsed since Mauperin promulgated his intention to assume the name of Villacourt, and no one has contested his right. But on the eve of the wedding day the last of the Villacourts turns up. He is a rude, rustic nobleman, a mighty hunter and drinker, who lives in the woods, and never looks at the newspapers, even when posted to him by pretty feminine hands. The journal sent by Renée, however, has at last come under his dreamy eyes. He springs up in wrath, hastens to Paris, bursts into Mauperin's apartment, and by way of counter-claim smites him in the face. In the duel which follows Mau-perin is killed, and Renée, with her brother's blood on her conscience, wastes away to death in a series of attitudes most gracefully described by MM. de Goncourt. Renée, as I have said, with her Parisian wit and her generous temper, is a very agreeable creation. Her talk throughout is excellent, though it is extremely difficult to translate. The following may serve as a specimen: "What a bore it is to be a young person—don't you think so? I would like to see you try it!" (She is bathing in the Seine, in company with a young man to whom these remarks are addressed. But of this anon.) "You would see what that bore comes to—the bore of being 'proper.' Suppose we were dancing now, eh? Do you think we can talk with our partner? Yes, no, yes, no—that's all. We must stick to monosyllables. That's proper! That's the pleasure of life for us. And for everything it's the same. The only thing that is really proper is to sit and swing our heels. I don't know how. And then to sit and tittle-tattle with persons of one's own sex. If we have the misfortune to let them go for a man—oh, mamma has blown me up for that! Another thing that isn't at all proper is to read. It is only these last two years that they allow me the *feuilletons* in the newspapers. There are some of the crimes in the 'faits divers' that they make me skip; they are not sufficiently proper. It's like our 'accomplishments'; they must not go beyond a certain little mark. Beyond duets on the piano and heads in crayon, it becomes professional; one sets up for something. For instance, I paint in oil, and my family are in despair. I ought to do nothing but roses in water-colors." When "Renée Mauperin" first appeared, the opening pages (from which my quotation is made) had a great success. The description of the young girl in the water is very felicitous, and is also worth quoting. "The young girl and the young man who were talking thus were in the water. Tired of swimming, drawn along by the current, they had hooked themselves to a rope which fastened one of the great boats, alongside the island. The force of the water swayed them softly to and fro at the end of the tense and quivering rope. They sank a little, then rose again. The water broke against the breast of the young girl, rose in her woollen dress as high as her neck, and threw against her from behind a little wave which a moment later was nothing but a dewdrop ready to fall from her ear. Clasping the rope a little higher than the young man, her arms were raised and her wrists turned in, to hold the cable better; her back was against the black wood of the boat. Naturally, every moment, her body floated away from that of the young man, carried against her by the current. In this hanging, retreating posture she resembled those figures of sea gods twisted by wood-carvers along the sides of galleys. A little tremor, coming from the movement of the river and the cold of the bath, seemed to give her something of the undulation of the water."

That is admirable; we seem to see it. MM. de Goncourt have possessed themselves of every literary secret; they have made a devout study of style. "Sœur Philomène," as a piece of writing and of visual observation, is a masterpiece; refinement of observation, an unerring scent for the curious and morbid, can hardly go further. The book is worth reading, from beginning to end, for its exquisite art—although the art is, to my mind, superficial, and the subject both morally and physically unsavory. It required great skill to interest us during a whole volume in the comings and goings of a simple and ignorant man, around the sickbeds of a roomful of paupers. The authors have "got up" their subject, as the phrase is, with extraordinary care; I do not know what their personal experience of hospital wards has been, but the reader might suppose that they had spent years in one. MM. de Goncourt are *dilettanti*; they are *raffinés* and they write for *raffinés*; but they are worth attention because they are highly characteristic of contemporary French culture. They are even more characteristic than some stronger writers; for they are not men of genius; they are the product of the atmosphere that surrounds them; their great talent is in great part the result of sympathy, and contact, and emulation. They represent the analysis of sensation raised to its highest power, and that is apparently the most original thing that the younger French imaginative literature has achieved. But from them as from Gustave Flaubert the attentive reader receives an indefinable impression of perverted ingenuity and wasted power. The sense of the picturesque has somehow killed the spiritual sense; the moral side of the work is dry and thin. I can hardly explain it, but such a book as "Sœur Philomène," with all its perfection of manner, gives me an impression of something I can find no other name for than cruelty. There are some things which should be sacred even to art, and art, when she is truly prosperous, is comfortably contented to let them alone. But when she begins to overhaul the baser forms of suffering and the meaner forms of vice, to turn over and turn again the thousand indecencies and impurities of life, she seems base and hungry, starving, desperate, and we think of her as one who has wasted her substance in riotous living.

I said that MM. de Goncourt did not strike me as men of genius, and I can think of but two names in the list of those whom I have called the minor French novelists that suggest the idea of genius. The first is that of Erckmann-Chatrian and the second that of Gustave Droz. The two associated storytellers known to the world under the former of these names constitute surely a genius of the purest water. Of all the French romancers of the day they are the most simply delightful, and their exquisite sense of the decent, wholesome, human side of reality, ought to balance a multitude of infectious researches in the opposite direction. It is natural to believe, and it is impossible not to hope, that "Le Conscrit de 1813," "Le Blocus," "L'Ami Fritz," "Le Joueur de Clarinette" will be read by our children's children. Gustave Droz is not by any means so clear or so complete a genius, but he has that spark of magic in his fancy, that something lightly and easily human in his humor, which are kindled in the glow of the sacred fire. One at least of the tales of M. Droz ought to stand. "Le Cahier Bleu de Mlle. Cibot" is a masterpiece, and a capital example of the charm that intense reality may have when it is reached by divination, by the winged fancy, rather than by a system more or less ingenious. After this, there are the brilliant talents—Octave Feuillet, Edmond About, Victor Cherbuliez. These writers are all prodigiously clever, but the cleverness of M. Cherbuliez overtops that of his companions. They are clever by nature, and he is clever by art, and yet he wears his cleverness with a grace and gallantry that quite eclipses theirs. He has deliberately learned how to write novels, and he writes them incomparably well. Unfortunately he seems of late to have come to the end of his lesson; his last two tales are almost painfully inferior to their predecessors. Five-and-twenty years ago, before the writers of whom these pages treat had (with one exception) presented themselves to the public, Mme. Sand was the first of French romancers. Five-and-twenty years have elapsed; these writers have exhibited all their paces, and Mme. Sand is still unsurpassed. Each of the novelists I have mentioned can do something which she cannot; but she, at her best, has resources which exceed the total aggregation of theirs. (I say advisedly at her best, for between her best and her second best there is a gulf.) She has the true, the great imagination—the metaphysical imagination. She conceives more largely and executes more nobly; she is easy and universal and—above all—agreeable.

Galaxy, February 1876

Victor Cherbuliez

Meta Holdenis. Par Victor Cherbuliez. Paris: Hachette, 1873.

WE HARDLY KNOW to what extent M. Cherbuliez is known and admired by English readers in general; to ourselves, we confess, he is an old friend, and a new novel from his hand has all the dignity of a literary event. Our friendship for him was formed more than ten years ago, over his *Comte Kostia*, the work by which he made his mark among the French romancers of the day. We doubt if this charming romance has ever become popular, but we are safe to say that it has had no indifferent or ungrateful readers. To our sense it seemed full of brilliant promise; it was impossible that so genuine an artist should not do more and better. M. Cherbuliez has done more, and has given his early master-piece half a dozen successors; but we have often vainly wondered whether, on the whole, he has done better. We inclined to think not, and this *Meta Holdenis*, clever as it is, has put an end to our doubts. The author's talent has become more and more flexible and polished, and, in the way of mere manner, the volume before us is still a masterpiece; but it has parted—parted fatally, we think, in the present case—with a certain essential charm,—a turn of fancy in which spontaneity and culture went hand in hand with singular grace. M. Cherbuliez's career, through his several novels, would be a study for a penetrating analyst, and demands more space than we can bestow. His talent is peculiarly delicate, and its development very much a matter of fine shades; but to trace these shades would be suggestive of many things, possibly of some reflections not altogether cheerful. A certain melancholy element there is in the history of all marked talents: the fact, we mean, that the growth of skill is always attended with the loss of simplicity. The genius ripens, but—unlike peaches and plums—it hardens. An author's first really strong work (especially when it is a work of imagination) is always more or less *classic*, as compared with works produced after he has caused something to be expected of him; it has a more virile compactness, it is more simply and contentedly itself. *Vanity Fair* is classic as compared with the *Newcomes*; *Oliver Twist* is classic as compared with *David Copperfield*; and *Adam Bede*, to our mind, is signally classic as compared with *Middlemarch*. So, to proceed from greater things to lesser, the *Comte Kostia* is classic as compared with *Meta Holdenis*. The charm of the former tale is difficult to describe, and we recommend our readers to taste it at first-hand. The story is perfectly a romance, and yet it is profoundly real. It is a piece of the finest artistic polish, and yet it bristles with "sensations"; it is the work at once of a master of style and of a consummate storyteller. But its great merit in this age of dingy realism is that it is simply beautiful, and that the author has ventured to remember that it is not precisely amiss that a work of art should be lighted with a ray of idealism. The book is an excellent example of the discreet use of this ingredient; it leaves the story, mechanically, as perfect as possible; it only furnishes an atmosphere for the mechanism to work in. M. Cherbuliez is a Swiss, his native city of Geneva playing a part in most of his tales; and although we may be sure, in the light of his last performance, that he will not thank us for doing so, we may nevertheless express a sense of the characteristically Genevese complexion of his talent in its earlier form,—a mental complexion lighted, indirectly perhaps, but none the less visibly, from Germany as well as from France. The Genevese mind, in so far as a stranger may guess at it, is less vivacious than the French, and says things incomparably less agreeably; but it feels them strongly enough, and, whatever they are, it has a way of taking them more seriously. This serious way of taking things we have always regarded as a result of its having a side-light open to German influences. How many Parisians of average culture can read Goethe in the original? This is a very common accomplishment in Geneva. M. Cherbuliez had read Goethe to good purpose, and his first two novels were the work of a man who took things seriously. *Meta Holdenis* is written to prove that German seriousness is very likely to be a humbug; it may be or may not; what remains true is, that the discerning reader of the *Comte Kostia* and *Paule Méré* felt himself in contact with an imagination whose poetically blue horizon, in one direction at least, lay well beyond the Rhine. The second of these tales is an attempted exposure, rather youthful in its unsparing ardor, of the narrowness and intolerance of Genevese society. How true the picture is, we are unable to say; but the story is admirably touching, and it has an aroma much less of the Parisian asphalt than of the cropped and drying grass on the mountain slopes that descend into the Lake of Geneva. The heroine is a delightfully tender conception, and though perhaps she is not absolutely natural, we prefer her, taking one piece of false drawing with another, to Meta Holdenis. In spite of the relative *naïveté* of imagination that we have touched upon, the author's first two tales were clever enough to leave us no surprise at the cleverness of the *Roman d'une Honnête Femme*; and what we felt, beside the pleasure of reading a very interesting story, was a certain suspicious regret at the eclipse of this same *naïveté*. The blue German mountains on the horizon had become extremely vague, and the book had much less a perfume of Goethe than of Octave Feuillet. M. Cherbuliez has remained, to our taste, a writer of an intellectual force which would not be represented by an addition of twenty Octave Feuillets; the greater pity that he has come at last to pitch his tone in the same key,—a note skilfully modulated, certainly, but a falsetto for all that. Of this intellectual force his two next tales—*Prosper Randoce* and *L'Aventure de Ladislas Bolski*—gave brilliant evidence. Each is an extremely ingenious study of an eccentric character: one of a man essentially a rascal, in spite of many gifts; the other of a poor fellow essentially a hero, in spite of many follies. Prosper Randoce is a Parisian scribbler, with a genius three parts tinsel to a fourth part silver, and a *morale* containing very little pure metal indeed. He is a portrait from the general type on which two powerful French novels have been based,—the "Horace" of George Sand, and the *Grand Homme de Province* of Balzac; the type of the self-deceiving charlatan, with now and then an honest impulse just so timed as fatally to confound the light and shade of his character, and extort the credulity which is foredoomed to repentance. The picture is admirably ironical, and the tone of the rabid realist of recent French poetry and fiction is burlesqued with extraordinary wit. *Ladislas Bolski* is the history of an infatuated young Pole, whose reason has succumbed to the tribulations incurred by the fantastic impetuosity of his temperament, related by himself in an interval of sanity. It is the most ingenious of the author's conceptions, and perhaps the most profound; in its attitude of detailed and sustained psychological introspection it resembles one of Mr. Browning's dramatic monologues. The author always rises to the level of his opportunity when he deals with a poetic element. His unbalanced but heroic young Pole, the dupe of his generosity and the victim of his passionate illusions, is a very poetic creation. When M. Cherbuliez gives the rein to his imagination, he does finer things than when he allows *carte blanche* to his wit and his remarkable skill in epigram. His imagination is always generous, and we pay it none too ponderous a compliment in adding, agreeably philosophical; his wit is apt to savor of an incisive but narrow irony, than which, says an authority in his own tongue, no attitude of the mind has less to do with philosophy. *Ladislas Bolski* is a tragedy, and marches roundly to a picturesquely dark *dénouement*. In this, as in all his tales, M. Cherbuliez is an admirable narrator; and if he gives the reader a constant literary pleasure, it is quite without detriment to the surprises and sensations attendant upon all properly regulated novels. In this respect the tale preceding the present one, *La Revanche de Joseph Noirel*, is perhaps his most powerful performance, as it is indeed in every way his most brilliant one. It is more than entertaining, and more even than characteristically clever; it has a certain imaginative elevation, which recalls the best elements of the *Comte Kostia*. If in *Meta Holdenis* he did not seem to us to have lost ground, we should say that in *Joseph Noirel* he had taken a fresh start. Here again he has selected an eccentric type of character, and has unfolded it with elaborate ingenuity. Joseph Noirel is a young Genevese mechanic, of the most sordid origin, but of a temperament which throws him into ardent sympathy with red radicalism, the International, and the Commune. He falls in love with his master's daughter, but is brought to a bitter sense that she is not for such as him,—a conclusion which fatally aggravates his moral irritability. She, meanwhile,—and a singularly enchanting and appealing figure the author has made of her,—is married in zealous haste by her parents to a Frenchman of title, but of enigmatic antecedents. The enigma is found in the course of time to have a very dark answer, and the young wife becomes entangled in sufferings and terrors, amid which she is very glad to receive the advice and assistance of the despised Joseph. Here begins his *revanche*; it is overwhelming and complete, and his compensation is even more fatal to his happiness than his disappointment was. The incidents will hardly bear repetition, and it takes all the author's tact and skill to make them probable. Probable or not, they are vastly thrilling, and it is really a novel pleasure to see situations such as would delight the heart of Mr. Wilkie Collins unfolded with such intellectual mastery. The novel appeared originally in the *Revue des Deux Mondes*, and we well remember as one of the most poignant sensations of our career as a novel-reader the absolutely *balked* state in which the imagination was left at the close of the last number but one. The characters were in a situation from which the compass of a single number could disentangle them only by some expedient of really heroic ingenuity. M. Cherbuliez's device is powerful, and his whole *dénouement* one of the most effective in the range of modern fiction. We have heard its probability, its logic, its taste, its decency, all earnestly discussed; but we must again refer the reader to the tale itself for an opinion. He can hardly fail to be struck with the forcibly discriminated portraiture of the aggressive, brooding, bilious, declamatory little artisan, who dreams of overturning society, and yet cannot keep himself on his feet. He is a singularly vivid image, and yet he is no caricature, but a conception belonging essentially to the day, to the hour.

The heroine of *Meta Holdenis* is, in two words, a German Becky Sharpe. The author assures us, at least, that she is a German, but this is just the point on which his story provokes discussion. With regard to German matters, one would say that he was not a man to deal in cheap burlesques; he knows the country and its literature, and has published some brilliant papers on several German writers; notably, an admirable one on Lessing. The presumption is, therefore, that he tells the truth, and it would carry us far if it did not encounter the adverse evidence of the very tone of the book itself. M. Cherbuliez's story is altogether a *pièce de circonstance*, a really rabid anti-Teutonic pamphlet in the disguise of a novel. We have read it with the dissatisfaction naturally produced by seeing an indifferent partisan spoil an excellent romancer. What need is there, we have even ventured to demand, for M. Cherbuliez's being a partisan at all? Let him stick to disinterested verity, and to an honest German point of view, and leave M. Dumas *fils* unaccompanied in his amazing enterprise of showing us that his *Femme de Claude* was a modern Messalina, because she was the daughter of the "Baron de Fieradlen,—*de très vieille famille bavaroise*." If Meta Holdenis is not exactly a Messalina, she is very nearly as nefarious a personage, and she is held up to our opprobrium with an almost Juvenalian acerbity. The story is told by the hero to a supposititious female friend (a German, to do her justice), who has tried to persuade him into matrimony with a pair of *yeux célestes*. This heavenly pair of eyes warns him off, and reminds him of the penalty he paid for falling in love with those of Meta Holdenis. He was a poor art-student, and she the eldest daughter of a pious and prosperous hardware merchant, who had lately emigrated from Elberfeld to Geneva. She is not pretty, and yet she is altogether too handsome to be ugly, and her striking and expressive physiognomy is very happily rendered. She cuts bread-and-butter for her numerous brothers and sisters, she sings hymns with a delicious voice, and she effectually fascinates the hero. They are betrothed under a very unctuous parental blessing, and, in the expansion of his confidence, the young man invests ten thousand francs (twelve are the modest amount of his fortune) in his prospective father-in-law's business. The virtuous Holdenis immediately suspends payment, and refers his indignant dupe to the Scriptures for consolation. The daughter plays him false with a grotesque little German baron, and he leaves Geneva in disgust and despair. But his despair makes a man of him, and he works to such good purpose that six years later he is well on the way to wealth and fame. We find him at this moment domesticated with a certain M. de Maussere, a French diplomatist, who has retired from public life to outweather the scandal of having eloped with a married woman. The fruit of this escapade is an intractable little girl, who is about to be committed to the care of a very superior governess. The governess arrives, and Tony (the hero) recognizes the faithless Meta. She is more ambiguously and dangerously handsome than ever, and has brought her genius for duplicity to perfection. The rest of the tale is occupied with her attempts to win a matrimonial prize,—attempts so zealous that she plays a double game, and tries at once to re-entangle Tony and to fascinate M. de Mauserre. She brings both schemes very nearly to a happy conclusion, and lies and plots and counterplots with touching plausibility; but she goes too far, overreaches herself, and is brought to dreadful confusion at the eleventh hour. She departs in wrath, joins a Protestant sisterhood, and talks of the hero and his friend her employer to whoever will listen to her, as a couple of horrible Frenchmen who had tried to seduce her.

M. Cherbuliez's design has been to create anything but a vulgar figure, and his imagination has doubtless dwelt as complacently on Meta Holdenis as on his Prosper Randoce or his Joseph Noirel. But the figure, nevertheless, can only be called, at best, a clever failure, partly because there is nothing so difficult as to draw a hypocrite (particularly a religious hypocrite), but especially because the writer's art is vitiated and vulgarized, made dry and hard, by his obtrusive *parti pris*. He starts with the thesis that a German is in nine cases out of ten a Pharisee and a humbug; a person fond of sentimentalizing about the stars and the angels, the Scriptures and his conscience, but excessively sly and tenacious in his pursuit of the main chance. This view of the German character is nowhere formally stated, but it is constantly implied, often, certainly, in a very witty manner. The hero's reflections on his attempt to paint Meta's portrait are a very good specimen of the author's epigrammatic touch:—

"Ce n'est pas tout: il y avait dans cette angélique figure autre chose encore que j'aurais bien voulu rendre. Il y a, madame, anges et anges. Ceux qu'on voit en Allemagne ne ressemblent point aux autres; leurs yeux, qui sont souvent de la couleur des turquoises, ont ceci de particulier, que sans qu'il s'en doutent, ils promettent dans une langue mystique des plaisirs qui ne le sont pas. Quiconque a voyagé dans votre pays comprendra ce que je veux dire; il y a sûrement rencontré d'adorables candeurs qui respirent la volupté qu'elles ignorent, de virginales innocences, capables de convertir un libertin au mariage et à la vertu, parcequ'il lui semble qu'il y trouvera son compte, et pour tout dire, des anges qui ne savent rien, mais que rien n'étonnera."

How far M. Cherbuliez is right on this point hardly matters, though we doubt that he is right enough to justify his indefatigably sarcastic tone; a satirist, he ought to remember, should be very right indeed, and we fancy that the sham morality of the Fraulein Holdenis would not have seemed so very typical if the Emperor William had not been so careful to thank God at the end of his bulletins. He little thought that he was going to make a clever novelist misconceive a masterpiece. The desire to make his heroine vividly typical has been fatal to the freedom of the author's hand, to that certainty of touch which is so conspicuous in his other tales. She is rigid, forced, illogical, seen altogether from without. German or not, we very little care: we wish to feel the living, breathing woman, in her virtues or in her vices. We greatly wonder that an artist of M. Cherbuliez's habitual tact and taste should not have seen the vice of his attitude of *showing up* his heroine, of forever working at the reader over her shoulder. It gives an uncommon smartness and pertness to his narrative, but it makes it small art instead of large. Thackeray described the adventures of Becky Sharpe in a very different way, and certainly Thackeray had temptation enough to be satirical. But his satire, where Becky is concerned, always goes hand in hand with a certain tender, sympathetic comprehension of her, with the thoroughly human tone which belongs to perfect insight. M. Cherbuliez, on the contrary, treats us to a kind of brutal exposure of his heroine, which has not even the merit of seeming tragic, for the reason that we don't see her, feel her, believe in her. She is made to order,—made to supply the extraordinary Parisian demand for evidence that German morality is a whited sepulchre, and the German conscience a delicious joke. The demand, as it has chiefly found expression, seems to us unspeakably puerile, and the author's alacrity in ministering to it has an air of unwisdom really disappointing to those who owe him great enjoyment. It seems rather a melancholy matter that this should have been *his* contribution to the moral situation of France and Germany. The truth is, we fear, that M. Cherbuliez is fatally clever, and that he will not believe he has grown unwise so long as he remains so very consciously readable. His polemic impulse in the present case has given a magical point to his pen and an admirable neatness to his style; anything lighter, more impertinent, than the whole movement of his tale, it would be difficult to imagine. But it is a sad falling off for the author of the *Comte Kostia* now to be stringing clever sneers, and offering them to us as a novel. The hard, metallic glitter of his style is a disagreeable substitute for the charming atmosphere of his early works. It is not unfair to speak of the ironical side of his tale as the whole substance of it, for the portraiture of the persons opposed to Meta has caught the infection of her own superficiality. There is an odd sort of levity in the whole picture of the situation of M. and Madame de Mauserre. In his emulation of the tone of novelists more trivial than himself he certainly hits the mark. Does he really see nothing indelicate in the walk and conversation of Madame de Mauserre, or does he simply put a brave face on it because prudery is a German virtue? This lady is living in what, out of a French novel, you will hardly find called by a politer term than concubinage with the gentleman whose name she has exchanged for that of her husband. Her conduct is irregular, but, if the author insists upon it, we are willing to believe that she is the most estimable person in the world. When, however, receiving, before half a dozen people, a letter announcing her husband's death, and making it possible to legitimate her union, she overflows into an amorous ecstasy, and calls upon every one to share her joy, we rather retract our admiration, and incline to think that she lacked a certain sense of the becoming, without which a lady's charms are precarious. This is simply a slight detail in evidence of the fact that every detail is perverted when the central idea is inharmonious. In a work pitched in a different key, we should, perhaps, have forgiven Madame de Mauserre her want of reserve. Heaven preserve us, says the author in conclusion, from *les consciences subtiles*. The subtlety of the conscience makes half its virtue, and we are afraid that M. Cherbuliez says more than he means,—or more than, as a disinterested student of human nature, he ought to mean. What, in fact, does all this prove, but that art should be before all things disinterested, and that a beautiful imagination may show to very poor advantage when impressed into the service of a transitory aim?

North American Review, October 1873

Miss Rovel. Par Victor Cherbuliez. New York: F. W. Christern; Boston: Estes & Lauriat (Translation.), 1875.

M. VICTOR CHERBULIEZ IS probably unknown to that large number of readers to whom the mystic words "a French novel" suggest a production of the school of Emile Gaboriau or Ponson du Terrail; but if reputation is measured by quality rather than extent, few writers of the day stand so high. It is Shelley, we believe, who has been called the poet of poets; and in a similar fashion M. Cherbuliez may be called the novelist of literary people. He is prized by those readers who, while they have a due esteem for a telling intrigue, are inclined to assign a primary place to consummate literary art—to art which, if need be, is even a trifle obtrusive and self-conscious. For those readers the author of 'Miss Rovel' has been for the last fifteen years a very important personage, and the appearance of each of his half-dozen novels a literary event. The charm of his tales has been that they seemed written by a scholar who knew the world. The usual clever novel of commerce bears few traces of an intellect generally brilliant—an intellect which, in other fields than the flowery meads of fiction, has any rights that a critic is bound to respect. But M. Cherbuliez has always beaten the regular romancer on his own ground and has given us, into the bargain, a style which it was a pure intellectual luxury to encounter. He has exhibited an acuteness and finish of mind which made us feel that if he were not good-naturedly devoting himself to story-telling he might do great things in history and philosophy. M. Cherbuliez began, in fact, as we believe, with very solid studies, and laid the foundations of a thoroughly superior culture. His circumstances, too, were such as to give him a ballast of due weight; he was a Genevese, born and brought up among academic and literary traditions, and his first venture was a most ingenious essay on Greek æsthetics. If to these advantages he added the novelist's faculty—observation raised to the degree of a passion—and if imagination too was not wanting, a critic with half an eye might feel that here would be a prince of story-tellers. And, indeed, very much one of these charming potentates M. Cherbuliez has actually been. His dominion has been small and his reign has been brief; but Athens, under Pericles, was neither vast nor long-lived. It is a sad fact that the reign of M. Cherbuliez has come to an end by his own unwisdom; the united voice of his once loyal subjects pronounces his *déchéance*. We might make a long story, if we had space, of the history of our author's talent as revealed in his successive novels—of its transformations, its moods, its inflections, its lights and shades. It would be a story of varying hopes and fears on the part of those who watched him closely and judged him sympathetically. This might be represented, quite dramatically, as a visible contest between a good and evil principle, with victory tossing like a shuttlecock from one side to the other.

The evil principle with M. Cherbuliez has been simply—paradoxical as it sounds—that he was dangerously clever. The germ of decay in his talent might have been found in a little black spot which casually looked harmless enough, or rather seemed positively to set off the expression of his literary physiognomy, like the patches worn by ladies in the last century. We allude to an exaggerated relish for epigram. This had given us some alarm in the author's earlier novels, but we never expected to see it acquire such prodigious proportions as in this unfortunate 'Miss Rovel.' Of course it is not every one who can make epigrams by the hundred; one needs to be clever, and we have said that M. Cherbuliez is inordinately so. But one day he had a great misfortune: he went to Paris—whether in person or not hardly matters, but at any rate intellectually. He went there—judging on the apparent evidence—for the particular purpose of proving that a Genevese is not a provincial, and that if he gives his mind to it he may be as good a Parisian as the best. In this undertaking M. Cherbuliez has expended an incalculable number of epigrams, and, like all converts and late-comers to a faith, he has been fanatically, indefatigably devout. He has proved his point a hundred times over; if being Parisian means having a certain tone which one must be a Parisian to describe, though one may perhaps recognize and appreciate it on easier terms, M. Cherbuliez is superabundantly, overwhelmingly Parisian. We wish now he would unstring his bow a little, rest upon his laurels, send his imagination to pasture among the flower-strewn Alpine meadows whose influences are his birthright, and tell us another story with the easy, natural grace of his masterpiece, the 'Comte Kostia.' We call this work his master-piece because it stands at the opposite end of the scale from 'Miss Rovel.' The latter is not a felicitous performance, and if we were not afraid of seeming to take the rubs of life unman-fully hard, we would say that we had passed some very dark hours in reading it. It offers, to speak frankly, the most strik-ing example of the eclipse of a great talent that we have ever encountered, and we doubt whether, while still in the mid-season of life, a clever man has often fallen so far below him-self. The author's cleverness is there; the story is smart, alert, effective at any cost; but it bears the same relation to the best of his former works as (to risk a trivial comparison) the in-tolerable stuff called bottled lemonade does to the agreeable compound it emulates. Miss Rovel, the author informs us, is a young English girl of eccentric antecedents, who, through a series of amazing escapades, ensnares the affections of a cyni-cal but attractive French *savant*, by whom she is ultimately led to the altar. M. Cherbuliez assures us, we say, that his heroine is English; but in spite of his representations we insist on it that the language of Shakspere was unknown to her, and that she was born in the Paris boulevard, where she sprang up from some noxious literary seed dropped into a crack of the asphalt. But her nationality is of little conse-quence, for we venture to pronounce her a totally impossible young lady, and, what is worse, a very detestable one. We can forgive a fantastic heroine when she is pleasing, but we resent being launched in a balloon in the company of a damsel we dislike. Why cannot a French novelist draw, with any ap-proach to verisimilitude, a young girl brought up in the An-glo-Saxon fashion? This question in itself would form the text of a disquisition, and we have only space to add that, as we should have said beforehand that M. Cherbuliez was the one writer of his craft in France capable of achieving the difficult feat we have mentioned, his signal failure is extremely disappointing. He has cruelly sacrificed his hero; for Miss Rovel was, in plain English, a very low-minded young woman.

Nation, June 3, 1875

Père Chocarne

The Inner Life of the Very Reverend Père Lacordaire, of the Order of Preachers. Translated from the French of the Rev. Père Chocarne, O. P. Dublin, 1867.

IT WAS THE OPINION of the late Father Lacordaire, formed during a visit to England, and at the sight of the flourishing condition of certain Catholic foundations in that country, that the Catholic Church was destined in the course of time to reassert its sway over the stronghold of Protestantism, and, indeed, that all the forms of modern scepticism concentrating themselves in a single camp, and all the forms of faith collecting about the Catholic standard, the contest would be reduced to a battle between these two armies, in which the latter would be victorious. It is, moreover, the opinion of the author of this volume that the influence of Father Lacordaire in particular is destined rapidly to expand until all weak and wandering souls have felt its fortifying virtue, and until the uttermost ends of the earth have confessed its celestial efficacy. Under these circumstances, it seems not unsuitable to make some enquiry into the character and history of the remarkable man who entertained such ardent hopes and communicated them to others, the more especially as Father Lacordaire is in any event a singularly interesting object of study. He was a combination of the most dissimilar qualities and tendencies. His character was made up of elements partially hostile to each other, which, by the intensity of his will, he had reduced to unity and consistency. One of his disciples qualified him happily enough as "an ancient Christian in a modern man." He was a mediæval monk and a political liberal. His sympathies, one may say, dwelt in the future and his ideas in the past. He subjected his body to the most rigorous austerities known to the cloister at the same time that he protested against religious persecution, and raised his voice in favor of personal and political liberty. He revived in France that monastic order whose members were the most active servants of the Inquisition, and he founded and conducted a school in which an ample freedom of conscience was allowed to pupils. And, moreover, in all things his sincerity was without reproach. Whatever he did, he did with the accent of conviction.

Jean-Baptiste-Henri Lacordaire was born in a small village in Burgundy in the year 1802—the year in which the Church emerged from the eclipse from which it had suffered during the régime of the Revolution. He was educated at Dijon under the care of an excellent mother. In his early years he showed signs of that passion for religious oratory which was to become the great resource of his manhood by preaching sermons to his nurse over the back of a chair. But as he grew older, and yielded himself to the discipline of public schools, his religious instincts died away, and were to be awakened again only by a personal experience of the vanity of earthly satisfactions. In 1822 he went up to Paris with the intention of studying law. He entered the office of an eminent advocate, worked hard, and was finally called to the bar, where he immediately gave evidence of his pronounced faculty for public speaking. But the very first sweets of professional success turned bitter upon his conscience. He gave himself up to religious meditations, and in May, 1824, proclaimed himself converted. His experience of the world had been brief—he was only twenty-two—but it had been intense. His feelings, indeed, were all intense, his nature was passionate, and he went in all things to extremities. To become a priest was to his mind the logical result of becoming a Christian, just as to become a monk was subsequently the logical result of becoming a priest. He entered the Seminary of St. Sulpice, began his theological studies, was ordained *abbé*, and spent several years in a state of strong religious and political fermentation. It was not in his nature to be idle; he longed for occupation and action, and at one time was on the point of starting as missionary to the United States, a country for which he always entertained a high esteem. The motive feeling of all his subsequent career was a desire for the perfect independence of the Church under the state, and he found his conception satisfied by the situation of the Church in this country. He was detained in France by an invitation to take part in the conduct of the *Avenir* newspaper, founded in 1830 by M. de Lamennais, and devoted to the maintenance of this programme as well as to that of various other liberal measures. The fate of the *Avenir* and its conductors has since become notorious. The latter carried their doctrines to an extreme which challenged the disapproval of the Papacy. They were summoned to Rome, and invited to retract. Lacordaire offered an immediate and total submission, and Lamennais held his ground, reiterated his views, and forthwith became for a time the black sheep of Catholic Christendom. Whatever may be the real value of the course taken by Lamennais, certain it is that Lacordaire was guilty of profound inconsistency, and that it is vain to attempt to prove, in the manner of the author of the volume before us, that there is no breach in the unity of his conduct. This is more than Lacordaire himself would have claimed. Absolute submission was in his eyes a duty whenever demanded by an ecclesiastical superior, but he would assuredly have admitted that it was a rupture with one's own development, and not a consummation and sanctification of it. He might, however, make express and isolated submission *ad infinitum*; he was unable to abjure the essential liberalism of his mind. On his return from Rome he began the series of "conferences" or sermons from the pulpit of Notre Dame, in Paris, which inaugurated and established his reputation and his influence as a sacred orator. During the years which ensued he conceived and matured the plan of reviving on French soil one of the extinct orders of monks, and finally decided in favor of the branch of the order of St. Dominic consecrated to preaching. This scheme offered a great variety of obstacles, but with courage, tact, and perseverance he successively overcame them, and in 1843 opened at Nancy the first of the new Dominican convents. He had passed his own novitiate in one of the Italian convents, and in 1840 had pronounced the solemn monastic vows which consecrated his final rupture with the world. But, in truth, to take leave of the world was for Lacordaire but to take possession of himself and his own genius. As a shaven and sandalled monk he was now to arrive at the perfection of his own development. He had recruited a considerable number of young men passionately desirous to embrace the Dominican career. He had in each case tested the soundness of their vocation, and when he had opened the house at Nancy he was able, as one may say, to stock it with persons of exemplary worth. At the close of 1840 he had reappeared in the pulpit of Notre Dame in his monastic habit, and had thereby authoritatively demanded and obtained tolerance for his order. Public opinion was the tribunal to which at all times Father Lacordaire ultimately appealed, and as, thanks to his irresistible eloquence as a speaker, he exercised a powerful sway upon the public temper, he seldom appealed in vain. The interval until 1854 was occupied with establishing new convents, to the number of four in all, preaching in various cities, and fostering with unwearied diligence the growth and influence of his order. In 1848 he was returned by the city of Marseilles as a member of the Constitutional Assembly of the new republic, a position which he occupied with no increase of reputation, and from which he speedily retired. One may say that throughout his career Father Lacordaire showed an indifference to superficial consistency of action, and a disposition to sacrifice it to the essential interests of the truth at stake, which do real credit to his sincerity. A good example of this tendency is offered by his acceptance of his election to the French Academy—an act which was thought at the time to be at flagrant variance with the character of an ascetic monk, but which he justified on the ground that he diverted the honor to the collective glory of his order, and that he made it a matter of conscience to repudiate no testimony that the monastic character was no obstacle to public consideration. In 1852 he had made a journey to England, and received from the spectacle of the three Dominican convents established in that country the gratifying impressions indicated at the outset of our remarks. Shortly after his return he entered upon the third and (to our mind) decidedly the most interesting phase of his career. He proceeded to the foundation of two houses of education, the colleges, namely, of Oullins and Lorège, in the neighborhood of Toulouse. For a very charming account of the latter establishment—the one over which he presided in person—we refer the reader to Mr. Matthew Arnold's little book, "A French Eton." In 1854 he had resigned the generalship of the French province of his order, and from that moment to his death had devoted himself to his pupils. He died in 1861.

His influence was exerted through three channels: his "conferences," his published writings, and, finally, his school. Belonging as we do to the profane and Protestant half of society, we are naturally able to form no estimate of the large spiritual empire which he is said to have exerted over the members of his order, his pupils, and those who placed themselves under his direction. His present biographer relates a number of instances of the spiritual efficacy of his contact and conversation. We can readily believe that he possessed the authority which accompanies great intensity of will, as well as the irresistible charm which belongs to passionate tenderness of feeling. Lacordaire had both of these gifts; and no small portion of his influence is logically explained by the fact that, besides being a most sagacious guide and an eloquent preacher, he was also a perfect exemplar and model of the spiritual virtues. He subjected his own person and character to the action of his will quite as much, and, indeed, decidedly more than he exerted it upon the lives of others. At the very outset of his career he seems to have reconciled himself by a prodigious moral effort to the utmost possible extremity of spiritual submission, so that never for an instant was he found wanting in perfect obedience, and so that, moreover, he never hesitated to enforce in all its rigor a virtue of which he was so completely the master. Nevertheless, severe as he was in his own regard, he was not so severe but that one is tempted to apply the simple term *impudence* to certain manifestations of his sacred fervor in the assumed interest of his friends. Of his own personal austerities, concerning which Father Chocarne gives some very curious details whereof we shall presently speak, one may hold such opinion as one finds it most natural to form; but what is one to think of such an anecdote as the following? A certain young man of wealth, satiated with pleasure, and longing for spiritual light and repose, had presented himself to the reverend father in quest of these treasures. Lacordaire had prescribed a retreat and meditation in a religious house, and ultimately the assumption of the Dominican habit; but the young man's friends had interfered and by their importunities had prevented him from acting upon this advice. The unhappy gentleman accordingly had spent a year in the utmost distress and irresolution of mind, yearning, and yet fearing, to break with the world and seek for peace in the cloister. At the end of this period he received a note from Lacordaire, summoning him to the apartment which he occupied when in Paris at the house of the Carmelites. The rev-

erend father received him with great severity and rebuked him
sternly for his weakness and cowardice. Then, suddenly inflamed by a sacred ardor, he commanded him to fall on his
knees and lay bare his shoulders. The young man felt that it
was not in him to disobey. Lacordaire seized a discipline of
leathern thongs and inflicted a sound scourging. With the
first blow the happy victim felt an ecstatic sense of relief. He
had received his baptism. He rose with a fortified spirit and a
complete absence of all doubts of his vocation. To perform
such acts as this one certainly needs that sacred audacity
which is a result of grace, but one also needs a little of that
grosser sort of assurance which is merely a gift of nature.

The writings of Father Lacordaire may be fairly pronounced, on the testimony of the most impartial critics,
works of no great value. His reading was extensive in certain
directions, but his information was not large, and his compositions exhibit that poverty of thought which smites with
its hideous barrenness all those works which come to the
world through seminaries and cloisters. We do not of course
mean to pass a sweeping condemnation on such works, we
only mean that, to be read with satisfaction, they should be
read also in seminaries and cloisters. It is only when the
sound of the world's mighty life is shut out from our ears,
and the fruits of its ceaseless labor hidden from our eyes, that
we can forgive the want of criticism, the want of the faculty
of appreciation, the want of *reality*—in a word, the intellectual insufficiency of books like our author's lives of Saint
Dominic and Saint Mary Magdalen. We can enjoy them in
our actual circumstances in a considerable degree, but this is
not what the author asks. We must be moved, enlightened,
converted. Ah! we exclaim, what a far different thing is the
light of our profane desire. What we say of Father Lacordaire's writings holds good of his sermons as we now possess
them. The reader is surprised that they should have stirred
vast multitudes and awakened so many sleeping consciences.
But here, as in the case of so many famous orators whom we
know only by their printed discourses, we are obliged to fall
back upon the delivery. There can be no doubt that there was
a magic virtue in his utterance, manner, and aspect, and that
it was in these things strictly that his eloquence lay.

Père Chocarne, the author of the volume before us, is simply an unquestioning enthusiast and devotee, from whom it would be folly to require any intelligent appreciation of the subject of his biography. His book is interesting, however, as an exhibition of the sort of profound attachment, and the kind of impression of absolute personal sanctity and value, which it was in the power of Father Lacordaire to produce. It justifies, moreover, its title by a full account of Lacordaire's private devotions and austerities. This remarkable man possessed so great a force of will that one is constantly in doubt as to where, in his career, passion ceased and volition began—as to when he was acting from inspiration and when he was acting on theory. We are quite unable to satisfy ourselves as to how far his assumption of the monastic character was a spiritual necessity, and how far a spiritual luxury—how far a matter of humility and how far a matter of pride. They order these things much better in the Catholic Church than we do in the world. Happy beings, the reader exclaims, as he peruses this record of the Dominican revival; happy beings, who could get such satisfaction out of your souls! who, burdened with this heavy, mortal necessity of a conscience, were able so cunningly to make it pay for its prerogative. Certain it is, however, that having once entered upon a monastic life, Father Lacordaire resolved to be a monk indeed. "A modern man," as one of his disciples pronounced him; but in no degree a modern monk. He plunged deep into the heart of the monastic ideal. "The hidden source of all his heroic resolutions," says his biographer, "the explanation of his whole life, (was) his love for Jesus Christ crucified. . . . Strange to say, even before his conversion, this idea of the cross of the Son of God seemed to pursue him. On the 15th of March, 1824, not being yet in possession of the faith, he writes: '*I should wish to be fastened alive to a wooden cross.*'" He passionately cherished through life the idea of the actual physical crucifixion, and constantly strove to keep fresh in his mind the thought of its anguish by a variety of ingenious mechanical devices. At one time he actually had himself crucified for three hours by means of ropes. But at all times he practised the most painful and degrading mortifications—such as causing himself to be lashed to a column and scourged, having his brother monks spit in his face, washing and kissing their feet—if, indeed, the kissing did not come first. Infinitely revolting, one says of these things, but apparently Lacordaire found his account in them. They possessed an exquisite adaptation to the species of culture to which he had subjected himself, and there is no species of culture that this marvellous human nature of ours will not patiently endure. One thing is plain, that, whether very proud or very humble, Father Lacordaire is made, in the volume before us, the object of an intensity of homage which in these days falls to the lot of very few persons. He was, in truth, a very remarkable man, but he was less remarkable than at first sight he appears to be. Father Chocarne exhibits to us all that he possessed; but who will exhibit all that he lacked? No one, assuredly, is competent to the task. We have but to look about to the world, to the age, and to the swarming elements of our own lives, and we will get a faint impression of it. Cut a man off from all human responsibilities, from society, and from his time—free him from the shackles and embarrassments which wait upon the moments of him who honestly attempts to *live*—simplify his career to this degree, and he will be a sad weakling if he cannot show you some fair achievement as the fruit of his hours. From the beginning to the end of these records of Father Lacordaire's life, there is hardly a faint echo of the sounds and movements of our age. He ignored it. He averted his head and cried that it was not worth looking at. One may say, therefore, that he quite failed to understand it, and that the most vigorous attempts to work upon it from his standpoint will be of necessity mere sword-thrusts in water. For our own part, accordingly, we feel no uncertainty as to the worth of Father Chocarne's estimate of the destinies of his friend's influence.

Nation, January 16, 1868

Alphonse Daudet

Three French Books.— *La Fille de Roland.* Drama en Quatre Actes en Vers. Par le Vicomte Henri de Bornier. Paris: Dentu, 1875. *Fromont Jeune et Risler Aîné.* Par Alphonse Daudet. Paris: Charpentier, 1874. *Jeanne d'Arc.* Par H. Wallon. Paris: Hachette, 1875.

LITERARY EVENTS of the first magnitude are rare in France at the present time. The great writers of the so-called "generation of 1830" have for the most part been gathered to their fathers, and the few that remain—Victor Hugo and George Sand—have passed into the condition of venerable shadows. They still write, but time in each case has rendered the well of inspiration rather shallow. The younger men, on the other hand, seem for the most part to have come rather prematurely to their tether's end, and the youngest men of all—the generation whose *début* in literature was contemporaneous with the war—offer us no names of appreciable promise. This is particularly the case in imaginative literature and in that charming branch the novel, in which the French have formerly done such great things. Edmond About is altogether silent. Octave Feuillet writes little, and that little is below his earlier level; and two authors of more recent fame, held in the highest esteem by true connoisseurs—Gustave Droz and Victor Cherbuliez—have each just inflicted a heavy blow on their admirers by the publication of a work of fiction in which the talent offers but a feeble, perverted echo of their original power. The "Revue des Deux Mondes," the classic and time-honored medium of publication of novels of the first rank, is reduced in this sterile season to putting forth translations of American tales which are almost wholly without honor in their own country. In this state of things a small success does duty as a great one. This is in a manner, we suppose, why M. de Bornier's drama "La Fille de Roland" has found such prosperity at the Théâtre-Français. In France a serious play, to succeed, must have literary qualities as well as theatrical ones, and those which do succeed run through a number of editions proportionate to the number of representations on the stage. "La Fille de Roland" has had a liberal share both of editions and representations. It is a very agreeable work, but it is perhaps rather a light performance to have made so much noise. Three or four considerations, however, help to explain its prosperity—for there are other reasons besides the dearth of stronger works. One is that France is just now morally in a mood of almost morbid patriotism. She has an exceptional relish for everything in her past and her possible future which savors of compensation for the shames and miseries of the "terrible year," 1870–71, and she is devoutly thankful to any one who will play, at all skilfully, on this patriotic chord and set its memories and hopes a-murmuring. This M. de Bornier has done, with a very graceful touch; his drama has a kind of aroma of ideal Gallicism which would be sure to go a great way with an intelligent audience. And then, moreover (and this is the most interesting point), the success of the piece throws a vivid psychological light upon the temper of the French mind. The French have always claimed (more than has been allowed them) that as a nation, and more than any other, they have been disinterested, generous, imaginative, capable of acting for an idea. They can in fact point to some examples, but their neighbors can match them with others of a different sort. However this may be, in a national sense, of the people who produced Louis XIV. and Napoleon, we think there is no doubt that privately they have a keen enjoyment of all exhibitions of heroic, exaggerated, chimerical virtue. Here again invidious neighbors may respond with familiar proverbs—may proclaim that charity begins at home, and talk about the people who strain at a gnat and swallow a camel. Allowing due weight to these reflections, we feel tempted to rejoin that the French have in fact a capacity for personal self-sacrifice to which their critics do not always render justice. They show it in their lives; in the way in which the individual habitually pays his tribute to the credit and honor of his family and his name; in the way in which parents clip their narrow incomes, for a series of years, to furnish marriage-portions for their children; in the almost superstitious respect that Frenchmen, legally emancipated, entertain for the parental authority (especially that of the mother and grandmother; for in the case of the latter personage it often becomes an "idea" pure and simple—an idea with which an Anglo-Saxon, if the old lady herself were aggressively possessed with it, would have a very short patience).

They show it, more abstractly, in their fondness for seeing people in novels and plays placed in sentimental situations of a subtilized and etherized sort. Nothing is more true, surely, than that in such matters one man's meat is, if not another man's poison, at any rate his least relished nutriment. "Your moral," one nation is always capable of saying to another, "is not our moral; you put your conscience into one thing; you are very welcome; we put it in another." The French, we might perhaps say, if we ventured to formulate the matter, put it into the exercise of the superfluous virtues—the virtues which, as their own phrase has it, are *de luxe*. Certain it is, at all events, that they can swallow a far greater amount of fine-spun sentiment than we Anglo-Saxons. The daughter of Roland is a charming young woman named Berthe, who is also niece of Charlemagne. Her father, the noblest of the great Emperor's peers, has perished on the fatal day of Roncesvalles, betrayed to the Saracens through the perfidious jealousy of his brother knight, Ganelon, who was also his step-father, the second husband of his mother. The traitor Ganelon, horrified at his crime as soon as it is perpetrated, disappears from men's eyes and wears away his days in the pangs of remorse—alleviated only by the prosperous growth and development in all youthful graces and knightly arts of his single son Gerald, whom he has brought up in blissful ignorance of his shame. The chances of mediæval adventure bring Berthe and Gerald into contact and a mutual passion is the very proper result. The play pivots upon the conduct of all concerned in this painful entanglement—upon the question of whether Berthe shall or shall not marry the son of her father's betrayer. Charlemagne in person makes his appearance, with a good deal of poetic picturesqueness; Gerald learns his father's sombre secret; Ganelon himself drains to the dregs the bowl of contrition and penance. Charlemagne forgives him. Berthe stands firm, and it might be supposed, therefore, that young Gerald would accept the situation, and not, as it were, look his gift-horse in the mouth. But Gerald takes the ideal view. He says it is all very kind in the others to remove difficulties and remit penalties. He prefers to pay penalties; he adores Berthe (who, played at the Théâtre-Français by Mlle. Sarah Bernhardt, must certainly have been adorable), but he prefers to renounce her and to offer an extremely refined expiation of his father's crime. To this decision the whole court of Charlemagne bows its head, and the portentous old monarch himself thus utters the last lines of the play:

> "Barons, princes, inclinez vous
> Devant celui qui part: il est plus grand que nous."

This is all very beautiful, but though Ganelon had been a great rascal, it is morally a trifle fantastic—it is drawing the thread rather fine. M. de Bornier handles his thread, however, with very artful fingers, and writes very picturesque, harmonious verses. The dramatic interest of the play is not intense, but its success is perhaps the more pleasing from the very fact that the interest is literary and sentimental. It is not, alas! for us, on any grounds, to pick faults in it. On the day when the English stage can convoke great audiences to witness a successful new drama which is at the same time a finished literary work, we can better afford to cheapen a success like that of M. de Bornier.

In the absence of anything better in the way of a novel, M. Alphonse Daudet's "Fromont Jeune et Risler Aîné" has passed rapidly into its fourth edition. There could perhaps be no better proof that the French genius, in this line, has lost its earlier glow. M. Daudet's novel has literary qualities of a considerable sort, but the whole execution of the book is, to our sense, painfully labored and cold. Like almost every one else nowadays—there are exceptions: M. de Bornier, for instance, of whom we have just been speaking, is one of them—M. Daudet goes in, as the phrase is, for realism. He is a disciple of M. Flaubert—though we suppose he makes claim to possessing a moral savor which M. Flaubert lacks. He is, indeed, a good deal of a sentimentalist, and he has, unlike his master, an eye for shades of feeling as well as for variations of texture and differences of surface. He would do well, we think, to cultivate his talent in this line—in which, if we are not mistaken, he has already achieved some success. His aspiration toward the laurels of realism seems to prove that the appetite for this sort of thing in France has not yet begun to fail. We think it a pity it should not, for the ground worked by the school of M. Flaubert yields at last nothing but stones and brambles. M. Daudet drives in his spade with extraordinary good will, and sweats and palpitates over his task; but his patient efforts only prove the aridity of the soil. The contrast between the literary skill expended upon themes cognate to that of the present novel, the elaboration, the fancy, the fineness of touch, the felicity of incidental detail, and the essential baseness and flimsiness of the theme itself, is very curious, and at times, if one reflects on the matter, very melancholy. M. Daudet has proposed to narrate the career, the *decensus Averni*, of a young woman of depraved and licentious instincts. Sidonie Chèbe is a child of the *pavé de Paris*, as the phrase is—the daughter of a broken-down tradesman. She makes an unexpectedly brilliant marriage, having secured the affections, without in the least repaying them, of the junior partner in a prosperous manufactory of wall-papers. Her fall dates from the moment of her rise. She is cold, false, vicious, luxurious, essentially corrupt. She seduces her husband's partner, she seduces her brother-in-law, another member of the firm, and by her extravagant demands upon these gentlemen she drags an honorable mercantile house to the verge of bankruptcy. She runs through the whole gamut of falsity and depravity, and disappears from sight as a third-rate singer of loose songs at a *café chantant*. She is a person for one to qualify by a single homely epithet, and dismiss from one's thought. But M. Daudet waits upon her steps with unwearying patience, analyzes her idiosyncrasies, and records her adventures with extravagant minuteness. It had all been done a thousand times before; it had been done one day, in an hour of inspiration that has never come back to him, by the author of "Madame Bovary;" and surely the edifying and the entertaining properties of the subject have been alike exhausted. M. Daudet is at pains to tell us that his heroine was by no means a Mme. Bovary; that she was an interesting variation of the type; that she had an originality of her own; that she possessed this, and that, and the other remarkable idiosyncrasy. At night all cats are gray, says the proverb, and past a certain level all women of the habits of Mesdames Bovary and Risler may be lumped together. If we are to write the natural history of the prostitute on this extended scale, on what scale shall we handle that of her betters? But in France, apparently, as we say, the supply of information on these points is not in excess of the demand. M. Daudet's novel contains some very pretty episodes; the whole picture of the social *entourage* of his heroine in the old shabby-genteel quarter of the Marais, is a very skilful piece of literary genre painting. There is, in especial, a certain M. Delobelle, an old actor out of employment, who is determined not to retire from the stage nor give up the struggle (he has not been before the footlights in some twenty years), and who is supported meanwhile in a career of picturesquely attired *flânerie*, by a devoted wife and daughter, on the proceeds of a trade which consists of furbishing up and making over the little stuffed birds and insects used in Parisian millinery. The picture of his impecunious but adoring household is quite admirable; though we think it would have lacked much of its *chiaroscuro* if M. Daudet had not been a great student of Dickens. We may say of him, on the whole, that he is an artist gone astray.

We may perhaps find further evidence that the French public is in the humor for making the most of the brighter episodes of its history in the fact that M. Wallon's excellent monograph on Jeanne d'Arc has been crowned by the Academy and reached its third edition. It is gratifying to see an historical work in two substantial volumes competing in popularity with the biography of Madame Risler. M. Wallon is at present Minister of Public Instruction, and he is a highly orthodox and estimable writer; but he is agreeable as well as erudite, and he has done liberal justice to his extremely interesting subject. His book will remain, for general readers, the final, conclusive account of the matter. It had at last become possible that the last word on Jeanne d'Arc should be said. M. Quicherat, the most learned of mediævalists, had published the complete reports of her two trials; materials abounded, and the only question was to use them sagaciously. M. Wallon, to our sense, is on some points rather timorous; he is afraid to take frankly, when it is needed, the psychological view; he considers his heroine too much from the standpoint of orthodox Catholicism, and attaches undue importance to the fact that she has never been canonized, though, at last, there is very good hope that she will be. But he combines ardor with impartiality, and he is, in feeling, thoroughly intimate with his subject. Evidence upon Jeanne's career has been brought together in enormous quantities, and each successive step in it is now almost as vividly illuminated as if—say—she had been a resident of Brooklyn. M. Wallon renews most powerfully one's sense of the impressiveness of her story. Its wonders had become one of the commonplaces of history, but they are here presented in a clearer light than ever. Few episodes in human annals compare with this in interest; we are tempted to say that there is only one that exceeds it. Narrating the capture of the Maid beneath the walls of Compiègne, M. Wallon risks the expression that now her Passion had begun. Even if the reader does not believe, with M. Wallon, that Jeanne was directly inspired, he will not resent this association. Certainly only in that other case is there such an example of a person being lifted up from the lowest fortune to the highest. The author, intimating his belief that his heroine was divinely commissioned, in the sense that the saints were, finds, from his own point of view, some assistance in understanding her. But if one is puzzled to see why, if Providence specifically appointed her to her task, and qualified her for it, Providence should have afterward allowed her to be for months in chains and then be roasted alive, one forfeits this desirable aid. And yet, without it, Jeanne's career is insolubly strange; the marvellous element in it is simply overwhelming. "Never," says the author, "did a theme seem more worthy of high poetry; it unites in itself the two conditions of the epic: a national subject, a supernatural action. But never did subject tempt poets less fortunately. Poetry lives upon fictions, and the figure of Jeanne submits to no foreign adornment. Her grandeur suffices to itself; she is more beautiful in her simplicity." This, in one sense, is very true; and yet the term "simplicity," in relation to her, is decidedly misleading. It was simplicity of this calibre: "Jeanne had already encountered many resistances to the accomplishment of her mission. She had encountered all kinds; at Domrémy, at Vaucouleurs, at Chinon, at Poitiers. She had triumphed then, but without yet persuading. As they had let her go to Chinon they sent her to Orleans; but mistrust followed her. If the people had faith in her, those in power used her without believing her. They put her forward and decided without her

knowledge, whether it was a question of the march of the provision train, or of the attack on the English fortresses. She had
to begin by doing them violence, in order to force the English
from their batteries, and drive them out of Orleans. The deliv-
erance of Orleans, which was more than a victory, had lent an
immense impulse to all minds. It only needed to be kept up
and followed; it was allowed to sink, and Jeanne had to struggle again against both inertia and malevolence. She demanded
the journey to Rheims; they offer her a campaign on the
Loire. She accepts it as if as a stop-gap; and we have seen with
what rapidity she finishes it. The 11th June she attacks Jargeau,
and takes it the 12th; the 13th she is at Orleans, where she ral-
lies her troops; the 15th she occupies the bridge of Meurs; the
16th she attacks Baugency, which surrenders on the 17th. The
English, who have started to the assistance of Jargeau, arrive
at Meurs on the day Baugency capitulates; they arrive only to
retreat, but not so fast but that they are overtaken and beaten
on the 18th at Patay. A week has ended all."

The extraordinary thing about Jeanne from the first hour
was the perfect definiteness of her ideas. She had no vagueness, no extravagance, nothing unpractical. She knew exactly
what she wished; her undertaking was mapped out before
her. Her good sense, her discretion were never at fault. Her
sense of detail was extraordinary; she had from the first the
military *coup d'œil*. Her sobriety never left her; her homely
good sense bore her company through the dreary tribulations
of her trial. M. Wallon's second volume is chiefly occupied
with a detailed report of this scandalous process; and in spite
of one's constant resentment of its odious travesty of justice,
there is almost a sort of entertainment in the confounding
felicity of her answers in cross examination. "The judge," says
M. Wallon, " who had not lost sight of her speech, 'Without
the grace of God I would do nothing,' asked her whether she
knew if she was in grace—a formidable question which excited remonstrances and murmurs even in the midst of that
assembly of prejudiced men. No one knows, says the Scrip-
ture, whether he is worthy of love or of hatred, and they
desired a poor, ignorant girl to say yes or no, whether she
was in the grace of God! One of the accusers ventured to say
to her that she was not obliged to reply. 'You had better have

held your tongue,' said the Bishop with acerbity, having thought that his prey was already in his grasp: for his question contained an argument with two edges: 'Do you know yourself to be in grace?' If she said no, what an admission! If she said yes, what pride! She answered, 'If I am not in grace, may God put me there; if I am there, may He keep me there!' "

"Her figure," as M. Wallon says, "great though it is, has no need of great formulas." And yet some sort of a formula one instinctively seeks for it. She was the highest conceivable embodiment of the passion of patriotism. The presence of the English on French soil wounded her soul as some cruel physical pressure would have wounded her body, and she would not rest until she had pulled out the sharp weapon. The extraordinary thing is that lonely daughter of the soil as she was, living among hinds and serfs and tending sheep in the fields, she should have measured and comprehended the English occupation as a national calamity. This proves that long before newspapers and telegrams there was such a thing as public opinion. And then our formula, such as it is, is disturbed by the great fact of her visions, her "voices." We think it is by no means impossible to account for these subjectively. They were the natural outgrowth of a mind wholly unaccustomed to deal with abstractions and, as reflection ardently pressed upon it, beguiled into expressing its emotions to itself, as it were, in images, and in the highest images it knew, the painted images of St. Michael and St. Margaret in the church windows. Patriotism is generally deemed one of the secondary, the acquired, the relative virtues; but in Jeanne's temperament it was apparently thoroughly primordial. We prefer to think of her as inspired, if you will, but inspired by familiar human forces. Her brief career is a monument to the possible triumphs of a powerful will.

Galaxy, August 1875

Mon Frère et Moi: Souvenirs d'Enfance et de Jeunesse. Par Ernest Daudet. Paris: Plon., 1882.

THE FRENCH HAVE about many matters a way of feeling that is not ours, and M. Ernest Daudet's little volume illustrates some of these differences. He is the brother of the brilliant author of the Lettres de mon Moulin, the Rois en Exil, and Numa Roumestan, and it has seemed to him natural to celebrate his kinship with so charming a writer in a volume published while the latter is yet in his prime, and in which biography and eulogy, admiration and tenderness, are gracefully blended. In England or in America, an artist's brother would, we think, hold himself less designated than another to discourse to the public about the great man of the family. The artist would be sure to dislike it, and the brother would have an awkward, and possibly morbid, fear of making two honest men ridiculous. But the French have never worshiped at the shrine of reticence, and it is fortunate that there should be a race of people who acquit themselves gracefully of delicate undertakings, and who have on all occasions the courage of their emotion. The French do such things because they *can*; we abstain because we have not that art. M. Ernest Daudet admires his brother as much as he loves him, and as he presumably knows him better than any one else, he may have regarded himself as the ideal biographer. His delightful volume is, to speak grossly, just a trifle too much of a *puff*; but if he was able to settle the matter with Alphonse Daudet (for whom he claims complete irresponsibility), we see no obstacle to his settling it with the public and with his own conscience. Our principal regret is the regret expressed by the subject of the work in a letter from which, in the preface, the author quotes a passage. M. Alphonse Daudet, who was in Switzerland at the time the chapters of which the present volume is composed were put forth in a periodical, protested against "being treated as people treat only the dead. I am living, and very living," he wrote, "and you make me enter rather too soon into history. I know people who will say that I have got my brother to advertise me." Alphonse Daudet is living, and very living; that is his great attraction. But after all, his too zealous biographer has not killed him. We hold, all the same, that there is little to please us in the growing taste of the age for revelations about the private life of the persons in whose works it is good enough to be interested. In our opinion, the life and the works are two very different matters, and an intimate knowledge of the one is not at all necessary for a genial enjoyment of the other. A writer who gives us his works is not obliged to throw his life after them, as is very apt to be assumed by persons who fail to perceive that one of the most interesting pursuits in the world is to read between the lines of the best literature. Alphonse Daudet is but forty-two years of age, and we hope to read a more definitive life of him thirty years hence. By that time we shall know whether we really need it.

Once grant M. Ernest Daudet his premises, he tells his story with taste as well as with tenderness. The story is perhaps not intrinsically remarkable, but there is something so ingratiating in the personality of the hero that we follow his small adventures with a kind of affectionate interest. His youth was the youth of nineteen out of twenty French artists and men of letters, and he served the usual apprenticeship to poverty and disappointment. Born in a small provincial city, of parents more or less acquainted with chill penury, he picks up a certain amount of heterogeneous knowledge at the communal college or the *lycée*; becomes conscious of talents or of ambition; struggles more or less, in a narrow interior, with a family circle which fails to appreciate these gifts; and finally, with empty pockets and immense curiosities, comes up to Paris to seek a fortune. Nineteen out of twenty of these slender beginners never get any further; they never succeed in breaking open their little envelope of obscurity. Daudet was the twentieth, who takes all the prizes. He deserved them, if suffering is a title; for his childhood, in spite of a few happy accidents,—the brightness and sweetness both of his birthplace and of his temperament,—had been difficult, almost cruel. He was born in that wonderful Provence which he has so frequently and so vividly, though perhaps not so accurately, described; he came into the world in the picturesque old city of Nîmes, the city of Roman remains, of fragrant gardens, of beautiful views, of sun and dust, of Southern dullness and Southern animation. Much of his childhood, however, thanks to his father's reverses and embarrassments (his family had been engaged in the weaving of silk), was spent at Lyons, among gray, damp, sordid, sickening impressions,—a period described with touching effect in M. Daudet's first long story, the exquisite memoirs of Le Petit Chose. M.

Ernest Daudet relates the annals of his family, which appears
to have numbered several vigorous and even distinguished
members, and makes no secret of the fact that in his own
childhood its once considerable honors had been much curtailed. This period, for the two brothers, contained many dismal passages, and Alphonse, while still a mere boy (at least,
in appearance), was obliged to earn a wretched livelihood as
ill-paid usher in a small provincial college. We do not mean,
however, to retrace the chapters of his life; we take him as we
find him to-day, in the full enjoyment of his powers and his
rewards, and we attempt, in a few rapid strokes, to sketch his
literary physiognomy.

If we were asked to describe it in two words, we should
say that he is beyond comparison the most *charming* story-
teller of the day. He has power as well as charm, but his
happy grace is what strikes us most. No one is so light and
keen, so picturesque; no one pleases so by his manner, his
movement, his native gayety, his constant desire to please. We
confess to an extreme fondness for M. Alphonse Daudet; he
is very near to our heart. The bright light, the warm color,
the spontaneity and loquacity, of his native Provence have entered into his style, and made him a talker as well as a novelist. He tells his stories as a talker; they have always something
of the flexibility and familiarity of conversation. The conversation, we mean, of an artist and a Frenchman; the conversation of a circle in which the faculty of vivid and discriminating speech exists as it has existed nowhere else. This
charming temper, touched here and there with the sentiment
of deeper things, is the sign of his earlier productions. As
time has gone on, he has enlarged his manner,—enlarged
with his field of observation. The Parisian has been added to
the Provençal, fortunately without crowding him out. It is
not M. Daudet's longest things that we like best, though we
profess a great fondness for Les Rois en Exil. The Lettres de
mon Moulin, the Contes du Lundi, Le Petit Chose, the exquisitely amusing history of Tartarin de Tarascon, the charming series of letters entitled Robert Helmont,—these contain,
to our sense, the cream of the author's delicate and indescribable talent. Daudet sketches in perfection; he does the little
piece— *il fait le morceau*, as the French call it—with a facility

all his own. No one has such an eye for a subject; such a perception of "bits," as the painters in water-colors say. It is indeed as if he worked in water-colors, from a rich and liquid palette; his style is not so much a literary form as a plastic form. He is a wonderful observer of all external things,—of appearances, objects, surface, circumstances; but what makes his peculiarity is that the ray of fancy, the tremor of feeling, always lights up the picture. This perception of material objects is not uncommon to-day, and it has never been rare among the French, in whom quickness of vision, combined with a talent for specifying and analyzing what they see, is a national characteristic. The new fashion of realism has indeed taught us all that in any description of life the description of places and things is half the battle. But to describe them we must see them, and some people see, on the same occasion, infinitely more than others. Alphonse Daudet is one of those who see most. Among the French, moreover, the gift is cultivated, and the first canon of the "young school" of to-day is that to write a novel you must take notes on the spot. Balzac took notes, Gustave Flaubert took notes, Emile Zola takes notes. We are sure that Alphonse Daudet takes them, too, though in his constitution there is a happy faculty for which all the notes in the world are an insufficient substitute, namely, the faculty of feeling as well as seeing. He feels what he sees, and the feeling expresses itself in quick, light irony, in jocosity, in poetry. M. Daudet never sees plain prose. He discovers everywhere the shimmer and murmur of the poetic. He has described in a great many places the Provençal turn of mind, the temperament of the man of the South; his last novel in particular—Numa Roumestan—being an elaborate picture of this genial type, for which M. Daudet does not profess an unlimited respect. He feels it so strongly, perhaps, because he feels it in himself; it is not to be denied that his own artistic nature contains several of the qualities on which he has expended his most charming satire. The weak points of the man of the South, in M. Daudet's view, are the desire to please at any cost, and, as a natural result of this, a brilliant indifference to the truth. There is a good deal of all this, in its less damaging aspects, in the author of Numa Roumestan. We have spoken of his desire to please, which is surely not an

unpardonable fault in an artist, though M. Zola holds it to be
so. M. Daudet likes to entertain, to beguile, to gratify, to
mystify, to purchase immediate applause. For ourselves, we
give the applause without the slightest reluctance. May it be
a fault in a writer of fiction to be very fond of fiction? In this
case it seems to us that M. Daudet is distinctly culpable. M.
Zola, to quote him again, holds that the love of fiction is the
most evil passion of the human heart; and yet he has most
inconsistently found many civil things to say of his *confrère*
Daudet, whom he would represent as one of the standard-
bearers of naturalism. M. Daudet is fond of fiction as Dickens
was fond of it,—he is fond of the picturesque. His taste is
for oddities and exceptions, for touching *dénoûments*, for situations slightly factitious, for characters surprisingly genial.
There is nothing uncompromising, nothing of a depressing
integrity, in his love of the real. Left to himself, he takes only
those parts of it that happen to commend themselves to his
fancy, which, as we have already said, is, in his intellectual
economy, the mistress of the house. But he has not always
been left to himself. He has lived in Paris, he has become a
disciple of Balzac, he has frequented Flaubert, he has known
Zola, he has been made to feel that there are such things as
responsibilities. There are, indeed,—those terrible responsibilities which M. Zola carries with such a ponderous tread.
He himself recalls Alphonse Daudet to a sense of them in a
passage which we may quote from his lately published volume, entitled Une Campagne. He is more troubled, we suspect, than he ventures to say by Daudet's taint of the
factitious, and he speaks with a good deal of point of the very
different aspect which the Provence of Numa Roumestan
wears from the Provence of his own young memories,—he
being also a son of that soil. "Alphonse Daudet seems to me
to see the country of Provence in one of the gilded falsehoods
of his hero. I don't speak of the inhabitants, whom he treats
with even too much cruelty; I speak of the look of the land,
of that perpetual dream of sunshine, which he manages to fill
with all the romance of the troubadours. He softens down
the very *mistral*, which he calls 'the wholesome, vivifying
blast, spreading its jovial influence to the furthest edge of the
horizon.' My own Provence, that of which the heated harsh-

ness still blows into my face, is a much rougher affair, and the mistral cracks my lips, burns my skin, fills the valley with a devastation so terrible that the blue sky grows pale. I remember the extinguished look of the sun in the pure, bleached air, through that roaring breath which sometimes ruins the country-side in a day. The Provence of Alphonse Daudet is therefore, for my sensations, too good-natured; I should like it stronger and more scorched, with that perfume of which the violence turns to bitterness under the hard and cloudless blue."

It was inevitable, we suppose, that our author should sooner or later become a Parisian; should attempt to master the great city, in the manner of successful Frenchmen. This capitalization of his talent, as we may call it, has been extremely fruitful, has produced a multitude of admirable chapters; but, on the other hand, it has made Alphonse Daudet much less perfect. The sketches and stories we mentioned at the beginning of this article all have the stamp of perfection. There is nothing to add to them, nothing to take from them, nothing to correct in them. In his later and larger works there have been great inequalities, though the successful portions, we admit, have become more and more brilliant. It is an odd thing that though it is as a peculiarly imaginative writer that we reckon him, he is not at his best when he gives his imagination the reins. At such moments he is very apt to become false and unnatural; his charming fancy is an excellent companion, but an uncertain guide. His great successes (in his longer works) have been portraits of known individuals. Fromont Jeune et Risler Aîné, the first in date of these later things, and perhaps the most popular, is by no means the one we prefer; with all its keenness of touch, it has perhaps even more than its share of the disparities of which we speak. The accessories, the details, the setting of the scene, the art of presentation, the three or four subordinate characters, furnish the strong points of the book. The portrait of the depraved and dangerous heroine (there is a virtuous female figure to balance her) is wanting to our sense in solidity, and the main interest of the novel suffers from thinness. Sidonie Chèbe strikes us as a study at once elaborate and shallow; and indeed the elaboration of the frivolous and perfidious wife, in French fiction, has grown to be inevitably and indefinably stale. The best figure in the book is the old humbugging tragedian De-lobelle,—a type of which we have had glimpses elsewhere. In Delobelle and in his daughter Désirée, English readers find an echo, at once gratifying and tormenting, of our own inimitable Dickens. Dickens is dying, they say; Dickens is dead (though we don't believe it), and nothing is more generally admitted than that Dickens's absent qualities were as striking as those he had. But on his own ground he was immeasurable, and when we are reminded of him by another writer, the comparison suggested is not likely to be to the advantage of the latter. We speak, of course, from the point of view of a generation impregnated with Dickens's humor, and our remark has no application to French readers, who have no idea, when they smile or sigh over the fortunes of the famille Joyeuse (in Le Nabab), or drop a tear upon the childish miseries of Jack, that they are tasting of an ingenious dilution of the violent humor of Nickleby and Copperfield. We do not mean in the least that Alphonse Daudet is a conscious copyist of Dickens; he has denied the charge, we believe, in definite terms. But the English writer is certainly one of his sympathies, and we suspect that if he had never opened (even in a translation) one of those volumes which constitute the great cockney epic, one of the effective notes of his scale would be absent. In Jack the influence of Dickens is very visible, and it has not, we think, made the story more natural. That falsetto note, in pathos, which was the fatal danger of the author of Dombey and Son, is sounded with a good deal of frequency in Jack, and the portrayal of innocent suffering, through the intensification of the innocence, is also overdone. Neither do we care very much for the famille Joyeuse, in Le Nabab, finding in them, as we do, too sensible a reflection of that rather voluntary glow of satisfaction with which Dickens invites us to contemplate such people as the Brothers Cheeryble. Le Nabab, is on the whole, however, a brilliant production, and contains some of the author's strongest pages. It is a gallery of portraits, like all of his later stories,—portraits of contemporary Parisian figures, in which the intelligent reader is always able to detect a more or less distinguished model. The hero himself is a study of the "man of the South," but in his more robust and fruitful aspects, and is an exceedingly vivid picture of a great industrial and commercial *parvenu*. The picture takes a tragical turn, for the great fortune of M. Daudet's ex-dock porter crumbles away through a series of events as remarkable as those which have helped to build it up. It is the analysis of a coarse, powerful, vulgar, jovial, florid, energetic temperament, which has known the two extremes of human experience; and it is no secret that the author has reproduced the history—or at least the physiognomy—of the remarkable M. Bravais, whose rapid rise and fall were one of the innumerable queer incidents of the later years of the Empire.

This period is embodied even more effectively in the figure of the Duc de Mora,—a thin modification of the once impressive title of the Duc de Morny, who is presented in M. Daudet's pages in company with several members of his circle. This is the historical novel applied to the passing hour. The author has expended his best pains on the portrait of the Duc de Mora, and if the picture fails of vividness it is not for want of the multiplication of fine touches. It has great color and relief,—the mark of that brush-like quality of pen which is a specialty of M. Daudet. Is Felicia Ruys intended for Mademoiselle Sarah Bernhardt? The answer to the question hardly matters, for the personage belongs to the rank of the author's half-successes. We mention her, because, like the other characters, she is an example of the manner which Alphonse Daudet may be said to have invented. This manner, the reproduction of actualities under a transparent veil, the appropriation of a type embodied in a living specimen, with the peculiarities much accentuated, is an inspiration which, when it is most fruitful, Alphonse Daudet induces rather to condone than to welcome. Cultivated by a writer of his tact and talent, it would probably produce a plentiful crop of vulgarities. M. Daudet is never vulgar, but he is sometimes rather false. Many of his readers doubtless hold that his best guarantee against falsity is this very practice of drawing not only from life, but from the special case. They remark, justly enough, that in Le Nabab, in the Rois en Exil, the best things are the things for which he has had chapter and verse in the world around him. When he has attempted to generalize, as in the more technically romantic episodes, he has gone astray, and become fantastic. We incline to agree to this, though it may seem to contradict what we have said about his great charm being his element of fancy. We should explain that we have not used fancy here in the sense of invention; we have used it to denote the faculty which projects the unexpected, irresponsible, illuminating day upon material supplied out of hand. If there were nothing else to distinguish Alphonse Daudet from Emile Zola, his delicate, constant sense of beauty would suffice. Zola of course consoles himself, though he does not always console others, with his superior sense of reality. Daudet is a passionate observer,—an observer not perhaps of the deepest things of life, but of the whole realm of the immediate, the expressive, the actual. This faculty, enriched by the most abundant exercise and united with the feeling of the poet who sees all the finer relations of things and never relinquishes the attempt to charm, is what we look for in the happiest novelist of our day. Ah, the things he sees,—the various, fleeting, lurking, delicate, nameless human things! We have spoken of his remarkable vision of accessories and details; but it is difficult to give an idea of the artistic "go" with which it is exercised. This beautiful vivacity finds its most complete expression in Les Rois en Exil, a book that could have been produced only in one of these later years of grace. Such a book is intensely modern, and the author is in every way an essentially modern genius. With the light, warm, frank Provençal element of him, he is, in his completeness, a product of the great French city. He has the nervous tension, the intellectual eagerness, the quick and exaggerated sensibility, the complicated, sophisticated judgment, which the friction, the contagion, the emulation, the whole spectacle, at once exciting and depressing, of our civilization at its highest, produces in susceptible natures. There are tears in his laughter, and there is a strain of laughter in his tears; and in both there is a note of music. What could be more modern than his style, from which every shred of classicism has been stripped, and which moves in a glitter of images, of discoveries, of verbal gymnastics, animated always by the same passion for the concrete? With his merits and shortcomings combined, Alphonse Daudet is the charming writer we began by declaring him, because he is so intensely living. He is a thoroughly special genius, and in our own sympathies he touches a very susceptible spot. He is not so serious, not to say so solemn, as Emile Zola, and we suspect that in his heart he finds the doctrine of naturalism a good deal of a bore. He is free from being as deep and wise and just as the great Turgenieff. But with his happy vision, his abundant expression, his talent for episodes and figures that detach themselves, his sense of intimate pleasures and pains, his good-humor, his gayety, his grace, and that modern quality of intensity that he throws into everything, he is really a great little novelist.

Atlantic Monthly, June 1882

ALPHONSE DAUDET

I

THE NOVEL OF MANNERS grows thick in England, and there are many reasons for it. In the first place it was born there, and a plant always flourishes in its own country." So wrote M. Taine, the French critic, many years ago. But those were the years of Dickens and Thackeray (as a prelude to a study of the latter of whom the remark was made); and the branch of literature mentioned by M. Taine has no longer, in the soil of our English-speaking genius, so strong a vitality. The French may bear the palm to-day in the representation of manners by the aid of fiction. Formerly, it was possible to oppose Balzac and Madame Sand to Dickens and Thackeray; but at present we have no one, either in England or in America, to oppose to Alphonse Daudet. The appearance of a new novel by this admirable genius is to my mind the most delightful literary event that can occur just now; in other words Alphonse Daudet is at the head of his profession. I say of his profession advisedly, for he belongs to our modern class of trained men of letters; he is not an occasional or a desultory poet; he is a novelist to his finger-tips—a soldier in the great army of constant producers. But such as he is, he is a master of his art, and I may as well say definitely that if I attempt to sketch in a few pages his literary countenance, it will be found that the portrait is from the hand of an admirer. We most of us feel that among the artists of our day certain talents have more to say to us and others less; we have our favourites, and we have our objects of indifference. The writer of these remarks has always had a sympathy for the author of the *Lettres de mon Moulin*; he began to read his novels with a prejudice in their favour. This prejudice sprang from the Letters aforesaid, which do not constitute a novel, but a volume of the lightest and briefest tales. They had, to my mind, an extraordinary charm; they put me quite on the side of Alphonse Daudet, whatever he might do in the future. One of the first things he did was to publish the history of *Fromont Jeune et Risler Aîné*. It is true that this work did not give me the pleasure that some of its successors have done, and though it has been crowned by the French Academy, I still think it weaker than *Les Rois en Exil* and *Numa Roumestan*. But I liked it better on a second reading than on a first; it contains some delightful things. After that came *Jack* and *Le Nabab*, and the two novels I have just mentioned, and that curious and interesting tale of *L'Evangéliste*, which appeared a few months since, and which proves that the author's genius, though on the whole he has pressed it hard, is still nervous, fresh, and young. Each of these things has been better than the last, with the exception, perhaps, of *L'Evangéliste*, which, to my taste, is not superior to *Numa Roumestan*. *Numa Roumestan* is a masterpiece; it is really a perfect work; it has no weakness, no roughness; it is a compact and harmonious whole. Daudet's other works have had their inequalities, their infirmities, certain places where, if you tapped them, they sounded hollow. His danger has always been a perceptible tendency to the factitious; sometimes he has fallen into the trap laid for him by a taste for superficial effects. In *Fromont Jeune*, for instance, it seems to me difficult to care much for the horrid little heroine herself, carefully as she is studied. She has been pursued, but she has not been caught, for she is not interesting (even for a *coquine*), not even human. She is a mechanical doll, with nothing for the imagination to take hold of. She is one more proof of the fact that it is difficult to give the air of consistency to vanity and depravity, though the portraiture of the vicious side of life would seem, from the pictorial point of view, to offer such attractions. The reader's quarrel with Sidonie Chèbe is not that she is bad, but that she is not *felt*, as the æsthetic people say. In *Jack* the hollow spot, as I have called it, is the episode of Doctor Rivals and his daughter Cécile, which reminds us of the more genial parts of Dickens. It is perhaps because to us readers of English speech the figure of the young girl, in a French novel, is almost always wanting in reality—seems to be thin and conventional; in any case poor Jack's love-affair, at the end of the book, does not produce the illusion of the rest of his touching history. In *Le Nabab* this artificial element is very considerable; it centres about the figure of Paul de Géry and embraces the whole group of M. Joyeuse and his blooming daughters, with their pretty attitudes—taking in also the very shadowy André Maranne, so touchingly re-united to his mother, who had lived for ten years with an Irish doctor to whom she was not married. In *Les Rois en Exil*, Tom Lévis and the diabolical Séphora seem to me purely fanciful creations, without any relation to reality; they are the inferior part of the book. They are composed by a master of composition, and the comedian Tom is described with immense spirit, an art which speaks volumes as to a certain sort of Parisian initiation. But if this artistic and malignant couple are very clever water-colour, they are not really humanity. Ruffians and rascals have a certain moral nature, as well as the better-behaved; but in the case I have mentioned M. Daudet fails to put his finger upon it. The same with Madame Autheman, the evil genius of poor Eline Ebsen, in the *L'Evangéliste*. She seems to me terribly, almost grotesquely, void. She is an elaborate portrait of a fanatic of Protestantism, a bigot to the point of monstrosity, cold-blooded, implacable, cruel. The figure is painted with Alphonse Daudet's inimitable art; no one that handles the pen to-day is such a pictorial artist as he. But Madame Autheman strikes me as quite automatic; psychologically she is a blank. One does not see the operation of her character. She must have had a soul, and a very curious one. It was a great opportunity for a piece of spiritual portraiture; but we know nothing about Madame Autheman's inner springs, and I

think we fail to believe in her. I should go so far as to say
that we get little more of an inside view, as the phrase is, of
Eline Ebsen; we are not shown the spiritual steps by which
she went over to the enemy—vividly, admirably as the outward signs and consequences of this disaster are depicted. The
logic of the matter is absent in both cases, and it takes all the
magic of the author's legerdemain to prevent us from missing
it. These things, however, are exceptions, and the tissue of
each of his novels is, for all the rest, really pure gold. No one
has such grace, such lightness and brilliancy of execution; it
is a fascination to see him at work. The beauty of *Numa Roumestan* is that it has no hollow places; the idea and the picture
melt everywhere into one. Emile Zola, criticising the work in
a very friendly spirit, speaks of the episode of Hortense Le
Quesnoy and the Provençal *tambourinaire* as a false note, and
declares that it wounds his sense of delicacy. Valmajour is a
peasant of the south of France; he is young, handsome, wears
a costume, and is a master of the rustic fife and tambourine—
instruments that are much appreciated in his part of the country. Mademoiselle Le Quesnoy, living in Paris, daughter of a
distinguished member of the French judiciary—"le premier
magistrat de France"—young, charming, imaginative, romantic, marked out for a malady of the chest, and with a certain
innocent perversity of mind, sees him play before an applaud-
ing crowd in the old Roman arena at Nîmes, and forthwith
conceives a secret, a singular but not, under the circumstances, an absolutely unnatural passion for him. He comes
up to Paris to seek his fortune at the "variety" theatres, where
his feeble and primitive music quite fails to excite enthusiasm.
The young girl, reckless and impulsive, and full of sympathy
with his mortification, writes him in three words (upon one
of her little photographs) an assurance of her devotion; and
this innocent missive, falling soon into the hands of his rapacious and exasperated sister (a wonderful figure, one of the
most living that has ever come from Daudet's pen), becomes
a source of infinite alarm to the family of Mademoiselle Le
Quesnoy, who see her compromised, calumniated and black-
mailed, and finally of complete humiliation to poor Hortense
herself, now fallen into a rapid consumption, and cured of her
foolish infatuation by a nearer view of the vain and ignorant

Valmajour. An agent of the family recovers the photograph (with the aid of ten thousand francs), and the young girl, with the bitter taste of her disappointment still in her soul, dies in her flower.

This little story, as I say, is very shocking to M. Zola, who cites it as an example of the folly of a departure from consistent realism. What is observed, says M. Zola, on the whole very justly, is strong; what is invented is always weak, especially what is invented to please the ladies. "See in this case," he writes, "all the misery of invented episodes. This love of Hortense, with which the author has doubtless wished to give the impression of something touching, produces a discomfort, as if it were a violation of nature. It is therefore the pages written for the ladies that are repulsive—even to a man accustomed to the saddest dissections of the human corpse." I am not of M. Zola's opinion—delightful as it would be to be of that opinion when M. Zola's sense of propriety is ruffled. The incident of Hortense and Valmajour is not (to my sense) a blot upon *Numa Roumestan*; on the contrary, it is perfectly conceivable, and is treated with admirable delicacy. "This romantic stuff," says M. Zola, elsewhere, "is as painful as a pollution. That a young girl should lose her head over a tenor, that may be explained, for she loves the operatic personage in the interpreter. She has before her a young man sharpened and refined by life, elegant, having at least certain appearances of talent and intelligence. But this tambourinist, with his drum and penny-whistle, this village dandy, a poor devil who doesn't even know how to speak! No, life has not such cruelties as that, I protest, I who certainly, as a general thing, am not accustomed to give ground before human aberrations!" This objection was worth making; but I should look at the matter in another way. It seems to me much more natural that a girl of the temper and breeding that M. Daudet has described should take a momentary fancy to a prepossessing young rustic, bronzed by the sun of Provence (even if it be conceded that his soul was vulgar), than that she should fasten her affections upon a "lyric artist," suspected of pomatum and paint, and illuminated by the footlights. These are points which it is vain to discuss, however, both because they are delicate and because they are details. I have come so far simply from a desire to justify my high admiration of *Numa Roumestan*. But Emile Zola, again, has expressed this feeling more felicitously than I can hope to do. "This, moreover, is a very slight blemish in a work which I regard as one of those, of all Daudet's productions, that is most personal to himself. He has put his whole nature into it, helped by his southern temperament, having only to make large draughts upon his innermost recollections and sensations. I do not think that he has hitherto reached such an intensity either of irony or of geniality. . . . Happy the books which arrive in this way, at the hour of the complete maturity of a talent! They are simply the widest unfolding of an artist's nature; they have in happy equilibrium the qualities of observation and the qualities of style. For Alphonse Daudet *Numa Roumestan* will mark this interfusion of a temperament and a subject that are made for each other, the perfect plenitude of a work which the writer exactly fills."

II

As I say, however, these are details, and I have touched them prematurely. Alphonse Daudet is a charmer, and the effect of his brilliant, friendly, indefinable genius is to make it difficult, in speaking of him, to take things in their order or follow a plan. In writing of him some time ago, in another place, I so far lost my head as to remark, with levity, that he was "a great little novelist." The diminutive epithet then, I must now say, was nothing more than a term of endearment, the result of an irresistible impulse to express a sense of personal fondness. This kind of feeling is difficult to utter in English, and the utterance of it, so far as this is possible, is not thought consistent with the dignity of a critic. If we were talking French, nothing would be simpler than to say that Alphonse Daudet is adorable, and have done with it. But this resource is denied me, and I must arrive at my meaning by a series of circumlocutions. I am not able even to say that he is very "personal"; that epithet, so valuable in the vocabulary of French literary criticism, has, when applied to the talent of an artist, a meaning different from the sense in which we use it. "A novelist so personal and so penetrating," says Emile Zola, speaking of the author of *Numa Roumestan*. That phrase, in English, means nothing in particular; so that I must add to it that the charm of Daudet's talent comes from its being charged to an extraordinary degree with his temperament, his feelings, his instincts, his natural qualities. This, of course, is a charm, in a style, only when nature has been generous. To Alphonse Daudet she has been exceptionally so; she has placed in his hand an instrument of many chords. A delicate, nervous organisation, active and indefatigable in spite of its delicacy, and familiar with emotion of almost every kind, equally acquainted with pleasure and with pain; a light, quick, joyous, yet reflective, imagination, a faculty of seeing images, making images, at every turn, of conceiving everything in the visible form, in the plastic spirit; an extraordinary sensibility to all the impressions of life and a faculty of language which is in perfect harmony with his wonderful fineness of perception — these are some of the qualities of which he is the happy possessor, and which make his equipment for the work he has undertaken exceedingly rich. There are others besides; but enumerations are ponderous, and we should avoid that danger in speaking of a genius whose lightness of touch never belies itself. His elder brother, who has not his talent, has written a little book about him in which the word *modernité* perpetually occurs. M. Ernest Daudet, in *Mon Frère et Moi*, insists upon his possession of the qualities expressed by this barbarous substantive, which is so indispensable to the new school. Alphonse Daudet is, in truth, very modern; he has all the newly-developed, the newly-invented, perceptions. Nothing speaks so much to his imagination as the latest and most composite things, the refinements of current civilisation, the most delicate shades of the actual. It is scarcely too much to say that (especially in the Parisian race), modern manners, modern nerves, modern wealth, and modern improvements, have engendered a new sense, a sense not easily named nor classified, but recognisable in all the most characteristic productions of contemporary art. It is partly physical, partly moral, and the shortest way to describe it is to say that it is a more analytic consideration of appearances. It is known by its tendency to resolve its discoveries into pictorial form. It sees the connection between feelings and external conditions, and it expresses such relations as they have not been expressed hitherto. It deserves to win victories, because it has opened its eyes well to the fact that the magic of the arts of representation lies in their appeal to the associations awakened by things. It traces these associations into the most unlighted corners of our being, into the most devious paths of experience. The appearance of things is constantly more complicated as the world grows older, and it needs a more and more patient art, a closer notation, to divide it into its parts. Of this art Alphonse Daudet has a wonderfully large allowance, and that is why I say that he is peculiarly modern. It is very true that his manner is not the manner of patience—though he must always have had a great deal of that virtue in the preparation of his work. The new school of fiction in France is based very much on the taking of notes; the library of the great Flaubert, of the brothers de Goncourt, of Emile Zola, and of the writer of whom I speak, must have been in a large measure a library of memorandum-books. This of course only puts the patience back a stage or two. In composition Daudet proceeds by quick, instantaneous vision, by the happiest divination, by catching the idea as it suddenly springs up before him with a whirr of wings. What he mainly sees is the great surface of life and the parts that lie near the surface. But life is, immensely, a matter of surface, and if our emotions in general are interesting, the *form* of those emotions has the merit of being the most definite thing about them. Like most French imaginative writers (judged, at least, from the English standpoint), he is much less concerned with the moral, the metaphysical world, than with the sensible. We proceed usually from the former to the latter, while the French reverse the process. Except in politics, they are uncomfortable in the presence of abstractions, and lose no time in reducing them to the concrete. But even the concrete, for them, is a field for poetry, which brings us to the fact that the delightful thing in Daudet's talent is the inveterate poetical touch. This is what mainly distinguishes him from the other lights of the realistic school—modifies so completely in his case the hardness of consistent realism. There is something very hard, very dry, in Flaubert, in Edmond de Goncourt, in the robust Zola; but there is something very soft in Alphonse Daudet. "Benevolent nature," says Zola, "has placed him at that exquisite point where poetry ends and reality begins." That is happily said; Daudet's great characteristic is this mixture of the sense of the real with the sense of the beautiful. His imagination is constantly at play with his theme; it has a horror of the literal, the limited; it sees an object in all its intermingled relations—on its sentimental, its pathetic, its comical, its pictorial side. Flaubert, in whom Alphonse Daudet would probably recognise to a certain degree a literary paternity, is far from being a simple realist; but he was destitute of this sense of the beautiful, destitute of facility and grace. He had, to take its place, a sense of the strange, the grotesque, to which *Salammbo, La Tentation de Saint-Antoine*, his indescribable posthumous novel of *Bouvard et Pécuchet*, abundantly testify. The talent of the brothers Goncourt strikes us as a talent that was associated originally with a sense of beauty; but we receive an impression that this feeling has been perverted and warped. It has ceased to be natural and free; it has become morbid and peevish, has turned mainly to curiosity and mannerism. And these two authors are capable, during a whole book (as in *Germinie Lacerteux* or *La Fille Elisa*), of escaping from its influence altogether. No one would probably ever think of accusing Emile Zola of having a perception of the beautiful. He has an illimitable, and at times a very valuable, sense of the ugly, of the unclean; but when he addresses himself to the poetic aspect of things, as in *La Faute de l'Abbé Mouret*, he is apt to have terrible misadventures.

III

IT IS for the expressive talents that we feel an affection, and Daudet is eminently expressive. His manner is the manner of talk, and if the talk is sincere, that makes a writer touch us. Daudet expresses many things; but he most frequently expresses himself—his own temper in the presence of life, his own feeling on a thousand occasions. This personal note is especially to be observed in his earlier productions—in the *Lettres de mon Moulin*, the *Contes du Lundi, Le Petit Chose*; it is also very present in the series of prefaces which he has undertaken to supply to the octavo edition of his works. In these

prefaces he gives the history of each successive book—relates
the circumstances under which it was written. These things
are ingenuously told, but what we are chiefly conscious of in
regard to them, is that Alphonse Daudet must express himself. His brother informs us that he is writing his memoirs,
and this will have been another opportunity for expression.
Ernest Daudet, as well (as I have mentioned), has attempted
to express him. *Mon Frère et Moi* is one of those productions
which it is difficult for an English reader to judge in fairness:
it is so much more confidential than we, in public, ever venture to be. The French have, on all occasions, the courage of
their emotion, and M. Ernest Daudet's leading emotion is a
boundless admiration for his junior. He lays it before us very
frankly and gracefully—not, on the whole, indiscreetly; and I
have no quarrel whatever with his volume, for it contains a
considerable amount of information on a very interesting subject. Indirectly, indeed, as well as directly, it helps us to a
knowledge of his brother. Alphonse Daudet was born in
Provence; he comes of an expansive, a confidential race. His
style is impregnated with the southern sunshine, and his talent has the sweetness of a fruit that has grown in the warm,
open air. He has the advantage of being a Provençal converted, as it were—of having a southern temperament and a
northern reason. We know what he thinks of the southern
temperament—*Numa Roumestan* is a vivid exposition of that.
"*Gau de carriero, doulou d'oustau,*" as the Provençal has it;
"*joie de rue, douleur de maison*—joy in the street and pain in
the house"—that proverb, says Alphonse Daudet, describes
and formulates a whole race. It has given him the subject of
an admirable story, in which he has depicted with equal force
and tenderness the amiable weaknesses, the mingled violence
and levity of the children of the clime of the fig and olive. He
has put before us, above all, their mania for talk, their irrepressible chatter, the qualities that, with them, render all passion, all purpose, inordinately vocal. Himself a complete
"*produit du Midi,*" like the famille Mèfre in *Numa Roumestan*,
he has achieved the feat of becoming objective to his own
vision, getting outside of his ingredients and judging them.
This he has done by the aid of his Parisianised conscience, his
exquisite taste, and that finer wisdom which resides in the

artist, from whatever soil he springs. Successfully as he has done it, however, he has not done it so well but that he too does not show a little of the heightened colour, the super-abundant statement, the restless movement of his compatriots. He is nothing if not demonstrative; he is always in a state of feeling; he has not a very definite ideal of reserve. It must be added that he is a man of genius, and that genius never spends its capital; that he is an artist, and that an artist always has a certain method and order. But it remains characteristic of his origin that the author of *Numa Roumestan*, one of the happiest and most pointed of satires, should have about him the aroma of some of the qualities satirised. There are passages in his tales and in his prefaces that are genuine "produits du Midi," and his brother's account of him could only have been written by a Provençal brother.

To be *personnel* to that point, transparent, effusive, gushing, to give one's self away in one's books, has never been, and will never be, the ideal of us of English speech; but that does not prevent our enjoying immensely, when we meet it, a happy example of this alien spirit. For myself, I am free to confess, half my affection for Alphonse Daudet comes from the fact that he writes in a way in which I would not write even if I could. There are certain kinds of feeling and observation, certain impressions and ideas, to which we are rather ashamed to give a voice, and yet are ashamed not to have in our scale. In these matters Alphonse Daudet renders us a great service: he expresses such things on our behalf. I may add that he usually does it much better than the cleverest of us could do even if we were to try. I have said that he is a Provençal converted, and I should do him a great injustice if I did not dwell upon his conversion. His brother relates the circumstances under which he came up to Paris, at the age of twenty (in a threadbare overcoat and a pair of india-rubbers), to seek his literary fortune. His beginnings were difficult, his childhood had been hard, he was familiar with poverty and disaster. He had no adventitious aid to success—his whole fortune consisted in his exquisite organisation. But Paris was to be, artistically, a mine of wealth to him, and of all the anxious and eager young spirits who, on the battle-field of uncarpeted *cinquièmes*, have laid siege to the indifferent city,

none can have felt more deeply conscious of the mission to
take possession of it. Alphonse Daudet, at the present hour,
is in complete possession of Paris; he knows it, loves it, uses
it; he has assimilated it to its last particle. He has made of it
a Paris of his own—a Paris like a vast crisp water-colour, one
of the water-colours of the school of Fortuny. The French
have a great advantage in the fact that they admire their capital very much as if it were a foreign city. Most of their artists,
their men of letters, have come up from the provinces, and
well as they may learn to know the metropolis, it never ceases
to be a spectacle, a wonder, a fascination for them. This
comes partly from the intrinsic brilliancy and interest of the
place, partly from the poverty of provincial life, and partly
from the degree to which the faculty of appreciation is developed in Frenchmen of the class of which I speak. To Daudet,
at any rate, the familiar aspects of Paris are endlessly pictorial,
and part of the charm of his novels (for those who share his
relish for that huge flower of civilisation) is in the way he
recalls it, evokes it, suddenly presents it, in parts or as a
whole, to our senses. The light, the sky, the feeling of the air,
the odours of the streets, the look of certain vistas, the silvery,
muddy Seine, the cool, grey tone of colour, the physiognomy
of particular quarters, the whole Parisian expression, meet you
suddenly in his pages, and remind you again and again that if
he paints with a pen he writes with a brush. I remember that
when I read *Le Nabab* and *Les Rois en Exil* for the first time,
I said to myself that this was the *article de Paris* in supreme
perfection, and that no reader could understand such productions who had not had a copious experience of the scene. It
is certain, at any rate, that those books have their full value
only for minds more or less Parisianised; half their meaning,
their magic, their subtlety of intention is liable to be lost. It
may be said that this is a great limitation—that the works of
the best novelists may be understood by all the world. There
is something in that; but I know not, all the same, whether
the fact I indicate be a great limitation. It is certainly a very
illustrative quality. Daudet has caught the tone of a particular
pitch of manners; he applies it with the lightest, surest hand,
and his picture shines and lives. The most generalised representation of life cannot do more than that.

I shrink very much from speaking of systems, in relation to such a genius as this: I should incline to believe that Daudet's system is simply to be as vivid as he can. Emile Zola has a system—at least he says so; but I do not remember, on the part of the author of *Numa Roumestan*, the smallest technical profession of faith. Nevertheless, he has taken a line, as we say, and his line is to sail as close as possible to the actual. The life of Paris being his subject, his attempt, most frequently, is to put his finger upon known examples; so that he has been accused of portraying individuals instead of portraying types. There are few of his figures to which the name of some celebrity of the day has not been attached. The Nabob is François Bravais; the Duc de Mora is the Duc de Morny. The Irish Doctor Jenkins is an English physician who flourished in Paris from such a year to such another; people are still living (wonderful to say), who took his little pills *à base arsénicale*. Félicia Ruys is Mademoiselle Sarah Bernhardt; Constance Crenmitz is Madame Taglioni; the Queen of Illyria is the Queen of Naples; the Prince of Axel is the Prince of Orange; Tom Lévis is an English house-agent (*not* in the Rue Royale, but hard by); Elysée Méraut is a well-known journalist, and Doctor Bouchereau a well-known surgeon. Such is the key, we are told, to these ingenious mystifications, and to many others which I have not the space to mention. It matters little, to my mind, whether in each case the cap fits the supposed model; for nothing is more evident than that Alphonse Daudet has proposed to himself to represent not only the people but the persons of his time. The conspicuity of certain individuals has added to the force with which they speak to his imagination. His taste is for salient figures, and he has said to himself that there is no greater proof of being salient than being known. The temptation to "put people into a book" is a temptation of which every writer of fiction knows something, and I hold that to succumb to it is not only legitimate but inevitable. Putting people into books is what the novelist lives upon; the question in the matter is the question of delicacy, for according to that delicacy the painter conjures away recognition or insists upon it. Daudet has been accused of the impertinence of insisting, and I believe that two or three of his portraits have provoked a protest. He is charged with ingratitude for having produced an effigy of the Duke of Morny, who had been his benefactor, and employed him as a secretary. Such a matter as this is between M. Daudet and his conscience, and I am far from pretending to pronounce upon it. The uninitiated reader can only say that the figure is a very striking one—such a picture as (it may be imagined) the Duc de Morny would not be displeased to have inspired. It may fairly be conceded, however, that Daudet is much more an observer than an inventor. The invented parts of his tales, like the loves of Jack and of Paul de Géry and the machinations of Madame Autheman (the theological vampire of *L'Evangéliste*, to whom I shall return for a moment), are the vague, the ineffective as well as the romantic parts. (I remember that in reading *Le Nabab*, it was not very easy to keep Paul de Géry and André Maranne apart.) It is the real— the transmuted real—that he gives us best; the fruit of a process that adds to observation what a kiss adds to a greeting. The joy, the excitement of recognition, are keen, even when the object recognised is dismal. They are part of his spirit— part of his way of seeing things. *L'Evangéliste* is the saddest story conceivable; but it is lighted, throughout, by the author's irrepressibly humorous view of the conditions in which its successive elements present themselves, and by the extraordinary vivacity with which, in his hands, narration and description proceed. His humour is of the finest; it is needless to say that it is never violent nor vulgar. It is a part of the high spirits—the animal spirits, I should say, if the phrase had not an association of coarseness—that accompany the temperament of his race; and it is stimulated by the perpetual entertainment which so rare a visual faculty naturally finds in the spectacle of life, even while encountering there a multitude of distressing things. Daudet's gaiety is a part of his poetry, and his poetry is a part of everything he touches. There is little enough gaiety in the subject of *Jack*, and yet the whole story is told with a smile. To complete the charm of the thing, the smile is full of feeling. Here and there it becomes an immense laugh, and the result is a delightful piece of drollery. *Les Aventures Prodigieuses de Tartarin de Tarascon* contains all his high spirits; it is one of his few stories in which laughter and tears are not intermingled.

This little tale, which is one of his first, is, like *Numa Roumestan*, a satire on a southern foible. Tartarin de Tarascon is an excellent man who inhabits the old town on the Rhone over which the palace of the good King René keeps guard; he has not a fault in the world except an imagination too vivid. He is liable to visions, to hallucinations; the desire that a thing shall happen speedily resolves itself into the belief that the thing will happen—then that it is happening—then that it *has* happened. Tartarin accordingly presents himself to the world (and to himself) as a gentleman to whom all wonders are familiar; his experience blooms with supposititious flowers. The coveted thing for a man of his romantic mould is that he shall be the bravest of the brave, and he passes his life in a series of heroic exploits, in which, as you listen to him, it is impossible not to believe. He passes over from Marseilles to Algiers, where his adventures deepen to a climax, and where he has a desperate flirtation with the principal ornament of the harem of a noble Arab. The lady proves at the end to be a horribly improper little Frenchwoman, and poor Tartarin, abused and disabused, returns to Tarascon to meditate on what might have been. Nothing could be more charming than the light comicality of the sketch, which fills a small volume. This is the most mirthful, the most completely diverting of all Daudet's tales; but the same element, in an infinitely subtler form, runs through the others. The essence of it is the wish to please, and this brings me back to the point to which I intended to return. The wish to please is the quality by which Daudet persuades his readers most; it is this that elicits from them that friendliness, that confession that they are charmed, of which I spoke at the beginning of these remarks. It gives a sociability to his manner, in spite of the fact that he describes all sorts of painful and odious things. This contradiction is a part of his originality. He has no pretension to being simple, he is perfectly conscious of being complex, and in nothing is he more modern than in this expressive and sympathetic smile—the smile of the artist, the sceptic, the man of the world—with which he shows us the miseries and cruelties of life. It is singular that we should like him for that—and doubtless many people do not, or think they do not. What they really dislike, I believe, is the things he relates, which are often lamentable.

IV

THE first of these were slight and simple, and for the most part cheerful; little anecdotes and legends of Provence, impressions of an artist's holidays in that strange, bare, lovely land, and of wanderings further afield, in Corsica and Algeria; sketches of Paris during the siege; incidents of the invasion, the advent of the Prussian rule in other parts of the country. In all these things there is *la note émue*, the smile which is only a more synthetic sign of being moved. And then such grace of form, such lightness of touch, such alertness of observation! Some of the chapters of the *Lettres de mon Moulin* are such perfect vignettes, that the brief treatment of small subjects might well have seemed, at first, Alphonse Daudet's appointed work. He had almost invented a manner, and it was impossible to do better than he the small piece, or even the passage. Glimpses, reminiscences, accidents, he rendered them with the brilliancy of a violinist improvising on a sudden hint. The *Lettres de mon Moulin*, moreover, are impregnated with the light, with the fragrance of a Provençal summer; the rosemary and thyme are in the air as we read, the white rocks and the grey foliage stretch away to an horizon of hills—the Alpilles, the little Alps—on which colour is as iridescent as the breast of a dove. The Provence of Alphonse Daudet is a delightful land; even when the mistral blows there it has a music in its whistle. Emile Zola has protested against this; he too is of Provençal race, he passed his youth in the old Languedoc, and he intimates that his fanciful friend throws too much sweetness into the picture. It is beyond contradiction that Daudet, like Tartarin de Tarascon and Numa Roumestan, exaggerates a little; he sees with great intensity, and is very sensitive to agreeable impressions. *Le Petit Chose*, his first long story, reads to-day like the attempt of a beginner, and of a beginner who had read and enjoyed Dickens. I risk this allusion to the author of *Copperfield* in spite of a conviction that Alphonse Daudet must be tired of hearing that he imitates him. It is not imitation; there is nothing so gross as imitation in the length and breadth of Daudet's work; but it is conscious sympathy, for there is plenty of that. There are pages in his tales which seem to say to us that at one moment of his life Dickens had been a revelation to him—pages more particularly in *Le Petit Chose*, in *Fromont Jeune* and in *Jack*. The heroine of the first of these works (a very shadowy personage) is never mentioned but as the "black eyes"; some one else is always spoken of as the *dame de grand mérite*; the heroine's father, who keeps a flourishing china-shop, never opens his mouth without saying "C'est le cas de le dire." These are harmless, they are indeed sometimes very happy, Dickensisms. We make no crime of them to M. Daudet, who must have felt as intelligently as he has felt everything else the fascinating form of the English novelist's drollery. *Fromont Jeune et Risler Aîné* is a study of life in the old quarter of the Marais, the Paris of the seventeenth century, whose stately *hôtels* have been invaded by the innumerable activities of modern trade. When I say a study, I use the word with all those restrictions with which it must be applied to a genius who is truthful without being literal, and who has a pair of butterfly's wings attached to the back of his observation. If sub-titles were the fashion to-day, the right one for *Fromont Jeune* would be— *or the Dangers of Partnership*. The action takes place for the most part in a manufactory of wall-papers, and the persons in whom the author seeks to interest us are engaged in this useful industry. There are delightful things in the book, but, as I intimated at the beginning of these remarks, there are considerable inequalities. The pages that made M. Daudet's fortune—for it was with *Fromont Jeune* that his fortune began—are those which relate to the history of M. Delobelle, the superannuated tragedian, his long-suffering wife, and his exquisite lame daughter, who makes butterflies and humming-birds for ladies' head-dresses. This eccentric and pathetic household was an immense hit, and Daudet has never been happier than in the details of the group. Delobelle himself, who has not had an engagement for ten years, and who never will have one again, but who holds none the less that it is his duty not to leave the stage, "not to give up the theatre," though his platonic passion is paid for by the weary eyesight of his wife and daughter, who sit up half the night attaching bead-eyes to little stuffed animals— the blooming and sonorous Delobelle, ferociously selfish and fantastically vain, under the genial forms of melodrama, is a beautiful representation of a vulgarly factitious nature. The book revealed a painter; all the descriptive passages, the pictorial touches, had the truest felicity. No one better than Daudet gives what we call the feeling of a place. The story illustrates, among other things, the fact that a pretty little woman who is consumed with the lowest form of vanity, and unimpeded in her operations by the possession of a heart, may inflict an unlimited amount of injury upon people about her, if she only have the opportunity. The case is well demonstrated, and Sidonie Chèbe is an elaborate study of flimsiness; her papery quality, as I may call it, her rustling dryness, are effectively rendered. But I think there is a limit to the interest which the English-speaking reader of French novels can take to-day in the adventures of a lady who leads the life of Madame Sidonie. In the first place he has met her again and again—he knows exactly what she will do and say in every situation; and in the second there always seems to him to be in her vices, her disorders, an element of the conventional. There is a receipt among French novelists for making little high-heeled reprobates. However this may be, he has at least a feeling that at night all cats are grey, and that the particular tint of depravity of a woman whose nature has the shallowness of a sanded floor is not a very important *constatation*. Daudet has expended much ingenuity in endeavouring to hit the particular tint of Sidonie; he has wished to make her a type—the type of the daughter of small unsuccessful shopkeepers (narrow-minded and self-complacent to imbecility), whose corruption comes from the examples, temptations, opportunities of a great city, as well as from her impure blood and the infection of the meanest associations. But what all this illustrates was not worth illustrating.

The early chapters of *Jack* are admirable; the later ones suffer a little, I think, from the story being drawn out too much, like an accordion when it wishes to be plaintive. Jack is a kind of younger brother of the Petit Chose, though he takes the troubles of life rather more stoutly than that delicate and diminutive hero; a poor boy with a doting and disreputable mother, whose tenderness is surpassed by her frivolity, and who sacrifices her son to the fantastic egotism of an unsuccessful man of letters with whom she passes several years of her life. She is another study of *coquinerie*—she is another shade; but she is a more apprehensible figure than Sidonie Chèbe—she is, indeed, a very admirable portrait. The success of the book, however, is the figure of her lover, that is of her protector and bully, the unrecognised genius aforesaid, author of *Le Fils de Faust*, an uncirculated dramatic poem in the manner of Goethe, and centre of a little group of *ratés*—a collection of dead-beats, as we say to-day, as pretentious, as impotent, as envious and as bilious as himself. He conceives a violent hatred of the offspring of his amiable companion, and the subject of *Jack* is the persecution of the boy by this monstrous charlatan. This persecution is triumphantly successful; the youthful hero dies on the threshold of manhood, broken down by his tribulations and miseries: he has been thrown upon the world to earn his bread, and among other things seeks a livelihood as a stoker on an Atlantic steamer. Jack has been taken young, and though his nature is gentle and tender, his circumstances succeed in degrading him. He is reduced at the end to a kind of bewildered brutishness. The story is simply the history of a juvenile martyrdom, pityingly, expansively told, and I am afraid that Mr. Charles Dudley Warner, who, in writing lately about "Modern Fiction,"[1] complains of the abuse of pathetic effects in that form of composition, would find little to commend in this brilliant paraphrase of suffering. Mr. Warner's complaint is eminently just, and the fault of *Jack* is certainly the abuse of pathos. Mr. Warner does not mention Alphonse Daudet by name, but it is safe to assume that in his reflections upon the perversity of those writers who will not make a novel as comfortable as one's stockings, or as pretty as a Christmas card, he was thinking of the author of so many uncompromising *dénouements*. It is true that this probability is diminished by the fact that when he remarks that surely "the main object in the novel is to entertain," he appears to imply that the writers who furnish his text are faithless to this duty. It is possible he would not have made that implication if he had had in mind the productions of a story-teller who has the great peculiarity of being "amusing," as the old-fashioned critics say, even

---

[1] In the *Atlantic Monthly*, for April 1883.

when he touches the source of tears. The word entertaining
has two or three shades of meaning; but in whatever sense it
is used I may say, in parenthesis, that I do not agree with Mr.
Warner's description of the main object of the novel. I should
put the case differently: I should say that the main object of
the novel is to represent life. I cannot understand any other
motive for interweaving imaginary incidents, and I do not
perceive any other measure of the value of such combinations.
The *effect* of a novel—the effect of any work of art—is to
entertain; but that is a very different thing. The success of a
work of art, to my mind, may be measured by the degree to
which it produces a certain illusion; that illusion makes it appear to us for the time that we have lived another life—that
we have had a miraculous enlargement of experience. The
greater the art the greater the miracle, and the more certain
also the fact that we have been entertained—in the best
meaning of that word, at least, which signifies that we have
been living at the expense of some one else. I am perfectly
aware that to say the object of a novel is to represent life does
not bring the question to a point so fine as to be uncomfortable for any one. It is of the greatest importance that there
should be a very free appreciation of such a question, and the
definition I have hinted at gives plenty of scope for that. For,
after all, may not people differ infinitely as to what constitutes
life—what constitutes representation? Some people, for instance, hold that Miss Austen deals with life, that Miss Austen
represents. Others attribute these achievements to the accomplished Ouida. Some people find that illusion, that enlargement of experience, that miracle of living at the expense of
others, of which I have spoken, in the novels of Alexandre
Dumas. Others revel in them in the pages of Mr. Howells.

V

M. DAUDET's unfortunate Jack, at any rate, lives altogether at
his own cost—that of his poor little juvenile constitution,
and of his innocent affections and aspirations. He is sent to
the horrible Gymnase Moronval, where he has no beguiling
works of fiction to read. The Gymnase Moronval is a Dothe-
boys' Hall in a Parisian "passage"—a very special class of

academy. Nothing could be more effective than Daudet's picture of this horrible institution, with its bankrupt and exasperated proprietors, the greasy penitentiary of a group of
unremunerative children whose parents and guardians have
found it convenient to forget them. The episode of the
wretched little hereditary monarch of an African tribe who
has been placed there for a royal education, and who, livid
with cold, short rations, and rough usage, and with his teeth
chattering with a sense of dishonour, steals away and wanders
in the streets of Paris, and then, recaptured and ferociously
punished, surrenders his little dusky soul in the pestilential
dormitory of the establishment—all this part of the tale is a
masterpiece of vivid description. We seem to assist at the terrible soirées where the *ratés* exhibit their talents (M. Moronval is of course a *raté*), and where the wife of the principal, a
very small woman with a very big head and a very high forehead, expounds the wonderful Méthode-Décostère (invented
by herself and designated by her maiden name), for pronouncing the French tongue with elegance. My criticism of
this portion of the book, and indeed of much of the rest of
it, would be that the pathetic element is too intentional, too
voulu, as the French say. And I am not sure that the reader
enters into the author's reason for making Charlotte, Jack's
mother, a woman of the class that we do not specify in American magazines. She is an accommodating idiot, but her good
nature is unfortunately not consecutive, and she consents, at
the instigation of the diabolical d'Argenton, to her child's
being brought up like a pauper. D'Argenton, like Delobelle,
is a study of egotism pushed to the grotesque; but the portrait is still more complete, and some of the details are inimitable. As regards the infatuated Charlotte, who sacrifices her
child to the malignity of her lover, I repeat that certain of the
features of her character appear to me a mistake, judged in
relation to the effect that the author wishes to produce. He
wishes to show us all that the boy loses in being disinherited—if I may use that term with respect to a situation in
which there is nothing to inherit. But his loss is not great
when we consider that his mother had, after all, very little to
give him. She had divested herself of important properties.
Bernard Jansoulet, in *Le Nabab*, is not, like the two most suc-

cessful figures that Daudet has previously created, a representation of full-blown selfishness. The unhappy nabob is generous to a fault; he is the most good-natured and free-handed of men, and if he has made use of all sorts of means to build up his enormous fortune, he knows an equal number of ways of spending it. This voluminous tale had an immense success; it seemed to show that Daudet had found his manner, a manner that was perfectly new and remarkably ingenious. As I have said, it held up the mirror to contemporary history, and attempted to complete for us, by supplementary revelations, those images which are projected by the modern newspaper and the album of photographs. *Les Rois en Exil* is an historical novel of this pattern, in which the process is applied with still more spirit. In these two works Daudet enlarged his canvas surprisingly, and showed his ability to deal with a multitude of figures.

The distance traversed artistically from the little anecdotes of the *Lettres de mon Moulin* to the complex narrative of *Le Nabab* and its successor, are like the transformation—often so rapid—of a slim and charming young girl into a blooming and accomplished woman of the world. The author's style had taken on bone and muscle, and become conscious of treasures of nervous agility. I have left myself no space to speak of these things in detail, and it was not part of my purpose to examine Daudet's novels piece by piece; but I may say that it is the items, the particular touches, that make the value of writing of this kind. I am not concerned to defend the process, the system, so far as there is a system; but I cannot open either *Le Nabab* or *Les Rois en Exil*, cannot rest my eyes upon a page, without being charmed by the brilliancy of execution. It is difficult to give an idea, by any general terms, of Daudet's style—a style which defies convention, tradition, homogeneity, prudence, and sometimes even syntax, gathers up every patch of colour, every colloquial note, that will help to illustrate, and moves eagerly, lightly, triumphantly along, like a clever woman in the costume of an eclectic age. There is nothing classic in this mode of expression; it is not the old-fashioned drawing in black and white. It never rests, never is satisfied, never leaves the idea sitting half-draped, like patience on a monument; it is always panting, straining, fluttering, trying to add a little more, to produce the effect which shall make the reader see with his eyes, or rather with the marvellous eyes of Alphonse Daudet. *Le Nabab* is full of episodes which are above all pages of execution, triumphs of translation. The author has drawn up a list of the Parisian solemnities and painted the portrait—or given a summary—of each of them. The opening day at the Salon, a funeral at Père-la-Chaise, a debate in the Chamber of Deputies, the *première* of a new play at a favourite theatre, furnish him with so many opportunities for his gymnastics of observation. I should like to say how rich and entertaining I think the figure of Jansoulet, the robust and good-natured son of his own works (originally a dock-porter at Marseilles), who, after amassing a fabulous number of millions in selling European luxuries on commission to the Bey of Tunis, comes to Paris to try to make his social fortune as he has already made his financial, and after being a nine-days' wonder, a public joke, and the victim of his boundless hospitality; after being flattered by charlatans, rifled by adventurers, belaboured by newspapers, and "exploited" to the last penny of his coffers and the last pulsation of his vanity by every one who comes near him, dies of apoplexy in his box at the theatre, while the public hoots him for being unseated for electoral frauds in the Chamber of Deputies, where for a single mocking hour he has tasted the sweetness of political life. I should like to say, too, that however much or however little the Duc de Mora may resemble the Duc de Morny, the character depicted by Daudet is a wonderful study of that modern passion, the love of "good form." The chapter that relates the death of the Duke, and describes the tumult, the confusion, of his palace, the sudden extinction of the rapacious interests that crowd about him, and to which the collapse of his splendid security comes as the first breath of a revolution—this chapter is famous, and gives the fullest measure of what Daudet can do when he fairly warms to his work.

Les Rois en Exil, however, has a greater perfection; it is simpler, more equal, and it contains much more of the beautiful. In *Le Nabab* there are various lacunæ and a certain want of logic; it is not a sustained narrative, but a series of almost diabolically clever pictures. But the other book has more largeness of line—a fine tragic movement which deepens and presses to the catastrophe. Daudet had observed that several dispossessed monarchs had taken up their residence in the French capital—some of them waiting and plotting for a restoration, and chafing under their disgrace; others indifferent, resigned, relieved, eager to console themselves with the pleasures of Paris. It occurred to him to suppose a drama in which these exalted personages should be the actors, and which, unlike either of his former productions, should have a pure and noble heroine. He was conscious of a dauntless little imagination, the idea of making kings and queens talk among themselves had no terror for him; he had faith in his good taste, in his exquisite powers of divination. The success is worthy of the spirit—the gallant artistic spirit—in which it was invoked. *Les Rois en Exil* is a finished picture. He has had, it is true, to simplify his subject a good deal to make it practicable; the court of the king and queen of Illyria, in the suburb of Saint-Mandé, is a little too much like a court in a fairytale. But the amiable depravity of Christian, in whom conviction, resolution, ambition, are hopelessly dead, and whose one desire is to enjoy Paris with the impunity of a young man about town; the proud, serious, concentrated nature of Frederica, who believes ardently in her royal function, and lives with her eyes fixed on the crown, which she regards as a symbol of duty; both of these conceptions do M. Daudet the utmost honour, and prove that he is capable of handling great situations—situations which have a depth of their own, and do not depend for their interest on amusing accidents. It takes perhaps some courage to say so, but the feelings, the passions, the view of life, of royal personages, differ essentially from those of common mortals; their education, their companions, their traditions, their exceptional position, take sufficient care of that. Alphonse Daudet has comprehended the difference; and I scarcely know, in the last few years, a straighter flight of imagination. The history of the queen of Illyria is a tragedy. Her husband sells his birthright for a few millions of francs, and rolls himself in the Parisian gutter; her child perishes from poverty of blood; she herself dries up in her despair. There is nothing finer in all Daudet than the pages, at the end of the book, which describe her visits to the great physician Bouchereau, when she takes her poor half-blind child by the hand, and (wishing an opinion unbiassed by the knowledge of her rank) goes to sit in his waiting-room like one of the vulgar multitude. Wonderful are the delicacy, the verity, the tenderness of these pages; we always point to them to justify our predilection. But we must stop pointing. We will not say more of *Numa Roumestan* than we have already said; for it is better to pass so happy a work by than to speak of it inadequately. We will only repeat that we delight in *Numa Roumestan*. Alphonse Daudet's last book is a novelty at the time I write; *L'Evangéliste* has been before the public but a month or two. I will say but little of it, partly because my opportunity is already over, and partly because I have found that, for a fair judgment of one of Daudet's works, the book should be read a second time, after a certain interval has elapsed. This interval has not brought round my second perusal of *L'Evangéliste*. My first suggests that with all the author's present mastery of his resources the book has a grave defect. It is not that the story is painful; that is a defect only when the sources of this element are not, as I may say, abundant. It treats of a young girl (a Danish Protestant) who is turned to stone by a Medusa of Calvinism, the sombre and fanatical wife of a great Protestant banker. Madame Autheman persuades Eline Ebsen to wash her hands of the poor old mother with whom up to this moment she has lived in the closest affection, and go forth into strange countries to stir up the wicked to conversion. The excellent Madame Ebsen, bewildered, heart-broken, desperate, terrified at the imagined penalties of her denunciation of the rich and powerful bigot (so that she leaves her habitation and hides in a household of small mechanics to escape from them—one of the best episodes in the book), protests, struggles, goes down on her knees in vain; then, at last, stupefied and exhausted, desists, looks for the last time at her inexorable, impenetrable daughter, who has hard texts on her lips and no recognition in her eye, and who lets her pass away, without an embrace, for ever. The incident in itself is perfectly conceivable: many well-meaning persons have held human relationships cheap in the face of a religious call. But Daudet's weakness has been simply a want of acquaintance with his subject. Proposing to

himself to describe a particular phase of French Protestantism, he has "got up" certain of his facts with commendable
zeal; but he has not felt nor understood the matter, has
looked at it solely from the outside, sought to make it above
all things grotesque and extravagant. Into these excesses it
doubtless frequently falls; but there is a general human verity
which regulates even the most stubborn wills, the most perverted lives; and of this saving principle the author, in quest
of striking pictures, has rather lost his grasp. His pictures are
striking, as a matter of course; but to us readers of Protestant
race, familiar with the large, free, salubrious life which the
children of that faith have carried with them over the globe,
there is almost a kind of drollery in these fearsome pictures of
the Protestant temperament. The fact is that M. Daudet has
not (to my belief) any natural understanding of the religious
passion; he has a quick perception of many things, but that
province of the human mind cannot be *fait de chic*—experience, there, is the only explorer. Madame Autheman is not a
real bigot; she is simply a dusky effigy, she is undemonstrated.
Eline Ebsen is not a victim, inasmuch as she is but half alive,
and victims are victims only in virtue of being thoroughly
sentient. I do not easily perceive her spiritual joints. All the
human part of the book, however, has the author's habitual
felicity; and the reader of these remarks knows what I hold
that to be. It may seem to him, indeed, that in making the
concession I made just above—in saying that Alphonse Daudet's insight fails him when he begins to take the soul into
account—I partly retract some of the admiration I have expressed for him. For that amounts, after all, to saying that he
has no high imagination, and, as a consequence, no ideas. It
is very true, I am afraid, that he has not a great number of
ideas. There are certain things he does not conceive—certain
forms that never appear to him. Imaginative writers of the
first order always give us an impression that they have a kind
of philosophy. We should be embarrassed to put our finger
on Daudet's philosophy. "And yet you have praised him so
much," we fancy we hear it urged; "you have praised him as
if he were one of the very first." All that is very true, and yet
we take nothing back. Determinations of rank are a delicate
matter, and it is sufficient priority for an author that one likes

him immensely. Daudet is bright, vivid, tender; he has an intense artistic life. And then he is so free. For the spirit that moves slowly, going carefully from point to point, not sure whether this or that or the other will "do," the sight of such freedom is delightful.

Century Magazine, August 1883
Reprinted in *Partial Portraits*, 1888

TRANSLATOR'S PREFACE

Alphonse Daudet's *Port Tarascon: The Last Adventures of the Illustrious Tartarin.*

THE THREE GREAT EPISODES in the career of Alphonse Daudet's genial and hapless hero form together so vivid a picture and so complete a history, are so full of reciprocal reference and confirmation, that it is scarcely fair to fix our attention on one of them without bearing the others in mind. They have this quality of the great classic trilogies, that each of them gains in interest by being read in the light of the others, so that the whole work becomes, in its way, a high example of artistic consistency. If the reader turn back to *Tartarin of Tarascon*, of which the main subject is the worthy bachelor's passion for the pursuit of imaginary beasts—of course he is incapable of killing a fly—he will see how the author has vivified the conception from the first, putting into it an intensity of life that could only throb on, hilariously, into new exuberances. Those readers to whom Tartarin's earlier adventures have not been definitely revealed—his visit to Algeria in pursuit of the lion of the Atlas, his wonderful appearance in Switzerland, where he qualifies himself, by rare and grotesque achievements, for the presidency of the Alpine Club of Tarascon, an office in regard to which the bilious Costecalde is his competitor—such uninstructed persons had better turn immediately to the first and second parts of the delightful record. They will there acquire a further insight into some of the matters tantalizingly alluded to in *Port Tarascon*—the baobab and the camel, the lion-skins, the poisoned arrows, the alpenstock of honor, the critical hours passed in a damp dungeon in the Chateau de Chillon.

We must praise, moreover, not only the evocation of the sonorous and sociable little figure of Tartarin himself—broad of shoulder and bright of eye, bald of head, short of beard, belted on a comfortable scale for all exploits—but the bright image of the wonderfully human little town which he has made renowned, and in which the charming art of touching up the truth—the poor, bare, shabby facts of things—is represented as flourishing more than anywhere else upon earth. A compendium of all the droll idiosyncrasies of his birthplace, Tartarin makes them epic and world-famous, hands them down to a warm immortality of condonation. Daudet has humorously described in a "definitive" preface (just as he alludes to them in the opening pages of *Port Tarascon*) some of the consequences, personal to himself, of this accident of his having happened to point his moral as well as adorn his tale with the little patch of Provence that sits opposite to Beaucaire by the Rhone. Guided in his irrepressible satiric play by his haunting sense of the French "Midi," his own provoking, engaging clime, it was quite at hazard that in his quest of the characteristic he put his hand on Tarascon. What he wanted was some little Southern community that he could place in comic and pathetic, at times almost in tragic, opposition to the colder, grayer Northern stripe in the national temperament. Tarascon resented at first such compromising patronage. She shook her plump brown shoulders and tried to wriggle out of custody. The quarrel, however, has now been more than made up, for the sensitive city, weighing the shame against the glory, has not, in the long-run, been perverse enough to pretend that the affair has cost her too much. It was, in fact, in regard to sweet old dusty Roman Nîmes, his native town, that he had permitted himself, in intention, the worst of his irreverences. At any rate, what most readers will say is that if the Tarascon of fact is not like the Tarascon of art, so much the worse for the former.

It is impossible not to ask one's self whether the author foresaw from the first the sequel and the conclusion of Tartarin's life; whether the first episode was a part of a conscious plan. The reason of this curiosity is that everything fits and corresponds so beautifully with everything else—the later developments are contained so in germ in the earlier. But curiosity as to the way exquisite things are produced in literature is an attitude as to which the profit is mainly in the healthy exercise of the faculty; for the questions it presses most eagerly are the most unanswerable. They are not, at any rate, the questions the man of genius himself most confidently meets. It is probable that Tartarin's full possibilities glimmered before his biographer even in the early chapters, but that they remained vague, in their vividness, till they were attempted—just as the lair of the lion and the land of the glacier both attracted and eluded the prudent Tartarin himself, till the rising growl of public opinion put him really on his mettle. The rest of the whole work—its general harmony and roundness—is neatness and tact of execution.

Tartarin's word about himself, quoted from his historian, that he is Don Quixote in the skin of Sancho Panza, is the best summary of his contradictions. The author's treatment of these contradictions is of the happiest; he keeps the threads of the tangle so distinct, and with so light a hand. Whenever life is caught in the fact with this sort of art, what shines out even more than the freshness of the particular case is its general correspondence with our experience. It becomes typical and suggestive and confirmatory in all sorts of ways, and that is how it becomes supremely interesting. The fat little boastful bachelor by the Rhone-side, with his poisoned arrows and his baobab, his perfect candor and his tremendous lies, his good intentions and his perpetual mistakes, presents to us a kind of eternal, essential ambiguity, an antagonism which many fallible souls spend their time trying to simplify. What is this ambiguity but the opposition of the idea and the application—the beauty one would like to compass in life and the innumerable snippets by which that beauty is abbreviated in the business of fitting it to our personal measure? There are two men in Tartarin, and there are two men in all of us; only, of course, to make a fine case, M. Daudet has zigzagged the line of their respective oddities. As he says so amusingly in *Tartarin of Tarascon*, in his comparison of the very different promptings of these inner voices, when the Don Quixote sounds the appeal, "Cover yourself with glory!" the Sancho Panza murmurs the qualification, "Cover yourself with flannel!" The glory is everything the imagination regales itself with as a luxury of reputation—the *regardelle* so prettily described in the last pages of *Port Tarascon*; the flannel is everything that life demands as a tribute to reality—a gage of self-preservation. The glory reduced to a tangible texture too often turns out to be mere prudent underclothing.

Tarascon was inordinately fond of glory. It was this love of glory at bottom that dragged it across the seas, where it so speedily became conscious of a greater need for flannel than its individual resources could supply. Delightful was M. Daudet's idea of illustrating the grotesque and inevitable compromise by the life of a whole community. We have had them all before; they all peep out in the first book of the series—Bézuquet and Pascalon, Bompard and Bravida, Costecalde and Escourbaniès, Mademoiselle Tournatoire and her brother, the blood-letting doctor. We have listened to the mingled nasality and sonority of their chatter, and admired in several cases the bold brush of their mustaches. We move in the aroma of garlic that constitutes their social atmosphere, and that suffuses somehow with incongruous picturesqueness the Gallo-Roman mementos of their civic past. We have already, in *Tartarin of Tarascon*, seen poor Mademoiselle Tournatoire, at her casement, with a face like a white horse, fixing fond eyes, as he passes, on her heroic fellow-townsman. We have heard the shrill of the cicadas on the "Walk Round," and the pipe of the little bootblacks before Tartarin's little gate. We know everything possible about the great man, down to the details of his personal habits and the peculiarities of his pronunciation, and how he knotted his bandanna before he went to bed, and where he kept the poisoned arrows, and where he could put his hand upon Captain Cook, and where upon Bougainville. We have lived with him so intimately that it makes a great difference to us that he has at last played his part out.

The only defect of *Port Tarascon* is that it leaves no more to come; it exhausts the possibilities. But the idea is vivid in it to the end, and poetic justice is vindicated. If the drama is over, it is the drama of the contending spirits. From the moment one of these spirits wins the victory and destroys the equilibrium, there is nothing left for Tartarin but to retire to Beaucaire, and Beaucaire, of course, is extinction. When the

Sancho Panza sees his romantic counterpart laid utterly low—
I needn't mention where the victory lies, nor take the edge
from the reader's own perception of the catastrophe; it is
enough to say that the thrill of battle could only be over from
the moment such abundant and discouraging evidence was
produced of the quantity of compromise it takes to transmute
our dreams into action, our inspiration into works—even
Sancho Panza, for all his escape, his gain of security, weeps
for the prostrate hidalgo. Tartarin is betrayed by his compromises; they rise up and jeer at him and denounce him. But he
granted them in good faith; he was unconscious of them at
the time. Indeed, he would have perished without them only
less promptly than he perishes with them; they were as necessary to save him for an hour as they were predestined to
lose him forever.

For all this, it can hardly be said that a book dissuades,
however humorously and paradoxically, from action, from the
deed to be done, when it is itself a performance so accomplished, so light and bright and irresistible, as the three
chronicles of Tartarin. Therefore the last moral of all is, that
however many traps life may lay for us, tolerably firm ground,
at any rate, is to be found in perfect art.

Harper's New Monthly Magazine, June 1890
New York: Harper & Brothers, 1890

ALPHONSE DAUDET

IN ALPHONSE DAUDET passed away nine days ago the last
eminent member but one of the French literary group
that—with great differences of date indeed—had arrived at
manhood and entered into activity under the second Empire.
He was much the junior of Taine, of Renan, of Flaubert and
Leconte de Lisle; but he had found them all on the stage, and
they had given him, as it were, a hand. Emile Zola is still
present as a younger representative of that strong company,
and his robust literary talent is still, happily, a promise of
duration; but, for the rest, so far as "the last new French
book" continues to have a message for our curiosity, it is a

fruit of trees that have come to bearing in the current spacious times. Distinguished as are two or three of the talents
of the new generation—generations in truth are rapid in
France and sometimes cease to be new before they have
ceased to be young—it sufficiently comes home to us that the
muster of high accomplishment is now comparatively thin.
Alphonse Daudet was not fifty-eight, though the limit of his
full production happened, through the grave failure of his
health, to have been for some years reached; and yet his extinction represents not only the removal of an admirable talent, but almost, already, the close of a tradition, the seal of
something that may very well soon begin to pass for positive
classicism. There was a time when, with his wonderful hand,
his bolder foreshortenings, his sharper penetrations and more
promiscuous vocabulary, he struck us all as intensely modern;
but in the light of Anatole France and Maurice Barrès—to
mention only two of the lately-risen stars—he has grown virtually antique, indirectly ancestral.

The effect was achieved in the short compass of some fifteen years of exquisite activity, during which, with sharp
stroke upon stroke, every stroke immensely counting and
none falling wide, he added brilliant book to book. These
things gave him, at the end, a place ineffaceably his own, an
artistic identity of the sharpest. He was really more personal,
more individual and more inimitable than any one. None of
the various descendants of Balzac who were to find in any
degree the fortune that, under Balzac's great impulse, they
often went so far to seek has even perhaps equally arrived at
that special success which consists in having drawn from one's
talent, from one's whole organization and every attendant circumstance, every drop they were capable of giving. To have
followed Daudet closely is to have been lost in admiration of
the way he worked his heritage and his experience. Not a
grain of the gold was lost for art or for effect; every grain was
saved and polished and beaten out. He produces the impression of having planted his garden up to the last inch of its
soil. There was nothing of his outfit, of his accidents or his
possibilities, that was not professionally convertible and converted. It may be said even in the face of his final long subjection to suffering that it would have been difficult to meet a

completer or a more charming case of success. His race, his origin, his nerves, all his sensibilities and idiosyncrasies, the southern sun in his blood and the southern sound in his ears, were always frankly and bravely his material, or at any rate, at the least, his form. His sense of everything that his southern air produced, whether in the shape of delightful nonsense or of perversities more dangerous, was inexhaustible, and he was especially wonderful as to the constant double use he contrived to make of it. It was at once, with him, the thing to be shown and the way to show it, the picture and the point of view. The first of these elements was not really more *méridional* than the second, and yet it was at the expense of the first that the second could so admirably perform and flourish. We should perhaps have had something of the sort in our literature if we had ever had an Irish painter of Irish manners endowed with an irony and an art as fine as that of the author of "Numa Roumestan." But for irony, in that direction, we happen mostly to have had, from Thackeray down, English irony, and in the way of sentiment we have had, whether English or Irish, mainly the cheap. We feel of Daudet and his Provence that, for literary purposes, he was almost an inventor. He emptied Keats's "beaker," at all events, drained it dry, and closed the chapter. There will be little envy of those who touch the "Midi" after him.

This was a part of that effect of being consummately *done* that infallibly attached to anything he attempted; and the effect came doubtless, in its measure, from his having so completely accepted and adopted the particular fact of his spontaneity and sensibility. He let himself vibrate as he would, and as he had at the same time a literary instinct of the rarest and acutest, as the artist in him was exquisitely alive and vigilant, this supreme "doing" inevitably attended his work; as to which we calculate, moreover, that he is one of those who will not have been cheated of their reward. There is not an inch of waste—everything tells and "comes off." Certain things are wanting to his view, many sides of the play of character, of the life of the will, the idea, the private soul; but what is there is extraordinarily vivid and warm, extraordinarily observed and peculiarly touching. He had the great democratic fancy. No genius with so much of the inevitable chill of a special manner remains so on the level with his reader, becomes so personal and intimate, takes him so into his confidence. He is at the opposite pole, in this respect, from Flaubert, with whom a kind of grand, measured distance from his canvas—paced as if for a duel—was an ideal, and who seemed to attack his subject with a brush twenty feet long. Daudet's charm is precisely in his agitation and his nerves—that is in a set of nerves that could make so for creation. His style is a matter of talking, gesticulating, imitating—of impressionism carried to the last point; but his surrender to all this cultivated familiarity never leaves us in a moment's doubt of his being, all the more, a master. What could be at once more personal, more whimsically and consentingly human, and yet more historical and responsible, so to express it, than such things as "L'Immortel" and "Les Rois en Exil"? We have had other cases, cases enough, of treatment by talk, but only to see the subject, as a result of it, stray further and further and lose itself. Daudet catches it in the finest net of talk, and this fine net is his marvellous style. It plays into the happy undiscernible instinct which is his triumphant substitute for composition, the instinct which saves him from the penalty of his want of connexion and continuity, his love of jumps and gaps, of the glimpse and the episode. He positively gains indeed by this last tendency; it makes him the novelist with the greatest number of wonderful "bits" to show, of beautiful sharp vignettes, of pages complete in themselves. To think of one of his books is to see a little gilded gallery with red sofas and small modern masterpieces.

He gives us thus, essentially, the concrete and the palpable, sensations and contacts, images, appearances, touches for the eye and ear, evocations of detail of which his unsurpassable article on the death of Edmond de Goncourt is perhaps the most brilliant specimen. But while we are under the charm we feel him to be one of the first of all observers of the things humanly nearest to us, nearest, above all, to our most amused or our most tender tolerance. He fairly makes us sensitive, and I like him, for myself, best of all the novelists who have not the greater imagination, the imagination of the moralist. He has even this faculty perhaps in flashes—there is something of it, for instance, in the sustained artistic flight of "Sapho," which makes us live the thing and think it, descend, ourselves, into the intimacy and the abyss; but, for the most part, his vision is of the brighter and weaker things, weaker natures, about us, the people, the passions, the complications that we either commiserate or laugh at, and as to which it is too pompous, and, indeed cruel and in bad taste, to sit up over the lesson. The lesson, for Daudet, was taught by laughter and by tears, of neither of which was he ever in the smallest degree ashamed. The former, perhaps, failed him perceptibly as he went on, but he took more complete refuge in pity, in melancholy that was not quite pensive, in pessimism that was not quite bitter. It would be difficult enough to fix the proportions in which his sense of drollery and his sense of evil united to form a friendly poetry; and this mystery, no doubt, even if there were none other, would be just one of the reasons of his distinction. The mixture, the poetry, had in the man himself an irresistible charm, for in the long years of illness in which his life closed he had become as acquainted with pain as he had remained faithful to fancy. The sun in his blood had never burnt out, and if it were necessary to characterize in a single word the quality that, either as artist or as man, he most distilled, one would speak unhesitatingly of his warmth. He was as warm as the south wall of a garden or as the flushed fruit that grows there. Of all consummate artists he was the most natural. Every impression he gave out passed through the imagination, but only to take from it more of common truth.

Literature, December 25, 1897

Ximenes Doudan

PARIS, June 9.—To people who are fond of good letters I recommend those of the late M. Doudan, which have just been published by the Comte d'Haussonville, one of his principal correspondents. Good letters are the most entertaining reading (to my sense) in the world, and in these two (it must be confessed rather formidably massive) volumes this branch of literature, so exceptionally rich in France, has received a delightful accession. M. Doudan was not known to fame, and his letters will not make him famous, inasmuch as their interest is of a very tranquil order and their charm of a sort to be appreciated only by people of delicate taste, who are always in the minority. But they are very exquisite and they testify eloquently to the culture, the intelligence, and the intellectual good manners of the circle of which their author was a member, and of which they form as it were simply the written conversations. M. Doudan was one of those men (every one has known a specimen) whose friends speak of them and their powers in superlative terms, but whom, as there is little to show for these same powers, the outside world must take on trust—the men of whom, to the end of their days, it is said that they might do great things if they only would. They pass away without having done anything, and the brutal world shrugs its shoulders and observes that when people *can* do something, they manage sooner or later to do it, and that if a man stands all his life on the brink of the stream it is safe to conclude that he does not know how to swim. Sainte-Beuve somewhere speaks of M. Doudan as one of the *"supremes délicats"* whose ideal is placed so high that they give up ever trying to reach it. A great many clever men doubtless belong to this category, as well as a great many charlatans; but we must not forget the homely proverb which says that to make an omelette you must break your eggs. To write a good book one must hang one's ideal on a peg where one can reach it. M. Doudan passed the greater part of his life in the family of Broglie, to which he had been introduced through being engaged as preceptor to young M. de Rocca, the son of Madame de Staël by her second marriage. He was an intimate friend of the Duchess de Broglie, the daughter of Madame de Staël; I believe that this lady was a saint, and that the intimacy was observed to go as far as an intimacy between a saint and an agreeable man may go. His correspondents in these volumes are chiefly her children and her son-in-law, M. d'Haussonville. The letters range from the year 1827 to the year 1872, the period of the author's death; many of them, year after year, are dated from that charming chateau of Coppet, on the Lake of Geneva, in which Madame de Staël spent her years of exile, and to which her descendants have continued to resort. M. Doudan was pre-eminently a literary man; literature was his passion, and two-thirds of his allusions in these volumes are to books; but he wrote very little and published less—the editor informing us that even his *magnum opus*, a brief and extremely condensed treatise on the art of style and the principles of literary composition, which he had spent a great deal of time in polishing and perfecting, never left his portfolio. I believe, however, that it is now to be given to the world. I don't know what M. Doudan's theories were, but his practice is admirable. His own style is charming, and the amount of excellent, of exquisite writing buried in these essentially familiar letters may excite the surprise of a generation whose epistolary manner threatens to savor more and more of the telegram and the postal card. There are letters and letters; those of M. Doudan are decidedly "old-fashioned," but they are not in the least ponderous. They are not formal dissertations on the one hand, nor on the other are they marked by the desperate vivacity of many of those social scribes who know that their letters are to be read aloud and handed about. They touch upon everything—events of the day, people, books, abstract questions; some readers will perhaps complain that they contain too little gossip, and absolutely no scandal. They have a great deal of humor, pitched in the minor key; it is never quite absent, but it never rises to the hight (or sinks to the depth) of the comic. I had marked a great many passages for quotation, but I must use the privilege scantily. Every now and then there is something excellently said—as when, speaking of foreign literatures, and declaring that one never, really enters into them, or cares to enter into them, as the natives do, that they have always a strangeness for us, M. Doudan affirms that "at bottom there are only two things that really please us, the ideal or our own likeness." Excellent too is this about Rousseau: "I am not surprised that he has displeased you. There is nothing sadder to see than this lively imagination, with its strength and severity, governed by vulgar inclinations. He wished sincerely to live according to the ideal which he saw floating before him, but his nature rebelling too strongly, he squeezed into his ideal all the pitiable qualities of his personal nature, by conscience, by insanity, and also by a certain perversity." And St. Augustine, he adds (whom his correspondent appears also to have been reading), "his confessions make one think of everything. They are like a fine night of Africa. Great shadows, vast spaces, and the eternal stars." M. Doudan had, as a young man, paid a short visit to Italy, and his Italian memories kept him company for life. His allusions to Italian things are constant, and they have an almost passionate tenderness. "A young Roman girl of the bourgeoisie has her confessor lodging behind St. Peter's, and in passing she thinks neither of the dome of St. Peter's, nor of the Egyptian obelisk, nor of the statues of Bernini, nor of the lions of Canova; but all these things are mingled confusedly with her real life. She is a bright little flower on the walls of a great monument. The sun of Rome has given her her brightness, but she doesn't know it. An old English lady declaims as she gazes on the Roman horizon, the catacombs, and the pines of the Villa Pamfili; and while the old English lady remains ugly and pale and declamatory, the little Roman bourgeoisie, who has never been so wise, grows up and becomes beautiful without thinking of the Tarquins or the Gracchi. M. de Langsdorf," he adds, "means soon to sail; but for my part, fond as I am of nature, I shouldn't care to go into those unsettled parts of America. I would rather see Königsberg or Nüremberg, under their grey sky, than all those virgin forests which have never been looked at but by lumber dealers. I am like my old English lady of just now: I like to declaim over old times, but if to-day I could be eighteen years old and have been born in Rome, even in the Via Babuino, I would give up forever all present and future declamations. But you can't be eighteen for wishing it, and if ever I am eighteen again

I shall stay so." A short time before the Roman revolution of 1848 he writes: "I lay my curse in advance upon all Italians who are not of an extreme moderation in these hard days. But patience and moderation are rare virtues. I don't know why they give the name of hero to those who mount a ladder under fire and plant a flag on a wall in the midst of balls. It's a matter of half an hour, after which you may go and lie down on a bed of laurels freshly cut. It is only those who have real patience and moderation who should be called heroes. Those are the great battles—battles that last long. You have to lie for years on peach-kernels, with doubt on your right hand and on your left the crowd, who informs you that you have no blood in your veins, and, to ascertain it, wants every now and then to cut your throat." Lastly—apropos of M. Renan's brilliant first literary performances: "The truth is he is like a young colt; he is fond of kicking up his heels. . . . A man must certainly have some vague ideas; a clever man who has none but clear ones is a fool, who will never come to anything; but nevertheless there must be some solid bones to hold a living being together when he is not of the race of the snakes. I don't see M. Renan's bones." M. Doudan's letters, in short, present an interesting image of a quiet, sensitive, fastidious man, living by preference on the shady side of life, possessing the most delicate perceptions and tastes, as well as the most agreeable culture, but haunted by a melancholy sense of his ineffectiveness. His gayety is subdued; there is a cast of autumnal haze in his sunshine. I may add that he appears to have been a voracious reader of English books, and to have had, in particular, an insatiable appetite for British fiction. On this last point he was a flattering exception to his countrymen; most French people to whom I have spoken of English novels have made up a very wry face.

New York Tribune, July 1, 1876

Mélanges et Lettres de X. Doudan. Avec une Introduction par M. le Comte d'Haussonville, etc. Tomes iii and iv. Paris: Calmann Lévy; New York: F. W. Christern, 1877.

T HE SECOND INSTALMENT of M. Doudan's letters proves as substantial as the first. M. Doudan was a copious as well as excellent letter-writer, and the success of the enterprise undertaken by M. d'Haussonville has been such as to make his correspondents yield up the remainder of their treasures. The letters here offered us do not belong to a new period of the author's life: they coincide in date with those already published (the first are of the year 1832); they are the result, in part, it may be supposed, of a second shifting, a second picking over of the basket, as we may say, and in part of the accession of fresh material. The first volumes contained perhaps the best things; but the difference is not very great, and people who, like ourselves, took a fancy to M. Doudan, will find these very well worth reading. The effect of them is not to present us with a new or in any degree modified portrait of the author, but to pass the pencil over the old outline and make it a trifle more definite. Here, as in the former publication, his delicacy, discrimination, discretion are the striking and charming features. A quiet scholar who was at the same time in a very sufficient degree a man of the world, and whose life was passed in the best society, who preferred observation to action, and with whom observation always implied conversation—conversation of the most expansive and reciprocal kind—such is the figure that detaches itself from these pages. His letters are simply his conversation, pen in hand, and they have all the alertness and lightness of his talk, as we may be sure that his talk had much of the neatness and natural smoothness of his letters. These, we must add, are not only the portrait of a single mind; they are also, in a sense, the portrait of a society. In this respect the picture, just as it stands, is certainly a very pleasing one. We may say that it is not complete, but what there is of it is extremely flattering. It represents a group of people whose life appears to be primarily the liberal play of their intelligence or their curiosity and interest in regard to all the events and productions of their time and of other times, and their desire to arrive at just and comprehensive opinions about them. These people, it will be remembered, were, more immediately, the family of the Duc de Broglie, the father of the recent highly conservative adviser of the President of the French Republic. The present Duc de Broglie was an intimate friend of M. Doudan, though it is to be observed that very few of the letters in the volumes before us are addressed to him; M. Doudan had been, in a measure, his preceptor, his guide, and philosopher.

It is impossible for the reader of these pages not to reflect that the blindly repressive policy which lately characterized the Ministry of which the Duc de Broglie was the most eminent member is not a very satisfactory offshoot of the teachings of M. Doudan. People who think M. Doudan has been somewhat overrated—and there are of course such people—have only to point to the exploits of his "favorite pupil." We ourselves, however, should not accept this as a refutation of our claims; for we should hesitate to assert that, if he had lived to the present hour, M. Doudan would not have sided with the policy of the recent Government. We are, on the contrary, very glad to mark in this manner our sense of his limitations. He was an intense conservative; the reader feels that on every page. Temperance and moderation were indeed his divinities, and he would certainly not have found them in the camp of MM. Fourtou and De Broglie. But it is plain that, as time went on, he became more and more an alarmist; he had a certain fund of liberalism, but he had emptied the cup. One of the few places in these letters in which he speaks with anger and acrimony is that in which he resents the right of the English newspapers to suggest that the justice of the Versailles Government towards the persons accused of complicity with the Commune be tempered with mercy. (It is very true that in another place he expressly advocates moderation.) His intelligence, his taste and wisdom, his lightness and alertness of imagination, are all most beautiful; but we confess that with much that is constantly first-rate, and worthy of all admiration, in his judgments and perceptions, he is always liable to give us a glimpse of the chain—a golden chain, if you will—that binds him to the old classical, conventional, and partial standpoint. He remains, in politics and morals as well as in literature, the man who can see no merit whatever in the poetry of Victor Hugo, but who is charmed with the lucubrations (he always kept an eye on the new English books) of the 'Country Parson.'

But we feel like apologizing for dealing with M. Doudan otherwise than by simply quoting him. His letters are a running commentary upon all the important things that happen

around him—of the small things he speaks little—and we
have only to choose the subject that we may desire his opinion of. What he says is always suggestive, especially because
he has found the point he starts from itself suggestive. He
always enlarges the topic, always passes toward some general
reflection, some higher point of view. We only regret our
want of space. M. Doudan's great passion—his only passion—was for literature; he was a *reader*, to his finger-tips.
Perhaps the best things he says are the things suggested by
books, which are his usual topic. "There are people who in
their whole life," he says, "have never read four pages in a
year, and who tell you with assurance that reviews are a very
superficial sort of reading." M. Doudan read a great many
reviews, as well as other things, and he was not superficial.
Apropos of Mrs. Gaskell's novel of 'Cranford' (he was very
fond of English novels) he launches into a dissertation upon
the drawbacks of the theological habit of mind—upon its
making us lose sight of the *vrai fond* of human nature. His
remarks are excellent, but he ends with apologizing for them,
and wonders what they have to do with 'Cranford.' But "j'ai
la fureur," he says, "des idées générales." He says elsewhere
that he had known an English military surgeon who had been
surgeon of the Duke of Wellington, and who had carried
about with him in all his campaigns a library of two hundred
volumes. "There is a man by whom one would like to be
looked after in an illness, and by whom one would gladly
have a leg amputated." Some of his best literary judgments
are in the later letters. "As for M. Victor Cousin, they say
that in all this he admires the genius of our Emperor. . . .
He bows down before the greatest politician of our time; so
he expressed himself the other day. . . . At the end of his
life his mind will be very weary of all these gambols through
the finite and the infinite. Socrates will have something to say
to him in the other world upon the duties of the profession
of a philosopher." Here is something very good apropos of
Madame Sand:

"Her misfortune at present is to pursue ideas. This rage
for having ideas has been the ruin of many writers who had
talent and a happy imagination. She deforms her people in

order to squeeze them into the lines of her systems. There would not be so many living beings in Shakspere if he had done this way. Nature, having larger views than the mind of man, makes people who are not simply a republican, a royalist, an officer, and a priest. Man has, in all senses, a something superfluous which corresponds probably to plans wider than our conceptions. It is for that reason, indeed, that people who have too much the stamp of their profession seem rather like fools."

In the former volumes there were two or three allusions to M. Renan of a rather irreverent sort, and here the tone of reference to the author of the 'Life of Jesus' is always ironical. "I have never seen in a theologian so great an acquaintance with the Oriental flora. He is a very much better landscapist than St. Augustine and Bossuet. He sows geraniums, anemones, and buttercups to reap incredulity." There is an excellent and very appreciative judgment upon Sainte-Beuve, which is too long to quote, in which M. Doudan speaks of his combining "the industry of a Benedictine with the penetrating imagination of a nervous woman." Here are two lines which are a very good example of the quiet penetration of the author's literary instinct. The allusion is again to Madame Sand: "Read the 'Comtesse de Rudolstadt,' in order to see how it does not resemble Bohemia. But, to say so in passing, I hold that if, in portrayal, exactness is a great virtue, we must yet not be too severe upon writers whose reveries produce fine pictures of distant countries of which they only know the general features." This remark, which is deeper than it appears, would seem to have come from a man who had himself tried imaginative writing. But M. Doudan had a great deal of imagination. Here, too, is a declaration which comes apparently from a man who has the "inside view": "I believe that the men who write are the men who profit by odd moments. One has never one's time before one as a housewife has a long piece of cloth. Life only gives us little squares of stuff; but of these little squares industrious people make great counterpanes which hold very well together."

There is almost always with M. Doudan a strain of melancholy and latent depression, and in the later letters this is especially noticeable. He is at times irritable and invidious; he takes a dark view of the future of France. It must be remembered that he was always an invalid, a valetudinarian. "If you believe I have no more fears," he writes in 1843, "you are in a very great error. I should like very much to see those people who tell me in a great, strong voice that I am perfectly well— I should like to see them obliged to handle this little network of spider-webs that is my own person." Like M. de Broglie to-day, M. Doudan was (already in 1850) haunted by the prospective "demagogy." "Since it has been discovered that Trouville is a solitary place, the whole nation has thrown itself upon this unhappy spot. Excursion trains vomit forth the scum of the capital and its suburbs. . . . They represent pretty well what France will be when the demagogic level shall have radically flattened it down." We are sorry to say that, in 1866, M. Doudan sympathized so far with what he himself admits to be the national "Chauvinism" as to think that the French were very great fools for allowing Germany to resolve herself into a nation. He was not for war, he says, at that moment, but for war eventually, as an anticipatory and preventive measure. M. Doudan, dying in 1872, lived through the siege of Paris and the Commune, and the letters of this period are of course full of sadness. He had always, apparently, had a friendly and familiar feeling toward England; he was versed in English literature. (His great sympathy, it must be said, however, was for Italy; his pages are full of charming passages about Italy.) But at the last he rarely alludes to England without bitterness. We have mentioned his indignation at the plea for moderation after the suppression of the Commune, dictated by her "pedantry of apparent liberalism." "What life are you leading in London?" he asks of a friend. "Do you go much into the *beau monde*? A poor Frenchman must have a first moment of embarrassment when he goes into a drawing-room full of people to whom no such things as these have happened since the invasion of the Danes. And even then!"

The last of these volumes terminates with the promised essay on the 'Revolutions of Taste,' the little dissertation which was circulated among M. Doudan's friends, but which he never consented to publish. It will, perhaps, now be found a little disappointing. It contains much ingenuity and many happy judgments; but in form, at least, it illustrates rather the rigid and conventional side of the author's own taste, and in felicity of expression it is very inferior to the letters.

Nation, January 24, 1878

Gustave Droz

Around a Spring. By Gustave Droz. Translated by MS. New York: Holt and Williams, 1871.

F RANCE HAS NOT VANISHED from among the nations, though at moments we are tempted to think so. It is a peculiar satisfaction, in this era of eclipse and confusion, to meet a genuine example of the better genius of the land. Such an example is furnished us in this excellent novel of M. Gustave Droz, which is here carefully translated. When the sanguinary mist obscuring that motley swarm which lived and prospered a few months since in the broad hot glare of the Empire shall have faded away; when the blood-stains shall have been washed out (in so far as blood-stains may) and the ashes swept up, our eyes will rest upon an altered stage and a modified *mise en scène*. We may hope that behind that lurid war-cloud the sheep have been sifted from the goats. Among those who may have survived for the sake of art, to keep the pledges given in more joyous days, we hopefully number the author of *Mademoiselle Cibot* and *Autour d'une Source*. His works—these two novels at least—belong to the best and ripest fruits of that huge literary harvest of recent France, amid which so many products were of monstrous and morbid growth. Reading over his novels in the light of late events, they acquire an interest quite independent of this matter of their intrinsic merits. The one before us has already something of the value of an historical document. It is impregnated with the flavor of the Empire. Balzac dreamed of transmitting to future ages a perfect image of the France of his day, and erected for the purpose that ponderous mechanism among whose cranks and derricks and scaffolds and ladders we wander now as among the pillars and arches of a dim cathedral. But M. Gustave Droz, going more simply and lightly to work, has resolved the social forces of his own brief hour into a clearer essence than his great predecessor. The light literature of recent France has always seemed to us to reflect the central lustre of the Empire very much as a heap of broken bottles reflects the noonday sun,—with the same cheap, untempered glare. It was the pretension of the system

which perished at Sedan to pervade and invade all things,—
to set the tune, to pitch the universal voice, to leave its visible
stamp in every corner. On the top of the page, in every clever
French novel of the last ten years, you seem to read that mystical *N.* which greeted you endlessly from the cornices of the
Louvre. Novelists, feuilletonists, critics, outscampered each
other in the panting effort to keep pace with the tendency of
which it was the symbol, to urge it in its headlong course, to
re-echo its phraseology, its morality. Up to the very edge of
the great silence of the past year,—the silence which among
arms falls upon letters as well as laws,—you hear the swelling
of this vast concert of Imperial harmonies; up to the very
verge of that collapse which fell as suddenly as the "driving
in" of Comus and his rout. M. Gustave Droz was one of the
freshest and clearest of these concerted voices; he gives us the
latest social news of the France of the past.

His great merit is that he gives it so intelligently. Of all the
amuseurs of pre-Communal Paris, he seems to us to have been
the most open-eyed. We speak, not of his philosophy,—we
doubt if he boasts of one,—but of his singularly clear and
penetrating perception. Through the mask of the jester and
conteur we see the gleam of a sagacious human eye. In him
the latter French generations have assuredly had a "chiel"
among them taking notes. These notes were first gathered
into those two amusing volumes, *Monsieur, Madame et Bébé*
and *Entre Nous.* The field occupied by M. Droz in these little
books is not wide. His task has been to turn the laugh on
good society, to satirize the manners and customs of the mon-
eyed aristocracy of the current year of grace, to reflect in the
minutest detail its passing follies and fashions and infatuations. Social Paris of the last few years will find itself more
lastingly embalmed, we imagine, in these light pages than in
many works of larger pretensions. They are flavored with that
old Gallic salt of humor which is ground in the mills of Rabelais and Molière. It is often too pungent for our Anglo-
Saxon palate, but it comes from the best bag. We might say
of M. Droz, that he is the wittiest of humorists. The deep
smile and the broad laugh, as you read, contend for precedence. Of pure comicality he is a genuine master; though perhaps personally we enjoy him most in his lighter forms of

irony. The delicacy of his touch at these moments, the mod-
ulation of his tone, the refinement of his phrase, are those of
an accomplished artist. We recommend him to the consideration of some of our own heavy-handed jokers and satirists.
But especially noticeable, as we say, is the penetrating nice-
ness of his observation. This has been more striking in each
successive volume, and has grappled in each with more substantial facts. It revels for the most part in the finer shades of
truth, and is most at home in that cool *demi-jour* of well-
appointed drawing-rooms, in which the accustomed eye finds
it of profit to detect and compare the subtler gradations of
social fact. His discrimination, his intuitions, his innuendoes,
are as delicately uttered as the vocal flourishes, the trills, the
roulades, of a fine singer. All this excellent perception, however, is, in the two volumes of sketches, lavished on very
flimsy subjects. In his novels M. Droz approaches with a firm
step the serious side of life, and converts himself from a clever
trifler into a real inventor and dramatist. It is pleasant to see
a writer proceed so resolutely from small things to great;
nothing offers such promise of his having a career to run.
Mademoiselle Cibot deserves, to our minds, to stand among
the very best fictions of recent years. It belongs to really superior art. In its rapid brevity, its density of texture, its unity
of effect, its admirable neatness of execution, it is a model of
narrative tragedy. It is tragic, as a matter of course; for, as a
matter of course, the story deals with the Seventh Commandment,—the breach, naturally, not the observance. The subject
was ready-made to the author's hand; it has the faded, threadbare quality of things overworn; but his presentation of it, his
figures, his details, his "tone," as painters say, are peculiarly
original and vivid. We hardly remember in fiction a figure
more incisively outlined, more potently realized, more
shaped, as Wordsworth says, "to haunt, to startle and waylay," than the terrible little invalid husband of the heroine.
Rarely, either, have we been admitted into the personal confidence of a fictitious character with that palpable closeness
which we enjoy in our conception of the unhappy woman
herself. We have seen her, known her, lived though the dreary
hours of her miserable life. M. Droz is a master of what we
may call sensuous detail; he thoroughly understands the rela-

tion between the cultivated fancy and the visible, palpable facts of the world. On one side of his talent he is an excellent *genre* painter. His work, moreover, suggests the interesting reflection that intelligent realism, in art, is sure to carry with it its own morality. Told in the vulgarly sentimental manner, the history of *Mademoiselle Cibot* might mean nothing at all; told in its hard material integrity, as our author tells it, it enforces a valuable truth,—the truth that sooner or later, here if not there, love demands its own; that under all its forms it remains the same imperative and incorruptible need; and that if it finds in its path no idol of marble and gold, it will turn into evil places and make one of mud and straw. There is an admirably sagacious irony in the contrast between the clear, deep-welling passion of Adèle and the shallow, cynical self-possession of the lover on whose condescension she lives and from whose indifference she dies.

In his second novel M. Droz has been more ambitious; he has chosen a broad, fresh subject, and treated it with a freer hand. The work lacks the simplicity and compactness of its predecessor; it is more diffuse and ponderous; but it indicates a proportionate growth of power. *Autour d'une Source* is the history of the origin of a watering-place,—an unfolding of those personal passions and motive accidents which lurk beneath the surface of broad public facts, like the little worms and insects we find swarming on the earthward face of a stone. The fable is extremely ingenious; it has the advantage of a moulded plot, turning on a central pivot, as distinguished from those mere measured chains of consecutive incident which suggest a yard-stick as their formative implement. The hero is a poor *curé* of an obscure village among the mountains of (presumably) Franche Comté and the Jura. Perched on the mountain-side is the old abandoned castle of the Counts of Manteigney, former lords of the land. The degenerate scion of this noble race, a *petit crevé* of the latest pattern, domiciled in Paris, having repaired his shrunken fortunes by a marriage with the sole daughter and heiress of an ex-vendor of water-cocks, enriched by prosperous traffic, comes with this shrewd father-in-law and his charming young wife to resume possession of his crumbling towers. The château is restored, refurbished, modernized; the curé, a man still young and stalwart enough to know the pangs of passion, but too good a son of the Church to endure them without protest, becomes entangled in relations with his new neighbors and of course with the pretty Countess in especial; and the retired faucet-maker, with plenty of comfortable leisure for dreams of quintupling his millions, wanders through the innocent country-side, seeking what he may devour. This M. Larreau is perhaps the most finished figure in the work; a Frenchman of the Yankee type (not the best), self-made, sharp as a razor, "genial," ambitious, bent on finding an "operation" in all things. He descries in Grand-Font-le-Haut the capacities of a Wiesbaden or a Vichy,—save and except the medicinal springs, alas! But by wondering intently enough whether the soil may not contain the precious fluid, he ends by causing it to flow. The central episode of the book is the victimization, in the interest of M. Larreau's scheme, of the poor curé as accessory to a kind of "bogus" miracle, by which, as it filters and reverberates through the superstitious peasantry, the outer world is to be charmed into a wondering suspicion of the merits of the locality. The mineral spring, in M. Larreau's argument, is to make the fortune of Grand-Font; and to make the fortune of the spring there can be nothing like a good Catholic legend. The Abbé Roche, by a fatal accident, finds himself implicated in an impious fraud which he detests and despises, and the secret burden of which he shares with the Countess. This latter fact (the result of circumstances too complex to relate, but extremely well devised) forbids him to exculpate himself: a word of explanation will "compromise" the lady. The weak point here is not far to seek,—the excessive sensitiveness, namely, of the heroine's reputation. To English minds, at least, the Abbé's scruples and all that comes of them seem suspended by a hair. "Speak, speak, and risk it," we should say. But in French tradition this weak point seems strong enough. For the sake of the Countess, at all events, the Abbé is silent; for her sake he sustains unaided the brunt of obloquy. When the inevitable reaction sets in, and the half-hatched miracle becomes an addled egg to pelt him withal, he suffers for her sake to the bitter end, and endures expulsion, disgrace, and ultimate martyrdom. The main element of the tale is this troubled passion of the honest priest for the charming reckless Countess, with her Parisian graces and follies and dazzling audacities,—the strife between his generous native manhood and his rigid clerical conscience. It is the temptation of St. Anthony, transferred from legend into prosaic fact. The situation is admirably rendered; with force, with color and sympathy, and yet with notable purity of tone. The Countess herself is, like all our author's women, a peculiarly vivid creation. M. Droz has measured the Frenchwoman of the period. He knows her secrets, he enters into her personality; she is scarcely more of a heroine for him than, borrowing a hint from the commoner adage, we may suppose her to be for her *femme de chambre*. The figure of the Countess lingers gratefully in the mind, in spite of the cynicism of the author's last touches. Madame de Monteigney is meant for better things; she judges her position, she despises her follies; she is in a manner, like the Abbé, the victim of a destiny she is too weak to combat; but she has drunk of a maddening wine, and we see her, hurried along in the turbid current of vanity, fling over one by one the light fragments of her maiden's conscience, till she passes from our eyes tossed in feverish unrest on the crest of the wave of pleasure,—like Mazeppa bound helpless on his unguided steed. The supreme interest of the story, however, is lodged in the large and dusky soul of the stalwart Abbé, lighted only by the votive taper of his simple primitive faith. In this connection it becomes extremely deep and poignant. What situation indeed is more tragical than to be condemned to dumbness just in proportion as you cease to be blind, as need and occasion for speech urge you the more harshly; to be forced to watch through a fiery mist of tears the hurrying, unpitying, consuming progression of fate; the fruitless strife of the old and familiar, the loved and consecrated, with the new, the unsparing, the elements of that cold future from which we shall be absent? The fierce irruption of modern life into the little mountain parish of the poor curé produces a cruel confusion of his life-long notions of duty and faith. His vague spiritual doubts and anxieties, his personal temptations and tribulations, are reproduced with a skill which sets a seal upon the masterly character of the work. Occasionally the metaphysical side of the matter, as we may call it, is somewhat meagre and pale; but considering the author's beginnings, we can only congratulate him on his success. The situation is one which demanded real analytic imagination for its treatment, and something very like this has been used. It would not be easy to find anything as much like it among the younger French romancers. As an artist M. Droz has all, and more than all, the common gifts; as a humorist he is peculiarly rich and exuberant; as a moralist, even, he is not to be dismissed in silence. This last term may have an irrelevant sound. What we mean is, that he will be unlikely ever to write a tale which will not project a certain moral deposit and leave the reader, after many broad smiles, in a musing mood. Such is the effect of all really analytic work. That he will write many tales we confidently hope. His two novels are surely the beginning of a career, not the end. It cannot fail to be brilliant. M. Droz was in the Empire, but not of it.

Atlantic Monthly, August 1871

Alexandre Dumas

Alexandre Dumas, *Affaire Clémenceau: Mémoire de l'Accusé*. Paris: Michel Lévy, 1866.

M. ALEXANDRE DUMAS, THE YOUNGER, having established a reputation as one of the most ingenious of playwrights, and the most unflinching in his adherence to certain morbid social types, has now, at one stroke, affixed his name to the list of the greater French novelists. He had, indeed, written a number of clever stories; but in none of them was there discernible a claim to arrest the public attention. In the "Affaire Clémenceau" this claim is apparent from the first page to the last; or, in other words, the work bears signal marks of being, before all things, *serious*. It is for this reason that we feel justified in speaking of it.

The story is cast into the shape of a memorial, drawn up for the use of his advocate by a man under indictment for the murder of his wife. It proposes to relate the history of their connection and to trace out, step by step, every link in a long chain of provocation. It aims, in fact, at putting the lawyer— or, in other words, the reader—as nearly as possible in the position of the accused. It is not a piece of special pleading; it is a patient, intelligent statement of facts. It is not, indeed, a mere dry *catalogue raisonné* of incidents governed only by the spirit of chronology; for the hero is, on the face of the matter, a man of the deepest feeling and the richest understanding. Although the narrative confines itself to facts, these are dealt with in a fashion which of late days it has been agreed to call physiological. Metaphysics have been for some time turning to physiology; novels are following their example. The author concerns himself with motives and with causes, but his process is the reverse of transcendental. He bores his way so keenly and so successfully into the real, that one is tempted to fear that he will come out on the other side, as the French Revolution is said to have done with regard to liberty. In speaking of his book, it behooves the critic honestly to take note of the direction towards which he sets his face. It is evident from the outset that he will deal with things as they are; that he will speak without intellectual prudery and without bravado; that, having to tell a story containing ele-

275

ments the most painful and the most repulsive, he will pursue
the one course which may justify his choice: that of exhibiting
these elements in their integrity. To adopt such a course, so
considerately, so consciously, and yet with so little of that
aggressive dogmatism which would be sure to betray the
mixed intention of an inferior writer; to pursue it so steadily,
so relentlessly, and with so sincere and manful an intelligence
of the interests at stake; to do this is, in our opinion, to have
accomplished a great work, and to have come very near being
a great writer.

Pierre Clémenceau is the natural son of an industrious and
successful *lingère*. His misfortunes begin with his going to
school, where the circumstances of his birth make him an object of general obloquy. The sufferings of childhood have
formed the stock of the first volume of many an English
novel, but we do not remember to have read any account of
a school-boy's tribulations so natural in outline and so severely sober in color as the bald recital of young Clémenceau's
persecution. It has been said, and doubtless with justice, in
criticisms of this part of the book, that M. Dumas has fallen
quite beside the mark in localizing such a system of moral
reprobation in a Parisian school. Let us American readers,
then, take it home to ourselves; we shall not have translated
the book for nothing. On leaving school, Clémenceau evinces
a lively inclination for modelling in clay; some of his figures
are shown to a famous sculptor, who gives him hearty encouragement, and kindly consents to receive him as a pupil.
From this moment his worldly fortunes prosper. His vocation
is plain, he works hard, his talent obtains due recognition. He
is still a very young man, however, when he meets at a fancy-
dress party, given by a literary lady of the Bohemian order, a
singular couple, whose destinies are forthwith interwoven
with his own: a showy, middle-aged woman, dressed as Marie
de Médicis, and her little daughter, radiant with velvet and
childish loveliness, as her page. The child, worn out with late
hours, falls asleep in an arm-chair; while she sleeps, Clémenceau, with an artist's impulse, attempts to sketch her figure,
and, while he sketches, loses his heart. The child awakes, asks
to see the picture, and then asks to possess it. Clémenceau
promises to add a few touches at his leisure, and to bring it

to her the next morning. This whole scene has been aptly cited as an instance of the author's resolute devotion to the actual and the natural. Nothing could be less ideal, less pastoral, than the dawning of the hero's passion. No privacy, no solitude, no fresh air, no glimpse of nature; but, instead, a shabby-genteel masquerade on a rainy night, the odors of the *pot-au-feu*, an infant phenomenon, and a mamma in hired finery. The acquaintance thus begun soon becomes an intimacy. Madame Dobronowska is a Polish lady who has had misfortunes, and who is leading a hand-to-mouth existence in Paris, in anticipation of the brilliant future to which she regards her daughter's beauty as the key. There follows an elaborate picture of the household of these two ladies, of their mingled poverty and vanity, of the childish innocence and incipient coquetry of the daughter, of the magnificent visions and the plausible garrulity of the mother. Madame Dobronowska is an adventuress, more false and mercenary than the fancy can readily conceive, but gifted for the ruin of her victims with a certain strong perfume of frankness, motherliness, and *bonhomie*, which is the more fatal because it is partly natural. There is something equally pathetic and hideous in her jealous adoration of her child's beauty and her merely prudential vigilance. "Have you seen her hands?" she asks of Clémenceau, when he comes with his sketch. "Yes." "Look at them by daylight." "She raised her daughter's hand and showed me its truly remarkable transparency by flattening it, so to speak, against the light; and then, taking it between her own, she kissed it with a sort of frenzy, crying, *'Tu es belle ça!'* These words produced upon the child the effect of a cordial; the color came to her cheeks, she smiled, she had got back her strength." Clémenceau executes a bust of the young girl, and makes himself useful to the mother. Before many weeks, however, his friends leave Paris to seek their fortunes in Russia. For three years Clémenceau sees nothing more of them, although he occasionally receives a letter from Iza (the daughter) describing the vicissitudes of their career. Failing in her attempt to secure for her daughter the notice of the Crown Prince at St. Petersburg, Madame Dobronowska removes to Warsaw, and commences operations afresh. As time elapses, however, these operations prove to be of a nature detrimental to her daughter's honor; and Iza, horrified by her mother's machinations, which she is now of an age to comprehend, applies for assistance to Clémenceau, as her only friend. The young man replies by a declaration of love, which Iza receives with rapture, and forthwith makes her escape to Paris. She is now seventeen years old, and in the perfection of beauty; Clémenceau's mother is admitted into the secret, and they are married. For a long time their married life is without a cloud; but at last Iza becomes a mother, Madame Dobronowska arrives, a reconciliation takes place, Clémenceau's own mother wastes away from an inexplicable malady, and a number of his friends show signs of leaving him. Finally comes upon him like a thunder-clap the revelation of a long course of exorbitant infidelity on the part of his wife. The woman who has been for him the purest of mortals has long been, for all the world beside, a prodigy of impudicity. Clémenceau breaks with her on the spot, and takes the edge from his frenzy by fighting a duel with the last of her many lovers. He provides for the maintenance of his child, and suffers himself to be led to Rome by one of his friends. Here, in the study of the great monuments of art, he awaits the closing of the wound which has been inflicted upon his honor and upon the deepest passions of his soul. His better wishes, however, are not answered; day by day the desire for revenge, the fury of resentment, gathers instead of losing force. Hearing at last that, after a short term of seclusion, his wife has appeared before the world in a blaze of splendor, as the presumed mistress of a foreign potentate, he hastily returns to Paris and presents himself at the mansion occupied by Iza at the cost of her royal protector. She receives him with the cynical good nature of a soul utterly bereft of shame, and he stabs her to the heart.

Such is a rapid outline of M. Dumas's story. It traces the process of the fatal domination acquired by a base and ignoble soul over a lofty and generous one. No criticism can give an idea of the mingled delicacy and strength of the method by which we are made to witness the unfolding of the heroine's vicious instincts. There is in one of Balzac's novels a certain Valérie Marneffe, who may be qualified as the poetry of Thackeray's Becky Sharp. Iza Dobronowska is the poetry of

Valérie Marneffe. The principle of her being is an absolute delight in her own corporeal loveliness; this principle, taking active force, leads her into the excesses which arrest her career.

We are content to sum up the defects of the "Affaire Clémenceau" in the statement that its ultimate effect is to depress the reader's mind, to leave it with no better compensation for the patient endurance of so many horrors than a grave conviction of the writer's prodigious talent, and a certain vague, irritating suspicion that his own depression is even deeper than ours. In the way of compensation this is not enough. To be completely great, a work of art must lift up the reader's heart; and it is the artist's secret to reconcile this condition with images of the barest and sternest reality. Life is dispiriting, art is inspiring; and a story-teller who aims at anything more than a fleeting success has no right to tell an ugly story unless he knows its beautiful counterpart. The impression that he should aim to produce on the reader's mind with his work must have much in common with the impression originally produced on his own mind by his subject. If the effect of an efficient knowledge of his subject had been to fill his spirit with melancholy, and to paralyze his better feelings, it would be impossible that his work should be written. Its existence depends on the artist's reaction against the subject; and if the subject is morally hideous, of course this reaction will be in favor of moral beauty. The fault of M. Dumas's book, in our judgment, is not that such a reaction has not occurred in his own mind, or even that it has been slight, but that it is but faintly reflected in the constitution of the story. There is in the author's tone an unpleasant suggestion of cynicism. It may be, however, that there is but just enough to show us how seriously, how solemnly even, he has taken the miseries which he describes. There is enough, at any rate, to establish an essential difference between the "Affaire Clémenceau" and such a book as M. Edmond About's "Madelon." It may be, taking high ground, a fault that the former work is depressing; but is it not a greater fault that the latter, considering what it is, is amusing? The work before us thrills and interests the reader from beginning to end. It is hard to give it more liberal praise than to say that, in spite of all its crudities, all its audacities, his finer feelings are never for an instant in abeyance, and although, to our nervous Anglo-Saxon apprehensions, they may occasionally seem to be threatened, their interests are never actually superseded by those of his grosser ones. Since the taste of the age is for realism, all thanks for such realism as this. It fortifies and enlarges the mind; it disciplines the fancy. Since radicalism in literature is the order of the day, let us welcome a radicalism so intelligent and so logical. In a season of careless and flippant writing, and of universal literary laxity, there are few sensations more wholesome than to read a work so long considered and so severely executed as the present. From beginning to end there is not a word which is accidental, not a sentence which leaves the author's pen without his perfect assent and sympathy. He has driven in his stake at the end as well as at the beginning. Such writing is reading for men.

Nation, October 11, 1866

Octave Feuillet

Camors: or, Life Under the New Empire. From the French of M. Octave Feuillet. New York: Blelock & Co., 1868.

THIS LATEST NOVEL of M. Octave Feuillet is already a year old, but we take occasion, from the recent appearance of an American translation of the work, to offer a few English comments. Let us say, to begin with, that the translation is perfectly bad; that it is equally pretentious, vulgar, and incorrect; and that we recommend no reader who has the smallest acquaintance with the French tongue to resort to it either for entertainment or for edification. M. Octave Feuillet has been known in France for the past fifteen years as a superior writer of light works—tales, proverbs, and comedies. Those of his plays which have been acted are among the most successful of the modern French theatre, and on perusal, indeed, they exhibit a rare union of strength and elegance. A couple of years ago M. Feuillet was admitted—on the plea, we fancy, rather of his elegance than of his strength—to the French Academy. He has apparently wished to justify his election by the production of a masterpiece. In "M. de Camors" he has contributed another novel to the superior literature of his country.

One of the most interesting things about M. Feuillet's career, to our mind, is his steady improvement, or, rather, his growth, his progression. His early works treat almost wholly of fine ladies, and seem as if they were meant to be read by fine ladies—to be half-languidly perused in the depths of a satin arm-chair, between a Sèvres coffee-cup and the last number of *Le Follet*, with the corner of a velvet prayer-book peeping out beneath it. M. Feuillet has a natural delight in elegance—elegance even of the most artificial kind—and this "M. de Camors," the ripest fruit of his genius, with all its nervous strength and energy, is one of the most highly elegant novels we have ever read. But whereas, in his first literary essays, elegance was ever the presiding spirit, she is now relegated to the second rank, and gazes serenely over the shoulders of force. M. Feuillet has gradually enlarged his foundations and introduced into his scheme of society a number of those natural factors which we find in real life to play as large a part as the artificial and conventional. Not that he has not retained, however, all his primitive arts and graces; only, they have lost their excessive perfume, and are reduced to comparative insignificance by being worn abroad in the open air of the world. The long play of "Rédemption" was much better than his short ones; "Dalila" was better still; and "Montjoie" and "M. de Camors" are best of all. Nevertheless, we confess that there is not one of M. Feuillet's comedies and proverbs—"scenes," as he calls them—that we have not read with extreme delight and that we are not willing to read again. It must have been from the first an earnest of future power for the close observer that the author, in spite of the light and unsubstantial character of his materials and the superficial action of his mind, should yet be so excellent a master of dramatic form; but for this excellence—a thoroughly masculine quality—there might have been some truth in the charge that M. Feuillet was a feminine writer. But women assuredly have no turn for writing plays. A play is action, movement, decision; the female mind is contemplation, repose, suspense. In "M. de Camors" the author has simply redeemed the promise, liberally interpreted, of the strong dramatic instincts of "Le Village" and "Alix."

In this work M. Feuillet has attempted to draw a picture of what he calls "one of the most brilliant Parisian lives of our time." He has endeavored to pull off the veil of brilliancy, and to show us his hero in all the nakedness of his moral penury. He has wished to effect a contrast between that face of a man's destiny which he presents to the world and that far other face which meets the eyes of his own soul. He has contrived for this purpose a narrative so dramatic and interesting that we shall briefly repeat its main outline. M. de Camors is the only son of the Count de Camors, who on the threshold of old age finds himself utterly disenchanted with the world. Feeling that he has come to the end of all things, and that his soul is equally indifferent to pleasure and to profit, he indites a long, didactic letter to his son and blows out his brains. This letter—an extremely clever performance—is the profession of faith of an aristocratic cynic. It declares that there are no such things as virtue and vice, and that the sole rule of life is the pursuit of agreeable physical sensations and the maintenance of a perfect equanimity. To be absolutely and consistently selfish is to come as near as possible to being happy. Wealth is essential to comfort and women are useful for pleasure. Children are an unmitigated nuisance—which, by the way, is not very civil to the count presumptive. "To be loved by women," writes the count, "to be feared by men, to be as impassible as a god before the tears of the former and the blood of the latter, to end your life in a tempest—this is the destiny which I have failed to grasp and which I bequeath to you." To cast off all natural ties, instincts, affections, sympathies, as so many shackles on his liberty; to marry only for valid reasons of interest and on no account to have children or friends, to perfect his fencing, to keep his temper, never to cry, and to laugh a little—these are the final injunctions of M. de Camors to his son. They are in many ways cold and pedantic, but they are conceived and expressed with great ingenuity. The young Count de Camors receives his father's bequest as a sacred deposit, and the story relates his attempts to apply practically these select principles. While his father has been occupied in drawing up his last will, he has been engaged in an act of supreme *rouerie* in the house of an intimate friend. So happy a start in the career of egotism is not to be thrown away, and M. de Camors says amen to the voice from beyond the grave. He forthwith prepares to enter political life and, betaking himself with this view to a small estate in the country, presents himself as candidate for the Chamber of Deputies. In this region he meets two women—the heroines of the tale. The younger, his cousin, a poor girl in a servile position, and a great beauty, appeals to the reader's interest from the first by offering her hand in marriage to M. de Camors—an overture which he feels compelled to arrest. The young lady subsequently makes a splendid match with an old general of immense wealth. The second of M. de Camors' female friends is Mme. de Tècle, a young widow, a charming woman and an admirably-finished portrait. M. de Camors wins the love of Mme. de Tècle and returns it, but is unable, for good reasons, to obtain her hand, which he is not yet sufficient master of his emotions to abstain from soliciting. Mme. de Tècle, to whom virtue is comparatively easy, determines to stifle her passion, or at least to keep it smouldering, by means of a very odd and ingenious device. She offers to bring up her little daughter as the wife of M. de Camors, who in eight years' time, when the girl has arrived at maturity, will have reached the marrying age of a man of his society. This idea and the scene in which Mme. de Tècle unfolds it are, as we say, ingenious; delicate also, and almost poetical; but strike us as unreal, unnatural, and morbid. M. de Camors is by no means enchanted by his friend's proposition; he assents coldly and vaguely and takes his departure, thanking his stars, after all, that Mme. de Tècle had the wit to refuse him.

He becomes engaged in political life and lays the foundation of a large fortune by industrial manœuvres. He works hard, keeps his terms with elegant dissipation, and cherishes the cold precepts of his father. After a lapse of three or four years he renews his relations with his beautiful cousin, now Mme. de Campvallar, but in so depraved (although so dramatic) a fashion that we need not enter into particulars. Mme. de Campvallar is by nature, and with a splendid feminine insolence and grace, just such an audacious and heartless soul as M. de Camors has well-nigh become by culture. The two unite their sympathies, their passions, and their lives. Finally, however, their intrigue is on the point of being discovered by the husband of Mme. de Campvallar—a *naïf* and honest old warrior, the soul of purity and honor, who esteems with an almost equal warmth his wife and his wife's lover—and an exposure is averted only by the tact and presence of mind of the impenitent marquise. Her husband is concealed and listening: Camors is expected. A motive for their meeting must be improvised within the minute, and a full intelligence of the situation flashed from her eyes into those of her lover. The latter arrives radiant. The pretext is ready. Mme. de Campvallar has sworn that she will not let M. de Camors depart until he has promised to marry—whom?—Mlle. de Tècle. In this way the prayers of Mme. de Tècle are fulfilled, and a third heroine is introduced—a third, and the most charming of all. The scene just indicated is in a dramatic sense, we may add, extremely effective; and if M. Feuillet ever converts his novel into a play (as it is the fashion to do in France), here is a situation made to his hand, strong enough, by itself, to ensure the success of the piece, and admirably fitted to exhibit good

acting. M. de Camors, then, marries Mlle. de Tècle and loves
Mme. de Campvallar. This is well enough for the latter lady;
but the other (who has a passionate childish admiration of
her rival) speedily discovers the facts of the matter, and signally fails to reconcile herself to them. M. de Campvallar,
whose suspicions, once dispelled, have begun once more to
congregate, eventually encounters the most damning confirmation of their truth, and expires under the hideous shock.
Mme. de Camors and her mother, more and more alienated
from the count, and infected with the most painful impressions touching his relations to the death of M. de Campvallar,
no longer conceal their open horror of his character. M. de
Camors, on his own side, weary of his mistress, writhing under the scorn of his wife, whose merits he has learned to appreciate, sick of the world and of his own life, dies, without
remorse and without hope.

The reader may perceive nothing in this sad story, as we
have told it, to justify us in deeming it worthy of repetition;
but it is certain that, told by M. Feuillet with all the energy
of his great talent, it makes a very interesting tale. The author,
indeed, has aimed at making it something more—at writing
a work with a high moral bearing. In this we think he has
signally failed. To stir the reader's moral nature, and to write
with truth and eloquence the moral history of superior men
and women, demand more freedom and generosity of mind
than M. Feuillet seems to us to possess. Like those of most
of the best French romancers, his works wear, morally, to
American eyes, a decidedly thin and superficial look. Men and
women, in our conception, are deeper, more substantial,
more self-directing; they have, if not more virtue, at least
more conscience; and when conscience comes into the game
human history ceases to be a perfectly simple tale. M. Feuillet
is not in the smallest degree a moralist, and, as a logical consequence, M. de Camors is a most unreal and unsubstantial
character. He is at the best a well appointed fop—what the
French call a *poseur*. The lesson of his life is that you cannot
really prosper without principles, and that although the strict
observance of "honor"—the only principle which M. de Camors recognizes—is a very fine thing in its way, there are
sore straits in life from which the only issue is (M. Feuillet

would say) through the portals of the Church; or, in other words, that our lives are in our own hands, and that religion is essential to happiness. This is, doubtless, very true; but somehow it is none the truer for M. Feuillet's story. To be happy, M. de Camors apparently needed only to strike a becoming attitude. When M. de Campvallar discovers him in the small hours of the night in his wife's apartment and marches on him furious, he remembers to fold his arms. Another man might have done it instinctively; but we may be sure that M. de Camors did it consciously. And so with Mme. de Campvallar. She is essentially cold, artificial, and mechanical. She is pedantically vicious. For these reasons and many others; from our inability to sympathize either with the delusions or the mortifications of his hero, M. Feuillet's book strikes us simply, as a novel, like any other. Its chief merit, we think, lies in the portraits of Mme. de Tècle and her daughter. Here, too, the author is superficial; but here, at least, he is charming. The virtues—the virtue, we may say, of these two ladies is above all things elegant, but it has a touch of the breadth and depth of nature. The work as a whole is cold and light; but it is neither vulgar nor trivial, and would amply repay perusal if only as a model of neat, compact, and elaborate dramatic writing.

Nation, July 30, 1868

Les Amours de Philippe. Par Octave Feuillet. Paris: Calmann Lévy; New York: F. W. Christern, 1877.

M. OCTAVE FEUILLET'S new novel reaches an eighth edition within a few weeks of its appearance; and this circumstance, combined with the reputation of the author, may fairly be held to indicate that it is worth reading. M. Feuillet usually lays his hand upon an interesting fable, and his execution is always extremely neat and artistic. His defect is a too obvious desire to be what we call in English a "fashionable" novelist. He relates exclusively the joys and sorrows of the aristocracy; the loves of marquises and countesses alone appear worthy of his attention, and heroes and heroines can hope to make no figure in his pages unless they have an extraordinary number of quarterings. But there are few storytellers of our day who know how to tell their story better than M. Octave Feuillet, though we must add that it may sometimes be a question whether his story was worth telling. This one is about a young man of very ancient lineage, who is predestined by his family to a union with a young girl of a proportionate pedigree. The young girl is his cousin; he is brought up side by side with her, and, knowing that she expects to be his wife, he conceives a violent aversion to her. This rebellious sentiment is so strong that when he comes of age he declares he will never look at her again, and departs for Paris, greatly to the distress of his aristocratic father. In Paris he takes a fancy to turn playwright, and manufactures an heroic drama, with a part especially intended for a brilliant and celebrated young actress with whom he has fallen violently in love. In the portrait of Mary Gerald M. Feuillet has evidently meant to suggest the figure of an actual artist, about whom "legend" has clustered thickly—Mlle. Sarah Bernhardt—but the image is rather vague; it lacks detail, and we should have advised the author either not to go so far or to go further. Philippe, however, goes very far in the company of his young actress. She takes a fancy to his play and to his person, and, staking everything upon the success of his drama, he mortgages his financial future on her behalf. The drama proves a colossal failure, and Mary Gerald ceases to care for a lover who has been hissed.

Philippe has a cruel awakening, but the war of 1870 breaks out in time to distract his attention. He serves in it gallantly, and on the return of peace falls in love with Mme. de Talyas, the wife of an intimate friend. This lady is a fiend incarnate and a monster of corruption, but she has charms which are so highly appreciated by Philippe that he becomes her reluctant but abject slave. Mme. de Talyas is very cleverly described by M. Feuillet, who in the portraiture of diabolical fine ladies has a very skilful touch and a very practised hand. Meanwhile Philippe's cousin and intended, the amiable Jeanne de la Roche-Ermel, is pining away at the château, deeply attached to the young man, and sorrowing over the *spretæ injuria formæ*. Mme. de Talyas has learned from Philippe that his marriage with her has been the dream of both their families, but that he has a positive repugnance to the young girl. The moment comes when she commands him, in these circumstances, to pretend to have reconciled himself to the project, in order to throw dust into the eyes of her husband. He obeys her, and the result of his obedience is that, weary of Mme. de Talyas, and disgusted at the dishonorable part he is playing, both as regards his friend, her husband, and as regards Jeanne, he falls honestly and earnestly in love with Mlle. de la Roche-Ermel. Caught in her own trap, the unscrupulous Mme. de Talyas tries first to stop the marriage, and then to bring about the death of Jeanne. At the moment when she has almost succeeded in the latter attempt Philippe comes on the scene, and seeing his fiancée in a very bad way (her rival, having invited her out to walk, has tried to push her into a lake), demands an explanation. Jeanne looks at Mme. de Talyas for a moment, and then utters one of those magnanimous fibs in which, from Victor Hugo down, French romancers delight. She says that she has by her own awkwardness slipped into the water, and that Madame has tried to save her. Madame, overwhelmed and humiliated by such generosity, retires, leaving the coast clear.

Such are the loves of Philippe, which, if they are not very pretty, are very prettily told. The faults of the tale are a certain disjointedness, the want of connection between the episode of Mary Gerald and that of Mme. de Talyas, and the very unsubstantial and inestimable character of the hero. The author tells us that he looked like one of the *mignons* of the court of the Valois king; and he really is hardly less contemptible. But French novelists are always addicted to making their heroes too unscrupulous first and too comfortable afterwards.

Gustave Flaubert

La Tentation de Saint Antoine. Par Gustave Flaubert. Paris: Charpentier; New York: F. W. Christern, 1874.

SAINT ANTHONY, as most readers know, was an Egyptian monk who, toward the end of the third century, hid himself in the desert to pray, and was visited by a series of hallucinations painfully irrelevant to this occupation. His visions and his stout resistance to them have long been famous—so famous that here is M. Gustave Flaubert, fifteen hundred years afterwards, publishing a large octavo about them, and undertaking to describe them in every particular. This volume, we confess, has been a surprise to us. Announced for publication three or four years ago, it seemed likely to be a novel of that realistic type which the author had already vigorously cultivated, with Saint Anthony and his temptation standing simply as a symbol of the argument. We opened it with the belief that we were to find, not a ragged old cenobite struggling to preserve his virtue amid Egyptian sands, but a portrait of one of the author's own contemporaries and fellow-citizens engaged in this enterprise in the heart of the French capital. M. Flaubert's strong side has not been hitherto the portrayal of resistance to temptation, and we were much in doubt as to whether the dénouement of the novel was to correspond to that of the legend; but it was very certain that, whatever the upshot, the temptation itself would be elaborately represented. So, in fact, it has been; but it is that of the dim-featured founder of monasticism, and not of a gentleman beset by our modern importunities. The work has the form of a long monologue by the distracted saint, interrupted by voluminous pictorial representations of his visions and by his imagined colloquies with the creatures who people them. We may frankly say that it strikes us as a ponderous failure; but it is an interesting failure as well, and it suggests a number of profitable reflections.

In so far as these concern M. Gustave Flaubert himself, they are decidedly melancholy. Many American readers probably have followed his career, and will readily recall it as an extraordinary example of a writer outliving his genius. There have been poets and novelists in abundance who are people of a single work, who have had their one hour of inspiration, and gracefully accept the certainty that it would never strike again. There are other careers in which a great success has been followed by a period of inoffensive mediocrity, and, if not confirmed, at least not flagrantly discredited. But we imagine there are few writers who have been at such extraordinary pains as M. Flaubert to undermine an apparently substantial triumph. Some fifteen years ago he published 'Madame Bovary,' a novel which, if it cannot be said exactly to have taken its place in the "standard literature" of his country, must yet have fixed itself in the memory of most readers as a revelation of what the imagination may accomplish under a powerful impulse to mirror the unmitigated realities of life. 'Madame Bovary,' we confess, has always seemed to us a great work, and capable really of being applied to educational purposes. It is an elaborate picture of vice, but it represents it as so indefeasibly commingled with misery that in a really enlightened system of education it would form exactly the volume to put into the hands of young persons in whom vicious tendencies had been distinctly perceived, and who were wavering as to which way they should let the balance fall.

The facts in 'Madame Bovary' were elaborate marvels of description, but they were also, by good luck, extremely interesting in themselves, whereas the facts in 'Salammbô,' in 'L'Education Sentimentale,' and in the performance before us, appeal so very meagrely to our sympathy that they completely fail in their appeal to our credulity. And yet we would not for the world have had M. Flaubert's novels unwritten. Lying there before us so unmistakably still-born, they are a capital refutation of the very dogma in defence of which they appeared. The fatal charmlessness of each and all of them is an eloquent plea for the ideal. M. Flaubert's peculiar talent is the description—minute, incisive, exhaustive—of material objects, and it must be admitted that he has carried it very far. He succeeds wonderfully well in making an image, in finding and combining just the words in which the *look* of his object resides. The scenery and properties in his dramas are made for the occasion; they have not served in other pieces. "The sky [in St. Anthony's landscape] is red, the earth completely black; under the gusts of wind the sand-drifts rise up like shrouds and then fall down. In a gap, suddenly, pass a flight of birds in a triangular battalion, like a piece of metal, trembling only on the edges." This is a specimen, taken at random, of the author's constant appeal to observation; he would claim, doubtless, for his works that they are an unbroken tissue of observations, that this is their chief merit, and that nothing is further from his pretension than to conclude to philosophize or to moralize. He proceeds upon the assumption that these innumerable marvels of observation will hold together without the underlying moral unity of what is called a "purpose," and that the reader will proceed eagerly from point to point, stopping just sufficiently short of complete hallucination to remember the author's cleverness.

The reader has, at least, in 'La Tentation de Saint Antoine,' the satisfaction of expecting a subject combining with a good deal of chance for color a high moral interest. M. Flaubert describes, from beginning to end, the whole series of the poor hermit's visions; the undertaking implies no small imaginative energy. In one sense, it has been bravely carried out; it swarms with ingenious, audacious, and erudite detail, and leaves nothing to be desired in the way of completeness. There is generally supposed to be a certain vagueness about visions; they are things of ambiguous shapes and misty edges. But vagueness of portrayal has never been our author's failing, and St. Anthony's hallucinations under his hands become a gallery of photographs, executed with the aid of the latest improvements in the art. He is visited successively by all the religions, idolatries, superstitions, rites and ceremonies, priests and potentates, of the early world—by Nebuchadnezzar and the Queen of Sheba, the Emperor Constantine and the Pope Calixtus, the swarm of the early Christian fanatics, martyrs, and philosophers—Origen, Tertullian, Arius, Hermogenes, Ebionites and Encratites, Theodotians and Marcosians, by Helen of Troy and Apollonius of Rhodes, by the Buddha in person, by the Devil in person, by Ormuzd and Ahriman, by Diana of the Ephesians, by Cybele, Atys, Isis, by the whole company of the gods of Greece and by Venus in particular, by certain unnamable Latin deities, whom M. Flaubert not only names but dramatizes, by the figures of Luxury and Death, by the Sphinx and the Chimæra, by the Pigmies and the Cynocephali, by the "Sadhuzag" and the unicorn, by all the beasts of the sea, and finally by Jesus Christ. We are not precisely given to understand how much time is supposed to roll over the head of the distracted anchorite while these heterogeneous images are passing before him, but, in spite of the fact that he generally swoons away in the *entr'acte*, as it were, we receive an impression that he is getting a good deal at one sitting, and that the toughest part of his famous struggle came off on a single night. To the reader who is denied the occasional refreshment of a swoon, we recommend taking up the book at considerable intervals. Some of the figures in our list are minutely described, others are briefly sketched, but all have something to say. We fancy that both as a piece of description and a piece of dramatization M. Flaubert is especially satisfied with his Queen of Sheba:

"Her dress, in golden brocade, divided regularly by furbelows of pearls, of jet, and of sapphire, compresses her waist into a narrow boddice, ornamented with applied pieces in color representing the twelve signs of the zodiac. She wears very high skates, of which one is black and spangled with silver stars, with the crescent of the moon, while the other is white, and covered with little drops in gold, with the sun in the middle. Her wide sleeves, covered with emeralds and with the feathers of birds, expose the nakedness of her little round arm, ornamented at the wrist by a bracelet of ebony; and her hands, laden with rings, terminate in nails so pointed that the ends of her fingers look almost like needles. A flat gold chain, passing under her chin, ascends beside her cheeks, rolls in a spiral around her hair, which is powdered with blue powder, then, falling, grazes her shoulder and comes and fastens itself on her bosom in a scorpion in diamonds, which thrusts out its tongue between her breasts. Two great blood pearls drag down her ears. The edges of her eyelids are painted black. She has on her left cheek-bone a natural brown mole, and she breathes, opening her mouth, as if her boddice hurt her. She shakes, as she walks, a green parasol surrounded with gilt bells, and twelve little woolly-headed negroes carry the long train of her dress, held at the end by a monkey, who occasionally lifts it up. She says: '*Ah, bel ermite, bel ermite! mon cœur défaille!*' "

This is certainly a "realistic" Queen of Sheba, and Nebuchadnezzar is almost equally so. Going on from figure to figure and scene to scene in this bewildering panorama, we ask ourselves exactly what it is that M. Flaubert has proposed to accomplish. Not a prose-poem from the saint's own moral point of view, with his spiritual sufferings and vagaries for its episode, and his ultimate expulsion of all profane emotions for its dénouement; for St. Anthony throughout remains the dimmest of shadows, and his commentary upon his hallucination is meagre and desultory. Not, on the other hand, a properly historical presentment of the various types he evokes, for fancy is called in at every turn to supplement the scanty testimony of history. What is M. Flaubert's historic evidence for the mole on the Queen of Sheba's cheek and the blue powder in her hair? He has simply wished to be tremendously pictorial, and the opportunity for spiritual analysis has been the last thing in his thoughts. It is matter of regret that a writer with the pluck and energy to grapple with so pregnant a theme should have been so indifferent to its most characteristic side. It is probable that, after M. Flaubert's big volume, we shall not have, in literature, for a long time, any more 'Temptations of St. Anthony'; and yet there is obviously a virtue in the subject which has by no means been exhausted. Tremendously pictorial M. Flaubert has certainly succeeded in being, and we stand amazed at his indefatigable ingenuity. He has accumulated a mass of curious learning; he has interfused it with a mass of still more curious conjecture; and he has resolved the whole into a series of pictures which, considering the want of models and precedents, may be said to be very handsomely executed. But what, the reader wonders, has been his inspiration, his motive, his *souffle*, as the French say? Of any abundant degree of imagination we perceive little in the work. Here and there we find a touch of something like poetry, as in the scene of the Christian martyrs huddled in one of the vaults of the circus, and watching through the bars of the opposite vault the lions and tigers to whom they are about to be introduced. Here and there is a happy dramatic turn in the talk of the hermit's visionary interlocutor or a vague approach to a "situation" in the attitude of the saint. But for the most part M. Flaubert's picturesque is a strangely artificial and cold-blooded picturesque—abounding in the grotesque and the repulsive, the abnormal and the barely conceivable, but seeming to have attained to it all by infinite labor, ingenuity, and research—never by one of the fine intuitions of a joyous and generous invention. It is all hard, inanimate, superficial, and inexpressibly disagreeable. When the author has a really beautiful point to treat—as the assembly of the Greek deities fading and paling away in the light of Christianity—he becomes singularly commonplace and ineffective.

His book being, with its great effort and its strangely absent charm, the really painful failure it seems to us, it would not have been worth while to call attention to it if it were not that it pointed to more things than the author's own deficiencies. It seems to us to throw a tolerably vivid light on the present condition of the French literary intellect. M. Flaubert and his contemporaries have pushed so far the education of the senses and the cultivation of the grotesque in literature and the arts that it has left them morally stranded and helpless. In the perception of the materially curious, in fantastic refinement of taste and marked ingenuity of expression, they seem to us now to have reached the limits of the possible. Behind M. Flaubert stands a whole society of æsthetic *raffinés*, demanding stronger and stronger spices in its intellectual diet. But we doubt whether he or any of his companions can permanently satisfy their public, for the simple reason that the human mind, even in indifferent health, does after all need to be *nourished*, and thrives but scantily on a regimen of pigments and sauces. It needs sooner or later—to prolong our metaphor—to detect a body-flavor, and we shall be very much surprised if it ever detects one in 'La Tentation de Saint Antoine.'

Nation, June 4, 1874

Correspondance de Gustave Flaubert. Quatrième Série. Paris, 1893.

IN THE YEAR 1877 Gustave Flaubert wrote to a friend: "You speak of Balzac's letters. I read them when they appeared, but with very little enthusiasm. The man gains from them, but not the artist. He was too much taken up with business. You never meet a general idea, a sign of his caring for anything beyond his material interests. . . . What a lamentable life!" At the time the volumes appeared (the year before) he had written to Edmond de Goncourt: "What a preoccupation with money and how little love of art! Have you noticed that he never *once* speaks of it? He strove for glory, but not for beauty."

The reader of Flaubert's own correspondence, lately given to the world by his niece, Madame Commanville, and which, in the fourth volume, is brought to the eve of his death—the student of so much vivid and violent testimony to an intensely exclusive passion is moved to quote these words for the sake of contrast. It will not be said of the writer that he himself never once speaks of art; it will be said of him with a near approach to truth that he almost never once speaks of anything else. The effect of contrast is indeed strong everywhere in this singular publication, from which Flaubert's memory receives an assault likely to deepen the air of felicity missed that would seem destined henceforth to hang over his personal life. "May I be skinned alive," he writes in 1854, "before I ever turn my private feelings to literary account." His constant refrain in his letters is the impersonality, as he calls it, of the artist, whose work should consist exclusively of his subject and his style, without an emotion, an idiosyncrasy that is not utterly transmuted. Quotation does but scanty justice to his rage for this idea; almost all his feelings were such a rage that we wonder what form they would have borrowed from a prevision of such posthumous betrayal. "It's one of my principles that one must never write down *one's self*. The artist must be present in his work like God in creation, invisible and almighty, everywhere felt, but nowhere seen." Such was the part he allotted to form, to that rounded detachment which enables the perfect work to live by its own life, that he regarded as indecent and dishonorable the production of any impression that was not intensely calculated. "Feelings" were necessarily crude, because they were inevitably unselected, and selection (for the picture's sake) was Flaubert's highest morality.

This principle has been absent from the counsels of the editor of his letters, which have been given to the world, so far as they were procurable, without attenuation and without scruple. There are many, of course, that circumstances have rendered inaccessible, but in spite of visible gaps the revelation is full enough and remarkable enough. These communications would, of course, not have been matter for Flaubert's highest literary conscience; but the fact remains that in our merciless age ineluctable fate has overtaken the man in the world whom we most imagine gnashing his teeth under it. His ideal of dignity, of honor and renown, was that nothing should be known of him but that he had been an impeccable writer. "I feel all the same," he wrote in 1852, "that I shall not die before I've set a-roaring somewhere (*sans avoir fait rugir quelque part*) such a style as hums in my head, and which may very well overpower the sound of the parrots and grasshoppers." This is a grievous accident for one who could write that "the worship of art contributes to pride, and of pride one has never too much." Sedentary, cloistered, passionate, cynical, tormented in his love of magnificent expression, of subjects remote and arduous, with an unattainable ideal, he kept clear all his life of vulgarity and publicity and newspaperism only to be dragged after death into the middle of the marketplace, where the electric light beats fiercest. Madame Commanville's publication hands him over to the Philistines with every weakness exposed, every mystery dispelled, every secret betrayed. Almost the whole of her second volume, to say nothing of a large part of her first, consists of his love-letters to the only woman he appears to have addressed in the accents of passion. His private style, moreover, was as unchastened as his final form was faultless. The result happens to be deeply interesting to the student of the famous "artistic temperament"; it can scarcely be so for a reader less predisposed, I think, for Flaubert was a writers' writer as much as Shelley was a "poets' poet"; but we may ask ourselves if the time has not come when it may well cease to be a leading feature of our homage to a distinguished man that we shall sacrifice him with sanguinary rites on the altar of our curiosity. Flaubert's letters, indeed, bring up with singular intensity the whole question of the rights and duties, the decencies and discretions of the insurmountable desire to *know*. To lay down a general code is perhaps as yet impossible, for there is no doubt that to know is good, or to want to know, at any rate, supremely natural. Some day or other surely we shall all agree that everything is relative, that facts themselves are often falsifying, and that we pay more for some kinds of knowledge than those particular kinds are worth. Then we shall perhaps be sorry to have had it drummed into us that the author of calm, firm masterpieces, of "Madame Bovary," of "Salammbô," of "Saint-Julien l'Hospitalier," was narrow and noisy, and had not personally and morally, as it were, the great dignity of his literary ideal.

When such revelations are made, however, they are made, and the generous attitude is doubtless at that stage to catch them in sensitive hands. Poor Flaubert has been turned inside out for the lesson, but it has been given to him to constitute practically—on the demonstrator's table with an attentive circle round—an extraordinary, a magnificent "case." Never certainly in literature was the distinctively literary idea, the fury of execution, more passionately and visibly manifested. This rare visibility is probably the excuse that the responsible hand will point to. The letters enable us to note it, to follow it from phase to phase, from one wild attitude to another, through all the contortions and objurgations, all the exaltations and despairs, tensions and collapses, the mingled pieties and profanities of Flaubert's simplified yet intemperate life. Their great interest is that they exhibit an extraordinary singleness of aim, show us the artist not only disinterested, but absolutely dishumanized. They help us to perceive what Flaubert missed almost more than what he gained, and if there are many questions in regard to such a point of view that they certainly fail to settle, they at least cause us to turn them over as we have seldom turned them before. It was the lifelong discomfort of this particular fanatic, but it is our own extreme advantage, that he was almost insanely excessive. "In literature," he wrote in 1861, "the best chance one has is by following out one's temperament and exaggerating it." His own he could scarcely exaggerate; but it carried him so far that we seem to see on distant heights his agitations outlined against the sky. "Impersonal" as he wished his work to be, it was his strange fortune to be the most expressive, the most vociferous, the most spontaneous of men. The record of his temperament is therefore complete, and if his ambiguities make the illuminating word difficult to utter, it is not because the picture is colorless.

Why was such a passion, in proportion to its strength, after all so sterile? There is life, there is blood in a considerable measure in "Madame Bovary," but the last word about its successors can only be, it seems to me, that they are splendidly and infinitely curious. Why may, why *must*, indeed, in certain cases, the effort of expression spend itself, and spend itself in success, without completing the circle, without coming round again to the joy of evocation? How can art be so genuine and yet so unconsoled, so unhumorous, so unsociable? When it is a religion, and therefore an authority, why should it not be, like other authorities, a guarantee? How can it be such a curse without being also a blessing? What germ of treachery lurks in it to make it, not necessarily, but so easily that there is but a hair-line to cross, delusive for personal happiness? Why, in short, when the struggle is success, should the success not be at last serenity? These mysteries and many others pass before us as we listen to Flaubert's loud plaint, which is precisely the profit we derive from his not having, with his correspondents, struck, like Balzac, only the commercial note. Nothing in his agitated and limited life, which began at Rouen in 1821, is more striking than the prompt, straightforward way his destiny picked him out and his conscience handed him over. As most young men have to contend with some domestic disapproval of the muse, so this one had rather to hang back on the easy incline and to turn away his face from the formidable omens. It was only too evident that he would be free to break his heart, to *gueuler*, as he fondly calls it, to spout, to mouth and thresh about, to that heart's content. No career was ever more taken for granted in its intensity, nor any series of tribulations more confidently invited. It was recognized from the first that the tall and splendid youth, green-eyed and sonorous (his stature and aspect were distinguished), was born to *gueuler*, and especially his own large cadences.

His father, a distinguished surgeon, who died early, had purchased near Rouen, on the Seine, the small but picturesque property of Croisset; and it was in a large five-windowed corner room of this quiet old house, his study for forty years, that his life was virtually spent. It was marked by two great events: his journey to the East and return through the south of Europe with Maxime du Camp in 1849, and the publication of "Madame Bovary" (followed by a train of consequences) in 1857. He made a second long journey (to Algeria, Tunis, and the site of Carthage) while engaged in writing "Salammbô"; he had before his father's death taken part in a scanted family pilgrimage to the north of Italy, and he appears once to have spent a few weeks on the Righi, and at another time a few days in London, an episode, oddly enough, of which there is but the faintest, scarcely a recognizable echo in his correspondence. For the rest, and save for an occasional interlarding of Paris, his years were spent at his patient table in the room by the rural Seine. If success in life (and it is the definition open perhaps to fewest objections) consists of achieving in maturity the dreams of one's prime, Flaubert's measure may be said to have been full. M. Maxime du Camp, in those two curious volumes of "Impressions Littéraires," which in 1882 treated a surprised world and a scandalized circle to the physiological explanation of his old friend's idiosyncrasies, declares that exactly as that friend was with intensity at the beginning, so was he with intensity in the middle and at the end, and that no life was ever simpler or straighter in the sense of being a case of growth without change. Doubtful, indeed, were the urgency of M. du Camp's revelation and the apparent validity of his evidence; but whether or no Flaubert was an epileptic subject, and whether or no there was danger in our unconsciousness of the question (danger to any one but M. Maxime du Camp), the impression of the reader of the letters is in complete conformity with the pronouncement to which I allude. The Flaubert of fifty differs from the Flaubert of twenty only in size. The difference between "Bouvard et Pécuchet" and "Madame

Bovary" is not a difference of spirit; and it is a proof of the author's essential continuity that his first published work, appearing when he had touched middle life and on which his reputation mainly rests, had been planned as long in advance as if it had been a new religion.

"Madame Bovary" was five years in the writing, and the "Tentation de Saint-Antoine," which saw the light in 1874, but the consummation of an idea entertained in his boyhood. "Bouvard et Pécuchet," the intended epos of the blatancy, the comprehensive *bêtise*, of mankind, was in like manner the working-out at the end of his days of his earliest generalization. It had literally been his life-long dream to crown his career with a panorama of human ineptitude. Everything in his literary life had been planned and plotted and prepared. One moves in it through an atmosphere of the darkest, though the most innocent, conspiracy. He was perpetually laying a train, a train of which the inflammable substance was "style." His great originality was that the long siege of his youth was successful. I can recall no second case in which poetic justice has interfered so gracefully. He began "Madame Bovary" from afar off, not as an amusement or a profit or a clever novel or even a work of art or a *morceau de vie*, as his successors say to-day, not even, either, as the best thing he could make it; but as a premeditated classic, a masterpiece pure and simple, a thing of conscious perfection and a contribution of the first magnitude to the literature of his country. There would have been every congruity in his encountering proportionate failure and the full face of that irony in things of which he was so inveterate a student. A writer of tales who should have taken the extravagance of his design for the subject of a sad "novelette" could never have permitted himself any termination of such a story but an effective anticlimax. The masterpiece at the end of years would inevitably fall very flat and the overweening spirit be left somehow to its illusions. The solution, in fact, was very different, and as Flaubert had deliberately sown, so exactly and magnificently did he reap. The perfection of "Madame Bovary" is one of the commonplaces of criticism, the position of it one of the highest a man of letters dare dream of, the possession of it one of the glories of France. No calculation was ever better fulfilled,

nor any train more successfully laid. It is a sign of the indefeasible bitterness to which Flaubert's temperament condemned him and the expression of which, so oddly, is yet as
obstreperous and boyish as that of the happiness arising from
animal spirits—it is a mark of his amusing pessimism that so
honorable a first step should not have done more to reconcile
him to life. But he was a creature of transcendent dreams and
unfathomable perversities of taste, and it was in his nature to
be more conscious of one broken spring in the couch of fame,
more wounded by a pin-prick, more worried by an assonance,
than he could ever be warmed or pacified from within. Literature and life were a single business to him, and the "torment of style," that might occasionally intermit in one place,
was sufficiently sure to break out in another. We may polish
our periods till they shine again, but over the style of life our
control is necessarily more limited.

To such limitations Flaubert resigned himself with the
worst possible grace. He polished ferociously, but there was
a side of the matter that his process could never touch. Some
other process might have been of use; some patience more
organized, some formula more elastic, or simply perhaps
some happier trick of good-humor; at the same time it must
be admitted that in his deepening vision of the imbecility of
the world any remedy would have deprived him of his prime,
or rather of his sole, amusement. The *bêtise* of mankind was
a colossal comedy, calling aloud to heaven for an Aristophanes to match, and Flaubert's nearest approach to joy was in
noting the opportunities of such an observer and feeling
within himself the stirrings of such a genius. Towards the end
he found himself vibrating at every turn to this ideal, and if
he knew to the full the tribulation of proper speech no one
ever suffered less from that of proper silence. He broke it in
his letters, on a thousand queer occasions, with all the luxury
of relief. He was blessed with a series of correspondents with
whom he was free to leave nothing unsaid; many of them
ladies, too, so that he had in their company all the inspiration
of gallantry without its incidental sacrifices. The most interesting of his letters are those addressed between 1866 and 1876
to Madame George Sand, which, originally collected in 1884,
have been re-embodied in Madame Commanville's publica-

tion. They are more interesting than ever when read, as we are now able to read them, in connection with Madame Sand's equally personal and much more luminous answers, accessible in the fifth and sixth volumes of her own copious and strikingly honorable "Correspondance." No opposition could have been more of a nature to keep the ball rolling than that of the parties to this candid commerce, who were as united by affection and by common interests as they were divided by temper and their way of feeling about those interests. Living, each of them, for literature (though Madame Sand, in spite of her immense production, very much less exclusively for it than her independent and fastidious friend), their comparison of most of the impressions connected with it could yet only be a lively contrast of temperaments. Flaubert, whose bark indeed (it is the rule) was much worse than his bite, spent his life, especially the later part of it, in a state of acute exasperation; but her unalterable serenity was one of the few irritants that were tolerable to him.

Their letters are a striking lesson in the difference between good humor and bad, and seem to point the moral that either form has only to be cultivated to become our particular kind of intelligence. They compared conditions, at any rate, her expansion with his hard contraction, and he had the advantage of finding in a person who had sought wisdom in ways so many and so devious one of the few objects within his ken that really represented virtue and that he could respect. It gives us the pattern of his experience that Madame Sand should have stood to him for so much of the ideal, and we may say this even under the impression produced by a reperusal of her total correspondence, a monument to her generosity and variety. Poor Flaubert appears to us to-day almost exactly by so much less frustrated as he was beguiled by this happy relation, the largest he ever knew. His interlocutress, who in the evening of an arduous life accepted refreshment wherever she found it and who could still give as freely as she took, for immemorial habit had only added to each faculty, his correspondent, for all her love of well-earned peace, offered her breast to his aggressive pessimism; had motherly, reasoning, coaxing hands for it; made, in short, such sacrifices that she often came to Paris to go to brawling Magny dinners to meet him and wear, to please him, as I have heard one of the diners say, unaccustomed peach-blossom dresses. It contributes to our sense of what there was lovable at the core of his effort to select and his need to execrate that he should have been able to read and enjoy so freely a writer so fluid; and it also reminds us that imagination is, after all, for the heart, the safest quality. Flaubert had excellent honest inconsistencies, crude lapses from purity in which he could like the books of his friends. He was susceptible of painless amusement (a rare emotion with him) when his imagination was touched, as it was infallibly and powerfully, by affection. To make a hard rule never to be corrupted, and then to make a special exception for fondness, is of course the right attitude.

He had several admirations, and it might always be said of him that he would have admired if he could, for he could like a thing if he could be proud of it, and the act adapted itself to his love of magnificence. He could like, indeed, almost any one he could say great colored things about: the ancients, almost promiscuously, for they never wrote in newspapers, and Shakespeare (of whom he could not say fine things enough) and Rabelais and Montaigne and Goethe and Victor Hugo (his biggest modern enthusiasm) and Leconte de Lisle and Renan and Théophile Gautier. He did scant justice to Balzac and even less to Alfred de Musset. On the other hand, he had an odd and interesting indulgence for Boileau. Balzac and Musset were not, by his measure, "writers," and he maintains that, be it in verse, be it in prose, it is only so far as they "write" that authors live; between the two categories he makes a fundamental distinction. The latter, indeed, the mere authors, simply did not exist for him, and with Mr. Besant's Incorporated Society he would have had nothing whatever to do. He declares somewhere that it is only the writer who survives in the poet. In spite of his patience with the "muse" to whom the majority of the letters in the earlier of the volumes before us were addressed, and of the great invidious *coup de chapeau* with which he could here and there render homage to versification, his relish for poetry as poetry was moderate. Far higher was his estimate of prose as prose, which he held to be much the more difficult art of the two, with more maddening problems and subtler rhythms, and on whose behalf he found it difficult to forgive the "proud-sister" attitude of verse. No man at any rate, to make up for scanty preferences, can have had a larger list of literary aversions. His eye swept the field in vain for specimens untainted with the "modern infection," the plague which had killed Théophile Gautier and to which he considered that he himself had already succumbed. If he glanced at a *feuilleton* he saw that Madame Sarah Bernhardt was "a social expression," and his resentment of this easy wisdom resounded disproportionately through all the air he lived in. One has always a kindness for people who detest the contemporary tone if they have done something fine; but the baffling thing in Flaubert was the extent of his suffering and the inelasticity of his humor. The jargon of the newspapers, the slovenliness of the novelists, the fatuity of Octave Feuillet, to whom he was exceedingly unjust, for that writer's love of magnificence was not inferior to his critic's, all work upon him with an intensity only to be explained by the primary defect of his mind, his want of a general sense of proportion. That sense stopped apparently when he had settled the relation of the parts of a phrase, as to which it was exquisite.

Fortunately he had confidants to whom he could cry out when he was hurt, and whose position, as he took life for the most part as men take a violent toothache, was assuredly no sinecure. To more than one intense friendship were his younger and middle years devoted; so close was his union with Louis Bouilhet, the poet and dramatist, that he could say in 1870: "I feel no longer the need to write, because I wrote especially for a being who is no more. There's no taste in it now—the impulse has gone." As he wrote for Bouilhet, so Bouilhet wrote for him. "There are so few people who like what I like or have an idea of what I care for." That was the indispensable thing for him in a social, a personal relation, the existence in another mind of a love of literature sufficiently demonstrated to relieve the individual from the great and damning charge, the charge perpetually on Flaubert's lips in regard to his contemporaries, the accusation of malignantly hating it. This universal conspiracy he perceived, in his own country, in every feature of manners, and to a degree which may well make us wonder how high he would have piled the indictment if he had extended the inquiry to the manners of ours. We draw a breath of relief when we think to what speedier suffocation he would have yielded had he been materially acquainted with the great English-speaking peoples. When he declared, naturally enough, that liking what he liked was a condition of intercourse, his vision of this community was almost destined, in the nature of things, to remain unachievable; for it may really be said that no one in the world ever liked anything so much as Flaubert liked beauty of style. The mortal indifference to it of empires and republics was the essence of that "modern infection" from which the only escape would have been to *ne faire que de l'art*. Mankind, for him, was made up of the three or four persons, Ivan Turgenieff in the number, who perceived what he was trying for, and of the innumerable millions who didn't. Poor M. Maxime du Camp, in spite of many of the leading characteristics of a friend, was one of this multitude, and he pays terribly in the pages before us for his position. He pays, to my sense, excessively, for surely he had paid enough and exactly in the just and appropriate measure, when, in the introduction contributed to the "definitive" edition of "Madame Bovary," M. Guy de Maupassant, avenging his master by an exquisite stroke, made public the letter of advice and remonstrance addressed to Flaubert by M. du Camp, then editor of the *Revue de Paris*, on the eve of the serial appearance of the former's first novel in that periodical. This incomparable effusion, with its amazing reference to excisions, and its suggestion that the work be placed in the hands of an expert and inexpensive corrector who will prepare it for publication, this priceless gem will twinkle forever in the setting M. de Maupassant has given it, or we may, perhaps, still more figuratively say in the forehead of the masterpiece it discusses. But there was surely a needless, there was surely a nervous and individual ferocity in such a vindictive giving to the world of every passage of every letter in which the author of that masterpiece has occasion to allude to his friend's want of tact. It naturally made their friendship unsuccessful that Flaubert disliked M. du Camp, but it is a monstrous imputation on his character to assume that he was small enough never to have forgiven and forgotten the other's mistake. Great people never should be avenged; it diminishes their privilege. What M. du Camp, so far as an outsider may judge, had to be punished for was the tone of his reminiscences. But the tone is unmistakably the tone of affection. He may have felt but dimly what his old comrade was trying for, and even the latent richness of "L'Education Sentimentale," but he renders full justice to Flaubert's noble independence. The tone of Flaubert's own allusions is a different thing altogether. It is not unfair to say that all this disproportionate tit-for-tat renders the episode one of the ugliest little dramas of recent literary history. The irony of a friend's learning after long years and through the agency of the press how unsuspectedly another friend was in the habit of talking of him, is an irony too cruel for impartial minds. The disaster is absolute, and our compassion goes straight to the survivor. There are other survivors who will have but little more reason to think that the decencies have presided over such a publication.

It is only a reader here and there in all the wide world who understands to-day, or who ever understood, what Gustave Flaubert tried for; and it is only when such a reader is also a writer, and a tolerably tormented one, that he particularly cares. Poor Flaubert's great revenge, however, far beyond that of any editorial treachery, is that when this occasional witness does care he cares very peculiarly and very tenderly, and much more than he may be able successfully to say. Then the great irritated style-seeker becomes, in the embracing mind, an object of interest and honor; not so much for what he altogether achieved, as for the way he strove and for the inspiring image that he presents. There is no reasoning about him; the more we take him as he is the more he has a special authority. "Salammbô," in which we breathe the air of pure æsthetics, is as hard as stone; "L'Education," for the same reason, is as cold as death; "Saint-Antoine" is a medley of wonderful bristling metals and polished agates, and the drollery of "Bouvard et Pécuchet" (a work as sad as something perverse and puerile done for a wager) about as contagious as the smile of a keeper showing you through the wards of a madhouse. In "Madame Bovary" alone emotion is just sufficiently present to take off the chill. This truly is a qualified report, yet it leaves Flaubert untouched at the points where he is most himself, leaves him master of a province in which, for many of us, it will never be an idle errand to visit him. The way to care for him is to test the virtue of his particular exaggeration, to accept for the sake of his æsthetic influence the idiosyncrasies now revealed to us, his wild gesticulation, his plaintive, childish side, the side as to which one asks one's self what has become of ultimate good-humor, of human patience, of the enduring *man*. He pays and pays heavily for his development in a single direction, for it is probable that no literary effort so great, accompanied with an equal literary talent, ever failed on so large a scale to be convincing. It convinces only those who are converted, and the number of such is very small. It is an appeal so technical that we may say of him still, but with more resignation, what he personally wailed over, that nobody takes his great question seriously. This is indeed why there may be for each of the loyal minority a certain fine scruple against insistence. If he had had in his nature a contradiction the less, if his indifference had been more forgiving, this is surely the way in which he would have desired most to be preserved.

To no one at any rate need it be denied to say that the best way to appreciate him is, abstaining from the clumsy process of an appeal and the vulgar process of an advertisement, exclusively to *use* him, to feel him, to be privately glad of his message. In proportion as we swallow him whole and cherish him as a perfect example, his weaknesses fall into their place as the conditions about which, in estimating a man who has been original, there is a want of tact in crying out. There is, of course, always the answer that the critic is to be suborned only by originalities that fertilize; the rejoinder to which, of equal necessity, must ever be that even to the critics of unborn generations poor Flaubert will doubtless yield a fund of amusement. To the end of time there will be something flippant, something perhaps even "clever" to be said of his immense ado about nothing. Those for some of whose moments, on the contrary, this ado will be as stirring as music, will belong to the group that has dabbled in the same material and striven with the same striving. The interest he presents, in truth, can only be a real interest for fellowship, for initiation of the practical kind; and in that case it becomes a sentiment, a sort of mystical absorption or fruitful secret.

The sweetest things in the world of art or the life of letters are the irresponsible sympathies that seem to rest on divination. Flaubert's hardness was only the act of holding his breath in the reverence of his search for beauty; his universal renunciation, the long spasm of his too-fixed attention, was only one of the absurdest sincerities of art. To the participating eye these things are but details in the little square picture made at this distance of time by his forty years at the battered table at Croisset. Everything lives in this inward vision of the wide room on the river, almost the cell of a monomaniac, but consecrated ground to the faithful, which, as he tried and tried again, must so often have resounded with the pomp of a syntax addressed, in his code, peremptorily to the ear. If there is something tragi-comic in the scene, as of a tenacity in the void or a life laid down for grammar, the impression passes when we turn from the painful process to the sharp and splendid result. Then, since if we like people very much we end by liking their circumstances, the eternal chamber and the dry Benedictine years have a sufficiently palpable offset in the *repoussé* bronze of the books.

An incorruptible celibate and *dédaigneux des femmes* (as, in spite of the hundred and forty letters addressed to Madame Louise Colet, M. de Maupassant styles him and, in writing to Madame Sand, he confesses himself), it was his own view of his career that, as art was the only thing worth living for, he had made immense sacrifices to application—sacrificed passions, joys, affections, curiosities, and opportunities. He says that he shut his passions up in cages, and only at long intervals, for amusement, had a look at them. The *orgie de littérature*, in short, had been his sole form of excess. He knew best, of course, but his imaginations about himself (as about other matters) were, however justly, rich, and to the observer at this distance he appears truly to have been made of the very stuff of a Benedictine. He compared himself to the camel, which can neither be stopped when he is going nor moved when he is resting. He was so sedentary, so averse to physical exercise, which he speaks of somewhere as an *occupation funeste*, that his main alternative to the chair was, even by day, the bed, and so omnivorous in research that the act of composition, with him, was still more impeded by knowledge than by taste.

"I have in me," he writes to the imperturbable Madame Sand, "a *fond d'ecclésiastique* that people don't know"—the clerical basis of the Catholic clergy. "We shall talk of it," he adds, "much better *vivâ voce* than by letter"; and we can easily imagine the thoroughness with which between the unfettered pair, when opportunity favored, the interesting subject was treated. At another time, indeed, to the same correspondent, who had given him a glimpse of the happiness of being a grandmother, he refers with touching sincerity to the poignancy of solitude to which the "radical absence of the feminine element" in his life had condemned him. "Yet I was born with every capacity for tenderness. One doesn't shape one's destiny, one undergoes it. I was pusillanimous in my youth— I was *afraid* of life. We pay for everything." Besides, it was his theory that a "man of style" should never stoop to action. If he had been afraid of life in fact, I must add, he was preserved from the fear of it in imagination by that great "historic start," the sensibility to the *frisson historique*, which dictates the curious and beautiful outburst, addressed to Madame Colet, when he asks why it had not been his lot to live in the age of Nero. "How I would have talked with the Greek rhetors, travelled in the great chariots on the Roman roads, and in the evening, in the hostelries, turned in with the vagabond priests of Cybele! . . . I *have* lived, all over, in those directions; doubtless in some prior state of being. I'm sure I've been, under the Roman empire, manager of some troop of strolling players, one of the rascals who used to go to Sicily to buy women to make actresses, and who were at once professors, panders, and artists. These scoundrels have wonderful 'mugs' in the comedies of Plautus, in reading which I seem to myself to remember things."

He was an extreme admirer of Apuleius, and his florid inexperience helps doubtless somewhat to explain those extreme sophistications of taste of which "La Tentation de Saint-Antoine" is so elaborate an example. Far and strange are the refuges in which such an imagination seeks oblivion of the immediate and the ugly. His life was that of a pearl-diver, breathless in the thick element while he groped for the priceless word, and condemned to plunge again and again. He passed it in reconstructing sentences, exterminating repetitions, calculating and comparing cadences, harmonious *chutes de phrase*, and beating about the bush to deal death to the abominable assonance. Putting aside the particular ideal of style which made a pitfall of the familiar, few men surely have ever found it so difficult to deal with the members of a phrase. He loathed the smug face of facility as much as he suffered from the nightmare of toil; but if he had been marked in the cradle for literature it may be said without paradox that this was not on account of any native disposition to write, to write at least as he aspired and as he understood the term. He took long years to finish his books, and terrible months and weeks to deliver himself of his chapters and his pages. Nothing could exceed his endeavor to make them all rich and round, just as nothing could exceed the unetherized anguish in which his successive children were born. His letters, in which, inconsequently for one who had so little faith in any rigor of taste or purity of perception save his own, he takes everybody into his most intimate literary confidence, the pages of the publication before us are the record of everything that retarded him. The abyss of reading answered to the abyss of writing; with the partial exception of "Madame Bovary" every subject that he treated required a rising flood of information. There are libraries of books behind his most innocent sentences. The question of "art" for him was so furiously the question of form, and the question of form was so intensely the question of rhythm, that from the beginning to the end of his correspondence we scarcely ever encounter a mention of any beauty but verbal beauty. He quotes Goethe fondly as to the supreme importance of the "conception," but the conception remains for him essentially the plastic one.

There are moments when his restless passion for form strikes us as leaving the subject out of account altogether, as if he had taken it up arbitrarily, blindly, preparing himself the years of misery in which he is to denounce the grotesqueness, the insanity of his choice. Four times, with his *orgueil*, his love of magnificence, he condemned himself incongruously to the modern and familiar, groaning at every step over the horrible difficulty of reconciling "style" in such cases with truth and dialogue with surface. He wanted to do the battle of Thermopylæ, and he found himself doing "Bouvard et Pécuchet." One of the sides by which he interests us, one of the sides that will always endear him to the student, is his extraordinary ingenuity in lifting without falsifying, finding a middle way into grandeur and edging off from the literal without forsaking truth. This way was open to him from the moment he could look down upon his theme from the position of *une blague supérieure*, as he calls it, the amused freedom of an observer as irreverent as a creator. But if subjects were made for style (as to which Flaubert had a rigid theory: the idea was good enough if the expression was), so style was made for the ear, the last court of appeal, the supreme touchstone of perfection. He was perpetually demolishing his periods in the light of his merciless *gueulades*. He tried them on every one; his *gueulades* could make him sociable. The horror, in particular, that haunted all his years was the horror of the *cliché*, the stereotyped, the thing usually said and the way it was usually said, the current phrase that passed muster. Nothing, in his view, passed muster but freshness, that which came into the world, with all the honors, for the occasion. To use the ready-made was as disgraceful as for a self-respecting cook to buy a tinned soup or a sauce in a bottle. Flaubert considered that the dispenser of such wares was indeed the grocer, and, producing his ingredients exclusively at home, he would have stabbed himself for shame like Vatel. This touches on the strange weakness of his mind, his puerile dread of the grocer, the *bourgeois*, the sentiment that in his generation and the preceding misplaced, as it were, the spirit of adventure and the sense of honor, and sterilized a whole province of French literature. That worthy citizen ought never to have kept a poet from dreaming.

He had for his delectation and for satiric purposes a large collection of those second-hand and approximate expressions which begged the whole literary question. To light upon a perfect example was his nearest approach to natural bliss. "Bouvard et Pécuchet" is a museum of such examples, the cream of that "Dictionnaire des Idées Reçues" for which all his life he had taken notes and which eventually resolved itself into the encyclopædic exactitude and the lugubrious humor of the novel. Just as subjects were meant for style, so style was meant for images; therefore as his own were numerous and

admirable he would have contended, coming back to the
source, that he was one of the writers to whom the significance of a work had ever been most present. This significance
was measured by the amount of style and the quantity of metaphor thrown up. Poor subjects threw up a little, fine subjects
threw up much, and the finish of his prose was the proof of
his profundity. If you pushed far enough into language you
found yourself in the embrace of thought. There are, doubtless, many persons whom this account of the matter will fail
to satisfy, and there will indeed be no particular zeal to put it
forward even on the part of those for whom, as a writer,
Flaubert most vividly exists. He is a strong taste, like any
other that is strong, and he exists only for those who have a
constitutional need to feel in some direction the particular
æsthetic confidence that he inspires. That confidence rests on
the simple fact that he carried execution so far and nailed it
so fast. No one will care for him at all who does not care for
his metaphors, and those moreover who care most for these
will be discreet enough to admit that even a style rich in similes is limited when it renders only the visible. The invisible
Flaubert scarcely touches; his vocabulary and all his methods
were unadjusted and alien to it. He could not read his French
Wordsworth, M. Sully-Prudhomme; he had no faith in the
power of the moral to offer a surface. He himself offers such
a flawless one that this hard concretion is success. If he is
impossible as a companion he is deeply refreshing as a reference; and all that his reputation asks of you is an occasional
tap of the knuckle at those firm thin plates of gold which
constitute the leaves of his books. This passing tribute will
yield the best results when you have been prompted to it by
some other prose.

In other words, with all his want of *portée*, as the psychological critics of his own country would say of him, poor
Flaubert is one of the artists to whom an artist will always go
back. And if such a pilgrim, in the very act of acknowledgment, drops for an instant into the tenderness of compassion,
it is a compassion singularly untainted with patronage or with
contempt; full, moreover, of mystifications and wonderments,
questions unanswered and speculations vain. Why was he so
unhappy if he was so active; why was he so intolerant if he

was so strong? Why should he not have accepted the circumstance that M. de Lamartine also wrote as his nature impelled,
and that M. Louis Enault embraced a convenient opportunity
to go to the East? The East, if we listen to him, should have
been closed to one of these gentlemen and literature forbidden to the other. Why does the inevitable perpetually infuri-
ate him, and why does he inveterately resent the ephemeral?
Why does he, above all, in his private, in other words his
continuous epistolary, despair, assault his correspondents
with malodorous comparisons? The bad smell of the age was
the main thing he knew it by. Naturally therefore he found
life a *chose hideuse*. If it was his great merit and the thing we
hold on to him for that the artist and the man were welded
together, what becomes, in the proof, of a merit that is so
little illuminating for life? What becomes of the virtue of the
beauty that pretends to be worth living for? Why feel, and
feel genuinely, so much about "art," in order to feel so little
about its privilege? Why proclaim it on the one hand the holy
of holies, only to let your behavior confess it on the other a
temple open to the winds? Why be angry that so few people
care for the real thing, since this aversion of the many leaves
a luxury of space? The answer to these too numerous questions is the final perception that the subject of our observations failed of happiness, failed of temperance, not through
his excesses, but absolutely through his barriers. He passed
his life in strange oblivion of the circumstance that, however
incumbent it may be on most of us to do our duty, there is,
in spite of a thousand narrow dogmatisms, nothing in the
world that any one is under the least obligation to *like*—not
even (one braces one's self to risk the declaration) a particular
kind of writing. Particular kinds of writing may sometimes,
for their producers, have the good fortune to please; but
these things are windfalls, pure luxuries, not resident even in
the cleverest of us as natural rights. Let Flaubert always be
cited as one of the devotees and even, when people are fond
of the word, as one of the martyrs of the plastic idea; but let
him be still more considerately preserved and more fully presented as one of the most conspicuous of the faithless. For it
was not that he went too far, it was on the contrary that he
stopped too short. He hovered forever at the public door, in

the outer court, the splendor of which very properly beguiled him, and in which he seems still to stand as upright as a sentinel and as shapely as a statue. But that immobility and even that erectness were paid too dear. The shining arms were meant to carry further, the other doors were meant to open. He should at least have listened at the chamber of the soul. This would have floated him on a deeper tide; above all it would have calmed his nerves.

Macmillan's Magazine, March 1893
Reprinted in *Essays in London and Elsewhere*, 1893

GUSTAVE FLAUBERT

THE FIRST THING I find to-day and on my very threshold[1] to say about Gustave Flaubert is that he has been reported on by M. Émile Faguet in the series of Les Grands Écrivains Français with such lucidity as may almost be taken to warn off a later critic. I desire to pay at the outset my tribute to M. Faguet's exhaustive study, which is really in its kind a model and a monument. Never can a critic have got closer to a subject of this order; never can the results of the approach have been more copious or more interesting; never in short can the master of a complex art have been more mastered in his turn, nor his art more penetrated, by the application of an earnest curiosity. That remark I have it at heart to make, so pre-eminently has the little volume I refer to not left the subject where it found it. It abounds in contributive light, and yet, I feel on reflection that it scarce wholly dazzles another contributor away. One reason of this is that, though I enter into everything M. Faguet has said, there are things— things perhaps especially of the province of the artist, the fellow-craftsman of Flaubert—that I am conscious of his not having said; another is that inevitably there are particular possibilities of reaction in our English-speaking consciousness that hold up a light of their own. Therefore I venture to fol-

[1] On the occasion of these prefatory remarks to a translation of "Madame Bovary," appearing in A Century of French Romance, under the auspices of Mr. Edmund Gosse and Mr. William Heinemann, in 1902.

low even on a field so laboured, only paying this toll to the latest and best work because the author has made it impossible to do less.

Flaubert's life is so almost exclusively the story of his literary application that to speak of his five or six fictions is pretty well to account for it all. He died in 1880 after a career of fifty-nine years singularly little marked by changes of scene, of fortune, of attitude, of occupation, of character, and above all, as may be said, of mind. He would be interesting to the race of novelists if only because, quite apart from the value of his work, he so personally gives us the example and the image, so presents the intellectual case. He was born a novelist, grew up, lived, died a novelist, breathing, feeling, thinking, speaking, performing every operation of life, only as that votary; and this though his production was to be small in amount and though it constituted all his diligence. It was not indeed perhaps primarily so much that he was born and lived a novelist as that he was born and lived literary, and that to be literary represented for him an almost overwhelming situation. No life was long enough, no courage great enough, no fortune kind enough to support a man under the burden of this character when once such a doom had been laid on him. His case was a doom because he felt of his vocation almost nothing but the difficulty. He had many strange sides, but this was the strangest, that if we argued from his difficulty to his work, the difficulty being registered for us in his letters and elsewhere, we should expect from the result but the smallest things. We should be prepared to find in it well-nigh a complete absence of the signs of a gift. We should regret that the unhappy man had not addressed himself to something he might have found at least comparatively easy. We should singularly miss the consecration supposedly given to a work of art by its having been conceived in joy. That is Flaubert's remarkable, his so far as I know unmatched distinction, that he has left works of an extraordinary art even the conception of which failed to help him to think in serenity. The chapter of execution, from the moment execution gets really into the shafts, is of course always and everywhere a troubled one—about which moreover too much has of late been written; but we frequently find Flaubert cursing his subjects themselves, wishing he had not chosen them, holding himself up to derision for having done so, and hating them in the very act of sitting down to them. He cared immensely for the medium, the task and the triumph involved, but was himself the last to be able to say why. He is sustained only by the rage and the habit of effort; the mere *love* of letters, let alone the love of life, appears at an early age to have deserted him. Certain passages in his correspondence make us even wonder if it be not hate that sustains him most. So, successively, his several supremely finished and crowned compositions came into the world, and we may feel sure that none others of the kind, none that were to have an equal fortune, had sprung from such adversity.

I insist upon this because his at once excited and baffled passion gives the key of his life and determines its outline. I must speak of him at least as I feel him and as in his very latest years I had the fortune occasionally to see him. I said just now, practically, that he is for many of our tribe at large *the* novelist, intent and typical, and so, gathered together and foreshortened, simplified and fixed, the lapse of time seems to show him. It has made him in his prolonged posture extraordinarily objective, made him even resemble one of his own productions, constituted him as a subject, determined him as a figure; the limit of his range, and above all of his reach, is after this fashion, no doubt, sufficiently indicated, and yet perhaps in the event without injury to his name. If our consideration of him cultivates a certain tenderness on the double ground that he suffered supremely in the cause and that there is endlessly much to be learned from him, we remember at the same time that, indirectly, the world at large possesses him not less than the *confrère*. He has fed and fertilised, has filtered through others, and so arrived at contact with that public from whom it was his theory that he was separated by a deep and impassable trench, the labour of his own spade. He is none the less more interesting, I repeat, as a failure however qualified than as a success however explained, and it is as so viewed that the unity of his career attaches and admonishes. Save in some degree by a condition of health (a liability to epileptic fits at times frequent, but never so frequent as to have been generally suspected,) he was not out-wardly hampered as the tribe of men of letters goes—an anxious brotherhood at the best; yet the fewest possible things appear to have ever succeeded in happening to him. The only son of an eminent provincial physician, he inherited a modest ease and no other incumbrance than, as was the case for Balzac, an over-attentive, an importunate mother; but freedom spoke to him from behind a veil, and when we have mentioned the few apparent facts of experience that make up his landmarks over and beyond his interspaced publications we shall have completed his biography. Tall, strong, striking, he caused his friends to admire in him the elder, the florid Norman type, and he seems himself, as a man of imagination, to have found some transmission of race in his stature and presence, his light-coloured salient eyes and long tawny moustache.

The central event of his life was his journey to the East in 1849 with M. Maxime Du Camp, of which the latter has left in his "Impressions Littéraires" a singularly interesting and, as we may perhaps say, slightly treacherous report, and which prepared for Flaubert a state of nostalgia that was not only never to leave him, but that was to work in him as a motive. He had during that year, and just in sufficient quantity, his revelation, the particular appropriate disclosure to which the gods at some moment treat the artist unless they happen too perversely to conspire against him: he tasted of the knowledge by which he was subsequently to measure everything, appeal from everything, find everything flat. Never probably was an impression so assimilated, so positively transmuted to a function; he lived on it to the end and we may say that in "Salammbô" and "La Tentation de Saint-Antoine" he almost died of it. He made afterwards no other journey of the least importance save a disgusted excursion to the Rigi-Kaltbad shortly before his death. The Franco-German War was of course to him for the time as the valley of the shadow itself; but this was an ordeal, unlike most of his other ordeals, shared after all with millions. He never married—he declared, toward the end, to the most comprehending of his confidants, that he had been from the first "afraid of life"; and the friendliest element of his later time was, we judge, that admirable comfortable commerce, in her fullest maturity, with Madame

George Sand, the confidant I just referred to; which has been preserved for us in the published correspondence of each. He had in Ivan Turgenieff a friend almost as valued; he spent each year a few months in Paris, where (to mention everything) he had his natural place, so far as he cared to take it, at the small literary court of the Princess Mathilde; and, lastly, he lost toward the close of his life, by no fault of his own, a considerable part of his modest fortune. It is, however, in the long security, the almost unbroken solitude of Croisset, near Rouen, that he mainly figures for us, gouging out his successive books in the wide old room, of many windows, that, with an intervening terrace, overlooked the broad Seine and the passing boats. This was virtually a monastic cell, closed to echoes and accidents; with its stillness for long periods scarce broken save by the creak of the towing-chain of the tugs across the water. When I have added that his published letters offer a view, not very refreshing, of his youthful entanglement with Madame Louise Colet—whom we name because, apparently not a shrinking person, she long ago practically named herself—I shall have catalogued his personal vicissitudes. And I may add further that the connection with Madame Colet, such as it was, rears its head for us in something like a desert of immunity from such complications.

His complications were of the spirit, of the literary vision, and though he was thoroughly profane he was yet essentially anchoretic. I perhaps miss a point, however, in not finally subjoining that he was liberally accessible to his friends during the months he regularly spent in Paris. Sensitive, passionate, perverse, not less than *immediately* sociable—for if he detested his collective contemporaries this dropped, thanks to his humanising shyness, before the individual encounter—he was in particular and superexcellently not *banal*, and he attached men perhaps more than women, inspiring a marked, a by no means colourless shade of respect; a respect not founded, as the air of it is apt to be, on the vague presumption, but addressed almost in especial to his disparities and oddities and thereby, no doubt, none too different from affection. His friends at all events were a rich and eager *cénacle*, among whom he was on occasion, by his picturesque personality, a natural and overtopping centre; partly perhaps because he was so much and so familiarly at home. He wore, up to any hour of the afternoon, that long, colloquial dressing-gown, with trousers to match, which one has always associated with literature in France—the uniform really of freedom of talk. Freedom of talk abounded by his winter fire, for the *cénacle* was made up almost wholly of the more finely distinguished among his contemporaries; of philosophers, men of letters and men of affairs belonging to his own generation and the next. He had at the time I have in mind a small perch, far aloft, at the distant, the then almost suburban, end of the Faubourg Saint-Honoré, where on Sunday afternoons, at the very top of an endless flight of stairs, were to be encountered in a cloud of conversation and smoke most of the novelists of the general Balzac tradition. Others of a different birth and complexion were markedly not of the number, were not even conceivable as present; none of those, unless I misremember, whose fictions were at that time "serialised" in the Revue des Deux Mondes. In spite of Renan and Taine and two or three more, the contributor to the Revue would indeed at no time have found in the circle in question his foot on his native heath. One could recall if one would two or three vivid allusions to him, not of the most quotable, on the lips of the most famous of "naturalists"—allusions to him as represented for instance by M. Victor Cherbuliez and M. Octave Feuillet. The author of these pages recalls a concise qualification of this last of his fellows on the lips of Émile Zola, which that absorbed auditor had too directly, too rashly asked for; but which is alas not reproducible here. There was little else but the talk, which had extreme intensity and variety; almost nothing, as I remember, but a painted and gilded idol, of considerable size, a relic and a memento, on the chimney-piece. Flaubert was huge and diffident, but florid too and resonant, and my main remembrance is of a conception of courtesy in him, an accessibility to the human relation, that only wanted to be sure of the way taken or to take. The uncertainties of the French for the determination of intercourse have often struck me as quite matching the sharpness of their certainties, as we for the most part feel these latter, which sometimes in fact throw the indeterminate into almost touching relief. I have thought of them at such times as the people in

the world one may have to go more of the way to meet than
to meet any other, and this, as it were, through their being
seated and embedded, provided for at home, in a manner that
is all their own and that has bred them to the positive pre-
acceptance of interest on their behalf. We at least of the Anglo-American race, more abroad in the world, perching
everywhere, so far as grounds of intercourse are concerned,
more vaguely and superficially, as well as less intelligently, are
the more ready by that fact with inexpensive accommodations, rather conscious that these themselves forbear from the
claim to fascinate, and advancing with the good nature that is
the mantle of our obtuseness to any point whatever where
entertainment may be offered us. My recollection is at any
rate simplified by the fact of the presence almost always, in
the little high room of the Faubourg's end, of other persons
and other voices. Flaubert's own voice is clearest to me from
the uneffaced sense of a winter week-day afternoon when I
found him by exception alone and when something led to his
reading me aloud, in support of some judgment he had
thrown off, a poem of Théophile Gautier's. He cited it as an
example of verse intensely and distinctively French, and
French in its melancholy, which neither Goethe nor Heine
nor Leopardi, neither Pushkin nor Tennyson nor, as he said,
Byron, could at all have matched in *kind*. He converted me
at the moment to this perception, alike by the sense of the
thing and by his large utterance of it; after which it is dreadful to have to confess not only that the poem was then new
to me, but that, hunt as I will in every volume of its author,
I am never able to recover it. This is perhaps after all happy,
causing Flaubert's own full tone, which was the note of the
occasion, to linger the more unquenched. But for the rhyme
in fact I could have believed him to be spouting to me something strange and sonorous of his own. The thing really rare
would have been to hear him do that—hear him *gueuler*, as
he liked to call it. Verse, I felt, we had always with us, and
almost any idiot of goodwill could give it a value. The value
of so many a passage of "Salammbô" and of "L'Éducation"
was on the other hand exactly such as gained when he allowed himself, as had by the legend ever been frequent *dans
l'intimité*, to "bellow" it to its fullest effect.

GUSTAVE FLAUBERT

One of the things that make him most exhibitional and most describable, so that if we had invented him as an illustration or a character we would exactly so have arranged him, is that he was formed intellectually of two quite distinct compartments, a sense of the real and a sense of the romantic, and that his production, for our present cognisance, thus neatly and vividly divides itself. The divisions are as marked as the sections on the back of a scarab, though their distinctness is undoubtedly but the final expression of much inward strife. M. Faguet indeed, who is admirable on this question of our author's duality, gives an account of the romanticism that found its way for him into the real and of the reality that found its way into the romantic; but he none the less strikes us as a curious splendid insect sustained on wings of a different coloration, the right a vivid red, say, and the left as frank a yellow. This duality has in its sharp operation placed "Madame Bovary" and "L'Éducation" on one side together and placed together on the other "Salammbô" and "La Tentation." "Bouvard et Pécuchet" it can scarce be spoken of, I think, as having placed anywhere or anyhow. If it was Flaubert's way to find his subject impossible there was none he saw so much in that light as this last-named, but also none that he appears to have held so important for that very reason to pursue to the bitter end. Posterity agrees with him about the impossibility, but rather takes upon itself to break with the rest of the logic. We may perhaps, however, for symmetry, let "Bouvard et Pécuchet" figure as the tail—if scarabs ever have tails—of our analogous insect. Only in that case we should also append as the very tip the small volume of the "Trois Contes," preponderantly of the deepest imaginative hue.

His imagination was great and splendid; in spite of which, strangely enough, his masterpiece is not his most imaginative work. "Madame Bovary," beyond question, holds that first place, and "Madame Bovary" is concerned with the career of a country doctor's wife in a petty Norman town. The elements of the picture are of the fewest, the situation of the heroine almost of the meanest, the material for interest, considering the interest yielded, of the most unpromising; but these facts only throw into relief one of those incalculable incidents that attend the proceedings of genius. "Madame

Bovary" was doomed by circumstances and causes—the freshness of comparative youth and good faith on the author's part being perhaps the chief—definitely to take its position, even though its subject was fundamentally a negation of the remote, the splendid and the strange, the stuff of his fondest and most cultivated dreams. It would have seemed very nearly to exclude the free play of the imagination, and the way this faculty on the author's part nevertheless presides is one of those accidents, manœuvres, inspirations, we hardly know what to call them, by which masterpieces grow. He of course knew more or less what he was doing for his book in making Emma Bovary a victim of the imaginative habit, but he must have been far from designing or measuring the total effect which renders the work so general, so complete an expression of himself. His separate idiosyncrasies, his irritated sensibility to the life about him, with the power to catch it in the fact and hold it hard, and his hunger for style and history and poetry, for the rich and the rare, great reverberations, great adumbrations, are here represented together as they are not in his later writings. There is nothing of the near, of the directly observed, though there may be much of the directly perceived and the minutely detailed, either in "Salammbô" or in "Saint-Antoine," and little enough of the extravagance of illusion in that indefinable last word of restrained evocation and cold execution "L'Éducation Sentimentale." M. Faguet has of course excellently noted this—that the fortune and felicity of the book were assured by the stroke that made the central figure an embodiment of helpless romanticism. Flaubert himself but narrowly escaped being such an embodiment after all, and he is thus able to express the romantic mind with extraordinary truth. As to the rest of the matter he had the luck of having been in possession from the first, having begun so early to nurse and work up his plan that, familiarity and the native air, the native soil, aiding, he had finally made out to the last lurking shade the small sordid sunny dusty village picture, its emptiness constituted and peopled. It is in the background and the accessories that the real, the real of his theme, abides; and the romantic, the romantic of his theme, accordingly occupies the front. Emma Bovary's poor adventures are a tragedy for the very reason that in a world unsuspecting, unassisting, unconsoling, she has herself to distil the rich and the rare. Ignorant, unguided, undiverted, ridden by the very nature and mixture of her consciousness, she makes of the business an inordinate failure, a failure which in its turn makes for Flaubert the most pointed, the most *told* of anecdotes.

There are many things to say about "Madame Bovary," but an old admirer of the book would be but half-hearted—so far as they represent reserves or puzzlements—were he not to note first of all the circumstances by which it is most endeared to him. To remember it from far back is to have been present all along at a process of singular interest to a literary mind, a case indeed full of comfort and cheer. The finest of Flaubert's novels is to-day, on the French shelf of fiction, one of the first of the classics; it has attained that position, slowly but steadily, before our eyes; and we seem so to follow the evolution of the fate of a classic. We see how the thing takes place; which we rarely can, for we mostly miss either the beginning or the end, especially in the case of a consecration as complete as this. The consecrations of the past are too far behind and those of the future too far in front. That the production before us *should* have come in for the heavenly crown may be a fact to offer English and American readers a mystifying side; but it is exactly our ground and a part moreover of the total interest. The author of these remarks remembers, as with a sense of the way such things happen, that when a very young person in Paris he took up from the parental table the latest number of the periodical in which Flaubert's then duly unrecognised masterpiece was in course of publication. The moment is not historic, but it was to become in the light of history, as may be said, so unforgettable that every small feature of it yet again lives for him: it rests there like the backward end of the span. The cover of the old Revue de Paris was yellow, if I mistake not, like that of the new, and "Madame Bovary: Mœurs de Province," on the inside of it, was already, on the spot, as a title, mysteriously arresting, inscrutably charged. I was ignorant of what had preceded and was not to know till much later what followed; but present to me still is the act of standing there before the fire, my back against the low beplushed and begarnished French chimney-piece and taking in what I might of that instalment, taking it in with so surprised an interest, and perhaps as well such a stir of faint foreknowledge, that the sunny little salon, the autumn day, the window ajar and the cheerful outside clatter of the Rue Montaigne are all now for me more or less in the story and the story more or less in them. The story, however, was at that moment having a difficult life; its fortune was all to make; its merit was so far from suspected that, as Maxime Du Camp—though verily with no excess of contrition—relates, its cloth of gold barely escaped the editorial shears. This, with much more, contributes for us to the course of things to come. The book, on its appearance as a volume, proved a shock to the high propriety of the guardians of public morals under the second Empire, and Flaubert was prosecuted as author of a work indecent to scandal. The prosecution in the event fell to the ground, but I should perhaps have mentioned this agitation as one of the very few, of any public order, in his short list. "Le Candidat" fell at the Vaudeville Theatre, several years later, with a violence indicated by its withdrawal after a performance of but two nights, the first of these marked by a deafening uproar; only if the comedy was not to recover from this accident the misprised lustre of the novel was entirely to reassert itself. It is strange enough at present—so far have we travelled since then—that "Madame Bovary" should in so comparatively recent a past have been to that extent a cause of reprobation; and suggestive above all, in such connections, as to the large unconsciousness of superior minds. The desire of the superior mind of the day—that is the governmental, official, legal—to distinguish a book with such a destiny before it is a case conceivable, but conception breaks down before its design of making the distinction purely invidious. We can imagine its knowing so little, however face to face with the object, what it had got hold of; but for it to have been so urged on by a blind inward spring to publish to posterity the extent of its ignorance, that would have been beyond imagination, beyond everything but pity.

And yet it is not after all that the place the book has taken is so overwhelmingly explained by its inherent dignity; for here comes in the curiosity of the matter. Here comes in especially its fund of admonition for alien readers. The dignity of its substance is the dignity of Madame Bovary herself as a vessel of experience—a question as to which, unmistakably, I judge, we can only depart from the consensus of French critical opinion. M. Faguet for example commends the character of the heroine as one of the most living and discriminated figures of women in all literature, praises it as a field for the display of the romantic spirit that leaves nothing to be desired. Subject to an observation I shall presently make and that bears heavily in general, I think, on Flaubert as a painter of life, subject to this restriction he is right; which is a proof that a work of art may be markedly open to objection and at the same time be rare in its kind, and that when it is perfect to this point nothing else particularly matters. "Madame Bovary" has a perfection that not only stamps it, but that makes it stand almost alone; it holds itself with such a supreme unapproachable assurance as both excites and defies judgment. For it deals not in the least, as to unapproachability, with things exalted or refined; it only confers on its sufficiently vulgar elements of exhibition a final unsurpassable form. The form is in *itself* as interesting, as active, as much of the essence of the subject as the idea, and yet so close is its fit and so inseparable its life that we catch it at no moment on any errand of its own. That verily is to *be* interesting—all round; that is to be genuine and whole. The work is a classic because the thing, such as it is, is ideally *done*, and because it shows that in such doing eternal beauty may dwell. A pretty young woman who lives, socially and morally speaking, in a hole, and who is ignorant, foolish, flimsy, unhappy, takes a pair of lovers by whom she is successively deserted; in the midst of the bewilderment of which, giving up her husband and her child, letting everything go, she sinks deeper into duplicity, debt, despair, and arrives on the spot, on the small scene itself of her poor depravities, at a pitiful tragic end. In especial she does these things while remaining absorbed in romantic intention and vision, and she remains absorbed in romantic intention and vision while fairly rolling in the dust. That is the triumph of the book as the triumph stands, that Emma interests us by the nature of her consciousness and the play of her mind, thanks to the reality and beauty with which those

sources are invested. It is not only that they represent *her*
state; they are so true, so observed and felt, and especially so
shown, that they represent the state, actual or potential, of all
persons like her, persons romantically determined. Then her
setting, the medium in which she struggles, becomes in its
way as important, becomes eminent with the eminence of art;
the tiny world in which she revolves, the contracted cage in
which she flutters, is hung out in space for her, and her companions in captivity there are as true as herself.

I have said enough to show what I mean by Flaubert's having in this picture expressed something of his intimate self,
given his heroine something of his own imagination: a point
precisely that brings me back to the restriction at which I just
now hinted, in which M. Faguet fails to indulge and yet
which is immediate for the alien reader. Our complaint is that
Emma Bovary, in spite of the nature of her consciousness and
in spite of her reflecting so much that of her creator, is really
too small an affair. This, critically speaking, is in view both of
the value and the fortune of her history, a wonderful circumstance. She associates herself with Frédéric Moreau in "L'Éducation" to suggest for us a question that can be answered, I
hold, only to Flaubert's detriment. Emma taken alone would
possibly not so directly press it, but in her company the hero
of our author's second study of the "real" drives it home.
Why did Flaubert choose, as special conduits of the life he
proposed to depict, such inferior and in the case of Frédéric
such abject human specimens? I insist only in respect to the
latter, the perfection of Madame Bovary scarce leaving one
much warrant for wishing anything other. Even here, however, the general scale and size of Emma, who is small even
of her sort, should be a warning to hyperbole. If I say that in
the matter of Frédéric at all events the answer is inevitably
detrimental I mean that it weighs heavily on our author's
general credit. He wished in each case to make a picture of
experience—middling experience, it is true—and of the
world close to him; but if he imagined nothing better for his
purpose than such a heroine and such a hero, both such limited reflectors and registers, we are forced to believe it to have
been by a defect of his mind. And that sign of weakness remains even if it be objected that the images in question were

addressed to his purpose better than others would have been: the purpose itself then shows as inferior. "L'Éducation Sentimentale" is a strange, an indescribable work, about which there would be many more things to say than I have space for, and all of them of the deepest interest. It is moreover, to simplify my statement, very much less satisfying a thing, less pleasing whether in its unity or its variety, than its specific predecessor. But take it as we will, for a success or a failure— M. Faguet indeed ranks it, by the measure of its quantity of intention, a failure, and I on the whole agree with him—the personage offered us as bearing the weight of the drama, and in whom we are invited to that extent to interest ourselves, leaves us mainly wondering what our entertainer could have been thinking of. He takes Frédéric Moreau on the threshold of life and conducts him to the extreme of maturity without apparently suspecting for a moment either our wonder or our protest—"Why, why *him*?" Frédéric is positively too poor for his part, too scant for his charge; and we feel with a kind of embarrassment, certainly with a kind of compassion, that it is somehow the business of a protagonist to prevent in his designer an excessive waste of faith. When I speak of the faith in Emma Bovary as proportionately wasted I reflect on M. Faguet's judgment that she is from the point of view of deep interest richly or at least roundedly representative. Representative of what? he makes us ask even while granting all the grounds of misery and tragedy involved. The plea for her is the plea made for all the figures that live without evaporation under the painter's hand—that they are not only particular persons but types of their kind, and as valid in one light as in the other. It is Emma's "kind" that I question for this responsibility, even if it be inquired of me why I then fail to question that of Charles Bovary, in its perfection, or that of the inimitable, the immortal Homais. If we express Emma's deficiency as the poverty of her consciousness for the typical function, it is certainly not, one must admit, that she is surpassed in this respect either by her platitudinous husband or by his friend the pretentious apothecary. The difference is none the less somehow in the fact that they are respectively studies but of their character and office, which function in each expresses adequately *all* they are. It may be, I concede, because Emma is the only woman in the book that she is taken by M. Faguet as *femininely* typical, typical in the larger illustrative way, whereas the others pass with him for images specifically conditioned. Emma is this same for myself, I plead; she is conditioned to such an excess of the specific, and the specific in her case leaves out so many even of the commoner elements of conceivable life in a woman when we are invited to see that life as pathetic, as dramatic agitation, that we challenge both the author's and the critic's scale of importances. The book is a picture of the middling as much as they like, but does Emma attain even to *that*? Hers is a narrow middling even for a little imaginative person whose "social" significance is small. It is greater on the whole than her capacity of consciousness, taking this all round; and so, in a word, we feel her less illustrational than she might have been not only if the world had offered her more points of contact, but if she had had more of these to give it.

We meet Frédéric first, we remain with him long, as a *moyen*, a provincial bourgeois of the mid-century, educated and not without fortune, thereby with freedom, in whom the life of his day reflects itself. Yet the life of his day, on Flaubert's showing, hangs together with the poverty of Frédéric's own inward or for that matter outward life; so that, the whole thing being, for scale, intention and extension, a sort of epic of the usual (with the Revolution of 1848 introduced indeed as an episode,) it affects us as an epic without air, without wings to lift it; reminds us in fact more than anything else of a huge balloon, all of silk pieces strongly sewn together and patiently blown up, but that absolutely refuses to leave the ground. The discrimination I here make as against our author is, however, the only one inevitable in a series of remarks so brief. What it really represents—and nothing could be more curious—is that Frédéric enjoys his position not only without the aid of a single "sympathetic" character of consequence, but even without the aid of one with whom we can directly communicate. Can we communicate with the central personage? or would we really if we could? A hundred times no, and if he himself can communicate with the people shown us as surrounding him this only proves him of their kind. Flaubert on his "real" side was in truth an ironic painter, and ironic to a tune that makes his final accepted state, his present literary dignity and "classic" peace, superficially anomalous. There is an explanation to which I shall immediately come; but I find myself feeling for a moment longer in presence of "L'Éducation" how much more interesting a writer may be on occasion by the given failure than by the given success. Successes pure and simple disconnect and dismiss him; failures—though I admit they must be a bit qualified—keep him in touch and in relation. Thus it is that as the work of a "grand écrivain" "L'Éducation," large, laboured, immensely " written," with beautiful passages and a general emptiness, with a kind of leak in its stored sadness, moreover, by which its moral dignity escapes—thus it is that Flaubert's ill-starred novel is a curiosity for a literary museum. Thus it is also that it suggests a hundred reflections, and suggests perhaps most of them directly to the intending labourer in the same field. If in short, as I have said, Flaubert is the novelist's novelist, this performance does more than any other toward making him so.

I have to add in the same connection that I had not lost sight of Madame Arnoux, the main ornament of "L'Éducation," in pronouncing just above on its deficiency in the sympathetic. Madame Arnoux is exactly the author's one marked attempt, here or elsewhere, to represent beauty otherwise than for the senses, beauty of character and life; and what becomes of the attempt is a matter highly significant. M. Faguet praises with justice his conception of the figure and of the relation, the relation that never bears fruit, that keeps Frédéric adoring her, through hindrance and change, from the beginning of life to the end; that keeps her, by the same constraint, forever immaculately "good," from youth to age, though deeply moved and cruelly tempted and sorely tried. Her contacts with her adorer are not even frequent, in proportion to the field of time; her conditions of fortune, of association and occupation are almost sordid, and we see them with the march of the drama, such as it is, become more and more so; besides which—I again remember that M. Faguet excellently notes it—nothing in the nature of "parts" is attributed to her; not only is she not presented as clever, she is scarce invested with a character at all. Almost nothing that she says is repeated, almost nothing that she does is shown. She is an image none the less beautiful and vague, an image of passion cherished and abjured, renouncing all sustenance and yet persisting in life. Only she has for real distinction the extreme drawback that she is offered us quite preponderantly through Frédéric's vision of her, that we see her practically in no other light. Now Flaubert unfortunately has not been able not so to discredit Frédéric's vision in general, his vision of everyone and everything, and in particular of his own life, that it makes a medium good enough to convey adequately a noble impression. Madame Arnoux is of course ever so much the best thing in his life—which is saying little; but his life is made up of such queer material that we find ourselves displeased at her being "in" it on whatever terms; all the more that she seems scarcely to affect, improve or determine it. Her creator in short never had a more awkward idea than this attempt to give us the benefit of such a conception in such a way; and even though I have still something else to say about that I may as well speak of it at once as a mistake that gravely counts against him. It is but one of three, no doubt, in all his work; but I shall not, I trust, pass for extravagant if I call it the most indicative. What makes it so is its being the least superficial; the two others are, so to speak, intellectual, while this is somehow moral. It was a mistake, as I have already hinted, to propose to register in so mean a consciousness as that of such a hero so large and so mixed a quantity of life as "L'Éducation" clearly intends; and it was a mistake of the tragic sort that is a theme mainly for silence to have embarked on "Bouvard et Pécuchet" at all, not to have given it up sooner than be given up by it. But these were at the worst not wholly compromising blunders. What *was* compromising—and the great point is that it remained so, that nothing has an equal weight against it—is the unconsciousness of error in respect to the opportunity that would have counted as his finest. We feel not so much that Flaubert misses it, for that we could bear; but that he doesn't *know* he misses it is what stamps the blunder. We do not pretend to say how he might have shown us Madame Arnoux better—that was his own affair. What is ours is that he really thought he was showing her as well as he could, or as she might be shown;

at which we veil our face. For once that he had a conception quite apart, apart I mean from the array of his other conceptions and more delicate than any, he " went," as we say, and spoiled it. Let me add in all tenderness, and to make up for possibly too much insistence, that it is the only stain on his shield; let me even confess that I should not wonder if, when all is said, it is a blemish no one has ever noticed.

Perhaps no one has ever noticed either what was present to me just above as the partial makeweight there glanced at, the fact that in the midst of this general awkwardness, as I have called it, there is at the same time a danger so escaped as to entitle our author to full credit. I scarce know how to put it with little enough of the ungracious, but I think that even the true Flaubertist finds himself wondering a little that some flaw of taste, some small but unfortunate lapse by the way, *should* as a matter of fact not somehow or somewhere have waited on the demonstration of the platonic purity prevailing between this heroine and her hero—so far as we do find that image projected. It is alike difficult to indicate without offence or to ignore without unkindness a fond reader's apprehension here of a possibility of the wrong touch, the just perceptibly false note. I would not have staked my life on Flaubert's security of instinct in such a connection—as an absolutely fine and predetermined security; and yet in the event that felicity has settled, there is not so much as the lightest wrong breath (speaking of the matter in this light of tact and taste) or the shade of a crooked stroke. One exclaims at the end of the question "Dear old Flaubert after all—!" and perhaps so risks seeming to patronise for fear of not making a point. The point made for what it is worth, at any rate, I am the more free to recover the benefit of what I mean by critical "tenderness" in our general connection—expressing in it as I do our general respect, and my own particular, for our author's method and process and history, and my sense of the luxury of such a sentiment at such a vulgar literary time. It is a respect positive and settled and the thing that has most to do with consecrating for us that loyalty to him as the novelist of the novelist—unlike as it is even the best feeling inspired by any other member of the craft. He may stand for our operative conscience or our vicarious sacrifice; animated by a sense of literary honour, attached to an ideal of perfection, incapable of lapsing in fine from a self-respect, that enable us to sit at ease, to surrender to the age, to indulge in whatever comparative meannesses (and no meanness in art is so mean as the sneaking economic,) we may find most comfortable or profitable. May it not in truth be said that we practise our industry, so many of us, at relatively little cost just *because* poor Flaubert, producing the most expensive fictions ever written, so handsomely paid for it? It is as if this put it in our power to produce cheap and thereby sell dear; as if, so expressing it, literary honour being by his example effectively secure for the firm at large and the general concern, on its whole esthetic side, floated once for all, we find our individual attention free for literary and esthetic indifference. All the while we thus lavish our indifference the spirit of the author of "Madame Bovary," in the cross-light of the old room above the Seine, is trying to the last admiration for the thing itself. That production puts the matter into a nutshell: "Madame Bovary," subject to whatever qualification, is absolutely the most literary of novels, so literary that it covers us with its mantle. It shows us once for all that there is no *intrinsic* call for a debasement of the type. The mantle I speak of is wrought with surpassing fineness, and we may always, under stress of whatever charge of illiteracy, frivolity, vulgarity, flaunt it as the flag of the guild. Let us therefore frankly concede that to surround Flaubert with our consideration is the least return we can make for such a privilege. The consideration moreover is idle unless it be real, unless it be intelligent enough to measure his effort and his success. Of the effort as mere effort I have already spoken, of the desperate difficulty involved for him in making his form square with his conception; and I by no means attach general importance to these secrets of the workshop, which are but as the contortions of the fastidious muse who is the servant of the oracle. They are really rather secrets of the kitchen and contortions of the priestess of *that* tripod—they are not an upstairs matter. It is of their specially distinctive importance I am now speaking, of the light shed on them by the results before us.

They all represent the pursuit of a style, of the ideally right one for its relations, and would still be interesting if the style had not been achieved. "Madame Bovary," "Salammbô," "Saint-Antoine," "L'Éducation" are so written and so composed (though the last-named in a minor degree) that the more we look at them the more we find in them, under this head, a beauty of intention and of effect; the more they figure in the too often dreary desert of fictional prose a class by themselves and a little living oasis. So far as that desert is of the complexion of our own English speech it supplies with remarkable rarity this particular source of refreshment. So strikingly is that the case, so scant for the most part any dream of a scheme of beauty in these connections, that a critic betrayed at artless moments into a plea for composition may find himself as blankly met as if his plea were for trigonometry. He makes inevitably his reflections, which are numerous enough; one of them being that if we turn our back so squarely, so universally to this order of considerations it is because the novel is so preponderantly cultivated among us by women, in other words by a sex ever gracefully, comfortably, enviably unconscious (it would be too much to call them even suspicious,) of the requirements of form. The case is at any rate sharply enough made for us, or against us, by the circumstance that women are held to have achieved on all our ground, in spite of this weakness and others, as great results as any. The judgment is undoubtedly founded: Jane Austen was instinctive and charming, and the other recognitions—even over the heads of the ladies, some of them, from Fielding to Pater—are obvious; without, however, in the least touching my contention. For signal examples of what composition, distribution, arrangement can do, of how they intensify the life of a work of art, we have to go elsewhere; and the value of Flaubert for us is that he admirably points the moral. This is the explanation of the "classic" fortune of "Madame Bovary" in especial, though I may add that also of Hérodias and Saint-Julien l'Hospitalier in the "Trois Contes," as well as an aspect of these works endlessly suggestive. I spoke just now of the small field of the picture in the longest of them, the small capacity, as I called it, of the vessel; yet the way the thing is done not only triumphs over the question of value but in respect to it fairly misleads and confounds us. Where else shall we find in anything proportionately so small such an air of dignity of size? Flaubert *made* things big—it was his way, his ambition and his necessity; and I say this while remembering that in "L'Éducation" (in proportion I mean again,) the effect has not been produced. The subject of "L'Éducation" is in spite of Frédéric large, but an indefinable shrinkage has overtaken it in the execution. The exception so marked, however, is single; "Salammbô" and "Saint-Antoine" are both at once very "heavy" conceptions and very consistently and splendidly high applications of a manner.

It is in this assured manner that the lesson sits aloft, that the spell for the critical reader resides; and if the conviction under which Flaubert labours is more and more grossly discredited among us his compact mass is but the greater. He regarded the work of art as *existing* but by its expression, and defied us to name any other measure of its life that is not a stultification. He held style to be accordingly an indefeasible part of it, and found beauty, interest and distinction as dependent on it for emergence as a letter committed to the post-office is dependent on an addressed envelope. Strange enough it may well appear to us to have to apologise for such notions as eccentric. There are persons who consider that style comes of itself—we see and hear at present, I think, enough of them; and to whom he would doubtless have remarked that it goes, of itself, still faster. The thing naturally differs in fact with the nature of the imagination; the question is one of proprieties and affinities, sympathy and proportion. The sympathy of the author of "Salammbô" was all with the magnificent, his imagination for the phrase as variously noble or ignoble in itself, contributive or destructive, adapted and harmonious or casual and common. The worse among such possibilities have been multiplied by the infection of bad writing, and he denied that the better ever do anything so obliging as to come of themselves. They scarcely indeed for Flaubert "came" at all; their arrival was determined only by fasting and prayer or by patience of pursuit, the arts of the chase, long waits and watches, figuratively speaking, among the peaks or by the waters. The production of a book was of course made inordinately slow by the fatigue of these measures; in illustration of which his letters often record that it has taken him three days[1] to arrive at one right sentence, tested by the pitch of his ideal of the right for the suggestion aimed at. His difficulties drew from the author, as I have mentioned, much resounding complaint; but those voices have ceased to trouble us and the final voice remains. No feature of the whole business is more edifying than the fact that he in the first place never misses style and in the second never appears to have beaten about for it. That betrayal is of course the worst betrayal of all, and I think the way he has escaped it the happiest form of the peace that has finally visited him. It was truly a wonderful success to be so the devotee of the phrase and yet never its victim. Fine as he inveterately desired it should be he still never lost sight of the question Fine for what? It is always so related and associated, so properly part of something else that is in turn part of something other, part of a reference, a tone, a passage, a page, that the simple may enjoy it for its least bearing and the initiated for its greatest. That surely is to be a writer of the first order, to resemble when in the hand and however closely viewed a shapely crystal box, and yet to be seen when placed on the table and opened to contain innumerable compartments, springs and tricks. One is ornamental either way, but one is in the second way precious too.

The crystal box then figures the style of "Salammbô" and "Saint-Antoine" in a greater degree than that of "Bovary," because, as the two former express the writer's romantic side, he had in them, while equally covering his tracks, still further to fare and still more to hunt. Beyond this allusion to their completing his duality I shall not attempt closely to characterise them; though I admit that in not insisting on them I press

[1]It was true, delightfully true, that, extravagance in this province of his life, though apparently in no other, being Flaubert's necessity and law, he deliberated and hung fire, wrestled, retreated and returned, indulged generally in a tragi-comedy of waste; which I recall a charming expression of on the lips of Edmond de Goncourt, who quite recognised the heroic legend, but prettily qualified it: "Il faut vous dire qu'il y avait là-dedans beaucoup de coucheries et d'école buissonière." And he related how on the occasion of a stay with his friend under the roof of the Princess Mathilde, the friend, missed during the middle hours of a fine afternoon, was found to have undressed himself and gone to bed to think!

most lightly on the scale into which he had in his own view cast his greatest pressure. He lamented the doom that drove him so oddly, so ruefully, to choose his subjects, but he lamented it least when these subjects were most pompous and most exotic, feeling as he did that they had then after all most affinity with his special eloquence. In dealing with the near, the directly perceived, he had to keep down his tone, to make the eloquence small; though with the consequence, as we have seen, that in spite of such precautions the whole thing mostly insists on being ample. The familiar, that is, under his touch, took on character, importance, extension, one scarce knows what to call it, in order to carry the style or perhaps rather, as we may say, sit with proper ease in the vehicle, and there was accordingly a limit to its smallness; whereas in the romantic books, the preferred world of Flaubert's imagination, there was practically no need of compromise. The compromise gave him throughout endless trouble, and nothing would be more to the point than to show, had I space, why in particular it distressed him. It was obviously his strange predicament that the only spectacle open to him by experience and direct knowledge was the bourgeois, which on that ground imposed on him successively his three so intensely bourgeois themes. He was obliged to treat these themes, which he hated, because his experience left him no alternative; his only alternative was given by history, geography, philosophy, fancy, the world of erudition and of imagination, the world especially of this last. In the bourgeois sphere his ideal of expression laboured under protest; in the other, the imagined, the projected, his need for facts, for matter, and his pursuit of them, sat no less heavily. But as his style all the while required a certain exercise of pride he was on the whole more at home in the exotic than in the familiar; he escaped above all in the former connection the associations, the disparities he detested. He could be frankly noble in "Salammbô" and "Saint-Antoine," whereas in "Bovary" and "L'Éducation" he could be but circuitously and insidiously so. He could in the one case cut his coat according to his cloth— if we mean by his cloth his predetermined tone, while in the other he had to take it already cut. Singular enough in his life the situation so constituted: the comparatively meagre human

consciousness—for we must come back to that in him—
struggling with the absolutely large artistic; and the large artistic half wreaking itself on the meagre human and half seeking a refuge from it, as well as a revenge against it, in
something quite different.

Flaubert had in fact command of two refuges which he
worked in turn. The first of these was the attitude of irony,
so constant in him that "L'Éducation" bristles and hardens
with it and "Bouvard et Pécuchet"—strangest of "poetic" jus-
tices—is made as dry as sand and as heavy as lead; the second
only was, by processes, by journeys the most expensive, to get
away altogether. And we inevitably ask ourselves whether, eschewing the policy of flight, he might not after all have
fought out his case a little more on the spot. Might he not
have addressed himself to the human still otherwise than in
"L'Éducation" and in "Bouvard"? When one thinks of the
view of the life of his country, of the vast French community
and its constituent creatures, offered in these productions,
one declines to believe it could make up the *whole* vision of a
man of his quality. Or when all was said and done was he
absolutely and exclusively condemned to irony? The second
refuge I speak of, the getting away from the human, the congruously and measurably human, altogether, perhaps becomes
in the light of this possibility but an irony the more. Carthage
and the Thebaid, Salammbô, Spendius, Matho, Hannon,
Saint Anthony, Hilarion, the Paternians, the Marcosians and
the Carpocratians, what are all these, inviting because queer,
but a confession of supreme impatience with the actual and
the near, often queer enough too, no doubt, but not consol-
ingly, not transcendently? Last remains the question whether,
even if our author's immediate as distinguished from his remote view had had more reach, the particular gift we claim
for him, the perfection of arrangement and form, would have
had in certain directions the acquired flexibility. States of
mind, states of soul, of the simpler kind, the kinds supposable
in the Emma Bovarys, the Frédérics, the Bouvards and the
Pécuchets, to say nothing of the Carthaginians and the Eremites—for Flaubert's eremites are eminently artless—these
conditions represent, I think, his proved psychological range.
And that throws us back remarkably, almost confoundingly,

upon another face of the general anomaly. The "gift" was of the greatest, a force in itself, in virtue of which he is a consummate writer; and yet there are whole sides of life to which it was never addressed and which it apparently quite failed to suspect as a field of exercise. If he never approached the complicated character in man or woman—Emma Bovary is not the least little bit complicated—or the really furnished, the finely civilised, was this because, surprisingly, he could not? *L'âme française* at all events shows in him but ill.

This undoubtedly marks a limit, but limits are for the critic familiar country, and he may mostly well feel the prospect wide enough when he finds something positively well enough done. By disposition or by obligation Flaubert selected, and though his selection was in some respects narrow he stops not too short to have left us three really "cast" works and a fourth of several perfect parts, to say nothing of the element of perfection, of the superlative for the size, in his three *nouvelles*. What he attempted he attempted in a spirit that gives an extension to the idea of the achievable and the achieved in a literary thing, and it is by this that we contentedly gauge the matter. As success goes in this world of the approximate it may pass for success of the greatest. If I am unable to pursue the proof of my remark in "Salammbô" and "Saint-Antoine" it is because I have also had to select and have found the questions connected with their two companions more interesting. There are numerous judges, I hasten to mention, who, showing the opposite preference, lose themselves with rapture in the strange bristling archæological picture—yet all amazingly vivified and co-ordinated—of the Carthaginian mercenaries in revolt and the sacred veil of the great goddess profaned and stolen; as well in the still more peopled panorama of the ancient sects, superstitions and mythologies that swim in the desert before the fevered eyes of the Saint. One may be able, however, at once to breathe more freely in "Bovary" than in "Salammbô" and yet to hope that there is no intention of the latter that one has missed. The great intention certainly, and little as we may be sweetly beguiled, holds us fast; which is simply the author's indomitable purpose of fully pervading his field. There are countries beyond the sea in which tracts are allowed to settlers on condition that they will really, not nominally, cultivate them. Flaubert is on his romantic ground like one of these settlers; he makes good with all his might his title to his tract, and in a way that shows how it is not only for him a question of safety but a question of honour. Honour demands that he shall set up his home and his faith there in such a way that every inch of the surface be planted or paved. He would have been ashamed merely to encamp and, after the fashion of most other adventurers, knock up a log hut among charred stumps. This was not what would have been for him taking artistic possession, it was not what would have been for him even personal honour, let alone literary; and yet the general lapse from integrity was a thing that, wherever he looked, he saw not only condoned but acclaimed and rewarded. He lived, as he felt, in an age of mean production and cheap criticism, the practical upshot of which took on for him a name that was often on his lips. He called it the hatred of literature, a hatred in the midst of which, the most literary of men, he found himself appointed to suffer. I may not, however, follow him in that direction—which would take us far; and the less that he was for himself after all, in spite of groans and imprecations, a man of resources and remedies, and that there was always his possibility of building himself in.

This he did equally in all his books—built himself into literature by means of a material put together with extraordinary art; but it leads me again to the question of what such a stiff ideal imposed on him for the element of exactitude. This element, in the romantic, was his merciless law; it was perhaps even in the romantic that—if there could indeed be degrees for him in such matters—he most despised the loose and the more-or-less. To be intensely definite and perfectly positive, to know so well what he meant that he could at every point strikingly and conclusively verify it, was the first of his needs; and if in addition to being thus synthetically final he could be strange and sad and terrible, and leave the cause of these effects inscrutable, success then had for him its highest savour. We feel the inscrutability in those memorable few words that put before us Frédéric Moreau's start upon his vain course of travel, "Il connût alors la mélancholie des paquebots;" an image to the last degree comprehensive and embracing, but which haunts us, in its droll pathos, without our quite knowing why. But he was really never so pleased as when he could be both rare and precise about the dreadful. His own sense of all this, as I have already indicated, was that beauty comes with expression, that expression is creation, that it *makes* the reality, and only in the degree in which it *is*, exquisitely, expression; and that we move in literature through a world of different values and relations, a blest world in which we know nothing except by style, but in which also everything is saved by it, and in which the image is thus always superior to the thing itself. This quest and multiplication of the image, the image tested and warranted and consecrated for the occasion, was accordingly his high elegance, to which he too much sacrificed and to which "Salammbô" and partly "Saint-Antoine" are monstrous monuments. Old cruelties and perversities, old wonders and errors and terrors, endlessly appealed to him; they constitute the unhuman side of his work, and if we have not the bribe of curiosity, of a lively interest in method, or rather in evocation just *as* evocation, we tread our way among them, especially in "Salammbô," with a reserve too dry for our pleasure. To my own view the curiosity and the literary interest are equal in dealing with the non-romantic books, and the world presented, the aspects and agents, are less deterrent and more amenable both to our own social and expressional terms. Style itself moreover, with all respect to Flaubert, never *totally* beguiles; since even when we are so queerly constituted as to be ninety-nine parts literary we are still a hundredth part something else. This hundredth part may, once we possess the book—or the book possesses us—make us imperfect as readers, and yet without it should we want or get the book at all? The curiosity at any rate, to repeat, is even greatest for me in "Madame Bovary," say, for here I can measure, can more directly appreciate, the terms. The aspects and impressions being of an experience conceivable to me I am more touched by the beauty; my interest gets more of the benefit of the beauty even though this be not intrinsically greater. Which brings back our appreciation inevitably at last to the question of our author's lucidity.

    I have sufficiently remarked that I speak from the point of

view of his interest to a reader of his own craft, the point of view of his extraordinary technical wealth—though indeed when I think of the general power of "Madame Bovary" I find myself desiring not to narrow the ground of the lesson, not to connect the lesson, to its prejudice, with that idea of the "technical," that question of the way a thing is done, so abhorrent, as a call upon attention, in whatever art, to the wondrous Anglo-Saxon mind. Without proposing Flaubert as the type of the newspaper novelist, or as an easy alternative to golf or the bicycle, we should do him less than justice in failing to insist that a masterpiece like "Madame Bovary" may benefit even with the simple-minded by the way it has been done. It derives from its firm roundness that sign of all rare works that there is something in it for every one. It may be read ever so attentively, ever so freely, without a suspicion of how it is written, to say nothing of put together; it may equally be read under the excitement of these perceptions alone, one of the greatest known to the reader who is fully open to them. Both readers will have been transported, which is all any can ask. Leaving the first of them, however that may be, to state the case for himself, I state it yet again for the second, if only on this final ground. The book and its companions represent for us a practical solution, Flaubert's own troubled but settled one, of the eternal dilemma of the painter of life. From the moment this rash adventurer deals with his mysterious matter at all directly his desire is not to deal with it stintedly. It at the same time remains true that from the moment he desires to produce forms in which it shall be preserved, he desires that these forms, things of *his* creation, shall not be, as testifying to his way with them, weak or ignoble. He must make them complete and beautiful, of satisfactory production, intrinsically interesting, under peril of disgrace with those who know. Those who don't know of course don't count for him, and it neither helps nor hinders him to say that every one knows about life. Every one does not—it is distinctly the case of the few; and if it were in fact the case of the many the knowledge still might exist, on the evidence around us, even in an age of unprecedented printing, without attesting itself by a multiplication of masterpieces. The question for the artist can only be of doing the artistic utmost,

and thereby of *seeing* the general task. When it is seen with
the intensity with which it presented itself to Flaubert a lifetime is none too much for fairly tackling it. It must either be
left alone or be dealt with, and to leave it alone is a comparatively simple matter.

To deal with it is on the other hand to produce a certain
number of finished works; there being no other known
method; and the quantity of life depicted will depend on this
array. What will this array, however, depend on, and what
will condition the number of pieces of which it is composed?
The "finish," evidently, that the formula so glibly postulates
and for which the novelist is thus so handsomely responsible.
He has on the one side to feel his subject and on the other
side to render it, and there are undoubtedly two ways in
which his situation may be expressed, especially perhaps by
himself. The more he feels his subject the more he *can* render
it—that is the first way. The more he renders it the more he
can feel it—that is the second way. This second way was unmistakeably Flaubert's, and if the result of it for him was a
bar to abundant production he could only accept such an incident as part of the game. He probably for that matter would
have challenged any easy definition of "abundance," contested
the application of it to the repetition, however frequent, of
the thing not "done." What but the "doing" makes the thing,
he would have asked, and how can a positive result from a
mere iteration of negatives, or wealth proceed from the simple addition of so many instances of penury? We should here,
in closer communion with him, have got into his highly characteristic and suggestive view of the fertilisation of subject by
form, penetration of the sense, ever, by the expression—the
latter reacting creatively on the former; a conviction in the
light of which he appears to have wrought with real consistency and which borrows from him thus its high measure of
credit. It would undoubtedly have suffered if his books had
been things of a loose logic, whereas we refer to it not only
without shame but with an encouraged confidence by their
showing of a logic so close. Let the phrase, the form that the
whole is at the given moment staked on, be beautiful and
related, and the rest will take care of itself—such is a rough
indication of Flaubert's faith; which has the importance that

it was a faith sincere, active and inspiring. I hasten to add indeed that we must most of all remember how in these matters everything hangs on definitions. The "beautiful," with our author, covered for the phrase a great deal of ground, and when every sort of propriety had been gathered in under it and every relation, in a complexity of such, protected, the idea itself, the presiding thought, ended surely by being pretty well provided for.

These, however, are subordinate notes, and the plain question, in the connection I have touched upon, is of whether we would really wish him to have written more books, say either of the type of "Bovary" or of the type of "Salammbô," and not have written them so well. When the production of a great artist who has lived a length of years has been small there is always the regret; but there is seldom, any more than here, the conceivable remedy. For the case is doubtless predetermined by the particular kind of great artist a writer happens to be, and this even if when we come to the conflict, to the historic case, deliberation and delay may not all have been imposed by temperament. The admirable George Sand, Flaubert's beneficent friend and correspondent, is exactly the happiest example we could find of the genius constitutionally incapable of worry, the genius for whom style "came," for whom the sought effect was ever quickly and easily struck off, the book freely and swiftly written, and who consequently is represented for us by upwards of ninety volumes. If the comparison were with this lady's great contemporary the elder Dumas the disparity would be quadrupled, but that ambiguous genius, somehow never really caught by us in the *fact* of composition, is out of our concern here: the issue is of those developments of expression which involve a style, and as Dumas never so much as once grazed one in all his long career, there was not even enough of that grace in him for a fillip of the finger-nail. Flaubert is at any rate represented by six books, so that he may on that estimate figure as poor, while Madame Sand, falling so little short of a hundred, figures as rich; and yet the fact remains that I can refer the congenial mind to him with confidence and can do nothing of the sort for it in respect to Madame Sand. She is loose and liquid and iridescent, as iridescent as we may undertake to find her; but

I can imagine compositions quite without virtue—the virtue I mean, of sticking together—begotten by the impulse to emulate her. She had undoubtedly herself the benefit of her facility, but are we not left wondering to what extent *we* have it? There is too little in her, by the literary connection, for the critical mind, weary of much wandering, to rest upon. Flaubert himself wandered, wandered far, went much roundabout and sometimes lost himself by the way, but how handsomely he provided for our present repose! He found the French language inconceivably difficult to write with elegance and was confronted with the equal truths that elegance is the last thing that languages, even as they most mature, seem to concern themselves with, and that at the same time taste, asserting rights, insists on it, to the effect of showing us in a boundless circumjacent waste of effort what the absence of it may mean. He saw the less of this desert of death come back to that—that everything at all saved from it for us since the beginning had been saved by a soul of elegance within, or in other words by the last refinement of selection, by the indifference on the part of the very idiom, huge quite other than "composing" agent, to the individual pretension. Recognising thus that to carry through the individual pretension is at the best a battle, he adored a hard surface and detested a soft one—much more a muddled; regarded a style without rhythm and harmony as in a work of pretended beauty no style at all. He considered that the failure of complete expression so registered made of the work of pretended beauty a work of achieved barbarity. It would take us far to glance even at his fewest discriminations; but rhythm and harmony were for example most menaced in his scheme by repetition—when repetition had not a positive grace; and were above all most at the mercy of the bristling particles of which our modern tongues are mainly composed and which make of the desired surface a texture pricked through, from beneath, even to destruction, as by innumerable thorns.

On these lines production was of course slow work for him—especially as he met the difficulty, met it with an inveteracy which shows how it *can* be met; and full of interest for readers of English speech is the reflection he causes us to make as to the possibility of success at all comparable among ourselves. I have spoken of his groans and imprecations, his interminable waits and deep despairs; but what would these things have been, what would have become of him and what of his wrought residuum, had he been condemned to deal with a form of speech consisting, like ours, as to one part, of "that" and "which"; as to a second part, of the blest "it," which an English sentence may repeat in three or four opposed references without in the least losing caste; as to a third face of all the "tos" of the infinitive and the preposition; as to a fourth of our precious auxiliaries "be" and "do"; and as to a fifth, of whatever survives in the language for the precious art of pleasing? Whether or no the fact that the painter of "life" among us has to contend with a medium intrinsically indocile, on certain sides, like our own, whether this drawback accounts for his having failed, in our time, to treat us, arrested and charmed, to a single case of crowned classicism, there is at any rate no doubt that we in some degree owe Flaubert's counterweight for that deficiency to *his* having, on his own ground, more happily triumphed. By which I do not mean that "Madame Bovary" is a classic because the "thats," the "its" and the "tos" are made to march as Orpheus and his lute made the beasts, but because the element of order and harmony works as a symbol of everything else that is preserved for us by the history of the book. The history of the book remains the lesson and the important, the delightful thing, remains above all the drama that moves slowly to its climax. It is what we come back to for the sake of what it shows us. We see—from the present to the past indeed, never alas from the present to the future—how a classic almost inveterately grows. Unimportant, unnoticed, or, so far as noticed, contested, unrelated, alien, it has a cradle round which the fairies but scantly flock and is waited on in general by scarce a hint of significance. The significance comes by a process slow and small, the fact only that one perceptive private reader after another discovers at his convenience that the book is rare. The addition of the perceptive private readers is no quick affair, and would doubtless be a vain one did they not—while plenty of other much more remarkable books come and go—accumulate and count. They count by their quality and continuity of attention; so they have gathered for

"Madame Bovary," and so they are held. That is really once more the great circumstance. It is always in order for us to feel yet again what it is we are held by. Such is my reason, definitely, for speaking of Flaubert as the novelist's novelist. Are we not moreover—and let it pass this time as a happy hope!—pretty well all novelists now?

Introduction to *Madame Bovary*,
London: Heinemann, 1902
Reprinted in *Notes on Novelists*, 1914

Eugène Fromentin

A Study of Rubens and Rembrandt. *Les Maîtres d'Autrefois. Belgique-Holland.* Par Eugène Fromentin. New York: F. W. Christern, 1876.

IT WILL NOT SURPRISE the readers of M. Fromentin's earlier compositions to learn that this is a very interesting book. Those persons who remember his two strangely pictorial little volumes on the East—'Un Été dans le Sahara,' 'Une Année dans le Dakhel'—will have retained a vivid impression of his descriptive powers and his skill in evoking figures and localities; while the admirers of the charming novel of 'Dominique'—a singularly exquisite and perfect work, which has had no successor—must have kept an equally grateful record of his art of analyzing delicate moral and intellectual phenomena. These three modest volumes have hitherto constituted what is called in France the author's literary baggage. The work whose title we have transcribed, and which is somewhat more massive than its predecessors, has just been added to the list, and upon this evidence ('Les Maîtres d'Autrefois' has attracted great attention) M. Fromentin the other day presented himself as a candidate for the French Academy. He was not elected, and one may, while admiring his writings, think perhaps that his application was a trifle premature. The quality of his productions is exquisite, but the quantity is as yet slender. It must be added, however, that M. Fromentin has had occupations other than literary. He is a distinguished painter, and a great many of his refined, if somewhat pallid, renderings of Eastern scenes have been seen in America. We prefer his books to his pictures, and we have greatly enjoyed the volume before us. We recommend it to those lovers of art who have visited the great Dutch and Flemish pictures in the cities in which they were painted; and we recommend it even more to persons who have the journey through Holland and Belgium still before them. It would be even more useful, perhaps, as an incitement than as a reminder.

M. Fromentin begins with Rubens, to whom he devotes the longest section in his volume, talks briefly of Vandyck, passes on to Jacob Ruysdael and the principal Dutch genre-painters, expatiates largely upon Rembrandt, and touches

347

finally (returning to Belgium) upon Van Eyck and Memling. We repeat that his whole volume is extremely interesting, but it strikes us as curious rather than valuable. We have always had a decided mistrust of literary criticism of works of plastic art; and those tendencies which have suggested this feeling are exhibited by M. Fromentin in their most extreme form. He would deny, we suppose, that his criticism is literary and assert that it is purely pictorial—the work of a painter judging painters. This, however, is only half true. M. Fromentin is too ingenious and elaborate a writer not to have taken a great deal of pleasure in the literary form that he gives to his thoughts; and when once the literary form takes the bit into its teeth, as it does very often with M. Fromentin, the effect, at least, of over-subtlety and web-spinning is certain to be produced. This over-subtlety is M. Fromentin's fault: he attempts to say too many things about his painters, to discriminate beyond the point at which discriminations are useful. A work of art has generally been a simpler matter, for the painter, than a certain sort of critic assumes, and M. Fromentin, who has painted pictures, ought to know that they are meant before all things to be enjoyed. The excess into which he falls is not of the same sort as that which is so common with Mr. Ruskin—the attribution of various incongruous and arbitrary intentions to the artist; it is rather a too eager analysis of the material work itself, a too urgent description of it, a too exhaustive enumeration of its constituent particles. Nothing can well be more fatal to that *tranquil* quality which is the very essence of one's enjoyment of a work of art. M. Fromentin, like most French writers on æsthetic or indeed on any other matters, abounds in his own sense. He can say so much so neatly and so vividly, in his admirable French style, that he loses all respect for the unsayable—the better half, we think, of all that belongs to a work of art. But his perception is extraordinarily just and delicate, and his power of entering into a picture is, in a literary critic, very rare. He enters too much, in our opinion, into the technical side, and he expects of his readers to care much more than should be expected even of a very ardent art-lover for the mysteries of the process by which the picture was made. There is a certain sort of talk which should be confined to manuals and note-books and studio records; there is something impertinent in pretending to work it into literary form—especially into the very elegant and rather self-conscious literary form of which M. Fromentin is master. It is narrow and unimaginative not to understand that a very deep and intelligent enjoyment of pictures is consistent with a lively indifference to this "inside view" of them. It has too much in common with the reverse of a tapestry, and it suggests that a man may be extremely fond of good concerts and yet have no relish for the tuning of fiddles. M. Fromentin is guilty of an abuse of it which gives his book occasionally a somewhat sickly and unmasculine tone. He is, besides, sometimes too inconclusive; he multiplies his descriptive and analytic touches, but we are at loss to know exactly what he has desired to prove.

This is especially the case in the pages upon Rubens, which contain a great many happy characterizations of the painter, but lack a "general drift," an argument. M. Fromentin indulges in more emotion on the subject of Rubens than we have ever found ourselves able to do, and his whole dissertation is a good example of the vanity of much of the criticism in the super-subtle style. We lay it down perplexed and bewildered, with a wearied sense of having strained our attention in a profitless cause. There is a limit to what it is worth while to attempt to say about the greatest artists. Michael Angelo and Raphael bid defiance to more than a moderate amount of "keen analysis." Either Rubens was a first-rate genius, and in this case he may be trusted to disengage himself freely from his admirers' impressions; or else he was not, and in this case it is not worth while to split hairs about him. M. Fromentin, speaking roughly, takes Rubens too seriously by several shades. There are fine painters and coarse painters, and Rubens belonged to the latter category: he reigned in it with magnificent supremacy. One may as well come to this conclusion first as last, for all the ingenuity in the world will not avert it. Rubens was, in painting, an incomparable *improvvisatore*; almost always a great colorist, often extremely happy in composition, he never leaves us without a sense that the particular turn the picture has taken, the cast of a certain face, the attitude of a certain figure, the flow of a drapery or the choice of a gesture, has been an accident of the moment.

Hence we have in Rubens a constant sense of something superficial, irreflective, something cheap, as we say nowadays. His intentions had often great energy, but they had very little profundity, and his imagination, we suspect, less delicacy than M. Fromentin attributes to it. He belongs, certainly, to the small group of the world's greatest painters, but he is, in a certain way, the vulgarest of the group. No other of its members has produced anything like the same amount of work of which the quality discredits and compromises the remaining and superior portion. M. Fromentin has some excellent remarks about his portraits, of which he recognizes the coarseness and the limited value. "Suppose Holbein," he says, " with Rubens's *clientèle*, and you immediately see before you a new human gallery, very interesting for the moralist, equally admirable for the history of life and the history of art, and which Rubens, one must admit, would not have enriched by a single type." M. Fromentin has, however, a charming paragraph about the magnificent "St. George" of the Church of St. James of Antwerp—the church containing the tomb of the painter; a paragraph we are glad to quote as an example of the admirable way in which the author often says things:

"One day, towards the end of his life, in the midst of his glory, in the midst, perhaps, of his repose, under an august title, under the invocation of the Virgin, and of the only one of all the saints to whom it seemed to him lawful to give his own image, it pleased him to paint in a small frame (about two yards square) what there had been venerable and seductive in the beings whom he had loved. He owed this last tribute to those of whom he was born, to those women [his two wives] who had shared and embellished his beautiful and laborious career, charmed it, ennobled it, perfumed it with grace, tenderness, and fidelity. He gave it to them as richly and in as masterly a way as was to be expected from his affectionate hand and his genius in the fulness of its power. He put into it his science, his piety, and a rarer degree of care. He made of the work what you know—a marvel, infinitely touching as the work of a son, a father, and a husband, and for ever memorable as a work of art."

M. Fromentin has some admirable pages upon the origin of Dutch art, and the conditions upon which it came into being: "Genius shall consist in prejudging nothing, in not knowing that you know, in letting yourself be taken by surprise by your model, in asking of it alone how it shall be represented. As for embellishing, never; ennobling, never; chastening, never; these are so many lies as so much useless trouble. Is there not in every artist worthy of the name a certain something which takes upon it this care naturally and without effort?" His chapters upon Paul Potter, Cuyp, Ruysdael, Terburg, and Metsu are in our opinion the most felicitous in the volume; they are full of just discrimination and interesting suggestion. He ranks Ruysdael immediately after Rembrandt, a classification of this enchanting painter with which we have no quarrel; but we are not sure that with regard to him, too, he may not be accused of looking for mid day (as the French say) *à quatorze heures*. But he characterizes him charmingly. He says very justly that there are a great many things which we should like to know about his life and person which it is impossible to ascertain; his history is obscure, and the questions are unanswerable. But would the idea come to us, he adds, of asking such questions about any of the other Dutch painters? "Brilliant and charming, they painted, and it seems as if this were enough. Ruysdael painted, but he lived, and this is why it is desirable to know how he lived. I know but three or four men who are to this degree personally interesting—Rembrandt, Ruysdael, Paul Potter, perhaps Cuyp. This is more than enough to class them." Upon Rembrandt M. Fromentin expatiates largely and very ingeniously; but we should say of these chapters as of his remarks upon Rubens, that the author goes through a great critical motion without arriving at any definite goal. He strikes a great many matches, and often rather bedims the subject. The great picture at Amsterdam, best known by its French name of the "Ronde de Nuit," is a very strange work if you will, but nothing is gained by making it out stranger than it is and exhausting the vocabulary of hopeless æsthetic conjecture on its behalf. The note of M. Fromentin's view of Rembrandt is struck by his saying that he "revealed one of the unknown corners of the human soul," and by his adding, at the close of his remarks, that he was "a pure spiritualist—an ideologist." Some readers, doubtless, will be more struck with the felicity of this definition than we have been. It is not the unknown, we should say, that Rembrandt represents, but the known, the familiar, the common, the homely. His subjects, his scenes, his figures are almost all taken from common life, and where they are not they are brought into it. He was an alchemist: he presents them in that extraordinary envelope of dense light and shade which is the familiar sign of his manner; but in this it is the execution that is rare to our sense—incomparably rare, certainly—rather than the conception. But to whatever degree in detail M. Fromentin's readers may dissent from him, they will do justice to the brilliancy of his work. Its acuteness and delicacy of perception are altogether remarkable and its manner most exquisite. It has a peculiar charm.

Nation, July 13, 1876

Théophile Gautier

Tableaux de Siège: Paris 1870 –1871. Par Théophile Gautier. Paris, 1871.

AMONG THE innumerable volumes dealing with the great events of the last eighteen months, in their various phases, none has a more peculiar interest than this collection of "Tableaux de Siège," by Théophile Gautier. The interest is of a less melancholy sort than belongs to many of these productions, for M. Gautier treats chiefly of the picturesque aspect of his country's troubles. Good patriot though he is, he preserves, through the mist of filial tears, a searching eye for "effects," and in these, bloodshed, fire, and famine, whatever other merits they may lack, are richly prolific. We have in English no literary analogue of Théophile Gautier. No English writer has as yet taken stock of the capacity of our language for light descriptive prose; and indeed, for that matter, the turn for light analytical description is decidedly less common in the English than in the French mind. M. Gautier is the apostle of visual observation—the poet of the look of things. His pen is almost a brush. Shut up in Paris during the first siege, and one of the host of anxious refugees at Versailles during the second, he remained a *feuilletoniste* through all; turned his enforced leisure to account, walked about, looked, noted, and wrote. His manner reaches perfection in these little sketches, originally printed for the most part in the miniature journals issued during the siege, when news was scanty, and the *feuilleton* ungrudged. He has rarely hit the vivid word and the pictorial phrase with more felicity. His style is such a perpetual tissue of images and pictures, that it is almost as unfair to detach examples from the context as it would be to make an excision in one of Titian's canvases for a specimen of his color. Here, however, are two or three hints. Of a certain emaciated dog, during the hungry days: "He was seen walking along the rampart as if he were going the rounds, rawboned, dissected by leanness, his spinal column like a rosary of beads, the tuberosities of his joints nearly piercing his skin, his sides like a series of hoops, his hide as rugged and rough as dry turf. . . . He was the ghostly shadow of a dog—two profiles glued together, with no more thickness than cut-paper." Of the fasting lions in the Jardin des Plantes: "One of them went vaguely to and fro with an air of *ennui*, beating his thighs with his tail; the other was lying in his cage, one fore-paw outstretched, the other folded under his breast, his head shining like a human mask, with its straight nose, its broad brow, its stiff moustaches, like silver threads, and its dishevelled, tawny mane. The yellow look of his fixed eyes was full of melancholy. Perhaps, in his famished dreams, he was thinking of the antelopes who came, towards evening, to drink at the fountain. . . . But a still more touching spectacle was a poor sick lioness, of an almost diaphanous leanness, who seemed consumptive and in the last stage of a decline. Attenuated, hollowed out like a greyhound, she had assumed a sort of ideal elegance, and looked like those lions rampant on ancient coats of arms, half ornament, half chimæra, of cursive and extravagant outline, which the heraldic art used to imprint on a groundwork of metal or of color—'tongue and claws gules.' Her hide, of a pale yellow, took the light and relieved her against the dusky background of her cage; she stood fixed on her four paws, whose muscles, still powerful, lay in furrows beneath the skin. Homesickness for the desert and the scorching rocks of Atlas was stamped in her chilled and languid *pose*; illness had given to her eyes a sort of unwonted softness—a harrowing look. Stripped of her strength, she seemed to beg for human pity. . . ." Lastly, of the park at Versailles: "At the end of the alleys which open in a fan around the basin near Trianon, as in the fugitive blue distances of the parks of Watteau, hovered those light fumes which deepen with their mists the aerial perspective. *The spring, like a timid landscapist, who advances with little strokes in his foliage, had begun to lay on the branches, with a sparse and sober brush, a few touches of tender green*." The readers will see that the author's style plays over into a sort of jocose and conscious exaggeration; he is always "humoristic," as the French say. Not the least of his charms, to our mind, has always been a certain sensuous serenity, the imperturbable levity of a mind utterly unhaunted by the metaphysics of things. Even in the presence of the Prussian ravages, he retains a fair share of good-nature. But we must pay for everything. Just as his visual perception and his happy verbal instinct have grown strong, his power of thought has declined. There is the oddest contrast between his descriptive *brio* and grace and the feeble note of reflection which from time to time crops through it. In this matter M. Gautier is little better than one of those Philistines of taste whom he despises. The chapter with which he closes his book (*Paris-Capitale*) reveals a moral levity so transcendent and immeasurable as to amount really to a psychological curiosity. It is a strange spectacle to see exquisite genius conditioned, as it were, upon such moral aridity. If M. Gautier's *confrères*, as a rule, remain as grossly unillumined as himself by the lurid light of their country's woes, the fact bodes ill for the future of France. The ineffable frivolity of his peroration recalls irresistibly that sternly unsavory Scriptural image of the dog and his vomit. It is enough to disgust one with the pursuit of local color.

Nation, January 25, 1872

Théâtre de Théophile Gautier: Mystères, Comédies, et Ballets. Paris: Charpentier, 1872.

THERE VERY RECENTLY DIED in Paris a man of genius whom his eulogists all made haste to proclaim a true poet. Many of them, indeed, spoke of Théophile Gautier as a great poet, and one, we remember, mentioned his last little volume, "Tableaux de Siège," as the crowning glory of the resistance to the Prussians. Gautier was indeed a poet and a strongly representative one—a French poet in his limitations even more than in his gifts; and he remains an interesting example of how, even when the former are surprisingly great, a happy application of the latter may produce the most delightful works. Completeness on his own scale is to our mind the idea he most instantly suggests. Such as his finished task now presents him, he is almost sole of his kind. He has had imitators who have imitated everything but his spontaneity and his temper; and as they have therefore failed to equal him, we doubt whether the literature of our day presents so naturally perfect a genius. We say this with no desire to transfer Gautier to a higher pedestal than he has fairly earned—a poor service, for the pedestal sometimes sadly dwarfs the figure. His great merit was that he understood himself so perfectly and handled himself so skilfully. Even more than Alfred de Musset (with whom the speech had a shade of mock-modesty) he might have said that, if his glass was not large, at least it was all his own glass. As an artist, he never knew an hour's weakness or failed to strike the note that should truly render his idea. He was, indeed, of literary artists the most accomplished. He was not of the Academy, but he completes not unworthily the picturesque group, gaining relief from isolation, of those eminent few—Molière, Pascal, Balzac, Béranger, George Sand—who have come near making it the supreme literary honour in France not to be numbered among the Forty. There are a host of reasons why we should not compare Gautier with such a poet as Browning; and yet there are several why we should. If we do so, with all proper reservations, we may wonder whether we are the richer, or, at all events, the better entertained, as a poet's readers should before all things be, by the clear, undiluted strain of Gautier's minor key, or by the vast, grossly commingled volume of utterance of the author of "Men and Women." This, perhaps, is an idle question; and the artificer of "Émaux et Camées" was presumably of opinion that it is idle at all times to point a moral. But if there are sermons in stones, there are profitable reflections to be made even on Théophile Gautier; notably this one—that a man's supreme use in the world is to master his intellectual instrument and play it in perfection.

There is, perhaps, scant apparent logic in treating a closed career more tenderly than an open one; but we suspect it belongs to the finer essence of good criticism to do so, and, at any rate, we find our judgment of the author of the "Voyage en Espagne" and the "Capitaine Fracasse" turning altogether to unprotesting kindness. We had a vague consciousness of lurking objections; but on calling them to appear they gave no answer. Gautier's death, indeed, in the nature of things could not but be touching and dispose one to large allowances. The world he left was the sum of the universe for him, and upon any other his writings throw but the dimmest light—project, indeed, that contrasted darkness which surrounds the edges of a luminous surface. The beauty and variety of our present earth and the insatiability of our earthly temperament were his theme, and we doubt whether these things have ever been placed in a more flattering light. He brought to his task a sort of pagan *bonhomie* which makes most of the descriptive and pictorial poets seem, by contrast, a goup of shivering ascetics or muddled metaphysicians. He excels them by his magnificent good temper and the unquestioning serenity of his enjoyment of the great spectacle of nature and art. His style certainly is one of the latest fruits of time; but his mental attitude before the universe has an almost Homeric simplicity. His world was all material, and its outlying darkness hardly more suggestive, morally, than a velvet canopy studded with silver nails. To close his eyes and turn his back on it must have seemed to him the end of all things; death, for him, must have been as the sullen dropping of a stone into a well. His faculty of visual discrimination was extraordinary. His observation was so penetrating and his descriptive instinct so unerring, that one might have fancied grave Nature, in a fit of coquetry, or tired of receiving but half-justice, had determined to construct a genius with senses of a finer strain than the mass of the human family. Gautier, as an observer, often reminds us of those classic habitués of the opera who listen with a subtler sense than their neighbours and register with a murmured *brava* the undistinguishable shades of merit in a prima donna's execution. He was for many years a diligent theatrical critic, faithful to his post in all dramatic weathers, so that one has only to extend the image a little to conceive him as always in an orchestra-stall before the general stage, watching a lamplit performance—flaring gas in one case, the influence of his radiant fancy in the other. "Descriptive" writing, to our English taste, suggests nothing very enticing—a respectable sort of padding, at best, but a few degrees removed in ponderosity from downright moralizing. The prejudice, we admit, is a wholesome one, and the limits of verbal portraiture of all sorts should be jealously guarded. But there is no better proof of Gautier's talent than that he should have triumphantly reformed this venerable abuse and, in the best sense, made one of the heaviest kinds of writing one of the lightest. Of his process and his success we could give an adequate idea only by a long series

of citations, and these we lack the opportunity to collect.
The reader would conclude with us, we think, that Gautier
is an inimitable model. He would never find himself condemned to that thankless task of pulling the cart up hill—
retouching the picture—which in most descriptions is fatal to
illusion. The author's manner is so light and true, so really
creative, his fancy so alert, his taste so happy, his humour so
genial, that he makes illusion almost as contagious as laughter; the image, the object, the scene, stands arrested by his
phrase with the wholesome glow of truth overtaken. Gautier's native gift of expression was extremely rich, and he cultivated and polished it with a diligence that may serve to give
the needed balance of gravity to his literary character. He enriched his picturesque vocabulary from the most recondite
sources; it has a most robust comprehensiveness. His favourite reading, we have somewhere seen, was the dictionary; he
loved words for themselves—for their look, their aroma, their
colour, their fantastic intimations. He kept a supply of the
choicest constantly at hand and introduced them at effective
points. In this respect he was a sort of immeasurably lighter-
handed Rabelais, whom, indeed, he resembled in that sensuous exuberance of temperament which his countrymen are
fond of calling peculiarly "Gaulois." He had an almost Rabelaisian relish for enumerations, lists, and catalogues—a sort
of grotesque delight in quantity. We need hardly remind the
reader that these are not the tokens of a man of thought, and
Gautier was none. In the line of moral expression his phrase
would have halted sadly; and when occasionally he emits a
reflection he is a very Philistine of Philistines. In his various
records of travel, we remember, he never takes his seat in a
railway train without making a neat little speech on the marvels of steam and the diffusion of civilization. If it were not
in a Parisian *feuilleton* it might proceed from Mr. Barlow, and
be addressed to Harry Sandford and Tommy Merton. These
genial commonplaces are Gautier's only tributes to philosophy. It seems as absurd to us as that very puerile performance
itself that the philosophic pretensions of the famous preface
to "Mademoiselle de Maupin" should have provoked any
other retort than a laugh. Gautier was incapable of looking,

for an appreciable duration of time, at any other than the superficial, the picturesque, face of a question. If you find him glancing closer, you may be sure, with all respect, that the phenomenon will last just as long as a terrier will stand on his hind-legs.

To raise on such a basis so large a structure was possible only to a Frenchman, and to a Frenchman inordinately endowed with the national sense of form and relish for artistic statement. Gautier's structure is composed of many pieces. He began, in his early youth, with "Mademoiselle de Maupin." It has seemed to us rather a painful exhibition of the prurience of the human mind that, in most of the recent notices of the author's death (those, at least, published in England and America) this work alone should have been selected as the critic's text. It is Gautier's one disagreeable performance; how it came to be written it is of small profit at this time to inquire. In certain lights the book is almost ludicrously innocent, and we are at a loss what to think of those critics who either hailed or denounced it as a serious profession of faith. With faith of any sort Gautier strikes us as slenderly furnished. Even his æsthetic principles are held with a good-humoured laxity that allows him, for instance, to say in a hundred places the most delightfully sympathetic and pictorial things about the romantic or Shakespearean drama, and yet to describe a pedantically classical revival of the "Antigone" at Munich with the most ungrudging relish. The only very distinct statement of intellectual belief that we remember in his pages is the singularly perfect little poem which closes the collection of chiselled and polished verses called "Émaux et Camées." It is a charming example of Gautier at his best, and we shall be pardoned for quoting it.

L'ART.

Oui, l'œuvre sort plus belle
D'une forme au travail
    Rebelle,
Vers, marbre, onyx, émail.

Point de contraintes fausses!
Mais que pour marcher droit
    Tu chausses,
Muse, un cothurne étroit.

Fi du rhythme commode,
Comme un soulier trop grand,
    Du mode
Que tout pied quitte et prend!

Statuaire, repousse
L'argile que pétrit
    Le pouce,
Quand flotte ailleurs l'esprit;

Lutte avec le carrare,
Avec le paros dur
    Et rare,
Gardiens du contour pur;

Emprunte à Syracuse
Son bronze où fermement
    S'accuse
Le trait fier et charmant;

D'une main délicate
Poursuis dans un filon
    D'agate
Le profil d'Apollon.

Peintre, fuis l'aquarelle,
Et fixe la couleur
    Trop frêle
Au four de l'émailleur;

Fais les sirènes bleues,
Tordant de cent façons
    Leurs queues;
Les monstres des blasons;

Dans son nimbe trilobe
La Vierge et son Jésus;
    Le globe
Avec la croix dessus.

Tout passe.—L'art robuste
Seul a l'éternité.
    Le buste
Survit à la cité.

Et la médaille austère
Que trouve un laboreur
    Sous terre
Révèle un empereur.

Les dieux eux-mêmes meurent,
Mais les vers souverains
    Demeurent
Plus forts que les airains.

Sculpte, lime, cisèle;
Que ton rêve flottant
    Se scelle
Dans le bloc résistant.

These admirable verses seem to us to be almost tinged with intellectual passion. It is a case of an æsthetic, an almost technical, conviction, glowing with a kind of moral fervour. They vividly reflect, in our opinion, the great simplicity of the author's mind. We doubt whether life often addressed him a more puzzling question than the one he has so gracefully answered here. He had, of course, his likes and dislikes; and, as the poet of the luxuries of life, he naturally preferred those paternal governments which pay heavy subventions to opera-houses, order palace frescoes by the half-mile, and maintain various picturesque sinecures. He was sensuously a conservative; although, after all, as an observer and describer, he was the frankest of democrats. He had a glance for everything and a phrase for everything on the broad earth, and all that he asked of an object, as a source of inspiration, was that it should have length, breadth and colour. Much of Gautier's poetry is of the same period as "Mademoiselle de Maupin," and some of it of the same quality; notably the frantically picturesque legend of "Albertus," written in the author's twenty-first year, and full of the germs of his later flexibility of diction. "Émaux et Camées," the second volume of his collected verses, contains, evidently, his poetic bequest. In this chosen series every poem is a masterpiece; it has received the author's latest and fondest care; all, as the title indicates, is goldsmiths' work. In Gautier's estimation, evidently, these exquisite little pieces are the finest distillation of his talent; not one of them but ought to have outweighed a dozen Academic blackballs. Gautier's best verse is neither sentimental, satirical, narrative, nor even lyrical. It is always pictorial and plastic— a matter of images, "effects," and colour. Even when the motive is an idea—of course, a slender one—the image absorbs and swallows it, and the poem becomes a piece of rhythmic imitation. What is this delightful little sonnet—the "Pot de Fleurs"—but a piece of self-amused imagery?

> Parfois un enfant trouve une petite graine,
> Et tout d'abord, charmé de ses vives couleurs,
> Pour la planter, il prend un pot de porcelaine
> *Orné de dragons bleus et de bizarres fleurs.*
>
> Il s'en va. La racine en couleuvres s'allonge,
> Sort de terre, fleurit et devient arbrisseau;
> Chaque jour, plus avant, son pied chevelu plonge
> Tant qu'il fasse éclater le ventre du vaisseau.
>
> L'enfant revient; surpris, il voit la plante grasse
> Sur les débris du pot brandir ses verts poignards;
> Il la veut arracher, mais la tige est tenace;
> Il s'obstine, et ses doigts s'ensanglantent aux dards.
>
> Ainsi germa l'amour dans mon âme surprise;
> Je croyais ne semer qu'une fleur de printemps:
> C'est un grand aloès dont la racine brise
> Le pot de porcelaine aux dessins éclatants.

We may almost fancy that the whole sonnet was written for the sake of the charming line we have marked—a bit of Keats Gallicized. Gautier's first and richest poetry, however, is to be found in his prose—the precious, artistic prose which for forty years he lavished in newspaper feuilletons and light periodicals. Here the vivid, plastic image is his natural, constant formula; he scatters pictures as a fine singer roulades; every paragraph is the germ of a sonnet, every sentence a vignette. "It is pure Lacrima-Christi," as Sainte-Beuve says, *"qu'on vous verse au coin d'une borne."* The twenty-five volumes or so into which this long daily labour has been gathered—feuilletons and sketches, novels and tales, records of travel, reports of "damned" plays and unsold pictures—form a great treasury of literary illustration. When Gautier, according to present promise, begins to be remembered mainly as the author of an indecent novel whose title is circulated in the interest of virtue, needy poets may deck their wares for the market with unmissed flowers of description from his blooming plantations. He has commemorated every phase and mood and attribute of nature and every achievement and possibility of art; and you have only to turn his pages long enough to find the perfect presentment of your own comparatively dim and unshaped vision.

Early in life he began to travel—to travel far for a Frenchman—and, of course, to publish his impressions. They relate altogether to the *look* of the countries he visited—to landscape, art-collections, street-scenery and costume. On the "institutions" of foreign lands he is altogether silent. His delightful vividness on his chosen points is elsewhere unapproached, and his "Voyage en Espagne," his "Constantinople," his "Italia," and his "Voyage en Russie," seem to us his most substantial literary titles. No other compositions of the same kind begin to give us, in our chair, under the lamp, the same sense of standing under new skies, among strange scenes. With Gautier's readers the imagination travels in earnest and makes journeys more profitable in some respects than those we really undertake. He has the broad-eyed, universal, almost innocent gaze at things of a rustic at a fair, and yet he discriminates them with a shrewdness peculiarly his own. We renew over his pages those happiest hours of youth when we have strolled forth into a foreign town, still sprin-

kled with the dust of travel, and lost ourselves deliciously in
the fathomless sense of local difference and mystery. Gautier
had a passion for material detail, and he vivifies, illuminates,
interprets it, woos it into relief, resolves it into pictures, with
a joyous ingenuity which makes him the prince of *ciceroni*.
His "Voyage en Espagne" is, in this respect, a masterpiece and
model. It glows, from beginning to end, with an overcharged
verisimilitude in which we seem to behold some intenser essence of Spain—of her light and colour and climate, her
expression and personality. All this borrows a crowning vivacity from the author's genial unpretentiousness, his almost
vainglorious triviality. A "high standard" is an excellent thing;
but we sometimes fancy it takes away more than it gives, and
that an untamed natural faculty of enjoying at a venture is a
better conductor of æsthetic light and heat. Gautier's superbly
appreciative temperament makes him, at the least, as solid an
observer as the representative German doctor in spectacles,
bristling with critical premises. It is signally suggestive to
compare his lusty tribute to San Moïsè at Venice, in his
"Italia," with Ruskin's stern dismissal of it in his "Stones of
Venice"—Ruskin so painfully unable to see the "joke" of it
and Gautier, possibly, so unable to see anything but the joke.
We may, in strictness, agree with Ruskin, but we envy Gautier. It was to be expected of such a genius that he should
enjoy the East; and Gautier professed a peculiar devotion to
it. He was fond of pretending that he was really an Oriental
come astray into our Western world. He has described Eastern scenery and manners, Eastern effects of all kinds, with
incomparable gusto; and, on reading the *libretti* to the three
or four ballets included in the volume we have named, we
wonder whether his natural attitude was not to recline in the
perfumed dusk of a Turkish divan, puffing a chibouque and
forecasting the successive episodes of a Mohammedan immortality. This pretension, however, did him injustice: and such
a book as the "Voyage en Russie;" such chapters as his various notes on the Low Countries, their landscape and their
painters; such a sketch, indeed, as his wonderful *humoristique*
history of a week in London, in his "Caprices et Zigzags"—
prove abundantly that he had more than one string to his
bow. He shot equally far with them all. Each of his chapters

of travel has a perfect tone of its own and that unity of effect
which is the secret of the rarest artists. The "Voyage en Espagne" is a masterly mixture of hot lights and warm shadows;
the "Constantinople" is an immense verbal Decamps, as one
may say; and the "Voyage en Russie," compounded of effects
taken from the opposite end of the scale, is illuminated with
the cold blue light of the North. Gautier's volumes abound
in records of the most unadventurous excursions—light
sketches of a feuilletonist's holidays. His fancy found its account in the commonest things as well as the rarest—in Cal-
lot as well as in Paul Veronese—and these immediate notes
are admirable in their multicoloured reflections of the perpetual entertainment of Nature. Gautier found Nature supremely
entertaining; this seems to us the shortest description of him.
She had no barren places for him, for he rendered her poverty
with a *brio* that made it as picturesque as her wealth. He professed always to care for nothing but beauty. "Fortunio," he
says, in the preface to this grotesquely meretricious production, "is a hymn to Beauty, Wealth, and Happiness—the only
three divinities we recognise. It celebrates gold, marble, and
purple." But, in fact, he was too curious an artist not to enjoy
ugliness very nearly as much, and he drew from it some of his
most striking effects. We recommend to the reader the account of a stroll among the slaughter-houses and the asylums
of lost dogs and cats in the Paris *banlieue*, in the "Caprices et
Zigzags;" his elaborate pictures, several times repeated, of
Spanish bull-fights (which show to what lengths *l'art pour
l'art* can carry the kindliest tempered of men), and a dozen
painful passages in his "Tableaux de Siège." This little volume, the author's last, is a culminating example of his skill. It
is a common saying with light littérateurs, that to describe a
thing you must not know it too well. Gautier knew Paris—
picturesque Paris—with a forty years' knowledge; yet he has
here achieved the remarkable feat of suppressing the sense of
familiarity and winning back, for the sake of inspiration, a
certain freshness of impression. The book was written in evil
days; but nothing from Gautier's hand is pleasanter; and the
silvery strain of his beautiful rhetoric, after so long a season
of thunderous bulletins and proclamations, suggests the high,
clear note of some venerable nightingale after a summer

storm. Deprived of his customary occupation he became a forced observer of certain vulgarly obvious things, and discovered that they, too, had their poetry, and that, if you only look at it closely, everything is remunerative. He found poetry in the poor rawboned lions and tigers of the Jardin des Plantes; in the hungry dogs in the street, hungrily eyed; in a trip on a circular railway and on the penny steamers on the Seine; in that delicacy of vanished seasons, a pat of fresh butter in Chevet's window. Beneath his touch these phenomena acquire the finely detailed relief of the accessories and distances in a print of Albert Dürer's; we remember no better example of the magic of style. But the happiest performance in the book is a series of chapters on Versailles, when the whirligig of time had again made its splendid vacancy an active spot in the world's consciousness. No one should go there now without Gautier's volume in his pocket. It was his good fortune that his autumn was as sound as his summer and his last writing second to none before it. The current of diction in this final volume is as full and clear as in the "Voyage en Espagne."

Gautier's stories and novels belong, for the most part, to his prime; he reached his climax as a storyteller ten years ago, with "Le Capitaine Fracasse." His productions in this line are not numerous, for dramatic invention with him was evidently not abundant. As was to be supposed, the human interest in his tales is inferior to the picturesque. They remind us of those small cabinet paintings of the contemporary French school, replete with archæological details as to costume and furniture, which hang under glass in immense gilt frames and form the delight of connoisseurs. Gautier's figures are altogether pictorial; he cared for nothing and knew nothing in men and women but the epidermis. With this, indeed, he was marvellously acquainted, and he organized in its service a phraseology as puzzlingly various as the array of pots and brushes of a coiffeur. His attitude towards the human creature is, in a sublimated degree, that of a barber or tailor. He anoints and arranges and dresses it to perfection; but he deals only in stuffs and colours. His fable is often pretty enough; but one imagines it always written in what is called a studio light—on the corner of a table littered with brushes and frip-

pery. The young woman before the easel, engaged at forty
sous a sitting to take off her dress and let down her hair, is
obviously the model for the heroine. His stories are always
the measure of an intellectual need to express an ideal of the
exquisite in personal beauty and in costume, combined with
that of a certain serene and full-blown sensuality in conduct,
and accompanied with gorgeous visions of upholstery and architecture. Nothing classifies Gautier better, both as to the
individual and the national quality of his genius, than the perfect frankness of his treatment of the human body. We of English speech pass (with the French) for prudish on this point;
and certain it is that there is a limit to the freedom with
which we can comfortably discourse of hair and skin, and
teeth and nails, even to praise them. The French, on the other
hand, discuss their physical texture as complacently as we discuss that of our trousers and boots. The Parisians profess, we
believe, to have certain tendencies in common with the old
Athenians; this unshrinking contemplation of our physical
surfaces might be claimed as one of them. Practically, however, it gives one a very different impression from the large
Greek taste for personal beauty; for the French type, being as
meagre as the Greek was ample, has been filled out with the
idea of "grace," which, by implying that the subject is conscious, makes modesty immediately desirable and the absence
of it vicious. Gautier, in this respect, is the most eloquent of
our modern Athenians, and pays scantiest tribute to our English scruples. Flesh and blood, noses and bosoms, arms and
legs were a delight to him, and it was his mission to dilate
upon them. For any one who has glanced at the dusky background of Parisian life, with its sallow tones and close odours,
among which no Athenian sky makes a blue *repoussoir* either
for statues or mortals, there is something almost touchingly
heroic in Gautier's fixed conception of sublime good looks.
He invents unprecedented attributes, and it is nothing to say
of his people that they are too good to live. In "Une Nuit de
Cléopâtre," the hero, inflamed with a hopeless passion for the
Egyptian queen, has been pursuing her barge in a little skiff,
and rowing so fast, under an Egyptian sun, that he has overtaken her fifty oarsmen. "He was a beautiful young man of
twenty, with hair so black that it seemed blue, a skin blond

as gold, and proportions so perfect that he might have been taken for a bronze of Lysippus. Although he had been rowing some time, he betrayed no fatigue, and *had not on his brow a single drop of sweat.*" Gautier's heroines are always endowed with transparent finger tips. These, however, are his idler touches. His real imaginative power is shown in his masterly evocation of localities, and in the thick-coming fancies that minister to his inexhaustible conception of that pictorial "setting" of human life which interested him so much more than human life itself. In the "Capitaine Fracasse," the "Roman de la Momie," "Le Roi Candaule," "Une Nuit de Cléopâtre," and "Aria Marcella" he revels in his passion for scenic properties and backgrounds. His science, in so far as it is archæological, is occasionally at fault, we suspect, and his facts slightly fantastic; but it all sounds very fine and his admirable pictorial instinct makes everything pass. He reconstructs the fabulous splendours of old Egypt with a magnificent audacity of detail, and rivals John Martin, of mezzotinto fame, in the energy with which he depicts the light of torches washing the black basalt of palace stairs. If the portrait is here and there inaccurate, so much the worse for the original. The works we have just mentioned proceed altogether by pictures. No reader of the "Roman de la Momie" will have forgotten the portentous image of the great Pharaoh, who sits like a soulless idol upon his palace roof and watches his messengers swim across the Nile and come and lie on their faces (some of them dying) at his feet. Such a picture as the following, from "Une Nuit de Cléopâtre," may be rather irresponsible archæology, but it is admirable imagery:—

Le spectacle changeait à chaque instant; tantôt c'était de gigantesques propylées qui venaient mirer au fleuve leurs murailles en talus, plaquées de larges panneaux de figures bizarres; des pylônes aux chapiteaux évasés, des rampes côtoyées de grands sphinx accroupis, coiffés du bonnet à barbe cannelée, et croisant sous leurs mamelles aiguës leurs pattes de basalte noir; des palais démesurés, faisant saillir sur l'horizon les lignes horizontales et sévères de leur entablement, où le globe emblématique ouvrait les ailes mystérieuses comme un aigle à l'envergure démesurée; des temples aux colonnes énormes, grosses comme des tours, où se détachait sur un fond d'éclatante blancheur des processions des figures hieroglyphiques; toutes les prodigiosités de cette architecture de Titans; tantôt des passages d'une aridité désolante; des collines formées par des petits éclats de pierre provenant des fouilles et des constructions, miettes de cette gigantesque débauche de granit qui dura plus de trente siècles; des montagnes exfoliées de chaleur, déchiquetées et zébrées de rayures noires, semblables aux cautérizations d'une incendie; des tertres bossus et difformes, accroupis comme le creocéphale des tombeaux, et découpant au bord du ciel leur attitude contrefaite; des marnes verdâtres, des ochres roux, des tufs d'un blanc farineux, et, de temps à autre, quelque escarpement de marbre couleur rose-sèche, où bâillaient les bouches noires des carrières.

If, as an illustration, we could transfuse the essence of one of Gautier's best performances into this colourless report, we should choose the "Capitaine Fracasse." In this delightful work Gautier surpassed himself, and produced the model of picturesque romances. The story was published, we believe, some twenty-five years after it was announced—and announced because the author had taken a fancy to the title and proposed to write "up" to it. We cannot say how much of the long interval was occupied with this endeavour; but certainly the "Capitaine Fracasse" is as good as if a quarter of a century had been given to it. Besides being his most ambitious work it bears more marks of leisure and meditation than its companions. M. Meissonier might have written it, if, with the same talent and a good deal more geniality, he had chosen to use the pen rather than the brush. The subject is just such a one as Gautier was born to appreciate—a subject of which the pictorial side emphasizes itself as naturally as that of "Don Quixote." It is borrowed, indeed, but as great talents borrow—for a use that brings the original into fashion again. Scarron's "Roman Comique," which furnished Gautier with his starting-point, is as barren to the eye as "Gil Blas" itself, besides being a much coarser piece of humour. The sort of memory one retains of the "Capitaine Fracasse" is hard to express, save by some almost physical analogy. We remember the perusal of most good novels as an intellectual pleasure—a pleasure which varies in degree, but is as far as it goes an affair of the mind. The hours spent over the "Capitaine Fracasse" seem to have been an affair of the senses, of personal experience, of observation and contact as illusory as those of a peculiarly vivid dream. The novel presents the adventures of a company of strolling players of Louis XIII.'s time,—their vicissitudes collective and individual, their miseries and gayeties, their loves and squabbles, and their final apportionment of worldly comfort—very much in that symmetrical fashion in which they have so often stood forth to receive it at the fall of the curtain. It is a fairy-tale of Bohemia, a triumph of the picaresque. In this case, by a special extension of his power, the author has made the dramatic interest as lively as the pictorial, and lodged good human hearts beneath the wonderfully-painted rusty doublets and tarnished satins of his maskers. The great charm of the book is a sort of combined geniality of feeling and colouring, which leaves one in doubt whether the author is the most joyous of painters or the cleverest of poets. It is a masterpiece of good-humour—a good-humour sustained by the artist's indefatigable relish for his theme. In artistic "bits," of course, the book abounds; it is a delightful gallery of portraits. The models, with their paint and pomatum, their broken plumes and threadbare velvet, their false finery and their real hunger, their playhouse manners and morals, are certainly not very choice company; but the author handles them with an affectionate, sympathetic jocosity of which we so speedily feel the influence that, long before we have finished, we seem to have drunk with them one and all out of the playhouse goblet to the confusion of respectability and life before the scenes. If we incline to look for deeper meanings, we can fancy the work in the last analysis an expression of that brotherly sympathy with the social position of the comedian which Gautier was too much what the French call an *homme de théâtre* not to entertain as an almost poetic sentiment. The "Capitaine Fracasse" ranks, in our opinion, with the first works of imagination produced in our day.

Of Gautier as a critic there is not much to say that we have not said of him as a traveller and storyteller. Rigid critic he was none; it was not in his nature to bring himself to fix a standard. The things he liked he spoke well of; of the things he disliked, a little less well. His brother critics, who would have preferred to count on him to substantiate their severities, found him unpardonably "genial." We imagine that, in the long run, he held a course nearer the truth than theirs, and did better service. His irresistible need for the positive in art, for something describable—phrasable, as we may say—often led him to fancy merit where it was not, but more often, probably, to detect it where it lurked. He was a constructive commentator; and if the work taken as his text is often below his praise, the latter, with its magical grasp of the idea, may serve as a sort of generous lesson. His work as a critic is very abundant and has been but partially collected. For many years he reported elaborately on the annual Salon and produced a weekly review of the theatre. His accounts of the Salon, which have yet to be republished, form, probably, the best history—if also the least didactic—of modern French art. When pictures and statues have passed out of sight, it is rather meagre entertainment to peruse amendments to their middle distance and to the finer points in their anatomy. Gautier's pages preserve what was best in them—the attempt, the image, the vision. His criticism illustrates more pointedly, perhaps, than his poems and tales, his native incapacity to moralize. Occasionally, we think, a promising subject comes near being sacrificed to it. We were lately struck, in reading the delightful "Correspondance" of Henri Regnault, whose herald-in-chief Gautier constituted himself, with the latter's fatally shallow conception of the duties of an æsthetic guide, philosopher and friend. Gautier, possibly, claimed no such office; but, at any rate, he spoke with authority; and the splendid, unmeasured flattery which he pours out on the young painter gives us something of the discomfort with which we should see an old man plying a young lad with strong wine. Regnault, fortunately, had a strong head; but the attitude, in Gautier, is none the less immoral. He repaints the young man's pictures, verbally, with almost superior power, and

consecrates their more ominous eccentricities by his glowing
rhetoric. To assure a youth of genius, by sound of trumpet,
that his genius is infallible, is, doubtless, good comradeship,
but, from a high point of view, it is poor æsthetics.

The first half of Gautier's theatrical feuilletons have been
gathered into six volumes, under the ambitious title—a device, evidently, of the publishers rather than the author—of
"L'Histoire de l'Art Dramatique en France." In the theatre,
as at the Salon, he is the most good-natured of critics, and
enjoys far less picking a feeble drama to pieces than sketching fine scenery and good acting. The book, however, is an
excellent one; its tone is so easy, its judgments so happy and
unpedantic, its good taste so pervasive, its spirit so whole-
somely artistic. But we confess that what has most struck us,
in turning it over, has been the active part played by the
stage in France during these forty years, its incalculable fertility and its insatiable absorption of talent and ingenuity.
Buried authors and actors are packed away in Gautier's
pages as on the shelves of an immense mausoleum; and if,
here and there, they exhibit the vivifying touch of the em-
balmer, the spectacle is on the whole little less lugubrious. It
takes away one's breath to think of the immense consumption of witticisms involved in the development of civilization. Gautier's volumes seem an enormous monument to the
shadowy swarm of jokes extinct and plots defunct—dim-featured ghosts, still haunting the lawless circumference of literature in pious confidence that the transmigration of souls
will introduce them to the foot-lights again. Gautier's dealings with the theatre were altogether those of a spectator;
for the little comedies collected in the volume which forms
the text of our remarks are not of the sort approved by managers. They are matters of colour, not of structure, and masterpieces of style rather than of "effect." The best of them,
the "Tricorne Enchanté, Bastonnade en un Acte, et en Vers,
Mêlée d'un Couplet," has been represented since the author's death, but, we believe, with only partial success. The
piece is a *pastiche*, suggested by various sources—Molière,
Goldoni, the old prints of the figures in the conventional
Italian farce. The style is a marvel of humorous ingenuity
and exhales a delightful aroma of the grotesque stage-world

of jealous guardians and light-fingered valets, saucy waiting-
maids and modest *ingénues*. The verse occasionally emulates
Molière with the happiest vivacity. Géronte, having lost his
valet, determines to serve himself.

> Quel est donc le fossé, quelle est donc la muraille
> Où gît, cuvant son vin, cette brave canaille?
> O Champagne! es-tu mort? As-tu pris pour cercueil
> Un tonneau défoncé de brie ou d'argenteuil?
> Modèle des valets, perle des domestiques,
> Qui passais en vertu les esclaves antiques,
> Que le ciel avait fait uniquement pour moi,—
> Par qui remplacer, comment vivre sans toi?
> —Parbleu! Si j'essayais de me servir moi-même?
> Ce serait la façon de trancher le problème.
> Je me commanderais et je m'obéirais.
> Je m'aurais sous la main, et quand je me voudrais,
> Je n'aurais pas besoin de me pendre aux sonnettes.
> Nul ne sait mieux que moi que j'ai des mœurs honnêtes,
> Que je me suis toujours conduit loyalement.
> Ainsi donc je m'accepte avec empressement.
> Ah, Messieurs les blondins, si celui-là me trompe,
> Vous le pourrez aller crier à son de trompe:
> J'empocherai votre or, et me le remettrai:
> Vos billets pleins de musc, c'est moi qui les lirai.
> D'ailleurs, je prends demain, qu'on me loue ou me blâme,
> Mademoiselle Inez, ma pupille, pour femme.
> Elle me soignera dans mes quintes de toux,
> Et près d'elle couché, je me rirai de vous,
> Les Amadis transis, les coureurs de fortune,
> Gelant sous le balcon par un beau clair de lune!
> Et, quand j'apercevrai mon coquin de neveu,
> De deux ou trois seaux d'eau j'arroserai son feu!

The little piece called "Une Larme du Diable," to which
the author has affixed the half-apologetic qualification of
"Mystère," is one of his cleverest and most characteristic performances. None illustrates better, perhaps, what we have
called the simplicity of his mind—the way in which he conceived the most exalted ideas as picturesque and picturesque

only. "Une Larme du Diable" is a light *pastiche* of a mediæval miracle-play, just as the "Tricorne Enchanté" is an imitation of a seventeenth-century farce. The scene is alternately in heaven and on earth. *Satanas* is the hero, and *le Bon Dieu* and *Christus*, grotesquely associated with Othello and Desdemona, are among the minor characters. *Christus* himself, conversing in heaven, manifests a taste for the picturesque. *"Ce matin je me suis déguisé en mendiant, je leur* (the two heroines) *ai demandé l'aumône; elles ont déposé dans ma main lépreuse, chacune à leur tour, une grosse pièce de cuivre, toute glacée de vert-de-gris."* These copper coins, glazed with verdigris, are a sort of symbol of the drama—a drama in which the celestial mind has a turn for bric-à-brac. Shrewdly fantastic as is the whole composition, it is a capital example of the weakness of an imagination dependent wholly upon the senses. That Gautier's fancy should have prompted him to write "Une Larme du Diable" is up to a certain point to its credit; that it should have carried him through the task suggests unutterable things as to his profundity. He had evidently no associations with divine images that it cost him a moment's hesitation to violate; and one may say of him that he was incapable of blasphemy because he was incapable of respect. He is compounded of consistent levity. These are strange things to find one's self saying of a poet, and they bring us back to our first remark —that our author's really splendid development is inexorably circumscribed. Infinite are the combinations of our faculties. Some of us are awkward writers and yearning moralists; others are masters of a perfect style which has never reflected a spiritual spark. Gautier's disposition served him to the end, and enabled him to have a literary heritage perfect of its kind. He could look every day at a group of beggars sunning themselves on the Spanish Steps at Rome, against their golden wall of mouldering travertine, and see nothing but the fine brownness of their rags and their flesh-tints—see it and enjoy it for ever, without an hour's disenchantment, without a chance of one of those irresistible revulsions of mood in which the "mellowest" rags are but filth, and filth is poverty, and poverty a haunting shadow, and picturesque squalor a mockery. His unfaltering robustness of vi-

sion—of appetite, one may say—made him not only strong
but enviable.

North American Review, April 1873
Reprinted under title "Théophile Gautier"
in *French Poets and Novelists*, 1878

Théophile Gautier, Souvenirs Intimes. Par Ernest Feydeau. Paris: E. Plon, 1874. *Histoire
du Romantisme, Suivie de Notices Romantiques, etc.* Par Théophile Gautier. Paris: Charpentier, 1874.

THE ADMIRERS OF Théophile Gautier will be pleased to
hear that a well-earned honor is to be bestowed on his
literary remains. The immense number of short articles—criticisms, *feuilletons*, sketches, notices—scattered through the
newspapers and magazines in which he earned his daily bread
are to be gathered into volumes and given to the world under
an intelligent and sympathetic editorial supervision. Two volumes have already appeared: one entitled *Les Jeunes-France*,
the second and more important baptized for the occasion as
we have indicated. We ourselves rejoice greatly in this undertaking, for we confess to a peculiar and, in its nature, almost
inexpressible kindness for the author of the *Voyage en Espagne*
and *Emaux et Camées*. His writings present themselves with
such modest pretensions that it is easy to underestimate them.
He wrote from day to day, from hour to hour (in the morning paper and the evening paper), his exquisite prose, flanked
on one side by the telegraphic gossip of the Agence Havas,
and on the other by the advertisement of the Révalescière
Dubarry. His work was a lifelong, ceaseless, restless improvisation, and his themes for the most part, at best, but a nine
days' wonder. And yet it may really be said of him, that he
has hardly written a line that is not worth reprinting. We
never read ten consecutive lines from his pen,—tossed off
though they may have been on the most trivial occasion,—
without feeling irresistibly charmed, without seeming to hear
the tread of the Muse, if in but a single foot-fall. Gautier was
blessed with a perception of material beauty so intense and
comprehensive that he was unable to write five lines without
creating a lovely image or ministering in some odd fashion to

the delight of the eyes. Art was his divinity, and he worshipped her by example as well as by dogma. He forged himself, at the outset of his career, a perfect style, and his lavish application of it has always reminded us of the conduct of the heroes of old-fashioned romances, who pay their debts by breaking off a bit of their gold chain. Gautier paid out his chain, as it were, in larger and smaller pieces, but the fragment, whatever its size, always contained a portion of the original metal. For many minds—minds of an ascetic and utilitarian temper—he will always have a limited interest, or rather an unlimited repulsiveness; but for the happy majority, as we imagine it, who are blessed with an eternal relish for the pictorial, whether rendered by the pen or by the brush, this projected complement to his published volumes will give a larger outline to his genius. As we recede from him with the lapse of time, and his figure is lighted by this intensified glow, we more freely perceive how rare and perfect a genius it was. Nothing probably is easier than to exaggerate Gautier's merits, or rather to pervert his claims; but to our sense we should lose more by making light of them than by commemorating them in unstinted measure. In his own way, Gautier was simply perfect, and we have had not many great talents in these latter years of whom the same can be said. Few have been so wholly of one piece, of so unmingled a strain: so pure, compact, serene, so in tune with themselves. This was the case with Gautier from the first, and there is something extremely respectable in the way in which through forty years of possible intellectual corruption he preserved the beautiful unity of his inspiration. He had an extraordinary intellectual simplicity. The late M. Feydeau, in a volume of *Souvenirs Intimes*, painfully compounded of triviality and pretentiousness, has attempted to render his friend the cruel service of establishing the contrary. He talks of him as a great thinker and a profound scholar. M. Feydeau's indiscreet adulation will provoke a smile in those who have breathed the atmosphere, so unweighted with a moral presence, so unstirred by the breath of reflection, which pervades equally our author's most ardent verse and most deliberate prose. Gautier's simplicity is his alpha and his omega, and the all-sufficient explanation of much that, in a complex nature, would have savored of offence. He never judged morality: he knew no more about it than a Fiji-Islander about coal-smoke. His sole mission in the world was to make pictures, and he discharged it with a singleness of sympathy which even his possibly more spiritualized ghost will shudder to see his posthumous eulogists attempting to discredit. His pictorial faculty was unsurpassed; he was one of the first of descriptive poets. This surely is glory enough, and in the very interest of refined enjoyment we protest against all extension or qualification of it. For it is not in the least paradoxical to say that Gautier would have been a much less estimable writer if he had been in the least a more edifying one. Nature had furnished him with an unequalled apparatus for æsthetic perception and verbal portraiture, and she had attempted, in the intellectual line, to do nothing else. To preserve the balance she had contented herself with giving him an imperturbable moral amenity. Those who have read to any purpose the *Voyage en Espagne* and the *Capitaine Fracasse*, to say nothing of that tremendous monument of juvenile salubrity, *Mademoiselle de Maupin*, in which the attempt to seem vicious is like a pair of burnt-cork mustaches smirched over lips still redolent of a mother's milk, will know what we mean when we say that Gautier is almost grotesquely *good*. His temperament is as full of *bonhomie* as his imagination of refinement. He occasionally pointed a period with a dash of sarcasm; but such a missile, in his hands, did execution hardly less gentle than a feather pillow. This almost helpless-looking moral simplicity and benignity in Gautier, as it shows in union with his life-long appeal to all the delightful material influences of life, is the source of that part of our good-will for our author which we just now called inexpressible. In one's admiration for him, in this spirit, there is something of compassion. He seems to be, in a manner, the unretributed sport of Nature. He gives her all his attention, his love, and his zeal; year in and year out he gazes at her, waits on her, catches her every image and mood and tone; and she, sitting there in her splendors and seeing herself mirrored in a style which never ceased to develop till its polished surface had reflected her from head to foot, never drops into his conscience, by way of reward, a single vivifying germ; never by her grateful breath transforms

him for a day from the poet who merely observes and describes into the poet who conceives and creates. All this, to
our sense, if we are not over-fanciful, gives Gautier an odd
sort of isolated, unsupported, unfriended air in the midst of
the beautiful material world to which he spent his life in paying exquisite compliments. We do not really react upon natural impressions and assert our independence, until these
impressions have been absorbed into our moral life and become a mysterious part of moral passion. Poor Gautier seems
to stand forever in the chill external air which blows over the
surface of things; above his brilliant horizon there peeped no
friendly refuge of truth purely intellectual, where he could
rake over the embers of philosophy, and rest his tired eyes
among the shadows of the unembodied.

M. Feydeau was, according to his own account, for many
years an intimate friend of Gautier and the confidant of his
most personal pleasures and pains. It was his habit to take
notes during this period of all noteworthy incidents, and he
aspires in his little volume to play the part of a miniature
Boswell. Unfortunately, we get a more lively sense of M. Feydeau's own personality than of that of his weightier friend;
and we may say in parenthesis, and without an infraction of
clarity, considering on this and on other occasions the frankness of the author's self-exposure, that a less attractive personality has rarely sought to exhibit itself in literature. His
volume, however, reminds us pertinently enough of the intellectual atmosphere in which Gautier lived and worked. It was
an atmosphere which imperiously urged all who breathed it
to the cultivation of the picturesque in some form or other, —
painting or the drama, the *feuilleton* or the novel. "Art," says
M. Flaubert, was his friend's master-passion: his life was
passed in the zealous appreciation of clever pictures and new
plays; in going from the studio to the theatre and from the
theatre to the printing-office. There have doubtless been circles far more prolific in valuable generalizations about art, —
circles in Berlin and Düsseldorf, in which the philosophy of
the matter was opened up in a far more abysmal fashion over
pipes and *Schoppen* any night in the year; but there has probably been in our time no more exquisite and penetrating a
sentiment of the subject than was to be found in the half-

Bohemian *coterie* of which M. Feydeau's "Théo" was the high-priest. From this *coterie* every human consideration not immediately bearing upon some possible artistic interpretation of sensuous pleasure seems to have been unanimously excluded. "Politics" were religiously tabooed, the sense of the company being unexceptionally that producers in their line should have a good strong money-spending, picture-ordering government to take care of them and guard them well against the rising tide of democracy and utilitarianism, but never be bothered with principles and details. When, on the close of the war (which brought to Gautier a good deal of personal misfortune), he has occasion, like any other good citizen, to treat his friend to a little talk (very sensible talk) about the prospects of France, the duties of Frenchmen, and the question of the "*revanche*," he thinks it necessary, according to M. Feydeau's report, to make an elaborate apology for venturing upon such unfamiliar ground, even in the freedom of a *tête-à-tête*. But perhaps the strongest impression we get from M. Feydeau is of the uninterrupted laboriousness of our author's career. Gautier was to the end a poor man. His exquisite literary work, though relished by the delicate of taste all over the world, never procured him anything but a decent subsistence. He could never treat himself to that supreme luxury of the artist,—the leisure to do a certain fine thing to please himself. He was chained to the newspapers; to the hour of his death he was hammering with his golden mallet on the resonant anvil of the daily press. His vivid images, his charming fancies, his wealth of color and metaphor and perception, his polished perfection and unerring felicity of style, through all of which, as we read, there seems to circulate such a current of joyous spontaneity and leisurely appreciation, were to the writer's own sense all mere daily drudgery, paid for by the line,—the goaded effort of a mind haunted by visions of hungry mouths and unpaid bills. In this daily pressure of labor and need, it is immensely to Gautier's credit that he never, for three words together, was false to his own rigid literary conscience. The work, under the spur, was not only done, but perfectly done. It was often done in the printing-office on the edge of a smutted table, with a dozen people talking; but there is never a case in which the reader of the finished article is not free to fancy it may have been excogitated in luxurious leisure, amid the fumes of a perfumed pipe, by a genius in a Persian dressing-gown reclining under a bower of roses. The conjunction of Gautier's hurried, overworked, oppressed manner of life with the indescribably exquisite, chiselled quality ("chiselled" is the word that always comes to us) of his prose, is one of the interesting facts of literature. It is just such a fact as the Academy was bound to take cognizance of, but he knocked more than once in vain at the door of rusty hinges; it remained his privilege to complete, with Balzac and Madame Sand for his companions, the trio of the great excluded imaginative writers.

We should like to quote, for curiosity's sake, a few lines from a letter of M. Gustave Flaubert, the author of *Madame Bovary*. M. Flaubert was an intimate friend of Gautier, and M. Feydeau prints a note received from him at the time of the poet's death:—

> "Je ne plains pas notre ami défunt. Au contraire, je l'envie profondément. Que ne suis-je à pourrir à sa place? Pour l'agrément qu'on a dans ce bas monde, autant s'en aller le plus vite possible. Le 4 Septembre a inauguré un état de choses qui ne nous regarde plus. *Nous sommes de trop*. On nous hait et on nous méprise. Voilà le vrai. Donc, bonsoir! Pauvre cher Théo! C'est de cela qu'il est mort (du dégoût de l'infection moderne). C'était un grand lettré et un grand poëte."

M. Feydeau gives his friend's letter with the reverse of an invidious intention, but its effect is the same as that of his own reflections throughout his volume when he quotes himself or speaks *in propria persona*. Gautier's younger comrades are a corrupt generation, and their arid cynicism only serves to throw into relief the admirable geniality of the elder writer,—the happy salubrity of a temperament which could spend forty years in the lap of tendencies predestined to all manner of ultimate morbid efflorescence, and yet preserve its sweetness to the end. MM. Feydeau and Flaubert, M. Dumas *fils*, and a dozen others are the dregs of a school,—the running to seed of the famous generation of 1830. Gautier had the good fortune to belong to the elder race, and to enjoy the

good health which, if it came from nothing else, would come
from his being original. The second of the volumes which
serves as the text of our remarks may be regarded as his contribution to the history of that extraordinary literary revolution. A "History of Romanticism" is a rather ambitious title
for what is hardly more than a string of picturesque anecdotes
and reminiscences of the author's early comrades, reinforced
by a series of obituary notices of the veterans in the grand
army, published as they dropped one by one out of the march.
But it was to the picturesque side of the movement of 1830
that Gautier was especially attached, and its hundred outward
eccentricities could not have found a more sympathetic and
amusing chronicler. The great flood-tide which, with the coming in of Louis Philippe, detached from their immemorial an-
chorage so many of the old divinities and dogmas in French
art and letters has, by this time, wellnigh subsided; has, in
fact, in great part retreated into various quiet coves and corners, under watch of the declining star of genius which has
earned its rest. But it behooves us to remember well what a
mighty tide it was, and what a wondrous work it achieved.
The eighteen years of the reign of Louis Philippe were certainly, for art and letters, one of the great moments of the human mind, and quite worthy, proportions observed, to rank
with the age of Pericles, the age of Elizabeth, or the Florentine
Renaissance. It offers a splendid list of names, as Gautier here
strings them together: "Lamartine, Victor Hugo, Alexandre
Dumas, Alfred de Musset, George Sand, Balzac, Sainte-
Beuve, Auguste Barbier, Delacroix, Louis Boulanger, Ary
Scheffer, Dévéria, Decamps, David d'Angers, Barye, Hector
Berlioz, Frédéric Lemaitre, and Madame Dorval." He omits
Prosper Mérimée, Michelet, and himself from the writers,
Horace Vernet from the painters, and Mademoiselle Rachel
from the actors. All these great talents worked together, lived
together very much, and had a multitude of common passions, hopes, and aspirations. They were young and poor, and
conscious of their strength: all herded together in the attics
and *entresols* of a brilliant, inspiring capital, and inflamed with
a generous comradeship as well as with artistic ardor. The
band of the young *romantiques* had its wild oats to sow, and it
scattered a plentiful crop; but English readers, in judging the

explosive temper of this Parisian *Sturm und Drang*, must remember how long art and letters in France had groaned under the weight of inanimate tradition. Literature was like Sindbad the Sailor with the Old Man of the Sea on his back. It resorted naturally enough to the most frolicsome pace and most fantastic gambols to unseat the monstrous incubus. Gautier says, in all but perfect earnest, that the old French theatre contained but two picturesque lines. Corneille had risked

"Cette obscure clarté qui tombe des étoiles."

And in Molière's Tartuffe Cléante had remarked that

"La campagne à présent n'est pas beaucoup fleurie."

To protest against the uniform grayness of classicism, it seemed to Gautier himself but half enough to write the glowing pictorial scenes of *Albertus* and take the liberties of *Mademoiselle de Maupin*; to be consistent, he thought it proper to let his hair grow down to his waist, to wear yellow Turkish slippers in the street, and to go to the first representation of Victor Hugo's *Hernani* in the crimson waistcoat which afterwards became legendary. He gives in the present volume the history of the crimson waistcoat, disentangled from legendary perversion, and informs us that the garment in question was composed of the finest scarlet satin and was laced behind like a woman's corset. Of information of this calibre the present chapters are largely composed; they make no pretensions to being a philosophic history. Philosophy, indeed, was so scantily represented either at that or at any period in the career of literary romanticism, that we wonder, as we think of it, whence came the saving discretion which kept it from submersion in its own excesses. All the intellectual force of the movement seemed concentrated in a passionate sense of the "plastic,"—of a plastic which should especially embody color. But all this unballasted æstheticism gives one a lively idea of the quantity of clear genius diffused through the group. The intuitive, instinctive side of art was magnificently exemplified. In spite of the lightness of Gautier's treatment of his theme, his chapters may provoke a good deal of serious reflection.

The list of the romanticists who drew the prize and grasped the laurel is very short, compared with that of their innumerable comrades who, as the French say, never "arrived." Gautier's allusions to these abortive careers are rather melancholy reading: so many were called, and so few chosen; so many were young and ardent and confident, and so few, relatively, lived and matured to exchange the young confidence for the old certainty. But we see here, as in the history of every important intellectual movement, that the failures fertilized the soil for success, that nothing great is done without a school, and that to produce a hundred finished masterpieces there must be ten thousand vain attempts. However many the masterpieces, it is always a pity there are not more; but one must nevertheless pronounce happy in its day the generation which, while the verdict was yet in abeyance, cared so universally and ardently to win the good cause. We have had great pleasure, we may say in conclusion, in reading the last division of the present volume, the *Tableau des Progrès de la Poésie Française depuis 1830*. The work was drawn up by request of the Imperial government with a series of cognate reports from other hands on the occasion of the Exhibition of 1867. It was perfectly in character that it should be "genial," and the place of criticism is kept throughout by exquisite, sympathetic, and, in the literal sense of the word, imaginative description. It is not often, we suppose, that in a government report one stumbles on such a passage as these lines upon Théodore de Banville:—

"La chaste pâleur et le contour tranquille des marbres ne suffisaient pas à ce coloriste. Les déesses étalaient dans l'onde ou dans la nuée des chairs de nacre, veinées d'azur, fouettées de rose, inondées de chevelures rutilantes au ton d'ambre et de topaze, et des rondeurs d'une opulence qu'eût évité l'art grec. Les roses, les lys, l'azur, l'or, la pourpre, l'hyacinthe abondent chez Banville; il revêt tout ce qu'il touche d'un voile tramé de rayons, et ses idées, comme des princesses de féeries, se promènent dans les prairies d'émeraude, avec des robes couleur du temps, couleur du soleil, et couleur de la lune."

North American Review, October 1874

A Winter in Russia. From the French of Théophile Gautier. By M.M. Ripley. New York: Henry Holt & Co., 1874.

WE HAVE OBSERVED for some time past an increasing mania for translations.

It is a very good fashion, but even the best things may be overdone. Of course, dull books should never be translated, but it by no means follows that because a book is clever it should be interpreted into another tongue. A book may be very clever in French or in German and very dull in English, and translation, intended as a compliment, may become in fact an unpardonable injury. There are certain cases, indeed, in which it seems to us really immoral; when it deliberately encumbers a foreign language, namely, with books of a light and trivial order. Natives have a certain property in their language, and though we may regret their using it for frivolous purposes, one can hardly pretend to legislate against them. As a general thing, a people may be trusted to produce its own padding, and there is no good reason why our groaning English idiom should be weighted with exotic commonplaces. A great many things are said in society which it is very well to hear once, if you happen to be sitting near the speaker; but he would be a very officious master of ceremonies who should insist on repeating and propagating them. In so far as we may lay down a general rule in the case we should say that the books translatable were books of *matter*, and books untranslatable books of *manner*. If the substance of a book is light and its chief attraction is in the way things are said, it had certainly better be left in the closely-fitting garment of the original. This, of course, limits very much the translation of merely entertaining and amusing books, but the restriction in such cases is especially wholesome. If a writer has nothing but sweetened froth to offer the public, it is well that he should at least have been at pains to beat his froth into the finest possible consistency; and just so it is well that readers who have an appetite for the compound should be forced, to take such exercise as is involved in a walk to the confectioner's. To read such a writer as Théophile Gautier, for instance, is pure diversion, and a healthy-minded reader ought to pay for his pastime by making the very moderate effort required for reading him in the original. It is true that readers are becoming such abandoned Sybarites, and the aversion of the public at large to anything which compels attention to pause for an instant and touch her feet to the earth is so strikingly on the increase, that the "healthy mind" in question can be but rarely postulated. Gautier is precisely one of the writers who are everything in their own tongue, and nothing, or almost nothing, out of it. He is what the French call a *fantaisiste*, and his fantasies are four-fifths verbal to one-fifth intellectual. Half the charm of his writing is in the mere curl and flutter of his phrase, as he unreels it in long bright-colored ribands; but in an English version the air of spontaneity soon disappears, and this ceaseless play of style becomes rigid and awkward. Moreover, Gautier chose his words with an extraordinary fineness of instinct, and in his pictures, as they stand, every hair-stroke tells. A translator rarely chooses the foreign equivalent with the care with which such an artist as Gautier selects the original term, so that the phrase must often be at best but a rough approximation to the author's. In each case the deflection is slight, but the difference in the whole is enormous. The house when it is finished is found to stand crooked. The translation before us is executed with commendable skill; its only fault is that it *is* a translation. It will have rendered a service, however, if it sends a few readers to its untranslated companions.

The 'Voyage en Russie' is one of Gautier's later works and not one of his best. It is not as full and compact as the 'Voyage en Espagne' or 'Italia,' the former of which has become in its way a sort of classic. Most of the writing is spread rather thin, and the art of the bookmaker is a trifle obvious. But the book is a charming one, and nothing approaching it in merit has been written on the outward face of things in Russia. Gautier was so true an artist that everything he wrote has a singular unity, and one may trust it from beginning to end to contain no false notes. And then the true notes are struck with such a masterly hand! As you close the 'Voyage en Russie' you seem to have before your eyes a sort of symbolic physical image composed of the white of glittering snows and the steely blue of northern air. The book is a verbal symphony on the theme *frost*. Gautier's winter in Russia was apparently one of the happiest seasons of his life, and the reader feels the contagion of his deep good-humor—of his luxurious enjoyment of his holiday, his fine friends and their dusky hot-house drawing-rooms, and his sleigh-rides beside pretty "Hyperborean" countesses, muffled in twenty thousand francs' worth of fur. He is the prince of travellers, taking the word in its simplest sense. He neither enquires nor investigates, nor dissents nor theorizes; he doesn't care a straw for politics, and if you had no notions of your own on the subject, you would never learn from his pages whether the Muscovite Empire is an absolute monarchy or a radical republic. He simply travels— that is, he looks and enjoys. His business is only with what comes within the jurisdiction of the eyes; but never were a pair of eyes so vigilant. One feels that from the moment he takes his seat in the railway carriage, facing the engine and next to a window, it behooves Mother Nature to be on her good behavior: Burns's "chiel" taking notes was nothing to this. He sees pictures where most people find mere dead surfaces, and where common eyes find the hint of a picture he constructs a complete work of art. His fancy is always on the alert. If he goes into an old crypt in the Kremlin at Moscow, he reflects that "here it was that, in an atmosphere heated to excess, the women, crouched in Oriental fashion upon piles of cushions, used to pass the long hours of the Russian winter looking out through the little windows to see the snow sparkle upon the gilded cupolas, and the ravens describe wild spirals around the belfries." He was an admirable descriptive poet, but we lately heard it truly, although somewhat uncivilly said, that his powers of reflection were about equivalent to those of an intelligent poodle. There is something characteristic in the way he here brings his journey and his book to a close—the way that, the play being over and the curtain dropped, the writer's mind feels no impulse towards a moment's musing—towards pointing any other moral than that "a coupé awaited me at the (Paris) station, and a quarter of an hour later I found myself surrounded by old friends and pretty women, before a table brilliant with lights, on which a fine supper was smoking, and my return was celebrated gaily until the morning." But if Gautier was not a moralist he was an incomparable painter, and there is no such good picture as this of St. Petersburg and Moscow.

Nation, November 12, 1874

Constantinople. From the French of Théophile Gautier. By Robert Howe Gould, M.A. New York: Henry Holt & Co., 1875.

WE HAD OCCASION, some months ago, on the appearance of the translation of Théophile Gautier's 'Russia,' to express our opinion as to the wisdom of depriving this extraordinary descriptive genius of the benefit of his own tongue. Gautier is above all a man of style, and one has no right to divest him of his own style without giving him another in exchange. The 'Winter in Russia' seemed to us carefully and not unskilfully translated, but the gentleman who has undertaken to do the present work into English has had a very imperfect idea of his responsibilities. To translate Gautier in the off-hand fashion in which you would transfer from one language to another the gist of a newspaper paragraph strikes us as a literary misdemeanor of the first magnitude, and yet of no less an offence has Mr. Robert Howe Gould, M.A., been guilty. 'Constantinople' is, next after the 'Voyage en Espagne,' its author's masterpiece, and to translate it with perfect verbal felicity would not have been easy. But to translate it with care, zeal, and respect was the least to be required of one who should put his hand to the task. Mr. Gould should, in the first place, have notified his readers that what he was giving them was an abbreviated and mutilated edition of the original. Omission in translation is rarely absolutely unjustifiable; but some intimation should always be given of the extent to which the privilege has been used. Mr. Gould uses it freely and constantly—indeed, we may say that whenever a passage is at all difficult to render he leaves it out. Many passages, it is true, were better left out than rendered as badly and flatly as Mr. Gould renders them. His infelicities swarm even in the opening pages of the book. The great point with Gautier was to use at any hazard what he calls the *mot propre*—to make an image. When he speaks of the country round Marseilles as "ces beaux rochers couleur de liège et de pain grillé"—the "color of cork and of toast"—Mr. Gould insipidly renders it "rocks of rich brown." This is indeed not only insipid, but false, inasmuch as it was obviously the idea of dry and arid brown that the author wished to convey. When he says that at Malta "il fait véritablement clair"—"it is really light"—the best that Mr. Gould can do is to say the "atmosphere is really clear." When the author uses so special and picturesque a phrase as the sea being "gaufré de moires par la brise," Mr. Gould translates vulgarly, "broken into ripples." Mr. Gould always gives the vague epithet instead of the special one. "Un bloc de rochers fauves, fendillés de sécheresse, calcinés de chaleur," is a vivid picture: "a mass of rocks, tawny, consumed by drought, burned by heat," is relatively none. Why shuffle away the admirably expressive term *fendillé*—split into chinks, cracked, chapped? Why in the next page interpolate bodily a threadbare line from Byron which does not exist in the original? In the chapter on the Golden Horn there is an admirable passage about certain old houses—"ces bonnes vieilles murailles empâtées, égratignées, lépreuses, chancies, moisies, affritées, que la truelle de Decamps maçonne avec tant de bonheur dans ses tableaux d'Orient, et qui donnent un si haut ragoût aux masures." This is Gautier at his best, but as to render the passage requires some little ingenuity, the translator quietly drops it out. A still finer passage, a description of a dervish, is worth quoting, with Mr. Gould's version of it: "Je n'oublierai jamais ce masque court, camard, élargi, qui semblait s'être écrasé sous la pression d'une main puissante, comme ces grotesques de caoutchouc qu'on fait changer d'expression en appuyant le pouce dessus; de grosses lèvres bleuâtres, épaisses comme celles d'un nègre; des yeux de crapaud, ronds, fixes, saillants; un nez sans cartilage, une barbe courte, rare et frisée, un teint de cuir fauve, glacé de tons rances et plus culotté de ton qu'un Espagnolet. . . ." What Mr. Gould offers us instead of this is: "His whole aspect and the mould of his features were among the most remarkable, as well as the most hideous, that I have ever beheld." Even for a single word the translator will not brighten his wit a little. If a casket of jewels is scattered "dans un désordre chatoyant," for Mr. Gould it is merely a "picturesque disorder." We have encountered those inexcusable shortcomings in a very rapid examination of the volume. It is evident that a vast number more may be found. The work, in short, has been translated by a person totally destitute of appreciation of his author, and in whose hands its essential merit, its vividness, its incisiveness, its gaiety, have evaporated. No one reads Gautier for information; we read him for the vivacity of his phrase, for his imagery. If you suppress this, you deliberately suffocate him. It is to be hoped that if it is intended to offer a translation of the 'Voyage en Espagne,' the services of some other literary artist than Mr. Gould will be obtained. A good translation might be made by a person who would give care, and taste, and imagination to it; but to subject the work to the process which has spoiled this unfortunate 'Constantinople' would be simply cruel.

Nation, July 15, 1875

Marie-Thérèse Rodet Geoffrin

Correspondance inédite du Roi Stanislas Auguste Poniatowski et de Mme. Geoffrin. (1764–1777.) Par M. Charles de Mouy. Paris: Plon et Cie, 1875.

MADAME GEOFFRIN'S NAME is familiar to all those who have glanced into the records of the French society of the last century, and especially familiar in its somewhat enigmatic aspect. She played a part in the world which it is not an exaggeration to call eminent, and yet there is nothing whatever to show in explanation of her success. She had neither birth, nor beauty, nor wit; she had no conversational talent, no specialty, no secret charm. She could do nothing particular; so far from being able to write, she could not even spell. And yet she was hand and glove with the people of her day; her house was a sort of intellectual headquarters; she scolds the King of Poland in her ill-spelled epistles; she travels across Europe to Warsaw, and her journey is a "European" event; she lodges in the King's palace, and speaks her mind to him face to face; she sees Catharine of Russia entreat her in vain to honor St. Petersburg with a visit; she passes through Vienna and sits holding the hand of Maria Theresa for an hour, while the Emperor of Austria gets out of his coach into the mud, and comes to make his obeisance to her. Meanwhile she remains a plain-faced old woman, with a close white cap tied under her chin, who draws a large income from a manufactory of looking-glasses. She was the daughter of a *valet de chambre* about the court, and she was married at fifteen years of age to a rich but insignificant tradesman, who was so illiterate that he was one day found reading the double-columned page of a dictionary straight across from margin to margin. Mme. Geoffrin made her way with the sole assistance of her tranquil but robust ambition, her native tact, and her extreme good sense. Though she was no talker herself, she knew how to make others talk; she knew apparently how to preside at a brilliant conversation, and in the highly intellectual circle which she brought about her she performed the office of moderator, or, to express it in parliamentary phrase, of speaker. Moreover, she was extremely benevolent and humane; she was a kind of maternal providence to the

whole sensitive and needy race—the *genus irritable*—of artists and men of letters. She was rich and hospitable, a great
giver of dinners, and above all she was discriminating. She
understood human nature, read character, and (except sometimes in her epistolary judgments, as when she falls foul of
Frederick the Great, and declares that in fifty years his name
will be utterly forgotten among men) she never made mistakes. She had a genius for good sense; we have the word of
Horace Walpole for it, and he, though he did not understand
everything, often understood men and women. She was a
person of excellent counsel, and her opinion on most matters
was well worth having. All this in a measure accounts for the
position she had made for herself, but it fails to solve the
whole case. A mysterious element remains, which the letters
before us do little toward clearing up. They give no glimpse
of that possible "hidden charm" which we spoke of just now,
as a necessary explanation of such an influence as Mme. Geoffrin's. They contain plenty of good sense, but they contain
also plenty of silliness, and on the whole they strike us as
quite below the average of publishable French letters. The
chance always is that a French letter will be charming, and
these of Mme. Geoffrin are rather common and dry. Such
persons as have cherished an historical devotion to the memory of the lady must have pronounced them disappointing.
One merit, however, they would have if they had no other,
and one service they would render—they would do something toward blunting the edge of our admiration for the
eighteenth century, of our envy of it as a kind of golden age
of "society," in so far as these feelings are at all tinged with
superstition. Posterity has agreed to bow very low to the
French *salons* of 1750—to admit that their wit, their intellectual brilliancy, their urbanity of tone, are, as it were, a broken
mould. Talleyrand said that a man who had not lived before
the French revolution could form no idea of how charming a
thing life could be; and we have always assumed that it savors
desirably of "culture" to agree with him. But in the light of
this closer familiarity with Mme. Geoffrin, who was one of
the dispensers of the charm commemorated by Talleyrand, we
are warranted in revising our regrets. Putting aside what belongs to the more primitive character of her time, and judging

the lady in herself, she strikes us as a rather uninspired priestess of the amenities. A single example will suffice. She declares to the King of Poland in one of her letters, that she never reads the "gazettes" and that "les raisonnements politiques" are so much Greek to her. The heroic proportions of her image are immediately somewhat curtailed, and she becomes simply a comfortable matron, who takes care that her guest's plates are filled, and prefers the shallow waters to the deep. Such a woman may be very agreeable, but we do not need a Talleyrand to tell us so.

The present volume, however, is published much less in the interest of Mme. Geoffrin than of Stanislaus Augustus, whose collateral descendants, the Poniatowski family, have opened their archives to the editor. Young Count Poniatowski came to Paris in 1753, at twenty years of age, was presented to Mme. Geoffrin, and was subsequently indebted to her intervention with his creditors for release from some of the penalties of too lavish an enjoyment of the pleasures of the capital. At twenty-five he was appointed Polish ambassador to the Russian court, where he made a lively impression upon the susceptible heart of the Empress Catharine, and had the honor of being one of her many lovers. In the midst of his good fortune, however, he was recalled, and it is apparent that he remained more faithful to the memory of the episode we have mentioned than the mighty Empress herself. It was always a sort of feather in his cap. The crown of Poland was elective, and on the death of Augustus III. young Poniatowski was presented to the Diet as a candidate—presented by Frederick II. and by Catharine, who was at least disposed to render the ex-ambassador this service. It was a questionable one, for the young nobleman was elected to a very uneasy throne. The nation itself seems to have had a very slender voice in the affair. In this, however, there was reason; for the Polish people appears, during the last years of its independence, to have been in a political sense little less than insane. Internal conflicts were unending, and rebellion was in a manner legitimated and rendered permanent by the custom of the country. The Diet was fanatically Catholic, among other things, and would allow of no possible *modus vivendi* with members of the Protestant and Greek communions. Frederick and Catharine again interfered to enforce the rights of the dissenters, occupied the country with their troops, deprived the King, who was being ground between two millstones, of everything but his name, and finally, with the assistance of Austria, proceeded to transact the first partition.

Stanislaus Augustus had retained a warm affection for Mme. Geoffrin, and a tender memory of her maternal assistance in his hour of youthful need in Paris. He had corresponded with her ever since that period, but the earlier letters are lost. The correspondence is preserved only from the moment of his ascending the throne, and this through Mme. Geoffrin having sent him back his letters in one of her frequent fits of irritation. It terminates only with her death in 1777, thus covering in the volume before us a space of thirteen years. During this time it had been subjected to some brief interruptions. The most important, if not the longest, was caused by Mme. Geoffrin's visit to Warsaw. This was a great event at the time, and was indeed a sufficiently remarkable occurrence. Mme. Geoffrin was sixty-seven years of age, and was the most sedentary of women; she had not slept out of Paris in years, and a journey to Warsaw, which in our own day has a slightly formidable sound, was in the last century, for an old *bourgeoise*, very fond of her fireside and her ease, a really heroic undertaking. It becomes heroic, indeed, or it becomes at least beautiful, when one regards the sentiment which lies at the bottom of it. Mme. Geoffrin's relation to the King of Poland was not a love affair; she was almost double his age, and he never calls her anything but "maman." But it was a great tenderness and an extreme devotion, a deep interest in his prosperity, a strong desire that he should make no mistakes of any kind, and a lively sympathy with his eventual misfortunes. Besides, she was of course proud of their intimacy; to be the "maman" of the King of Poland was a high distinction. Her visit, at any rate, was only partially a success; they fell out more than once during her sojourn in the palace, and on her return there is an after taste of acrimony in her letters. She was sensitive, suspicious, and a trifle jealous; and indeed her moral tone, as we call it nowadays, does not in general strike us as particularly high. She was too violent and too perverse a partisan. Stanislaus Augustus himself, however, produces the impression of an altogether genial and generous nature, and his letters are finer than Mme. Geoffrin's. He was a decidedly ineffectual king, but this arose in a measure from his very virtues. He was a man of a rather feminine type, and he hoped to overcome all his difficulties by patience, tact, and discretion. He was full of good will and good intention, and he evidently had a sincere love for his country; but he was too light a weight to ride so dangerous a steed. He had plenty of delicacy, but he lacked force, and while Poland is being carved into morsels, and the treasury is empty, he is busy writing to Mme. Geoffrin to send him pictures and busts, and assuring her, with amiable optimism, that all is for the best. One feels that in the same situation a man of a different temper might have done something to control events. All that he can do is to resort to the last expedient of misplaced monarchs and suffer picturesquely.

We had noted as we read a number of quotable passages in these letters, but have not allowed ourselves space to reproduce them. Glancing over them, we feel as if we may have seemed to exaggerate the want of merit in the letters of Mme. Geoffrin; for here and there her thought has much elevation, and her expression a certain homely felicity. She is, moreover, always very downright and emphatic, and she perfectly knows her own mind on every possible subject. She dislikes Voltaire, and when a subscription is opened to erect a statue to him, she declines to put down her name, and has a perfectly definite answer. She thinks him good enough for a bust or a medallion, but not good enough for a statue. The book, we should add, is admirably edited. It is preceded by a copious and lucid introduction, narrating in full the dark chapter of Polish history of which Stanislaus Augustus was hero, and it is enriched with a multitude of exact and compact notes, in which no ambiguous allusion or undefined figure fails to be made clear. By readers fond of the period, the book will be found not only interesting but entertaining.

Émile de Girardin

LETTER FROM PARIS: *Grandeur ou Déclin de la France*

PARIS, Feb. 11.—I have just been looking through a new book by M. Émile de Girardin, a heavy octavo of 750 pages, entitled "Grandeur ou Déclin de la France." There is a great deal of good sense in it, and if there were more Frenchmen of this author's highly reasonable temper the future of France would be less problematical. M. de Girardin, who has always been before the public in one way or another, has been more than once called a turncoat and a weathercock, but he has really been quite self-consistent, for his constant principle has been to ask for all the liberty that was possible under the circumstances. He glories in the fact that he has never been an "irreconcilable;" he has accepted the situation under every government, and exerted himself to get all the good that was possible out of it. This long book—which is but a collection of his newspaper articles of the last two years, and which does not contain a single word of sterile recrimination against Germany, or even of acrimonious allusion—is an ardent appeal to his countrymen to sink party differences in a frank acceptance of the Republic. It may be said that his demonstration of the issueless character of both monarchy and empire is more successful than any insurance he has to offer against the perils of that straining radicalism which the Republic carries in its flanks; but he does not claim that the Republic is the millennium, only that it is relative repose. Above all he wants things settled upon their intrinsic merits, and not by party considerations, and he is probably one of the few Frenchmen who would have the courage to write, "If such a prince is better for such an office than such a radical, let us without hesitating take the prince; but if such a radical is better than such a prince, let us take the radical." But in truth, in France, when the radical shall lie down with the prince, I imagine that the millennium really will have arrived. M. de Girardin has the further audacity to recommend forgiveness of the Prussians—to deprecate, that is, in the strongest terms, all thoughts of a *revanche*. He hopes for a peaceful one some day, by diplomatic and equitable means, and meantime he wishes France to shake herself free of her military incubus. He deliberately entreats her to give up arming, and he maintains that if she does it Germany will be enchanted to do likewise. I do not know that he is absolutely right, but there is certainly something to be said in that sense. I have a suspicion, however, that M. de Girardin does not privately care for the *revanche* as much as a purely ideal patriotism would seem to recommend; his dream is to see France the greatest commercial and industrial country. The sanest men have their hobbies, and that of the editor of the *France* is that his country, if it only wills it, may become a great maritime power and cover the seas with her merchant fleets. Certainly there are things enough under the sun France can do, if she will only set her house in order and give her mind—her admirable mind—to them. I had marked as worth quoting a couple of extracts which M. de Girardin makes from two Bonapartist publications, but I have space only to allude to them. One of these volumes is by M. Georges Lachaud, and it consists of an exemplification of the programme contained in these words: "The condemnation of the French people to gayety in perpetuity." "Persuaded as we are," says M. Georges Lachaud, on behalf of the Empire, "that a dictatorship alone, by disembarrassing the French people of its grave cares, can restore to it its lightness and its grace, we await with impatience the hour in which France will transfer to the shoulders of a master the burden that renders her thoughtful. Let our future master bring the 'imperial corruption' into honor again! And if ever his detractors accuse him of degrading the people, and bring forward to outrage him the old Roman device, *panem et circenses*, on that day the chief of the state may say with pride that he is really a great sovereign!" "The great duty of the Empire," M. Lachaud adds—and the formula seems to me an exquisite *trouvaille* (it is worthy to have been put into circulation by Napoleon III. himself, who had a genius for the invention of phrases with just that sound)—"the great duty of the empire is to *extirper le pessimisme*." Delightful idea! But things are not looking well for M. Lachaud's optimism, and it seems as if he and his friends were more likely to be extirpated.

New York Tribune, March 4, 1876

Comte Joseph Arthur de Gobineau

Nouvelles Asiatiques. Par le Comte de Gobineau. Paris: Didier & Co.; New York: F. W. Christern, 1876.

WE NOTICED IN THESE COLUMNS a couple of years since M. de Gobineau's remarkable novel of 'Les Pléiades'— a work by no means formed to achieve popularity, but destined to awaken a peculiar degree, and, indeed, a peculiar quality, of interest, in the minds of a few readers. Such readers will be certain to give speedy attention to a new work of imagination from the same hand, and we think we can assure them that the volume of 'Nouvelles Asiatiques' now before us will not disappoint their just expectations. It is not too much to say of M. de Gobineau that he is a fascinating writer. His merit is not the usual French merit of form; he does not present that hard, smooth surface, as flawless as that of the delicate white porcelain manufactured in France and known as *biscuit*—as flawless and about as individual—which is offered us by the usual French story-teller; his charm is much more that of substance. He is a man of thought, of deep observation, of a taste for general truths, and he is intellectually less after the French pattern than any Frenchman of his day. To Oriental studies M. de Gobineau has devoted much of his life, and his excellent work entitled 'Les Religions de l'Asie' is probably much better known than any of his attempts in the line of fiction are likely to be. In this collection of tales he sums up some of his personal impressions of the Oriental character. He is evidently deeply versed in Asiatic manners; he has lived in the midst of them. In fact, although M. de Gobineau is at present French Minister to Sweden, he formerly occupied more than one diplomatic post in the East. He pays, in an interesting introduction to his volume, a compliment to an English book which was much read forty years ago, but is now almost wholly forgotten. Morier's novel of 'Hajji-Baba'—the novel-readers of the first half of this century will remember it—is, according to M. de Gobineau, "assuredly the best book that has been written upon the temperament of an Asiatic nation." "It is a matter of course," he immediately adds, "that the 'Arabian Nights' are here counted

397

out; they remain incomparable, they are the truth itself, and they will never be equalled. But this masterpiece excepted, 'Hajji-Baba' holds the first rank. . . . What it depicts is the levity, the inconsistency of mind, the tenuity of moral ideas among the Persians." We may ask in parenthesis whether now—in the days of 'Daniel Deronda,' that is—that fiction and "culture" are, like the lion and the lamb, lying down together, and the contemplation of race-questions is very much the fashion, it would not be worth some publisher's trouble to reprint Morier's charming tale? It was reprinted in the far-away days when English fiction reached us almost exclusively by way of Philadelphia; but the Philadelphia pamphlet, happily for modern eyesight, will not be easy to find.

"It has not only been my design," says M. de Gobineau, "to bring out, after Morier, the more or less conscious immorality of the Asiatics, and the spirit of lies which governs them; I have tried that too, but that was not enough. It seemed to me to the purpose not to leave in the shade the bravery of some and the sincerely romantic temper of others; the native goodness of these, the fundamental honesty of those; among certain ones the passion of patriotism pushed to its last excesses; among certain others complete generosity, devotion, affection; among all an incomparable *laissez-aller* and the absolute tyranny of the first impulse, whether it be good or whether it be the worst possible."

The author has endeavored to be as characteristic as possible, and to select types and cases which shall be intensely illustrative. The local color of the East in its material sense has probably been overdone during the last thirty years. What M. de Gobineau has tried to reproduce is the local color of the Oriental mind and soul. He is a very acute psychologist, and he handles the subtle threads of the Eastern character with singularly unerring fingers. He puts himself as far as possible into the Asiatic skin, looks at things from his heroes' and heroines' point of view, never comments nor protests, but contents himself with relating exactly how his characters felt and acted in the circumstances which he has devised for them. His tales are six in number, and they are perhaps of unequal merit; two, at least, of which the scene is laid in Persia—'The

Story of Gamber-Ali' and 'The War of the Turcomans'—are genuine masterpieces. 'The Dancing-Girl of Shamakha' is a story of the Russian Caucasus, and is a very curious and touching study of the female character in regions where the aspirations of the softer sex have not that elevated tone which they have attained among ourselves. The figure of Omm-Djéhâne is indeed an admirable portrait of a formidable but doubtless very possible original. The word "Tartar" has passed into English speech with a very invidious meaning, which, it must be confessed, is completely justified by M. de Gobineau's vivid representation of a passionate Tartar maiden. And, in speaking of this tale, we may note the singular fact that M. Gobineau, when he has occasion to introduce a European hero, never selects one of his own countrymen. In 'Les Pléiades' the two heroes were English and German; the heroines were English, German, and Russian. In 'La Danseuse de Shamakha' the interesting young European whom he makes the object of the hopeless passion of his fascinating Calmuck is a Spaniard; and in the last tale in the book, the 'Vie de Voyage,' desiring to represent the emotions of a civilized young couple who undertake to travel in an immense caravan, he selects two Italians. It may almost be said that with M. de Gobineau any reference to his native land is conspicuous by its absence. This, however, is a detail. The second story, 'L'illustre Magicien,' is perhaps the least interesting, though it doubtless touches a very characteristic point, being the history of a most exemplary and amiable young Persian, married to a wife in every way worthy of him, and enjoying the fullest domestic bliss and prosperity, who leaves his happy home to follow a squalid Dervish and learn the great secret of truth.

'Gamber-Ali,' as we have said, is admirable, and, as a sympathetic and irresponsible picture of unconscious rascality, is hardly inferior to one of Browning's dramatic monologues. (It should be noted that the author always tells his story exactly as a fellow-townsman of his hero would tell it—with the same moral tone.) Gamber-Ali is a young man about town at Shiraz, remarkable for his personal beauty and his love of amusement, whose entrance into active life the author relates in detail. The details are taken, as the French say, *sur*

le vif, and afford an interesting picture of the state of manners
and morals in the land of Firdousi and of the jewelled monarch whom the kingdoms of Europe outstrove each other
three years since to entertain. Gamber-Ali is the child of epicurean parents, and the Bohemian ménage of the shiftless
painter Hassan-Kahn and his terrible wife, Bibi Djanem, is
very happily touched off. Their dissipated son, in a drunken
scrimmage in a tavern, has the good fortune to pass for having diverted a few blows from the portly person of one of the
hangers on of the palace of the governor, and the gratitude
of this flurried functionary proves the stepping-stone of the
young man's fortunes. He becomes a sort of Persian Gil Blas,
obtains a place in the governor's suite, learns all the tricks of
the trade, lies and steals triumphantly, and lines his pocket
with the bribes of all applicants for justice or favor. But his
avidity proves his ruin, or nearly so, inasmuch as he fails to
share his booty with his employers, to whom, properly, a
handsome percentage of all profits is due. This brings him
into contempt and disgrace, and finally, having stabbed to
death one of his fellow-servants, he is obliged to flee for his
life, and takes refuge in a mosque erected over the tomb of
an eminent saint. The account of his sojourn in this inviolable
asylum is the best part of the story. He is represented as being
in an insurmountable agony of fear as to what will be done
to him if he is taken, and the picture of his frank, expansive,
absorbing terror completes admirably the whole portrait of
his smoothness, softness, impudence, luxuriousness, and, as it
were, feminine rascality. The most solemn assurances that he
will be allowed to escape in safety cannot induce him to
budge. He becomes an object of extreme interest to all the
faithful who frequent the mosque, and who cover him with
admiration and sympathy. The ladies of the locality "go on"
about him as if he were a handsome tenor or light comedian
in New York, and a perpetual chorus of feminine lamentation
and adulation surrounds his resting-place. At last the King of
Kings, in person, comes to visit the mosque, and the terror
of Gamber-Ali, lest the mighty monarch should detach him
by force from his refuge, becomes such that he clings to the
walls of the monument (the tomb of the saint) as a drowning
man to a spar. He is pointed out to the king, who conde-

scends to converse with him, tries to persuade him that he may go in peace, and finally gives his royal word that not a hair of his head shall be touched. But Gamber-Ali, stupid with terror, only clings the closer and trembles the harder, and the monarch marches off in disgust. Then the chorus of admiration from the ladies deepens, and the young refugee is almost mobbed by the fair spectators. At last the sentiment of the assemblage finds expression in the energetic conduct of a great lady, who makes her way into the sacred enclosure and fairly kidnaps Gamber-Ali, now too exhausted with inanition to resist, having been afraid to touch the cakes and sweetmeats offered him by his admirers lest they should poison him. The lady in question carries him off in her coach-and-four, comforts and consoles him, and makes him her chief steward; in which character he may now be seen riding about in state, more beautiful than ever, supremely happy, covered with jewels, and adored by all observers.

'La Guerre des Turcomans' is a picture of Persian optimism, or, at least, of the amiable serenity with which persons of that enviable race may endure the most odious tribulations. Ghoulam-Hussein relates his own adventures, and his tone is a wonderful mixture of patience and humility in the individual, and complacency and impudence in the race. There is an extraordinary air of truth in his wife's repeated experiments in matrimony—for in offering facilities for such experiments Persia appears almost to compete with certain sections of our own country—and in his easily-accepted miseries and easily-enjoyed mitigations during his life in the army and his captivity by the foe. "Les Amants de Kandahar" is striking, but it is more romantic, less ironical, and less entertaining than its companions. "La Vie de Voyage" is hardly a tale; it is a sketch of homesickness, of what a young European woman feels when she is launched in a great caravan with a two months' journey before her; of the oppressive strangeness and isolation, amounting almost to terror, which finally forces her to persuade her husband to retreat in the first caravan they encounter bound for Europe. We had marked for quotation from these pages an admirable description of the aspect, march, and movement of a great promiscuous caravan, but we have exceeded our space. All M. de Gobineau's pages, moreover, are worth reading; they are the work of a rich and serious mind, of a really philosophic observer.

Nation, December 7, 1876

Edmond de Goncourt

La Fille Elisa. Paris, 1877.

THE GREAT SUCCESS of Emile Zola's remarkable and repulsive novel, 'L'Assommoir,' which was lately described
in these columns, has been, if not equalled, at least emulated,
by 'La Fille Elisa' of M. Edmond de Goncourt. 'L'Assommoir,' we believe, is going on forwards its thirtieth edition,
while the last copy of 'La Fille Elisa' that we have seen is
stamped with the fainter glory of a tenth. On the other hand,
M. Zola's novel had by some weeks the start of its companion,
and the adventures of M. de Goncourt's heroine (a prostitute
who murders a soldier) may after all be as widely disseminated
as those of the fair protagonist of 'L'Assommoir,' the washerwoman who dies of drink. M. Edmond de Goncourt has gone
into these matters in a more amateurish sort of way than his
rival, who is thoroughly professional and business-like; and
'La Fille Elisa' is very inferior in ability to the history of Gervaise and Coupeau. It is equal, however, or perhaps even superior, in audacity. Edmond de Goncourt, we may remind the
reader, is the elder and survivor of the two brothers De Goncourt, who, during the lifetime of the younger, Jules, published several novels of the realistic sort and several substantial
works upon the history of France in the last century. 'La Fille
Elisa' is the first production upon the title-page of which the
name of one of the brothers has stood alone; and, curiously
enough, it offers some enlightenment (for such readers as
have wondered over the matter) as to the mystery of French
"collaboration." The book is feebler, thinner, less clever than
its predecessors; it seems to prove that there are some talents
that need to "collaborate," and that they are fully themselves
only on this condition. Like M. Zola, the author of the tale in
question has written a preface, in which he calls attention to
the edifying properties of his book—his "livre austère et
chaste." Speaking seriously, the preface is the best part of the
work. M. de Goncourt says, very justly, that it is an unwar-
rantable pretension on the part of certain critics to forbid the
school of novelists to which he belongs—"la jeune école
sérieuse"—to write anything but what may be read by young

ladies in railway trains. This is really what the prohibitory legislation amounts to. The author asserts that the young serious school, if not interfered with, stands ready to divest the novel of its traditional frivolity, and make it co-operate with history and scientific research in the task of enlightening and instructing mankind. As an example, M. de Goncourt devotes himself to showing up the horrors of the régime of silence in prisons—the system which he appears to consider it the peculiar infamy of the American penal establishments to have invented and propagated. His heroine, convicted of manslaughter, is imprisoned for life, and, being never allowed to speak, becomes after a certain number of years idiotic and dies of a sort of chronic stupor. This part of the book, the last third, dealing with her prison life, shows most ability, and has doubtless a certain value. The author has evidently "studied up" his subject. The preceding chapters, which describe minutely the career of the unfortunate Elisa as a street-walker of the lowest class, and include an account of the circumstances of her childhood—as daughter of a *sage-femme* also of the lowest class—are not practically agreeable, however valid the theory upon which they have been composed. As we read them we wonder what is becoming of the French imagination, and we say that even readers who have flattered themselves that they knew the French mind tolerably well find that it has some surprisingly unpleasant corners. M. de Goncourt's theory is perfectly respectable; novelists are welcome to become as serious as they please; but are the mysteries of such a career as Elisa's the most serious thing in the list? M. de Goncourt's fault is not that he is serious or historical or scientific or instructive, but that he is intolerably unclean. The proof of the pudding is in the eating, and, in spite of its elevated intentions, "La Fille Elisa" must be profoundly distasteful to healthy appetites.

Nation, May 10, 1877

THE JOURNAL OF THE BROTHERS DE GONCOURT

I CAN SCARCELY FORBEAR beginning these limited remarks on an interesting subject with a regret—the regret that I had not found the right occasion to make them two or three years ago. This is not because since that time the subject has become less attaching, but precisely because it has become more so, has become so absorbing that I am oppressively conscious of the difficulty of treating it. It was never, I think, an easy one; inasmuch as for persons interested in questions of literature, of art, of form, in the general question of the observation of life for an artistic purpose, the appeal and the solicitation of Edmond and Jules de Goncourt were essentially not simple and soothing. The manner of this extraordinary pair, their temper, their strenuous effort and conscious system, suggested anything but a quick solution of the problems that seemed to hum in our ears as we read; suggested it almost as little indeed as their curious, uncomfortable style, with its multiplied touches and pictorial verbosity, was apt to evoke an immediate vision of the objects to which it made such sacrifices of the synthetic and the rhythmic. None the less, if one liked them well enough to persist, one ended by making terms with them; I allude to the liking as conditional, because it appears to be a rule of human relations that it is by no means always a sufficient bond of sympathy for people to care for the same things: there may be so increasing a divergence when they care for them in different ways. The great characteristic of the way of the brothers De Goncourt was that it was extraordinarily "modern"; so illustrative of feelings that had not yet found intense expression in literature that it made at last the definite standpoint, the common ground and the clear light for taking one's view of them. They bristled (the word is their own) with responsible professions, and took us farther into the confidence of their varied sensibility than we always felt it important to penetrate; but the formula that expressed them remained well in sight. They were historians and observers who were painters; they composed biographies, they told stories, with the palette always on their thumb.

Now, however, all that is changed and the case is infinitely more complicated. M. Edmond de Goncourt has published, at intervals of a few months, the Journal kept for twenty years by his brother and himself, and the Journal makes all the difference. The situation was comparatively manageable before, but now it strikes us as extremely embarrassing. M. Edmond de Goncourt has mixed the cards in the most extraordinary way; he has shifted his position with a carelessness of consequences of which I know no other example. Who can recall an instance of an artist's having it in his power to deprive himself of the advantage of the critical perspective in which he stands, and being eager to use that power?

That MM. de Goncourt should have so faithfully carried on their Journal is a very interesting and remarkable fact, as to which there will be much to say; but it has almost a vulgarly usual air in comparison with the circumstance that one of them has judged best to give the document to the light. If it be true that the elder and surviving brother has held a part of it back, that only adds to the judicious, responsible quality of the act. He has selected, and that indicates a plan and constitutes a presumption of sanity. There has been, so to speak, a method in M. Edmond de Goncourt's madness. I use the term madness because it so conveniently covers most of the ground. How else indeed should one express it when a man of talent defaces with his own hand not only the image of himself that public opinion has erected on the highway of literature, but also the image of a loved and lost partner who can raise no protest and offer no explanation? If instead of publishing his Journal M. de Goncourt had burned it up we should have been deprived of a very curious and entertaining book; but even with that consciousness we should have remembered that it would have been impertinent to expect him to do anything else. Barely conceivable would it have been had he withheld the copious record from the flames for the perusal of a posterity who would pass judgment on it when he himself should be dust. That would have been an act of high humility—the sacrifice of the finer part of one's reputation; but, after all, a man can commit suicide only in his lifetime, and the example would have had its distinction on the part of a curious mind moved by sympathy with the curiosity of a coming age.

If I suggest that if it were possible to us to hear Jules de Goncourt's voice to-day it might convey an explanation, this perhaps represents an explanation as more possible than we see it as yet. Certainly it is difficult to see it as graceful or as conciliatory. There is scarcely any account we can give of the motive of the act that doesn't make it almost less an occasion for complacency than the act itself. (I still refer, of course, to the publication, not to the composition, of the Journal. The composition, for nervous, irritated, exasperated characters, may have been a relief—though even in this light its operation appears to have been slow and imperfect. Indeed, it occurs to one that M. Edmond de Goncourt may have felt the whimsical impulse to expose the fond remedy as ineffectual.) If the motive was not humility, not mortification, it was something else—something that we can properly appreciate only by remembering that it is not enough to be proud, and that the question inevitably comes up of what one's pride is about. If MM. de Goncourt were two almost furious *névrosés*, if the infinite vibration of their nerves and the soreness of their sentient parts were the condition on which they produced many interesting books, the fact was pathetic and the misfortune great, but the legitimacy of the whole thing was incontestable. People are made as they are made, and some are weak in one way and some in another. What passes our comprehension is the state of mind in which their weakness appears to them a source of glory or even of dolorous general interest. It may be an inevitable, or it may even for certain sorts of production be an indispensable, thing to be a *névrosé*; but in what particular juncture is it a communicable thing? M. de Goncourt not only communicates the case, but insists upon it; he has done personally what M. Maxime du Camp did a few years ago for Gustave Flaubert (in his "Souvenirs Littéraires") when he made known to the world that the author of "Madame Bovary" had epileptic fits. The differences are great, however, for if we are disposed to question M. du Camp's right to put another person's secret into circulation, we must admit that he does so with compunction and mourning. M. de Goncourt, on the other hand, waves the banner of the infirmity that his *collaborateur* shared with him and invites all men to listen to the details. About his right, I hasten to add, so far as he speaks for himself, there is nothing dubious, and this puts us in a rare position for reading and enjoying his book. We are not accomplices and our honor is safe. People are betrayed by their friends, their enemies, their biographers, their critics, their editors, their publishers, and so far as we give ear in these cases we are not quite without guilt; but it is much plainer sailing when the burden of defence rests on the very sufferers. What would have been thought of a friend or an editor, what would have been thought even of an enemy, who should have ventured to print the Journal of MM. de Goncourt?

The reason why it must always be asked in future, with regard to any appreciation of these gentlemen, "Was it formed before the Journal or after the Journal?" is simply that this publication has obtruded into our sense of their literary performance the disturbance of a revelation of personal character. The scale on which the disturbance presents itself is our ground for surprise, and the nature of the character exhibited our warrant for regret. The complication is simply that if today we wish to judge the writings of the brothers De Goncourt freely, largely, historically, the feat is almost impossible. We have to reckon with a prejudice—a prejudice of our own. And that is why a critic may be sorry to have missed the occasion of testifying to a liberal comprehension before the prejudice was engendered. Almost impossible, I say, but fortunately not altogether; for is it not the very function of criticism and the sign of its intelligence to acquit itself honorably in embarrassing conditions and track the idea with patience just in proportion as it is elusive? The good method is always to sacrifice nothing. Let us therefore not regret too much either that MM. de Goncourt did not burn their Journal if they wished their novels to be liked, or that they did not burn their novels if they wished their Journal to be forgotten. The difficult point to deal with as regards this latter production is that it is a journal of pretensions; for is it not a sound generalization to say that when we speak of pretensions we always mean pretensions exaggerated? If the Journal sets them forth, it is in the novels that we look to see them justified. If the justification is imperfect, that will not disgust us, for what does the disparity do more than help to characterize our authors? The importance of their being characterized depends largely on their talent (for people engaged in the same general effort and interested in the same questions), and of a poverty of talent even the reader most struck with the unamiable way in which, as diarists, they for the most part use their powers will surely not accuse MM. de Goncourt. They express, they represent, they give the sense of life; it is not always the life that such and such a one of their readers will find most interesting, but that is his affair and not theirs. Theirs is to vivify the picture. This art they unmistakably possess, and the Journal testifies to it still more than "Germinie Lacerteux" and "Manette Salomon"; infinitely more, I may add, than the novels published by M. Edmond de Goncourt since the death of his brother.

I do not pronounce for the moment either on the justice or the generosity of the portrait of Sainte-Beuve produced in the Journal by a thousand small touches, entries made from month to month and year to year, and taking up so much place in the whole that the representation of that figure (with the Princess Mathilde, Gavarni, Théophile Gautier, and Gustave Flaubert thrown in a little behind) may almost be said to be the main effect of the three volumes. What is incontestable is the intensity of the vision, the roundness of the conception, and the way that the innumerable little parts of the image hang together. The Sainte-Beuve of MM. de Goncourt may not be the real Sainte-Beuve, but he is a wonderfully possible and consistent personage. He is observed with detestation, but at least he is observed, and the faculty is welcome and rare. This is what we mean by talent—by having something fresh to contribute. Let us be grateful for anything at all fresh so long as our gratitude is not chilled—a case in which it has always the resource of being silent. It is obvious that this check is constantly at hand in our intercourse with MM. de Goncourt, for the simple reason that, with the greatest desire in the world to see all round, we cannot rid ourselves of the superstition that, when all is said and done, art is most in character when it most shows itself amiable. It is not amiable when it is narrow and exclusive and jealous, when it makes the deplorable confession that it has no secret for resisting exasperation. It is not the sign of a free intelligence or a rich life to be hysterical because somebody's work whom you don't like affirms itself in opposition to that of somebody else whom you do; but this condition is calculated particularly little to please when the excitement springs from a comparison more personal. It is almost a platitude to say that the artistic passion will ever most successfully assuage the popular suspicion that there is a latent cruelty in it when it succeeds in not appearing to be closely connected with egotism. The uncalculated trick played by our authors upon their reputation was to suppose that their name could bear such a strain. It is tolerably clear that it can't, and this is the mistake we should have to forgive them if we proposed to consider their productions as a whole. It doesn't cover all the ground to say that the injury of their mistake is only for themselves: it is really in some degree for those who take an interest in the art they practise. Such eccentrics, such passionate seekers, may not, in England and America, be numerous; but even if they are a modest band, their complaint is worth taking account of. No one can ever have been nearly so much interested in the work of Edmond and Jules de Goncourt as these gentlemen themselves; their deep absorption in it, defying all competition, is one of the honorable sides of their literary character. But the general brotherhood of men of letters may very well have felt humiliated by the disclosure of such wrath in celestial, that is, in analogous minds. It is, in short, rather a shock to find that artists who could make such a miniature of their Sainte-Beuve have not carried their delicacy a little further. It is always a pain to perceive that some of the qualities we prize don't imply the others.

What makes it important not to sacrifice the Journal (to speak for the present only of that) is this very illustration of the degree to which, for the indefatigable diarists, the things of literature and art are the great realities. If every genuine talent is for the critic a "case" constituted by the special mixture of elements and faculties, it is not difficult to put one's finger on the symptoms in which that of these unanimous brothers resides. It consists in their feeling life so exclusively as a theme for descriptive pictorial prose. Their exclusiveness is, so far as I know, unprecedented; for if we have encountered men of erudition, men of science as deeply buried in learning and in physics, we have never encountered a man of letters (our authors are really one in their duality) for whom his profession was such an exhaustion of his possibilities. Their friend and countryman Flaubert doubtless gave himself up to "art" with as few reservations, but our authors have over him exactly the superiority that the Journal gives them: it is a proof the more of their concentration, of their having drawn breath only in the world of subject and form. If they are not more representative, they are at least more convenient to refer to. Their concentration comes in part from the fact that it is the meeting of two natures, but this also would have counted in favor of expansion, of leakage. "Collaboration" is always a mystery, and that of MM. de Goncourt was probably close beyond any other; but we have seen the process successful several times, so that the real wonder is not that in this case the parties to it should have been able to work together, to divide the task without dividing the effect, but rather that nature should have struck off a double copy of a rare original. An original is a conceivable thing, but a pair of originals who are original in exactly the same way is a phenomenon embodied so far as I know only in the authors of "Manette Salomon." The relation borne by their feelings on the question of art and taste to their other feelings (which they assure us were very much less identical), this peculiar proportion constitutes their originality. In whom was ever the group of "other feelings" proportionately so small? In whom else did the critical vibration (in respect to the things cared for, limited in number, even very limited, I admit) represent so nearly the totality of emotion? The occasions left for MM. de Goncourt to vibrate differently were so few that they scarcely need be counted.

The manifestation of life that most appeals to them is the manifestation of Watteau, of Lancret, of Boucher, of Fragonard; they are primarily critics of pictorial art (with sympathies restricted very much to a period) whose form of expression happens to be literary, but whose sensibility is the sensibility of the painter and the sculptor, and whose attempt, allowing for the difference of the instrument, is to do what the painter and the sculptor do. The most general stricture to be made on their work is probably that they have not allowed enough for the difference of the instrument, have persisted in the effort to render impressions that the plastic artist renders better, neglecting too much those he is unable to render. From time to time they have put forth a volume which is really an instructive instance of misapplied ingenuity. In "Madame Gervaisais," for example, a picture of the visible, sketchable Rome of twenty-five years ago, we seem to hear the voice forced to sing in a register to which it doesn't belong, or rather (the comparison is more complete) to attempt effects of sound that are essentially not vocal. The novelist competes with the painter and the painter with the novelist, in the treatment of the aspect and figure of things; but what a happy tact each of them needs to keep his course straight, without poaching on the other's preserves! In England it is the painter who is apt to poach most, and in France the writer. However this may be, no one probably has poached more than have MM. de Goncourt.

Whether it be because there is something that touches us in pious persistence in error, or because even when it prevails there may on the part of a genuine talent be the happiest hits by the way, I will not pretend to declare; certain it is that the manner in which our authors abound in their own sense and make us feel that they would not for the world care for anything but what exactly they do care for, raises the liveliest presumption in their favor. If literature is kept alive by a passion loyal even to narrowness, MM. de Goncourt have rendered real services. They may look for it on the one side in directions too few, and on the other in regions thankless and barren; their Journal, at all events, is a signal proof of their good faith. Wonderful are such courage and patience and industry; fatigued, displeased, disappointed, they never intermit their chronicle nor falter in their task. We owe to this remarkable feat the vivid reflection of their life for twenty years, from the *coup d'état* which produced the Second Empire to the death of the younger brother on the eve of the war with Germany; the history of their numerous books, their articles, their studies, studies on the social and artistic history of France during the latter half of the last century—on Mme. de Pompadour, Mme. du Barry, and the other mistresses of Louis XV., on Marie Antoinette, on society and *la femme* during the Revolution and the Directory; the register, moreover, of their adventures and triumphs as collectors (collectors of the furniture, tapestries, drawings of the last century), of their observations of every kind in the direction in which their nature and their *milieu* prompt them to observe, of their talks, their visits, their dinners, their physical and intellectual states, their projects and visions, their ambitions and collapses, and, above all, of their likes and dislikes. Above all of their dislikes, perhaps I should say, for in this sort of testimony the Journal is exceedingly rich. The number of things and of people obnoxious to their taste is extremely large, especially when we consider the absence of variety, as the English reader judges variety, in their personal experience. What strikes an English reader, curious about a society in which acuteness has a high development and thankful for a picture of it, is the small surface over which the career of MM. de Goncourt is distributed. It seems all to take place in a little ring, a coterie of a dozen people. Movement, exercise, travel, other countries, play no part in it; the same persons, the same places, names, and occasions perpetually recur; there is scarcely any change of scene or any enlargement of horizon. The authors rarely go into the country, and when they do they hate it, for they find it *bête*. To the English mind that item probably describes them better than anything else. We end with the sensation of a closed room, of a want of ventilation; we long to open a window or two and let in the air of the world. The Journal of MM. de Goncourt is mainly a record of resentment and suffering, and to this circumstance they attribute many causes; but we suspect at last that the real cause is for them too the inconvenience from which we suffer as readers—simply the want of space and air.

Though the surface of the life represented is, as I have said, small, it is large enough to contain a great deal of violent reaction, an extraordinary quantity of animadversion, indignation, denunciation. Indeed, as I have intimated, the simplest way to sketch the relation of disagreement of our accomplished diarists would be to mention the handful of persons and things excepted from it. They are "down" absolutely on Sainte-Beuve and strongly on MM. Taine and Schérer. But I am taking the wrong course. The great exceptions then, in addition to the half-dozen friends I have mentioned (the Princess, Gavarni, Théophile Gautier, Flaubert, and Paul de Saint-Victor, though the two last named with restrictions which finally become in the one case considerable and in the other very marked), are the artistic production of the reign of Louis XV. and some of the literary, notably that of Diderot, which they oppose with a good deal of acrimony to that of Voltaire. They have also no quarrel with the wonderful figure of Marie Antoinette, unique in its evocation of luxury and misery, as is proved by the elaborate monograph which they published in 1858. This list may appear meagre, but I think it really exhausts their positive sympathies, so far as the Journal enlightens us. That is precisely the interesting point and the fact that arrests us, that the Journal, copious as a memorandum of the artistic life, is in so abnormally small a degree a picture of enjoyment. Such a fact suggests all sorts of reflections, and in particular an almost anxious one as to whether the passionate artistic life necessarily excludes enjoyment. I say the passionate because this makes the example better; it is only passion that gives us revelations and notes. If the artist is necessarily sensitive, does that sensitiveness form in its essence a state constantly liable to shade off into the morbid? Does this liability, moreover, increase in proportion as the effort is great and the ambition intense? MM. de Goncourt have this ground for expecting us to cite their experience in the affirmative, that it is an experience abounding in revelations. I don't mean to say that they are all, but only that they are preponderantly, revelations of suffering. In the month of March, 1859, in allusion to their occupations and projects, they make the excellent remark, the fruit of acquired wisdom, that "In this world one must do a great deal, one must intend a great deal." That is refreshing, that is a breath of air. But as a general thing what they commemorate as workers is the simple break-down of joy.

"Tell us," they would probably say, " where you will find an analysis equally close of the cheerfulness of creation, and then we will admit that our testimony is superficial. Many a record of a happy personal life, yes; but that is not to the point. The question is how many windows are opened, how many little holes are pierced, into the consciousness of the artist. Our contention would be that we have pierced more little holes than any other gimlet has achieved. Doubtless there are many people who are not curious about the consciousness of the artist and who would look into our little holes—if the sense of a kind of indelicacy, even of indecency in the proceeding were not too much for them—mainly with some ulterior view of making fun of them. Of course the better economy for such people is to let us alone. But if you *are* curious (there are a few who happen to be), where will you get to the same degree as in these patient pages the particular sensation of having your curiosity stimulated and fed? Will you get it in the long biography of Scott, in that of Dickens, in the autobiography of Trollope, in the letters of Thackeray? An intimation has reached us that in reading the letters of Thackeray you are moved, on the contrary, to wonder by what trick certain natural little betrayals of the consciousness of the artist have been conjured away. Very likely (we see you mean it) such betrayals are 'natural' only when people have a sense of responsibility. This sense may very well be a fault, but it is a fault to which the world owes some valuable information. Ah! of course if you don't think our information valuable, there is no use talking." The most convenient answer to this little address would probably be the remark that valuable information is supplied by the artist in more ways than one, and that we must look for it in his finished pieces as well as in his note-books. If we should see a flaw in this supposititious plea of our contentious friends it would be after turning back to "Germinie Lacerteux" and "Manette Salomon." Distinguished and suggestive as these performances are, they do not illustrate the artistic view so very much more than the works of those writers whose neglect of the practice of keeping a diary of protest lays them open to the imputation of levity.

In reading the three volumes pencil in hand, I have marked page after page as strongly characteristic, but I find in turning them over that it would be difficult to quote from them without some principle of selection. The striking passages or pages range themselves under three or four heads—the observation of persons, the observation of places and things (works of art, largely), the report of conversations, and the general chapter of the subjective, which, as I have hinted, is the general chapter of the *saignant*. "During dinner," I read in the second volume, "*nous avons l'agacement* of hearing Sainte-Beuve, the fine talker, the fine connoisseur in letters, talk art in a muddled manner, praise Eugène Delacroix as a philosophical painter," etc. These words, *nous avons l'agacement*, might stand as the epigraph of the Journal at large, so exact a translation would they be of the emotion apparently most frequent with the authors. On every possible and impossible occasion they have the annoyance. I hasten to add that I can easily imagine it to have been an annoyance to hear the historian of Port Royal talk, and talk badly, about Eugène Delacroix. But on whatever subject he expressed himself he seems to have been to the historians of Manette Salomon even as a red rag to a bull. The aversion they entertained for him, a plant watered by frequent intercourse and protected by punctual notes, has brought them good luck; in this sense, I mean, that they have made a more living figure of him than of any name in their work. The taste of the whole evocation is, to my mind and speaking crudely, atrocious; there is only one other case (the portrait of Madame de Païva) in which it is more difficult to imagine the justification of so great a license. Nothing of all this is quotable by a cordial admirer of Sainte-Beuve, who, however, would resent the treachery of it even more than he does if he were not careful to remember that the scandalized reader has always the resource of opening the "Causeries du Lundi." MM. de Goncourt write too much as if they had forgotten that. The thirty volumes of that wonderful work contain a sufficiently substantial answer to their account of the figure he cut when they dined with him as his invited guests or as fellow-members of a brilliant club. Impression for impression, we have that of the Causeries to set against that of the Journal, and it takes the larger hold of us. The reason is that it belongs to the finer part of Sainte-Beuve; whereas the picture from the Goncourt gallery (representing him, for instance, as a *petit mercier de province en partie fine*) deals only with his personal features. These are important, and they were unfortunately anything but superior; but they were not so important as MM. de Goncourt's love of art, for art makes them, nor so odious surely when they were seen in conjunction with the nature of his extraordinary mind. Upon the nature of his extraordinary mind our authors throw no more light than his washerwoman or his shoemaker might have done. They may very well have said, of course, that this was not their business, and that the fault was the eminent critic's if his small and ugly sides were what showed most in his conversation. Their business, they may contend, was simply to report that conversation and its accompaniment of little, compromising personal facts as minutely and vividly as possible; to attempt to reproduce for others the image that moved before them with such infirmities and limitations. Why for others? the reader of these volumes may well ask himself in this connection as well as in many another; so clear does it appear to him that *he* must have been out of the question of Sainte-Beuve's private relations—just as he feels that he was never included in that of Madame de Païva's or the Princess Mathilde's. We are confronted afresh with the whole subject of critical discretion, the responsibility of exposure, and the strange literary manners of our day. The Journal of MM. de Goncourt will have rendered at least the service of fortifying the blessed cause of occasional silence. If their ambition was to make Sainte-Beuve odious, it has suffered the injury that we are really more disagreeably affected by the character of the attack. That is more odious even than the want of private dignity of a demoralized investigator. And in this case the question the reader further asks is, Why even for themselves? and what superior interest was served by the elaboration week by week of this minute record of an implacable animosity? Keeping so patiently-written, so crossed and dotted and dated a register of hatred is a practice that gives the queerest account of your own nature, and indeed there are strange lights thrown throughout these pages on that of MM. de Goncourt. There is a kind of ferocity in the way the reporter that abides in them (how could they have abstained from kicking him out of doors with a "You're very clever, but you're really a bird of night"?) pursues the decomposing *causeur* to the end, seeking effects of grotesqueness in the aspects of his person and the misery of his disease.

All this is most unholy, especially on the part of a pair of *délicats*. MM. de Goncourt, I know, profess a perfect readiness to relinquish this title in certain conditions; they consider that there is a large delicacy and a small one, and they remind us of the fact that they could never have written "Germinie Lacerteux" if they had been afraid of being called coarse. In

fact they imply, I think, that for people of masculine observation the term has no relevancy at all; it is simply non-obser-
vant in its associations and exists for the convenience of the
ladies—a respectable function, but one of which the importance should not be overrated. This idea is luminous, but it
will probably never go far without plumping against another,
namely, that there is a reality in the danger of *feeling* coarsely,
that the epithet represents also a state of perception. Does it
come about, the danger in question, in consequence of too
prolonged a study, however disinterested, of the uglinesses
and uncleannesses of life? It may occur in that fashion and it
may occur in others; the point is that we recognize its ravages
when we encounter them, and that they are a much more
serious matter than the accident—the source of some silly reproach to our authors—of having narrated the history of an
hysterical servant-girl. That is a detail ("Germinie Lacerteux"
is a very brilliant experiment), whereas the catastrophe I speak
of is of the very essence. We know it has taken place when we
begin to notice that the artist's instrument has parted with
the quality which is supposed to make it most precious—the
fineness to which it owed its sureness, its exemption from
mistakes. The spectator's disappointment is great, of course,
in proportion as his confidence was high. The fine temper of
MM. de Goncourt has inspired us with the highest; their
whole attitude had been a protest against vulgarity. Mere
prettiness of subject—we were aware of the very relative
place they give to that; but, on the other hand, had they not
mastered the whole gamut of the shades of the aristocratic
sense? Was not a part of the charm of execution of "Germinie
Lacerteux" the glimpse of the taper fingers that wielded the
brush? It was not perhaps the brush of Vandyck, but might
Vandyck not have painted the white hand that held it? It is
no white hand that holds, alas, this uncontrollably querulous
and systematically treacherous pen. "Mémoires de la Vie Littéraire" is the sub-title of their Journal; but what sort of a life
will posterity credit us with having led and for what sort of
chroniclers will they take the two gentlemen who were assiduous attendants at the Diner Magny only to the end that they
might smuggle in, as it were, the uninvited (that is, you and
me who read), and entertain them at the expense of their col-

leagues and comrades? The Diner Magny was a club, the club is a high expression of the civilization of our time; but the way in which MM. de Goncourt interpret the institution makes them singular participants of that civilization. It is a strange performance, when one thinks of the performers— celebrated representatives of the refinement of their age. "If this was the best society," our grandchildren may say, "what could have been the *procédés* in that which was not so good?"

It is the firm conviction of many persons that literature is not doing well, that it is even distinctly on the wane, and that before many years it will have ceased to exist in any agreeable form, so that those living at that period will have to look far back for any happy example of it. May it not occur to us that if they look back to the phase lately embodied by MM. de Goncourt it will perhaps strike them that their loss is not cruel, since the vanished boon was, after all, so far from guar- anteeing the amenities of things? May the moral not appear pointed by the authors of the Journal rather than by the *con- frères* they have sacrificed? We of the English tongue move here already now in a region of uncertain light, where our proper traditions and canons cease to guide our steps. The portions of the work before us that refer to Madame de Païva, to the Princess Mathilde Bonaparte, leave us absolutely with- out a principle of appreciation. If it be correct according to the society in which they live, we have only to learn the lesson that we have no equivalent for some of the ideas and stan- dards of that society. We read on one page that our authors were personal friends of Madame de Païva, her guests, her interlocutors, recipients of her confidence, partakers of her hospitality, spectators of her splendor. On the next we see her treated like the last of the last, with not only her character but her person held up to our irreverent inspection, and the dec- laration that "elle s'est toute crachée," in a phrase which showed one day that she was purse-proud. Is it because the lady owed her great wealth to the favors of which she had been lavish that MM. de Goncourt hold themselves free to turn her friendship to this sort of profit? If Madame de Païva was good enough to dine, or anything else, with, she was good enough either to speak of without brutality or to speak of not at all. Does not this misdemeanor of MM. de Gon-

court perhaps represent, where women are concerned, a national as well as a personal tendency—a tendency which
introduces the strangest of complications into the French theory of gallantry? Our Anglo-Saxon theory has only one face,
while the French appears to have two; with "Make love to
her," as it were, on one side, and "Tue-la" on the other. The
French theory, in a word, involves a great deal of killing, and
the ladies who are the subject of it must often ask themselves
whether they do not pay dearly for this advantage of being
made love to. By "killing" I allude to the exploits of the pen
as well as to those of the directer weapons so ardently advo-
cated by M. Dumas the younger. On what theory has M.
Edmond de Goncourt handed over to publicity the whole
record of his relations with the Princess Mathilde? He stays
in her house for days, for weeks together, and then portrays
for our entertainment her person, her clothes, her gestures,
and her *salon*, repeating her words, reproducing her language,
relating anecdotes at her expense, describing the freedom of
speech used towards her by her *convives*, the racy expressions
that passed her own lips. In one place he narrates (or is it his
brother?) how the Princess was unable to resist the impulse
to place a kiss upon his brow. The liberty taken is immense,
and the idea of gallantry here has undergone a transmutation
which lifts it quite out of measurement by any scale or scruple
of ours. I repeat that the plea is surely idle that the brothers
are accomplished reporters to whom an enterprising newspaper would have found it worth while to pay a high salary;
for that cleverness, that intelligence, are simply the very standard by which we judge them. The betrayal of the Princess is
altogether beyond us.

Would Théophile Gautier feel that he is betrayed? Probably
not, for Théophile Gautier's feelings, as represented by MM.
de Goncourt, were nothing if not eccentric, his judgment
nothing if not perverse. His two friends say somewhere that
the sign of his conversation was *l'énormité dans le paradoxe*.
He certainly then would have risen to the occasion if it were
a question of maintaining that his friends had rendered a service to his reputation. This to my mind is contestable, though
their intention (at least in publishing their notes on him) was
evidently to do so, for the greater part of his talk, as they

repeat it, owes most of its relief to its obscenity. That is not fair to a man really clever—they should have given some other examples. But what strongly strikes us, however the service to Gautier may be estimated, is that they have rendered a questionable service to themselves. He is the finest mind in their pages, he is ever the object of their sympathy and applause. That is very graceful, but it enlightens us as to their intellectual perspective, and I say this with a full recollection of all that can be urged on Gautier's behalf. He was a charming genius, he was an admirable, a delightful writer. His vision was all his own and his brush was worthy of his vision. He knew the French color-box as well as if he had ground the pigments, and it may really be said of him that he did grind a great many of them. And yet with all this he is not one of the first, for his poverty of ideas was great. *Le sultan de l'épithète* our authors call him, but he was not the emperor of thought. To be light is not necessarily a damning limitation. Who was lighter than Charles Lamb, for instance, and yet who was wiser for our immediate needs? Gautier's defect is that he had veritably but one idea: he never got beyond the superstition that real literary greatness is to bewilder the *bourgeois*. Flaubert sat, intellectually, in the same everlasting twilight, and the misfortune is even greater for him, for his was the greater spirit. Gautier had other misfortunes as well—the struggle that never came to success, the want of margin, of time to do the best work, the conflict, in a hand-to-mouth, hackneyed literary career, between splendid images and peculiarly sordid realities. Moreover, his paradoxes were usually genial and his pessimism was amiable—in the poetic glow of many of his verses and sketches you can scarcely tell it from optimism. All this makes us tender to his memory, but it does not blind us to the fact that MM. de Goncourt classify themselves when they show us that in the literary circle of their time they find him the most typical figure. He has the supreme importance, he looms largest and covers most ground. This leaves Gautier very much where he was, but it tickets his fastidious friends.

"Théophile Gautier, who is here for some days, talks opera-dancers," they note in the summer of 1868. "He describes the white satin shoe which, for each of them, is strengthened by

a little cushion of silk in the places where the dancer feels that
she bears and presses most; a cushion which would indicate
to an expert the name of the dancer. And observe that this
work is always done by the dancer herself." I scarcely know
why, but there is something singularly characteristic in this
last injunction of MM. de Goncourt, or of MM. de Goncourt
and Théophile Gautier combined: "Et remarquez—!" The
circumstance that a ballet-girl cobbles her shoes in a certain
way has indeed an extreme significance. "Gautier begins to
rejudge *The Misanthrope*, a comedy for a Jesuit college on the
return from the holidays. Ah! the pig—what a language! it *is*
ill-written!" And Gautier adds that he can't say this in print;
people would abuse him and it would take the bread out of
his mouth. And then he falls foul of Louis XIV. "A hog, pock-
marked like a colander, and short! He was not five feet high,
the great king. Always eating and—" My quotation is nipped
in the bud: an attempt to reproduce Gautier's conversation in
English encounters obstacles on the threshold. In this case we
must burn pastilles even to read the rest of the sketch, and we
cannot translate it at all. "*Les bourgeois*—why, the most enormous things go on *chez les bourgeois*," he remarks on another
occasion. "I have had a glimpse of a few interiors. It is the
sort of thing to make you veil your face." But again I must
stop. M. Taine on this occasion courageously undertakes the
defence of the *bourgeois*, of their decency, but M. Paul de
Saint-Victor comes to Gautier's support with an allusion impossible even to paraphrase, which apparently leaves those
gentlemen in possession of the field. The effort of our time
has been, as we know, to disinter the details of history, to see
the celebrities of the past, and even the obscure persons, in
the small facts as well as in the big facts of their lives. In his
realistic evocation of Louis XIV. Gautier was in agreement
with this fashion; the historic imagination operated in him by
the light of the rest of his mind. But it is through the nose
even more than through the eyes that it appears to have operated, and these flowers of his conversation suggest that,
though he was certainly an animated talker, our wonder at
such an anomaly as that MM. de Goncourt should apparently
have sacrificed almost every one else to their estimate of him
is not without its reasons.

There are lights upon Flaubert's conversation which are somewhat of the same character (though not in every case) as those projected upon Gautier's. Gautier himself furnishes one of the most interesting of them when he mentions that the author of "Madame Bovary" had said to him of a new book, "It is finished; I have a dozen more pages to write, but I have the fall of every phrase." Flaubert had the religion of rhythm, and when he had caught the final cadence of each sentence— something that might correspond, in prose, to the rhyme— he filled in the beginning and middle. But Gautier makes the distinction that his rhythms were addressed above all to the ear (they were "mouthers," as the author of "Le Capitaine Fracasse" happily says); whereas those that he himself sought were ocular, not intended to be read aloud. There was no style worth speaking of for Flaubert but the style that required reading aloud to give out its value; he *mouthed* his passages to himself. This was not in the least the sort of prose that MM. de Goncourt themselves cultivated. The reader of their novels will perceive that harmonies and cadences are nothing to them, and that their rhythms are, with a few rare exceptions, neither to be sounded nor to be seen. A page of "Madame Gervaisais," for instance, is an almost impossible thing to read aloud. Perhaps this is why poor Flaubert ended by giving on their nerves when on a certain occasion he invited them to come and listen to a manuscript. They could endure the structure of his phrase no longer, and they alleviate themselves in their diary. It accounts for the great difference between their treatment of him and their treatment of Gautier: they accept the latter to the end, while with the author of "Salammbô" at a given moment they break down.

It may appear that we *have* sacrificed MM. de Goncourt's Journal, in contradiction to the spirit professed at the beginning of these remarks; so that we must not neglect to give back with the other hand something presentable as the equivalent of what we have taken away. The truth is our authors are, in a very particular degree, specialists, and the element of which, as they would say, *nous avons l'agacement* in this autobiographic publication is largely the result of a disastrous attempt, undertaken under the circumstances with a strangely good conscience, to be more general than nature intended them. Constituted in a remarkable manner for receiving impressions of the external, and resolving them into pictures in which each touch looks fidgety, but produces none the less its effect—for conveying the suggestion (in many cases, perhaps in most, the derisive or the invidious suggestion) of scenes, places, faces, figures, objects, they have not been able to deny themselves in the page directly before us the indulgence of a certain yearning for the abstract, for conceptions and ideas. In this direction they are not happy, not general and serene; they have a way of making large questions small, of thrusting in their petulance, of belittling even the religion of literature. *Je vomis mes contemporains*, one of them somewhere says, and there is always danger for them that an impression will act as an emetic. But when we meet them on their own ground, that of the perception of feature and expression, that of translation of the printed and published text of life, they are altogether admirable. It is mainly on this ground that we meet them in their novels, and the best pages of the Journal are those in which they return to it. There are, in fact, very few of these that do not contain some striking illustration of the way in which every combination of objects about them makes a picture for them, and a picture that testifies vividly to the life led in the midst of it. In the year 1853 they were legally prosecuted as authors of a so-called indecent article in a foolish little newspaper; the prosecution was puerile, and their acquittal was a matter of course. But they had to select a defender, and they called upon a barrister who had been recommended to them as "safe." "In his drawing-room he had a flower-stand of which the foot consisted of a serpent in varnished wood climbing in a spiral up to a bird's nest. When I saw this flower-stand I felt a chill in my back. I guessed the sort of advocate that was to be our lot." The object, rare or common, has on every occasion the highest importance for them; when it is rare it gives them their deepest pleasure, but when it is common it represents and signifies, and it is ever the thing that signifies most.

Théophile Gautier's phrase about his own talent has attained a certain celebrity ("Critics have been so good as to reason about me overmuch—I am simply a man for whom the visible world exists"), but MM. de Goncourt would have had every bit as good a right to utter it. People for whom the visible world doesn't "exist" are people with whom they have no manner of patience, and their conception of literature is a conception of something in which such people have no part. Moreover, oddly enough, even as specialists they pay for their intensity by stopping short in certain directions; the country is a considerable part of the visible world, but their Journal is full of little expressions of annoyance and disgust with it. What they like is the things they can do something with, and they can do nothing with woods and fields, nothing with skies that are not the ceiling of crooked streets or the "glimmering square" of windows. However, we must, of course, take men for what they have, not for what they have not, and the good faith of the two brothers is immensely fruitful when they project it upon their own little plot. What an amount of it they have needed, we exclaim as we read, to sustain them in such an attempt as "Madame Gervaisais"—an attempt to trace the conversion of a spirit from scepticism to Catholicism through contact with the old marbles and frescos, the various ecclesiastical bric-à-brac of Rome. Nothing could show less the expert, the habitual explorer of the soul than the purely pictorial plane of the demonstration. Of the attitude of the soul itself, of the combinations, the agitations, of which it was traceably the scene, there are no picture and no notation at all. When the great spiritual change takes place for their heroine, the way in which it seems to the authors most to the purpose to represent it is by a wonderful description of the confessional, at the Gesù, to which she goes for the first time to kneel. A deep Christian mystery has been wrought within her, but the account of it in the novel is that

"The confessional is beneath the mosaic of the choir, held and confined between the two supports carried by the heads of angels, with the shadow of the choir upon its brown wood, its little columns, its escutcheoned front, the hollow of its blackness detaching itself dark from the yellow marble of the pilasters, from the white marble of the wainscot. It has two steps on the side for the knees of the penitent; at the height for leaning a little square of copper trellis-work, in the middle of which the whisper of lips and

the breath of sins has made a soiled, rusty circle; and above
this, in a poor black frame, a meagre print, under which is
stamped *Gesù muore in croce*, and the glass of which receives
a sort of gleam of blood from the flickering fire of a lamp
suspended in the chapel beside it."

The weakness of such an effort as "Madame Gervaisais" is
that it has so much less authority as the history of a life than
as the exhibition of a palette. On the other hand, it expresses
some of the aspects of the most interesting city in the world
with an art altogether peculiar, an art which is too much, in
places, an appeal to our patience, but which says a hundred
things to us about the Rome of our senses a hundred times
better than we could have said them for ourselves. At the risk
of seeming to attempt to make characterization an affair of as
many combined and repeated touches as MM. de Goncourt
themselves, or as the cumulative Sainte-Beuve, master of aggravation, I must add that their success, even where it is
great, is greatest for those readers who are submissive to description and even to enumeration. The process, I say, is an
appeal to our patience, and I have already hinted that the
image, the evocation, is not immediate, as it is, for instance,
with Guy de Maupassant: our painters believe, above all, in
shades, deal essentially with shades, have a horror of anything
like rough delineation. They arrive at the exact, the particular;
but it is, above all, on a second reading that we see them
arrive, so that they perhaps suffer a certain injustice from
those who are unwilling to give more than a first. They select,
but they see so much in things that even their selection contains a multiplicity of items. The Journal, none the less, is full
of aspects caught in the fact. In 1867 they make a stay in Auvergne, and their notes are perhaps precisely the more illustrative from the circumstance that they find everything odious.

"Return to Clermont. We go up and down the town.
Scarcely a passer. The flat Sabbatical gloom of *la province*,
to which is added here the mourning of the horrible stone
of the country, the slate-stone of the Volvic, which resembles the stones of dungeons in the fifth act of popular melodramas. Here and there a *campo* which urges suicide, a little
square with little pointed paving-stones and the grass of the

court of a seminary growing between them, where the dogs yawn as they pass. A church, the cathedral of colliers, black without, black within, a law-court, a black temple of justice, an Odeon-theatre of the law, academically funereal, from which one drops into a public walk where the trees are so bored that they grow thin in the wide, mouldy shade. Always and everywhere the windows and doors bordered with black, like circulars conveying information of a demise. And sempiternally, on the horizon, that eternal Puy de Dôme, whose bluish cone reminds one so, grocer-fashion, of a sugar-loaf wrapped in its paper."

A complete account of MM. de Goncourt would not close without some consideration of the whole question of, I will not say the legitimacy, but the discretion, of the attempt on the part of an artist whose vehicle is only collocations of words to be nothing if not plastic, to do the same things and achieve the same effects as the painter. Our authors offer an excellent text for a discourse on that theme, but I may not pronounce it, as I have not in these limits pretended to do more than glance in the direction of that activity in fiction on which they appear mainly to take their stand. The value of the endeavor I speak of will be differently rated according as people like to "see" as they read, and according as in their particular case MM. de Goncourt will appear to have justified by success a manner of which it is on every occasion to be said that it was handicapped at the start. My own idea would be that they have given this manner unmistakable life. They have had an observation of their own, which is a great thing, and it has made them use language in a light of their own. They have attempted an almost impossible feat of translation, but there are not many passages they have altogether missed. Those who feel the spectacle as they feel it will always understand them enough, and any writer—even those who risk less—may be misunderstood by readers who have not that sympathy. Of course the general truth remains that if you wish to compete with the painter prose is a roundabout vehicle, and it is simpler to adopt the painter's tools. To this MM. de Goncourt would doubtless have replied that there is *no* use of words that is not an endeavor to "render," that lines of division are arrogant and arbitrary, that the point at which the pen should give way to the brush is a matter of appreciation, that the only way to see what it can do, in certain directions of ingenuity, is to try, and that they themselves have the merit of having tried and found out. What they have found out, what they show us, is not certainly of the importance that all the irritation, all the envy and uncharitableness of their Journal would seem to announce for compositions brought forth in such throes; but the fact that they themselves make too much of their genius should not lead us to make too little. Artists will find it difficult to forgive them for introducing such a confusion between æsthetics and ill-humor. That is compromising to the cause, for it tends to make the artistic spirit synonymous with the ungenerous. When one has the better thoughts one doesn't print the worse. We have never been ignorant of the fact that talent may be considerable even when character is peevish; that is a mystery which we have had to accept. It is a poor reward for our philosophy that Providence should appoint MM. de Goncourt to insist upon the converse of the proposition during three substantial volumes.

Fortnightly Review, October 1888
Reprinted in *Essays in London and Elsewhere*, 1893

Eugénie de Guérin

The Journal of Eugénie de Guérin. Translated by G. S. Trébutien. London: Simpkin & Marshall, 1865.

IF MADEMOISELLE DE GUÉRIN, transcribing from the fulness of her affection and her piety her daily record of one of the quietest lives that ever was led by one who had not formally renounced the world, could have foreseen that within a few years after her death, her love, her piety, her character, her daily habits, her household cares, her inmost and freest thoughts, were to be weighed and measured by half the literary critics of Europe and America, she would, doubtless, have found in this fact a miracle more wonderful than any of those to which, in the lives of her favorite saints, she accorded so gracious a belief. The history of a man or woman of genius prolongs itself after death; and one of the most pleasing facts with regard to that of Mlle. de Guérin is that it was her fate to know nothing of her fame. One of the most unselfish of women, she was spared the experience of that publicity which was the inevitable result of her talents. Genius is not a private fact: sooner or later, in the nature of things, it becomes common property. Mlle. de Guérin pays from her present eminence the penalty of her admirable faculties. If there be in the seclusion, the modesty, the cheerful obscurity and humility of her life, an essential incongruity with the broad light of actual criticism, we may console ourselves with the reflection that, in so far as it might, fortune has dealt with her in her own spirit. It has respected her noble unconsciousness. Her life and her fame stand apart. Between her own enjoyment of the work and the world's enjoyment of it intervenes that fact of her death which completes the one and excuses the other.

Our own excuse for speaking of Mlle. de Guérin at this somewhat late day lies in the recent issue of an English translation of her journal. This translation is apparently as good as it was likely to be. In the matter of style, it is our opinion that Mlle. de Guérin loses as much by translation as her great countrywoman, Mme. de Sévigné; and as it is for her style especially that we personally value Mlle. de Guérin, we cannot but think that an English version of her feelings would fail, in a very important particular, to represent her—her journal being, indeed, nothing more than a tissue of feelings, woven as simply, as easily, as closely, as rapidly, with the same interrupted continuity, as a piece of fireside knitting-work. It is probable, nevertheless, that the book will prove acceptable from its character of piety; and for those who are not acquainted with the original, it may even, through the translator's faithful sympathy, possess a certain literary charm.

Mlle. de Guérin's journal begins in 1834, when she was twenty-nine years of age, and ceases in 1840. It was strictly a series of daily letters addressed to her brother Maurice, and consigned to a number of blank-books, which he read when each was filled. It may be divided into two parts: the first, covering less than five years, extending to the death of Maurice de Guérin; and the second, covering a year and a half, extending from this event to what we may almost call the real death of Mlle. de Guérin herself—that is, the cessation of that practice of daily communion with her brother which had so long absorbed her most lively energies. She actually survived her brother nine years, a period of which she has left us only that beginning of a record formed by those few pages of her journal which she has inscribed to his departed soul. Her admirers will hardly regret the absence of a more extended chronicle of these weary years. Mlle. de Guérin's thoughts had always been half for heaven and half for Maurice. When Maurice died they reverted, by a pious compromise, to heaven alone, and assumed an almost painful monotony.

The chief figure in Mlle. de Guérin's life, accordingly, is not her own, but that of her brother. He, too, has become famous; he, too, had his genius. The sisterly devotion expressed and implied in every line of Mlle. de Guérin's writing needs, indeed, no such fact as this to explain it. She was nothing of a critic; and for the readers of the journal alone, the simple presumption that Maurice de Guérin was a lovable man is sufficient to account for his supremacy in the life of a woman who lived exclusively in her natural affections. For her, then, he was simply the dearest of her brothers; for us, if we had the space, he would be a most interesting object of study. But we can spare him but a few words. He was by several years

Eugénie's junior. Sent to school at a distance at an early age, and compelled subsequently to earn his living in Paris by teaching and writing, his life was passed in comparative solitude, and his relations with his family maintained by letters. His first plan had been to enter the church, and with this view he had attached himself to a small community of theological students organized and governed by Lamennais. The dispersion of this community, however, arrested and diverted his ecclesiastical aspirations; and if he never thoroughly abandoned himself to the world as it stands opposed to the church, his habitual seclusion and temperance are marked by a strictly secular tone. After several years of Paris drudgery, he contracted a marriage with a young girl of some fortune. He died at the age of twenty-eight. To ourselves, Maurice de Guérin is a more interesting person than his sister. We cannot, indeed, help regarding the collection recently made of his letters and literary remains as a most valuable contribution to our knowledge of the human mind. What he would have accomplished if time had been more generous towards him, it is difficult to say; but as it is, little can be claimed for him on the ground of his positive achievements. To say that he is chiefly interesting as a *phenomenon* seems but a cold way of looking at one who, in all that we know of his character, inspires us with the most tender affection; and yet so it is that we are tempted to speak of Maurice de Guérin. So it is that we are led to look at every man who is deficient in *will*. This was the case with Guérin. His letters, his diary, his verses, are one long record of moral impotency. He was one of the saddest of men. That he had genius, we think his little prose-poem, entitled "The Centaur," conclusively proves; not a splendid, a far-reaching genius, but nevertheless a source of inspiration which was all his own. His sensibility, his perceptions, were of the deepest. He put imagination into everything that he said or wrote. He has left descriptions of nature which have probably never been excelled, because, probably, nature has never been more delicately perceived. And yet we may be sure that for posterity he will live rather in his sister than in himself. For he is essentially an *imperfect* figure; and what the present asks of the past is before all things completeness. A man is only remembered beyond his own generation

by his *results*; and the most that Guérin has left us is a heritage of processes. If he had lived and grown great, we should
assuredly be delighted to peruse the record of his moral and
religious *tâtonnements*. But as his whole life was but a fragment, his fragmentary efforts lack that character of unity
which is essential to whomsoever, in morals or in letters, is
destined to become anything of a classic. Maurice de Guérin's
only unity is in his sister.

The singular unity of her own genius, indeed, is such as
almost to qualify her for this distinction. As her brother was
all complexity, she was all simplicity. As he was all doubt, she
was all faith. It seems to us that we shall place Mlle. de
Guérin on her proper footing, and obviate much possible
misconception, if we say that hers was an essentially *finite*
nature. We just now mentioned Mme. de Sévigné. The great
charm of Mme. de Sévigné's style is her perfect ability to say
whatever she pleases. But as she was chiefly an observer of
fashionable society, she was not often tempted to utter very
composite truths. Now, Mlle. de Guérin, perpetually engaged
in the contemplation of the Divine goodness, finds the right
word and the right phrase with the same delightful ease as
her great predecessor. With her, as with Mme. de Sévigné,
style was a natural gift. Many of the causes of this perfection
are doubtless identical in both cases. Both Mme. de Sévigné
and Mlle. de Guérin were women of taste and of tact, who,
under these conditions, wrote from the heart. They wrote
freely and familiarly, without any pre-occupation whatever.
They were both women of birth, both *ladies*, as we say now-
a-days. To both of them there clings an air of purely natural
distinction, of implicit subordination to the fact of race, a silent sense of responsibility to the past, which goes far to explain the positive character of their style. When we add to
this that in both of them the imaginative faculty was singularly limited, we shall have indicated those features which they
possessed in common, and shall have helped to confirm our
assertion of the finite quality of Mlle. de Guérin's mind. It
was not that she was without imagination; on the contrary,
she unmistakably possessed it; but she possessed it in very
small measure. Religion without imagination is piety; and
such is Mlle. de Guérin's religion. Her journal, taken as a

whole, seems to us to express a profound contentment. She was, indeed, in a certain sense, impatient of life, but with no stronger impatience than such as the church was able to allay. She had, of course, her moments of discouragement; but, on the whole, she found it easy to believe, and she was too implicit a believer to be unhappy. Her peculiar merit is that, without exaltation, enthusiasm, or ecstacy, quietly, steadily, and naturally, she entertained the idea of the Divine goodness. The truth is that she was strong. She was a woman of character. Thoroughly dependent on the church, she was independent of everything else.

Nation, December 14, 1865

Lettres d'Eugénie de Guérin. Paris: Didier, 1866. *Letters of Eugénie de Guérin*. New York: Alexander Strahan & Co., 1866.

Now that the friends and correspondents of Mademoiselle de Guérin have consented to the publication of her letters, there remains no obstacle to a thorough acquaintance not only with the facts of her external life, but with her thoughts and feelings—the life of her soul. It can have been the fortune of few persons to become so widely and intimately known as the author of these letters, and to have evoked sentiments of such unalloyed admiration and tenderness. How small is the proportion either of men or of women who could afford to have the last veil of privacy removed from their daily lives; not for an exceptional moment, a season of violent inspiration or of spasmodic effort, but constantly, uninterruptedly, for a period of seventeen years. Mlle. de Guérin's letters confirm in every particular the consummately pleasing impression left by her journal. A delicate mind, an affectionate heart, a pious soul—the gift of feeling and of expression in equal measure—and this not from the poverty of the former faculty, but from the absolute richness of the latter. The aggregation of these facts again resolves itself under the reader's eyes into a figure of a sweetness so perfect, so uniform, and so simple that it seems to belong rather to the biography of a mediæval saint than to the complex mechanism of our actual life. And, indeed, what was Mlle. de Guérin, after all, but a mediæval saint? No other definition so nearly covers the union of her abundant gentleness and her perfect simplicity. There are saints of various kinds—passionate saints and saints of pure piety. Mlle. de Guérin was one of the latter, and we cannot but think that she needed but a wider field of action to have effectually recommended herself to the formal gratitude of the Church. This collection of her letters seems to us to have every quality requisite to place it beside those *livres édifiants* of which she was so fond—unction, intensity, and orthodoxy.

We have called Mlle. de Guérin a saint perhaps as much from a sense of satisfaction in being able to apply a temporary definition to our predicate as from the desire to qualify our subject. What is a saint? the reader may ask. A saint, we hasten to reply, is—Mlle. de Guérin; read her letters and you will discover. If you are disappointed, the reason will lie not in this admirable woman, but in the saintly idea. Such as this idea is, she answers it—and we have called her, moreover, a mediæval saint. It is true that the organization of society during these latter years has not been favorable to a direct and extensive action on the part of personal sanctity, and that, as we associate the idea of a successful exercise of this distinction with social conditions which have long ceased to exist, it seems almost illogical to imply that saintship is possible among our contemporaries. Yet it is equally certain that men and women of extraordinary purity of character constantly attain to a familiarity with divine things as deep and undisturbed as Mlle. de Guérin's. Her peculiar distinction—that fact through which she evokes the image of an earlier stage of the world's history—is the singular simplicity of her genius and of her circumstances. Nowhere are exquisite moral rectitude and the spirit of devotion more frequent than in New England; but in New England, to a certain extent, virtue and piety seem to be nourished by vice and skepticism. A very good man or a very good woman in New England is an extremely complex being. They are as innocent as you please, but they are anything but ignorant. They travel; they hold political opinions; they are accomplished Abolitionists; they read magazines and newspapers, and write for them; they read novels and police reports; they subscribe to lyceum lectures and to great libraries; in a word, they are enlightened. The result of this freedom of enquiry is that they become profoundly self-conscious. They obtain a notion of the relation of their virtues to a thousand objects of which Mlle. de Guérin had no conception, and, owing to their relations with these objects, they present a myriad of reflected lights and shadows. For Mlle. de Guérin there existed but two objects— the church and the world, of neither of which did it ever occur to her to attempt an analysis. One was all good, the other all evil—although here, perhaps, her rich natural charity arrested in some degree her aversion. Such being her attitude toward external things, Mlle. de Guérin was certainly not enlightened. But she was better than this—she was light itself. Her life—or perhaps we should rather say her faith— is like a small, still taper before a shrine, flickering in no fitful air-current, and steadily burning to its socket.

To busy New Englanders the manners and household habits exhibited in these letters are stamped with all the quaintness of remote antiquity. But for a couple of short sojourns in Paris and in the Nivernais, a journey to Toulouse, and a visit to the Pyrenees shortly before her death, Mlle. de Guérin's life was passed in an isolated château in the heart of an ancient province, without visitors, without books, without diversions; with no society but that of her only sister, a brother, the senior of Maurice, and her father, whom the reader's fancy, kindled by an occasional allusion, depicts as one of the scattered outstanding gentlemen of the old *régime*—proud, incorruptible, austere, devout, and affectionate, and, with his small resources, a keen wine-grower. It is no wonder that, in the social vacuity of her life, Mlle. de Guérin turned so earnestly to letter-writing. Her only other occupations were to think about her brother Maurice, to spin by the kitchen fireside, to read the life of a saint, or at best a stray volume of Scott or Lamartine, or Bernardin de Saint-Pierre; to observe zealously the fasts and festivals and sacraments of the church, and to visit sick peasants. Her greatest social pleasure seems to have been an occasional talk with an ecclesiastic; for to her perception all priests were wise and benignant, and never commonplace. "To-morrow," she writes, "I shall talk sermon.

We are to hear the Abbé Roques. He is always my favorite preacher. *It is n't that the others are not excellent.*" There is something very pathetic in the intellectual penury with which Mlle. de Guérin had to struggle, although there is no doubt that the unsuspecting simplicity of vision which charms us in her writing is largely owing to the narrow extent of her reading. The household stock of books was small; it was difficult, both on account of the exiguity of the means of the family and its remoteness from a large town, to procure new ones; and in the case of Mlle. de Guérin herself, the number of available works was further limited by her constant scruples as to their morality. It must be owned that she knew few works of the first excellence. She read St. Augustine and Fénelon and Pascal, but for the most part she got her thoughts very far from the source. Some one gives her Montaigne, but, although she is no longer a young girl, she discreetly declines to open him. "I am reading for a second time," she writes, "Bernardin de Saint-Pierre, an amiable and simple author, whom it is good to read in the country. After this I should like 'Notre Dame de Paris;' but I am afraid. These novels make such havoc that I dread their passage; it terrifies me simply to see their effect on certain hearts. Mine, now so calm, would like to remain as it is." So, instead of the great men, she contents herself with the small. "You see," she else-where says, "we are keeping the Month of Mary. I have bought for this purpose at Albi a little book, 'The New Month of Mary,' by the Abbé Le Gaillan; a little book of which I am very fond—soft and sweet, like May itself, and full of flowers of devotion. Whoever should take it well to heart would be agreeable to God and *en admiration aux anges*. . . . . Read it; it is something celestial."

It is difficult to give an idea of the intimacy, the immediacy, of Mlle. de Guérin's relations with the practice of piety. Not an incident but is a motive, a pretext, an occasion, for religious action or reflection of some kind. She looks at the world from over the top of her *prie-dieu*, with her finger in her prayer-book. "Mlle. d'H.," she writes, "comes to edify me every second day; she reaches church early, confesses herself, and takes the communion with an *air d'ange* that ravishes and desolates me. *How I envy her her soul!* . . . . . Her brothers, too, are little saints. The eldest, etc. . . . . . Is n't it very edifying?" And again: "I am in every way surrounded with edification, fed upon sermons and discourses. Such a good Lent as I have passed!" Describing to a dear friend, a young lady of her own age, a peculiar ceremony which she had witnessed on a young girl's taking conventual vows: "They say," she concludes, "that everything the novice asks of God at this moment is granted her. One asked to die; she died. Do you know what I would ask? *That you should be a saint.*" The reader will, of course, be prepared to find Mlle. de Guérin a very consistent Catholic—a perfect, an absolute one. This fact explains her, and we may even say excuses her. So complete a spiritual submission, so complete an intellectual self-stultification, would be revolting if they were a matter of choice. It is because they are a matter of authority and necessity, things born to and implicitly accepted, that the reader is able to put away his sense of their fundamental repulsiveness sufficiently to allow him to appreciate their incidental charms. It is the utter consistency of Mlle. de Guérin's faith, the uninterrupt-edness of her spiritual subjection, that make them beautiful. A question, a doubt, an act of will, the least shadow of a claim to *choice*—these things would instantly break the charm, deprive the letters of their invaluable distinction, and transform them from a delightful book into a merely readable one. That distinction lies in the fact that they form a work of pure, unmitigated *feeling*. The penalty paid by Mlle. de Guérin and those persons who are educated in the same principles, for their spiritual and mental security, is that they are incapable of entertaining or producing ideas. There is not, to our belief, a single idea, a single thought, in the whole of these pages. On the other hand, one grand, supreme idea being tacitly understood and accepted throughout—the idea, namely, of the Church—and a particular direction being thus given to emotion, there is an incalculable host of feelings. Judge how matters are simplified. Genius and pure feeling! No wonder Mlle. de Guérin writes well! There are, doubtless, persons who would be ill-natured enough to call her a bigot; but never would the term have been so ill applied. Is a pure sceptic a bigot? Mlle. de Guérin was the converse of this, a pure believer. A pure sceptic doubts all he knows; Mlle. de

Guérin believes all she knows. She knows only the Catholic
Church. A bigot refuses; she did nothing all her life but
accept.

The two great events of Mlle. de Guérin's life were her visit
to Paris on the occasion of the marriage of her brother Maurice, and his death, in Languedoc, eight months afterwards.
Paris she took very quietly, as she took everything. What
pleased her most was the abundance and splendor of the
churches, in which she spent a large portion of her time. She
had changed her sky, but she did not change her mind. The
profoundest impression, however, that she was destined to
receive was that caused by her brother's death. He died on
the best of terms with the Church, from which he had suffered a temporary alienation. Her letters on the occasion of
this event have an accent of intense emotion which nothing
else could arouse. We cannot do better than translate a portion of one, which seems to us to possess a most painful
beauty:

"For a week now since he has left us—since he is in
heaven and I am on earth—I have n't been able to speak
to you of him, to be with you, to unite with you, my tender friend, also so dearly loved. Shall we never be disabused
of our affections? Neither sorrows, nor rupture, nor
death—nothing changes us. We love, still love—love into
the very tomb, love ashes, cling to the body which has
borne a soul; but the soul, we know that is in heaven. Oh,
yes! there above, where I see thee, my dear Maurice; where
thou art awaiting me and saying, 'Eugénie, come hither to
God, where one is happy.' My dear friend, all happiness on
earth is at an end; I told you so; I have buried the life of
my heart; I have lost the charm of my existence. I did not
know all that I found in my brother, nor what happiness I
had placed in him. Prospects, hopes, my old life beside his,
and then a soul that understood me. He and I were two
eyes in the same head. Now we 're apart. God has come
between us. His will be done! God stood on Calvary for
the love of us; let us stand at the foot of the cross for the
love of him. This one seems heavy and covered with
thorns, but so was that of Jesus. Let him help me to carry

mine. We shall at last get to the top, and from Calvary to heaven the road is n't long. Life is short, and indeed what should we do on earth with eternity? My God! so long as we are holy, that we profit by the grace that comes from trials, from tears, from tribulations and anguish, treasures of the Christian! Oh, my friend! you have only to look at these things, this world, with the eye of faith, and all changes. Happy Father Trubert, who sees this so eminently! How I should like to have a little of his soul, so full of faith, so radiant with love! . . . How things change! Let us change, too, my friend; let us disabuse ourselves of the world, of its creatures, of everything. I only ask for complete indifference."

Nation, September 13, 1866

Maurice de Guérin

The Journal of Maurice de Guérin. Translated by Edward Thornton Fisher. New York: Leypoldt & Holt, 1867.

WE HAVE HAD OCCASION more than once, in these columns, to speak of Eugénie de Guérin, and in so doing to touch upon her less famous but even more remarkable brother. The opportunity is to-day afforded us to dwell at greater length upon Maurice de Guérin. A gentleman well fitted for the task has executed a translation of the most valuable portion of Guérin's literary remains—his "Journal"—and promises us a version of his letters and his fragmentary pieces. When these shall have been published, American readers who are acquainted with the writings of Eugénie de Guérin, and whose curiosity has been stimulated by the important although silent part played therein by her brother, will find themselves in possession of all such evidence as exists of the young man's extraordinary powers. Let us say immediately a good word for the present translation. It bears marks of fidelity, sympathy, and intelligence, the three essential requisites of a translator; and it strikes us, moreover, as the work of one possessing a good English style. We have observed two or three slight aberrations from the lines of the French text, where it is somewhat ambiguous; but these are pardonable, since the spirit of the whole is not falsified. We should add that the editor has prefixed to the "Journal" a translation of Sainte-Beuve's "Causerie" on Guérin, an example of his best manner; and Mr. Matthew Arnold's essay, an example of his poorest. It was chiefly for the good taste of his selections—always one of Mr. Arnold's great merits—that his essay was valuable; and as Mr. Fisher has suppressed the extracts and given us only the commentary, the character of the essay suffers not a little.

The facts of Guérin's life are soon told. He was born at the château of Cayla, in Languedoc, in the year 1810, of a family noble, religious, and poor. His first studies were prosecuted at the *petit seminaire* of Toulouse; his subsequent ones, from the age of thirteen, at the Collège Stanislas, in Paris. On the completion of these latter, he spent a short interval in Paris, undecided as to a profession and in search of temporary work; but, finally, in mid-winter of 1832, in accordance with the wishes of his family, he entered a small quasi-religious brotherhood, founded and governed by La Mennais, at La Chenaie, in Brittany. This step was taken with a view of preparing himself for an ecclesiastical career. Guérin possessed the least conceivable fitness (short of positive aversion) for such a career. There is every appearance, however, that he derived great benefit from his sojourn and his daily contact with La Mennais. These were brought to a sudden conclusion by La Mennais' dissension with the Church and the consequent dispersion of his little group of disciples. Guérin's attitude throughout this critical period is that of cordial sympathy with his instructor. Nine months of religious seclusion and study, however, have convinced him that the Church is not his vocation, and he is again thrown upon the world for support. Before returning to Paris, he spends a number of weeks in the house of a friend on the coast of Brittany, and it is here that some of the finest passages of his journal are written. In January, 1834, he takes up his residence in Paris, where he remains until his early death in 1839. Destitute of all resources save such as he himself creates, his life during this interval is one of hard and often distasteful labor. He gives lessons of Latin and Greek and contributes articles to magazines and newspapers. His lessons, however, are ill paid and his literary connections not extensive, and the first real ease which he knows he obtains through a marriage which he allows to be arranged for him in his twenty-eighth year. Judging from the evidence of his letters and of those of his sister, these words do not misrepresent the nature of Guérin's marriage. His wife was young, charming, and mistress of an income, but Guérin did not live to enjoy his good fortune. He died of consumption in the course of a few months.

Such are the external facts of his history—facts few and simple. To what does he owe, it may be asked, the reputation which, twenty-seven years after his death, causes his writings to be translated into a foreign tongue? What are the names of his works? What idea has he given to the world? There is something very odd in the answer to these questions. Guérin's "works" are a private journal of a hundred duodecimo pages; a half-dozen copies of verses, some twenty-odd letters, and two short prose compositions on mythological subjects. He produced, moreover, a number of book-notices and of miscellaneous articles for periodicals, but these have never been disentombed, and it is by the scanty relics of his private history that his reputation is upheld. So solid a reputation has seldom rested on a basis so accidental. As for Guérin's "ideas," the task of enumeration is easy; or, rather, it is impossible. We are unable to associate a single idea with his name. His gift to the world was the gift of himself, of his own history; or, in other words, of the documents in which this history is reflected—documents as exquisite in quality as they are few in number.

Guérin's history may be briefly described as that of a melancholy man who overcomes his melancholy. The reader of his journal and letters is made a spectator of this delicate process of self-education. He watches the gradual decline of the writer's sadness, the successive diminution of each of its multifold elements, its backward retreat before the advance of the positive cares of life, and its final extinction at the moment when the young man engages in the most rational of marriages and embraces for the second time the most paternal and comfortable of creeds. It may be that Guérin's struggles were not really over at this moment, but it is certain that the reader's perception of them is satisfied.

When we speak of Guérin's sadness, of his melancholy, of his *tristesse*, we feel straightway bound to qualify our language and to explain the force of these terms. Save in a single particular, Guérin was not built on a large scale; he possessed an extraordinary sense of style; he was a master of the use of words. His melancholy has nothing profound and organic. It is not complicated with intellectual curiosity and intellectual doubts. His objects of interest are few in number, and easily approached. His dejection, therefore, is not the prodigious sadness of Pascal, nor, to take another example from among his own countrymen, the ceaseless weariness of Rousseau. It is an egotistical, a sentimental sadness. It is not the apprehension that the world is wrong, that life is worthless, that everything is nothing; it is the impression that *he* is wrong, that his own life is worthless, that his own powers are null. From the beginning to the end of his journal there is no trace of that penetrating (and penetrated) observation of the manners and motives of men which imparts a large portion of their value to the pages of Pascal and Rousseau. Guérin's outward gaze is for physical nature alone. When it deserts this field it reverts to his own mind. Here it lingers with a patience, a vigilance, which have never been surpassed. We quote an illustration:

> "Day before yesterday, in the evening, I had passed my arm round the trunk of a lilac and was singing softly J. J.'s song, 'Que le jour me dure.' This touching, melancholy air, my posture, the calm of evening, and, more than all, this habit that belongs to my soul of taking up at evening all its sadness, of surrounding itself with pale clouds towards the end of the day, threw me back upon the deep vast consciousness of my inner poverty. I saw myself miserable, very miserable, and utterly incapable of a future. At the same time, I seemed to hear murmuring, far and high above my head, that world of thought and poetry toward which I so often spring without the power ever to attain to it."

On this occasion he experiences a reaction; that is, he extracts a species of consolation, a whisper of encouragement, from the very depths of his dejection. At other times his depression is complete:

> "My soul shrinks and recoils upon itself like a leaf touched by the cold; it has abandoned all the positions from which it looked out. After some days of struggle against social realities, I have been obliged to fall back and retire within. Here I am circumscribed and blockaded until my thought, swollen by a new inundation, rises above the dike and flows freely over all the banks. I know of few events of my internal life so formidable for me as this sudden contraction of my being after extreme expansion. In this condensation, the most active faculties, the most unquiet, the most bitter elements find themselves seized and condemned to inaction, *but without paralysis, without decrease of vitality*; all their vehemence is confined and com-

pressed with them. Pressed and crowded, they struggle against each other and altogether against their barrier. At these times all the feeling of life I have is reduced to a deep dull irritation, alternating with paroxysms; it is the fermentation of so many various elements, becoming inflamed and exasperated by their forced contact, and making repeated efforts to burst forth. All the faculties which place me in communication with outside space, with distance—those bright and faithful messengers of the soul, which go and come continually from the soul to nature and from nature to the soul—finding themselves pent within, I remain isolated, cut off from full participation in universal life. I become, like an infirm old man deficient in all his senses, alone and excommunicated from the world of nature."

These lines strike us as a forcible example of clear insight into moral phenomena, and of clear and masculine writing. We might multiply examples on both of these points, but want of space forbids us. The value and interest attached to Guérin's introspective habits reside in the fact that his self-scrutiny was so honest and unsparing, and that he really brought back positive data from his incursions into his soul. But perhaps the source of their main interest is in the intimate connection which existed between his constant self-appreciation and his sympathies with the world of external nature. It is upon this last phase of his character that Mr. Matthew Arnold chiefly dwells; and it is to the exquisite delicacy of his feeling for the life of the earth that we owe some of the finest pages of his journal. Many of them have been quoted and requoted, so that we hardly know which to choose. It is not, in our opinion, when he deliberately describes in its fulness a landscape or a bit of scenery that his style attains to its greatest beauty; this happens more particularly when a vague and general sense of the bounding, inexhaustible forces of nature, as contrasted with his own slow-beating pulses, imparts an almost special rhythm to his language, or when an irresistible memory of spring or of midsummer breaks into the tissue of his prose and suffuses it with light and heat and sound:

"Leave there," he cries at the end of a noble passage in which he registers an impression of growing strength,

through the contact of the spreading idea of liberty,—
"leave there those men and their sayings, and steep yourself
in the memory of those days of freedom when you roamed
at will through the country, with your heart swollen with
joy, and singing full-voiced hymns to liberty; or when you
spent a day all idleness from one end to the other, from the
joyous breezes of morning to the warm odors of evening;
lying under a pear tree, careless of everything, and bidding
defiance in your insolent ease to the tyrants of every kind,
bound like vultures upon the flanks of the human race."

Here is another fine passage:

"Let us abjure the worship of idols; let us turn our backs
on all the deities of art, decked with paint and false finery,
on all these images with mouths that speak not. Let us
adore nature, frank, ingenuous, and in no respect exclusive.
Great God! how can men make poetry in face of the broad
poem of the universe? Your poetry! The Lord has made it
for you; it is the created world."

But it is in the short prose poem entitled "The Centaur"
that we find the richest fruits of Guérin's constant communion with the silent processes of nature, and of his unquenchable curiosity as to her secrets. The centaur relates the story
of his long life, recalls the memories of his early years, and
enumerates his sensations, at once so simple and so complex.
Guérin's style in this composition reaches a breadth and elevation which are truly remarkable when we consider the age
at which it was written. There is no loose flinging of epithets,
no confounding of crude colors. The whole piece is marked
by a classical unity and simplicity. What poetry is more impetuous at once and more serene than this?

"My glances travelled freely and reached the most distant
points. Like the shores of rivers, for ever wet, the mountain
ranges in the west remained stamped with spaces of light,
but half wiped out by the shadows. There, in the pale clearness, survived the pure, bare peaks. There I saw at one time
the descent of the god Pan, always alone, and at another
the choir of the secret divinities, or the passage of some
mountain nymph, intoxicated by the night. Sometimes the

eagles of Mount Olympus crossed the upper sky and vanished among the far-off constellations or in the depths of the inspired woods. The presence of the gods, overtaken by sudden trouble, would break the quiet of the old oaks."

There is a hyper-criticism which consists in burrowing for small beauties quite as offensive as that which consists in picking out insignificant faults; but we trust we shall not be held guilty of this vice when we say that the simple words "always alone," in the above passage, taken in their connection, strike us as more thoroughly imbued with the spirit of poetry than the brightest of those floral chains of adjectives with which the poets of a later day have grown used to festoon the naked surface of their verse. Guérin was, in truth, an incomparable writer, and it is for this reason that his name deserves to stand. It is great praise to say of a man, deceased at the age of twenty-eight, that his style possesses something of that authority which will enable one to imitate it with impunity; but this praise may be given to Guérin. With so much about him that was weak, he must have felt that here he was strong. He has written pages which will live as long as his language.

Nation, March 7, 1867

Victor Hugo

Les Travailleurs de la Mer. Par Victor Hugo. Bruxelles: A. Lacroix, Verboeckhoven et Cie.; New York: F. W. Christern, 1866.

"RELIGION, SOCIETY, and nature," says M. Victor Hugo in his preface, "such are the three struggles of man. . . . Man deals with difficulty under the form superstition, under the form prejudice, and under the form element. A triple *anankè* weighs upon us: the *anankè* of dogmas, the *anankè* of laws, the *anankè* of things. In 'Notre Dame de Paris' the author has denounced the first; in 'Les Misérables' he has pointed out the second; in the present work he indicates the third."

Great programmes and intentions, even though they be *à posteriori*, are one of M. Victor Hugo's liveliest characteristics. It will, therefore, not surprise any of his old readers to find him calling what a writer less fond of magnificent generalizations would have been content to describe as "a tale of the sea," a picture of "the *anankè* of things." But M. Victor Hugo is a poet, and he embarks upon the deep in a very different spirit from the late Captain Marryatt. He carries with him provisions for a voyage all but interminable; he touches at foreign lands whose existence has never been suspected; and he makes discoveries of almost fabulous importance.

The scene of "Les Travailleurs de la Mer" is laid in M. Hugo's adopted home of Guernsey, or rather in great part in— yes, literally *in*—the circumjacent ocean. The story is a very small one in spite of its enormous distensions and inflations. An inhabitant of the island, the proprietor of a very pretty niece, becomes also proprietor, in the early days of the invention, of a very pretty steamer, with which he establishes communication with the coast of France. He employs as captain one Sieur Clubin, a man long noted on the island for his exquisite probity and virtue. One of his chief recommendations to the esteem of his employer is the fact that in former years, when the latter had admitted to partnership a person of doubtful antecedents, by name Rantaine, he had, out of the fulness of his integrity, divined this gentleman's

447

rascality, and had forewarned his master that some fine day
Rantaine would decamp with the cash-box. This catastrophe
is, indeed, not slow in happening. Rantaine suddenly departs
for regions unknown, taking with him fifty thousand francs
more than his share of the capital. These three persons,
Lethierry, the proprietor of the steamer, Rantaine, and the
captain, Clubin, are all described with a minuteness very disproportionate to any part they play in the story. But when
M. Victor Hugo picks up a supernumerary he is not wont
to set him down until he has bedecked him with more epigrams, anecdotes, formulas, and similes than would furnish
forth a dozen ordinary heroes. Lethierry is famous for his
alacrity in rescuing the victims of shipwrecks. In heavy
weather he paces the shore, scanning the horizon, and if he
descries a craft of any species or degree in need of assistance,
he is soon seen from afar "upright on the vessel, dripping
with rain, mingled with the lightning, with the face of a lion
who should have a mane of sea foam." After a day spent in
this exercise, he goes home and knits a pair of stockings. He
was a savage, says the author, but he had his elegances. The
chief of these is that he is very fastidious about women's
hands. The reason that he had never married was probably
that he had never found a pretty enough pair of hands in his
own station of life. He brings up his niece, Déruchette, to
take care, above all things, of her hands. About this young
lady M. Hugo says an enormous number of extravagant and
pretty things. We all know what to expect, however, when
M. Hugo enters upon the chapter *jeune fille*. "To have a
smile," he says at the close of a rhapsody on this subject,
"which, one knows not how, lightens the weight of the
enormous chain dragged in common by all the living, is—
what else can I call it but divine? Déruchette had this smile.
We will say more. Déruchette *was* this smile." Rantaine, the
villain, is a most formidable creature. He is a mass of incongruities. He has been everywhere and everything. "He was
capable of all things, and of worse." "He had passed his life
in making eclipses—appearing, disappearing, re-appearing.
He was a rascal with a revolving light." "He used to say, '*Je
suis pour les mœurs*'—I go in for morals." Sieur Clubin is the
reverse of Rantaine. His life is all above-board. He is piety,

honesty, decency incarnate. To suspect him is to make one's self suspected. He is like the ermine; he would die of a stain. As we have said, he sails the little steamer from Guernsey to Saint Malo. One of his idiosyncrasies is never to forget a face he has seen. At the latter place, accordingly, he recognizes after a number of years the *ci-devant* humbug, Rantaine. He procures a revolver, surprises him on the cliff, just after (unfortunately, as you might say) he has confirmed his identity by pushing a coast-guard over into the sea; he faces him, and coolly demands a restitution of the fifty thousand francs. Such is his address that the formidable Rantaine complies like a child, and hands over the little box containing the money. Finding a surplus of ten thousand francs, Clubin returns them, pockets the balance, and dismisses the criminal. All that Clubin desires is to restore to his impoverished employer his dues. Forthwith, accordingly, he gets up steam, and departs for Guernsey, with his fifty thousand francs secured in a belt about his waist. On the Guernsey coast, however, the steamer enters a heavy fog, which soon obscures all progress; and, to make matters worse at this critical moment, the pilot is drunk. The captain takes the helm and advances boldly through the fog. But a sudden break in the sky shows the vessel to be close upon a terrible shoal, and before it can be avoided a terrific shock indicates that the steamer has struck. The passengers are huddled into a boat, but the captain, who has conducted himself throughout with admirable presence of mind, announces his intention of remaining with the vessel until it goes down. This ideal of heroism is vainly combated; the boat moves away, and the disinterested Clubin is left alone with the ocean, the wreck, and—do you see the point?—the fifty thousand francs. Doubtless, you do not see it yet; for, in the first place, the Sieur Clubin cannot use the money if he will, and then, as we know, he would not if he could. But here comes a grand *coup de théâtre*, one of M. Hugo's own. What if the virtuous Clubin should, after all, be no better than the iniquitous Rantaine, no better than a life-long hypocrite, the would-be murderer of a ship-load of innocents?

The author develops this hypothesis in a wonderful chapter entitled "The interior of a soul illumined." A very dark soul indeed is this of Clubin, needing all the rockets and bonfires of M. Hugo's speech to penetrate its dusky recesses. Left alone on the dreadful ocean, this monstrous being bursts into a wicked laugh. He folds his arms and tastes his solitude. He is free, he is rich, he has succeeded. Now he is going to begin. He has "eliminated the world." "There are caverns in the hypocrite," adds the author; "or rather, the whole hypocrite is a single cavern. When Clubin found himself alone his cavern opened. He ventilated his soul." "He had been," we furthermore read, "the Tantalus of cynicism." He now looks upon his honesty as a serpent looks upon his old skin; and as he does so he laughs a second time. But in these delights he does not forget the practical. His plan is to swim ashore (he is a marvellous swimmer), to remain hidden on the coast until a smuggling vessel picks him up, and then to make his way to America. His exultation, however, is but short-lived. As he looks the fog is rent in twain, and he sees that he has lost his way more effectually than he had intended. The fog has served him but too well. He has not struck the small shoal which he had, as he fancied, steered for, but a much larger one further distant from the shore. Instead of having a mile to swim, he has fifteen. Nevertheless he strips and plunges. As he touches bottom he feels his foot seized. Meanwhile the small boat has been picked up by a sloop, and the passengers have brought the evil tidings into the port of Saint Sampson. The good proprietor of the steamer is overwhelmed with grief for the loss of his precious, his unique, his laboriously wrought machinery. It is suggested, however, that it may still be recovered, that it may be disengaged from the double embrace of the wreck and the rocks, and successfully brought ashore. Whereupon Miss Déruchette steps forth and declares that she will marry the man who shall accomplish this herculean labor. Now this young lady has long been adored in silence by a young *amateur* of the ocean, a strange, brooding, melancholy, ill-reputed fellow, a kind of amphibious Werther, whose only outlet for his passion has been, for a number of years, to serenade his mistress with an instrument which M. Hugo repeatedly denominates a "bug-pipe." He accepts the challenge, and straightway betakes himself, alone and unaided, to the fatal shoal between which the hapless vessel stands wedged. Here begins M. Hugo's version of the struggle of man with the elements, "the *ananke* of things" promised in his preface, and a wonderful version it is.

The whole of the second book is devoted to the labors of this new Hercules in wrenching with his single hands the machinery of the steamer from the angry clutch of nature. Gilliatt (such is the hero's name) encamps upon the summit of a great rock hard by the field of his operations, one of a brace of strong brothers which just hold their chins out of water. Here, under the stars, surrounded by the world of waves, he spends the nights of two long months, during which, through hurricane and cold and fever and hunger, thirst, and despair, he gradually, by a combination of cranks and cross-beams and pulleys which, we doubt not, are as admirably self-consistent as the famous camel which the German philosopher evolved from the depths of his moral consciousness, he finally, we say, disenthralls the machinery from the shattered authority of the wreck. To believe so big a story you must understand what an extraordinary personage was this Gilliatt. M. Hugo has smoothed the way by a full analysis of his nature and habits at the opening of the work; but we protest in all gravity that we utterly fail to comprehend him. Physically, he is of those days when there were giants; morally, he is the product of too much reading of M. de Lamartine, Alfred de Musset, and M. Victor Hugo himself. "*La somme,*" says the author, "he was simply a poor man who knew how to read and write." Elsewhere, he is "a great troubled mind and a great wild heart." He has thus a certain affiliation with Mr. Carlyle. Again, while he is defying the tempests and tides for the love of Déruchette, he is "a kind of Job of the ocean. But a Job militant, a Job conqueror, a Job Prometheus." There is a vast deal in this long description of his daily battle with the elements which we should like to quote, had we the space. A great deal we should quote for the reader's amusement; but for a few passages we should expect his admiration. Never, we believe, has mere writing gone so far: that is, never was nature so effectually ousted from its place, in its own nominal interest. We have room only for half-a-dozen sentences relative to Gilliatt's adventure with a certain hideous marine animal, called by M. Hugo the *pieuvre*: an enlarged jelly-fish, with tentacles, and eyes of hideous expression. This obscene creature will become famous through M. Hugo's magnificent hyperbole. "Compared with the *pieuvre*," he says, "the old hydras provoke a smile. Homer and Hesiod could only make the Chimæra. God has made the *pieuvre*. When God wishes, he excels in the execrable."

The author then proceeds with solemn iteration to rehearse all the monsters, fabulous and veritable, which have ever been the terror of man, together with their respective death-dealing attributes. The *pieuvre* has none of all these—none of these vulgar agencies of dread. "What, then, is the *pieuvre*? It is a sucker. It is, in appearance, a mere rag floating under water. When at rest it is dust-colored. But enraged it grows violet. Then it throws itself upon you. Fearful sensation! it is soft." Its tentacular thongs garrote you; its contact paralyzes. "It looks scorbutic, gangrenescent. It is disease arranged into a monstrosity." But we will leave M. Hugo the fine illustrations of his own tongue. *"Une viscosité qui a une volonté, quoi de plus effrayable? De la glu pétrie de haine."* This irresistible creature devours you in such a way as to elicit from M. Hugo the following remark: "Beyond the terrible, being eaten alive, is the ineffable, being drunk alive." This is followed by some characteristic ratiocinations on physiology. Gilliatt comes near being absorbed into the *pieuvre*; but, for the matter of that, we all go into each other. *"Pourriture, c'est nourriture.* Fearful cleaning of the globe! Carnivorous man is an entomber; and life is made of death. . . . We are sepulchres." In spite of this general law, however, Gilliatt defers his burial by decapitating the *pieuvre*. Shortly afterwards he discovers, in a very nearly submarine cavern, a human skeleton, girded about with a money belt, inside of which is written *Sieur Clubin*. It was not in vain, therefore, that this unfaithful servant had been detained beneath the waters. Gilliatt appropriates, provisionally, the belt, and ultimately arrives at a successful solution of his problem in mechanics. His interruptions, his perils, his sufferings, his visions, must be read in detail. There is a long description of a storm which grazes the sublime and jostles the ridiculous. Detached from its context, any example of the former would, we fear, fail to justify itself to the reader; and, indeed, the nearest approach to greatness in this whole episode is not to be found in particular passages, but in the very magnificent intention of the whole. As for the ridiculous, we cannot but think that it is amply represented by everything that follows Gilliatt's successful return with the rescued and renovated vessel. While Déruchette's uncle is digesting his surprise, gratitude, and joy, Déruchette herself is engaged in a very sentimental *tête-à-tête* in the garden with a young Anglican divine. An involuntary witness of their emotions, Gilliatt immediately withdraws his claims. More than this, he personally superintends the marriage of the young couple, and sees them on board the vessel which, after the wedding, is to convey them to England. And after this, says the superficial reader, he of course goes home and smokes a pipe. But little has such a reader fathomed the depths of this heroic nature. He betakes himself to a well-known spot on the side of a cliff, where a depression in the rock forms, at low tide, a sort of natural chair. Here he seats himself in time to witness the passage of the vessel bearing away Déruchette and her husband. It almost "grazed the cliff," says M. Hugo. There on the deck, in a bar of sunshine, sit the happy young couple, lost in mutual endearments. The vessel moves away toward the horizon, while the tide rises to Gilliatt's feet. As the vessel travels before his unwinking eye, so gradually the water surges about him. It reaches his knees, his waist, his shoulders, his chin: but he moves not. The little birds call to him warningly, but he heeds them not. He sits open-eyed, gazing at the sloop. His eye, says the author, "resembled nothing that can be seen on this earth. That calm and tragic pupil contained the inexpressible." As the distant sloop disappears from the horizon, the eye is hidden, the head is covered, the ocean reigns alone.

Such is M. Victor Hugo's story. The reader will see that, dramatically, it is emphatically *not* what, from the title, it was likely pre-eminently to be—a study from nature. Nature is nowhere: M. Victor Hugo is everywhere; and his work will add very little to our knowledge of anything but himself. It is, in our opinion, the work of a decline. We have not hesitated to speak of it with levity, because we believe it to have been written exclusively from the head. This fact we deeply regret, for we have an enormous respect for M. Victor Hugo's heart.

Nation, April 12, 1866

Quatrevingt-treize. Par Victor Hugo. Paris: Michel Lévy, 1874. *Ninety-three*. By Victor Hugo. Translated by Frank Lee Benedict. New York: Harper & Bros., 1874.

A NEW WORK FROM Victor Hugo may be considered a literary event of some magnitude. If the magnitude of the event, indeed, were measured by that of the work in chapters, books, and volumes, we should need one of the author's own mouth-filling epithets to qualify it. The present performance is apparently but a fragment—the first *"récit"* of a romance destined to embody on a vast scale the history of a single year. Like all the author's novels, it abounds in subdivisions and minor headings, which serve as a kind of mechanical symbolism of his passion for the moral enormous. It is nevertheless complete enough to give us a solid reminder of his strangely commingled strength and weakness. The 'Misérables,' we suppose, may have been called a great triumph; but we doubt if its successors—the 'Travailleurs de la Mer' and 'L'Homme qui Rit'—found many readers who were constant to the end. The verdict on the present work, however, so far as it has been pronounced, has been eminently favorable, and we are assured that M. Hugo has rekindled his smoldering torch at the pure flame of inspiration. The reader, indeed, has only to open the volume at hazard to find that M. Hugo is himself again with a vengeance. "Cimourdain was a conscience pure but sombre. He had within him the absolute. He had been a priest, which is grave. Man can, like the sky, have a black serenity; it is enough that something should have made night within him. The priesthood had made night in Cimourdain. Who has been a priest, is one." Or further: "We approach the great peak.—Here is the Convention.—The gaze becomes fixed in the presence of this summit.—Nothing higher has ever appeared on the horizon of man.—There is the Himalayah and there is the Convention." Or elsewhere, of the cry of a mother who sees her children in danger: "Nothing is more ferocious and nothing is more touching. When a woman utters it, you think you hear a wolf: when a wolf utters it, you think you hear a woman. . . . . Hecuba barked, says Homer." These few lines suffice to show that the author has not flinched from his chosen path, and that he walks escorted between the sublime and the ridiculous as resolutely as his own most epic heroes. In truth, at M. Hugo's venerable age, and with one's forehead aching with laurels, it is not to be expected that one should ever drop a glance at the swarm of nameless satirists; but the moral of the matter is that the luxurious cultivation of his own peculiar manner, for which our author continues remarkable, seems now not only the natural thing, but on the whole the sagacious one. If you are sure of your strength, the lesson seems to read, cleave to your ideal, however arrogant, however perverted, however indifferent to the ideals of others, and in the end even the fastidious will accept you. We confess to a conservative taste in literary matters—to a relish for brevity, for conciseness, for elegance, for perfection of form. M. Hugo's manner is as diffuse as that of the young woman in the fairy tale who talked diamonds and pearls would alone have a right to be, and as shapeless and formless as if it were twenty times the "grande improvisation" which is his definition of the French Revolution. His prolixity, moreover, has the further defect of giving one a nearly intolerable impression of conceit; few great rhetoricians have the air of listening so reverently to their own grandiloquence. And yet we frankly admit that the effect of these volumes has been to make us submit to the inevitable, and philosophically accept the author whose shoulders sustain so heavy a load of error. To many persons our experience will have a familiar air. There comes a time, in most lives, when points of difference with friends and foes and authors dwindle, and points of contact expand. We have a vision of the vanity of remonstrance and of the idleness of criticism. We cease to look for what we know people cannot give us—as we have declared a dozen times—and begin to look for what they can. To find this last and enjoy it undisturbedly is one of the most agreeable of intellectual sensations. We are doubtless wrong in breaking our yard-stick; for what is to become of the true and the beautiful without a "high standard"? We only say that we are natural, and we simply pretend that in this natural fashion we have been enjoying 'Quatrevingt-treize.'

M. Hugo has chosen a subject in which his imagination may revel at its ease; his inordinate relish for the huge and the horrible may feast its fill upon the spectacle of the French Revolution. One might have wondered indeed that he should not long ago have made it his own; but he has shown the instinct of the genuine epicure in such matters in keeping it in reserve. He has drawn from it effects of the most sinister picturesqueness, and, judging his work from the picturesque point of view merely, he is certainly to be congratulated on his topic. Judged from the rational point of view, the theme seems to us much less fortunate. If the French people could forget their Revolution for fifty years and forego all manner of allusion to it, we are sure the result would be most favorable to their intellectual health. The moral has been drawn again and again, for seventy years, the lesson has been learned, the last drop of sweetness has been drained from the hideous sediment of blood and error. The better part of the Revolution is by this time a divided heritage; European society has been living on it, paying its daily expenses with it, as we may say, for the last twenty years. Nothing could better illustrate the strange moral irresponsibility which is so often combined with a rich imagination than the reckless glee with which our author kindles the blue fire, touches off the rockets, and sets a-whizzing the catherine-wheels of this new apotheosis. If anything were wanted to prove that, as a philosopher, M. Hugo has nothing of the smallest consequence to say, the extraordinary intellectual levity with which he faces the unsolved problems of his theme would amply suffice. He has not attempted, however, to give us a picture of the whole Revolution, but, choosing a salient episode, has dramatized with characteristic vividness the sanguinary strife of the Royalists of Brittany and the Republican troops. As a story, M. Hugo's work as yet is meagre; it has no hero, no heroine, no central figure, none of the germs of a regular drama. The hero properly is the Republican army, the heroine the fanatical horde of the Vendéans. We are shifted from place to place, hurried through deserts of declamation and oceans of paradox, tossed, breathless, from a bewildering antithesis to an astounding "situation" with all that energy to which, from of old, M. Hugo's readers have received notice that they must accommodate their intellectual pace. Our author's characters are always more or less monstrous, either in virtue or vice, and he has given us here the usual proportion of heroic grotesques. Robespierre, Danton, and Marat figure, in their estimable persons, and we are treated to a conference in which, in the back shop of a café, they settle the affairs of the nation. We have seen this called one of the strong episodes of the work, but it is very disappointing. The leading members of the Committee of Public Safety talk altogether in disjointed epigrams and bristling antitheses, any one of which would be highly in keeping with M. Hugo himself on the frequent occasions when he appears as chorus to the drama. This scene, in which an immense effort has been attended with a meagre result, is ushered in by an elaborate picture of the streets of Paris during the high-pressure time of the Revolution. The author has collected an extraordinary multitude of small facts and anecdotes, and he strings them together with the effectiveness of a great painter. The chapter is well worth reading. Less vivid, but curious enough, is the account of the hall of session of the National Convention in the Tuileries and its surrounding precinct. In these pictures M. Hugo makes Revolutionary Paris really palpable to our senses. If he would only give us more pictures and fewer disquisitions! His pictures, however, are vitiated by an affectation of the Rabelaisian fashion of long catalogues; we are deluged with proper names and useless enumerations.

The main action of the story consists of the adventures of a Paris battalion sent into Brittany to confront a certain Marquis de Lantenac, a superb old fanatic for the Royal cause, invincible among his savage peasantry, and conspiring to help the English fleet to effect a landing. The handful of tried Parisians is commanded by a nephew of the Marquis, a young Viscomte de Gauvain, who has torn up his pedigree and cast his lot with the Republic. From Paris, despatched by Robespierre to hold the young nobleman, whose thoroughgoing rigidity is suspected, to a strict account, is a certain Cimourdain, a *ci-devant* priest and actual radical of the deepest dye—

one of the duskiest and most colossal of all M. Hugo's dusky and colossal heroes. Cimourdain is bound to Gauvain by ties of old affection, having been his preceptor and more than a father to him. Gauvain, in fact, is the apple of his eye; he loves him better even than the Revolution. Just so, Gauvain is bound to the Marquis de Lantenac, on whose head he sets a price, by ties of blood, and the relations of the three individuals are as fertile as may be expected in those terrific conflicts between the voice of nature and a cruel outward force which have formed the majority of our author's great dramatic situations. Out of all this comes an abundance of tragic suspense—and sometimes of comic surprise. For the rest, the story is chiefly a compound of blood and gunpowder, of long descriptions, geographical and genealogical, which are frequently mere strings of proper names drawn out through pages, and of infinite discourse on things in general by M. Hugo. The only really charming element in the work is the occasional apparition of three little children, whose adventures indeed are the *nodus* of the action. Very charming it is, and lighted up with the author's brightest poetry. With a genius at once powerful and eccentric, like M. Hugo, if one has great disappointments, one has great compensations. A writer in whom the poetic heat is so intense that he must be sublime under all circumstances and at any cost, makes many a strange alliance and produces many a monstrosity; but every now and then it befalls him to flash his lantern upon an object which, as one may say, receives transfiguration gracefully. These little children, whose poor peasant-mother is supposed to have been shot in a bloody *battue* of the Royalists, are picked up and adopted by the Parisian battalion. They are subsequently carried off by the Royalists, kept as hostages, and confined in an old feudal tower, in which Lantenac with a handful of men is besieged by the Parisians. The latter break into the castle, to which the others, escaping through a subterranean passage, have succeeded in setting fire. The children are left behind, but although we see them, in their rosy innocence, nestling in what the author happily calls a "grotto of flame," of course they are not destroyed. They are reserved obviously for future volumes, where their presence is the more needful that Gauvain and Cimourdain perish on the same occasion in all the sublimity of melodrama. If the work contained nothing else than the chapter in which the three chubby babies are described as playing, amid the impending carnage, in the old dusty library of the château, it would not have been ineffectually written.

The whole work is a mine of quotations—nuggets of substantial gold and strange secretions of the mere overflow of verbiage. M. Hugo's pretension is to say many things in the grand manner—to fling down every proposition like a ringing medal stamped with his own image. Hence, for the reader, an intolerable sense of effort and tension; he seems to witness the very contortions of ingenuity. But, as we say, the contortions are often those of the inspired sybil, and the poet utters something worth hearing. We care little for the Marquis de Lantenac and less for the terrible Cimourdain; but the author's great sense of the sad and tragic has rarely been exercised more effectively than in the figures of Michelle Fléchard, the poor stupid starving peasant-mother of the three children, and of Tellemarch, the philosophic beggar who gives her shelter in her desperate quest. Here the author deals with the really human and not with the mechanical and monstrous, aping the human. All this is Victor Hugo at his best. One judges a work of these dimensions and pretensions, however, not by its parts, better or worse, but by its general tone, by the spirit of the whole, by its leading idea. Expressed with perfect frankness, the leading idea of 'Quatrevingt-treize' seems to us to be that the horrible—the horrible in crime and suffering and folly, in blood and fire and tears—is a delightful subject for the embroidery of fiction. After this there is no denying that M. Hugo is really fond of horrors. He is an old man; he has written much and seen much; he may be supposed to know his own mind; yet he dives into this sea of blood for the pearl of picturesqueness with a truly amazing freshness of appetite. If we were inclined to interpret things rigidly, we might find a very sombre meaning in the strange complacency with which his imagination contemplates the most atrocious details of his subject. His fellow-countrymen lately took occasion to remind the world forcibly that they were of the same stock as their ancestors, and that when once they had warmed to the work again they could burn and kill

on the same extensive scale. One would have said that, to a
reflective mind, it might have seemed that the blood-stains
and ashes of French history had, for some years to come, better be consigned to obscurity. The sublimely clear conscience
with which M. Hugo drags them into the light proves, to say
the least, an inordinate share of national vanity. To say, in
combination with this, that we have enjoyed the work, may
seem but an admission that we have been passing through an
atmosphere of corrupting paradox. But what we have enjoyed
is neither Cimourdain nor Marat, nor the woman-shootings
of the Royalists, nor the ambulant guillotine of the Republi-
cans. It is M. Hugo himself as a whole, the extraordinary genius that shines through the dusky confusion of repulsive
theme and erratic treatment. It is the great possibilities of his
style and the great tendencies of his imagination. The latter
sometimes leads him astray; but when it leads him aright he
is great.

Nation, April 9, 1874

Légende des Siècles. Paris, 1877.

FROM THE VERY flattering notices which the English journals have accorded to the new volumes of Victor Hugo's 'Légende des Siècles,' it is apparent that the writer has
lately become almost the fashion in England—a fact to be
attributed in a measure to the influence of the "æsthetic"
school, or, to speak more correctly, probably, of Mr. Swinburne, who, as we know, swears by Victor Hugo, and whose
judgments seem to appeal less forcibly to the English sense of
humor than they do to a corresponding quality on this side
of the Atlantic. Be this as it may, however, Victor Hugo's
new volumes are as characteristic as might have been expected—as violent and extravagant in their faults, and in their
fine passages as full of imaginative beauty. Apropos of the
sense of humor, the absence of this quality is certainly Victor
Hugo's great defect—the only limitation (it must be confessed it is a very serious one) to his imaginative power. It
should teach him occasionally to kindle Mr. Ruskin's "lamp

of sacrifice." This "nouvelle série" of the 'Légende des Siècles' is not a continuation of the first group of poems which appeared under this name; it is rather a return to the same ground, the various categories under which the first poems appeared being supplied with new recruits. These categories are too numerous to be mentioned here; they stretch from the creation of the world to the current year of grace. It is an immense plan, and shows on the author's part not only an extraordinary wealth of imagination, but a remarkable degree of research. It is true that Victor Hugo's researches are often rather pedantically exhibited; no poet was ever so fond of queer proper names, dragged together from dusty corners of history and legend, and strung together rhythmically—often with a great deal of ingenuity. He is too fond of emulating Homer's catalogue of the ships. But he has what the French call an extraordinary *scent* for picturesque subjects. These two volumes contain many examples of it; the story, for instance, of a certain king of Arragon who gives his son a blow on the cheek, whereupon the proud and sensitive young man, outraged, retires into the desert. The father, aggrieved at his desertion and greatly sorrowing, descends into the sepulchral crypt where his own father is buried, and there, apostrophizing the bronze statue on his tomb, complains of the young man's ingratitude and weeps. After this has gone on some time he feels, in the darkness, the statue stroke his cheek tenderly with its great hand. "L'Aigle de Casque," one of the best things in the two volumes, is the tale of a certain Northumbrian baron of the dark ages, Lord Tiphaine—Victor Hugo's English names are always very queer. He has a duel with a young Scotch noble—a delicate stripling many years his junior, and on the latter taking fright and fleeing from him, he pursues him a whole summer's day, over hill and dale, and at last overtakes him and murders him. The story of the chase and its various episodes is a specimen of Victor Hugo at his best. When the brutal Northumbrian has hacked his victim to death the brazen eagle perched upon his helmet suddenly becomes animate, utters in a rancorous scream its detestation of the dead, bends over and with its beak and talons tears his face to pieces, and then spreading its wings sails majestically away. Victor Hugo excels in leading a long narrative piece of verse up to a startling climax of this kind, related in the half-dozen closing lines. These volumes contain the usual proportion of fulsome adulation of Paris and of the bloodiest chapters in its history—that narrow Gallomania which makes us so often wonder at times, not whether the author is, after all, a great poet, but whether he is not very positively and decidedly a small poet. But, outside of this, this new series of what is probably his capital work contains plenty of proofs of his greatness—passages and touches of extraordinary beauty. No poet has written like Victor Hugo about children, and the second of these volumes contains a masterpiece of this kind. "Petit Paul" is simply the history of a very small child whose mother dies and whose father takes a second wife—a coarse, hard woman, who neglects the little boy. Before his father's second marriage he has been much with his grandfather, who delights in him—"Oh! quel céleste amour entre ces deux bonshommes." The grandfather dies and is buried, to Paul's knowledge, in the village churchyard. The stepmother comes; the child's life is miserably changed, and at last, one winter's night, he starts out, and, not having been missed, is found the next morning dead in the snow at the closed gate of the cemetery. We must quote the lines in which the author describes him while he is meditating this attempt to rejoin his grandfather, the other *bonhomme*; on hearing his step-mother caress his step-brother, lately born:

> "Paul se souvenait avec la quantité
> De mémoire qu'auraient les agneaux et les roses
> Qu'il s'était entendu dire les mêmes choses.
> Il prenait dans un coin, à terre, ses repas;
> Il était devenu muet, ne parlait pas,
> Ne pleurait plus. L'enfance est parfois sombre et forte,
> Souvent il regardait lugubrement la porte."

Nation, May 3, 1877

Joseph Joubert

Pensées of Joubert. Selected and translated, with the original French appended. By Henry Attwell. London and New York: Macmillan & Co., 1878.

MANY READERS WILL REMEMBER the graceful sketch of Joubert in Mr. Matthew Arnold's 'Essays in Criticism,' and the claim for urbanity, sweet reasonableness, the academic quality, and other cognate virtues made by the English critic on behalf of his French precursor. The impression of most of such readers will perhaps have been that Joubert was a singularly ingenious and delicate writer—a literary man of exquisite taste—but that he was not quite the high authority which Mr. Matthew Arnold appeared to deem him. The latter writer, however, has hitherto remained the chief source of information for English readers about the author of these carefully-elaborated 'Pensées.' To-day Mr. Attwell publishes a version in our own less pensive tongue of the maxims and reflections which are Joubert's chief title to distinction. Assuming that it was wise to attempt to translate them, the work has been very neatly and happily performed. The translator has evidently weighed his English equivalents patiently, and has rarely contented himself with a vague or a rough rendering. At the same time that he has been literal, he has succeeded in making Joubert's superior epigrams appear natural and free, and as he has reprinted the French originals at the end of his pretty volume, we are able to measure his fidelity as we go.

We question to a certain extent, however, whether the task was worth performing, and whether Joubert's aphorisms may not be said to do a certain violence, at the best, to English ways of thinking and expressing things. English, as compared with French, is a very unepigrammatic tongue, and it was to the resources of his native language for epigram that Joubert constantly appealed. How abundant these are is proved by the degree to which the writing of maxims and aphorisms has always flourished in France. It is a favorite amusement of what may be called amateur thinkers; where an English mind relieves itself in a copy of verses, a thoughtful French person, of either sex, is very likely to commit to paper a dozen or two of more or less pregnant and studiously concise prose reflections. Of course Joubert was not what we have called an amateur; he was rather a professional producer of maxims. "If ever," he says, "a man was tormented by the accursed ambition of putting a whole book into a page, a whole page into a phrase, and that phrase into a word, I am that man." The skill with which he compresses a great deal of suggestion into a very few words is often most noticeable. He is extremely serious; if he is not so serious as Pascal, he strikes us as much more serious than La Rochefoucauld; but it must be said that his aphorisms also strike us as being sometimes much more fanciful than substantial.

This, however, is inevitable in all makers of *pensées*, and Joubert made a great many on many different subjects, though what Mr. Attwell has published is but a selection. A real *pensée*, like a real lyric, should be born of a particular occasion or of a strong emotion. But a great many of those of Joubert are real. "There is in the soul a taste for the good" (*un gout qui aime le bien*), says Joubert, "just as there is in the soul an appetite for enjoyment." "One may err once—nay, a hundred times—without being double-minded (*sans avoir l'esprit faux*); there can never be mental duplicity where there is sincerity." "We may convince others by our arguments; we can only persuade them by their own." "The simple-hearted and sincere never do more than half deceive themselves." "The punishment of bad princes is to be thought worse than they really are." These are specimens of Joubert's happy hits, as we may say—things in which the neatness and what the French call the *justesse* are equal. The thought which follows the last quoted, by the way, runs in the original, "Toute autorité légitime doit aimer son étendue et ses limites"; or, as we should put it, "All legitimate authority should take satisfaction in its limits as well as in its extent." Mr. Attwell's rendering—"Every legitimate authority should *respect* its extent and its limits"—makes the idea more trivial than need have been. Sometimes, on the other hand, Joubert strikes us rather as playing with words than as really thinking thoughts; as, for instance, "It is good and beautiful that thoughts irradiate; but they should rarely glitter. It is best that they shine." For the most part, however, his *pensées* highly repay thinking over again. This is especially the case with the thoughts upon literary subjects, many of which are exceedingly sagacious and penetrating. As we said at the beginning, if Joubert's reflections have, in the translator's hands, lost their verbal foreignness, they have often kept a certain foreignness of essence; but this volume would still be welcome, if on no other grounds than for the pages containing the original *pensées*.

Horace de Lagardie

"FRENCH NOVELS AND FRENCH LIFE"

THE MARCH NUMBER of *Macmillan's* contains a noticeable article on "French Novels and French Life," signed by a name which a few years since made a slight mark in French journalism. Horace de Lagardie is, we believe, the pseudonym of a clever lady, the author of two volumes of 'Chroniques (or Causeries) Parisiennes,' published some years since by Charpentier. If the article we speak of is not a translation, Horace de Lagardie writes English almost as well as French; and if it is, he may at least profess to know England exceptionally well. His purpose is to point out the fact that French novels do not form an accurate portrait of French life in anything like the sense in which English novels are faithful in their portraiture of English life. This was worth pointing out, for French literature is very much better known than French society, and French novels are read all over the world by people who are likely to have as little opportunity as possible to correct the erroneous impressions they derive from them. We had long ago been struck with the very limited correspondence that exists in France between fiction and manners, but we had always supposed that its limitations were very obvious. We felt that there was an immense deal of humbug in French novels, but we fancied that every one perceived it. In fact, in France every one does perceive it, and it continues to flourish only under that extraordinary rule which, in the country of Balzac, gives validity to the " we know and you know, and you know that we know" system. French fiction, in other words, rests upon a certain number of conventions, which authors and readers agree together, for mysterious reasons, to pretend to take *au sérieux*. We say the reasons are mysterious, but they are probably connected with the desire, so strong in the French mind, to have certain types and categories and general heads definitely established. The author of the paper in *Macmillan's* points out some of the conventions we speak of. It is a convention that young girls living in châteaux roam the country alone on horseback; it is a convention that young *gentilshommes*, disappointed in love, embark on an extensive course of foreign travel; it is a convention that these same *gentilshommes* spend large sums of money, or have it habitually to spend. In fact, young girls in France are not errant equestrians, and young men, of whatever position and in whatever state of their affections, go abroad as little as possible. But these and a great many other things form part of the general romancer's stock, of which the novelist, with a propitiatory wink, as it were, invites the reader, for the sake of having a neat, artistic, well-rounded tale, to *assume* the reality. Horace de Lagardie points out the great difference between the novel-writing classes in England and France, and the way in which in the latter country novelists come to have very little knowledge of what is called good society. They belong to the literary class exclusively, and the literary class is apt to be poor, dingy, shabby, Bohemian. The novel is far less cultivated in France than in England, and is a form of literature to which people are rather ashamed to give much attention. Those clever amateurs—men and women of the world—who supply the fiction market so industriously in England have no correlative class in France. There the class which forms the greatest body in our novel-reading public— the young girls—are suppressed at a stroke: in France young girls never read novels. In England governesses write novels; but in France the *institutrice* who should permit herself such an intellectual escapade would have little regard for assured employment. Presuming that he is writing for young girls in England, we suppose, Horace de Lagardie does not touch upon the most salient of the romancer's conventions in the list we have mentioned. We mean the convention of the inveteracy of the rupture of the seventh commandment.

Nation, March 29, 1877

Auguste Laugel

Italie, Sicile, Bohême: Notes de Voyage. Par Auguste Laugel. Paris: Henri Plon; New York: F. W. Christern, 1872.

WE HAVE ALWAYS CONSIDERED the observations of an intelligent traveller worth recording, even when his experience is confined to the beaten track and repeats that of innumerable others. We find something eternally fresh and delightful in all first impressions of foreign scenes, and we confess that the outpourings of even the most ingenuous tourists always strike in us a sympathetic chord. Of course these productions are very likely to be diffuse and trivial—to neglect the essential for the accidental, and to hold the minute detail so close to the eye as to conceal the general view. These are common faults with literary tourists; but M. Auguste Laugel, in his charming little volume on Italy and Bohemia, seems to us to have completely escaped them. His book is a model for travellers inclined to publish their "impressions." Brief, compact, rapid in style, and yet expansive enough to be occasionally very vivid and pictorial, it is equally free from idle detail on the one hand and pretentious generalization on the other. In the art of putting literary material into form the French certainly excel us, and M. Laugel's volume is a capital example of this accomplishment. He has selected, condensed, retouched, and harmonized with extreme taste and discretion, and the result is one of those infrequent performances in which every sentence counts and there is not a sentence too much. M. Laugel is a general observer; he appreciates and describes the picturesque aspect of things with as much force and point as if they were his especial study, and yet he constantly strikes the moral note, the note of reflection, with a felicity unusual in the devotees of the picturesque—especially in France, where these gentlemen are fond of passing for unbridled Pagans. Of the deeper thoughts—not all cheerful—suggested in Italy at every turn, he is a particularly eloquent interpreter. We have rarely found the moral impression of Naples, for instance, as happily defined as in the few lines in which he resumes it:

468

"Beneath this admirable sky, before this nature with its pure forms and solemn lines, this blue sea which nothing can pollute, lives a people without ideal, indifferent to the morrow, begging, crying, gesticulating, never still, whose religion is all in feasts and images, with no art, no country, debased by absolutism and servitude, with no gods but chance and force, vile, miserable, foul in its sensuality. Can liberty ever give back the least nobleness to this degenerate race? So long as the *frutti di mare* are cheap on the quay of Santa Lucia, so long as the *improvvisatori* are there to entertain them, as there are jugglers and tumblers to make them laugh, a sun to dry their rags, music, processions, and feasts to amuse them—do they need anything more? Their life is a long laugh, a perpetual grin. From the windows of the convent of San Martino, which overhangs the city from such a height, you hear the deafening hum of this shrill street life, tumultuous as the sound of a powerful tide. The great line stretches round the vast gulf; the houses are hung upon the rocks, among *cacti*, oranges, and aloes; you must raise your eyes to the summits of Vesuvius and to the highest crests of the Somma to find a space that man has respected. And yet, go down from these heights through the crooked streets which slope away in every direction, and in this large city you will not find a corner, an asylum, a church, a palace, a work to arrest your eyes—not one that reflects in its forms and lines the admirable splendor of this beautiful sky and of this nature eternally young and fair. . . . Naples is not, like Venice, Florence, and Rome, one of the cities of the soul. You are too constantly deafened; reverie and contemplation are perpetually interrupted; you must get out on the bay or shut yourself up with the silent company of the statues; you cannot live in the past; you are too much jostled; you are overcome by the continual fever, the sterile activity, the indefatigable and idle curiosity which stir so many thousand beings."

Of Venice, too, of which everything would seem to have been said, M. Laugel says excellent things, and at the close of his chapter some very pretty ones, for which we must refer the reader to his book. Of Rome his enjoyment is keen, and his notes have many happy descriptive touches. No reader who has stood in St. Peter's but will feel how exactly the author renders, in its finer points, the sensuous impression of the place:

"I came in with my mind full of distrust of Bernini, on the defensive; I felt myself disarmed by so much spaciousness, by this unheard of luxury, which yet looks natural and does not weary you. Brutal size here acts as an æsthetic element; the immensity envelops details, melts them, drowns them; the light plays on the fine gilded cornices, on the multicolored marbles; it comes down through the azure, as it were, of the high dome, where the saints and angels are sitting in their motionless rings; it sparkles on the gold embroideries which twine about the bronze columns of the great altar; it flashes back from the immense glory which shines like a sun in the depth of the choir. The marble pavement, without a bench or chair to disturb its perspective, stretches away like a great lake. You take pleasure, without knowing why, in this vastness, in this order so obvious, in spite of the profusion of ornaments. Immensity produces here not the impression of terror, but a sort of contentment which makes you indulgent for all the pretentious tombs, the gigantic smirking attitudinizing saints of either sex, the white marble draperies twisted and blown by the impertinent wind that comes from nowhere, for the angels thrust into every corner—cupids of Christianity! The luxury is all so ample, so grandiose, so joyous! The sun comes in by the broad openings, and its rays, glancing back in every direction from polished angles, glittering mouldings, precious stones, and the gold of the mosaics, forms a sort of aureole which seems to lift and sustain the immense pillars and the colossal vaults. This formidable luxury, which exceeds all private or princely fortunes, has nothing which shocks or astonishes; you feel here none of the terrors and the sublime anxieties of Gothic art; you are far, too, from the robust and sombre simplicity of the basilicas; you assist at the definitive triumph of Catholicism—at its apotheosis."

The longest section is devoted to Sicily, where we are unable to compare impressions with the author. But this picture of the beauty and the misery of this once imperial island, its shrines and temples, its mountains and sea, its almost cruelly smiling nature, and its helpless and hopeless humanity, is forcible enough to beguile us into a half-sense of knowledge. His whole account of the ruined temples is admirable; it is that at once of an artist and a scholar. The author's errand in Bohemia was to visit the battlefields of the Seven Weeks' War—in distinguished company; that of the Orleans princes. We have sometimes fancied our intellect impenetrable to all allusions to military movements; but we have almost understood M. Laugel's. The tone of the whole book is grave, we might almost say melancholy. The reader may judge by the closing paragraph, suggested by a glance at some of the great Frederic's scenes of victory:

"And yet for what strange heroes history works! Providence, the unknown God, has taken for his representative the old King of Prussia, and given a revolutionary task to a born enemy of the Revolution! What a jest is history, if you look only at the outside—at the stage-setting! But there is a secret, terrible force which sets in motion all the gods and demi-gods of the earth; an unconscious force tending as a still more unconscious force drives it; history is an ordered succession of chances; it moves always towards something necessary; it uses everything, tribunes and kings, monarchies and republics, barbarism and civilization. Whither is it leading us? Whither is aged, worn-out Europe going? Whither our Latin races? Whither France, so vile and so charming, so cunning and so easy to cheat, so full of hatred and of sweetness, so brave and timid, so unjust to those who have loved her, so generous to those who have injured; insane nation, loved and hated, sole of her kind, who may be vanquished but not equalled, mastered but not subdued, who bids defiance to all measurement by the suppleness of her elusive and ungoverned genius? She is not only inconstant; she is tormented with a sort of perverse logic, which demonstrates to her the falsity of all things. Between all things and herself she places her mocking doubt and her incurable irony."

Nation, February 27, 1873

La France Politique et Sociale. Par Auguste Laugel. Paris: Germer Baillière; New York: F. W. Christern, 1877.

M. AUGUSTE LAUGEL, who is known to our readers as the author of several interesting historical studies, has just published a volume to which the peculiarly critical position of affairs in France gives a particular importance. It offers us, in combination, a résumé of the salient points in the historical process of which the France of to-day is the result, and a sort of general psychological view of the French national character. There are no people of any pretentions to liberal culture, of whatever nationality, to whom the destiny of the most brilliant nation in the world is a matter of indifference; and at a moment like the present, when she seems to stand at the parting of the ways and to be about to make a supreme choice between the habit of revolution and the experiment of tranquillity, any well-considered words that may elucidate the mystery of her recurrent dilemmas are sure to find a hearing. M. Laugel writes with a certain tone of condensed and refined patriotism which will command the sympathy of the generous reader: but it must be added that the impression left by his book is not cheerful. He is not an optimist, and he is not at any great pains to pass for one.

The author first devotes a chapter to an account of the formation of the French race, and then another to the formation of the nation. Any review of the elements of which the race gradually composed itself must lead us to assent to M. Laugel's affirmation that "its genius is the richest that can be imagined, inasmuch as it has taken something from all the superior races of humanity": more from the Celtic and Latin races, that is, than England and Germany—more from the Germanic than Italy and Spain. He points out afresh that in spite of the general interfusion, of the rising and spreading of the Roman tide in the south, and the propagation in the opposite quarter of the Norman and German elements, it was in that middle region "of which Touraine is the centre and the core" that the distinctively French character began to define itself. "The first flowering of a really French art took place on the banks of the Loire. . . . The more literature became really French, the more she drew near also to the centre and the heart of France." M. Laugel devotes a series of pages to the characteristics of the French race, in which the reader will perceive that he pays it a great many handsome compliments, to not a few of which, however, the reader will find himself disposed to assent. The author has spoken of the "strange docility" of the French character and its want of the political instinct—its tendency to make the people "spectators rather than actors in the drama of public affairs," its social rather than political genius. As regards docility, M. Laugel remarks that the terrible disorders in which the French have so often steeped themselves have arisen from the submission of the mass of the people to a few "audacieux." "The armies of the League and of the Huguenots were never numerous; the men who maintained throughout France the Reign of Terror were perhaps not five thousand in number." The French are an irritable and quick-tempered people, but this same "strange docility" is certainly one of the things most striking to the stranger who lives among them. The first and last object that he perceives at the frontier is an official sign indicating a "défense" to do some particular thing—a "défense" patiently and inveterately submitted to by the public. He feels, however, that the author is very right in saying that the French national character is not servile. "The race is protected against baseness (*bassesse*) by the grace and fineness of its mind, by its laborious tastes, by that spirit of economy which gives to every one the sentiment of a relative independence. At the great periods of our history we must imagine a host of narrowly-established lives, arranged according to rule, animated with humble ambitions, happy with a little, parsimonious; sustained in their monotonous effort by a natural gaiety, by the pleasures of the mind, by the love of the family, and, finally, by the vision and the brightness of the national glory. . . . Everything combines, from childhood upward," he adds, "to accustom the Frenchman to take a designated place in a *grand et bel en-*

semble; ideas of order and submission are in the air he breathes." It must be added that these are the characteristics of the classical and traditional Frenchman—of that old French type which there is some reason to think we are gradually seeing superseded.

It is apparently M. Laugel's belief that these more beautiful and familiar things are passing away. He writes in his latter pages as if, as regards these matters, the fountains of the deep were opened and some of the best attributes of the French race might not impossibly be submerged. These pages are perhaps the most interesting and most eloquent in the volume before us; but we must mention the series of chapters by which they are connected with the passages to which we have already alluded. The one upon the characteristics of the French nobility points out very forcibly the reasons why it has never played the great part to which some of its brilliant qualities might have entitled it. It was a military much more than a territorial aristocracy—an aristocracy in which the younger and older members alike attached themselves to the sword, and never tried to make their fortunes by commerce or by peaceful professions. Moreover, as the author says, "there was always in France a natural tendency to divide property, and, in consequence, to weaken and ruin the nobility." The younger sons obtained a portion of the patrimony, which, in spite of its smallness, they made the source of a title. They separated themselves from the people by their titles, and thus the people grew used to seeing them both exclusive and poor. The power and weight of the nobility, therefore, became, in a large measure, simply a matter of the imagination. The author traces the enormous multiplication of titles of nobility through the seventeenth and eighteenth centuries, when, according to the classification of De Tocqueville, even the peerage, the highest rank in the scale, had fallen from the category of real forces into that of "vanities." He relates the stages by which the crown depressed and disfranchised the peerage to the advantage of the magistracy, and he gives a picture of the extraordinary redundancy of noble or ennobled families at the end of the last century. "There were four thousand administrative offices which conferred nobility and all its privileges." The author has a fine passage, which we shall venture to quote, upon the sacrifice of its feudal rights made by the French nobility in the States-General of 1789:

"The greatness with which it was made is well known; it was even too complete. . . . The French nobility was, on this famous night, faithful to its historic character; it showed itself the most generous nobility in Europe, the least grossly attached to money, to the earth, to everything that is material; the fruits of conquest which others have known how to preserve with so jealous, and sometimes so cruel, a care, melted away in its fingers. It was too fond of the life of adventures, of play, of war, of hazard and exposure; its passions were too juvenile and too feminine, and it thought it could sufficiently defend itself against the encroachments of the baser sort by ironical pleasantry and scorn. . . . It was the last representative of the chivalric spirit; it has always had a certain *emportement* in its fidelity, in its devotion, in its courage, in its vices and virtues alike. It cannot be accused of having been too grasping and too hard; it has ever preferred light and delicate pleasures to the solid advantages bestowed by power, strength, and wealth; we must see in it the flower of French society rather than the trunk or the root; but what Frenchman could ever erect this into a reproach? Where will the world find more accomplished models of taste, dignity, and ease; anything more exquisite in its kindness, more simple in misfortune, more dignified before the insults of destiny? In other countries there clings even to the great people something vulgar; whereas the French nobility has brought feelings and manners to such a refinement that for a long time now there has been nothing low even in the people."

We may hazard the conjecture that in this agreeable portrait of the French aristocracy the author has not been without a secret intention of portraying also, by implication, the aristocracy of a neighboring country, where this class is remarkable for the success with which it has retained territorial dominion and political power. He speaks, with a detail into which we have not space to follow him, of the characteristics of the French monarchy, of those which marked the Reformation in

France, and of those of the French church. Many people have amused themselves with wondering what would have been the effect of Protestantism obtaining in France a large and permanent foothold—the effect, it may be said, to a certain extent, of the non-occurrence of the Massacre of St. Bartholomew. Few speculations are more interesting or more vain; but M. Laugel appears to think that the action of the Reformation in France was essentially limited. In the first place, it was aristocratic; and in the second place, it was anti-patriotic—it had no scruples about bringing in foreign allies. He comments upon the faint trace it has left in French literature; it is associated with but a single eminent name—that of Agrippa d'Aubigné. Of the French church the author speaks with deference and moderation, and to the purity of character of the clergy of our day he pays a liberal tribute. He notes the extinction of the Gallican church, and the increasing ultramontane tendencies of actual French ecclesiasticism; but these tendencies do not appear to excite his alarm. "France has filled great missions in this world; she is busy, perhaps, to-day with some great work of spiritual unity of which future ages will see the accomplishment." Upon the Revolution and its consequences M. Laugel has, of course, much to say; but the reader will probably agree with him that everything has been said about the Revolution. It is interesting to observe that, from the point of view of a Liberal, M. Laugel deems that in 1789 the Tiers-Etat "failed of generosity and of political foresight; it refused to sacrifice its resentments to the cause of liberty; it wished to humiliate at any price the crown and the nobility." M. Laugel does not believe in that cardinal doctrine of a certain school of Liberals—the *inevitableness* of the Revolution; he thinks that in 1789 a liberal and constitutional monarchy might easily have been founded. It is to be noted that the doctrine in question does not enjoy, in various quarters, the credit which for so many years attached to it; as regards the dogma that the Revolution was a necessary evil, it is becoming the fashion to suppress the adjective and emphasize the noun.

We have left ourselves too little opportunity to speak of the pages in which the author discusses the present condition and the future of France. We confess that the latter does not strike us as quite so darkly uncertain as the image of it foreshadowed by M. Laugel. Within the last six years the country has given to an admiring world the most extraordinary proofs of robust vitality, and appears only to desire the opportunity to pursue, undisturbed, the same really impressive exhibition. The dangers of the "demagogy" of which the author speaks are not peculiar to France; they are common to civilization in general, and France has, perhaps more than other countries, some of the qualities that are most opposed to them. M. Laugel, while recognizing the deeply democratic character of the French nation, points out the somewhat anomalous fact that the democracy of the future, in France, must of necessity be an armed one. It is a new problem that presents itself to the political philosopher. "What rules of legislation and government may not be applied to a great democratic, centralized and, by necessity, military nation?" He admits that his chief hope for the France of the future is in the army. The army can best be trusted to preserve the purity of the national character, its ideal, the exemption from the insidious passions of a populace at once refined and depraved, and from the levity of that prosperous and sceptical bourgeoisie of which, on page 297, the author draws an admirably vivid picture. If the army should be false to this mission, says M. Laugel, "France would have nothing left but to wrap her head in the folds of her political purple and to wait for death!"

Nation, October 18, 1877

John Lemoinne

LETTER FROM PARIS: The Reception of John Lemoinne at the Academy—
His Characteristics as a Journalist—The Variable Merits of Academicians

PARIS, March 10.—Except the assembling of the Senate and the Chamber I can think of no event of importance of recent occurrence here save the reception of M. John Lemoinne at the Academy, which took place a week since. M. John Lemoinne is the eminent journalist—the bright particular star of the *Débats*—and journalism has received in his person at the hands of the Academy a compliment of which, if she particularly desires to, she may be proud. It was a proud day at least for the *Journal des Débats*. John Lemoinne replaces Jules Janin, who spent 40 years in the "basement," as they call it, of that honorable sheet—turned off every Monday during that period the dramatic feuilleton which graces the bottom of its otherwise somewhat austere first two pages. He pronounced the customary eulogy of his departed *confrère*, and M. Cuvillier-Fleury replied to him at very great length with a eulogy of himself, M. Cuvillier-Fleury being the principal literary critic of the *Journal des Débats*. It was therefore, for this journal, quite a *fête de famille*. M. John Lemoinne is a very clever man; he possesses in perfection the French "art of saying," and if the Academy was designed simply to represent good writing, he has an eminent claim to a place in it. (It is singular, by the way, that M. John Lemoinne should, as a writer, be of so pure a French strain. He was born in England, and, in a measure, educated there, and he speaks our language irreproachably.) If, however, to reward good thinking and good feeling is a part of the Academy's mission, M. Lemoinne's right of entrance does not seem so unquestionable. Brilliant, incisive, and trenchant as he always is, I have never been able to resist the feeling that there is something very dry and sterile in his political criticism. To say acrimonious and contemptuous things in a masterly manner appears to be the sum of his ambition. He is essentially what the French call a *frondeur*—a faultfinder; his criticism is always restrictive and denunciatory, never suggestive or inspiring, and he lacks supremely Matthew Arnold's famous

478

requisite of "sweetness." This is the greater pity, as he has evidently plenty of "light." He seems to proceed by fits of irritation. He appears in the *Débats* not daily, but at intervals; suddenly darts forth, whirling his sling and letting fly his sharp flints. When he has quite darkened the air with them he retires to his tent—feeling better himself, for the time, I hope—to await a fresh reëxasperation of his wrath. It is all nervous, capricious, splenetic. M. John Lemoinne's chief stock in trade is his peculiarly insidious hatred of England; and, indeed, during the past Winter, exciting as the political situation has been, it is only the perfidy of Albion that has been able to rouse him to utterance. At the time of the purchase of the Khedive's shares he came out, as the phrase is, very strong, and produced two or three articles in which the expression of withering enmity could not have been surpassed. England, for M. Lemoinne, is a shabby country at the best, but her unpardonable sin was her failure to come to the rescue of France when the latter was bleeding to death in the gripe of Prussia—her "standing watching us stretched on the earth like gladiators." And yet even this is not sufficient to account for such a perennial freshness of hostility. The reader cannot rid himself of a feeling that M. John Lemoinne is avenging a personal injury; where does the shoe pinch, he wonders; whom has he in his mind—*à qui en veutil?* These conjectures are probably fantastic, and they are certainly vain.

The fact remains, however, that M. Lemoinne's England is very much an affair of his imagination; it is, as *The London Times* said the other day, an *article de Paris*. I may add that the sturdiest Anglo-Saxon must have had last week a kindly feeling for the new Academician, in seeing him undertake the heroic task of eulogizing (I was going to say apologizing for) Jules Janin. M. John Lemoinne did his best, but unless I am very much mistaken one hears the creaking of the pump. There have been many strange Academicians, but I think there has been none quite so strange as the dramatic critic of the *Débats*. There have been Academicians whose literary titles were of the slenderest, and who were admitted for reasons of state—thinly disguised motives of convenience and propriety; there have been—heaven knows!—dull, dreary, insipid Academicians, authors of classical, respectable, unreadable prose and verse. There have also been flimsy and futile Academicians, whose literature was of a vaporous and imponderable sort. But there was none before M. Jules Janin who had erected futility into a system and raised flimsiness to a fine art.

There are writers in whom mannerism has gone very far, but there are none in whom it has become the all-in-all to the same degree as in Janin. His mannerism in his later years attained the proportions of a monstrosity. Such a shuffling away of substance, such a juggling with thought, partook really of the nature of the magical. He was the great master of the type of criticism that speaks of everything but the subject, and that spins its phrases faster in proportion as it has less and less to say. Janin ended very early by having nothing in life to say, and the rattle and clatter he made in saying it was to all healthy intellectual men the most intolerable noise conceivable. If the Academy has any meaning, one would say that its meaning should be exactly that its honors are not for writers of the Janin family. But has the Academy any meaning? Two or three incidents have lately occurred which make the inquiry proper. The most striking was certainly the admission among the sacred party, last Spring, of Alexandre Dumas fils. M. Dumas is supremely clever, and he has composed dramas which it is impossible, on certain sides, too highly to admire; but it seems to me that he has about as much business in the Academy as in the Cabinet of the Emperor of China. He is a man with a fixed idea—a monomaniac. He can see nothing in life but the "unfortunate" woman; she is the pivot of his imagination—all his inspiration, his allusions and metaphors are drawn from her. If the Academy were an intellectual asylum, with wards, cells, and keepers, M. Dumas might very well appeal to its hospitality; but as it is, there is something grotesque in his presence there. The prime duty of the Academy ought to be to distinguish between the cracked vessel and the sound; and it seems to me that if she had observed this duty, she would have said to Jules Janin, and Alexandre Dumas, alike (dissimilar in talent as they are), that they were welcome to be clever, and popular, and brilliant, but that they were made of precisely the stuff she could not wear—they were deformed, erratic, mistaken. "Here is a certain straight line," she should have said, "you and I can never be on the same side of it."

New York Tribune, April 1, 1876

Pierre Loti

A FEW YEARS AGO the author of these remarks received from an observant friend then in Paris (not a Frenchman) a letter containing a passage which he ventures to transcribe. His correspondent had been to see a celebrated actress—the most celebrated actress of our time—in a new and successful play.

"She is a wonderful creature, but how a being so intelligent as she can so elaborate what has so little moral stuff in it to work upon I don't comprehend. The play is hard and sinister and horrible without being in the least degree tragic or pathetic; one felt when it was over like an accomplice in some cold-blooded piece of cruelty. I am moved to give up the French and call to my own species to stand from under and let their fate overtake them. Such a disproportionate development of the external perceptions and such a perversion of the natural feelings must work its Nemesis in some way."

These simple lines, on account of their general, not of their special application, have come back to me in reading over the several volumes of the remarkable genius who wears in literature the name of Pierre Loti, as well as in refreshing my recollection of some of the pages of his contemporaries. An achievement in art or in letters grows more interesting when we begin to perceive its connections; and, indeed, it may be said that the study of connections is the recognized function of intelligent criticism. It is a comparatively poor exercise of the attention (for the critic always, I mean) to judge a book all by itself, even if it happen to be a book as independent, as little the product of a school and a fashion, as "Le Mariage de Loti" or "Mon Frère Yves" or "Pêcheur d'Islande." Each of these works is interesting as illustrating the talent and character of the author, but they become still more interesting as we note their coincidences and relations with other works, for then they begin to illustrate other talents and other characters as well: the plot thickens, the whole spectacle expands. We seem to be studying not simply the genius of an individual, but, in a living manifestation, that of a nation or of a conspicuous group; the nation or the group becomes a great figure operating on a great scale, and the drama of its literary production (to speak only of that) a kind of world-drama, lighted by the universal sun, with Europe and America for the public, and the arena of races, the battle-field of their inevitable contrasts and competitions, for the stage. Is not the entertainment, moreover, a particularly good bill, as they say at the theatre, when it is a question of the performances of France? Will not the connoisseur feel much at his ease, in such a case, about the high capacity of the actor, settle himself in his stall with the comfortable general confidence that he is to listen to a professional and not to an amateur? Whatever benefits or injuries that great country may have conferred upon mankind, she has certainly rendered them the service of being always, according to her own expression, *bien en scène*. She commits herself completely and treats us to extreme cases; her cases are test-cases, her experiments heroic and conclusive. She has educated our observation by the finish of her manner, and whether or no she has the best part in the play we feel that she has rehearsed best.

A writer of the ability of Alphonse Daudet, of that of Guy de Maupassant, or of that of the brothers De Goncourt, can never fail to be interesting by virtue of that ability, the successive manifestations of which keep our curiosity alive; but this curiosity is never so great as after we have noted, as I think we almost inveterately do, that the strongest gift of each of them is the strongest gift of all: a remarkable art of expressing the life, of picturing the multitudinous, adventurous experience, of the senses. We recognize this accomplishment with immense pleasure as we read—a pleasure so great that it is not for some time that we make the other observation that inevitably follows on its heels. That observation is somewhat to this effect: that in comparison the deeper, stranger, subtler inward life, the wonderful adventures of the soul, are so little pictured that they may almost be said not to be pictured at all. We end with an impression of want of equilibrium and proportion, and by asking ourselves (so coercive are

the results of comparative criticism) whether such a sacrifice
be quite obligatory. The value of the few words in the letter
I just cited is simply that they offer a fresh, direct, almost
startled measure of the intensity of the sacrifice, accompanied
with the conviction that it must sooner or later be paid for,
like every other extravagance, and that if the payment be on
the scale of the aberration it will make an eddy of which those
who are wise in time should keep clear. This profuse development of the external perceptions—those of the appearance,
the sound, the taste, the material presence and pressure of
things, will at any rate, I think, not be denied to be the mas-
ter-sign of the novel in France as the first among the younger
talents show it to us to-day. They carry into the whole business of looking, seeing, hearing, smelling, into all kinds of
tactile sensibility and into noting, analyzing, and expressing
the results of these acts, a seriousness much greater than that
of any other people. Their tactile sensibility is immense, and
it may be said in truth to have produced a literature. They are
so strong on this side that they seem to me to be easily masters, and I cannot imagine that their supremacy should candidly be contested.

An acute sense of aspect and appearance is not common,
for the only sense that most people have is of the particular
matter with which, on any occasion, their business, their interest or subsistence is bound up; but it is less uncommon in
some societies than in others, and it flourishes conspicuously
in France. Such is the witness borne by the very vocabulary
of the people, which abounds in words and idioms expressing
shades and variations of the visible. I once in Paris, at a café,
heard a gentleman at a table next to my own say to a companion, speaking of a lady who had just entered the establishment, "A quoi ressemble-t-elle donc?" "Mon Dieu, à une
poseuse de sangsues." The reply struck me as a good example
of prompt exactness of specification. If you ask a French hat-
ter which of two hats is the more commendable, he will tell
you that one of them *dégage mieux la physionomie*. The judgment of his English congener may be as good (we ourselves
perhaps are pledged to think it better), but it will be more
dumb and pointless—he will have less to say about disengaging the physiognomy. Half the faculty I speak of in the

French is the expressive part of it. The perception and the expression together have been worked to-day (for the idiosyncrasy is noticeably modern) with immense vigor, and from Balzac to Pierre Loti, the latest recruit to the band of painters, the successful workers have been the novelists. There are different ways of working, and Flaubert, Edmond and Jules de Goncourt, Zola, Daudet, Maupaussant, and the writer to whom I more particularly refer, have each had a way of his own. There are story-tellers to-day in France who are not students, or at any rate not painters, of the mere palpable—but then they are not conspicuously anything else. I can think of but one writer whose foremost sign, though his literary quality is of the highest, does not happen to be visual curiosity. M. Paul Bourget looks much more within than without, and notes with extraordinary closeness the action of life on the soul, especially the corrosive and destructive action. Many people in England hold that corrosion and destruction are not worth noting; but it should be added that they are probably not as a general thing people to whom one would go for information on the subject—I mean on the subject of the soul. M. Paul Bourget, however, is peculiar in this, that he is both master and pupil; he is alone, *parmi les jeunes*; and, moreover, there are other directions in which he is not isolated at all, those of tactile sensibility, or isolated only because he follows them so far.

The case was not always as I have here attempted to indicate it, for Madame George Sand had an admirable faculty of looking within and a comparatively small one of looking without. Attempting, some months ago, at Venice, to read over "Consuelo," I was struck on the spot with the very small degree to which the author troubled herself about close representation, the absence of any attempt at it or pretension to it; and I could easily understand the scorn with which that sort of irresponsibility (reaching at times on Madame Sand's part a truly exasperating artlessness) has always filled the votaries of the reproductive method. M. Octave Feuillet turns his polished glass on the life of the spirit, but what he finds in the spirit is little more (as it strikes me) than the liveliest phenomena of the flesh. His heroes and heroines are lined on the under side with the same stuff as on the upper—a curious

social silken material, adapted only, as we are constantly reminded, to the contacts of patricians. If the soul, for the moralizing observer, be a romantic, moonlighted landscape, with
woods and mountains and dim distances, visited by strange
winds and murmurs, for M. Octave Feuillet it is rather a
square French salon in white and gold, with portraits of the
king and queen and the pope, a luminary in old Sèvres and
plenty of *bibelots* and sofas. I hasten to add that it is an apartment in which one may spend an hour most agreeably. Even
at present there are distinguished variations, if we look outside the group of novelists. If there were not a poet like Sully-
Prudhomme or a moralist like M. Renan, the thesis that the
French imagination has none but a sensual conscience would
be made simpler than it ever is to prove anything.

We perceive, on the other hand, that the air of initiation
fails as soon as the inward barrier is crossed, and the diminution of credit produced by this failure is, I confess, the only
Nemesis in which for the present I have confidence. It appears to me, indeed, all-sufficient—it appears ideal; and if the
writers I have named deserve chastisement for their collective
sin against proportion (since sin it shall be held), I know not
how a more terrible one could have been invented. The penalty they pay is the heaviest that can be levied, the most summary writ that can be served, upon a great talent—great
talents having, as a general thing, formidable defences—and
consists simply in the circumstance that, when they lay their
hands upon the spirit of man, they cease to seem expert. This
would be a great humiliation if they recognized it. They rarely
do, however, so far as may be observed; which is a proof that
their defences *are* formidable. There is a distinct transition, at
any rate, in the case I mention, and assuredly a distinct descent. As painters they go straight to the mark, as analysts
they only scratch the surface. We leave authority on one side
of the line, and encounter on the other a curiously complacent and unconscious provincialism. Such is the impression
we gather in every case, though there are some cases in which
the incongruity is more successfully dissimulated than in others. What makes it grow, when once we perceive it, is the
large and comprehensive pretensions of the writers—the
sense they give us of camps and banners, war-cries and watch-

fires. The "Journal" of the brothers De Goncourt, of which two volumes have lately been put forth, is a very interesting publication and suggests many thoughts; but the first remark to be made about it is that it makes a hundred claims to penetration, to profundity. At the same time it is a perfect revelation of the visual passion and of the way it may flourish (not joyously indeed in this case, but with an air of jealous, nervous, conscious tension), at the expense of other passions and even other faculties. Perhaps the best illustration of all would be the difference between the superiority of Gustave Flaubert as a painter of aspects and sensations, and his lapses and limitations, his general insignificance, as a painter of ideas and moral states. If you feel the talent that abides in his style very much (and some people feel it immensely and as a sort of blinding glory), you are bribed in a measure to overlook the inequality; but there comes a moment when the bribe, large as it is, is ineffectual. His imagination is so fine that we take some time to become conscious that almost none of it is moral or even human. "Bouvard et Pécuchet," even as an unfinished work, has merits of execution that could only spring from a great literary energy; but "Bouvard et Pécuchet" is surely, in the extreme juvenility of its main idea, one of the oddest productions for which a man who had lived long in the world was ever responsible. Flaubert, indeed, was the very apostle of surface, and an extraordinary example of a sort of transposition of the conscience. If for "perversion of the natural feelings" (the phrase of the letter I quoted) we read inaction rather, and inexperience and indifference in regard to the phenomena of character and the higher kinds of sensibility, he will appear to represent the typical disparity at its maximum. The brothers De Goncourt strike us as knowing as little about these matters as he, but somehow it is not suggested to us in the same degree that they might have known more. His gift is not their gift, and it is his gift that makes us measure him by a high standard. "Germinie Lacerteux," indeed, without being so fine as "Madame Bovary," has great ability; but nothing else they have written has an equal ability with "Germinie Lacerteux."

One of the consequences of the generalization I have ventured to make is that when a new French talent mounts above the horizon we watch with a kind of anxiety to see whether it will present itself in a subversive and unaccommodating manner. M. Pierre Loti is a new enough talent for us still to feel something of the glow of exultation at his having not contradicted us. He has in fact done exactly the opposite. He has added more than we had dared to hope to the force of our generalization and removed every scruple of a magnanimous sort that we might have felt in making it. By scruples of a magnanimous sort I mean those that might have been engendered by a sense of favors intensely enjoyed. At the moment we are under the spell of such a talent as Alphonse Daudet's or Emile Zola's or Guy de Maupassant's or (to give variety to the question) that of so rare and individual a genius as this exquisite Loti, it takes no great sophistry to convince us of the indelicacy, of the ingratitude even, of turning an invidious eye on anything so irrelevant as deficiencies. But the spell is foredoomed to fluctuations, to lapses, and we end by seeming to perceive with perplexity that even literary figures so brilliant as these may have too happy, too insolent a lot. Are they after all to enjoy their honors without paying for them? How *we* should have to pay for them if *we* were to succeed in plucking them and wearing them! The fortunate Frenchmen give us the sense of a kind of fatuity in impunity, a kind of superficiality in distinction, a kind of irritating mastery of the trick of eating your cake and having it. Such is one of the reflections to which Pierre Loti eventually leads us. In common with his companions he performs so beautifully as to kick up a fine golden dust over the question of what he contains—or of what he doesn't. The agility of all their movements makes up for the thinness of so much of their inspiration. To be so constituted as to expose one's self to the charge of vulgarity of spirit and yet to have a charm that successfully snaps its fingers at all "charges," is to be so lucky that those who work in harder conditions surely may allow themselves the solace of small criticisms. It may be said that if we indulge in small criticisms we resist our author's charm after all; but the answer to this is that the effort to throw off our enthralment even for an hour is an almost heroic struggle with a sweet superstition. The whole second-rate element in Loti, for instance, becomes an absolute stain if we think much about it. But practically (and this is his first-rate triumph) we *don't* think much about it, so unreserved is our surrender to irresistible illusion and contagious life.

To be so rare that you can be common, so good that you can be bad without loss of caste, be a mere sponge for sensations and yet not forfeit your human character—secure, on the contrary, sympathy and interest for it whenever you flash *that* facet into the sun—and then on top of all write, as Goldsmith wrote, like an angel—that surely is to wear the amulet to some purpose, the literary feather with a swagger that becomes pardonable. This rarity of the mixture, which makes such a literary unity of such a personal duality, is altogether in Pierre Loti a source of fascination. He combines aptitudes which seldom sit down to the same table, and combines them with singular facility and naturalness, an air of not caring whether he combines them or not. He may not be as ignorant of literature as he pretends (he protests perhaps a little too much that he never opens a book), but it is very clear that what is at the bottom of his effect is not (in a degree comparable at least to the intensity of the effect) the study of how to produce it. What he studies is a very different matter, and I know no case in which literature, left to come off as it can, comes off so beautifully. To be such a rover of the deep, such a dabbler in adventure as would delight the soul of Mr. Robert Louis Stevenson, and yet to have at one's command a sensitive and expressive apparatus separated by the whole scale from that of Jim Hawkins and John Silver, is to have little need of "cultivating" originality, as M. Guy de Maupassant the other day recommended us to do. An officer in the French navy, perpetually circumnavigating the globe, M. Loti has spent most of his life (though its duration, I believe, has not yet been considerable) in strange waters and far lands, and his taste for foreign contacts and free manners, for the natural, personal life, has led him to cultivate most of his opportunities. That taste and those opportunities are among soldiers and sailors common enough; but what is not so in the same connection is the spirit of the artist, which in M. Loti is as natural as all the rest. There is a reflection in regard to the distribution of earthly advantages which is probably familiar to most men of letters, and which at any

rate often occurs to the writer of these lines. The persons who
see the great things are terribly apt not to be persons who can
write or even talk about them; and the persons who can write
about them, reproduce them in some way, are terribly apt not
to be persons who see them. The "chance" is with the blind
or the dumb, and the immortal form, waiting for a revelation
that doesn't come, is with the poor sedentary folk who bewail
the waste of chances. Many an artist will have felt his heart
sink on questioning some travelled friend in vain. The travelled friend has not noticed or has nothing to say about
things which must have had an inestimable suggestiveness. So
we frame a sort of ideal of success, in which the man of action
and the man of observation melt into each other. The transcendent result is a precious creature who knows the sea as
well as Captain Marryat, and writes about it as well—I can
only say as well as Pierre Loti.

> "She flew before the weather, the *Marie* [a fishing-boat
> in the Icelandic waters], flew faster and faster, and the
> weather flew as well, as before something mysterious and
> terrible. The gale, the sea, the *Marie* herself, were all taken
> with the same madness of flight and speed in the same di-
> rection. What scurried the fastest was the wind; then the
> great surges of the swell, slower and heavier, rushing after
> it; then the *Marie*, borne along in the universal motion.
> The waves pursued her with their blanched crests, rolling
> in a perpetual fall, and she, forever caught, forever left be-
> hind, got away from them, all the same, by the clever fur-
> row she made in her wake, which sucked their rage away.
> And in this flying pace what they were conscious of above
> all was the sense of lightness; they felt themselves spring,
> without trouble or effort. When the *Marie* rose on the bil-
> lows it was without a shock, as if the wind had lifted her;
> and then her descent was like a slide. . . . She seemed to
> be sliding backwards, the fleeing mountain falling away
> from under her to rush onward, while she dropped into
> one of the great hollows that were also rushing. She
> touched its terrible bottom without a hurt, in a splash of
> water which didn't even wet her, but which fled like all the
> rest—fled and fainted ahead, like smoke, like nothing. In

the depth of these hollows it was darker, and after each wave had passed they watched the next coming on behind—the next bigger and higher, green and transparent, which hurried up with furious contortions, scrolls almost closing over and seeming to say, 'Wait till I catch you—till I swallow you up!' But it didn't catch you; it only lifted you as you lift a feather in shrugging your shoulders, and you felt it pass under you almost gently, with its gushing foam, the crash of a cascade."

"Mon Frère Yves" and "Pêcheur d'Islande" are full of pages as vivid as that, which seem to us to place the author among the very first of sea-painters.

"You made out thousands of voices [in the huge clamor of a storm in Northern seas], those above either shrill or deep and seeming distant from being so big: that was the wind, the great soul of the uproar, the invisible power that carried on the whole thing. It was dreadful, but there were other sounds as well, closer, more material, more bent on destruction, given out by the torment of the water, which crackled as if on live coals. And it grew and still grew. In spite of their flying pace the sea began to cover them, to 'eat them up,' as they said; first the spray, whipping them from aft, then great bundles of water hurled with a force that might smash everything. The waves grew higher and still crazily higher, and yet they were ravelled as they came and you saw them hanging about in great green tatters, which were the falling water scattered by the wind. It fell in heavy masses on the deck, with the sound of a whack, and then the *Marie* shuddered all over, as if in pain. Now you could make out nothing more, on account of this drift of white slobber; when the gusts groaned afresh you saw it borne in thicker clouds, like the dust on the roads in summer. A heavy rain which had come on now passed aslant, almost horizontal, and all these things hissed together, lashing and wounding like stripes."

The English reader may see in such passages as these what the English reader is rather apt to see in any demonstrative view of difficulty or danger, any tendency to insist that a storm is bad or a mountain steep—a nervous exaggeration, the emotion of one who is not as Englishmen are. But Pierre Loti has many other things to say of the ocean than that it is a terrible place, and of strange countries than that it is a mercy one ever gets there, and the descriptions I have quoted are chosen at hazard. "It always came to an end suddenly [the hot, tropical rain]; the black curtain drew away slowly, dragging its train over the turquoise-tinted sea; the splendid light came forth more astounding after the darkness, and the great equatorial sun drank up fast all the water we had taken; the sails, the wood of the ship, the awnings recovered their whiteness in the sunshine; the *Sibyl* put on altogether the bright color of a dry thing in the midst of the great blue monotony that stretched around her." Pierre Loti speaks better than of anything else of the ocean, the thing in the world that, after the human race, has most intensity and variety of life; but he renders with extraordinary felicity all the poetry of association, all the touching aspects and suggestions in persons, places, and objects connected with it, whose essential character is that they are more or less its sport and its victims. There is always a charming pity and a kind of filial passion in his phrase when it rests upon the people and things of his windswept and wave-washed Brittany. The literature of our day contains nothing more beautiful than the Breton passages, as they may be called, of "Mon Frère Yves" and "Pêcheur d'Islande." There is a sentence in the former of these tales, in reference to the indefinable sweetness of the short-lived Breton summer, which constitutes a sort of image of the attraction of his style. "A compound of a hundred things; the charm of the long, mild days, rarer than elsewhere and sooner gone; the deep, fresh grasses, with their extreme profusion of pink flowers; and then the sense of other years which sleeps there, spread through everything." All this is in Pierre Loti, the mildness and sadness, the profusion of pink flowers, and that implication of *other* conditions at any moment, which is the innermost note of the voice of the sea. When Gaud, in "Pêcheur d'Islande," takes her walk to the dreary promontory where she hopes she may meet her lover, "there were no more trees at all now, nothing but the bare heath, with its green furze, and here and there the divine crucified cutting out the great arms of their crosses against the sky and making the whole region look like an immense place of justice." Too long to quote in their fulness are the two admirable pages in the early part of the history of Gaud and Yann about the winter festival of the *pardon* of the fishermen, with Paimpol full of "the sound of bells and the chant of priests, the rude and monotonous songs of the taverns—old airs to cradle sailors, old *complaintes* brought from the sea, brought from I know not where, from the deep night of time"; full of "old granite houses, shutting in the swarm of the crowd; old roofs that told the story of their centuries of struggle against the west winds, the salt spray, the rains, everything that the sea brings to bear; the story, too, of the warm episodes they had sheltered, old adventures of daring and love." Easier to reproduce, in its concision, is the description of the day, the last day, before Yann Gaos goes forth on the ill-starred expedition from which he never returns:

"There was no wind from any quarter. The sea had turned very gentle; it was everywhere of the same pale blue and remained perfectly quiet. The sun shone with a great white brightness, and the rough Breton land soaked itself in the light as in something fine and rare; it seemed to feel a cheer and a refreshment even to its far-away distances. The air was deliciously tepid and smelt of summer; you would have said that it had stilled itself forever, that there never again would be dark days or tempests. The capes, the bays, without the changing shadows of the clouds, drew out in the sunshine their great motionless lines. They, too, appeared given up to endless rest and tranquillity. . . . On the edges of the ways you saw little hasty flowers, primroses and violets, pale and without scent."

"Madame Chrysanthème," the history of a summer spent in very curious conditions at Nagasaki, the latest of the author's productions and the most distinctively amusing, has less spontaneity than its predecessors, and seems more calculated, more made to order; but it abounds in unsurpassable little vignettes, of which the portrait of certain Japanese ladies of quality whom he met at the photographer's is a specimen:

"I couldn't satiate my desire to look at these two creatures; they captivated me like incomprehensible things that
one had never seen. Their fragile bodies, outlandishly
graceful in posture, are drowned in stiff materials and redundant sashes, of which the ends droop like tired wings.
They make me think, I don't know why, of great, rare insects; the extraordinary patterns on their garments have
something of the dark bedizenment of night-butterflies.
Above all, there is the mystery of their quite small eyes,
drawn back and up so far that the lids are tight and they
can scarcely open; the mystery of their expression, which
seems to denote inner thoughts of a cold, vague complacency of absurdity—a world of ideas absolutely closed to
ourselves."

It may be that many an English reader will not recognize
Pierre Loti as a man of action who happens to have a genius
for literary expression, the account he himself gives of his exploits not being such as we associate with that character. The
term action has a wide signification, but there are some kinds
of life which it represents to us certainly much less than others. The exploits of the author of "Madame Chrysanthème,"
of "Ayizadé," of "Rarahu," of "Le Roman d'un Spahi," and
"Pasquala Ivanovitch," are—I hardly know what to call them,
for we scarcely mention achievements of this order in English—more relaxing on the whole than tonic. An author less
tonic than Pierre Loti can indeed not well be imagined, and
the English reader ought already to have been notified (the
plainest good faith requires it and I have delayed much too
long) that a good deal of what he has to tell us relates mainly
to his successes among the ladies. We have a great and I think
a just dislike to the egotistic-erotic, to literary confidences on
such points, and when a gentleman abounds in them the last
thing we take him for is a real man of action. It must be
confessed that Pierre Loti abounds, though his two best
books are not autobiographical, and there is simply nothing
to reply to any English reader who on ascertaining this circumstance may declare that he desires to hold no commerce
with him; nothing, that is, but the simple remark that such a
reader will lose a precious pleasure. This warning, however,

is a trifle to the really scandalized. I maintain my epithet, at any rate, and I should desire no better justification for it than such an admirable piece as the "Corvée Matinale," in the volume entitled "Propos d'Exil," which describes how the author put off at dawn from a French ship of war, in a small boat with a handful of men, to row up a river on the coast of Anam and confer, with a view of bringing them promptly to terms, with the authorities of the queerest of little Asiatic towns. A writer is to my sense quite man of action enough when he has episodes like that to relate; they give a sufficient perfection to the conjunction of the "chance" and the pictorial view. Danger has nothing to do with it; the manner in which M. Loti gives us on this occasion the impression of an almost grotesque absence of danger, of ugly mandarins superfluously frightened as well as of the color and temperature of the whole scene, the steaming banks of the river, with flat Asiatic faces peeping out of the rushes, the squalid, fetid crowds, the shabby, contorted pagodas, with precious little objects glimmering in the shade of their open fronts—the vividness of all these suggestions is the particular sign of this short masterpiece. The same remark applies to the "Pagodes Souterraines," in the same volume—the story, told with admirable art, of an excursion, while the ship lingers exasperatingly on the same hot, insufferable coast, to visit certain marvellous old tombs and temples, hewn out of a mountain of pink marble, filled with horrible monstrous effigies and guarded by bonzes almost as uncanny. The appreciation of the exotic, which M. Jules Lemaître marks as Loti's distinguishing sign, finds perfect expression in such pages as these.

There are many others of the same sort in the "Propos d'Exil," which is a chaplet of pearls; but perhaps the book is above all valuable for the sketch entitled "Un Vieux"—the picture of the old age, dreary and lamentable, of a worn-out mariner who has retired on his pension to a cottage in the suburbs of Brest. It has delicate sentiment as well as an extraordinary objective reality; but it is not sentimental, for it is characterized by an ineffable pessimism and a close, fascinated notation of the inexorable stages by which lonely and vacant old age moulders away, with its passions dying, dying very hard. "Un Vieux" is singularly ugly, and "Pêcheur d'Islande" is singularly beautiful; but I should be tempted to say that in Pierre Loti's work "Un Vieux" is the next finest thing to "Pêcheur d'Islande." "Mon Frère Yves" is full of beauty, but it carries almost to a maximum the author's characteristic defect, the absence of composition, the *décousu* quality which makes each of his productions appear at first a handful of flying leaves. "Un Vieux" has a form as a whole, though it occurs to me that, perhaps, it is surpassed in this respect by another gem of narration or description, the best pages of the "Fleurs d'Ennui." (We hesitate for a word when it is a question mainly of rendering, as Loti renders it, the impression, of giving the material illusion, of a strange place and strange manners.) I leave to the impartial reader to judge whether "Les Trois Dames de la Kasbah," the gem in question (it has been extracted from the "Fleurs d'Ennui" and published in a pretty little volume by itself), is more or only is less ugly than "Un Vieux." That will depend a good deal on whether he be shocked by the cynicism of the most veracious of all possible representations of the adventures of a band of drunken sailors during a stuffy night at Algiers. Such, and nothing more (the adventures are of the least edifying, and the *dénoûment* is not even mentionable to ears polite), is the subject of "Les Trois Dames de la Kasbah, Conte Oriental"; and yet the life, the spirit, the color, the communicative tone, the truth and poetry of this little production are such that one cannot conscientiously relegate it (one wishes one could) to a place even of comparative obscurity.

If our author's ruling passion is the appreciation of the exotic, it is not in his first works that he confines his quest to funny calls on nervous mandarins, to the twilight gloom of rheumatic old sailors or the vulgar pranks of reckless young ones. "Le Roman d'un Spahi," "Ayizadé," and "Rarahu" each contain the history of a love-affair with a primitive woman or a combination of primitive women. There is a kind of complacent animalism in them which makes it difficult to speak of them as the perfection of taste, and I profess to be able to defend them on the ground of taste only so long as they are not attacked. The great point is that they will not be attacked by any one who is capable of feeling the extraordinary power of evocation of (for instance) "Le Mariage de Loti" (another name for "Rarahu"), at the same time that he recognizes the abnormal character of such a performance, a character the more marked as the feeling of youth is strong in these early volumes, and the young person has rarely M. Loti's assurance as a *viveur*. He betrays a precocity of depravity which is disconcerting. I write the gross word depravity because we must put the case against him (so many English readers would feel it that way) as strongly as it can be put. It doesn't put it strongly enough to say that the serene surrender to polygamous practices among coral-reefs and in tepid seas is a sign much rather of primitive innocence, for there is an element in the affair that vitiates the argument. This is simply that the serenity (which, I take it, most makes the innocence) cannot under the circumstances be adequate. The pen, the talent, the phrase, the style, the note-book take care of that and change the whole situation; they invalidate the plea of the primitive. They introduce the conscious element, and that is the weak side of Loti's spontaneities and pastorals. What saves him is that his talent never falters, and this is but another illustration of his interesting double nature. His customs and those of his friends at Tahiti, at Stamboul, on the east coast of the Adriatic, or again, according to his latest work, at Nagasaki, are not such as we associate in the least with high types; and yet when we close these various records of the general activity known as the attitude of "conquest," the impression that abides with us is one of surpassing delicacy. The facts are singularly vulgar, in spite of the exotic glow that wraps them up; but the subjective side of the business, the author's imagination, has an extraordinary light. Few things could suggest more the value that we instinctively attach to a high power of evocation—the degree to which we regard it as precious in itself.

What makes the facts vulgar, what justifies us in applying to Loti's picture of himself an ironic epithet or two, is his almost inveterate habit of representing the closest and most intimate personal relations as unaccompanied with any moral feeling, any impulse of reflection or reaction. He has so often the air of not seeming to talk of affection when he talks of love—that oddest of all French literary characteristics, and one to which we owe the circumstance that whole volumes have been written on the latter of these principles without an allusion to the former. There is a moral feeling in the singular friendship of which "Mon Frère Yves" is mainly a masterly commemoration, and also a little in the hindered passion which at last unites, for infinite disaster, alas! the hero and heroine of "Pêcheur d'Islande." These are the exceptions; they are admirable and reassuring. The closer, the more intimate is a personal relation the more we look in it for the human drama, the variations and complications, the note of responsibility for which we appeal in vain to the loves of the quadrupeds. Failing to satisfy us in this way, such a relation is not, as Mr. Matthew Arnold says of American civilization, *interesting*. M. Pierre Loti is too often guilty of the simplicity of assuming that when exhibited on his own part it *is* interesting. I should make a point of parenthesizing that the picture of the passion which holds together in an immortal embrace the two great figures of "Pêcheur d'Islande" is essentially a picture of affection. "Rarahu" is a wonderful extension of the reader's experience—a study of the *nonchalance* of the strange, attractive Maori race and the private life of Polynesia. The impression is irresistible and the transfusion of our consciousness, as one may say, effected without the waste of a drop. The case is the same with "Ayizadé," and the transfusion this time is into a more capacious recipient. "Ayizadé" relates the adventures of a French naval officer who spends a winter, at Salonica and Constantinople, in the tolerably successful effort to pass (not only in the eyes of others but in his very own) for a Turk, and a Turk of the people moreover, with the ingrained superstitions and prejudices. He secures in this experiment the valuable assistance of sundry unconventional persons (for his ideal is the Bohemian Turk, if the expression may be used), foremost of whom is the lady, the wife of a rich and respectable Mussulman, who gives her name to the book. It is for M. Loti himself to have judged whether the results were worth the trouble; the great point is that his reader feels that *he* has them, in their reality, without the trouble, and is beholden to the author accordingly for one of the greatest of literary pleasures. M. Jules Lemaître, whom it is difficult not to quote in speaking of any writer of whom he has spoken, gives "Ayizadé" the high praise of being the finest case of enlarged sympathy that he knows, and the most

successful effort at changing one's skin. Commendation of
this order it doubtless deserves, equally with "Le Mariage de
Loti," in spite of the infirmity I have hinted at, the fact that
the interest is supposed largely to be attached to a close personal relation which is not quite human, which is too simplified, too much like the loves of the quadrupeds. The desire to
change his skin is frequent with M. Loti, and it has this oddity that his preference is almost always for a dusky one. We
rarely see him attempt to assume the complexion of one of
the fairer races—of the English for instance, the fairest perhaps of all. He indulges indeed in the convenient fiction that
the personage of whom Loti was originally the *nom de guerre*
is Mr. Harry Grant, a midshipman in her Majesty's service;
but this device is perfunctory and the identity is not maintained. Nothing could illustrate more our author's almost impertinent amateurishness and laxity of composition, as well as
the circumstance that we forgive it at every step, than the
artless confusion which runs through all his volumes in regard
to such identities. They don't signify, and it is all, as his own
idiom has it, sewn with white thread. Loti is at once the pseudonym of M. Julien Viaud and the assumed name of the hero
of a hundred more or less scandalous anecdotes. Suddenly he
ceases to be Harry Grant and becomes an officer in the
French navy. The brother Yves is one person in the charming
book which bears his name, and another (apparently) in "Madame Chrysanthème." The name becomes generic and represents any convivial Breton sailor. A curious shadow called
Plumkett—a naval comrade—wanders vaguely in and out of
almost all the books, in relations incompatible with each
other. The odd part of it is that this childish confusion does
not only not take from our pleasure, but does not even take
from our sense of the author's talent. It is another of the
things which prove Loti's charm to be essentially a charm absolute, a charm outside of the rules, outside of logic, and independent of responsibility.

In "Madame Chrysanthème" the periodical experiment is
Japanese, the effort on Loti's part has been to saturate with
the atmosphere of Nipon that oft-soaked sponge to which I
have ventured to compare his imagination. His success has
not been so great as in other cases, for the simple reason that

the Japanese have not rubbed off on him as freely as the Turks and the Tahitians. The act of sympathy has not taken place, the experiment is comparatively a failure. The wringing-out of the sponge leaves rather a turbid deposit. The author's taste is for the primitive and beautiful, the large and free, and the Japanese strike him as ugly and complicated, tiny and conventional. His attitude is more profane than our own prejudice can like it to be; he quite declines to take them seriously. The reproach, in general, to which many people would hold him to be most open, is that he takes seriously people and things which deserve it less. I may be altogether mistaken, but we treat ourselves to the conviction that he fails of justice to the wonderful little people who have renewed, for Europe and America, the whole idea of Taste. It occurs to us for the first time that he is partially closed, slightly narrow, he whose very profession it is to be accessible to extreme strangeness, and we feel, as devoted readers, a certain alarm. We ask ourselves whether the sponge has been so often dipped that it has lost its retentive property, and with an anxious desire for reassurance on this point we await his next production.

It is, however, singularly out of place to talk of what Pierre Loti may next produce when I have not interrupted my general remarks to mention in detail the high claims of "Mon Frère Yves" and "Pêcheur d'Islande." It is of these things above all the friendly critic must speak if he wishes to speak to friendly ears. If our author had written his other books and not written these he would have been a curious and striking figure in literature; but the two volumes I have last named give him a different place altogether, and if I had not read and re-read them I should not have put forth this general plea. "Mon Frère Yves" is imperfect (it is notably, for what it is, too long), and "Pêcheur d'Islande" is to my sense perfect, yet they have almost an equal part in contributing to their author's name an association of supreme beauty. The history of Marguerite Mével and Yann Gaos strikes me as one of the very few works of imagination of our day completely and successfully beautiful. The singular thing is that these two tales, with their far finer effect, differ only in degree from their predecessors, differ not at all in kind. The part of them that deals with the complicated heart is still the weakest element;

it is still, as in the others, the senses that vibrate most (to every impression of air and climate and color and weather and season); the feeling is always the feeling of the great earth—the navigator's earth—as a constant physical solicitation. But the picture in each case has everything that gives a lift to that susceptibility and nothing that draws it down, and the susceptibility finds a language which fits it like a glove. The impulse to be human and reflective—the author has felt it, indeed, strongly in each case; but it is still primitive humanity that fascinates him most, and if Yves and Yann and Silvestre and Gaud and the old grandmother Moan are more complicated than Ayizadé and Samuel and Achmet and Fatou-gaye and Rarahu, they are infinitely less so than the young people of either sex who supply the interest of most valid works of fiction. "Pêcheur d'Islande" is the history of a passion, but of a passion simplified, in its strength, to a sort of community with the winds and waves, the blind natural forces hammering away at the hard Breton country where it is enacted. "Mon Frère Yves" relates the history of an incorrigible drunkard and *coureur*, a robust, delightful Breton sailor who, in his better moments, reads "Le Marquis de Villemer" and weeps over it. (There is a sort of mystification, I should remark, in this production, for the English reader at least, the book being in a large degree the representation of an intimate friendship between the sailor and his superior officer, the spectator of his career and chronicler of his innumerable relapses. Either the conditions which permit of this particular variation of discipline are not adequately explained or the rigor of the hierarchy is less in the French service than in others.) What strikes me in "Pêcheur d'Islande" is the courage which has prompted him to appeal to us on behalf of a situation worn so smooth by generations of novelists that there would seem to be nothing left in it to hook our attention to, not to mention the scarcely less manifest fact that it is precisely this artless absence of suspicion that he was attempting a *tour de force* which has drawn down the abundance of success. Yann Gaos is a magnificent young fisherman—magnificent in stature and strength, and shy and suspicious in temper—whose trade is to spend his summer hauling up millions of cod in the cold and dangerous waters of the North.

He meets among the coast-folk of his home a very clever and pretty girl who receives from him an even deeper impression than she gives, but with whom he completely fails to come to an understanding. The understanding is delayed for two years (thanks largely to an absence of "manner" on either side), during which the girl's heart comes near to breaking. At last, quite suddenly, they find themselves face to face, she confessing her misery and he calling himself a dolt. They are married in a hurry, to have a short honeymoon before he starts for his annual cruise (the idea of which fills her with an irresistible foreboding), and he sails away to Iceland with his mates. She waits in vain for his return, and he never, never comes back. This is all the tale can boast in the way of plot; it is the old-fashioned "love-story" reduced to a paucity of terms. I am sure M. Loti has no views nor theories as to what constitutes and does not constitute a plot; he has taken no precautions, he has not sacrificed to any irritated divinity, and yet he has filled the familiar, the faded materials with freshness and meaning. He has appealed to us on "eternal" grounds, and besides the unconscious *tour de force* of doing so in this particular case successfully we impute to him the even more difficult feat of having dispensed with the aid of scenery. His scenery is exactly the absence of scenery; he has placed his two lovers in the mere immensity of sea and sky, so that they seem suspended in a gray, windy void. We see Yann half the time in the perfect blank of fog and darkness. A writer with a story to tell that is not very fresh usually ekes it out by referring as much as possible to surrounding objects. But in this misty medium there are almost no surrounding objects to refer to, and their isolation gives Yann and Gaud a kind of heroic greatness. I hasten to add that, of course, the author would not have conjured so well had he not been an incomparable painter of the sea. The book closes with a passage of strange and admirable eloquence, which it seems to me that no critic speaking of it has a right to omit to quote. I should say, as a preliminary, that in the course of the tale Yann Gaos, "chaffed" by his comrades on the question of his having a sweetheart and marrying her, has declared that for him there is no woman, no wife, no bride, none but the ocean to which he is already betrothed. Also that a vivid and touching incident (as the figure is also itself wonderfully charming) is that of the young fisherman Sylvestre Moan, a cousin of Gaud and a great friend, though younger, of Yann, who, called to serve in the navy, is mortally wounded at Tonquin, and, on the fetid transport that brings him home, dies, suffocating, in the tropics. The author relates how he is buried on the way, in a rank, bright cemetery, during a short disembarkment at Singapore.

"Yann never came home. One August night, out there off the coast of Iceland, in the midst of a great fury of sound, were celebrated his nuptials with the sea—with the sea who of old had also been his nurse. She had made him a strong and broad-chested youth, and then had taken him in his magnificent manhood for herself alone. A deep mystery had enveloped their monstrous nuptials. Dusky veils all the while had been shaken above them, curtains inflated and twisted, stretched there to hide the feast; and the bride gave voice continually, made her loudest horrible noise to smother the cries. He, remembering Gaud, his wife of flesh, had defended himself, struggling like a giant, against this spouse who was the grave, until the moment when he let himself go, his arms open to receive her, with a great, deep cry like the death-roar of a bull, his mouth already full of water, his arms open, stretched and stiff forever. And they were all at his wedding—all those whom he had bidden of old, all except Sylvestre, who, poor fellow, had gone off to sleep in enchanted gardens far away on the other side of the earth."

If it be then a matter of course in France that a fresh talent should present its possessor mainly as one more *raffiné* in the observation of external things, and also, I think I may add, as one more pessimist in regard to the nature of man and of woman, and if such a presumption appears to have been confirmed by an examination of Pierre Loti, in spite of the effort of poor Yves to cultivate his will and of the mutual tenderness of Yann and Gaud, our conclusion, all the same, will not have escaped the necessity of taking into account the fact that there still seems an inexhaustible life for writers who obey this particular inspiration. The Nemesis remains very much what I

attempted to suggest its being at the beginning of these remarks, but somehow the writers over whom it hovers enjoy
none the less remarkable health on the side on which they are
strong. If they have almost nothing to show us in the way of
the operation of character, the possibilities of conduct, the
part played in the world by the *idea* (you would never guess,
either from Pierre Loti or from M. Guy de Maupassant, that
the idea has any force or any credit in the world); if man, for
them, is the simple sport of fate, with suffering for his main
sign—either suffering or one particular satisfaction, always
the same—their affirmation of all this is still, on the whole,
the most complete affirmation that the novel at present offers
us. They have on their side the accident, if accident it be, that
they never cease to be artists. They will keep this advantage
till the optimists of the hour, the writers for whom the life of
the soul is equally real and visible (lends itself to effects and
triumphs, challenges the power to "render"), begin to seem
to them formidable competitors. On that day it will be very
interesting to see what line they take, whether they will throw
up the battle, surrendering honorably, or attempt a change of
base. Many intelligent persons hold that for the French a
change of base is impossible and that they are either what
they incessantly show themselves or nothing. This view, of
course, derives sanction from that awkward condition which
I have mentioned as attached to the work of those among
them who are most conspicuous—the fact that their attempts
to handle the life of the spirit are comparatively so ineffectual.
On the other hand, it is terribly compromising when those
who do handle the life of the spirit with the manner of experience fail to make *their* affirmation complete, fail to make us
take them seriously as artists, and even go so far (some of
them are capable of that) as to introduce the ruinous suggestion that there is perhaps some essential reason (I scarcely
know how to say it) why observers who are of that way of
feeling should be a little weak in the conjuring line. To be
even a little weak in representation is, of course, practically
and for artistic purposes, to be what schoolboys call a duffer,
and I merely glance, shuddering, at such a possibility. What
would be *their* Nemesis, what penalty would such a group
have incurred in their failure to rebut triumphantly so dam-

aging an imputation? Who would then have to stand from under? It is not Pierre Loti, at any rate, who makes the urgency of these questions a matter only for the materialists (as it is convenient to call them) to consider. He only adds to our suspicion that, for good or for evil, they have still an irrepressible life, and he does so the more notably that, in his form and seen as a whole, he is a renovator, and, as I may say, a refresher. He plays from his own bat, imitating no one, not even nearly or remotely, to my sense—though I have heard the charge made—Châteaubriand. He arrives with his bundle of impressions, but they have been independently gathered in the world, not in the school, and it is a coincidence that they are of the same order as the others, expressed in their admirable personal way and with an indifference to the art of transitions which is at once one of the most striking cases of literary irresponsibility that I know and one of the finest of ingratiation. He has settled the question of his own *superficies* (even in the pathos of the sacred reunion of his lovers in "Pêcheur d'Islande" there is something inconvertibly carnal), but he has not settled the other, the general question of how long and how far accomplished and exclusive—practically exclusive—impressionism will yet go, with its vulture on its back and feeding on it. I hope I appear not to speak too apocalyptically in saying that the problem is still there to minister to our interest and perhaps even a little to our anxiety.

Fortnightly Review, May 1888
Reprinted in *Essays in London and Elsewhere*, 1893

PIERRE LOTI

I MAY AS WELL ADMIT at the outset that in speaking of Pierre Loti I give way to an inclination of the irresistible sort, express indeed a lively obligation. I am conscious of owing him that amount and that kind of pleasure as to which hesitation resides only in the difficulty of statement. He has been for me, from the hour of my making his acquaintance, one of the joys of the time, and the fact moreover of his being of the time has often, to my eyes, made it seem to suffer less

from the presence of writers less delightful yet more acclaimed. It is a part of the joy I speak of that, having once for
all, at the beginning, caused the critical sense thoroughly to
vibrate, he has ever since then let it alone, brought about in
my mind a state of acceptance, a state of gratitude, in which
I have been content not to discriminate. Critically, on first
knowing him, I surrendered—for it has always seemed to me
that the inner chamber of taste opens only to that key; but,
the surrender being complete—the chamber never again
closed—I feel that, like King Amasis with the ring, I have
thrown the key into the deep. He is extremely unequal and
extremely imperfect. He is familiar with both ends of the scale
of taste. I am not sure even that on the whole his talent has
gained with experience as much as was to have been expected,
that his earlier years have not been those in which he was
most to endear himself. But these things have made little difference to a reader so committed to an affection.

It has been a very simple case. At night all cats are grey,
and I have liked him so much in general that there has always
been a perch, a margin left when the special case has for the
moment cut away a little of the ground. The love of letters
renders us no greater service—certainly opens to us no
greater satisfaction—than in putting us from time to time
under some such charm. There need never be a fear, I think,
of its doing so too often. When the charm, in such a manner,
fixes itself, what has happened is that the effect, the operative
gift, has become to us simply a value, and that an experience
more or less bitter has taught us never, in literature, to sacrifice any value we may have been fortunate enough to light
upon. Such discoveries are too happy, such values too great.
They do for us what nothing else does. There are other
charms and other surrenders, but those have their action in
another air. What the mind feels in any form of magic is a
particular extension of the contact with life, and no two forms
give us exactly the same. Every artist who really touches us
becomes in this way an individual instrument, the fiddler, the
improviser of an original tune. The inspiration may sometimes fail, the notes sound weak or false; but to break, on
that account, the fiddle across one's knee is surely—given, as

we look about the much-mixed field, the other "values"—a strange æsthetic economy.

II.

I read and relish him whenever he appears, but his earlier things are those to which I most return. It took some time, in those years, quite to make him out—he was so strange a mixture for readers of our tradition. He was a "sailor-man" and yet a poet, a poet and yet a sailor-man. To a marked division of these functions we had always been accustomed, looking as little for sensibility in the seaman as perhaps for seamanship in the man of emotion. So far as we were at all conscious of the uses of sensibility it was not to the British or the American tar that we were in the habit of applying for it. Tobias Smollett, Captain Marryat, Tom Cringle, Fenimore Cooper had taught us another way, and in general our enjoyment of what we artlessly term adventure had not been associated, either as a fact or as an idea, with the privilege of a range of feeling. There was from the first in Loti the experience of the navigator, and yet there was the faculty, the necessity of expression. The experience had doubtless not been prodigious, but it had been at least of a sort that among writers of our race has mostly, for some reason, seemed positively to preclude expression. He introduced confusion, as I have elsewhere had occasion to say, into our assumption, so consecrated by time, that adventures are mainly for those who lack the fiddle-bow and the fiddle-bow all for those condemned to chamber-music. This was his period of most beautiful production—the period of *Mon Frère Yves*, *Pêcheur d'Islande*, *Fleurs d'Ennui*, *Aziyadé*, *Le Roman d'un Spahi*, *Le Mariage de Loti*; which are not here enumerated in their order of appearance. They presented themselves as the literary recreations—flowers of reminiscence and imagination, not always flowers of lassitude—of a young officer in the navy, a native of Rochefort and of old Huguenot race, whose private name has so completely lost itself in his public that I shall mention him but this once as M. Julien Viaud. They made their full mark only on the publication of *Mon Frère Yves*, but from that moment Loti was placed.

I hasten to add that from that moment also the sea-rover has been less visible in him than the man of expression; without detriment, however, to the immense good fortune of his having betimes, in irresponsible youth, possessed himself of the mystery of the sea. The sense of it and the love of it, with the admirable passion they make, are the background of most of his work, and of all French writers of the day he is the one from whom Paris, with its screen of many folds, least shuts off the rest of the globe. He mentions Paris not even to curse it, and the rest of the globe—but mainly the watery wastes— has been his hunting-ground. It is largely in fact as if he had been kept afloat by the very reasons that conduce to the frequent disembarkment of the Englishman in quest of impressions. He had in these years, as a Frenchman, fewer places to land. When he did land, however, the impressions came thick and are mainly presented in the intensely personal form. They are autobiographic without reserve, for reserve, in spite of his extraordinary faculty of selection and compression, his special genius for summarising, is not his strong point. Whenever Loti landed, in short, he made love, and whenever he made love he appears to have told of it. That would be our main stick to beat him with if his principal use for us had been to inspire us—as I believe it has inspired some readers—with the desire to beat. The limits of that desire on my own part I have sufficiently hinted at, and I feel that I should have had no use of him at all had I not at an early stage arrived at some sort of adequate view of his necessity for "telling." It is the telling, above all, I judge, that is the lion in the path of those whom he displeases. I have never supposed, at any rate, that we can enjoy the special gift of others altogether on terms made by ourselves; it seems to me that when such a gift is real we should take it in any way we can get it—take it and be thankful. Of course—by the most blessed of all laws—we are always free not to take, not even to read, and I dare say that for many persons the non-perusal of reminiscences such as these constitutes a positive pleasure. There are writers, there are voyagers who tell nothing, and for the best of reasons. Loti's singular power to tell is exactly his value, and to attempt to make a law for it might easily be, for readers and critics, a rash adventure. His striking of the notes we delight in may be, for all we know, conditioned on his striking of others we don't. And then—and then: what can one say after all but that we leave him his liberty? Not that we would leave it to everyone. There are sympathies, in short, and impunities; so that I have been careful to make with the erotics both of *Le Mariage de Loti* and of *Madame Chrysanthème* such terms as would not spoil for me the rest of the message. This rest, in Loti, has always one meaning. It is the part *not* about his love-making.

We are most of all free from care, accordingly, in those of his volumes in which the story he has to tell is the story of someone else—the delightful brother Yves, the magnificent Yann of Brittany, Ramuntcho the bold young Basque, or even the doleful little hero of *Matelot*. It is difficult not to regret that these stories of someone else, all with so special a beauty, are not the most numerous in the list; I would gladly have given for another *Pêcheur d'Islande*, indeed for another *Ramuntcho* or another *Matelot*, a dozen things of the complexion of *L'Exilée*, of *Fantôme d'Orient*, of *Le Roman d'un Enfant*. In *L'Exilée* he "tells" with a vengeance and quite too much; too much, I mean, of what he feels for the troubled, misplaced, accomplished Queen of whose splendid hospitality and confidence the volume is a record: too much also, doubtless, of what he knows of the personal appearance and habits and private affairs—oh, of a delicacy!—of her principal lady-in-waiting. These are Loti's mystifying moments, other specimens of which confront us in the singular publicity given by *Le Livre de la Pitié et de la Mort* to the last illness, the last hours, the laying out and interment of one of the nearest and most loved of his female relatives. Stranger than strange as well, in the pages in question, are the simplicity and solemnity of his expatiation on the favourite cats and other inmates, the domestic arrangements and intimate trifles of the home of his youth. It is odd that a mere matter of shading—for in such things it is only that—should make so much difference; but these are the errors as to which it may be said not so much that the hand would be stayed in the commission of them by the presence of a sense of humour as that this presence would in general have rendered them insupposable. They proceed after all largely, from one of the most marked features of the French literary mind of the day—that intense professionalism which is in its turn the result of conscious and cultivated art. To work as hard as the countrymen of Loti for the most part work their language—work their perceptions, their emotions and sensibilities, their sense of form, of style, of the shade, the effect, their analysis alike of subject and of tone—to do all this is to thrust the torch assuredly into every corner of experience and to drop every grain of observation into the literary mill.

Nothing, in consequence, is more striking than the failure of any sense—as we ourselves understand it—of a division between the public and the private: the writer becomes primarily a writer and ceases in the same proportion to be anything else. His soul, his life and its pulsations are mere wheels and springs in the machinery of expression, and the man, as a man, can treat himself to no distinctive experience, reserve no garden-plot for wasteful human use. There are precious kinds of silence that he ceases to be able to afford, luxuries of simple choice, happy failures of logic, for ever banished from his budget. Full of suggestion on this head, for instance, is the manner in which the brothers Goncourt live, in their extraordinary *Journal*, up to the last penny of that part of their income which might have been supposed to be most peculiarly personal; paying it out, on the spot, without, as one may say, so much as passing it through their moral bank. The French writer, on the other hand—I speak most, of course, of the creators, as we perhaps a trifle fatuously call them— can afford an expenditure of expression, particularly in prose, that causes his English-speaking brother to appear by contrast to carry on a very small business. The literary establishment of the latter is indeed in comparison but meagrely mounted. Such is far from the case with Loti's, which offers perhaps, through the peculiar profusion of the personal note, as striking an example as can be named of the rattling spiritual *train de maison* to which I allude. I am lost in admiration of such an economy; wonderstruck, as I reflect, as I measure it, at his employment of his means. Three fourths of his work are the most charming egotism; the portion that is finest, the four or five more or less constructed and conducted tales, is the minor portion. And yet the egotism lives and blooms too, scatters the rarest fragrance and throws out pages like great strange flowers. It all comes from the fact that he uses all his impressions. There are many impressions he never has, but he gives us for all they are worth those with which he is favoured—never misses them on the wing nor shirks the catching; and of the lightest, loosest yet cunningest interweaving of these his curious prose mainly consists. It consists of the happiest conceivable utterance of feelings about aspects. What he may well have assured himself at the start was of his probably being one of the persons in the world to whom aspects had most to say. Wonderful and beautiful is the language in which they speak to him, and that language, as he has reported it, has made his literary fortune. Knowledge of the finer, or at any rate the unpersonal sort, reflection of the deeper, the power to compose, in the larger sense, or truly to invent, have had the smallest hand in the business. At the same time he has been subject to the law that nothing in art, however capricious, can be done without love, and he has continually loved two things—one of them the great watery globe and the other the nature of man.

These two things are what, in an exquisite way, both *Pêcheur d'Islande* and *Mon Frère Yves* consist of; the first the simplest, deepest little story of love and death, the other the largest, tenderest, brightest picture of friendship and life. The persons concerned are all sailor-folk, and the setting of the drama—so far as not the great void of the sea-spaces, against which his figures magnificently stand up—is the landscape and colouring, the village scenery of Brittany, for which no one has had so fine and sincere a touch. With however much appreciation any lover of Loti may once have spoken of these books, there can never fail to be a freshness in coming back to them; they belong so to the class of the happiest literary things. And yet, essentially, one must speak of them mainly for old acquaintance—without the power of really naming their charm. The beauty of the author at his best is something too unnameable, something that seems a kind of secret between himself and his reader. That indeed perhaps is what we feel for all the authors who give us the finer joy: we feel it to be quite enough if *they* know what we like them for. When others don't know, that, somehow, at moments, practically adds to the reason. None of the famous "love-stories" of the world are, at any rate, more charged than this history of Yann and Gaud with the particular exquisite, the mixture of beauty and misery, that we require of the type—which, to commend itself to the right corner of our memory, must always have its final terror and tragedy. Made up of two main forces, human passion, human hope and effort, pain and defeat, and the wonderfully vivified presence of nature in ambush and waiting only to devour, the whole thing hangs together and drives home its effect with an admirable artistic economy. Loti's manner is so all his own—the manner of intimate confidence in his reader, of talk, of anecdote, of sequences neglected and lost, a part of the work obligingly done for him—that quite equally at his best and at his middling he offers the constant interest of a thorough concealment of his means. I can imagine at once no more unqualified success and no model more to be deprecated. The only thing possible was to *be* Loti; let us pray to be protected from any attempt to emulate him by any shorter cut. He offers himself expressly enough as the least literary of writers, and one grants him that without a protest so long as he remains one of the most literary of pleasures. He is of course only what is vulgarly called "deep," and at the very bottom of his depth—like the purse in the consciousness of the pickpocket looking innocently the other way—lies the finest little knowledge of exactly how to do it. A small gold thread, perfectly palpable to himself, guides him through his gaps and breaks, the sweet wild garden of his conspicuous want of plan. This serves him extraordinarily in *Mon Frère Yves*, in which there is so much delightful clearness and so little concatenation. There are times indeed when we feel him to hold his happy instinct on terms scarcely fair; it does so for him whatever he wants and yet gives, on our part, a positive air of pedantry to all technical inquiries.

What touches deepest in his tales—and indeed in his every page—is, as should be mentioned without delay, the general pity of almost everything. It need hardly be said that he is not of the complexion of the moralist, and the light leading him through the tribulations of his people is as little as possible any reference to what they "had better" have done. We can never at all imagine them to have done anything different, so little can it come up for them to follow anything but their immediate social instincts. When they pay for that only in sorrow or shame, this becomes precisely for ourselves the spring of an added interest. Loti's philosophy is the philosophy of imagination—of likes and dislikes, of indulgence for weakness and compassion for accident, of kindly tolerance for unguarded or unbalanced good faith. His people have come into the world mainly to feel, and he, upon their heels, mainly to feel *for* them. So, with all this, he feels even more than they. That is his most individual note—that he has carried his sensibility, so unquenched and on the whole so little vulgarised, so much about the great globe. The subjects of it in his two earlier novels and in *Matelot* and *Ramuntcho* are the simplest of simple folk, the poorest of the poor. They are all young and fresh and strong, all beautiful and natural, kind and stricken; they earn their living in labour and sorrow, and their joys are the scant breathing-times in the hard battle of life. The humility of their condition is perhaps what most of all—given the admirable tenderness of his treatment of them—makes us think of Loti as the last of the *raffinés*. It gives the measure of his admirable sense of sociability, gives the natural note to the delicacy of his human tone, to all his heart-softenings and his cultivation of pathos. The strange little tale of *Matelot* is nothing in the world but heart-softening; I call it strange for the simple reason of its being *a priori* so unexpected a stroke on the part of a member of his profession. It depicts the career of a small sensitive sailor-boy who feels everything really too much and in regard to whom we are ourselves, doubtless, in this way—though it is almost brutal to say so—drawn on to participations that are excessive. He dies, of course, in sight of home, of a fever contracted in torrid eastern seas, and the whole affair is but a merciless performance on the finest fiddlestring. Yet the good Lotist, as I may say, can only swallow *Matelot* whole: I should even guage his goodness by his capacity to do so. But if the thing is irresistible it is also calculated, transparent; it unscrews the stopper of tears with a positively audible creak. What then is the reason that its tone is exquisite and its pathos practically profound? I am glad to suppose the answer to such a question to lie beyond my analysis. The reason is where the best reason always is, in the very air of the picture—of which a particular breath, for instance, is in the eloquence, the rare delicacy of presentation, of the episode of the young man's innocent friendship, blighted by fate, with the mild Madeleine of Quebec, the charm of such a passage—Loti at his melancholy happiest—as that in which the author strikes the last note of this adventure. "So it had come to their loving each other with a tenderness that was equally pure for each. She, ignorant of the things of love and reading her Bible every night; she, destined to keep her useless freshness and youth for a few more springtimes not less pale and then to grow old and fade in the narrowing round of these same streets and these same walls. He, already spoiled with kisses and with other arms, having the world for his changing abode and called to start off perhaps to-morrow, never again to come back—only to leave his body in distant seas."

Fully characteristic of Loti is this mention of his sailor-boy as "spoiled"—spoiled by contacts after all supposedly familiar to sailor-boys. That is but a touch of his usual pessimism, and practically our comment on it as we read consists in not believing it: being spoiled is a process his delightful people are in general so little the worse for. The reason of which, I take it, just brings us close to the general explanation of the author's largest magic, the beauty of his dealings with sun and wind and space. These are the elements with which, whether spoiled or not, his characters mainly live and which he renders for them with a breadth that never fails. They remain somehow, throughout, globe-creatures, with the great arch of the sky for two-thirds of their consciousness, becoming no uglier by anything that may happen to them than birds become by the traps and missiles of man. If they were mewed and stewed in close rooms, in dark towns, it might be a different matter. None of them circulate with more ease and grace than Ramuntcho, the hero of his latest tale, expert, in his character of bright young Basque, at Pyreneean tennis, Pyreneean smuggling and climbing, Pyreneean love-making, too, not least. If here and there, from book to book, the charm had suffered a chill, in *Ramuntcho* it all comes back—the thing is wholly admirable. And yet what is it?—what that would commend it to readers who like their mouthful of "story" big? Perfect is the bravery of the author's indifference to these and possibly the thing that I most like him for. It is impossible not to admire a man whose general assurance and his faith in his particular star permit him to set sail with so small a provision of plot. The beauty of such an outfit as Loti's is in its positively never leaving him without a subject. Cast ashore on strands the most desert, he is sufficiently nourished by the delicacy of his senses. They play in and out of *Ramuntcho* with the effect of the chequering of the sun in a wood, and our enjoyment of the tale—one can speak at least of one's own—is simply our recognition of the intensity of all the presences. We look into the eyes of the people, we sit with them in the boat, and spring with them on the turf, and racket with them at the game, and sweat with them in the great hot sun, smelling the woods and tasting the wine and hearing the cries—enjoying at every turn the colour and the rustle and the light. We live with their simplicity and we generally love their ways. Above all we love their loves, and there is no one like Loti for making us fond of his lovers. So moments and pictures stand out for us, all with the freshness of odours, contacts, the tone of white walls and brown interiors caught, in glimpses, as we take our ascent through chestnut-woods. It is all experience and memory, and yet all glamour and grace.

III.

In the volumes, the most numerous, that are simply the record of impressions, of change of place, we come back perpetually to that tremor of the fiddlestring. No other word renders so well the fine vibration in Loti of what he sees and what he makes us see. This fineness is his charming quality and arrived at without affectation or contortion. The spasm of the descriptive alternates in the case of too many other travellers with mere visual apathy, and our choice is on the whole mainly between those who are without observation and those who are without expression. But to Loti things come with the sun and the wind and the chance of the spot and the moment; his perception is a sensitive plate on which aspects are forever at play. He is the companion, beyond all others, of my own selection, for the simple reason that none other shows me so easily such far and strange things. He has readers, of a certainty, whom he more than consoles for the humdrum nature of their fate; as positively, with this affection for him, it is better to have had no adventures of one's own. It is simpler—and I say so quite without irony—not to have travelled, not to have trodden with heavier feet the ground over which we follow him. It is of the scenes I shall never visit that I like to read descriptions, and nothing, for that matter, would induce me to interfere with any impression happily received from him. The description in fact for the most part only mystifies and irritates when memory is really in possession. I prefer his memory to my own, and am ready to think it no hard rule of life to have had, in my chair, to take so much of the more wonderful world from a little lemon-covered book. We can only, at the best, be transported, and the author of *Propos d'Exil*, of *Au Maroc*, of *Japoneries d'Automne* delivers us infallibly, by a process of his own, at the right door in the wall. He has not been an explorer and is not of that race, but his perception so penetrates that he has only to take me round the corner to give me the sense of exploring. I have been assured that *Madame Chrysanthème* is as preposterous, as benighted a picture of Japan as if a stranger, disembarking at Liverpool, had confined his acquaintance with England to a few weeks spent in disreputable female society in a vulgar suburb of that city. But the moral of this truth, if a truth it be, would really seem all to the writer's advantage: I should delight in any observer in whom the gift of observation, the sense of appearances, might be such as to make Birkenhead, say, give him, and by his delightful intervention give *me*, a picture so charming and so living. Whether Loti tells us or no what we want is a question that we certainly never put; what we want becomes for the time just whatever he has to tell us. To turn him over again as I write these lines is, none the less, scarcely to know where, for examples, to pick and choose. We always meet side by side, to begin with, specimens of his innocence and specimens of his craft. This collection of *Figures et Choses qui Passaient*, opens with a succession of pages embodying, on the occasion of the death of the baby of his servant, the sort of emotion that we others flatter ourselves we keep—when we have it to keep—veiled and hushed; but it goes on to the admirable *Trois Journées de Guerre*, an impression of the French attack on the Anam forts in the summer of 1883, which gives the reader exactly the sense of blinking, wondering, perspiring participation in the presence of endless queerness—the sense of seeing, hearing, touching, smelling the whole hot, grotesque little horror. No one approaches Loti for reconstituting such an episode as this—and in the most off-hand, jotted, anecdotic way—as a presented personal impression. Such notes are doubtless journalism, but journalism exquisite. "In the midst of the morning light, which was fresh and blue, these flames" (a village was on fire) " were of an extraordinary red; they cast no light, but were as dark as blood. You saw them twisted and mixing, saw everything instantly consumed; the smoke-clouds, intensely black, diffused a sharp musty stench. On the roofs of the pagodas, in the midst of their devilries, among the darts of all the forked tails and outspread claws, the rush of the fire-tongues seemed at first natural enough. But all the little plaster monsters had begun to crackle and burst, scattering to right and left the blue porcelain of their scales and the crystal balls of their wicked eyes, then had crumbled, with the beams, into the gaping holes of the temples."

Loti's East is, throughout, of all Easts the most beguiling, though, for the most part—unless perhaps in the case of *Au Maroc*, where he appears to have been peculiarly initiated—it seldom ceases to be the usual, accessible East, the East of Cook, of tickets and time-tables, of the English and American swarm. The swarm, at any rate, never taints Loti's air, and we remain, in his caravan, as disconnected from everything else as it need occur to us to desire. If he has been only where they all have been, he has at least brought back what they all have not, what indeed, for my imagination, none other has done—the fine, strange flower of the thing, the element that continues to haunt us, the sweetest, saddest secret it whispers to the mind. When the innumerable others—further pushers, doubtless, and sharper penetrators—shall offer us notes of this quality, then, only then, shall we grant that they have been as far. It would of course never be easy to find in any caravan a pilgrim with so absolute an esteem for his own emotions. Loti belongs to the precious few who are not afraid of being ridiculous; a condition not in itself perhaps constituting positive wealth, but speedily raised to that value when the naught in question is on the right side of certain other figures. His attitude is that whatever, on the spot and in the connection, he may happen to feel is suggestive, interesting and human, so that his duty with regard to it can only be essentially to utter it. The duty of not being ridiculous is one to which too many travellers of our own race assign the high position that he attributes to right expression, to right expression alone. It has led him, this gallant point of honour, to say, at Jerusalem—in the volume with that title—too many things about himself, even to appear indeed to have made the wondrous pilgrimage too much in search of a presentable figure which is not quite the one we might have guessed. Yet here too his sympathetic "self" still includes a more sensible vision of a hundred other and very different things than many a record—of the type that leaves us unstirred—accompanied with more precautions. *Jerusalem*, on the other hand, I admit, is a trifle spoiled for the rigid Lotist by being, in all the list, the book that gives out most wandering airs, most echoes already heard, of "literature." That the author has not been from beginning to end intensely literary let me not for a moment do his prodigious legerdemain the wrong to suggest, for his particular shade of the natural was surely never arrived at without much choosing and comparing. His lightness is the lightness of knowledge and his ease the ease of practice. But he covers his tracks, as I have hinted, consummately; it is the perfect pointing of the watch without, discoverably, the mechanism. In *Jerusalem* we seem a little to hear the tick.

But I have been reading again *Au Maroc*, in which, figuratively as well as literally, there is not the least rumble of wheels. The author here wanders over his subject with a step as independent of the usual literary macadam as the march of his caravan, in the roadless land, found itself perforce of any other; and nothing is more delightful than to keep him company through such a mixture of wondrous matter and incalculable talk. Such a volume as this expresses him at his best, for the special adventure gives most chance to his admirable curiosity, his undiscourageable passion for putting on as many as possible of the queer forms of consciousness encountered in other races and under other skies, of living—though not perhaps for so very long—into conditions exotic and uncomfortable, the inner sense of the strangeness of which he more beguilingly than ever communicates. The inner sense seems to me always to begin where the finest *flair* of most travellers stops, and this exquisite *Au Maroc* is all made up of it. His evocation of the almost unutterable Fez, his description of the days spent there apart from the other members of the mission in which he was included, his picture, perhaps even more, of his further push to the gruesome, melancholy Mekinez—the warm vividness of these things takes on for the fond reader the intensity of some private romance. Loti, in short, becomes thus—to put it only at that, and where his wandering sensibility is concerned—the rarest of tale-tellers. He drinks, in this character, so deep of impressions that places where he has passed are left dry: there are none, I repeat, we pay him the questionable compliment of wishing to visit after him. We are content to go nowhere—which is a much greater tribute. When I say we are content I mean perhaps we are determined, for he leaves us, in a way all his own, with a fear of finding strange things themselves not so true as *he* is true to their surprising essence. Droll, in a manner, yet without injury to their charm, are the pages of his attempt— condemned, one must recognise, to a success mainly superficial—to live a little the life of any corner that happens to strike him as extraordinary and in particular to dress in its draperies, droll perhaps above all his frank delight in these last aids to illusion and very expressive, at all events, of the joy of masquerading as an Oriental that appears to have been from the first his harmless revenge on his having been born a mere Huguenot. This he was not the man to think sufficient. We forgive any millinery that still leaves the standpoint of the painter as free as, for instance, in such a passage as this: "Toward two in the afternoon a halt in some place or other, from which this image remains with me: the perpetual boundless plain, flowered over as never a garden, and alone there, a little way off, our old exhausted Caïd down on his knees at prayer. We are in a zone of white daisies mixed with pink poppies. The old man, close to his end, has an earthen face, a beard as blanched as lichen, a dress of the same freshness of colour as the poppies and daisies around, the kaftan of pink cloth showing through the long white mufflers. His white horse, with its high red saddle, browses beside him and plunges its head into the grass. He himself, half sunk among the flowers, the white and pink flowers that are circled, beneath the deep blue of the summer sky, by the infinite desert of the immense flowery level—he himself, prostrate on the earth in which he will soon be laid, begs for the mercy of Allah with the fervour of prayer given by the feeling of annihilation at hand." That is pure, essential Loti—poetry in observation, felicity in sadness.

Introduction to *Impressions*, by Pierre Loti.
Westminster: Archibald Constable & Co., 1898

Guy de Maupassant

I

THE FIRST ARTISTS, in any line, are doubtless not those whose general ideas about their art are most often on their lips—those who most abound in precept, apology, and formula and can best tell us the reasons and the philosophy of things. We know the first usually by their energetic practice, the constancy with which they apply their principles, and the serenity with which they leave us to hunt for their secret in the illustration, the concrete example. None the less it often happens that a valid artist utters his mystery, flashes upon us for a moment the light by which he works, shows us the rule by which he holds it just that he should be measured. This accident is happiest, I think, when it is soonest over; the shortest explanations of the products of genius are the best, and there is many a creator of living figures whose friends, however full of faith in his inspiration, will do well to pray for him when he sallies forth into the dim wilderness of theory. The doctrine is apt to be so much less inspired than the work, the work is often so much more intelligent than the doctrine. M. Guy de Maupassant has lately traversed with a firm and rapid step a literary crisis of this kind; he has clambered safely up the bank at the further end of the morass. If he has relieved himself in the preface to *Pierre et Jean*, the last-published of his tales, he has also rendered a service to his friends; he has not only come home in a recognisable plight, escaping gross disaster with a success which even his extreme good sense was far from making in advance a matter of course, but he has expressed in intelligible terms (that by itself is a ground of felicitation) his most general idea, his own sense of his direction. He has arranged, as it were, the light in which he wishes to sit. If it is a question of attempting, under however many disadvantages, a sketch of him, the critic's business therefore is simplified: there will be no difficulty in placing him, for he himself has chosen the spot, he has made the chalk-mark on the floor.

I may as well say at once that in dissertation M. de Maupassant does not write with his best pen; the philosopher in
his composition is perceptibly inferior to the story-teller. I
would rather have written half a page of *Boule de Suif* than
the whole of the introduction to Flaubert's *Letters to Madame
Sand*; and his little disquisition on the novel in general, attached to that particular example of it which he has just put
forth,* is considerably less to the point than the masterpiece
which it ushers in. In short, as a commentator M. de Maupassant is slightly common, while as an artist he is wonderfully rare. Of course we must, in judging a writer, take one
thing with another, and if I could make up my mind that M.
de Maupassant is weak in theory, it would almost make me
like him better, render him more approachable, give him the
touch of softness that he lacks, and show us a human flaw.
The most general quality of the author of *La Maison Tellier*
and *Bel-Ami*, the impression that remains last, after the others
have been accounted for, is an essential hardness—hardness
of form, hardness of nature; and it would put us more at ease
to find that if the fact with him (the fact of execution) is so
extraordinarily definite and adequate, his explanations, after
it, were a little vague and sentimental. But I am not sure that
he must even be held foolish to have noticed the race of critics: he is at any rate so much less foolish than several of that
fraternity. He has said his say concisely and as if he were saying it once for all. In fine, his readers must be grateful to him
for such a passage as that in which he remarks that whereas
the public at large very legitimately says to a writer, "Console
me, amuse me, terrify me, make me cry, make me dream, or
make me think," what the sincere critic says is, "Make me
something fine in the form that shall suit you best, according
to your temperament." This seems to me to put into a nutshell the whole question of the different classes of fiction,
concerning which there has recently been so much discourse.
There are simply as many different kinds as there are persons
practising the art, for if a picture, a tale, or a novel be a direct
impression of life (and that surely constitutes its interest and

* *Pierre et Jean*. Paris: Ollendorff, 1888.

value), the impression will vary according to the plate that takes it, the particular structure and mixture of the recipient.

I am not sure that I know what M. de Maupassant means when he says, "The critic shall appreciate the result only according to the nature of the effort; he has no right to concern himself with tendencies." The second clause of that observation strikes me as rather in the air, thanks to the vagueness of the last word. But our author adds to the definiteness of his contention when he goes on to say that any form of the novel is simply a vision of the world from the standpoint of a person constituted after a certain fashion, and that it is therefore absurd to say that there is, for the novelist's use, only one reality of things. This seems to me commendable, not as a flight of metaphysics, hovering over bottomless gulfs of controversy, but, on the contrary, as a just indication of the vanity of certain dogmatisms. The particular way we see the world is our particular illusion about it, says M. de Maupassant, and this illusion fits itself to our organs and senses; our receptive vessel becomes the furniture of *our* little plot of the universal consciousness.

"How childish, moreover, to believe in reality, since we each carry our own in our thought and in our organs. Our eyes, our ears, our sense of smell, of taste, differing from one person to another, create as many truths as there are men upon earth. And our minds, taking instruction from these organs, so diversely impressed, understand, analyse, judge, as if each of us belonged to a different race. Each one of us, therefore, forms for himself an illusion of the world, which is the illusion poetic, or sentimental, or joyous, or melancholy, or unclean, or dismal, according to his nature. And the writer has no other mission than to reproduce faithfully this illusion, with all the contrivances of art that he has learned and has at his command. The illusion of beauty, which is a human convention! The illusion of ugliness, which is a changing opinion! The illusion of truth, which is never immutable! The illusion of the ignoble, which attracts so many! The great artists are those who make humanity accept their particular illusion. Let us, therefore, not get angry with any one theory, since every theory is the generalised expression of a temperament asking itself questions."

What is interesting in this is not that M. de Maupassant happens to hold that we have no universal measure of the truth, but that it is the last word on a question of art from a writer who is rich in experience and has had success in a very rare degree. It is of secondary importance that our impression should be called, or not called, an illusion; what is excellent is that our author has stated more neatly than we have lately seen it done that the value of the artist resides in the clearness with which he gives forth that impression. His particular organism constitutes a *case*, and the critic is intelligent in proportion as he apprehends and enters into that case. To quarrel with it because it is not another, which it could not possibly have been without a wholly different outfit, appears to M. de Maupassant a deplorable waste of time. If this appeal to our disinterestedness may strike some readers as chilling (through their inability to conceive of any other form than the one they like—a limitation excellent for a reader but poor for a judge), the occasion happens to be none of the best for saying so, for M. de Maupassant himself precisely presents all the symptoms of a "case" in the most striking way, and shows us how far the consideration of them may take us. Embracing such an opportunity as this, and giving ourselves to it freely, seems to me indeed to be a course more fruitful in valid conclusions, as well as in entertainment by the way, than the more common method of establishing one's own premises. To make clear to ourselves those of the author of *Pierre et Jean*—those to which he is committed by the very nature of his mind—is an attempt that will both stimulate and repay curiosity. There is no way of looking at his work less dry, less academic, for as we proceed from one of his peculiarities to another, the whole horizon widens, yet without our leaving firm ground, and we see ourselves landed, step by step, in the most general questions—those explanations of things which reside in the race, in the society. Of course there are cases and cases, and it is the salient ones that the disinterested critic is delighted to meet.

What makes M. de Maupassant salient is two facts: the first of which is that his gifts are remarkably strong and definite, and the second that he writes directly *from* them, as it were: holds the fullest, the most uninterrupted—I scarcely know what to call it—the boldest communication with them. A case is poor when the cluster of the artist's sensibilities is small, or they themselves are wanting in keenness, or else when the personage fails to admit them—either through ignorance, or diffidence, or stupidity, or the error of a false ideal—to what may be called a legitimate share in his attempt. It is, I think, among English and American writers that this latter accident is most liable to occur; more than the French we are apt to be misled by some convention or other as to the sort of feeler we *ought* to put forth, forgetting that the best one will be the one that nature happens to have given us. We have doubtless often enough the courage of our opinions (when it befalls that we have opinions), but we have not so constantly that of our perceptions. There is a whole side of our perceptive apparatus that we in fact neglect, and there are probably many among us who would erect this tendency into a duty. M. de Maupassant neglects nothing that he possesses; he cultivates his garden with admirable energy; and if there is a flower you miss from the rich parterre, you may be sure that it could not possibly have been raised, his mind not containing the soil for it. He is plainly of the opinion that the first duty of the artist, and the thing that makes him most useful to his fellow-men, is to master his instrument, whatever it may happen to be.

His own is that of the senses, and it is through them alone, or almost alone, that life appeals to him; it is almost alone by their help that he describes it, that he produces brilliant works. They render him this great assistance because they are evidently, in his constitution, extraordinarily alive; there is scarcely a page in all his twenty volumes that does not testify to their vivacity. Nothing could be further from his thought than to disavow them and to minimise their importance. He accepts them frankly, gratefully, works them, rejoices in them. If he were told that there are many English writers who would be sorry to go with him in this, he would, I imagine, staring, say that that is about what was to have been expected of the Anglo-Saxon race, or even that many of them probably could not go with him if they would. Then he would ask how our authors can be so foolish as to sacrifice such a *moyen*, how they can afford to, and exclaim, "They must be pretty works, those they produce, and give a fine, true, complete account of life, with such omissions, such lacunæ!" M. de Maupassant's productions teach us, for instance, that his sense of smell is exceptionally acute—as acute as that of those animals of the field and forest whose subsistence and security depend upon it. It might be thought that he would, as a student of the human race, have found an abnormal development of this faculty embarrassing, scarcely knowing what to do with it, where to place it. But such an apprehension betrays an imperfect conception of his directness and resolution, as well as of his constant economy of means. Nothing whatever prevents him from representing the relations of men and women as largely governed by the scent of the parties. Human life in his pages (would this not be the most general description he would give of it?) appears for the most part as a sort of concert of odours, and his people are perpetually engaged, or he is engaged on their behalf, in sniffing up and distinguishing them, in some pleasant or painful exercise of the nostril. "If everything in life speaks to the nostril, why on earth shouldn't we say so?" I suppose him to inquire; "and what a proof of the empire of poor conventions and hypocrisies, *chez vous autres*, that you should pretend to describe and characterise, and yet take no note (or so little that it comes to the same thing) of that essential sign!"

Not less powerful is his visual sense, the quick, direct discrimination of his eye, which explains the singularly vivid concision of his descriptions. These are never prolonged nor analytic, have nothing of enumeration, of the quality of the observer, who counts the items to be sure he has made up the sum. His eye *selects* unerringly, unscrupulously, almost impudently—catches the particular thing in which the character of the object or the scene resides, and, by expressing it with the artful brevity of a master, leaves a convincing, original picture. If he is inveterately synthetic, he is never more so than in the way he brings this hard, short, intelligent gaze to bear. His vision of the world is for the most part a vision of ugliness, and even when it is not, there is in his easy power to generalise a certain absence of love, a sort of bird's-eye-view contempt. He has none of the superstitions of observation, none of our English indulgences, our tender and often imaginative superficialities. If he glances into a railway carriage bearing its freight into the Parisian suburbs of a summer Sunday, a dozen dreary lives map themselves out in a flash.

"There were stout ladies in farcical clothes, those middle-class goodwives of the *banlieue* who replace the distinction they don't possess by an irrelevant dignity; gentlemen weary of the office, with sallow faces and twisted bodies, and one of their shoulders a little forced up by perpetual bending at work over a table. Their anxious, joyless faces spoke moreover of domestic worries, incessant needs for money, old hopes finally shattered; for they all belonged to the army of poor threadbare devils who vegetate frugally in a mean little plaster house, with a flower-bed for a garden." . . .

Even in a brighter picture, such as the admirable vignette of the drive of Madame Tellier and her companions, the whole thing is an impression, as painters say nowadays, in which the figures are cheap. The six women at the station clamber into a country cart and go jolting through the Norman landscape to the village.

"But presently the jerky trot of the nag shook the vehicle so terribly that the chairs began to dance, tossing up the travellers to right, to left, with movements like puppets, scared grimaces, cries of dismay suddenly interrupted by a more violent bump. They clutched the sides of the trap, their bonnets turned over on to their backs, or upon the nose or the shoulder; and the white horse continued to go, thrusting out his head and straightening the little tail, hairless like that of a rat, with which from time to time he whisked his buttocks. Joseph Rivet, with one foot stretched upon the shaft, the other leg bent under him, and his elbows very high, held the reins and emitted from his throat every moment a kind of cluck which caused the animal to prick up his ears and quicken his pace. On either side of the road the green country stretched away. The colza, in flower, produced in spots a great carpet of undulating yellow, from which there rose a strong, wholesome smell, a smell penetrating and pleasant, carried very far by the breeze. In the tall rye the cornflowers held up their little azure heads, which the women wished to pluck; but M. Rivet refused to stop. Then, in some place, a whole field looked as if it were sprinkled with blood, it was so crowded with poppies. And in the midst of the great level, taking colour in this fashion from the flowers of the soil, the trap passed on with the jog of the white horse, seeming itself to carry a nosegay of richer hues; it disappeared behind the big trees of a farm, to come out again where the foliage stopped and parade afresh through the green and yellow crops, pricked with red or blue, its blazing cartload of women, which receded in the sunshine."

As regards the other sense, the sense *par excellence*, the sense which we scarcely mention in English fiction, and which I am not very sure I shall be allowed to mention in an English periodical, M. de Maupassant speaks for that, and of it, with extraordinary distinctness and authority. To say that it occupies the first place in his picture is to say too little; it covers in truth the whole canvas, and his work is little else but a report of its innumerable manifestations. These manifestations are not, for him, so many incidents of life; they are life itself, they represent the standing answer to any question that we may ask about it. He describes them in detail, with a familiarity and a frankness which leave nothing to be added; I should say with singular truth, if I did not consider that in regard to this article he may be taxed with a certain exaggeration. M. de Maupassant would doubtless affirm that where the empire of the sexual sense is concerned, no exaggeration is possible: nevertheless it may be said that whatever depths may be discovered by those who dig for them, the impression of the human spectacle for him who takes it as it comes has less analogy with that of the monkeys' cage than this admirable writer's account of it. I speak of the human spectacle as we Anglo-Saxons see it—as we Anglo-Saxons pretend we see it, M. de Maupassant would possibly say.

At any rate, I have perhaps touched upon this peculiarity sufficiently to explain my remark that his point of view is almost solely that of the senses. If he is a very interesting case, this makes him also an embarrassing one, embarrassing and mystifying for the moralist. I may as well admit that no writer of the day strikes me as equally so. To find M. de Maupassant a lion in the path—that may seem to some people a singular proof of want of courage; but I think the obstacle will not be made light of by those who have really taken the measure of the animal. We are accustomed to think, we of the English faith, that a cynic is a living advertisement of his errors, especially in proportion as he is a thorough-going one; and M. de Maupassant's cynicism, unrelieved as it is, will not be disposed of off-hand by a critic of a competent literary sense. Such a critic is not slow to perceive, to his no small confusion, that though, judging from usual premises, the author of *Bel-Ami* ought to be a warning, he somehow is not. His baseness, as it pervades him, ought to be written all over him; yet somehow there are there certain aspects—and those commanding, as the house-agents say—in which it is not in the least to be perceived. It is easy to exclaim that if he judges life only from the point of view of the senses, many are the noble and exquisite things that he must leave out. What he leaves out has no claim to get itself considered till after we have done justice to what he takes in. It is this positive side of M. de Maupassant that is most remarkable—the fact that his literary character is so complete and edifying. "Auteur à peu près irréprochable dans un genre qui ne l'est pas," as that excellent critic M. Jules Lemaître says of him, he disturbs us by associating a conscience and a high standard with a temper long synonymous, in our eyes, with an absence of scruples. The situation would be simpler certainly if he were a bad writer; but none the less it is possible, I think, on the whole, to circumvent him, even without attempting to prove that after all he is one.

The latter part of his introduction to *Pierre et Jean* is less felicitous than the beginning, but we learn from it—and this is interesting—that he regards the analytic fashion of telling a story, which has lately begotten in his own country some such remarkable experiments (few votaries as it has attracted among ourselves), as very much less profitable than the simple epic manner which "avoids with care all complicated explanations, all dissertations upon motives, and confines itself to making persons and events pass before our eyes." M. de Maupassant adds that in his view "psychology should be hidden in a book, as it is hidden in reality under the facts of existence. The novel conceived in this manner gains interest, movement, colour, the bustle of life." When it is a question of an artistic process, we must always mistrust very sharp distinctions, for there is surely in every method a little of every other method. It is as difficult to describe an action without glancing at its motive, its moral history, as it is to describe a motive without glancing at its practical consequence. Our history and our fiction are what we do; but it surely is not more easy to determine where what we do begins than to determine where it ends—notoriously a hopeless task. Therefore it would take a very subtle sense to draw a hard and fast line on the borderland of explanation and illustration. If psychology be hidden in life, as, according to M. de Maupassant, it should be in a book, the question immediately comes up, "From whom is it hidden?" From some people, no doubt, but very much less from others; and all depends upon the observer, the nature of one's observation, and one's curiosity. For some people motives, reasons, relations, explanations, are a part of the very surface of the drama, with the footlights beating full upon them. For me an act, an incident, an attitude, may be a sharp, detached, isolated thing, of which I give a full account in saying that in such and such a way it came off. For you it may be hung about with implications, with relations, and conditions as necessary to help you to recognise it as the clothes of your friends are to help you know them in the street. You feel that they would seem strange to you without petticoats and trousers.

M. de Maupassant would probably urge that the right thing is to know, or to guess, how events come to pass, but to say as little about it as possible. There are matters in regard to which he feels the importance of being explicit, but that is not one of them. The contention to which I allude strikes me as rather arbitrary, so difficult is it to put one's finger upon the reason why, for instance, there should be so little mystery about what happened to Christiane Andermatt, in *Mont-Oriol*, when she went to walk on the hills with Paul Brétigny, and so much, say, about the forces that formed her for that gentleman's convenience, or those lying behind any other odd collapse that our author may have related. The rule misleads, and the best rule certainly is the tact of the individual writer, which will adapt itself to the material as the material comes to him. The cause we plead is ever pretty sure to be the cause of our idiosyncrasies, and if M. de Maupassant thinks meanly of "explanations," it is, I suspect, that they come to him in no great affluence. His view of the conduct of man is so simple as scarcely to require them; and indeed so far as they are needed he *is*, virtually, explanatory. He deprecates reference to motives, but there is one, covering an immense ground in his horizon, as I have already hinted, to which he perpetually refers. If the sexual impulse be not a moral antecedent, it is none the less the wire that moves almost all M. de Maupassant's puppets, and as he has not hidden it, I cannot see that he has eliminated analysis or made a sacrifice to discretion. His pages are studded with that particular analysis; he is constantly peeping behind the curtain, telling us what he discovers there. The truth is that the admirable system of simplification which makes his tales so rapid and so concise (especially his shorter ones, for his novels in some degree, I think, suffer from it), strikes us as not in the least a conscious intellectual effort, a selective, comparative process. He tells us all he knows, all he suspects, and if these things take no account of the moral nature of man, it is because he has no window looking in that direction, and not because artistic scruples have compelled him to close it up. The very compact mansion in which he dwells presents on that side a perfectly dead wall.

This is why, if his axiom that you produce the effect of truth better by painting people from the outside than from the inside has a large utility, his example is convincing in a much higher degree. A writer is fortunate when his theory and his limitations so exactly correspond, when his curiosities may be appeased with such precision and promptitude. M. de Maupassant contends that the most that the analytic novelist can do is to put himself—his own peculiarities—into the costume of the figure analysed. This may be true, but if it applies to one manner of representing people who are not ourselves, it applies also to any other manner. It is the limitation, the difficulty of the novelist, to whatever clan or camp he may belong. M. de Maupassant is remarkably objective and impersonal, but he would go too far if he were to entertain the belief that he has kept himself out of his books. They speak of him eloquently, even if it only be to tell us how easy—how easy, given his talent of course—he has found this impersonality. Let us hasten to add that in the case of describing a character it is doubtless more difficult to convey the impression of something that is not one's self (the constant effort, however delusive at bottom, of the novelist), than in the case of describing some object more immediately visible. The operation is more delicate, but that circumstance only increases the beauty of the problem.

On the question of style our author has some excellent remarks; we may be grateful indeed for every one of them, save an odd reflection about the way to "become original" if we happen not to be so. The recipe for this transformation, it would appear, is to sit down in front of a blazing fire, or a tree in a plain, or any object we encounter in the regular way of business, and remain there until the tree, or the fire, or the object, whatever it be, become different for us from all other specimens of the same class. I doubt whether this system would always answer, for surely the resemblance is what we wish to discover, quite as much as the difference, and the best way to preserve it is not to look for something opposed to it. Is not this indication of the road to take to become, as a writer, original touched with the same fallacy as the recommendation about eschewing analysis? It is the only *naïveté* I have encountered in M. de Maupassant's many volumes. The best originality is the most unconscious, and the best way to describe a tree is the way in which it has struck us. "Ah, but we don't always know how it has struck us," the answer to that may be, "and it takes some time and ingenuity—much fasting and prayer—to find out." If we do not know, it probably has not struck us very much: so little indeed that our inquiry had better be relegated to that closed chamber of an artist's meditations, that sacred back kitchen, which no *a priori* rule can light up. The best thing the artist's adviser can do in such a case is to trust him and turn away, to let him fight the matter out with his conscience. And be this said with a full appreciation of the degree in which M. de Maupassant's observations on the whole question of a writer's style, at the point we have come to to-day, bear the stamp of intelligence and experience. His own style is of so excellent a tradition that the presumption is altogether in favour of what he may have to say.

He feels oppressively, discouragingly, as many another of his countrymen must have felt—for the French have worked their language as no other people have done—the penalty of coming at the end of three centuries of literature, the difficulty of dealing with an instrument of expression so worn by friction, of drawing new sounds from the old familiar pipe. "When we read, so saturated with French writing as we are that our whole body gives us the impression of being a paste made of words, do we ever find a line, a thought, which is not familiar to us, and of which we have not had at least a confused presentiment?" And he adds that the matter is simple enough for the writer who only seeks to amuse the public by means already known; he attempts little, and he produces "with confidence, in the candour of his mediocrity," works which answer no question and leave no trace. It is he who wants to do more than this that has less and less an easy time of it. Everything seems to him to have been done, every effect produced, every combination already made. If he be a man of genius, his trouble is lightened, for mysterious ways are revealed to him, and new combinations spring up for him even after novelty is dead. It is to the simple man of taste and talent, who has only a conscience and a will, that the situation may sometimes well appear desperate; he judges himself as he goes, and he can only go step by step over ground where every step is already a footprint.

If it be a miracle whenever there is a fresh tone, the miracle has been wrought for M. de Maupassant. Or is he simply a man of genius to whom short cuts have been disclosed in the watches of the night? At any rate he has had faith—religion has come to his aid; I mean the religion of his mother tongue, which he has loved well enough to be patient for her sake.

He has arrived at the peace which passeth understanding, at a kind of conservative piety. He has taken his stand on simplicity, on a studied sobriety, being persuaded that the deepest science lies in that direction rather than in the multiplication of new terms, and on this subject he delivers himself with superlative wisdom. "There is no need of the queer, complicated, numerous, and Chinese vocabulary which is imposed on us to-day under the name of artistic writing, to fix all the shades of thought; the right way is to distinguish with an extreme clearness all those modifications of the value of a word which come from the place it occupies. Let us have fewer nouns, verbs and adjectives of an almost imperceptible sense, and more different phrases variously constructed, ingeniously cast, full of the science of sound and rhythm. Let us have an excellent general form rather than be collectors of rare terms." M. de Maupassant's practice does not fall below his exhortation (though I must confess that in the foregoing passage he makes use of the detestable expression "stylist," which I have not reproduced). Nothing can exceed the masculine firmness, the quiet force of his own style, in which every phrase is a close sequence, every epithet a paying piece, and the ground is completely cleared of the vague, the ready-made and the second-best. Less than any one to-day does he beat the air; more than any one does he hit out from the shoulder.

II

HE has produced a hundred short tales and only four regular novels; but if the tales deserve the first place in any candid appreciation of his talent it is not simply because they are so much the more numerous: they are also more characteristic; they represent him best in his originality, and their brevity, extreme in some cases, does not prevent them from being a collection of masterpieces. (They are very unequal, and I speak of the best.) The little story is but scantily relished in England, where readers take their fiction rather by the volume than by the page, and the novelist's idea is apt to resemble one of those old-fashioned carriages which require a wide court to turn round. In America, where it is associated pre-

eminently with Hawthorne's name, with Edgar Poe's, and
with that of Mr. Bret Harte, the short tale has had a better
fortune. France, however, has been the land of its great prosperity, and M. de Maupassant had from the first the advantage of addressing a public accustomed to catch on, as the
modern phrase is, quickly. In some respects, it may be said,
he encountered prejudices too friendly, for he found a tradition of indecency ready made to his hand. I say indecency
with plainness, though my indication would perhaps please
better with another word, for we suffer in English from a lack
of roundabout names for the *conte leste*—that element for
which the French, with their *grivois*, their *gaillard*, their *égril-
lard*, their *gaudriole*, have so many convenient synonyms. It is
an honoured tradition in France that the little story, in verse
or in prose, should be liable to be more or less obscene (I can
think only of that alternative epithet), though I hasten to add
that among literary forms it does not monopolise the privilege. Our uncleanness is less producible—at any rate it is less
produced.

For the last ten years our author has brought forth with
regularity these condensed compositions, of which, probably,
to an English reader, at a first glance, the most universal sign
will be their licentiousness. They really partake of this quality,
however, in a very differing degree, and a second glance
shows that they may be divided into numerous groups. It is
not fair, I think, even to say that what they have most in
common is their being extremely *lestes*. What they have most
in common is their being extremely strong, and after that
their being extremely brutal. A story may be obscene without
being brutal, and *vice versâ*, and M. de Maupassant's contempt for those interdictions which are supposed to be made
in the interest of good morals is but an incident—a very large
one indeed—of his general contempt. A pessimism so great
that its alliance with the love of good work, or even with the
calculation of the sort of work that pays best in a country of
style, is, as I have intimated, the most puzzling of anomalies
(for it would seem in the light of such sentiments that nothing is worth anything), this cynical strain is the sign of such
gems of narration as *La Maison Tellier*, *L'Histoire d'une Fille
de Ferme*, *L'Ane*, *Le Chien*, *Mademoiselle Fifi*, *Monsieur Pa-*

rent, *L'Héritage*, *En Famille*, *Le Baptême*, *Le Père Amable*. The author fixes a hard eye on some small spot of human life, usually some ugly, dreary, shabby, sordid one, takes up the particle, and squeezes it either till it grimaces or till it bleeds. Sometimes the grimace is very droll, sometimes the wound is very horrible; but in either case the whole thing is real, observed, noted, and represented, not an invention or a castle in the air. M. de Maupassant sees human life as a terribly ugly business relieved by the comical, but even the comedy is for the most part the comedy of misery, of avidity, of ignorance, helplessness, and grossness. When his laugh is not for these things, it is for the little *saletés* (to use one of his own favourite words) of luxurious life, which are intended to be prettier, but which can scarcely be said to brighten the picture. I like *La Bête à Maître Belhomme*, *La Ficelle*, *Le Petit Fût*, *Le Cas de Madame Luneau*, *Tribuneaux Rustiques*, and many others of this category much better than his anecdotes of the mutual confidences of his little *marquises* and *baronnes*.

Not counting his novels for the moment, his tales may be divided into the three groups of those which deal with the Norman peasantry, those which deal with the *petit employé* and small shopkeeper, usually in Paris, and the miscellaneous, in which the upper walks of life are represented, and the fantastic, the whimsical, the weird, and even the supernatural, figure as well as the unexpurgated. These last things range from *Le Horla* (which is not a specimen of the author's best vein—the only occasion on which he has the weakness of imitation is when he strikes us as emulating Edgar Poe) to *Miss Harriet*, and from *Boule de Suif* (a triumph) to that almost inconceivable little growl of Anglophobia, *Découverte*—inconceivable I mean in its irresponsibility and ill-nature on the part of a man of M. de Maupassant's distinction; passing by such little perfections as *Petit Soldat*, *L'Abandonné*, *Le Collier* (the list is too long for complete enumeration), and such gross imperfections (for it once in a while befalls our author to go woefully astray), as *La Femme de Paul*, *Châli*, *Les Sœurs Rondoli*. To these might almost be added as a special category the various forms in which M. de Maupassant relates adventures in railway carriages. Numerous, to his imagination, are the pretexts for enlivening fiction afforded by first, second, and third class compartments; the accidents (which have nothing to do with the conduct of the train) that occur there constitute no inconsiderable part of our earthly transit.

It is surely by his Norman peasant that his tales will live; he knows this worthy as if he had made him, understands him down to the ground, puts him on his feet with a few of the freest, most plastic touches. M. de Maupassant does not admire him, and he is such a master of the subject that it would ill become an outsider to suggest a revision of judgment. He is a part of the contemptible furniture of the world, but on the whole, it would appear, the most grotesque part of it. His caution, his canniness, his natural astuteness, his stinginess, his general grinding sordidness, are as unmistakable as that quaint and brutish dialect in which he expresses himself, and on which our author plays like a virtuoso. It would be impossible to demonstrate with a finer sense of the humour of the thing the fatuities and densities of his ignorance, the bewilderments of his opposed appetites, the overreachings of his caution. His existence has a gay side, but it is apt to be the barbarous gaiety commemorated in *Farce Normande*, an anecdote which, like many of M. de Maupassant's anecdotes, it is easier to refer the reader to than to repeat. If it is most convenient to place *La Maison Tellier* among the tales of the peasantry, there is no doubt that it stands at the head of the list. It is absolutely unadapted to the perusal of ladies and young persons, but it shares this peculiarity with most of its fellows, so that to ignore it on that account would be to imply that we must forswear M. de Maupassant altogether, which is an incongruous and insupportable conclusion. Every good story is of course both a picture and an idea, and the more they are interfused the better the problem is solved. In *La Maison Tellier* they fit each other to perfection; the capacity for sudden innocent delights latent in natures which have lost their innocence is vividly illustrated by the singular scenes to which our acquaintance with Madame and her staff (little as it may be a thing to boast of), successively introduces us. The breadth, the freedom, and brightness of all this give the measure of the author's talent, and of that large, keen way of looking at life which sees the pathetic and the droll, the stuff of which the whole piece is made, in the queerest and humblest patterns. The tone of *La Maison Tellier* and the few compositions which closely resemble it, expresses M. de Maupassant's nearest approach to geniality. Even here, however, it is the geniality of the showman exhilarated by the success with which he feels that he makes his mannikins (and especially his womankins) caper and squeak, and who after the performance tosses them into their box with the irreverence of a practised hand. If the pages of the author of *Bel-Ami* may be searched almost in vain for a manifestation of the sentiment of respect, it is naturally not by Mme. Tellier and her charges that we must look most to see it called forth; but they are among the things that please him most.

Sometimes there is a sorrow, a misery, or even a little heroism, that he handles with a certain tenderness (*Une Vie* is the capital example of this), without insisting on the poor, the ridiculous, or, as he is fond of saying, the bestial side of it. Such an attempt, admirable in its sobriety and delicacy, is the sketch, in *L'Abandonné*, of the old lady and gentleman, Mme. de Cadour and M. d'Apreval, who, staying with the husband of the former at a little watering-place on the Normandy coast, take a long, hot walk on a summer's day, on a straight, white road, into the interior, to catch a clandestine glimpse of a young farmer, their illegitimate son. He has been pensioned, he is ignorant of his origin, and is a commonplace and unconciliatory rustic. They look at him, in his dirty farmyard, and no sign passes between them; then they turn away and crawl back, in melancholy silence, along the dull French road. The manner in which this dreary little occurrence is related makes it as large as a chapter of history. There is tenderness in *Miss Harriet*, which sets forth how an English old maid, fantastic, hideous, sentimental, and tract-distributing, with a smell of india-rubber, fell in love with an irresistible French painter, and drowned herself in the well because she saw him kissing the maid-servant; but the figure of the lady grazes the farcical. Is it because we know Miss Harriet (if we are not mistaken in the type the author has had in his eye) that we suspect the good spinster was not so weird and desperate, addicted though her class may be, as he says, to "haunting all the *tables d'hôte* in Europe, to spoiling Italy, poisoning Switzerland, making the charming towns of the

Mediterranean uninhabitable, carrying everywhere their queer little manias, their *mœurs de vestales pétrifiées*, their indescribable garments, and that odour of india-rubber which makes one think that at night they must be slipped into a case?" What would Miss Harriet have said to M. de Maupassant's friend, the hero of the *Découverte*, who, having married a little Anglaise because he thought she was charming when she spoke broken French, finds she is very flat as she becomes more fluent, and has nothing more urgent than to denounce her to a gentleman he meets on the steamboat, and to relieve his wrath in ejaculations of "Sales Anglais"?

M. de Maupassant evidently knows a great deal about the army of clerks who work under government, but it is a terrible tale that he has to tell of them and of the *petit bourgeois* in general. It is true that he has treated the *petit bourgeois* in *Pierre et Jean* without holding him up to our derision, and the effort has been so fruitful, that we owe to it the work for which, on the whole, in the long list of his successes, we are most thankful. But of *Pierre et Jean*, a production neither comic nor cynical (in the degree, that is, of its predecessors), but serious and fresh, I will speak anon. In *Monsieur Parent*, *L'Héritage*, *En Famille*, *Une Partie de Campagne*, *Promenade*, and many other pitiless little pieces, the author opens the window wide to his perception of everything mean, narrow, and sordid. The subject is ever the struggle for existence in hard conditions, lighted up simply by more or less *polissonnerie*. Nothing is more striking to an Anglo-Saxon reader than the omission of all the other lights, those with which our imagination, and I think it ought to be said our observation, is familiar, and which our own works of fiction at any rate do not permit us to forget: those of which the most general description is that they spring from a certain mixture of good-humour and piety—piety, I mean, in the civil and domestic sense quite as much as in the religious. The love of sport, the sense of decorum, the necessity for action, the habit of respect, the absence of irony, the pervasiveness of childhood, the expansive tendency of the race, are a few of the qualities (the analysis might, I think, be pushed much further) which ease us off, mitigate our tension and irritation, rescue us from the nervous exasperation which is almost the commonest element of life as depicted by M. de Maupassant. No doubt there is in our literature an immense amount of conventional blinking, and it may be questioned whether pessimistic representation in M. de Maupassant's manner do not follow his particular original more closely than our perpetual quest of pleasantness (does not Mr. Rider Haggard make even his African carnage pleasant?) adheres to the lines of the world we ourselves know.

Fierce indeed is the struggle for existence among even our pious and good-humoured millions, and it is attended with incidents as to which after all little testimony is to be extracted from our literature of fiction. It must never be forgotten that the optimism of that literature is partly the optimism of women and of spinsters; in other words the optimism of ignorance as well as of delicacy. It might be supposed that the French, with their mastery of the *arts d'agrément*, would have more consolations than we, but such is not the account of the matter given by the new generation of painters. To the French we seem superficial, and we are certainly open to the reproach; but none the less even to the infinite majority of readers of good faith there will be a wonderful want of correspondence between the general picture of *Bel-Ami*, of *Mont-Oriol*, of *Une Vie*, *Yvette* and *En Famille*, and our own vision of reality. It is an old impression of course that the satire of the French has a very different tone from ours; but few English readers will admit that the feeling of life is less in ours than in theirs. The feeling of life is evidently, *de part et d'autre*, a very different thing. If in ours, as the novel illustrates it, there are superficialities, there are also qualities which are far from being negatives and omissions: a large imagination and (is it fatuous to say?) a large experience of the positive kind. Even those of our novelists whose manner is most ironic pity life more and hate it less than M. de Maupassant and his great initiator Flaubert. It comes back I suppose to our good-humour (which may apparently also be an artistic force); at any rate, we have reserves about our shames and our sorrows, indulgences and tolerances about our Philistinism, forbearances about our blows, and a general friendliness of conception about our possibilities, which take the cruelty from our self-derision and operate in the last resort as a sort of tribute to our freedom. There is a horrible, admirable scene in *Monsieur Parent*, which is a capital example of triumphant ugliness. The harmless gentleman who gives his name to the tale has an abominable wife, one of whose offensive attributes is a lover (unsuspected by her husband), only less impudent than herself. M. Parent comes in from a walk with his little boy, at dinner-time, to encounter suddenly in his abused, dishonoured, deserted home, convincing proof of her misbehaviour. He waits and waits dinner for her, giving her the benefit of every doubt; but when at last she enters, late in the evening, accompanied by the partner of her guilt, there is a tremendous domestic concussion. It is to the peculiar vividness of this scene that I allude, the way we hear it and see it, and its most repulsive details are evoked for us: the sordid confusion, the vulgar noise, the disordered table and ruined dinner, the shrill insolence of the wife, her brazen mendacity, the scared inferiority of the lover, the mere momentary heroics of the weak husband, the scuffle and somersault, the eminently unpoetic justice with which it all ends.

When Thackeray relates how Arthur Pendennis goes home to take pot-luck with the insolvent Newcomes at Boulogne, and how the dreadful Mrs. Mackenzie receives him, and how she makes a scene, when the frugal repast is served, over the diminished mutton-bone, we feel that the notation of that order of misery goes about as far as we can bear it. But this is child's play to the history of M. and Mme. Caravan and their attempt, after the death (or supposed death) of the husband's mother, to transfer to their apartment before the arrival of the other heirs certain miserable little articles of furniture belonging to the deceased, together with the frustration of the manœuvre not only by the grim resurrection of the old woman (which is a sufficiently fantastic item), but by the shock of battle when a married daughter and her husband appear. No one gives us like M. de Maupassant the odious words exchanged on such an occasion as that: no one depicts with so just a hand the feelings of small people about small things. These feelings are very apt to be "fury"; that word is of strikingly frequent occurrence in his pages. *L'Héritage* is a drama of private life in the little world of the Ministère de la Marine—a world, according to M. de Maupassant, of dreadful little jealousies and ineptitudes. Readers of a robust complexion should learn how the wretched M. Lesable was handled by his wife and her father on his failing to satisfy their just expectations, and how he comported himself in the singular situation thus prepared for him. The story is a model of narration, but it leaves our poor average humanity dangling like a beaten rag.

Where does M. de Maupassant find the great multitude of his detestable women? or where at least does he find the courage to represent them in such colours? Jeanne de Lamare, in *Une Vie*, receives the outrages of fate with a passive fortitude; and there is something touching in Mme. Roland's *âme tendre de caissière*, as exhibited in *Pierre et Jean*. But for the most part M. de Maupassant's heroines are a mixture of extreme sensuality and extreme mendacity. They are a large element in that general disfigurement, that *illusion de l'ignoble, qui attire tant d'êtres*, which makes the perverse or the stupid side of things the one which strikes him first, which leads him, if he glances at a group of nurses and children sunning themselves in a Parisian square, to notice primarily the *yeux de brute* of the nurses; or if he speaks of the longing for a taste of the country which haunts the shopkeeper fenced in behind his counter, to identify it as the *amour bête de la nature*; or if he has occasion to put the boulevards before us on a summer's evening, to seek his effect in these terms: "The city, as hot as a stew, seemed to sweat in the suffocating night. The drains puffed their pestilential breath from their mouths of granite, and the underground kitchens poured into the streets, through their low windows, the infamous miasmas of their dishwater and old sauces." I do not contest the truth of such indications, I only note the particular selection and their seeming to the writer the most *apropos*.

Is it because of the inadequacy of these indications when applied to the long stretch that M. de Maupassant's novels strike us as less complete, in proportion to the talent expended upon them, than his *contes* and *nouvelles*? I make this invidious distinction in spite of the fact that *Une Vie* (the first of the novels in the order of time) is a remarkably interesting experiment, and that *Pierre et Jean* is, so far as my judgment goes, a faultless production. *Bel-Ami* is full of the bustle and the crudity of life (its energy and expressiveness almost bribe one to like it), but it has the great defect that the physiological explanation of things here too visibly contracts the problem in order to meet it. The world represented is too special, too little inevitable, too much to take or to leave as we like— a world in which every man is a cad and every woman a harlot. M. de Maupassant traces the career of a finished blackguard who succeeds in life through women, and he represents him primarily as succeeding in the profession of journalism. His colleagues and his mistresses are as depraved as himself, greatly to the injury of the ironic idea, for the real force of satire would have come from seeing him engaged and victorious with natures better than his own. It may be remarked that this was the case with the nature of Mme. Walter; but the reply to that is—hardly! Moreover the author's whole treatment of the episode of Mme. Walter is the thing on which his admirers have least to congratulate him. The taste of it is so atrocious, that it is difficult to do justice to the way it is made to stand out. Such an instance as this pleads with irresistible eloquence, as it seems to me, the cause of that salutary diffidence or practical generosity which I mentioned on a preceding page. I know not the English or American novelist who could have written this portion of the history of *Bel-Ami* if he would. But I also find it impossible to conceive of a member of that fraternity who would have written it if he could. The subject of *Mont-Oriol* is full of queerness to the English mind. Here again the picture has much more importance than the idea, which is simply that a gentleman, if he happen to be a low animal, is liable to love a lady very much less if she presents him with a pledge of their affection. It need scarcely be said that the lady and gentleman who in M. de Maupassant's pages exemplify this interesting truth are not united in wedlock—that is with each other.

M. de Maupassant tells us that he has imbibed many of his principles from Gustave Flaubert, from the study of his works as well as, formerly, the enjoyment of his words. It is in *Une Vie* that Flaubert's influence is most directly traceable, for the thing has a marked analogy with *L'Education Sentimentale*. That is, it is the presentation of a simple piece of a life (in this case a long piece), a series of observations upon an episode *quelconque*, as the French say, with the minimum of arrangement of the given objects. It is an excellent example of the way the impression of truth may be conveyed by that form, but it would have been a still better one if in his search for the effect of dreariness (the effect of dreariness may be said to be the subject of *Une Vie*, so far as the subject is reducible) the author had not eliminated excessively. He has arranged, as I say, as little as possible; the necessity of a "plot" has in no degree imposed itself upon him, and his effort has been to give the uncomposed, unrounded look of life, with its accidents, its broken rhythm, its queer resemblance to the famous description of "Bradshaw"—a compound of trains that start but don't arrive, and trains that arrive but don't start. It is almost an arrangement of the history of poor Mme. de Lamare to have left so many things out of it, for after all she is described in very few of the relations of life. The principal ones are there certainly; we see her as a daughter, a wife, and a mother, but there is a certain accumulation of secondary experience that marks any passage from youth to old age which is a wholly absent element in M. de Maupassant's narrative, and the suppression of which gives the thing a tinge of the arbitrary. It is in the power of this secondary experience to make a great difference, but nothing makes any difference for Jeanne de Lamare as M. de Maupassant puts her before us. Had she no other points of contact than those he describes?—no friends, no phases, no episodes, no chances, none of the miscellaneous *remplissage* of life? No doubt M. de Maupassant would say that he has had to select, that the most comprehensive enumeration is only a condensation, and that, in accordance with the very just principles enunciated in that preface to which I have perhaps too repeatedly referred, he has sacrificed what is uncharacteristic to what is characteristic. It characterises the career of this French country lady of fifty years ago that its long gray expanse should be seen as peopled with but five or six figures. The essence of the matter is that she was deceived in almost every affection, and that essence is given if the persons who deceived her are given.

The reply is doubtless adequate, and I have only intended my criticism to suggest the degree of my interest. What it really amounts to is that if the subject of this artistic experiment had been the existence of an English lady, even a very dull one, the air of verisimilitude would have demanded that she should have been placed in a denser medium. *Une Vie* may after all be only a testimony to the fact of the melancholy void of the coast of Normandy, even within a moderate drive of a great seaport, under the Restoration and Louis Philippe. It is especially to be recommended to those who are interested in the question of what constitutes a "story," offering as it does the most definite sequences at the same time that it has nothing that corresponds to the usual idea of a plot, and closing with an implication that finds us prepared. The picture again in this case is much more dominant than the idea, unless it be an idea that loneliness and grief are terrible. The picture, at any rate, is full of truthful touches, and the work has the merit and the charm that it is the most delicate of the author's productions and the least hard. In none other has he occupied himself so continuously with so innocent a figure as his soft, bruised heroine; in none other has he paid our poor blind human history the compliment (and this is remarkable, considering the flatness of so much of the particular subject) of finding it so little *bête*. He may think it, here, but comparatively he does not say it. He almost betrays a sense of moral things. Jeanne is absolutely passive, she has no moral spring, no active moral life, none of the edifying attributes of character (it costs her apparently as little as may be in the way of a shock, a complication of feeling, to discover, by letters, after her mother's death, that this lady has not been the virtuous woman she has supposed); but her chronicler has had to handle the immaterial forces of patience and renunciation, and this has given the book a certain purity, in spite of two or three "physiological" passages that come in with violence—a violence the greater as we feel it to be a result of selection. It is very much a mark of M. de Maupassant that on the most striking occasion, with a single exception, on which his picture is not a picture of libertinage it is a picture of unmitigated suffering. Would he suggest that these are the only alternatives?

The exception that I here allude to is for *Pierre et Jean*, which I have left myself small space to speak of. Is it because in this masterly little novel there is a show of those immaterial forces which I just mentioned, and because Pierre Roland is one of the few instances of operative character that can be recalled from so many volumes, that many readers will place M. de Maupassant's latest production altogether at the head of his longer ones? I am not sure, inasmuch as after all the character in question is not extraordinarily distinguished, and the moral problem not presented in much complexity. The case is only relative. Perhaps it is not of importance to fix the reasons of preference in respect to a piece of writing so essentially a work of art and of talent. *Pierre et Jean* is the best of M. de Maupassant's novels mainly because M. de Maupassant has never before been so clever. It is a pleasure to see a mature talent able to renew itself, strike another note, and appear still young. This story suggests the growth of a perception that everything has not been said about the actors on the world's stage when they are represented either as helpless victims or as mere bundles of appetites. There is an air of responsibility about Pierre Roland, the person on whose behalf the tale is mainly told, which almost constitutes a pledge. An inquisitive critic may ask why in this particular case M. de Maupassant should have stuck to the *petit bourgeois*, the circumstances not being such as to typify that class more than another. There are reasons indeed which on reflection are perceptible; it was necessary that his people should be poor, and necessary even that to attenuate Madame Roland's misbehaviour she should have had the excuse of the contracted life of a shopwoman in the Rue Montmartre. Were the inquisitive critic slightly malicious as well, he might suspect the author of a fear that he should seem to give way to the *illusion du beau* if in addition to representing the little group in *Pierre et Jean* as persons of about the normal conscience he had also represented them as of the cultivated class. If they belong to the humble life this belittles and—I am still quoting the supposedly malicious critic—M. de Maupassant *must*, in one way or the other, belittle. To the English reader it will appear, I think, that Pierre and Jean are rather more of the cultivated class than two young Englishmen in the same social position. It belongs to the drama that the struggle of the elder brother—educated, proud, and acute—should be partly with the pettiness of his opportunities. The author's choice of a *milieu*, moreover, will serve to English readers as an example of how much more democratic contemporary French fiction is than that of his own country. The greater part of it— almost all the work of Zola and of Daudet, the best of Flaubert's novels, and the best of those of the brothers De Goncourt—treat of that vast, dim section of society which, lying between those luxurious walks on whose behalf there are easy presuppositions and that darkness of misery which, in addition to being picturesque, brings philanthropy also to the writer's aid, constitutes really, in extent and expressiveness, the substance of any nation. In England, where the fashion of fiction still sets mainly to the country house and the hunting-field, and yet more novels are published than anywhere else in the world, that thick twilight of mediocrity of condition has been little explored. May it yield triumphs in the years to come!

It may seem that I have claimed little for M. de Maupassant, so far as English readers are concerned with him, in saying that after publishing twenty improper volumes he has at last published a twenty-first, which is neither indecent nor cynical. It is not this circumstance that has led me to dedicate so many pages to him, but the circumstance that in producing all the others he yet remained, for those who are interested in these matters, a writer with whom it was impossible not to reckon. This is why I called him, to begin with, so many ineffectual names: a rarity, a "case," an embarrassment, a lion in the path. He is still in the path as I conclude these observations, but I think that in making them we have discovered a legitimate way round. If he is a master of his art and it is discouraging to find what low views are compatible with mastery, there is satisfaction, on the other hand in learning on what particular condition he holds his strange success. This condition, it seems to me, is that of having totally omitted one of the items of the problem, an omission which has made the problem so much easier that it may almost be described as a short cut to a solution. The question is whether it be a fair cut. M. de Maupassant has simply skipped the whole reflective part of his men and women—that reflective part which governs conduct and produces character. He may say that he does not see it, does not know it; to which the answer is, "So much the better for you, if you wish to describe life without it. The strings you pull are by so much the less numerous, and you can therefore pull those that remain with greater promptitude, consequently with greater firmness, with a greater air of knowledge." Pierre Roland, I repeat, shows a capacity for reflection, but I cannot think who else does, among the thousand figures who compete with him—I mean for reflection addressed to anything higher than the gratification of an instinct. We have an impression that M. d'Apreval and Madame de Cadour reflect, as they trudge back from their mournful excursion, but that indication is not pushed very far. An aptitude for this exercise is a part of disciplined manhood, and disciplined manhood M. de Maupassant has simply not attempted to represent. I can remember no instance in which he sketches any considerable capacity for conduct, and his women betray that capacity as little as his men. I am much mistaken if he has once painted a gentleman, in the English sense of the term. His gentlemen, like Paul Brétigny and Gontran de Ravenel, are guilty of the most extraordinary deflections. For those who are conscious of this element in life, look for it and like it, the gap will appear to be immense. It will lead them to say, "No wonder you have a contempt if that is the way you limit the field. No wonder you judge people roughly if that is the way you see them. Your work, on your premises, remains the admirable thing it is, but is your 'case' not adequately explained?"

The erotic element in M. de Maupassant, about which much more might have been said, seems to me to be explained by the same limitation, and explicable in a similar way wherever else its literature occurs in excess. The carnal side of man appears the most characteristic if you look at it a great deal; and you look at it a great deal if you do not look at the other, at the side by which he reacts against his weaknesses, his defeats. The more you look at the other, the less the whole business to which French novelists have ever appeared to English readers to give a disproportionate place—the business, as I may say, of the senses—will strike you as the only typical one. Is not this the most useful reflection to make in regard to the famous question of the morality, the decency, of the novel? It is the only one, it seems to me, that will meet the case as we find the case to-day. Hard and fast rules, *a priori* restrictions, mere interdictions (you shall not speak of this, you shall not look at that), have surely served their time, and will in the nature of the case never strike an energetic talent as anything but arbitrary. A healthy, living and growing art, full of curiosity and fond of exercise, has an indefeasible mistrust of rigid prohibitions. Let us then leave this magnificent art of the novelist to itself and to its perfect freedom, in the faith that one example is as good as another, and that our fiction will always be decent enough if it be sufficiently general. Let us not be alarmed at this prodigy (though prodigies are alarming) of M. de Maupassant, who is at once so licentious and so impeccable, but gird ourselves up with the conviction that another point of view will yield another perfection.

Fortnightly Review, March 1888
Reprinted in *Partial Portraits*, 1888

GUY DE MAUPASSANT

IT IS SO EMBARRASSING to speak of the writers of one country to the readers of another that I sometimes wonder at the complacency with which the delicate task is entered upon. There are cases in which the difficult art of criticism becomes doubly difficult, inasmuch as they compel the critic to forfeit what I may call his natural advantages. The first of these natural advantages is that those who read him shall help him by taking a great many things for granted; shall allow him his general point of view and his terms—terms which he is not obliged to define. The relation of the American reader to the French writer, for instance, is, on the contrary, so indirect that it gives him who proposes to mediate between them a great deal more to do. Here he has in a manner to define his terms and establish his point of view.

The first simplification he is prompted to effect is therefore to ask the reader to make the effort to approach the author as nearly as possible in the supposed spirit of one of his own (one of the author's) fellow-countrymen. If the author be French, remember that as it is to Frenchmen he addresses himself, it is profitless to read him without a certain displacement of tradition. If he be German, reflect in the same way that it was far from his business to write in such a manner as would conciliate most the habits and prejudices of the English-speaking mind. There are doubtless many people all ready to regard themselves as injured by a suggestion that they should for the hour, and even in the decent privacy of the imagination, comport themselves as creatures of alien (by which we usually understand inferior) race. To them it is only to be answered that they had better never touch a foreign book on any terms, but lead a contented life in the homogeneous medium of the dear old mother-speech. That life, by compensation, they will of course endeavor to make as rich as possible; and there is one question they will always be able to ask without getting an immediate answer, so that the little inquiry will retain more or less its triumphant air, "Why should we concern ourselves so much about French literature, when those who produce it concern themselves so little about ours?"

That strong argument will always be in order, especially among those who do not really know how little the French are, as they say, preoccupied with English and American work; and on some occasions it will be supported by the further inquiry: "Is not the very perfection of French literature to-day an exemplary consequence of the fact that its principal exponents stay at home and mind their business—shut their doors and 'take care of' (soigner) their form? They don't waste time," it will be added, "in superficial excursions, nor have they any confidence in the lessons that are to be learned beyond the frontier. Watch them a little and you will see plenty of examples of that want of confidence. They accept their own order of things as their limit, and in that order they dig, as we know, very deep. To speak only of fiction, there are multitudes of tales by English and American writers which profess to deal with French and with Italian life, yet probably not one of which, unless it be George Eliot's *Romola*, has any verisimilitude or any value for Frenchmen or for Italians. Few indeed are the works of fiction which they on their side have dedicated to the portraiture of the Anglo-Saxon world; and great, doubtless, do they deem the artistic *naïveté* of a race which can content itself with that sort of stuff as a substitute for thoroughness." Thus, it will be seen, the very "perfection" of French literature (which a hundred observers will also of course contest) may, oddly enough, be offered as a reason for having nothing to do with it.

These are the embroilments of a flirtation—an expression which is really the only proper one to apply to our interest in the "sort of stuff" which has enabled such a writer as M. Guy de Maupassant, whose name I have prefixed to these remarks, to be possible. To a serious and well-regulated union with such a writer the American public must, in the nature of things, shrink from pretending; but nothing need prevent it—not even the sense of danger (often, it must be said, much rather an incentive)—from enjoying those desultory snatches of intercourse which represent in the world of books the broken opportunities of Rosina or Juliet. These young ladies, it is true, eventually went much further, and the situation of the Anglo-Saxon reader, when craning over the creaking fourth or fifth floor balcony of a translation, must be understood as that to which the romance of curiosity would have been restricted if the Guardian and the Nurse—in other words, public opinion—had succeeded in keeping the affair within limits. M. de Maupassant is an Almaviva who strums his guitar with the expectation of raising the street, and he performs most skilfully under those windows from which the flower of attention at any price is flung down to him. If he is a capital specimen of the foreign writer with whom the critic has most trouble, there could at the same time be no better exhibition of the force which sets this inquiring, admiring spirit in motion.

The only excuse the critic has for braving the embarrassments I have mentioned is that he wishes to perform a work of recommendation, and indeed there is no profit in talking in English of M. de Maupassant unless it be in the sense of recommending him. One should never go out of one's way to differ; and translation, interpretation, the business of adjusting to another medium, are a going out of one's way. Silence is the best disapproval; and to take people up with an earnest grip, only to put them down, is to add to the vain gesticulation of the human scene. That reader will therefore be most intelligent who, if he does not leave M. de Maupassant quite alone, makes him a present, as it were, of the conditions. My purpose was to enumerate these, but I shall not accomplish it properly if I fail to recognize that they are manifold.

The first of them to be mentioned is, doubtless, that he came into the literary world, as he himself has related, under the protection of the great Flaubert. This was but a dozen years ago, for Guy de Maupassant belongs, among the distinguished Frenchmen of his period, to the new generation. His celebrity has been gathered in a short career, and his experience, which in certain ways suggests the helping hand of time, in a rapid life, inasmuch as he was born in 1850. These things go fast in France, and there is already a newer generation still, with its dates and its notabilities; but we need scarcely yet open a parenthesis for the so-called *décadents*: they have produced no talent that seems particularly alive; to do so would, indeed, be a disloyalty to their name. Besides the link of the same literary ideal, Gustave Flaubert had with his young pupil a strong community of local sense—the sap of the rich old Norman country was in the veins of both. It is not too much to say that there is a large element in Maupassant that the reader will care for in proportion as he has a kindly impression of the large, bountiful Norman land, with its abbeys and its nestling farms, its scented hedges and hard white roads, where the Sunday blouse of the rustic is picked out in color, its succulent domestic life, and its canny and humorous peasantry. There is something in the accumulated heritage of such a province which may well have fed the imagination of an artist whose vision was to be altogether of this life.

That is another of M. de Maupassant's conditions: what is clearest to him is the immitigability of our mortal predicament, with its occasional beguilements and its innumerable woes. Flaubert would have been sorry to blur this sharpness, and indeed he ministered to it in helping to place his young friend in possession of a style which completely reflects it. Guy de Maupassant, from his own account (in the preface to

Pierre et Jean), devoted much time to the moral that to prove that you have a first-rate talent you must have a first-rate style. He therefore learned to write, and acquired an instrument which emits no uncertain sound. He is wonderfully concise and direct, yet at the same time it would be difficult to characterize more vividly. To have color and be sober with it is an ideal, and this ideal M. de Maupassant constantly touches. The complete possession of his instrument has enabled him to attack a great variety of subjects—usually within rigid limits of space. He has accepted the necessity of being brief, and has made brevity very full, through making it an energetic selection. He has published less than half a dozen novels and more than a hundred tales; and it is upon his tales that his reputation will mainly rest. The short tale is infinitely relished in France, which can show in this form an array of masterpieces; and no small part of Maupassant's success, I think, comes from his countrymen's pride in seeing him add to a collection which is already a national glory. He has done so, as I say, by putting selection really upon its mettle—by going in every picture straight to the strongest ingredients, and to them alone.

The turn of his mind has helped him to do this, an extraordinary perceptive apparatus of the personal, material, immediate sort. M. de Maupassant takes his stand on everything that solicits the sentient creature who lives in his senses; gives the impression of the active, independent observer who is ashamed of none of his faculties, describes what he sees, renders, with a rare reproduction of tone, what he hears, and is more anxious to see and to hear than to make sure, in advance, of propping up some particular theory of things. He has indeed a theory to the effect that they are pretty bad, but practically the air of truth in the given case is almost never sacrificed to it. His strong, hard, cynical, slightly cruel humor can scarcely be called a theory; what one may say of this rather is that his drollery is a direct emanation from the facts, and especially from the rural facts, which he knows with extraordinary knowledge. His most brilliantly clever tales deal with the life, pervaded, for the most part, by a strong smell of the barn-yard and the wine-shop, of the Norman cottage and market-place. Such a little picture as "La Ficelle" ("The

Piece of String") is a pure gem, so caught in the fact are the whimsicalities of the thick-witted rustic world.

For the last ten years M. de Maupassant has contributed an almost weekly *nouvelle* to some Parisian sheet which has allowed him a luxurious liberty. They have been very unequal, too numerous, and occasionally bad enough to be by an inferior hand (an inevitable accident in copious production), but they have contained an immense element of delightful work. Taken all together, they are full of life (of life as the author conceives it, of course—he is far from having taken its measure in all directions), and between the lines of them we seem to read of that partly pleasant and wholly modern invention, a roving existence in which for art no impression is wasted. M. de Maupassant travels, explores, navigates, shoots, goes up in balloons, and writes. He treats of the North and of the South, evidently makes "copy" of everything that happens to him, and in the interest of such copy and such happenings, ranges from Étretat to the depths of Algeria. Lately he has given signs of adding a new cord to his bow—a silver cord of intenser vibration. His last two novels, *Pierre et Jean* and *Fort comme la Mort*, deal with shades of feeling and delicacies of experience to which he had shown himself rather a stranger. They are the work of an older man, and of a man who has achieved the feat of keeping his talent fresh when other elements have turned stale. In default of other convictions it may still for the artist be an adequate working faith to turn out something fine. Guy de Maupassant is a striking illustration of this curious truth and of the practical advantage of having a first-rate ability. Such a gift may produce surprises in the mere exercise of its natural health. The dogmatist is never safe with it.

Harper's Weekly, October 19, 1889

Charles de Mazade

M. CHARLES DE MAZADE, one of the most active contributors to the *Revue des Deux Mondes*, has lately
published in that periodical an article entitled "La Littérature
et nos Désastres," in which he discusses an interesting topic,
though he perhaps throws no very intense light upon it. The
gist of his article is the question, "What did the Empire do
for French literature?" His conclusion appears to be that it
did little—a conclusion in which many persons will agree
with him. It behooves such persons to remember, however,
that it is hard at all times to measure what, for good or for
ill, the political administration of a country does for its literary tone. If the government is corrupt, it is very likely that
the books of the day will be poor; but this is rather because
the people who put up with a corrupt government are the
sort of people to write poor books than because the political
régime exerts any very direct pressure upon literature. M. de
Mazade reminds us of the brilliant beginnings of contemporary French literature during the period from 1830 to 1848,
and then asks what it has come to in the hands of such writers
as MM. Feydeau and Zola. It is very true that the "generation
of 1830" offered an extraordinary reunion of genius and enthusiasm, and that it produced a series of masterpieces; but
the generation of 1830 had been preceded by the despotic
First Empire and the narrow régime of the Restoration, and
although the reign of Louis Philippe was comparatively, for
Frenchmen, a very comfortable one, its tone was certainly not
particularly inspiring or nourishing. However that may be, it
is incontestable that as the powerful talents who had passed
their maturity dropped away, their places, under the Empire,
were never filled. We can think of but two eminent writers
who rose to conspicuity after the *coup d'état* of whom it may
be said that their talent is of an elevated order: we allude to
MM. Renan and Taine. A great many clever writers sprang
into activity, but their cleverness had always a vicious strain
in it. The "moral" writers under the Empire were extremely
feeble and unreadable. The Empire had decidedly a taste of

its own, and that taste was a very bad one. The books of the day have its stamp, but it is very possible that they gave as much as they took. The Empire had indeed a literary style which was as bad as possible—the pretentious, hollow, insincere style of Napoleon III. in his speeches and addresses, the "official" French of the *Moniteur*. In so far as this insufferable phraseology rubbed off on other productions it was of course most baleful. French talents and cleverness were, we believe, as great as ever under the Empire; it was what underlies talent—thought, feeling, conviction, substance—that was wanting. Everything ran to form, and the successful books were apt to resemble little vases, skilfully moulded and chiselled, into which unclean things have been dropped. It was not always, indeed, that the successful books had form to recommend them; M. de Mazade accuses the "sovereigns" of reading 'Rocambole' at their villas. Apart from the other many excellent reasons for hoping for the continuance of the Republic in France we have this additional ground for deprecating the resurrection of the Empire—the permanence of the Republic will help, namely, to solve a curious intellectual problem: how far can a government really "encourage or discourage good literature." If under the Republic the chiselled and gilded empty shell of French literary form really finds a living soul again, we shall almost begin to believe in the old traditions about the "protection" of literature.

Nation, December 30, 1875

The Life of Count Cavour. Translated from the French of Charles de Mazade. New York: G. P. Putnam's Sons, 1877.

IN THIS SUBSTANTIAL VOLUME M. Charles de Mazade has related in a very interesting manner the history of an extraordinarily interesting career. Cavour's career was a short one—the space of eleven years covers the whole of it, and the shorter space of six years witnessed its most striking achievements—but it was nevertheless one of the most remarkable and most active in the annals of statesmanship. Clearly and harmoniously unfolded as it is in these pages, it reads indeed like a romance or a fairy-tale: there seems almost an element of magic in Cavour's inveterate successes. M. de Mazade is a passionate admirer of his hero, and the story loses in his hands none of its brilliancy of coloring. But it needs no re-touching: the naked facts themselves are a drama, with all the necessary requisites—the large and moving argument, the skilful performers, the thickening plot, the moment of suspense, the happy dénouement, the attentive auditory. The work accomplished by Cavour had a peculiar completeness and unity: it was a single, consistent task cut out for him by circumstances. It is sometimes said of him that circumstances had more part in the result than the man himself, and that if they had not happened to combine themselves again and again in a peculiarly favorable manner the liberator of Italy would not have been known beyond the limits of the quiet little kingdom of Piedmont. But M. de Mazade points out that Cavour's greatness was precisely in his marvellous talent for making his occasion—for knowing just the way in which to take hold of circumstances. From the day on which, of his own moment and as the first step in a far-seeing plan, he sent, in the face of domestic opposition, a Piedmontese contingent to the Crimean war, he pursued this vigilant culture of opportunity without faltering or going astray. M. de Mazade characterizes him as an extraordinary mixture of prudence and boldness; and these qualities with him always went hand in hand. He knew equally well how to wait and when to act. But it is the element of discretion, the art of sailing with the current of events, that enabled him to effect a great revolution by means that were, after all, in relation to the end in view, not violent—by measures that were never reckless, high-handed or of a character to force from circumstances more than they could naturally yield. For M. de Mazade, Cavour is the model of the moderate and conservative liberal. Liberal he was, as a friend said of him, "as he was fair-complexioned, lively and witty—by birth." But M. de Mazade constantly emphasizes the fact that his liberalism was untinged by the radical leaven, and that if he was a liberator, he had nothing in common with some of the gentry who aspire to this title. All this is very obvious. Cavour was not only the champion of his country: he was also the servant of his king, and his

dream was to see Italy not only united, but brought under
the sway of the old Piedmontese crown. He often said, according to M. de Mazade, that no republic can give as much
liberty, and as real liberty, as a constitutional monarchy that
operates regularly. It is noticeable that, keeping in view his
hero's conservative side, M. de Mazade relates in considerable
detail the story of the liberation of Italy, with no allusion to
Mazzini beyond speaking of him two or three times as a vulgar and truculent conspirator, and with a regrettable tendency
to stint the mixture of praise to the erratic but certainly, during a most important period, efficient Garibaldi. But Cavour's
nature was a wonderfully rich and powerful one; and there is
something very striking in such religious devotion to an idea
when it is unaccompanied with fanaticism or narrowness of
view, and tempered with good sense and wit and the art of
taking things easily.

Cavour had had his idea from the first: he cherished it for
a long time very quietly: he was awaiting his opportunity.
"We will do something," he said one day in 1850, rubbing his
hands—his legendary gesture—as he looked across Lago
Maggiore to the Austrian shore. It was not till 1855 that the
first serious opportunity came, but he attached himself to this
with the quiet zeal and obstinacy of a man who feels that he
is driving in the narrow end of the wedge. There were all
sorts of telling objections to be made to the co-operation of
Piedmont in the Crimean war, and Cavour was at the disadvantage, for a man who was rigidly and supremely practical,
of having to defend his course on ideal and far-fetched
grounds. But his idealism proved to be plain good sense: it
brought little Piedmont to the notice of Europe, and gave her
the right to call attention to her affairs. The young Italian
officer spoke the truth who said to a poor soldier struggling
with the mud in the Crimean trenches, "Never mind—make
the best of it: with this mud we are making Italy!" As Piedmont had had a hand in the war, so she had a seat at the
Congress of Paris which followed it; and here Cavour, finding
his auditory ready made to his hand, introduced—a little perhaps by the shoulders—the then comparatively novel "Italian
question." This was his second opportunity. The emperor
Napoleon had asked him, from an impulse of imperial civility,

"If there was anything he could do for Italy?" and Cavour, taking him at his word, and more than his word, had instantly drawn up a list of *desiderata*. M. de Mazade gives a detailed and very interesting account of the gradual adoption by the emperor of his Italian policy—of the various phases through which it passed, of its complications and interruptions, and of Napoleon's curiously fitful, illusive and at times evasive attitudes. Cavour's relations with Napoleon III. may serve as the best example of his disposition to use the best instruments and opportunities that offered themselves, and not quarrel with them because they were not ideally perfect. This was what the Italian "patriots" of the mere romantic type could never forgive: that Italy should appeal for liberation to the oppressor of France was to them a displeasing and monstrous anomaly. But Cavour had a lively sense of reality in human affairs, and for him the best thing was the best possible thing. It was enough that—for reasons best known to himself—the "Man of December" had taken a fancy to this idea of lending a hand to the oppressed Peninsula: his own duty was to fan the flame. The emperor's sympathy with Italian independence is certainly the most interesting and honorable feature in his career, and its mingled motives and mysterious fluctuations present a very curious study. The desire to do something for Italy was, however, steadfast, and had been an early dream; and the reader of M. de Mazade's pages can easily believe that Cavour's personal influence and magnetism had something—had even a good deal—to do with bringing it to a climax. Napoleon appreciated the Piedmontese statesman, and felt his superiority. From a certain ideal point of view there is something displeasing in seeing the advocate of so noble a cause dancing attendance upon an unscrupulous adventurer, and hanging as it were upon his lips; but we know not what other ways there may have been: we only know that, in fact, a great deal of generous French blood was shed upon the plains of Lombardy.

After the Congress of Paris, Cavour spent two years of eager, anxious waiting and of the most active private agitation. It was by the aid of England and France combined that he proposed to compass his aim, but he had, in the case of England, to content himself with a strictly Platonic sympathy.

His mingled ardor and tact during this period, his tension of purpose, and yet his self-restraint, his inveterate skill in turning events to his advantage, are vividly narrated by M. de Mazade. At last, in the summer of 1858, Napoleon sent for him to Plombières, drove him out in a dog-cart, and during the drive told him that he was now ready to "do something" for Italy. Then and there the outline of the war of 1859 was resolved upon. The abrupt conclusion of the war was, at least momentarily, a profound disappointment to Cavour: the Peace of Villafranca, which left half its fruits ungathered, seemed to the Italian party almost an act of treachery on the part of the French emperor. Napoleon was, in fact, alarmed at his work: he had been almost too successful, and he determined to throw up the game. Cavour, in irritation, disgust and despair, immediately withdrew from the ministry, his place being taken by Urbano Rattazzi. The new minister presided at that great breaking-up throughout the rest of Italy for which the expulsion of the Austrians from Lombardy had given the signal, and which took place under the direct patronage of Piedmont. The attitude of the latter state was a very difficult one, and Rattazzi proved but half master of the situation: at the end of six months Cavour was recalled to power. From this point in his work one step succeeds another with a sort of dramatic effectiveness. He was confronted with the constant necessity of presenting an unflinching front to Austria; the necessity, equally imperious, of checking reactionary excesses in Parma and Modena, Bologna and Tuscany; the need of keeping what had been gained, and at the same time reaching forth for more; of keeping on good terms with France, who had drawn back almost as far as she first advanced; of remaining free, especially, from the reproach of meddling with the papacy—an enterprise for which the occasion was not ripe; of stimulating England, who had advanced in proportion as France withdrew; and of being supremely careful, generally, to commit no faults. The cession of Savoy and Nice brought down upon Cavour a storm of denunciation, but he had counted the cost, and the resolution with which he paid the price of Napoleon's assistance was extremely characteristic of him. It was apparently equally characteristic of Garibaldi, born at Nice and her most illus-

trious son, that he felt it a mortal affront that by this diplomatic bargain he should have been "deprived of a country."
M. de Mazade characterizes very happily Cavour's attitude
during Garibaldi's invasion of the Two Sicilies—his silent
complicity, his skill in giving his terrible associate rope, as it
were, and yet keeping him in hand. Cavour did not live to
see the last two acts of his great drama—the occupation of
Venetia and of Rome—but they were only, as it were, the
epilogue: they were implied in what had gone before. He
died of overwork—broke down in the midst of his labors.
Great innovator as he had been, he was remarkable for the
moderation of his attitude toward the Church; and the last
words he uttered to the good friar who attended his deathbed
were a repetition of his famous formula—"Libera chiesa in
libero stato."

Lippincott's Magazine, December 1877

Prosper Mérimée

Dernières Nouvelles de Prosper Mérimée, de L'Académie Française. Paris: Michel Lévy; New York: F. W. Christern, 1873.

EDMOND ABOUT somewhere speaks of Madame Sand and Prosper Mérimée, "the two greatest French writers." Without exactly agreeing with M. About, the reader interested in literary matters in France may have a high enough opinion of the author of 'Colomba' and the 'Double Méprise' to be thankful for this posthumous volume of tales. Unfortunately, the stories before us will add little weight to the opinion; though, indeed, they remind us agreeably of the author's limited but singularly perfect talent. Mérimée had long ago given the measure of his power as a story-teller, and it was hardly to be hoped that this little collection of literary remnants would place it in a new light. His first successes date from the early years of the century; the 'Théâtre de Clara Gazul' and 'Colomba,' his masterpiece, as most people think, are already ancient literature. In the subject-matter of his tales he was a precursor of the *romantiques* of 1830, and it is greatly to be wished that they had taken example by his manner as well. Victor Hugo would have been none the worse poet for a little of Mérimée's conscious sobriety, and Madame Sand would have been none the less readable for occasionally emulating his extraordinary conciseness. That M. About should couple the author of 'Lélia' with Mérimée, in the estimate just quoted, indicates a taste determined to be comprehensive at any cost; for the shortest way to describe Mérimée would perhaps be to say that he is the absolute reverse of Madame Sand. He is unlike her in the *quantity* of his genius as well as the quality, his fecundity being as limited as hers has been excessive. He wrote very short tales, and produced them, one by one, at long intervals. Many years before his death he ceased to produce stories at all, and confined himself to publishing occasionally a short historical or archæological sketch, so that a complete collection of his tales would fill but three or four small volumes, and might be read in a day. Such as they are, however, we confess that Mérimée's chiselled and polished little fictions, and, indeed, the whole manner and system of the author, have always had a great fascination for us. He is, perhaps, the most striking modern example of zealous artistic conciseness—of the literary artist who works in detail, by the line, by the word. There have been poets who scanned their rhythm as narrowly as Mérimée, but we doubt whether there has ever been a prose writer. His effort was to compress as large an amount of dramatic substance as possible into a very narrow compass, and the result is that, though his stories are few and short, one may read them again and again, and perceive with each reading a greater force of meaning. Some of the earlier ones are most masterly in this pregnant brevity; the story seems to say its last word, as the reader lays it down, with a kind of magical after-resonance. We have often thought a selection might be made from these tales, and presented to young narrators as a sort of manual of their trade—a guide for the avoidance of prolixity. Mérimée's subjects are always of the romantic and picturesque order, dealing in action, not in sentiment. They almost always hinge on a violent adventure or chain of adventures, and are strongly seasoned with bloodshed and general naughtiness. There are a great many sword-thrusts and pistol-shots, and a good deal of purely carnal love-making. At the beginning of his career the author had a great relish for Spanish local color, and several of his early works are richly charged with it. The 'Théâtre de Clara Gazul,' written, we believe, before he was twenty-three, is a series of short tragic dramas on the picturesque cruelties and immoralities of Old Spain. One of his masterpieces, 'Carmen,' published later, is the history of a wonderful *gitanilla*—a princess among the heroines who have dared much for love. With his brutal subjects and his cynical style, Mérimée is doubtless thoroughly disagreeable to such readers as are not fascinated by his artistic skill. To tell a terrible little story without flinching—without expressing a grain of reprobation for the clever rascal who escapes under cover of the scuffle in which his innocent rival has his brains blown out, or a grain of compassion for the poor guilty lady whose husband or father, brought upon the scene by the crack of pistols, condemns her to a convent-cell for life; not to be sentimental, not to be moral, not to be rhetorical, but to have simply a sort of gentlemanly, epicurean relish for the bitter-

ness of the general human lot, and to distil it into little polished silver cups—this was Mérimée's conscious effort, and
this was his rare success.

Some of his best stories are those in which a fantastic or
supernatural element is thrown into startling relief against a
background of hard, smooth realism. An admirable success in
this line is the 'Venus d'Ille'—a version of the old legend of
a love-pledge between a mortal and an effigy of the goddess.
Mr. Morris has treated the theme with his usual somewhat
prolix imagery in his 'Earthly Paradise.' Mérimée, making his
heroine an antique bronze statue, disinterred in the garden of
a little château in Gascony, and her victim the son of the old
provincial antiquarian who discovered her, almost makes us
believe in its actuality. This was the first known to us of Mérimée's tales, and we shall never forget our impression of its
admirable art. The first and much the best of the stories in
the present volume, "Lokis," deals with a subject as picturesquely unnatural. A Polish lady is seized by a bear, and
dragged for five minutes toward his hiding-place. She is rescued in time to save her life, but her reason has succumbed
to her terror, and she remains for ever a monomaniac. A few
months after her disaster she gives birth to a son. Mérimée
tells us the son's story. We recommend it to readers not averse
to a good stiff horror. Our author's last years were very silent,
though "Lokis," indeed, was published shortly before his
death. He broke his silence in a flimsier cause in producing
the mildly scandalous tale of the 'Chambre Bleue.' Among the
papers found at the Tuileries after the flight of the Empress,
as the story goes, was the MS., tied with blue ribbons, of this
little performance à la Crébillon Fils. Worthy, perhaps, of the
circle for which it was composed, it adds little to the reputation of one of the "first French writers." But we strongly suspect that Mérimée's best things will be valued for many years
to come. Among writers elaborately perfect in a somewhat
narrow line he will hold a high place; he will always be admired by the votaries of "manner." Twenty years hence,
doubtless, clever young men, reading him for the first time,
will, in the flash of enthusiasm, be lending his volumes to
appreciative female friends, and having them promptly returned, with the observation that they are "coarse." Where-

upon, we suppose, the clever young men will fall to reading them over, and reflecting that it is quite right, after all, that men should have their distinctive pleasures, and that a good story by Mérimée is not the least of these. We should add that our author gave some attention to Russian literature, and that the best thing in the present volume, after "Lokis," the extremely energetic little tale called "Le Coup de Pistolet," is a translation from Pushkin.

Nation, February 12, 1874

MÉRIMÉE'S LETTERS

THE MANY READERS who take pleasure in clever French books have found themselves of late deploring the sadly diminished supply of this commodity. The past few years have brought forth no new literary names of the first rank in France and have witnessed the decline and extinction of most of the elder talents. It is a long time now since a French book has made a noise on valid grounds. Here, at last, however, is a publication which, in six weeks, has reached a fourth edition and which most people of taste are talking about. But, though new in subject, the two volumes to which we allude belong to the literature of thirty years ago. They are the last contribution to literature of a writer whose reputation was made in the early part of the century. We recently heard it declared by a competent critic that they contain the best writing (as simple writing) that has appeared in France since Voltaire. This is strong language; but the reader of the easy, full-flavoured, flexible prose to which Mérimée treats his correspondent will certainly feel the charm that prompted it. Prosper Mérimée's title to fame has hitherto consisted in a couple of dozen little tales, varying from ten to a hundred pages in length. They have gradually come to be considered perfect models of the narrative art; and we confess our own admiration for them is such that we feel like declaring it a capital offence in a young story-teller to put pen to paper without having read them and digested them. It was a very handsome compliment to pure quality (to the sovereignty of form)

when Mérimée, with his handful of little stories, was elected
to the French Academy. The moral element in his tales is such
as was to be expected in works remarkable for their pregnant
concision and for a firmness of contour suggesting hammered
metal. In a single word they are not sympathetic. Sympathy
is prolix, sentiment is diffuse, and our author, by inexorably
suppressing emotion, presents his facts in the most salient relief. These facts are, as a general thing, extremely disagreeable—murder and adultery being the most frequent and the
catastrophe being always ingeniously tragical. Where sentiment never appears, one gradually concludes that it does not
exist; and we had mentally qualified this frigid artist as a natural cynic. A romancer with whom bloodshed and tears were
so abundant and subjective compassion so rare had presumably a poor opinion of the stock from which heroes and heroines spring. Many years ago M. Mérimée ceased to publish
stories and devoted himself to archæology and linguistics. We
have often wondered how during all these years he employed
his incisive imagination. The "Lettres à une Inconnue" inform
us.

They consist of a series of familiar—often singularly familiar—epistles, addressed during more than thirty years to a
lady of whom nothing is generally known. The letters begin
apparently about 1838; the last is written in September 1870,
two hours before the author's death, in the prime of his
country's recent disasters. Love-letters we suppose they are
properly to be called; but the reader may judge from a few
extracts whether they seem superficially to belong to this category. In his private as well as his public compositions Mérimée was an enemy to fine phrases; and here, instead of
burning incense at the feet of his beloved, he treats her to
such homely truths as these: "The cakes you eat with such
appetite to cure you of the backache you got at the opera
surprised me still more. But it isn't that among your defects I
don't place coquetry and gluttony in the first rank." "The affection that you have for me is only a sort of *jeu d'esprit*. You
are all *esprit*. You are one of those 'chilly women of the
North.' You only live by your head." He is forever accusing
her of coquetry, heartlessness, duplicity, mendacity. "Why, after we have been what we are to each other so long, do you

take several days to answer the simplest question?" After her marriage he tells her it is all nonsense for her to say that she is a better person than she was before. "You seem to me prettier; but you have acquired, on the other hand, a pretty dose of selfishness and hypocrisy." It is true that in the beginning of their acquaintance he disclaims the ambition of being her lover. "Perhaps you'll gain a real friend; and I, perhaps, shall find in you what I have been looking for so long—a woman with whom I am not in love and in whom I can have confidence." One doubts whether he was gratified. "You grow every day more imperious and you have scandalous refinements of coquetry." And yet one wonders, too, whether to attribute to friendship or love this vigorous allusion to a walk with his correspondent: "For myself, contrary to my habit, I have no distinct recollections. I am like a cat who licks his whiskers a long time after drinking milk." We owe our knowledge of these letters to the lady herself, who has published them with a frankness more common in France than among ourselves. She has, however, taken every pains to draw the veil about her identity, and it may be said on her behalf that it is none of our business who she was or what she was. But only a very unimaginative reader will spare his conjectures. There is something extremely provoking to curiosity in the image, however shadowy, of a woman clever enough to have all this cleverness addressed to her. The author tells her early in the book that she has "a nature so *raffinée*"—something more than our "refined"—"as to be for him the summing-up of a civilization." It is not, apparently, without reason that he writes to her: "Between your head and your heart I never know which is to carry the day. You don't know yourself; but you always give the victory to your head." She had a head worth favouring. Constantly busy himself with philological studies, he recommends her to learn Greek as a pastime, and tells her how to set to work. It soon appears that she has taken his advice, and in the course of time we find her enjoying Homer and the tragedians. Later, when, with the privilege of a twenty years' friendship, he utters all the crudities that come into his head—and they grow very numerous as he grows older—he scolds her for being alarmed at what she finds in Aristophanes. The burden of his complaint from the first is her reserve, her calculations, her never obeying the first impulse. She had carried so far refusing to see him, for fear of getting tired of him, that he estimates that they have spent but three or four hours together in the course of six or seven years. This is Platonism with a vengeance and Mérimée makes an odd figure in it. He constantly protests, and begs for a walk in the Champs Elysées or a talk in the gallery of the Louvre. The critic to whom we just alluded and whose impression differs from our own in that these volumes have made him like the writer more than before, rather than less, maintains that we have a right to be very severe toward the heroine. She was cold, he affirms; she was old-maidish and conventional; she had no spontaneous perceptions. When Mérimée is not at hand to give her a cue her opinions are evidently of the flimsiest. When she travels he exhorts her almost fiercely to observe and inquire, to make a note of everything curious in manners and morals, and he invariably scolds her for the inefficiency of her *compte-rendu*. This is probably true enough. She had not the unshrinking glance of her guide, philosopher and friend. But we confess that our own sentiment with regard to her partakes of vague compassion. Mérimée's tone and general view of things, judged in a vivid moral light, were such as very effectually to corrupt a pliable and dependent nature; and what we perceive in his correspondent's reserve—her reluctance, in common phrase, to make herself cheap—is the natural effort to preserve a certain ideal dignity in her own eyes. "Each time we meet," he declares, in 1843, "it seems as if there were a new formation of ice to break through. Why don't I find you the same as I left you? If we met oftener, this wouldn't happen. I am like an old opera for you, which you need to forget to hear it again with any pleasure." He numbers this annoying self-possession, apparently, among the machinations of what he calls her "infernal coquetry." His conception of the feminine character, though it had sunk a deep shaft in a single direction, was strikingly narrow. In the later letters, where he appears altogether in his dressing-gown and slippers, he is for ever berating his old friend for her "prudery." He can think of no other name for the superficiality of her investigation of certain points of harem-life, during a sojourn in Algiers; and he showers the same accusation upon her when, on his having lent her books unfamiliar to most women, she alludes to their peculiar character in returning them. One is anxious to know where he drew the line between "prudery" and modesty, or whether he really thought the distinction not worth making. And yet it was not that his friendship had not a masculine delicacy of its own. He says innumerable tender things, in which his ardour is anything but cynical. Here is an allusion to a Spanish greeting with which she had begun a letter: "I wish I had seen you when you were writing *amigo de mi alma*. When you have your portrait taken for me, say that to yourself, instead of *'petite pomme d'api,'* as the ladies say who wish to make their mouths look pretty." The nearest approach in the book to the stuff that love-letters are generally made of is an allusion to the pains of the tender passion. "Several times it has come into my head not to answer you and to see you no more. This is very reasonable and a great deal can be said for it. The execution is more difficult."

Gradually, however, sentiment of the tenderer sort disappears—but by absorption, as one may say, and not by evanescence. After a correspondence of ten years the writer's devotion may be taken for granted. His letters become an irremissible habit, an intellectual need, a receptacle for his running commentary on life. The second volume of the "Lettres à une Inconnue" contains less that is personal to the lady, and more allusions to other people and things, more anecdotes and promiscuous reflections. Mérimée became more and more a man of the world. He was member of two Academies, inspector and conservator of national monuments (a very active post, apparently), a senator of the Empire and an intimate friend of his sovereigns. He travels constantly from Moscow to Madrid, makes regular archæological surveys through the length and breadth of France, and pays frequent visits to England. He meets every one and knows most people—most great people, at least. In the midst of these things he despatches constant notes to his correspondent, flashing his lantern fitfully over his momentary associates and over events of the hour. There is a multitude of entertaining opinions, characterizations and anecdotes; but we lack space for quotations. Everything he says is admirably said; his phrase, in its mingled brevity and laxity, is an excellent "fit" for his thought. He tells anecdotes as vividly as Madame de Sévigné and in much fewer words. His judgments are rarely flattering and his impressions rarely genial; and, as proper names have been retained throughout, with unprecedented audacity, many of his opinions must have aroused a sufficiently inharmonious echo. He goes again and again to England; but familiarity seems to breed something very much akin to contempt. "I am beginning to have enough of *ce pays-ci*. I am satiated with perpendicular architecture and the equally perpendicular manners of the natives. I passed two days at Cambridge and at Oxford in the houses of 'reverends,' and, the matter well considered, I prefer the Capuchins. I gave (at Salisbury) half-a-crown to a person in black who showed me the cathedral, and then I asked him the address of a gentleman to whom I had a letter from the Dean. It turned out that it was to him the letter was addressed. He looked like a fool, and I too; but he kept the money." The most interesting thing throughout the later letters is not, however, the witty anecdotes and the raps at the writer's *confrères*, but the development of his scepticism and cynicism. He took his stand early in life on his aversion to florid phrases (one must remember, in palliation, that he was a Frenchman of the so-called generation of 1830), and he fell a victim ultimately to what we may call a dogmatization of his temperament. His dislike for fine names led him at last to a total disbelief in fine things. He had found a great many pretty puppets stuffed with sawdust or nothing at all; so he concluded that all sentiment was hollow and flattered himself that he had pricked the bubble. We have noted but a single instance of his speaking of a case of moral ardour without raillery more or less explicit; and even here it is a question to what extent the ardour is in fact moral. "Since there have been so many romances and poems of the passionate or would-be passionate sort every woman pretends to have a heart. Wait a little yet. When you have a heart in good earnest, you will let me know. You will regret the good time when you lived only by your head, and you will see that the evils you suffer from now are but pin-pricks compared to the dagger-blows that will rain down on you when the time of passions comes." M. Taine, in a masterly preface to these volumes, has laid his finger on the weak spot in Mérimée's character. "For fear of being dupe, he *mistrusted* in life, in love, in science, in art; and *he was dupe of his mistrust.* One is always dupe of something." This latter sentence may be true; but Mérimée's fallacy was, of all needful illusions, the least remunerative while it lasted, for it eventually weakened an intellect which had every reason for being strong. The letters of his latter years are sad reading. His wit loses none of its edge; but what the French call *sécheresse* had utterly invaded his soul. His health breaks down, and his short notes are hardly more than a record of reiterated ailments and contemptuous judgments. Most forms of contempt are unwise; but one of them seems to us peculiarly ridiculous—contempt for the age one lives in. Men with but a tithe of Mérimée's ingenuity have been able, and have not failed, in every age, to make out a deplorable case for mankind.

Poor Mérimée, apparently, long before his death, ceased to enjoy anything but the sunshine and a good dinner. His imagination faded early, and it is certainly a question whether this generous spirit, half-sister, at least, to Charity, will remain under a roof in which the ideal is treated as uncivilly as Mérimée treated it. He was constantly in the Imperial train at Fontainebleau, Compiègne and Saint Cloud; but he does little save complain of the discomforts of grandeur in general and of silk tights in especial. He was, however, as the event proved, a sincere friend of the Emperor and Empress, and not a mere mercenary courtier. He always speaks kindly of them and sharply of every one else except Prince Bismarck, whom he meets at Biarritz and who takes his fancy greatly. The literature of the day he considers mere rubbish. Half a dozen of his illustrious contemporaries come in for hard knocks; but M. Renan and his *paysages* are his pet aversion. The manners of the day are in his opinion still worse and the universal world is making a prodigious fool of itself. The collapse of the Empire, in which he believed as much as he believed in anything, set the seal to his pessimism, and he died, most consentingly, as one may suppose, as the Germans were marching upon Paris. His effort had been to put as little as possible of his personal self into his published writings; but fortune and his correspondent have betrayed him, and after reading these letters we feel that we know him. This fact, added to their vigour, their vivacity and raciness, accounts for their great success. There had been lately a great many poems and novels, philosophies and biographies, abounding in more or less fantastic *simulacra* of human creatures; but here is a genuine, visible, palpable *man*, with a dozen limitations but with a most distinct and curious individuality.

Independent, April 9, 1874
Reprinted in *French Poets and Novelists*, 1878

Lettres à une autre Inconnue. Par Prosper Mérimée, de l'Académie Française. Avant-propos par H. Blaze de Bury. Paris: Michel Lévy; New York: F. W. Christern, 1875.

OUR READERS HAVE probably not forgotten the review of Mérimée's 'Lettres à une Inconnue' which appeared in these columns some year and a half ago. The book had been largely read, but it was variously appreciated. Some people thought it very trivial, others deemed it very deep; upon its being entertaining, however, most people were agreed. Amid the criticism to which it gave rise, there was not a little animadversion upon the audacity of the lady to whom the letters were addressed, who, when her admirer had passed away, had not scrupled to make public some thirty years of their common very private history. We hardly know if it makes this lady's frankness more surprising or more natural to find another person capable of the same intrepidity. Here is another "unknown" with another bundle of confidential epistles. She has apparently very sagaciously reflected that to have been a correspondent of Mérimée is just now a remunerative situation, and that since the ice has been broken there is no harm in making a few more holes. About Mérimée himself everything worth saying seems to us by this time to have been said; he has received his dues, and more than his dues. So small an investment of talent has certainly never brought in a higher interest of fame. He wrote a dozen tales which will last, but there is something really paradoxical in talking much about them—so very reticent, and spare, and frugal of eloquence are they themselves. M. Blaze de Bury, a writer who is a great talker (and it must be added a very entertaining one), has endeavored in a long preface to the present volume to say something new about the author of 'Colomba,' but most of his novelties are of a sort that would evaporate in quotation. He has made one good point, however, on the subject of that masterly reserve for which Mérimée has been so much praised. Mérimée never describes, he only narrates, and there is certainly often something very eloquent in his studied sobriety. It has always been assumed that if he did not describe it is because he would not, and not because he could not; but M. Blaze de Bury reminds us that there is another side to the question, and that there is such a thing as glorifying negative merits too highly. In the 'Chronique de Charles IX.,' when the king comes in, the author, who is apparently about to give a sketch of his person, suddenly stops short. "His portrait?—wait. Really you had better go and see it in the Museum at Angoulême; it is in the second room; number 98." "This is a convenient way of getting out of it," says M. Blaze de Bury; "is it the best way? Mérimée was a sly fox, depend upon it, and he had no need of La Fontaine and his fables to characterize the grapes that one cannot reach." It is certain, with all deference to what is called economy of effect, that the phrase above quoted could not have been written by a man of a rich genius, and Mérimée decidedly was not a man of a rich genius. There is fortunately a golden mean between bathos and blankness.

It is not, however, for their undue reticence that these new letters are remarkable. Mérimée's pen, in addressing his fair correspondents, was neither prudish nor cautious, and there are several passages in this little volume which seem to belong to a date much earlier than our modern proprieties. They will afford an extra satisfaction to those connoisseurs who consider Mérimée the last of the French writers who has to some extent preserved the last-century traditions of style. These letters are fifty in number; they are very short; and they are really not valuable. Persons seriously interested in the author will find in them something to complete their mental image of him; but those who should read them without having been otherwise introduced to Mérimée, would scarcely suppose them to be the productions of a superior man. They run, at wide intervals, through a space of five years, from 1865 to 1870, and the person to whom they were addressed is less of a mystery than the first unknown. She was a Polish lady of high rank, who seems to have been, like her correspondent, on a footing of familiarity at the court of Napoleon III. The Empress, during those laboriously brilliant years that preceded the war, had established certain "courts of love" for the entertainment of her social circle, and Mérimée's correspondent was "president," or judge, at one of these. Whether she had ever had to pass sentence on Mérimée as an offender is more than we can say, but it is in this character that he always addresses her. He deals chiefly in court gossip, and alludes to the trifles of the hour. Such slender value as the letters possess belongs to the fact that the Imperial court, having become so thoroughly a thing of the past, a theme for the historian and the moralist, Mérimée's anecdotes and *cancans* have a sort of historical savor. "We have the happiness occasionally of seeing the Empress of Mexico. She is a *maîtresse-femme*, and as like as two peas to Louis Philippe. She has some ladies of honor with flaming eyes, but complexions like gingerbread, and a sort of look of orang-outangs. We expected to see the houris of Mahomet! It is supposed that her majesty has come to ask for money and soldiers; but I fancy they will give her nothing but fêtes, for which she seems to care little." That seems very far away from the present moment in France. Most of the proper names have been retained; the reader may judge of the practical results in some cases. "The Princess of Metternich is, on the contrary, all grace and amiability. Only, she has thrown herself into painting. I mean the *Samojivopistro* (the painting of one's self); and how this science has progressed! She has lips of the most delightful flame-color, with which she can drink tea without leaving them on the cup." Here is another specimen, from Biarritz: "We have here the Grand-Duchess Marie of Russia, and the Grand-Duke of Leuchtenberg, who is a very handsome fellow, and who would make ravages on this shore if there were a few beauties less thoroughly known than those we possess. Madame de Talleyrand, whose hair has become blond, the Duchess of Frias—such are the highest temptations we can offer. I don't speak of

Madame Korsakof, in a yellow dress and a black jacket, black stockings, and boots with yellow rosettes, who leads about a great black dog (without any yellow), and a gentleman to protect her. She has still a charming figure, and with her back turned makes a great many conquests." The following is more interesting: "We have brought back the Emperor in very good health. He took long tramps on foot with us, which quite used us up. In truth, the more I see of princes, the more I perceive that they are made of another paste than common mortals. For myself, I have no fitness whatever for the profession, and I abstain absolutely from all pretension to sovereignty—even to that of Greece or the Moldo-Wallachian Principalities."

On the whole, the unprejudiced reader may conclude that, if these letters add nothing to Mérimée's reputation, they were at least good enough for the person to whom they were addressed, and who has seen fit to give them to the world.

Nation, January 27, 1876

PROSPER MÉRIMÉE

FOR SPEAKING TO-DAY by way of a change—a marked change—of Prosper Mérimée, the two admirable volumes lately published by M. Augustin Filon offer me the happiest occasion. Yet I must none the less not take time for admiring the art with which the author, treating his subject firstly and secondly—in the latter case, after an interval of four years—for the brilliant series of Hachette's Grands Écrivains Français has kept the two forms of his service distinct and managed, on repetition, to be just different enough. Such a feat is especially remarkable with a subject not yielding space for wide evolutions. Mérimée may be one of the immortal, as the immortal nowadays go, but he is not one of the infinite. My concern with his biographer, however, is mainly a matter of gratitude for being just turned again to the man himself and feeling the revival—a remembrance infinitely agreeable—of an old literary love. That one should ever have "loved" Mérimée seems perhaps odd, but that, at any rate, is the light in which I like now to recover eagerness of early appreciation. It was definitely rekindled, this memory,

by M. Filon's other volume, the *Mérimée et ses Amis*, which
perhaps implied a promise of richer revelations to come than
the conditions of a "series" properly permit. M. Filon has all
the air—the graceful, enviable authority—of a conscious de-
positary, and may, for all I know, have still a card or two up
his sleeve. There are conspicuously several cards—precious
groups of unpublished letters—yet to be played. But meanwhile there is plenty of interest in those already on the table.

Mérimée is a writer—and, more generally, a personal figure—singularly provoking to the critical sense, even though
he be, in the matter of expression, not by any means of the
family of the many-sided. Limited and hard, he yet affects us
as complete—which is partly, doubtless, because he was in
the worldly way a success, and led his life much as he chose.
Though he is superficial, he makes us wonder how he is put
together. That, at all events, I perfectly recall, was his action,
years and years ago, on a reader barely adolescent and not of
the writer's own race. This sensitive spirit found itself, one
unforgettable summer's day, fluttering deliciously—quite as
if with a sacred terror—at the touch of *La Vénus d'Ille*. That
was the first flush of a sentiment destined to last for many a
year and of which the ashes are not even at present completely
cold. *La Vénus d'Ille* struck my immaturity as a masterpiece
of art and offered to the young curiosity concerned that
sharpest of all challenges for youth, the challenge as to the
special source of the effect. It may in these days sound monstrous, but there are readers who, while still schoolboys, wonder more even how the thing is done than how the tangle
will come out. With Mérimée it always came out, to the particular attention I speak of, as sharp as a pirate's blade or an
Indian torture, and that was quite enough. So everything else
in another volume—the volume was *Colomba*, the product of
the imagination by which Mérimée mainly lives—contributed
to show. It brought home as nothing else had done—for
prose, for the life of our time—the lesson of a mysterious
selection and concision. M. Filon very happily compares these
things—Mérimée's tales and dramatic morsels in general—to
the neatest medals, and it was doubtless, though then unnameable, just a part of the glad impression that, as one handled them, the hard bronze pieces seemed to rattle together

and click. The poison of the "short story" was evidently in one's blood when *Tamango*, *Matteo Falcone*, *L'Enlèvement de la Redoute* had the magic of an edge so fine and a surface so smooth. There is a pleasure at last, however this be, of noting any obligation of the awakening intelligence, of picking it out of the dust-heap of the years. The very young person I speak of supposed it to be of great artistic profit to translate the first two of the stories just mentioned and offer them, for insertion, to an illustrated weekly periodical. So long ago struck, for him, the hour of precarious appeals. He can see at this moment the rejected MS., cast at his feet again by the post, unroll, ironically, its anxious neatness—for in those days of comparative amenity contributions appear to have been bodily returned; and there must have glimmered before him his first vision of the difference between the taste of the "caterers" for the public and the taste of the brooding critic. Certain it is that from that moment he was sure Mérimée was distinguished; perhaps there even dawned in him an apprehension of the germs, on the part of that author's victim, of the same complaint.

After that, with the *Chronique de Charles IX.*, with *Le Vase Etrusque* and *La Double Méprise*, with *Carmen*, *Arsène Guillot*, *L'Abbé Aubain*, above all with *Clara Gazul* and various other matters—after that it became a thorough superstition, of which there is now a charm in retracing the rites and portents, the fevers and fits. The glamour was doubtless in the perception that, somehow, more than any one else in the same line, equally near at hand, Mérimée was an "artist." The way the thing was done was the dead secret, the hidden treasure. If I was still at a loss as to what the artist might be, I had only to look straight before me for the answer. The artist was simply Mérimée, and it was a blessing so to be able to rest. If this was a tribute to his remarkable faculty for keeping the number of his touches down and making each one unerringly tell—his instinct for incorruptible selection, in other words, in view of his effect—what he essentially suggested was that that was the fine way to write. There came in time and little by little a change in this view: it was the fine way to write—such a truth had lost none of its force, but after a while arrived the wonder of why then it was not more satisfying. It was firm and sharp and penetrating; yet perhaps, more and more, it struck the unfolding mind as meagre. Then there came a light: it was the best way to write, yes—but was it, altogether, the best way to *be*? The question only made the author more interesting—opened up vistas as to the connexion, as it were, between the talent and the soul. It took a long time, I hasten to add, to move in that direction a distance at present worth speaking of; but I well remember how, when many years had come and gone, the general subject, in relation to the individual Mérimée, was refreshed by the publication of the letters to the Inconnue.

The value of these admirable volumes was greatest of all for those who had early been mystified. They scattered a lapful of answers, and every page the author had directly addressed to the public appeared to have been but a preparation for the surprise and the success of his Correspondence. This was to make him the partaker of a literary good fortune very superior to the odd, marked demi-reputation that his works of fiction and of research, so few and so brief, had had to content themselves with achieving for him. His reputation is made whole by his letters, his case beautifully arranged. The mixture of the strong and the thin in his previous volumes presented him as a puzzle, but the puzzle has been cleared up, and the result has the highest price. I mean not indeed for the aid and comfort of mankind in general, but for that of the critic desirous really to possess himself of the figure before him. This figure seems, to-day, removed not by a quarter, but by the whole of a century, and to belong to a tradition that the present literary manners of its country have made almost as alien as some passing fashion of Siam or some faded classic of China. But it is precisely in this rococo element—with what the various volumes of his letters enable us to read into it—that there is a special, indescribable unity; so sharp a light does Mérimée throw, in his way, on the whole "classic" business in France, showing us both what queer things, in the old order, could go with it and what indispensable ones it could go without. Here come in his contradictions and harsh inconsistencies— of surface, at all events; the whole range of anomaly illustrated by the sterility of his rare talent, flowering into a mere handful of small pieces, and by his having at once so much curiosity and so much prejudice. If there was a character that above all he desired to exhibit, it was that of a man of the world, and yet as a mere man of the world even he might have got a glimpse of what was finally reserved for a literary taste that consisted almost wholly in the dread of emotion and the abuse of sobriety. This conscious sobriety—the absence of redundancy, of loose ends, of twaddle—that, given strong subjects, made the distinction of his best tales, was, after all, a horse that was not to take him far.

It was really, to all appearance, as if the artist in him had been killed by the man, by the personal character and its strong and not particularly sweet idiosyncracies, its great mark in particular, its horror of the air of innocence. Mérimée, coarse in temperament and in imagination, in spite of the high type of his cultivation and accomplishment, was scarcely innocent of anything, and could well have afforded, having so much of the reality, not to encumber himself with the affectation of experience. But he was blighted, as other men have been, with that worst kind of priggishness, the priggishness of perversity. Strange it must have seemed to him to have produced in youth a little row—for it was not a case of a single "fluke"—of prose pieces destined to live on and on, and yet to find himself, during his long after-time, powerless to add to it. If we can imagine that the artist *might*, in conditions, have lived and was simply sacrificed to a certain vulgar element—incongruous as the term may sound—in the man's love of life, the case would be admirable as the subject of an apologue. But I doubt if in fact Mérimée ever put his finger on the spot or guessed that the artist had really almost better feign an innocence than try to get on with so little. Oddest of all—I mean as keeping company with so general an absence of illusions—was his one life-long *entêtement* on the question of what romanticism was doing for French prose. He apparently never arrived at a suspicion that it could do anything—there is no sophistication so complete but it leaves somewhere a verdant spot. Mérimée's blindness in respect to the whole of the new movement, from Victor Hugo down, remained to the end his verdancy. None the less, was it not, at bottom, just in order to console himself for his doom of productive meagreness that he "lived"—more particularly in the sense that his countrymen attach to the word—with so much energy and variety—one might be tempted to add with so much brutality? That is the way it is almost irresistible to see him—as thoroughly conscious of his case, yet, in spite of his extreme acuteness, unable to help himself and accordingly "taking it out" of everything else to make up for disappointed ambition.

He arrived indeed, and in profusion, at gratifications as well, and everything in the picture falls into its place. The whole view makes him an illustration singularly outlined and concrete of a period already beginning to wear, as it recedes, the sort of special note by which we recognise a dead and buried age. The first Empire had this note under the second, and the old *régime* had it under the first. To-day the second Empire has it; that period is already old France—it will do for that. Mérimée's interesting intimacy, from an early time, with Mme. de Montijo bore signal fruit from the moment the daughter of that lady, the born heroine of a fairy-tale, found herself upon the throne of France. He had known from baby-hood the Empress that was to be, and the miracle of her ex-altation "placed" him for the rest of his life. The favour, the attachment of the two Sovereigns, his particular position at court, his senatorship, his emoluments, his general inspector-ship of historical monuments, enabled him to carry out to the full his character of man of the world. The word, even so lately, had scarce been invented, but, almost without knowing it, he was a modern cosmopolite. He knew English so well that there are no mistakes in his letters—and I mean not only no mistakes of spelling. He was in and out of London and of Scotland, and, with his *goguenard* turn of fancy and the wide range of his irony, that is just another of his many incongru-ities. How he breathed in a "British" medium, save so far as London tailors could help him, it would seem to defy the acutest criticism to say. That he not only, in fact, breathed, but almost revelled, is to the credit, I think, of every one con-cerned, and not least to that of his English friends, who must have been good-natured folk. Of course, I surmise, with his Correspondence for proof, he was, in intercourse, abundantly witty—how witty was perhaps, here, not always clear to every one. M. Filon expresses with remarkable felicity the truth, about him, that prompts most to reflection—the manner in which the Correspondence is his long-delayed but wonderful revenge. He died, intellectually speaking, of dryness, too young, only at last to come to life again in a form in which the dryness—figuring so as purely personal and whimsical—was not only not fatal, but was susceptible of an extraordinary renovation. The perpetual irony which, breaking down as an aid to what we now call creation, threw him mainly into sensations and spectatorship, could reap a harvest from the moment he had, instead of creating, only to enjoy, to observe and to talk. This evolution demanded, of course, a great many happy accidents and "good things"—an ample competence, ample leisure, ample honours, plenty of society, of attractive women, of good cooks. It would have failed, I am afraid, had the subject of it not been so fortunate, not been, as it were, so handsomely set up in business. It is difficult to imagine the correspondent of the Inconnue addressing her from humble lodgings or after a bad dinner. As the case stands, at all events, we have come in for a literary treasure. And the treasure, clearly, is to be augmented—the prospect is of the richest. M. Filon holds out the hope—or so I read him—that we shall ultimately have, among all the letters as yet held back, the many addressed to Mme. de Montijo. Then, no doubt, we shall be still more struck with that difference in the writer's favour on which his biographer insists—the way that he outshines in this field, among his countrymen, the other celebrities of his class and time. M. Filon very justly contrasts their poverty and vulgarity as letter-writers with Mérimée's liberality and inimitability. But they had not, the leisureless Balzacs and Gautiers, his arrears to make up.

Literature, July 23, 1898

Gustave de Molinari

Lettres sur les Etats-Unis et le Canada. Par M. G. de Molinari. Paris: Hachette; New York: F. W. Christern, 1876.

M. DE MOLINARI, a well-known political and economical writer attached to the *Journal des Débats*, addressed last summer to that sheet a series of letters descriptive of a rapid tour through the United States. He has just gathered these letters into a volume in which American readers will find a good deal of entertainment and a certain amount of instruction. M. de Molinari, in his capacity of French journalist, is of course lively and witty; but his vivacity is always in excellent taste. He is moreover extremely observant, and he often renders his impressions with much felicity. He had apparently the advantage of coming to America without strong preconceptions in any direction; he was not pledged to find democratic institutions purely delightful, nor had he it on his conscience to lay in a stock of invidious comfort for oppressed Europeans. We have had in America too many observers of each of these categories. M. de Molinari's conclusions seem disinterested and liberal, especially when we remember that they were addressed to a journal which is not remarkable (save when M. Laboulaye writes in it) for a deferential consideration of American affairs. They are, in the gross, very much the reflections with which sensible Americans themselves point the moral of their contemporary history. M. de Molinari's weak point appears to have been that he had not time or inclination to look beneath the external surface of American manners, and that he was but scantily acquainted with the language of the people whom he had undertaken to examine. He usually writes his English words faultily—it is startling, for instance, to see a gentleman who has passed three months in America talking of "pilgrims fathers"—and he confesses himself unqualified for conversation. He reproaches us with our ignorance of foreign tongues; but we doubt whether even the American sentiment of the facility of things is likely to produce a volume upon French institutions by a Transatlantic traveller unfamiliar with the language which M. de Molinari writes so well. We hasten to add, however, that the author has made a great many happy guesses, and has been guilty of fewer serious errors than might have been expected. He says somewhere that every people has certainly its quantum of national vanity, but that that of the Americans towers far above all others. Granting the truth of this assertion, we must yet say that we have in this country this symptom of modesty, that we are always rather surprised when an entertaining book is written about us. Addicted as we are to lamenting the absence of "local color" within our borders, we are astonished to see a foreigner find so many salient points and so much characteristic detail.

M. de Molinari was present at the opening ceremonies of the Centennial Exhibition, to which he devotes a letter; and he devotes a letter also to the Exhibition itself, by which he seems to have been duly impressed. But we are at a loss to imagine to what class of the population he alludes when he affirms, after observing the multitude at Philadelphia, that the taste for button-hole decorations "is perhaps still more pronounced" among us than in Europe. The only orders we can think of are those of the rosebud and the pink. M. de Molinari has some observations of New York at midsummer, and, considering the circumstances, speaks of this city with extreme kindness. He goes to Coney Island, witnesses the phenomenon of "flirtation" between young persons of opposite sexes, and comments upon it with less imaginative wealth than his countrymen, having a chance at the subject, have sometimes shown. In the train on the way to Baltimore he makes these extremely just reflections:

"One is struck, moreover, with the real politeness of American manners, in spite of the want of ceremony in habits and behavior. All the indications that I am obliged to ask—in what an English, ah heaven!—are given me with perfect courtesy. One perceives immediately that there exists in this country, as a rule, neither an aristocracy nor a populace; one is afflicted nowhere with the exhibition of grossness or bad morals, . . . but the absence of refinement and elegance in the manners is not less striking. The contact of the superior class has raised the level of the masses; but perhaps the contact of the masses has, on the other hand, lowered the level of the superior class. Manners form thus a sort of something middling, equally distant from extreme coarseness and extreme refinement."

At Washington, having occasion to apply at the Capitol for two or three Congressional Reports, M. de Molinari is overcome by the matter-of-course way in which the employee presents them to him out of hand, and, without even asking his name, offers to have them made into a parcel free of expense:

"It was impossible to believe! . . . We leave at last this hospitable Capitol, in which the arrangements for parliamentary comfort are only surpassed by the politeness of the employees of every order, and the singular desire to be agreeable to the public which they manifest upon every occasion. The world turned upside down!"

The author looks into Canada, where he is agreeably impressed with the respectable, if not the particularly brilliant, character of the French population, on whose behalf he makes an appeal to the sympathies of the mother-country—an appeal which, we are afraid, will fall upon perfectly deaf ears. He laments the uninstructed and extremely provincial state of culture of the French Canadians, as compared with their English fellow-citizens, and asks why France should not resume—of course without any political afterthought—a "tutelary part" corresponding, among the French population, to that of England. Why should not the French banks have branches at Quebec, as the English banks have them at Montreal? M. de Molinari repeats these interrogatories when he becomes acquainted with the solid remnant of the French establishment in Louisiana. But we are afraid that he himself gives the answer. "It is certain that we do not suspect the existence of this living branch of the old French root." The French do not suspect the existence of it, and do not care to do so. We doubt that it is within the power of human ingenuity to quicken their consciousness on this point.

M. de Molinari visits Lake George and the "ravishing Hotel Fort William Henry," and spends a day at Saratoga, where, though at midnight his bed was not made up, nor his boots blacked, he generously pronounces the Grand Union Hotel "a colossal manufactory of comfort, and one of the most characteristic creations of American genius." He makes a rapid visit to the South, and is greatly struck with the desolate appearance of many localities; but he finds the Southern whites very "braves gens," and lends a favoring—perhaps a too favoring—ear to their version of their sufferings. He reproduces the Southern account of the situation in a long speech, in which slavery is painted in rose-color and the North is very roughly handled; but he adds that he does not find these arguments wholly satisfactory, inasmuch as before the war it used to be unlawful to teach blacks to read and as Northerners were apt to be tarred and feathered. He despairs of the negroes, thinks apparently that there may have been a good deal in slavery after all, and tells a singular tale of Sherman's army (" which renewed the exploits of the landsknechts and black bands of the Middle Ages") having "violated the tombs in the cemeteries to rob the dead of the jewels with which it is the pious but imprudent custom to bury them"! With all respect to the propriety of the author's sympathy for the hard fate of the Southern States, we suspect that the inhabitants in this part of the country "got round" him more successfully than they did elsewhere. We hear of a "delicious miss" at Savannah, who has "eyes as blue as corn-flowers, fine and delicate features, a complexion of dead whiteness, an opulent golden mane, and that indefinable something feminine which is lacking to her Northern sisters, brought up with boys."

Finding the country in the midst of its Presidential campaign, the author of course made many reflections upon American politics. He gives a sufficiently correct account of each of the platforms, but declares that he has no faith in good results coming from either of them:

> "I greatly fear that neither Tilden nor Hayes is capable of reforming a state of things which arises from the vicious attitude (*l'assiette vicieuse*) and the flagrant defects of American institutions. And as neither the politicians nor the passive multitude of the citizens appear to me disposed to seek and recognize the true sources of the evil, the natural

course of things can only aggravate this critical situation. Must I say all? I cannot resist the fear that, in the course of a few years, the crisis will terminate, European fashion, in the dictatorship of a 'General' who will undertake, with the support of the Republican party, to bring back a certain order into this disorganized democracy."

M. de Molinari repairs to Cambridge in search of a university "libre et libérale," and finds this ideal realized in Harvard College. He gives of this institution a flattering—we will not say a flattered—portrait. He visits, of course, the Library, "of which the *personnel* is composed in great part of young misses. Observe that this library is almost for the exclusive use of the students of the University. But the young misses of Cambridge *sont des personnes savantes et sages*; they have studied Latin, ay, and Greek too, and I am assured that they have no passion for anything but the Catalogue. It is true that this catalogue is a marvel of method and clearness." And then the author describes the little drawers of the Harvard Library, which, deservedly, are becoming famous the world over. The last pages of M. de Molinari's volume are devoted to various public institutions in New York and to a summing-up of his impressions. He draws a liberal picture of the great things that have been achieved in America—of the energy and audacity which have built up the material prosperity of the country. As we look at this picture " we are penetrated with admiration; for never has so colossal an effort been accomplished, and never have results so prodigious been obtained by human industry. The levees of the Mississippi alone have exacted more work than the dykes of Holland [we may perhaps question the exactitude of this statement], and the network of railways in the United States is almost as extensive as that of Europe." But M. de Molinari observes that social and intellectual culture has remained much behind—we make excellent pianos but no musicians—and that political morality is further behind still. Upon our political abuses, upon the unworthy character of our professional politicians, and the scandalous nature of much of our political machinery, he makes all those reflections of which even extreme familiarity has not diminished the pertinence. But in speaking of our political machinery he becomes somewhat fantastical. The fallibility of the spectator who must run as he reads is here amusingly evident. Flag-raisings and torch-light processions have gone to M. de Molinari's head and disordered his judgment. He regards these frolicsome phenomena as the prime agency in the electoral process, and the chief instrument by which the wicked politicians beguile the easily-bamboozled people into working their will. The gravity with which he unfolds this charge, which forms the last and apparently the principal clause in his indictment of American politics, is really startling:

"The orators at the meetings talk in the midst of garlands of Chinese lanterns, their faces illumined by projections of electric light; the booming of the big drum and the clash of copper, at a rate to rouse the dead, mark time to their speeches. Besides, these orators are well-dressed and polished gentlemen. . . . And this is how the American elections have finished by resembling the practical jokes of a carnival or the parade of a company of mountebanks. This is how, to my ineffable stupefaction, I saw the election of the future chief of one of the most powerful and civilized nations of the earth prepared with the same apparatus which serves at fairs to attract the crowd to the Siren of the Tropics or the Albinos of Madagascar."

And he considers that the first lesson to be drawn from "the reverse of the medal of the great republic" is that "it is not sufficient to go to our electoral reunions costumed as Troubadours and Turks to ameliorate seriously the composition of our political class." Let those whom the shoe pinches take notice, and let the American elector in general take care how he suffers the Troubadours and Turks to twist him around their fingers.

Nation, February 22, 1877

Émile Montégut

Souvenirs de Bourgogne. Par Emile Montégut. Paris: Hachette; New York: F. W. Christern, 1874.

AMONG THE FRENCH WRITERS of the past twenty years, M. Emile Montégut is not the most conspicuous. The *rôle effacé*, as the French say, which he has been willing to play, has indeed in a measure helped to characterize his gifts. His articles, extremely numerous and various, and treating often of English themes, must be sought out in the back volumes of the *Revue des Deux Mondes*, for he has never thought it worth his while to republish them. We have often wondered why, and have finally concluded that this inflexible modesty is but another form of the subtle fastidiousness which is the most striking quality in his writings. His only large literary enterprise has been a prose translation of Shakspere, but it must be confessed that this is a task of handsome proportions. He has also published French versions of Macaulay's History and of Emerson's earlier essays. His philosophy as a critic and commentator is rather of the pessimistic sort; it is at least a philosophy in which resignation, appreciation, and a kind of mellow stoicism, finding its *point d'appui* in culture for culture's sake, stand instead of certain more boisterous forms of hope and faith. It is difficult to define so peculiar a literary temperament as that of M. Montégut, but the attempt would be worth making for the sake of enlarging our conception of intellectual delicacy. To succeed in it, one would really need our author's own faculty of super-subtle analysis. We most rapidly hit the mark, perhaps, in saying that he is, to our sense, a fruit of pure culture, refined to an intellectual mellowness beside which the inspiration proceeding from genius seems crude and cold. Whether M. Montégut is a man of genius or not is again a case for an æsthetic casuist like himself to deal with, and he lacks, certainly, the more aggressive attributes of talent. He has neither the weight and mass and emphasis of M. Taine, nor the bristling malice—the critical *scratch*, as one may call it—of Sainte-Beuve. Many readers, we imagine, find him tame and dull, and his best friends must be those contemplative minds who care more for the journey than for the goal—more to look out of the window than to arrive. His characteristic fault is a tendency to prolixity, but this prolixity is so sincere, so suggestive, so charged with information and reflection, that we rarely desire to abridge it. Each of M. Montégut's essays, indeed, reads like a series of excursions from the broad highway; his main idea has generally the lightness and *finesse* of those butterflies of thought which flit across the path of more dogmatic minds, but rarely tempt them so far afield in pursuit. Little by little our author's slow-moving, wide-glancing manner diffuses itself over his subject like a soft autumnal atmosphere— an atmosphere in which the muffled melancholy which resounds through all deep science plays the part of the grey autumnal haze. In this atmosphere we have spent many an agreeable hour, and we have had pleasure in finding it, in the volume before us, as salutary and soothing as ever.

A few years since, M. Montégut published a volume of notes of travel in Belgium and Holland, and showed that he was as ingenious a critic of painting and architecture as of literature and morals. He now follows with a substantial record of a really exhaustive tour of contemplation, we should call it, rather than of inspection, through one of the rich provinces of France—the thrice-historic Burgundy. In a preface animated not altogether rationally by the petulance of wounded patriotism, he offers his fellow-countrymen a plea for their now broad land as a field for the tourist. It now behoves Frenchmen, he says, to shut themselves up from a world which has measured out such scanty sympathy to their disasters and look for consolations at home. "Let us make of Normandy our England; of Provence our Italy; of Béarn and Roussillon our Spain; and let us look for Germany only in those provinces which force has taken from us." If M. Montégut's countrymen in general possessed the admirable tourist-temperament with which he has been gifted, they might certainly discover a limitless source of entertainment and consolation; and if they possessed his singular faculty of suggestive and vivifying description, they would add at the same time to the entertainment of their neighbors. A tourist so redolent of varied culture as M. Montégut is in this indirect fashion, a most agreeable companion; and there is something

really affecting in witnessing the contact of a mind infinitely
refined, and exquisitely prepared by years of discriminating
bookishness, with the material treasures of civilization. In
fact, M. Montégut's impressions of landscapes and monuments strike us often like the response of a deep-toned musical instrument to the touch of authoritative fingers. His
cultivated imagination gives out in the historic Burgundian
atmosphere a kind of constant murmur of appreciation—a
tremor of perception and reflection. The book reads like the
record of an intellectual holiday; but such only are the holidays of those with whom knowledge is a passion which consents at most to shift its opportunities. Happy the observer
who passes on his way with a mind at once so fertilized and
so unfatigued by the gathered lore of things, and happy the
cities and sites that receive the tribute of so much patient ingenuity, of such a genial passion for reviving and interpreting,
cross-questioning ghosts and shadows and echoes, healing
and repairing the general injury of time! M. Montégut's volume has suggested to us more reflections than we have space
for. Several of these have touched upon the charm of the sort
of writing to which his book belongs. We have always been
fond of the record of spontaneous personal impressions of the
objects which share with ourselves the privilege of dotting the
earth's surface, and which differ from us mainly in being but
a trifle more passive than we; and these pages confirm our
partiality by proving that such a record may be a perfectly
graceful vehicle for the most general and most comprehensive
reflections. It is true that to manage it well we should possess
that combination of qualities which in their high development make the rare originality of M. Montégut—the sense of
the artist, the joy in material forms, and the conscience of the
moralist, the care for spiritual meanings. Both as connoisseur
and as moralist, M. Montégut is equally ingenious and penetrating, equally conjectural, fanciful, adventurous, incapable
of remaining inert and irresponsive before *any* manifestation
of what was once a living force. Painters will not care for his
criticisms on pictures—they will call them too fantastic and
far-fetched and literary; and moralists of the sterner sort will
not care for his meditations—they will call them too æsthetic,
too disinterested, too much tainted with that spirit to which

the nature of a creed differs only in degree from that of the ornamental stonework of the church which commemorates it; but we are safe in saying that the "general reader" will find in the 'Souvenirs de Bourgogne' a fund of serious and yet not oppressive diversion.

Nation, July 23, 1874

Alfred de Musset

Selections from the Prose and Poetry of Alfred de Musset. Translated by Sarah Butler Wister. New York: Hurd and Houghton, 1870.

MRS. OWEN WISTER has made a commendable effort to introduce a much-loved French poet to the English-reading public, and the measure of her success is much larger, it strikes us, than that of the ordinary translator from the same difficult language. If Alfred de Musset is greatest as a lyric poet,—and he certainly seems so to the Anglo-Saxon critic,—Mrs. Wister has done wisely in making her "Selections" with a kind of lyric purpose even as to the prose. However startling it might sound in Gallic ears, very little is hazarded in the remark that the present translator has done her readers greater service, and the poet too, by giving them *Mimi Pinson* and "The White Black Bird" than she would have done by serving up to them the whole of *La Confession d'un Enfant du Siècle*. That unequal performance of his younger years may seem De Musset's masterpiece to those who can understand all of his more sober poetry, but the English reader, we venture to say, will see more to admire and to be thankful for in the portrayal of Mimi Pinson's exquisite French human nature than in all the raptures of Octave and Madame Brigitte, or the calmer sentimentalities of the "honnête Smith." It is to be feared that Mrs. Bridget would be as prosaically unromantic as her name, if translated into our literature, and that the triumphant Smith would be only a plain Mr. Smith in English garments.

Of the two other pieces of prose with which Mrs. Wister has favored us, the little two-act comedy of "Fantasio" perhaps reads the better. Her rendering of *On ne badine pas avec l'Amour* ("No trifling with Love") does not fall short so much from any lack in her; it is as well done as the former; but the fault may be said to lie in the charming little comedy itself. Those who have seen it played as only French actors can play such pieces will understand why any reading of it in English or French must seem unsatisfactory. Published twenty-seven years before it was thought worth while to represent it, scarcely ever was there a play that shows so much better on

592

the stage than it does in print. Indeed, after an evening of *On ne badine pas avec l'Amour* at the Théâtre Français, in Paris, De Musset's original language reads like a translation.

If Mrs. Wister's success in the rendering of the nine poems which conclude her volume is not quite equal, it is certainly striking in some instances. All things considered, the poem in which the translator has best caught and conveyed the spirit of the original is perhaps that entitled "Advice to a Gay Lady" (*Conseils à une Parisienne*). Here Mrs. Wister has, in our opinion, wisely made up for what she may have lost in the movement of the French verse, by changing the succession of the rhymes:—

> "Yes, were I a woman, charming and pretty,
>   I think I should do,
>   Fair Julia, as you;
> Without fear or favor, distinction or pity,
>   Smile and make eyes
>   At all 'neath the skies."

> "Oui, si j'étais femme, aimable et jolie,
>   Je voudrais, Julie,
>   Faire comme vous;
> Sans peur ni pitié, sans choix ni mystère,
>   A toute la terre
>   Faire les yeux doux."

This, we think, is very happily turned. It is, indeed, more within the possibilities of translation than the more heroic or the most vivacious of French poetry. The following from Mimi Pinson's song is less successful, though it is so perhaps because perfect success there would have been almost impossible. It is very doubtful whether Mimi's elfin gayety could be got into English words. Her exquisite vivacity is at least taken off here with her solitary dress:—

> "Mimi Pinson is a blonde of renown;
>   But one gown and cap has she;
>   The Grand Turk has surely more!
> Heaven gave her small store,

Meaning her discreet to be.
None can pawn Mimi Pinson's only gown."

"Mimi Pinson est une blonde,
    Une blonde que l'on connaît,
    Elle n'a qu'une robe au monde,
      Landerirette!
      Et qu'un bonnet.
Le Grand Turc en a davantage.
Dieu voulut de cette façon
      La rendre sage.
On ne peut pas la mettre en gage,
La robe de Mimi Pinson."

The next morning after the student banquet at which Mimi Pinson had sung her song she proved that it was not true, and in a way which illustrates the winning, contradictory nature of the lively grisette. The passage in which this is related gives a fair sample of the manner of Mrs. Wister's translation from De Musset's prose: —

"'Mademoiselle has gone to church,' said the woman who answered the door, to the two students, when they reached Mademoiselle Pinson's lodgings.

"'To church!' repeated Eugene with surprise.

"'To church!' echoed Marcel. 'That is impossible; she is not out. Let us in, we are old friends.'

"'I assure you, sir,' said the woman, 'that she went to church about three quarters of an hour ago.'

"'To what church did she go?'

"'To St. Sulpice, as usual; she never misses a morning.'

"'Yes, yes, I know that she says her prayers, but it seems odd that she should be out to-day.'

"'There she comes, sir; she is turning the corner; you can see her for yourself.'

"It really was Mademoiselle Pinson coming home from church. Marcel no sooner caught sight of her than he rushed toward her, impatient to examine her toilet. She had on, in lieu of a gown, a petticoat of dark calico, half hidden by a green serge curtain, of which she had contrived to make herself a sort of shawl. From this singular costume, which, however, owing to its dark tone, did not attract attention, peeped her graceful head in its white cap, and her little feet in gaiter-boots. She had wrapped herself in her curtain with so much art and care that it really looked like an old shawl, and the border could hardly be seen. In short, she contrived to be charming even in this toggery, and to prove, for the thousandth time, that a pretty woman is always pretty.

" 'How do I look?' said she to the young men, opening her curtain a little and giving them a glimpse of her slender waist.

" 'You look charming!' cried Marcel. 'Upon my soul, I never would have believed anybody could look so well in a window-curtain.'

" 'Do you really think so?' returned Mademoiselle Pinson. 'I look a little bunchy, though.'

" 'Like a bunch of roses!' replied Marcel. 'I am almost sorry now that I brought you back your dress.'

" 'My dress? Where did you find it?'

" 'Where you left it, most likely.'

" 'And have you rescued it from captivity?'

" 'Yes, by Jove, I paid its ransom. Do you resent the liberty?'

" 'No indeed! provided you will let me do as much for you some day. I'm glad enough to see my dress again, for, to tell the truth, we have lived together for a long while, and I have insensibly become attached to it.'

"As she spoke, Mademoiselle Pinson ran briskly up the five flights of stairs which led to her little room, which the two friends entered with her.

" 'But I can only give you back the dress upon one condition,' said Marcel.

" 'Fie!' exclaimed the grisette. 'For shame! Conditions? I won't have it.'

" 'I have a wager,' continued Marcel. 'And you must tell us honestly why you pawned your gown.' "

Then it comes out that Mimi has pawned her only dress to save from starvation another grisette, with whom she had feasted sumptuously a week before, and with whom two days afterward she was feasting more sumptuously and expensively than ever,—on probably the last franc sent to their relief by sympathizing friends.

In the poem "On Three Steps of Rose-colored Marble,"
which as a whole is very well rendered, we notice that the
name of the Greek painter Praxiteles is used with the penult
improperly long; and in the very next poem, and on the next
page but one, the same word is given with its proper quantity, the antepenult long. Here and there, too, is a word or
phrase which does not exactly convey De Musset's meaning,
but there are many more in which it is hit off in an idiomatic
way truly admirable. Indeed, it is hardly fair to dwell on the
few minor blemishes which, after all, it is much easier to pick
out than to have avoided in a work so difficult.

If, as Sainte-Beuve has said, Alfred de Musset entered the
lyric sanctuary through the window, "Spécialité d'absinthe"
must have been inscribed on the back door through which he
went out. George Sand by her scandalous portrayal, and his
brother Paul equally by his scathing denial, have made the fail-
ings of the unfortunate poet only too well known to the world;
and no small measure of gratitude, we take it, is due to the
American lady who has so well contributed her share toward
doing what Madame Sand and his brother would both better
have done, namely, let Alfred de Musset speak for himself.

Atlantic Monthly, September 1870

Biographie de Alfred de Musset: sa Vie et ses Œuvres. Par Paul de Musset. Paris: Charpentier, 1877. *Alfred de Musset.* Von Paul Lindau. Berlin: Hofmann, 1877.

IT HAD BEEN KNOWN for some time that M. Paul de Musset
was preparing a biography of his illustrious brother, and
the knowledge had been grateful to Alfred de Musset's many
lovers; for the author of "Rolla" and the "Lettre à Lamartine"
has lovers. The book has at last appeared—more than twenty
years after the death of its hero. It is probably not unfair to
suppose that a motive for delay has been removed by the recent death of Madame Sand. M. Paul de Musset's volume
proves, we confess, rather disappointing. It is a careful and
graceful but at the same time a very slight performance, such
as was to be expected from the author of "Lui et Elle" and of
the indignant refutation (in the biographical notice which ac-

companies the octavo edition of Alfred de Musset's works) of M. Taine's statement that the poet was addicted to walking about the streets late at night. As regards this latter point, M. Paul de Musset hastened to declare that his brother had no such habits—that his customs were those of a *gentilhomme*; by which the biographer would seem to mean that when the poet went abroad after dark it was in his own carriage, or at least in a hired cab, summoned from the nearest stand. M. Paul de Musset is a devoted brother and an agreeable writer; but he is not, from the critic's point of view, the ideal biographer. This, however, is not seriously to be regretted, for it is little to be desired that the ideal biography of Alfred de Musset should be written, or that he should be delivered over, bound hand and foot, to the critics. Those who really care for him would prefer to judge him with all kinds of allowances and indulgences—sentimentally and imaginatively. Between him and his readers it is a matter of affection, or it is nothing at all; and there is something very happy, therefore, in M. Paul de Musset's fond fraternal reticences and extenuations. He has related his brother's life as if it were a pretty "story;" and indeed there is enough that was pretty in it to justify him. We should decline to profit by any information that might be offered us in regard to its prosaic, its possibly shabby side. To make the story complete, however, there appears simultaneously with M. Paul de Musset's volume a publication of a quite different sort—a biography of the poet by a clever German writer, Herr Paul Lindau. Herr Lindau is highly appreciative, but he is also critical, and he says a great many things that M. Paul de Musset leaves unsaid. As becomes a German biographer, he is very minute and exhaustive, and a stranger who should desire a "general idea" of the poet would probably get more instruction from his pages than from the French memoir. Their fault is indeed that they are apparently addressed to persons whose mind is supposed to be a blank with regard to the author of "Rolla." The exactions of bookmaking alone can explain the long analyses and prose paraphrases of Alfred de Musset's comedies and tales to which Herr Lindau treats his readers—the dreariest kind of reading when an author is not in himself essentially inaccessible. Either one has not read Alfred de Musset's comedies or not felt the charm of them—in which case one will not be likely to resort to Herr Lindau's memoirs—or one has read them in the charming original, and can therefore dispense with an elaborate German summary.

In saying just now that M. Paul de Musset's biography of his brother is disappointing, we meant more particularly to express our regret that he has given us no letters—or given us at least but two or three. It is probable, however, that he had no more in his hands. Alfred de Musset lived in a very compact circle; he spent his whole life in Paris, and his friends lived in Paris near him. He was little separated from his brother, who appears to have been his best friend (M. Paul de Musset was six years Alfred's senior) and much of his life was passed under the same roof with the other members of his family. Seeing his friends constantly, he had no occasion to write to them; and as he saw little of the world (in the larger sense of the phrase) he would have had probably but little to write about. He made but one attempt at travelling— his journey to Italy, at the age of twenty-three, with George Sand. "He made no important journeys," says Herr Lindau, "and if one excepts his love affairs, he really had no experiences." But his love affairs, as a general thing, could not properly be talked about. M. de Musset shows good taste in not pretending to narrate them. He mentions two or three of the more important episodes of this class, and with regard to the others he says that when he does not mention them they may always be taken for granted. It is perhaps indeed in a limited sense that Alfred de Musset's love affairs may be said to have been in some cases more important than in others. It was his own philosophy that in this matter one thing is about as good as another—

> "Aimer est le grand point; qu'importe la maîtresse?
> Qu'importe le flacon pourvu qu'on ait l'ivresse?"

Putting aside the "ivresse," which was constant, Musset's life certainly offers little material for narration. He wrote a few poems, tales, and comedies, and that is all. He *did* nothing, in the sterner sense of the word. He was inactive, indolent, idle; his record has very few dates. Two or three times the occasion to do something was offered him, but he shook his head and let it pass. It was proposed to him to accept a place as *attaché* to the French embassy at Madrid, a comfortable salary being affixed to the post. But Musset found no inspiration in the prospect. He had written about Spain in his earlier years—he had sung in the most charming fashion about Juanas and Pepitas, about señoras in mantillas stealing down palace staircases that look "blue" in the starlight. But the desire to see the picturesqueness that he had dreamt of proved itself to have none of the force of a motive. This is the fact in Musset's life which the writer of these lines finds most regrettable—the fact of his contented smallness of horizon—the fact that on his own line he should not have cared to go farther. There is something really exasperating in the sight of a picturesque poet wantonly slighting an opportunity to go to Spain—the Spain of forty years ago. It does violence even to that minimum of intellectual eagerness which is the portion of a contemplative mind. It is annoying to think that Alfred de Musset should have been meagrely contemplative. This is the weakness that tells against him, more than the weakness of what would be called his excesses. From the point of view of his own peculiar genius it was a good fortune for him to be susceptible and tender, sensitive and passionate. The trouble was not that he was all this, but that he was lax and soft; that he had too little energy and curiosity. Shelley was at least equally tremulous and sensitive—equally a victim of his impressions, and an echo, as it were, of his temperament. But even Musset's fondest readers must feel that Shelley had within him a firm, divinely-tempered spring, against which his spirit might rebound indefinitely. As regards intense sensibility—that fineness of feeling which is the pleasure and pain of the poetic nature—M. Paul de Musset tells two or three stories of his brother which remind one of the anecdotes recorded of the author of the "Ode to the West Wind." "One of the things that he loved best in the world was a certain exclamation of Racine's Phædra, which expresses by its *bizarrerie* the trouble of her sickened heart:

'Ariane, ma sœur, de quel amour blessée,
  Vous mourûtes aux bords où vous fûtes laissée!'

When Rachel used to murmur forth this strange, unexpected plaint, Alfred always took his head in his two hands and turned pale with emotion."

The author describes the poet's early years, and gives several very pretty anecdotes of his childhood. Alfred de Musset was born in 1810, in the middle of old Paris, on a spot familiar to those many American visitors who wander across the Seine, better and better pleased as they go, to the museum of the Hôtel de Cluny. The house in which Musset's parents lived was close to this beautiful monument—a happy birthplace for a poet; but both the house and the street have now disappeared. M. Paul de Musset does not relate that his brother began to versify in his infancy; but Alfred was indeed hardly more than an infant when he achieved his first success. The poems published under the title of "Contes d'Espagne et d'Italie" were composed in his eighteenth and nineteenth years; he had but just completed his nineteenth when the volume into which they had been gathered was put forth. There are certainly—if we consider the quality of the poems—few more striking examples of literary precocity. The cases of Chatterton and Keats may be equally remarkable but they are not more so. These first boyish verses of Musset have a vivacity, a brilliancy, a freedom of feeling and of fancy which may well have charmed the little *cénacle* to which he read them aloud—the group of littérateurs and artists which clustered about Victor Hugo, who, although at this time very young, was already famous. M. Paul de Musset intimates that if his brother was at this moment (and as we may suppose, indeed, always) one of the warmest admirers of the great author of "Hernani" and those other splendid productions which project their violent glow across the threshold of the literary era of 1830, and if Victor Hugo gave kindly audience to "Don Paez" and "Mardoche," this kindness declined in proportion as the fame of the younger poet expanded. Alfred de Musset was certainly not fortunate in his relations with his more distinguished contemporaries. Victor Hugo "dropped" him; it would have been better for him if George Sand had never taken him up; and Lamartine, to whom, in the shape of a passionate epistle, he addressed the most beautiful of his own, and one of the most beautiful of all, poems, acknowledged the compliment only many years after it was paid. The *cénacle* was all for Spain, for local colour, for serenades, and daggers, and Gothic arches. It was nothing if not audacious (it was in the van of the Romantic movement), and it was partial to what is called in France the "humoristic" as well as to the ferociously sentimental. Musset produced a certain "Ballade à la Lune" which began—

> "C'était dans la nuit brune
> Sur le clocher jauni
>   La lune
> Comme un point sur un i!"

This assimilation of the moon suspended above a church spire to a dot upon an *i* became among the young Romanticists a sort of symbol of what they should do and dare; just as in the opposite camp it became a by-word of horror. But this was only playing at poetry, and in his next things, produced in the following year or two, Musset struck a graver and more resonant chord. The pieces published under the title of "Un Spectacle dans un Fauteuil" have all the youthful grace and gaiety of those that preceded them; but they have beyond this a suggestion of the quality which gives so high a value to the author's later and best verses—the accent of genuine passion. It is hard to see what, just yet, Alfred de Musset had to be passionate about; but passion, with a poet, even when it is most genuine, is very much an affair of the imagination and the personal temperament (independently, we mean, of strong provoking causes) and the sensibilities of this young man were already exquisitely active. His poems found a great many admirers, and these admirers were often women. Hence for the young poet, says M. Paul de Musset, a great many romantic and "*Boccaciennes*" adventures. "On several occasions I was awaked in the middle of the night to give my opinion on some question of high prudence. All these little stories having been confided to me under the seal of secrecy, I have been obliged to forget them; but I may affirm that more than one of them would have aroused the envy of Bassompierre and Lauzun. Women at that time were not wholly absorbed in their care for luxury and dress. To hope to please,

young men had no need to be rich; and it served a purpose
to have at nineteen years of age the prestige of talent and
glory." This is very pretty, as well as very Gallic; but it is
rather vague, and we may without offence suspect it to be, to
a certain extent, but that conventional *coup de chapeau* which
every self-respecting Frenchman renders to actual or potential, past, present, or future gallantry. Doubtless, however,
Musset was, in the native phrase, *lancé*. He lived with his
father and mother, his brother and sister; his purse was
empty; Seville and Granada were very far away; and these
"Andalusian passions," as M. Paul de Musset says, were mere
reveries and boyish visions. But they were the visions of a boy
who was all ready to compare reality with romance, and who,
in fact, very soon acceded to a proposal which appeared to
offer a peculiar combination of the two. It is noticeable, by
the way, that from our modest Anglo-Saxon point of view
these same "Andalusian passions," dealing chiefly with ladies
tumbling about on disordered couches, and pairs of lovers
who take refuge from an exhausted vocabulary in *biting* each
other, are an odd sort of thing for an ingenuous lad, domiciled in the manner M. Paul de Musset describes, and hardly
old enough to have a latch-key, to lay on the family breakfast-
table. But this was very characteristic all round the circle.
Musset was not a didactic poet, and he had no time to lose
in going through the preliminary paces of one. His business
was to talk about love in unmistakable terms, to proclaim its
pleasures and pains with all possible eloquence; and he would
have been quite at a loss to understand why he should have
blushed or stammered in preluding to so beautiful a theme.
Herr Lindau thinks that even in the germ Musset's inspiration is already vicious—that "his wonderful talent was almost
simultaneously ripe and corrupted." But Herr Lindau speaks
from the modest Saxon point of view; a point of view, however, from which, in such a matter, there is a great deal to be
said.

The great event in Alfred de Musset's life, most people
would say, was his journey to Italy with George Sand. This
event has been abundantly—superabundantly—described,
and Herr Lindau, in the volume before us, devotes a long
chapter to it and lingers over it with peculiar complacency.

Our own sentiment would be that there is something extremely displeasing in the publicity which has attached itself to the episode; that there is indeed a sort of colossal indecency in the way it has passed into the common fund of literary gossip. It illustrates the base, the weak, the trivial side of all the great things that were concerned in it—fame, genius and love. Either the Italian journey was in its results a very serious affair for the remarkable couple who undertook it—in which case it should be left in that quiet place in the history of the development of the individual into which public intrusion can bring no light, but only darkness—or else it was a piece of levity and conscious self-display; in which case the attention of the public has been invited to it on false grounds. If there ever was an affair it should be becoming to be silent about, it was certainly this one; but neither the actors nor the spectators have been of this way of thinking; one may almost say that there exists a whole literature on the subject. To this literature Herr Lindau's contribution is perhaps the most ingenious. He has extracted those pages from Paul de Musset's novel of "Lui et Elle" which treat of the climax of the relations of the hero and heroine, and he has printed the names of George Sand and Alfred de Musset instead of the fictitious names. The result is perhaps of a nature to refresh the jaded vision of most lovers of scandal.

We must add that some of his judgments on the matter happen to have a certain felicity. M. Paul de Musset has narrated the story more briefly—having, indeed, by the publication of "Lui et Elle," earned the right to be brief. He mentions two or three facts, however, the promulgation of which he may have thought it proper, as we said before, to postpone to Madame Sand's death. One of them is sufficiently dramatic. Musset had met George Sand in the summer of 1833, about the time of the publication of "Rolla"—seeing her for the first time at a dinner given to the contributors of the "Revue des Deux Mondes," at the restaurant of the Trois Frères Provençaux. George Sand was the only woman present. Sainte-Beuve had already endeavoured to bring his two friends together, but the attempt had failed, owing to George Sand's reluctance, founded on an impression that she should not like the young poet. Alfred de Musset was twenty-three years of age; George Sand, who had published "Indiana," "Valentine," and "Lélia," was close upon thirty. Alfred de Musset, as the author of "Rolla," was a very extraordinary young man—quite the young man of whom Heinrich Heine could say "he has a magnificent past before him." Upon his introduction to George Sand, an intimacy speedily followed—an intimacy commemorated by the lady in expansive notes to Sainte-Beuve, whom she kept informed of its progress. When the winter came the two intimates talked of leaving Paris together, and, as an experiment, paid a visit to Fontainebleau. The experiment succeeded, but this was not enough, and they formed the project of going to Italy. To this project, as regarded her son, Madame de Musset refused her consent. (Alfred's father, we should say, had died before the publication of "Rolla," leaving his children without appreciable property, though during his lifetime, occupying a post in a government office, he had been able to maintain them comfortably.) His mother's opposition was so vehement that Alfred gave up the project and countermanded the preparations that had already been made for departure.

"That evening toward nine o'clock," says M. Paul de Musset, "our mother was alone with her daughter by the fireside, when she was informed that a lady was waiting for her at the door in a hired carriage and begged urgently to speak with her. She went down accompanied by a servant. The unknown lady named herself; she besought this deeply grieved mother to confide her son to her, saying that she would have for him a maternal affection and care. As promises did not avail, she went so far as sworn vows. She used all her eloquence, and she must have had a great deal, since her enterprise succeeded. In a moment of emotion the consent was given." The author of "Lélia" and the author of "Rolla" started for Italy together. M. Paul de Musset mentions that he accompanied them to the mail coach "on a sad, misty evening, in the midst of circumstances that boded ill." They spent the winter at Venice, and M. Paul de Musset and his mother continued to hear regularly from Alfred. But toward the middle of February his letters suddenly stopped, and for six weeks they were without news. They were on the point of starting for Italy, to put an end to their suspense, when they received a melancholy epistle informing them that their son and brother was on his way home. He was slowly recovering from an attack of brain fever, but as soon as he should be able to drag himself along he would seek the refuge of the paternal roof.

On the 10th of April he reappeared alone. A quarter of a century later, and a short time after his death, Madame Sand gave to the world, in the guise of a novel, an account of the events which had occupied this interval. The account was highly to her own advantage and much to the discredit of her companion. Paul de Musset immediately retorted with a little book which is decidedly poor as fiction, but tolerably good, probably, as history. As a devoted brother, given all the circumstances, it was perhaps the best thing he could do. It is believed that his reply was more than, in the vulgar phrase, Madame Sand had bargained for; inasmuch as he made use of documents of whose existence she had been ignorant. Alfred de Musset, suspecting that her version of their relations would be given to the world, had, in the last weeks of his life, dictated to his brother a detailed statement of those incidents to which misrepresentation would chiefly address itself, and this narrative Paul de Musset simply incorporated in his novel. The gist of it is that the poet's companion took advantage of his being seriously ill, in Venice, to be flagrantly unfaithful, and that, discovering her infidelity, he relapsed into a brain fever which threatened his life, and from which he rose only to make his way home with broken wings and a bleeding heart. Madame Sand's version of the story is that his companion's infidelity was a delusion of the fever itself and the charge was but the climax of a series of intolerable affronts and general fantasticalities.

Fancy the great gossiping, vulgar-minded public, deliberately invited to ponder this delicate question! The public should never have been appealed to; but once the appeal made, it administers perforce a rough justice of its own. According to this rough justice, the case looks badly for Musset's fellow-traveller. She was six years older than he (at that time of life a grave fact); she had drawn him away from his mother, taken him in charge, assumed a responsibility. Their two literary physiognomies were before the world, and she was, on the face of the matter, the riper, stronger, more reasonable nature. She had made great pretensions to reason, and it is fair to say of Alfred de Musset that he had made none whatever. What the public sees is that the latter, unreasonable though he may have been, comes staggering home, alone and forlorn, while his companion remains quietly at Venice and writes three or four highly successful romances. Herr Lindau, who analyzes the affair, comes to the same conclusion as the gross, synthetic public; and he qualifies certain sides of it in terms of which observant readers of George Sand's writings will recognise the justice. It is very happy to say "she was something of a Philistine;" that at the bottom of all experience with her was the desire to turn it to some economical account; and that she probably irritated her companion in a high degree by talking too much about loving him as a mother and a sister. (This, it will be remembered, is the basis of action with Thérèse, in "Elle et Lui." She becomes the hero's mistress in order to retain him in the filial relation, after the fashion of Rousseau's friend, Madame de Warens). On the other hand, it seems hardly fair to make it one of Musset's grievances that his comrade was industrious, thrifty and methodical; that she had, as the French say, *de l'ordre*; and that, being charged with the maintenance of a family, she allowed nothing to divert her from producing her daily stint of "copy."

It is easy to believe that Musset may have tried the patience of a tranquil associate. George Sand's Jacques Laurent in "Elle et Lui," is a sufficiently vivid portrait of a highly endowed, but hopelessly petulant, unreasonable and dissipated egotist. We are far from suspecting that the portrait is perfectly exact; no portrait by George Sand is perfectly exact. Whatever point of view she takes, she always abounds too much in her own sense. But it evidently has a tolerably solid foundation in fact. Herr Lindau holds that Alfred de Musset's life was literally blighted by the grief that he suffered in Italy, and that the rest of his career was a long, erratic, unprofitable effort to drown the recollection of it. Our own inclination would be to judge him at once with more and with less indulgence. Whether deservedly or no, there is no doubt that his suffering was great; his brother quotes a passage from a document written five years after the event, in which Alfred affirms that, on his return to Paris, he spent four months shut up in his room in incessant tears—tears interrupted only by a "mechanical" game of chess in the evening. But Musset, like all poets, was essentially a creature of impressions; as with all poets, his sentimental faculty needed constantly to renew itself. He found his account in sorrow, or at least in emotion, and we may say, in differing from Herr Lindau, that he was not a man to let a grievance grow stale. To feel permanently the need of smothering sorrow is in a certain sense to be sobered by it. Musset was never sobered (a cynical commentator would say he was never sober). Emotions bloomed again lightly and brilliantly on the very stem on which others had withered. After the catastrophe at times his imagination saved him, distinctly, from permanent depression; and on a different line, this same imagination helped him into dissipation.

M. Paul de Musset mentions that in 1837 his brother conceived a "passion sérieuse" for an attractive young lady, and that the *liaison* lasted two years—"two years during which there was never a quarrel, a storm, a cooling-off; never a pretext for umbrage or jealousy. This is why," he adds, "there is nothing to be told of them. Two years of love without a cloud cannot be narrated." It is noticeable that this is the third "passion sérieuse" that M. Paul de Musset alludes to since the dolorous weeks which followed the return from Venice. Shortly after this period another passion had come to the front, a passion which, like that which led him to Italy, was destined to have a tragical termination. This particular love affair is commemorated, in accents of bitter melancholy, in the "Nuit de Décembre," just as the other, which had found its catastrophe at Venice, figures, by clear allusion, in the "Nuit de Mai," published a few months before. It may provoke a philosophic smile to learn, as we do from M. Paul de Musset—candid biographer!—that the "motives" of these two poems are not identical, as they have hitherto been assumed to be. It had never occurred to the reader that one disillusionment could follow so fast upon the heels of another. When we add that a short time afterward—as the duration of great intimacies of the heart is measured—Alfred de Musset was ready to embark upon "two years of love without a cloud" with still another object—to say nothing of the brief interval containing another sentimental episode of which our biographer gives the prettiest account—we seem to be justified in thinking that, for a "blighted" life, that of Alfred de Musset exhibited a certain germinal vivacity.

During his stay in Italy he had written nothing; but the five years which followed his return are those of his most active and brilliant productiveness. The finest of his verses, the most charming of his tales, the most original of his comedies, belong to this relatively busy period. Everything that he wrote at this time has a depth and intensity that distinguish it from the jocosely sentimental productions of his commencement and from the somewhat mannered and vapidly elegant compositions which he put forth, at wide intervals, during the last fifteen years of his life. This was the period of Musset's intellectual virility. He was very precocious, but he was at the same time, at first, very youthful. On the other hand, his decline began early; in most of his later things, especially in his verses (they become very few in number) the inspiration visibly runs thin. "Mon verre n'est pas grand, mais je bois dans mon verre," he had said, and both clauses of the sentence are true. His glass held but a small quantity; the best of his verses—those that one knows by heart and never wearies of repeating—are very soon counted. We have named them when we have mentioned "Rolla," the "Nuit de Mai," the "Nuit d'Août," and the "Nuit d'Octobre"; the "Lettre à Lamartine," and the "Stances à la Malibran." These, however, are perfection; and if Musset had written nothing else he would have had a right to say that it was from his own glass that he drank. The most beautiful of his comedies, "Il ne faut pas badiner avec l'Amour," dates from 1834, and to the same year belongs the "Lorenzaccio," the strongest, if not the most exquisite, of his dramatic attempts. His two most agreeable *nouvelles*, "Emmeline" and "Fréderic et Bernerette," appeared about the same time. But we have not space to enumerate his productions in detail. During the fifteen last years of his life, as we have said, they grew more and more rare; the poet had, in a certain sense, out-lived himself. Of these last years Herr Lindau gives a rather realistic and unflattered sketch; picturing him especially as a figure publicly familiar to Parisian loungers, who were used to observe him as "an unfortunate with an interesting face, dressed with extreme care," with the look of youth and the lassitude of age, seated in a corner of a café and gazing blankly over a marble table on which "a half empty bottle of absinthe and a quite empty glass" stood before him. M. Paul de Musset, in describing his brother's later years, is mindful of the rule to glide, not to press; with a very proper fraternal piety, he leaves a great many foibles and transgressions in the shade. He mentions, however, Alfred's partiality for stimulants—a taste which had defined itself in his early years. Musset made an excessive use of liquor; in plain English, he got drunk. Sainte-Beuve, somewhere in one of his merciless, but valuable foot-notes, alludes to the author of "Rolla" coming tipsy to the sittings of the French Academy. Herr Lindau repeats a pun which was current on such occasions. "Musset s'absente trop," said some one. "Il s'absinthe trop," replied some one else. He had been elected to the Academy in 1852. His speech on the occasion of his reception was a disappointment to his auditors. Herr Lindau attributes the sterility of his later years to indolence and perversity; and it is probable that there is not a little justice in the charge. He was unable to force himself; he belonged to the race of gifted people who must do as it pleases them. When a literary task was proposed to him and he was not in the humour for it, he was wont to declare that he was not a maid-of-all-work but an artist. He must write when the fancy took him; the fancy took him, unfortunately, less and less frequently. With a very uncertain income and harassed constantly by his debts, he scorned to cultivate a pecuniary inspiration. He died in the arms of his brother in the spring of 1857.

He was beyond question one of the first poets of our day. If the poetic force is measured by the *quality* of the inspiration—by its purity, intensity, and closely personal savour— Alfred de Musset's place is surely very high. He was, so to speak, a thoroughly *personal* poet. He was not the poet of nature, of the universe, of reflection, of morality, of history; he was the poet simply of a certain order of personal emotions, and his charm is in the frankness and freedom, the grace and harmony, with which he expresses these emotions. The affairs of the heart—these were his province; in no other verses has the heart spoken more characteristically. Herr Lindau says very justly that if he was not the greatest poet among his contemporaries, he was at any rate the most poetically constituted nature. A part of the rest of Herr Lindau's judgment is worth quoting:

"He has remained the poet of youth. No one has sung so truthfully and touchingly its aspirations and its sensibilities, its doubts and its hopes. No one has comprehended and justified its follies and its amiable idiosyncrasies with a more poetic irony, with a deeper conviction. His joy was young, his sorrow was young, and young was his song. To youth he owed all happiness, and in youth he sang his brightest chants. But the weakness of youth was his fatal enemy, and with youth faded away his joy in existence and in creation."

This is exactly true. Half the beauty of Musset's writing is its simple suggestion of youthfulness—of something fresh and fair, slim and tremulous, with a tender epidermis. This quality, with some readers, may seem to deprive him of a certain proper dignity; and it is very true that he was not a Stoic. You may even call him unmanly. He cries out when he is hurt; he resorts frequently to tears, and he talks much about his tears. (We have seen that after his return from Venice they formed, for four months, his principal occupation). But his defence is that if he does not bear things like a man, he at least, according to Shakespeare's distinction, feels them like a man. What makes him valuable is just this gift for the expression of that sort of emotion which the conventions and proprieties of life, the dryness of ordinary utterance, the stiffness of most imaginations, leave quite in the vague, and yet which forms a part of human nature important enough to have its exponent. If the presumption is against the dignity of deeply lyric utterance, poor Musset is, in the vulgar phrase, nowhere—he is a mere grotesque sound of lamentation. But if in judging him you do not stint your sympathy, you will presently perceive him to have an extraordinarily precious quality—a quality equally rare in literature and in life. He has passion. There is in most poetry a great deal of reflection, of wisdom, of grace, of art, of genius; but (especially in English poetry) there is little of this peculiar property of Musset's. When it occurs we feel it to be extremely valuable; it touches us beyond anything else. It was the great gift of Byron, the quality by which he will live in spite of those weaknesses and imperfections which may be pointed out by the dozen. Alfred de Musset in this respect resembled the poet whom he appears most to have admired—living at a time when it had not begun to be the fashion to be ashamed to take Byron seriously. Mr. Swinburne in one of his prose essays speaks of him with violent scorn as Byron's "attendant dwarf," or something of that sort. But this is to miss the case altogether. There is nothing diminutive in generous admiration, and nothing dwarfish in being a younger brother; Mr. Swinburne's charge is too coarse a way of stating the position. Musset resembles Byron in the fact that the beauty of his verse is somehow identical with the feeling of the writer—with his immediate, sensible warmth—and not dependent upon that reflective stage into which, to produce its great effects, most English poetic expression instantly passes, and which seems to chill even while it nobly beautifies. Musset is talked of nowadays in France very much as Byron is talked of among ourselves; it is noticed that he often made bad verses, and he is accused of having but half known his trade. This sort of criticism is eminently just, and there is a weak side of the author of "Rolla" which it is easy to attack.

Alfred de Musset, like Mr. Murray's fastidious correspondent, wrote poetry as an amateur—wrote it, as they say in France, *en gentilhomme.* It is the fashion, I believe, in some circles, to be on one's guard against speaking foreign tongues too well (the precaution is perhaps superfluous) lest a marked proficiency should expose one to be taken for a teacher of languages. It was a feeling of this kind, perhaps, that led Alfred de Musset to a certain affectation of negligence and laxity: though he wrote for the magazines, he could boast a long pedigree, and he had nothing in common with the natives of Grub Street. Since his death a new school of poets has sprung up—of which, indeed, his contemporary, Théophile Gautier, may be regarded as the founder. These gentlemen have taught French Poetry a multitude of paces of which so sober-footed a damsel was scarcely to have been supposed capable; they have discovered a great many secrets that Musset appears never to have suspected, or (if he did suspect them) to have thought not worth finding out. They have sounded the depths of versification, and beside their refined, consummate *facture* Musset's simple devices and good-natured prosody seem to belong to a primitive stage of art. It is the difference between a clever performer on the tight rope and a gentleman strolling along on soft turf with his hands in his pockets. If people care supremely for form, Musset will merely but half satisfy them. It is very pretty, they will say; but it is confoundedly unbusinesslike. His verse is not chiselled and pondered, and in spite of an ineffable natural grace it lacks the positive qualities of cunning workmanship—those qualities which are found in such high perfection in Théophile Gautier. To our own sense Musset's exquisite feeling more than makes up for one-half the absence of "chiselling," and the ineffable grace we spoke of just now makes up for the other half. His sweetness of passion, of which the poets who have succeeded him have so little, is a more precious property than their superior science. His grace is often something divine; it is in his grace that we must look for his style. Herr Lindau says that Heine speaks of "truth, harmony, and grace" being his salient qualities. (By the first, we take it, he meant what we have called Musset's passion.) His harmony, from the first, was often admirable; the rhythm of even some of his earliest verses makes them haunt the ear after one has murmured them aloud.

> Ulric, des mers nul œil n'a mesuré l'abîme,
> Ni les hérons plongeurs, ni les vieux matelots;
> Le soleil vient briser ses rayons sur leur cime,
> Comme un soldat vaincu brise ses javelots.

Musset's grace, in its suavity, freedom, and unaffectedness, is altogether peculiar; though it must be said that it is only in the poems of his middle period that it is at its best. His latest things are, according to Sainte-Beuve, *colifichets*—baubles; they are too much in the rococo, the Dresden china, style. But as we have said before, with his youth Musset's inspiration failed him. It failed him in his prose as well as in his verse. "Il faut qu'une Porte soit ouverte ou fermée," one of the last of his dramatic proverbs, is very charming, very perfect in its way; but compared with the tone of the "Caprices de Marianne," the "Chandelier," "Fantasio," the sentiment is thin and the style has rather a simper. It is what the French call *marivaudage*. There can, however, be no better example of the absoluteness of the poetic sentiment, of its justifying itself as it goes, of lyrical expression being as it were not only a means, but an end, than the irresistible beauty of such effusions as the "Lettre à Lamartine" and the "Nuit d'Août."

> Poëte, je t'écris pour te dire que j'aime!

—that is all, literally, that Musset has to say to the "amant d'Elvire"; and it would be easy to make merry at the expense of so simply candid a piece of "gush." But the confidence is made with a transparent ardour, a sublime good faith, an audible, touching tremour of voice, which, added to the enchanting harmony of the verse, make the thing one of the most splendid poems of our day.

> Ce ne sont pas des chants, ce ne sont que des larmes,
> Et je ne te dirai que ce que Dieu m'a dit!

Musset has never risen higher. He has, in strictness, only one idea—the idea that the passion of love and the act of loving are the divinest things in a miserable world; that love has a thousand disappointments, deceptions, and pangs, but that for its sake they are all worth enduring, and that as Tennyson has said, more curtly and reservedly,

> 'Tis better to have loved and lost
> Than never to have loved at all.

Sometimes he expresses this idea in the simple epicurean fashion, with gaiety and with a more or less cynical indifference to the moral side of the divine passion. Then he is often pretty, picturesque, fanciful, but he remains essentially light. At other times he feels its relation to the other things that make up man's destiny, and the sense of aspiration mingles with the sense of enjoyment or of regret. Then he is at his best; then he seems an image of universally sentient youth.

> Je ne puis; malgré moi, l'infini me tourmente,
> Je n'y saurais songer sans crainte et sans espoir;
> Et quoiqu'on en ait dit, ma raison s'épouvante
> De ne pas le comprendre, et pourtant de le voir.

While we may suspect that there is something a little over-coloured in M. Paul de Musset's account of the degree to which his brother was haunted by the religious sentiment—by the impulse to grope for some philosophy of life—we may also feel that with the poet's sense of the "divineness" of love there went a conviction that ideal love implies a divine object. This is the feeling expressed in the finest lines of the "Lettre à Lamartine"—in lines at least which, if they are not the finest, are fine enough to quote:

> Eh bien, bon ou mauvais, inflexible ou fragile,
> Humble ou gai, triste ou fier, mais toujours gémissant,
> Cet homme, tel qu'il est, cet être fait d'argile,
> Tu l'a vu, Lamartine, et son sang est ton sang.
> Son bonheur est le tien; sa douleur est la tienne;
> Et des maux qu'ici bas il lui faut endurer,
> Pas un qui ne te touche et qui ne t'appartienne;
> Puisque tu sais chanter, ami, tu sais pleurer.
> Dis-moi, qu'en penses-tu dans tes jours de tristesse?
> Que t'a dit le malheur quand tu l'as consulté?
> Trompé par tes amis, trahi par ta maîtresse,
> Du ciel et de toi-même as-tu jamais douté?
> Non, Alphonse, jamais. La triste expérience
> Nous apporte la cendre et n'éteint pas le feu.
> Tu respectes le mal fait par la Providence;
> Tu le laisses passer et tu crois à ton Dieu.
> Quelqu'il soit c'est le mien; il n'est pas deux croyances.
> Je ne sais pas son nom: j'ai regardé les cieux;
> Je sais qu'ils sont à lui, je sais qu'ils sont immenses,
> Et que l'immensité ne peut pas être à deux.
> J'ai connu, jeune encor, de sévères souffrances;
> J'ai vu verdir les bois et j'ai tenté d'aimer.

Je sais ce que la terre engloutit d'espérances,
Et pour y recueillir ce qu'il y faut semer.
Mais ce que j'ai senti, ce que je veux t'écrire,
C'est ce que m'ont appris les anges de douleur;
Je le sais mieux encor et puis mieux te le dire,
Car leur glaive, en entrant, l'a gravé dans mon cœur.

And the rest of the poem is a lyrical declaration of belief in immortality.

We have called the "Lettre à Lamartine" Musset's highest flight, but the "Nuit de Mai" is almost as fine a poem—full of imaginative splendour and melancholy ecstasy. The series of the "Nuits" is altogether superb; with an exception made, perhaps, for the "Nuit de Décembre," which has a great deal of sombre beauty, but which is not, like the others, in the form of dialogue between the Muse and the poet—the Muse striving to console the world-wounded bard for his troubles and urging him to take refuge in hope and production.

Poëte, prends ton luth et me donne un baiser;
La fleur de l'églantier sent ses bourgeons éclore.
Le printemps naît ce soir; les vents vont s'embraser;
Et la bergeronnette, en attendant l'aurore,
Aux premier buissons verts commence à se poser.
Poëte, prends ton luth et me donne un baiser.

That is impregnated with the breath of a vernal night. The same poem (the "Nuit de Mai") contains the famous passage about the pelican—the passage beginning—

Les plus désespérés sont les chants les plus beaux,
Et j'en sais d'immortels qui sont de purs sanglots—

in which the legend of the pelican opening his breast to feed his starving young is made an image of what the poet does to entertain his readers:

Poëte, c'est ainsi que font les grands poëtes.
Ils laissent s'égayer ceux qui vivent un temps;
Mais les festins humains qu'ils servent à leurs fêtes
Ressemblent la plupart à ceux des pélicans.

This passage is perhaps—unless we except the opening verses of "Rolla"—Musset's noblest piece of poetic writing. We must place next to it—next to the three "Nuits"—the admirably passionate and genuine "Stanzas to Malibran"—a beautiful characterization of the artistic disinterestedness of the singer who suffered her genius to consume her—who sang herself to death. The closing verses of the poem have a wonderful purity; to rise so high, and yet in form, in accent, to remain so still and temperate, belongs only to great poetry; as it would be well to remind the critic who thinks the author of the "Stanzas to Malibran" dwarfish. There is another sort of verse in which violence of movement is more sensible than upwardness of direction.

So far in relation to Musset's lyric genius—though we have given but a brief and inadequate account of it. He had besides a dramatic genius of the highest beauty, to which we have left ourself space to devote only a few words. It is true that the drama with Musset has a decidedly lyrical element, and that though his persons always talk prose, they are constantly saying things which would need very little help to fall into the mould of a stanza or a sonnet. In his dramas as in his verses his weakness is that he is amateurish; they lack construction; their merit is not in their plots, but in what, for want of a better term, we may call their sentimental perfume. The earliest of them failed upon the stage, and for many years it was supposed they could not be played. Musset supposed so himself, and took no trouble to encourage the experiment. He made no concessions to contemporary "realism." But at last they were taken up—almost by accident—and it was found that, in the hands of actors whose education enabled them to appreciate their delicacy, this delicacy might become wonderfully effective. If feeling is the great quality in his verses, the case is the same in his strange, fantastic, exquisite little *comédies*; comedies in the literal English sense of the word we can hardly call them, for they have almost always a melancholy or a tragical termination. They are thoroughly sentimental; he puts before us people who convince us that they really feel; the drama is simply the history of their feeling. In the emotions of Valentin and Perdican, of Fantasio and Fortunio, of Célio and Octave, of Carmosine and Bettine, there is something contagious, irresistibly touching. But the great charm is Musset's dramatic world itself, the atmosphere in which his figures move, the element they breathe.

It seems at first a reckless thing to say, but we will risk it: in the *quality* of his fancy Musset always reminds us of Shakespeare. His little dramas go forward in the country of "As You Like It" and the "Winter's Tale"; the author is at home there, like Shakespeare himself, and he moves with something of the Shakespearean lightness and freedom. His fancy loves to play with human life, and in the tiny mirror that it holds up we find something of the depth and mystery of the object. Musset's dialogue, in its mingled gaiety and melancholy, its sweetness and irony, its allusions to real things and its kinship with a romantic world, has an altogether indefinable magic. To utter it on the stage is almost to make it coarse. Once Musset attempted a larger theme than usual; in "Lorenzaccio" he wrote an historical drama on the scale of Shakespeare's histories; that is, with multitudes of figures, scenes, incidents, illustrations. He laid his hand on an admirable subject—the story of a certain Lorenzino de' Medici, who played at being a debauchee and a poltroon in order better to put the tyrant of Florence (his own cousin) off his guard, and serve his country by ridding her of him. The play shows an extraordinary abundance and vivacity of imagination, and really, out of those same "histories" of Shakespeare, it is hard to see where one should find an equal spontaneity in dealing with the whole human furniture of a period. Alfred de Musset, in "Lorenzaccio," has the air of being as ready to handle a hundred figures as a dozen—of having imagination enough for them all. The thing has the real creative inspiration, and if it is not the most perfect of his productions it is probably the most vigorous.

We have not spoken of his tales; their merit is the same as of the *comédies*—that of spontaneous feeling, and of putting people before us in whose feelings we believe. Besides this, they have Musset's grace and delicacy in a perhaps excessive degree; they are the most mannered of his productions. Two or three of them, however—"Emmeline," "Les Deux Maîtresses," "Frédéric et Bernerette"—are masterpieces; this last epithet is especially to be bestowed upon the letter written by the heroine of the last-mentioned tale (an incorrigibly *volage* grisette) to her former lover on the occasion of his marrying and settling. The incoherency, the garrulity, the mingled resignation and regret of an amiable flirt of the lower orders, divided between the intensity of her emotion and the levity of her nature, are caught in the act. And yet it is not fair to say of anything represented by Musset that it is caught in the act. Just the beauty and charm of it is that it is not the exact reality, but a something seen by the imagination—a tinge of the ideal, a touch of poetry. We must try to see Musset himself in the same way; his own figure needs to a certain extent the help of our imagination. And yet, even with such help taken, we cannot but feel that he is an example of the wasteful way in which nature and history sometimes work—of their cruel indifference to our personal standards of economy—of the vast amount of material they take to produce a little result.

Alfred de Musset's superfine organization, his exaltations and weaknesses, his pangs and tears, his passions and debaucheries, his intemperance and idleness, his years of unproductiveness, his innumerable mistresses (with whatever pangs and miseries it may seem proper to attribute to *them*), his quarrel with a woman of genius, and the scandals, exposures, and recriminations that are so ungracefully bound up with it—all this was necessary in order that we should have the two or three little volumes into which his *best* could be compressed. It takes certainly a great deal of life to make a little art! In this case, however, we must remember, that little is exquisite.

Galaxy, June 1877
Reprinted in *French Poets and Novelists*, 1878

Henri Regnault

Correspondance de Henri Regnault, recueillie et annotée par M. Arthur Duparc. Paris: Charpentier; New York: F. W. Christern, 1872.

THERE ARE NO MORE striking works in the Luxembourg Museum than two large pictures recently placed there, side by side: one an immense equestrian portrait of General Prim, the Spanish revolutionist; the other a Moorish executioner, wiping on the hem of his garment the scimetar with which he has just dissevered the head and body which lie gushing blood at his feet. The pictures arrest attention by the singular brilliancy and audacity of their coloring, their massive breadth of execution, and, above all, a certain unmistakable glow of youth and genius. They are signed by Henri Regnault, a name already a little known in America, where one of the artist's few finished works—the "Automedon"—is owned, but deserving of a wider knowledge now that the volume whose title we have transcribed has established the record of his rapid, brilliant, and touching career. The portrait of Prim was painted in his twenty-sixth, and its companion in his twenty-seventh year. Six months later, on the 19th of January, 1871, Regnault fell at Buzenval, before the walls of Paris, victim of the last shot possibly fired before the surrender of the city. It could hardly have extinguished a life of greater promise. During the previous months of national distress he had written these lines:

> "We have lost many men; we must supply their places with better and stronger ones. We must learn the lesson. We must cease to be relaxed by facile pleasures. We have no longer the right to live for ourselves alone. It was the fashion not long since to believe in nothing but enjoyment and in all the bad passions. Selfishness must depart, and take with it that fatal bravado of contempt for all that is honest and good. . . . The Republic now demands of us a pure, honorable, serious life, and we must all pay to our country, and beyond our country to free humanity, our debt of body and soul. We owe them what both these may produce together. All our energies must concur to the well-being of

the great family, through the practice for ourselves, and the example for others, of the feelings of honor and the love of work."

In spite of its brevity, there is something singularly complete in Regnault's career, and we may almost expect that, as time goes on, it will become poetized and etherealized, and assume a sort of legendary hue. He had almost every gift, and his talent with the brush was but the finest of a dozen accomplishments. He was an excellent musician, and his beautiful voice was the delight of his friends. He relates in one of his letters from Rome that M. Hébert, the director of the French Academy there, giving a sort of official dinner to a company of princesses and duchesses, and having engaged for their entertainment certain operatic artists, who broke their contract at the eleventh hour, came to him in distress and begged him to furnish the whole musical diversion. Regnault consented modestly, but successfully. He was a devoted horseman, and an impassioned observer and painter of the animal. He was an accomplished gymnast, and not the least picturesque episode of his picturesque residence in Spain is his story of having *épaté* (flattened out) a company of Madrid *gitanos* by walking on his hands and leaping five chairs in a row. As a writer he is admirable, and even if his paintings were of much less value, his delightful letters would amply serve to keep his memory sweet. He made the utmost of his life while it lasted, for though at moments he bitterly accuses himself of recklessness and waste of time, yet he *lived* incessantly in a way altogether foreign to characters of a less generous temper—with an intensity of perception and enjoyment, and a rapidity of development, which make a kind of breathless effort of the perusal of his letters. He succeeded from the first, and made a brilliant impression. He travelled much, and when he had fairly got command of his talent, struck blow upon blow. He made innumerable friends, who speak of the charm of his talent as second only to that of his character. The reader receives from the volume before us an irresistible impression of both. At last, so that no touching and appealing point should be wanting in his history, he becomes engaged to a young girl whom he had long loved, and while waiting for a brighter day to marry receives a bullet through his brain for his country. One of his many friends has here collected his letters, which reflect his well-filled days with admirable vividness. The reader will thank us for allowing him to speak for himself.

In 1866 Regnault received a *prix de Rome* from the *Ecole des Beaux Arts*, and early in the following year took up his residence at that Villa Medici on the Pincian, a chance, however remote, of being promoted to whose academic shades ought to stand nowadays, it seems to us, against many prospective tribulations of *la jeune France*. His letters begin with his journey and are admirable from the first—full of observation and expression, alacrity and energy. Rome disappoints him—especially the churches and the small scale of certain famous buildings and ruins, the Capitol, the Forum, and the Arch of Titus, which he thinks altogether below the reputation of the Ancient Romans. He has a good word for the Coliseum, however, and many admiring ones for Michael Angelo.

> "I'm back from the Vatican. I got on my knees to the paintings of the 'Sistine Chapel' and the 'Stanze.' I'm crushed. That giant of a Michael Angelo has left me half dead. That ceiling is a thunder-stroke. It's above everything conceivable by the imagination of a painter, a sculptor, and a poet, and can never lose its fascination. I confess that in the presence of this ceiling, the wonder of wonders, I was unable to look at the 'Last Judgment.' "

It was some time before he got to work. In reply to some remarks from his father on the subject of his delay, he declares that he is intentionally idle; that he wishes to take a general view, to absorb impressions, to prepare his mind. He makes innumerable excursions, takes long rides on the Campagna, talks music with the Abbé Liszt, pays a flying visit to Naples, and, on his return, decides to make a visit to Paris, where the great Exhibition of 1867 had just opened. Up to this point, if Regnault were not a real genius, we might almost fancy him an imitation, but in Paris he begins his first important work— the portrait of a lady in red velvet on a red background. He took his picture back to Rome with him, finished it laboriously, and, sending it to the Salon of 1868, found himself suddenly almost famous.

Théophile Gautier, as if in prevision of Regnault's brief harvest of laurels, blew the trumpet of praise with magnificent resonance, and published the first of those articles, not less rich in color than the pictures themselves, with which he did honor to each of the young painter's successive performances. On his return to Rome Regnault made a second excursion to Naples to see Vesuvius in eruption; but from this moment he begins to work in earnest, and till he enters upon his military duties during the siege of Paris the brush is hardly out of his hand. He begins two ambitious pictures: a "Judith and Holofernes" and an "Automedon" with the horses of Achilles. The latter is his first *envoi* to the annual exhibition in Paris of the works of the pupils at Rome, and his description of his design is worth quoting:

> "It's a free translation; Automedon may be anything you want, and I have aimed, in my horses, not at the cut of the mane of the Thessalian horses, but at whatever there is most noble and most frightful in the horse—at what might make the historical horse, the horse that spoke, the horse that foresaw the death of his master Achilles. . . . The sky is overladen with clouds; a leaden sea begins to toss, dumbly, though on the surface it still seems to sleep. A ray of melancholy sunshine casts a pallid light along the horizon upon a naked, rocky shore. The horses, knowing that their master is leading them to battle, that this battle will be his last, and will cost him his life, wrestle and struggle against the servant who has come to fetch them from pasture. One of them, a dark bay, rears like a great dark phantom in relief against the sky. I have tried to express in the picture a foreboding of calamity. But have I expressed all I wished?"

The conception is somewhat boyish, and the picture (judging by an engraving) is even more so; but both are sufficiently imaginative and vigorous to promise better things. Regnault defines himself from the first a *picturesque* painter. He was a born draughtsman, and with his pencil felt his strength; but what he consciously sought and ardently studied was color and its infinite mysteries and suggestions. It is characteristic and significant that, at the same time that he protests of his boundless admiration for Michael Angelo, he holds off stoutly from him and contents himself with worshipping at a distance:

> "What would you have a man do when he finds himself staring point-blank at that formidable giant of the Sistine Chapel? . . . Michael Angelo is a god whom one is afraid to touch, lest fire should issue from him. For the time, at any rate, I haven't the courage to approach him; I foresee that he would do me more harm than good, and I'm satisfied with paying him a contemplative worship. I confess that I don't feel as if I had the strength to attack him with my arms in my hand."

Regnault had strength enough and the sense of strength; the truth, as we take it, was that Michael Angelo was, in a single word, too *austere*. To copy a figure from the Sistine roof is an eminently chastening process, and Regnault's tendency was altogether toward license. It had begun to be true of him that, as a discriminating critic (M. Paul de Saint-Victor) wrote of him two years later, *apropos* of his masterpiece, the "Salome," "we may admire but we must mistrust, also, such a *rouerie de pinceau* in so young a man." The term *rouerie de pinceau* is severe, but Regnault, with all his generous breadth of talent, was too essentially a Parisian not to have incurred it, at least as a caution. In the early summer of 1868, Regnault was thrown by a vicious horse with a violence which nearly proved fatal. His recovery was slow; to hasten it a change of climate was recommended, and he accordingly started with alacrity for Spain, which, much more than Italy, had always been the land of his imagination. He came back to the Villa Medici again; but intellectually he had turned his back upon Rome; prematurely, we should have perhaps said, had he lived. For the long run Rome would have had much to teach him; but the prodigious impulse he received in Spain more than served him for his crowded remnant of life. In Spain he found color in something of the strength he had dreamed of, and he found, too, Velasquez, a master after his own heart. His attitude toward the great Spaniard is very different from the respectful reluctance with which he honored Michael Angelo. Not only he began with ardor to copy the "Surrender of Breda"; but his portrait of Prim is almost an imitation of Velasquez. His letters from Madrid are numerous and of really enchanting interest; extracts more copious than we have space for could alone do them justice. The expulsion of Isabella took place during his stay there, and he describes the revolution, as he saw it in the streets, with admirable humor and intelligence. His observation was not confined to the streets, for he was introduced to several of the leaders and men of the day. Prim, he writes, has been very gracious, and he has undertaken his portrait—without sittings as yet—but with the hope of *one* for the face. Prim, unhappily, was not gracious to the end; if he was a good revolutionist, at least he was a poor critic. The portrait is really in the grand manner, and any model however exalted might be proud of making such an appearance before posterity. But Prim perceived only an "*homme indécent*, who hadn't washed his face, and who looked very absurd without his cap." The General's bare head is half the beauty of the picture. Regnault would make no alterations, and he foresaw that if he surrendered his work Prim would consign it to the garret. "Garret for garret," he writes, "I prefer my own," and he sends a respectful note to his illustrious model politely expressing this preference. Thus it is that Regnault's garret has become the Luxembourg Museum. He had depended on the price of the portrait to pay his Madrid color-man and carry him back to Rome; but in the end he had to make the journey "like a pauper, regretting that there was no sixth-class on the railways and steamboats, and obliged to content myself with the third." Yet in spite of these tribulations his winter in Madrid, if he had lived, would have remained delightfully memorable. His time was richly occupied.

"To-morrow," he writes, "I sha'n't have a minute to myself. At a quarter to eight, a beggar to finish, a study begun to-day; at half-past eleven, a visit to the Fomento, to see a fine Goya; at one, a sitting for the little portrait I'm painting of Madame de B. in a Spanish dress of pink and black—which, by the way, becomes her vastly; at four o'clock, dusk, errand at the *Calle di Toledo* to see an old *gitano* mantle, and buy it, doubtless; at five, my guitar lesson, so that I can scratch tolerably a *jaleo* or a *malaguena* of some sort; dinner at six; at seven, model again in the studio. So it is every day, and so ought it always to have been every day. *Si jeunesse savait!*"

He describes in several charming pages, which deepen one's impression of his rare personal attractiveness, the success with which he fraternized with the *gitanos* of Madrid. Of the natural amenity and capacity of these people, and of the Spaniards generally, he formed the highest opinion:

"I confess that Italy, after Spain," he writes on his return to Rome, "seems to me very dull, very commonplace, very *exploitée*. The Italians, male and female, bore me; their dresses look black, colorless, or glaring, always inharmonious. What a difference from Spain, which yet is but a stepping-stone! It is the East I call for, I demand, I insist on! There only, I believe, I shall feel that I am something."

Elsewhere he says that Rome seems to him lit by a nightlight (*une veilleuse*). His "Prim" appeared at the Paris Salon of 1869, and made a great sensation. Théophile Gautier blew a louder blast than before, and Paul de Saint-Victor multiplied his strictures. The present editor gives the articles of each critic, and it is interesting to see how they correct and amend each other. The truth is between them; but it little mattered to Regnault how they shared it, for he remained in Rome, working hard, in obedience to an impulse altogether original. He was rapidly finishing his "Judith" and his "Salome," and preparing for a return to Spain and a further excursion to Morocco. To the artist who, at twenty-six, had achieved these two extraordinary performances in colors, our Western world had surely little more to offer. The shining East alone could yield to him "motives" intense enough. The month of September found him established with a friend at Granada, spending busy, rapturous days in the Alhambra. His admiration for the Moorish architecture knew no bounds; it affected him like a revelation:

"Let the earth stop turning," he writes, "let the stars fall, let cities crumble, let the mountains become valleys—it will matter little, so long as the Alhambra is saved and our friends can see it. . . . I am plunging for the moment into water-colors of the most fantastic difficulty. You must know what I think of Granada, the beauty of beauties, Granada with its sky of lapis, its rosy towers and fortresses, its Alhambra of gold, of silver, of diamonds—of the richest things in the world. I was for several days unable to work; I saw nothing but fire."

He adds later in the same letter strangely: "Clairin [his companion] and I are destined to be short-lived. We lead a life *trop vagabonde*, we strive too hard, we have too much ambition, too many desires, to live long."

His doubts were transient, however, in the joy of such visions as these:

"Every morning we go a few steps off, to the Alcazar, to the divine Alhambra, where the walls in the morning are a lace-work of amethysts and roses, of diamonds at noon, and of green gold and red copper at sunset. We stay there till the moon comes to see us, and when she has sent us a few kisses and put to sleep the shadows of the fairies and genies who chiselled this wondrous palace, we go sadly away turning back at every step, unable to tear our eyes from the columns of rosy marble which take at moments the pearly hues of the lustrous body of a goddess, and are at once our bliss and our despair."

On this visit to Spain Regnault seemed to enter into full possession of his genius, and even more of his ambition. His letters give an irresistible impression of the concentrated ardor and passionate ferment of youthful genius. Promise is stamped on every line. Every hour during these months was a golden lesson; every glance and pencil stroke a forward stride. The more he saw, the more he wished to see; his imagination outstripped experience, and he dreamed restlessly of the uttermost East. In describing to a friend an immense Moorish subject which he had determined to paint:

"The doors open," he writes, "on a gallery whose steps are bathed by a river or a lake, on whose edge my palace is built. I evade criticism in making neither the Alhambra nor the Alcazar, *but a palace not surrounded by water is no palace for me*."

He had already become superbly fastidious. In December he went to Gibraltar and crossed to Tangiers, where he found a splendor of light approaching his ideal—approaching, but not realizing it, however. He adds, in the letter from which we have just quoted, still speaking of his picture:

"In short, it must be a *work*. Then I can take up my bag and go and adore Brahma and Siva! . . . Don't forget India; it's from there we must come back men. Till now, I have learned only to walk, to eat. . . . Be ready for the autumn of 1871. We must start *young* to be moved, to assimilate and drink the sun, to endure the dazzle of marbles and stuffs; and we must come back *young* to create with force."

He established himself at Tangiers for the winter and following summer, in the most picturesque and oriental of studios, and worked ardently and happily. The "Moorish Execution" at the Luxembourg was painted here, and served as his third "Envoi de Rome" (the "Judith" having been the second); the "Salome," too, carried everything before it at the Salon of 1870. Happily, we have said, Regnault worked; toward the end his happiness was fatally overshadowed by the disasters of his country in the field. When the investment of Paris began, he hurried home and enrolled himself in the National Guard. He remained in the ranks to the end, in spite of urgent offers of promotion, doing a soldier's utmost duty, and sharing the common lot of darkness and danger, cold, sleet, and sordid circumstance of every kind. Brahma and Siva had forgotten their worshipper! Close upon the end and the hour of release he fell, with but a tithe of his secrets told. His death, as the climax of the narrative formed by his letters, is terribly, ineffably touching, and will always deepen the vivid interest of his works. These, with various limitations, have the supreme merit of a sort of immeasurable strength. Regnault would not have stopped half way. He had the artistic temperament in very much the same degree as the great Italian masters of the Renaissance. He might not have equalled the greatest of these, but he would have recalled them; and, indeed, we may say that, like them, he is already historical.

Nation, January 2, 1873

Ernest Renan

W E ENCOUNTERED in some journal several weeks ago the rather surprising statement that "M. Ernest Renan was at Ischia writing a novel." It appears that at the time it was published the first half of this statement was true; M. Renan had indeed the felicity of being at Ischia. Whether he was writing a novel or not, we are unable to say; but he was writing something very nearly as entertaining. He has just published in the *Revue des Deux Mondes*, in the form of a letter from Ischia, a singularly interesting account of some of the doings of the late learned Congress of Palermo. It is written in the exquisite style usual with M. Renan, and it will well repay reading. At the close of the Congress, Signor Bonghi, the Italian Minister of Public Instruction, organized a ten days' excursion to the various ruins and historical sites of Sicily. Every one present seems to have had very little time to spare, and the party travelled at high pressure beneath a Sicilian September sun. M. Renan says that he did not sleep during the whole ten days, and that at last fatigue overwhelmed him; but he saw everything, and, thanks to his large erudition, understood everything. As an honored guest, he takes a rather rose-colored view of Sicily; we hear not a word about brigands; it is all a population of "braves gens." Here is an interesting passage:

"A surprising ease, occasionally a little presumption, are the fruit of the high sense of his nobleness of origin which is the characteristic of the Sicilian. The idea that he is inferior to any one in the world never occurs to him. The petty tricks that we call reserve and discretion are in us the relic of a long social inequality. The Greek is equally unacquainted with these timidities. At first I was surprised at the innumerable letters, at the cosmogonies and treatises on the universe and the nature of things, at the projects of universal reform, that I received every day. It is not often that with us a stranger comes to you and says, 'Your philosophy is mine,' or, 'You are one of the small number of persons who have arrived at the just conception of the created.' Then you remember that you are in Greece, that things took place in this way in the time of Empedocles, and that it is owing to this awakening that humanity began to institute a search for causes. Sicily is perhaps the country where a taste for speculation is most natural. If anything can still give us the idea of a country in which, as in Greece, the taste for beautiful things was the care of a whole people, and in which the difference of culture between the inferior classes and the upper ones existed only in degree, we must look for it in Sicily. What seems to us *naïf* is simply antique. The joyous greeting given in the country districts to the Congress was a spectacle that no other country in Europe could have offered."

It is agreeable to hear all this about regions from which the principal news lately has been the doings of the *mafia* and the impossibility of getting juries to convict murderers. Upon the great ruins—Syracuse, Agrigentum, and Taormina— M. Renan is of course very eloquent and interesting.

Nation, December 30, 1875

LETTER FROM PARIS: CURRENT LITERATURE

Paris, March 21.— The only literary event of first-rate importance that has occurred in Paris during the Winter has been the publication of Taine's "Ancien Régime," of which, at the time, I made mention. In so sterile a season I suppose that the appearance in the last number of the *Revue des Deux Mondes* of the first installment of Ernest Renan's "Souvenirs d'Enfance" may be spoken of as a salient event. The article appears to have attracted much attention, but to have caused some disappointment. It consists of two parts—a few pages of personal reminiscence by M. Renan himself, and a narrative taken down—with considerable embellishment—from the lips of his mother. The story is tame and of slender significance; but M. Renan's own memoirs are enchanting. His touch is more exquisite, his style more magical, surely, than any others of the day. The death of Daniel Stern (Mme. d'Agoult) and that of Mme. Louise Colet may also be spoken of as literary incidents. Mme. d'Agoult was a serious writer and Mme. Colet a light one, but both ladies had had beauty and adventures. Of these adventures the Abbé Liszt was the hero in one case, and Alfred de Musset in the other. I saw quoted the other day from Mme. d'Agoult a felicitous sentence: "An agreeable mind is a mind that is affirmative only in the measure strictly necessary." This dictum is characteristic of a writer who was also a very skillful *maitresse de salon*. Mme. Colet never said anything so good as that. Some years ago, when Mme. Sand published her very ill-advised "Elle et Lui," and Paul de Musset (the brother of the presumptive original of the hero) retorted with "Lui et Elle," Mme. Colet cried like Correggio, *"Anch' io son pittore!"* and put forth a tale entitled "Lui," the purpose of which was to prove, as I remember it, that she used to roam in the Bois de Boulogne in the small hours of the night in a low-necked dress, while "He," roaming hand in hand with her, showered kisses upon her shoulders. "Orpheus and the Bacchantes" these contributions to erotic history were happily called. Poor Orpheus!

New York Tribune, April 22, 1876

LETTER FROM PARIS: M. ERNEST RENAN'S NEW VOLUME

PARIS, May 27.—M. Ernest Renan has just published a new volume, which will not fail to find its way speedily into the hands of all lovers of good writing. A new volume by Renan is an intellectual feast; if he is not the first of French writers, I don't know who may claim the title. In these "Dialogues et Fragments Philosophiques," indeed, it is the dialogues alone that are new; they occupy but half of the volume, the rest of which is composed of reprinted pieces. The dialogues are a sort of *jeu d'esprit*, but a *jeu d'esprit* of a very superior kind—the recreation of a man of elevated genius. They are prefaced by a few pages breathing a very devoted patriotism, and proving that the author's exorbitant intellectual reveries have not relaxed his sense of the plain duties of citizenship. To win back that esteem which he appears willing to concede that they have in some degree forfeited, he exhorts his fellow-countrymen above all things to work. Let each, he says, surpass himself in his own particular profession, "so that the world may still cry of us, 'These Frenchmen are still the sons of their fathers; eighty years ago Condorcet, in the midst of the Reign of Terror, waiting for death in his hiding-place in the Rue Servandoni, wrote his Sketch of the Progress of the Human Mind.'" M. Renan imagines a group of friends, who assemble in a quiet corner of a park of Versailles, to exchange reflections upon the "ensemble de l'Univers." The subject is extensive, and it may well take half a dozen talkers to cover the ground. Three persons, however, take the lead, each one of whom unfolds his particular view of the Cosmos. These three views are classed by M. Renan under the respective heads of Certainties, Probabilities, and Reveries. He disclaims them all as a representation of his own opinions, and says that he has simply entertained himself with imagining what might be urged and argued in each direction. It is probable, however, that if his convictions and feelings are not identical with those of either of his interlocutors, they have a great deal in common with the whole mass of the discussion, and that Philalethes, Theophrastus, and Theoctistes are but names for certain moods of M. Renan's mind. If so, one can only congratulate him upon the extraordinary ingenuity and fertility of his intellect and the entertaining company of his thoughts. These pages are full of good things admirably said, of brilliant and exquisite suggestions, and of happy contributions to human wisdom. Their fault is the fault which for some time has been increasing in M. Renan's writing—a sort of intellectual foppishness, a love of paradox and of distinction for distinction's sake. His great merit has always been his natural distinction, but now, in this same distinction, in the affectation of views which are nothing if not exquisite, views sifted and filtered through an infinite intellectual experience, there is something rather self-conscious and artificial. The reader cannot help wishing that M. Renan might be brought into more immediate contact with general life itself —general life as distinguished from that horizon of pure learning which surrounds the *cabinet de travail* of a Parisian scholar—suspecting that, if this could happen, some of his fine-spun doubts and perplexities would find a very natural solution, and some of his fallacies die a very natural death.

Philalethes, the exponent of M. Renan's "Certainties," is not so certain about some things as his friends might have expected; but his skepticism is narrowed down to a point just fine enough to be graceful. "In fact," he says, "if I had been a priest, I should never have been willing to accept a fee for my mass; I should have been afraid of doing as the shopkeeper who delivers for money an empty bag. Just so I should have had a scruple about drawing a profit from my religious beliefs. I should have been afraid of seeming to distribute false notes and to prevent poor people, by putting them off with dubious hopes, from claiming their portion in this world. These things are substantial enough for us to talk about them, to live by them, to think of them always; but they are not certain enough to enable us to be sure that in pretending to teach them we are not mistaken as to the quality of the goods delivered." Theophrastus, who discourses on "Probabilities," takes, on the whole, a cheerful view of the future—it must be confessed with considerable abatements. He agrees probably in a great measure with Theoctistes, who remarks, "I have never said that the future was cheerful. Who knows whether the truth is not sad?" Theophrastus thinks that the maturity of the world is to arrive by the expansion of science—on condition, indeed, that the mechanical theory of heat succeeds within five or six hundred years in inventing a substitute for coal. If it fails—and the failure is quite probable—"humanity will enter into a sort of mediocrity from which she will hardly have the means to emerge." It must be added that Theophrastus is prepared to see art and beauty (as we have hitherto understood it) disappear; "the day will perhaps come (we already see its dawn) when a great artist, a virtuous man, will be antiquated, almost useless things."

The speculations of Theoctistes, however, are much the most curious. He imagines a development of science so infinite and immeasurable that it will extend our relations beyond the limits of the planet on which we dwell, and he deems the function of this perfected machine to be above all the production of great men. The great men may be so selected and sifted and improved that human perfection may at last concentrate itself in one extremely superior being, who will hold all the universe in cheerful and grateful subordination. This is what Theoctistes calls "God being realized." With these sentiments it is not surprising that he should not expect that God will be realized by a democracy. He gets into deeper water than he can always buffet, but his style is the perfection of expression. I must quote a few lines more. "For myself, I relish the universe through that sort of general sentiment to which we owe it that we are sad in a sad city, gay in a gay city. I enjoy thus the pleasures of those given up to pleasure, the debauchery of the debauchee, the worldliness of the worldling, the holiness of the virtuous man, the meditations of the *savant*, the austerity of the ascetic. By a sort of sweet sympathy I imagine to myself that I am their consciousness. The discoveries of the *savant* are my property; the triumphs of the ambitious are my festival. I should be sorry that anything should be missing in this world, for I have the consciousness of all that it contains. My only displeasure is that the age has fallen so low that it no longer knows how to enjoy. Then I take refuge in the past—in the sixteenth century, in the seventeenth, in antiquity; everything that has been beautiful, amiable, noble, just, makes a sort of paradise for me. With this I defy misfortune to touch me; I carry with me the charming garden of the variety of my thoughts." This paragraph seems to me magnificent; one would like to have written it. The charm of M. Renan's style is hard to define; it is ethereal as a perfume. It is a style above all things urbane, and, with its exquisite form, is suggestive of moral graces, amenity, delicacy, generosity. Now that Sainte-Beuve is dead, it strikes me as the most perfect vehicle of expression actually in operation in France. The only style to be compared to it is that of Mme. Sand; but for pure quality even this must yield the palm. Mme. Sand's style is, after all (with all respect), a woman's style.

New York Tribune, June 17, 1876

Souvenirs d'Enfance et de Jeunesse. Par Ernest Renan, Membre de l'Institut, etc. Paris: Calmann Lévy, 1883.

THERE HAS always been an element of the magical in the style of M. Ernest Renan—an art of saying things in a way to make them beautiful. At the present moment he is the first writer in France; no one has in an equal degree the secret of fairness of expression. His style is fair in both the senses in which we use the word—in that of being temperate and just, and in that of being without a flaw; and these Reminiscences of his younger years, lately collected from the Revue des Deux Mondes, are perhaps the most complete revelation of it. His problem here was unusually difficult, and his success has been proportionately brilliant. He proposed to talk uninterruptedly about himself, and yet he proposed—or rather he was naturally disposed—to remain a model of delicacy. M. Renan is the great apostle of the delicate; he upholds this waning fashion on every occasion. His mission is to say delicate things, to plead the cause of intellectual good manners, and he is wonderfully competent to discharge it. No one today says such things so well, though in our own language Mr. Matthew Arnold often approaches him. Among his own countrymen, Sainte-Beuve cultivated the same art, and there was nothing too delicate for Sainte-Beuve to attempt to say. But he spoke less simply—his delicacy was always a greater complexity. M. Renan, on the other hand, delivers himself of those truths which he has arrived at through the fineness of his perception and the purity of his taste with a candid confidence, an absence of personal precautions, which leave the image as perfect and as naked as an old Greek statue. It is needless to say that there is nothing crude in M. Renan; but the soft serenity with which, in the presence of a mocking world, he leaves his usual plea for the ideal to any fate that may await it is an example of how extremes may sometimes meet. It is not enough to say of him that he has the courage of his opinions; for that, after all, is a comparatively frequent virtue. He has the resignation; he has the indifference; he has, above all, the good humor. He combines qualities the most diverse, and, lighted up as he is by the interesting confessions of the volume before us, he presents himself as an extraordinary figure. He makes the remark that in his opinion less importance will be attached to talent as the world goes on; what we shall care for will be simply truth. This declaration is singular in many ways, among others in this: that it appears to overlook the fact that one of the great uses of talent will always be to discover truth and present it; and that, being an eminently personal thing, and therefore susceptible of great variety, it can hardly fail to be included in the estimate that the world will continue to make of persons. M. Renan makes light of his own talent—he can well afford to; if he appears to be quite conscious of the degree in which it exists, he minimizes as much as possible the merit that attaches to it. This is a part of that constant play of taste which animates his style, governs his judgments, colors all his thought; for nothing can be in better taste, of course, than to temper the violence with which you happen to strike people. To make your estimate of your own gifts as low as may seem probable is a form of high consideration for others; it corresponds perfectly with that canon of good manners which requires us to take up a moderate space at table. At the feast of existence we may not jostle our neighbors, and to be considerate is for M. Renan an indefeasible necessity. He informs us of this himself; it is true that we had long ago guessed it. He places the fact before us, however, in a relation to other facts, which makes it doubly interesting; he gives us the history of his modesty, his erudition, his amiability, his temperance of appetite, his indifference to gain. The reader will easily perceive the value that must attach to such explanations on the part of a man of M. Renan's intelligence. He finds himself in constant agreement with the author, who does nothing but interpret with extraordinary tact the latent impressions of his critic.

M. Renan carries to such a high point the art of pleasing that we enter without a protest into the pleasantness of the account he gives of himself. He is incapable of evil, learned, happy, cheerful, witty, devoted to the ideal, indifferent to every vulgar aim. He demonstrates all this with such grace, such discretion and good humor, that the operation, exempt from vulgar vanity, from motives of self-interest, M. Renan being at that point of literary eminence where a writer has nothing more to gain, seems to go on in the pure ether of the abstract, among the causes of things and above all questions of relative success. Speaking of his ancestors in Brittany, whom he traces back to the fifth century, simple tillers of the earth and fishers of the sea, he says, with great felicity, "There they led for thirteen hundred years a life of obscurity, saving up their thoughts and sensations into an accumulated capital, which has fallen at last to me. I feel that I think for them and that they live in me. . . . My incapacity to be bad, or even to appear so, comes to me from them." Many men would hesitate to speak so freely of their incapacity to be bad; others, still more of their incapacity to appear so. But M. Renan has polished to such clearness the plate of glass through which he allows us to look at him that we are quite unable to charge him with deceiving us. If we fail to see in him so much good as that, it is simply that our vision is more dim, our intelligence less fine. "I have a strong taste for the people, for the poor. I have been able, alone in my age, to understand Jesus and Francis of Assisi." There is a great serenity in that, and though, detached from the text, it may startle us a little, it will not seem to the reader who meets it in its place to be a boastful note. M. Renan does not indeed mean to say that he has been the only Christian of his time; he means that he is not acquainted with any description of the character of Jesus containing as much historic truth as the Life he published in 1864. The passage is curious, however, as showing the lengths to which a man of high delicacy may go when he undertakes to be perfectly frank. That, indeed, is the interest of the whole volume. Many of its pages are rare and precious, in that they offer us together certain qualities that are almost never combined. The aristocratic intellect is not prone to confess itself, to take other minds into its confidence. M. Renan believes in a caste of intellectual nobles, and of course does not himself belong to any inferior order. Yet in these volumes he has alighted from his gilded coach, as it were; he has come down into the streets and walked about with the multitude. He has, in a word, waived the question of privacy—a great question for such a man as M. Renan to waive. When the impersonal becomes personal the change is great, and it is interesting to see that sooner or later it must become so. Naturally, for us English readers, the difference of race renders such a fact more difficult to appreciate; for we have a traditional theory that when it comes to making confidences a Frenchman is capable of almost anything. He is certainly more gracefully egotistic than people of other stock, though he may have more real reserve than his style would indicate.

His modesty is individual, his style is generic; he writes in a language which makes everything definite, including confessions and other forms of self-reference. The truth is that he talks better than other people, and that the genius of talk carries him far. There is nothing into which it carries people more naturally than egotism. M. Renan's volume is a prolonged *causerie*, and he has both the privileges and the success of the talker.

There are many things in his composition and many things in his writing; more than we have any hope of describing in their order. "I was not a priest in profession; I was a priest in mind. All my defects are owing to that: they are the defects of the priest." The basis of M. Renan's character and his work is the qualities that led him to study for the priesthood, and the experience of a youth passed in Catholic seminaries. "Le pli était pris—the bent was taken," as he says; in spite of changes, renunciations, a rupture with these early aspirations as complete as it was painful, he has remained indefinably, ineffaceably, clerical. The higher education of a Catholic priest is an education of subtleties, and subtlety is the note, as we say to-day, of M. Renan's view of things. But he is a profane philosopher as well as a product of the seminary, and he is in the bargain a Parisian and a man of letters; so that the groundwork has embroidered itself with many patterns. When we add to this the high scholarship, the artistic feeling, the urbanity, the amenity of temper, that quality of ripeness and completeness, the air of being permeated by civilization, which our author owes to his great experience of human knowledge, to his eminent position in literature and science, to his association with innumerable accomplished and distinguished minds—when we piece these things together we feel that the portrait he has, both by intention and by implication, painted of himself has not wanted an inspiring model. The episode which M. Renan has had mainly to relate in these pages is of course the interruption of his clerical career. He has made the history so suggestive, so interesting, and given such a charm to his narrative, that we have little hesitation in saying that these chapters will rank among the most brilliant he has produced. We are almost ashamed to express ourselves in this manner, for, as we have said, M. Renan makes very

light of literary glory, and cares little for this kind of commendation. Indeed, when we turn to the page in which he
gives us the measure of his indifference to successful form we
feel almost tempted to blot out what we have written. "I do
not share the error of the literary judgments of our time.
. . . I tried to care for literature for a while only to gratify
M. Sainte-Beuve, who had a great deal of influence over me.
Since his death I care no longer. I see very well that talent has
a value only because the world is childish. If it had a strong
enough head it would content itself with truth. . . . I have
never sought to make use of this inferior quality [literary
skill], which has injured me more as a *savant* than it has
helped me for itself. I have never in the least rested on
it. . . . I have always been the least literary of men." The
reader may be tempted to ask himself whether these remarks
are but a refinement of coquetry; whether a faculty of expression so perfect as M. Renan's was ever a simple accident. He
will do well, however, to decide that the writer is sincere, for
he speaks from the point of view of a seeker of scientific truth.
M. Renan is deeply versed in the achievements of German
science: he knows what has been done by scholars who have
not sacrificed to the graces, and in the presence of these great
examples he would fain persuade himself that he has not, at
least consentingly, been guilty of that weakness. In spite of
this he will continue to pass for one of the most characteristic
children of the race that is preëminent in the art of statement.
It is a proof of the richness of his genius that we may derive
so much entertainment from those parts of it which he regards as least essential. We do not pretend in this place to
speak, with critical or other intention, of the various admirable works which have presented M. Renan to the world as
one of the most acute explorers of the mysteries of early
Christian history; we take for granted the fact that they have
been largely appreciated, and that the writer, as he stands before us here, has the benefit of all the authority which a great
task executed in a great manner can confer. But we venture
to say that, fascinating, touching, as his style, to whatever
applied, never ceases to be, none of the great subjects he has
treated has taken a more charming light from the process than
these evocations of his own laborious past.

And we say this with a perfect consciousness that the volume before us is after all, in a certain sense, but an elaborate *jeu d'esprit*. M. Renan is a philosopher, but he is a sportive philosopher; he is full of soft irony, of ingenious fancy, of poetic sympathies, of transcendent tastes. He speaks more than once of his natural gayety, and of that quality in members of the Breton race which leads them to move freely in the moral world and to divert themselves with ideas, with sentiments. Half of the ideas, the feelings, that M. Renan expresses in these pages (and they spring from under his pen with wonderful facility) are put forward with a smile which seems a constant admission that he knows that everything that one may say has eventually to be qualified. The qualification may be in one's tact, one's discretion, one's civility, one's desire not to be dogmatic; in other considerations, too numerous for us to mention. M. Renan has a horror of dogmatism; he thinks that one should always leave that to one's opponent, as it is an instrument with which he ends by cutting himself. He has a high conception of generosity, and though his mind contains several very positive convictions, he is of the opinion that there is always a certain grossness in insistence. Two or three curious passages throw light upon this disposition. "Not having amused myself when I was young, and yet having in my character a great deal of irony and gayety, I have been obliged, at the age at which one sees the vanity of everything, to become extremely indulgent to foibles with which I had never had to reproach myself: so that various persons, who perhaps have not behaved so well as I, have sometimes found themselves scandalized at my complaisance. In political matters, above all, people of a Puritan turn cannot imagine what I am about; it is the order of things in which I like myself best, and yet ever so many persons think my laxity in this respect extreme. I cannot get it out of my head that it is perhaps, after all, the libertine who is right and who practices the true philosophy of life. From this source have sprung in me certain surprises, certain exaggerated admirations. Sainte-Beuve, Théophile Gautier, pleased me a little too much. Their affectation of immorality prevented me from seeing how little their philosophy hung together (*le décousu de leur philosophie*)." There is a certain stiffly literal sense in which, of course, these lines are not to be taken; but they are a charming specimen of what one may call delicacy of confession. The great thing is to have been able to afford to write them; on that condition they are delightfully human and charged with the soft irony of which I have spoken—the element to which M. Renan alludes in a passage that occurs shortly after the one I have quoted, and in which he mentions that, "save the small number of persons with whom I recognize an intellectual fraternity, I say to every one what I suppose must give him pleasure." He says that he expresses himself freely only with people " whom I know to be liberated from any opinion, and to be able to take the stand-points of a kindly universal irony." "For the rest," he remarks, "I have sometimes, in my conversation and my correspondence, *d'étranges défaillances*. . . . My inanity with people I meet in society exceeds all belief. . . . Devoted on a kind of system to an exaggerated politeness, the politeness of the priest, I try to find out what my interlocutor would like me to say to him. . . . This is the result of a supposition that few men are sufficiently detached from their own ideas not to be wounded if you say something different from what they think." We should not omit to explain that what we have just quoted applies only to M. Renan's conversation and letters. "In my published writings I have been of an absolute sincerity. Not only have I not said anything that I do not think, but, a much more rare and more difficult thing, I have said all that I think." It will be seen that M. Renan tells us a good deal about himself.

His Reminiscences are ushered in by a preface which is one of the happiest pieces of writing that has ever proceeded from his pen, and in which he delivers himself of his opinion on that very striking spectacle, the democratization of the world. He is preëminently a man of general views. Few men have more of them at their command; few men face the occasion for speech with greater serenity, or avail themselves of it with more grace. His prefaces have always been important and eloquent; readers of the first collection of his critical essays, published upwards of thirty years ago, will not have forgotten the enchanting pages that introduced it. We feel a real obligation to quote the opening lines of the preface before us;

from the point of view of style they give the key of the rest of the volume. We must add that it is not easy to transport their exquisite rhythm into another tongue. "Among the legends most diffused in Brittany is that of a so-called town of Is, which at an unknown period must have been engulfed by the sea. They show you, in sundry places on the coast, the site of this fabled city, and the fishermen tell you strange stories about it. They assure you that on days of storm the tip of the spires of its churches may be seen in the hollow of the waves; that on days of calm you may hear the sound of its bells come up from the deeps, intoning the hymn of the day. It seems to me often that I have in the bottom of my heart a city of Is, which still rings bells that persist in gathering to sacred rites the faithful who no longer hear. At times I stop to lend an ear to these trembling vibrations, which appear to me to come from infinite depths, like the voices of another world. On the limits of old age, above all, I have taken pleasure in collecting together such echoes of an Atlantis that has passed away." It may have been that M. Renan wrote these harmonious lines with the same ignorance of what he was about that characterized M. Jourdain; in this case he is only to be congratulated the more. The city of Is represents his early education, his early faith, a state of mind that was peopled with spires and bells, but has long since sunk deep into the sea of time. He explains in some degree the manner in which he has retraced this history, choosing to speak of certain things and to pass in silence over others, and then proceeds, by those transitions through which no one glides so gracefully as he, to sundry charming considerations upon the present state of mankind and the apparent future of our society. We call his reflections charming, because M. Renan's view of life always strikes us as a work of art, and we naturally apply to it the epithets which we should use in speaking of any delightful achievement. As a votary of the ideal, a person who takes little interest in the practical, a distinguished member of that beneficent *noblesse* of intellect of which we have spoken, it would be natural that M. Renan should tend to conservative opinions; and he expresses such opinions, in various later pages, with exquisite humor and point: "In other terms, our great democratic machines exclude the polite man.

I have long since given up using the omnibus; the conductors ended by taking me for a passenger of no intentions. . . . I was made for a society founded upon respect, in which one is saluted, classified, placed, according to his costume, and has not to protect himself. . . . The habit that I found in the East of walking only preceded by a forerunner suited me not ill; for one's modesty receives a lift from the apparatus of force. It is well to have under one's orders a man armed with a scourge which one prevents him from using. I should not be sorry to have the right of life and death, so that I might never put it into practice; and I should be very glad to own a few slaves, in order to be extremely mild with them and make them adore me." There is a certain dandyism of sensibility, if we may be allowed the expression, in that; but the author's perfect good-humor carries it off, as it always carries off the higher flights of his fastidiousness, making them seem simply a formal, a sort of cheerfully hopeless, protest in the name of the ideal. M. Renan is always ready to make the practical concession, and he shows that it is a great thing to have a fine taste, which tells us when to yield as well as when to resist, and points out, moreover, the beauty of passing things by. "One should never write save about what one likes. Forgetfulness and silence are the punishment that we inflict on what we find ugly or common in the walk that we take through life." This discretion helps M. Renan to feel that, though the immense material progress of this century is not favorable to good manners, it is a great mistake to put ourselves in opposition to what our age may be doing. "It does it without us, and probably it is right. The world moves toward a sort of Americanism, which wounds our refined ideas, but which, once the crisis of the present hour is passed, may very well be no worse than the old *régime* for the only thing that matters; that is, the emancipation and the progress of the human mind." And M. Renan develops the idea that, in spite of all that the votaries of disinterested speculation may find wanting in a society exclusively democratic and industrial, and however much they may miss the advantages of belonging to a protected class, their security is greater, on the whole, in the new order of things. "Perhaps some day the general vulgarity will be a condition of the happiness of the elect. The American vulgarity [*sic*] would not burn Giordano Bruno, would not persecute Galileo. . . . People of taste live in America, on the condition of not being too exacting." So he terminates with the declaration that the best thing one can do is to accept one's age, if for no other reason than that it is after all a part of the past that one looks back to with regret. "All the centuries of a nation are the leaves of the same book." And in regard to this intelligent resignation, which fortifies itself with curiosity, M. Renan says several excellent things: "There will always be an advantage in having lighted on this planet as late as possible. . . . One must never regret that one sees a little better." M. Renan's preface is a proof that he possesses the good spirits which he notes as an ingredient of his character. He is a *raffiné*, and a raffiné with an extraordinary gift of putting his finger on sensitive spots; with a reasoned ideal of the millennium. But a raffiné without bitterness is a very harmless person.

The first chapters of this volume are not the most vivid, though they contain a very interesting picture of the author's birthplace, the little dead town of Tréguier, a gray cluster of convents and churches on the coast of Catholic Brittany. Tréguier was intensely conventual, and the young Renan was, as a matter of course, predestined to the church. "This strange set of circumstances has given me for historic studies those qualities that I may possess. The essence of criticism is to be able to understand states very different from those in which we live. I have seen the primitive world. In Brittany, before 1830, the most distant past was still alive." The specimens which M. Renan gives of this primitive world are less happily sketched than the general picture; the coloring is rather pale; some of the anecdotes—that of the little Noémi, that of the Bonhomme Système—are perhaps slightly wanting in point. He remarks somewhere, in regard to the opposition, about which so much used to be said, between the classic and the romantic, that, though he fully admits the latter, he admits it only as subject—not in the least as a possible form. To his mind there is only one form, which is the classic. And in another place he speaks of Flaubert, the novelist—"ce pauvre Flaubert"—as being quite unable to conceive of anything abstract. Putting these things together, we see a certain reason why M. Renan's personal portraits (with the exception of the picture of himself) should be wanting in reality. They are too general, too white; the author, wonderfully at home in the abstract, has rather neglected the concrete. "Ce pauvre Flaubert" would be revenged for M. Renan's allusion, if it were possible to him to read the episode of the Flax-Grinder—revenged (an exquisite revenge for an artist) by simply finding it flat. It is when he comes to dip into his own spiritual history that M. Renan shows himself a masterly narrator. In that region of abstractions, where the most tangible thing was the palpitating conscience, he moves with the firmest step. The chapters on the two seminaries in which he spent the first years of his residence in Paris, Saint Nicholas du Chardonnet and Saint Sulpice, are full of the most acute notation of moral and intellectual conditions. The little Breton seminarist moved too fast, and, to speak briefly, very soon transcended his instructors. He had a passion for science, and his great aptitude for philology promptly defined itself. He traces with singular art the process by which, young, simple, devout, dedicated to the church from his infancy, the object of maternal and pastoral hopes, he found himself confronted with the fact that he could no longer be a Catholic. He also points out well that it was the rigidity of the Catholic system that made continuance impossible, it being all of one piece, so that dissent as to one point involved rejection of the whole. "It is not my fault if my masters had taught me logic, and by their pitiless argumentations had converted my mind into a steel blade. I took seriously what I had learned—the scholastic philosophy, the rules of the syllogism, theology, Hebrew. I was a good scholar; I can never be damned for that." M. Renan holds, moreover, that little was wasted of his elaborate religious education. "I left their hands [those of the priests] with a moral sentiment so prepared for every test that Parisian levity could afterwards put a surface on this jewel without hurting it. I was so effectually made up for the good, for the true, that it would have been impossible for me to follow any career not directed to the things of the soul. My masters rendered me so unfit for all temporal work that I was stamped with an irrevocable mark for the spiritual life. . . . I persist in believing that existence is the most frivolous thing in the world, if one does not conceive it as a great and continual duty." This moral richness, these spiritual aspirations, of M. Renan's, of which we might quote many other examples, pervade all his utterances, even when they are interfused with susceptibilities which strike us at times as those of a dilettante; with refinements of idealism which suggest to us occasionally that they correspond to no possible reality, and even that the natural corrective for this would be that reality, in some of the forms which we children of less analytic race are obliged to make our peace with it, would impose itself a little more absolutely upon our critic. To what extent M. Renan's nature has been reduplicated, as it were, by his intellectual curiosity may be gathered from his belief, recorded in these pages, that he would have gone much further in the exploration of the universe if he had not taken his inspiration from the historical sciences. "Physiology and the natural sciences would have carried me along; and I may certainly say it, the extreme ardor which these vital sciences excited in my mind makes me believe that if I had cultivated them in a consecutive manner I should have arrived at several of the results of Darwin, of which I had had glimpses. . . . I was drawn [instead] toward the historical sciences—little conjectural sciences which are pulled down as often as they are set up, and which will be neglected a hundred years hence." We know not what M. Renan may have missed, and we know not what may be the ultimate fate of historical conjecture and of the hapless literary art, in both of which he so brilliantly excels; but what such a volume as these mingled, but on the whole delightful, Reminiscences represents in the way of attainment, suggestion and sympathy is a sum not easily to be calculated. With his extraordinarily composite nature, his much-embracing culture, he is a most discriminating critic of life. Even his affectations are illuminating, for they are either exaggerations of generosity or ingenuities of resignation.

Atlantic Monthly, August 1883

Madame de Sabran

Correspondance Inédite de la Comtesse de Sabran et du Chevalier de Boufflers. Paris: Plon, 1875.

THE PRESENT CENTURY in France has been the golden age of editors. It might have been supposed that the mine of literary wealth bequeathed to that country by the eighteenth century had been exhausted, and that the occupation of the exhibitory fraternity was gone. The mine has been worked with extraordinary industry and with the most perfect appliances of erudition and criticism, and its contents have been brought to light in particles of all dimensions—in massive boulders, such as only the more skilled engineers might safely transport, in fragments convenient for immediate use, and in barely ponderable powder and dust. More even than our own time the eighteenth century was an age of scribbling. This indeed is untrue if taken in the sense that the amount of published writing, in proportion to the size of society, was larger than in our own day; but it is true if we speak with an eye to the quality of production. In proportion to the size of society, we suspect that there were more things written in private between 1720 and 1790 which might go to press without professional revision (save in the matter of orthography) than between 1800 and 1875. There was in other words, so far as form was concerned, less merely wasted and squandered literary effort than we witness nowadays. The distinction between padding and substance had not then been invented; and it is not only more charitable but more accurate to say that all the writing (so far as it went) was substance rather than padding. There are vast quantities of it that we cannot read—that we should not be able to read even if our own age made no appeal to us; but this is in a great measure because the whole body of civilisation has taken a jump, and we are wofully out of relation with our ancestors. We are a thousand times more clever; but it may be questioned whether, just as the Venetians in the sixteenth century knew something about the art of painting that all our cleverness will not put us into possession of, the ladies and gentlemen who sowed the ultimate seeds of the French Revolution had not a natural sense of agreeable literary expression which is quite irrecoverable by our straining modern wit. Comparisons, however, are odious, and it is certain that our ancestors had their bores and that we have our charmers. What we may say is that people of the eighteenth century wrote much and wrote well—so much that some lost or unsuspected yellow manuscript is still constantly drawn from hiding, and so well that the presumption is always in favour of its being very readable.

The best society at least wrote in those days more than it does now, and the obvious reason is that it had vastly more time on its hands. It had nothing to do with trade; the men who composed it had no daily duties in "stores" and counting rooms. The gentlemen of the eighteenth century were either in the Army, the Church, the diplomatic service, or the civil service; and these are all eminently sociable professions. The occupations of women were proportionately less exacting, for women's lives have always been fashioned in that portion of the piece, as one may say, which remains after men's have been cut out. Ladies, therefore, wrote a great deal, and at a first glance at the field it seems as if every woman of good fashion had produced certain volumes of letters, of reminiscences, of memoirs, of maxims, or of madrigals. Since Madame de Sévigné French gentlewomen have been excellent letter writers, and those lessons in easy style to which allusion was made above may often be culled from their ill-spelled gossip with their absent friends. (They all spelled very much at random. Even Madame du Châtelet, the learned coquette with whom Voltaire lived so many years, and who edited Newton and competed for the prizes of the Academy of Sciences, gained appreciably as a correspondent by being charitably read aloud.) French society in the eighteenth century was indeed very small, and we know it nowadays with surprising minuteness; we know it almost as well as if a brilliant Balzac of that age had laboriously constructed it and, with all the pains in the world, had not been able to make his people seem really more multitudinous than a pre-Raphaelite painter does the leaves of his trees. It is a multitude, but it is a multitude that we can count. For an historic group its outlying edges have very little nebulosity or mystery—very little of the look of continuity with the invisible. The fierce light that beats upon the subject-matter of French *études critiques* has illumined every corner and crevice of it. The people who are fond of remarking that, after all, the world is very small, must make their assertion with emphasis after a course of French memoirs, with an eye to the notes, or simply after reading Sainte-Beuve's "Causeries." The same names, the same figures, the same anecdotes, the same allusions, constantly recur; it is a dense cross web of relations, distinctly circumscribed. It is hardly too much to say that for all purposes save those of specialists the time is all contained in Sainte-Beuve's forty volumes. A collection of newspaper articles fairly comprehends it, even to many of its *minutiæ*.

The situation has a certain resemblance to those portions of modern Rome and Athens in which there are still chances of disinterring Greek statues. Excavation has been so systematically pursued that we may reasonably suppose there are now many more maimed divinities above ground than beneath it; and yet the explorer's spade still rings against a masterpiece often enough to maintain us in hopeful attention. It was but the other day—compared to the duration of its mouldy concealment—that the beautiful mailed Augustus of the Vatican was restored to the light, and it was but yesterday that MM. de Magnieu and Prat put forward, in a beautiful and substantial volume, the letters of Madame de Sabran. This excellent publication belongs to a class to which there is good reason for expecting more recruits. Madame de Sabran's letters are love-letters, and in such missives the female hand has at all times been prolific. The author was not in her day a woman of eminent distinction; she moved in the best society, she was known to be clever, and those who corresponded with her had a high appreciation of her epistolary talent. But she never published anything (although she alludes to a work on the Conduct of Life which she has in hand), and you will not find her name in the "Biographie Universelle." She was one of the multitudinous minor satellites of the French court; she represents the average clever woman of quality of her time. Many other women were presumably esteemed equally clever, and many others must have left letters as voluminous and, on some grounds, as valuable as hers. Many such, as we know, have already seen the light. This is not said to depre-

ciate the merit of Madame de Sabran's epistles, but simply to
note the fact that, charming as they are, they belong to a
numerous family. Madame de Sabran's letters were piously
preserved by her son, recently deceased (of whose childhood
they contain much mention), and are published in execution
of his testamentary injunctions. For him at least his mother
had claims to renown. Few readers of the volume before us
will fail to agree with him. In France it has been highly relished, and the relations of Madame de Sabran and the Chevalier de Boufflers have taken their place as one of the most
touching episodes in the history of the old French society.
The writer of these lines has read the book with extreme pleasure, and he cannot resist the temptation to prolong his pleasure and share it with such readers as have a taste for delicate
things.

Madame de Sabran, who was born in 1750, married with
the usual docility of the young women of her country. M. de
Sabran was an officer in the navy, fifty years his wife's senior,
and possessed of a meagre fortune, though also of what we
call nowadays a handsome "record." She speaks of her marriage in the very charming account which she gives, in 1787,
of her daughter's wedding: "My heart has never beaten so
hard as at the moment I placed her on the *prie-dieu* where she
was going to utter that famous *yes* that one can never unsay
when once it is said, much as one may sometimes wish it. My
own did not produce such an effect upon me; and yet what a
difference! I was about to marry an infirm old man, of whom
I was to be rather the sick-nurse than the wife, and she a
young man full of grace and merit. But it is that then I felt
the consequences so little; everything seemed to me equally
well, equally good; as I loved nothing, everything seemed to
me worthy of being loved, and I felt toward my *bonhomme de
mari* very much as toward my father and my grandfather—a
feeling very sweet at that time, and that my heart found sufficient. Time has undeceived me; I have lost my faith in happiness; so in spite of myself, during the whole service, I wept
a flood of tears." Her married life lasted but a short time; M.
de Sabran died of apoplexy, leaving his wife among social ties
that might have beguiled an even less consolable widowhood.
The Abbé Delille, the horticultural poet, taught her Latin,

and the great Turgot prized her conversation. Several years later she made the acquaintance of the Chevalier de Boufflers, and her first letter, in the volume before us, is of the date of 1778. Madame de Sabran was a woman of culture and M. de Boufflers was a patron of arts and letters; he also passed for one of the most agreeable men of his time, and he figures not infrequently in its chronicles. They became intimate, and Madame de Sabran's friendship ripened into a passion of which the present letters are the flickering but always ardent utterance. At a certain moment (apparently in 1781) she begins to address her correspondent with the *thou* and to call him "my child." Up to this moment it had been "my brother." M. de Boufflers was altogether a man of the world, and of the gayest world, and his roving disposition was a constant interruption to his attentions to his friend. In 1785 he was appointed governor of the colony of Senegal, and during his sojourn in Africa Madame de Sabran continued her letters in the form of a journal. He was absent but eighteen months, but after a short visit to France he returned to his post and remained there two years. Madame de Sabran resumed her diary, and M. de Boufflers also kept, for her entertainment, a journal which is hardly less charming than that of his mistress. He married Madame de Sabran in 1797, when he was sixty years old and his bride was forty-seven. This long delay is but insufficiently accounted for by his desire to be able to offer his wife a fortune and a great position. M. de Boufflers enjoyed many of the advantages of matrimony without its encumbrances. The division was not equal, for Madame de Sabran seems to have had all the anxieties of a wife and none of the guarantees. The couple emigrated during the Revolution and their marriage took place in Germany. The Chevalier de Boufflers died in Paris in 1815, and his widow survived him twelve years. A certain reticence on the part of the editors prompts the adventurous reader to wonder whether, in its later stages, this intimacy was not touched by the ravages of time; but the conjecture is almost impertinent, decidedly cynical and, inasmuch as there is no visible answer to the question, utterly vain.

What have we here, then, is something very light—the passionate, unstudied jottings of an amiable and intelligent woman who loves a man whose affection she is conscious of possessing, but whose absences and delays and preoccupations and admirations and social dissipations, and duties of all kinds, are a constant irritant to the impatience, the jealousies, the melancholy, of which her own affection, in its singularly delicate texture, is all indivisibly composed. It is hard to say why we should be interested in these very personal affairs of an obscure French lady of a hundred years ago, and if a stern logician should accuse us of frivolous tastes we should find it difficult to justify our enthusiasm. Madame de Sabran's letters have in the direct way but a slender historical value, for they allude to but few of the important events of the time. They throw no very vivid light on contemporary manners; for there is little in them to refer them to their actual date. Their psychological and dramatic interest cannot be said to be profound; they have none of the dignity of tragedy. Their compass of feeling is not wide, and the persons concerned in them are not, in any very striking way, at the mercy of events. They portray no terrible suffering, no changes of fortune; the most important event related is that Madame de Sabran marries her daughter. If they are passionate, it is passion in the minor key, without any great volume or resonance. Yet for all that they are charming, simply because so far as they go they are perfect. Madame de Sabran had an exquisite talent for the expression of feminine tenderness, and a gift like this has an absolute value. Two appreciable causes throw it here into a sort of picturesque relief. One is the fascination of the background our sense of the peculiar atmosphere of the eighteenth century; the other is the extremely dramatic form in which, in this case, the usual contrast between the man's life and the woman's is presented to us—the opposition between the heart for which any particular passion was but one of many and the heart for which all passion resolved itself into a single unquenchable flame. As regards the eighteenth century, it is rather late in the day, perhaps, to talk about that; but so long as we read the books of the time, so long will our sense of its perplexing confusion of qualities retain a certain freshness. No other age appeals at once so much and so little to our sympathies, or provokes such alternations of curiosity and repugnance. It is near enough to us to seem to partake of many of our current feelings, and yet it is divided from us by an impassable gulf. For many persons it will always have in some ways an indefinable charm—a charm that they will entertain themselves in looking for even in the faded and mouldering traces of its material envelope—its costumes, its habits, its scenic properties. There are few imaginations possessed of a desultory culture that are not able to summon at will the dim vision of a high saloon, panelled in some pale colour, with oval medallions over the doors, with a polished, uncarpeted floor, with thin-legged chairs and tables, with Chinese screens, with a great glass door looking out upon a terrace where clipped shrubs are standing in square green boxes. It is peopled with men and women whose style of dress inspires both admiration and mistrust. There is a sort of noble amplitude in the cut of their garments and a richness of texture in the stuff; breeches and stockings set off the manly figure, and the stiffly-pointed waists of the women serve as a stem to the flower-like exuberance of dazzling bosoms. As we glance from face to face the human creature seems to be in an expansive mood; we receive a lively impression of vigour of temperament, of sentimental fermentation, of moral curiosity. The men are full of natural gallantry and the women of natural charm, and of forms and traditions they seem to take and leave very much what they choose. It is very true that they by no means always gain by minute inspection. An acute sense of untidiness is brought home to us as we move from group to group. Their velvets and brocades are admirable, but they are worn with rather too bold a confidence in their intrinsic merit, and we arrive at the conviction that powder and pomatum are not a happy combination in a lady's tresses, and that there are few things less attractive than soiled satin and tarnished embroidery. In the same way we gather an uneasy impression of moral cynicism; we overhear various phrases which make us wonder whither our steps have strayed. And yet, as we retreat, we cast over the threshold a look that is on the whole a friendly one; we say to ourselves that after all these people are singularly human. They care intensely for the things of the mind and the heart, and though they often make a very foolish use of them they strike here and there a light by whose aid we are now reading certain psychological mysteries. They have the psychological passion, and if they expose themselves in morbid researches it is because they wish to learn by example as well as precept and are not afraid to pay for their knowledge. "The French age *par excellence*," an acute French critic has said, "it has both our defects and our qualities. Better in its intelligence than in its behaviour, more reasoning than philosophical, more moralistic than moral, it has offered the world lessons rather than examples, and examples rather than models. It will be ever a bad sign in France when we make too much of it or too little; but it would be in especial a fatal day were we to borrow its frivolity and its corruption and leave aside its noble instincts and its faculty of enthusiasm." A part of our kindness for the eighteenth century rests on the fact that it paid so completely the price of both corruptions and enthusiasms. As we move to and fro in it we see something that our companions do not see—we see the sequel, the consummation, the last act of the drama. The French Revolution rounds off the spectacle and renders it a picturesque service which has also something besides picturesqueness. It casts backward a sort of supernatural light, in the midst of which, at times, we seem to see a stage full of actors performing fantastic antics for our entertainment. But retroactively, too, it seems to exonerate the generations that preceded it, to make them irresponsible and give them the right to say that, since the penalty was to be exorbitant, a little pleasure more or less would not signify. There is nothing in all history which, to borrow a term from the painters, "composes" better than the opposition, from 1600 to 1800, of the audacity of the game and the certainty of the reckoning. We all know the idiom which speaks of such reckonings as "paying the piper." The piper here is the People. We see the great body of society executing its many-figured dance on its vast polished parquet; and in a dusky corner, behind the door, we see the lean, gaunt, ragged Orpheus filling his hollow reed with tunes in which every breath is an agony.

The opening lines of the first of Madame de Sabran's letters are characteristic both of the time and of the woman. The time was sceptical and priests were out of fashion, except for such assistance as they might render at a lady's toilet; but

Madame de Sabran's most amiable quality is a certain instinctive moderation. "I really need to talk with you to-day, my brother, to cheer myself up and divert myself from a certain visit I have been making. And what a visit! A visit that one makes only at certain times, to the knees of a certain man, to confess certain things which I won't tell you. I am still very weary and ashamed with it. I don't at all like that ceremony. They tell us it is very salutary, and I submit, like a respectable woman." It is not in our power to say what sins Madame de Sabran had to confess; she gives an account of her life at Anisy, the residence of her uncle the Bishop of Laon, where she regularly spent her summers, which seems to allow a margin for none but venial aberrations: "I get up every morning at eight, and read and write till eleven; then I set myself at painting till dinner time. I am doing a superb oil picture which I have composed for myself and which I will show you. . . . I read in Latin the original letters of Héloïse and Abélard, and I have a good mind to translate some of the most coherent ones—not those of Abélard, for they are most tiresomely dry and pedantic, but those of poor Héloïse." In everything that Madame de Sabran says there is a certain closely personal accent, and at last we have a complete portrait, formed by a multitude of desultory touches. The total is something we like so much that we do not feel disposed to call the weak spots by their specific names. Is it vanity when she frankly pronounces her oil painting "superb"? "Apropos, I have not yet spoken to you of the portrait of the Countess Auguste that I made while she was staying here; it is a little masterpiece. It is a perfect likeness. It is full length, a table beside her, with books and papers. It is a charming picture, and it will be a pleasure to me to show it to you." Is this vanity, or is it the unaffected frankness of a person who is conscious of genuine talent? We have no means of taking the measure of Madame de Sabran's talent; but she was a very clever woman, and it is not hard to believe that her pictures were charming and that the musical airs which she is constantly composing and sending to M. de Boufflers were infinitely sweet. But in dealing with people of this race and society, especially at that time, we Anglo-Saxons are constantly reminded of the necessity of weighing virtues and vices in an adjusted scale. Words and things, ideas and feelings, have a different value. There are French vanities that are very innocent and English humilities that are not at all so; French corruptions that, *mutatis mutandis*, are by no means damning. For instance, M. de Boufflers, writing from Africa, tells Madame de Sabran of the condition of her portrait, which she has given him. "As by a special grace, I have been left alone a moment. I have just left my letter to go and kiss you. You are behind certain cross-pieces of wood, intended to fix the picture in its case, and you look like your pretty Delphine in her convent parlour—though if there is a difference, I know very well to whose advantage it is." Here is a gallant gentleman trying to be agreeable to a superior woman by telling her that she is prettier than her own daughter. The inference is, that M. de Boufflers thought he was saying something very charming and that Madame de Sabran received his compliment in a sympathetic spirit. And yet Madame de Sabran was a devoted mother. M. de Boufflers in the next sentence speaks with the tenderest solicitude of Mademoiselle de Sabran, and in the following letter he sends a most graceful message to his friend's children. "Kiss your charming children for me. My heart bleeds when I think that I cannot press them against my breast and prove to them what it is in my eyes to be born of you." The portrait mentioned by M. de Boufflers is apparently not the charming picture by Mme. Vigée le Brun of which a capital reproduction in aqua-fortis is prefixed to the Correspondence. Madame de Sabran was called a beauty, but we should say that, if this picture is to be trusted, this was just what she was not. It is an intensely French physiognomy and quite the one that shapes itself in our mind's eye out of the perusal of the letters. But half its interest is in the way it pleases in spite of its irregularity. It is extraordinarily sympathetic, and offers a singular combination of wit and amiability.

In the letter but one preceding that one which has been mentioned as indicating the moment of expansion, as it were, in Madame de Sabran's friendship, she evidently defends herself against such contingencies. She has been scolding her friend for delay in writing. "You can have no idea what I have suffered, and I am so frightened at it myself that there is

nothing I wouldn't do to recover my reason, even to going
to the moon in search of it on the back of a hippogriff. But
meanwhile I take the firm resolution to trouble myself no
more about your silence, your absence, and even your indifference; to live a little for you, a great deal for myself, and to
be always gay and contented whatever befalls me. In the
midst of all this fine philosophy, however," she adds, "I rejoice in your return"; and her philosophy henceforth was destined to play a very secondary part. There are times when she
summons it to her aid—for as regards all things in which M.
de Boufflers was not concerned it was very alert and competent; but when she plays at resignation or indifference, stoicism or epicureanism, she hardly even pretends that she
deceives herself. She had indeed a strain of melancholy in her
disposition which is constantly cropping up; she was afraid of
the deeper currents of life, and she thought that when one
felt one's feet touching bottom it was the part of wisdom to
stand still. "I don't rejoice as you do in the discovery of *truth*.
I am afraid it will hurt me. All those people will turn your
head and, in conducting you to happiness, they will spoil this
happiness of ours. We are comfortable; let us rest upon that;
what do we need more? I don't care for a science which is of
no use to our love and which may on the contrary be injurious to it." M. de Boufflers had sent home a little blacka-
moor as a present to a friend who had taken the interesting
stranger to see the aunt of the donor. Shortly afterward Madame de Sabran called upon this lady, who denounced the
little negro as an ill-bred monster. "As soon as he saw her he
uttered horrible cries and threw himself upon the ground
with signs of the greatest fright, while he had been caressing
every one else. On his being asked why, he replied that she
made up a face at him. The Maréchale never suspected that
he had reasons for finding her different from other people,
and she has given him no thanks for his frankness. It makes
one shudder to see how little we know ourselves. Is it a
good?—is it an evil? I can't decide. But I believe that illusion
is useful in all things, and for myself all that I fear in this
world is the truth. The truth is almost always sad and she
leaves almost no consolation behind her. Happily every individual has a common interest in being cheated, and the hu-

man race in this respect doesn't spare itself. What is most to be desired is to be *well* cheated, till one's last day." In one place, however, she relates how her mind has taken a flight into the very empyrean of philosophy. "At the degree of elevation at which my spirit travelled, objects grew so small to my imagination that you also seemed no more to me than a worm, and I was indignant that so little an animal could do me so much harm and make me see things so crookedly."

One feature of this correspondence—and I suppose we may dignify it with the name of historical, for it is probable that in love-letters exchanged in aristocratic circles at the present day such allusions are rare—is the manner in which both Madame de Sabran and M. de Boufflers expatiate on the state of their health and upon their drugs and doses. "Meanwhile," the former writes, "I will take no more pills, since they make *you* so sick at your stomach"; and she adduces this concession as a proof of her lover's empire over her mind. Could there be a more touching illustration of intimate union than this phenomenon of a lover being acted upon by his mistress's medicine? Madame de Sabran's health was delicate and she paid frequent visits to various healing springs. "These two days," she writes from Spa, "I have been in my bed with fever. I shall get off with a bad cold, which I owe to the Princess of Orange, who did me the honour—I don't know by what fantasy—to choose me out of a thousand to accompany her in a ride on horseback, which she performed throughout at a great gallop, beneath a fearful sun, and with an abominable wind. I came back tired half to death, coughing, with my ribs and thighs broken, cursing all the princesses on earth, who never do anything like other people." On leaving Spa on this occasion Madame de Sabran made an excursion into the Low Countries, of which she gives a most humorous and entertaining account. "We are making this journey like plain goodwives, by the public vehicles, under assumed names; whereby it will cost us almost nothing, we shall be much better, and be restored to Spa within a week. But don't go and speak to any one of this project; I wish to tell it to you alone for a thousand thousand reasons. You must know that I am called Mme. de Jobert, and Mme. d'Andlau Mme. Bertin. We came hither from Brussels in a barge which was quite like

Noah's ark, as regards all that it contained. I amused myself all day with sketching the queer people who were with us, and among others two Capuchins, whom I painted so like life that every one admired them; which gave me a great reputation and success in the assembly. I effected immediately the conquest of a young English merchant, who never left us during the voyage, and who, from time to time, treated my companion and me to beer, to refresh us, almost making us tipsy, for in politeness we were afraid to refuse it." "The journey to Holland," she writes later, " was not a success [as regards her health], but it vastly amused us. No one knew who we were; we were taken now for saleswomen on their way to the Haarlem fair, now for ladies from Friesland, now for singing-women. We were treated sometimes very well and sometimes very ill; we often dined at the public table. We travelled sometimes on foot, sometimes in a phaëton, sometimes in a sail-boat. We passed one night on the highway and another at the city-gate. It would be impossible to see and do more things in a week. We went as far as Amsterdam, where the sight of the port amazed us; for neither of us had ever seen a ship. They are superb contrivances, but I should be very sorry to be shut up in one, unless it were with you."

Madame de Sabran's letters are so vaguely dated that we are often in ignorance of her whereabouts; but considering that in theory she led a very quiet life she seems to have spent a good deal of time on the road. She made excursions if not journeys. To meet M. de Boufflers away from home was often the purpose of her wanderings. It would be part of the entertainment afforded by these letters to understand the logic of Madame de Sabran's goings and comings; to know to what extent it was part of her scheme to conceal from the world the extent of her intimacy with her friend. Such intimacies may in those days have been concealable, but they certainly were not generally concealed. Madame de Sabran lived half the year, however, with a great clerical dignitary. She was a bishop's niece, and this doubtless put her somewhat in the position of Cæsar's wife. It is not unfair to M. de Boufflers, however, to imagine that his society was often to be enjoyed only on his own terms, and that there were moments when he would rather go ten miles to meet his friend than thirty.

Was it not in his character to commingle a due appreciation of the bird in the hand with a lively attention to the bird in the bush? Madame de Sabran, who professed in general a high relish for illusions, appears to have judged her friend in some points without them. We cannot say whether she was jealous of the past: if she was, she gave a very amiable turn to her jealousy. Writing in 1787 from Nancy, where M. de Boufflers had formerly been in garrison, "I have not stopped thinking of you all day," she says, "and I am tired to death with it. It must be that the air of this place is impregnated with certain little atoms that come and fasten themselves to me by sympathy. I don't pass through a street without thinking how often you have walked there. I don't see a house without imagining it is inhabited by one of the Dulcineas who formerly vied with each other for the happiness of pleasing you. I was present at the session of the Academy on the day of Saint Louis, where I saw all kinds of these same Dulcineas and was greatly entertained. I tried to read in their faces and their eyes some traces of love for you; for at present, contrary to old times, I want every one to love you. But I saw in them the traces of time much more than of love; they were all frightfully old and ugly." Madame de Sabran is generous, and this little scratch at the end is the least possible tribute to human weakness. She saw another indubitable Dulcinea at the theatre at Valenciennes. "Looking at her with other eyes than mine, she has really very few charms. . . . She amused me a thousand times more than the play. She was extremely occupied with two officers, who kept her in continual motion from right to left, to make neither jealous; she laughed and talked louder than the actors. This time I was jealous, not of her successes, but of her happiness, and I said to myself, 'She knew that poor African; she loved him; she did more, and yet she has been able to forget him and love others. How can she do it?' I should like to have her receipt—*pauvre bête* that I am, consuming myself in vain regrets and, a thousand leagues away from him, seeing only with his eyes, hearing him only, able to think of him only, making the past the present for the love of him, and giving up the present to sadness and despair. My life will not be longer than hers; yet she turns hers to profit and I throw mine out of the window."

The reader, as he goes, marks certain passages as signs of the times; the first thunder-growls of the French Revolution affect one as the strokes of the bell that rings up the curtain at a tragedy. "People talk of nothing but taxes and cutting down pensions: it is the paying the piper—*le quart d'heure de Rabelais*. People live with the edge of their teeth." And elsewhere: "The poor Marshal [de Soubise] died this morning. His sister the *dévote* is in despair—all the more that he died without confession and without consciousness to ask pardon of God for his millions of mortal sins. He was the Solomon of our age, minus the wisdom. His whole seraglio is at present in tears and misery, even to the sultana Validé. The King inherits five hundred thousand livres of income; it comes in the nick of time, for in spite of the notables and their sage counsels, he doesn't know where to thrust his head." Madame de Sabran was in the tree that the tempest had begun to shake; she was on an honourable footing of familiarity at court. Her little son Elzéar was at Versailles with his uncle. "He has already," she writes, "great success at court. The Queen found him on her passage and kissed him on his two little pink cheeks. This morning she said to me, 'Do you know that I kissed a gentleman yesterday?' 'I know it, madame, for he boasts of it.'"

The journal kept by M. de Boufflers during his second sojourn in Senegal is appended to these letters of his friend. M. de Boufflers is known on other evidence, but this charming record of homeward thoughts in exile completes his portrait—completes it very favourably. He is not positively an edifying figure, but he is, in his way, a decidedly interesting one. He was an eminent specimen of the "charming man," as this fortunate mortal flourished in favourable social conditions. Those of the last century in France placed him much more in relief, and enabled him to develop on a more imposing scale, than the pre-occupied, democratic, commercial society of our own day. M. de Boufflers was a gentleman in the large picturesque sense; it is striking at what a cost his gentility was kept up—on what a copious diet it had to be fed. He had an admirable vigour of temperament and he was thoroughly at home in the world. He was the son of a king's mistress and the incumbent of an ecclesiastical living of forty thousand livres, by the bounty of the king himself (the deposed Stanislaus I. of Poland, to whom as a comfort for his old age Louis XV.—his son-in-law—made over the duchy of Lorraine, where the little court of Lunéville was a vastly less splendid, but an easier and cosier, Versailles). Boufflers had signalized his period of probation at the seminary of Saint Sulpice by the production of certain *contes galants*, which, though abbés in those days could go far, transgressed even the ecclesiastical licence. So he turned from priest to knight of Malta, went to the German wars, amused himself on a great scale, squandered his money, and at middle age, to repair his wasted substance, had to solicit a colonial governorship. In Africa, characteristically, his vigour and vivacity did him service; he took his duties in hand and really administered his government. All this time he dabbled in letters and made love *à l'envi*. There are several anecdotes about him in Grimm's "Correspondance," but all that I know of his literature is a short tale in verse, in two alternating rhymes, quoted by Grimm, and chiefly remarkable for its frank indecency. On his return from Africa he went as deputy to the States-General and, after the Revolution, entered the French Academy and completed the circle of his activity by composing a very dull book on Free Will. The Boufflers of these letters is the full-blown Boufflers of middle life, largely versed in men, women and things, and possessed of a great acquired flexibility of sentiment and wit. He strikes one as a shrewd epicurean, with a decided mind to eat his cake and have it. It is nothing new to observe that when men and women spin the web of sentiment together, the finest threads are generally the woman's, and it doubtless cannot be said, in this particular case, that M. de Boufflers abused the lover's usual right to be less exquisite than his mistress. Certain however it is that the reader cannot rid himself of the feeling that not a little of what is exquisite in Madame de Sabran is wasted, given simply to the air, exhaled into the elements. M. de Boufflers balanced his account in the gross, and of a certain proportion of this amiable woman's articulate heartbeats no note was ever made. But probably we make these reflections simply because we are jealous of the extravagant Chevalier. The reader is himself in love with Madame de Sabran and he judges M. de

Boufflers but grudgingly. Speaking impartially, these two hundred pages of his journal are delightful reading. His gaiety, his wit, his ardour, his tenderness, his mingled impatience and resignation, his marital invocations and ejaculations, his delicate natural compliments, make the tone of this fragmentary diary a real model of manly grace.

There is a sketch of M. de Boufflers in one of Madame de Sabran's letters which should already have been quoted: "No, my child, I have no use for illusion on your part; our love has no need of it; it was born without it and it will subsist without it; for it was surely not my charms, which had ceased to exist when you knew me, that fixed you near me; neither is it your *manières de Huron*, your absent, surly air, your stinging, truthful sallies, your great appetite, and your profound sleep when one wishes to talk with you, that have made me love you to distraction; it is a certain nameless something that puts our souls into unison, a certain sympathy that makes me feel and think like you. For beneath this rude envelope you conceal the spirit of an angel and the heart of a woman. You unite all contrasts and there is no being in heaven or on earth more lovable and more loved than you. Come and see me, *à cause de cela*, as soon as you can." It implies no want of sagacity to imagine that the unflattering lines in this picture are only finer and subtler caresses. M. de Boufflers could at times express himself with an implicit tenderness of which an angel, since Madame de Sabran would have it so, need hardly have been ashamed. "A thing that no one suspects, not even you, is that I am forty-eight years old to-day. Here is a vast amount of time lost; for there have been nothing but minutes well spent. I leave you to guess them. But, *ma fille*, this number of forty-eight—doesn't it impress you with respect? I let you off of the respect in advance, for it seems to me that I leave half of my years here, as I leave half of my luggage, not wanting it all on my voyage. Besides, I have grown so used to the idea of being loved by you, in spite of youth, in spite of old age, that I think much less of my age as it goes on. You remember, perhaps, that portrait that I loved so before I dared to speak to the original; that widow's dress which I wished you to retain in my honour. My age makes me think of it, but it doesn't make me think of your change; it is only matter that changes in us, and there is so little in you that it seems to me that I have nothing to fear. Farewell, my daughter. I have struck out two or three lines which would have saddened you. Let us love life and not fear death, for souls don't die, but love for ever." This was written on his ship, as he was approaching the shores of France, and he adds the next day: "I see France drawing near, and I am like the little girl of a fairy story when they told her, There is a kingdom; in the kingdom there is a town; in the town there is a house; in the house there is a room. . . . Here are forty days thrown overboard," he says later, recording adverse winds. "Forty days! that is almost the life of a man, if one counts in life only the moments worth counting." It is to be hoped that he found reason to reckon time less wastefully after his reunion with his friend.

These few extracts from Madame de Sabran's letters can have given but an imperfect idea of those things by which she irresistibly pleases. Her grace, her tempered vivacity, her softened intensity, her admirable mixture of passion and reason, her happy, natural, flexible style, are all forcible appeals to our sympathy. It seemed in place just now to say that some of these charming qualities had been squandered; but I must hasten to unsay it when I reflect that, in this foreign land and in this alien age, we restlessly appreciative moderns are almost reverently inhaling their faint, sweet perfume.

Galaxy, October 1875
Reprinted in *French Poets and Novelists*, 1878

Charles Augustin Sainte-Beuve

Portraits of Celebrated Women. By C. A. Sainte-Beuve. Translated from the French by H. W. Preston. Boston: Roberts Bros., 1868.

THE ESSAYS COLLECTED in the volume introduced to American readers by Miss Preston in this very agreeable translation (to which the translator has prefixed a well-written and discriminating preface) belong to the early period of the distinguished writer's career, and may be said, moreover, to treat of persons not especially dear to the American public. And yet on this occasion we have no hesitation in speaking of the book and its author; for M. Sainte-Beuve still lives and writes, and so long as he has not gone to join those illustrious departed spirits to whom in this modern world he has given a voice and a shape, he may be deemed in literature one of the subjects of the day. Miss Preston's translation, we say, is agreeable; but is it always exactly faithful? In the article on Mme. de Sévigné, the author, commenting in a note on a description of his heroine by a contemporary, writes: *"Que c'est bien elle!"* etc., which Miss Preston renders, "This is worth while." This is the first error on which our eyes fell; we have not pursued the search; perhaps it is the only one.

Of the nine women whose lives are here sketched, three alone are known even by name to American ears—Mesdames de Sévigné, Roland, and De Staël. Who is Mme. de Duras, Mme. de Krüdener, Mme. de Rémusat? Each of these ladies, in the early part of our century, wrote two or three novels which thirty years ago—the date of these articles—were in a fair way to be forgotten in France. M. Sainte-Beuve, in his inimitable manner, said a good word for each; but did he arrest the wave of oblivion? On the contrary, his word was doubtless felt to be the last word, and his heroines received their quietus. It is not as that of a novelist that the mystical Krüdener's ghost of a name appears to us. To read and enjoy his various articles must have seemed to ordinary readers an all-sufficient tribute to these departed women of talent. They read M. Sainte-Beuve's extracts, and this was quite enough. Who nowadays sits down to a perusal of "Edouard" or "Valérié?" M. Sainte-Beuve himself, in the current year, would admit that we can make a better use of our time. There is, to our sensibilities, something sad and spectral in the sight of these poor old French ladies, summoned from their quiet graves, deep in the warm and comfortable soil of oblivion, and clad afresh in the chilly drapery of our American speech. With all deference to the translator's opinion, we cannot help thinking that this was not a book to translate. For our own part, we should have wholly deprecated any translation at all; but if such a work had been determined upon, we should have suggested a selection of articles from the immense repository of the "Causeries du Lundi," where the translator would have found at once greater perfection of manner and heroines more generally interesting. The article on Mme. Roland in the present collection is extremely good, but it is wholly inferior to the admirable paper on the new edition of her memoirs contained in the eighth volume of the "Nouveaux Lundis." And so any one of the essays before us, with the exception of the first, the fourth, and the fifth, might have ceded its place to the sketch in the "Derniers Portraits" of Mme. de Staal-Delaunay, the author of one of the most deeply-interesting volumes of memoirs ever written. To induce an intelligent reader to go through the memoirs of Mme. de Staal-Delaunay would be a better service than to lead him (or her, we may say, as Miss Preston chiefly covets female readers) to rest content with a few extracts from three or four feeble and elegant tales of fifty years ago. Let us add the expression of our regret that the translator has judged best to omit the article on Mme. de Charrière, a lady no better known indeed than her sisters, but far more deserving of our modern attention. This person, a Dutchwoman by birth, and for a long time a resident in Switzerland—it is doubted that she ever visited Paris—was perfect mistress of a delightful French style, in which she composed two excellent novels as well as several inferior ones. From these two works M. Sainte-Beuve gives a number of extracts, all remarkable for strength and truthfulness. Mme. de Charrière looks like the first of the realists. But with the realists, as we have learned, one must proceed cautiously, and it is very possible that with all her merits Mme. de Charrière could not logically hope to figure in these chastened English pages.

"The quiet fairness," says Miss Preston in her preface, "with which M. Sainte-Beuve estimates feminine effort and achievement in letters, as contrasted alike with the indulgent praise and considerate blame which they ordinarily receive, is to a woman, at least, absolutely affecting." This is doubtless perfectly true, and yet after all the author's tone is by no means the pure judicial one. On the title-page of the French edition of the work before us is the following bit of dialogue, by way of an epigraph: " 'Have you ever been a woman, sir, that you should pretend in this way to know us?' 'No, madam, I am not Tiresias the soothsayer; I am only a humble mortal who has loved you much.' " He has loved them much—this is the motive and the secret of M. Sainte-Beuve's deep appreciation of the characteristics of women. To our mind it is not his fairness that is affecting, but his devotion; the exquisite humility of his intellect—its servility, one may call it—under the charm of feminine grace and talent. In one sense it is a deeper and more disinterested devotion than that of the great poets and romancers. These writers construct lovely women by the dozen, and lose their hearts to their own creations; but their heroines are emphatically their creatures; they bear the stamp of their own passions and prejudices; they flatter their genius. M. Sainte-Beuve takes women as they come, neither ideally beautiful nor ideally gifted, full of foibles and disenchantments and incompleteness, and places his faculties at their service to act upon society; waits upon them, interprets them, exhibits them, repeats their faint accents in a louder key. It is decidedly as they are—as they have been, even in the past—and not as they may be and as many of them wish to be, that he studies and admires them. The translator, we think, forces a point when she intimates that M. Sainte-Beuve has caught a glimpse of that luminous future which shines from afar in the eyes of the more sober and strenuous of her sex. She even goes so far—*horrescimus referentes*—as to mention in this connection the word suffrage. This term suggests an order of facts and ideas to which we may be sure that the mind of the illustrious critic is a stranger. We may best ex-

CHARLES AUGUSTIN SAINTE-BEUVE 667

press at once the extent and the limitation of his conception of the feminine nature—of *das ewige Weibliche*—by saying that he deals only with women as established in society, and that he uses the word society in its artificial and modern sense of *good company*. If we regard this circumstance in connection with the fact indicated in the epigraph—the fact that he maintains an emphatically sentimental relation to the ladies of his choice—we shall see that it is no easy task to enlist him on the side of reform, progress, emancipation, or any tendency foreshadowed in these formidable words. Society, in the sense necessarily attached to the word by M. Sainte-Beuve, does not exist, and is not likely to exist, in this country. To M. Sainte-Beuve it has, as much as anything can have, probably, an absolute sanctity and meaning. In France, from the time of Madame de Sévigné down to the present day, it has gradually assumed form and substance, and has constituted the only possible medium of life and action for superior women. Each of the ladies described in the present volume was a woman of the world—of the nine no less than seven were members of what is called the great world, of the inner circle of society. This inner circle was composed of many elements, among which it would be unfair not to mention literature. But the further one penetrates into it, it seems to us, the more those complex elements tend to reduce themselves to two simple ones—in the first place the *salon*, and in the second place love, or, as it would be more correct to say, lovers. Miss Preston admits, correctly, that what our author chiefly values in woman is the "capacity for passion." Of course the love indicated in our quotation is not all on one side. M. Sainte-Beuve repays himself for his own effusion of sentiment by detecting and pursuing the emotion in the lives of his heroines. Assuredly, it is not directed towards himself; but this is of small account. Provided it is really the process, the act of love, he is quite content to be but a spectator. The translator has, of necessity, omitted from her volume the last of the original portraits, a sketch of a certain Madame de Pontivy. This lady, who flourished in the first half of the last century, was in no sense of the word a celebrated woman; she was not even a literary woman, and we remain in ignorance of the documents in which her history is revealed. Her sole claim to our interest is her love-story—the fact that for a large number of years, a whole lifetime indeed, in the midst of a faithless and licentious society, she maintained privately, and yet in all its fulness, a passion of the most exquisite quality. There is nothing in the story but that; no wit, nor wisdom, nor action—nothing but happy love, pure and simple. M. Sainte-Beuve relates it with excellent skill, and with the most generous sympathy and unction. But that he should relate such a story in such a manner is conclusive evidence that he is very little of a moralist and, in a really liberal sense of the word, not overmuch of a thinker. We are half sorry that the translator might not have ventured to retain the sketch. To a serious mind it offers perhaps more matter for reflection than any of the other essays.

What we ourselves most enjoy in the writings of M. Sainte-Beuve is their numerous literary merits. The literary merit of the present volume so far exceeds its merits in other particulars that it seems futile to look upon it as anything but a contribution to pure literature. A writer and a psychologist— an empiric, if you will, in each case, but a most successful one—these seem to us the terms which best describe M. Sainte-Beuve. We admit that it is dangerous to assume aught of a trenchant tone in speaking of the constitution of his genius. He contains a little of so many things in a degree that sadly puzzles the critic's mind and leads him to forswear the attempt to classify and label him. He is a little of a poet, a little of a moralist, a little of a historian, a little of a philosopher, a little of a romancer. But successively, with patience and care, you detect each of these characters in its littleness— you detect the wonderful man in flagrant default of imagination, of depth, of sagacity, of constructive skill, and you feel that he is reduced to logical proportions. At the same time you feel that there is another element of his mind which looks small from no point of view, but which remains immeasurable, original, and delightful. This is his passion for literature—in which we include both his insatiable curiosity and his eternal gift of expression—his style.

Nation, June 4, 1868

Premiers Lundis. Par C. A. Sainte-Beuve, de l'Académie Française. Tome I. Paris: Michel Lévy; New York: F. W. Christern, 1874.

THE ACUTEST CRITIC the world has seen spent much of the latter part of his life in revising his published writings, amending them, minutely annotating, and generally re-editing them. Everything that had ever come from his pen retained his interest to the last, and he thought that anything that was worth doing at all was worth doing well. He had a passion for exactitude, and he wished, as it were, to make a certain toilet for his productions, on their appearance before posterity. This is the sentiment of a man who feels that he has done good work; it is only solid objects that will bear free handling, and Sainte-Beuve had a comfortable sense that in his essays and *causeries* there was no want of pegs to hang notes and appendices upon. He prepared, therefore, during his last years, a series of "authorized editions" of all his principal performances—beginning with the later and proceeding back to the earlier ones. The editor of the present volume quotes from him a passage in which he expresses his general theory on these undertakings:

"I save what I can of the damaged baggage; I wish that what I reject might perish wholly and leave no trace. Unfortunately, this cannot absolutely be; what one collects into stout volumes is not saved by that fact, and what remains in scattered sheets is not so completely lost that it does not drag in one's track and weigh down, if need be, one's literary march and, later, one's memory (if a memory there is to be), with a multitude of confused and straggling reminiscences. It is proper, then, to answer only for what one has admitted, and, without disavowing the rest, to send it to the bottom. In a word, if one has a care for the future; if, without having the vanity of believing in anything in the way of glory, one feels at least the lawful desire to be in some rank or other an honorable witness to one's time, one has all precautions to take: one cannot too much act as a ship (*faire navire*), and keep one's course straight, to pass, without foundering, the perilous straits."

Sainte-Beuve republished his early poems and his youthful novel 'Volupté,' but he did not live to collect his first critical articles, his groping experiments in the line in which he subsequently became a master. It is a vast pity that, since they were to be exhumed, he himself should not have presided at the ceremony. He would have supplied them with a number of entertaining notes, and given many valuable glimpses of the history of the formation of his opinions. It is a strange and uncomfortable thing to find one's self reading Sainte-Beuve uncommented by himself; the absence of the familiar footnotes, generally more characteristic and pointed than the text itself, has something melancholy and almost cruel; it reminds one afresh of his departure, and is like seeing a person thrust half-dressed into company. The present volume has been put together by one of his literary executors, and the work has apparently been carefully done, as far as the searching out and identification of his pieces are concerned. Sainte-Beuve had, after much solicitation, announced his intention of doing this work himself; they seem to come under the head of those things which would not go to the bottom, even if one threw them overboard. They were contributed to the *Globe* newspaper during a series of years beginning with 1824, when the author was a half-hearted medical student of twenty. The title of 'Lundis' is of course a device of the publisher, but the subjects are the same in character as those he treated later—literary figures of the day, and of the seventeenth and eighteenth centuries.

It is interesting to observe his first trustful impressions of writers on whom he subsequently expatiated with such ripe sagacity and, in some cases, with such polished irony. This especially strikes us in reading his youthfully glowing tribute to the early poetry of Victor Hugo and Lamartine. As to Victor Hugo indeed, as years advanced, Sainte-Beuve maintained a portentous silence; he let him alone, as he let alone Madame Sand and Balzac (to the latter of whom he never did justice), and when he withheld an opinion one might know there was a good reason for it. But Lamartine, on various occasions, he handled with unsparing acerbity; the poet had relaxed and the critic had hardened. The merit of these papers is evidently greater than was to be expected; they seem to us to contain the distinct promise of the author's future. There are things excellently said throughout, and which would be worth quoting; but the main thing is the general manner, the general firmness, the certainty and maturity of touch. The author writes as if he felt that, without abrupt transitions, he was going to become a master; if we had been his editor we should certainly have kept an eye on him. The article on the Memoirs of Madame de Genlis is, for a young man of twenty-two, extremely remarkable, and if he does not yet speak with the authority with which, many years after, he alluded to the lady's being *de veine verbeuse et mensongère*, there is no lack of a really penetrating perception of her foibles. The talent for incisive irony is apparent from the first. "At Modena, the Prime Minister, M. de Lascaris, threw himself at her feet, with a little air of triumph which she contrived very well to repress. At Rome, she saw the Cardinal de Bernis, whom they called there the King of Rome. . . . He assisted regularly at the baths of Madame de Genlis, and enlivened them by his charming conversation. The Chevalier de Bernis, his nephew, was her guide in her nocturnal promenades among the ruins of the Coliseum, but 'he was at least fifty years old.' At Naples, she ravished the whole court by the sound of her harp—and the queen especially, who kissed her hands; she saw also some lazzaroni, all naked, and some superb figs and pineapples—and there ends the journey in Italy." These lines, from a charming paper on Diderot, of the date of 1830, might have been written at the close of the author's life; they have quite his final tone and rhythm: "That Diderot should grow fat, that his paunch should define itself, that he should have indigestion and take medicine, that Mlle. Voland herself should 'pay a bad fortnight for a little glass of wine and the thigh of a partridge too much,' this shocks us, in turn, for a long time, and spoils for us many effusions still living, many fresh reminiscences of love. For noble, ideal love, as for poetry, there are but two periods of life, youth and old age; in the interval, when profound and passionate love exists, it must hide itself and beware of witnesses; it does not easily interest a third person; it is complicated with a thousand petty miseries of body and mind, with obesity, with ambition; one can hardly believe in it, one can't admire it." These reflections savor of the wisdom that comes of much observation of the world, and, if anything might have qualified our

confidence in the wisdom of the shrewd young critic, it
would have been the suspicion that he was *too* shrewd, too
old, too *posé*; that his taste was too good. Youthful genius is,
traditionally at least, a trifle more erratic.

English readers will glance with especial interest at the articles on Scott's 'Life of Napoleon' and on Fenimore Cooper.
The former is remarkable for its very delicate and sympathetic
discrimination between Scott's charm as a romancer and his
culpable weaknesses as a historian. For a young Frenchman
of 1827 to declare so eloquently that he esteemed the author
of 'The Bride of Lammermoor,' *as such*, none the less for having compiled that melancholy work, 'The Life of Napoleon,'
indicates a striking measure of critical generosity. But young
Frenchmen of that period took romancers on easy terms if we
may judge by the extreme friendliness of the author's remarks
on 'Le Corsaire Rouge'—that fast friend of our school-days,
'The Red Rover.' Cooper's magnificent popularity in France
has always seemed to us a half-amusing, half-touching spectacle, and there could be no better proof that people, in judging a foreigner, should never be sure they have not made a
mistake in *proportion*. The "cultivated American" at the present day has an old-time fondness for Cooper, which makes
the smile in which he indulges on finding that there are people who still read him a very kindly smile; but though we
have a healthy disposition to make the most of our literary
luminaries, we are not commonly addicted to speaking of the
author of the 'Last of the Mohicans' as a first-rate man, and
we are puzzled on finding ardent allusions to him in such
writers as Balzac and Madame Sand. But, of course, if we take
his trappers and his Indians in good faith, Europeans could
hardly do less, and the prairie and the virgin forest, as he
portrayed them, had, when contemplated from the Boulevard, a prodigiously natural air. We are inclined to believe,
however, that Sainte-Beuve made, first and last, almost no
other mistake than this, and these slight papers give us, as we
have hinted, an impression of almost formidable sagacity. We
confess that, touching such a man as Sainte-Beuve, our curiosity is infinite; we feel as if we could never learn enough
about him. His intellectual fecundity was so unbounded that
one imagines that the history of his individual opinions

would throw a preternaturally brilliant light upon the laws of the human mind at large. We are thankful to learn from his present editor that such a history is to receive a valuable contribution in the publication of his letters, as completely as possible. We had a couple of years since a taste of his epistolary faculty in his published notes to the Princess Mathilde. These were not elaborate letters; they were emphatically notes—notes on life, on people, on books—but they had a point, an acuteness, a savor which make one eager for the sequel. They will set the seal of completeness on a truly magnificent literary record. We may add that there is apparently to be another volume of these 'Nouveaux Lundis,' and that there is much so-called "ripe criticism" at the present hour which has less flavor than these verdant first-fruits of a man of extraordinary genius. The grasp may here and there lack firmness, but the hand is already the hand of a master.

Nation, February 18, 1875

English Portraits. By C. A. Sainte-Beuve. Edited and Translated from the *Causeries de Lundi*. With an Introductory Chapter on Sainte-Beuve's Life and Writings. New York: Henry Holt & Co., 1875.

IT MAY BE SAID that if it is of no particular profit to translate Sainte-Beuve into English, it at least does no harm. Those who care to read him will be sure to be able, and to prefer, to read him in his own tongue, and those who do not will let him alone, as before. To this may be answered, we think, that a performance like the present volume sins in being a spurious rather than a real service to culture; that Sainte-Beuve, of all men, was devoted to culture in its purest and most incorruptible forms; and that it is therefore paying him a poor compliment to present him in a fashion based on a compromise with sound taste. Sainte-Beuve's was not in the least an English mind, in spite of his partially English ancestry; he was a Frenchman to his finger-tips; and his intellect, his erudition, his taste, his tone, his style, were of a deeply national stamp. It cannot be said that he spoke without authority on any subject whatever; but his authority in speaking of foreign writers was diminished by half. He spoke of them rarely; he *happened*, so to say, at wide intervals to have touched upon Franklin, Chesterfield, Gibbon, Cowper, and Pope. The articles are charming, but even in the original they are not among his best; and in the present translation (which is yet extremely good) they offer an almost painfully dim and ineffective image of the brilliant qualities familiar to those who greatly admire him. The part of culture—the part of that penetrating and initiated taste of which Sainte-Beuve was so eminent a representative—is to say: "You are not really reading the great critic in this form; you are only half reading him; you are seeing him through a glass, very darkly; you are not doing him justice." The part of the translator of these essays, on the other hand, of the compiler of the volume for which circulation and popularity are sought, is to say, naturally: "You *are* doing him justice; the glass is a glass, but it is very clear; what you lose is, after all, not the essential." And this is why to serve up half-a-dozen of Sainte-Beuve's second-best *Causeries* as an English book is to be at odds with the very spirit of Sainte-Beuve. We may be thought rather cynically fastidious; but we may affirm that if there is a touch of ill-humor in our restrictions we are not without an excuse for it. If the voluminous introductory essay prefixed to the present volume had been a strikingly felicitous performance—had offered us any new information or any especially suggestive reflections—we do not think that we should have been less disposed to hold the translator to an account. But the essay strikes us as having little value. It is both meagre and clumsy—extremely diffuse in manner and yet very chary of real characterization, of that finer, subtler characterization of which one strikes the note in the simple mention of Sainte-Beuve's name. The author alludes to a great many books and writers, and institutes a vast number of laborious, commonplace comparisons and *rapprochements*, but we honestly think that a reader whose sole knowledge of the great critic should be derived from these pages would carry away an extremely vague and formless image. And why should the translator utter a judgment so unaccountable as the following? "Though it is hardly doubtful that Sainte-Beuve's 'Causeries du Lundi' will gratify and inform future generations of Frenchmen, yet the universality and endurance of his renown might have been still better assured had he produced one work, of moderate compass, supplying a complete impression of his power." If the 'Causeries' do not supply a complete impression of his powers, these are even larger than our large estimate of them, and if through "one work of moderate compass" he would have become more easily the intellectual companion, the ever-present, suggestive, inspiring friend of those who love letters, surely the admirably consistent, available, unimportunate form of the 'Causeries' is ingenuity sadly wasted. We are grateful to the author, however, for his quotation from Taine, which, in its admirable definiteness, stands out in high relief in the midst of his own vague portraiture.

If M. Taine has succeeded in portraying Sainte-Beuve, it is not that the task was an easy one. He himself was more complex than any figure he ever drew, and he could only have been adequately painted in colors from his own palette. There are so many things to say about him that one hardly knows where to begin, and whatever we say, we feel that we have omitted something essential. The truly essential thing, we take it, is that he worked, as Taine happily says, "for lettered and delicate men." These are Sainte-Beuve's real public—the public which would find something indelicate in Sainte-Beuve Anglicized. But even this is true only if taken in a certain cautious sense. The great critic had as much of what is called human nature as of erudition, and the proof of his genius was the fashion in which he made them go hand-in-hand. He was a man of books, and yet in perception, in divination, in sympathy, in taste, he was consummately a man of the world. It is a marvel to see the way in which he effects this subtle interfusion of science and experience. He appeals to the cultured man, to the highly civilized and finished social unit, but he appeals to him in behalf of something which demands no sacrifice of points of contact with the world, but an increase and a higher sensibility in each. Most erudition beside Sainte-Beuve's seems sterile and egoistic; none was ever turned to such infinite account, so put to use, so applied, so controlled by life. These are his general characteristics, and the portrait would be only more interesting in going down into detail. Then would appear his patience, his religious exactitude, his marvellous memory, his exquisite fancy—all the accomplishments and virtues and graces of the literary passion. On the other hand, we should touch in a dozen different directions his limitations and his defects, and these perhaps would be most interesting of all. They would be limitations of temper, of morality, of generosity, and they would also now and then be limitations of taste. This it takes some courage to say; but readers who have really suffered in a tender part of their mental organism from certain baser moments, as they may call them, in the great critic, will feel as if they had paid for the right to be positive. We allude here to the vices of temper, to his two volumes on Chateaubriand, to such an episode, for instance, as the long, interpolated diatribe against poor Gustave Planche—against his personal habits, his ugliness, his poverty—in the series of papers (in the *Nouveaux Lundis*) on Horace Vernet; as well as to many a thrust and scratch, quite out of the rules of the game, in the author's innumerable foot-notes. We should fancy that among the people of the day, within range of Sainte-Beuve's reference, there must have been a certain special, well-known physical sensation associated with a glimpse of their names in these terrible notes. There was no knowing what was coming: he never spoke save by book; what documents had he got hold of now? Sainte-Beuve's faults of taste were those of omission, not of commission. Anything he admired was in some degree admirable; but there were also things to which he was constitutionally unable to do justice. He flourished side by side with Balzac, whom he detested, without ever suspecting, apparently, the colossal proportions of the great novelist's genius. It is true that what we all dislike in Balzac Sainte-Beuve disliked with an acuteness, with a power to measure the extent of its aberration, which few of us possess. He liked Pope and Cowper, as the present volume shows, more than the mind of the "period" just now finds easy. It would be most interesting to follow through his writings the vein of old French conservatism of taste—to see it wind and twist and double, making occasionally a startling deflection into dangerous places, taking a plunge into turbid waters, but never altogether, as simple *taste*, losing a certain remote family likeness to Philistinism. Sainte-Beuve, as a whole, is the least of a Philistine conceivable; but to the end of his life, in spite of passing fancies and sudden enthusiasms, in spite of his immense and constant intellectual hospitality and flexibility, what he most relished was temperance, perfect taste, measure. This fact of necessity makes him a partial and inadequate witness to English literature. All these points will be elucidated, harmonized, balanced against each other, when a really conclusive and adequate portrait is produced—a better portrait than that which M. d'Haussonville has lately been contributing to the *Revue des Deux Mondes* with so much pretended, and so little real, liberality. M. d'Haussonville's last word is that Victor Cousin once said to him, as the conclusion of a comparison they had been making together (they might have been better employed!) of Sainte-Beuve and Mérimée: "Mérimée is a *gentilhomme*, and Sainte-Beuve is not: that is why Mérimée is superior to Sainte-Beuve." This is as valueless as the majority of epigrams. Carlyle says of Mirabeau that he had swallowed all formulas; and we may say of Sainte-Beuve that he had swallowed all *gentilshommes*—M. Cousin, certainly, *quâ* gentilhomme, included. Sainte-Beuve's defects, we think, are not to be analyzed in that line, but on an even deeper and subtler one. The best essays in the present volume are those upon Franklin and Gibbon. It is also very well to see what an acute Frenchman can say on behalf of Chesterfield, who has been too long the victim of the pure Johnsonian view. The article on Mary Stuart is, in the present state of learning, rather antiquated. That on Taine's English literature is chiefly a sympathetic disquisition upon Pope. Even if Sainte-Beuve were, at the worst, twice the Philistine he escapes being, it would still be delightful to see a conservative opinion uttered with such happy tact as this:

"But apropos of Boileau, can I then accept this strange judgment of a clever man, this opinion which M. Taine assumes, and does not fear to take on his shoulders as he goes? 'There are two sorts of verses in Boileau: the most numerous, which seem by a good sophomore; the least numerous, which seem by a good senior.' The clever man who so speaks (M. Guillaume Guizot) does not feel Boileau as a poet, and I will go further and say that he does not feel any poet as a poet. I quite understand that you should not make all poetry lie in the *métier*, but I do not at all understand that when you are treating of an art you should take no account of the art itself, and should depreciate to this point the perfect workmen who excel in it. Suppress at a stroke all poetry in verse—that would be more expeditious; otherwise speak with esteem of those who have possessed its secrets. Boileau was of the small number of these; Pope equally."

Nation, April 15, 1875

LETTER FROM PARIS. Recent Books: *Chroniques Parisiennes* and *Cahiers de Sainte-Beuve*

PARIS, April 22.—I have on my table three or four books of which I had meant to speak, but I have as usual left myself little space for literature. The literary remains of Sainte-Beuve are being brought to light with merciless energy—the "Chroniques Parisiennes" and the "Cahiers de Sainte-Beuve" having appeared within two or three weeks of each other. I use the word "merciless" rather with regard to the great critic's victims than to his own reputation. The emptying of table-drawers and memoranda after an eminent writer's death has always a disagreeable and painful side, but if this posthumous rummaging is ever justifiable, it may pass in the case of Sainte-Beuve. His literary house was always in such good order that an irregular visit will discover no untidiness, and moreover he belonged to that only small order of minds for which it may be claimed that their lightest thoughts and utterances have a value. But some of his friends and acquaintances will be more interested than gratified to read the notes and observations he made upon their conversation and talents for his own use. He was sharp enough in his *causeries* with the public, but he was sharper still in *tête-à-tête* with himself. It is interesting to have a glimpse of his literary practices—to see how he lived pen in hand and took notes not only upon what he read but upon what he heard, thought, felt, and dreamed. Never was there so literary a life.

New York Tribune, May 13, 1876

Correspondance de C. A. Sainte-Beuve (1822–69). Paris: Calmann Lévy, 1878.

WHEN, IN PUBLISHING some years since the small collection of letters which Sainte-Beuve had addressed to his gracious and appreciative friend the Princess Mathilde, his last secretary, M. Troubat, announced his intention of getting together and bringing to the light the general correspondence of the great critic, the thing seemed a capital piece of literary good news. After a considerable interval the editor has redeemed his promise, and we have two substantial volumes of Sainte-Beuve's letters. The result may be said, on the whole, to be very interesting—our prospect of high entertainment was not illusory. The letters extend from the year 1822 to the autumn of 1869, the moment of the writer's death, and are naturally most abundant during the closing years of his career—the second volume occupying entirely the period from 1865. The editor mentions that during the passage of the second volume through the press a number of letters of whose existence he had not been aware came into his hands. These he has reserved for a supplementary volume; the reader will have to interpolate them at their proper dates. I do not longer await the appearance of this volume—it was promised several months ago—in order to speak of its predecessors, for these are complete in themselves, and are so rich in interesting matter that I shall be able to do them but scanty justice.

Sainte-Beuve's letters do nothing but complete a picture which was already a very vivid one. He had already painted his own portrait, painted it in a myriad fine, unerring, cumulative touches; no writer was ever more personal, more certain, in the long run, to infuse into his judgments of people and things those elements out of which an image of himself might be constructed. The whole of the man was in the special work—he was *all* a writer, a critic, an appreciator. He was literary in every pulsation of his being, and he expressed himself totally in his literary life. No character and no career were ever more homogeneous. He had no disturbing, perverting tastes; he suffered no retarding, embarrassing accidents. He lost no time, and he never wasted any. He was not even married; his literary consciousness was never complicated with the sense of an unliterary condition. His mind was never diverted or distracted from its natural exercise—that of looking in literature for illustrations of life, and of looking in life for aids to literature. Therefore it is, as I say, that his work offers a singularly complete image of his character, his tastes, his temper, his idiosyncrasies. It was from himself always that he spoke—from his own personal and intimate point of view. He wrote himself down in his published pages, and what was left for his letters was simply to fill in the details, to supply a few missing touches, a few inflections and shades. As a matter of course he was not an elaborate letter-writer. He had always his pen in his hand, but it had little time for long excursions. His career was an intensely laborious one—his time, attention and interest, his imagination and sympathies were unceasingly mortgaged. The volumes before us contain almost no general letters, pages purely sociable and human. The human and sociable touch is frequent, is perpetual; to use his own inveterate expression, he "slips it in" wherever there is an opening. But his occasions are mostly those of rapid notes dictated by some professional or technical pretext. There is very little overflow of his personal situation, of his movements and adventures, of the incidents of his life. Sainte-Beuve's adventures, indeed, were not numerous, and the incidents in his life were all intellectual, moral, professional incidents—the publication of his works, the changes, the phases, the development of his opinions. He never traveled; he had no changes of place, of scenery, of society, to chronicle. He once went to Liège, in Flanders, to deliver a course of lectures, and he spent a year at Lausanne for the same purpose; but, apart from this, his life was spent uninterruptedly in Paris.

Of course, when one makes the remark that a man's work is in a peculiar degree the record of a mind, the history of a series of convictions and feelings, the reflection of a group of idiosyncrasies, one does not of necessity by that fact praise it to the skies. Everything depends on what the mind may have been. It so happened that Sainte-Beuve's was extraordinary, was so rich and fine and flexible, that this personal accent, which sounds everywhere in his writings, acquired a superior value and an exquisite rarity. He had indeed a remarkable combination of qualities, and there is something wondrous in his way of reconciling certain faculties which are usually held to be in the nature of things opposed to each other. He had, to begin with, two passions, which are commonly assumed to exclude each other—the passion for scholarship and the passion for life. He was essentially a creature of books, a *literatus*; and yet to his intensely bookish and acquisitive mind nothing human, nothing social or mundane was alien. The simplest way to express his particular felicity is to say that, putting aside the poets and novelists, the purely imaginative and inventive authors, he is the student who has brought into the study the largest element of reflected life. No scholar was ever so much of an observer, of a moralist, a psychologist; and no such regular and beguiled *abonné* to the general spectacle was ever so much of a scholar. He valued life and literature equally for the light they threw upon each other; to his mind one implied the other; he was unable to conceive of them apart. He made use in literature, in an extraordinary manner, of the qualities that are peculiarly social. Some one said of him that he had the organization of a nervous woman and the powers of acquisition of a Benedictine. Sainte-Beuve had nerves assuredly; there is something feminine in his tact, his penetration, his subtlety and pliability, his rapidity of transition, his magical divinations, his sympathies and antipathies, his marvelous art of insinuation, of expressing himself by fine touches and of adding touch to touch. But all this side of the feminine genius was re-enforced by faculties of quite another order—faculties of the masculine stamp; the completeness, the solid sense, the constant reason, the moderation, the copious knowledge, the passion for exactitude and for general considerations In attempting to appreciate him it is impossible to keep these things apart; they melt into each other like the elements of the atmosphere; there is scarcely a stroke of his pen that does not contain a little of each of them. He had ended by becoming master of a style of which the polished complexity was a complete expression of his nature—a style which always reminds one of some precious stone that has been filed into a hundred facets by the skill of a consummate lapidary. The facets are always all there; the stone revolves and exhibits them in the course of a single paragraph. When I speak of attempting to appreciate him I know it is not an easy matter, and I have no intention of undertaking a task for which his own resources would have been no more than sufficient. He might have drawn himself, intendingly, from head to foot, but no other artist holds in his hand the fine-tipped, flexible brushes with which such a likeness should be pointed and emphasized.

Various attempts, nevertheless, have been made to appraise him, as was eminently natural and inevitable. He spent his life in analyzing and pondering other people, and it was a matter of course that he also should be put into the scales. But, as a general thing, on these occasions they were not held with a very even hand; as too often happens in France, the result was disfigured by party passion. This is especially the case with the judgments of hostility, of which the number, as may well be imagined, is not small. Sainte-Beuve had wounded too many susceptibilities and vanities—had taken upon himself functions too thankless and invidious—to find the critic's couch a bed of roses. And he not only offended individuals, he offended societies and "sets," who, as a general thing, never forgave him, and who took their revenge according to their lights and their means. The very pivot of his intellectual existence was what he would have called the liberty of appreciation; it was upon this he took his stand—it was in the exercise of this privilege that his career unfolded itself. Of course he did not claim a monopoly of the privilege, and he would never have denied that the world was at liberty to appreciate Sainte-Beuve. The greater wisdom, to my mind, was on his side; his great qualities—his intense interest in the truth of any matter, his desire to arrive at the most just and comprehensive perception of it, his delight in the labor involved in such attempts, and his exquisite skill in presenting the results of such labor—these things have never been impugned. Into the innumerable hostilities and jealousies of which he was the object—the resentments more or less just, the reproaches more or less valid, the calumnies more or less impudent—no stranger, fortunately, need pretend to penetrate. These are matters of detail, and here the details are altogether too numerous. Sainte-Beuve's greatest admirers are not obliged to accept him unconditionally. Like every one else he had the defects of his qualities. He had a very large dose of what the French call "malice"—an element which was the counterpart of his subtlety, his feminine fineness of perception. This subtlety served him not only as a magical clew to valuable results, but it led him sometimes into small deviations that were like the lapses, slightly unholy, of the tempted. It led him to analyze motives with a minuteness which was often fatal to their apparent purity; it led him to slip in—to *glisser*, as he always says—the grain of corrosive censure with the little parcel of amenities. For feats of this kind his art was instinctive; he strikes the reader as more than feminine—as positively feline. It is beyond question that he has at times the feline scratch. The truth is, that his instrument itself—his art of expression—was almost a premium upon the abuse of innuendo. The knowledge that he could leave the impression without having said the thing must frequently have been an intellectual temptation. Besides, it may be said that his scratch was really, on the whole, defensive, or, at the worst, retributive; it was, to my belief, never wanton or aggressive. We each have our defensive weapon, and I am unable to see why Sainte-Beuve's was not a legitimate one. He had the feline agility and pliancy; nothing was more natural than that he should have had the feline claw. But he apprehended the personality, the moral physiognomy of the people to whom he turned his attention—Victor Cousin, for instance, Lamartine, Villemain, Balzac, Victor Hugo, Chateaubriand—with an extraordinary clearness and sharpness; he took intellectual possession of it and never relaxed his grasp. The image was always there, with all its features, for familiar reference; it illuminated and colored every allusion he had occasion to make to the original. "What will you have?" he would have said; "I am so intensely impressible, and my impressions are so vivid, so permanent. One can go but by one's impressions; those are mine. Heaven knows how the plate has been polished to take them!" He was very apt to remember people's faults in considering their merits. He says in one of his letters that he is more sensitive to certain great faults than to certain great merits. And then, with his passion for detail, for exactitude and completeness, for facts and examples, he thought nothing unimportant. To be vague was the last thing possible to him, and the deformities or misdemeanors of people he had studied remained in his eyes as definite as the numbers of a "sum" in addition or subtraction.

His great justification, however, it seems to me, is, that the cause he upheld was the most important, for it was simply the cause of liberty, in which we are all so much interested. This, in essence, is what I mean by saying that certain of those habits of mind which made many people dislike him were defensive weapons. It was doubtless not always a question of defending his own character, but it was almost always a question of defending his position as a free observer and appreciator. This is the fine thing about him, and the only thing with which, as strangers, happily detached from that imbroglio of rival interests and ambitions in which his lot was cast, we need greatly concern ourselves. In a society that swarmed with camps and coteries, with partisans and advocates, he was more than any one else the independent individual, pinning his faith to no emblazoned standard and selling his vote to no exclusive group. The literary atmosphere in France has always been full of watchwords and catchwords, the emblems and tokens of irreconcilable factions and of what may be called vested literary interests. His instinct, from the beginning of his career, was to mistrust any way of looking at things which should connect the observer with a party pledged to take the point of view most likely to minister to its prosperity. He cared nothing for the prosperity of parties; he cared only for the ascertainment of the reality and for hitting the nail on the head. He only cared to look freely—to look all round. The part he desired to play was that of the vividly intelligent, brightly enlightened mind, acting in the interest of literature, knowledge, taste, and spending itself on everything human and historic. He was frankly and explicitly a critic; he attributed the highest importance to the critical function, and he understood it in so large a way that it gives us a lift to agree with him. The critic, in his conception, was not the narrow lawgiver or the rigid censor that he is often assumed to be; he was the student, the inquirer, the interpreter, the taker of notes, the active, restless commentator, whose constant aim was to arrive at justness of characterization. Sainte-Beuve's own faculty of characterization was of the rarest and most remarkable; he held it himself in the highest esteem; his impression was the thing in the world he most valued. There is something admirable in his gravity, consistency and dignity on this point. I know nothing more finely characteristic of him than a phrase which occurs in one of the volumes before me in the course of his correspondence with Madame Christine de Fontanes on the subject of the biographical notice he had undertaken to supply for a new edition of her father's works. The whole correspondence is most interesting and shows him at his best—full of urbanity and tact, but full also of firmness and reason, knowing exactly what he wishes and means and adhering to it absolutely. M. de Fontanes, whose reputation has sensibly faded now, was a critic and poet of eminence under the First Empire and the Restoration; his daughter was editing a "definitive" collection of his writings, and Sainte-Beuve had sent her his own article to read before insertion. The tone of the article was respectful and sympathetic (it is included at present among his "Portraits Littéraires"), but to certain points in his judgment of her father the Comtesse de Fontanes had taken exception. He offered to withdraw the article altogether, but he refused to alter a word. "Upon anything else in the world I would yield," he says; *"pas sur les choses de la plume quand une fois je crois avoir* DIT*"* (not on things of the pen when once I think I have hit it) ". . . That's my weakness," he adds; "can you forgive me?" For my own part, I can forgive him easily; I should have found it hard to forgive him if he had acted otherwise. All Sainte-Beuve is in those few words—all his famous "method," which has been so much talked about, and, one may almost say, all his philosophy. His method was to "hit it"—to "say it," as he says—to express it, to put his fingers on the point; his philosophy was to accept and make the best of truths so discriminated. He goes on to give Madame Christine de Fontanes several examples of what he means. "I wrote a biographical notice of M. Ampère the elder, from private documents supplied by the son, my friend. I did n't read him the notice. He only saw it printed, and he was content, save with a word that I had slipped in upon something that I believed to be a weakness of character in M. Ampère with regard to great people. He said to me, 'I was pleased with it all, except that word, which I would have begged you to leave out if I had seen it beforehand.' It was just for that that I had not submitted my article to him. *If I had not been free to write that word I would not have written the notice. . . .* When I wrote upon Madame de Staël," he goes on, "Madame de Broglie [her daughter] sent for me, and, with all that authority of grace and virtue which was hers, prescribed to me certain limits; she desired me to communicate my article in advance; I was unwilling to do so. When she came to read it she was pleased, except with regard to a page which nothing in the world would have induced me to withdraw, for it consisted of my reserves and my insinuations (with regard to the 'romantic' life at Coppet)." Nothing could be more characteristic and delightful than this frank allusion to his insinuations. To "insinuate" was a part of his manner, and was to his sense a perfectly legitimate way of dealing with a subject. Granting certain other of the conditions, he was assuredly right. And indeed there is nothing intrinsically unlawful in an insinuation; everything depends on the rest of the tone, and also on the thing insinuated. "From all this," he pursues, after various other remarks upon the points at issue with Madame de Fontanes, "I conclude that it is impossible that the notice should go into the edition. On your side is your duty; on mine is a feeling which I don't know how to name, *mais qui est ma nature même.*" It was in fact Sainte-Beuve's "very nature" to trust his perception and to abide by what he considered his last analysis of a matter. He knew with what quality of intelligence he had aimed at point—he knew the light, the taste, the zeal, the experience he had brought to bear upon it. A certain side of his feeling about criticism is strikingly expressed in one of the later letters (in date) of this collection. The page is so excellent, so full of a sense of the realities of life as distinguished from the shadows, that I quote the greater part of it. It contains an allusion, by the way, which helps to understand the little discussion of which I have just partly given an account. He is writing to M. Ernest Bersot:

"Is it not necessary," he asks, "to break with that false conventionality, that system of cant, which declares that we shall judge a writer not only by his intentions, but by his pretensions? It is time that this should come to an end. I will take the critics as instances. What! am I to see nothing of M. de Fontanes but the great master, polished, noble, elegant, trimmed with fur, religious—not the quick, impetuous, abrupt, sensual man that he was? What! La Harpe shall be but a man of taste, eloquent in his academic chair, and I shall not see him of whom Voltaire used to say, '*Le petit se fâche!*' And for the present, come now—I talk to you without circumlocution—I have no animosity at heart, and I appreciate those who have been, in whatever degree, my masters; but here are five-and-thirty years, and more, that I live before Villemain, the great talent, the fine mind, so draped and decorated with generous, liberal, philanthropic, Christian, civilizing sentiments, etc., and in fact the most sordid soul—*le plus méchant singe qui existe.* What must one do, in definitive—how must one conclude with respect to him? Must one go on praising his noble, lofty sentiments, as is done invariably all round him? And, as this is the reverse of the truth, must one be a dupe and continue to dupe others? Are men of letters, historians and moralistic preachers nothing more than comedians, whom one has no right to take outside of the *rôle* that they have arranged for themselves? Must one see them only on the stage and look at them only while they are there? Or else is it permitted, when the subject is known, to come boldly, though at the same time discreetly, and slip in the scalpel and show the weak point of the breastplate—show the *seam*, as it were, between the talent and the soul; to praise the one, but to mark also the defect of the other, perceptible even in the talent itself and in the effect that it produces in the long run? Will literature lose by this? It is possible; but moral science will gain. That 's where we are going, fatally. *There is no longer such a thing as an isolated question of taste.* When I know the man, then only can I explain to myself the talker, and especially that species of talker who is the most artful of all—the one who prides himself on having nothing of the mere talker left. And the great men (you will say), and the respect one owes them, and the reputation that must be so dearly paid for? Very true; every man who competes for praise and celebrity is devoted to every infamy by that very fact. It is the law. Molière is insulted by Bossuet, Goethe by the first rowdy that comes along; only yesterday Renan and

Littré by Dupanloup—and insulted in his character, in his morality. What is to be done about it? It is n't by cuddling one's self that one can escape from it. One must *be* something or some one; and in that case one resists—one has one's army—one counts in spite of one's detractors. As soon as you penetrate a little under the veil of society, as in nature, you see nothing but wars, struggles, destructions and recompositions. This Lucretian view of criticism is n't a cheerful one; but, once we attain to it, it seems preferable, even with its high sadness, to the worship of idols."

If it be needful to admit that the harsher side of Sainte-Beuve's temperament comes out in such a passage as I have just quoted, it may be added that these volumes are by no means without testimony to the extreme acuteness with which he could feel irritation and the inimitable neatness and lucidity with which he could express it. The letter to M. Villemain, of the date of September, 1839, and that to Victor Cousin, of July, 1843, are highly remarkable in this respect, and remarkable, too, for the manner in which they appeal to the sympathy of a reader who is totally unacquainted with the merits of the quarrel. The delicate acerbity of the tone, the absence of passion, of violence, of confusion, produce an impression of beauty, and our intellectual relish of the perfection with which he says what he desires suffices by itself to place us on his side. There are various examples of his skill in that process known to the French as telling a person *son fait*. "I only ask of you one thing," he writes to Madame Louise Colet, who had pestered him to publish a critical appreciation of her literary productions, "to admire you in silence, without being obliged to point out to the public just where I cease to admire you." In the letters to the Princess Mathilde there occurs a very entertaining episode, related by Sainte-Beuve to his sympathetic correspondent. A lady had sent him her manuscript commonplace-book to read, with the request that he would give an opinion upon the literary value of its contents. Turning it over, Sainte-Beuve encountered a passage relating to himself and not present to the lady's mind when she sent him the volume—a passage of a highly calumnious character, attributing to him the most unattractive qualities and accusing him of gross immorality. He copies out for the Princess the letter with which he has returned the manuscript of his imprudent friend and in which, after administering a rebuke of the most ingeniously urbane character, he concludes by begging her "to receive the assurance of an esteem which he shall never again have occasion to express." The whole letter should be read. Even in perfectly friendly letters his irrepressible "malice" crops out—it has here and there even a slightly diabolical turn. A most interesting letter to Charles Baudelaire, of the year 1858, is full of this quality, especially in the closing lines: ". . . It is n't a question of compliments. I am much more disposed to scold [Baudelaire had just sent him "Les Fleurs du Mal"], and if I were walking with you on the edge of the sea, along a cliff, without pretending to play the Mentor, I would try and trip you up, my dear friend, and throw you suddenly into the water, so that, as you know how to swim, you should henceforth take your course out there in the sunshine and the tide." The most interesting parts of the contents of these volumes, however, I have found to be the graver and more closely personal ones. In the history of such a mind every autobiographical touch has a high interest. There are a number of autobiographical touches bearing on his material life and illustrating his extreme frugality and the modesty—the more than modesty—of his literary income. "From 1830 to 1840," he says, "I lived in a student's room (in the Cour du Commerce) on a fourth floor, and at the rate of *twenty-three francs* a month, my breakfasts included." In 1840 he was appointed titular librarian at the Bibliothèque Mazarine, and then "I found myself rich, or at my ease, for the first time in my life. I began to study again, I learned Greek; my work contains indications of this increase of leisure and of my being able to do it as I chose. Then came the Academy, towards 1843; I became a member of the committee of the Dictionary, and really I had hard work to spend my income. To do so, I had to buy rare books, for which the taste came to me little by little . . . I have *never* had a debt in my life . . . they attack me there on my strong side. I have my weaknesses, I have told you so: they are those which gave to King Solomon the disgust of everything and the satiety of life. I may have regretted feeling sometimes that they quenched my ardor—but they never perverted my heart."

Of autobiographical touches of the other sort—those that bear upon his character and his opinions—there are a considerable number—a number which, however, would be a good deal larger if the letters written before the year 1860 had been more carefully preserved by his correspondents. I have marked a great many of these passages, but I must content myself with a few extracts. There was an element of philosophic stoicism in Sainte-Beuve, which is indicated in his earliest letters; the note is struck at intervals throughout the correspondence. "Take care of yourself," he says to one of his friends, in a letter written at the age of twenty-four; "pass the least time possible in regrets; resign yourself to having had no youth, no past, no future; I don't tell you not to suffer from it, not to die of it even, at the end; but I tell you not to lose your temper over it, nor to let it make you stand still and stamp." This is quite the same man who found himself impelled to write in 1864: "The more I go on the more indifferent I become; only, judgments take form within me, and, once established, after being shaken and tested two or three times, they never leave me. I believe, moreover, that I have no animosity. Observe that I have no time for that; animosities themselves need to be cultivated. Obliged as I am to change so often the direction of my mind and my interest, to fasten and make them sink into writings and authors so different, trying to find in each of these the greatest possible amount of truth, I grow case-hardened to pricks and irritations, and after a little while I don't even know what they are meant for. But, I repeat to you—and it is the misfortune and also a little the honor of the critical spirit—my judgments abide with me." That is the Sainte-Beuve of my predilection—I may almost say of my faith—the Sainte-Beuve whose voice was incapable of the note of vulgarity, whose vision was always touched with light. I see no element of narrowness or obstinacy in the declaration I have just quoted; I only see the perceptive mind, the ripe intelligence. There is an expression of this ripe intelligence, this faculty of perception resting upon a sense of experience, in a letter of 1863 to a female friend. "We are getting ready for a great battle, in which philosophic minds will be known by true marks. I am one of them, after all. I went in for a little Christian mythology in my day, but that has evaporated. It was like the swan of Leda, a means of getting at the fair and wooing them in a more tender fashion. Youth has time and makes use of everything. Now I am old and I have chased away all the clouds. I mortify myself less, and I see *plus juste*. It is a pity that all this can not last, and that the moment when one is most master of one's self and one's thoughts should be that at which they are nearest faltering and finishing." I don't know at what period Sainte-Beuve disentangled himself from the "Christian mythology," but already in 1845 he makes a striking allusion to what he deems to be the collapse of his power to feel at the seat of feeling. "Your letter touched me, honored me; but I always find myself without words before your praise, feeling so little worthy of it, passed as I have into the state of a pure critical intelligence, and assisting as I do with a melancholy eye at the death of my heart. I judge myself, and I rest calm, cold, indifferent. I am dead, and I see myself dead—but without emotion or confusion. Whence comes this strange state? Alas! there are causes old and deep. Here I am talking to you suddenly as to a confessor; but I know you are so friendly, so *charitable*—and it is this, this last point, which is everything, and which the world calls the heart, that is dead in me. The intellect shines over the graveyard like a dead moon." This is strongly stated; apparently Sainte-Beuve is speaking of a certain special function of the heart which, after forty, is supposed to have seen its best days. Of a certain intellectual cordiality, the power of tender, of sympathetic understanding, he gave full proof during the remainder of his long career. If his heart was dead its ghost at least very restlessly walked. Moreover, the heart can hardly be said to die. In some cases it has never existed, and in these it is not likely to spring into being. But when it has once existed the imagination, in spite of what surgeons call the removal, does some of the work. The house may be closed, but the garden still goes on.

It was to be expected that the letters of a great critic should contain a great deal of good criticism, and in this respect these volumes will not be found disappointing. They contain a great variety of fragmentary judgments and of characteristic revelations and sidelights. With his great breadth of view, his general intelligence and his love of seeing "juste," Sainte-

Beuve was nevertheless a man of strong predispositions, of vigorous natural preferences. He never repudiated the charge of having strong "bents" of taste. This indeed would have been most absurd; for one's taste is an effect, more than a cause, of one's preferences; it is indeed the result of a series of particular tastes. With Sainte-Beuve, as with every one else, it grew more and more flexible with time; it adapted itself and opened new windows and doors. He achieved in his last years feats that may fairly be called extraordinary in the way of doing justice to writers and works of an intensely "modern" stamp—to Baudelaire and Flaubert, to Feydeau and the brothers Goncourt. There is even in the second of these volumes a letter, on the whole appreciative, to the young writer whose vigorous brain, in later years, was to give birth to the monstrous "Assommoir." But originally Sainte-Beuve's was not a mind that appeared likely, even at a late stage of its evolution, to offer hospitality to M. Émile Zola. He was always a man of his time; he played his part in the romantic movement; Joseph Delorme and the novel of "Volupté" are creations eminently characteristic of that fermentation of opinion, that newer, younger genius which produced the great modern works of French literature. Sainte-Beuve, in other words, was essentially of the generation of Lamartine and Victor Hugo, of Balzac and George Sand. But he was, if not more weighted, more anchored than some of his companions; he was incapable of moving in a mass; he never was a violent radical. He had a high tenderness for tradition, for the old models, for classic ideas. In 1845 he was open to the charge of "reactionary" taste; it must be remembered that the critics and commentators cannot, in the nature of things, afford to run the risks and make the bold experiments of the poets and producers. "I have *never* liked the modern drama as Hugo and Dumas have made it, and I have never recognized in it, the least in the world, the ideal that I conceive in this respect. . . . I should be unable to express to you what I feel with regard to the enormities which have partly defeated our hopes, but there are points on which I hold my ground, and I flatter myself that I have never deserted my early convictions. It is all the same to me that Madame de Girardin should come and tell me that I am going in for reaction pure and simple, and I don't give myself the trouble even of heeding it; but, if you say it, I permit myself to answer *no*, and to tell you that you are completely mistaken, which is the result, perhaps, of your not attaching the same importance as I to purely literary points—points on which I have remained very much the same." Sainte-Beuve here defends himself against the charge of having dropped out of the line; he intimates that it is he who has adhered to the pure "romantic" tradition, and that the eccentric movement refers itself to the two writers he mentions. They were not the only ones of whom he failed to approve; it is unfortunately a substantial fact that he never rendered half justice to Balzac, and that to George Sand he rendered but half at the most. There is an interesting passage bearing upon this in a letter of 1866, written to a critic who had published an appreciative notice of Sainte-Beuve's long and delightful article upon Gavarni. "You have indeed put your finger upon the two delicate points. At bottom, I know, Musset had *passion* and Théo [Théophile Gautier] did n't have it; and one warms people up only by having a flame one's self. And then Balzac, I know too, with defects that I feel too much (being of quite another family), had *power*, and Gavarni only had an infinitude of wit, elegance and observation. But Gavarni had taste and *le trait juste*—things I greatly value. That being said, I have my private idea, not as an advocate, but as a critic of conviction, which is, namely, that in our day there is too much water carried to the river, too much admiration *quand même*, too little real judging. Once the word genius is pronounced, everything is accepted and proclaimed. Musset's worst verses are quoted as proverbs; they are admired on trust. So for the great novelist. It would seem that there had been no observer but he; that Eugène Sue, Frédéric Soulié—all those big fellows—have ceased to exist, have been absorbed by him. But it is, above all, when it is a question of the great men of the past, that I am unable to accept the high figure at which they put his genius. This is the bottom of my thought, and it doubtless judges me myself. . . ." And it is here that he goes on to add the remark I have quoted, to the effect that he is more sensitive to certain great defects than to a certain order of qualities. He had, in his latter years, an occasional caprice

or slight perversity of judgment; he took two or three very
incongruous literary fancies. Such was the high relish which,
for a certain period, he professed for the few first productions
of M. Ernest Feydeau, and such the serious attention that he
appears to have bestowed upon the literary activity of Charles
Baudelaire. Both of these writers had their merits, but one
would have said that Sainte-Beuve, who discriminated so
closely, would not have found his account in them. He writes
to M. Feydeau, in 1860, on the occasion of this gentleman
having put the finishing touches to a novel on a peculiarly
repulsive theme, which was a very light literary matter into
the bargain: "It will be very nice of you to tell me when 'Syl-
vie' will be worthy in your eyes to make her début in my
faubourg; I shall be all eyes, all ears, to receive her."

But he paid so many tributes of a different kind that it is
out of place to do more than touch upon that one. Here is
quite another note. "If you knew English," he writes to a
clerical friend who had sent him some poetic attempts, "you
would have a treasure-house upon which you could draw.
They have a poetic literature very superior to ours—and,
above all, more healthy, more full. Wordsworth is not translated; one does n't translate those things; one goes and drinks
them at the fount. Let me enjoin upon you to learn English.
. . . In a year or two you would be master of it, and you
would have a private poetic treasure for your own use. Be a
poet—I was only a little rivulet from those beautiful poetic
lakes, with all their gentleness and melancholy." What I have
found most interesting in these pages is the mark of the expert, as I may call it—the definiteness and clearness, the ripe
sagacity, of the writer's critical sense. When it is a case of
giving advice, of praising or of blaming, of replying to a question or an appeal, there is something delightful in our impression of the perfect competence. He always knows so well the
weak point, always touches in passing upon the remedy. "The
day on which you shall be willing to sacrifice a little to that
French taste which you know so well, to our need of a frame
and a border, you will have the value of all your essential
qualities." He writes that to his distinguished fellow critic M.
Schérer, whose culture he deemed a little too Germanic; and
it would have been impossible to give him in a single sentence

better practical advice. There is an admirable letter to M. Taine, on the appearance of the latter's rather infelicitous attempt at satire—the volume of impressions of M. Graindorge. This letter should be read by every one who has read the book—it is impossible to express more felicitously the feeling of discomfort produced by seeing a superior man make a great mistake. I have spoken of Sainte-Beuve's letter to Émile Zola; it is full of exquisite good sense (the writer's great quality), and the closing lines are worth quoting as an illustration of the definite and practical character of the critical reflections that he offered his correspondents. The allusion is to M. Zola's first novel, "Thérèse Raquin." "You have done a bold act; you have, in your work, braved both the public and the critics. Don't be surprised at certain indignations—the battle has begun; your name has been sounded. Such struggles terminate, when an author of talent is so minded, by another work equally bold, but a little less on the stretch, in which the public and the critics fancy they see a concession to their own sense; and the affair is wound up by one of those treaties of peace which consecrate one more reputation." It must be added that this was not the advice that M. Émile Zola took. He has never, that I know of, signed a treaty of peace; and, though his reputation is great, it can hardly be said to have been "consecrated." But I must make no more quotations; I must do no more than recommend these two volumes to all those readers for whom our author may have been at any time a valued companion. They will find a complete reflection of the man and the writer—the materials for a living image. They will find too a large confirmation of their confidence. Sainte-Beuve's was a mind of a thousand sides, and it is possible sometimes to meet it at a disconcerting or displeasing angle. But as regards the whole value I should never for an instant hesitate. If it is a question of taking the critic or leaving him—of being on his "side" or not—I take him, definitively, and on the added evidence of these letters, as the very genius of observation, discretion and taste.

North American Review, January 1880
Revised and reprinted in *American Literary Criticism*,
ed. William Morton Payne. New York:
Longmans, Green and Co., 1904

George Sand

Mademoiselle Merquem: A Novel. By Madame George Sand. New York: G. W. Carleton & Co., 1868.

MADAME SAND'S LAST NOVEL—the last in a very long list, the reader will remember—is decidedly not one of the best of her works; but as it has enjoyed the rare fortune of being translated in this country, a few critical remarks may not fall amiss. The time was when Madame Sand's novels were translated as fast as they appeared, and circulated, half surreptitiously, as works delightful and intoxicating, but scandalous, dangerous, and seditious. To read George Sand in America was to be a socialist, a transcendentalist, and an abolitionist. You may obtain from the biography of Margaret Fuller an impression of the sort of influence which she exercised in certain circles, and of the estimation in which she was held; of the large credit attached to her philosophical and didactic pretensions, which seem to us somewhat vain; and of the apparent indifference bestowed upon her vast imaginative and descriptive powers. One of Miss Fuller's first acts on reaching Paris, we learn from her life, was to call upon Madame Sand, effecting thereby, as it seems to you in reading the life, a very curious and anomalous conjunction. It may be added, however, that although George Sand figures in Miss Fuller's memoirs, the brilliant American is not mentioned in those of her illustrious sister. For ourselves, the first occasion on which Madame Sand became to us something more than a name was on the perusal of a chapter in Thackeray's "Paris Sketch Book," in which the author, in a moralizing mood, pulls to pieces one of her novels. The work in question was "Spiridion," from which, unfortunately for his intent, he translates a passage of some length. We cherished the passage in our memory—and indeed the writer admits its great beauty—but we retained a very vague impression of the drift of Mr. Thackeray's sermon. The impression was vivid enough, however, when subsequently we came to read "Spiridion" (which we must premise to be a tale of a purely religious cast, without incidents and without love, without the mention, indeed, throughout of a woman's name), forcibly to

suggest the reflection that it was a piece of signal impertinence in the author of the "Sketch Book," holding, as he
obviously did, the lightest and most superficial religious opinions, to measure his flimsy convictions against the serious and
passionate ideas propounded in Madame Sand's work. We can
perfectly well understand that Thackeray should not have
liked "Spiridion"—to ourselves it is not an agreeable book—
but there can be no better instance of that superficial and ma-
terialistic quality of mind which constantly chafes the serious
reader of his novels, than his gross failure to appreciate the
relative dignity of Madame Sand's religious attitude and of
his own artificial posture. But these are things of the past, and
possibly best forgotten. The last of Madame Sand's novels
translated in America was one of her prettiest tales, "Teverino," which, we believe, had but little success. Since "Teverino" the author has produced a vast number of romances,
and exhibited a greater fecundity, we think, considering the
quality of her work, than any writer of our day. With all
her precipitation, not one of her tales (we believe we have
read them all) can be said to have forfeited the claim to literary excellence. This is certainly more than can be said for
the productions of her *confrères*, Messrs. Dumas and Eugene
Sue.

Your foremost impression, we fancy, on reading the work
before us, "Mademoiselle Merquem," is of the extraordinary
facility in composition begotten by the author's incessant
practice. Never has a genius obtained a more complete and
immediate mastery of its faculties. In the pages before us they
seem to move not, as in common minds, at its express behest
and injunction, but in harmony with its very instincts, and
simultaneously with the act of inspiration. This perfect unity
of the writer's intellectual character, the constant equilibrium
of the powers reigning within its precinct, the confidence
with which the imagination appeals to the faculty of utterance, and the radiant splendor which the latter reflects so
gratefully from the imagination—these things, more than any
great excellence of form in particular works, constitute the
author's real claim to admiration and gratitude. These things
it is which bestow an incomparable distinction on this actual
"Mademoiselle Merquem" far more than any felicity of selec-

tion in the way of events and characters. The narrative gushes along copious and translucent as a deep and crystalline stream, rolling pebbles and boulders and reflecting all the convex vault of nature. Madame Sand's style, as a style, strikes us as so far superior to that of other novelists, that while the impression of it is fresh in your memory, you must make up your mind to accept her competitors wholly on the ground of their merits of substance, and remit for the time the obligation of writing properly. The great difference between the author of "Consuelo" and "Mademoiselle Merquem," and the authors (let us say) of "The Newcomes" and of "David Copperfield," is, that whereas the latter writers express in a satisfactory manner certain facts, certain ideas of a peculiar and limited order, Madame Sand expresses with equal facility and equal grace ideas and facts the most various and the most general. The things which we can imagine Thackeray and Dickens attempting to say will be found on reflection, if we are not mistaken, to be but so many variations of a small number of stock ideas and images. Thackeray will say nothing that cannot be said humorously, colloquially, and lightly—in the light sentimental manner, at best. Dickens will say nothing that cannot be said specifically—applied to a particular person or thing. But the movement of Madame Sand's thoughts seems to us as free as the air of heaven. They progress with equal ease to the right hand and to the left, and she considers and contemplates all things with a superior and impartial mind. You do not feel that she looks at the world in any degree as a specialist. She handles men and women, the rich and the poor, the peasant and the noble, the passionate and the joyous, with equal sympathy and power. This characteristic gives to her descriptions of natural scenery and of personal character a breadth and profundity which we miss in corresponding passages in other novelists. We shall perhaps be excused for attempting to illustrate the sense of our words; and we choose for the purpose a short description of mountain scenery in "Teverino," premising that it is one of a dozen in the same work, and that it appears to be flung upon the paper absolutely without effort and without the consciousness of doing a fine thing:

"Our travellers had reached the summit of a long and painful ascent, and on emerging from the bed of rock in which they had been confined they saw an immense valley stretched out beneath them at a giddy depth. From the plateau on which they stood gigantic rocks, crowned with snow, still lifted themselves towards heaven. Nature was bare, grotesque, frightfully romantic; but before them the road, descending with a rapid inclination, plunged in a thousand picturesque contortions toward the gradual slopes of a region fertile, smiling, and richly colored. What could have been more beautiful than such a spectacle at sunset, when through the angular framework of the Alpine scenery you discovered the splendor of the fruitful soil, the blooming sides of the intermediate hills, all glowing with the western fires, the gulfs of greenness unrolled into space, the enkindled streams and lakes scattered like burning-glasses through the mighty picture, and, further still, the belts of blue, mingling but unconfounded, the violet horizon, and the sky sublime with light and transparency."

There are in modern novels descriptions more elaborate than this, more *précieuses*, as the French say, but none, we imagine, more free, comprehensive, and sincere. The mind producing it seems not to have isolated and contracted itself in the regions of perception, but to expand with longing and desire.

Madame Sand's literary career has been, as the reader knows, a very long and eventful one. It is marked by a vast number of moral and intellectual stages or stations, and now, towards its close, it assumes a form in which the sagacity and serenity of age are very finely blended with the freshness and lightness of an immortal imagination. "Mademoiselle Merquem" bears the stamp of an intellect weary of the contemplation of disorder, and of an inventive faculty for which, not to move and act—not to frolic through space like another Ariel—is simply to die. Herein resides both the strength and the weakness of Madame Sand's imagination. It is indefatigable, inexhaustible; but it is restless, nervous, and capricious; it is, in short, the imagination of a woman. The romance before us is conceived and executed with a heartiness, a good faith, a spontaneity, which assuredly justify our use of the word "immortal." Madame Sand will die, but not her imagination. "Teverino," from which we have quoted, bears the date of 1845. Now there is no story which, as a composition, more truly than "Teverino" lives and breathes, unless it be "Mademoiselle Merquem."

The author's faculties seem not merely to have preserved themselves, but to have undergone a positive rejuvenescence. Nevertheless, we confess that we prefer her earlier works. Her later novels are almost too limpid, too fluent, too liquid. The creative spirit is well-nigh too impersonal, too impartial, too ethereal. A couple of years ago Madame Sand published a tale, "Le Dernier Amour," which, in spite of a very disagreeable subject, seemed to us as we read it the last word of narrative art. The progression of the story was as noiseless, as unrelenting, as the luminous growth of the moon. Nevertheless, as we say, we have a vague preference for the earlier tales, in which an occasional crudity or a fitful turgidity of diction appeared to remind us that we were dealing with literary and not with vital phenomena. Madame Sand's masterpieces, however, are scattered throughout her career, and in many cases stand cheek to cheek with some of her most trivial works. "Simon" appeared in the same year with "Mauprat," and "Les Beaux Messieurs de Bois-Doré" about the same time as that marvellous romance of "La Daniella." But taking it as a whole, and judging it in a liberal fashion, what a splendid array does this career exhibit! What a multitude of figures, what an infinite gallery of pictures! What a world of entertainment and edification! From our own point of view there has been none in modern years to compare with it, and to find a greater magician we must turn to the few supreme names in literature. Madame Sand is said to have celebrated but a single passion—the passion of love. This is in a great measure true; but in depicting it she has incidentally portrayed so many others that she may be said to have pretty thoroughly explored the human soul. The writer who has amply illustrated the passion of love has, by implication, thrown a great deal of light on the rest of our nature. In the same way, the writer who has signally failed to achieve an adequate conception of this vast object, must be said to remain an incomplete and partial witness. This is the case with Balzac, in so many respects Madame Sand's superior, and who is never to be considered as slighted by any praise bestowed upon his comrade. Balzac's merits form a very long story, and he is not to be dealt with in a parenthesis. An intelligent reader of both authors will, at times, be harassed with the feeling that it behooves him to choose between them and take up his stand with the one against the other. But, in fact, they are not mutually inimical, and the wise reader, we think, will take refuge in the reflection that choosing is an idle business, inasmuch as we possess them both. Balzac, we may say, if the distinction is not too technical, is a novelist, and George Sand a romancer. There is no reason why they should not subsist in harmony. A large portion of the works of both will eventually be swept into oblivion, but several of the best productions of each will, we imagine, survive for the delight of mankind. Let us softly add the expression of our belief that for Balzac, booked as he is for immortality or thereabouts, this is a very happy circumstance. You may read "Consuelo" and "Mauprat," and not be ashamed to raise your eyes from the book to the awful face of Nature. But when you have been reading "Le Père Goriot" or "Un Ménage de Garçon," you emphatically need to graduate your return to life. Who at such a moment better than George Sand can beguile the remorseful journey, and with "Consuelo" and "Mauprat," or even with "L'Homme de Neige" and "Mademoiselle Merquem," reconcile you to your mortal lot?

Nation, July 16, 1868

LETTER FROM PARIS: THE LATE GEORGE SAND

Paris, June 9.—Since I began my letter the news has come of a great loss to literature—the death of George Sand. She died in that rustic chateau of Nohant, in the old province of Berry, which she had so often and so picturesquely described. She had been painfully and alarmingly ill for a number of days, and the public was prepared for the event. It is the close of a very illustrious and very interesting career, of which I must defer speaking at length to my next writing. Mme. Sand is not, as was at first affirmed, to be buried at Paris, but at Nohant, to which (as I believe) somewhat inaccessible spot a numerous deputation from the literary world has piously repaired. It has been proposed, says the *Figaro*, to Alexandre Dumas to pronounce her funeral oration. I hope he will decline. Madame Sand, admire her with what modification we will, deserves a better fate than to serve as a pretext for this gentleman's self-complacent epigrams. Madame Sand was 72 years of age. She had of late lived almost exclusively in the country, and at the time of her death had not been to Paris for two Winters. I have heard her this Winter much spoken of by persons who knew her well, and always with great esteem. Her life had had many phases, but the longest was that of her old age, which was very tranquil and reasonable; so much so as to efface the memory of certain others which had preceded it, and which had been of a more questionable cast. She had always been a singular mixture of quietude and turbulence. I am told that she was fearfully shy; her books are certainly of all books the least shy. She had little conversation, and yet her books are singularly loquacious and confidential. Her fertility was most extraordinary, and her admirers will be anxious to learn whether it has not bequeathed some documents—memoirs, reminiscences, or narratives more explicitly fictitious—which are yet to see the light.

New York Tribune, July 1, 1876

LETTER FROM PARIS: George Sand. Incidents of Her Career—Her Tireless Industry—M. Renan's Tribute to Her Genius—Characteristics of Her Earlier and Later Works.

PARIS, June 28.—The newspapers, for the last fortnight, have contained a certain number of anecdotes about Madame Sand; but they have been generally of a rather trivial sort, and I have not gathered any that are worth repeating. Private life in France—more fortunate than among ourselves—is still acknowledged to have some rights which the reporter and the interviewer are bound to respect. A Frenchman often makes surprising confidences to the public about himself, but as a rule he is not addicted to telling tales about his neighbor. Madame Sand, in the memoirs which she published 20 years ago, lifted the vail from her personality with a tolerably unshrinking hand (though to the admirers of what is called scandal she gave very little satisfaction); and yet for the last 30 years of her life she was one of the most shade-loving and retiring of celebrities. Her life, indeed, was almost entirely in her books, and it is there that one must look for it. She was essentially a scribbler; she wrote unceasingly from the publication of her first novel to the day of her death, and she had always been fond above all things of a quiet life, even during that portion of her career in which our Anglo-Saxon notions of "quietness" are supposed to have been most effectively violated. She was very intimate at one time with Alfred de Musset, and I have heard that this charming poet, by right of his membership of the *genus irritabile*, sometimes found it more than his nerves could endure to see the author of "Consuelo" sit down to her perpetual manuscript at the most critical hours of their somewhat troubled friendship. But Madame Sand wrote for her bread, and her remarkable power of imaginative abstraction must help to explain the very large amount of work that she achieved. She was also very intimate with Prosper Mérimée, and I have been told that very early one cold Winter morning he perceived her, with a handkerchief on her head, lighting the fire to resume her literary tasks. He also, it appears, had nerves; the spectacle disturbed them—he himself was not thinking of getting about his labors yet awhile—and from that moment the intimacy ceased. Madame Sand had spent a large portion of her life at Nohant, in the Berry, in the plain old country-house, which she described so charmingly in "L'Histoire de ma Vie," and for which and for its (I believe) rather meager setting of natural beauty she appears to have had a singularly intense affection. As she advanced in life, Nohant became more and more her home, and her visits to Paris were brief. Her house was very hospitable, and under her own roof she was never without society. She had worked very hard, and she had made no fortune; she still earned her income—an income which at the bottom, as they say, of an old French province is still considered easy, but which in America, as in England, would not be thought in fair proportion to the writer's industry and eminence. Madame Sand made, I believe, between six and seven thousand dollars a year. She was very silent, and had little assurance of manner. People who knew her well have told me that she looked a great deal on the ground, and seemed preoccupied; that one felt shut off from her by a sort of vail or film. Occasionally this vail was lifted, she found her voice, and talked to very good purpose. This characterization corresponds with a phrase which one of her heroes, in I forget what novel, applies to one of her heroines—the heroine being an idealized portrait of Madame Sand herself. He calls her a *sphinx bon enfant*—"a good-natured sphinx." In spite of her advanced age—she was 72—Madame Sand's vigor had not failed at the time of the sudden illness which ended in her death. Her activity was great, and her faculties unimpaired. I saw a letter, the other day, written a few weeks before she died, in which she declared that her eyesight was better than when she was 50, and that she went up stairs as fast as her dog. She was carried off by an acute attack of a malady which she had at first neglected. Her last audible words on her deathbed were characteristic of one who had loved nature passionately, and described it almost incomparably—"*Laissez verdure.*—" The allusion was apparently to some wild herbage in the corner of the village churchyard in which she expressed a wish to rest. In spite of her complete rupture, early in life, with Catholicism—in spite of "Spiridion," "Mademoiselle La Quintinie," and numberless other expressions of religious independence—Madame Sand was buried from the little church of Nohant, and the curé performed the service. Her family had the good taste to ask permission of the Bishop of Bourges, and the Bishop had the good taste to answer that if she had not positively refused the sacraments he saw no objection. What made it good taste in Madame Sand's family (it was poor logic), was the fact that she was greatly beloved by the country people, that she had been held in great esteem by the prior generation, that these people were numerically her chief mourners, and that it would have perplexed and grieved them not to see her buried in the only fashion of which they recognized the impressiveness. Alexandre Dumas did not pronounce a funeral oration, though he was, with Prince Napoleon, one of the pall-bearers. A short address by Victor Hugo was read—he not being personally present. It had all of his latter-day magniloquence, but it contained no phrase so happy in its eloquence as one that I find in a letter from Ernest Renan, published in the *Temps* a few days after Madame Sand's death. The last lines she had written were a short notice of M. Renan's new book, the "Dialogues Philosophiques." "I am touched to the bottom of my heart," he says, "to have been the last to produce a vibration of that sonorous soul which was, as it were, the Æolian harp of our time." Persons who have read Madame Sand with a certain amount of sympathy will find it just, as well as fanciful, to call her soul "sonorous." It is an excellent description of her intellectual temperament. A few other fine lines in M. Renan's letter are worth quoting: "Madame Sand went through all visions, smiled at them all, believed in them all; her practical judgment may occasionally have gone astray, but as an artist she never deceived herself. Her works are truly the echo of our age. When this poor nineteenth century which we abuse so much is gone, it will be heard and eagerly looked into, and much one day will be forgiven it. George Sand then will rise up as our interpreter. The age has not had a wound with which her heart has not bled, not an ailment of which she has not harmoniously complained." I suspect that M. Renan has not perused any very great number of Madame Sand's fictions, but this is none the less very finely said.

I have been refreshing my memory of some of George Sand's earlier novels, which I confess I do not find as easy reading as I once did. But—taking the later ones as well— they are a very extraordinary and splendid series, and certainly one of the great literary achievements of our time. Some people, I know, cannot read Madame Sand; she has no illusion for them and but a moderate amount of charms; but I think such people are to be pitied—they lose a great pleasure. She was an *improvisatrice*, raised to a very high power; she told stories as a nightingale sings. No novelist answers so well to the childish formula of "making up as you go along." Other novels seem meditated, pondered, calculated, thought out and elaborated with a certain amount of trouble; but the narrative with Madame Sand always appears to be an invention of the moment, flowing from a mind which a constant process of quiet contemplation, absorption and reverie keeps abundantly supplied with material. It is a sort of general emanation, an intellectual evaporation. There had been plenty of improvisation before the author of "Consuelo," but it had never been—and it has never been in other hands—of so fine a quality. She had a natural gift of style which is certainly one of the most remarkable of our day; her diction from the first was ripe and flexible, and seemed to have nothing to learn from practice. The literary form of her writing has always been exquisite, and this alone would have sufficed to distinguish it from the work of the great body of clever scribblers who spin their two or three plots a year. Some of her novels are very inferior to others; some of them show traces of weariness, of wandering attention, of a careless choice of subject; but the manner, at the worst, never sinks below a certain high level—the tradition of good writing is never lost. In this bright, voluminous envelope, it must be confessed that Madame Sand has sometimes wrapped up a rather flimsy kernel; some of her stories will not bear much thinking over. But her great quality from the first was the multiplicity of her interests and the activity of her sympathies. She passed through a succession of phases, faiths and doctrines—political, religious, moral, social, personal—and to each she gave a voice which the conviction of the moment made eloquent. She gave herself up to each as if it were to be final, and in every case she turned her steps behind her. Sainte-Beuve, who as an artist relished her but slenderly, says somewhere, in allusion to her, that "no one had ever played more fairly and openly at the great game of life." It has been said wittily, in reference to Buffon's well-known axiom that "the style is the man," (which by the way is a misquotation,) that of no one was this dictum ever so true as of Madame Sand; but I incline to believe, with the critic in whose pages I find this *mot*, that at bottom the man was always Madame Sand herself. She accepted as much of every influence as suited her, and when she had written a novel or two about it she ceased to care about it. This proves her, doubtless, to have been a decidedly superficial moralist; but it proves her to have been a born ro-

mancer. It is by the purely romantic side of her productions
that she will live. It is a misfortune that she pretended to
moralize to the extent that she did, for about moral matters
her head was not at all clear. It had now and then capital
glimpses and inspirations, but her didacticism has always
seemed to me what an architectural drawing would be, executed by a person who should turn up his nose at geometry.
Madame Sand's straight lines are straight by a happy
chance—and for people of genius there are so many happy
chances. She was without a sense of certain differences—the
difference between the pure and the impure—the things that
are possible for people of a certain delicacy, and the things
that are not. When she struck the right notes, and so long as
she continued to strike them, the result was charming, but a
sudden discord was always possible. Sometimes the right note
was admirably prolonged—as for instance in her masterpiece,
"Consuelo," in which during three long volumes, if I remember rightly, the charming heroine adheres strictly to the
straight line. After all, Madame Sand's "tendency" novels, as
the Germans call such works, constitute but the minor part of
her literary bequest; as she advanced in life she wrote her stories more and more for the story's sake, and attempted to
prove nothing more alarming than that human nature is on
the whole tolerably noble and generous. After this pattern she
produced a long list of master-pieces. Her imagination
seemed gifted with perpetual youth: the freshness of her invention was marvelous. Her novels have a great many faults;
they lack three or four qualities which the realistic novel of
the last thirty or forty years, with its great successes, has
taught us to consider indispensable. They are not exact nor
probable; they contain few living figures; they produce a limited amount of illusion. Madame Sand created no figures that
have passed into common life and speech; her people are usually only very picturesque, very voluble, and very "high-
toned" shadows. But the shadows move to such a persuasive
music that we watch them with interest. The art of narration
is extraordinary. This was Madame Sand's great art. The recital moves along with an evenness, a lucidity, a tone of
seeing, feeling, knowing everything, a reference to universal
things, a sentimental authority, which makes the reader care

for the characters in spite of his incredulity and feel anxious about the story in spite of his impatience. He feels that the author holds in her hands a stringed instrument composed of the chords of the human soul.

New York Tribune, July 22, 1876

GEORGE SAND

AMONG THE EULOGIES and dissertations called forth by the death of the great writer who shared with Victor Hugo the honour of literary pre-eminence in France, quite the most valuable was the short notice published in the "Journal des Débats," by M. Taine. In this notice the apostle of the "milieu" and the "moment" very justly remarked that George Sand is an exceptionally good case for the study of the pedigree of a genius—for ascertaining the part of prior generations in forming one of those minds which shed back upon them the light of glory. What renders Madame Sand so available an example of the operation of heredity is the fact that the process went on very publicly, as one may say; that her ancestors were people of qualities at once very strongly marked and very abundantly recorded. The record has been kept in a measure by George Sand herself. When she was fifty years old she wrote her memoirs, and in this prolix and imperfect but extremely entertaining work a large space is devoted to the heroine's parents and grandparents.

It was a very picturesque pedigree—quite an ideal pedigree for a romancer. Madame Sand's great-grandfather was the Maréchal Maurice de Saxe, one of the very few generals in the service of Louis XV. who tasted frequently of victory. Maurice de Saxe was a royal bastard, the son of Augustus II., surnamed the Strong, Elector of Saxony and King of Poland, and of a brilliant mistress, Aurore de Königsmark. The victories of the Maréchal de Saxe were not confined to the battlefield; one of his conquests was an agreeable actress much before the Parisian public. This lady became the mother of Madame Sand's grandmother, who was honourably brought up and married at a very early age to the Comte de

Horn. The Comte de Horn shortly died, and his widow, after an interval, accepted the hand of M. Dupin de Francueil, a celebrity and a very old man. M. Dupin was one of the brilliant figures in Paris society during the period immediately preceding the Revolution. He had a large fortune, and he too was a conqueror. A sufficiently elaborate portrait of him may be found in that interesting, if disagreeable, book, the "Mémoires" of Madame d'Epinay. This clever lady had been one of his spoils of victory. Old enough to be his wife's grandfather, he survived his marriage but a few years, and died with all his illusions intact, on the eve of the Revolution, leaving to Madame Dupin an only son. His wife outweathered the tempest, which, however, swept away her fortune; though she was able to buy a small property in the country—the rustic Château de Nohant, which George Sand has so often introduced into her writings. Here she settled herself with her son, a boy of charming promise, who was in due time drawn into the ranks of Napoleon's conquering legions. Young Dupin became an ardent Bonapartist and an accomplished soldier. He won rapid promotion. In one of the so-called "glorious" Italian campaigns he met a young girl who had followed the army from Paris, from a personal interest in one of its officers; and falling very honestly in love with her he presently married her, to the extreme chagrin of his mother. This young girl, the daughter of a bird-catcher, and, as George Sand calls her, an "enfant du vieux pavé de Paris," became the mother of the great writer. She was a child of the people and a passionate democrat, and in the person of her daughter we see the confluence of a plebeian stream with a strain no less (in spite of its irregularity) than royal. On the paternal side Madame Sand was cousin (in we know not what degree) to the present Bourbon claimant of the French crown; on the other she was affiliated to the stock which, out of the "vieux pavé," makes the barricades before which Bourbons go down.

This may very properly be called a "picturesque" descent; it is in a high degree what the French term *accidenté*. Its striking feature is that each conjunction through which it proceeds is a violent or irregular one. Two are illegitimate—those of the King of Poland and his son with their respective mistresses; the other two, though they had the sanction of law, may be called in a manner irregular. It was irregular for the fresh young Comtesse de Horn to be married to a man of seventy; it was irregular in her son, young Dupin, to make a wife of another man's mistress, often as this proceeding has been reversed. If it is a fair description of Madame Sand to say that she was, during that portion of her career which established her reputation, an apostle of the rights of love *quand même*, a glance at her pedigree shows that this was a logical disposition. She was herself more sensibly the result of a series of love-affairs than most of us. In each of these cases the woman had been loved with a force that asserted itself in contradiction to propriety or to usage.

We may observe moreover, in this course of transmission, the opposition of the element of insubordination and disorder (which sufficiently translated itself in outward acts in Madame Sand's younger years) and the "official" element, the respectable, conservative, exclusive strain. Three of our author's ancestresses were light women—women at odds with society, defiant of it, and, theoretically at least, discountenanced by it. The grand-daughter of the Comtesse de Königsmark and of Mademoiselle Verrières, the daughter of Madame Dupin the younger, could hardly have been expected not to take up this hereditary quarrel. It is striking that on the feminine side of the house what is called respectability was a very relative quality. Madame Dupin the elder took it very hard when her only and passionately loved son married a *femme galante*. She did not herself belong to this category, and her opposition is easily conceivable; but the reader of "L'Histoire de ma Vie" cannot help smiling a little when he reflects that this irreconcilable mother-in-law was the offspring of two illegitimate unions, and that her mother and grandmother had each enjoyed a plurality of lovers. At the same time, if there is anything more striking in George Sand, as a literary figure, than a certain traditional Bohemianism, it is that other very different quality which we just now called official, and which is constantly interrupting and complicating her Bohemianism. "George Sand immoral?" I once heard one of her more conditional admirers exclaim. "The fault I find with her is that she is so insufferably virtuous." The military and aristocratic side of her lineage is attested by this "virtuous" property—by her constant tendency to edification and didacticism, her love of philosophizing and preaching, of smoothing and harmonizing things, and by her great literary gift, her noble and imperturbable style, the style which, if she had been a man, would have seated her in that temple of all the proprieties, the French Academy.

It is not the purpose of these few pages to recapitulate the various items of George Sand's biography. Many of these are to be found in "L'Histoire de ma Vie," a work which, although it was thought disappointing at the time of its appearance, is very well worth reading. It was given to the world day by day, as the feuilleton of a newspaper, and, like all the author's compositions, it has the stamp of being written to meet a current engagement. It lacks plan and proportion; the book is extremely ill made. But it has a great charm, and it contains three or four of the best portraits—the only portraits, we were on the point of saying—that the author has painted. The story was begun, but was never really finished; this was the public's disappointment. It contained a great deal about Madame Sand's grandmother and her father—a large part of two volumes are given to a transcript of her father's letters (and very charming letters they are). It abounded in anecdotes of the writer's childhood, her playmates, her pet animals, her school-adventures, the nuns at the Convent des Anglaises by whom she was educated; it related the juvenile unfolding of her mind, her fits of early piety, and her first acquaintance with Montaigne and Rousseau; it contained a superabundance of philosophy, psychology, morality and harmless gossip about people unknown to the public; but it was destitute of just that which the public desired—an explicit account of the more momentous incidents of the author's maturity. When she reaches the point at which her story becomes peculiarly interesting (up to that time it has simply been agreeable and entertaining) she throws up the game and drops the curtain. In other words, she talks no scandal—a consummation devoutly to be rejoiced in.

The reader nevertheless deems himself unfairly used, and takes his revenge in seeing something very typical of the author in the shortcomings of the work. He declares it to be a nondescript performance, which has neither the value of truth nor the illusion of fiction; and he inquires why the writer should preface her task with such solemn remarks upon the edifying properties of autobiography, and adorn it with so pompous an epigraph, if she meant simply to tell what she might tell without trouble. It may be remembered, however, that George Sand has sometimes been compared to Goethe, and that there is this ground for the comparison—that in form "L'Histoire de ma Vie" greatly resembles the "Dichtung und Wahrheit." There is the same charming, complacent expatiation upon youthful memories, the same arbitrary confidences and silences, the same digressions and general judgments, the same fading away of the narrative on the threshold of maturity. We should never look for analogies between George Sand and Goethe; but we should say that the lady's long autobiographic fragment is in fact extremely typical—the most so indeed of all her works. It shows in the highest degree her great strength and her great weakness— her unequalled faculty of improvisation, as it may be called, and her peculiar want of veracity. Every one will recognise what we mean by the first of these items. People may like George Sand or not, but they can hardly deny that she is the great *improvisatrice* of literature—the writer who best answers to Shelley's description of the skylark singing "in profuse strains of unpremeditated art." No writer has produced such great effects with an equal absence of premeditation.

On the other hand, what we have called briefly and crudely her want of veracity requires some explanation. It is doubtless a condition of her serene volubility; but if this latter is a great literary gift, its value is impaired by our sense that it rests to a certain extent upon a weakness. There is something very liberal and universal in George Sand's genius, as well as very masculine; but our final impression of her always is that she is a woman and a Frenchwoman. Women, we are told, do not value the truth for its own sake, but only for some personal use they make of it. My present criticism involves an assent to this somewhat cynical dogma. Add to this that woman, if she happens to be French, has an extraordinary taste for investing objects with a graceful drapery of her own contrivance, and it will be found that George Sand's cast of mind includes both the generic and the specific idiosyncrasy. We have more than once heard her readers say (whether it was professed fact or admitted fiction that they had in hand), "It is all very well, but I can't believe a word of it!" There is something very peculiar in this inability to believe George Sand even in that relative sense in which we apply the term to novelists at large. We believe Balzac, we believe Gustave Flaubert, we believe Dickens and Thackeray and Miss Austen. Dickens is far more incredible than George Sand, and yet he produces much more illusion. In spite of her plausibility, the author of "Consuelo" always appears to be telling a fairy-tale. We say in spite of her plausibility, but we might rather say that her excessive plausibility is the reason of our want of faith. The narrative is too smooth, too fluent; the narrator has a virtuous independence that the Muse of history herself might envy her. The effect it produces is that of a witness who is eager to tell more than is asked him, the worth of whose testimony is impaired by its importunity. The thing is beautifully done, but you feel that rigid truth has come off as it could; the author has not a high standard of exactitude; she never allows facts to make her uncomfortable. "L'Histoire de ma Vie" is full of charming recollections and impressions of Madame Sand's early years, of delightful narrative, of generous and elevated sentiment; but we have constantly the feeling that it is what children call "made up." If the fictitious quality in our writer's reminiscences is very sensible, of course the fictitious quality in her fictions is still more so; and it must be said that in spite of its odd mixture of the didactic and the irresponsible, "L'Histoire de ma Vie" sails nearer to the shore than its professedly romantic companions.

The usual objection to the novels, and a very just one, is that they contain no living figures, no people who stand on their feet, and who, like so many of the creations of the other great novelists, have become part of the public fund of allusion and quotation. As portraits George Sand's figures are vague in outline, deficient in detail. Several of those, however, which occupy the foreground of her memoirs have a remarkable vividness. In the four persons associated chiefly with her childhood and youth she really makes us believe. The first of these is the great figure which appears quite to have filled up the background of her childhood—almost to the exclusion of the child herself—that of her grandmother, Madame Dupin, the daughter of the great soldier. The second is that of her father, who was killed at Nohant by a fall from his horse, while she was still a young girl. The third is that of her mother—a particularly remarkable portrait. The fourth is the grotesque but softly-lighted image of Deschartres, the old pedagogue who served as tutor to Madame Sand and her half-brother; the latter youth being the fruit of an "amourette" between the Commandant Dupin and one of his mother's maids. Madame Dupin philosophically adopted the child; she dated from the philosophers of the preceding century. It is worth noting that George Sand's other playmate—the "Caroline" of the memoirs—was a half-sister on her mother's side, a little girl whose paternity antedated the Commandant Dupin's acquaintance with his wife.

In George Sand's account of her father there is something extremely delightful; full of filial passion as it is, and yet of tender discrimination. She makes him a charming figure—the ideal "gallant" Frenchman of the old type; a passionate soldier and a delightful talker, leaving fragments of his heart on every bush; clever, tender, full of artistic feeling and of Gallic gaiety—having in fair weather and foul always the *mot pour rire*. His daughter's publication of his letters has been called a rather inexpensive mode of writing her own biography; but these letters—charming, natural notes to his mother during his boyish campaigns—were well worth bringing to the light. All George Sand is in the author's portrait of her mother; all her great merit and all her strange defects. We should recommend the perusal of the scattered passages of "L'Histoire de ma Vie" which treat of this lady to a person ignorant of Madame Sand and desiring to make her acquaintance; they are an excellent measure of her power. On one side an extraordinary familiarity with the things of the mind, the play of character, the psychological mystery, and a beautiful clearness and quietness, a beautiful instinct of justice in dealing with them; on the other side a startling absence of delicacy, of reticence, of the sense of certain spiritual sanctities and reservations. That a woman should deal in so free-handed a fashion with a female parent upon whom nature and time have enabled her to look down from an eminence, seems at first a considerable anomaly; and the woman who does it must to no slight extent have shaken herself free from the bonds of custom. We do not mean that George Sand talks scandal and tittle-tattle about her mother; but that Madame Dupin having been a light woman and an essentially irregular character, her daughter holds her up in the sunshine of her own luminous contemplation with all her imperfections on her head. At the same time it is very finely done—very intelligently and appreciatively; it is at the worst a remarkable exhibition of the disinterestedness of a great imagination.

It must be remembered also that the young Aurore Dupin "belonged" much more to her grandmother than to her mother, to whom in her childhood she was only lent, as it were, on certain occasions. There is nothing in all George Sand better than her history of the relations of these two women, united at once and divided (after the death of the son and husband) by a common grief and a common interest; full of mutual jealousies and defiances, and alternately quarrelling and "making up" over their little girl. Jealousy carried the day. One was a patrician and the other a jealous democrat, and no common ground was attainable. Among the reproaches addressed by her critics to the author of "Valentine" and "Valvèdre" is the charge of a very imperfect knowledge of family life and a tendency to strike false notes in the portrayal of it. It is apparent that both before and after her marriage her observation of family life was peculiarly restricted and perverted. Of what it must have been in the former case this figure of her mother may give us an impression; of what it was in the latter we may get an idea from the somewhat idealized *ménage* in "Lucrezia Floriani."

George Sand's literary fame came to her very abruptly. The history of her marriage, which is briefly related in her memoirs, is sufficiently well known. The thing was done, on her behalf, by her relatives (she had a small property) and the husband of their choice, M. Dudevant, was neither appreciative nor sympathetic. His tastes were vulgar and his manners frequently brutal; and after a short period of violent dissension and the birth of two children, the young couple separated. It is safe to say, however, that even with an "appreciative" husband Madame Sand would not have ac-

cepted matrimony once for all. She represents herself as an
essentially dormant, passive and shrinking nature, upon which
celebrity and productiveness were forced by circumstances,
and whose unconsciousness of its own powers was dissipated
only by the violent breaking of a spell. There is evidently
much truth in these assertions; for of all great literary people
few strike us as having had a smaller measure of the more
vulgar avidities and ambitions. But for all that, it is tolerably
plain that even by this profoundly slumbering genius the
most brilliant matrimonial associate would have been utterly
overmatched.

Madame Sand, even before she had written "Indiana," was
too imperious a force, too powerful a machine, to make the
limits of her activity coincide with those of wifely submissiveness. It is very possible that for her to write "Indiana" and
become a woman of letters a spell had to be broken; only, the
real breaking of the spell lay not in the vulgarity of a husband,
but in the deepening sense, quickened by the initiations of
marriage, that outside of the quiet meadows of Nohant there
was a vast affair called *life*, with which she had a capacity for
making acquaintance at first hand. This making acquaintance
with life at first hand is, roughly speaking, the great thing
that, as a woman, Madame Sand achieved; and she was predestined to achieve it. She was more masculine than any man
she might have married; and what powerfully masculine person—even leaving genius apart—is content at five-and-
twenty with submissiveness and renunciation? "It was a mere
accident that George Sand was a woman," a person who had
known her well said to the writer of these pages; and though
the statement needs an ultimate corrective, it represents a
great deal of truth. What was feminine in her was the quality
of her genius; the *quantity* of it—its force, and mass, and
energy—was masculine, and masculine were her temperament and character. All this masculinity needed to set itself
free; which it proceeded to do according to its temporary
light. Her separation from her husband was judicial, and assured her the custody of her children; but as, in return for
this privilege, she made financial concessions, it left her without income (though in possession of the property of Nohant)

and dependent upon her labours for support. She had be-
taken herself to Paris in quest of labour, and it was with this
that her career began.

This determination to address herself to life at first hand—
this personal, moral impulse, which was not at all a literary
impulse—was her great inspiration, the great pivot on which
her history wheeled round into the bright light of experience
and fame. It is, strictly, as we said just now, the most interesting thing about her. Such a disposition was not customary,
was not what is usually called womanly, was not modest nor
delicate, nor, for many other persons, in any way comfortable. But it had one great merit: it was in a high degree original and active; and because it was this it constitutes the great
service which George Sand rendered her sex—a service in
which, we hasten to add, there was as much of fortune as of
virtue. The disposition to cultivate an "acquaintance with life
at first hand" might pass for an elegant way of describing the
attitude of many young women who are never far to seek,
and who render no service to their own sex—whatever they
may render to the other. George Sand's superiority was that
she looked at life from a high point of view, and that she had
an extraordinary talent. She painted fans and glove-boxes to
get money, and got very little. "Indiana," however—a mere
experiment—put her on her feet, and her reputation dawned.
She found that she could write, and she took up her pen
never to lay it down. Her early novels, all of them brilliant,
and each one at that day a literary event, followed each other
with extraordinary rapidity. About this sudden entrance into
literature, into philosophy, into rebellion, and into a great
many other matters, there are various different things to be
said. Very remarkable, indeed, was the immediate development of the literary faculty in this needy young woman who
lived in cheap lodgings and looked for "employment." She
wrote as a bird sings; but unlike most birds, she found it
unnecessary to indulge, by way of prelude, in twitterings and
vocal exercises; she broke out at once with her full volume
of expression. From the beginning she had a great style.
"Indiana," perhaps, is rather in falsetto, as the first attempts
of young, sentimental writers are apt to be; but in "Valen-

tine," which immediately followed, there is proof of the highest literary instinct—an art of composition, a propriety and harmony of diction, such as belong only to the masters.

One might certainly have asked Madame Sand, as Lord Jeffrey asked Macaulay on the appearance of his first contribution to the "Edinburgh Review," where in the world she had picked up that style. She had picked it up apparently at Nohant, among the meadows and the *traînes*—the deeply-sunken byroads among the thick, high hedges. Her language had to the end an odour of the hawthorn and the wild honeysuckle—the mark of the "climat souple et chaud," as she somewhere calls it, from which she had received "l'initiation première." How completely her great literary faculty was a matter of intuition is indicated by the fact that "L'Histoire de ma Vie" contains no allusion to it, no account of how she learned to write, no record of effort or apprenticeship. She appears to have begun at a stage of the journey at which most talents arrive only when their time is up. During the five-and-forty years of her literary career, she had something to say about most things in the universe; but the thing about which she had least to say was the writer's, the inventor's, the romancer's art. She possessed it by the gift of God, but she seems never to have felt the temptation to examine the pulse of the machine.

To the cheap edition of her novels, published in 1852–'3, she prefixed a series of short prefaces, in which she relates the origin of each tale—the state of mind and the circumstances in which it was written. These prefaces are charming; they almost justify the publisher's declaration that they form the "most beautiful examination that a great mind has ever made of itself." But they all commemorate the writer's extraordinary facility and spontaneity. One of them says that on her way home from Spain she was shut up for some days at an inn, where she had her children at play in the same room with her. She found that the sight of their play quickened her imagination, and while they tumbled about the floor near her table, she produced "Gabriel"—a work which, though inspired by the presence of infancy, cannot be said to be addressed to infants. Of another story she relates that she wrote it at Fontainebleau, where she spent all her days wandering about the forest, making entomological collections, with her son. At night she came home and took up the thread of "La Dernière Aldini," on which she had never bestowed a thought all day. Being at Venice, much depressed, in a vast dusky room in an old palace that had been turned into an inn, while the sea wind roared about her windows, and brought up the sound of the carnival as a kind of melancholy wail, she began a novel by simply looking round her and describing the room and the whistling of the mingled tumult without. She finished it in a week, and, hardly reading it over, sent it to Paris as "Léone Léoni"—a masterpiece.

In the few prefatory lines to "Isidora" I remember she says something of this kind: "It was a beautiful young woman who used to come and see me, and profess to relate her sorrows. I saw that she was attitudinizing before me, and not believing herself a word of what she said. So it is not her I described in 'Isidora.'" This is a happy way of saying how a hint—a mere starting point—was enough for her. Particularly charming is the preface to the beautiful tale of "André"; it is a capital proof of what one may call the author's limpidity of reminiscence, and want of space alone prevents me from quoting it. She was at Venice, and she used to hear her maidservant and her sempstress, as they sat at work together, chattering in the next room. She listened to their talk in order to accustom her ear to the Venetian dialect, and in so doing she came into possession of a large amount of local gossip. The effect of it was to remind her of the small social life of the little country town near Nohant. The women told each other just such stories as might have been told there, and indulged in just such reflections and "appreciations" as would have been there begotten. She was reminded that men and women are everywhere the same, and at the same time she felt homesick. "I recalled the dirty, dusky streets, the tumble-down houses, the poor moss-grown roofs, the shrill concerts of cocks, children and cats, of my own little town. I dreamed too of our beautiful meadows, of our perfumed hay, of our little running streams, and of the botany beloved of old which I could follow now only on the muddy mosses and the floating weeds that adhered to the sides of the gondolas. I don't know amid what vague memories of various types I set in motion the least complex and the laziest of fictions. These types belonged quite as much to Venice as to Berry. Change dress and language, sky, landscape and architecture, the outside aspect of people and things, and you will find that at the bottom of all this man is always the same, and woman still more, because of the tenacity of her instincts."

George Sand says that she found she could write for an extraordinary length of time without weariness, and this is as far as she goes in the way of analysis of her inspiration. From the time she made the discovery to the day of her death her life was an extremely laborious one. She had evidently an extraordinary physical robustness. It was her constant practice to write at night, beginning after the rest of the world had gone to sleep. Alexandre Dumas the younger described her somewhere, during her latter years, as an old lady who came out into the garden at midday in a broad-brimmed hat and sat down on a bench or wandered slowly about. So she remained for hours, looking about her, musing, contemplating. She was gathering impressions, says M. Dumas, absorbing the universe, steeping herself in nature; and at night she would give all this forth as a sort of emanation. Without using too vague epithets one may accept this term "emanation" as a good account of her manner.

If it is needless to go into biographical detail, this is because George Sand's real history, the more interesting one, is the history of her mind. The history of her mind is of course closely connected with her personal history; she is indeed a writer whose personal situation, at a particular moment, is supposed to be reflected with peculiar vividness in her work. But to speak of her consistently we must regard the events of her life as intellectual events, and its landmarks as opinions, convictions, theories. The only difficulty is that such landmarks are nearly as numerous as the trees in a forest. Some, however, are more salient than others. Madame Sand's account of herself is that her ideal of life was repose, obscurity and idleness—long days in the country spent in botany and entomology. She affirms that her natural indolence was extreme, and that the need of money alone induced her to take her pen into her hand. As this need was constant, her activity was constant; but it was a perversion of the genius of a kind, simple, friendly, motherly, profoundly unambitious woman, who would have been amply content to take care of her family, live in slippers, gossip with peasants, walk in the garden and listen to the piano. All this is certainly so far true as that no person of equal celebrity ever made fewer explicit pretensions. She philosophized upon a great many things that she did not understand, and toward the close of her life, in especial, was apt to talk metaphysics, in writing, with a mingled volubility and vagueness which might have been taken to denote an undue self-confidence. But in such things as these, as they come from George Sand's pen, there is an air as of not expecting any one in particular to read them. She never took herself too much *au sérieux*—she never postured at all as a woman of letters. She scribbled, she might have said—scribbled as well as she could; but when she was not scribbling she never thought of it; though she liked to think of all the great things that were worth scribbling about—love and religion and science and art, and man's political destiny. Her reader feels that she has no vanity, and all her contemporaries agree that her generosity was extreme.

She calls herself a *sphinx bon enfant*, or says at least that she looked like one. Judgments may differ as to what degree she was a sphinx; but her good nature is all-pervading. Some of her books are redolent of it—some of the more "objective" ones: "Consuelo," "Les Maîtres Sonneurs," "L'Homme de Neige," "Les beaux Messieurs de Bois-Doré." She is often passionate, but she is never rancorous; even her violent attacks upon the Church give us no impression of small acrimony. She has all a woman's loquacity, but she has never a woman's shrillness; and perhaps we can hardly indicate better the difference between great passion and small than by saying that she never is hysterical. During the last half of her career, her books went out of fashion among the new literary generation. "Realism" had been invented, or rather propagated; and in the light of "Madame Bovary" her own facile fictions began to be regarded as the work of a sort of superior Mrs. Radcliffe. She was antiquated; she belonged to the infancy of art. She accepted this destiny with a cheerfulness which it would have savoured of vanity even to make explicit. The Realists were her personal friends; she knew that they did not, and could not, read her books; for what could Gustave Flaubert make of "Monsieur Sylvestre," what could Ivan Turgénieff make of "Césarine Dietrich"? It made no difference; she contented herself with reading their productions, never mentioned her own, and continued to write charming, improbable romances for initiated persons of the optimistic class.

After the first few years she fell into this more and more; she wrote stories for the story's sake. Among the novels produced during a long period before her death I can think of but one, "Mademoiselle La Quintinie," that is of a controversial cast. All her early novels, on the other hand, were controversial—if this is not too mild a description of the passionate contempt for the institution of marriage expressed in "Indiana," "Valentine," "Lélia," and "Jacques." Her own acquaintance with matrimony had been of a painful kind, and the burden of three at least of these remarkable tales ("Lélia" stands rather apart) is the misery produced by an indissoluble matrimonial knot. "Jacques" is the story of an unhappy marriage from which there is no issue but by the suicide of one of the partners; the husband throws himself into an Alpine crevasse in order to leave his wife to an undisturbed enjoyment of her lover.

It very soon became apparent that these matters were handled in a new and superior fashion. There had been plenty of tales about husbands, wives, and "third-parties," but since the "Nouvelle Héloïse" there had been none of a high value or of a philosophic tone. Madame Sand, from the first, was nothing if not philosophic; the iniquity of marriage arrangements was to her mind but one of a hundred abominations in a society which needed a complete overhauling, and to which she proceeded to propose a loftier line of conduct. The passionate eloquence of the writer in all this was only equalled by her extraordinary self-confidence. "Valentine" seems to us even now a very eloquent book, and "Jacques" is hardly less so; it is easy to imagine their having made an immense impression. The intellectual freshness, the sentimental force of "Valentine," must have had an irresistible charm; and we say this with a full sense of what there is false and fantastical in the substance of both books. Hold them up against the light of a certain sort of ripe reason, and they seem as porous as a pair of sieves; but subject them simply to the literary test, and they hold together very bravely.

The author's philosophic predilections were at once her merit and her weakness. On the one side it was a great mind, curious about all things, open to all things, nobly accessible to experience, asking only to live, expand, respond; on the other side stood a great personal volition, making large exactions of life and society and needing constantly to justify itself—stirring up rebellion and calling down revolution in order to cover up and legitimate its own agitation. George Sand's was a French mind, and as a French mind it had to theorize; but if the positive side of its criticism of most human institutions was precipitate and ill-balanced, the error was in a great measure atoned for in later years. The last half of Madame Sand's career was a period of assent and acceptance; she had decided to make the best of those social arrangements which surrounded her—remembering, as it were, the homely native proverb which declares that when one has not got what one likes one must like what one has got. Into the phase of acceptance and serenity, the disposition to admit that even as it is society *pays*, according to the vulgar locution, our author passed at about the time that the Second Empire settled down upon France. We suspect the fact we speak of was rather a coincidence than an effect. It is very true that the Second Empire may have seemed the death-knell of "philosophy"; it may very well have appeared profitless to ask questions of a world which anticipated you with such answers as that. But we take it rather that Madame Sand was simply weary of criticism; the pendulum had swung into the opposite quarter—as it is needless to remark that it always does.

We have delayed too long to say how far it had swung in the first direction; and we have delayed from the feeling that it is difficult to say it. We have seen that George Sand was by the force of heredity projected into this field with a certain violence; she took possession of a portion of it as a conqueror, and she was never compelled to retreat. The reproach brought against her by her critics is that, as regards her particular advocacy of the claims of the heart, she has for the most part portrayed vicious love, not virtuous love. But the reply to this, from her own side, would be that she has at all events portrayed something which those who disparage her activity have not portrayed. She may claim, that although she has the critics against her, the writers of her own class who represent virtuous love have not pushed her out of the field. She has the advantage that she has portrayed a *passion*, and those of the other group have the disadvantage that they have not. In English literature, which, we suppose, is more especially the region of virtuous love, we do not "go into" the matter, as the phrase is (we speak of course of English prose). We have agreed among our own confines that there is a certain point at which elucidation of it should stop short; that among the things which it is possible to say about it, the greater number had on the whole better not be said. It would be easy to make an ironical statement of the English attitude, and it would be, if not easy, at least very possible, to make a sound defence of it. The thing with us, however, is not a matter of theory; it is above all a matter of practice, and the practice has been that of the leading English novelists. Miss Austen and Sir Walter Scott, Dickens and Thackeray, Hawthorne and George Eliot, have all represented young people in love with each other; but no one of them has, to the best of our recollection, described anything that can be called a passion—put it into motion before us and shown us its various paces. To say this is to say at the same time that these writers have spared us much that we consider disagreeable, and that George Sand has not spared us; but it is to say furthermore that few persons would resort to English prose fiction for any information concerning the ardent forces of the heart—for any ideas upon them. It is George Sand's merit that she has given us ideas upon them—that she has enlarged the novel-reader's conception of them and proved herself in all that relates to them an authority. This is a great deal. From this standpoint Miss Austen, Walter Scott and Dickens will appear to have omitted the erotic sentiment altogether, and George Eliot will seem to have treated it with singular austerity. Strangely loveless, seen in this light, are those large, comprehensive fictions "Middlemarch" and "Daniel Deronda." They seem to foreign readers, probably, like vast, cold, commodious, respectable rooms, through whose window-panes one sees a snow-covered landscape, and across whose acres of sober-hued carpet one looks in vain for a fireplace or a fire.

The distinction between virtuous and vicious love is not particularly insisted upon by George Sand. In her view love is always love, is always divine in its essence and ennobling in its operation. The largest life possible is to hold one's self open to an unlimited experience of this improving passion. This, I believe, was Madame Sand's practice, as it was certainly her theory—a theory to the exposition of which one of her novels, at least, is expressly dedicated. "Lucrezia Floriani" is the history of a lady who, in the way of love, takes everything that comes along, and who sets forth her philosophy of the matter with infinite grace and felicity. It is probably fortunate for the world that ladies of Lucrezia Floriani's disposition have not as a general thing her argumentative brilliancy. About all this there would be much more to say than these few pages afford space for. Madame Sand's plan was to be open to *all* experience, all emotions, all convictions; only to keep the welfare of the human race, and especially of its humbler members, well in mind, and to trust that one's moral and intellectual life would take a form profitable to the same. One was therefore not only to extend a great hospitality to love, but to interest one's self in religion and politics. This Madame Sand did with great activity during the whole of the reign of Louis Philippe. She had broken utterly with the Church, of course, but her disposition was the reverse of sceptical. Her religious feeling, like all her feelings, was powerful and voluminous, and she had an ideal of a sort of etherealized and liberated Christianity, in which unmarried but affectionate couples might find an element friendly to their "expansion." Like all her feelings, too, her religious sentiment was militant; her ideas about love were an attack upon marriage; her faith was an attack upon the Church and the clergy; her socialistic sympathies were an attack upon all present political arrangements. These things all took hold of her by turn—shook her hard, as it were, and dropped her, leaving her to be played upon by some new inspiration; then, in some cases, returned to her, took possession of her afresh and sounded another tune. M. Renan, in writing of her at the time of her death, used a fine phrase about her; he said that she was "the Æolian harp of our time;" he spoke of her "sonorous soul." This is very just; there is nothing that belonged to her time that she had not a personal emotion about—an emotion intense enough to produce a brilliant work of art—a novel that had bloomed as rapidly and perfectly as the flower that the morning sun sees open on its stem. In her care about many things during all these years, in her expenditure of passion, reflection, and curiosity, there is something quite unprecedented. Never had philosophy and art gone so closely hand in hand. Each of them suffered a good deal; but it had appeared up to that time that their mutual concessions must be even greater. Balzac was a far superior artist; but he was incapable of a lucid reflection.

We have already said that mention has been made of George Sand's analogy with Goethe, who claimed for his lyrical poems the merit of being each the result of a particular incident in his life. It was incident too that prompted Madame Sand to write; but what it produced in her case was not a short copy of verses, but an elaborate drama, with a plot and a dozen characters. It will help us to understand this extraordinary responsiveness of mind and fertility of imagination to remember that inspiration was often embodied in a concrete form; that Madame Sand's "incidents" were usually clever, eloquent, suggestive men. "Le style c'est l'homme"—of her, it has been epigramatically said, that is particularly true. Be this as it may, these influences were strikingly various, and they are reflected in works which may be as variously labelled: amatory tales, religious tales, political, æsthetic, pictorial, musical, theatrical, historical tales. And it is to be noticed that in whatever the author attempted, whether or no she succeeded, she appeared to lose herself. The "Lettres d'un Voyageur" read like a writer's single book. This melancholy, this desolation and weariness, might pass as the complete distillation of a soul. In the same way "Spiridion" is exclusively religious and theological. The author might, in relation to this book, have replied to such of her critics as reproach her with being too erotic, that she had performed the very rare feat of writing a novel not only containing no love save divine love, but containing not one woman's figure. We can recall but one rival to "Spiridion" in this respect—Godwin's "Caleb Williams."

But if other things come and go with George Sand, amatory disquisition is always there. It is of all kinds, sometimes very noble and sometimes very disagreeable. Numerous specimens of the two extremes might be cited. There is to our taste a great deal too much of it; the total effect is displeasing. The author illuminates and glorifies the divine passion, but she does something which may be best expressed by saying that she cheapens it. She handles it too much; she lets it too little alone. Above all she is too positive, too explicit, too business-like; she takes too technical a view of it. Its various signs and tokens and stages, its ineffable mysteries, are all catalogued and tabulated in her mind, and she whisks out her references with the nimbleness with which the doorkeeper at an exhibition hands you back your umbrella in return for a check. In this relation, to the English mind, discretion is a great point—a virtue so absolute and indispensable that it speaks for itself and cannot be analysed away; and George Sand is judged from our point of view by one's saying that for her discretion is simply non-existent. Its place is occupied by a sort of benevolent, an almost conscientious disposition to sit down, as it were, and "talk over" the whole matter. The subject fills her with a motherly loquacity; it stimulates all her wonderful and beautiful self-sufficiency of expression—the quality that we have heard a hostile critic call her "glibness."

We can hardly open a volume of George Sand without finding an example of what we mean. We glance at a venture into "Teverino," and we find Lady G., who has left her husband at the inn and gone out to spend a day with the more fascinating Léonce, "passing her beautiful hands over the eyes of Léonce, *peut-être par tendresse naïve,* perhaps to convince herself that it was really tears she saw shining in them." The *peut-être* here, the *tendresse naïve,* the alternatives, the impartial way in which you are given your choice, are extremely characteristic of Madame Sand. They remind us of the heroine of "Isidora," who alludes in conversation to "une de mes premières fautes." In the list of Madame Sand's more technically amatory novels, however, there is a distinction to be made; the earlier strike us as superior to the later. The fault of the earlier—the fact that passion is too intellectual, too pedantic, too sophistical, too much bent upon proving itself abnegation and humility, maternity, fraternity, humanity, or some fine thing that it really is not and that it is much simpler and better for not pretending to be—this fault is infinitely exaggerated in the tales written after "Lucrezia Floriani." "Indiana," "Valentine," "Jacques," and "Mauprat" are, comparatively speaking, frankly and honestly passionate; they do not represent the love that declines to compromise with circumstances as a sort of eating of one's cake and having it too—an eating it as pleasure and a having it as virtue. But the stories of the type of "Lucrezia Floriani," which indeed is the most argumentative,[1] have an indefinable falsity of tone. Madame Sand had here begun to play with her topic intellectually; the first freshness of her interest in it had gone, and invention had taken the place of conviction. To acquit one's self happily of such experiments, one must certainly have all the gifts that George Sand possessed. But one must also have two or three that she lacked. Her sense of purity was certainly defective. This is a brief statement, but it means a great deal, and of what it means there are few of her novels that do not contain a number of illustrations.

There is something very fine, for instance, about "Valentine," in spite of its contemptible hero; there is something very sweet and generous in the figure of the young girl. But why, desiring to give us an impression of great purity in her heroine, should the author provide her with a half-sister who is at once an illegitimate daughter and the mother of a child born out of wedlock, and who, in addition, is half in love with Valentine's lover? though George Sand thinks to better the matter by representing this love as partly maternal. After Valentine's marriage, a compulsory and most unhappy one, this half-sister plots with the doctor to place the young wife and the lover whom she has had to dismiss once more *en rapport*. She hesitates, it is true, and inquires of the physician if their scheme will not appear unlawful in the eyes of the world. But the old man reassures her, and asks, with a "sou-

---

[1] "Constance Verrier," "Isidora," "Pauline," "Le dernier Amour," "La Daniella," "Francia," "Mademoiselle Merquem."

rire malin et affectueux," why she should care for the judgment of a world which has viewed so harshly her own
irregularity of conduct. Madame Sand constantly strikes these
false notes; we meet in her pages the most startling confusions. In "Jacques" there is the oddest table of relations between the characters. Jacques is possibly the brother of Silvia,
who is probably, on another side, sister of his wife, who is
the mistress of Octave, Silvia's dismissed *amant*! Add to this
that if Jacques be *not* the brother of Silvia, who is an illegitimate child, he is convertible into her lover. *On s'y perd.* Silvia,
a clever woman, is the guide, philosopher, and friend of this
melancholy Jacques; and when his wife, who desires to become the mistress of Octave (*her* discarded lover), and yet,
not finding it quite plain sailing to do so, weeps over the
crookedness of her situation, she writes to the injured husband that she has been obliged to urge Fernande not to take
things so hard: "je suis forcée de la consoler et de la relever à
ses propres yeux." Very characteristic of Madame Sand is this
fear lest the unfaithful wife should take too low a view of
herself. One wonders what had become of her sense of humour. Fernande is to be "relevée" before her fall, and the operation is somehow to cover her fall prospectively.

Take another example from "Léone Léoni." The subject of
the story is the sufferings of an infatuated young girl, who
follows over Europe the most faithless, unscrupulous and ignoble, but also the most irresistible of charmers. It is "Manon
Lescaut," with the incurable fickleness of Manon attributed to
a man; and as in the Abbé Prévost's story the touching element is the devotion and constancy of the injured and deluded Desgrieux, so in "Léone Léoni" we are invited to feel
for the too closely-clinging Juliette, who is dragged through
the mire of a passion which she curses and yet which survives
unnameable outrage. She tells the tale herself and yet it might
have been expected that, to deepen its effect, the author
would have represented her as withdrawn from the world and
cured of her excessive susceptibility. But we find her living
with another charmer, jewelled and perfumed; in her own
words, she is a *fille entretenue*, and it is to her new lover that
she relates the story of the stormy life she led with the old.
The situation requires no comment beyond our saying that

the author had morally no taste. Of this want of moral taste we remember another striking instance. Mademoiselle Merquem, who gives her name to one of the later novels, is a young girl of the most elevated character, beloved by a young man, the intensity of whose affection she desires to test. To do this she contrives the graceful plan of introducing into her house a mysterious infant, of whose parentage she offers an explanation so obtrusively vague, that the young man is driven regretfully to the induction that its female parent is none other than herself. We forget to what extent he is staggered, but, if we rightly remember, he withstands the test. We do not judge him, but it is permitted to judge the young lady.

We have called George Sand an *improvisatrice*, and in this character, where she deals with matters of a more "objective" cast, she is always delightful; nothing could be more charming than her tales of mystery, intrigue, and adventure. "Consuelo," "L'Homme de Neige," "Le Piccinino," "Teverino," "Le Beau Laurence" and its sequel, "Pierre qui Roule," "Antonia," "Tamaris," "La Famille de Germandre," "La Filleule," "La dernière Aldini," "Cadio," "Flamarande"—these things have all the spontaneous inventiveness of the romances of Alexandre Dumas, his open-air quality, his pleasure in a story for a story's sake, together with an intellectual refinement, a philosophic savour, a reference to spiritual things, in which he was grotesquely deficient.

We have given, however, no full enumeration of the author's romances, and it seems needless to do so. We have lately been trying to read them over, and we frankly confess that we have found it impossible. They are excellent reading for once, but they lack that quality which makes things classical—makes them impose themselves. It has been said that what makes a book a classic is its style. We should modify this, and instead of style say *form*. Madame Sand's novels have plenty of style, but they have no form. Balzac's have not a shred of style, but they have a great deal of form. Posterity doubtless will make a selection from each list, but the few volumes of Balzac it preserves will remain with it much longer, we suspect, than those which it borrows from his great contemporary. We cannot easily imagine posterity travelling with "Valentine" or "Mauprat," "Consuelo" or the

"Marquis de Villemer" in its trunk. At the same time we can imagine that if these admirable tales fall out of fashion, such of our descendants as stray upon them in the dusty corners of old libraries will sit down on the bookcase ladder with the open volume and turn it over with surprise and enchantment. What a beautiful mind! they will say; what an extraordinary style! Why have we not known more about these things? And as, when that time comes, we suppose the world will be given over to a "realism" that we have not as yet begun faintly to foreshadow, George Sand's novels will have, for the children of the twenty-first century, something of the same charm which Spenser's "Fairy Queen" has for those of the nineteenth. For a critic of to-day to pick and choose among them seems almost pedantic; they all belong quite to the same intellectual family. They are the easy writing which makes hard reading.

In saying this we must immediately limit our meaning. All the world can read George Sand once and not find it in the least hard. But it is not easy to return to her; putting aside a number of fine descriptive pages, the reader will not be likely to resort to any volume that he has once laid down for a particular chapter, a brilliant passage, an entertaining conversation. George Sand invites reperusal less than any mind of equal eminence. Is this because after all she was a woman, and the laxity of the feminine intellect could not fail to claim its part in her? We will not attempt to say; especially as, though it may be pedantic to pick and choose among her works, we immediately think of two or three that have as little as possible of intellectual laxity. "Mauprat" is a solid, masterly, manly book; "André" and "La Mare au Diable" have an extreme perfection of form. M. Taine, whom we quoted at the beginning of these remarks, speaks of our author's rustic tales (the group to which the "Mare au Diable" belongs[1]) as a signal proof of her activity and versatility of mind. Besides being charming stories, they are in fact a real study in philology—such a study as Balzac made in the "Contes Drôlatiques," and as Thackeray made in "Henry Esmond." George Sand's attempt to return to a more artless and archaic stage of the language which she usually handled in so

[1] "François le Champi," "La Petite Fadette."

modern and voluminous a fashion was quite as successful as
that of her fellows. In "Les Maîtres Sonneurs" it is extremely
felicitous, and the success could only have been achieved by
an extraordinarily sympathetic and flexible talent. This is one
of the impressions George Sand's reader—even if he have
read her but once—brings away with him. His other prevailing impression will bear upon that quality which, if it must
be expressed in a single word, may best be called the generosity of her genius. It is true that there are one or two things
which limit this generosity. We think, for example, of Madame Sand's peculiar power of self-defence, her constant need
to justify, to glorify, to place in a becoming light, to "arrange," as we said at the outset, those errors and weaknesses
in which her own personal credit may be at stake. She never
accepts a weakness as a weakness; she always dresses it out as
a virtue; and if her heroines abandon their lovers and lie to
their husbands, you may be sure it is from motives of the
highest morality. Such productions as "Lucrezia Floriani" and
"Elle et Lui" may be attributed to an ungenerous disposition—both of them being stories in which Madame Sand is
supposed to have described her relations with distinguished
men who were dead, and whose death enabled her without
contradiction to portray them as monsters of selfishness,
while the female protagonist appeared as the noblest of her
sex. But without taking up the discussion provoked by these
works, we may say that, on the face of the matter, there is a
good deal of justification for their author. She poured her
material into the crucible of art, and the artist's material is of
necessity in a large measure his experience. Madame Sand
never described the actual; this was often her artistic weakness, and as she has the reproach she should also have the
credit. "Lucrezia Floriani" and "Elle et Lui" were doubtless
to her imagination simply tales of what might have been.

   It is hard not to feel that there is a certain high good conscience and passionate sincerity in the words in which, in one
of her prefaces, she alludes to the poor novel which Alfred de
Musset's brother put forth as an incriminative retort to "Elle
et Lui." Some of her friends had advised her not to notice the
book; "but after reflection she judged it to be her duty to
attend to it at the proper time and place. She was, however,

by no means in haste. She was in Auvergne following the imaginary traces of the figures of her new novel along the scented byways, among the sweetest scenes of spring. She had brought the pamphlet with her to read it; but she did not read it. She had forgotten her herbarium, and the pages of the infamous book, used as a substitute, were purified by the contact of the wild flowers of Puy-de-Dôme and Sancy. Sweet perfumes of the things of God, who to you could prefer the memory of the foulnesses of civilization?"

It must, however, to be just all round, be farther remembered that those persons and causes which Madame Sand has been charged first and last with misrepresenting belonged to the silent, inarticulate, even defunct class. She was always the talker, the survivor, the adversary armed with a gift of expression so magical as almost to place a premium upon sophistry. To weigh everything, we imagine she really *outlived* experience, morally, to a degree which made her feel, in retrospect, as if she were dealing with the history of another person. "Où sont-ils, où sont-ils, nos amours passés?" she exclaims in one of her later novels. (What has become of the passions we have shuffled off?—into what dusky limbo are they flung away?) And she goes on to say that it is a great mistake to suppose that we die only once and at last. We die piecemeal; some part of us is always dying; it is only what is left that dies at last. As for our "amours passés," where are they indeed? Jacques Laurent and the Prince Karol may be fancied, in echo, to exclaim.

In saying that George Sand lacks truth the critic more particularly means that she lacks exactitude—lacks the method of truth. Of a certain general truthfulness she is full to overflowing; we feel that to her mind nothing human is alien. We should say of her, not that she *knew* human nature, but that she felt it. At all events she loved it and enjoyed it. She was contemplative; but she was not, in the deepest sense, observant. She was a very high order of sentimentalist, but she was not a moralist. She perceived a thousand things, but she rarely in strictness judged; so that although her books have a great deal of wisdom, they have not what is called weight. With the physical world she was as familiar as with the human, and she knew it perhaps better. She would probably at any time have

said that she cared much more for botany, mineralogy and astronomy, than for sociology. "Nature," as we call it—landscape, trees and flowers, rocks and streams and clouds—plays
a larger part in her novels than in any others, and in none are
they described with such a grand general felicity. If Turner
had written his landscapes rather than painted them he might
have written as George Sand has done. If she was less truthful
in dealing with men and women, says M. Taine, it is because
she had too high an ideal for them; she could not bear not to
represent them as better than they are. She delights in the representation of virtue, and if we sometimes feel that she has not
really measured the heights on which she places her characters, that so to place them has cost little to her understanding,
we are nevertheless struck with the nobleness of her imagination. M. Taine calls her an idealist; we should say, somewhat
more narrowly, that she was an optimist. An optimist "lined,"
as the French say, with a romancer, is not the making of a
moralist. George Sand's optimism, her idealism, are very
beautiful, and the source of that impression of largeness, luminosity and liberality which she makes upon us. But we suspect that something even better in a novelist is that tender
appreciation of actuality which makes even the application of
a single coat of rose-colour seem an act of violence.

Galaxy, July 1877
Reprinted in *French Poets and Novelists*, 1878

Dernières Pages. Par George Sand. Paris: Calmann Lévy, 1877.

MADAME SAND'S INDUSTRY was equal to her talent, and
the quantity of her work was not less remarkable than
the quality. Her diligence did not decline with age; the latter
years of her life were indeed even more productive than the
earlier ones. She wrote a large number of newspaper articles,
and she was not above performing in this line the most
modest functions. Obituary notices, short reviews of books,
prefaces, fragmentary reminiscences—these things flowed
constantly from her pen, and had always a certain value from
being signed with her name. This was not their only value,

for in every utterance of George Sand, however brief, there is always an appreciable touch of wisdom and grace of style. Every scrap that fell from her pen has now been collected, and these 'Dernières Pages' contain the very last possible gleanings. Most of them are very slight, but the book is worth glancing through, for the author had this characteristic of a great mind, that her touch was never vulgar or vulgarizing, and that every now and then, even when the topic is the slightest, it strikes a charming gleam. Only three of the short articles of which this volume is composed deserve specification—the rest are mere trifles. One of these is of the most rambling character: beginning with an account of a walk in the woods in midwinter, and of some curious botanical observations, it terminates in an interesting and discriminating appreciation of the personal character of Napoleon III., who at the time the article was written was on his death-bed. Madame Sand judges the late Emperor partly from personal impressions; she relates that, at one period, having twice had an interview with him on behalf of an unfortunate person (apparently a political prisoner), she made up her mind that he was deluding her with false pretensions and not keeping faith, and left Paris abruptly, without presenting herself at a third audience. She afterwards received news not that (as in the anecdote of Louis XIV.) the King had almost waited, but that the Emperor had waited altogether. She judges him leniently and liberally, thinks him above all a dreamer, a kind of sinister Don Quixote, and says, very justly, that the French people owes it to its own self-respect not to try to make out that the sovereign to whom they submitted for twenty years was an unmitigated villain. This is what Victor Hugo so loudly proclaims; and in this case, what does Victor Hugo make of complaisant Paris, the most amiable, the most high-toned, the most exemplary city in the world?

In another article Madame Sand gives an entertaining account of her granduncle, the Abbé de Beaumont, who figures in the early pages of 'L'Histoire de ma Vie,' and upon whose portrait, having received some fresh documentary evidence about her ancestor, she desires to bestow a few flattering touches. He was the robust and handsome bastard of a great nobleman of the old régime (the Duc de Bouillon), whose only legitimate child was a helpless and peevish cripple, and the account of his unrequited devotion to his at once more and less fortunate brother is sufficiently affecting. But the most charming thing in these pages is the history of the theatre of marionettes—in plain English, the puppet-show—which has been for many years a brilliant feature of the author's home at Nohant. Madame Sand has written few more delightful pages. There are puppet-shows and puppet-shows; Madame Sand takes the institution very seriously and earnestly pleads the cause of *fantoccini* as a domestic amusement. The account she gives of the gradual elaboration and finally brilliant perfection of the troupe of marionettes of which her son had constituted himself operator is peculiarly interesting, and all that she says about the possible extension of the development of the entertainment is full of a characteristic appreciation, both of artistic and human things. We recommend the perusal of these pages, and we urge their being acted upon. Or must we be French and frivolous to care about ingenious and artistic pastimes? We should almost recommend that the article be translated, and circulated as a tract, for the benefit of domestic circles infected with what Matthew Arnold calls "dreariness."

Nation, October 25, 1877

SHE AND HE: RECENT DOCUMENTS

I HAVE BEEN READING in the Revue de Paris for November 1st, 1896, some fifty pages, of an extraordinary interest, which have had in respect to an old admiration a remarkable effect. Undoubtedly for other admirers too who have come to fifty year—admirers, I mean, once eager, of the distinguished woman involved—the perusal of the letters addressed by George Sand to Alfred de Musset in the course of a famous friendship will have stirred in an odd fashion the ashes of an early ardour. I speak of ashes because early ardours for the most part burn themselves out, while the place they hold in our lives varies, I think, mainly according to the degree of tenderness with which we gather up and preserve their dust; and I speak of oddity because in the present case it is difficult to say whether the agitation of the embers results at last in a returning glow or in a yet more sensible chill. That indeed is perhaps a small question compared with the simple pleasure of the reviving emotion. One reads and wonders and enjoys again, just for the sake of the renewal. The small fry of the hour submit to further shrinkage, and we revert with a sigh of relief to the free genius and large life of one of the greatest of all masters of expression. Do people still handle the works of this master—people other than young ladies studying French with "La Mare au Diable" and a dictionary? Are there persons who still read "Valentine"? Are there others capable of losing themselves in "Mauprat"? Has "André," the exquisite, dropped out of knowledge, and is any one left who remembers "Teverino"? I ask these questions for the mere sweet sound of them, without the least expectation of an answer. I remember asking them twenty years ago, after Madame Sand's death, and not then being hopeful of the answer of the future. But the only response that matters to us perhaps is our own, even if it be after all somewhat ambiguous. "André" and "Valentine" then are rather on our shelves than in our hands, but in the light of what is given us in the "Revue de Paris" who shall say that we do not, and with avidity, "read" George Sand? She died in 1876, but she lives again intensely in these singular pages, both as to what in her spirit was most attaching and what most disconcerting. We are vague as to what they may represent for the generation that has come to the front since her death; nothing, I dare say, very imposing or even very pleasing. But they give out a great deal to a reader for whom thirty years ago—the best time to have taken her as a whole—she was a high clear figure, a great familiar magician. This impression is a strange mixture, but perhaps not quite incommunicable; and we are steeped as we receive it in one of the most curious episodes in the annals of the literary race.

I

It is the great interest of such an episode that, apart from its proportionate place in the unfolding of a personal life it has a wonderful deal to say on the relation between experience and art at large. It constitutes an eminent special case, in which the workings of that relation are more or less uncovered; a case too of which one of the most striking notes is that we are in possession of it almost exclusively by the act of one of the persons concerned. Madame Sand at least, as we see to-day, was eager to leave nothing undone that could make us further acquainted than we were before with one of the liveliest chapters of her personal history. We cannot, doubtless, be sure that her conscious purpose in the production of "Elle et Lui" was to show us the process by which private ecstasies and pains find themselves transmuted in the artist's workshop into promising literary material—any more than we can be certain of her motive for making toward the end of her life earnest and complete arrangements for the ultimate publication of the letters in which the passion is recorded and in which we can remount to the origin of the volume. If "Elle et Lui" had been the inevitable picture, postponed and retouched, of the great adventure of her youth, so the letters show us the crude primary stuff from which the moral detachment of the book was distilled. Were they to be given to the world for the encouragement of the artist-nature—as a contribution to the view that no suffering is great enough, no emotion tragic enough to exclude the hope that such pangs may sooner or later be esthetically assimilated? Was the whole proceeding, in intention, a frank plea for the intellectual and in some degree even the commercial profit, to a robust organism, of a store of erotic reminiscence? Whatever the reasons behind the matter, that is to a certain extent the moral of the strange story.

It may be objected that this moral is qualified to come home to us only when the relation between art and experience really proves a happier one than it may be held to have proved in the combination before us. The element in danger of being most absent from the process is the element of dignity, and its presence, so far as that may ever at all be hoped for in an appeal from a personal quarrel, is assured only in proportion as the esthetic event, standing on its own feet, represents a noble gift. It was vain, the objector may say, for our author to pretend to justify by so slight a performance as "Elle et Lui" that sacrifice of all delicacy which has culminated in this supreme surrender. "If you sacrifice all delicacy," I hear such a critic contend, "show at least that you were right by giving us a masterpiece. The novel in question is no more a masterpiece," I even hear him proceed, "than any other of the loose liquid lucid works of its author. By your supposition of a great intention you give much too fine an account on the one hand of a personal habit of incontinence and on the other of a literary habit of egotism. Madame Sand, in writing her tale and in publishing her love-letters, obeyed no prompting more exalted than that of exhibiting her personal (in which I include her verbal) facility, and of doing so at the cost of whatever other persons might be concerned; and you are therefore—and you might as well immediately confess it— thrown back for the element of interest on the attraction of her general eloquence, the plausibility of her general manner and the great number of her particular confidences. You are thrown back on your mere curiosity or sympathy—thrown back from any question of service rendered to 'art.' " One might be thrown back doubtless still further even than such remarks would represent if one were not quite prepared with the confession they propose. It is only because such a figure is interesting—in every manifestation—that its course is marked for us by vivid footprints and possible lessons. And to enable us to find these it scarcely need have aimed after all so extravagantly high. George Sand lived her remarkable life and drove her perpetual pen, but the illustration that I began by speaking of is for ourselves to gather—if we can.

I remember hearing many years ago in Paris an anecdote for the truth of which I am far from vouching, though it professed to come direct—an anecdote that has recurred to me more than once in turning over the revelations of the Re-vue de Paris, and without the need of the special reminder (in the shape of an allusion to her intimacy with the hero of the story) contained in those letters to Sainte-Beuve which are published in the number of November 15th. Prosper Mérimée was said to have related—in a reprehensible spirit—that during a term of association with the author of "Lélia" he once opened his eyes, in the raw winter dawn, to see his compan-ion, in a dressing-gown, on her knees before the domestic hearth, a candlestick beside her and a red *madras* round her head, making bravely, with her own hands, the fire that was to enable her to sit down betimes to urgent pen and paper. The story represents him as having felt that the spectacle chilled his ardour and tried his taste; her appearance was unfortunate, her occupation an inconsequence and her industry a reproof—the result of all of which was a lively irritation and an early rupture. To the firm admirer of Madame Sand's prose the little sketch has a very different value, for it presents her in an attitude which is the very key to the enigma, the answer to most of the questions with which her character confronts us. She rose early because she was pressed to write, and she was pressed to write because she had the greatest instinct of expression ever conferred on a woman; a faculty that put a premium on all passion, on all pain, on all experience and all exposure, on the greatest variety of ties and the smallest reserve about them. The really interesting thing in these posthumous *laideurs* is the way the gift, the voice, carries its possessor through them and lifts her on the whole above them. It gave her, it may be confessed at the outset and in spite of all magnanimities in the use of it, an unfair advantage in every connection. So at least we must continue to feel till—for our appreciation of this particular one—we have Alfred de Musset's share of the correspondence. For we shall have it at last, in whatever faded fury or beauty it may still possess—to that we may make up our minds. Let the galled jade wince, it is only a question of time. The greatest of literary quarrels will in short, on the general ground, once more come up—the quarrel beside which all others are mild and arrangeable, the eternal dispute between the public and the private, between curiosity and delicacy.

This discussion is precisely all the sharper because it takes place for each of us within as well as without. When we wish to know at all we wish to know everything; yet there happen to be certain things of which no better description can be given than that they are simply none of our business. "What *is* then forsooth of our business?" the genuine analyst may always ask; and he may easily challenge us to produce any rule of general application by which we shall know when to push in and when to back out. "In the first place," he may continue, "half the 'interesting' people in the world have at one time or another set themselves to drag us in with all their might; and what in the world in such a relation is the observer that he should absurdly pretend to be in more of a flutter than the object observed? The mannikin, in all schools, is at an early stage of study of the human form inexorably superseded by the man. Say that we are to give up the attempt to understand: it might certainly be better so, and there would be a delightful side to the new arrangement. But in the name of common-sense don't say that the continuity of life is not to have some equivalent in the continuity of pursuit, the renewal of phenomena in the renewal of notation. There is not a door you can lock here against the critic or the painter, not a cry you can raise or a long face you can pull at him, that are not quite arbitrary things. The only thing that makes the observer competent is that he is neither afraid nor ashamed; the only thing that makes him decent—just think!—is that he is not superficial." All this is very well, but somehow we all equally feel that there is clean linen and soiled and that life would be intolerable without some acknowledgment even by the pushing of such a thing as forbidden ground. M. Émile Zola, at the moment I write, gives to the world his reasons for rejoicing in the publication of the physiological *enquête* of Dr. Toulouse—a marvellous catalogue or handbook of M. Zola's outward and inward parts, which leaves him not an inch of privacy, so to speak, to stand on, leaves him nothing about himself that is *for* himself, for his friends, his relatives, his intimates, his lovers, for discovery, for emulation, for fond conjecture or flattering deluded envy. It is enough for M. Zola that everything is for the public and no sacrifice worth thinking of when it is a question of presenting to the open mouth of that apparently gorged but still gaping monster the smallest spoonful of truth. The truth, to his view, is never either ridiculous or unclean, and the way to a better life lies through telling it, so far as possible, about everything and about every one.

There would probably be no difficulty in agreeing to this if it didn't seem on the part of the speaker the result of a rare confusion between give and take, between "truth" and information. The true thing that most matters to us is the true thing we have most use for, and there are surely many occasions on which the truest thing of all is the necessity of the mind, its simple necessity of feeling. Whether it feels in order to learn or learns in order to feel, the event is the same: the side on which it shall most feel will be the side to which it will most incline. If it feels more about a Zola functionally undeciphered it will be governed more by that particular truth than by the truth about his digestive idiosyncrasies, or even about his "olfactive perceptions" and his "arithmomania or impulse to count." An affirmation of our "mere taste" may very supposedly be our individual contribution to the general clearing up. Nothing often is less superficial than to ignore and overlook, or more constructive (for living and feeling at all) than to want impatiently to choose. If we are aware that in the same way as about a Zola undeciphered we should have felt more about a George Sand unexposed, the true thing we have gained becomes a poor substitute for the one we have lost; and I scarce see what difference it makes that the view of the elder novelist appears in this matter quite to march with that of the younger. I hasten to add that as to being of course asked why in the world with such a leaning we have given time either to M. Zola's physician or to Musset's correspondent, this is only another illustration of the bewildering state of the subject.

When we meet on the broad highway the rueful denuded figure we need some presence of mind to decide whether to cut it dead or to lead it gently home, and meanwhile the fatal complication easily occurs. We have *seen*, in a flash of our own wit, and mystery has fled with a shriek. These encounters are indeed accidents which may at any time take place, and the general guarantee in a noisy world lies, I judge, not so much in any hope of really averting them as in a regular organisation of the struggle. The reporter and the reported have duly and equally to understand that they carry their life in their hands. There are secrets for privacy and silence; let them only be cultivated on the part of the hunted creature with even half the method with which the love of sport—or call it the historic sense—is cultivated on the part of the investigator. They have been left too much to the natural, the instinctive man; but they will be twice as effective after it begins to be observed that they may take their place among the triumphs of civilisation. Then at last the game will be fair and the two forces face to face; it will be "pull devil, pull tailor," and the hardest pull will doubtless provide the happiest result. Then the cunning of the inquirer, envenomed with resistance, will exceed in subtlety and ferocity anything we to-day conceive, and the pale forewarned victim, with every track covered, every paper burnt and every letter unanswered, will, in the tower of art, the invulnerable granite, stand, without a sally, the siege of all the years.

II

It was not in the tower of art that George Sand ever shut herself up; but I come back to a point already made in saying that it is in the citadel of style that, notwithstanding rash *sorties*, she continues to hold out. The outline of the complicated story that was to cause so much ink to flow gives, even with the omission of a hundred features, a direct measure of the strain to which her astonishing faculty was exposed. In the summer of 1833, as a woman of nearly thirty, she encountered Alfred de Musset, who was six years her junior. In spite of their youth they were already somewhat bowed by the weight of a troubled past. Musset, at twenty-three, had that of his confirmed libertinism—so Madame Arvède Barine, who has had access to materials, tells us in the admirable short biography of the poet contributed to the rather markedly unequal but very interesting series of Hachette's Grands Ecrivains Français. Madame Sand had a husband, a son and a daughter, and the impress of that succession of lovers—Jules Sandeau had been one, Prosper Mérimée another—to which she so freely alludes in the letters to Sainte-Beuve, a friend more disinterested than these and qualified to give much counsel in exchange for much confidence. It cannot be said that the situation of either of our young persons was of good omen for a happy relation, but they appear to have burnt their ships with much promptitude and a great blaze, and in the December of that year they started together for Italy. The following month saw them settled, on a frail basis, in Venice, where the elder companion remained till late in the summer of 1834 and where she wrote, in part, "Jacques" and the "Lettres d'un

Voyageur," as well as "André" and "Léone-Léoni," and gathered the impressions to be embodied later in half-a-dozen stories with Italian titles—notably in the delightful "Consuelo."
The journey, the Italian climate, the Venetian winter at first
agreed with neither of the friends; they were both taken ill
—the young man very gravely—and after a stay of three
months Musset returned, alone and much ravaged, to Paris.

In the meantime a great deal had happened, for their union
had been stormy and their security small. Madame Sand had
nursed her companion in illness (a matter-of-course office, it
must be owned) and her companion had railed at his nurse in
health. A young physician, called in, had become a close
friend of both parties, but more particularly a close friend of
the lady, and it was to his tender care that on quitting the
scene Musset solemnly committed her. She took up life with
Pietro Pagello—the transition is startling—for the rest of her
stay, and on her journey back to France he was no inconsiderable part of her luggage. He was simple, robust and kind—
not a man of genius. He remained, however, but a short time
in Paris; in the autumn of 1834 he returned to Italy, to live on
till our own day but never again, so far as we know, to meet
his illustrious mistress. Her intercourse with her poet was, in
all its intensity, one may almost say its ferocity, promptly renewed, and was sustained in that key for several months
more. The effect of this strange and tormented passion on the
mere student of its records is simply to make him ask himself
what on earth is the matter with the subjects of it. Nothing
is more easy than to say, as I have intimated, that it has no
need of records and no need of students; but this leaves out
of account the thick medium of genius in which it was foredoomed to disport itself. It was self-registering, as the phrase
is, for the genius on both sides happened to be the genius of
eloquence. It is all rapture and all rage and all literature. The
"Lettres d'un Voyageur" spring from the thick of the fight;
"La Confession d'un Enfant du Siècle" and "Les Nuits" are
immediate echoes of the concert. The lovers are naked in the
market-place and perform for the benefit of society. The matter with them, to the perception of the stupefied spectator, is
that they entertained for each other every feeling in life but
the feeling of respect. What the absence of that article may do

for the passion of hate is apparently nothing to what it may do for the passion of love.

By our unhappy pair at any rate the luxury in question—the little luxury of plainer folk—was not to be purchased, and in the comedy of their despair and the tragedy of their recovery nothing is more striking than their convulsive effort either to reach up to it or to do without it. They would have given for it all else they possessed, but they only meet in their struggle the inexorable *never*. They strain and pant and gasp, they beat the air in vain for the cup of cold water of their hell. They missed it in a way for which none of their superiorities could make up. Their great affliction was that each found in the life of the other an armoury of weapons to wound. Young as they were, young as Musset was in particular, they appeared to have afforded each other in that direction the most extraordinary facilities; and nothing in the matter of the mutual consideration that failed them is more sad and strange than that even in later years, when their rage, very quickly, had cooled, they never arrived at simple silence. For Madame Sand, in her so much longer life, there was no hush, no letting alone; though it would be difficult indeed to exaggerate the depth of relative indifference from which, a few years after Musset's death, such a production as "Elle et Lui" could spring. Of course there had been floods of tenderness, of forgiveness; but those, for all their beauty of expression, are quite another matter. It is just the fact of our sense of the ugliness of so much of the episode that makes a wonder and a force of the fine style, all round, in which it is offered us. That force is in its turn a sort of clue to guide, or perhaps rather a sign to stay, our feet in paths after all not the most edifying. It gives a degree of importance to the somewhat squalid and the somewhat ridiculous story, and, for the old George-Sandist at least, lends a positive spell to the smeared and yellowed paper, the blotted and faded ink. In this twilight of association we seem to find a reply to our own challenge and to be able to tell ourselves why we meddle with such old dead squabbles and waste our time with such grimacing ghosts. If we were superior to the weakness, moreover, how should we make our point (which we must really make at any cost) as to the so valuable vivid proof that a great talent is the best guarantee—that it may really carry off almost anything?

The rather sorry ghost that beckons us on furthest is the rare personality of Madame Sand. Under its influence—or that of old memories from which it is indistinguishable—we pick our steps among the *laideurs* aforesaid: the misery, the levity, the brevity of it all, the greatest ugliness in particular that this life shows us, the way the devotions and passions that we see heaven and earth called to witness are over before we can turn round. It may be said that, for what it was, the intercourse of these unfortunates surely lasted long enough; but the answer to that is that if it had only lasted longer it wouldn't have been what it was. It was not only preceded and followed by intimacies, on one side and the other, as unadorned by the stouter sincerity, but was mixed up with them in a manner that would seem to us dreadful if it didn't still more seem to us droll, or rather perhaps if it didn't refuse altogether to come home to us with the crudity of contemporary things. It is antediluvian history, a queer vanished world—another Venice from the actually, the deplorably familiarised, a Paris of greater bonhomie, an inconceivable impossible Nohant. This relegates it to an order agreeable somehow to the imagination of the fond quinquegenarian, the reader with a fund of reminiscence. The vanished world, the Venice unrestored, the Paris unextended, is a bribe to his judgment; he has even a glance of complacency for the lady's liberal *foyer*. Liszt, one lovely year at Nohant, "jouait du piano au rez-de-chaussée, et les rossignols, ivres de musique et de soleil, s'égosillaient avec rage sur les lilas environnants." The beautiful manner confounds itself with the conditions in which it was exercised, the large liberty and variety overflow into admirable prose, and the whole thing makes a charming faded medium in which Chopin gives a hand to Consuelo and the small Fadette has her elbows on the table of Flaubert.

There is a terrible letter of the autumn of 1834 in which our heroine has recourse to Alfred Tattet on a dispute with the bewildered Pagello—a disagreeable matter that involved a question of money. "À Venise il comprenait," she somewhere says, "à Paris il ne comprend plus." It was a proof of remarkable intelligence that he did understand in Venice, where he had become a lover in the presence and with the exalted approval of an immediate predecessor—an alternate representative of the part, whose turn had now, on the removal to Paris, come round again and in whose resumption of office it was looked to him to concur. This attachment—to Pagello—had lasted but a few months; yet already it was the prey of complication and change, and its sun appears to have set in no very graceful fashion. We are not here in truth among very graceful things, in spite of superhuman attitudes and great romantic flights. As to these forced notes Madame Arvède Barine judiciously says that the picture of them contained in the letters to which she had had access, and some of which are before us, "presents an example extraordinary and unmatched of what the romantic spirit could do with beings who had become its prey." She adds that she regards the records in question, "in which we follow step by step the ravages of the monster," as "one of the most precious psychological documents of the first half of the century." That puts the story on its true footing, though we may regret that it should not divide these documentary honours more equally with some other story in which the monster has not quite so much the best of it. But it is the misfortune of the comparatively short and simple annals of conduct and character that they should ever seem to us somehow to cut less deep. Scarce—to quote again his best biographer—had Musset, at Venice, begun to recover from his illness than the two lovers were seized afresh by *le vertige du sublime et de l'impossible*. "Ils imaginèrent les déviations de sentiment les plus bizarres, et leur intérieur fut le théâtre de scènes qui égalaient en étrangeté les fantaisies les plus audacieuses de la littérature contemporaine;" that is of the literature of their own day. The register of virtue contains no such lively items—save indeed in so far as these contortions and convulsions were a conscious tribute to virtue.

Ten weeks after Musset has left her in Venice his relinquished but not dissevered mistress writes to him in Paris: "God keep you, my friend, in your present disposition of heart and mind. Love is a temple built by the lover to an object more or less worthy of his worship, and what is grand

in the thing is not so much the god as the altar. Why should
you be afraid of the risk?"—of a new mistress she means.
There would seem to be reasons enough why he should have
been afraid, but nothing is more characteristic than her eagerness to push him into the arms of another woman—more
characteristic either of her whole philosophy in these matters
or of their tremendous, though somewhat conflicting, effort
to be good. She is to be good by showing herself so superior
to jealousy as to stir up in him a new appetite for a new
object, and he is to be so by satisfying it to the full. It appears
not to occur to either one that in such an arrangement his
own honesty is rather sacrificed. Or is it indeed because he
has scruples—or even a sense of humour—that she insists
with such ingenuity and such eloquence? "Let the idol stand
long or let it soon break, you will in either case have built a
beautiful shrine. Your soul will have lived in it, have filled it
with divine incense, and a soul like yours must produce great
works. The god will change perhaps, the temple will last as
long as yourself." "Perhaps," under the circumstances, was
charming. The letter goes on with the ample flow that was
always at the author's command—an ease of suggestion and
generosity, of beautiful melancholy acceptance, in which we
foresee, on her own horizon, the dawn of new suns. Her simplifications are delightful—they remained so to the end; her
touch is a wondrous sleight-of-hand. The whole of this letter
in short is a splendid utterance and a masterpiece of the shade
of sympathy, not perhaps the clearest, which consists of wishing another to feel as you feel yourself. To feel as George
Sand felt, however, one had to be, like George Sand, of the
true male inwardness; which poor Musset was far from being.
This, we surmise, was the case with most of her lovers, and
the truth that makes the idea of her *liaison* with Mérimée,
who *was* of a consistent virility, sound almost like a union
against nature. She repeats to her correspondent, on grounds
admirably stated, the injunction that he is to give himself up,
to let himself go, to take his chance. That he took it we all
know—he followed her advice only too well. It is indeed not
long before his manner of doing so draws from her a cry of
distress. "Ta conduite est déplorable, impossible. Mon Dieu,
à quelle vie vais-je te laisser? l'ivresse, le vin, les filles, et en-

core et toujours!" But apprehensions were now too late; they would have been too late at the very earliest stage of this celebrated connection.

III

The great difficulty was that, though they were sublime, the couple were really not serious. But on the other hand if on a lady's part in such a relation the want of sincerity or of constancy is a grave reproach the matter is a good deal modified when the lady, as I have mentioned, happens to be—I may not go so far as to say a gentleman. That George Sand just fell short of this character was the greatest difficulty of all; because if a woman, in a love affair, may be—for all she is to gain or to lose—what she likes, there is only one thing that, to carry it off with any degree of credit, a man may be. Madame Sand forgot this on the day she published "Elle et Lui"; she forgot it again more gravely when she bequeathed to the great snickering public these present shreds and relics of unutterably personal things. The aberration refers itself to the strange lapses of still other occasions—notably to the extraordinary absence of scruples with which she in the delightful "Histoire de ma Vie" gives away, as we say, the character of her remarkable mother. The picture is admirable for vividness, for breadth of touch; it would be perfect from any hand not a daughter's, and we ask ourselves wonderingly how through all the years, to make her capable of it, a long perversion must have worked and the filial fibre—or rather the general flower of sensibility—have been battered. Not this particular anomaly, however, but many another, yields to the reflection that as just after her death a very perceptive person who had known her well put it to the author of these remarks, she was a woman quite by accident. Her immense plausibility was almost the only sign of her sex. She needed always to prove that she had been in the right; as how indeed could a person fail to who, thanks to the special equipment I have named, might prove it so brilliantly? It is not too much to say of her gift of expression—and I have already in effect said so—that from beginning to end it floated her over the

real as a high tide floats a ship over the bar. She was never
left awkwardly straddling on the sandbank of fact.

For the rest, in any case, with her free experience and her
free use of it, her literary style, her love of ideas and questions, of science and philosophy, her comradeship, her
boundless tolerance, her intellectual patience, her personal
good-humour and perpetual tobacco (she smoked long before
women at large felt the cruel obligation), with all these things
and many I don't mention she had more of the inward and
outward of the other sex than of her own. She had above all
the mark that, to speak at this time of day with a freedom for
which her action in the matter of publicity gives us warrant,
the history of her personal passions reads singularly like a
chronicle of the ravages of some male celebrity. Her relations
with men closely resembled those relations with women that,
from the age of Pericles or that of Petrarch, have been complacently commemorated as stages in the unfolding of the
great statesman and the great poet. It is very much the same
large list, the same story of free appropriation and consumption. She appeared in short to have lived through a succession
of such ties exactly in the manner of a Goethe, a Byron or a
Napoleon; and if millions of women, of course, of every condition, had had more lovers, it was probable that no woman
independently so occupied and so diligent had had, as might
be said, more unions. Her fashion was quite her own of extracting from this sort of experience all that it had to give her
and being withal only the more just and bright and true, the
more sane and superior, improved and improving. She strikes
us as in the benignity of such an intercourse even more than
maternal: not so much the mere fond mother as the supersen-
suous grandmother of the wonderful affair. Is not that practically the character in which Thérèse Jacques studies to
present herself to Laurent de Fauvel? the light in which "Lucrezia Floriani" (a memento of a friendship for Chopin, for
Liszt) shows the heroine as affected toward Prince Karol and
his friend? George Sand is too inveterately moral, too preoccupied with that need to do good which is in art often the
enemy of doing well; but in all her work the story-part, as
children call it, has the freshness and good faith of a monastic
legend. It is just possible indeed that the moral idea was the

real mainspring of her course—I mean a sense of the duty of avenging on the unscrupulous race of men their immemorial selfish success with the plastic race of women. Did she wish above all to turn the tables—to show how the sex that had always ground the other in the volitional mill was on occasion capable of being ground?

However this may be, nothing is more striking than the inward impunity with which she gave herself to conditions that are usually held to denote or to involve a state of demoralisation. This impunity (to speak only of consequences or features that concern us) was not, I admit, complete, but it was sufficiently so to warrant us in saying that no one was ever less demoralised. She presents a case prodigiously discouraging to the usual view—the view that there is no surrender to "unconsecrated" passion that we escape paying for in one way or another. It is frankly difficult to see where this eminent woman conspicuously paid. She positively got off from paying—and in a cloud of fluency and dignity, benevolence, competence, intelligence. She sacrificed, it is true, a handful of minor coin—suffered by failing wholly to grasp in her picture of life certain shades and certain delicacies. What she paid was this irrecoverable loss of her touch for them. That is undoubtedly one of the reasons why to-day the picture in question has perceptibly faded, why there are persons who would perhaps even go so far as to say that it has really a comic side. She doesn't know, according to such persons, her right hand from her left, the crooked from the straight and the clean from the unclean: it was a sense she lacked or a tact she had rubbed off, and her great work is by the fatal twist quite as lopsided a monument as the leaning tower of Pisa. Some readers may charge her with a graver confusion still—the incapacity to distinguish between fiction and fact, the truth straight from the well and the truth curling in steam from the kettle and preparing the comfortable tea. There is no word oftener on her pen, they will remind us, than the verb to "arrange." She arranged constantly, she arranged beautifully; but from this point of view, that of a general suspicion of arrangements, she always proved too much. Turned over in the light of it the story of "Elle et Lui" for instance is an attempt to prove that the mistress of Laurent de Fauvel was little less than a prodigy of virtue. What is there not, the intemperate admirer may be challenged to tell us, an attempt to prove in "L'Histoire de ma Vie"?—a work from which we gather every delightful impression but the impression of an impeccable veracity.

These reservations may, however, all be sufficiently just without affecting our author's peculiar air of having eaten her cake and had it, been equally initiated in directions the most opposed. Of how much cake she partook the letters to Musset and Sainte-Beuve well show us, and yet they fall in at the same time, on other sides, with all that was noble in her mind, all that is beautiful in the books just mentioned and in the six volumes of the general "Correspondance: 1812–1876," out of which Madame Sand comes so immensely to her advantage. She had, as liberty, all the adventures of which the dots are so put on the i's by the documents lately published, and then she had, as law, as honour and serenity, all her fine reflections on them and all her splendid busy literary use of them. Nothing perhaps gives more relief to her masculine stamp than the rare art and success with which she cultivated an equilibrium. She made from beginning to end a masterly study of composure, absolutely refusing to be upset, closing her door at last against the very approach of irritation and surprise. She had arrived at her quiet elastic synthesis—a good-humour, an indulgence that were an armour of proof. The great felicity of all this was that it was neither indifference nor renunciation, but on the contrary an intense partaking; imagination, affection, sympathy and life, the way she had found for herself of living most and living longest. However well it all agreed with her happiness and her manners, it agrees still better with her style, as to which we come back with her to the sense that this was really her *point d'appui* or sustaining force. Most people have to say, especially about themselves, only what they can; but she said— and we nowhere see it better than in the letters to Musset— everything in life that she wanted. We can well imagine the effect of that consciousness on the nerves of this particular correspondent, his own poor gift of occasional song (to be so early spent) reduced to nothing by so unequalled a command of the last word. We feel it, I hasten to add, this last word, in all her letters: the occasion, no matter which, gathers it from her as the breeze gathers the scent from the garden. It is always the last word of sympathy and sense, and we meet it on every page of the voluminous "Correspondance." These pages are not so "clever" as those, in the same order, of some other famous hands—the writer always denied, justly enough, that she had either wit or presence of mind—and they are not a product of high spirits or of a marked avidity for gossip. But they have admirable ease, breadth and generosity; they are the clear quiet overflow of a very full cup. They speak above all for the author's great gift, her eye for the inward drama. Her hand is always on the fiddle-string, her ear is always at the heart. It was in the soul, in a word, that she saw the drama begin, and to the soul that, after whatever outward flourishes, she saw it confidently come back. She herself lived with all her perceptions and in all her chambers—not merely in the showroom of the shop. This brings us once more to the question of the instrument and the tone, and to our idea that the tone, when you are so lucky as to possess it, may be of itself a solution.

By a solution I mean a secret for saving not only your reputation but your life—that of your soul; an antidote to dangers which the unendowed can hope to escape by no process less uncomfortable or less inglorious than that of prudence and precautions. The unendowed must go round about, the others may go straight through the wood. Their weaknesses, those of the others, shall be as well redeemed as their books shall be well preserved; it may almost indeed be said that they are made wise in spite of themselves. If you have never in all your days *had* a weakness worth mentioning, you can be after all no more, at the very most, than large and cheerful and imperturbable. All these things Madame Sand managed to be on just the terms she had found, as we see, most convenient. So much, I repeat, does there appear to be in a tone. But if the perfect possession of one made her, as it well might, an optimist, the action of it is perhaps more consistently happy in her letters and her personal records than in her "creative" work. Her novels to-day have turned rather pale and faint, as if the image projected—not intense, not absolutely concrete—failed to reach completely the mind's eye. And the odd point is that the wonderful charm of expression is not really a remedy for this lack of intensity, but rather an aggravation of it through a sort of suffusion of the whole thing by the voice and speech of the author. These things set the subject, whatever it be, afloat in the upper air, where it takes a happy bath of brightness and vagueness or swims like a soap-bubble kept up by blowing. This is no drawback when she is on the ground of her own life, to which she is tied by a certain number of tangible threads; but to embark on one of her confessed fictions is to have—after all that has come and gone, in our time, in the trick of persuasion—a little too much the feeling of going up in a balloon. We are borne by a fresh cool current and the car delightfully dangles; but as we peep over the sides we see things—as we usually know them—at a dreadful drop beneath. Or perhaps a better way to express the sensation is to say what I have just been struck with in the re-perusal of "Elle et Lui"; namely that this book, like others by the same hand, affects the reader—and the impression is of the oddest—not as a first but as a second echo or edition of the immediate real, or in other words of the subject. The tale may in this particular be taken as typical of the author's manner; beautifully told, but told, as if on a last remove from the facts, by some one repeating what he has read or what he has had from another and thereby inevitably becoming more general and superficial, missing or forgetting the "hard" parts and slurring them over and making them up. Of everything but feelings the presentation is dim. We recognise that we shall never know the original narrator and that the actual introducer is the only one we can deal with. But we sigh perhaps as we reflect that we may never confront her with her own informant.

To that, however, we must resign ourselves; for I remember in time that the volume from which I take occasion to speak with this levity is the work that I began by pronouncing a precious illustration. With the aid of the disclosures of the Revue de Paris it was, as I hinted, to show us that no mistakes and no pains are too great to be, in the air of art, triumphantly convertible. Has it really performed this function? I thumb again my copy of the limp little novel and wonder what, alas, I shall reply. The case is extreme, for it was the case of a suggestive experience particularly dire, and the literary flower that has bloomed upon it is not quite the full-blown rose. "Oeuvre de rancune" Arvède Barine pronounces it, and if we take it as that we admit that the artist's distinctness from her material was not ideally complete. Shall I not better the question by saying that it strikes me less as a work of rancour than—in a peculiar degree—as a work of egotism? It becomes in that light at any rate a sufficiently happy affirmation of the author's infallible form. This form was never a more successful vehicle for the conveyance of sweet reasonableness. It is all superlatively calm and clear; there never was a kinder, balmier last word. Whatever the measure of justice of the particular representation, moreover, the picture has only to be put beside the recent documents, the "study," as I may call them, to illustrate the general phenomenon. Even if "Elle et Lui" is not the full-blown rose we have enough here to place in due relief an irrepressible tendency to bloom. In fact I seem already to discern that tendency in the very midst of the storm; the "tone" in the letters too has its own way and performs on its own account—which is but another manner of saying that the literary instinct, in the worst shipwreck, is never out of its depth. The worker observed at the fire by Mérimée could be drowned but in an ocean of ink. Is that a sufficient account of what I have called the laying bare of the relation between experience and art? With the two elements, the life and the genius, face to face— the smutches and quarrels at one end of the chain and the high luminosity at the other—does some essential link still appear to be missing? How do the graceless facts after all confound themselves with the beautiful spirit? They do so, incontestably, before our eyes, and the mystification remains. We try to trace the process, but before we break down we had better perhaps hasten to grant that—so far at least as George Sand is concerned—some of its steps are impenetrable secrets of the grand manner.

Yellow Book, January 1897
Reprinted under the title "George Sand, 1897,"
in *Notes on Novelists*, 1914

GEORGE SAND: THE NEW LIFE

THOSE AMONG US comfortably conscious of our different usage—aware, some would say, of our better conscience—may well have remarked the general absence from French practice of biographic commemoration of extinct worthies. The Life as we understand it, the prompt pious spacious record and mirror of the eminent career, rarely follows the death. The ghost of the great man, when he happens to have been a Frenchman, "sits" for such portraiture, we gather, with a confidence much less assured than among ourselves, and with fewer relatives and friends to surround the chair. The manner in which even for persons of highest mark among our neighbours biography either almost endlessly hangs back or altogether fails, suggests that the approach is even when authorised too often difficult. This general attitude toward the question, it would thus appear, implies for such retrospects the predominance of doors bolted and barred. Hesitation is therefore fairly logical, for it rests on the assumption that men and women of great gifts will have lived with commensurate intensity, and that as regards some of the forms of this intensity the discretion of the inquirer may well be the better part of his enthusiasm. The critic can therefore only note with regret so much absent opportunity for the play of perception and the art of composition. The race that produced Balzac—to say nothing of Sainte-Beuve—would surely have produced a Boswell, a Lockhart and a Trevelyan if the fashion had not set so strongly against it. We have lately had a capital example of the encounter of an admirable English portraitist and an admirable English subject. It is not irrelevant to cite such a book as Mr. Mackail's "Life of William Morris" as our high-water mark—a reminder of how we may be blessed on both faces of the question. Each term of the combination appears supposable in France, but only as distinct from the other term. The artist, we gather, would there have lost his chance and the sitter his ease.

It completes in an interesting way these observations, which would bear much expansion, to perceive that when we at last have a Life of George Sand—a celebrity living with the imputed intensity, if ever a celebrity did—we are indebted for it to the hand of a stranger. No fact could more exactly point the moral of my few remarks. Madame Sand's genius and renown would have long ago made her a subject at home if alacrity in such a connection had been to be dreamed of. There is no more significant sign of the general ban under which alacrity rests. Everything about this extraordinary woman is interesting, and we can easily imagine the posthumous honours we ourselves would have hastened to assure to a part taken, in literature and life, with such brilliancy and sincerity. These demonstrations, where we should most look for them, have been none the less as naught—save indeed, to be exact, for the publication of a number of volumes of letters. It is just Madame Sand's letters, however—letters interesting and admirable, peculiarly qualified to dispose the reader in her favour—that in England or in America would have quickened the need for the rest of the evidence. But now that, as befalls, we do at last have the rest of the evidence as we never have had it before, we are of course sufficiently enlightened as to the reasons for a special application of the law of reserves and delays. It is not in fact easy to see how a full study of our heroine could have been produced earlier; and even at present there is a sensible comfort in its being produced at such a distance as practically assigns the act to a detached posterity. Contemporaneously it was wise to forbear; but to-day, and in Russia, by good luck, it is permitted to plunge.

Mme. Wladimir Karénine's extraordinarily diffuse, but scarcely less valuable, biography, of which the first instalment,[1] in two large volumes, brings the story but to the year 1838, reaches us in a French version, apparently from the author's own hand, of chapters patiently contributed to Russian periodicals. Were it not superficially ungrateful to begin with reserves about a book so rich and full, there might be some complaint to make of this wonderful tribute on grounds of form and taste. Ponderous and prolix, the author moves in a mass, escorted by all the penalties of her indifference to selection and compression. She insists and repeats, she wanders wide; her subject spreads about her, in places, as rather a pathless waste. Above all she has produced a book which manages to be at once remarkably expert and singularly provincial. Our innocence is perhaps at fault, but we are moved to take the mixture for characteristically Russian. Would in-

---

[1] "George Sand, sa Vie et ses Œuvres, 1804–1876." Paris, 1899.

deed any but that admirable "Slav" superiority to prejudice of which we have lately heard so much have availed to handle the particular facts in this large free way? Nothing is at all events more curious than the union, on the part of our biographer, of psychological intelligence and a lame esthetic. The writer's literary appreciations lag in other words half a century behind her human and social. She treats us to endless disquisitions on pages of her author to which we are no longer in any manageable relation at all—disquisitions pathetic, almost grotesque, in their misplaced good faith. But her attitude to her subject is admirable, her thoroughness exemplary, the spirit of service in her of the sort that builds the monument stone by stone. When we see it reared to the summit, as we are clearly to do, we shall feel the structure to be solid if not shapely. Nothing is more possible meanwhile than that a culture more homogeneous—a French hand or a German—could not have engaged in the work with anything like the same sincerity. An English hand—and the fact, for *our* culture, means much—would have been incapable of touching it. The present scale of it at all events is certainly an exotic misconception. But we can take of it what concerns us.

The whole thing of course, we promptly reflect, concerns at the best only those of us who can remount a little the stream of time. The author of "L'Histoire de ma Vie" died in 1876, and the light of actuality rests to-day on very different heads. It may seem to belittle her to say that to care for her at all one must have cared for her from far back, for such is not in general the proviso we need to make on behalf of the greatest figures. It describes Madame Sand with breadth, but not with extravagance, to speak of her as a sister to Goethe, and we feel that for Goethe it can never be too late to care. But the case exemplifies perhaps precisely the difference even in the most brilliant families between sisters and brothers. She was to have the family spirit, but she was to receive from the fairies who attended at her cradle the silver cup, not the gold. She was to write a hundred books but she was not to write "Faust." She was to have all the distinction but not all the perfection; and there could be no better instance of the degree in which a woman may achieve the one and still fail of the other. When it is a question of the rare originals who have either she confirms us, masculine as she is, in believing that it takes a still greater masculinity to have both. What she had, however, she had in profusion; she was one of the deepest voices of that great mid-century concert against the last fine strains of which we are more and more banging the doors. Her work, beautiful, plentiful and fluid, has floated itself out to sea even as the melting snows of the high places are floated. To feel how she has passed away as a "creator" is to feel anew the immense waste involved in the general ferment of an age, and how much genius and beauty, let alone the baser parts of the mixture, it takes to produce a moderate quantity of literature. Smaller people have conceivably ceased to count; but it is strange for a member of the generation immediately succeeding her own that she should have had the same fate as smaller people: all the more that such a mourner may be ruefully conscious of contributing not a little himself to the mishap. Does he still read, re-read, can he to-day at all deal with, this wonderful lady's novels? It only half cheers him up that on the occasion of such a publication as I here speak of he finds himself as much interested as ever.

The grounds of the interest are difficult to give—they presuppose so much of the old impression. If the old impression therefore requires some art to sustain and justify itself we must be content, so far as we are still under the charm, to pass, though only at the worst, for eccentric. The work, whether we still hold fast to it or not, has twenty qualities and would still have an immense one if it had only its style; but what I suppose it has paid for in the long-run is its want of plastic intensity. Does any work of representation, of imitation, live long that is predominantly loose? It may live in spite of looseness; but that, we make out, is only because closeness has somewhere, where it has most mattered, played a part. It is hard to say of George Sand's productions, I think, that they show closeness anywhere; the sense of that fluidity which is more than fluency is what, in speaking of them, constantly comes back to us, and the sense of fluidity is fundamentally fatal to the sense of particular truth. The thing presented by intention is never the stream of the artist's inspiration; it is the deposit of the stream. For the things presented by George Sand, for the general picture, we must look elsewhere, look at her life and her nature, and find them in the copious documents in which these matters and many others are now reflected. All *this* mass of evidence it is that constitutes the "intensity" we demand. The mass has little by little become large, and our obligation to Madame Karénine is that she makes it still larger. She sets our face, and without intending to, more and more in the right direction. Her injudicious analyses of forgotten fictions only confirm our discrimination. We feel ourselves in the presence of the extraordinary author of the hundred tales, and yet also feel it to be not by reason of them that she now presents herself as one of the most remarkable of human creatures. By reason then of what? Of everything that determined, accompanied, surrounded their appearance. They formed all together a great feature in a career and a character, but the career and the character are the real thing.

Such is far from usually the case, I hasten to recognise, with the complete and consistent artist. Poor is the art, a thing positively to be ashamed of, that, generally speaking, is not far more pressing for this servant of the altar than anything else, anything outside the church, can possibly be. To have been the tempered and directed hammer that makes the metal hard: if that be not good enough for such a ministrant, we may know him by whatever he has found better—we shall not know him by the great name. The immense anomaly in Madame Sand was that she freely took the form of being, with most zest, quite another sort of hammer. It testifies sufficiently to her large endowment that, given the wide range of the rest of her appetite, she should seem to us to-day to have sacrificed even superficially to *any* form of objective expression. She had in spite of herself an imagination almost of the first order, which overflowed and irrigated, turning by its mere swift current, without effort, almost without direction, every mill it encountered, and launching as it went alike the lightest skiff and the stateliest ship. She had in especial the gift of speech, speech supreme and inspired, to which we particularly owe the high value of the "case" she presents. For the case was definitely a bold and direct experiment, not at all in "art," not at all in literature, but conspicuously and repeatedly in the business of living; so that our profit of it is before anything else that it was conscious, articulate, vivid—recorded, reflected, imaged. The subject of the experiment became also at first hand the journalist—much of her work being simply splendid journalism—commissioned to bring it up to date. She interviewed nobody else, but she admirably interviewed herself, and this is exactly our good fortune. Her autobiography, her letters, her innumerable prefaces, all her expansive parentheses and excursions, make up the generous report. We have in this form accordingly a literary title for her far superseding any derived from her creative work. But that is the result of a mere betrayal, not the result of an intention. Her masterpiece, by a perversity of fate, is the thing she least sat down to. It consists—since she is a case—in the mere notation of her symptoms, in help given to the study of them. To this has the author of "Consuelo" come.

But how in the world indeed was the point so indicated *not* to be the particular cross-road at which the critic should lie in wait for a poor child of the age whom preceding ages and generations had almost infernally conspired to trap for him, to give up, candidly astray, to his hands? If the element of romance for which our heroine's name stands is best represented by her personal sequences and solutions, it is sufficiently visible that her heredity left her a scant alternative. Space fails me for the story of this heredity, queer and complicated, the very stuff that stories are made of—a chain of generations succeeding each other in confidence and joy and with no aid asked of legal or other artificial sanctions. The facts are, moreover, sufficiently familiar, though here as elsewhere Madame Karénine adds to our knowledge. Presented, foreshortened, stretching back from the quiet Nohant funeral of 1876 to the steps of the throne of King Augustus the Strong of Poland, father of Maurice de Saxe, great-great-grandfather of Aurore Dupin, it all hangs together as a cluster of components more provocative than any the great novelist herself ever handled. Her pre-natal past was so peopled with *dramatis personæ* that her future was really called on to supply them in such numbers as would preserve the balance. The tide of illegitimacy sets straight through the series. No one to speak of—Aurore's father is an exception—seems to have had a "regular" paternity. Aurore herself squared with regu-

larity but by a month or two; the marriage of her parents
gave her a bare escape. She was brought up by her paternal
grandmother between a son of her father and a daughter of
her mother born out of wedlock. It all moves before us as a
vivid younger world, a world on the whole more amused and
more amusing than ours. The period from the Restoration to
the events of 1848 is the stretch of time in which, for more
reasons than we can now go into, French life gives out to
those to whom its appeal never fails most of its charm—
most, at all events, of its ancient sociability. Happy is our
sense of the picturesque Paris unconscious of a future all "avenues" and exhibitions; happy our sense of these middle years
of a great generation, easy and lusty despite the ensanguined
spring that had gone before. They live again, piecing themselves ever so pleasantly and strangely together, in Madame
Sand's records and references; almost as much as the conscious close of the old régime so vaunted by Talleyrand they
strike us as a season it would have been indispensable to
know for the measure of what intercourse could richly be.

The time was at any rate unable to withhold from the wonderful young person growing up at Nohant the conditions
she was so freely to use as measures of her own. Though the
motto of her autobiography is *Wahrheit und Dichtung* quite
as much as it had been that of Goethe's, there is a truth beyond any projected by her more regular compositions in her
evocation of the influences of her youth. Upon these influences Madame Karénine, who has enjoyed access through her
heroine's actual representatives to much evidence hitherto unpublished, throws a hundred interesting lights. Madame Dupin de Francueil and Madame Dupin the younger survive and
perform for us, "convince" us as we say, better than any Lélia
or any Consuelo. Our author's whole treatment of her remarkable mother's figure and history conveniently gives the
critic the pitch of the great fact about her—the formation
apparently at a given moment, yet in very truth, we may be
sure, from far back, of the capacity and the determination to
live with high consistency for herself. What she made of this
resolve to allow her nature all its chances and how she carried
on the process—these things are, thanks to the immense illustration her genius enabled her to lend them, the essence of

her story; of which the full adumbration is in the detached pictorial way she causes her mother to live for us. Motherhood, daughterhood, childhood, embarrassed maturity, were phenomena she early encountered in her great adventure, and nothing is more typical of her energy and sincerity than the short work we can scarce help feeling she makes of them. It is not that she for a moment blinks or dodges them; she weaves them straight in—embarks with them indeed as her principal baggage. We know to-day from the pages before us everything we need to know about her marriage and the troubled years that followed; about M. Casimir Dudevant and his possible points of view, about her separation, her sharp secession, rather, as it first presents itself, and her discovery, at a turn of the road as it can only be called, of her genius.

She stumbled on this principle, we see, quite by accident and as a consequence of the attempt to do the very humblest labour, to support herself from day to day. It would be difficult to put one's finger more exactly upon a case of genius unaided and unprompted. She embarked, as I have called it, on her great voyage with no grounds of confidence whatever; she had obscurely, unwittingly the spirit of Columbus, but not so much even as his exiguous outfit. She found her gift of improvisation, found her tropic wealth, by leaping—a surprised *conquistador* of "style"—straight upon the coral strand. No awakened instinct, probably, was ever such a blessing to a writer so much in need. This instinct was for a long time all her initiation, practically all her equipment. The curious thing is that she never really arrived at the fruit of it as the result of a process, but that she started with the whole thing as a Patti or a Mario starts with a voice which *is* a method, which *is* music, and that it was simply the train in which she travelled. It was to render her as great a service as any supreme faculty ever rendered its possessor, quite the same service as the strategic eye renders a commander in the field or instant courage the attacking soldier: it was to carry her through life still more inimitably than through the career of authorship. Her books are all rich and resonant with it, but they profit by it meagrely compared with her character. She walks from first to last in music, that is in literary harmonies, of her own making, and it is in truth sometimes only, with her present biographer to elbow us a little the way, that these triumphant sounds permit us a near enough approach to the procession to make out quite exactly its course.

No part of her career is to my sense so curious as this particular sudden bound into the arena. Nothing but the indescribable heredity I have spoken of appears traceably to have prepared it. We have on one side the mere poverty and provinciality of her marriage and her early contacts, the crudity of her youth and her ignorance (which included so small a view of herself that she had begun by looking for a future in the bedaubing, for fancy-shops, of little boxes and fans); and on the other, at a stride, the full-blown distinction of "Valentine" and "Jacques," which had had nothing to lead up to it, we seem to make out, but the very rough sketch of a love-affair with M. Jules Sandeau. I spoke just now of the possible points of view of poor M. Dudevant; at which, had we space, it might be of no small amusement to glance—of an amusement indeed large and suggestive. We see him, surely, in the light of these records, as the most "sold" husband in literature, and not at all, one feels, by his wife's assertion of her freedom, but simply by her assertion of her mind. He appears to have married her for a nobody approved and guaranteed, and he found her, on his hands, a sister, as we have seen, of Goethe—unless it be but a figure to say that he ever "found" her anything. He appears to have lived to an advanced age without having really—in spite of the lawsuits he lost—comprehended his case; not the least singular feature of which had in fact positively been the deceptive delay of his fate. It was not till after several years of false calm that it presented itself in its special form. We see him and his so ruthlessly superseded name, never to be gilded by the brilliant event, we see him reduced, like a leaf in a whirlwind, to a mere vanishing-point.

We deal here, I think, with something very different from the usual tittle-tattle about "private" relations, for the simple reason that we deal with relations foredoomed to publicity by the strange economy involved in the play of genius itself. Nothing was ever less wasted, from beginning to end, than all this amorous experience and all this luxury of woe. The parties to it were to make an inveterate use of it, the principal party most of all; and what therefore on that marked ground concerns the critic is to see what they were appreciably to get out of it. The principal party, the constant one through all mutations, was alone qualified to produce the extract that affects us as final. It was by the publication four years since of her letters to Alfred de Musset and to Sainte-Beuve, by the appearance also of Madame Arvède Barine's clear compact biography of Musset, that we began to find her personal history brought nearer to us than her own communications had in her lifetime already brought it. The story of her relations with Musset is accordingly so known that I need only glance at the fact of her having—shortly after the highest degree of intimacy between them had, in the summer of 1833, established itself in Paris—travelled with him to Italy, settled with him briefly in Venice, and there passionately quarrelled and parted with him—only, however, several months later, on their return to France, to renew again, to quarrel and to part again, all more passionately, if possible, even than before. Madame Karénine, besides supplying us with all added light on this episode, keeps us abreast of others that were to follow, leaves us no more in the dark about Michel de Bourges, Félicien Mallefille and Chopin than we had already been left about their several predecessors. She is commendably lucid on the subject of Franz Liszt, impartially examines the case and authoritatively dismisses it. Her second volume brings her heroine to the eve of the historic departure with Chopin for Majorca. We have thus in a convenient form enough for one mouthful of entertainment, as well as for superabundant reflection.

We have indeed the whole essence of what most touches us, for this consists not at all of the quantity of the facts, nor even of their oddity: they are practically all there from the moment the heroine's general attitude defines itself. That is the solid element—the details to-day are smoke. Yet I hasten to add that it was in particular by taking her place of an autumn evening in the southward-moving diligence with Alfred de Musset, it was on this special occasion that she gave most the measure of her choice of the consistent, even though it so little meant the consequent, life. She had reached toward such a life obviously in quitting the conjugal roof in 1831—had attacked the experiment clumsily, but according to her light, by throwing herself on such material support as faculties yet untested might furnish, and on such moral as several months of the *intimité* of Jules Sandeau and a briefer taste of that of Prosper Mérimée might further contribute. She had done, in other words, what she could; subsequent lights show it as not her fault that she had not done better. With Musset her future took a long stride; emotionally speaking it "looked up." Nothing was wanting in this case—independently of what might then have appeared her friend's equal genius—quite ideally to qualify it. He was several years her junior, and as she had her husband and her children, he had, in the high degree of most young Frenchmen of sensibility, his mother. It is recorded that with this lady on the eve of the celebrated step she quite had the situation, as the phrase is, out; which is a note the more in the general, the intellectual lucidity. The only other note in fact to be added is that of the absence of funds for the undertaking. Neither partner had a penny to spare; the plan was wholly to "make money," on a scale, as they went. A great deal was in the event, exactly speaking, to be made—but the event was at the time far from clear to them. The enterprise was in consequence purely and simply, with a rounded perfection that gives it its value for the critic, an affair of the heart. That the heart, taking it as a fully representative organ, should fail of no good occasion completely and consistently to engage itself was the definite and, as appeared, the promising assumption on which everything rested. The heart was real life, frank, fearless, intelligent and even, so far as might be, intelligible life; everything else was stupid as well as poor, muddle as well as misery. The heart of course might be misery, for nothing was more possible than that life predominantly was; but it was at all events the misery that is least ignoble.

This was the basis of Madame Sand's personal evolution, of her immense moral energy, for many a year; it was a practical system, applied and reapplied, and no "inquiry" concerning her has much point save as settling what, for our enlightenment and our esteem, she made of it. The answer meets us, I think, after we have taken in the facts, promptly enough and with great clearness, so long as we consider that it is not, that it cannot be in the conditions, a simple one. She made of it then intellectually a splendid living, but she was able to do this only because she was an altogether exceptional example of our human stuff. It is here that her famous heredity comes in: we see what a race-accumulation of "toughness" had been required to build her up. Monstrous monarchs and bastards of kings, great generals and bastards of bastards, courtesans, dancers supple and hard, accomplished men and women of the old dead great world, seasoned young soldiers of the Imperial epic, grisettes of the *pavé de Paris*, Parisian to the core; the mixture was not quite the blood of people in general, and obviously such a final flower of such a stem might well fix the attention and appeal to the vigilance of those qualified to watch its development. These persons would, doubtless, however, as a result of their observation, have acquired betimes a sense of the high vitality of their young friend. Formed essentially for independence and constructed for resistance and survival she was to be trusted, as I have hinted, to take care of herself: this was always the residuary fact when a passion was spent. She took care of Musset, she took care of Chopin, took care, in short, through her career, of a whole series of nurslings, but never failed, under the worst ingratitude, to be by her own elasticity still better taken care of. This is why we call her anomalous and deprecate any view of her success that loses sight of the anomaly. The success was so great that but *for* the remainder she would be too encouraging. She was one in a myriad, and the cluster of circumstances is too unlikely to recur.

It is by her success, none the less, we must also remember, that we know her; it is this that makes her interesting and calls for study. She had all the illumination that sensibility, that curiosity, can give, and that so ingeniously induces surrender to it; but the too numerous weaknesses, vulgarities and penalties of adventure and surrender she had only in sufficient degree to complete the experience before they shaped themselves into the eloquence into which she could always reascend. Her eloquence—it is the simplest way to explain her—fairly *made* her success; and eloquence is superlatively rare. When passion can always depend upon it to vibrate passion becomes to that extent action, and success is nothing but action repeated and confirmed. In Madame Sand's particular case the constant recurrence of the malady of passion promoted in the most extraordinary way the superior appearance, the general expression, of health. It is of course not to be denied that there are in her work infirmities and disfigurements, odd smutches even, or unwitting drolleries, which show a sense on some sides enfeebled. The sense of her characters themselves for instance is constantly a confused one; they are too often at sea as to what is possible and what impossible for what we roughly call decent people. Her own categories, loose and liberal, are yet ever positive enough; when they err it is by excess of indulgence and by absence of the humorous vision, a nose for the ridiculous—the fatal want, this last almost always, we are reminded, the heel of Achilles, in the sentimental, the romantic estimate. The general validity of her novels, at any rate, I leave impugned, and the feature I have just noted in them is but one of the points at which they fail of reality. I stick to the history of her personal experiment, as the now so numerous documents show it; for it is here, and here only, that her felicity is amusing and confounding; amusing by the quaintness of some of the facts exposed, and yet confounding by reason of the beauty mixed with them.

The "affair" with Musset for example has come to figure, thanks to the talent of both parties, as one of the great affairs in the history of letters; and yet on the near view of it now enjoyed we learn that it dragged out scarce more than a year. Even this measure indeed is excessive, so far as any measure serves amid so much that is incoherent. It supposed itself to have dropped for upwards of six months, during which another connection, another imperious heart-history, reigned in its stead. The enumeration of these trifles is not, I insist, futile; so that while we are about it we shall find an interest in being clear. The events of Venice, with those that immediately preceded and followed them, distinctly repay inspection as an epitome, taken together, of the usual process. They appear to contain, as well as an intensity all their own, the essence of all that of other occasions. The young poet and the young novelist met then, appear to have met for the first time, toward the end of June 1833, and to have become finally intimate in the month of August of that year. They started together for Italy at the beginning of the winter and were settled—if settled be not too odd a word to use—by the end of January in Venice. I neglect the question of Musset's serious illness there, though it is not the least salient part of the adventure, and observe simply that by the end of March he had started to return to Paris, while his friend, remaining behind, had yielded to a new affection. This new affection, the connection with Pietro Pagello, dates unmistakably from before Musset's departure; and, with the completion of "Jacques" and the composition of the beautiful "André," the wonderful "Léone-Léoni" and some of the most interesting of the "Lettres d'un Voyageur," constituted the main support of our heroine during the spring and early summer. By midsummer she had left Italy with Pagello, and they arrive in Paris on August 14th. This arrival marks immediately the term of their relations, which had by that time lasted some six or seven months. Pagello returned to Italy, and if they ever met again it was the merest of meetings and after long years.

In October, meanwhile, the connection with Musset was renewed, and renewed—this is the great point—because the sentiments still entertained by each (in spite of Pagello, in spite of everything) are stronger even than any awkwardness of which either might have been conscious. The whole business really is one in which we lose our measure alike of awkwardness and of grace. The situation is in the hands of comedy—or *would* be, I should rather say, were it not so distinctly predestined to fall, as I have noted, into those of the nobler form. It is prolonged till the following February, we make out, at furthest, and only after having been more than once in the interval threatened with violent extinction. It bequeaths us thus in a handful of dates a picture than which probably none other in the annals of "passion" was ever more suggestive. The passion is of the kind that is called "immortal"—and so called, wonderful to say, with infinite reason and justice. The poems, the letters, the diaries, the novels, the unextinguished accents and lingering echoes that commemorate it are among the treasures of the human imagination. The literature of the world is appreciably the richer for it. The noblest forms, in a word, on both sides, marked it for their own; it was born, according to the adage, with a silver spoon in its mouth. It was an affection in short transcendent and sublime, and yet the critic sees it come and go before he can positively turn round. The brief period of some seventeen or eighteen months not only affords it all its opportunity, but places comfortably in its lap a relation founded on the same elements and yet wholly distinct from it. Musset occupied in fact but two-thirds of his mistress's time. Pagello overlapped him because Pagello also appealed to the heart; but Pagello's appeal to the heart was disposed of as expeditiously. Musset, in the same way, succeeded Pagello at the voice of a similar appeal, and this claim, in its turn, was polished off in yet livelier fashion.

Liveliness is of course the tune of the "gay" career; it has always been supposed to relegate to comedy the things to which it puts its mark—so that as a series of sequences amenable mainly to satire the approximations I have made would fall neatly into place. The anomaly here, as on other occasions of the same sort depicted in Madame Karénine's volumes, is that the facts, as we are brought near to them, strike us as so out of relation to the beautiful tone. The effect and the achieved dignity are those of tragedy—tragedy rearranging, begetting afresh, in its own interest, all the elements of ecstasy and despair. How can it not be tragedy when this interest is just the interest, which I have touched on, of exemplary eloquence? There are lights in which the material, with its want of nobleness, want of temper, want even of manners, seems scarcely life at all, as the civilised conscience understands life; and yet it is as the most magnanimous of surrenders to life that the whole business is triumphantly reflected in the documents. It is not only that "La Nuit d'Octobre" is divine, that Madame Sand's letters are superb and that nothing can exceed, in particular, the high style of the passage that we now perceive Musset to have borrowed from one of them for insertion in "On ne Badine pas avec l'Amour"—to the extreme profit of the generation which was, for many years thereafter, to hear Delaunay exquisitely declaim it at the Théâtre Français; it is that, strange to say, almost the finest flower of the bouquet is the now-famous written "declaration" addressed to Pagello one evening by the lady. Musset was ill in bed; he was the attendant doctor; and while, watching and ignorant of French, he twirled his thumbs or dipped into a book, his patient's companion, on the other side of the table and with the lamp between them, dashed off (it took time) a specimen of her finest prose, which she then folded and handed to him, and which, for perusal more at leisure, he carried off in his pocket. It proved neither more nor less than one of the pontoon bridges which a force engaged in an active campaign holds itself ready at any time to throw across a river, and was in fact of its kind a stout and beautiful structure. It happily spanned at all events the gulf of a short acquaintance.

The incident bears a family resemblance to another which our biographer finds in her path in the year 1837. Having to chronicle the close of the relation with Michel de Bourges, from which again her heroine had so much to suffer, she has also to mention that this catastrophe was precipitated, to all appearance, by the contemporaneous dawn of an affection "plus douce, moins enthousiaste, moins âpre aussi, et j'espère plus durable." The object of this affection was none other than the young man then installed at Nohant as preceptor to Madame Sand's children—but as to whom in the event we ask ourselves what by this time her notion of measure or durability can have become. It is just this element that has positively least to do, we seem to make out, with "affection" as so practised. Affection in any sense worth speaking of *is* durability; and it is the repeated impermanence of those manifestations of it on behalf of which the high horse of "passion" is ridden so hard that makes us wonder whether such loves and such licences, in spite of the quality of free experience they represent, had really anything to do with it. It was surely the last thing they contained. Félicien Mallefille may be, to his heart's content, of 1837 and even of a portion of 1838; it is Chopin who is of the rest of the year and—let us hope our biographer will have occasion to show us—of at least the whole of the following. It is here that, as I have mentioned, she pauses.

One of the most interesting contributions to her subject is the long letter from Balzac to his future wife, Madame Hanska, now reproduced in the most substantial of the few volumes of his correspondence ("Lettres à l'Étrangère, 1833–

1842," published 1899) and printed by Madame Karénine. The
author, finding himself near Nohant in the spring of 1838,
went over to pay his illustrious colleague a visit and spent
more than a day in sustained conversation with her. He had
the good fortune to find her alone, so that they could endlessly talk and smoke by the fire, and nothing can be all at
once more vivid, more curious and more judicious than his
immediate report of the occasion. It lets into the whole question of his hostess's character and relations—inevitably more
or less misrepresented by the party most involved—air and
light and truth; it fixes points and re-establishes proportions.
It shows appearances confronted, in a word, with Balzac's
strong sense of the real and offers the grateful critic still another chance to testify for that precious gift. This same critic's
mind, it must be added, rests with complacency on the vision
thus evoked, the way that for three days, from five o'clock in
the afternoon till five in the morning, the wonderful friends
must have had things out. For once, we feel sure, fundamental questions were not shirked. As regards his comrade at any
rate Balzac puts his finger again and again on the truth and
the idiosyncrasy. "She is not *aimable* and in consequence will
always find it difficult to be loved." He adds—and it is here
that he comes nearest straightening the question—that she
has in character all the leading marks of the man and as few
as possible those of his counterpart. He implies that, though
judged as a woman she may be puzzling enough, she hangs
together perfectly if judged as a man. She *is* a man, he repeats, "and all the more that she wants to be, that she has
sunk the woman, that she isn't one. Women attract, and she
repels; and, as I am much of a man, if this is the effect she
produces on me she must produce it on men who are like
me—so that she will always be unhappy." He qualifies as
justly, I may parenthesise, her artistic side, the limits of
which, he moreover intimates, she had herself expressed to
him. "She has neither intensity of conception, nor the constructive gift, nor the faculty of reaching the truth"—Balzac's
own deep dye of the truth—"nor the art of the pathetic. But
she holds that, without knowing the French language, she has
style. And it's true."

The light of mere evidence, the light of such researches as

Madame Karénine's, added to her so copious correspondence and autobiography, makes Madame Sand so much of a riddle that we grasp at Balzac's authoritative word as at an approach to a solution. It is, strange to say, by reading another complexity into her image that we finally simplify it. The riddle consists in the irreconcilability of her distinction and her vulgarity. Vulgar somehow in spite of everything is the record of so much taking and tasting and leaving, so much publicity and palpability of "heart," so much experience reduced only to the terms of so many more or less greasy males. And not only vulgar but in a manner grotesque—from the moment, that is, that the experience is presented to us with any emphasis in the name of terror and pity. It was not a passive but an active situation, that of a nature robust and not too fastidious, full at all times of resistance and recovery. No history gives us really more ground to protest against the new fashion, rife in France, of transporting "love," as there mainly represented, to the air of morals and of melancholy. The fashion betrays only the need to rejuvenate, at a considerable cost of falsity, an element in connection with which levity is felt either to have exhausted itself or to look thin as a motive. It is in the light of levity that many of the facts presented by Madame Karénine are most intelligible, and that is the circumstance awkward for sensibility and for all the graces it is invited to show.

The scene quite changes when we cease to expect these graces. As a man Madame Sand was admirable—especially as a man of the dressing-gown and slippers order, easy of approach and of *tutoiement*, rubbing shoulders with queer company and not superstitiously haunted by the conception of the gentleman. There have been many men of genius, delightful, prodigal and even immortal, who squared but scantly with that conception, and it is a company to which our heroine is simply one of the most interesting of recruits. She has in it all her value and loses none of her charm. Above all she becomes in a manner comprehensible, as any frank Bohemian is comprehensible. We have only to imagine the Bohemian really endowed, the Bohemian, that is, both industrious and wise, to get almost all her formula. She keeps here and there a feminine streak—has at moments an excess of volubility and too great an insistence on having been in the right; but for the rest, as Balzac says, the character, confronted with the position, is an explanation. "Son mâle," he tells Madame Hanska, "était rare"—than which nothing could have been more natural. Yet for this masculine counterpart—so difficult to find—she ingenuously spent much of her early life in looking. That the search was a mistake is what constitutes, in all the business of which the Musset episode is the type, the only, the real melancholy, the real moral tragedy.

For all such mistakes, none the less, the whole lesson of the picture is precisely in the disconcerting success of her system. Everything was at the start against that presumption; but everything at the end was to indicate that she was not to have been defeated. Others might well have been, and the banks of the stream of her career are marked, not invisibly, with mouldering traces of the less lucky or the less buoyant; but her attitude as life went on was more and more that of showing how she profited of all things for wisdom and sympathy, for a general expertness and nobleness. These forces, all clarified to an admirable judgment, kept her to the last day serene and superior, and they are one of the reasons why the monument before us is felt not to be misplaced. There should always be a monument to those who have achieved a prodigy. What greater prodigy than to have bequeathed in such mixed elements, to have principally made up of them, the affirmation of an unprecedented intensity of life? For though this intensity was one that broke down in each proposed exhibition the general example remains, incongruously, almost the best we can cite. And all we can say is that this brings us back once more to the large manner, the exceptional energy and well-nigh monstrous vitality, of the individual concerned. Nothing is so absurd as a half-disguise, and Madame Sand's abiding value will probably be in her having given her sex, for its new evolution and transformation, the real standard and measure of change. This evolution and this transformation are all round us unmistakable; the change is in the air; women are turned more and more to looking at life as men look at it and to getting from it what men get. In this direction their aim has been as yet comparatively modest and their emulation low; the challenge they have hitherto picked up is but the challenge of the "average" male. The approximation of the extraordinary woman has been practically, in other words, to the ordinary man. George Sand's service is that she planted the flag much higher—her own approximation at least was to the extraordinary. She reached him, she surpassed him, and she showed how, with native dispositions, the thing could be done. So far as we have come these new records will live as the precious text-book of the business.

North American Review, April 1902
Reprinted under the title "George Sand, 1899"
in *Notes on Novelists*, 1914

George Sand: Sa Vie et ses Œuvres, vol. iii. (1838–1848). Par Wladimir Karénine. Paris: Plon, 1912.

It has much occurred to us, touching those further liberations of the subordinate sex which fill our ears just now with their multitudinous sound, that the promoters of the great cause make a good deal less than they might of one of their very first contentious "assets," if it may not indeed be looked at as quite the first; and thereby fail to pass about, to the general elation, a great vessel of truth. Is this because the life and example of George Sand are things unknown or obscure to the talkers and fighters of to-day—present and vivid as they were to those of the last mid-century, or because of some fear that to invoke victory in her name might, for particular, for even rueful reasons, not be altogether a safe course? It is difficult to account otherwise for the fact that so ample and embossed a shield, and one that shines too at last with a strong and settled lustre, is rather left hanging on the wall than seen to cover advances or ward off attacks in the fray. Certain it is that if a lapse of tradition appeared at one time to have left a little in the lurch the figure of the greatest of all women of letters, of Letters in truth most exactly, as we hold her surely to have been, that explanation should have begun to fail, some fourteen years ago, with the publication of the first volume of Madame Wladimir Karénine's biography, and even in spite of the fact that this singularly interesting work was not till a twelvemonth ago to arrive at the dignity of a third, which leaves it, for all its amplitude, still incomplete. The latest instalment, now before us, follows its predecessors after an interval that had alarmed us not a little for the proper consummation; and the story is even now carried but to the eve of the Revolution of 1848, after which its heroine (that of the Revolution, we may almost say, as well as of the narrative) was to have some twenty-seven years to live. Madame Karénine appears to be a Russian critic writing under a pseudonym; portions of her overbrimming study have appeared dispersedly, we gather, in Russian periodicals, but the harmonious French idiom, of which she is all-sufficient mistress, welds them effectively together, and the result may already be pronounced a commemorative monument of all but the first order. The first order in such attempts has for its sign a faculty of selection and synthesis, not to say a sense of composition and proportion, which neither the chronicler nor the critic in these too multiplied pages is able consistently to exhibit; though on the other hand they represent quite the high-water mark of patience and persistence, of the ideal biographic curiosity. They enjoy further the advantage of the documented state in a degree that was scarce to have been hoped for, every source of information that had remained in reserve—and these proved admirably numerous—having been opened to our inquirer by the confidence of the illustrious lady's two great-granddaughters, both alive at the time the work was begun. Add to this that there has grown up in France a copious George Sand literature, a vast body of illustrative odds and ends, relics and revelations, on which the would-be propagator of the last word is now free to draw—always with discrimination. Ideally, well-nigh overwhelmingly informed we may at present therefore hold ourselves; and were that state all that is in question for us nothing could exceed our advantage.

I

Just the beauty and the interest of the case are, however, that such a condition by no means exhausts our opportunity, since in no like connection could it be less said that to know most is most easily or most complacently to conclude. May we not decidedly feel the sense and the "lesson," the suggestive spread, of a career as a thing scarce really to be measured when the effect of more and more acquaintance with it is simply to make the bounds of appreciation recede? This is why the figure now shown us, blazed upon to the last intensity by the lamplight of investigation, and with the rank oil consumed in the process fairly filling the air, declines to let us off from an hour of that contemplation which yet involves discomfiture for us so long as certain lucidities on our own part, certain serenities of assurance, fail correspondingly to play up. We feel ourselves so outfaced, as it were; we somehow want in any such case to meet and match the assurances with which the subject himself or herself immitigably bristles, and are nevertheless by no means certain that our bringing up premature forces or trying to reply with lights of our own may not check the current of communication, practically without sense for us unless flowing at its fullest. At our biographer's rate of progress we shall still have much to wait for; but it can meanwhile not be said that we have not plenty to go on with. To this may be added that the stretch of "life," apart from the more concrete exhibition, already accounted for by our three volumes (if one may discriminate between "production" and life to a degree that is in this connection exceptionally questionable), represents to all appearance the most violently and variously agitated face of the career. The establishment of the Second Empire ushered in for Madame Sand, we seem in course of preparation to make out, the long period already more or less known to fame, that is to criticism, as the period of her great placidity, her more or less notorious appeasement; a string of afternoon hours as hazily golden as so many reigns of Antonines, when her genius had mastered the high art of acting without waste, when a happy play of inspiration had all the air, so far as our spectatorship went, of filling her large capacity and her beautiful form to the brim, and when the gathered fruit of what she had dauntlessly done and been heaped itself upon her table as a rich feast for memory and philosophy. So she came in for the enjoyment of all the *sagesse* her contemporaries (with only such exceptions as M. Paul de Musset and Madame Louise Colet and the few discordant pleaders for poor Chopin) finally rejoiced on their side to acclaim; the sum of her aspects "composing," arranging themselves in relation to each other, with a felicity that nothing could exceed and that swept with great glosses and justifications every aspect of the past. To few has it been given to "pay" so little, according to *our* superstition of payment, in proportion to such enormities of ostensibly buying or borrowing—which fact, we have to recognise, left an existence as far removed either from moral, or intellectual, or even social bankruptcy as if it had proceeded from the first but on the most saving lines.

That is what remains on the whole most inimitable in the picture—the impression it conveys of an art of life by which the rough sense of the homely adage that we may not both eat our cake and have it was to be signally falsified; this wondrous mistress of the matter strikes us so as having consumed *her* refreshment, her vital supply, to the last crumb, so far as the provision meant at least freedom and ease, and yet having ever found on the shelf the luxury in question undiminished. Superlatively interesting the idea of how this result was, how it *could* be, achieved—given the world as we on our side of the water mainly know it; and it is as meeting the mystery that the monument before us has doubtless most significance. We shall presently see, in the light of our renewed occasion, how the question is solved; yet we may as well at once say that this will have had for its conclusion to present our heroine—mainly figuring as a novelist of the romantic or sentimental order once pre-eminent but now of shrunken credit—simply as a supreme case of the successful practice of life itself. We have to distinguish for this induction after a fashion in which neither Madame Sand nor her historian has seemed at all positively concerned to distinguish; the indifference on the historian's part sufficiently indicated, we feel, by the complacency with which, to be thorough, she explores even the most thankless tracts of her author's fictional activity, telling the tales over as she comes to them on much the same scale on which she unfolds the situations otherwise documented. The writer of "Consuelo" and "Claudie" and a hundred other things is to this view a literary genius whose output, as our current term so gracefully has it, the exercise of an inordinate personal energy happens to mark; whereas the exercise of personal energy is for ourselves what most reflects the genius—

recorded though this again chances here to be through the inestimable fact of the possession of style. Of the action of that perfect, that only real preservative in face of other perils George Sand is a wondrous example; but her letters alone suffice to show it, and the style of her letters is no more than the breath of her nature, her so remarkable one, in which expression and aspiration were much the same function. That is what it is really to *have* style—when you set about performing the act of life. The forms taken by this latter impulse then cover everything; they serve for your adventures not less than they may serve at their most refined pitch for your Lélias and your Mauprats.

This means accordingly, we submit, that those of us who at the present hour "feel the change," as the phrase is, in the computation of the feminine range, with the fullest sense of what it may portend, shirk at once our opportunity and our obligation in not squeezing for its last drop of testimony such an exceptional body of illustration as we here possess. It has so much to say to any view—whether, in the light of old conventions, the brightest or the darkest—of what may either glitter or gloom in a conquest of every license by our contemporaries of the contending sex, that we scarce strain a point in judging it a provision of the watchful fates for this particular purpose and profit: its answers are so full to most of our uncertainties. It is to be noted of course that the creator of Lélia and of Mauprat was on the one hand a woman of an extraordinary gift and on the other a woman resignedly and triumphantly voteless—doing without that boon so beautifully, for free development and the acquisition and application of "rights," that we seem to see her sardonically smile, before our present tumults, as at a rumpus about nothing; as if women need set such preposterous machinery in motion for obtaining things which she had found it of the first facility, right and left, to stretch forth her hand and take. There it is that her precedent stands out—apparently to a blind generation; so that some little insistence on the method of her appropriations would seem to be peculiarly in place. It was a method that may be summed up indeed in a fairly simple, if comprehensive, statement: it consisted in her dealing with life exactly as if she had been a man—exactly not being too much

to say. Nature certainly had contributed on her behalf to this
success; it had given her a constitution and a temperament,
the kind of health, the kind of mind, the kind of courage, that
might most directly help—so that she had but to convert
these strong matters into the kind of experience. The writer
of these lines remembers how a distinguished and intimate
friend of her later years, who was a very great admirer, said
of her to him just after her death that her not having been
born a man seemed, when one knew her, but an awkward
accident: she had been to all intents and purposes so fine and
frank a specimen of the sex. This anomalous native turn, it
may be urged, can have no general application—women cannot be men by the mere trying or by calling themselves "as
good"; they must have been provided with what we have just
noted as the outfit. The force of George Sand's exhibition
consorts, we contend, none the less perfectly with the logic
of the consummation awaiting us, if a multitude of signs are
to be trusted, in a more or less near future: that effective repudiation of the *distinctive*, as to function and opportunity, as
to working and playing activity, for which the definite removal of immemorial disabilities is but another name. We are
in presence already of a practical shrinkage of the distinctive,
at the rapidest rate, and that it must shrink till nothing of it
worth mentioning be left, what is this but a war-cry (presenting itself also indeed as a plea for peace) with which our ears
are familiar? Unless the suppression of the distinctive, however, is to work to the prejudice, as we may fairly call it, of
men, drawing them over to the feminine type rather than
drawing women over to theirs—which is not what seems
most probable—the course of the business will be a virtual
undertaking on the part of the half of humanity acting ostensibly for the first time in freedom to annex the male identity,
that of the other half, so far as may be at all contrivable, to
its own cluster of elements. Individuals are in great world and
race movements negligible, and if that undertaking must inevitably appeal to different recruits with a differing cogency, its
really enlisting its army or becoming reflected, to a perfectly
conceivable vividness, in the mass, is all our demonstration
requires. At that point begins the revolution, the shift of the
emphasis from the idea of woman's weakness to the idea of

her strength—which is where the emphasis has lain, from far back, by his every tradition, on behalf of man; and George Sand's great value, as we say, is that she gives us the vision, gives us the particular case, of the shift achieved, displayed with every assurance and working with every success.

The answer of her life to the question of what an effective annexation of the male identity may amount to, amount to in favouring conditions certainly, but in conditions susceptible to the highest degree of encouragement and cultivation, leaves nothing to be desired for completeness. This is the moral of her tale, the beauty of what she does for us—that at no point whatever of her history or her character do their power thus to give satisfaction break down; so that what we in fact on the whole most recognise is not the extension she gives to the feminine nature, but the richness that she adds to the masculine. It is not simply that she could don a disguise that gaped at the seams, that she could figure as a man of the mere carnival or pantomime variety, but that she made so virile, so efficient and homogeneous a one. Admirable child of the old order as we find her, she was far from our late-coming theories and fevers—by the reason simply of her not being reduced to them; as to which nothing about her is more eloquent than her living at such ease with a conception of the main relevance of women that is viewed among ourselves as antiquated to "quaintness." She could afford the traditional and sentimental, the old romantic and historic theory of the function most natural to them, since she entertained it exactly as a man would. It is not that she fails again and again to represent her heroines as doing the most unconventional things—upon these they freely embark; but they never in the least do them for themselves, themselves as the "sex," they do them altogether for men. Nothing could well be more interesting thus than the extraordinary union of the pair of opposites in her philosophy of the relation of the sexes—than the manner in which her immense imagination, the imagination of a man for range and abundance, intervened in the whole matter for the benefit, absolutely, of the so-called stronger party, or to liberate her sisters up to the point at which men may most gain and least lose by the liberation. She read the relation essentially in the plural term—the relations, and her

last word about these was as far as possible from being that
they are of minor importance to women. Nothing in her view
could exceed their importance to women—it left every other
far behind it; and nothing that could make for authority in
her, no pitch of tone, no range of personal inquiry nor wealth
of experience, no acquaintance with the question that might
derive light from free and repeated adventure, but belonged
to the business of driving this argument home.

II

Madame Karénine's third volume is copiously devoted to
the period of her heroine's intimacy with Chopin and to the
events surrounding this agitated friendship, which largely fill
the ten years precedent to '48. Our author is on all this
ground overwhelmingly documented, and enlisted though
she is in the service of the more successful party to the association—in the sense of Madame Sand's having heartily outlived and survived, not to say professionally and brilliantly
"used," it—the great composer's side of the story receives her
conscientious attention. Curious and interesting in many
ways, these reflections of George Sand's middle life afford
above all the most pointed illustration of the turn of her personal genius, her aptitude for dealing with men, in the intimate relation, exactly after the fashion in which numberless
celebrated men have contributed to their reputation, not to
say crowned their claim to superiority, by dealing with
women. This being above all the note of her career, with its
vivid show of what such dealing could mean for play of mind,
for quickening of gift, for general experience and, as we say,
intellectual development, for determination of philosophic
bent and education of character and fertilisation of fancy, we
seem to catch the whole process in the fact, under the light
here supplied us, as we catch it nowhere else. It gives us in
this application endlessly much to consider—it is in itself so
replete and rounded a show; we at once recognise moreover
how comparatively little it matters that such works as "Lucrezia Floriani" and "Un Hiver à Majorque" should have proceeded from it, cast into the shade as these are, on our
biographer's evidence, by a picture of concomitant energies

still more attaching. It is not here by the force of her gift for rich improvisation, beautiful as this was, that the extraordinary woman holds us, but by the force of her ability to act herself out, given the astounding quantities concerned in this self. That energy too, we feel, was in a manner an improvisation—so closely allied somehow are both the currents, the flow of literary composition admirably instinctive and free, and the handling power, as we are constantly moved to call it, the flow of a splendid intelligence all the while at its fullest expressional ease, for the *actual* situations created by her, for whatever it might be that vitally confronted her. Of how to bring about, or at the least find one's self "in for," an inordinate number of situations, most of them of the last difficulty, and then deal with them on the spot, in the narrowest quarters as it were, with an eloquence and a plausibility that does them and one's own nature at once a sort of ideal justice, the demonstration here is the fullest—as of what it was further to have her unfailing verbal as well as her unfailing moral inspiration. What predicament could have been more of an hourly strain for instance, as we cannot but suppose, than her finding herself inevitably accompanied by her two children during the stay at Majorca made by Chopin in '38 under her protection? The victory of assurance and of the handling power strikes us as none the less never an instant in doubt, that being essentially but over the general *kind* of inconvenience or embarrassment involved for a mother and a friend in any real consistency of attempt to carry things off male fashion. We do not, it is true, see a man as a mother, any more than we easily see a woman as a gentleman —and least of all perhaps in either case as an awkwardly placed one; but we see Madame Sand as a sufficiently bustling, though rather a rough and ready, father, a father accepting his charge and doing the best possible under the circumstances; the truth being of course that the circumstances never *can* be, even at the worst, or still at the best, the best for parental fondness, so awkward for him as for a mother.

What call, again, upon every sort of presence of mind could have been livelier than the one made by the conditions attending and following the marriage of young Solange Dudevant to the sculptor Clésinger in 1846, when our heroine, summoned by the stress of events both to take responsible action and to rise to synthetic expression, in a situation, that is in presence of a series of demonstrations on her daughter's part, that we seem to find imaginable for a perfect dramatic adequacy only in that particular home circle, fairly surpassed herself by her capacity to "meet" everything, meet it much incommoded, yet undismayed, unabashed and unconfuted, and have on it all, to her great advantage, the always prodigious last word? The elements of this especial crisis claim the more attention through its having been, as a test of her powers, decidedly the most acute that she was in her whole course of life to have traversed, more acute even, because more complicated, than the great occasion of her rupture with Alfred de Musset, at Venice in '35, on which such a wealth of contemplation and of ink has been expended. Dramatic enough in their relation to each other certainly those immortal circumstances, immortal so far as immortalised on either side by genius and passion: Musset's return, ravaged and alone, to Paris; his companion's transfer of her favour to Pietro Pagello, whom she had called in to attend her friend medically in illness and whose intervention, so far from simplifying the juncture, complicated it in a fashion probably scarce paralleled in the history of the erotic relation; her retention of Pagello under her protection for the rest of her period in Venice; her marvellously domesticated state, in view of the literary baggage, the collection of social standards, even taking these but at what they were, and the general amplitude of personality, that she brought into residence with her; the conveyance of Pagello to Paris, on her own return, and the apparent signification to him at the very gate that her countenance was then and there withdrawn. This was a brilliant case for her—of coming off with flying colours; but it strikes us as a mere preliminary flourish of the bow or rough practice of scales compared to the high virtuosity which Madame Karénine's new material in respect to the latter imbroglio now enables us ever so gratefully to estimate. The protagonist's young children were in the Venetian crisis quite off the scene, and on occasions subsequent to the one we now glance at were old enough and, as we seem free to call it, initiated enough not to solicit our particular concern for them; whereas at the

climax of the connection with Chopin they were of the perfect age (which was the fresh marriageable in the case of Solange) to engage our best anxiety, let alone their being of a
salience of sensibility and temper to leave no one of their aspects negligible. That their parent should not have found herself conclusively "upset," sickened beyond repair, or otherwise
morally bankrupt, on her having to recognise in her daughter's hideous perversity and depravity, as we learn these
things to have been, certain inevitabilities of consequence
from the social air of the maternal circle, is really a monumental fact in respect to our great woman's elasticity, her instinct
for never abdicating by mere discouragement. Here in especial we get the broad male note—it being so exactly the
manly part, and so very questionably the womanly, not to
have to draw from such imputations of responsibility too
crushing a self-consciousness. Of the extent and variety of
danger to which the enjoyment of a moral tone could be exposed and yet superbly survive Madame Karénine's pages give
us the measure; they offer us in action the very ideal of an
exemplary triumph of character and mind over one of the
very highest tides of private embarrassment that it is well possible to conceive. And it is no case of that *passive* acceptance
of deplorable matters which has abounded in the history of
women, even distinguished ones, whether to the pathetic or
to the merely scandalous effect; the acceptance is active, constructive, almost exhilarated by the resources of affirmation
and argument that it has at its command. The whole instance
is sublime in its sort, thanks to the acuteness of *all* its illustrative sides, the intense interest of which loses nothing in the
hands of our chronicler; who perhaps, however, reaches off
into the vast vague of Chopin's native affiliations and references with an energy with which we find it a little difficult to
keep step.

In speaking as we have done of George Sand's "use" of
each twist of her road as it came—a use which we now recognise as the very thriftiest—we touch on that principle of
vital health in her which made nothing that might by the
common measure have been called one of the graver dilemmas, that is one of the checks to the continuity of life, really
matter. What this felicity most comes to in fact is that doing

at any cost the work that lies to one's hand shines out again and yet again as the saving secret of the soul. She affirmed her freedom right and left, but her most characteristic assertion of it throughout was just in the luxury of labour. The exhaustive account we at any rate now enjoy of the family life surrounding her during the years here treated of and as she had constituted it, the picture of all the queer conflicting sensibilities engaged, and of the endless ramifications and reflections provided for these, leaves us nothing to learn on that congested air, that obstructive medium for the range of the higher tone, which the lady of Nohant was so at her "objective" happiest, even if at her superficially, that is her nervously, most flurried and depressed, in bravely breasting. It is as if the conditions there and in Paris during these several years had been consistently appointed by fate to throw into relief the applications of a huge facility, a sort of universal readiness, with a rare intelligence to back it. Absolutely nothing was absent, or with all the data *could* have been, that might have bewildered a weaker genius into some lapse of eloquence or of industry; everything that might have overwhelmed, or at least have disconcerted, the worker who could throw off the splendid "Lucrezia Floriani" in the thick of battle came upon her at once, inspiring her to show that on her system of health and cheer, of experiential economy, as we may call it, to be disconcerted was to be lost. To be lacerated and calumniated was in comparison a trifle; with a certain sanity of reaction these things became as naught, for the sanity of reaction was but the line of consistency, the theory and attitude of sincerity kept at the highest point. The artist in general, we need scarcely remind ourselves, is in a high degree liable to arrive at the sense of what he may have seen or felt, or said or suffered, by working it out as a subject, casting it into some form prescribed by his art; but even here he in general knows limits—unless perchance he be loose as Byron was loose, or possess such a power of disconnection, such a clear stand-off of the intelligence, as accompanied the experiments of Goethe. Our own experiments, we commonly feel, are comparatively timid, just as we can scarce be said, in the homely phrase, to serve our esthetic results of them hot and hot; we are too conscious of a restrictive instinct about the conditions we may, in like familiar language, let ourselves in for, there being always the question of what we should be able "intellectually" to show for them. The life of the author of "Lucrezia Floriani" at its most active may fairly be described as an immunity from restrictive instincts more ably cultivated than any we know. Again and yet again we note the positive premium so put upon the surrender to sensibility, and how, since the latter was certain to spread to its maximum and to be admired in proportion to its spread, some surrender was always to have been worth while. "Lucrezia Floriani" ought to have been rather measurably bad—lucidity, harmony, maturity, definiteness of sense, being so likely to fail it in the troubled air in which it was born. Yet how can we do less than applaud a composition throwing off as it goes such a passage as the splendid group of pages cited by Madame Karénine from the incident of the heroine's causing herself to be rowed over to the island in her Italian lake on that summer afternoon when the sense of her situation had become sharp for her to anguish, in order to take stock of the same without interruption and see, as we should say to-day, where she is? The whole thing has the grand manner and the noblest eloquence, reaching out as it does on the spot to the lesson and the moral of the convulsions that have been prepared in the first instance with such complacency, and illustrating in perfection the author's faculty for the clear reemergence and the prompt or, as we may call it, the paying reaction. The case is put for her here as into its final nutshell: you may "live" exactly as you like, that is live in perfect security and fertility, when such breadth of rendering awaits your simply sitting down to it. Is it not true, we say, that without her breadth our wonderful woman would have been "nowhere"?—whereas with it she is effectively and indestructibly at any point of her field where she may care to pretend to stand.

This biographer, I must of course note, discriminates with delicacy among her heroine's felicities and mistakes, recognising that some of the former, as a latent awkwardness in them developed, inevitably parted with the signs that distinguished them from the latter; but I think we feel, as the instances multiply, that no regret could have equalled for us that of our not having the display vivid and complete. Once all the elements of the scarce in advance imaginable were there it would have been a pity that they should not offer us the show of their full fruition. What more striking show, for example, than that, as recorded by Madame Karénine in a footnote, the afflicted parent of Solange should have lived to reproduce, or rather, as she would herself have said, to "arrange" the girlish character and conduct of that young person, so humiliating at the time to any near relation, let alone a mother, in the novel of "Mademoiselle Merquem," where the truth to the original facts and the emulation of the graceless prime "effects" are such as our author can vouch for? The fiction we name followed indeed after long years, but during the lifetime of the displeasing daughter and with an ease of reference to the past that may fairly strike us as the last word of superiority to blighting association. It is quite as if the close and amused matching of the character and its play in the novel with the wretched old realities, those that had broken in their day upon the scared maternal vision, had been a work of ingenuity attended with no pang. The example is interesting as a measure of the possible victory of time in a case where we might have supposed the one escape to have been by forgetting. Madame Sand remembers to the point of gratefully—gratefully as an artist—reconstituting; we in fact feel her, as the irrepressible, the "healthy" artist, positively to enjoy so doing. Thus it clearly defined itself for her in the fulness of time that, humiliating, to use our expression, as the dreadful Solange might have been and have incessantly remained, she herself had never in the least consented to the stupidity or sterility of humiliation. So it could be that the free mind and the free hand were ever at her service. A beautiful indifferent agility, a power to cast out that was at least proportioned to the power to take in, hangs about all this and meets us in twenty connections. Who of her readers has forgotten the harmonious dedication—her inveterate dedications have always, like her clear light prefaces, the last grace—of "Jeanne," so anciently, so romantically readable, to her faithful Berrichon servant who sits spinning by the fire? "Vous ne savez pas lire, ma paisible amie," but that was not to prevent the association of her name with the book, since both her own daughter and the author's are in happy possession of the art and will be able to pass the entertainment on to her. This in itself is no more than a sign of the writer's fine democratic ease, which she carried at all times to all lengths, and of her charming habit of speech; but it somehow becomes further illustrational, testifying for the manner in which genius, if it be but great enough, lives its life at small cost, when we learn that after all, by a turn of the hand, the "paisible amie" was, under provocation, bundled out of the house as if the beautiful relation had not meant half of what appeared. Françoise and her presence were dispensed with, but the exquisite lines remain, which we would not be without for the world.

III

The various situations determined for the more eminent of George Sand's intimate associates would always be independently interesting, thanks to the intrinsic appeal of these characters and even without the light reflected withal on the great agent herself; which is why poor Chopin's figuration in the events of the year 1847, as Madame Karénine so fully reconstitutes them, is all that is wanted to point their almost nightmare quality. Without something of a close view of them we fail of a grasp of our heroine's genius—her genius for keeping her head in deep seas morally and reflectively above water, though but a glance at them must suffice us for averting this loss. The old-world quality of drama, which throughout so thickens and tones the air around her, finds remarkable expression in the whole picture of the moment. Every connection involved bristles like a conscious consequence, tells for all it is worth, as we say, and the sinister complexity of reference—for all the golden clearings-up that awaited it on the ideal plane—leaves nothing to be desired. The great and odd sign of the complications and convulsions, the alarms and excursions recorded, is that these are all the more or less direct fruits of sensibility, which had primarily been indulged in, under the doom of a preparation of them which no preparation of anything else was to emulate, with a good faith fairly touching in presence of the eventual ugliness. Madame Sand's wonderful mother, commemorated for us in "L'His-

toire de ma Vie" with the truth surely attaching in a like degree to no mother in all the literature of so-called confession,
had had for cousin a "fille entretenue" who had married a
mechanic. This Adèle Brault had had in the course of her
adventures a daughter in whom, as an unfortunate young relative, Madame Dupin had taken an interest, introducing her
to the heiress of Nohant, who viewed her with favour—she
appears to have been amiable and commendable—and eventually associated her with her own children. She was thus the
third member of that illegitimate progeny with which the Nohant scene was to have become familiar, George Sand's natural brother on her father's side and her natural sister on her
mother's representing this element from the earlier time on.
The young Augustine, fugitive from a circle still less edifying,
was thus made a companion of the son and the daughter of
the house, and was especially held to compare with the latter
to her great advantage in the matter of character, docility and
temper. These young persons formed, as it were, with his
more distinguished friend, the virtual family of Chopin during those years of specifically qualified domestication which
affect us as only less of a mystification to taste than that phase
of the unrestricted which had immediately preceded them.
Hence a tangled tissue of relations within the circle that became, as it strikes us, indescribable for difficulty and "delicacy," not to say for the perfection of their impracticability,
and as to which the great point is that Madame Sand's having
taken them so robustly for granted throws upon her temperamental genius a more direct light than any other. The whole
case belongs doubtless even more to the hapless history of
Chopin himself than to that of his terrible friend—terrible for
her power to flourish in conditions sooner or later fatal to
weaker vessels; but is in addition to this one of the most striking illustrations possible of that view or theory of social life
handed over to the reactions of sensibility almost alone
which, while ever so little the ideal of the Anglo-Saxon world,
has largely governed the manners of its sister societies. It has
been our view, very emphatically, in general, that the sane
and active social body—or, for that matter, the sane and active individual, addressed to the natural business of life—goes
wrongly about it to *encourage* sensibility, or to do anything

on the whole but treat it as of no prime importance; the traps it may lay for us, however, being really of the fewest in a race to which the very imagination of it may be said, I think, to have been comparatively denied. The imagination of it sat irremovably, on the other hand, and as a matter of course, at the Nohant fireside; where indeed we find the play and the ravage chiefly interesting through our thus seeing the delicate Chopin, whose semi-smothered appeal remains peculiarly pathetic, all helpless and foredoomed at the centre of the whirl. Nothing again strikes us more in the connection than the familiar truth that interesting persons make everything that concerns them interesting, or seldom fail to redeem from what might in another air seem but meanness and vanity even their most compromised states and their greatest wastes of value. Every one in the particular Nohant drama here exposed loses by the exposure—so far as loss could be predicated of amounts which, in general, excepting the said sensibility, were so scant among them; every one, that is, save the ruling spirit of all, with the extraordinary mark in her of the practical defiance of waste and of her inevitable enrichment, for our measure, as by reflection from the surrounding shrinkage. One of the oddest aspects of the scene is also one of the wretchedest, but the oddity makes it interesting, by the law I just glanced at, in spite of its vulgar side. How could it not be interesting, we ask as we read, to feel that Chopin, though far from the one man, was the one gentleman of the association, the finest set of nerves and scruples, and yet to see how little that availed him, in exasperated reactions, against mistakes of perverted sympathy? It is relevant in a high degree to our view of his great protectress as reducible at her best to male terms that she herself in this very light fell short, missed the ideal safeguard which for her friend had been preinvolved—as of course may be the peril, ever, with the creature so transmuted, and as is so strikingly exemplified, in the pages before us, when Madame Karénine ingenuously gives us chapter and verse for her heroine's so unqualified demolition of the person of Madame d'Agoult, devotee of Liszt, mother to be, by that token, of Richard Wagner's second wife, and sometime intimate of the author of "Isidora," in which fiction we are shown the parody perpetrated. If women rend each other on occasion with sharper talons than seem to belong on the whole to the male hand, however intendingly applied, we find ourselves reflect parenthetically that the loss of this advantage may well be a matter for them to consider when the new approximation is the issue.

The great sign of the Nohant circle on all this showing, at any rate, is the intense personalism, as we may call it, reigning there, or in other words the vivacity, the acuity and irritability of the personal relations—which flourished so largely, we at the same time feel, by reason of the general gift for expression, that gift to which we owe the general superiority of every letter, from it scarce matters whom, laid under contribution by our author. How could people not feel with acuity when they could, when they had to, write with such point and such specific intelligence?—just indeed as one asks how letters could fail to remain at such a level among them when they incessantly generated choice matter for expression. Madame Sand herself is of course on this ground easily the most admirable, as we have seen; but every one "knows how" to write, and does it well in proportion as the matter in hand most demands and most rewards proper saying. Much of all this stuff of history seems indeed to have been susceptible of any amount of force of statement; yet we note all the while how in the case of the great mistress of the pen at least some shade of intrinsic beauty attends even the presentation of quite abominable facts. We can only see it as abominable, at least, so long as we have Madame Sand's words—which are somehow a different thing from her word—for it, that Chopin had from the first "sided" with the atrocious Solange in that play of her genius which is characterised by our chronicler as wickedness for the sake of wickedness, as art for the sake of art, without other logic or other cause. "Once married," says Madame Karénine, "she made a double use of this wickedness. She had always hated Augustine; she wished, one doesn't know why, to break off her marriage, and by calumnies and insinuations she succeeded. Then angry with her mother she avenged herself on her as well by further calumnies. Thereupon took place at Nohant such events that"— that in fine we stop before them with this preliminary shudder. The cross-currents of violence among them would take more keeping apart than we have time for, the more that everything comes back, for interest, to the intrinsic weight of the tone of the principal sufferer from them—as we see her, as we wouldn't for the world not see her, in spite of the fact that Chopin was to succumb scarce more than a year later to multiplied lacerations, and that she was to override and reproduce and pre-appointedly flourish for long years after. If it is interesting, as I have pronounced it, that Chopin, again, should have consented to be of the opinion of Solange that the relations between her brother Maurice and the hapless Augustine were of the last impropriety, I fear I can account no better for this than by our sense that the more the *genius loci* has to feed her full tone the more our faith in it, as such a fine thing in itself, is justified. Almost immediately after the precipitated marriage of the daughter of the house has taken place, the Clésinger couple, avid and insolent, of a breadth of old time impudence in fact of which our paler day has lost the pattern, are back on the mother's hands, to the effect of a vividest picture of Maurice well-nigh in a death-grapple with his apparently quite monstrous "bounder" of a brother-in-law, a picture that further gives us Madame Sand herself smiting Clésinger in the face and receiving from him a blow in the breast, while Solange "coldly," with an iciness indeed peculiarly her own, fans the rage and approves her husband's assault, and while the divine composer, though for that moment much in the background, approves the wondrous approval. He still approves, to all appearance, the daughter's interpretation of the mother's wish to "get rid" of him as the result of an amorous design on the latter's part in respect of a young man lately introduced to the circle as Maurice's friend and for the intimate relation with whom it is thus desirable that the coast shall be made clear. How else than through no fewer consistencies of the unedifying on the part of these provokers of the expressional reaction should we have come by innumerable fine epistolary passages, passages constituting in themselves verily such adornments of the tale, such notes in the scale of all the damaged dignity redressed, that we should be morally the poorer without them? One of the vividest glimpses indeed is not in a letter but in a few lines from "L'Histoire de ma Vie," the composition of which was begun toward the end of this period and while its shadow still hung about—early in life for a projected autobiography, inasmuch as the author had not then reached her forty-fifth year. Chopin at work, improvising and composing, was apt to become a prey to doubts and depressions, so that there were times when to break in upon these was to render him a service.

> But it was not always possible to induce him to leave the piano, often so much more his torment than his joy, and he began gradually to resent my proposing he should do so. I never ventured on these occasions to insist. Chopin in displeasure was appalling, and as with me he always controlled himself it was as if he might die of suffocation.

It is a vision of the possibilities of vibration in such organisms that does in fact appal, and with the clash of vibrations, those both of genius and of the general less sanctioned sensibility, the air must have more than sufficiently resounded. Some eight years after the beginning of their friendship and the year after the final complete break in it she writes to Madame Pauline Viardot:

> Do you see Chopin? Tell me about his health. I have been unable to repay his fury and his hatred by hatred and fury. I think of him as of a sick, embittered, bewildered child. I saw much of Solange in Paris, the letter goes on, and made her my constant occupation, but without finding anything but a stone in the place of her heart. I have taken up my work again while waiting for the tide to carry me elsewhere.

All the author's "authority" is in these few words, and in none more than in the glance at the work and the tide. The work and the tide rose ever as high as she would to float her, and wherever we look there is always the authority. "I find Chopin *magnificent*," she had already written from the thick of the fray, "to keep seeing, frequenting and approving Clésinger, who struck me because I snatched from his hands the hammer he had raised upon Maurice—Chopin whom every one talks of as my most faithful and devoted friend." Well indeed may our biographer have put it that from a certain date in May 1847 "the two *Leitmotive* which might have been called in the terms of Wagner the *Leitmotif* of soreness and the *Leitmotif* of despair—Chopin, Solange—sound together now in fusion, now in a mutual grip, now simply side by side, in all Madame Sand's unpublished letters and in the few (of the moment) that have been published. A little later a third joins in—Augustine Brault, a motive narrowly and tragically linked to the *basso obligato* of Solange." To meet such a passage as the following under our heroine's hand again is to feel the whole temper of intercourse implied slip straight out of our analytic grasp. The allusion is to Chopin and to the "defection" of which he had been guilty, to her view, at the time when it had been most important that she might count on him. What we have first, as outsiders, to swallow down, as it were, is the state of things, the hysteric pitch of family life, in which any ideal of reticence, any principle, as we know it, of minding one's business, for mere dignity's sake if for none other, had undergone such collapse.

I grant you I am not sorry that he has withdrawn from me the government of his life, for which both he and his friends wanted to make me responsible in so much too absolute a fashion. His temper kept growing in asperity, so that it had come to his constantly blowing me up, from spite, ill-humour and jealousy, in presence of my friends and my children. Solange made use of it with the astuteness that belongs to her, while Maurice began to give way to indignation. Knowing and seeing *la chasteté de nos rapports*, he saw also that the poor sick soul took up, without *wanting to* and perhaps without being able to help it, the attitude of the lover, the husband, the proprietor of my thoughts and actions. He was on the point of breaking out and telling him to his face that he was making me play, at forty-three years of age, a ridiculous part, and that it was an abuse of my kindness, my patience, and my pity for his nervous morbid state. A few months more, a few days perhaps, of this situation, and an impossible frightful struggle would have broken out between them. Foreseeing the storm, I took advantage of Chopin's predilection for Solange and left him to sulk, without an effort to bring him round. We have not for three months exchanged a word in writing, and I don't know how such a cooling-off will end.

She develops the picture of the extravagance of his sick irritability; she accepts with indifference the certainty that his friends will accuse her of having cast him out to take a lover; the one thing she "minds" is the force of evil in her daughter, who is the centre of all the treachery. "She will come back to me when she needs me, that I know. But her return will be neither tender nor consoling." Therefore it is when at the beginning of the winter of this same dreadful year she throws off the free rich summary of what she has been through in the letter to M. Charles Poncy already published in her Correspondence we are swept into the current of sympathy and admiration. The preceding months had been the heaviest and most painful of her life.

I all but broke down under them utterly, though I had for long seen them coming. But you know how one is not always overhung by the evil portent, however clear one may read it—there are days, weeks, even whole months, when one lives on illusion and fondly hopes to divert the blow that threatens. It is always at last the most probable ill that surprises us unarmed and unprepared. To this explosion of unhappy underground germs joined themselves sundry contributive matters, bitter things too and quite unexpected; so that I am broken by grief in body and soul. I believe my grief incurable, for I never succeed in throwing it off for a few hours without its coming upon me again during the next in greater force and gloom. I nevertheless struggle against it without respite, and if I don't hope for a victory which would have to consist of not feeling at all, at least I have reached that of still bearing with life, of even scarcely feeling ill, of having recovered my taste for work and of not showing my distress. I have got back outside calm and cheer, which are so necessary for others, and everything in my life seems to go on well.

We had already become aware, through commemorations previous to the present, of that first or innermost line of defence residing in George Sand's splendid mastery of the letter, the gift that was always so to assure her, on every issue, the enjoyment of the first chance with posterity. The mere cerebral and manual activity represented by the quantity no less than the quality of her outflow through the post at a season when her engagements were most pressing and her anxieties of every sort most cruel is justly qualified by Madame Karénine as astounding; the new letters here given to the world heaping up the exhibition and testifying even beyond the finest of those gathered in after the writer's death—the mutilations, suppressions and other freedoms then used, for that matter, being now exposed. If no plot of her most bustling fiction ever thickened at the rate at which those agitations of her inner circle at which we have glanced multiplied upon her hands through the later 'forties, so we are tempted to find her rather less in possession of her great *moyens* when handling the artificial presentation than when handling what we may call the natural. It is not too much to say that the long letter addressed to the cynical Solange in April '52, and which these pages give us *in extenso*, would have made the fortune of any mere interesting "story" in which one of the characters might have been presented as writing it. It is a document of the highest psychological value and a practical summary of all the elements of the writer's genius, of all her indefeasible advantages; it is verily the gem of her biographer's collection. Taken in connection with a copious communication to her son, of the previous year, on the subject of his sister's character and vices, and of their common experience of these, it offers, in its ease of movement, its extraordinary frankness and lucidity, its splendid apprehension and interpretation of realities, its state, as it were, of saturation with these, exactly the kind of interest for which her novels were held remarkable, but in a degree even above their maximum. Such a letter is an effusion of the highest price; none of a weight so baffling to estimation was probably ever inspired in a mother by solicitude for a clever daughter's possibilities. Never surely had an accomplished daughter laid under such contribution a mother of high culture; never had such remarkable and pertinent things had to flow from such a source; never in fine was so urgent an occasion so admirably, so inimitably risen to. Marvellous through it all is the way in which, while a common recognition of the "facts of life," as between two perfectly intelligent men of the world, gives the whole diapason, the abdication of moral authority and of the rights of wisdom never takes place. The tone is a high implication of the moral advantages that Solange had inveterately enjoyed and had decided none the less to avail herself of so little; which advantages we absolutely believe in as we read — *there* is the prodigious part: such an education of the soul, and in fact of every faculty, such a claim for the irreproachable, it would fairly seem, do we feel any association with the great fluent artist, in whatever conditions taking place, inevitably, necessarily to have been. If we put ourselves questions we yet wave away doubts, and with whatever remnants of prejudice the writer's last word may often have to clash, our own is that there is nothing for grand final rightness like a sufficiently *general* humanity — when a particularly beautiful voice happens to serve it.

Quarterly Review, April 1914
Living Age, June 13, 1914
Reprinted in *Notes on Novelists*, 1914

Jules Sandeau

Jean de Thommeray; Le Colonel Evrard. Par Jules Sandeau, de l'Académie Française. Paris: Michel Lévy; New York: F. W. Christern, 1873.

NOW THAT, as one may say without unkindness, the sun of Madame Sand's genius has dipped pretty well into the horizon, and M. Gustave Flaubert seems to have told the one good story he had to tell, and M. Octave Feuillet breaks his long silences to no great purpose, and M. Dumas *fils*, who has produced at least one very clever tale, has taken to writing prefaces to his own and other people's masterpieces—in this not very brilliant state of affairs we know no French novelist whom we prefer on the whole to M. Jules Sandeau. His novels, some time ago, brought him into the Academy, which was natural enough, as they rigorously respect all the proprieties, moral and literary. M. Sandeau is a writer with a finished and perhaps slightly conscious style, but with a good deal of graceful invention. His two last *nouvelles* have just been republished, and 'Jean de Thommeray' has met with great success. We recommend it to such American readers as are not above looking for something in a novel besides the "story," in the belief that it will provoke them to some entertaining reflection. Jean de Thommeray is a young man of old Breton family, and, with a natural aptitude for everything beautiful and honorable, brought up in the faith of his ancestors, and wishing only for a noble cause—preferably in the æsthetic line—to take service in. He comes up to Paris at twenty, full of ingenuous ardor and literary hero-worship, and discovers that morally he is terribly out of the fashion. A clever young man, who is very much in it, writes a jesting squib about him in a *petit journal*; the inevitable duel ensues. Thommeray is seriously wounded, and is ordered to Italy to recover. The author of the impertinent parody had been an ostensible friend; but under the sky of Pisa the young man's shattered faith in fine things begins also to mend, and beguiles him into a misplaced passion for a young Parisian lady of the first fashion, whom he most erroneously fancies an angel. His pious and tender mother, who has come to nurse him, vainly combats his delusion; he is fascinated and perverted; he shakes off the poor mother and follows the profligate Countess. The latter deceives him, betrays him, swindles him, literally, in an episode very skilfully related, whereupon he flings the last of his young superstitions to the winds, and plunges into shameless dissipation. He becomes a professional gambler, lives publicly with a certain Fiametta, and passes for a prince of rakes. His parents, of whom he had been the especial darling, are bowed to the earth with grief and shame; he abjures every vestige of filial tenderness, and they mourn him in bitterness as one morally dead. He is fatally corrupted—as hard as a stone. Meanwhile, the war with Germany breaks out, and Jean de Thommeray does not hesitate to declare that patriotism is all stuff; that the country may take care of herself; that he means to take himself off with his dressing-case and weather the storm on safer shores. He makes this declaration in the street to the friend who figures as narrator of the tale. The latter blows him up for an abandoned coward, and Thommeray shrugs his shoulders. Suddenly, as they stand there—on the Quai Voltaire, beside the Seine—the sound of martial music is heard. Thommeray listens; it is an air of his native Brittany, played on the Breton *biniou*. The Breton *gardes mobiles* are entering Paris. At the head of the troop rides his father; behind the old *gentilhomme* ride his two other sons. At this moment Madame de Thommeray, the mother, appears on a neighboring balcony, waving her handkerchief. The young man stares; he seems changed into stone. His friend leaves him to the mercy of God. The next day, in the court of the Louvre, old M. de Thommeray marshals his battalion; a new-comer approaches and demands a place in the ranks. "Your name?" "Jean; a man who has lived ill and wishes to reform." A moment later the roll is called. "Jean de Thommeray!" cries the commander. A manly voice answers "Present!"

The purpose of M. Sandeau's tale is to show us a corrupted heart regenerated by patriotism. The operation is performed, certainly, in a very effective tableau, but at some cost, we think, of real human truth. The author has meant to be moral, but he seems to us to have been quite the contrary; and his *dénouement* strikes us as a very good example of the dangerous uses to which a moral idea may be put by a clever

French mind with a taste for "situations." It is of more importance (if we are to have a moral tale about it) that Jean de Thommeray and other headlong sinners should be left awhile to the gloomy impression that there is absolutely no redemption from luxurious vice than that their country should muster them under her banners. During the siege of Paris it was thought a very natural and irreproachable arrangement that wounded soldiers should be nursed in the houses, and at the expense, of the sisterhood of which our hero's Fiametta was an ornament—a view of things in which the ascent from Avernus seems really the easier path of the two. There is decidedly an abuse in France of the idea of "rehabilitation." M. Sandeau has told his story in a manner worthy of an Academician; but as a patriotic retrospect and invocation—the best an Academician could muster—our imagination does not warm to it. If we were a German professor of chemistry, in spectacles, who had lived through the siege of Paris, we are afraid we should laugh at it. But in that case, twenty to one we should be utterly insensitive to its charm of style. To 'Le Colonel Evrard' belongs this charm of style, though the tale is otherwise slight.

Nation, February 5, 1874

Edmond Schérer

Nouvelles Etudes sur la Littérature Contemporaine. Par Edmond Scherer. Paris, 1865.

To the first series of these literary studies, published two years ago, M. Scherer attached a preface which he doubtless intends shall serve also for this second volume. A short glance at this preface will initiate us into the author's view of the limits of his own work. "Custom exacts," says M. Scherer, "that a preface should sum up the doctrines of the book. But suppose the book has no doctrines? I find many subjects handled in these pages: philosophy, religion, literature, history, politics, morals—there is a little of all these. If, indeed, I start no ideas on these subjects, I speak of men who have done so. But in the midst of all this I look in vain for the least sign of a doctrine. Nay, what is worse, the book seems to me to be full of inconsistencies, or, as some might say, of contradictions. I find myself to-day all attitude, and to-morrow all indignation; now a rigid moralist, now a disinterested critic; now tolerant as a philosopher, now strenuous as a partizan." To the critic duly reproached with these inconsistencies, pursues M. Scherer, there remains this resource: to accept the reproach, and to reduce it to its proper value. This M. Scherer proceeds to do in his own case. At bottom, he affirms, rightly understood, no serious mind ever contradicts itself. To accuse a man of so doing is simply to display covertly your own ignorance. How can we know those secret reasons, those blind instincts, those confused motives, which the subject of them himself only half suspects? We think that a man has changed when he has only pursued or achieved his natural manifestation. There are in the tyranny of circumstances and the inherent inflexibility of ideas a hundred obstacles to the complete expression of feelings. These feelings, which constitute a man's real substance, his inclinations, his affections, his aspirations, never change. The nearest approach they make to it is to develop by a strictly logical process. In default of doctrines in a work—or, as we should say, in default of a system, of a consistent argument—there is always, accordingly, a certain irrepressible moral substance. This moral substance in his own work M. Scherer declares to be the love of liberty. He loves liberty as the necessary condition of truth, of thorough examination, of impartiality. "Contention, written and spoken," says M. Scherer, "the opposition and the fusion of opinions, errors, retractions, excuses, reactions: all these things are the formation of truth." And these things are only possible under liberty. "Truth," he continues, "is for me simply improvement; and liberty is scarcely more than another name for this constant process of improvement."

M. Scherer's merits, then, as a critic, are these: that he has no doctrines, and that in default of these he is prompted by as excellent a feeling as the love of liberty. It may seem questionable at first whether the former fact is really a merit. It is not that in reading M. Scherer's volume we do not find much that is positive: many opinions, much sympathy, much dissent, much philosophy, much strong feeling; for without these the reproach of inconsistency would be impossible. We find much that we can specifically approve or condemn. We find even plenty of theories. But this touches perhaps the very point. There are plenty of theories, but no theory. We find— and this is the highest praise, it seems to us, that we can give a critic—none but a moral unity: that is, the author is a liberal. It is hard to say, in reading M. Scherer's books, which is the most pleasing phenomenon, this intellectual eclecticism or this moral consistency. The age surely presents no finer spectacle than that of a mind liberal after this fashion; not from a brutal impatience of order, but from experience, from reflection, seriously, intelligently, having known, relished, and appropriated the many virtues of conservatism; a mind inquisitive of truth and of knowledge, accessible on all sides, unprejudiced, desirous above all things to examine directly, fearless of reputed errors, but merciless to error when proved, tolerant of dissent, respectful of sincerity, content neither to reason on matters of feeling nor to sentimentalize on matters of reason, equitable, dispassionate, sympathetic. M. Scherer is a solid embodiment of Mr. Matthew Arnold's ideal critic. Those who affirmed Mr. Arnold's ideal to be impracticable may here be refuted; those who thought it undesirable may perhaps be converted. For they will see that once granted M. Scherer's seriousness, his competency to the treatment of a given subject rests entirely upon his intellectual independence or irresponsibility. Of all men who deal with ideas, the critic is essentially the least independent; it behooves him, therefore, to claim the utmost possible incidental or extrinsic freedom. His subject and his stand-point are limited beforehand. He is in the nature of his function *opposed* to his author, and his position, therefore, depends upon that which his author has taken. If, in addition to his natural and proper servitude to his subject, he is shackled with a further servitude, outside of his subject, he works at a ridiculous disadvantage. This outer servitude may either be to a principle, a theory, a doctrine, a dogma, or it may be to a party; and it is against this latter form of subordination, as most frequent in his own country, that Mr. Arnold more especially protests. But as a critic, quite as much as any other writer, must have what M. Scherer calls an inspiration of his own, must possess a *unit* of sincerity and consistency, he finds it in his conscience. It is on this basis that he preserves his individuality, or, if you like, his self-respect. It is from this moral sense, and, we may add, from their religious convictions, that writers like Scherer derive that steadfast and delicate spiritual force which animates, coordinates, and harmonizes the mass of brief opinions, of undeveloped assertions, of conjectures, of fancies, of sentiments, which are the substance of this work.

There are, of course, degrees in criticism as in everything else. There is small criticism and there is great criticism. But great criticism seems to us to touch more or less nearly on pure philosophy. Pure criticsm must be of the small kind. Goethe is a great critic; M. Sainte-Beuve is a small one. Goethe has laid down general principles. M. Sainte-Beuve has laid down particular principles; and, above all, he has observed facts and stated results. Goethe frequently starts from an idea; M. Sainte-Beuve starts from a fact: Goethe from a general rule, M. Sainte-Beuve from a particular instance. When we reflect upon all the faculties and all the accomplishments needed by the literary critic in these days, we are almost tempted to say that he should unite in himself the qualities which are required for success in every other department of letters. But we may more strictly sum up his necessary character by saying that he is a compromise between the philosopher and the historian. We spoke of M. Sainte-Beuve, who, on the whole, may be called the first of living critics. He is a philosopher in so far as that he deals with ideas. He counts, weighs, measures, appraises them. But he is not a philosopher in so far as that he works with no supreme object. There results from his work no deliberate theory of life, of nature, of the universe. He is not, as the philosopher must ever be more or less, a partizan. When he pulls down, it lies in his discretion or his generosity to build up again; whereas the philosopher is for ever offering the better in exchange for the worse—that which is more true in exchange for that which is less. The philosopher's function is to compare a work with an abstract principle of truth; the critic's is to compare a work with itself, with its own concrete standard of truth. The critic deals, therefore, with parts, the philosopher with wholes. In M. Sainte-Beuve, however, it is the historian who is most generously represented. As a critic, he bears the same relation to facts that he does to ideas. As the metaphysician handles ideas with a preconceived theory, so the historian handles facts with a preconcerted plan. But with this theory or this plan, the critic has nothing to do. He works on the small scale, in detail, looking neither before him, behind him, nor on either side. Like Mr. Ruskin's model young painter with his landscape, M. Sainte-Beuve covers up all history but the small square field under his eye. On this field, however, he works with pre-Raphaelite minuteness; he exhausts it. Then he shifts his window-frame, as we may call it, and begins again. The essence of the practicability of history is in a constant obedience to proportion. M. Sainte-Beuve, like a true critic, ignores proportion. The reunion of his chapters, therefore, would make no history, any more than the reunion of the young pre-Raphaelite's studies would make a picture.

M. Scherer's place among the critics of the time is very high. If M. Sainte-Beuve has earned the highest place, M. Scherer has a claim to the next. For ourselves, we prefer M. Scherer. He has not M. Sainte-Beuve's unrivalled power of reproducing the physiognomy of a particular moment as of a particular figure of the past; he cannot pick out some obscure secondary figure of the seventeenth century—some forgotten *littérateur*, some momentary king's mistress—and in twenty pages place the person before you as a complete human being, to be for ever remembered, with a distinct personality, with a character, an expression, a face, a dress, habits, eccentricities. M. Scherer, we say, has not done this. But we prefer him because his morality is positive without being obtrusive; and because, besides the distinction of beauty and ugliness, the æsthetic distinction of right and wrong, there constantly occurs in his pages the moral distinction between good and evil; because, in short, we salute in this fact that wisdom which, after having made the journey round the whole sphere of knowledge, returns at last with a melancholy joy to morality.

If we have a complaint, indeed, to make of M. Sainte-Beuve, it is that with all his experience he is not more melancholy. On great subjects, subjects of the first order, M. Scherer is as efficient as the author of the "Causeries de Lundi." He has judged his contemporaries quite as keenly: witness his article on M. Veuillot. And in the volume under notice are two papers, one on Mme. de Sévigné, the other on Mme. Roland, which are delicate with all M. Sainte-Beuve's delicacy, and eloquent with more than his eloquence. If we were tempted to set another critic above M. Scherer, that critic would be M. Taine. But on reflection we conclude that M. Taine is not pre-eminently a critic. He is alternately a philosopher and a historian. His strong point is not to discriminate shades of difference. On the contrary, he is perpetually sacrificing shades to broad lines. He is valuable for his general views, his broad retrospects, his *résumés*. He passes indeed, incidentally, very shrewd literary judgments, as when, for instance, he says of Swift's poetry that instead of creating illusions it destroys them. But he is too passionate, too partial, too eloquent. The critic is useful in repairing the inevitable small injustices committed by other writers; in going over the ground after them and restoring the perverted balance of truth. Now in Taine's "History of English Literature," which is nominally a critical work, there is in each chapter abundant room for this supplementary process of the critic proper. In the work of M. Scherer there is room but for contradiction— which is in fact, a forcible making of room. With him, analysis has reached its furthest limits, and it is because he is more analytic than Mr. Taine—admitting, as we do, that he has not

his genius—that we place him higher as a critic. Of M. Scherer's religious character we have not explicitly spoken, because we cannot speak of it properly in these limits. We can
only say that in religion, as in everything else, he is a liberal;
and we can pay no higher tribute to his critical worth than
by adding that he has found means to unite the keenest theological penetration and the widest theological erudition with
the greatest spiritual tolerance.

Nation, October 12, 1865

Etudes Critiques de Littérature. Par Edmond Schérer. Sixième Série. Paris: Michel Lévy;
New York: F. W. Christern, 1876.

WE HAVE OFTEN WONDERED why M. Edmond Schérer,
a critic whose privilege it sometimes is, by the acuteness of his insight or the felicity of his expression, to remind
his readers of Saint-Beuve, has never undertaken a work of
larger proportions than the short journalistic articles in which
he has hitherto been content to record his opinions. Such an
enterprise seems at present more remote than ever, for M.
Schérer has for some time past been devoting himself with
increasing zeal to practical politics, and has lately been elected
one of the seventy-five life members (on the Republican side)
of the new French Senate. Moreover, the present volume perhaps explains in a measure why the author has remained a
desultory critic. Clever as he is, brilliant also, abundant in
knowledge and excellent in style, he stops short at a certain
point. He tends to fall within the limit that the reader has set
for him. He often disappoints, he lacks imagination, and he
is subject to odd lapses and perversities of taste. He is one of
the very few French writers who give the reader a sense of
any serious first-hand acquaintance with English literature;
and yet we remember his speaking some time since of the
remarkable faculty of the English people for agreeing at a
given moment to get excited or infatuated over a nothing or
a trifle, as the necessary explanation of the popularity of
Thackeray, "a cold, *ennuyeux* writer." A literary critic who
does not enjoy Thackeray has certainly a limp in his gait. This

impediment in his own carriage, however, M. Schérer manages on the whole very skilfully to conceal, and some of the best pages in the present volume are devoted to English authors. They contain, among other things, one of the best criticisms of Taine's 'English Literature' that we remember to have seen—that extraordinary work in which a superb energy has vainly done its best to conceal a fatal want of familiarity with the subject. M. Schérer resents this want of familiarity almost as roundly as a native Englishman, and has in particular some excellent remarks about the author's perverse magnification of Byron. There are indeed few things more singular than the way in which M. Taine steps over the heads of the whole literary group ushered in by the present century—Wordsworth, Shelley, Keats, Scott—and fastens himself upon Byron for the reason that he is more an "Englishman" than the others—more a Viking, a Berserker, a product of north-winds and sea-fog! M. Schérer well observes that, with regard to Byron, M. Taine stands just where French criticism stood thirty years ago. The author has a long, entertaining, and well-informed article upon Milton, whom he greatly admires, though perhaps the average English reader will wince at his summing-up of his judgment of 'Paradise Lost':

> " 'Paradise Lost' is a false, grotesque, tiresome poem; not one reader in a hundred can go, without smiling, through the ninth and tenth books, or without yawning through the eleventh and twelfth. It does not hold together, it is a pyramid balancing on its point, the most frightful of problems resolved by the most puerile of means. And yet, nevertheless, 'Paradise Lost' is immortal. It lives in virtue of some episodes which will remain for ever famous. In opposition to Dante, whom we must read altogether if we wish really to possess his beauties, we must read Milton only in fragments. But these fragments are part of the poetic patrimony of the human race."

In English we express the foregoing sentiments less trenchantly; every one is waiting for some one else to begin. But even among ourselves it has been for some time tacitly admitted that with regard to 'Paradise Lost' some of the cargo must be thrown overboard to save the ship. In an article on Bossuet and some of his recent editors, M. Schérer has some equally downright remarks upon sermons in general. "I conclude as I began: the sermon is a false style, and it is false in particular because it has grown old. It has so little human and general truth that it is difficult to interest one's self in it even retrospectively. In vain we consent to place ourselves at the desired point of view, make allowance for time and change, take tradition into account. We must be very fond of eloquence to enjoy it when it is in the condition of pure form— that is to say, of empty form, of rhetoric." On Bossuet in general M. Schérer makes some remarks which have a rather wholesome freshness as against the conventional, superstitious deference to their great classics which has so long prevailed among the French.

"The fact is that Bossuet has no *stock* (*pas de fonds*), or, what amounts to the same thing, that his stock doesn't belong to him. He is neither a *savant*, a thinker, nor a moralist. He never has what we call views, still less audacities. He lacks invention, observation, intelligence. He has a great imagination, a consummate knowledge of the oratorical style, an abundant, magnificent movement of phrase, but he uses these things only to paraphrase the commonplaces of the ecclesiastical dogma and the ecclesiastical morality. His exposition, in spite of its amplitude of form, remains essentially scholastic."

The longest of M. Schérer's papers, and the one we have found most interesting, is upon Goethe; its interest is the greater from the fact that it appeared after the Franco-Prussian war. Better than anything else, however, it illustrates what we have called the author's limitations and in particular his want of imagination. He remarks upon the fact that since the war the French have begun to pay a good deal of attention to German literature, and he thinks it an excellent sign.

"The Germans," to quote, "have revived against us the right of conquest; they have attacked us with envious hatred and cowardly insult; they have placed between us and themselves such offences as cannot be forgiven. But if it is just to detest Germany, it would be puerile on that account to seek to ignore her. It is at an end, we know; the charm that formerly drew us towards her is for ever broken; we shall no longer expect from her a single one of the ideas that elevate, of the sentiments that ennoble. So be it, we shall be but better placed to judge her. There had mingled itself with our inclination for German science and literature an enthusiasm which excluded discernment; in future it will be easier to see things in their true proportions. . . . If we are able to preserve ourselves from the other extreme—deliberate and intentional disparagement—we shall have obtained the noblest of enjoyments: that of judging impartially those who themselves defy all justice."

If M. Schérer has made an effort to be impartial, it is evident that it has cost him something. It may be said, too, that he decidedly exaggerates the "charm" which the French public found, before the war, in German literature. If he speaks of a small coterie of highly cultivated men, his observations have a certain justice; but French readers in general have certainly never given themselves the least trouble about the literature of the land of Goethe. If they find good reason to hate the Germans now, it is not that they ever loved them. The French have never been duped by the Germans or any one else; for to be duped implies attention and acquaintance. They have never been duped by any people but themselves. Upon Goethe M. Schérer says a great many discriminating and excellent things, and his article is a very vivid piece of portraiture. But he is guilty of a strange dulness of vision when he declares that he can see nothing but dreariness in 'Wilhelm Meister,' and, indeed, in all the author's literary works except the lyrics and 'Faust.' "Goethe remains none the less," he says in conclusion, "one of the greatest among the sons of men. 'After all,'" he said to one of his friends, " 'there are here and there some honest people who will be enlightened by my works, and whoever reads them and takes the trouble to understand me will recognize that he has gained by it a certain inward liberty.' I would write these words on the pedestal of Goethe's statue; one can give him no juster praise, and, indeed, one can make of no man a higher or more enviable eulogy." We alluded just now to Sainte-Beuve, and it is in place to add that we have often wished that he might have witnessed and survived the late war, if for no other purpose than to show us how he would have spoken of the Germans. The situation would have been a most interesting test of that subtilized and almost etherealized faculty of impartiality which had developed in him in his later years. It would have given play to all his *finesse*—to that strange mixture of fatal compliments and flattering blame. Unfortunately, Sainte-Beuve's acquaintance with German literature was very limited; one cannot know absolutely everything. He had written about Goethe and two or three other German authors, but he had evaded with characteristic skill any indication of whether he read them in translations or in the original.

Nation, April 6, 1876

Stendhal (*Marie Henri Beyle*)

Henry Beyle (otherwise De Stendahl). A Critical and Biographical Study. By Andrew Archibald Paton. London: Trübner & Co., 1874.

STENDAHL WAS a most singular character, but nothing surely in his destiny was so singular as having Mr. Paton write his life. Beyond his good-will and his industry, we are unable to perceive that the biographer has a single qualification for his task, and we should be curious to know whether it was undertaken spontaneously or to order. In speaking of the author's admirable 'Chroniques Italiennes,' and by implication of his masterpiece, the 'Chartreuse de Parme,' Mr. Paton remarks that Beyle was here quite off his beat, and that what he *might* have done was something in the "pleasant, gossiping manner of Louisa Mühlbach"! In his review of his hero's works, Mr. Paton devotes eleven pages to that forgotten fragment, the 'Vie de Rossini,' and not a line to this same 'Chartreuse de Parme,' now recognized as Beyle's chief title to the attention of posterity. Of the smallest capacity to appreciate the author either on his moral or intellectual side Mr. Paton is strikingly guiltless. He regards him as a shrewd, amusing, eccentric gossip, determined to have his laugh at everything, and to offer his readers at any cost a light, frothy entertainment—a judgment about on a level with his speaking incidentally of the "naïve Dutch realism of Balzac." A critic who finds Stendahl amusing and Balzac "naïf" must be left to his own devices. Mr. Paton is, as a commentator, quite worthless, and as a writer sadly slip-shod and vulgar. We have seldom seen a book more in need of a complete revision, both as to matter and to manner. It contains hardly an opinion which is not ludicrously erratic, and hardly a quotation, a foreign phrase, or a proper name which is not misspelled and misprinted. But the author writes with a garrulous *bonhomie*—that of an easy-going cosmopolite, well advanced, apparently, in years—which will soften the edge of the reader's displeasure; and he is to be thanked at any rate for bringing Beyle once more before the world, and giving occasion for that final sifting and summing up of opinion which the world finds it constantly more needful to practise expeditiously towards all claimants for permanent attention. But it seems, we repeat, the crowning stroke of that something perverse and melancholy which pervaded all Stendahl's career, that these last proceedings in judgment should take place in an English court and be carried on in English—and in English in which Mr. Paton has a voice. Beyle was the most French of Frenchmen, but he spent half his life in Italy, lauding the Italians and denouncing his countrymen. He caused "Arrigo Beyle, Milanese," to be inscribed upon his tombstone, and he falls victim, thirty years after his death, to a biographer who discourses upon him in a strange, slovenly English, flavored with Scotch and interlarded with disfigured fragments of French and Italian. By denying that he was the flippant feuilletonist represented by Mr. Paton, we do not mean to intimate that he was a dull writer. He is always interesting and often divertingly so, but his merit, to our sense, is not in his powers of entertainment, greater or less, but simply in his instinctive method. What this method was, and how instinctive it was, is suggested by this passage in a letter to his sister, written in his twenty-first year:

"I like *examples*, and not, like Montesquieu, Buffon, and Rousseau, systems. . . . Help me to know provincial manners and passions; describe me the manners in the drawing-room of Madame ——. I need examples and facts. Write quickly, without seeking fine phrases. . . . Contribute to my knowledge of women, facts, facts! I have a passionate desire to know human nature, and a great mind to live in a boarding-house, where people cannot conceal their real characters. . . . Borrow and read Sallust; you will find there thirty superb characters."

Later, he advises the same young lady to make a list of the good and bad passions, and then to write opposite each category a description of such examples as she had observed. By perseverance in this course, she would find that she had discovered treasures of knowledge of human nature. It was this absorbing passion for example, anecdote, and illustration that constituted Beyle's distinctive genius, and is the ground of the fresh claims put forth on his behalf by his recent eloquent apostle, M. Taine. Beyle felt, as soon as he began to observe, that character, manners, and civilization are explained by circumstances, and that in the way of observing and collecting circumstances there was a great work to be done. He devoted himself as far as possible to doing it, and on the whole, with his profound mistrust of systems, left the theory of the matter very much to take care of itself. M. Taine follows, with a genius for theory, and erects a symmetrical system on Beyle's unordered *data*. It is interesting to observe that in his attempts to theorize, Beyle is always flimsy and erratic; and that in his attempts to collect small facts in the manner of Beyle (as in 'Monsieur Graindorge'), M. Taine is generally ponderous and infelicitous.

The only value of Mr. Paton's volume is in its disinterring a good many obscure facts of Beyle's personal history, and, in particular, in its offering us a number of extracts from the copious and intimate correspondence which he carried on in his early years with his sister Pauline. With his genius for observation, fortune led Beyle, happily, to see a good deal of the world. He was born at Grenoble in the year 1783. His father occupied an honorable position in the law, but his means were moderate, and Beyle's money-troubles were unceasing to the day of his death. In his own line, he had a fine start in life in having opportunities for close observation of the great Napoleonic drama. He obtained by family influence a cavalry commission in the army, and afterwards occupied some responsible posts in the commissariat. He was at the battle of Marengo and in the retreat from Moscow (as the reader of any given five pages of his writing will not fail to discover). He also discharged various small administrative functions in Germany. In his Italian campaign, he formed that passion for Italy and all things Italian which provided him with the occupation of a lifetime. He returned to Milan in 1811, and from that time to his death made repeated visits, of varying duration, amounting in all to more than twenty years. His last ten years (though he died while on leave of absence in Paris) were spent as consul to Civita Vecchia—a passion for Italy cherished certainly under difficulties. He died in 1841. Mr. Paton will enable an ingenious reader to construct a tolerably vivid personal portrait. After the fall of the Empire, Beyle was continually poor, and his habits and tastes demanded money. His writings were not popular, and have come into favor since his death. He was extremely ugly, with a coarse, corpulent, plebeian ugliness. Mr. Paton says characteristically that by one of his friends "some rather offensive" traits are mentioned—"for instance, he wore stays." This is certainly not an Anglo-Saxon custom for gentlemen, but, except that, as Beyle was very fat, tight-lacing may have often been uncomfortable to him, we are at a loss to see to whom, besides himself, it was "offensive." Mr. Paton adds that the same witness, whose name he misprints, pronounces him "a *gentilhomme sans blason*," and translates the phrase "a would-be gentleman, without armorial bearings." It means, of course, the direct reverse—a real gentleman, though he could show no arms. This judgment affords some relief to the reader's imagination, which, by reflecting much upon Beyle's poverty and his ugliness, has found itself unable to view in as graceful a light as is desirable his unremitting and somewhat pretentious love-affairs. It is an especial ill-fortune for Beyle that his relations with women and his views on the whole matter of love should be presented for judgment at an English tribunal, unaccustomed to dealing either with such temperaments or with such opinions. Beyle's temperament was apparently the French temperament in a highly exaggerated form; and as for his opinions, they are scattered through all his writings, and especially embodied in his voluminous treatise 'De l'Amour'—his masterpiece, according to Mr. Paton, but to our taste that one of his books which, with the exception perhaps of 'Le Rouge et le Noir,' comes nearest to being absolutely unreadable. As is generally the case in regard to this matter in the lives of men of genius in which it plays a part, we know at once too much and too little. We know with more or less accuracy the number and succession of the ladies to whom these gentlemen have been devoted, and we know their published philosophy of such devotion, but we are not able, for want of a general light, to appreciate justly either the weak points in their philosophy or the strong points in their conduct.

Stendahl was apparently very industrious, though he worked in a desultory and disjointed manner, wrote (or published, at least) because he had to do so for bread, and affected to be as little as possible a littérateur by profession. He

ought to have considered, however, that the character was
made honorable by the danger which he persisted in fancying
attached to it. He published everything under a false name
(he had half a dozen), travestied his own on his tombstone,
and is known to fame by a disguise. He professed an entire
indifference to literary fame, except as consisting in mere conciseness. He boasts that the 'Chartreuse de Parme' is written
in the style of the Civil Code. He borrowed largely, especially
in his early writings, and transferred long passages from other
books without acknowledgment. One may say roughly that
his subject is always Italy. He had a number of affectations,
but his passion for Italy is evidently profoundly sincere, and
will serve to keep his memory sweet to many minds and his
authority unquestioned. This subject he treated under a number of different forms; most successfully, toward the end of
his life, in a novel which will always be numbered among the
dozen finest novels we possess; in a number of short tales,
founded on fact, and extracted from the manuscript archives
of Italian families, of many of whom Stendahl purchased the
privilege of transcribing for a certain number of mornings in
their libraries—just as in some parts of the Rhineland one
may obtain for a small fee the right to spend an hour in a
vineyard or orchard, and retire carrying as much fruit as possible about one's person, as the phrase is; and in a series of
loosely connected notes, descriptive, reflective, anecdotic, and
epigrammatic, on monuments and pictures, manners and
morals (such as 'Rome, Naples et Florence' and the 'Promenades dans Rome'). To these last may be added his 'Histoire
de la Peinture en Italie' and various pamphlets—the 'Vie de
Rossini' and 'Racine et Shakespeare.' The 'History of Painting' is an ambitious name for a string of desultory though
often acute and suggestive dissertations on matters nearly and
remotely connected with Italian art. It is no history, and, with
much suggestiveness, it has to our mind little value. Stendahl
as an art-critic is inveterately beside the mark, and it is striking evidence of the development of the science of taste within
the last forty years that with his extreme "sensibility," as he
would call it, and his excellent opportunities for study, he
should seem to us nowadays to belong to so false a school.

The letters placed in Mr. Paton's hands by Beyle's family,

and unfortunately offered us here only in translated and condensed extracts, add much to our sense of intimacy with our author, but help us little to understand him better. He was a strange mixture of genius and pretension, of amiability and arrogance, of fine intuitions and patent follies. He condemned his genius to utter more foolish things than it seems to us a wise man was ever before responsible for. He practised contempt on a wholesale, a really grotesque scale, and considered, or pretended to consider, all mankind an aggregation of "*sots,*" except a small class endowed like himself with "sensibility." We have spoken of his method; it was excellent, but we may say on the whole that it was better than any use he made of it—save only when he wrote the 'Chartreuse de Parme.' His notion was that *passion*, the power to surrender one's self sincerely and consistently to the feeling of the hour, was the finest thing in the world, and it seemed to him that he had discovered a mine of it in the old Italian character. In the French, passion was abortive, through the action of vanity and the fear of the neighbors' opinion—a state of things with which he is never weary of expressing his disgust. It is easy to perceive that this doctrine held itself quite irresponsible to our old moralistic canons, for *naïveté* of sentiment in any direction, combined with great energy, was considered absolutely its own justification. In the 'Chartreuse de Parme,' where every one is grossly immoral, and the heroine is a kind of monster, there is so little attempt to offer any other, that through the magnificently sustained pauses of the narrative we feel at last the influence of the writer's cynicism, regard it as amiable, and enjoy serenely his clear vision of the mechanism of character, unclouded by the mists of prejudice. Among writers called immoral there is no doubt that he best deserves the charge; the others, beside him, are spotlessly innocent. But his immorality seems vicious and harsh only according to the subjects he handles. 'Le Rouge et le Noir,' 'L'Amour,' and certain passages in his other writings have an air of unredeemed corruption—a quality which in the novel amounts to a positive blight and dreariness. For the rest, Stendahl professed a passionate love of the beautiful *per se*, and there is every reason to suppose that it was sincere. He was an entertaining mixture of sentiment and cynicism. He

describes his heroes and heroines in perfect good faith as
"sublime," in appearance and fact, in the midst of the most
disreputable actions, and it seems to him that one may perfectly well live a scandalous life and sit up half the night reading Dante in a glow of pure rapture. In repudiating Mr.
Paton's assumption that he is a light writer, we would fain
express that singular something which is fairly described neither as serious nor as solemn—a kind of painful tension of
feeling under the disguise of the coolest and easiest style. It is
the tension, in part, of conceit—the conceit which leads him
with every tenth phrase to prophesy in the most trenchant
manner the pass to which "les sots" will have brought things
within such and such a period—and in part of aspiration, of
deep enjoyment of some bold touch of nature or some fine
stroke of art. This bespeaks the restlessness of a superior
mind, and makes our total feeling for Beyle a kindly one. We
recommend his books to persons of "sensibility" whose moral
convictions have somewhat solidified.

Nation, September 17, 1874

Anne Sophie Swetchine

Life and Letters of Madame Swetchine. By Count de Falloux of the French Academy. Translated by H. W. Preston. Boston: Roberts Brothers, 1867.

THIS BOOK IS a translation of the first volume of a work published some six years ago under the title of *Madame Swetchine: sa Vie et ses Œuvres.* The work attracted great attention, and was followed by the publication of Mme. Swetchine's letters and literary fragments to the number of six volumes. The account of the author's life, which introduced this immense mass of literary matter, is particularly well written, and has been judged worthy of being laid before American readers. How American readers will like it we are at loss to conjecture; but we cannot help thinking that Mme. Swetchine's history will lose much of its charm and its interest in being transplanted into the alien atmosphere of the English tongue. Mme. Swetchine was the centre of a *coterie* narrowly limited in its extent and its influence, and generated by a form of society of which no likeness exists in America. This is so true, that, even in reading her biography and her letters in the original French, an American is acutely sensible of the remoteness of the ideas and the character which they present to his mind, and of the existence of an impassable barrier between the possibilities of American life and the charms and perfections of Mme. Swetchine's circle. In their English dress these things wear a very grotesque and anomalous look. If he wishes, therefore, to get the best possible notion of Mme. Swetchine, we advise the reader to have recourse to the French publications, and, if he cannot read French, not to meddle with her until he has acquired the language. Detract from this remarkable woman her *specific* element,—her French culture, her French style, and the various delicate associations which it invokes,—and you take from her what is by far best worth knowing. There can be no greater mistake in taste, in our opinion, than to claim for her virtues a general value, and for her example a general application. To do so, indeed, is to prove that one has studied her life to but little purpose. "If every bigoted disliker of the Roman Catholic Church," writes Mr. Alger, in his Preface, "could read this book, and, as a consequence, have his prejudices lessened, his sympathies enlarged, the result, so far from being deprecated, should be warmly welcomed." Such a result, assuredly, would have been welcomed neither by Mme. Swetchine nor by her associates. To enlarge peoples' sympathies was no part of her desire nor of her mission. If one were a good Catholic, one had always sympathies enough. What Mme. Swetchine would have welcomed would have been an exchange of the reader's actual sympathies for those which she herself indulged; but the indefinite extension of the moral and intellectual horizon indicated in Mr. Alger's words finds no place in her programme.

In spite of her having contributed half a dozen volumes octavo to French literature, and spent the greater part of her life in Paris, Mme. Swetchine was a Russian by birth and descent. Prolonged as her life was into the second half of the present century, the reader needs to remind himself that it began in the full tide of the old European society. She was born at Moscow in 1782, of the union of two distinguished families. Her father, M. Soymonof, being summoned to St. Petersburg while she was still a child, to occupy an important position at court, she was brought up in the best society and with every material advantage. In her sixteenth year she was appointed maid of honor to the Empress Mary, second wife of the Emperor Paul, son and successor of the great Catherine, and grandfather of the Emperor Nicholas. In her seventeenth year a marriage was arranged for her with General Swetchine, an officer of merit, but her senior by twenty-five years, he having reached the age of forty-two. To this arrangement Mlle. Soymonof accommodated herself with that perfect submissiveness to her constituted directors which was to be one of her main characteristics through life, and which, accompanied as it was by a perfect intelligence of the case in point, was to form in her career an element of no small strength. Mme. Swetchine was one of those firm and exquisitely tempered natures which can afford to bend; there was no fear of her breaking. Her marriage, in fact, was a happy one. With few sympathies in common, M. and Mme. Swetchine maintained, during a long succession of years, an implicit regard for each other's pursuits and convictions.

M. de Falloux gives an excellent picture of the complexion of the society about the Russian court during the first ten years of the century. The capital was largely frequented by French exiles, members of the French nobility, for whom there was no place under the *régime* of Napoleon. M. de Falloux is a charming writer, but he is a conservative, and he looks back with tender glances upon the persons and things of the French Monarchy. It is very possible, therefore, that he flings a rosy mantle over the dignity of this little circle of aristocratic fugitives. The group, however, certainly contained one important figure,—the illustrious Count Joseph de Maistre, Ambassador of the King of Sardinia, and the most impassioned and resolute of the defenders of religious ultramontanism. Accredited by a poverty-stricken court, and from a kingdom barely sure from day to day of its existence, without resources of his own, separated from his family, and oppressed by the influence of a climate as rigorous as that of his own country was mild, the Count de Maistre prolonged his stay in St. Petersburg through a hundred grievous embarrassments, with the constant purpose of keeping warm, on behalf of the national existence of his own countrymen, the animosity of the Russian government against Napoleon, and with such assistance and comfort as he derived from his studies and his religious convictions. He formed an intimate acquaintance with Mme. Swetchine, and repaid by an almost paternal tenderness and a sincere regard and esteem the admiration which she yielded to his distinguished gifts and character. To the end of her days, Mme. Swetchine kept apart in her memory a place for his image, and looked upon him as the author of much of that which eventually grew to be her great happiness.

The origin of a great movement is, of its whole history, the point most difficult to determine. Mme. Swetchine's conversion to Romanism fairly deserves, in a psychological sense, the name of a great movement; but its rise and growth can have been intimately known only to herself. Mme. Swetchine was nothing of an egotist; it was not her practice to descant to her friends upon the secret and exquisite process of her religious development. It is in her letters to Mlle. de Stourdza, a cherished friend attached to the person of the wife of the Emperor Alexander, that her doubts begin to betray themselves. One feels at least that her genius is beginning to expand; that religion is daily becoming a more imperious necessity in her life; and that although, as she says, from the age of nineteen (she is now thirty), when she threw herself into the arms of God, she has practised the most implicit and most fervent piety, she is at present prepared to bring to the subject the light of her ripened faculties, and the ardor of a soul which has fathomed the depth of worldly pleasures.

In the month of June, 1815, while all Europe was thrilling with the *dénouement* of the great Napoleonic drama, Mme. Swetchine took a step at once deeply significant of the intensity of her religious preoccupations, and prophetic of the position which she was from that moment forward to fill,—far aloft on the lonely heights of contemplation and remote from the surging, eddying current of the age, and the turmoil of our actual interests and tendencies. She had resolved upon a firm and patient effort to conjure faith out of her doubts, and to solve the problem of the relative merits of the Greek and Latin churches. She had determined not to content herself with data received at second-hand, but to examine personally the most minute existing evidence and the highest authorities. She obtained the use of a country-house near St. Petersburg, belonging to one of her friends, and thither she transported herself, with her books and her adopted daughter, Mlle. de Staëline, for all society. Her venture was of course criticised by such of her friends as were admitted to her confidence, and among others by the Count de Maistre, who would have had her take the matter more easily, and await the visitation of the Supreme truth, rather than embark on so arduous a journey in pursuit of it. He urged upon his young friend's consciousness the immensity of her enterprise in an intellectual sense, and its sterile and unprofitable character so far as moral and spiritual effects were concerned, and drew up a terrible map of the ground she would have to traverse, with all the Fathers and historians and Church records in the centre, and the Greek and Latin tongues at either end. "He supposed himself," says M. de Falloux, "to be uttering a defiance. He was but tracing a programme which was followed in detail." Mme. Swetchine listened, bent her head, smiled discreetly, and applied herself to her work. The amount of labor which she achieved during the ensuing summer is something truly remarkable. She had accurately measured her own powers; she felt that she had a strong head. She had, indeed, never been afraid of study. An immense collection of note-books, extracts, and memoranda of her early reading remains, to bear witness both to its serious character and its great extent. So in reading, writing, thinking, and praying she passed these weeks which were to remain the eventful weeks of her life, and to set the seal on the rest of her career. Later, Mme. Swetchine used to speak with enthusiasm of occasionally "plunging into a bath of metaphysics." It was during this memorable summer that she made good her right to speak with authority, both of the pleasures and pains of hard and continuous thought. How likely this course of study may have been thought beforehand to contain the germ of its actual results, we are not in a position to say. All we know with certainty is, that Mme. Swetchine came out from her retirement with a conviction of the validity of the claims of the Romish Church, of the force of the historical evidence of its divine establishment, and of its adherence to the sacred principles of its foundation, which she never afterwards allowed to be shaken. Not only in the present, but in the past and in the future, the Catholic Church was for Mme. Swetchine the sole reality—the omnipotent fact—in history. We may differ from her conclusions, but we are obliged to admit that they are indeed conclusions, and that they were purchased at the expense of her dearest treasure,—the essential energies of her mind and heart. Mme. Swetchine had staked her happiness upon the truth which she finally embraced. It is not uncommon for people to die for their faith: Mme. Swetchine lived emphatically for hers.

We have not the space to trace in detail the remainder of Mme. Swetchine's history. We will rapidly indicate its chief incidents. With her conversion and her consequent removal to Paris her life may be said really to begin; but it becomes at the same time so uniform in its character, and so monotonous in its expression, that it offers but a limited field for narration. Before her final settlement in the French capital, Mme. Swetchine made a journey to Italy, and subsequently two journeys to Russia: otherwise her time was spent, from the day of her arrival to that of her death, in her residence in the Faubourg St. Germain, in the discharge of her innumerable religious duties, in the practice of "good works," and above all in the maintenance of her *salon*. It was through her *salon*, during her lifetime, that her influence was chiefly exerted; she made no claims to literary distinction, and, although she was forever writing, she never published. Her social influence was of course gradually achieved. M. de Falloux gives a singularly perfect and graphic account of it, as it existed from 1820 to 1840. His narrative is of course that of an *habitué*, one of the initiated, one who was in a manner under the pledge and under the charm; but it may be cordially recommended to the reader on the condition that he will afterwards read the two articles of M. Sainte-Beuve, where he will find the subtile spirit of profane criticism carried into the very heart of the sanctuary, and twitching the consecrated garments of the priestess. M. Sainte-Beuve is doubtless the least bit malicious; but M. de Falloux is the least bit superstitious, and the two faults balance each other.

During these twenty years of active influence, Mme. Swetchine's life was one of real labor. Hard work seems to have been the great necessity of her being. She rose early, went to mass, visited certain of her poor, and was at home again by eight o'clock. From this hour to three she ostensibly shut herself up in her study, and applied herself to her books and papers; but we are assured that the importunity of her friends and pensioners was so great that these precious hours were constantly invaded. From three to six she threw open her *salon* to the first of her two categories of visitors. At six she dined. At nine she again received her friends, until the small hours of the night. Such was her daily programme,— diversified by frequent visits to the chapel, which, by special permission, she had established in an apartment adjoining her drawing-room. The relations between the chapel and the drawing-room were frequent and intimate, and we receive the impression of a constant gliding to and fro between the two apartments.

The reader will see to how large a degree Mme. Swetchine had simplified her life. She had eliminated the profane element, or at least reduced it to a narrow marginal relation to the great central object. Her originality, and her great merit, to our mind, is, that thoroughly attached as she was to the world to come, she maintained on its behalf the dignity of our actual life. It is difficult to say whether she had more of imagination or of tact, more of intellectual passion or of self-control. Her soul was the soul of an ardent devotee,—her reason was equally strong and subtile,—her mind was that of a woman of the world. Her religious conceptions are of the exquisitely transcendental sort; and one feels that, if she had surrendered herself to her imagination, she would have drifted into exalted asceticism and into a passionate indifference to a worldly equilibrium. Some of her letters reveal that heavy perfume of mysticism, that intensity of contemplation, in which one detects the fatal insanity of piety. But Mme. Swetchine was, after all, herself, and the juxtaposition of her chapel and her drawing-room symbolizes very well the constitution of her mind. She had practically reconciled the two spheres of our thought,—the natural and the supernatural,— and she made them play into each other's hands. She was a most efficient link between the Church and the world.

Of her literary character there is not a great deal to be said. She writes well, often with eloquence, and always with subtilty and neatness; but the general public need feel under no obligation to assist M. de Falloux and her friends in making her an author in spite of herself. Of the many volumes from her pen which have been given to the world, the first alone (her letters with M. de Falloux's connecting narrative) will repay the perusal of any but the really curious reader. Women of grosser spiritual texture and of a life less harmoniously balanced have written much better. Mme. Swetchine will linger in the memory chiefly as a person of an exquisite temper and of rich moral endowments. She will serve as an example of the large capacities of this poor human nature which she wished to hide from sight in the divine.

North American Review, July 1868

Hippolyte Taine

Italy: Rome and Naples. From the French of H. Taine. By John Durand. New York: Leypoldt & Holt, 1868.

A FEW YEARS SINCE M. Taine, appointed to a professorial chair in the School of Fine Arts in Paris, made a journey to Italy to put himself in the humor for his office. The result, in the course of time, in addition to his lectures, was two large volumes of notes, letters, and journals. The first of these, "Rome and Naples," has just been translated for the American public. Whether it will be largely read in this country we are unable to say; but it is certain that M. Taine deserves well of English readers. He is the author of a really valuable history of English literature, and he has taken the trouble to arrive at a more intimate knowledge of the English mind than members of one race often care to possess of the idiosyncrasies of another. Add to this that he is one of the most powerful writers of the day—to our own taste, indeed, the most powerful; the writer of all others who throws over the reader's faculties, for the time, the most irresistible spell, and against whose influence, consequently, the mental reaction is most violent and salutary—and you have an idea of his just claim on your attention. M. Taine's manner and style are extremely individual, and it is somewhat odd that being, as he is, a great stickler, in literary and historical problems, for the credit of national and local influences, he should personally be a signal example of their possible futility. He is scarcely a Frenchman. Not that he is anything else; but he is before all things the brilliant, dogmatic, sombre, and (from a reader's point of view) extremely heartless offspring of his own resolute will. His style, literally translated (and Mr. Durand is very literal), makes very natural English. It has an energy, an impetus, a splendor to which no words of ours can do justice. It is not delicate, courteous, and persuasive like that of several of the most eminent French writers of the day—notably MM. Sainte-Beuve, Renan, and Cousin—it is vehement, impetuous, uncompromising, arrogant—insolent, if you will. The affirmative movement of M. Taine's mind is always a ringing hammer-blow. Every proposition is fastened down with a tenpenny nail. Finally, of course, this is very fatiguing; your head aches with the metallic resonance of the process. It is the climax of dogmatism. There was something ironical in M. Taine's being appointed professor; he was professor from the first, by natural right. His whole tone is didactic; every sentence comes *ex cathedra*. But with the essential energy and originality of his mind he invests the character with a new dignity, and reconciles it to the temperament of a man still young and audacious.

He has, intellectually, nothing of professorial dryness or prudery. Of all writers he is the most broadly picturesque. He throws into his language a wealth of color and a fulness of sound which would set up in trade a hundred minor poets and story-tellers. The secret of the power which he exerts on the mind, or on many minds, at least, we take to be the union of this vast current of imagery, of descriptive vigor and splendor, and of sensuous susceptibility with great logical precision and large erudition. He describes a figure, a costume, a building, a picture, not only with all the richness of his imagination, but with the authority and *prestige* of his knowledge. The pictorial element in his style, its color and rhythm, is not the substance of his thought, as in so many charming second-class writers, but its mere vestment and gait. Nevertheless, we admit that, to our perception, in spite of his learning, his logic, and his merits as a metaphysician, or rather an anti-metaphysician (whatever they may be), he remains pre-eminently an artist, a *writer*. If we had doubted of the truth of this judgment, we should have been convinced by that singular work, recently published, "Notes sur Paris: Opinions de M. Thomas Graindorge." Of feeling in the work there is none; of ideas there are very few; but of images, pictures, description, style, a most overwhelming superabundance. The same relation between the two elements of his genius appears in the "History of English Literature." In his appreciation of certain writers, the faculty of perception, apprehension, without being absent, is quite lost to sight in the energy of the act of portraiture. There are a series of pages on Shakespeare which, although full of controvertible propositions and precipitate formulas, form to our mind a supremely valuable tribute to his genius, inasmuch as of all attempts to appreciate and measure it they are the most energetic, unreserved, and eloquent. They form a direct homage to the immensity of the theme; they are almost as vast as silence; they are, in short, on the Shakespearian scale. The nurse of *Juliet* is not assuredly distinguished on the immortal page by a more animated and furious loquacity than M. Taine exhibits on her behalf. But an example is more conclusive than our own logic, and we find one to our hand in a striking passage in the second volume (Florence and Venice) of the "Voyage en Italie." This passage is interesting as showing, as it seems to us, the thoroughly unreligious cast of the author's mind (for we know few writers who appear to find it more natural to speak of a religion—no matter which—from a distant external standpoint), and then its gravity, melancholy, and hopelessness, and then, finally, its supreme delight in the literary form. It begins, if we are not mistaken, in a moral key, and ends in an artistic one. It is tragical, but it is perfect, consciously perfect. We translate, premising that the author is speaking of the impression produced by certain primitive frescoes in various Italian churches, buried under the work of later painters, and restored to light by the excavation, as one may call it, of the subsequent applications of color:

"You raise your eyes then and find before you the four edifices of old Pisa, lonely on a square where the grass grows, with the dead paleness of their marbles outlined against the blue divine. What a mass of ruins; what a cemetery is history! How many human palpitations, of which there remains no trace but a form imprinted on a block of stone! What a careless smile is that of the peaceful sky; and what a cruel beauty dwells in that luminous dome, stretched over the decease of successive generations like a canopy at a common burial! We have read these ideas in books, and with the pride of youth we have treated them as mere talk; but when a man has gone over half of his career, and, retiring within himself, he counts up all the ambitions he has strangled, all the hopes he has plucked up, all the dead things he carries in his heart; the magnificence and the hardness of nature appear to him at once, and the heavy sob of his inward obsequies suggests to him a deeper

lamentation—that of the great human tragedy which unfolds itself from age to age to lay low so many strugglers
in a single tomb. He stops, feeling upon his own head, as
upon that of others, the hand of the fateful powers, and
comprehends his condition. This humanity, of which he is
a member, has its image in the 'Niobe' of Florence. Around
her, her daughters and her sons, all her loved ones, fall unceasingly beneath the bolts of invisible archers. One of
them is prostrate on his back, his bosom tremulous with a
piercing wound; another, still living, lifts her useless hands
toward the celestial murderers; the youngest hides her head
in the robe of her mother. She, meanwhile, cold and still,
erects herself hopeless, and, with her eyes raised to heaven,
gazes with wonder and horror upon the dazzling, deathly
nimbus, the outstretched arms, the inevitable arrows, and
the implacable serenity of the gods."

M. Taine may certainly be said to belong to the materialist
school of thinkers. He is no sentimentalist; in the way of sentiment he rarely treats us to anything lighter than the passage
just quoted. To his perception man is extremely interesting as
an object of study, but he is without sanctity or mystery of
any sort. He takes a positive satisfaction in reminding the
reader of the purely objective and finite character of his organization, and he uses for this purpose a special vocabulary.
"La tragédie, la comédie humaine," "la colonie humaine," "la
plante humaine," "la machine humaine," these expressions
continually recur. M. Taine, in effect, studies man as a plant
or as a machine. You obtain an intimate knowledge of the
plant by a study of the soil and climate in which it grows, and
of the machine by taking it apart and inspecting its component pieces. M. Taine applies this process to the human mind,
to history, art, and literature, with the most fruitful results.
The question remains, indeed, with each reader as to whether,
as the author claims, the description covers all the facts; as to
whether his famous theory of *la race, le milieu, le moment* is
an adequate explanation of the various complications of any
human organism—his own (the reader's) in particular. But
he will be willing, at least, to admit that the theory makes
incomparable observers, and that in choosing a travelling

companion he cannot do better than take him from the school of M. Taine. For, in fact, you can do your own moralizing and sentimentalizing; you can draw your own inferences and arrange your own creed; what you wish in a companion, a guide, is to help you accumulate *data*, to call your attention to facts. The present writer observes everything, and selects and describes the best.

M. Taine rapidly traversed Italy, and began his journey at Naples upward. The early portion of his book is pervaded by that strong feeling of joy natural to an ardent dogmatist at the prospect of an unexplored field. He describes the city of Naples with singular vividness; its radiant, transparent, natural loveliness, the latent tokens of its pure Greek origin, the traces of the Spanish dominion, the splendor and squalor, the sensuality in manners and art and religion. Nothing grand, nothing Gothic (even remotely, as in Northern Italy), nothing impressive and mysterious. Parisian light and gorgeousness, and careless joyousness and superstition, form the substance of his impressions. Having described a church bedizened with a wilderness of florid ornament in the artificial Italian style of the seventeenth century, he opens a vista to thought at the close of the chapter by touching with eloquent brevity upon a passionate and sombre Spanish painting: "The breath of the great period still stirs the machine; it is Euripides, if it is no longer Sophocles. Some of the pieces are splendid; among others, 'A Descent from the Cross,' of Ribera. The sun struck upon the head of Christ through the half-drawn curtain of red silk. The darksome background seemed the more mournful beside this sudden radiance of luminous flash, and the dolorous Spanish coloring; the expression, here mystical, there violent, of the passionate figures in the shadow gave to the scene the aspect of a vision, such as used to people the monastic, chivalrous brain of a Calderon or a Lope." These few lines are assuredly picturesque writing; but it seems to us that they serve to illustrate the difference between the picturesque as practised by a writer with his facts in hand, and one who has nothing but fancies. At Naples, however, M. Taine found but few paintings, and these were to be his principal concern. *En revanche*, he gives us, *apropos* of the Greek and Roman relics of the neighborhood, some admirable pages on "Homeric Life and the City of Antiquity." It is not until he reaches Rome, Florence, and Venice that he really plunges into his subject. Here we are unable to follow him. We can only recommend him to the attentive perusal of all persons interested in the history of art, and gratified by the spectacle of an indefatigable critical *verve*. M. Taine is guilty, doubtless, of many errors of judgment; but we strongly suspect that the great masters—Michael Angelo, Raphael, Leonardo, and Titian—have never been more correctly, as well as more ardently, estimated. Several of the great painters of the second rank—notably, Veronese and Tintoretto—are celebrated with a splendor of coloring and a breadth of design which recall the aspect of their own immortal works. Finally, we cannot help laying down our conviction that M. Taine's two volumes form a truly great production; great not in a moral sense, and very possibly not in a philosophical, but appreciably great as a contribution to literature and history. One feels at moments as if, before this writer, there had been no critics, no travellers, observers, or æsthetic inquisitors. This is, of course, a mistake, and we shall like no genuine critic the less (we personally, on the contrary, from the character of our sympathies, feel that we shall like him the more) for giving M. Taine his liberal dues. It is inexpressibly gratifying—fortifying, one may say—to see a writer, *armé en guerre*, fling himself into his subject with such energy, such fury. It is an admirable intellectual feat. M. Taine is a representative of pure intellect, and he exhibits the necessarily partial character of all purely intellectual estimates. But there are days when we resort instinctively to an intellectual standpoint. On such days our author is excellent reading.

Nation, May 7, 1868

Notes sur l'Angleterre. Par H. Taine. Paris: Hachette, 1872.

NOW THAT by the issue of an English version of his "English Literature" M. Taine has been made one of the topics of the day, this volume of "Notes on England" may expect a double welcome. Offering, as it does, a glimpse of the documents and materials on which the History rests, it is a valuable complementary sequel to that work. These notes were taken, the author informs us in a short preface, during two visits, in 1861 and 1862; they have been revised and modified from the impressions of a visit last year, and, as they stand, they present an extremely copious and comprehensive record of personal experience.

The reader's foremost impression will be that the author is a singularly vigilant and methodical observer. His note-book is never out of his hand, and facts, facts, is his constant demand. His work fairly bristles with them; his constant effort is to resolve his impression into a positive and definite statement. "I continue," he somewhere says, "to jot down conversations; nothing seems to me so pleasant as an evening passed in this way, with one or two interlocutors who are sincere, obliging, and unprejudiced, who have seen life and the world; national conceit does not interfere; you talk to learn, not to contend or shine. You venture to give the little characteristic fact, the precise, telling detail; each offers, as briefly as he can, the best of his experience. . . . My mind has never fed so largely nor so well; I remained catechizing and listening till one o'clock in the morning." And again: "When I feel an inference beginning to take shape in my mind, I carry it to two or three English friends who have travelled; I submit it to their judgment; we reason about it; it comes out of the discussion corrected or developed, and the next day I write it down as it stands." As to the value of some of M. Taine's inferences there will be various opinions, but his manner is the right manner, and his temper is excellent.

He begins with the *dehors*—the outside look of things; and by the energy and vivacity of his pictorial faculty reminds us afresh of what we have formerly suspected—that descriptive and not philosophical writing is his strong point. He visits docks and workhouses and churches; he goes to the Derby, walks the streets, and lounges indefatigably in the parks; questions, converses, gazes, crowds item upon item. The climate seems to him detestable; he returns to it again and again with undiminished hostility, and exhausts his vocabulary in the attempt to express its abominations. We think that he exaggerates its influence as a factor in English character; but correctness here is a matter of degree. One thing certainly may be said: that if national temper is the product of external influences to the extent contended for by M. Taine, a larger sense of external beauty than he recognizes would have been apportioned to the English; for their climate, if not the most cheerful, is surely the most picturesque and, so to speak, the most pictorial in Europe. For a single "effect" in landscape and interior scenery produced in France or Italy at a given moment by the play of light and shade, there are a hundred in England. There is a hiatus here, as at various other points in M. Taine's reasoning. The moist, darksome, shifting, marine atmosphere which in his theory helps so largely to account for the idiosyncrasies of the Flemish and Dutch painters—their lowness of tone, their patient science and finish—has produced under English conditions the gaudiest school of art in Europe—a school in which color is nothing if not "telling," and in which, as a general thing, science and finish are conspicuously absent. In fact, we imagine foreign observers are apt to lapse into an easy fallacy as regards the English climate. There is, in the first place, the peculiar atmospheric medium of London, Liverpool, and Manchester— a monstrous and indefinable compound of fog and coal smoke and the myriad fine exhalations of serried hundreds of thousands of human creatures, half of them the most squalid in the world; then there is, in the second place, the English climate proper—the climate of villages and lanes and parks, of the whole vast world of English ruralism, and this, to the eye of sense (putting aside the eye of sentiment), fairly swarms with æsthetic suggestions. On the whole, M. Taine finds little beauty in the outward aspect of English life. He is overwhelmed, like most foreigners, with the massiveness and hugeness and multitudinousness of the material civilization, and he is struck, like Hawthorne, with a certain broad analogy between the English and the Romans of the Empire. The same vast and multifarious needs, gratified on the same huge scale—in the one case by conquest, in the other by industry; the same immense development of practical and material resources. The Crystal Palace at Sydenham, with its gigantic aggregation of specimens and trophies and pastimes, vividly recalls the traditional image of the baths and circuses and mu-

seums of the antique sovereign people. The want of taste is
the salient fact: if it strikes an American, it must doubly offend a Frenchman; and it finds its most powerful expression
in the costume of the women. "Their excessive overdress suggests the *lorette* or the *parvenue*; one is amazed to see repu-
table young women decked out in such a fashion. At Hyde
Park, on Sunday, among the ladies and the young girls of the
wealthy middle-class, the intemperance of dress is shocking;
bonnets like piled-up tufts of rhododendrons, or else of
snowy whiteness and extraordinary smallness, with bundles of
red flowers and enormous ribbons; dresses of shiny violet silk,
with dazzling reflections, or of stiff tulle on a roundabout
cage of petticoats bristling with embroidery; immense shawls
of black lace falling to the heels, gloves of spotless white or
of vivid purple; chains of gold, belts of gold, with buckles of
gold; hair falling in a shining mass upon the back. . . . Their
heads are stiff on their necks, like those of beadles in a
church-march; their hair is either plastered flat or excessively
undone." And on top of all this, no grace of movement. To
the beauty of Englishwomen the author in various other
places does ample justice, and of their moral graces, their
steadfastness, their devotion, their precious domestic virtues,
he seems to have formed a most flattering opinion. But as
to their social faculty he makes the following happy discrimination:

"According to C., an Englishwoman is incapable of presiding in a drawing-room (*tenir un salon*) as skilfully as a
Frenchwoman; he knows but two or three women in this
country who could. The Englishwoman lacks the tact, the
promptitude, the pliancy, to enable her to accommodate
herself to people and things, to vary her greeting, to catch
a hint, slip in a compliment, make each guest the object of
a particular welcome. She is only affable; she has nothing
but kindness and calmness. For myself, I ask nothing more,
and I imagine nothing better. But it is plain that a woman
of the world, a woman who desires to make her house a
favored and valued place of reunion for distinguished people of all kinds, has need of a talent more complex and
more delicate. C. vastly admires the ease with which, with

us, a young wife learns the world. A month after her marriage, she knows how to do the honors of her home to all comers; and, in the same way, a little *bourgeoise* takes her place at the desk in the shop the day after her wedding, catches the trick of the trade, talks, smiles, keeps customers. I saw the contrast at Dieppe, in a restaurant. The husband, a Frenchman, always *empressé* and smiling, circulated among the tables with all kinds of civilities, and seemed to be waiting on people for his pleasure; the wife, an Englishwoman, stiff and serious, said in icy tones to people as they rose from table, '*Havé-vo payé, mosieur?*' "

For certain elderly gentlewomen of England he professes an especial relish. Here is a passage which at once expresses it, and indicates his admirable faculty for presenting his impressions as pictures:

"Two of these aged ladies have remained in my mind as a fine Dutch picture. It was in the country, in a lofty parlor, upholstered in white and pearl-gray; the high light was softened by the evening shadows. The broad middle window jutted out upon a series of flower-beds, showing masses of verdure through its brilliant panes. On a chair, near the light, a young girl—fair, intelligent, and cold— sat reading a little religious treatise. In the middle, two old ladies, before a tea-table, entertained their guest. Faces with large features, serene, decided, even imperious; in this single point they differed from the Flemish portraits. For dress, gowns of black silk, in large folds, lace at the throat and at the wrists, rich gauze caps, with streamers, white embroideries at the bosom, as in the figures of Mierevelt; the combination of severity and opulence which is displeasing in the adornments of the younger woman harmonized with their age and their gravity. Around them, the signs of ample fortune, unquestioned position, a well-balanced mind, a healthy soul, a worthy life."

Upon education there is a very interesting chapter, especially in its remarks on the public schools and on Oxford. English children seem to him essentially different from French—the grand distinction being that, as regards boys especially, there is no definite line of division, as in France, between the moral life of the child and that of the grown man. "School and society are on a level, without intermediate wall or moat: one prepares for the other and leads into it, and the boy enters life not from a forcing-house and special atmosphere. . . . The French collegian is *ennuyé*, embittered, over-refined, precocious—too precocious; he is kept in a cage, and his imagination ferments." The relation between English parents and children puzzles him, as it does most foreigners. The apparently reckless multiplication of offspring, the necessity not only of sons but of daughters shifting for themselves, the want of sentimental confidence between mothers and sons, are all at variance with French tradition. As to French habits under this last head, he mentions some facts which the unregenerate Anglo-Saxon mind hardly knows whether to pronounce very nice or (as Charles Lamb says) very nasty. He closes his account of Oxford with a reflection which admits us vividly into a certain bitter and, as it were, tragical phase of an intelligent Frenchman's consciousness—words which suggest afresh what so frequently occurs to students of French literature, that the rays of the sun of "glory" must, after all, be rather chilling ones:

> "I visit [at Oxford] two or three of the professors' residences; some recalling old French *hôtels*, others modern and delightful, all with gardens and flowers, outlooks noble or graceful. In the very oldest, beneath the portraits of former occupants, are gathered all the elements of modern comfort. I compare them to those of our *savants*—denlike lodgings in some third story, in a great city, or to the gloomy quarters of the Sorbonne, and I think of the meagre, colorless aspect of our Collége de France. Poor French! poor, indeed, living here and there as we can! We are of yesterday; we have been ruined from father to son by Louis XIV., Louis XV., by the Revolution, by the Empire. We had pulled down, and had to make over all things anew. Here the generation that follows never breaks with the generation that precedes; institutions are reformed by superposition, and the present, resting on the past, continues it."

Both the interest of M. Taine's work and the rigor of his method reach their climax in his chapter on "The English Mind." He has collected here a number of suggestive facts—such facts as a society rarely disengages by any spontaneous attempt at self-analysis, and for which it is generally indebted to the fresher vision of an alien. His main impression is that the characteristic English mind is indifferent and even hostile to ideas, and finds its almost exclusive pabulum in facts. The inside of an English head is like one of Murray's guide-books, crammed with facts, figures, statistics, maps, bits of historical information, useful-moral admonitions; it lacks *vues d'ensemble*, spontaneity of thought, the general harmonizing action of a sense of style and form. Society furnishes the young Englishman when he enters it with ready-made moulds (*cadres*) of thought; the religion is reasonable, the constitution excellent; the great lines of belief are distinctly traced. The author says elsewhere, we remember, that the Englishman who begins life finds on all things ready-made answers; the young Frenchman nothing but ready-made doubts. To theories, inferences, conclusions, to the more or less irresponsible play of conjecture, opinion, and invention, the Englishman turns the cold shoulder. His power of conclusion strikes the author as strangely unproportioned to his rate of information. M. Taine cites as an example a letter in Carlyle's "Life of Sterling," written by Sterling from the West Indies to his mother immediately after a fierce tornado had ravaged his estate and almost destroyed his house. The writer is an author, a poet, a man of fancy, but he confines himself to a naked statement of facts; he accumulates details, he draws a diagram, he suggests Gulliver and Robinson Crusoe. The point with M. Taine is that he makes no phrases, no attempt to embroider, generalize, or round off his picture. And this love of facts is the more striking, as it includes the taste for moral as well as material facts. M. Taine mentions two letters shown him by an English lady, from two young friends recently married, each considering herself the happiest woman in the world. One of these ladies gives an exhaustive account of her material circumstances—of her husband's appearance, manners, temper, of their house, their neighbors, their expenditure, their whole external economy. The other traces, in equal detail, the moral history of her courtship and honeymoon, and reveals a singular aptitude for psychological observation. The clearness, directness, and simplicity of each letter is the same; each is a string of special facts, without a hint of general reflection or conception.

M. Taine touches further upon the comparative paucity in English speech of abstract words and general terms. Nothing is more natural in French than such a formula as *le vrai*, *le beau et le bien*; nothing is less a matter of course in English than to allude to the True, the Beautiful, and the Good. M. Taine, we suppose, pretends here to be dealing only with those straws which show how the wind blows, so that we may suggest a case even more in point—the common currency in French speech of the term *la femme*, as compared with its English analogue. For twenty times that this agreeable entity figures in an average French conversation, it puts in but the shadow of an appearance in an English one. M. Taine's theory may be infinitely fortified by special examples, and Americans, as a general thing, if they are not sensibly more furnished with the conceptive turn of mind, as we may roughly term it, than the English, are sufficiently less oppressed by that indefinable social proscription which, in England, weighs upon the jauntily-theorizing tendency, to feel a certain kindly fellowship with our author in his effort to establish his distinction. There is that in the walk and conversation of the average self-respecting Briton which denotes the belief that it is a sign of inferior, or at best of foreign, breeding to indulge, in the glow of conversational confidence, the occasional impulse to extemporize a picturesque formula, or to harmonize fact with fact by the plastic solvent of an "idea." This idiosyncrasy, definitely stated, however, belongs to that class of allegations which immediately evokes as large a body of contradictory as of confirmatory testimony; and to our minds a juster, or at least a simpler, expression of the prime intellectual difference between the English and French is to be found in their unequal apportionment of the sense of form and shape. The French possess that lively æsthetic conscience which, on the whole, is such a simplifier. Upon this point our author also touches: "In our magazines an article, even on science or on political economy, should have an exordium, a peroration, an architecture; there occur few in the *Revue des*

Deux Mondes which are not preceded by a sort of porch of general ideas." That quality of the English mind on which M. Taine most insists—its imaginative force—might seem in some degree to undermine this charge of the want of intellectual agility; but in English imaginations it is the moral leaven that works most strongly; their home is the realm of psychology, and their fondest exercise not the elaboration of theories, but the exposition of the facts of human character, the mysteries and secrets of conscience and the innumerable incidents of life. The English genius for psychological observation has no correlative in France. Its vast range is indicated, in M. Taine's opinion, by that delicate scrutiny of the childish mind effected by so many English-writing novelists—Dickens, George Eliot, the author of the "Wide, Wide World." We may say, on the other hand, however, that the enquiry has perhaps been pushed at one end to its undue curtailment at the other. If there are no David Copperfields nor Tom Tullivers in French literature, there are no Madame Bovarys, Jacques, nor Mauprats in English.

It is in fiction and in painting that this characteristic comes out most strongly; and upon the English school of art M. Taine has several very interesting pages. The absence of form, of the sense of design and of beauty, and the rich suggestiveness on the moral and sentimental line, seem to him here equally conspicuous. He professes a deep though restricted relish for Wilkie and Mulready, Landseer and Leslie:

"It is impossible to be more expressive, to expend more effort to address the mind through the senses, to illustrate an idea or a truth, to collect into a surface of twelve square inches a closer group of psychological observations. What patient and penetrating critics! What connoisseurs of man! . . . I find here and there masterpieces of this kind—that of Johnston, for example—'Lord and Lady Russell receiving the Sacrament.' Lord Russell is about to ascend the scaffold; his wife looks at him full in the face to learn if he is reconciled with God. This intense gaze of the wife and Christian is admirable; she is satisfied now of her husband's salvation. What a pity that it should have been painted instead of being written!"

The reader who remembers the work in question (at Kensington) will agree that it is a singularly characteristic mixture of sentimental delicacy and pictorial ineffectiveness. We refer him to the author's remarks on the further idiosyncrasies of English art and on Mr. Ruskin's theories. They will yield some of the elements of that critical corrective without which Ruskin is so erratic, and with which he is so profitable, a monitor. The art in which the English have best succeeded is that of poetry; the deep impressibility of the moral *ego* feeds the sources of their verse with unequalled generosity:

> "No poetry equals theirs, speaks so strongly and distinctly to the soul, moves it more to the depths, carries in its diction a heavier burden of meaning, reflects better the shocks and the strivings of our inward being, grasps the mind more potently and effectively, and draws from the innermost chords of personality sounds so magnificent and so searching."

The reader will be surprised after this handsome compliment to find M. Taine citing "Aurora Leigh" with infinite admiration as a representative English poem. This choice is a capital example of that want of *initiation* which his history so constantly betrays, of his insensibility to the color and mystery, as we may say, of English diction, and of his consequent failure to apprehend the native code of æsthetics and do justice to a whole great province of the English mind. This province he has hardly visited; he might have gathered there on the outskirts many a Tennysonian, a Wordsworthian, or even a Byronic lyric, telling more in its twenty lines of the real genius of English verse than Mrs. Browning in her twenty thousand. Mrs. Browning, however, was certainly a poet of English temper, and we have no desire to cut the ground from under the feet of genuine admiration.

M. Taine, reviewing his impressions, briefly concludes that the English are better off than the French in three main points: the stability and liberality of their political system; the morality and healthy tone of their religion; the extent of their acquired wealth, and their greater ease in acquiring and producing. Against these advantages he places in France: the better climate; the more equal distribution of property; and the *vie de famille et de société.* You have in France the immense advantage that—

> "In talk, you can say anything—go to the end of your story or your theory. Fiction, criticism, art, philosophy, and general curiosity are not shackled, as on the other side of the Channel, by religion, morality, and the official proprieties. . . . These differences make the English stronger, the French happier."

A very obvious remark is that if, just now, the French can manage to be happy, we can but wonder and admire. But, in fact, French optimism has been pretty rudely tested through the whole course of French history. The "spirit of conversation" apparently holds its own. May it still stand firm and continue to produce talents as vigorous, as living, as national as that of M. Taine!

Nation, January 25, 1872

History of English Literature. By H. A. Taine. Translated by H. Van Laun. New York: Holt and Williams, 1871.

WE HESITATE TO EXPRESS perfect satisfaction at the appearance of an English version of M. Taine's massive essay. On the one hand, the performance is no more than a proper compliment to a highly complimentary work; but, on the other, it involves so effective a violation of the spirit of that work and so rude a displacement of its stand-point, as to interfere with a just comprehension of it. M. Taine himself, however, stands sponsor in a short Preface, and the liberal reception of the two volumes seems to indicate that English readers are not sensible of having unduly lost by the transfer. The English version may fairly demand success on its own merits, being careful, exact, and spirited. It errs, we think, on the side of a too literal exactness, through which it frequently ceases to be idiomatic. "He tore from his vitals, ..." for instance, "the idea which he had conceived," would render M. Taine's figure better than "he tore from his *entrails*." And it is surely in strong contradiction to the author's portrait of Lord

Macaulay to translate his allusion to the great historian's *physionomie animée et pensante* by "an animated and pensive face." No one, we fancy, not even M. Taine, ever accused Lord Macaulay of being pensive.

M. Taine's work is a history of our literature only in a partial sense of the term. "Just as astronomy," he says, "is at bottom a problem in mechanics, and physiology a problem in chemistry, so history at bottom is a problem in psychology." His aim has been "to establish the psychology of a people." A happier title for his work, therefore, save for its amplitude, would be, "A Comparative Survey of the English Mind in the leading Works of its Literature." It is a picture of the English intellect, with literary examples and allusions in evidence, and not a record of works nor an accumulation of facts. To philological or biographical research it makes no claim. In this direction it is altogether incomplete. Various important works are unmentioned, common tradition as to facts is implicitly accepted, and dates, references, and minor detail conspicuous by their absence. The work is wholly critical and pictorial, and involves no larger information than the perusal of a vast body of common documents. Its purpose is to discover in the strongest features of the strongest works the temper of the race and time; which involves a considerable neglect not only of works, but of features. But what is mainly to the point with the English reader (as it is of course excessively obvious in the English version) is that M. Taine writes from an avowedly foreign stand-point. The unit of comparison is throughout assumed to be the French mind. The author's undertaking strikes us, therefore, constantly as an *excursion*. It is not as if he and our English tongue were old friends, as if through a taste early formed and long indulged he had gradually been won to the pious project of paying his debt and embodying his impressions; but as if rather, on reaching his intellectual majority and coming into a handsome property of doctrine and dogma, he had cast about him for a field to conquer, a likely subject for experiment, and, measuring the vast capacity of our English record of expression, he had made a deliberate and immediate choice. We may fancy him declaring, too, that he would do the thing handsomely; devote five or six years to it, and spend five or six months in the country.

He has performed his task with a vigor proportionate to this sturdy resolve; but in the nature of the case his treatment of the subject lacks that indefinable quality of spiritual initiation which is the tardy consummate fruit of a wasteful, purposeless, passionate sympathy. His opinions are prompted, not by a sentiment, but by a design. He remains an interpreter of the English mind to the mind of another race; and only remotely, therefore,—only by allowance and assistance,—an interpreter of the English mind to itself. A greater fault than any of his special errors of judgment is a certain reduced, contracted, and limited air in the whole field. He has made his subject as definite as his method.

M. Taine is fairly well known by this time as a man with a method, the apostle of a theory,—the theory that "vice and virtue are products, like vitriol and sugar," and that art, literature, and conduct are the result of forces which differ from those of the physical world only in being less easily ascertainable. His three main factors—they have lately been reiterated to satiety—are the race, the medium, and the time. Between them they shape the phenomena of history. We have not the purpose of discussing this doctrine; it opens up a dispute as ancient as history itself,—the quarrel between the minds which cling to the supernatural and the minds which dismiss it. M. Taine's originality is not in his holding of these principles, but in his lively disposition to apply them, or, rather, in the very temper and terms in which he applies them. No real observer but perceives that a group of works is more or less the product of a "situation," and that as he himself is forever conscious of the attrition of infinite waves of circumstance, so the cause to which, by genius as by "fate," he contributes, is a larger deposit in a more general current. Observers differ, first, as to whether there are elements in the deposit which cannot be found in the current; second, as to the variety and complexity of the elements: maintaining, on the one side, that fairly to enumerate them and establish their mutual relations the vision of science is as yet too dim; and, on the other, that a complete analysis is at last decently possible, and with it a complete explanation. M. Taine is an observer of the latter class; in his own sole person indeed he almost includes it. He pays in his Preface a handsome tribute to the great service rendered by Sainte-Beuve to the new criticism. Now Sainte-Beuve is, to our sense, the better apostle of the two. In purpose the least doctrinal of critics, it was by his very horror of dogmas, moulds, and formulas, that he so effectively contributed to the science of literary interpretation. The truly devout patience with which he kept his final conclusion in abeyance until after an exhaustive survey of the facts, after perpetual returns and ever-deferred farewells to them, is his living testimony to the importance of the facts. Just as he could never reconcile himself to saying his last word on book or author, so he never pretended to have devised a method which should be a key to truth. The truth for M. Taine lies stored up, as one may say, in great lumps and blocks, to be released and detached by a few lively hammer-blows; while for Sainte-Beuve it was a diffused and imponderable essence, as vague as the carbon in the air which nourishes vegetation, and, like it, to be disengaged by patient chemistry. His only method was fairly to dissolve his attention in the sea of circumstance surrounding the object of his study, and we cannot but think his frank provisional empiricism more truly scientific than M. Taine's premature philosophy. In fact, M. Taine plays fast and loose with his theory, and is mainly successful in so far as he is inconsequent to it. There is a constantly visible hiatus between his formula and his application of it. It serves as his badge and motto, but his best strokes are prompted by the independent personal impression. The larger conditions of his subject loom vaguely in the background, like a richly figured tapestry of good regulation pattern, gleaming here and there in the author's fitful glance, and serving a picturesque purpose decidedly more than a scientific one. This is especially noticeable in the early chapters of the present work, where the changes are rung to excess upon a note of rather slender strain,—the common "Gothic" properties of history and fiction,—Norse blood, gloomy climate, ferocious manners, considered as shaping forces. The same remark applies, we imagine, to the author's volumes on Italy, where a thin soil of historical evidence is often made to produce some most luxuriant flowers of deduction. The historical position is vague, light, and often insecure, and the author's passage from the general conditions to the particular case is apt to be a flying leap of fancy, which, though admirable writing, is rather imperfect science.

We of course lack space to discuss his work in its parts. His portrayal of authors and works is always an attempt to fix the leading or motive faculty, and through his neglect of familiar details and his amplification of the intellectual essence which is the object of his search, his figures often seem out of drawing to English eyes. He distorts the outline, confounds the light and shade, and alters the coloring. His judgments are sometimes very happy and sometimes very erroneous. He proposes some very wise amendments to critical tradition; in other cases he enforces the common verdict with admirable point and vigor. For Spenser, for instance, we doubt whether the case has ever been stated with a more sympathetic and penetrating eloquence. His errors and misjudgments arise partly from his being so thoroughly a stranger to what we may call the intellectual climate of our literature, and partly from his passionate desire to simplify his conception and reduce it to the limits, not merely of the distinctly knowable, but of the symmetrically and neatly presentable. The leading trait of his mind, and its great defect, is an inordinate haste to conclude, combined with a passion for a sort of largely pictorial and splendidly comprehensive expression. A glance at the list of his works will show how actively he has kept terms with each of these tendencies. He is, to our sense, far from being a man of perceptions; the bent of his genius seems to be to generate ideas and images on two distinct lines. For ourselves, on the whole, we prefer his images. These are immensely rich and vivid, and on this side the author is a great artist. His constant effort is to reconcile and harmonize these two groups, and make them illumine and vivify each other. Where he succeeds his success is admirable, and the reader feels that he has rarely seen a truth so completely presented. Where he fails the violence of his diction only serves to emphasize the inadequacy of his conception. M. Taine's great strength is to be found close to his eminent fallibility as a critic,—in his magnificent power of eloquent and vivid statement and presentation. His style is admirable; we know of none that is at once more splendid and more definite, that has at once more structure and more color. Just as his natural preference is evidently for energy and vehemence in talent, his own movement is toward a sort of monstrous cumulative violence of expression; to clinch, to strike, to hit hard, to hit again, till the idea rings and resounds, to force color *à l'outrance* and make proportion massive, is his notion of complete utterance. This is productive of many effects splendid in themselves, but it is fatal to truth in so far as truth resides in fine shades and degrees.

In this intense constructive glow, M. Taine quite forgets his subject and his starting-point; the impetus of his rhetoric, the effort to complete his picture and reach forward to the strongest word and the largest phrase, altogether absorbs him. For ourselves, we confess that, as we read, we cease to hold him at all rigidly to his premises, and content ourselves with simply enjoying the superb movement of his imagination, thankful when it lights his topic at all truly, and mainly conscious of its radiance as color, heat, and force. Thus, while as a gallery of portraits the work demands constant revision and correction, as a sort of enormous *tableau vivant*, ingeniously and artificially combined, it is extremely rich and various. A phrase of very frequent occurrence with M. Taine, and very wholesome in its frequency, is *la grande invention*; his own tendency is to practise it. In effort and inclination, however, he is nothing if not impartial; and there is something almost touching in the sympathetic breadth of his admiration for a tone of genius so foreign to French tradition as the great Scriptural inspiration of Bunyan and of Milton. To passionate vigor he always does justice. On the other hand, when he deals with a subject simply because it stands in his path, he is far less satisfactory. His estimate of Swift is a striking example of his tendency to overcharge his portrait and make a picture at all hazards. Swift was a bitter and incisive genius, but he had neither the volume nor the force implied in M. Taine's report of him. We might add a hundred instances of the fatally defective perception of "values," as the painters say, produced by the author's foreign stand-point. M. Taine expresses altogether the "Continental" view of Byron, between which and the English view there is much the same difference as between the estimate Byron courted and the estimate he feared. A hundred special points may be conceded; but few modern Englishmen are prepared to accept him, as a whole, as the consistently massive phenomenon described by M. Taine. Touching the later poets, the author is extremely incomplete and fallacious; he pretends, indeed, merely to sketch general tendencies. On Wordsworth, however, he has some pertinent remarks from that protesting man-of-the-world point of view to which the great frugal bard drives most Englishmen for desperate refuge, let alone an epigrammatic Frenchman. We are tempted to say that a Frenchman who should have twisted himself into a relish for Wordsworth would almost have forfeited our respect. On Thackeray and Dickens he has two chapters of great suggestiveness to those who know the authors, but on the whole of excessively contracted outline. Of course, one cannot pronounce upon important literary figures, of whatever dimensions, without a certain work of elimination; but a valid charge against M. Taine is that, whereas your distinctly sensitive critic finds this process to be an effort, M. Taine has the air of finding it a relief. A compromise is perfectly legitimate so long as it is not offered as a synthesis.

With all abatements, and especially in spite of one most important abatement, M. Taine's work remains a very admirable performance. As a philosophical effort it is decidedly a failure; as the application of a theory it is ineffective; but it is a great literary achievement. The fruit of an extremely powerful, vivacious, and observant mind, it is rich in suggestive sidelights and forcible aids to opinion. With a great many errors of detail, as a broad expression of the general essence of the English genius it seems to us equally eloquent and just. M. Taine has felt this genius with an intensity and conceived it with a lucidity which, in themselves, form a great intellectual feat. Even under this head the work is not conclusive in the sense in which the author tenders it, but it is largely and vividly contributive, and we shall wait till we have done better ourselves before we judge it too harshly. It is, in other words, very entertaining provisional criticism and very perfect final art. It is, indeed, a more significant testimony to the French genius than to the English, and bears more directly upon the author's native literature than on our own. In its powerful, though arbitrary, unity of composition, in its sustained æsthetic temper, its brilliancy, variety, and symmetry, it is a really monumental accession to a literature which, whatever its limitations in the reach of its ideas, is a splendid series of masterly compositions.

Atlantic Monthly, April 1872

Notes on Paris. The Life and Opinions of M. Frederic-Thomas Graindorge, etc. By H. A. Taine. Translated by John Austin Stevens. New York: Henry Holt & Co., 1875.

THIS IS a very clever work, but it is by no means one of the author's most successful. Indeed, though a brilliant failure, no one, we believe, has ever pretended that it was anything but a failure. The author has tried a *tour de force*, and missed his effect. He has attempted to force his talent, but his talent has resisted and proved fatally inflexible. He has wished to be light and graceful, but he has succeeded only in being most elaborately and magnificently grave. For M. Taine to attempt lightness was, it seems to us, a most ill-advised undertaking. It is true that he has been charged, as the historian of English literature, with a certain presumptuous levity of judgment; but in form, at least, he is always solid, weighty, and majestic. There are few writers whom, as simple writers, we prefer; his style is full of color and muscle and savor; but we never suppose ourselves, in reading it, to be dabbling in light literature, and we rarely take it but in moderate quantities at a sitting. If M. Taine treats a subject at all, he bears heavily; the touch-and-go manner is a closed book to him. Here he has tried the touch-and-go manner, and the effect is very much like hearing a man with a deep bass voice trying to sing an air written for a thin tenor. There is such a thing as being too serious to succeed in a *jeu d'esprit*, and this has been M. Taine's trouble. A writer of half the value would have done much better with the same material, and, indeed, we remember that at the same time that M. Taine's work appeared, eight years ago, and was voted by all good critics a rather melancholy mistake, M. Gustave Droz was making his literary fortune with 'Monsieur, Madame et Bébé,' being acknowledged to have hit the nail on the head with his little silver hammer far more justly than the historian of English literature with his formidable battering-ram. Yet one reads the book, as a failure if not as success, and, all abatements made, we feel ourselves to be dealing with a man of extraordinary talent. It is very possible that it may have even more readers in English than in French, and to the American public seem decidedly entertaining. We apparently are capable of consuming an inordinate quantity of information, veracious or the reverse, about Paris, and the present volume is sufficiently free-spoken as to those social mysteries which are deemed typically Parisian. Many readers will take much satisfaction in reading in English what could not possibly with decency have originally been written in English. M. Taine is not easy to translate; but, well translated, he need be but a trifle less effective than in his own tongue. He loses very much less in a foreign version than his great fellow-critic Sainte-Beuve; for his chief characteristics are not subtlety and fugitive, idiomatic grace, but vigor and amplitude and a certain imaginative splendor, such as the English language is peculiarly qualified to render. To translate Taine, indeed, is in a measure to make him restore what he has borrowed, for there is a large English element in his style. The present translation has been very cleverly done, and the right word often found where some taste was required to select it.

Exactly what M. Taine desired to do we hardly know; what he has done is to produce a singular compound of Stendhal and Théophile Gautier. Stendhal, as all readers of our author know, is the divinity of whom M. Taine is the prophet. Stendhal invented a method of observation which, in M. Taine's opinion, renewed the whole science of literary and social criticism. This method M. Taine has constantly applied—first to authors and books, then to works of art, and at last, in this case, to men and women, to a society. It was in this last fashion that Stendhal himself chiefly used his method; he was not a literary critic, he was a practical psychologist; he lived most of his life in Italy, and his work was the study and description of human nature in Milan, Florence, and Rome. He accumulated facts and anecdotes; he judged that there were none too trivial to serve as a stroke in the portrait; and he has left a storehouse of good, bad, and indifferent ones. M. Taine has proposed to do for Paris what Stendhal did for Milan; but he has come fifty years later, and he is consequently much more complex and needs a great deal more machinery. He is picturesque, for instance, both by necessity and by taste, which Stendhal was not at all, in intention; his book overflows with the description of material objects—of face and hair, shoulders and arms, jewels, dresses, and furniture—and it is evident in all this description that, although M. Taine is a man of too individual a temperament to be an imitator, he has read Théophile Gautier, the master in this line, with great relish and profit. He is shooting in Gautier's premises, and when he brings down a bird we cannot help regarding it as Gautier's property.

M. Taine has endeavored to imagine a perfect observer, and he has given this gentleman's personality as a setting to his own extremely characteristic lucubrations. His observer is M. Frederic-Thomas Graindorge, a Frenchman, a bachelor, a man of fifty, who has made a fortune by hog-packing in Cincinnati, and returns to Paris in the afternoon of his days to take his ease, see the polite world in epitome, and systematize a little his store of observations. He has gone through the mill and been ground very fine; he was at school at Eton, as a boy; he was afterwards at the University of Jena; he has passed twenty years in our own great West, where his adventures have been of the most remarkable description. In his local color, as to this phase of his hero's antecedents, M. Taine is very much at fault; and this is the greater pity, as he has never failed to profess that one should speak only of that which one directly and personally knows. He knows the manners and customs of our Western States in a very roundabout and theoretical fashion; he seems to be under the impression, for instance, that the picturesque art of hog-packing (up to the time of our late war) was carried on in Cincinnati by slave-labor. "I desire only to listen and to look," says M. Graindorge; "I listen and I look; no woman is displeased at being looked at; nor any man at being listened to. Sometimes, as I button up my overcoat, an idea comes to me: I write it down when I go home; hence my notes. You see that this is not a literary matter." It is much more literary than M. Graindorge admits; and his notes have been for M. Taine quite as much an exercise of style as an expression of opinion. He writes admirably; he writes too well; he is simply the very transparent mask of the real author. He is, therefore, as a person, a decidedly ineffective creation, and it was hardly worth while to be at so much labor to construct him. But the point was that M. Taine desired full license to be sceptical and cynical, to prove that he had no prejudices; that he judged things not sentimentally but rationally; that he saw the workings of the *machine humaine* completely *à nu*, and he could do all this under cover of a fictitious M. Graindorge more gracefully than in his own person. M. Graindorge is the most brutal of materialists, and the more he watches the great Parisian spectacle, the greater folly it seems to him to be otherwise. He finds it all excessively ugly, except in so far as it is redeemed by a certain number of pretty women in beautiful dresses, cut very low. But though it is ugly, it is not depressing; exaltation and depression have nothing to do with it; the thing is to see—to see minutely, closely, with your own eyes, not to be a dupe, to find it very convenient that others are, to treat life and your fellow-mortals as a spectacle, to relish a good dinner, and keep yourself in as luxurious a physical good-humor as possible until the "machine" stops working. That of M. Graindorge ceases to operate in the course of the present volume, and the book closes with a statement of his "intimate" personal habits by his secretary, in lieu of a funeral oration.

Nation, May 6, 1875

LETTER FROM PARIS: *Les origines de la France contemporaine.* Paris, 1875.

PARIS, Dec. 18.—1 just now mentioned M. Taine's new book, which is the literary event of the day, and is very well worth speaking of. The history of the French Revolution, upon which he has so long been engaged, proves to be a work of the somewhat larger scope, which the title I quoted above would indicate. The first volume, a stout octavo of 550 pages, came out two or three days since; it is devoted to the "Ancien Régime." M. Taine has been so much translated that he has now, to English eyes, a tolerably distinct physiognomy. With the exception of M. Renan, he is now the most

brilliant French writer, albeit that he is not in the Academy.
But in truth, with his extraordinary store of general knowledge and his magnificent skill in that office, which is considered the peculiar function of academies—presentation,
exhibition, harmonious arrangement—M. Taine is an academy in himself. He is very far from infallible, and so are academies; but like them, right or wrong, he always speaks with a
certain accumulated authority. I speak of him advisedly as a
"writer," for although he is also a logician, a metaphysician,
a thinker, and a scholar, it is the literary quality of his genius
that I most highly relish. I suspect, moreover, that it is the
side that he most relishes himself, and that, on the whole, it
is the most valuable side. Some of his theories have been severely riddled by criticism, but at the worst he is capital reading. His style in his present work flows in as ample a current
as ever; one sees that it has been fed from many sources. His
theories here, moreover, are not obtrusive. His work has been
chiefly one of narration and exposition. He has given a complete picture of the structure and condition of the French society that preceded the Revolution—its organization, its
habits, its occupations, its public and private economy, its
diet, its costume, its temper, its ideas, its ways of feeling. The
picture is extraordinarily complete, and is executed with that
sustained vigor of which M. Taine only is capable. The eighteenth century in French literature has been turned inside out,
sifted and resifted, explored in its minutest detail; but the
thing has never been done with the method and energy of M.
Taine; there is no other such rich and vivid *résumé*. He has
disinterred new facts, possessed himself of new documents,
illuminated a variety of points with a stronger light, and made
a most interesting book. It is amazing how well we have
come to know the eighteenth century; there was never such a
labor of revivification. The defunct is standing upon his feet
again; he wears his clothes as he used to put them on himself,
and his wig as his valet used to powder it; he has the cares of
life in his cheeks and the look of sympathy in his eyes; not a
wrinkle on his brow, not a detail of his costume is wanting;
he can almost speak, or if he cannot speak he easily can listen.
If he listens to M. Taine he will hear some painful truths. M.
Taine is supposed to intend to take a reactionary view of the

French Revolution, and to devote himself chiefly to that somewhat neglected province of history, the injury it did to France. It is high time, certainly, that this work were done, from the liberal and philosophical standpoint. In this volume, however, the author is by no means reactionary; a more damning indictment than his picture of the social orders that the Revolution swept away cannot be imagined. The criticism of what it in turn established will come later. The book is a curious mine of facts about the old royal and aristocratic habits—about the expenditure of the court and of those who frequented it. I had marked a great many passages for quotation. Page after page is filled with accounts of the sinecures under Louis XIV. and Louis XV. Gentlemen and ladies drew ten and twenty thousand francs a year for performing functions which had not even a name, and others for performing functions which had names which we do not pronounce in English (they do in French), though the functions themselves were strictly nominal. The analysis of the temper and intellectual condition of society is as complete as might have been expected from so keen a psychologist as M. Taine. This is accompanied by a great many characteristic anecdotes. Louis XIV. loved to centralize; he wished the whole aristocracy to be perpetually at court, paying him its respects. He was therefore much gratified, I suppose, when a certain M. de Vardes (the name deserves to be preserved) remarked to him that, "When one is away from your Majesty, one is not only unhappy; one is ridiculous." One might be ridiculous, it appears, even within speaking distance of his Majesty. M. Taine speaks of course of the reign of "sensibility" which set in about the middle of the last century and continued during the Revolution, without the least detriment to that of Terror. It produced a great deal of vaporous sentimentality, but it sometimes gave a very delicate point to the feelings. "We meet thus," says our author, " with actions and expressions of a supreme grace, unique of their kind, like some tiny little masterpiece in Sèvres china." One day when the Countess Amélie de Bouffiers was speaking rather lightly of her husband, her mother-in-law said, "You forget that you are speaking of my son." "It is true," she answered, "I thought I was speaking only of your son-in-law." The virtuous and temperate Madame Elizabeth had sixty thousand dollars allowed her annually for her food. There was doubtless a good deal of reason in Talleyrand's saying that "He who had not lived before 1789 did not know the sweetness of living." There was another point of view, however: the last division of M. Taine's volume, and the most interesting, is on the people. But the whole book is to be read.

New York Tribune, January 8, 1876

M. Taine's Letter on George Sand in the *Journal des Débats*

M. TAINE has just published in the *Journal des Débats* an interesting critical letter upon George Sand. He observes, first, that she is a literary figure whom we have altogether exceptional facilities for knowing and describing.

"In no case can one better apply the method of Sainte-Beuve, who, to understand a great individual, employed physiology, noted the links of consanguinity, observed the parents and the ancestors. We know with details the father and the mother of George Sand, and her grandparents to the fourth generation; we have their letters, we know their private life, we can follow from the King Augustus [of Poland], through the Maréchal de Saxe, Madame Dupin, the *commandant* Dupin, down to George Sand herself, the transmission of an original temperament, of particular faculties which, exaggerated, attenuated, renewed, or transformed by successive 'crosses,' attained their highest development and their most perfect harmony in the final genius who summed them up. There is not in human history another example equally instructive, a collection of materials so rich and going back so far, a case so precious for the light it throws upon psychological heredity."

M. Taine adds that upon George Sand herself information is abundant, and that her 'Histoire de ma Vie' is a complete record of the growth of her mind as well as of her external circumstances during her younger years.

"Then come her novels and her whole work, more than a hundred volumes, of which the weakest deserves a study, for she never wrote simply to write. Even into a tale of thirty pages she put a thought. No one has ever more continually and more sincerely turned over grave questions; she was possessed and beset by them; and in following the series of her novels one might by their testimony write the moral and philosophic history of the age. With a very fixed stock of persistent beliefs and aspirations, she always continued to develop; among her contemporaries she is with Sainte-Beuve almost the only one who voluntarily and deliberately renewed herself, enlarged the circle of her ideas, refused to rest content with answers made once for all. Better still, and through the simple progress of an intelligence which was always active, she passed spontaneously from bad answers to good ones."

She passed, says M. Taine, from the stormy and rebellious temper of her younger years to the quiet conservatism of her later ones; "without lowering her ideal, she reconciled herself to the regular course of life," accepted "work, good sense, reason, society, marriage, the family, all useful, salutary, or necessary things." M. Taine says (justly to our mind) that if George Sand's novels have not the solid realism of those of Balzac, their species is a higher one. "Only, to relish them, you must put yourself at a certain point of view, interest yourself in the portrayal of a finer and better humanity. That of Madame Sand's novels is two or three degrees superior to ours; the men have more talent and genius, the women more heart and devotion, than among ourselves; they all talk better and more eloquently than we; they are framed in a finer scenery, surrounded by landscapes and apartments that have been artistically arranged; it is an ideal world, and to keep up our illusion the writer tones some things down, suppresses others, and often, instead of painting an individual figure, sketches a general outline." M. Taine goes on to say that another merit of her novels is that they each contain, as a groundwork, "a general idea, a philosophic, religious, or moral thesis, a problem of the heart or the conscience, or a problem of education." He adds (but perhaps his confidence on this point is erroneous) that "it is these abstractions, these *tirades*, that will obtain for George Sand a permanent and sympathetic attention when the minute copies of the cleverest painters will have ceased to be understood, or have become mere documents for the historian." Lastly, M. Taine pays a vigorous tribute to Madame Sand's style:

"It places her beyond comparison. . . No one, since the classics of the last two centuries, has had so much eloquence, and this eloquence is never misplaced, for it is the proper tone of an artist who is handling 'questions' and who intentionally gives his characters genius or talent. . . . Nothing is forced, wanton, unequal; everything is abundant, spontaneous, and sound. Towards the middle of her career she had worked herself free of a remnant of a tendency to declamation, and had ceased to think of 'la phrase'; it is probably to her rustic novels and her studies on simplicity of style that she owes this reform. By the same stroke she had discovered a new and exquisite literary form. To my mind, allowing for the distance between poetry and prose, her rustic tales are almost equal to the 'Hermann and Dorothea' of Goethe. Their style is unique—as Greek as that of Goethe, with this difference: that Goethe's verses seem imitated from Homer, and that George Sand's narrative appears to have been inspired by Xenophon."

He finds an analogy between her dialogues and those of the 'Cyropædia,' and he says in conclusion that "in a civilization like ours, beneath such an encumberment of abstractions and theories, in the midst of a literature so complicated and so composite, this creation, this renovation of the primitive tongue, is an unexampled *tour de force*. No portion of the immense work of George Sand gives so high an idea of the originality of her genius and the flexibility of her mind."

Nation, July 27, 1876

Victor Tissot

LETTER FROM PARIS: *Les Prussiens en Allemagne*. Paris, 1876.

PARIS, March 10.—There is a certain analogy between this brave burlesque and the lively travesty of actual things presented in M. Victor Tissot's second volume on his adventures in Germany. The book has been out but a few days, and it is already in its eighth edition. M. Victor Tissot is the author of the "Voyage aux Pays des Milliards," which was published a few months since, and is now in its twenty-second edition. He at present gives a sequel, "Les Prussiens en Allemagne," which I suppose will gain the same distinction as its predecessor—that of being placed under an interdict in Berlin. This last circumstance raises the one presumption in favor of M. Tissot's veracity. He is exceedingly clever, admirably observant, and his Teutophobia, as an exhibition of vivacity and energy, is really very fine. But, like M. Lemoinne's England, his Germany is quite an "article de Paris." I heard a gentleman of Germanic sympathies characterize an impertinent fable the other day as "du Tissot tout pur," and certainly M. Tissot's reader largely repunctuates his pages with interrogation marks. He should remember the proverb that he who wishes to prove too much proves nothing. The French, they say, are beginning to study Germany, but they had better not take M. Tissot's volumes for their text-books.

New York Tribune, April 1, 1876

Voyage aux Pays Annexés. Par Victor Tissot. Paris: Dentu; New York: F. W. Christern, 1877.

M. VICTOR TISSOT, since the Franco-German war, has been the authorized interpreter of Germany to his fellow-countrymen. Since his laborious investigations have been given to the world let no one say that the French are superficial. It being generally observed at the close of the war that, while the Germans were deeply versed in their neighbors' secrets, the French had been content to know little or nothing of the state of things beyond the Rhine, many Frenchmen

declared that they must change all that, and that, heroically
overmastering a natural antipathy to the subject, they must
study Germany even as Germany had studied them. They
must be serious, searching, thorough. M. Victor Tissot appears to have been, in an eminent degree, of this opinion; he
sallied forth in the van of the new explorers. He is a young
man who seems to have been prepared for his task by a brief
residence in a German university before the war. He therefore
has some acquaintance with the German language and literature—a sort of accomplishment which French investigators
of foreign parts have not always considered indispensable. He
pretends, according to the French phrase, to have paid with
his person—to have seen, heard, felt, and tasted all the abominations which he describes. His experiences were embodied,
to begin with, in the 'Voyage aux Pays des Milliards'—a volume which has reached its thirty-sixth edition. Then came
'Les Prussiens en Allemagne,' and now we have the volume
whose title we have transcribed. The 'Prussiens en Allemagne'
is in its twenty-sixth edition, and, doubtless, an equal prosperity is in store for the present work. M. Victor Tissot, well
as he has worked his ground, has by no means exhausted it.
He announces as in preparation 'Vienne et la Vie Viennoise'
and—what will probably be the gem of his collection—'L'Allemagne Amoureuse.' It is when this last volume appears that
the hypocritical Teutons will really "catch it."

   M. Victor Tissot is very clever; he is an accomplished book
maker, and his productions are, in form, very readable. But
they strike us as melancholy performances, and, without in
the least pretending to bend a servile knee to Prince Bismarck,
we regret that M. Tissot has not made a better use of his
cleverness. A considerable portion of the French public takes
him, doubtless, at his proper value; but the large sale of his
books seems to prove that that ignorance of German affairs
to which the French charge the calamities of their campaign
is incapable of being seriously modified. Whereas formerly it
was flavored with indifference, it is now seasoned with positive hatred; but this is the only change it has undergone. People appear to accept stories about the Germans very much as
they would receive statements about the South Sea Islanders;
there is nothing in the recipient's mind to exercise the least

control over the aberrations of the narrator. M. Tissot's plan has been perfectly simple—to be ferociously and consistently scurrilous and abusive. We do wrong perhaps to say "consistently"; for as the author accuses the Prussians of every conceivable vice and iniquity, there is sometimes less method in his madness than there should be—he violates the logic of vituperation itself. Few people, even Prussians, can have literally all the vices; few people can have all diseases at once. The Prussians, of course, are the object of M. Tissot's peculiar contempt; the fate which overtook the cities of the plain would be, to his mind, too good for them by half. His plan is to represent the more immediate subjects of M. de Brandebourg (as he is fond of calling the Emperor William) as plunged in horrible depravity, while the other Germans, without abatement of their own peculiar immoralities, groan over those of their oppressors. It is remarkable how the occasion always favors M. Tissot's own view of matters. In Bavaria, in Hanover, in Baden, the first person he speaks to, if it is only to ask what o'clock it is, immediately bursts into a diatribe against the ruling race. Just so in the haunts of the ruling race itself, every person or thing that M. Tissot's eyes rest upon, every word that he hears spoken, happens to be a capital example of Prussian brutality, indecency, and general baseness. But a specimen of M. Tissot's style is worth many descriptions. Here are some of his impressions of the Rhine. At Niederbreisig,

> "It has lost the grand, wild character which was formerly its beauty; the knightly river has become the river of grocers; . . . you smell cabbage-soup, burnt coffee, and cheese. The masters of Reineck and Argenfels stand shaving upon their towers, and spread out their flannel shirts in the sun. The mistresses ride on asthmatic hacks and give assignation to the officers of Cologne and Coblentz, who are as stiff in their corsets as great girls; and for madrigals to touch their heart, they must be wrapped up in bank-notes."

It is not remarkable that M. Tissot should have found the capital of such a population "a combination of a prison, a Terror, and a tomb." The last chapters of the volume before us treat of the author's observations in Alsace and Lorraine, where the "Kreis-Director," or sub-prefect, incurs his especial contumely. "He is invariably a *doctor*; they are all doctors, indeed, as in Paris all the Auvergnats are water-carriers. . . . He has rolled through the universities, played all the tricks, stolen dogs, beaten servant-girls, and fought duels. Before the war he wore out his only pair of patched breeches in an obscure post in Westphalia or Pomerania, where, to pass his time, he begat children." His wife is a match for him. A shoemaker told M. Tissot that a *Kreis-Directorin* used to come to him without any stockings to be measured for shoes. As we have said, fortune favors M. Tissot. He sits down to dinner on a Rhine steamboat, and a lady opposite asks the waiter for a small spoon. Immediately a gentleman beside him offers her his own. "I have finished," he says, "my coffee." But it is a pity, doubtless, to make too much of M. Tissot, for good or for evil. As a compiler of historical and literary odds and ends he resorts to rather cheap expedients, and as a narrator of things seen and heard he has not the art of impressing us with his veracity. The popularity of his volumes makes them worth noticing, however, with the reflection that it seems a pity that the perusal of this ingenious but essentially vulgar vituperation should appear to French readers the best way of arriving at that knowledge of the reality of things beyond the Rhine in which they have confessed themselves deficient. M. Tissot defeats his own end; he represents the late antagonists of France as a swarm of fabulous monsters—grotesque chimeras, not seriously to be reckoned with.

Nation, May 17, 1877

Émile Zola

LETTER FROM PARIS: *Son Excellence Eugène Rougon.*

PARIS, April 22.—Another book of the hour is Emile Zola's new novel, "Son Excellence Eugène Rougon," which has obtained a success not hitherto enjoyed by the productions of this remarkable young writer. The success of the present work is owing partly to its cleverness, partly to the fact that it is a presentation, through a transparent vail, of actual persons, and chiefly, I suspect, to its brutal indecency. Eugène Rougon is Eugène Rouher, M. de Marsy is M. de Morny, and the initiated will tell you who Clorinda Balbi, the heroine, is. This last is a most amazing portrait. Émile Zola, a "pupil" of Gustave Flaubert, is, as a novelist, the most thorough-going of the little band of the out-and-out realists. Unfortunately the real, for him, means exclusively the unclean, and he utters his crudities with an air of bravado which makes them doubly intolerable.

New York Tribune, May 13, 1876

Une Page d'Amour. Par Émile Zola. Paris: Charpentier; New York: F. W. Christern, 1878.

A NEW NOVEL by the author of 'L'Assommoir' is certain to attract a good deal of attention; but we think it is safe to say that the volume before us is not destined to achieve the peculiar vogue of that remarkable work. (We observe, however, that at the present writing, a very short time after its appearance, 'Une Page d'Amour' has reached a fourth edition.) M. Émile Zola has evidently proposed to himself in the present case to strike a different note from that of 'L'Assommoir,' and to show that he can treat of innocence and purity as well as of misery, vice, and uncleanness. For this purpose he has resorted to radical measures—he has taken for his heroine a little girl of eleven years of age. We cannot say that, however creditable it may be to M. Zola's higher motives, the device has been successful; for 'Une Page d'Amour' has neither the power, the brilliancy, nor the extraordinary technical qualities, as they may be called, of its predecessor. It must be added that the author's attempt to show that he appreciates purity of subject is attended with some remarkable incidents. We should say, however, before going farther, that in his preface M. Zola distinctly repudiates any such short-sighted motive as a desire to throw a sop to public opinion. He prefixes to the present tale the genealogical tree of the Rougon-Macquart family, of whose various members and off-shoots the eight novels of his great series already published embody a portion of the history. This history, says M. Zola, is to be unfolded in twelve more novels; and he declares that the genealogical tree in question has not been invented after the fact—at one of the later stages of the working-out of his remarkable scheme—but was completely prepared and elaborated in 1868, before a line of the first novel ('La Fortune des Rougon') was written. M. Zola publishes it now as a proof that every detail of his immense plan was settled in advance. This, to even moderately sympathetic readers, is perfectly credible; for whatever may be the author's defects, he gives us the impression of extraordinary elaborateness and patience of arrangement. This, indeed, is almost his strongest quality; he evidently sat himself down at the outset and tabulated, as it were, the enormous contents of his twenty novels— pigeon-holed his episodes and characters as if he had been a clerk in a post-office. When the twentieth is published he will certainly have performed an almost unprecedented task; his only rival will have been Balzac, and in some respects the laborious, and, as he would allege, scientific quality of his performance has hardly been equalled in the 'Comédie Humaine.' He requests that full judgment on each of his novels be not passed until the series is complete and the individual story may be examined according to its place in the scale.

A partial judgment, however, he admits that the reader is welcome to form; and it is by the light of this partial judgment that we feel justified in saying that the present episode in the history of the race of Rougon-Macquart is both disagreeable and dull. 'L'Assommoir' was prodigiously disagreeable, but it could not, on the whole, be pronounced dull. 'Une Page d'Amour' suggests, as we read, in a much less degree the need for disinfectants and deodorizers; but neither has it, on the other hand, the really magnificent reality of its companion. An "œuvre intime et de demi-teinte" M. Zola pronounces it in his preface; but, in spite of this gracefully-sounding qualification, the story has little that is positively agreeable. The author of 'L'Assommoir' has not an agreeable imagination; and let him select from life what objects he will, the light it projects upon them is, in the nature of the case, a turbid one. He puts before us here a certain Hélène Grandjean, of the stock of the Rougons, whose childhood has been touched upon in a former story. She is young, beautiful, and virtuous, and she has been left a widow, in Paris, with a small income and a little daughter, a child of a morbidly affectionate nature, of a jealous, suspicious, and fantastic disposition, and liable to convulsions, epileptic fits, and other grievous ailments. This little girl, who, as we have said, is properly the heroine of the tale, is apparently meant to appeal to our tenderest sentiments; but we feel bound to declare that, of all unhealthy children, she is represented by M. Zola as the most detestable, the most ill-bred, the most impossible to live with. She is constantly ill, and her mother is obliged frequently to call in the doctor; the consequence of which is that the doctor (who has a wife of his own) falls madly in love with Madame Grandjean, and that Madame Grandjean (who has become a good friend of the wife) reciprocates, and very soon gratifies, his passion. On one occasion, while she is occupied in gratifying it in the Rue Taitbout, the little girl, left at home alone naturally, conceives such grief, shame, and anger at her deserted condition and her mother's estrangement that she falls into a paroxysm which proves fatal, and to which she presently succumbs. Her illness and death are minutely described (and, it must be added, very powerfully; these pages are the most effective in the volume), together with the remorse and shame of her mother, who has immediately dismissed the doctor. Afterwards, Madame Grandjean marries a former suitor, "rentre," says M. Zola, by no means ironically, "dans l'orgueil de son honnêteté," visits the grave of the little girl in the cemetery at Passy, and quite washes her hands, morally, of the circumstances attending the child's death.

The matter, the *fonds*, of M. Zola's story strikes us as very weak and common, and, in so far as the tale is a history of the guilty mother, it is strangely ineffective. To this singular figure of the exceptionally virtuous widow, who throws herself into the arms of her daughter's physician, and then gets so bravely over it, the author has imparted neither solidity nor coherency. The doctor, too, remains simply a peculiarly unpleasant shadow—something like a bad odor. As a history of the child herself, 'Une Page d'Amour' exhibits a certain quantity of the author's skill in producing a sense of reality. There is a terrible abuse of description, but much of the description hits the mark; and probably only M. Zola could have written the thirty or forty pages, at the close, describing the little girl's last illness. It is probable that everything he produces will exhibit the same incongruity—the application of a remarkably complete and powerful method, an extremely solid literary instrument, to objects meanly and, as we may say, ignorantly chosen and bathed in an atmosphere of low-class Parisian cockneyism. If, with his talent and his resolution, he had what we may call a little more horizon, his work would be tripled in value. But, such as it is, he will certainly conduct it to its goal; he will fill out his programme, and, in doing so, he will have performed one of the most remarkable literary tasks of our day.

Nation, May 30, 1878

Nana. Paris, 1880.

M. ZOLA'S NEW NOVEL has been immensely talked about for the last six months; but we may doubt whether, now that we are in complete possession of it, its fame will further increase. It is a difficult book to read; we have to push our way through it very much as we did through *L'Assommoir*, with the difference that in *L'Assommoir* our perseverance, our patience, were constantly rewarded, and that in *Nana*, these qualities have to content themselves with the usual recompense of virtue, the simple sense of duty accomplished. I do not mean, indeed, by this allusion to duty that there is any moral obligation to read *Nana*; I simply mean that such an exertion may have been felt to be due to

M. Zola by those who have been interested in his general attempt. His general attempt is highly interesting, and *Nana* is the latest illustration of it. It is far from being the most successful one; the obstacles to the reader's enjoyment are numerous and constant. It is true that, if we rightly understand him, enjoyment forms no part of the emotion to which M. Zola appeals; in the eyes of "naturalism" enjoyment is a frivolous, a superficial, a contemptible sentiment. It is difficult, however, to express conveniently by any other term the reader's measure of the entertainment afforded by a work of art. If we talk of interest, instead of enjoyment, the thing does not better our case—as it certainly does not better M. Zola's. The obstacles to interest in *Nana* constitute a formidable body, and the most comprehensive way to express them is to say that the work is inconceivably and inordinately dull. M. Zola (if we again understand him) will probably say that it is a privilege, or even a duty, of naturalism to be dull, and to a certain extent this is doubtless a very lawful plea. It is not an absolutely fatal defect for a novel not to be amusing, as we may see by the example of several important works. *Wilhelm Meister* is not a sprightly composition, and yet *Wilhelm Meister* stands in the front rank of novels. *Romola* is a very easy book to lay down, and yet *Romola* is full of beauty and truth. *Clarissa Harlowe* discourages the most robust persistence, and yet, paradoxical as it seems, *Clarissa Harlowe* is deeply interesting. It is obvious, therefore, that there is something to be said for dullness; and this something is perhaps, primarily, that there is dullness and dullness. That of which *Nana* is so truly a specimen, is of a peculiarly unredeemed and unleavened quality; it lacks that human savor, that finer meaning which carries it off in the productions I just mentioned. What *Nana* means it will take a very ingenious apologist to set forth. I speak, of course, of the impression it produces on English readers; into the deep mystery of the French taste in such matters it would be presumptuous for one of these to attempt to penetrate. The other element that stops the English reader's way is that monstrous uncleanness to which—to the credit of human nature in whatever degree it may seem desirable to determine—it is probably not unjust to attribute a part of the facility with which the volume before us has reached, on the day of its being offered for sale by retail, a thirty-ninth edition. M. Zola's uncleanness is not a thing to linger upon, but it is a thing to speak of, for it strikes us as an extremely curious phenomenon. In this respect *Nana* has little to envy its predecessors. The book is, perhaps, not pervaded by that ferociously bad smell which blows through *L'Assommoir* like an emanation from an open drain and makes the perusal of the history of Gervaise and Coupeau very much such an ordeal as a crossing of the Channel in a November gale; but in these matters comparisons are as difficult as they are unprofitable, and *Nana* is, in all conscience, untidy enough. To say the book is indecent, is to make use of a term which (always, if we understand him), M. Zola holds to mean nothing and to prove nothing. Decency and indecency, morality and immorality, beauty and ugliness, are conceptions with which "naturalism" has nothing to do; in M. Zola's system these distinctions are void, these allusions are idle. The only business of naturalism is to be—natural, and therefore, instead of saying of *Nana* that it contains a great deal of filth, we should simply say of it that it contains a great deal of nature. Once upon a time a rather pretentious person, whose moral tone had been corrupted by evil communications, and who lived among a set of people equally pretentious, but regrettably low-minded, being in conversation with another person, a lady of great robustness of judgment and directness of utterance, made use constantly, in a somewhat cynical and pessimistic sense, of the expression, "the world—the world." At last the distinguished listener could bear it no longer, and abruptly made reply: "My poor lady, do you call that corner of a pig-sty in which you happen to live, *the world*?" Some such answer as this we are moved to make to M. Zola's naturalism. Does he call that vision of things of which *Nana* is a representation, *nature*? The mighty mother, in her blooming richness, seems to blush from brow to chin at the insult! On what authority does M. Zola represent nature to us as a combination of the cesspool and the house of prostitution? On what authority does he represent foulness rather than fairness as the sign that we are to know her by? On the authority of his predilections alone; and this is his great trouble and the weak point of his incontestably remarkable talent. This is the point that, as we said just now, makes the singular foulness of his imagination worth touching upon, and which, we should suppose, will do much towards preserving his works for the curious contemplation of the psychologist and the historian of literature. Never was such foulness so spontaneous and so complete, and never was it united with qualities so superior to itself and intrinsically so respectable. M. Zola is an artist, and this is supposed to be a safeguard; and, indeed, never surely was any other artist so dirty as M. Zola! Other performers may have been so, but they were not artists; other such exhibitions may have taken place, but they have not taken place between the covers of a book—and especially of a book containing so much of vigorous and estimable effort. We have no space to devote to a general consideration of M. Zola's theory of the business of a novelist, or to the question of naturalism at large—much further than to say that the system on which the series of *Les Rougons-Macquart* has been written, contains, to our sense, a great deal of very solid ground. M. Zola's attempt is an extremely fine one; it deserves a great deal of respect and deference, and though his theory is constantly at odds with itself, we could, at a pinch, go a long way with it without quarreling. What we quarrel with is his application of it—is the fact that he presents us with his decoction of "nature" in a vessel unfit for the purpose, a receptacle lamentably, fatally in need of scouring (though no scouring, apparently, would be really effective), and in which no article intended for intellectual consumption should ever be served up. Reality is the object of M. Zola's efforts, and it is because we agree with him in appreciating it highly that we protest against its being discredited. In a time when literary taste has turned, to a regrettable degree, to the vulgar and the insipid, it is of high importance that realism should not be compromised. Nothing tends more to compromise it than to represent it as necessarily allied to the impure. That the pure and the impure are for M. Zola, as conditions of taste, vain words, and exploded ideas, only proves that his advocacy does more to injure an excellent cause than to serve it. It takes a very good cause to carry a *Nana* on its back, and if realism breaks down, and the conventional comes in again with a rush, we may know the reason why. The real has not a single shade more affinity with an unclean vessel than with a clean one, and M. Zola's system, carried to its utmost expression, can dispense as little with taste and tact as the floweriest mannerism of a less analytic age. Go as far as we will, so long as we abide in literature, the thing remains always a question of taste, and we can never leave taste behind without leaving behind, by the same stroke, the very grounds on which we appeal, the whole human side of the business. Taste, in its intellectual applications, is the most human faculty we possess, and as the novel may be said to be the most human form of art, it is a poor speculation to put the two things out of conceit of each other. Calling it naturalism will never make it profitable. It is perfectly easy to agree with M. Zola, who has taken his stand with more emphasis than is necessary; for the matter reduces itself to a question of application. It is impossible to see why the question of application is less urgent in naturalism than at any other point of the scale, or why, if naturalism is, as M. Zola claims, a method of observation, it can be followed without delicacy or tact. There are all sorts of things to be said about it; it costs us no effort whatever to admit in the briefest terms that it is an admirable invention, and full of promise; but we stand aghast at the want of tact it has taken to make so unreadable a book as *Nana*.

To us English readers, I venture to think, the subject is very interesting, because it raises questions which no one apparently has the energy or the good faith to raise among ourselves. (It is of distinctly serious readers only that I speak, and *Nana* is to be recommended exclusively to such as have a very robust appetite for a moral.) A novelist with a system, a passionate conviction, a great plan—incontestable attributes of M. Zola—is not now to be easily found in England or the United States, where the storyteller's art is almost exclusively feminine, is mainly in the hands of timid (even when very accomplished) women, whose acquaintance with life is severely restricted, and who are not conspicuous for general views. The novel, moreover, among ourselves, is almost always addressed to young unmarried ladies, or at least always assumes them to be a large part of the novelist's public. This fact, to a French storyteller, appears, of course, a damnable restriction, and M. Zola would probably decline to take *au sérieux* any work produced under such unnatural conditions. Half of life is a sealed book to young unmarried ladies, and how can a novel be worth anything that deals only with half of life? How can a portrait be painted (in any way to be recognizable) of half a face? It is not in one eye, but in the two eyes together that the expression resides, and it is the combination of features that constitutes the human identity. These objections are perfectly valid, and it may be said that our English system is a good thing for virgins and boys, and a bad thing for the novel itself, when the novel is regarded as something more than a simple *jeu d'esprit*, and considered as a composition that treats of life at large and helps us to *know*. But under these unnatural conditions and insufferable restrictions a variety of admirable works have been produced; Thackeray, Dickens, George Eliot, have all had an eye to the innocent classes. The fact is anomalous, and the advocates of naturalism must make the best of it. In fact, I believe they have little relish for the writers I have mentioned. They find that something or other is grievously wanting in their productions—as it most assuredly is! They complain that such writers are not serious. They are not so, certainly, as M. Zola is so; but there are many different ways of being serious. That of the author of *L'Assommoir*, of *La Conquête de Plassans*, of *La Faute de L'Abbé Mouret* may, as I say, with all its merits and defects taken together, suggest a great many things to English readers. They must admire the largeness of his attempt and the richness of his intention. They must admire, very often, the brilliancy of his execution. *L'Assommoir*, in spite of its fetid atmosphere, is full of magnificent passages and episodes, and the sustained power of the whole thing, the art of carrying a weight, is extraordinary. What will strike the English reader of M. Zola at large, however, and what will strike the English reader of *Nana*, if he have stoutness of stomach enough to advance in the book, is the extraordinary absence of humor, the dryness, the solemnity, the air of tension and effort. M. Zola disapproves greatly of wit; he thinks it is an impertinence in a novel, and he would probably disapprove of humor if he *knew* what it is. There is no indication in all his works that he has a suspicion of this; and what tricks the absence of a sense of it plays him! What a mess it has made of this admirable *Nana*! The presence of it, even in a limited degree, would have operated, to some extent, as a disinfectant, and if M. Zola had had a more genial fancy he would also have had a cleaner one. Is it not also owing to the absence of a sense of humor that this last and most violent expression of the realistic faith is extraordinarily wanting in reality? Anything less illusory than the pictures, the people, the indecencies of *Nana*, could not well be imagined. The falling-off from *L'Assommoir* in this respect can hardly be exaggerated. The human note is completely absent, the perception of character, of the way that people feel and think and act, is helplessly, hopelessly at fault; so that it becomes almost grotesque at last to see the writer trying to drive before him a herd of figures that never for an instant stand on their legs. This is what saves us in England, in spite of our artistic levity and the presence of the young ladies—this fact that we are by disposition better psychologists, that we have, as a general thing, a deeper, more delicate perception of the play of character and the state of the soul. This is what often gives an interest to works conceived on a much narrower program than those of M. Zola—makes them more touching and more real, although the apparatus and the machinery of reality may, superficially, appear to be wanting. French novelists are at bottom, with all their extra freedom, a good deal more conventional than our own; and *Nana*, with the prodigious freedom that her author has taken, never, to my sense, leaves for a moment the region of the conventional. The figure of the brutal *fille*, without a conscience or a soul, with nothing but devouring appetites and impudences, has become the stalest of the stock properties of French fiction, and M. Zola's treatment has here imparted to her no touch of superior verity. He is welcome to draw as many figures of the same type as he finds necessary, if he will only make them human; this is as good a way of making a contribution to our knowledge of ourselves as another. It is not his choice of subject that has shocked us; it is the melancholy dryness of his execution, which gives us all the bad taste of a disagreeable dish and none of the nourishment.

Parisian, February 26, 1880

ÉMILE ZOLA

IF IT BE TRUE that the critical spirit to-day, in presence of the rising tide of prose fiction, a watery waste out of which old standards and landmarks are seen barely to emerge, like chimneys and the tops of trees in a country under flood— if it be true that the anxious observer, with the water up to his chin, finds himself asking for the *reason* of the strange phenomenon, for its warrant and title, so we likewise make out that these credentials rather fail to float on the surface. We live in a world of wanton and importunate fable, we breathe its air and consume its fruits; yet who shall say that we are able, when invited, to account for our preferring it so largely to the world of fact? To do so would be to make some adequate statement of the good the product in question does us. What does it do for our life, our mind, our manners, our morals—what does it do that history, poetry, philosophy may not do, as well or better, to warn, to comfort and command the countless thousands for whom and by whom it comes into being? We seem too often left with our riddle on our hands. The lame conclusion on which we retreat is that "stories" are multiplied, circulated, paid for, on the scale of the present hour, simply because people "like" them. As to why people *should* like anything so loose and mean as the preponderant mass of the "output," so little indebted for the magic of its action to any mystery in the making, is more than the actual state of our perceptions enables us to say.

This bewilderment might be our last word if it were not for the occasional occurrence of accidents especially appointed to straighten out a little our tangle. We are reminded that if the unnatural prosperity of the wanton fable cannot be adequately explained, it can at least be illustrated with a sharpness that is practically an argument. An abstract solution failing we encounter it in the concrete. We catch in short a new impression or, to speak more truly, recover an old one. It was always there to be had, but we ourselves throw off an oblivion, an indifference for which there are plenty of excuses. We become conscious, for our profit, of a *case*, and we see that our mystification came from the way cases had appeared for so long to fail us. None of the shapeless forms about us for the time had attained to the dignity of one. The one I am now conceiving as suddenly effective—for which I fear I must have been regarding it as somewhat in eclipse—is that of Émile Zola, whom, as a manifestation of the sort we are considering, three or four striking facts have lately combined to render more objective and, so to speak, more massive. His close connection with the most resounding of recent public quarrels; his premature and disastrous death; above all, at the moment I write, the appearance of his last-finished novel, bequeathed to his huge public from beyond the grave—these rapid events have thrust him forward and made him loom abruptly larger; much as if our pedestrian critic, treading the dusty highway, had turned a sharp corner.

It is not assuredly that Zola has ever been veiled or unapparent; he had, on the contrary been digging his field these thirty years, and for all passers to see, with an industry that kept him, after the fashion of one of the grand grim sowers or reapers of his brother of the brush, or at least of the canvas, Jean-François Millet, duskily outlined against the sky. He was there in the landscape of labour—he had always been; but he was there as a big natural or pictorial feature, a spreading tree, a battered tower, a lumpish round-shouldered useful hayrick, confounded with the air and the weather, the rain and the shine, the day and the dusk, merged more or less, as it were, in the play of the elements themselves. We had got used to him, and, thanks in a measure just to this stoutness of his presence, to the long regularity of his performance, had come to notice him hardly more than the dwellers in the marketplace notice the quarters struck by the town-clock. On top of all accordingly, for our skeptical mood, the sense of his work—a sense determined afresh by the strange climax of his personal history—rings out almost with violence as a reply to our wonder. It is as if an earthquake or some other rude interference had shaken from the town-clock a note of such unusual depth as to compel attention. We therefore once more give heed, and the result of this is that we feel ourselves after a little probably as much enlightened as we can hope ever to be. We have worked round to the so marked and impressive anomaly of the adoption of the futile art by one of the stoutest minds and stoutest characters of our time. This extraordinarily robust worker has found it good enough for him, and if the fact is, as I say, anomalous, we are doubtless helped to conclude that by its anomalies, in future, the bankrupt business, as we are so often moved to pronounce it, will most recover credit.

What is at all events striking for us, critically speaking, is that, in the midst of the dishonour it has gradually harvested by triumphant vulgarity of practice, its pliancy and applicability can still plead for themselves. The curious contradiction stands forth for our relief—the circumstance that thirty years ago a young man of extraordinary brain and indomitable purpose, wishing to give the measure of these endowments in a piece of work supremely solid, conceived and sat down to Les Rougon-Macquart rather than to an equal task in physics, mathematics, politics or economics. He saw his undertaking, thanks to his patience and courage, practically to a close; so that it is exactly neither of the so-called constructive sciences that happens to have had the benefit, intellectually speaking, of one of the few most constructive achievements of our time. There then, provisionally at least, we touch bottom; we get a glimpse of the pliancy and variety, the ideal of vividness, on behalf of which our equivocal form may appeal to a strong head. In the name of what ideal on its own side, however, does the strong head yield to the appeal? What is the logic of its so deeply committing itself? Zola's case seems to tell us, as it tells us other things. The logic is in its huge freedom of adjustment to the temperament of the worker, which it carries, so to say, as no other vehicle can do. It expresses fully and directly the whole man, and big as he may be it can still be big enough for him without becoming false to its type. We see this truth made strong, from beginning to end, in Zola's work; we see the temperament, we see the whole man, with his size and all his marks, stored and packed away in the huge hold of Les Rougon-Macquart as a cargo is packed away on a ship. His personality is the thing that finally pervades and prevails, just as so often on a vessel the presence of the cargo makes itself felt for the assaulted senses. What has most come home to me in reading him over is that a scheme of fiction so conducted is in fact a capacious vessel. It can carry anything—with art and force in the stowage; nothing in this case

will sink it. And it is the only form for which such a claim
can be made. All others have to confess to a smaller scope—
to selection, to exclusion, to the danger of distortion, explosion, combustion. The novel has nothing to fear but sailing
too light. It will take aboard all we bring in good faith to the
dock.

An intense vision of this truth must have been Zola's comfort from the earliest time—the years, immediately following
the crash of the Empire, during which he settled himself to
the tremendous task he had mapped out. No finer act of courage and confidence, I think, is recorded in the history of letters. The critic in sympathy with him returns again and again
to the great wonder of it, in which something so strange is
mixed with something so august. Entertained and carried out
almost from the threshold of manhood, the high project, the
work of a lifetime, announces beforehand its inevitable weakness and yet speaks in the same voice for its admirable, its
almost unimaginable strength. The strength was in the young
man's very person—in his character, his will, his passion, his
fighting temper, his aggressive lips, his squared shoulders
(when he "sat up") and overweening confidence; his weakness
was in that inexperience of life from which he proposed not
to suffer, from which he in fact suffered on the surface remarkably little, and from which he was never to suspect, I
judge, that he had suffered at all. I may mention for the interest of it that, meeting him during his first short visit to
London—made several years before his stay in England during the Dreyfus trial—I received a direct impression of him
that was more informing than any previous study. I had seen
him a little, in Paris, years before that, when this impression
was a perceptible promise, and I was now to perceive how
time had made it good. It consisted, simply stated, in his
fairly bristling with the betrayal that nothing whatever had
happened to him in life but to write Les Rougon-Macquart.
It was even for that matter almost more as if Les Rougon-
Macquart had written *him*, written him as he stood and sat,
as he looked and spoke, as the long, concentrated, merciless
effort had made and stamped and left him. Something very
fundamental was to happen to him in due course, it is true,
shaking him to his base; fate was not wholly to cheat him of

an independent evolution. Recalling him from this London hour one strongly felt during the famous "Affair" that his outbreak in connection with it was the act of a man with arrears of personal history to make up, the act of a spirit for which life, or for which at any rate freedom, had been too much postponed, treating itself at last to a luxury of experience.

I welcomed the general impression at all events—I intimately entertained it; it represented so many things, it suggested, just as it was, such a lesson. You could neither have everything nor be everything—you had to choose; you could not at once sit firm at your job and wander through space inviting initiations. The author of Les Rougon-Macquart had had all those, certainly, that this wonderful company could bring him; but I can scarce express how it was implied in him that his time had been fruitfully passed with *them* alone. His artistic evolution struck one thus as, in spite of its magnitude, singularly simple, and evidence of the simplicity seems further offered by his last production, of which we have just come into possession. "Vérité" truly does give the measure, makes the author's high maturity join hands with his youth, marks the rigid straightness of his course from point to point. He had seen his horizon and his fixed goal from the first, and no cross-scent, no new distance, no blue gap in the hills to right or to left ever tempted him to stray. "Vérité," of which I shall have more to say, is in fact, as a moral finality and the crown of an edifice, one of the strangest possible performances. Machine-minted and made good by an immense expertness, it yet makes us ask how, for disinterested observation and perception, the writer had used so much time and so much acquisition, and how he can all along have handled so much material without some larger subjective consequence. We really rub our eyes in other words to see so great an intellectual adventure as Les Rougon-Macquart come to its end in deep desert sand. Difficult truly to read, because showing him at last almost completely a prey to the danger that had for a long time more and more dogged his steps, the danger of the mechanical all confident and triumphant, the book is nevertheless full of interest for a reader desirous to penetrate. It speaks with more distinctness of the author's temperament, tone and manner than if, like several of his volumes, it achieved or enjoyed a successful life of its own. Its heavy completeness, with all this, as of some prodigiously neat, strong and complicated scaffolding constructed by a firm of builders for the erection of a house whose foundations refuse to bear it and that is unable therefore to rise—its very betrayal of a method and a habit more than adequate, on past occasions, to similar ends, carries us back to the original rare exhibition, the grand assurance and grand patience with which the system was launched.

If it topples over, the system, by its own weight in these last applications of it, that only makes the history of its prolonged success the more curious and, speaking for myself, the spectacle of its origin more attaching. Readers of my generation will remember well the publication of "La Conquête de Plassans" and the portent, indefinable but irresistible, after perusal of the volume, conveyed in the general rubric under which it was a first instalment, Natural and Social History of a Family under the Second Empire. It squared itself there at its ease, the announcement, from the first, and we were to learn promptly enough what a fund of life it masked. It was like the mouth of a cave with a signboard hung above, or better still perhaps like the big booth at a fair with the name of the show across the flapping canvas. One strange animal after another stepped forth into the light, each in its way a monster bristling and spotted, each a curiosity of that "natural history" in the name of which we were addressed, though it was doubtless not till the issue of "L'Assommoir" that the true type of the monstrous seemed to be reached. The enterprise, for those who had attention, was even at a distance impressive, and the nearer the critic gets to it retrospectively the more so it becomes. The pyramid had been planned and the site staked out, but the young builder stood there, in his sturdy strength, with no equipment save his two hands and, as we may say, his wheelbarrow and his trowel. His pile of material—of stone, brick and rubble or whatever—was of the smallest, but this he apparently felt as the least of his difficulties. Poor, uninstructed, unacquainted, unintroduced, he set up his subject wholly from the outside, proposing to himself wonderfully to get into it, into its depths, as he went.

If we imagine him asking himself what he knew of the "so-cial" life of the second Empire to start with, we imagine him also answering in all honesty: "I have my eyes and my ears— I have all my senses: I have what I've seen and heard, what I've smelled and tasted and touched. And then I've my curiosity and my pertinacity; I've libraries, books, newspapers, witnesses, the material, from step to step, of an *enquête*. And then I've my genius—that is, my imagination, my passion, my sensibility to life. Lastly I've my method, and that will be half the battle. Best of all perhaps even, I've plentiful lack of doubt." Of the absence in him of a doubt, indeed of his inability, once his direction taken, to entertain so much as the shadow of one, "Vérité" is a positive monument—which again represents in this way the unity of his tone and the meeting of his extremes. If we remember that his design was nothing if not architectural, that a "majestic whole," a great balanced façade, with all its orders and parts, that a singleness of mass and a unity of effect, in fine, were before him from the first, his notion of picking up his bricks as he proceeded becomes, in operation, heroic. It is not in the least as a record of failure for him that I note this particular fact of the growth of the long series as on the whole the liveliest interest it has to offer. "I don't know my subject, but I must live into it; I don't know life, but I must learn it as I work"—that attitude and programme represent, to my sense, a drama more intense on the worker's own part than any of the dramas he was to invent and put before us.

It was the fortune, it was in a manner the doom, of Les Rougon-Macquart to deal with things almost always in gregarious form, to be a picture of *numbers*, of classes, crowds, confusions, movements, industries—and this for a reason of which it will be interesting to attempt some account. The individual life is, if not wholly absent, reflected in coarse and common, in generalised terms; whereby we arrive precisely at the oddity just named, the circumstance that, looking out somewhere, and often woefully athirst, for the taste of fineness, we find it not in the fruits of our author's fancy, but in a different matter altogether. We get it in the very history of his effort, the image itself of his lifelong process, comparatively so personal, so spiritual even, and, through all its patience and pain, of a quality so much more distinguished than the qualities he succeeds in attributing to his figures even when he most aims at distinction. There can be no question in these narrow limits of my taking the successive volumes one by one—all the more that our sense of the exhibition is as little as possible an impression of parts and books, of particular "plots" and persons. It produces the effect of a mass of imagery in which shades are sacrificed, the effect of character and passion in the lump or by the ton. The fullest, the most characteristic episodes affect us like a sounding chorus or procession, as with a hubbub of voices and a multitudinous tread of feet. The setter of the mass into motion, he himself, in the crowd, figures best, with whatever queer idiosyncrasies, excrescences and gaps, a being of a substance akin to our own. Taking him as we must, I repeat, for quite heroic, the interest of detail in him is the interest of his struggle at every point with his problem.

The sense for crowds and processions, for the gross and the general, was largely the *result* of this predicament, of the disproportion between his scheme and his material—though it was certainly also in part an effect of his particular turn of mind. What the reader easily discerns in him is the sturdy resolution with which breadth and energy supply the place of penetration. He rests to his utmost on his documents, devours and assimilates them, makes them yield him extraordinary appearances of life; but in his way he too improvises in the grand manner, the manner of Walter Scott and of Dumas the elder. We feel that he *has* to improvise for his moral and social world, the world as to which vision and opportunity must come, if they are to come at all, unhurried and unhustled—must take their own time, helped undoubtedly more or less by blue-books, reports and interviews, by inquiries "on the spot," but never wholly replaced by such substitutes without a general disfigurement. Vision and opportunity reside in a personal sense and a personal history, and no short cut to them in the interest of plausible fiction has ever been discovered. The short cut, it is not too much to say, was with Zola the subject of constant ingenious experiment, and it is largely to this source, I surmise, that we owe the celebrated element of his grossness. He was *obliged* to be gross, on his system, or neglect to his cost an invaluable aid to representation, as well as one that apparently struck him as lying close at hand; and I cannot withhold my frank admiration from the courage and consistency with which he faced his need.

His general subject in the last analysis was the nature of man; in dealing with which he took up, obviously, the harp of most numerous strings. His business was to make these strings sound true, and there were none that he did not, so far as his general economy permitted, persistently try. What happened then was that many—say about half, and these, as I have noted, the most silvered, the most golden—refused to give out their music. They would only sound false, since (as with all his earnestness he must have felt) he could command them, through want of skill, of practice, of ear, to none of the right harmony. What therefore was more natural than that, still splendidly bent on producing his illusion, he should throw himself on the strings he might thump with effect, and should work them, as our phrase is, for all they were worth? The nature of man, he had plentiful warrant for holding, is an extraordinary mixture, but the great thing was to represent a sufficient part of it to show that it was solidly, palpably, commonly the nature. With this preoccupation he doubtless fell into extravagance—there was clearly so much to lead him on. The coarser side of his subject, based on the community of all the instincts, was for instance the more practicable side, a sphere the vision of which required but the general human, scarcely more than the plain physical, initiation, and dispensed thereby conveniently enough with special introductions or revelations. A free entry into this sphere was undoubtedly compatible with a youthful career as hampered right and left even as Zola's own.

He was in prompt possession thus of the range of sympathy that he *could* cultivate, though it must be added that the complete exercise of that sympathy might have encountered an obstacle that would somewhat undermine his advantage. Our friend might have found himself able, in other words, to pay to the instinctive, as I have called it, only such tribute as protesting taste (his own dose of it) permitted. Yet there it was again that fortune and his temperament served him. Taste as he knew it, taste as his own constitution supplied it, proved to have nothing to say to the matter. His own dose of the precious elixir had no perceptible regulating power. Paradoxical as the remark may sound, this accident was positively to operate as one of his greatest felicities. There are parts of his work, those dealing with romantic or poetic elements, in which the inactivity of the principle in question is sufficiently hurtful; but it surely should not be described as hurtful to such pictures as "Le Ventre de Paris," as "L'Assommoir," as "Germinal." The conception on which each of these productions rests is that of a world with which taste has nothing to do, and though the act of representation may be justly held, as an artistic act, to involve its presence, the discrimination would probably have been in fact, given the particular illusion sought, more detrimental than the deficiency. There was a great outcry, as we all remember, over the rank materialism of "L'Assommoir," but who cannot see to-day how much a milder infusion of it would have told against the close embrace of the subject aimed at? "L'Assommoir" is the nature of man—but not his finer, nobler, cleaner or more cultivated nature; it is the image of his free instincts, the better and the worse, the better struggling as they can, gasping for light and air, the worse making themselves at home in darkness, ignorance and poverty. The whole handling makes for emphasis and scale, and it is not to be measured how, as a picture of conditions, the thing would have suffered from timidity. The qualification of the painter was precisely his stoutness of stomach, and we scarce exceed in saying that to have taken in and given out again less of the infected air would, with such a resource, have meant the waste of a faculty.

I may add in this connection moreover that refinement of intention did on occasion and after a fashion of its own unmistakably preside at these experiments; making the remark in order to have done once for all with a feature of Zola's literary physiognomy that appears to have attached the gaze of many persons to the exclusion of every other. There are judges in these matters so perversely preoccupied that for them to see anywhere the "improper" is for them straightway to cease to see anything else. The said improper, looming supremely large and casting all the varieties of the proper quite into the shade, suffers thus in their consciousness a much greater extension than it ever claimed, and this consciousness becomes, for the edification of many and the information of a few, a colossal reflector and record of it. Much may be said, in relation to some of the possibilities of the nature of man, of the nature in especial of the "people," on the defect of our author's sense of proportion. But the sense of proportion of many of those he has scandalised would take us further yet. I recall at all events as relevant—for it comes under a very attaching general head—two occasions of long ago, two Sunday afternoons in Paris, on which I found the question of intention very curiously lighted. Several men of letters of a group in which almost every member either had arrived at renown or was well on his way to it, were assembled under the roof of the most distinguished of their number, where they exchanged free confidences on current work, on plans and ambitions, in a manner full of interest for one never previously privileged to see artistic conviction, artistic passion (at least on the literary ground) so systematic and so articulate. "Well, I on my side," I remember Zola's saying, "am engaged on a book, a study of the *mœurs* of the people, for which I am making a collection of all the 'bad words,' the *gros mots*, of the language, those with which the vocabulary of the people, those with which their familiar talk, bristles." I was struck with the tone in which he made the announcement—without bravado and without apology, as an interesting idea that had come to him and that he was working, really to arrive at character and particular truth, with all his conscience; just as I was struck with the unqualified interest that his plan excited. It was *on* a plan that he was working—formidably, almost grimly, as his fatigued face showed; and the whole consideration of this interesting element partook of the general seriousness.

But there comes back to me also as a companion-piece to this another day, after some interval, on which the interest was excited by the fact that the work for love of which the brave license had been taken was actually under the ban of the daily newspaper that had engaged to "serialise" it. Publication had definitively ceased. The thing had run a part of its course, but it had outrun the courage of editors and the curiosity of subscribers—that stout curiosity to which it had

evidently in such good faith been addressed. The chorus of
contempt for the ways of such people, their pusillanimity,
their superficiality, vulgarity, intellectual platitude, was the
striking note on this occasion; for the journal impugned had
declined to proceed and the serial, broken off, been obliged,
if I am not mistaken, to seek the hospitality of other columns,
secured indeed with no great difficulty. The composition so
qualified for future fame was none other, as I was later to
learn, than "L'Assommoir"; and my reminiscence has perhaps
no greater point than in connecting itself with a matter always
dear to the critical spirit, especially when the latter has not
too completely elbowed out the romantic—the matter of the
"origins," the early consciousness, early steps, early tribulations, early obscurity, as so often happens, of productions
finally crowned by time.

Their greatness is for the most part a thing that has originally begun so small; and this impression is particularly
strong when we have been in any degree present, so to speak,
at the birth. The course of the matter is apt to tend preponderantly in that case to enrich our stores of irony. In the eventual conquest of consideration by an abused book we
recognise, in other terms, a drama of romantic interest, a
drama often with large comic no less than with fine pathetic
interweavings. It may of course be said in this particular connection that "L'Assommoir" had not been one of the literary
things that creep humbly into the world. Its "success" may be
cited as almost insolently prompt, and the fact remains true if
the idea of success be restricted, after the inveterate fashion,
to the idea of circulation. What remains truer still, however,
is that for the critical spirit circulation mostly matters not the
least little bit, and it is of the success with which the history
of Gervaise and Coupeau nestles in *that* capacious bosom,
even as the just man sleeps in Abraham's, that I here speak.
But it is a point I may better refer to a moment hence.

Though a summary study of Zola need not too anxiously
concern itself with book after book—always with a partial
exception from this remark for "L'Assommoir"—groups and
varieties none the less exist in the huge series, aids to discrimination without which no measure of the presiding genius
is possible. These divisions range themselves to my sight,

roughly speaking, however, as scarce more than three in number—I mean if the ten volumes of the Œuvres Critiques and the Théâtre be left out of account. The critical volumes in especial abound in the characteristic, as they were also a wondrous addition to his sum of achievement during his most strenuous years. But I am forced not to consider them. The two groups constituted after the close of Les Rougon-Macquart—"Les Trois Villes" and the incomplete "Quatre Évangiles"—distribute themselves easily among the three types, or, to speak more exactly, stand together under one of the three. This one, so comprehensive as to be the author's main exhibition, includes to my sense all his best volumes—to the point in fact of producing an effect of distinct inferiority for those outside of it, which are, luckily for his general credit, the less numerous. It is so inveterately pointed out in any allusion to him that one shrinks, in repeating it, from sounding flat; but as he was admirably equipped from the start for the evocation of number and quantity, so those of his social pictures that most easily surpass the others are those in which appearances, the appearances familiar to him, are at once most magnified and most multiplied.

To make his characters swarm, and to make the great central thing they swarm about "as large as life," portentously, heroically big, that was the task he set himself very nearly from the first, that was the secret he triumphantly mastered. Add that the big central thing was always some highly representative institution or industry of the France of his time, some seated Moloch of custom, of commerce, of faith, lending itself to portrayal through its abuses and excesses, its idolface and great devouring mouth, and we embrace the main lines of his attack. In "Le Ventre de Paris" he had dealt with the life of the huge Halles, the general markets and their supply, the personal forces, personal situations, passions, involved in (strangest of all subjects) the alimentation of the monstrous city, the city whose victualling occupies so inordinately much of its consciousness. Paris richly gorged, Paris sublime and indifferent in her assurance (so all unlike poor Oliver's) of "more," figures here the theme itself, lies across the scene like some vast ruminant creature breathing in a cloud of parasites. The book was the first of the long series to show the full freedom of the author's hand, though "La Curée" had already been symptomatic. This freedom, after an interval, broke out on a much bigger scale in "L'Assommoir," in "Au Bonheur des Dames," in "Germinal," in "La Bête Humaine," in "L'Argent," in "La Débâcle," and then again, though more mechanically and with much of the glory gone, in the more or less wasted energy of "Lourdes," "Rome," "Paris," of "Fécondité," "Travail" and "Vérité."

"Au Bonheur des Dames" handles the colossal modern shop, traces the growth of such an organisation as the Bon Marché or the Magasin-du-Louvre, sounds the abysses of its inner life, marshals its population, its hierarchy of clerks, counters, departments, divisions and sub-divisions, plunges into the labyrinth of the mutual relations of its staff, and above all traces its ravage amid the smaller fry of the trade, of all the trades, pictures these latter gasping for breath in an air pumped clean by its mighty lungs. "Germinal" revolves about the coal-mines of Flemish France, with the subterranean world of the pits for its central presence, just as "La Bête Humaine" has for its protagonist a great railway and "L'Argent" presents in terms of human passion—mainly of human baseness—the fury of the Bourse and the monster of Credit. "La Débâcle" takes up with extraordinary breadth the first act of the Franco-Prussian war, the collapse at Sedan, and the titles of the six volumes of The Three Cities and the Four Gospels sufficiently explain them. I may mention, however, for the last lucidity, that among these "Fécondité" manipulates, with an amazing misapprehension of means to ends, of remedies to ills, no less thickly peopled a theme than that of the decline in the French birth-rate, and that "Vérité" presents a fictive equivalent of the Dreyfus case, with a vast and elaborate picture of the battle in France between lay and clerical instruction. I may even further mention, to clear the ground, that with the close of Les Rougon-Macquart the diminution of freshness in the author's energy, the diminution of intensity and, in short, of quality, becomes such as to render sadly difficult a happy life with some of the later volumes. Happiness of the purest strain never indeed, in old absorptions of Zola, quite sat at the feast; but there was mostly a measure of coercion, a spell without a charm. From these last-named productions of the climax everything strikes me as absent but quantity ("Vérité," for instance, is, with the possible exception of "Nana," the longest of the list); though indeed there is something impressive in the way his quantity represents his patience.

There are efforts here at stout perusal that, frankly, I have been unable to carry through, and I should verily like, in connection with the vanity of these, to dispose on the spot of the sufficiently strange phenomenon constituted by what I have called the climax. It embodies in fact an immense anomaly; it casts back over Zola's prime and his middle years the queerest grey light of eclipse. Nothing moreover—nothing "literary"—was ever so odd as in this matter the whole turn of the case, the consummation so logical yet so unexpected. Writers have grown old and withered and failed; they have grown weak and sad; they have lost heart, lost ability, yielded in one way or another—the possible ways being so numerous—to the cruelty of time. But the singular doom of this genius, and which began to multiply its symptoms ten years before his death, was to find, with life, at fifty, still rich in him, strength only to undermine all the "authority" he had gathered. He had not grown old and he had not grown feeble; he had only grown all too wrongly insistent, setting himself to wreck, poetically, his so massive identity—to wreck it in the very waters in which he had formally arrayed his victorious fleet. (I say "poetically" on purpose to give him the just benefit of all the beauty of his power.) The process of the disaster, so full of the effect, though so without the intention, of perversity, is difficult to trace in a few words; it may best be indicated by an example or two of its action.

The example that perhaps most comes home to me is again connected with a personal reminiscence. In the course of some talk that I had with him during his first visit to England I happened to ask him what opportunity to travel (if any) his immense application had ever left him, and whether in particular he had been able to see Italy, a country from which I had either just returned or which I was luckily—not having the Natural History of a Family on my hands—about to revisit. "All I've done, alas," he replied, " was, the other year, in the course of a little journey to the south, to my own *pays*—all

that has been possible was then to make a little dash as far as
Genoa, a matter of only a few days." "Le Docteur Pascal," the
conclusion of Les Rougon-Macquart, had appeared shortly
before, and it further befell that I asked him what plans he
had for the future, now that, still *dans la force de l'âge*, he had
so cleared the ground. I shall never forget the fine promptitude of his answer—"Oh, I shall begin at once Les Trois
Villes." "And which cities are they to be?" The reply was finer
still—"Lourdes, Paris, Rome."

It was splendid for confidence and cheer, but it left me, I
fear, more or less gaping, and it was to give me afterwards
the key, critically speaking, to many a mystery. It struck me
as breathing to an almost tragic degree the fatuity of those in
whom the gods stimulate that vice to their ruin. He was an
honest man—he had always bristled with it at every pore; but
no artistic reverse was inconceivable for an adventurer who,
stating in one breath that his knowledge of Italy consisted of
a few days spent at Genoa, was ready to declare in the next
that he had planned, on a scale, a picture of Rome. It flooded
his career, to my sense, with light; it showed how he had
marched from subject to subject and had "got up" each in
turn—showing also how consummately he had reduced such
getting-up to an artifice. He had success and a rare impunity
behind him, but nothing would now be so interesting as to
see if he could again play the trick. One would leave him, and
welcome, Lourdes and Paris—he had already dealt, on a
scale, with his own country and people. But was the adored
Rome also to be his on such terms, the Rome he was already
giving away before possessing an inch of it? One thought of
one's own frequentations, saturations—a history of long
years, and of how the effect of them had somehow been but
to make the subject too august. Was *he* to find it easy through
a visit of a month or two with "introductions" and a
Bædeker?

It was not indeed that the Bædeker and the introductions
didn't show, to my sense, at that hour, as extremely suggestive; they were positively a part of the light struck out by his
announcement. They defined the system on which he had
brought Les Rougon-Macquart safely into port. He had had
his Bædeker and his introductions for "Germinal," for "L'As-

sommoir," for "L'Argent," for "La Débâcle," for "Au Bonheur des Dames"; which advantages, which researches, had clearly been all the more in character for being documentary, extractive, a matter of *renseignements*, published or private, even when most mixed with personal impressions snatched, with *enquêtes sur les lieux*, with facts obtained from the best authorities, proud and happy to co-operate in so famous a connection. That was, as we say, all right, all the more that the process, to my imagination, became vivid and was wonderfully reflected back from its fruits. There *were* the fruits— so it hadn't been presumptuous. Presumption, however, was now to begin, and what omen mightn't there be in its beginning with such complacency? Well, time would show—as time in due course effectually did. "Rome," as the second volume of The Three Cities, appeared with high punctuality a year or two later; and the interesting question, an occasion really for the moralist, was by that time not to recognise in it the mere triumph of a mechanical art, a "receipt" applied with the skill of long practice, but to do much more than this—that is really to give a name to the particular shade of blindness that could constitute a trap for so great an artistic intelligence. The presumptuous volume, without sweetness, without antecedents, superficial and violent, has the minimum instead of the maximum of *value*; so that it betrayed or "gave away" just in this degree the state of mind on the author's part responsible for its inflated hollowness. To put one's finger on the state of mind was to find out accordingly what was, as we say, the matter with him.

It seemed to me, I remember, that I found out as never before when, in its turn, "Fécondité" began the work of crowning the edifice. "Fécondité" is physiological, whereas "Rome" is not, whereas "Vérité" likewise is not; yet these three productions joined hands at a given moment to fit into the lock of the mystery the key of my meditation. They came to the same thing, to the extent of permitting me to read into them together the same precious lesson. This lesson may not, barely stated, sound remarkable; yet without being in possession of it I should have ventured on none of these remarks. "The matter with" Zola then, so far as it goes, was that, as the imagination of the artist is in the best cases not only clarified but intensified by his equal possession of Taste (deserving here if ever the old-fashioned honour of a capital) so when he has lucklessly never inherited that auxiliary blessing the imagination itself inevitably breaks down as a consequence. There is simply no limit, in fine, to the misfortune of being tasteless; it does not merely disfigure the surface and the fringe of your performance—it eats back into the very heart and enfeebles the sources of life. When you have no taste you have no discretion, which is the conscience of taste, and when you have no discretion you perpetrate books like "Rome," which are without intellectual modesty, books like "Fécondité," which are without a sense of the ridiculous, books like "Vérité," which are without the finer vision of human experience.

It is marked that in each of these examples the deficiency has been directly fatal. No stranger doom was ever appointed for a man so plainly desiring only to be just than the absurdity of not resting till he had buried the felicity of his past, such as it was, under a great flat leaden slab. "Vérité" is a plea for science, as science, to Zola, is *all* truth, the mention of any other kind being mere imbecility; and the simplification of the human picture to which his negations and exasperations have here conducted him was not, even when all had been said, credible in advance. The result is amazing when we consider that the finer observation is the supposed basis of all such work. It is not that even here the author has not a queer idealism of his own; this idealism is on the contrary so present as to show positively for the falsest of his simplifications. In "Fécondité" it becomes grotesque, makes of the book the most muscular mistake of *sense* probably ever committed. Where was the judgment of which experience is supposed to be the guarantee when the perpetrator could persuade himself that the lesson he wished in these pages to convey could be made immediate and direct, chalked, with loud taps and a still louder commentary, the sexes and generations all convoked, on the blackboard of the "family sentiment?"

I have mentioned, however, all this time but one of his categories. The second consists of such things as "La Fortune des Rougon" and "La Curée," as "Eugène Rougon" and even "Nana," as "Pot-Bouille," as "L'Œuvre" and "La Joie de

Vivre." These volumes may rank as social pictures in the narrowest sense, studies, comprehensively speaking, of the manners, the morals, the miseries—for it mainly comes to that—of a bourgeoisie grossly materialised. They deal with the life of individuals in the liberal professions and with that of political and social adventures, and offer the personal character and career, more or less detached, as the centre of interest. "La Curée" is an evocation, violent and "romantic," of the extravagant appetites, the fever of the senses, supposedly fostered, for its ruin, by the hapless second Empire, upon which general ills and turpitudes at large were at one time so freely and conveniently fathered. "Eugène Rougon" carries out this view in the high colour of a political portrait, not other than scandalous, for which one of the ministerial *âmes damnées* of Napoleon III., M. Rouher, is reputed, I know not how justly, to have sat. "Nana," attaching itself by a hundred strings to a prearranged table of kinships, heredities, transmissions, is the vast crowded *epos* of the daughter of the people filled with poisoned blood and sacrificed as well as sacrificing on the altar of luxury and lust; the panorama of such a "progress" as Hogarth would more definitely have named—the progress across the high plateau of "pleasure" and down the facile descent on the other side. "Nana" is truly a monument to Zola's patience; the subject being so ungrateful, so formidably special, that the multiplication of illustrative detail, the plunge into pestilent depths, represents a kind of technical intrepidity.

There are other plunges, into different sorts of darkness; of which the esthetic, even the scientific, even the ironic motive fairly escapes us—explorations of stagnant pools like that of "La Joie de Vivre," as to which, granting the nature of the curiosity and the substance laboured in, the patience is again prodigious, but which make us wonder what pearl of philosophy, of suggestion or just of homely recognition, the general picture, as of rats dying in a hole, has to offer. Our various senses, sight, smell, sound, touch, are, as with Zola always, more or less convinced; but when the particular effect upon each of these is added to the effect upon the others the mind still remains bewilderedly unconscious of any use for the total. I am not sure indeed that the case is in this respect better

with the productions of the third order—"La Faute de l'Abbé
Mouret," "Une Page d'Amour," "Le Rêve," "Le Docteur Pascal"—in which the appeal is more directly, is in fact quite
earnestly, to the moral vision; so much, on such ground, was
to depend precisely on those discriminations in which the
writer is least at home. The volumes whose names I have just
quoted are his express tribute to the "ideal," to the select and
the charming—fair fruits of invention intended to remove
from the mouth so far as possible the bitterness of the ugly
things in which so much of the rest of his work had been
condemned to consist. The subjects in question then are
"idyllic" and the treatment poetic, concerned essentially to
please on the largest lines and involving at every turn that
salutary need. They are matters of conscious delicacy, and
nothing might interest us more than to see what, in the shock
of the potent forces enlisted, becomes of this shy element.
Nothing might interest us more, literally, and might positively affect us more, even very nearly to tears, though indeed
sometimes also to smiles, than to see the constructor of Les
Rougon-Macquart trying, "for all he is worth," to be fine
with fineness, finely tender, finely true—trying to be, as it is
called, distinguished—in face of constitutional hindrance.

The effort is admirably honest, the tug at his subject splendidly strong; but the consequences remain of the strangest,
and we get the impression that—as representing discriminations unattainable—they are somehow the price he paid. "Le
Docteur Pascal," for instance, which winds up the long
chronicle on the romantic note, on the note of invoked
beauty, in order to sweeten, as it were, the total draught—
"Le Docteur Pascal," treating of the erotic ardour entertained
for each other by an uncle and his niece, leaves us amazed at
such a conception of beauty, such an application of romance,
such an estimate of sweetness, a sacrifice to poetry and passion so little in order. Of course, we definitely remind ourselves, the whole long chronicle is explicitly a scheme, solidly
set up and intricately worked out, lighted, according to the
author's pretension, by "science," high, dry and clear; and
with each part involved and necessitated in all the other parts,
each block of the edifice, each "morceau de vie," *physiologically*
determined by previous combinations. "How can I help it,"

we hear the builder of the pyramid ask, "if experience (by which alone I proceed) shows me certain plain results—if, holding up the torch of my famous 'experimental method,' I find it stare me in the face that the union of certain types, the conflux of certain strains of blood, the intermarriage, in a word, of certain families, produces nervous conditions, conditions temperamental, psychical and pathological, in which nieces *have* to fall in love with uncles and uncles with nieces? Observation and imagination, for any picture of life," he as audibly adds, "know no light but science, and are false to all intellectual decency, false to their own honour, when they fear it, dodge it, darken it. To pretend to any other guide or law is mere base humbug."

That is very well, and the value, in a hundred ways, of a mass of production conceived in such a spirit can never (when robust execution has followed) be small. But the formula really sees us no further. It offers a definition which is no definition. "Science" is soon said—the whole thing depends on the ground so covered. Science accepts surely *all* our consciousness of life; even, rather, the latter closes maternally round it—so that, becoming thus a force within us, not a force outside, it exists, it illuminates only as we apply it. We do emphatically apply it in art. But Zola would apparently hold that it much more applies *us*. On the showing of many of his volumes then it makes but a dim use of us, and this we should still consider the case even were we sure that the article offered us in the majestic name is absolutely at one with its own pretension. This confidence we can on too many grounds never have. The matter is one of appreciation, and when an artist answers for science who answers for the artist—who at the least answers for art? Thus it is with the mistakes that affect us, I say, as Zola's penalties. We are reminded by them that the game of art has, as the phrase is, to be played. It may not with any sure felicity for the result be both taken and left. If you insist on the common you must submit to the common; if you discriminate, on the contrary, you must, however invidious your discriminations may be called, trust to them to see you through.

To the common then Zola, often with splendid results, inordinately sacrifices, and this fact of its overwhelming him is what I have called his paying for it. In "L'Assommoir," in "Germinal," in "La Débâcle," productions in which he must most survive, the sacrifice is ordered and fruitful, for the subject and the treatment harmonise and work together. He describes what he best feels, and feels it more and more as it naturally comes to him—quite, if I may allow myself the image, as we zoologically see some mighty animal, a beast of a corrugated hide and a portentous snout, soaking with joy in the warm ooze of an African riverside. In these cases everything matches, and "science," we may be permitted to believe, has had little hand in the business. The author's perceptions go straight, and the subject, grateful and responsive, gives itself wholly up. It is no longer a case of an uncertain smoky torch, but of a personal vision, the vision of genius, springing from an inward source. Of this genius "L'Assommoir" is the most extraordinary record. It contains, with the two companions I have given it, all the best of Zola, and the three books together are solid ground—or would be could I now so take them—for a study of the particulars of his power. His strongest marks and features abound in them; "L'Assommoir" above all is (not least in respect to its bold free linguistic reach, already glanced at) completely genial, while his misadventures, his unequipped and delusive pursuit of the life of the spirit and the tone of culture, are almost completely absent.

It is a singular sight enough this of a producer of illusions whose interest for us is so independent of our pleasure or at least of our complacency—who touches us deeply even while he most "puts us off," who makes us care for his ugliness and yet himself at the same time pitilessly (pitilessly, that is, for *us*) makes a mock of it, who fills us with a sense of the rich which is none the less never the rare. Gervaise, the most immediately "felt," I cannot but think, of all his characters, is a lame washerwoman, loose and gluttonous, without will, without any principle of cohesion, the sport of every wind that assaults her exposed life, and who, rolling from one gross mistake to another, finds her end in misery, drink and despair. But her career, as presented, has fairly the largeness that, throughout the chronicle, we feel as epic, and the intensity of her creator's vision of it and of the dense sordid life hanging about it is one of the great things the modern novel has been able to do. It has done nothing more completely constitutive and of a tone so rich and full and sustained. The tone of "L'Assommoir" is, for mere "keeping up," unsurpassable, a vast deep steady tide on which every object represented is triumphantly borne. It never shrinks nor flows thin, and nothing for an instant drops, dips or catches; the high-water mark of sincerity, of the genial, as I have called it, is unfailingly kept.

For the artist in the same general "line" such a production has an interest almost inexpressible, a mystery as to origin and growth over which he fondly but rather vainly bends. How after all does it so get itself *done?*—the "done" being admirably the sign and crown of it. The light of the richer mind has been elsewhere, as I have sufficiently hinted, frequent enough, but nothing truly in all fiction was ever built so strong or made so dense as here. Needless to say there are a thousand things with more charm in their truth, with more beguilement of every sort, more prettiness of pathos, more innocence of drollery, for the spectator's sense of truth. But I doubt if there has ever been a more totally *represented* world, anything more founded and established, more provided for all round, more organised and carried on. It is a world practically workable, with every part as functional as every other, and with the parts all chosen for direct mutual aid. Let it not be said either that the equal constitution of parts makes for repletion or excess; the air circulates and the subject blooms; deadness comes in these matters only when the right parts are absent and there is vain beating of the air in their place—the refuge of the fumbler incapable of the thing "done" at all.

The mystery I speak of, for the reader who reflects as he goes, is the wonder of the scale and energy of Zola's assimilations. This wonder besets us above all throughout the three books I have placed first. How, all sedentary and "scientific," did he get so *near?* By what art, inscrutable, immeasurable, indefatigable, did he arrange to make of his documents, in these connections, a use so vivified? Say he was "near" the subject of "L'Assommoir" in imagination, in more or less familiar impression, in temperament and humour, he could not after all have been near it in personal experience, and the

copious personalism of the picture, not to say its frank animalism, yet remains its note and its strength. When the note
had been struck in a thousand forms we had, by multiplication, as a kind of cumulative consequence, the finished and
rounded book; just as we had the same result by the same
process in "Germinal." It is not of course that multiplication
and accumulation, the extraordinary pair of legs on which he
walks, are easily or directly consistent with his projecting himself morally; this immense diffusion, with its appropriation of
everything it meets, affects us on the contrary as perpetually
delaying access to what we may call the private world, the
world of the individual. Yet since the individual—for it so
happens—is simple and shallow our author's dealings with
him, as met and measured, maintain their resemblance to
those of the lusty bee who succeeds in plumping for an
instant, of a summer morning, into every flower-cup of the
garden.

Grant—and the generalisation may be emphatic—that the
shallow and the simple are *all* the population of his richest
and most crowded pictures, and that his "psychology," in a
psychologic age, remains thereby comparatively coarse, grant
this and we but get another view of the miracle. We see
enough of the superficial among novelists at large, assuredly,
without deriving from it, as we derive from Zola at his best,
the concomitant impression of the solid. It is in general—I
mean among the novelists at large—the impression of the
cheap, which the author of Les Rougon-Macquart, honest
man, never faithless for a moment to his own stiff standard,
manages to spare us even in the prolonged sandstorm of
"Vérité." The Common is another matter; it is one of the
forms of the superficial—pervading and consecrating all
things in such a book as "Germinal"—and it only adds to the
number of our critical questions. How in the world is it
made, this deplorable democratic malodorous Common, so
strange and so interesting? How is it taught to receive into
its loins the stuff of the epic and still, in spite of that association with poetry, never depart from its nature? It is in the
great lusty game he plays with the shallow and the simple that
Zola's mastery resides, and we see of course that when values
are small it takes innumerable items and combinations to

make up the sum. In "L'Assommoir" and in "Germinal," to some extent even in "La Débâcle," the values are all, morally, personally, of the lowest—the highest is poor Gervaise herself, richly human in her generosities and follies—yet each is as distinct as a brass-headed nail.

What we come back to accordingly is the unprecedented case of such a combination of parts. Painters, of great schools, often of great talent, have responded liberally on canvas to the appeal of ugly things, of Spanish beggars, squalid and dusty-footed, of martyred saints or other convulsed sufferers, tortured and bleeding, of boors and louts soaking a Dutch proboscis in perpetual beer; but we had never before had to reckon with so literary a treatment of the mean and vulgar. When we others of the Anglo-Saxon race are vulgar we are, handsomely and with the best conscience in the world, vulgar all through, too vulgar to be in any degree literary, and too much so therefore to be critically reckoned with at all. The French are different—they separate their sympathies, multiply their possibilities, observe their shades, remain more or less outside of their worst disasters. They mostly contrive to get the *idea*, in however dead a faint, down into the lifeboat. They may lose sight of the stars, but they save in some such fashion as that their intellectual souls. Zola's own reply to all puzzlements would have been, at any rate, I take it, a straight summary of his inveterate professional habits. "It is all very simple—I produce, roughly speaking, a volume a year, and of this time some five months go to preparation, to special study. In the other months, with all my *cadres* established, I write the book. And I can hardly say which part of the job is stiffest."

The story was not more wonderful for him than that, nor the job more complex; which is why we must say of his whole process and its results that they constitute together perhaps the most extraordinary *imitation* of observation that we possess. Balzac appealed to "science" and proceeded by her aid; Balzac had *cadres* enough and a tabulated world, rubrics, relationships and genealogies; but Balzac affects us in spite of everything as personally overtaken by life, as fairly hunted and run to earth by it. He strikes us as struggling and all but submerged, as beating over the scene such a pair of wings as were not soon again to be wielded by any visitor of his general air and as had not at all events attached themselves to Zola's rounded shoulders. His bequest is in consequence immeasurably more interesting, yet who shall declare that his adventure was in its greatness more successful? Zola "pulled it off," as we say, supremely, in that he never but once found himself obliged to quit, to our vision, his magnificent treadmill of the pigeonholed and documented—the region we may qualify as that of experience by imitation. His splendid economy saw him through, he laboured to the end within sight of his notes and his charts.

The extraordinary thing, however, is that on the single occasion when, publicly—as his whole manifestation was public—life did swoop down on him, the effect of the visitation was quite perversely other than might have been looked for. His courage in the Dreyfus connection testified admirably to his ability to live for himself and out of the order of his volumes—little indeed as living at all might have seemed a question for one exposed, when his crisis was at its height and he was found guilty of "insulting" the powers that were, to be literally torn to pieces in the precincts of the Palace of Justice. Our point is that nothing was ever so odd as that these great moments should appear to have been wasted, when all was said, for his creative intelligence. "Vérité," as I have intimated, the production in which they might most have been reflected, is a production unrenewed and unrefreshed by them, spreads before us as somehow flatter and greyer, not richer and more relieved, by reason of them. They really arrived, I surmise, too late in the day; the imagination they might have vivified was already fatigued and spent.

I must not moreover appear to say that the power to evoke and present has not even on the dead level of "Vérité" its occasional minor revenges. There are passages, whole pages, of the old full-bodied sort, pictures that elsewhere in the series would in all likelihood have seemed abundantly convincing. Their misfortune is to have been discounted by our intensified, our finally fatal sense of the *procédé*. Quarrelling with all conventions, defiant of them in general, Zola was yet inevitably to set up his own group of them—as, for that matter, without a sufficient collection, without their aid in simplifying and making possible, how could he ever have seen his big ship into port? Art welcomes them, feeds upon them always; no sort of form is practicable without them. It is only a question of what particular ones we use—to wage war on certain others and to arrive at particular forms. The convention of the blameless being, the thoroughly "scientific" creature possessed impeccably of all truth and serving as the mouthpiece of it and of the author's highest complacencies, this character is for instance a convention inveterate and indispensable, without whom the "sympathetic" side of the work could never have been achieved. Marc in "Vérité," Pierre Froment in "Lourdes" and in "Rome," the wondrous representatives of the principle of reproduction in "Fécondité," the exemplary painter of "L'Œuvre," sublime in his modernity and paternity, the patient Jean Macquart of "La Débâcle," whose patience is as guaranteed as the exactitude of a well-made watch, the supremely enlightened Docteur Pascal even, as I recall him, all amorous nepotism but all virtue too and all beauty of life—such figures show us the reasonable and the good not merely in the white light of the old George Sand novel and its improved moralities, but almost in that of our childhood's nursery and school-room, that of the moral tale of Miss Edgeworth and Mr. Thomas Day.

Yet let not these restrictions be my last word. I had intended, under the effect of a reperusal of "La Débâcle," "Germinal" and "L'Assommoir," to make no discriminations that should not be in our hero's favour. The long-drawn incident of the marriage of Gervaise and Cadet-Cassis and that of the Homeric birthday feast later on in the laundress's workshop, each treated from beginning to end and in every item of their coarse comedy and humanity, still show the unprecedented breadth by which they originally made us stare, still abound in the particular kind and degree of vividness that helped them, when they appeared, to mark a date in the portrayal of manners. Nothing had then been so sustained and at every moment of its grotesque and pitiful existence lived into as the nuptial day of the Coupeau pair in especial, their fantastic processional pilgrimage through the streets of Paris in the rain, their bedraggled exploration of the halls of the Louvre museum, lost as in the labyrinth of Crete, and their arrival at last, ravenous and exasperated, at the *guinguette* where they sup at so much a head, each paying, and where we sit down with them in the grease and the perspiration and succumb, half in sympathy, half in shame, to their monstrous pleasantries, acerbities and miseries. I have said enough of the mechanical in Zola; here in truth is, given the elements, almost insupportably the sense of life. That effect is equally in the historic chapter of the strike of the miners in "Germinal," another of those illustrative episodes, viewed as great passages to be "rendered," for which our author established altogether a new measure and standard of handling, a new energy and veracity, something since which the old trivialities and poverties of treatment of such aspects have become incompatible, for the novelist, with either rudimentary intelligence or rudimentary self-respect.

As for "La Débâcle," finally, it takes its place with Tolstoi's very much more universal but very much less composed and condensed epic as an incomparably human picture of war. I have been re-reading it, I confess, with a certain timidity, the dread of perhaps impairing the deep impression received at the time of its appearance. I recall the effect it then produced on me as a really luxurious act of submission. It was early in the summer; I was in an old Italian town; the heat was oppressive, and one could but recline, in the lightest garments, in a great dim room and give one's self up. I like to think of the conditions and the emotion, which melt for me together into the memory I fear to imperil. I remember that in the glow of my admiration there was not a reserve I had ever made that I was not ready to take back. As an application of the author's system and his supreme faculty, as a triumph of what these things could do for him, how could such a performance be surpassed? The long, complex, horrific, pathetic battle, embraced, mastered, with every crash of its squadrons, every pulse of its thunder and blood resolved for us, by reflection, by communication from two of the humblest and obscurest of the military units, into immediate vision and contact, into deep human thrills of terror and pity—this bristling centre of the book was such a piece of "doing" (to come back to our word) as could only shut our mouths. That doubtless is why a generous critic, nursing the sensation, may desire to drop for a farewell no term into the other scale. That our author was clearly great at congruous subjects—this may well be our conclusion. If the others, subjects of the private and intimate order, gave him more or less inevitably "away," they yet left him the great distinction that the more he could be promiscuous and collective, the more even he could (to repeat my imputation) illustrate our large natural allowance of health, heartiness and grossness, the more he could strike us as penetrating and true. It was a distinction not easy to win and that his name is not likely soon to lose.

Atlantic Monthly, August 1903
Reprinted in *Notes on Novelists*, 1914

OTHER EUROPEAN
WRITERS

Contents

Moritz Busch

Graf Bismarck und seine Leute während des Krieges mit Frankreich. Leipzig, 1878.

THE LONDON *Times* lately published, in three instalments, a series of copious extracts from a publication which has excited no little attention in Germany—'Graf Bismarck und seine Leute während des Krieges mit Frankreich. Nach Tagebuchsblättern, von Dr. Moritz Busch.' M. Émile de Laveleye, in the December *Fortnightly*, devotes an entertaining article to the same record, which we shall see before long in an English translation. The book is only just out in Germany, where it has produced no small agitation and scandal; and while we await a more complete acquaintance with it we may find some profit in the specimens with which we have already been furnished. Dr. Moritz Busch, who appears to be a veritable Teutonic Boswell, was a practised journalist, in the employ of the Berlin Foreign Office, when he accompanied the great Chancellor, in the summer of 1870, to the seat of war. It may be added that his name figures as the translator of those American tales (by Messrs. Bret Harte, Howells, Aldrich, H. James, jr., etc.) which have lately been introduced in such profusion to German readers. He appears to have noted down, indefatigably, the conversation of his illustrious chief, and his book offers an almost complete record of Prince Bismarck's tabletalk and small-talk during the momentous months of the Franco-German war. The result is an extraordinary portrait, which, whether pleasing or not, has evidently the merit of minute fidelity. The Chancellor, in fact, paints himself, and his devoted diarist has done nothing but suspend the picture. It has presumably been given to the world with Prince Bismarck's own sanction, and this proceeding is only the conclusive, crowning instance of that tremendous audacity which is the most salient feature in the personality of the model. As regards everything and every one, Prince Bismarck is unsparingly, exhaustively, brutally frank. His opinion of the French nation is of the lowest; he speaks lightly even of M. Thiers:

> "He is a clever, attractive gentleman, witty, spirited, intellectual, but without talent for diplomacy. He is far too

sentimental for the profession. Though more manly and dignified than M. Favre, he is altogether unfit for the trade. He came to me as a negotiator when he had not gumption enough to know how to set about selling a horse. He is easily staggered, and he shows it."

Elsewhere, however, he is reported as having said to M. Thiers: "It is a pleasure to talk with so civilized a human being as you." In regard to the French love of phrases he says: "You may lay twenty-five lashes on a Frenchman's back with impunity, if only delivering the while a speech upon liberty and the dignity of mankind; the imaginative victim will not know he is being flogged." And the world will be interested to learn that, for every defect of the French, the Germans have a corresponding merit: "I am quite sure that the expression *politesse de cœur* is not French, but a translation from the German. This is a peculiar sort of politeness which I have met nowhere but in Germany. . . . The French certainly know nothing of the kind, being polite only from hatred or envy." One may be pardoned for wondering whether it was from *politesse de cœur* (even in the German original) that, as the Chancellor relates, the Princess Bismarck, in the autumn of 1870, " would have the French exterminated root and branch, only excepting the little children, who cannot be held responsible for having such atrocious parents." This edifying wish is one of those numerous passages for which it is almost inconceivable that Prince Bismarck should have desired the honors of publicity.

Nation, December 19, 1878

Gabriele D'Annunzio

The Triumph of Death. Translated by Georgina Harding. London: Heinemann, 1898; *Le Triomphe de la Mort.* Traduit de l'italien par G. Hérelle. Paris: Calmann Lévy, 1899; *The Virgins of the Rocks.* Translated by Agatha Hughes. London: Heinemann, 1899; *The Flame of Life.* Translated by Kassandra Vivaria. London: Heinemann, 1900; *Gioconda.* Translated by Arthur Symons. London: Heinemann, 1901; *Francesca da Rimini.* Translated by Arthur Symons. London: Heinemann, 1902.

THE GREAT FEAST-DAYS of all, for the restless critic, are those much interspaced occasions of his really meeting a "case," as he soon enough learns to call, for his convenience and assistance, any supremely contributive or determinant party to the critical question. These are recognitions that make up for many dull hours and dry contacts, many a thankless, a disconcerted gaze into faces that have proved expressionless. Always looking, always hoping for his happiest chance, the inquirer into the reasons of things—by which I mean especially into the reasons of books—so often misses it, so often wastes his steps and withdraws his confidence, that he inevitably works out for himself, sooner or later, some handy principle of recognition. It may be a rough thing, a mere home-made tool of his trade, but it serves his purpose if it keeps him from beginning with mistakes. He becomes able to note in its light the signs and marks of the possible precious identity, able to weigh with some exactitude the appearances that make for its reality. He ends, through much expenditure of patience, by seeing when, how, why, the "case" announces and presents itself, and he perhaps even feels that failure and felicity have worked together to produce in him a sense for it that may at last be trusted as an instinct. He thus arrives at a view of all the candidates, frequently interesting enough, who fall short of the effective title, because he has at need, perhaps even from afar, scented along the wind the strongest member of the herd. He may perhaps not always be able to give us the grounds of his certainty, but he is at least never without knowing it in presence of one of the full-blown products that are the joy of the analyst. He recognises as well how the state of being full-blown comes above all from the achievement of consistency, of that last consistency which springs from the unrestricted enjoyment of freedom.

Many of us will doubtless not have forgotten how we were witnesses a certain number of years since to a season and a society that had found themselves of a sudden roused, as from some deep drugged sleep, to the conception of the "esthetic" law of life; in consequence of which this happy thought had begun to receive the honours of a lively appetite and an eager curiosity, but was at the same time surrounded and manipulated by as many different kinds of inexpertness as probably ever huddled together on a single pretext. The spectacle was strange and finally was wearisome, for the simple reason that the principle in question, once it was proclaimed—a principle not easily formulated, but which we may conveniently speak of as that of beauty at any price, beauty appealing alike to the senses and to the mind—was never felt to fall into its place as really adopted and efficient. It remained for us a queer high-flavoured fruit from overseas, grown under another sun than ours, passed round and solemnly partaken of at banquets organised to try it, but not found on the whole really to agree with us, not proving thoroughly digestible. It brought with it no repose, brought with it only agitation. We were not really, not fully convinced, for the state of conviction is quiet. This was to have been the state itself—that is the state of mind achieved and established—in which we were to know ugliness no more, to make the esthetic consciousness feel at home with us, or learn ourselves at any rate to feel at home with *it*. That would have been the reign of peace, the supreme beatitude; but stability continued to elude us. We had mustered a hundred good reasons for it, yet the reasons but lighted up our desert. They failed to flower into a single concrete esthetic "type." One authentic, one masterful specimen would have done wonders for us, would at least have assuaged our curiosity. But we were to be left till lately with our curiosity on our hands.

This is a yearning, however, that Signor D'Annunzio may at last strike us as supremely formed to gratify; so promptly we find in him as a literary figure the highest expression of the reality that our own conditions were to fail of making possible. He has immediately the value of giving us by his mere logical unfolding the measure of our shortcomings in the same direction, that of our timidities and penuries and failures. He throws a straighter and more inevitable light on the esthetic consciousness than has, to my sense, in our time, reached it from any other quarter; and there is many a mystery that properly interrogated he may help to clear up for us, many an explanation of our misadventure that—as I have glanced at it—he may give. He starts with the immense advantage of enjoying the invoked boon by grace and not by effort, of claiming it under another title than the sweat of his brow and the aspiration of his culture. He testifies to the influence of things that have had time to get themselves taken for granted. Beauty at any price is an old story to him; art and form and style as the aim of the superior life are a matter of course; and it may be said of him, I think, that, thanks to these transmitted and implanted instincts and aptitudes, his individual development begins where the struggle of the mere earnest questioner ends. Signor D'Annunzio is earnest in his way, quite extraordinarily—which is a feature of his physiognomy that we shall presently come to and about which there will be something to say; but we feel him all the while in such secure possession of his heritage of favouring circumstance that his sense of intellectual responsibility is almost out of proportion. This is one of his interesting special marks, the manner in which the play of the esthetic instinct in him takes on, for positive extravagance and as a last refinement of freedom, the crown of solicitude and anxiety. Such things but make with him for ornament and parade; they are his tribute to civility; the essence of the matter is meanwhile in his blood and his bones. No mistake was possible from the first as to his being of the inner literary camp—a new form altogether of perceptive and expressive energy; the question was settled by the intensity and variety, to say nothing of the precocity, of his early poetic production.

Born at Pescara, in the Regno, the old kingdom of Naples, "toward" 1863, as I find noted by a cautious biographer, he had while scarce out of his teens allowed his lyric genius full opportunity of scandalising even the moderately austere. He defined himself betimes very much as he was to remain, a rare imagination, a poetic, an artistic intelligence of extraordinary range and fineness concentrated almost wholly on the life of the senses. For the critic who simplifies a little to state clearly, the only ideas he urges upon us are the erotic and the plastic, which have for him about an equal intensity, or of which it would be doubtless more correct to say that he makes them interchangeable faces of the same figure. He began his career by playing with them together in verse, to innumerable light tunes and with an extraordinary general effect of curiosity and brilliancy. He has continued still more strikingly to play with them in prose; they have remained the substance of his intellectual furniture. It is of his prose only, however, that, leaving aside the Intermezzo, L'Isottèo, La Chimera, Odi Navali and other such matters, I propose to speak, the subject being of itself ample for one occasion. His five novels and his four plays have extended his fame; they suggest by themselves as many observations as we shall have space for. The group of productions, as the literary industry proceeds among us today, is not large, but we may doubt if a talent and a temperament, if indeed a whole "view of life," ever built themselves up as vividly for the reader out of so few blocks. The writer is even yet enviably young; but this solidity of his literary image, as of something already seated on time and accumulation, makes him a rare example. Precocity is somehow an inadequate name for it, as precocity seldom gets away from the element of promise, and it is not exactly promise that blooms in the hard maturity of such a performance as "The Triumph of Death." There are certain expressions of experience, of the experience of the whole man, that are like final milestones, milestones for his possible fertility if not for his possible dexterity; a truth that has not indeed prevented "Il Fuoco," with its doubtless still ampler finality, from following the work just mentioned. And we have had particularly before us, in verse, I must add, "Francesca da Rimini," with the great impression a great actress has enabled this drama to make.

Only I must immediately in this connection also add that Signor D'Annunzio's plays are, beside his novels, of decidedly minor weight; testifying abundantly to his style, his romantic sense and his command of images, but standing in spite of their eloquence only for half of his talent, largely as he yet appears in "Il Fuoco" to announce himself by implication as an intending, indeed as a pre-eminent dramatist. The example is interesting when we catch in the fact the opportunity for comparing with the last closeness the capacity of the two rival canvases, as they become for the occasion, on which the picture of life may be painted. The closeness is never so great, the comparison never so pertinent, as when the separate efforts are but different phases of the same talent. It is not at any rate under this juxtaposition that the infinitely greater amplitude of portrayal resident in the novel strikes us least. It in fact strikes us the more, in this quarter, for Signor D'Annunzio, that his plays have been with one exception successes. We must none the less take "Francesca" but for a success of curiosity; on the part of the author I mean even more than on the part of the public. It is primarily a pictorial and ingenious thing and, as a picture of passion, takes, in the total collection, despite its felicities of surface and arrangement, distinctly a "back seat." Scarcely less than its companions it overflows with the writer's plenitude of verbal expression, thanks to which, largely, the series will always prompt a curiosity and even a tenderness in any reader interested precisely in this momentous question of "style in a play"—interested in particular to learn by what esthetic chemistry a play would as a work of art propose to eschew it. It is in any such connection so inexpugnable that we have only to be cheated of it in one place to feel the subject cry aloud for it, like a sick man forsaken, in another.

I may mention at all events the slightly perverse fact that, thanks, on this side, to the highest watermark of translation, Signor D'Annunzio makes his best appeal to the English public as a dramatist. Of each of the three English versions of other examples of his work whose titles are inscribed at the beginning of these remarks it may be said that they are adequate and respectable considering the great difficulty encountered. The author's highest good fortune has nevertheless been at the hands of his French interpreter, who has managed to keep constantly close to him—allowing for an occasional inconsequent failure of courage when the directness of the original *brave l'honnêteté*—and yet to achieve a tone not less idiomatic, and above all not less marked by "authority," than his own. Mr. Arthur Symons, among ourselves, however, has rendered the somewhat insistent eloquence of "La Gioconda" and the intricate and difficult verse of "Francesca" with all due sympathy, and in the latter case especially—a highly arduous task—with remarkably patient skill. It is not his fault, doubtless, if the feet of his English text strike us as moving with less freedom than those of his original; such being the hard price paid always by the translator who tries for correspondence from step to step, tries for an identical order. Even less is he responsible for its coming still more home to us in a translation that the meagre anecdote here furnishing the subject, and on which the large superstructure rests, does not really lend itself to those developments that make a full or an interesting tragic complexity. Behind the glamour of its immense literary association the subject of "Francesca" is for purposes of essential, of enlarged exhibition delusive and "short."

These, however, are for the moment side-issues; what is more relevant is the stride taken by our author's early progress in his first novel and his second, "Il Piacere" and "L'Innocente"; a pair from the freshness, the direct young energy of which he was, for some of his admirers, too promptly and too markedly to decline. We may take it as characteristic of the intensity of the literary life in him that his brief career falls already thus into periods and supplies a quantity of history sufficient for those differences among students by which the dignity of history appears mainly to be preserved. The nature of his prime inspiration I have already glanced at; and we are helped to a characterisation if I say that the famous enthroned "beauty" which operates here, so straight, as the great obsession, is not in any perceptible degree moral beauty. It would be difficult perhaps to find elsewhere in the same compass so much expression of the personal life resting so little on any picture of the personal character and the personal will. It is not that Signor D'Annunzio has not more than once pushed his furrow in this latter direction; but nothing is exactly more interesting, as we shall see, than the seemingly inevitable way in which the attempt falls short.

"Il Piacere," the first in date of the five tales, has, though with imperfections, the merit of giving us strongly at the outset the author's scale and range of view, and of so constituting a sort of prophetic summary of his elements. All that is done in the later things is more or less done here, and nothing is absent here that we are not afterwards also to miss. I propose, however, that it shall not be prematurely a question with us of what we miss; no intelligible statement of which, for that matter, in such considerations as these, is ever possible till there has been some adequate statement of what we find. Count Andrea Sperelli is a young man who pays, pays heavily, as we take it that we are to understand, for an unbridled surrender to the life of the senses; whereby it is primarily a picture of that life that the story gives us. He is represented as inordinately, as quite monstrously, endowed for the career that from the first absorbs and that finally is to be held, we suppose, to engulf him; and it is a tribute to the truth with which his endowment is presented that we should scarce know where else to look for so complete and convincing an account of such adventures. Casanova de Seingalt is of course infinitely more copious, but his autobiography is cheap loose journalism compared with the directed, finely-condensed iridescent epic of Count Andrea.

This young man's years have run but half their course from twenty to thirty when he meets and becomes entangled with a woman more infernally expert even than himself in the matters in which he is most expert—and he is given us as a miracle of social and intellectual accomplishment—the effect of whom is fatally to pervert and poison his imagination. As his imagination is applied exclusively to the employments of "love," this means, for him, a frustration of all happiness, all comfortable consistency, in subsequent relations of the same order. The author's view—this is fundamental—is all of a world in which relations of any other order whatever mainly fail to offer themselves in any attractive form. Andrea Sperelli, loving, accordingly—in the manner in which D'Annunzio's young men love and to which we must specifically return—a woman of good faith, a woman as different as possible from the creature of evil communications, finds the vessel of his spirit itself so infected and disqualified that it falsifies and dries up everything that passes through it. The idea that has virtually determined the situation appears in fact to be that the hero *would* have loved in another manner, or would at least have wished to, but that he had too promptly put any such fortune, so far as his capacity is concerned, out of court. We have our reasons, presently manifest, for doubting the possibility itself; but the theory has nevertheless given its direction to the fable.

For the rest the author's three sharpest signs are already unmistakable: first his rare notation of states of excited sensibility; second his splendid visual sense, the quick generosity of his response to the message, as we nowadays say, of aspects and appearances, to the beauty of places and things; third his ample and exquisite style, his curious, various, inquisitive, always active employment of language as a means of communication and representation. So close is the marriage between his power of "rendering," in the light of the imagination, and whatever he sees and feels, that we should much mislead in speaking of his manner as a thing distinct from the matter submitted to it. The fusion is complete and admirable, so that, though his work is nothing if not "literary," we see at no point of it where literature or where life begins or ends: we swallow our successive morsels with as little question as we swallow food that has by proper preparation been reduced to singleness of savour. It is brought home to us afresh that there is no complete creation without style any more than there is complete music without sound; also that when language becomes as closely applied and impressed a thing as for the most part in the volumes before us the fact of artistic creation is registered at a stroke. It is never more present than in the thick-sown illustrative images and figures that fairly bloom under D'Annunzio's hand. I find examples in "Il Piacere," as elsewhere, by simply turning the pages. "His will"— of the hero's weakness—"useless as a sword of base temper hung at the side of a drunkard or a dullard." Or of his own southern land in September: "I scarce know why, looking at the country in this season, I always think of some beautiful woman after childbirth, who lies back in her white bed, smiling with a pale astonished inextinguishable smile." Or the incision of this: "Where for him now were those unclean short-lived loves that left in the mouth the strange acidity of fruit cut with a steel knife?" Or the felicity of the following, of a southern night seen and felt from the terrace of a villa. "Clear meteors at intervals streaked the motionless air, running over it as lightly and silently as drops of water on a crystal pane." "The sails on the sea," he says of the same look-out by day, "were as pious and numberless as the wings of cherubim on the gold grounds of old Giottesque panels."

But it is above all here for two things that his faculty is admirable; one of them his making us feel through the windows of his situation, or the gaps, as it were, of his flowering wood, the golden presence of Rome, the charm that appeals to him as if he were one of the pilgrims from afar, save that he reproduces it with an authority in which, as we have seen, the pilgrims from afar have mainly been deficient. The other is the whole category of the phenomena of "passion," as passion prevails between his men and his women—and scarcely anything else prevails; the states of feeling, of ecstasy and suffering engendered, the play of sensibility from end to end of the scale. In this direction he has left no dropped stitches for any worker of like tapestries to pick up. We shall here have made out that many of his "values" are much to be contested, but that where they are true they are as fresh as discoveries; witness the passage where Sperelli, driving back to Rome after a steeplechase in which he has been at the supreme moment worsted, meets nothing that does not play with significance into his vision and act with force on his nerves. He has before the race had "words," almost blows, on the subject of one of the ladies present, with one of the other riders, of which the result is that they are to send each other their seconds; but the omens are not for his adversary, in spite of the latter's success on the course.

From the mail-coach, on the return, he overtook the flight toward Rome of Giannetto Rutolo, seated in a small two-wheeled trap, behind the quick trot of a great roan, over whom he bent with tight reins, holding his head down and his cigar in his teeth, heedless of the attempts of policemen to keep him in line. Rome, in the distance, stood up dark against a zone of light as yellow as sulphur; and the statues crowning St. John Lateran looked huge, above the zone, in their violet sky. *Then it was that Andrea fully knew the pain he was making another soul suffer.*

Nothing could be more characteristic of the writer than the way what has preceded flowers into that last reality; and equally in his best manner, doubtless, is such a passage as the following from the same volume, which treats of the hero's first visit to the sinister great lady whose influence on his soul and his senses is to become as the trail of a serpent. She receives him, after their first accidental meeting, with extraordinary promptitude and the last intimacy, receives him in the depths of a great Roman palace which the author, with a failure of taste that is, unfortunately for him, on ground of this sort, systematic, makes a point of naming. "Then they ceased to speak. Each felt the presence of the other flow and mingle with his own, with her own, very blood; till it was *her* blood at last that seemed to have become his life, and his that seemed to have become hers. The room grew larger in the deep silence; the crucifix of Guido Reni made the shade of the canopy and curtains religious; the rumour of the city came to them like the murmur of some faraway flood." Or take for an instance of the writer's way of showing the consciousness as a full, mixed cup, of touching us ourselves with the mystery at work in his characters, the description of the young man's leaving the princely apartments in question after the initiation vouchsafed to him. He has found the great lady ill in bed, with remedies and medicine-bottles at her side, but not too ill, as we have seen, to make him welcome. "Farewell," she has said. "Love me! Remember!"

It seemed to him, crossing the threshold again, that he heard behind him a burst of sobs. But he went on, a little uncertain, wavering like a man who sees imperfectly. The odour of the chloroform clung to his sense like some fume of intoxication; but at each step something intimate passed away from him, wasting itself in the air, so that, impulsively, instinctively, he would have kept himself as he was, have closed himself in, have wrapped himself up to prevent the dispersion. The rooms in front of him were deserted and dumb. At one of the doors "Mademoiselle" appeared, with no sound of steps, with no rustle of skirts, standing there like a ghost. "This way, signor conte. You won't find it." She had an ambiguous, irritating smile, and her curiosity made her grey eyes more piercing. Andrea said nothing. The woman's presence again disconcerted and troubled him, affected him with a vague repugnance, stirred indeed his wrath.

Even the best things suffer by detachment from their context; but so it is that we are in *possession* of the young man's exit, so it is that the act interests us. Fully announced from the first, among these things, was D'Annunzio's signal gift of never approaching the thing particularly to be done, the thing that so presents itself to the painter, without consummately doing it. Each of his volumes offers thus its little gallery of episodes that stand out like the larger pearls occurring at intervals on a string of beads. The steeplechase in "Il Piacere," the auction sale of precious trinkets in Via Sistina on the wet afternoon, the morning in the garden at Schifanoia, by the southern sea, when Donna Maria, the new revelation, first comes down to Andrea, who awaits her there in the languor of convalescence from the almost fatal wound received in the duel of which the altercation on the race-course has been the issue: the manner of such things as these has an extraordinary completeness of beauty. But they are, like similar pages in "Il Trionfo" and "Il Fuoco," not things for adequate citation, not things that lend themselves as some of the briefer felicities. Donna Maria, on the September night at Schifanoia, has been playing for Andrea and their hostess certain old quaint gavottes and toccatas.

It lived again wondrously beneath her fingers, the eighteenth-century music, so melancholy in its dance-tunes—tunes that might have been composed to be danced, on languid afternoons of some St. Martin's summer, in a deserted park, among hushed fountains and pedestals without their statues, over carpets of dead roses, by pairs of lovers soon to love no more.

Autobiographic in form, "L'Innocente" sticks closely to its theme, and though the form is on the whole a disadvantage to it the texture is admirably close. The question is of nothing less than a young husband's relation to the illegitimate child of his wife, born confessedly as such, and so born, marvellous to say, in spite of the circumstance that the wife adores him, and of the fact that, though long grossly, brutally false to her, he also adores his wife. To state these data is sufficiently to express the demand truly made by them for superiority of treatment; they require certainly two or three almost impossible postulates. But we of course never play the fair critical game with an author, never get into relation with him at all, unless we grant him his postulates. His subject is what is given him—given him by influences, by a process, with which we have nothing to do; since what art, what revelation, can ever really make such a mystery, such a passage in the private life of the intellect, adequately traceable for us? His treatment of it, on the other hand, is what he actively gives; and it is with what he gives that we are critically concerned. If there is nothing in him that effectually induces us to make the postulate, he is then empty for us altogether, and the sooner we have done with him the better; little as the truly curious critic enjoys, as a general thing, having publicly to throw up the sponge.

Tullio Hermil, who finally compasses the death of the little "innocent," the small intruder whose presence in the family life has become too intolerable, retraces with a master's hand each step of the process by which he has arrived at this sole issue. Save that his wife dumbly divines and accepts it his perpetration of the deed is not suspected, and we take the secret confession of which the book consists as made for the relief and justification of his conscience. The action all goes forward in that sphere of exasperated sensibility which Signor D'Annunzio has made his own so triumphantly that other story-tellers strike us in comparison as remaining at the door of the inner precinct, as listening there but to catch an occasional faint sound, while he alone is well within and moving through the place as its master. The sensibility has again in itself to be qualified; the exasperation of feeling is ever the essence of the intercourse of some man with some woman who has reduced him, as in "L'Innocente" and in "Il Trionfo," to homicidal madness, or of some woman with some man who, as in "Il Fuoco," and also again by a strange duplication of its office in "L'Innocente," causes her atrociously to suffer. The plane of the situation is thus visibly a singularly special plane; that, always, of the more or less insanely demoralised pair of lovers, for neither of whom is any other personal relation indicated either as actual or as conceivably possible. Here, it may be said on such a showing, is material rather alarmingly cut down as to range, as to interest and, not least, as to charm; but here precisely it is that, by a wonderful chance, the author's magic comes effectively into play.

Little in fact as the relation of the erotically exasperated *with* the erotically exasperated, when pushed on either side to frenzy, would appear to lend itself to luminous developments, the difficulty is surmounted each time in a fashion that, for consistency no less than for brilliancy, is all the author's own. Though surmounted triumphantly as to interest, that is, the trick is played without the least falsification of the luckless subjects of his study. They remain the abject victims of sensibility that his plan has originally made them; they remain exasperated, erotic, hysterical, either homicidally or suicidally determined, cut off from any personal source of life that does not poison them; notwithstanding all of which they neither starve dramatically nor suffer us to starve with them. How then is this seemingly inevitable catastrophe prevented? We ask it but to find on reflection that the answer opens the door to their historian's whole secret. The unfortunates are deprived of any enlarging or saving personal relation, that is of any beneficent reciprocity; but they make up for it by their relation both to the *idea* in general and to the whole world of the senses, which is the completest that the author can conceive for them. He may be described as thus executing on their behalf an artistic *volte-face* of the most effective kind, with results wonderful to note. The world of the senses, with which he surrounds them—a world too of the idea, that is of a few ideas admirably expressed—yields them such a crop of impressions that the need of other occasions to vibrate and respond, to act or to aspire, is superseded by their immense factitious agitation. This agitation runs its course in strangely brief periods—a singular note, the brevity, of every situation;

but the period is while it lasts, for all its human and social poverty, quite inordinately peopled and furnished. The innumerable different ways in which his concentrated couples are able to feel about each other and about their enclosing cage of golden wire, the nature and the art of Italy—these things crowd into the picture and pervade it, lighting it scarcely less, strange to say, because they are things of bitterness and woe.

It is one of the miracles of the imagination; the great shining element in which the characters flounder and suffer becomes rich and beautiful for them, as well as in so many ways for us, by the action of the writer's mind. They not only live in his imagination, but they borrow it from him in quantities; indeed without this charitable advance they would be poor creatures enough, for they have in each case almost nothing of their own. On the aid thus received they start, they get into motion; it makes their common basis of "passion," desire, enchantment, aversion. The essence of the situation is the same in "Il Trionfo" and "Il Fuoco" as in "L'Innocente": the temporarily united pair devour each other, tear and rend each other, wear each other out through a series of erotic convulsions and nervous reactions that are made interesting—interesting to *us*—almost exclusively by the special wealth of their consciousness. The medium in which they move is admirably reflected in it; the autumn light of Venice, the afterglow of her past, in the drama of the elderly actress and the young rhetorician of "Il Fuoco"; the splendour of the summer by the edge of the lower Adriatic in that of the two isolated erotomaniacs of "Il Trionfo," indissolubly linked at last in the fury of physical destruction into which the man drags the woman by way of retribution for the fury of physical surrender into which she has beguiled him.

As for "L'Innocente" again, briefly, there is perhaps nothing in it to match the Roman passages of "Il Piacere"; but the harmony of the general, the outer conditions pervades the picture; the sweetness of the villeggiatura life, the happiness of place and air, the lovability of the enclosing scene, all at variance with the sharpness of the inner tragedy. The inner tragedy of "L'Innocente" has a concentration that is like the carrying, through turns and twists, upstairs and down, of some cup filled to the brim, of which no drop is yet spilled;

such cumulative truth rules the scene after we have once accepted the postulate. It is true that the situation as exhibited involves for Giuliana, the young wife, the vulgarest of adventures; yet she becomes, as it unfolds, the figure of the whole gallery in whom the pathetic has at once most of immediate truth and of investing poetry. I much prefer her for beauty and interest to Donna Maria in "Il Piacere," the principal other image of faith and patience sacrificed. We see these virtues as still supreme in her even while she faces, in advance, her ordeal, in respect to which it has been her hope, in fact her calculation, that her husband will have been deceived about the paternity of her child; and she is so truthfully touching when this possibility breaks down that even though we rub our eyes at the kind of dignity claimed for her we participate without reserve in her predicament. The origin of the infant is frankly ignoble, whereas it is on the nobleness of Giuliana that the story essentially hinges; but the contradiction is wonderfully kept from disconcerting us altogether. What the author has needed for his strangest truth is that the mother shall feel exactly as the husband does, and that the husband shall after the first shock of his horror feel intimately and explicitly with the mother. They take in this way the same view of their woeful excrescence; and the drama of the child's advent and of the first months of his existence, his insistent and hated survival, becomes for them in respect to the rest of the world a drama of silence and dissimulation, in every step of which we feel a terror.

The effect, I may add, gains more than one kind of intensity from that almost complete absence of *other* contacts to which D'Annunzio systematically condemns his creatures; introducing here, however, just the two or three that more completely mark the isolation. It may doubtless be conceded that our English-speaking failure of insistence, of inquiry and penetration, in certain directions, springs partly from our deep-rooted habit of dealing with man, dramatically, on his social and gregarious side, as a being the variety of whose intercourse with his fellows, whatever forms his fellows may take, is positively half his interesting motion. We fear to isolate him, for we remember that as we see and know him he scarce understands himself save in action, action which inevitably mixes him with his kind. To see and know him, like Signor D'Annunzio, almost only in passion is another matter, for passion spends itself quickly in the open and burns hot mainly in nooks and corners. Nothing, too, in the picture is more striking than the manner in which the merely sentimental abyss—that of the couple brought together by the thing that might utterly have severed them—is consistently and successfully avoided. We should have been certain to feel it in many other hands yawning but a few steps off. We see the dreadful facts in themselves, are brought close to them with no interposing vaguenesses or other beggings of the question, and are forcibly reminded how much more this "crudity" makes for the communication of tenderness—what is aimed at—than an attitude conventionally more reticent. We feel what the tenderness can be when it rests on *all* the items of a constituted misery, not one of which is illogically blinked.

For the pangs and pities of the flesh in especial D'Annunzio has in all his work the finest hand—those of the spirit exist with him indeed only as proceeding from these; so that Giuliana for instance affects us, beyond any figure in fiction we are likely to remember, as living and breathing under our touch and before our eyes, as a creature of organs, functions and processes, palpable, audible, pitiful physical conditions. These are facts, many of them, of an order in pursuit of which many a spectator of the "picture of life" will instinctively desire to stop short, however great in general his professed desire to enjoy the borrowed consciousness that the picture of life gives us; and nothing, it may well be said, is more certain than that we have a right in such matters to our preference, a right to choose the kind of adventure of the imagination we like best. No obligation whatever rests on us in respect to a given kind—much light as our choice may often throw for the critic on the nature of our own intelligence. *There* at any rate, we are disposed to say of such a piece of penetration as "L'Innocente," there is a particular dreadful adventure, as large as life, for those who can bear it. The conditions are all present; it is only the reader himself who may break down. When in general, it may be added, we see readers do so, this is truly more often because they are shocked at really finding the last consistency than because they are shocked at missing it.

"Il Trionfo della Morte" and "Il Fuoco" stand together as the amplest and richest of our author's histories, and the earlier, and more rounded and faultless thing of the two, is not unlikely to serve, I should judge, as an unsurpassable example of his talent. His accomplishment here reaches its maximum; all his powers fight for him; the wealth of his expression drapes the situation represented in a mantle of voluminous folds, stiff with elaborate embroidery. The "story" may be told in three words: how Giorgio Aurispa meets in Rome the young and extremely pretty wife of a vulgar man of business, her unhappiness with whom is complete, and, falling in love with her on the spot, eventually persuades her—after many troubled passages—to come and pass a series of weeks with him in a "hermitage" by the summer sea, where, in a delirium of free possession, he grows so to hate her, and to hate himself for his subjection to her, and for the prostration of all honour and decency proceeding from it, that his desire to destroy her even at the cost of perishing with her at last takes uncontrollable form and he drags her, under a pretext, to the edge of a sea-cliff and hurls her, interlocked with him in appalled resistance, into space. We get at an early stage the note of that aridity of agitation in which the narrator has expended treasures of art in trying to interest us. "Fits of indescribable fury made them try which could torture each other best, which most lacerate the other's heart and keep it in martyrdom." But they understand, at least the hero does; and he formulates for his companion the essence of their *impasse*. It is not her fault when she tears and rends.

> Each human soul carries in it for love but a determinate quantity of sensitive force. It is inevitable that this quantity should use itself up with time, as everything else does; so that when it *is* used up no effort has power to prevent love from ceasing. Now it's a long time that you have been loving me; nearly two years!

The young man's intelligence is of the clearest; the woman's here is inferior, though in "Il Fuoco" the two opposed faculties are almost equal; but the pair are alike far from living in their intelligence, which only serves to bestrew with lurid gleams the black darkness of their sensual life. So far as the intelligence is one with the will our author fundamentally treats it as cut off from all communication with any other quarter—that is with the senses arrayed and encamped. The most his unfortunates arrive at is to carry their extremely embellished minds with them through these dusky passages as a kind of gilded glimmering lantern, the effect of which is merely fantastic and ironic—a thing to make the play of their shadows over the walls of their catacomb more monstrous and sinister. Again in the first pages of "Il Trionfo" the glimmer is given.

> He recognised the injustice of any resentment against her, because he recognised the fatal necessities that controlled them alike. No, his misery came from no other human creature; it came from the very essence of life. The lover had not the lover to complain of, but simply love itself. Love, toward which his whole being reached out, from within, with a rush not to be checked, love was of all the sad things of this earth the most lamentably sad. And to this supreme sadness he was perhaps condemned till death.

That, in a nutshell, is D'Annunzio's subject-matter; not simply that his characters see in advance what love is worth for them, but that they nevertheless need to make it the totality of their consciousness. In "Il Trionfo" and "Il Fuoco" the law just expressed is put into play at the expense of the woman, with the difference, however, that in the latter tale the woman perceives and judges, suffers in mind, so to speak, as well as in nerves and in temper. But it would be hard to say in which of these two productions the inexhaustible magic of Italy most helps the effect, most hangs over the story in such a way as to be one with it and to make the ugliness and the beauty melt together. The ugliness, it is to be noted, is continually *presumed* absent; the pursuit and cultivation of beauty—that fruitful preoccupation which above all, I have said, gives the author his value as our "case"—being the very ground on which the whole thing rests. The ugliness is an

accident, a treachery of fate, the intrusion of a foreign substance—having for the most part in the scheme itself no admitted inevitability. Against it every provision is made that
the most developed taste in the world can suggest; for, ostensibly, transcendently, Signor D'Annunzio's *is* the most developed taste in the world—his and that of the ferocious yet so
contracted *conoscenti* his heroes, whose virtual identity with
himself, affirmed with a strangely misplaced complacency by
some of his critics, one would surely hesitate to take for
granted. It is the wondrous physical and other endowments
of the two heroines of "Il Piacere," it is the joy and splendour
of the hero's intercourse with them, to say nothing of the
lustre of his own person, descent, talents, possessions, and of
the great general setting in which everything is offered us—
it is all this that makes up the picture, with the constant suggestion that nothing of a baser quality for the esthetic sense,
or at the worst for a pampered curiosity, might hope so much
as to live in it. The case is the same in "L'Innocente," a scene
all primarily smothered in flowers and fruits and fragrances
and soft Italian airs, in every implication of flattered embowered constantly-renewed desire, which happens to be a
blighted felicity only for the very reason that the cultivation
of delight—in the form of the wife's luckless experiment—
has so awkwardly overleaped itself. Whatever furthermore we
may reflectively think either of the Ippolita of "Il Trionfo" or
of her companion's scheme of existence with her, it is enchanting grace, strange, original, irresistible in kind and degree, that she is given us as representing; just as her material
situation with her young man during the greater part of the
tale is a constant communion, for both of them, with the
poetry and the nobleness of classic landscape, of nature consecrated by association.

The mixture reaches its maximum, however, in "Il Fuoco,"
if not perhaps in "The Virgins of the Rocks"; the mixture I
mean of every exhibited element of personal charm, distinction and interest, with every insidious local influence, every
glamour of place, season and surrounding object. The heroine
of the first-named is a great tragic actress, exquisite of aspect,
intelligence and magnanimity, exquisite for everything but for
being unfortunately middle-aged, battered, marked, as we are

constantly reminded, by all the after-sense of a career of promiscuous carnal connections. The hero is a man of letters, a poet, a dramatist of infinite reputation and resource, and their union is steeped to the eyes in the gorgeous medium of Venice, the moods of whose melancholy and the voices of whose past are an active part of the perpetual concert. But we see *all* the persons introduced to us yearn and strain to exercise their perceptions and taste their impressions as deeply as possible, conspiring together to interweave them with the pleasures of passion. They "go in" as the phrase is, for beauty at any cost—for each other's own to begin with; their creator, in the inspiring quest, presses them hard, and the whole effect becomes for us that of an organised general sacrifice to it and an organised general repudiation of everything else. It is not idle to repeat that the value of the Italian background has to this end been inestimable, and that every spark of poetry it had to contribute has been struck from it—with what supreme felicity we perhaps most admiringly learn in "The Virgins of the Rocks." To measure the assistance thus rendered, and especially the immense literary lift given, we have only to ask ourselves what appearance any one of the situations presented would have made in almost any Cisalpine or "northern" frame of circumstance whatever. Supported but by such associations of local or of literary elegance as *our* comparatively thin resources are able to furnish, the latent weakness in them all, the rock, as to final effect, on which they split and of which I shall presently speak, would be immeasurably less dissimulated. All this is the lesson of style, by which we here catch a writer in the very act of profiting after a curious double fashion. D'Annunzio arrives at it both by expression and by material—that is, by a whole side of the latter; so that with such energy at once and such good fortune it would be odd indeed if he had not come far. It is verily in the very name and interest of beauty, of the lovely impression, that Giorgio Aurispa becomes homicidal in thought and finally in act.

> She would in death become for me matter of thought, pure ideality. From a precarious and imperfect existence she would enter into an existence complete and definitive, for-

saking forever the infirmity of her weak luxurious flesh. Destroy to possess—there is no other way for him who seeks the absolute in love.

To these reflections he has been brought by the long, dangerous past which, as the author says, his connection with his mistress has behind it—a past of recriminations of which the ghosts still walk. "It dragged behind it, through time, an immense dark net, all full of dead things." To quote here at all is always to desire to continue, and "Il Trionfo" abounds in the illustrative episodes that are ever made so masterfully concrete. Offering in strictness, incidentally, the only exhibition in all the five volumes of a human relation other than the acutely sexual, it deals admirably enough with this opportunity when the hero pays his visit to his provincial parents before settling with his mistress at their hermitage. His people are of ancient race and have been much at their ease; but the home in the old Apulian town, overdarkened by the misdeeds of a demoralised father, is on the verge of ruin, and the dull mean despair of it all, lighted by outbreaks of helpless rage on the part of the injured mother, is more than the visitor can bear, absorbed as he is in impatiences and concupiscences which make everything else cease to exist for him. His terror of the place and its troubles but exposes of course the abjection of his weakness, and the sordid squabbles, the general misery and mediocrity of life that he has to face, constitute precisely, for his personal design, the abhorred challenge of ugliness, the interference of a call other than erotic. He flees before it, leaving it to make shift as it can; but nothing could be more "rendered" in detail than his overwhelmed vision of it.

So with the other finest passages of the story, notably the summer day spent by the lovers in a long dusty dreadful pilgrimage to a famous local miracle-working shrine, where they mingle with the multitude of the stricken, the deformed, the hideous, the barely human, and from which they return, disgusted and appalled, to plunge deeper into consoling but too temporary transports; notably also the incident, masterly in every touch, of the little drowned contadino, the whole scene of the small starved dead child on the beach, in all the beauty of light and air and view, with the effusions and vociferations and grimnesses round him, the sights and sounds of the quasi-barbaric life that have the relief of antique rites portrayed on old tombs and urns, that quality and dignity of looming larger which a great feeling on the painter's part ever gives to small things. With this ampler truth the last page of the book is above all invested, the description of the supreme moment—for some time previous creeping nearer and nearer—at which the delirious protagonist beguiles his vaguely but not fully suspicious companion into coming out with him toward the edge of a dizzy place over the sea, where he suddenly grasps her for her doom and the sense of his awful intention, flashing a light back as into their monstrous past, makes her shriek for her life. She dodges him at the first betrayal, panting and trembling.

"Are you crazy?" she cried with wrath in her throat. "Are you crazy?" But as she saw him make for her afresh in silence, as she felt herself seized with still harsher violence and dragged afresh toward her danger, she understood it all in a great sinister flash which blasted her soul with terror. "No, no, Giorgio! Let me go! Let me go! Another minute—listen, listen! Just a minute! I want to say——!" She supplicated, mad with terror, getting herself free and hoping to make him wait, to put him off with pity. "A minute! Listen! I love you! Forgive me! Forgive me!" She stammered incoherent words, desperate, feeling herself overcome, losing her ground, seeing death close. "Murder!" she then yelled in her fury. And she defended herself with her nails, with her teeth, biting like a wild beast. "Murder!" she yelled, feeling herself seized by the hair, felled to the ground on the edge of the precipice, lost. The dog meanwhile barked out at the scuffle. The struggle was short and ferocious, as between implacable enemies who had been nursing to this hour in the depths of their souls an intensity of hate. And they plunged into death locked together.

The wonder-working shrine of the Abruzzi, to which they have previously made their way, is a local Lourdes, the resort from far and wide of the physically afflicted, the evocation of

whose multitudinous presence, the description of whose unimaginable miseries and ecstasies, grovelling struggles and
supplications, has the mark of a pictorial energy for such matters not inferior to that of Émile Zola—to the degree even
that the originality of the pages in question was, if I remember rightly, rather sharply impugned in Paris. D'Annunzio's
defence, however, was easy, residing as it does in the fact that
to handle any subject successfully handled by Zola (his failures are another matter) is quite inevitably to walk more or
less in his footsteps, in prints so wide and deep as to leave
little margin for passing round them. To which I may add
that, though the judgment may appear odd, the truth and
force of the young man's few abject days at Guardiagrele, his
casa paterna, are such as to make us wish that other such
corners of life were more frequent in the author's pages. He
has the supremely interesting quality in the novelist that he
fixes, as it were, the tone of every cluster of objects he approaches, fixes it by the consistency and intensity of his reproduction. In "The Virgins of the Rocks" we have also a *casa
paterna*, and a thing, as I have indicated, of exquisite and
wonderful tone; but the tone here is of poetry, the truth and
the force are less measurable and less familiar, and the whole
question, after all, in its refined and attenuated form, is still
that of sexual pursuit, which keeps it within the writer's too
frequent limits. Giorgio Aurispa, in "Il Trionfo," lives in communion with the spirit of an amiable and melancholy uncle
who had committed suicide and made him the heir of his
fortune, and one of the nephew's most frequent and faithful
loyalties is to hark back, in thought, to the horror of his first
knowledge of the dead man's act, put before us always with
its accompaniment of loud southern resonance and confusion.
He is in the place again, he is in the room, at Guardiagrele,
of the original appalled vision.

He heard, in the stillness of the air and of his arrested
soul, the small shrill of an insect in the wainscot. And the
little fact sufficed to dissipate for the moment the extreme
violence of his nervous tension, as the puncture of a needle
suffices to empty a swollen bladder. Every particular of the
terrible day came back to his memory: the news abruptly

brought to Torretta di Sarsa, toward three in the afternoon, by a panting messenger who stammered and whimpered; the ride on horseback, at lightning speed, under the canicular sky and up the torrid slopes, and, during the rush, the sudden faintnesses that turned him dizzy in his saddle; then the house at home, filled with sobs, filled with a noise of doors slamming in the general scare, filled with the strumming of his own arteries; and at last his irruption into the room, the sight of the corpse, the curtains inflated and rustling, the tinkle on the wall of the little font for holy water.

This young man's great mistake, we are told, had been his insistence on regarding love as a form of enjoyment. He would have been in a possible relation to it only if he had learned to deal with it as a form of suffering. This is the lesson brought home to the heroine of "Il Fuoco," who suffers indeed, as it seems to us, so much more than is involved in the occasion. We ask ourselves continually why; that is we do so at first; we do so before the special force of the book takes us captive and reduces us to mere charmed absorption of its successive parts and indifference to its moral sense. Its defect is verily that it has no moral sense proportionate to the truth, the constant high style of the general picture; and this fact makes the whole thing appear given us simply because it has happened, because it was material that the author had become possessed of, and not because, in its almost journalistic "actuality," it has any large meaning. We get the impression of a direct transfer, a "lift," bodily, of something seen and known, something not really produced by the chemical process of art, the crucible or retort from which things emerge for a new function. Their meaning here at any rate, extracted with difficulty, would seem to be that there is an inevitable leak of ease and peace when a mistress happens to be considerably older than her lover; but even this interesting yet not unfamiliar truth loses itself in the great poetic, pathetic, psychologic ceremonial.

That matters little indeed, as I say, while we read; the two sensibilities concerned bloom, in all the Venetian glow, like wondrous water-plants, throwing out branches and flowers of which we admire the fantastic growth even while we remain, botanically speaking, bewildered. They are other sensibilities than those with which we ourselves have community—one of the main reasons of their appearing so I shall presently explain; and, besides, they are isolated, sequestrated, according to D'Annunzio's constant view of such cases, for an exclusive, an intensified and arid development. The mistress has, abnormally, none of the protection, the alternative life, the saving sanity of other interests, ties, employments; while the hero, a young poet and dramatist with an immense consciousness of genius and fame, has for the time at least only those poor contacts with existence that the last intimacies of his contact with his friend's person, her poor *corpo non più giovane*, as he so frequently repeats, represent for him. It is not for us, however, to contest the relation; it is in the penetrating way again in which the relation is rendered that the writer has his triumph; the way above all in which the world-weary interesting sensitive woman, with her infinite intelligence, yet with her longing for some happiness still among all her experiments untasted, and her genius at the same time for familiar misery, is marked, featured, individualised for us, and, with the strangest art in the world—one of those mysteries of which great talents alone have the trick—at once ennobled with beauty and desecrated by a process that we somehow feel to be that of exposure, to spring from some violation of a privilege. " 'Do with me,' " says the Foscarina on a certain occasion, " ' whatever you will'; and she smiled in her offered abjection. She belonged to him like the thing one holds in one's fist, like the ring on one's finger, like a glove, like a garment, like a word that may be spoken or not, like a draught that may be drunk or poured on the ground." There are some lines describing an hour in which she has made him feel as never before "the incalculable capacity of the heart of man. And it seemed to him as he heard the beating of his own heart and divined the violence of the other beside him that he had in his ears the loud repercussion of the hammer on the hard anvil where human destiny is forged." More than ever here the pitch of the personal drama is taken up by everything else in the scene—everything else being in fact but the immediate presence of Venice, her old faded colour and old vague harmonies, played with constantly as we might play with some rosy fretted faintly-sounding sea-shell.

It would take time to say what we play with in the silver-toned "Virgins of the Rocks," the history of a visit paid by a transcendent young man—always pretty much the same young man—to an illustrious family whose fortunes have tragically shrunken with the expulsion of the Bourbons from the kingdom of Naples, and the three last lovely daughters of whose house are beginning to wither on the stem, undiscovered, unsought, in a dilapidated old palace, an old garden of neglected pomp, a place of fountains and colonnades, marble steps and statues, all circled with hard bright sun-scorched volcanic scenery. They are tacitly candidates for the honour of the hero's hand, and the subject of the little tale, which deals with scarce more than a few summer days, is the manner of their presenting themselves for his admiration and his choice. I decidedly name this exquisite composition as my preferred of the series; for if its tone is thoroughly romantic the romance is yet of the happiest kind, the kind that consists in the imaginative development of observable things, things present, significant, related to us, and not in a weak false fumble for the remote and the disconnected.

It is indeed the romantic mind itself that makes the picture, and there could be no better case of the absolute artistic vision. The mere facts are soon said; the main fact, above all, of the feeble remnant of an exhausted race waiting in impotence to see itself cease to be. The father has nothing personal left but the ruins of his fine presence and of his old superstitions, a handful of silver dust; the mother, mad and under supervision, stalks about with the delusion of imperial greatness (there is a wonderful page on her parading through the gardens in her rococo palanquin, like a Byzantine empress, attended by sordid keepers, while the others are hushed into pity and awe); the two sons, hereditarily tainted, are virtually imbecile; the three daughters, candidly considered, are what we should regard in our Anglo-Saxon world as but the stuff of rather particularly dreary and shabby, quite unutterably idle old maids. Nothing, within the picture, occurs; nothing is done or, more acutely than usual, than everywhere, suffered; it is all a mere affair of the rich impression, the complexity of images projected upon the quintessential spirit of the hero, whose own report is what we have—an affair of the quality of observation, sentiment and eloquence brought to bear. It is not too much to say even that the whole thing is in the largest sense but a theme for style, style of substance as well as of form. Within this compass it blooms and quivers and shimmers with light, becomes a wonderful little walled garden of romance. The young man has a passage of extreme but respectful tenderness with each of the sisters in turn, and the general cumulative effect is scarcely impaired by the fact that "nothing comes" of any of these relations. Too little comes of anything, I think, for any very marked human analogy, inasmuch as if it is interesting to be puzzled to a certain extent by what an action, placed before us, is designed to show or to signify, so we require for this refined amusement at least the sense that some general idea *is* represented. We must feel it present.

Therefore if making out nothing very distinct in "Le Vergini" but the pictorial idea, and yet cleaving to the preference I have expressed, I let the anomaly pass as a tribute extorted by literary art, I may seem to imply that a book may have a great interest without showing a perfect sense. The truth is undoubtedly that I am in some degree beguiled and bribed by the particularly intense expression given in these pages to the author's esthetic faith. If he is so supremely a "case" it is because this production has so much to say for it, and says it with such a pride of confidence, with an assurance and an elegance that fairly make it the last conceivable word of such a profession. The observations recorded have their origin in the narrator's passionate reaction against the vulgarity of the day. All the writer's young men react; but Cantelmo, in the volume before us, reacts with the finest contempt. He is, like his brothers, a *raffiné* conservative, believing really, so far as we understand it, only in the virtue of "race" and in the grand manner. The blighted Virgins, with all that surrounds them, are an affirmation of the grand manner—that is of the shame and scandal of what in an odious age it has been reduced to. It consists indeed of a number of different things which I may not pretend to have completely fitted together, but which are, with other elements, the sense of the supremacy of beauty, the supremacy of style and, last not least, of the personal will, manifested for the most part as a cold insolence of attitude—not manifested as anything much more edifying. What it really appears to come to is that the will is a sort of romantic ornament, the application of which, for life in the present and the future, remains awkwardly vague, though we are always to remember that it has been splendidly forged in the past. The will in short *is* beauty, is style, is elegance, is art—especially in members of great families and possessors of large fortunes. That of the hero of "Le Vergini" has been handed down to him direct, as by a series of testamentary provisions, from a splendid young ancestor for whose memory and whose portrait he has a worship, a warrior and virtuoso of the Renaissance, the model of his spirit.

> He represents for me the mysterious meaning of the power of style, not violable by any one, and least of all ever by myself in my own person.

And elsewhere:—

> The sublime hands of Violante [the beauty and interest of hands play a great part, in general, in the picture], pressing out in drops the essence of the tender flowers and letting them fall bruised to the ground, performed an act which, as a symbol, corresponded perfectly to the character of my style; this being ever to extract from a thing its very last scent of life, to take from it all it could give and leave it exhausted. Was not this one of the most important offices of my art of life?

The book is a singularly rich exhibition of an inward state, the state of private poetic intercourse with things, the kind of current that in a given personal experience flows to and fro between the imagination and the world. It represents the esthetic consciousness, proud of its conquests and discoveries, and yet trying, after all, as with the vexed sense of a want, to look through other windows and eyes. It goes all lengths, as is of course indispensable on behalf of a personage constituting a case. "I firmly believe that the greatest sum of future dominion will be precisely that which shall have its base and its apex in Rome"—such being in our personage the confidence of the "Latin" spirit. Does it not really all come back to style? It was to the Latin spirit that the Renaissance was primarily vouchsafed; and was not, for a simplified statement, the last word of the Renaissance the question of taste? That is the esthetic question; and when the Latin spirit after many misadventures again clears itself we shall see how all the while this treasure has been in its keeping. Let us as frankly as possible add that there is a whole side on which the clearance may appear to have made quite a splendid advance with Signor D'Annunzio himself.

But there is another side, which I have been too long in coming to, yet which I confess is for me much the more interesting. No account of our author is complete unless we really make out what becomes of that esthetic consistency in him which, as I have said, our own collective and cultivated effort is so earnestly attempting and yet so pathetically, if not so grotesquely, missing. We are struck, unmistakably, early in our acquaintance with these productions, by the fact that their total beauty somehow extraordinarily fails to march with their beauty of parts, and that something is all the while at work undermining that bulwark against ugliness which it is their obvious theory of their own office to throw up. The disparity troubles and haunts us just in proportion as we admire; and our uneasy wonderment over the source of the weakness fails to spoil our pleasure only because such questions have so lively an interest for the critic. We feel ourselves somehow in presence of a singular incessant *leak* in the effect of distinction so artfully and copiously produced, and we apply our test up and down in the manner of the inquiring person who, with a tin implement and a small flame, searches our premises for an escape of gas. The bad smell has, as it were, to be accounted for; and yet where, amid the roses and lilies and pomegranates, the thousand essences and fragrances, can such a thing possibly be? Quite abruptly, I think, at last (if we have been much under the spell) our test gives us the news, not unaccompanied with the shock with which we see our escape of gas spring into flame. There is no mistaking it; the leak of distinction is produced by a positive element of the vulgar; and that the vulgar should flourish in an air so

charged, intellectually speaking, with the "aristocratic" element, becomes for us straightway the greatest of oddities and
at the same time, critically speaking, one of the most interesting things conceivable.

The interest then springs from its being involved for us in
the "case." We recognise so many suggested consequences if
the case is really to prove responsible for it. We ask ourselves
if there be not a connection, we almost tremble lest there
shouldn't be; since what is more obvious than that, if a high
example of exclusive estheticism—as high a one as we are
likely ever to meet—is bound sooner or later to spring a leak,
the general question receives much light? We recognise here
the value of our author's complete consistency: he would
have kept his bottom sound, so to speak, had he not remained
so long at sea. If those imperfect exponents of his faith whom
we have noted among ourselves fail to flower, for a climax, in
any proportionate way, we make out that they are embarrassed not so much by any force they possess as by a force—
a force of temperament—that they lack. The anomaly I speak
of presents itself thus as the dilemma in which Signor D'Annunzio's consistency has inexorably landed him; and the
disfigurement breaks out, strikingly enough, in the very
forefront of his picture, at the point where he has most lavished his colour. It is where he has most trusted and depended that he is most betrayed, the traitor sharing certainly
his tent and his confidence. What is it that in the interest of
beauty he most elaborately builds on if not on the love-affairs
of his heroes and heroines, if not on his exhibition of the free
play, the sincere play, the play closely studied and frankly represented, of the sexual relation? It is round this exercise, for
him, that expressible, demonstrable, communicable beauty
prevailingly clusters; a view indeed as to which we all generously go with him, subject to the reserve for each of us of our
own expression and demonstration. It is these things on his
part that break down, it is his discrimination that falls short,
and thereby the very kind of intellectual authority most implied by his pretension. There is according to him an immense amenity that can be saved—saved by style—from the
general wreck and welter of what is most precious, from the
bankruptcy determined more and more by our basely demo-

cratic conditions. As we watch the actual process, however, it is only to see the lifeboat itself founder. The vulgarity into which he so incongruously drops is, I will not say the space he allots to love-affairs, but the weakness of his sense of "values" in depicting them.

We begin to ask ourselves at an early stage what this queer passion may be in the representation of which the sense of beauty ostensibly finds its richest expression and which is yet attended by nothing else at all—neither duration, nor propagation, nor common kindness, nor common consistency with other relations, common congruity with the rest of life—to make its importance good. If beauty is the supreme need so let it be; nothing is more certain than that we can never get too much of it if only we get it of the right sort. It is therefore on this very ground—the ground of its own sufficiency—that Signor D'Annunzio's invocation of it collapses at our challenge. The vulgarity comes from the disorder really introduced into values, as I have called them; from the vitiation suffered—that we should have to record so mean an accident—by taste, impeccable taste, itself. The truth of this would come out fully in copious examples, now impossible; but it is not too much to say, I think, that in every principal situation presented the fundamental weakness causes the particular interest to be inordinately compromised.

I must not, I know, make too much of "Il Piacere"—one of those works of promising youth with which criticism is always easy—and I should indeed say nothing of it if it were also a work of less ability. It really, however, to my mind, quite gives us the key, all in the morning early, to our author's general misadventure. Andrea Sperelli is the key; Donna Maria is another key of a slightly different shape. They have neither of them the esthetic importance, any more than the moral, that their narrator claims for them and in his elaborate insistence on which he has so hopelessly lost his way. If they *were* important—by which I mean if they showed in any other light than that of their particular erotic exercise—they would justify the claim made for them with such superior art. They have no general history, since their history is only, and immediately and extravagantly, that of their too cheap and too easy romance. Why should the career of the young man be offered as a sample of pathetic, of tragic, of edifying corruption?—in which case it might indeed be matter for earnest exhibition. The march of corruption, the insidious influence of propinquity, opportunity, example, the ravage of false estimates and the drama of sterilising passion—all this is a thinkable theme, thinkable especially in the light of a great talent. But for Andrea Sperelli there is not only no march, no drama, there is not even a weakness to give him the semblance of dramatic, of plastic material; he is solidly, invariably, vulgarly strong, and not a bit more corrupt at the end of his disorders than at the beginning. His erudition, his intellectual accomplishments and elevation, are too easily spoken for; no view of him is given in which we can feel or taste them. Donna Maria is scarcely less signal an instance of the apparent desire on the author's part to impute a "value" defeated by his apparently not knowing what a value is. She is apparently an immense value for the occasions on which the couple secretly meet, but how is she otherwise one? and what becomes therefore of the beauty, the interest, the pathos, the struggle, or whatever else, of her relation—relation of character, of judgment, even of mere taste—to her own collapse? The immediate physical sensibility that surrenders in her is, as throughout, exquisitely painted; but since nothing operates for her, one way or the other, *but* that familiar faculty, we are left casting about us almost as much for what else she has to give as for what, in any case, she may wish to keep.

The author's view of the whole matter of durations and dates, in these connections, gives the scale of "distinction" by itself a marked downward tilt; it confounds all differences between the trivial and the grave. Giuliana, in "L'Innocente," is interesting because she has had a misadventure, and she is exquisite in her delineator's view because she has repented of it. But the misadventure, it appears, was a matter but of a minute; so that we oddly see this particular romance attenuated on the ground of its brevity. Given the claims of the exquisite, the attenuation should surely be sought in the very opposite quarter; since, where these remarkable affections are concerned, how otherwise than by the element of comparative duration do we obtain the element of comparative good faith, on which we depend for the element, in turn, of comparative dignity? Andrea Sperelli becomes in the course of a few weeks in Rome the lover of some twenty or thirty women of fashion—the number scarce matters; but to make this possible his connection with each has but to last a day or two; and the effect of that in its order is to reduce to nothing, by vulgarity, by frank grotesqueness of association, the romantic capacity in him on which his chronicler's whole appeal to us is based. The association rising before us more nearly than any other is that of the manners observable in the most mimetic department of any great menagerie.

The most serious relation depicted—in the sense of being in some degree the least suggestive of mere zoological sociability—is that of the lovers in "Il Fuoco," as we also take this pair for their creator's sanest and most responsible spirits. It is a question between them of an heroic affection, and yet the affection appears to make good for itself no place worth speaking of in their lives. It holds but for a scant few weeks; the autumn already reigns when the connection begins, and the connection is played out (or if it be not the ado is about nothing) with the first flush of the early Italian spring. It suddenly, on our hands, becomes trivial, with all our own estimate of reasons and realities and congruities falsified. The Foscarina has, on professional business, to "go away," and the young poet has to do the same; but such a separation, so easily bridged over by such great people, makes a beggarly climax for an intercourse on behalf of which all the forces of poetry and tragedy have been set in motion. Where then we ask ourselves is the weakness?—as we ask it, very much in the same way, in respect to the vulgarised aspect of the tragedy of Giorgio Aurispa. The pang of pity, the pang that springs from a conceivable community in doom, is in this latter case altogether wanting. Directly we lift a little the embroidered mantle of that gift for appearances which plays, on Signor D'Annunzio's part, such tricks upon us, we find ourselves put off, as the phrase is, with an inferior article. The inferior article is the hero's poverty of life, which cuts him down for pathetic interest just as the same limitation in "Il Piacere" cuts down Donna Maria. Presented each as victims of another rapacious person who has got the better of them, there is no process, no complexity, no suspense in their story; and thereby, we submit, there is no esthetic beauty. Why *shouldn't* Giorgio Aurispa go mad? Why shouldn't Stelio Effrena go away? We make the inquiry as disconcerted spectators, not feeling in the former case that we have had any communication with the wretched youth's sanity, and not seeing in the latter why the tie of all the passion that has been made so admirably vivid for us should not be able to weather change.

Nothing is so singular with D'Annunzio as that the very basis and subject of his work should repeatedly go aground on such shallows as these. He takes for treatment a situation that is substantially none—the most fundamental this of his values, and all the more compromising that his immense art of producing illusions still leaves it exposed. The idea in each case is superficially specious, but *where* it breaks down is what makes all the difference. "Il Piacere" would have meant what it seems to try to mean only if a provision had been made in it for some adequate "inwardness" on the part either of the nature disintegrated or of the other nature to which this poisoned contact proves fatal. "L'Innocente," of the group, comes nearest to justifying its idea; and I leave it unchallenged, though its meaning surely would have been written larger if the attitude of the wife toward her misbegotten child had been, in face of the husband's, a little less that of the dumb detached animal suffering in her simplicity. As a picture of such suffering, the pain of the mere dumb animal, the work is indeed magnificent; only its connections are poor with the higher dramatic, the higher poetic, complexity of things.

I can only repeat that to make "The Triumph of Death" a fruitful thing we should have been able to measure the triumph by its frustration of some conceivable opportunity at least for life. There is a moment at which we hope for something of this kind, the moment at which the young man pays his visit to his family, who have grievous need of him and toward whom we look to see some one side or other of his fine sensibility turn. But nothing comes of that for the simple reason that the personage is already dead—that nothing exists in him but the established *fear* of life. He turns his back on everything but a special sensation, and so completely shuts the door on the elements of contrast and curiosity. Death really triumphs, in the matter, but over the physical terror of the inordinate woman; a pang perfectly communicated to us, but too small a surface to bear the weight laid on it, which accordingly affects us as that of a pyramid turned over on its point. It is throughout one of D'Annunzio's strongest marks that he treats "love" as a matter not to be mixed with life, in the larger sense of the word, at all—as a matter all of whose other connections are dropped; a sort of secret game that can go on only if each of the parties has nothing to do, even on any *other* terms, with any one else.

I have dwelt on the fact that the sentimental intention in "Il Fuoco" quite bewilderingly fails, in spite of the splendid accumulation of material. We wait to the end to see it declare itself, and then are left, as I have already indicated, with a mere meaningless anecdote on our hands. Brilliant and free, each freighted with a talent that is given us as incomparable, the parties to the combination depicted have, for their affection, the whole world before them—and not the simple terraqueous globe, but that still vaster sphere of the imagination in which, by an exceptionally happy chance, they are able to move together on very nearly equal terms. A tragedy is a tragedy, a comedy is a comedy, when the effect, in either sense, is *determined* for us, determined by the interference of some element that starts a complication or precipitates an action. As in "Il Fuoco" nothing whatever interferes—or nothing certainly that need weigh with the high spirits represented— we ask why such precious revelations are made us for nothing. Admirably made in themselves they yet strike us as, esthetically speaking, almost cruelly wasted.

This general remark would hold good, as well, of "Le Vergini," if I might still linger, though its application has already been virtually made. Anatolia, in this tale, the most robust of the three sisters, declines marriage in order to devote herself to a family who have, it would certainly appear, signal need of her nursing. But this, though it sufficiently represents *her* situation, covers as little as possible the ground of the hero's own, since he, quivering intensely with the treasure of his "will," inherited in a straight line from the *cinque-cento*, only asks to affirm his sublimated energy. The temptation to affirm it erotically, at least, has been great for him in relation to each of the young women in turn; but it is for Anatolia that his admiration and affection most increase in volume, and it is accordingly for her sake that, with the wonderful moral force behind him (kept as in a Florentine casket,) we most look to see him justified. He has a fine image—and when has the author not fine images?—to illustrate the constant readiness of this possession. The young woman says something that inspires him, whereupon, "as a sudden light playing over the dusky wall of a room causes the motionless sword in a trophy to shine, so her word drew a great flash from my suspended *volontà*. There was a virtue in her," the narrator adds, " which could have produced portentous fruit. Her substance might have nourished a superhuman germ." In spite of which it never succeeds in becoming so much as a question that his affection for her shall *act*, that this grand imagination in him shall operate, that he himself is, in virtue of such things, exactly the person to come to her aid and to combine with her in devotion. The talk about the *volontà* is amusing much in the same way as the complacency of a primitive man, unacquainted with the uses of things, who becomes possessed by some accident of one of the toys of civilisation, a watch or a motor-car. And yet artistically and for our author the will *has* an application, since without it he could have done no rare vivid work.

Here at all events we put our finger, I think, on the very point at which his esthetic plenitude meets the misadventure that discredits it. We see just where it "joins on" with vulgarity. That sexual passion from which he extracts such admirable detached pictures insists on remaining for him *only* the act of a moment, beginning and ending in itself and disowning any representative character. From the moment it depends on itself alone for its beauty it endangers extremely its distinction, so precarious at the best. For what it represents, precisely, is it poetically interesting; it finds its extension and consummation only in the rest of life. Shut out from the rest of life, shut out from all fruition and assimilation, it has no more dignity than—to use a homely image—the boots and shoes that we see, in the corridors of promiscuous hotels, standing, often in double pairs, at the doors of rooms. Detached and unassociated these clusters of objects present, however obtruded, no importance. What the participants do with their agitation, in short, or even what it does with them, *that* is the stuff of poetry, and it is never really interesting save when something finely contributive in themselves makes it so. It is this absence of anything finely contributive in themselves, on the part of the various couples here concerned, that is the open door to the trivial. I have said, with all appreciation, that they present the great "relation," for intimacy, as we shall nowhere else find it presented; but to see it related, in its own turn, to nothing in the heaven above or the earth beneath, this undermines, we definitely learn, the charm of that achievement.

And so it is, strangely, that our esthetic "case" enlightens us. The only question is whether it be the only case of the kind conceivable. May we not suppose another with the elements differently mixed? May we not in imagination alter the proportions within or the influences without, and look with cheerfulness for a different issue? *Need* the esthetic adventure, in a word, organised for real discovery, give us no more comforting news of success? Are there not, so to speak, finer possible combinations? are there not safeguards against futility that in the example before us were but too presumably absent? To which the sole answer probably is that no man can say. It is Signor D'Annunzio alone who has really sailed the sea and brought back the booty. The actual case is so good that all the potential fade beside it. It has for it that it exists, and that, whether for the strength of the original outfit or for the weight of the final testimony, it could scarce thinkably be bettered.

Quarterly Review, April 1904
Reprinted under the title "Gabriele D'Annunzio, 1902"
in *Notes on Novelists*, 1914

Johann Wolfgang von Goethe

Wilhelm Meister's Apprenticeship and Travels. From the German of Goethe. By Thomas Carlyle. In Two Volumes. Boston: Ticknor and Fields, 1865.

THIS NEW EDITION of Goethe's great novel will give many persons the opportunity of reading a work which, although introduced to the English public forty years ago, is yet known to us chiefly by hearsay. We esteem it a matter for gratitude that it should now invite some share of attention as a novelty, if on no other ground; and we gladly take advantage of the occasion thus afforded to express our sense of its worth. We hope this republication may help to discredit the very general impression that *Wilhelm Meister* belongs to the class of the great unreadables. The sooner this impression is effaced, the better for those who labor under it. Something will have been gained, at least, if on experiment it should pass from a mere prejudice into a responsible conviction; and a great deal more will have been gained, if it is completely reversed.

To read *Wilhelm Meister* for the first time is an enviable and almost a unique sensation. Few other books, to use an expression which Goethe's admirers will understand, so steadily and gradually *dawn* upon the intelligence. In few other works is so profound a meaning enveloped in so common a form. The slow, irresistible action of this latent significance is an almost awful phenomenon, and one which we may vainly seek in those imaginative works in which the form of the narrative bears a direct, and not, as it appears here to do, an inverse, relation to its final import; or in which the manner appeals from the outset to the reader's sympathy. Whatever may be the lesson which Goethe proposes to teach us, however profound or however sublime, his means invariably remain homely and prosaic. In no book is the intention of elegance, the principle of selection, less apparent. He introduces us to the shabbiest company, in order to enrich us with knowledge; he leads us to the fairest goals by the longest and roughest roads. It is to this fact, doubtless, that the work owes its reputation of tediousness; but it justifies the reputation only when, behind the offensive detail, the patient reader fails to discover, not a glittering, but a steadily shining generality. Frequently the reader is unable to find any justification for certain wearisome *minutiæ*; and, indeed, many of the incidents are so "flat," that the reader who comes to his task with a vague inherited sense of Goethe's greatness is constrained, for very pity, to supply them with a hidden meaning. It would not, therefore, be difficult to demonstrate that the great worth of *Wilhelm Meister* is a vast and hollow delusion, upheld by a host of interested dupes. The book is, indeed, so destitute of the quality of cleverness, that it would be comparatively easy for a clever man to make out any given case whatsoever against it; do anything with it, in short, except understand it. The man who is only clever may do much; but he may not do this. It is perhaps one of the most valuable properties of *Wilhelm Meister* that it does not react against this kind of manipulation. We gladly admit, nay, we assert, that, unless seriously read, the book must be inexpressibly dull. It was written, not to entertain, but to edify. It has no factitious qualities, as we may call them; none of those innumerable little arts and graces by which the modern novel continually and tacitly deprecates criticism. It stands on its own bottom, and freely takes for granted that the reader cannot but be interested. It exhibits, indeed, a sublime indifference to the reader,—the indifference of humanity in the aggregate to the individual observer. The author, calmly and steadily guided by his purpose, has none of that preoccupation of *success* which so detracts from the grandeur of most writers at the present day, and leads us at times to decide sweepingly that all our contemporaries are of the second class.

Of plot there is in this book properly none. We have Goethe's own assertion that the work contains no central point. It contains, however, a central figure, that of the hero. By him, through him, the tale is unfolded. It consists of the various adventures of a burgher youth, who sets out on his journey through life in quest, to speak generally, of happiness,—that happiness which, as he is never weary of repeating, can be found only in the subject's perfect harmony with himself. This is certainly a noble idea. Whatever pernicious conclusions may be begotten upon it, let us freely admit that at the outset, in its virginity, it is beautiful. Meister conceives that he can best satisfy his nature by connecting himself with the theatre, the home, as he believes, potentially at least, of all noble aims and lessons. The history of this connection, which is given at great length, is to our mind the most interesting part of the whole work; and for these reasons: that those occasional discussions by which the action is so frequently retarded or advanced (as you choose to consider it), and of which, in spite of their frequency, we would not forfeit a single one, are here more directly suggestive than in subsequent chapters; and that the characters are more positive. The "Apprenticeship" is, in the first half, more of a story, or, to state it scientifically, more dramatic than in the last. If Goethe is great as a critic, he is at least equally great as a poet; and if *Wilhelm Meister* contains pages of disquisition which cannot be too deeply studied, it likewise contains men and women who cannot be forgotten. Meister's companions bear no comparison with the ingenious puppets produced by the great turning-lathe of our modern fancy.

There is the same difference between them and the figures of last month's successful novel, as there is between a portrait by Velasquez and a photograph by Brady. Which of these creations will live longest in your memory? Goethe's persons are not lifelike; that is the mark of our fashionable photographic heroes and heroines: they are life itself. It was a solid criticism of certain modern works of art, that we recently heard applied to a particular novelist: "He tells you everything except the very thing you want to know." We know concerning Philena, Aurelia, Theresa, Serlo, and Werner none of those things of which the clever story-teller of the present day would have made hot haste to inform us; we know neither their costume, nor their stature, nor the indispensable color of their eyes; and yet, for all that, they *live*,—and assuredly a figure cannot do more than that.

The women in *Wilhelm Meister* are, to our mind, truer even than the men. The three female names above mentioned stand for three persons, which abide in our memory with so unquestioned a right of presence that it is hard to believe that we have not actually known them. Is there in the whole range of fiction a more natural representation of a light-hearted coquette than that of the actress Philena,—she who, at the outset of an excursion into the country, proposes that a law be passed prohibiting the discussion of inanimate objects? Where, too, is there as perfect an example of an irretrievable sentimentalist as her comrade Aurelia, she who, as herself declares, bears hard upon all things, as all things bear hard upon her, and who literally dies for the sake of poetic consistency? What an air of solid truth, again, invests the practical, sensible, reasonable Theresa!

Wilhelm's purpose being exclusively one of self-culture, he is an untiring observer. He listens to every man, woman, and child, for he knows that from each something may be learned. As a character, he is vague and shadowy, and the results of his experience are generally left to the reader's inference. Indeed, as his lessons are mostly gathered from conversations for which he furnishes the original motive, the reader may place himself in the hero's position of an eminently respectful auditor, and judge of the latter's impressions by his own.

Although incidentally dramatic, therefore, it will be seen that, as a whole, *Wilhelm Meister* is anything but a novel, as we have grown to understand the word. As a whole, it has, in fact, no very definite character; and, were we not vaguely convinced that its greatness as a work of art resides in this very absence of form, we should say that, as a work of art, it is lamentably defective. A modern novelist, taking the same subject in hand, would restrict himself to showing the sensations of his hero during the process of education; that is, his hero would be the broad end, and the aggregate of circumstances the narrow end, of the glass through which we were invited to look; and we should so have a comedy or a tragedy, as the case might be. But Goethe, taking a single individual as a pretext for looking into the world, becomes so absorbed in the spectacle before him, that, while still clinging to his hero as a pretext, he quite forgets him as a subject. It may be here objected, that the true artist never forgets either himself or anything else. However that may be, each reader becomes his own Wilhelm Meister, an apprentice, a traveller, on his own account; and as his understanding is large or small, will Wilhelm and the whole work be real or the contrary. It is, indeed, to the understanding exclusively, and never, except in the episode of Mignon, to the imagination, that the author appeals. For what, as we read on, strikes us as his dominant quality? His love of the real. "It will astonish many persons," says a French critic, "to learn that Goethe was a great scorner of what we call the ideal. Reality, religiously studied, was always his muse and his inspiration."

The bearing of *Wilhelm Meister* is eminently practical. It might almost be called a treatise on moral economy,—a work intended to show how the experience of life may least be wasted, and best be turned to account. This fact gives it a seriousness which is almost sublime. To Goethe, nothing was vague, nothing empty, nothing trivial,—we had almost said, nothing false. Was there ever a book so dispassionate, or, as some persons prefer to call it, cold-blooded? In reading it, we learn the meaning of the traditional phrase about the author's calmness. This calmness seems nearly identical with the extraordinary activity of his mind, as they must both indeed have been the result of a deep sense of intellectual power. It is hard to say which is the truer, that his mind is without haste or without rest. In the pages before us there is not a ray of humor, and hardly a flash of wit; or if they exist, they are lost in the luminous atmosphere of justice which fills the book. These things imply some degree of passion; and Goethe's plan was *non flere, non indignari, sed intelligere*.

We do not know that in what we have said there is much to lead those who are strangers to this work to apply themselves to the perusal of it. We are well aware that our remarks are lamentably disproportionate to the importance of our subject. To attempt to throw a general light upon it in the limits here prescribed would be like striking a match to show off the *Transfiguration*. We would therefore explicitly recommend its perusal to all such persons, especially young persons, as feel that it behooves them to attach a meaning to life. Even if it settles nothing in their minds, it will be a most valuable experience to have read it. It is worth reading, if only to differ with it. If it is a priceless book to love, it is almost as important a one to hate; and whether there is more in it of truth or of error, it is at all events *great*. Is not this by itself sufficient? *Wilhelm Meister* may not have much else that other books have, but it has this, that it is the product of a great mind.

There are scores of good books written every day; but this one is a specimen of the grand manner.

North American Review, July 1865

Julius Rodenberg

England, Literary and Social, from a German Point of View. By Julius Rodenberg. London: Richard Bentley & Son, 1875.

HERR RODENBERG'S BOOK, though entertaining and worth printing, is rather disappointing. It is not, as its title seems to indicate, a study of contemporary manners, and it contains very little psychology. Neither is it in any especial sense written from the "German point of view." It is a collection of four long antiquarian essays by a man who knows and likes England so well that it is only to be divined from an occasional Teutonism of style that he is not an Englishman. It must be said, however, that the abundance of research and the paucity of personal observation are sufficiently characteristic of the author's nationality, and that only a German, probably, collecting impressions of a foreign country on the spot, would have looked for them almost exclusively in books. Herr Rodenberg knows his England perhaps better than M. Taine; but there is more of vivid portraiture—of the essence of the matter—in a single page of Taine's 'Notes' than in one of this author's long chapters. Herr Rodenberg writes upon "Kent and the Canterbury Tales," "Shakspeare's London," the "Coffee-Houses and Clubs of London," and the "Jews in England." To these lightly historic studies he affixes two chapters of inferior value, entitled "Pictures of English High-roads" and "Autumn on the English Lakes." These essays contain a great many curious reminders and allusions, and not a little unfamiliar information, presented in an easy, agreeable style, in which the "geniality" alone, perhaps, is a trifle overdone. Herr Rodenberg evidently knows English history and English literature with great exactness, and his manner of entering into them, the peculiar degree of his relish for the objects, persons, and places associated with them, are very remarkable in a foreigner. Beyond a certain point, generally, such facts become too minute for a foreigner's care; he is content to admire more in the gross. But Herr Rodenberg seems to feel a sort of intellectual birthright in the English past, and his intimate acquaintance with it may serve as an example to the English themselves, who certainly of all nations are, in the average, least acquainted with their own history and their own classics. For instance, it strikes us with a kind of respect for the thoroughness of a foreign observer that he should quote, apparently off-hand, some flat lines from the poet Akenside about Chaucer. How much must he have gone through, we reflect, before he arrived in the due course of things at drowsy Akenside! Herr Rodenberg, taking for his text the Kentish landscape and the streets of Canterbury, gossips very agreeably and eruditely upon Chaucer's life, and weighs one hypothesis against another as to certain contested points in it. The author's long prose synopsis of the contents of several of the Canterbury Tales might, however, have been profitably omitted from the work.

The article on "Shakspeare's London" contains a good deal of entertaining archæology and topography, and many curious details about the arrangement of the primitive English theatre. It is to be inferred, however, that the author's knowledge of the past is more exact than it occasionally appears to be of the present. After the play, in Shakspeare's day, he says, the troupe of actors stood forth in a semicircle and dismissed the audience by a prayer to the queen—"a custom which is maintained to the present day in England, where no play, opera, or concert is left before the National Anthem has been sung." But Herr Rodenberg's most entertaining pages are those upon the London coffee-houses and clubs, into which he compresses the savor of the whole literature of the subject. He calls attention, properly, to the singular anomaly of the fact that though coffee-houses began to flourish about 1650, the coffee of England is still the worst in Europe, having usually a strange, barbarous, experimental flavor. It is also very odd that in a country where coffee is made with the least appreciation of its merits and has always remained a decidedly exotic beverage, the dining-room at hotels should invariably be dubbed the coffee-room. This often seems to the breakfastless foreigner like a wanton addition of insult to injury. "It is remarkable," says Herr Rodenberg in a note, "that the smell of coffee seems so unpleasant to the true Briton. Each of the above-quoted pamphlets [broadsides and satires of the seventeenth century] calls it a 'stink.' " We must thank the author for reminding us of one of the most characteristic and amusing instances of Dr. Johnson's conversational brutality. Garrick had been proposed for election into the Literary Club, and Johnson, who was supposed to be his very good friend, protested against the nomination. "Sir," he said, "I love my little David heartily, more than all, or many, of his flatterer᾿ do; but surely in such a society as ours one should not sit elbowed *by players, pimps, and mimes!*" Almost the only pages of contemporaneous allusion in Herr Rodenberg's volume are his descriptions of the great clubs in Pall Mall, "the almost overpowering splendor" of the Reform, and "those deep, handsome basins, in which it is a delight to bathe one's face and hands." We have mentioned the paper on the history of the Jews in England, which traces their varying fortunes up to their present highly comfortable condition, and is written, if we mistake not, from the "Semitic consciousness." We must add an extract from the chapter on the "English High-roads": "A universal shout of revolt went through the British nation when, at the beginning of the last century, the improvement of the roads began and post-chaises came into use. Some declared that the national courage would be destroyed if a man who had been in the habit of riding on horseback through the country, and of maintaining at any rate a struggle with a highway robber, should now allow himself to sneak along in coaches." These objectors, if they had been prophetic, might have held their peace; they would have foreseen a system of locomotion which was to be, in some of its ultimate developments, quite as effective a test of the national courage as the danger of meeting Dick Turpin and Claude Duval.

Nation, March 16, 1876

Matilde Serao

F EW ATTENTIVE READERS, I take it, would deny that the English novelist—from whom, in this case, there happens to be even less occasion than usual for distinguishing the American—testifies in his art much more than his foreign comrade, from whatever quarter, to the rigour of convention. There are whole sides of life about which he has as little to say as possible, about which he observes indeed in general a silence that has visibly ended by becoming for the foreign comrade his great characteristic. He strikes the spectator as having with a misplaced humility consented once for all to be admonished as to what he shall or shall not "mention"—and to be admonished in especial by an authority altogether indefinite. He subscribes, when his turn comes round, to an agreement in the drawing-up of which he has had no hand; he sits down to his task with a certain received canon of the "proper" before his eyes. The critic I am supposing reproaches him, naturally, in this critic's way, with a marked failure ever to challenge, much less to analyse, that conception; with having never, as would appear, so much as put to himself in regard to most of the matters of which he makes his mystery the simple question "Proper to what?" How can any authority, even the most embodied, asks the exponent of other views, decide for us in advance what shall in any case be proper—with the consequent implication of impropriety—to our given subject?

The English novelist would, I imagine, even sometimes be led on to finding that he has practically had to meet such an overhauling by a further admission, though an admission still tacit and showing him not a little shy of the whole discussion—principles and formulas being in general, as we know, but little his affair. Would he not, if off his guard, have been in peril of lapsing into the doctrine—suicidal when reflected upon—that there may be also an *a priori* rule, a "Thou shalt not," if not a "Thou shalt," as to treatable subjects themselves? Then it would be that his alien foe might fairly revel in the sense of having him in a corner, laughing an evil laugh to hear him plead in explanation that it is exactly *most* as to the subject to be treated that he feels the need laid upon him to conform. What is he to do when he has an idea to embody, we might suspect him rashly to inquire, unless, frankly to ask himself in the first place of *all* if it be proper? Not indeed— we catch the reservation—that he is consciously often accessible to ideas for which that virtue may not be claimed. Naturally, however, still, such a plea only brings forth for his interlocutor a repetition of the original appeal: "Proper to what?" There is only one propriety the painter of life can ask of his morsel of material: Is it, or is it not, of the stuff of life? So, in simplified terms at any rate, I seem to hear the interchange; to which I need listen no longer than thus to have derived from it a word of support for my position. The question of our possible rejoinder to the scorn of societies otherwise affected I must leave for some other connection. The point is—if point I may expect to obtain any countenance to its being called—that, in spite of our great Dickens and, in a minor degree, of our great George Eliot, the limitations of our practice are elsewhere than among ourselves pretty well held to have put us out of court. The thing least conceded to us moreover is that we handle at all frankly—if we put forward such a claim—even our own subject-matter or in other words our own life. "Your own is all we want of you, all we should like to see. But that your system really touches your own is exactly what we deny. Never, never!" For what it really comes to is that practically we, of all people in the world, are accused of a system. Call this system a conspiracy of silence, and the whole charge is upon us.

The fact of the silence, whether or no of the system, is fortunately all that at present concerns us. Did this not happen to be the case nothing could be more interesting, I think, than to follow somewhat further several of the bearings of the matter, which would bring us face to face with some wonderful and, I hasten to add, by no means doubtless merely disconcerting truths about ourselves. It has been given us to read a good deal, in these latter days, about *l'âme Française* and *l'âme Russe*—and with the result, in all probability, of our being rather less than more penetrated with the desire, in emulation of these opportunities, to deliver ourselves upon the English or the American soul. There would appear to be nothing we are totally conscious of that we are less eager to reduce to the mere expressible, to hand over to publicity, current journalistic prose aiding, than either of these fine essences; and yet incontestably there are neighbourhoods in which we feel ourselves within scent and reach of them by something of the same sense that in thick forests serves the hunter of great game. He may not quite touch the precious presence, but he knows when it is near. So somehow we know that the "Anglo-Saxon" soul, the modern at least, is not far off when we frankly consider the practice of our race—comparatively recent though it be—in taking for granted the "innocence" of literature.

Our perhaps a trifle witless way of expressing our conception of this innocence and our desire for it is, characteristically enough, by taking refuge in another vagueness, by invoking the allowances that we understand works of imagination and of criticism to make to the "young." I know not whether it has ever officially been stated for us that, given the young, given literature, and given, under stress, the need of sacrificing one or the other party, it is not certainly by our sense of "style" that our choice would be determined: no great art in the reading of signs and symptoms is at all events required for a view of our probable instinct in such a case. That instinct, however, has too many deep things in it to be briefly or easily disposed of, and there would be no greater mistake than to attempt too simple an account of it. The account most likely to be given by a completely detached critic would be that we are as a race better equipped for action than for thought, and that to let the art of expression go by the board is through that very fact to point to the limits of what we mostly have to express. If we accept such a report we shall do so, I think, rather from a strong than from a weak sense of what may easily be made of it; but I glance at these things only as at objects almost too flooded with light, and come back after my parenthesis to what more immediately concerns me: the plain reflection that, if the element of compromise—compromise with fifty of the "facts of life"—be the common feature of the novel of English speech, so it is mainly indebted for this character to the sex comparatively without a feeling for logic.

Nothing is at any rate *a priori* more natural than to trace a connection between our general mildness, as it may conveniently be called, and the fact that we are likewise so generally feminine. Is the English novel "proper" because it is so much written by women, or is it only so much written by women because its propriety has been so firmly established? The intimate relation is on either determination all that is here pertinent—effect and cause may be left to themselves. What is further pertinent, as happens, is that on a near view the relation is not constant; by which I mean that, though the ladies are always productive, the fashion of mildness is not always the same. Convention in short has its ups and downs, and these votaries have of late years, I think, been as often seen weltering in the hollow of the wave as borne aloft on its crest. Some of them may even be held positively to have distinguished themselves most—whether or no in veils of anonymity—on the occasion of the downward movement; making us really wonder if their number might not fairly, under any steadier force of such a movement, be counted on to increase. All sorts of inquiries are suggested in truth by the sight. "Emancipations" are in the air, and may it not possibly be that we shall see two of the most striking coincide? If convention has, to the tune to which I just invited an ear, blighted our fiction, what shall we say of its admitted, its still more deprecated and in so many quarters even deplored, effect upon the great body under the special patronage of which the "output" has none the less insisted on becoming incomparably copious? Since the general inaptitude of women appears by this time triumphantly to have been proved an assumption particularly hollow, despoiled more and more each day of the last tatters of its credit, why should not the new force thus liberated really, in the connection I indicate, give something of its measure?

It is at any rate keeping within bounds to say that the novel will surely not become less free in proportion as the condition of women becomes more easy. It is more or less in deference to their constant concern with it that we have seen it, among ourselves, pick its steps so carefully; but there are indications that the future may reserve us the surprise of having to thank the very class whose supposed sensibilities have most oppressed us for teaching it not only a longer stride, but a healthy indifference to an occasional splash. It is for instance only of quite recent years that the type of fiction commonly identified as the "sexual" has achieved—for purposes of reference, so far as notices in newspapers may be held to constitute reference—a salience variously estimated. Now therefore, though it is early to say that all "imaginative work" from the female hand is subject to this description, there is assuredly none markedly so subject that is *not* from the female hand. The female mind has in fact throughout the competition carried off the prize in the familiar game, known to us all from childhood's hour, of playing at "grown-up;" finding thus its opportunity, with no small acuteness, in the more and more marked tendency of the mind of the other gender to revert, alike in the grave and the gay, to those simplicities which there would appear to be some warrant for pronouncing puerile. It is the ladies in a word who have lately done most to remind us of man's relations with himself, that is with woman. His relations with the pistol, the pirate, the police, the wild and the tame beast—are not these prevailingly what the gentlemen have given us? And does not the difference sufficiently point my moral?

Let me, however, not seem to have gone too far afield to seek it; for my reflections—general perhaps to excess—closely connect themselves with a subject to which they are quite ready to yield in interest. I have lately been giving a happy extension to an old acquaintance, dating from early in the eighties, with the striking romantic work of Matilde Serao; a writer who, apart from other successes, has the excellent effect, the sign of the stronger few, that the end of her story is, for her reader, never the end of her work. On thus recently returning to her I have found in her something much more to my present purpose than the mere appearance of power and ease. If she is interesting largely because she is, in the light of her free, her extraordinary Neapolitan temperament, a vivid painter and a rich register of sensations and impressions, she is still more so as an exceptionally compact and suggestive *case*, a case exempt from interference and presenting itself with a beautiful unconsciousness. She has had the good fortune—if it be, after all, not the ill—to develop in an air in which convention, in our invidious sense, has had as little to say to her as possible; and she is accordingly a precious example of the possibilities of free exercise. The questions of the proper and the improper are comfortably far from her; and though more than in the line of her sisters of English speech she may have to reckon with prescriptions as to form—a burden at which in truth she snaps her fingers with an approach to impertinence—she moves in a circle practically void of all pre-judgment as to subject and matter. Conscious enough, doubtless, of a literary law to be offended, and caring little in fact, I repeat—for it is her weakness— what wrong it may suffer, she has not even the agreeable incentive of an ability to calculate the "moral" shocks she may administer.

Practically chartered then she is further happy—since they both minister to ease—in two substantial facts: she is a daughter of the veritable south and a product of the contemporary newspaper. A Neapolitan by birth and a journalist by circumstance, by marriage and in some degree doubtless also by inclination, she strikes for us from the first the note of facility and spontaneity and the note of initiation and practice. Concerned, through her husband, in the conduct of a Neapolitan morning paper, of a large circulation and a radical colour, she has, as I infer, produced her novels and tales mainly in such snatches of time and of inspiration as have been left her by urgent day-to-day journalism. They distinctly betray, throughout, the conditions of their birth—so little are they to the literary sense children of maturity and leisure. On the question of style in a foreign writer it takes many contributive lights to make us sure of our ground; but I feel myself on the safe side in conceiving that this lady, full of perception and vibration, can not only not figure as a purist, but must be supposed throughout, in spite of an explosive eloquence, to pretend but little to distinction of form: which for an Italian is a much graver predicament than for one of our shapeless selves. That, however, would perhaps pass for a small quarrel with a writer, or rather with a talker and—for it is what one must most insist on—a *feeler*, of Matilde Serao's remarkable spontaneity. Her Neapolitan nature is by itself a value, to whatever literary lapses it may minister. A torch kindled at that flame can be but freely waved, and our author's arm has a fine action. Loud, loquacious, abundant, natural, happy, with luxurious insistences on the handsome, the costly and the fleshly, the fine persons and fine clothes of her characters, their satin and velvet, their bracelets, rings, white waistcoats, general appointments and bedroom furniture, with almost as many repetitions and as free a tongue, in short, as Juliet's nurse, she reflects at every turn the wonderful mixture that surrounds her—the beauty, the misery, the history, the light and noise and dust, the prolonged paganism and the renewed reactions, the great style of the distant and the past and the generally compromised state of the immediate and the near. These things were all in the germ for the reader of her earlier novels—they have since only gathered volume and assurance—so that I well remember the impression made on me, when the book was new (my copy, apparently of the first edition, bears the date of 1885), by the rare energy, the immense *disinvoltura*, of "La Conquista di Roma." This was my introduction to the author, in consequence of which I immediately read "Fantasia" and the "Vita e Avventure di Riccardo Joanna," with some smaller pieces; after which, interrupted but not detached, I knew nothing more till, in the course of time, I renewed acquaintance on the ground of "Il Paese di Cuccagna," then, however, no longer in its first freshness. That work set me straightway to reading everything else I could lay hands on, and I think therefore that, save "Il Ventre di Napoli" and two or three quite recent productions that I have not met, there is nothing from our author that I have not mastered. Such as I find her in everything, she remains above all things the signal "case."

If, however, she appears, as I am bound to note, not to have kept the full promise of her early energy, this is because it has suited her to move less in the direction—where so much might have awaited her—of "Riccardo Joanna" and "La Conquista" than in that, on the whole less happily symptomatic, of "Fantasia." "Fantasia" is, before all else, a study of "passion," or rather of the intenser form of that mystery which the Italian *passione* better expresses; and I hasten to confess that had she not so marked herself an exponent of this specialty I should probably not now be writing of her. I conceive none the less that it would have been open to her to favour more that side of her great talent of which the so powerful "Paese di Cuccagna" is the strongest example. There is by good fortune in this large miscellaneous picture of Neapolitan life no *passione* save that of the observer curiously and pityingly intent upon it, that of the artist resolute at any cost to embrace and reproduce it. Admirably, easily, convincingly objective, the thing is a sustained panorama, a chronicle of manners finding its unity in one recurrent note, that of the consuming lottery-hunger which constitutes the joy, the curse, the obsession and the ruin, according to Matilde Serao, of her fellow-citizens. Her works are thus divided by a somewhat unequal line, those on one side of which the critic is tempted to accuse her of having not altogether happily sacrificed to those on the other. When she for the most part invokes under the name of *passione* the main explanation of the mortal lot it is to follow the windings of this clue in the upper walks of life, to haunt the aristocracy, to embrace the world of fashion, to overflow with clothes, jewels and promiscuous intercourse, all to the proportionate eclipse of her strong, full vision of the more usually vulgar. "La Conquista" is the story of a young deputy who comes up to the Chamber, from the Basilicata, with a touching candour of ambition and a perilous ignorance of the pitfalls of capitals. His dream is to conquer Rome, but it is by Rome naturally that he is conquered. He alights on his political twig with a flutter of wings, but has reckoned in his innocence without the strong taste in so many quarters for sport; and it is with a charge of shot in his breast and a drag of his pinions in the dust that he takes his way back to mediocrity, obscurity and the parent nest. It is from the ladies—as was indeed even from the first to be expected with Serao—that he receives his doom; *passione* is in these pages already at the door and soon arrives; *passione* rapidly enough passes its sponge over everything not itself.

In "Cuore Infermo," in "Addio Amore," in "Il Castigo," in the two volumes of "Gli Amanti" and in various other pieces this effacement is so complete that we see the persons concerned but in the one relation, with every other circumstance, those of concurrent profession, possession, occupation, connection, interest, amusement, kinship, utterly superseded and obscured. Save in the three or four books I have named as exceptional the figures evoked are literally professional lovers, "available," as the term is, for *passione* alone: which is the striking sign, as I shall presently indicate, of the extremity in which her enjoyment of the freedom we so often have to envy has strangely landed our author. "Riccardo Joanna," which, like "La Conquista," has force, humour and charm, sounding with freshness the note of the general life, is such a picture of certain of the sordid conditions of Italian journalism as, if I may trust my memory without re-perusal, sharply and pathetically imposes itself. I recall "Fantasia" on the other hand as wholly *passione*—all concentration and erotics, the latter practised in this instance, as in "Addio Amore," with extreme cruelty to the "good" heroine, the person innocent and sacrificed; yet this volume too contributes its part in the retrospect to that appearance of marked discipleship which was one of the original sources of my interest. Nothing could more have engaged one's attention in these matters at that moment than the fresh phenomenon of a lady-novelist so confessedly flushed with the influence of Émile Zola. Passing among ourselves as a lurid warning even to workers of his own sex, he drew a new grace from the candid homage—all implied and indirect, but, as I refigure my impression, not the less unmistakable—of that half of humanity which, let alone attempting to follow in his footsteps, was not supposed even to turn his pages. There is an episode in "Fantasia"—a scene in which the relations of the hero and the "bad" heroine are strangely consolidated by a visit together to a cattle-show—in which the courage of the pupil has but little to envy the breadth of the master. The hot day and hot hour, the heavy air and the strong smells, the great and small beasts, the action on the sensibilities of the lady and the gentleman of the rich animal life, the collapse indeed of the lady in the presence of the prize bull—all these are touches for which luckily our author has the warrant of a greater name. The general picture, in "Fantasia," of the agricultural exhibition at Caserta is in fact not the worse at any point for a noticeable echo of more than one French model. Would the author have found so full an occasion in it without a fond memory of the immortal Comices of "Madame Bovary"?

These, however, are minor questions—pertinent only as connecting themselves with the more serious side of her talent. We may rejoice in such a specimen of it as is offered by the too brief series of episodes of "The Romance of the Maiden." These things, dealing mainly with the small miseries of small folk, have a palpable truth, and it is striking that, to put the matter simply, Madame Serao is at her best almost in direct proportion as her characters are poor. By poor I mean literally the reverse of rich; for directly they *are* rich and begin, as the phrase is, to keep their carriage, her taste totters and lapses, her style approximates at moments to that of the ladies who do the fashions and the letters from the watering-places in the society papers. She has acutely and she renders with excellent breadth the sense of benighted lives, of small sordid troubles, of the general unhappy youthful (on the part of her own sex at least) and the general more or less starved plebeian consciousness. The degree to which it testifies to all this is one of the great beauties of "Il Paese di Cuccagna," even if the moral of that dire picture be simply that in respect to the gaming-passion, the madness of "numbers," no walk of life at Naples is too high or too low to be ravaged. Beautiful, in "Il Romanzo della Fanciulla," are the exhibitions of grinding girl-life in the big telegraph office and in the State normal school. The gem of "Gli Amanti" is the tiny tale of "Vicenzella," a masterpiece in twenty small pages—the vision of what three or four afternoon hours could contain for a slip of a creature of the Naples waterside, a poor girl who picks up a living by the cookery and sale, on the edge of a parapet, of various rank dismembered polyps of the southern sea, and who is from stage to stage despoiled of the pence she patiently pockets for them by the successive small emissaries of her artful, absent lover, constantly faithless, occupied, not too far off, in regaling a lady of his temporary preference, and proportionately clamorous for fresh remittances. The moment and the picture are but a scrap, yet they are as large as life.

"Canituccia," in "Piccole Anime," may happily pair with "Vicenzella," Canituccia being simply the humble rustic guardian, in field and wood—scarce more than a child—of the still more tender Ciccotto; and Ciccotto being a fine young pink-and-white pig, an animal of endowments that lead, after he has had time to render infatuated his otherwise quite solitary and joyless friend, to his premature conversion into bacon. She assists, helplessly silent, staring, almost idiotic, from a corner of the cabin-yard, by night and lamplight, in the presence of gleaming knives and steaming pots and bloody tubs, at the sacrifice that deprives her of all company, and nothing can exceed the homely truth of the touch that finally rounds off the scene and for which I must refer my reader to the volume. Let me further not fail to register my admiration for the curious cluster of scenes that, in "Il Romanzo," bears the title of "Nella Lava." Here frankly, I take it, we have the real principle of "naturalism"—a consistent presentment of the famous "slice of life." The slices given us—slices of shabby hungry maidenhood in small cockney circles—are but sketchily related to the volcanic catastrophe we hear rumbling behind them, the undertone of all the noise of Naples; but they have the real artistic importance of showing us how little "story" is required to hold us when we get, before the object evoked and in the air created, the impression of the real thing. Whatever thing—interesting inference—has but effectively to *be* real to constitute in itself story enough. There is no story without it, none that is not rank humbug; whereas with it the very desert blooms.

This last-named phenomenon takes place, I fear, but in a minor degree in such of our author's productions as "Cuore Infermo," "Addio Amore," "Il Castigo" and the double series of "Gli Amanti"; and for a reason that I the more promptly indicate as it not only explains, I think, the comparative inanity of these pictures, but does more than anything else to reward our inquiry. The very first reflection suggested by Serao's novels of "passion" is that they perfectly meet our speculation as to what might with a little time become of our own fiction were our particular convention suspended. We see so what, on its actual lines, does, what *has*, become of it, and are so sated with the vision that a little consideration of the latent other chance will surely but refresh us. The effect then, we discover, of the undertaking to give *passione* its whole place is that by the operation of a singular law no place speedily appears to be left for anything else; and the effect of that in turn is greatly to modify, first, the truth of things, and second, with small delay, what may be left them of their beauty. We find ourselves wondering after a little whether there may not really be more truth in the world misrepresented according to our own familiar fashion than in such a world as that of Madame Serao's exuberant victims of Venus. It is not only that if Venus herself is notoriously beautiful her altar, as happens, is by no means always proportionately august; it is also that we draw, in the long run, small comfort from the virtual suppression, by any painter, of whatever skill—and the skill of this particular one fails to rise to the height—of every relation in life but that over which Venus presides. In "Fior di Passione" and the several others of a like connection that I have named the suppression is really complete; the common humanities and sociabilities are wholly absent from the picture.

The effect of this is extraordinarily to falsify the total show and to present the particular affair—the intimacy in hand for the moment, though the moment be but brief—as taking place in a strange false perspective, a denuded desert which experience surely fails ever to give us the like of and the action of which on the faculty of observation in the painter is anything but favourable. It strikes at the root, in the impression producible and produced, of discrimination and irony, of humour and pathos. Our present author would doubtless contend on behalf of the works I have mentioned that pathos at least does abound in them—the particular bitterness, the inevitable despair that she again and again shows to be the final savour of the cup of *passione*. It would be quite open to her to urge—and she would be sure to do so with eloquence—that if we pusillanimously pant for a moral, no moral really can have the force of her almost inveterate evocation of the absolute ravage of Venus, the dry desolation that in nine cases out of ten Venus may be perceived to leave behind her. That, however, but half meets our argument—which bears by no means merely on the desolation behind, but on the desolation before, beside and generally roundabout. It is not in short at all the moral but the fable itself that in the exclusively sexual light breaks down and fails us. Love, at Naples and in Rome, as Madame Serao exhibits it, is simply unaccompanied with any interplay of our usual conditions—with affection, with duration, with circumstances or consequences, with friends, enemies, husbands, wives, children, parents, interests, occupations, the manifestation of tastes. Who are these people, we presently ask ourselves, who love indeed with fury—though for the most part with astonishing brevity—but who are so without any suggested situation in life that they can only strike us as loving for nothing and in the void, to no gain of experience and no effect of a felt medium or a breathed air. We know them by nothing but their convulsions and spasms, and we feel once again that it is not the passion of hero and heroine that gives, that can ever give, the heroine and the hero interest, but that it is they themselves, with the ground they stand on and the objects enclosing them, who give interest to their passion. This element touches us just in proportion as we see it mixed with other things, with all the things with which it has to reckon and struggle. There is moreover another reflection with which the pathetic in this connection has to count, even though it undermine not a little the whole of the tragic effect of the agitations of *passione*. Is it, ruthlessly speaking, certain that the effect most consonant, for the spectator, with truth is half as tragic as it is something else? Should not the moral be sought in the very different quarter where the muse of comedy rather would have the last word? The ambiguity and the difficulty are, it strikes me, of a new growth, and spring from a perverse desire on the part of the erotic novelist to secure for the adventures he depicts a dignity that is not of the essence. To compass this dignity he has to cultivate the high pitch and beat the big drum, but when he has done so he has given everything the wrong accent and the whole the wrong extravagance. Why see it all, we ask him, as an extravagance of the solemn and the strained? Why make *such* an erotic a matter of tears and imprecations, and by so doing render so poor a service both to pleasure and to pain? Since by your own free showing it is pre-eminently a matter of folly, let us at least have folly with her bells, or when these must—since they must—sound knells and dirges, leave them only to the light hand of the lyric poet, who turns them at the worst to music. Matilde Serao is in this connection constantly lugubrious; even from the little so-called pastels of "Gli Amanti" she manages, with an ingenuity worthy of a better cause, to expunge the note of gaiety.

This dismal *parti pris* indeed will inevitably, it is to be feared, when all the emancipations shall have said their last word, be that of the ladies. Yet perhaps too, whatever such a probability, the tone scarce signifies—in the presence, I mean, of the fundamental mistake from which the author before us warns us off. That mistake, we gather from her warning, would be to encourage, after all, any considerable lowering of the level of our precious fund of reserve. When we come to analyse we arrive at a final impression of what we pay, as lovers of the novel, for such a chartered state as we have here a glimpse of; and we find it to be an exposure, on the intervention at least of such a literary temperament as the one before us, to a new kind of vulgarity. We have surely as it is kinds enough. The absence of the convention throws the writer back on tact, taste, delicacy, discretion, subjecting these principles to a strain from which the happy office of its presence is, in a considerable degree and for performers of the mere usual endowment, to relieve him. When we have not a very fine sense the convention appears in a manner to have it on our behalf. And how frequent to-day, in the hurrying herd of brothers and sisters of the pen, *is* a fine sense—of *any* side of their affair? Do we not approach the truth in divining that only an eminent individual here and there may be trusted for it? Here—for the case is our very lesson—is this robust and wonderful Serao who is yet not to be trusted at all. Does not the dim religious light with which we surround its shrine do more, on the whole, for the poetry of *passione* than the flood of flaring gas with which, in her pages, and at her touch, it is drenched? Does it not shrink, as a subject under treatment, from such expert recognitions and easy discussions, from its so pitiless reduction to the category of the familiar? It issues from the ordeal with the aspect with which it might escape from a noisy family party or alight from a crowded omnibus. It is at the category of the familiar that vulgarity begins. There may be a cool virtue therefore even for "art," and an appreciable distinction even for truth, in the grace of hanging back and the choice of standing off, in that shade of the superficial which we best defend by simply practising it in season. A feeling revives at last, after a timed intermission, that we may not immediately be quite able, quite assured enough, to name, but which, gradually clearing up, soon defines itself almost as a yearning. We turn round in obedience to it—unmistakably we turn round again to the opposite pole, and there before we know it have positively laid a clinging hand on dear old Jane Austen.

North American Review, March 1901
Reprinted in *Notes on Novelists*, 1914

Ivan Turgenev

Frühlingsfluthen. Ein König Lear des Dorfes. Zwei Novellen. Von Iwan Turgéniew. Mitau, 1873.

WE KNOW OF several excellent critics who to the question, Who is the first novelist of the day? would reply, without hesitation, Ivan Turgénieff. Comparisons are odious, and we propose to make none that shall seem merely invidious. We quote our friends' verdict as a motive for this brief record of our own impressions. These, too, are in the highest degree favourable; and yet we wish not to impose a conclusion, but to help well-disposed readers to a larger enjoyment. To many such Turgénieff is already vaguely known as an eminent Russian novelist. Twelve years ago he was little more than a name, even in France, where he perhaps now finds his most sympathetic readers. But all his tales, we believe without exception, have now been translated into French—several by the author himself; an excellent German version of the best is being published under his own supervision, and several very fair English versions have appeared in England and America. He enjoys what is called a European reputation, and it is constantly spreading. The Russians, among whom fiction flourishes vigorously, deem him their greatest artist. His tales are not numerous, and many of them are very short. He gives us the impression of writing much more for love than for lucre. He is particularly a favourite with people of cultivated taste; and nothing, in our opinion, cultivates the taste more than to read him.

I.

He belongs to the limited class of very careful writers. It is to be admitted at the outset that he is a zealous genius, rather than an abundant one. His line is narrow observation. He has not the faculty of rapid, passionate, almost reckless improvisation—that of Walter Scott, of Dickens, of George Sand. This is an immense charm in a story-teller; on the whole, to our sense, the greatest. Turgénieff lacks it; he charms us in other ways. To describe him in the fewest terms, he is a story-teller who has taken notes. This must have been a life-long habit. His tales are a magazine of small facts, of anecdotes, of descriptive traits, taken, as the phrase is, *sur le vif*. If we are not mistaken, he notes down an idiosyncracy of character, a fragment of talk, an attitude, a feature, a gesture, and keeps it, if need be, for twenty years, till just the moment for using it comes, just the spot for placing it. "Stachoff spoke French tolerably, and as he led a quiet sort of life, passed for a philosopher. Even as an ensign, he was fond of disputing warmly whether, for instance, a man in his life might visit every point of the globe, or whether he might learn what goes on at the bottom of the sea, and was always of the opinion that it was impossible." The writer of this description may sometimes be erratic, but he is never vague. He has a passion for distinctness, for bringing his characterization to a point, for giving you an example of his meaning. He often, indeed, strikes us as loving details for their own sake, as a bibliomaniac loves the books he never reads. His figures are all portraits; they have each something special, something peculiar, something that none of their neighbours have, and that rescues them from the limbo of the gracefully general. We remember, in one of his stories, a gentleman who makes a momentary appearance as host at a dinner-party, and after being described as having such and such a face, clothes, and manners, has our impression of his personality completed by the statement that the soup at his table was filled with little paste figures, representing hearts, triangles, and trumpets. In the author's conception, there is a secret affinity between the character of this worthy man and the contortions of his vermicelli. This habit of specializing people by vivid oddities was the gulf over which Dickens danced the tight-rope with such agility. But Dickens, as we say, was an improvisatore; the practice, for him, was a lawless revel of the imagination. Turgénieff, on the other hand, always proceeds by book. What could be more minutely appreciative, and at the same time less like Dickens, than the following portrait?

"People in St. Petersburg still remember the Princess R———. She appeared there from time to time at the period of which we speak. Her husband was a well-bred man, but rather stupid, and she had no children. The Princess used to start suddenly on long journeys, and then return suddenly to Russia. Her conduct in all things was very strange. She was called light, and a coquette. She used to give herself up with ardour to all the pleasures of society: dance till she dropped with exhaustion, joke and laugh with the young men she received before dinner in her darkening drawing-room, and pass her nights praying and weeping, without finding a moment's rest. She often remained till morning in her room stretching her arms in anguish; or else she remained bowed, pale and cold, over the leaves of a hymn-book. Day came, and she was transformed again into an elegant creature, paid visits, laughed, chattered, rushed to meet everything that could give her the smallest diversion. She was admirably shaped. Her hair, the colour of gold, and as heavy as gold, formed a tress that fell below her knees. And yet she was not spoken of as a beauty: she had nothing fine in her face except her eyes. This even, perhaps, is saying too much, for her eyes were grey and rather small; but their deep keen gaze, careless to audacity, and dreamy to desolation, was equally enigmatical and charming. Something extraordinary was reflected in them, even when the most futile speeches were passing from her lips. Her toilets were always too striking."

These lines seem to carry a kind of historical weight. It is the Princess R—— and no one else. We feel as if the author could show us documents and relics; as if he had her portrait, a dozen letters, some of her old trinkets. Or take the following few lines from the admirable tale called "The Wayside Inn": "He belonged to the burgher class, and his name was Nahum Ivanoff. He had a thick short body, broad shoulders, a big round head, long waving hair already grizzled, though he was not yet forty. His face was full and fresh-coloured; his forehead low and white. His little eyes, of a clear blue, had a strange look, at once oblique and impudent. He kept his head always bent, his neck being too short; he walked fast, and never let his hands swing, keeping them always closed. When he smiled, and he smiled often, but without laughing and as if by stealth, his red lips parted disagreeably, showing a row of very white, very close teeth. He spoke quickly, with a snarling tone." When fiction is written in this fashion, we believe as we read. The same vividly definite element is found in the author's treatment of landscape: "The weather continued to stand at set-fair; little rounded white clouds moved through the air at a great height, and looked at themselves in the water; the reeds were stirred by movements and murmurs produced by no wind; the pond, looking in certain places like polished steel, absorbed the splendid sunshine." There is an even greater reality, because it is touched with the fantastic, without being perverted by it, in this brief sketch of the Pontine Marshes, from the beautiful little story of "Visions":—

"The cloud before my eyes divided itself. I became aware of a limitless plain beneath me. Already, from the warm soft air which fanned my cheeks, I had observed that I was no longer in Russia. This plain, moreover, was not like our Russian plains. It was an immense dusky level, overgrown, apparently, with no grass, and perfectly desolate. Here and there, over the whole expanse, glittered pools of standing water, like little fragments of looking-glass. In the distance, the silent, motionless sea was vaguely visible. In the intervals of the broad beautiful clouds glittered great stars. A murmur, thousand-voiced, unceasing, and yet not loud, resounded from every spot; and strangely rang this penetrating, drowsy murmur, this nightly voice of the desert. . . . 'The Pontine Marshes,' said Ellis. 'Do you hear the frogs? Do you recognise the smell of sulphur?' "

This is a cold manner, many readers will say, and certainly it has a cold side; but when the character is one over which the author's imagination really kindles, it is an admirable vehicle for touching effects. Few stories leave on the mind a more richly poetic impression than "Hélène"; all the tenderness of our credulity goes forth to the heroine. Yet this exquisite image of idealized devotion swims before the author's vision in no misty moonlight of romance; she is as solidly fair as a Greek statue; his dominant desire has been to understand her, and he retails small facts about her appearance and habits with the impartiality of a judicial, or even a medical, summing up. The same may be said of his treatment of all his heroines, and said in evidence of the refinement of his art; for if there are no heroines we see more distinctly, there are none we love more ardently. It would be difficult to point, in the blooming fields of fiction, to a group of young girls more radiant with maidenly charm than M. Turgénieff's Hélène, his Lisa, his Katia, his Tatiana and his Gemma. For the truth is that, taken as a whole, he regains on another side what he loses by his apparent want of joyous invention. If his manner is that of a searching realist, his temper is that of a devoutly attentive observer, and the result of this temper is to make him take a view of the great spectacle of human life more general, more impartial, more unreservedly intelligent, than that of any novelist we know. Even on this line he proceeds with his characteristic precision of method; one thinks of him as having divided his subject-matter into categories, and as moving from one to the other—with none of the magniloquent pretensions of Balzac, indeed, to be the great showman of the human comedy—but with a deeply intellectual impulse toward universal appreciation. He seems to us to care for more things in life, to be solicited on more sides, than any novelist save George Eliot. Walter Scott cares for adventure and bravery and honour and ballad-figures and the humour of Scotch peasants; Dickens cares, on an immense, far-reaching scale, for picturesqueness; George Sand cares for love and mineralogy. But these writers care also, greatly, and indeed almost supremely, for their fable, for its twists and turns and surprises, for the work they have in hand of amusing the reader. Even George Eliot, who cares for so many other things besides, has a weakness for making a rounded plot, and often swells out her tales with mechanical episodes, in the midst of which their moral unity quite evaporates. The Bulstrode-Raffles episode in "Middlemarch," and the whole fable of "Felix Holt," are striking cases in point. M. Turgénieff lacks, as regards form, as we have said, this immense charm of absorbed inventiveness; but in the way of substance there is literally almost nothing he does not care for. Every class of society, every type of character, every degree of fortune, every phase of manners, passes through his hands; his imagination claims its property equally, in town and country, among rich and poor, among wise people and idiots, *dilettanti* and peasants, the tragic and the joyous, the probable and the grotesque. He has an eye for all our passions, and a deeply sympathetic sense of the wonderful complexity of our souls. He relates in "Mumu" the history of a deaf-and-dumb serf and a lap-dog, and he portrays in "A Strange Story" an extraordinary case of religious fanaticism. He has a passion for shifting his point of view, but his object is constantly the same—that of finding an incident, a person, a situation, *morally* interesting. This is his great merit, and the underlying harmony of his apparently excessive attention to detail. He believes in the intrinsic value of "subject" in art; he holds that there are trivial subjects and serious ones, that the latter are much the best, and that their superiority resides in their giving us absolutely a greater amount of information about the human mind. Deep into the mind he is always attempting to look, though he often applies his eye to very dusky apertures. There is perhaps no better evidence of his minutely psychological attitude than the considerable part played in his tales by simpletons and weak-minded persons. There are few novelists who have not been charmed by the quaintness and picturesqueness of mental invalids; but M. Turgénieff is attracted by something more—by the opportunity of watching the machinery of character, as it were, through a broken window-pane. One might collect from his various tales a perfect regiment of incapables, of the stragglers on life's march. Almost always, in the background of his groups of well-to-do persons there lurks some grotesque, under-witted poor relation, who seems to hover about as a vague memento, in his scheme, of the instability both of fortune and of human cleverness. Such, for instance, is Uvar Ivanovitsch, who figures as a kind of inarticulate chorus in the tragedy of "Hélène." He sits about, looking very wise and opening and closing his fingers, and in his person, in this attitude, the drama capriciously takes leave of us. Perhaps the most moving of all the author's tales—moving, not in the sense that it makes us shed easy tears, but as reminding us vividly of the solidarity, as we may say, of all human weakness—has for its hero a person made imbecile by suffering. The admirable little story of "The Brigadier" can only be spoilt by an attempt to retail it; we warmly recommend it to the reader, in the French version. Never did Romance stoop over a lowlier case of moral decomposition, but never did she gather more of the perfume of human truth. To a person able to read but one of M. Turgénieff's tales, we should perhaps offer this one as a supreme example of his peculiar power; for here the artist, as well as the analyst, is at his best. All rigid critical formulas are more or less unjust, and it is not a complete description of our author—it would be a complete description of no real master of fiction—to say that he is simply a searching observer. M. Turgénieff's imagination is always lending a hand and doing work on its own account. Some of this work is exquisite; nothing could have more of the simple magic of picturesqueness than such tales as "The Dog," "The Jew," "Visions," "The Adventure of Lieutenant Jergounoff," "Three Meetings," a dozen episodes in the "Memoirs of a Sportsman." Imagination guides his hand and modulates his touch, and makes the artist worthy of the observer. In a word, he is universally sensitive. In susceptibility to the sensuous impressions of life—to colours and odours and forms, and the myriad ineffable refinements and enticements of beauty—he equals, and even surpasses, the most accomplished representatives of the French school of story-telling; and yet he has, on the other hand, an apprehension of man's religious impulses, of the *ascetic* passion, the capacity of becoming dead to colours and odours and beauty, never dreamed of in the philosophy of Balzac and Flaubert, Octave Feuillet and Gustave Droz. He gives us Lisa in "A Nest of Noblemen," and Madame Polosoff in "Spring-Torrents." This marks his range. Let us add, in conclusion, that his merit of form is of the first order. He is remarkable for concision; few of his novels occupy the whole of a moderate volume, and some of his best performances are tales of thirty pages.

II.

M. Turgénieff's themes are all Russian; here and there the scene of a tale is laid in another country, but the actors are genuine Muscovites. It is the Russian type of human nature that he depicts; this perplexes, fascinates, inspires him. His works savour strongly of his native soil, like those of all great novelists, and give one who has read them all a strange sense of having had a prolonged experience of Russia. We seem to have travelled there in dreams, to have dwelt there in another state of being. M. Turgénieff gives us a peculiar sense of being out of harmony with his native land—of his having what one may call a poet's quarrel with it. He loves the old, and he is unable to see where the new is drifting. American readers will peculiarly appreciate this state of mind; if they had a native novelist of a large pattern, it would probably be, in a degree, his own. Our author *feels* the Russian character intensely, and cherishes, in fancy, all its old manifestations—the unemancipated peasants, the ignorant, absolute, half-barbarous proprietors, the quaint provincial society, the local types and customs of every kind. But Russian society, like our own, is in process of formation, the Russian character is in solution, in a sea of change, and the modified, modernized Russian, with his old limitations and his new pretensions, is not, to an imagination fond of caressing the old, fixed contours, an especially grateful phenomenon. A satirist at all points, as we shall have occasion to say, M. Turgénieff is particularly unsparing of the new intellectual fashions prevailing among his countrymen. The express purpose of one of his novels, "Fathers and Sons," is to contrast them with the old; and in most of his recent works, notably "Smoke," they have been embodied in various grotesque figures.

It was not, however, in satire, but in thoroughly genial, poetical portraiture, that our author first made his mark. "The Memoirs of a Sportsman" were published in 1852, and were regarded, says one of the two French translators of the work, as much the same sort of contribution to the question of Russian serfdom as Mrs. Stowe's famous novel to that of American slavery. This, perhaps, is forcing a point, for M. Turgénieff's group of tales strikes us much less as a passionate *pièce de circonstance* than as a disinterested work of art. But circumstances helped it, of course, and it made a great impression—an impression that testifies to no small culture on the part of Russian readers. For never, surely, was a work with a polemic bearing more consistently low in tone, as painters say. The author treats us to such a scanty dose of flagrant horrors that the moral of the book is obvious only to attentive readers. No single episode pleads conclusively against the "peculiar institution" of Russia; the lesson is in the cumulative testimony of a multitude of fine touches—in an after-sense of sadness that sets wise readers thinking. It would be difficult to name a work that contains better instruction for those heated spirits who are fond of taking sides on the question of "art for art." It offers a capital example of moral meaning giving a sense to form and form giving relief to moral meaning. Indeed, all the author's characteristic merits are to be found in the "Memoirs," with a certain amateurish looseness of texture which will charm many persons who find his later works too frugal, as it were, in shape. Of all his productions, this is indeed the most purely delightful. We especially recommend the little history of Foma, the forest keeper, who, one rainy night, when the narrator has taken refuge in his hut, hears a peasant stealing faggots in the dark, dripping woods; rushes forth and falls upon him, drags the poor wretch home, flings him into a corner, and sits on in the smoky hovel (with the author, whom we perceive there, noting, feeling, measuring it all), while the rain batters the roof and the drenched starveling howls and whines and imprecates. Anything more dismally real in a narrower compass we have never read—anything more pathetic, with less of the machinery of pathos. In this case, as at every turn with M. Turgénieff, "It is life itself," we murmur as we read, "and not this or that or the other story-teller's more or less clever 'arrangement' of life." M. Turgénieff deserves this praise in its largest application; for "life" in his pages is very far from meaning a dreary liability to sordid accidents, as it seems to mean with those writers of the grimly pathetic school who cultivate sympathy to the detriment of comprehension. He does equal justice—joyous justice—to all brighter accidents—to everything in experience that helps to keep it within the pale of legend. Two of the Sportsman's reminiscences are inexpressibly charming—the chapter in which he spends a warm summer night lying on the grass listening to the small boys who are sent out to watch the horses at pasture, as they sit chattering to each other of hobgoblins and fairies; and the truly beautiful description of a singing-match in a village ale-house, between two ragged serfs. The latter is simply a perfect poem. Very different, but in its way as characteristic, is the story of "A Russian Hamlet"—a poor gentle-man whom the Sportsman, staying overnight at a fine house where he has been dining, finds assigned to him as room-mate, and who, lying in bed and staring at him grotesquely over the sheets, relates his lugubrious history. This sketch, more than its companions, strikes the deep moral note that was to reverberate through the author's novels.

The story of "Rudin," which followed soon after, is per-haps the most striking example of his preference for a theme which takes its starting-point in character—if need be, in morbid character. We have had no recent opportunity to re-fresh our memory of the tale, but we have not forgotten the fine quality of its interest—its air of psychological truth, unencumbered with the usual psychological apparatus. The theme is one which would mean little enough to a coarse imagination—the exhibition of a character peculiarly un-rounded, unmoulded, unfinished, inapt for the regular ro-mantic attitudes. Dmitri Rudin is a moral failure, like many of the author's heroes—one of those fatally complex natures who cost their friends so many pleasures and pains; who might, and yet, evidently, might not, do great things; natures strong in impulse, in talk, in responsive emotion, but weak in will, in action, in the power to feel and do singly. Madame Sand's "Horace" is a broad, free study of this type of person, always so interesting to imaginative and so intolerable to ra-tional people; M. Turgénieff's hero is an elaborate miniature-portrait. Without reading Rudin we should not know just how fine a point he can give to his pencil. But M. Turgénieff, with his incisive psychology, like Madame Sand, with her ex-pansive synthesis, might often be a vain demonstrator and a very dull novelist if he were not so constantly careful to be a dramatist. Everything, with him, takes the dramatic form; he is apparently unable to conceive anything independently of it, he has no recognition of unembodied ideas; an idea, with him, is such and such an individual, with such and such a nose and chin, such and such a hat and waistcoat, bearing the same relation to it as the look of a printed word does to its meaning. Abstract possibilities immediately become, to his vi-sion, concrete situations, as elaborately defined and localized as an interior by Meissonier. In this way, as we read, we are always looking and listening; and we seem, indeed, at moments, for want of a running thread of explanation, to see rather more than we understand.

It is, however, in "Hélène" that the author's closely commingled realism and idealism have obtained their greatest triumph. The tale is at once a homely chronicle and a miniature epic. The scene, the figures, are as present to us as if we saw them ordered and moving on a lamp-lit stage; and yet, as we recall it, the drama seems all pervaded and coloured by the light of the moral world. There are many things in "Hélène," and it is difficult to speak of them in order. It is both so simple and so various, it proceeds with such an earnest tread to its dark termination, and yet it entertains and beguiles us so unceasingly as it goes, that we lose sight of its simple beauty in its confounding, entrancing reality. But we prize it, as we prize all the very best things, according to our meditative after-sense of it. Then we see its lovely unity melting its brilliant parts into a single harmonious tone. The story is all in the portrait of the heroine, who is a heroine in the literal sense of the word; a young girl of a will so calmly ardent and intense that she needs nothing but opportunity to become one of the figures about whom admiring legend clusters. She is a really elevated conception; and if, as we shall complain, there is bitterness in M. Turgénieff's imagination, there is certainly sweetness as well. It is striking that most of his flights of fancy are in his conceptions of women. With them only, occasionally, does he wholly forswear his irony and become frankly sympathetic. We hope it is not false ethnology to suppose that this is a sign of something, potentially at least, very fine in the character of his country-women. As fine a poet as you will would hardly have devised a Maria Alexandrovna (in "A Correspondence"), an Hélène, a Lisa, a Tatiana, an Irene even, without having known some very admirable women. These ladies have a marked family likeness, an exquisite something in common which we may perhaps best designate as an absence of frivolous passion. They are addicted to none of those *chatteries* which French romancers consider the "adorable" thing in women. The baleful beauty, in "Smoke," who robs Tatiana of her lover, acts in obedience to an impulse deeper than vulgar coquetry.

And yet these fair Muscovites have a spontaneity, an independence, quite akin to the English ideal of maiden loveliness. Directly, superficially, they only half please. They puzzle us almost too much to charm, and we fully measure their beauty only when they are called upon to act. Then the author imagines them doing the most touching, the most inspiring things.

Hélène's loveliness is all in unswerving action. She passes before us toward her mysterious end with the swift, keen movement of a feathered arrow. She finds her opportunity, as we have called it, in her sympathy with a young Bulgarian patriot who dreams of rescuing his country from Turkish tyranny; and she surrenders herself to his love and his project with a tranquil passion which loses none of its poetry in M. Turgénieff's treatment. She is a supreme example of his taste for "original" young ladies. She would certainly be pronounced *queer* in most quiet circles. She has, indeed, a fascinating oddity of outline; and we never lose a vague sense that the author is presenting her to us with a charmed expectancy of his own, as a travelled friend would show us some quaintly-feathered bird brought from beyond the seas, but whose note he had not yet heard. To appreciate Hélène's oddity, you must read of the orthodoxy of the people who surround her. All about the central episode the story fades away into illimitable irony, as if the author wished to prove that, compared with the deadly seriousness of Hélène and Inssaroff, everything else is indeed a mere playing at life. We move among the minor episodes in a kind of atmosphere of sarcasm: now kindly, as where Bersenieff and Schubin are dealt with; now unsparingly comical, as in the case of her foolish parents and their tardy bewilderment—that of loquacious domestic fowls who find themselves responsible for the hatching of an eagle. The whole story is charged with lurking meanings, and to retail them would be as elaborate a task as picking threads out of a piece of fine tapestry. What is Mademoiselle Zoe, for instance, the little German *dame de compagnie*, but a humorous sidelight upon Hélène's intensity—Mademoiselle Zoe, with the pretty shoulders, and her presence in the universe a sort of mere general rustle of muslin, accompanied, perhaps, by a faint toilet-perfume?

There is nothing finer in all Turgénieff than the whole matter of Bersenieff's and Schubin's relation to Hélène. They, too, in their vivid reality, have a symbolic value, as they stand watching the woman they equally love whirled away from them in a current swifter than any force of their own. Schubin, the young sculptor, with his moods and his theories, his exaltations and depressions, his endless talk and his disjointed action, is a deeply ingenious image of the artistic temperament. Yet, after all, he strikes the practical middle key, and solves the problem of life by the definite application of what he *can*. Bersenieff, though a less fanciful, is perhaps, at bottom, a still more poetical figure. He is condemned to inaction, not by his intellectual fastidiousness, but by a conscious, intelligent, intellectual mediocrity, by the dogged loyalty of his judgment. There is something in his history more touching than even in that of Hélène and Inssaroff. These two, and Schubin as well, have their consolations. If they are born to suffering, they are born also to rapture. They stand at the open door of passion, and they can sometimes forget. But poor Bersenieff, wherever he turns, meets conscience with uplifted finger, saying to him that though Homer may sometimes nod, the sane man never misreasons and the wise man assents to no mood that is not a working mood. He has not even the satisfaction of lodging a complaint against fate. He is by no means sure that he has one; and when he finds that his love is vain he translates it into friendship with a patient zeal capable almost of convincing his own soul that it is not a renunciation, but a consummation. Bersenieff, Schubin, Zoe, Uvar Ivanovitsch, the indigent house-friend, with his placid depths of unuttered commentary, the pompous egotist of a father, the feeble egotist of a mother—these people thoroughly animate the little world that surrounds the central couple; and if we wonder how it is that from half a dozen figures we get such a sense of the world's presence and complexity, we perceive the great sagacity of the choice of the types.

We should premise, in speaking of "A Nest of Noblemen" (the English translation bears, we believe, the simple title of "Lisa"), that of the two novels it was the earlier published. It

dates from 1858; "Hélène" from 1859. The theme is an unhappy marriage and an unhappy love. Fedor Ivanovitsch Lavretzky marries a pretty young woman, and after three years
of confident bliss finds himself grossly deceived. He separates
from his wife, returns from Paris, where his eyes have been
unsealed, to Russia, and, in the course of time, retires to his
patrimonial estates. Here, after the pain of his wound has
ached itself away and the health and strength of life's prime
have reaffirmed themselves, he encounters a young girl whom
he comes at last to love with the double force of a tender
heart that longs to redeem itself from bitterness. He receives
news of his wife's death, and immediately presumes upon his
freedom to express his passion. The young girl listens, responds, and for a few brief days they are happy. But the
report of Madame Lavretzky's death has been, as the
newspapers say, premature; she suddenly reappears, to remind her husband of his bondage and to convict Lisa almost
of guilt. The pathetic force of the story lies, naturally, in its
taking place in a country unfurnished with the modern facilities for divorce. Lisa and Lavretzky of course must part. Madame Lavretzky lives and blooms. Lisa goes into a convent,
and her lover, defrauded of happiness, determines at least to
try and be useful. He ploughs his fields and instructs his serfs.
After the lapse of years he obtains entrance into her convent
and catches a glimpse of her as she passes behind a grating,
on her way across the chapel. She knows of his presence, but
she does not even look at him; the trembling of her downcast
lids alone betrays her sense of it. "What must they both have
thought, have felt?" asks the author. "Who can know? who
can say? There are moments in life, there are feelings, on
which we can only cast a glance without stopping." With an
unanswered question his story characteristically closes. The
husband, the wife, and the lover—the wife, the husband, and
the woman loved—these are combinations in which modern
fiction has been prolific; but M. Turgénieff's treatment renews the youth of the well-worn fable. He has found its
moral interest, if we may make the distinction, deeper than
its sentimental one; a pair of lovers accepting adversity seem
to him more eloquent than a pair of lovers grasping at happiness. The moral of his tale, as we are free to gather it, is

that there is no effective plotting for happiness, that we must take what we can get, that adversity is a capable mill-stream, and that our ingenuity must go toward making it grind our corn. Certain it is that there is something very exquisite in Lavretzky's history, and that M. Turgénieff has drawn from a theme associated with all manner of uncleanness a story embalmed in a lovely aroma of purity. This purity, indeed, is but a pervasive emanation from the character of Lisaveta Michailovna. American readers of Turgénieff have been struck with certain points of resemblance between American and Russian life. The resemblance is generally superficial; but it does not seem to us altogether fanciful to say that Russian young girls, as represented by Lisa, Tatiana, Maria Alexandrovna, have to our sense a touch of the faintly acrid perfume of the New England temperament—a hint of Puritan angularity. It is the women and young girls in our author's tales who mainly represent strength of will—the power to resist, to wait, to attain. Lisa represents it in all that heroic intensity which says so much more to M. Turgénieff's imagination than feline grace. The character conspicuous in the same tale for feline grace—Varvara Pavlovna, Lavretzky's heartless wife—is conspicuous also for her moral flimsiness. In the integrity of Lisa, of Hélène, even of the more dimly shadowed Maria Alexandrovna—a sort of finer distillation, as it seems, of masculine honour—there is something almost formidable: the strongest men are less positive in their strength. In the keenly pathetic scene in which Marfa Timofievna (the most delightful of the elderly maiden aunts of fiction) comes to Lisa in her room and implores her to renounce her project of entering a convent, we feel that there are depths of purpose in the young girl's deferential sweetness that nothing in the world can overcome. She is intensely religious, as she ought to be for psychological truth, and nothing could more effectually disconnect her from the usual *ingénue* of romance than our sense of the naturalness of her religious life. Her love for Lavretzky is a passion in its essence half renunciation. The first use she makes of the influence with him which his own love gives her is to try and reconcile him with his wife; and her foremost feeling, on learning that the latter is not dead, as they had believed, is an

irremissible sense of pollution. The dusky, antique consciousness of sin in this tender, virginal soul is a combination which we seem somehow to praise amiss in calling it
picturesque, but which it would be still more inexact to
call didactic. Lisa is altogether a most remarkable portrait,
and one that readers of the heroine's own sex ought to
contemplate with some complacency. They have been
known to complain on the one hand that romancers abuse
them, and on the other that they insufferably patronise
them. Here is a picture drawn with all the tenderness of a
lover, and yet with an indefinable—an almost unprecedented—respect. In this tale, as always with our author,
the drama is quite uncommented; the poet never plays chorus; situations speak for themselves. When Lavretzky reads
in the *chronique* of a French newspaper that his wife is
dead, there is no description of his feelings, no portrayal of
his mental attitude. The living, moving narrative has so effectually put us in the way of feeling with him that we can
be depended upon. He had been reading in bed before
going to sleep, had taken up the paper and discovered the
momentous paragraph. He "threw himself into his clothes,"
the author simply says, "went out into the garden, and
walked up and down till morning in the same alley." We
close the book for a moment and pause, with a sense of
personal excitement. But of M. Turgénieff's genius for in-
fusing a rich suggestiveness into common forms, the character of Gottlieb Lemm, the melancholy German music-
master, is a perhaps surpassing example. Never was homely
truth more poetical; never was poetry more minutely veracious.

Lavretzky, sorely tried as he is, is perhaps the happiest of
our author's heroes. He suffers great pain, but he has not the
intolerable sense of having inflicted it on others. This is the
lot, both of the hero of "Smoke" and of the fatally passive
youth whose adventures we follow in the author's latest
work. On "Smoke" we are unable to linger, as its theme is
almost identical with that of "Spring-Torrents," and the latter
will be a novelty to a greater number of our readers.
"Smoke," with its powerful and painful interest, lacks, to our
mind, the underlying sweetness of most of its companions. It

has all their talent, but it has less of their spirit. It treats of a dangerous beauty who robs the loveliest girl in Russia of her plighted lover, and the story duly absorbs us; but we find that, for our own part, there is always a certain langour in our intellectual acceptance of the grand coquettes of fiction. It is obviously a hard picture to paint; we always seem to see the lady pushing about her train before the foot-lights, or glancing at the orchestra-stalls during her victim's agony. In the portrait of Irene, however, there are very fine intentions, and the reader is charmed forward very much as poor Litvinof was. The figure of Tatiana, however, is full of the wholesome perfume of nature. "Smoke" was preceded by "Fathers and Sons," which dates from ten years ago, and was the first of M. Turgénieff's tales to be translated in America. In none of them is the subject of wider scope or capable of having more of the author's insidious melancholy expressed from it; for the figures with which he has filled his foreground are, with their personal interests and adventures, but the symbols of the shadowy forces that are fighting for ever a larger battle—the battle of the old and the new, the past and the future, of the ideas that arrive with the ideas that linger. Half the tragedies in human history are born of this conflict; and in all that poets and philosophers tell us of it the clearest fact is still its perpetual necessity. The opposing forces in M. Turgénieff's novel are an elder and a younger generation; the drama can indeed never have a more poignant interest than when we see the young world, as it grows to a sense of its strength and its desires, turning to smite the old world which has brought it forth with a mother's tears and a mother's hopes. The young world, in "Fathers and Sons," is the fiercer combatant; and the old world in fact is simply for ever the *victa causa* that even stoics pity. And yet with M. Turgénieff, characteristically, the gaining cause itself is purely relative, and victors and vanquished are commingled in a common assent to fate. Here, as always, his rare discretion serves him, and rescues him from the danger of exaggerating his representative types. Few figures in his pages are more intelligibly human than Pavel Petrovitsch and Eugene Bazaroff—human each of them in his indefeasible weakness; the one in spite of his small allowances, the other in spite of his brutal claims. In the elder Kirsanoff the author has imaged certain things he instinctively values—the hundred fading traditions of which the now vulgarized idea of the "gentleman" is the epitome. He loves him, of course, as a romancer must, but he has done the most impartial justice to the ridiculous aspect of his position. Bazaroff is a so-called "nihilist"—a red-handed radical, fresh from the shambles of criticism, with Büchner's *Stoff und Kraft* as a text-book, and everything in nature and history for his prey. He is young, strong, and clever, and strides about, rejoicing in his scepticism, sparing nothing, human or divine, and proposing to have demolished the universe before he runs his course. But he finds there is something stronger, cleverer, longer-lived than himself, and that death is a fiercer nihilist than even Dr. Büchner. The tale traces the course of the summer vacation that he comes to spend in the country with a college friend, and is chiefly occupied with the record of the various trials to which, in this short period, experience subjects his philosophy. They all foreshadow, of course, the supreme dramatic test. He falls in love, and tries to deny his love as he denies everything else, but the best he can do is only to express it in a coarse formula. M. Turgénieff is always fond of contrasts, and he has not failed to give Bazaroff a foil in his young comrade, Arcadi Kirsanoff, who represents the merely impermanent and imitative element that clings to the skirts of every great movement. Bazaroff is silenced by death, but it takes a very small dose of life to silence Arcadi. The latter belongs to the nobility, and Bazaroff's exploits in his tranquil, conventional home are those of a lusty young bull in a cabinet of rococo china. Exquisitely imagined is the whole attitude and demeanour of Pavel Petrovitsch, Arcadi's uncle, and a peculiarly happy invention the duel which this perfumed conservative considers it his manifest duty to fight in behalf of gentlemanly opinions. The deeper interest of the tale, however, begins when the young Büchnerite repairs to his own provincial home and turns to a pinch of dust the tender superstitions of the poor old parental couple who live only in their pride in their great learned son and have not even a genteel prejudice, of any consequence, to oppose to his terrible positivism. M. Turgénieff has written nothing finer than this last half of his story; every touch is masterly, every detail is eloquent. In Vassili Ivanovitsch and Arina Vlassievna he has shown us the sentient heart that still may throb in disused forms and not be too proud to subsist a while yet by the charity of science. Their timid devotion to their son, their roundabout caresses, their longings and hopes and fears, and their deeply pathetic stupefaction when it begins to be plain that the world can spare him, all form a picture which, in spite of its dealing with small things in a small style, carries us to the uttermost limits of the tragical. A very noticeable stroke of art, also, is Bazaroff's ever-growing discontentment—a chronic moral irritation, provoked not by the pangs of an old-fashioned conscience, but, naturally enough, by the absence of the agreeable in a world that he has subjected to such exhaustive disintegration. We especially recommend to the reader his long talk with Arcadi as they lie on the grass in the midsummer shade, and Bazaroff kicks out viciously at everything propounded by his ingenuous companion. Toward him too he feels vicious, and we quite understand the impulse, identical with that which in a nervous woman would find expression in a fit of hysterics, through which the overwrought young rationalist, turning to Arcadi with an alarming appearance of real gusto, proposes to fight with him, "to the extinction of animal heat." We must find room for the portrait of Arina Vlassievna:—

She " was a real type of the small Russian gentry of the old *régime*; she ought to have come into the world two hundred years sooner, in the time of the grand-dukes of Moscow. Easily impressed, deeply pious, she believed in all signs and tokens, divinations, sorceries, dreams; she believed in the *Iourodivi* [half-witted persons, popularly held sacred], in familiar spirits, in those of the woods, in evil meetings, in the evil eye, in popular cures, in the virtue of salt placed upon the altar on Good Friday, in the impending end of the world; she believed that if the tapers at the midnight mass in Lent do not go out, the crop of buckwheat will be good, and that mushrooms cease to grow as soon as human eye has rested on them; she believed that the Devil likes places where there is water, and that all Jews have a blood-spot on their chests; she was afraid of mice, snakes, toads, sparrows, leeches, thunder, cold water, draughts of air, horses, goats, red-haired men and black cats, and considered crickets and dogs as impure creatures; she ate neither veal, nor pigeons, nor lobsters, nor cheese, nor asparagus, nor hare, nor watermelon (because a melon opened resembled the dissevered head of John the Baptist), and the mere idea of oysters, which she did not know even by sight, caused her to shudder; she liked to eat well, and fasted rigorously; she slept ten hours a day, and never went to bed at all if Vassili Ivanovitsch complained of a headache. The only book that she had read was called 'Alexis, or The Cottage in the Forest'; she wrote at most one or two letters a year, and was an excellent judge of sweetmeats and preserves, though she put her own hand to nothing, and, as a general thing, preferred not to move. . . . . She was anxious, was perpetually expecting some great misfortune, and began to cry as soon as she remembered anything sad. Women of this kind are beginning to be rare; God knows whether we should be glad of it."

The novel which we have chosen as the text of these remarks was published some six years since. It strikes us at first as a reproduction of old material, the subject being identical with that of "Smoke" and very similar to that of the short masterpiece called "A Correspondence." The subject is one of the saddest in the world, and we shall have to reproach M. Turgénieff with delighting in sadness. But "Spring-Torrents" has a narrative charm that sweetens its bitter waters, and we may add that, from the writer's point of view, the theme does differ by several shades from that of the tales we have mentioned. These treat of the fatal weakness of will that M. Turgénieff apparently considers the peculiar vice of the new generation in Russia; "Spring-Torrents" illustrates, more generally, the element of folly which mingles, in a certain measure, in all youthful spontaneity, and makes us grow to wisdom by the infliction of suffering. The youthful folly of Dmitri Sanin has been great, the memory of it haunts him for years and lays on him at last such an icy grip that his heart will break unless he can repair it. The opening sentences of the story indicate the key in which it is pitched. We may quote them as an example of the way in which M. Turgénieff almost invariably appeals at the outset to our distinctively *moral* curiosity, our sympathy with character. Something tells us, in this opening strain, that we are not invited to lend ear to the mere dead rattle that rises for ever from the surface of life:—

". . . . Towards two o'clock at night, he came back into his sitting-room. The servant who had lighted the candles he sent away, threw himself into a chair by the chimney-piece, and covered his face with his hands. Never had he felt such a weariness of body and soul. He had been spending the whole evening with graceful women, with cultivated men; some of the women were pretty, almost all the men were distinguished for wit and talent; he himself had talked with good effect, even brilliantly; and yet with all this, never had that *tædium vitæ*, of which the Romans already speak, that sense of disgust with life, pressed upon him and taken possession of him in such an irresistible fashion. Had he been somewhat younger, he would have wept for sadness, for ennui and overwrought nerves: a corroding, burning bitterness, like the bitterness of wormwood, filled his whole soul. Something inexpugnable—cold, sickening, oppressive—crowded in upon him from all sides like autumn dusk, and he knew not how he could free himself from this duskiness and bitterness. He could not count upon sleep; he knew he should not sleep. . . . . He began to muse—slowly, sadly, bitterly. . . . . He thought of the vanity, the uselessness, the common falsity of the whole human race. . . . . He shook his head, sprang up from his seat, walked several times up and down the room, sat down at his writing-table, pulled out one drawer after the other, and began to fumble among old papers, mostly letters in a woman's hand. He knew not why he did it—he was looking for nothing, he simply wished to seek refuge in an outward occupation from the thoughts that tormented him. . . . . He got up, went back to the fireplace, sank into his chair again, and covered his face with his hands. . . . . 'Why to-day, just to-day?' he thought; and many a memory from the long-vanished past rose up in him. He remembered—this is what he remembered."

On his way back to Russia from a foreign tour he meets, at Frankfort, a young girl of modest origin but extraordinary beauty—the daughter of an Italian confectioner. Accident brings them together, he falls in love with her, holds himself ardently ready to marry her, obtains her mother's consent, and has only, to make the marriage possible, to raise money on his Russian property, which is of moderate value. While he is revolving schemes he encounters an old schoolfellow, an odd personage, now married to an heiress who, as fortune has it, possesses an estate in the neighbourhood of Sanin's own. It occurs to the latter that Madame Polosoff may be induced to buy his land, and, as she understands "business" and manages her own affairs, he repairs to Wiesbaden, with leave obtained from his betrothed, to make his proposal. The reader of course foresees the sequel—the reader, especially, who is versed in Turgénieff. Madame Polosoff understands business and much else besides. She is young, lovely, unscrupulous, dangerous, fatal. Sanin succumbs to the spell, forgets honour, duty, tenderness, prudence, everything, and after three days of bewildered resistance finds himself packed into the lady's travelling-carriage with her other belongings and rolling toward Paris. But we foresee that he comes speedily to his senses; the spring-torrent is spent. The years that follow are as arid as brooding penitence can make them. Penitence, after that night of bitter memories, takes an active shape. He makes a pilgrimage to Frankfort and seeks out some trace of the poor girl he had deserted. With much trouble he obtains tidings, and learns that she is married in America, that she is happy, and that she serenely forgives him. He returns to St. Petersburg, spends there a short, restless interval, and suddenly disappears. People say he has gone to America. The spring torrents exhale themselves in autumn mists. Sanin, in the Frankfort episode, is not only very young, but very Russian; how young, how Russian, this charming description tells:—

"He was, to begin with, a really very good-looking

fellow. He had a tall, slender figure, agreeable, rather vague features, kindly blue eyes, a fair complexion suffused with a fresh red, and, above all, that genial, joyous, confiding, upright expression, which at the first glance, perhaps, seems to give an air of limitation, but by which, in former times, you recognised the son of a tranquil aristocratic family—a son of the 'fathers,' a good country gentleman, born and grown up, stoutly, in those fruitful provinces of ours which border on the steppe; then a somewhat shuffling gait, a slightly lisping way of speaking, a childlike laugh as soon as any one looked at him, ... health, in short, freshness and a softness,—a softness! . . . . there you have all Sanin. Along with this he was by no means dull, and had learnt a good many things. He had remained fresh in spite of his journey abroad; those tumultuous impulses that imposed themselves upon the best part of the young men of that day were little known to him."

If we place beside this vivid portrait the sketch, hardly less expressive, of Madame Polosoff, we find in the mere apposition the germ of a novel:—

"Not that she was a perfect beauty; the traces of her plebeian origin were perceptible enough. Her forehead was low, her nose rather thick and inclining to an upward inflection; she could boast neither of a fine skin nor of pretty hands and feet. But what did all this signify? Not before the 'sanctity of beauty'—to use Puschkin's words—would he who met her have stood lingering, but before the charm of the powerful half-Russian, half-Bohemian, blooming, womanly body—and he would not have lingered without a purpose."

Madame Polosoff, though her exploits are related in a short sixty-five pages, is unfolded in the large dramatic manner. We seem to be in her presence, to listen to her provoking, bewildering talk, to feel the danger of her audacious, conscious frankness. Her quite peculiar cruelty and depravity make a large demand on our credulity; she is perhaps a trifle too picturesquely vicious. But she is strangely, vividly natural, and our imagination goes with her in the same charmed mood as with M. Turgénieff's other evil-doers. Not without an effort, too, do we accept the possibility of Sanin's immediate infidelity to the object of the pure still passion with which his heart even yet overflows. But these are wonderful mysteries; its immediacy, perhaps, best accounts for it; spring torrents, the author would seem to intimate, *must* flow, and ravage their blooming channels. To give a picture of the immeasurable blindness of youth, of its eagerness of desire, its freshness of impression, its mingled rawness and ripeness, the swarming, shifting possibilities of its springtime, and to interfuse his picture with something of the softening poetizing harmony of retrospect—this has been but half the author's purpose. He has designed beside to paint the natural conflict between soul and sense, and to make the struggle less complex than the one he has described in "Smoke," and less brutal, as it were, than the fatal victory of sense in "A Correspondence." "When will it all come to an end?" Sanin asks, as he stares helpless at Maria Nikolaievna, and feels himself ignobly paralysed. "Weak men," says the author, "never themselves make an end,—they always wait for the end." Sanin's history is weighted with the moral that salvation lies in being able, at a given moment, to bring one's will down like a hammer. If M. Turgénieff pays his tribute to the magic of sense he leaves us also eloquently reminded that soul in the long run claims her own. He has given us no sweeter image of uncorrupting passion than this figure of Gemma, the frank young Italian nature blooming in northern air from its own mere wealth of joyousness. Yet, charming as Gemma is, she is but a half-sister to Lisa and Tatiana. Neither Lisa or Tatiana, we suspect, would have read popular comedy with her enchanting mimicry; but, on the other hand, they would have been withheld by a delicate, indefinable conscientiousness from caricaturing the dismissed lover of the day before for the entertainment of the accepted lover of the present. But Gemma is a charming piece of colouring, and all this only proves how many different ways there are of being the loveliest girl in the world. The accessories of her portrait are as happily rendered; the whole picture of the little Italian household, with its narrow back-shop life in the German town, has a mellow enclosed light in which the reader gratefully lingers. It touches the figure of the usual half-fantastic house-friend, the poor old ex-barytone Pantaleone Cippatola, into the most vivacious relief.

III.

We always desire more information about the writers who greatly interest us than we find in their works, and many American readers have probably a friendly curiosity as to the private personality of M. Turgénieff. We are reduced, however, to regretting our own meagre knowledge. We gather from his writings that our author is much of a cosmopolitan, a dweller in many cities and a frequenter of many societies, and, along with this, an indefinable sense of his being of a so-called "aristocratic" temperament; so that if a man's genius were visible to the eye, like his fleshly integument, that of M. Turgénieff would be observed to have, say, very shapely hands and feet, and a nose expressive of the patrician graces. A friend of ours, indeed, who has rather an irresponsible fancy, assures us that the author of "Smoke" (which he deems his masterpiece) is, personally, simply his own Pavel Kirsanoff. Twenty to one our friend is quite wrong; but we may nevertheless say that, to readers disposed now and then to risk a conjecture, much of the charm of M. Turgénieff's manner resides in this impalpable union of an aristocratic temperament with a democratic intellect. To his inquisitive intellect we owe the various, abundant, human substance of his tales, and to his fastidious temperament their exquisite form. But we must not meddle too freely with causes when results themselves are so suggestive. The great question as to a poet or a novelist is, How does he feel about life? what, in the last analysis, is his philosophy? When vigorous writers have reached maturity we are at liberty to look in their works for some expression of a total view of the world they have been so actively observing. This is the most interesting thing their works offer us. Details are interesting in proportion as they contribute to make it clear.

The foremost impression of M. Turgénieff's reader is that he is morbidly serious, that he takes life terribly hard. We move in an atmosphere of unrelieved sadness. We go from one tale to the other in the hope of finding something cheerful, but we only wander into fresh agglomerations of gloom. We try the shorter stories with a hope of chancing upon something pitched in the traditional key of "light reading," but they strike us alike as so many ingenious condensations of melancholy. "A Village Lear" is worse than "The Antchar"; "The Forsaken" is hardly an improvement on "A Correspondence"; "The Journal of a Superfluous Man" does little to lay the haunting ghost of "Three Portraits." The author has written several short dramas. Appealing to them to beguile us of our dusky vapours, we find the concentrated tragedy of "The Bread of Charity," and, by way of an after-piece, the lugubrious humour of "The Division." Sad beginnings, worse endings, good people ineffably wretched, happy ones hugely ridiculous; disappointment, despair, madness, suicide, degrading passions, and blighted hopes—these seem, on first acquaintance, the chief ingredients of M. Turgénieff's version of the human drama; and to deepen our sense of its bitterness we discover the author in the background winding up his dismal demonstration with a chuckle. We set him down forthwith as a cold-blooded pessimist, caring for nothing in life but its misery, and for nothing in misery but its picturesqueness—its capacity for furnishing cynical epigrams. What is each of the short tales we have mentioned, we ask, but a ruthless epigram, in the dramatic form, upon human happiness? Evlampia Charloff, in "A Village Lear," drives her father to madness and death by her stony depravity, and then joins a set of religious fanatics, among whom she plays a great part as the "Holy Mother of God." In "The Bread of Charity," a young heiress brings home to her estates her newly-wedded husband, and introduces him to her old neighbours. They dine with him, and one of them, an officious coxcomb, conceives the brilliant idea of entertaining him by an exhibition of a poor old gentleman who has long been hanging about the place as a pensioner of the late parents of the young wife, and is remarkable for a dumb canine attachment to herself. The heartless guest plies the modest old man with wine, winds him up and makes him play the fool. But suddenly Kusofkin, through the fumes of his potations, perceives that he is being laughed at, and breaks out into a passionate assurance that, baited and buffeted as he is, he is nothing less than the father of the mistress of the house. She overhears his cry, and though he, horrified at his indiscretion, attempts to retract it, she wins from him a confession of the fact that he had been her mother's lover. The husband, however, makes him swallow his words, and do public penance. He turns him out of the house with a small pension, and the curtain falls on the compliment offered this fine fellow by the meddlesome neighbour on his generosity: "You are a true Russian gentleman!" The most perfectly epigrammatic of our author's stories, however, is perhaps that polished little piece of misery, "A Correspondence." A young man, idle, discontented, and longing for better things, writes, for a pastime, to a young girl whom he has formerly slightly known and greatly esteemed, who has entertained an unsuspected and unrequited passion for him, and who lives obscurely in the country, among very common people. A correspondence comes of it, in the course of which they exchange confidences and unburden their hearts. The young girl is most pitiable, most amiable, in her sadness, and her friend begins to suspect that she, at last, may give a meaning to his aimless life. She, on her side, is compassionately interested, and we see curiosity and hope throbbing timidly beneath the austere resignation to which she has schooled herself, and the expression of which, mingled with our sense of her blooming beauty of character, makes of Maria Alexandrovna the most nobly fascinating, perhaps, of our author's heroines. Alexis Petrovitsch writes at last that he must see her, that he will come to her, that she is to expect him at such a date, and we imagine tenderly, in the unhastening current of her days, the gentle eddy of her expectation. Her next letter, after an interval, expresses surprise at his non-appearance; her next, several months later, is a last attempt to obtain news of him. The correspondence closes with his confession, written as he lies dying at Dresden. Just as he was starting to join her, he had encountered another woman, a dancing-girl at the opera, with whom he had fallen madly in love. She was low, stupid, heartless; she had nothing to recommend her to anything but his senses. It was ignoble, but so it was. His passion has led him such a life that his health is gone. He has brought on disease of the lungs, by waiting for the young lady at the opera-door in the winter nights. Now his hours are numbered, and this is the end of all! And on this lugubrious note the story closes. We read with intent curiosity, for the tale is a masterpiece of narration; but we wonder, in some vexation, what it all means. Is it a piece of irony for irony's sake, or is it a disinterested picture of the struggle between base passion and pure passion? Why, in that case, should it seem a matter of course for the author that base passion should carry the day? Why, as for Rudin, for Sanin, for the distracted hero of "Smoke," should circumstances also have been too many, as the phrase is, for poor Alexis Petrovitsch? If we pursue our researches, in the hope of finding some method in this promiscuous misery, examples continue to seem more numerous than principles. The author continues everywhere to imply that there is something essentially ridiculous in human nature, something indefeasibly vain in human effort. We are amazed, as we go, at the portentous number of his patent fools; no novelist has drawn a tenth as many. The large majority of his people are the people we laugh at, and a large fraction of the remainder the people we half disgustedly pity. There is little room left, therefore, for the people we esteem, and yet room enough perhaps, considering that our very benevolence is tempered with scepticism. What with the vicious fools and the well-meaning fools, the prosperous charlatans and the grotesque nonentities, the dead failures and the sadder failures that regret and protest and rebel, the demoralized lovers and the jilted maidens, the dusky pall of fatality, in a word, suspended over all human things, it may be inferred that we are not invited to a particularly exhilarating spectacle. Not a single person in the novel of "Fathers and Sons" but has, in some degree, a lurking ironical meaning. Every one is a more or less ludicrous parody on what he ought to have been, or an ineffectual regret at what he might have been. The only person who compasses a reasonable share of happiness is Arcadi, and even his happiness is a thing for strenuous minds to smile at—a happiness based on the *pot au feu*, the prospect of innumerable babies and the sacrifice of "views." Arcadi's father is a vulgar failure; Pavel Petrovitsch is a poetic failure; Bazaroff is a tragic failure; Anna Sergheievna misses happiness from an ungenerous fear of sacrificing her luxurious quietude; the elder Bazaroff and his wife seem a couple of ingeniously grotesque manikins, prepared by a melancholy *fantoccinista* to illustrate the mocking vanity of parental hopes. We lay down the book, and we repeat that, with all the charity in the world, it is impossible to pronounce M. Turgénieff anything better than a pessimist.

The judgment is just, but it needs qualifications, and it finds them in a larger look at the author's position. M. Turgénieff strikes us, as we have said, as a man disappointed, for good reasons or for poor ones, in the land that is dear to him. Harsh critics will say for poor ones, reflecting that a fastidious imagination has not been unconcerned in his discontentment. To the old Muscovite virtues, and especially the old Muscovite *naïveté*, his imagination filially clings, but he finds these things, especially in the fact that his country turns to the outer world, melting more and more every day into the dimness of tradition. The Russians are clever, and clever people are ambitious. Those with whom M. Turgénieff has seen himself surrounded are consumed with the desire to pass for intellectual cosmopolites, to know, or seem to know, everything that can be known, to be astoundingly modern and progressive and European. Madame Kukshin, the poor little literary lady with a red nose, in "Fathers and Sons," gives up George Sand as "nowhere" for her want of knowledge of embryology, and, when asked why she proposes to remove to Heidelberg, replies with "Bunsen, you know." The fermentation of social change has thrown to the surface in Russia a deluge of hollow pretensions and vicious presumptions, amid which the love either of old virtues or of new achievements finds very little gratification. It is not simply that people flounder laughably in deeper waters than they can breast, but that in this discord of crude ambitions the integrity of character itself is compromised and men and women make, morally, a very ugly appearance. The Russian colony at Baden-Baden, depicted in "Smoke," is a collection of more or less inflated profligates. Panschin, in "A Nest of Noblemen," is another example; Sitnikoff, in "Fathers and Sons," a still more contemptible one. Driven back, depressed and embittered, into his imagination for the edification which the social spectacle immediately before him refuses him, and shaped by nature to take life hard and linger among its shadows, our observer surrenders himself with a certain reactionary, irresponsible gusto to a sombre portrayal of things. An imaginative preference for dusky subjects is a perfectly legitimate element of the artistic temperament; our own Hawthorne is a signal case of its being innocently exercised; innocently, because with that delightfully unconscious genius it remained imaginative, sportive, inconclusive, to the end. When external circumstances, however, contribute to confirm it, and reality lays her groaning stores of misery at its feet, it will take a rarely elastic genius altogether to elude the charge of being morbid. M. Turgénieff's pessimism seems to us of two sorts—a spontaneous melancholy and a wanton melancholy. Sometimes in a sad story it is the problem, the question, the idea, that strikes him; sometimes it is simply the picture. Under the former influence he has produced his masterpieces; we admit that they are intensely sad, but we consent to be moved, as we consent to sit silent in a death-chamber. In the other case he has done but his second best; we strike a bargain over our tears, and insist that when it comes to being simply entertained, wooing and wedding are better than death and burial. "The Antchar," "The Forsaken," "A Superfluous Man," "A Village Lear," "Toc . . . toc . . . toc," all seem to us to be gloomier by several shades than they need have been; for we hold to the good old belief that the presumption, in life, is in favour of the brighter side, and we deem it, in art, an indispensable condition of our interest in a depressed observer that he should have at least tried his best to be cheerful. The truth, we take it, lies for the pathetic in poetry and romance very much where it lies for the "immoral." Morbid pathos is reflective pathos; ingenious pathos, pathos not freshly born of the occasion; noxious immorality is superficial immorality, immorality without natural roots in the subject. We value most the "realists" who have an ideal of delicacy and the elegiasts who have an ideal of joy.

"Picturesque gloom, possibly," a thick and thin admirer of M. Turgénieff's may say to us, "at least you will admit that it *is* picturesque." This we heartily concede, and, recalled to a sense of our author's brilliant diversity and ingenuity, we bring our restrictions to a close. To the broadly generous side of his imagination it is impossible to pay exaggerated homage, or, indeed, for that matter, to its simple intensity and fecundity. No romancer has created a greater number of the figures that breathe and move and speak, in their habits as they might have lived; none, on the whole, seems to us to have had such a masterly touch in portraiture, none has mingled so much ideal beauty with so much unsparing reality. His sadness has its element of error, but it has also its larger element of wisdom. Life *is*, in fact, a battle. On this point optimists and pessimists agree. Evil is insolent and strong; beauty enchanting but rare; goodness very apt to be weak; folly very apt to be defiant; wickedness to carry the day; imbeciles to be in great places, people of sense in small, and mankind generally, unhappy. But the world as it stands is no illusion, no phantasm, no evil dream of a night; we wake up to it again for ever and ever; we can neither forget it nor deny it nor dispense with it. We can welcome experience as it comes, and give it what it demands, in exchange for something which it is idle to pause to call much or little so long as it contributes to swell the volume of consciousness. In this there is mingled pain and delight, but over the mysterious mixture there hovers a visible rule, that bids us learn to will and seek to understand. So much as this we seem to decipher between the lines of M. Turgénieff's minutely written chronicle. He himself has sought to understand as zealously as his most eminent competitors. He gives, at least, no meagre account of life, and he has done liberal justice to its infinite variety. This is his great merit; his great defect, roughly stated, is a tendency to the abuse of irony. He remains, nevertheless, to our sense, a very welcome mediator between the world and our curiosity. If we had space, we should like to set forth that he is by no means our ideal story-teller—this honourable genius possessing, attributively, a rarer skill than the finest required for producing an artful *réchauffé* of the actual. But even for better romancers we must wait for a better world. Whether the world in its higher state of perfection will occasionally offer colour to scandal, we hesitate to pronounce; but we are prone to conceive of the ultimate novelist as a personage altogether purged of sarcasm. The imaginative force now expended in this direction he will devote to describing cities of gold and heavens of sapphire. But, for the present, we gratefully accept M. Turgénieff, and reflect that his manner suits the most frequent mood of the greater number of readers. If he were a dogmatic optimist we suspect that, as things go, we should long ago have ceased to miss him from our library. The personal optimism of most of us no romancer can confirm or dissipate, and our personal troubles, generally, place fictions of all kinds in an impertinent light. To our usual working mood the world is apt to seem M. Turgénieff's hard world, and when, at moments, the strain and the pressure deepen, the ironical element figures not a little in our form of address to those short-sighted friends who have whispered that it is an easy one.

North American Review, April 1874
Reprinted under the title "Ivan Turgénieff"
in *French Poets and Novelists*, 1878

TRANSLATION OF A SHORT POEM

Two or three of the Paris journals have lately published a translation of a short poem by the Russian novelist, Ivan Turgenef, which—we quote the *Figaro*—"has recently been recited before the Czarevitch, and has obtained a rapid popularity in Russia." We give an English version of the *Figaro's* translation:

"The Queen is sitting in her forest of Windsor, around her the ladies of her court play at a game which not long since came into fashion—a game called croquet. You roll little balls and you make them pass skilfully through little hoops. The Queen looks on and laughs; but suddenly she stops; her face grows deathly pale.

"It seems to her that, instead of shapely balls driven by the lightly-tapping mallet, there are hundreds of heads rolling along, all smeared with blood. Heads of women, of young girls, of children: faces with marks of dreadful tortures and bestial outrage, of the claws of beasts, and all the horror of death-pangs.

"And now the youngest daughter of the Queen, a gentle

maiden, pushes one of these heads further and further from the others, pushes it until it reaches her mother's feet. The head of a child with curly hair; its little livid mouth turns to murmur reproaches. The Queen utters a shriek of horror; an ineffable terror darkens her eyes.

" 'My doctor, quick, quick, let him come to me!' And she tells him her terrible vision. But he then answers: 'It doesn't surprise me; reading the newspapers has disturbed you. The *Times* explains to us so well how the Bulgarians have deserved the wrath of the Turks. Here is a draught; take it and your trouble will pass.' And the Queen goes back into her palace.

"She is alone, and she begins to muse. Her eyelids fall, and—oh! horror, the edge of her garment is befouled with a bloody stain. 'Let them take it away this instant—I wish to forget it. Wash it for me, rivers of England!' 'No, your Majesty, never shall the royal robe of England be washed of the stain of this innocent blood!' "

Nation, October 5, 1876

Terres Vierges. Par Ivan Tourguéneff. Traduit par E. Durand-Gréville. Paris, 1877; New York: F. W. Christern.

T HERE ARE ONLY two living novelists the appearance of whose new productions constitutes anything that can be called a literary event. If one of these writers is that blessing of reviewers the author of 'Daniel Deronda,' the other is certainly the distinguished Russian whose name we have inscribed at the head of these remarks, and who has now for some time been recognized, even among those people who are condemned to know him only in imperfect translations, as one of the profoundest of observers and one of the most fascinating of story-tellers. It had been known for some months past that Ivan Turgenef was engaged upon a new novel, which was to be in plan and purpose one of the most considerable of his productions, and the impatience of his admirers was increased by the fact that—Russian scholars being few—the book would be for some time before the world and yet be inaccessible. 'Nov' appeared in Russia during the first weeks of the present year; but it has been translated into French with commendable promptitude—with what degree of accuracy we are unable to say, though we may suppose that as the translation was made under the eyes of the author it is fairly satisfactory. This is a very good moment for a Russian novel to appear—at least out of Russia. As a *pièce de circonstance* we can imagine nothing except a Turkish novel which would be more opportune. We believe that in M. Turgenef's own country the prospective clash of arms has to a certain extent deadened the public ear to the voice of the artist; but among ourselves, disinterested yet observant spectators of what is going on in the East, we imagine the author will find the attention he commands has rather been quickened by circumstances. The designs, ambitions, prospects, and characteristics of Russia form a great spectacle, in which M. Turgenef's literary activity has its place. This is all the more the case that the subject of his new novel connects the work with an element in the spectacle which we hear a great deal about, and which is, perhaps, especially what appeals to our curiosity. The outside world knows in a vague way of the existence of certain "secret societies" in Russia, and of the belief entertained by some people that their revolutionary agitation forms a sufficient embarrassment at home to keep the Government of the Czar from extending his conquests abroad. Of one of these secret societies M. Turgenef has given a picture, though it must be said that the particular association he describes hardly appears to be of a nature seriously to alarm the powers of order. Whether it is because it is a characteristic of his genius to throw a sort of ironical light over all things— even to some extent over the things that have his deepest sympathy; to see with peculiar vividness the side on which human effort is comical, and helpless, and ineffectual; or whether it is that revolutionary propagandism in Russia is really too crude, and youthful, and vague to be, as the phrase is, counted with; certain it is, the impression left by Neshdanoff and Markeloff, by Ostrodumoff and Mashurina, even by Marianne and Solomin, is not so much of a sinister as a touching and melancholy, or even of a softly-exhilarating cast. Ivan Turgenef always shows his superiority in the choice of his subjects; his themes are never conventional and stale; he is certain to select a *donnée* which means and reveals something. He has shown this admirable instinct here—shown it much more strongly than by producing, as the mention of his subject may have suggested, a story of mysteries and surprises, excitements and escapes. He has approached his ground on the moral and psychological side, and made, as is usual with him, a profound study of character. The vulgar capacities of the theme have not been taken advantage of, but the finer ones have been handled in a masterly manner. The author's wisdom is shown in his deep perception of the fact that the clandestine movement of which he gives a sketch is particularly fertile in revelations of character—that it contains inevitably the seeds of an interesting psychological drama. The opposition of different natures convoked together by a common ideal—this ideal being one which appeals with peculiar force to youthful generosity, accompanied by a due share of that "little knowledge" which is a dangerous thing; such, roughly speaking, is the subject of 'Terres Vierges.'

The story is a picture of a certain portion of the "young generation" in Russia, the generation of which we had a glimpse in 'Fathers and Sons,' and of which the "nihilist" Bazaroff was so robust an exponent—the young people of liberal instincts who find no legitimate channel of expression, and who expend their ardor in aimless machinations, compounded in equal parts of puerility and heroism. The central figure in the present tale is a young man named Neshdanoff, selected, like most of the author's central figures, on account of his being a particularly good subject for irony. Ivan Turgenef's heroes are never heroes in the literal sense of the word, rather quite the reverse; their function is to be conspicuous as failures, interesting but impotent persons who are losers at the game of life. The utmost that the heroic can hope for is to be obscurely embodied in some secondary figure whose quiet robustness helps to satirize its companions. Upon M. Turgenef's predilection for failures, losers at the game, his acute observation and extensive knowledge of them, there would be a great deal to say; in the eyes of foreign readers he has almost made them the Russian type *par excellence*. We suspect that if they are not this, they are at least, in Russia, a very characteristic class of persons; though whether such persons are always as interesting as the art of Ivan Turgenef renders them is possibly doubtful. Their interest, in his hands, comes in a great measure from the fact that they are exquisitely conscious of their shortcomings, thanks to the fine and subtle intelligence, that "subjective" tendency, with which he represents all Russians who are not positive fools and grotesques as being endowed. His central figure is usually a person in a false position, generally not of his own making, which, according to the peculiar perversity of fate, is only aggravated by his effort to right himself. Such eminently is the case with young Neshdanoff, who is the natural son of a nobleman, not recognized by his father's family, and who, drifting through irritation and smothered rage and vague aspiration into the stream of occult radicalism, finds himself fatally fastidious and sceptical and "æsthetic"—more essentially an aristocrat, in a word, than any of the aristocrats he has agreed to conspire against. He has not the gift of faith, and he is most uncomfortably at odds with his companions, who have it in a high degree—these types of "faith" which surround Neshdanoff being most vividly portrayed. He accepts a place as resident tutor in the house of a certain Sipiagin, a liberal of the discreet and official sort, whose ideal of conduct, costume, and manner is the English country gentleman of large fortune, Parliamentary training, and "progressive" tendencies. One of the features of the story is the contrast between the passionate fermentation of the four young revolutionists and the urbane and patronizing sympathy with progress of this happy proprietor, whose liberalism is hardly more than an affair of the toilet. In his house lives his niece, Marianne Sinetzkaïa, who forms, with Neshdanoff, the connecting link between genteel society and the little group of propagandists. Turgenef's young girls are always remarkable creations, and this striking figure of the young lady by birth, who is an ardent democrat by temperament and aspiration, is perhaps the great success of 'Terres Vierges.' Like all Turgenef's heroines, Marianne is both very original and very real; never was there less of a portrait in pastel. She crops her hair short and keeps her own counsel; very soon, of course, living under the same roof with Neshdanoff, the preceptor of her little cousin, she discovers his propagandist affiliations and falls more or less in love with him. We say "of course"; but, in fact, in Turgenef's novels events never take the conventional and expected course; there is always some deeper complexity—some closer "twist." Marianne and Neshdanoff exchange ideas and expressions of sympathy, admire each other greatly, become very intimate, and have secret nocturnal interviews. At last they agree to leave the house together and throw themselves into the revolutionary movement, and they wander forth like brother and sister, hand in hand, like the Babes in the Wood, and take up their abode with a certain Solomin, a radical of the sturdy and practical type, who can bide his time. (This Solomin is an admirable portrait.) There is something very beautiful and very characteristic of Turgenef in the idea of the mutual purity of these two young people. They have started on a wild-goose chase, and would be quite at a loss to say what they propose to do, and how they propose to do it; but the delicacy of their enthusiasm is such that they do not even desire to possess each other, and in their moments of tenderest *épanchement* they only shake hands affectionately, like plighted comrades.

There is another young man, Markeloff by name, a character directly opposed to Neshdanoff—a revolutionist whose perceptions are narrow and whose faith is absolute, so that his attitude towards constituted powers and beliefs is very much that of a projectile emitted from a cannon-mouth. In his dogged, dusky, unlovely, but unshrinking and fatally consistent figure there is a certain tragic impressiveness. He has but one touch of inconsistency—he is in love with Marianne, and he therefore finds himself for a moment in apparent rivalry with the younger, handsomer, more agreeable Neshdanoff. The finest scene in the book is that in which his jealousy of Neshdanoff, who is engaged with him in a common and sacred cause, breaks out in the course of a jolting drive which they take together at night. One has, of course, read Turgenef to little purpose if one has not observed that the Russian character, as he portrays it, differs strikingly at a dozen points from that of other peoples with which we are more familiar; but we remember no incident in all his novels that more forcibly illustrates this difference. Markeloff, in his wrath, sud-

denly reminds Neshdanoff of his irregular birth, and declares
that his gaining Marianne's favor is nothing, after all, but the
"usual good luck of the d—d race of bastards!" This affront
is mortal, and is felt in the keenest manner by Neshdanoff,
who declares that it can only be washed out in blood, and
prepares immediately to part company with his companion.
But the latter has hardly uttered the words before he repents
of them; he entreats his rival to remain, and offers to go
down on his knees and beg his pardon. This is a most extraordinary scene, and it is evident that the author feels it to be
such. Neshdanoff shakes hands with his insulter, and the author explains that before three minutes were over the two
were addressing each other with *thee* and *thou*, as if nothing
had happened; all of which seems to prove that Russians have
not the idea of "honor" as strongly developed as some other
races, though in that very phase of their character upon which
this episode throws light there is something very interesting,
spontaneous, and human.

   We will not spoil the reader's entertainment by disclosing
the solution of poor Neshdanoff's difficulties further than to
say that it is a solution to which Ivan Turgenef's heroes have
more than once resorted. Of course, his career receives the
final tragic stamp; the "æsthetic" young man, venturing to
play with revolution, finds it a coarse, ugly, vulgar, and moreover very cruel thing; the reality makes him deadly sick. Very
happily invented is the incident which completes his disillusionment—his being brought home dead-drunk from a propagandist excursion among the peasantry, who have insisted
on his proving himself a good fellow by swallowing long
draughts of their pestilent brandy. Marianne, who is not
æsthetic nor addicted to hair-splitting, loses no illusions and
we feel that she never will. The author leaves her with the
excellent Solomin, in whom she finds her proper counterpart
as a type of one of the latent forces of the future, in a country
in which these will probably let themselves loose on a great
scale. Marianne, as we said, is very real so far as she goes; but
we confess that we find her the least agreeable of Ivan Turgenef's young girls; and this, we think, contrary to the author's intention. She lacks sweetness and softness; she is
somewhat too acrimonious, too pert, in her dealings with

Mme. Sipiagin, her highly uncongenial aunt. The book contains a great number of other figures, which we have not left ourselves space to pick out for especial commendation. Particularly good is the female devotee of the "common cause," Mashurina, who is big, ugly, and awkward, but profoundly pure and sincere. She has taken her diploma in obstetrics, and she is privately in love with Neshdanoff, who never knows it and would be horrified if he were to do so; she is one of those intensely individual figures which form Turgenef's great strength. We must also pass over Mme. Sipiagin, the lady remarkable for her resemblance to Raphael's Dresden Madonna, who represents the feminine side of cultivated liberalism—represents it in a manner to make the reader shudder. We have seen the episode of Zimushka and Zomushka, the grotesque old couple living among their rococo coffee-cups and snuff-boxes, condemned as a *hors d'œuvre*— an excrescence; but this strikes us as an inattentive judgment. The picture of their ancient superstitions, their quaintness, and mellowness and serenity, is intended as a dramatic offset to the crude and acrid unrest of the young radicals who come to see them; it has a "value," as the painters say. It is, moreover, very charming in itself. Subtle intentions are far from wanting in 'Terres Vierges'; there are always more of these in Ivan Turgenef than even the acutest critic can gather together the threads of. In the present work they all throw into relief the author's great quality—the union of the deepest reality of substance, of *fonds*, as the French say, with the most imaginative, most poetic, touches.

Nation, April 26, 1877

IVAN TURGÉNIEFF

WHEN THE MORTAL REMAINS of Ivan Turgénieff were about to be transported from Paris for interment in his own country, a short commemorative service was held at the Gare du Nord. Ernest Renan and Edmond About, standing beside the train in which his coffin had been placed, bade farewell in the name of the French people to the illustrious stranger who for so many years had been their honoured and grateful guest. M. Renan made a beautiful speech, and M. About a very clever one, and each of them characterised, with ingenuity, the genius and the moral nature of the most touching of writers, the most lovable of men. "Turgénieff," said M. Renan, "received by the mysterious decree which marks out human vocations the gift which is noble beyond all others: he was born essentially impersonal." The passage is so eloquent that one must repeat the whole of it. "His conscience was not that of an individual to whom nature had been more or less generous: it was in some sort the conscience of a people. Before he was born he had lived for thousands of years; infinite successions of reveries had amassed themselves in the depths of his heart. No man has been as much as he the incarnation of a whole race: generations of ancestors, lost in the sleep of centuries, speechless, came through him to life and utterance."

I quote these lines for the pleasure of quoting them; for while I see what M. Renan means by calling Turgénieff impersonal, it has been my wish to devote to his delightful memory a few pages written under the impression of contact and intercourse. He seems to us impersonal, because it is from his writings almost alone that we of English, French and German speech have derived our notions—even yet, I fear, rather meagre and erroneous—of the Russian people. His genius for us is the Slav genius; his voice the voice of those vaguely-imagined multitudes whom we think of more and more to-day as waiting their turn, in the arena of civilisation, in the grey expanses of the North. There is much in his writings to encourage this view, and it is certain that he interpreted with wonderful vividness the temperament of his fellow-countrymen. Cosmopolite that he had become by the force of circumstances, his roots had never been loosened in his native soil. The ignorance with regard to Russia and the Russians which he found in abundance in the rest of Europe—and not least in the country he inhabited for ten years before his death—had indeed the effect, to a certain degree, to throw him back upon the deep feelings which so many of his companions were unable to share with him, the memories of his early years, the sense of wide Russian horizons, the joy and pride of his mother-tongue. In the collection of short pieces, so deeply interesting, written during the last few years of his life, and translated into German under the name of *Senilia*, I find a passage—it is the last in the little book—which illustrates perfectly this reactionary impulse: "In days of doubt, in days of anxious thought on the destiny of my native land, thou alone art my support and my staff, O great powerful Russian tongue, truthful and free! If it were not for thee how should man not despair at the sight of what is going on at home? But it is inconceivable that such a language has not been given to a great people." This Muscovite, home-loving note pervades his productions, though it is between the lines, as it were, that we must listen for it. None the less does it remain true that he was not a simple conduit or mouthpiece; the inspiration was his own as well as the voice. He was an individual, in other words, of the most unmistakable kind, and those who had the happiness to know him have no difficulty to-day in thinking of him as an eminent, responsible figure. This pleasure, for the writer of these lines, was as great as the pleasure of reading the admirable tales into which he put such a world of life and feeling: it was perhaps even greater, for it was not only with the pen that nature had given Turgénieff the power to express himself. He was the richest, the most delightful, of talkers, and his face, his person, his temper, the thoroughness with which he had been equipped for human intercourse, make in the memory of his friends an image which is completed, but not thrown into the shade, by his literary distinction. The whole image is tinted with sadness: partly because the element of melancholy in his nature was deep and constant—readers of his novels have no need to be told of that; and partly because, during the last years of his life, he had been condemned to suffer atrociously. Intolerable pain had been his portion for too many months before he died; his end was not a soft decline, but a deepening distress. But of brightness, of the faculty of enjoyment, he had also the large allowance usually made to first-rate men, and he was a singularly complete human being. The author of these pages had greatly admired his writings before having the fortune to make his acquaintance, and this privilege, when it presented itself, was highly illuminating. The man and the writer together occupied from that moment a very high place in his affection. Some time before knowing him I committed to print certain reflections which his tales had led me to make; and I may perhaps, therefore, without impropriety give them a supplement which shall have a more vivifying reference. It is almost irresistible to attempt to say, from one's own point of view, what manner of man he was.

It was in consequence of the article I just mentioned that I found reason to meet him, in Paris, where he was then living, in 1875. I shall never forget the impression he made upon me at that first interview. I found him adorable; I could scarcely believe that he would prove—that any man could prove—on nearer acquaintance so delightful as that. Nearer acquaintance only confirmed my hope, and he remained the most approachable, the most practicable, the least unsafe man of genius it has been my fortune to meet. He was so simple, so natural, so modest, so destitute of personal pretension and of what is called the consciousness of powers, that one almost doubted at moments whether he were a man of genius after all. Everything good and fruitful lay near to him; he was interested in everything; and he was absolutely without that eagerness of self-reference which sometimes accompanies great, and even small, reputations. He had not a particle of vanity; nothing whatever of the air of having a part to play or a reputation to keep up. His humour exercised itself as freely upon himself as upon other subjects, and he told stories at his own expense with a sweetness of hilarity which made his peculiarities really sacred in the eyes of a friend. I remember vividly the smile and tone of voice with which he once repeated to me a figurative epithet which Gustave Flaubert (of whom he was extremely fond) had applied to him—an epithet intended to characterise a certain expansive softness, a comprehensive indecision, which pervaded his nature, just as it pervades so many of the characters he has painted. He enjoyed Flaubert's use of this term, good-naturedly opprobrious, more even than Flaubert himself, and recognised perfectly the element of truth in it. He was natural to an extraordinary degree; I do not think I have ever seen his match in this respect, certainly not among people who bear, as he did, at the same time, the stamp of the highest cultivation. Like all men of a large pattern, he was composed of many different pieces; and what was always striking in him was the mixture of simplicity with the fruit of the most various observation. In the little article in which I had attempted to express my admiration for his works, I had been moved to say of him that he had the aristocratic temperament: a remark which in the light of further knowledge seemed to me singularly inane. He was not subject to any definition of that sort, and to say that he was democratic would be (though his political ideal was a democracy), to give an equally superficial account of him. He felt and understood the opposite sides of life; he was imaginative, speculative, anything but literal. He had not in his mind a grain of prejudice as large as the point of a needle, and people (there are many) who think this a defect would have missed it immensely in Ivan Serguéitch. (I give his name, without attempting the Russian orthography, as it was uttered by his friends when they addressed him in French.) Our Anglo-Saxon, Protestant, moralistic, conventional standards were far away from him, and he judged things with a freedom and spontaneity in which I found a perpetual refreshment. His sense of beauty, his love of truth and right, were the foundation of his nature; but half the charm of conversation with him was that one breathed an air in which cant phrases and arbitrary measurements simply sounded ridiculous.

I may add that it was not because I had written a laudatory article about his books that he gave me a friendly welcome; for in the first place my article could have very little importance for him, and in the second it had never been either his habit or his hope to bask in the light of criticism. Supremely modest as he was, I think he attached no great weight to what might happen to be said about him; for he felt that he was destined to encounter a very small amount of intelligent appreciation, especially in foreign countries. I never heard him even allude to any judgment which might have been passed upon his productions in England. In France he knew that he was read very moderately; the "demand" for his volumes was small, and he had no illusions whatever on the subject of his popularity. He had heard with pleasure that many intelligent persons in the United States were impatient for everything that might come from his pen; but I think he was never convinced, as one or two of the more zealous of these persons had endeavoured to convince him, that he could boast of a "public" in America. He gave me the impression of thinking of criticism as most serious workers think of it—that it is the amusement, the exercise, the subsistence of the critic (and, so far as this goes, of immense use); but that though it may often concern other readers, it does not much concern the artist himself. In comparison with all those things which the production of a considered work forces the artist little by little to say to himself, the remarks of the critic are vague and of the moment; and yet, owing to the large publicity of the proceeding, they have a power to irritate or discourage which is quite out of proportion to their use to the person criticised. It was not, moreover (if this explanation be not more gross than the spectre it is meant to conjure away), on account of any esteem which he accorded to my own productions (I used regularly to send them to him) that I found him so agreeable, for to the best of my belief he was unable to read them. As regards one of the first that I had offered him he wrote me a little note to tell me that a distinguished friend, who was his constant companion, had read three or four chapters aloud to him the evening before and that one of them was written *de main de maître!* This gave me great pleasure, but it was my first and last pleasure of the kind. I continued, as I say, to send him my fictions, because they were the only thing I had to give; but he never alluded to the rest of the work in question, which he evidently did not finish, and never gave any sign of having read its successors. Presently I quite ceased to expect this, and saw why it was (it interested me much), that my writings could not appeal to him. He cared, more than anything else, for the air of reality, and my reality was not to the purpose. I do not think my stories struck him as quite meat for men. The manner was more apparent than the matter; they were too *tarabiscoté*, as I once heard him say of the style of a book—had on the surface too many little flowers and knots of ribbon. He had read a great deal of English, and knew the language remarkably well—too well, I used often to think, for he liked to speak it with those to whom it was native, and, successful as the effort always was, it deprived

him of the facility and raciness with which he expressed himself in French.

I have said that he had no prejudices, but perhaps after all
he had one. I think he imagined it to be impossible to a person of English speech to converse in French with complete
correctness. He knew Shakespeare thoroughly, and at one
time had wandered far and wide in English literature. His
opportunities for speaking English were not at all frequent,
so that when the necessity (or at least the occasion) presented
itself, he remembered the phrases he had encountered in
books. This often gave a charming quaintness and an unexpected literary turn to what he said. "In Russia, in spring, if
you enter a beechen grove"—those words come back to me
from the last time I saw him. He continued to read English
books and was not incapable of attacking the usual Tauchnitz
novel. The English writer (of our day) of whom I remember
to have heard him speak with most admiration was Dickens,
of whose faults he was conscious, but whose power of presenting to the eye a vivid, salient figure he rated very high. In
the young French school he was much interested; I mean, in
the new votaries of realism, the grandsons of Balzac. He was
a good friend of most of them, and with Gustave Flaubert,
the most singular and most original of the group, he was altogether intimate. He had his reservations and discriminations, and he had, above all, the great back-garden of his Slav
imagination and his Germanic culture, into which the door
constantly stood open, and the grandsons of Balzac were not,
I think, particularly free to accompany him. But he had much
sympathy with their experiment, their general movement, and
it was on the side of the careful study of life as the best line
of the novelist that, as may easily be supposed, he ranged
himself. For some of the manifestations of the opposite tradition he had a great contempt. This was a kind of emotion
he rarely expressed, save in regard to certain public wrongs
and iniquities; bitterness and denunciation seldom passed his
mild lips. But I remember well the little flush of conviction,
the seriousness, with which he once said, in allusion to a
novel which had just been running through the *Revue des
Deux Mondes*, "If I had written anything so bad as that, I
should blush for it all my life."

His was not, I should say, predominantly, or even in a high degree, the artistic nature, though it was deeply, if I may make the distinction, the poetic. But during the last twelve years of his life he lived much with artists and men of letters, and he was eminently capable of kindling in the glow of discussion. He cared for questions of form, though not in the degree in which Flaubert and Edmond de Goncourt cared for them, and he had very lively sympathies. He had a great regard for Madame George Sand, the head and front of the old romantic tradition; but this was on general grounds, quite independent of her novels, which he never read, and which she never expected him, or apparently any one else, to read. He thought her character remarkably noble and sincere. He had, as I have said, a great affection for Gustave Flaubert, who returned it; and he was much interested in Flaubert's extraordinary attempts at bravery of form and of matter, knowing perfectly well when they failed. During those months which it was Flaubert's habit to spend in Paris, Turgénieff went almost regularly to see him on Sunday afternoon, and was so good as to introduce me to the author of *Madame Bovary*, in whom I saw many reasons for Turgénieff's regard. It was on these Sundays, in Flaubert's little salon, which, at the top of a house at the end of the Faubourg Saint-Honoré, looked rather bare and provisional, that, in the company of the other familiars of the spot, more than one of whom[1] have commemorated these occasions, Turgénieff's beautiful faculty of talk showed at its best. He was easy, natural, abundant, more than I can describe, and everything that he said was touched with the exquisite quality of his imagination. What was discussed in that little smoke-clouded room was chiefly questions of taste, questions of art and form; and the speakers, for the most part, were in æsthetic matters, radicals of the deepest dye. It would have been late in the day to propose among them any discussion of the relation of art to morality, any question as to the degree in which a novel might or might not concern itself with the teaching of a lesson. They had settled these preliminaries long ago, and it would have been primitive and incongruous to recur to them.

[1] Maxime Du Camp, Alphonse Daudet, Emile Zola.

The conviction that held them together was the conviction that art and morality are two perfectly different things, and that the former has no more to do with the latter than it has with astronomy or embryology. The only duty of a novel was to be well written; that merit included every other of which it was capable. This state of mind was never more apparent than one afternoon when *ces messieurs* delivered themselves on the subject of an incident which had just befallen one of them. *L'Assommoir* of Emile Zola had been discontinued in the journal through which it was running as a serial, in consequence of repeated protests from the subscribers. The subscriber, as a type of human imbecility, received a wonderful dressing, and the Philistine in general was roughly handled. There were gulfs of difference between Turgénieff and Zola, but Turgénieff, who, as I say, understood everything, understood Zola too, and rendered perfect justice to the high solidity of much of his work. His attitude, at such times, was admirable, and I could imagine nothing more genial or more fitted to give an idea of light, easy, human intelligence. No one could desire more than he that art should be art; always, ever, incorruptibly, art. To him this proposition would have seemed as little in need of proof, or susceptible of refutation, as the axiom that law should always be law or medicine always medicine. As much as any one he was prepared to take note of the fact that the demand for abdications and concessions never comes from artists themselves, but always from purchasers, editors, subscribers. I am pretty sure that his word about all this would have been that he could not quite see what was meant by the talk about novels being moral or the reverse; that a novel could no more propose to itself to be moral than a painting or a symphony, and that it was arbitrary to lay down a distinction between the numerous forms of art. He was the last man to be blind to their unity. I suspect that he would have said, in short, that distinctions were demanded in the interest of the moralists, and that the demand was indelicate, owing to their want of jurisdiction. Yet at the same time that I make this suggestion as to his state of mind I remember how little he struck me as bound by mere neatness of formula, how little there was in him of the partisan or the pleader. What he thought of the relation of art to life his stories, after all, show better than anything else. The immense variety of life was ever present to his mind, and he would never have argued the question I have just hinted at in the interest of particular liberties—the liberties that were apparently the dearest to his French *confrères*. It was this air that he carried about with him of feeling all the variety of life, of knowing strange and far-off things, of having an horizon in which the Parisian horizon—so familiar, so wanting in mystery, so perpetually *exploité*—easily lost itself, that distinguished him from these companions. He was not all there, as the phrase is; he had something behind, in reserve. It was Russia, of course, in a large measure; and, especially before the spectacle of what is going on there to-day, that was a large quantity. But so far as he was on the spot, he was an element of pure sociability.

I did not intend to go into these details immediately, for I had only begun to say what an impression of magnificent manhood he made upon me when I first knew him. That impression, indeed, always remained with me, even after it had been brought home to me how much there was in him of the quality of genius. He was a beautiful intellect, of course, but above all he was a delightful, mild, masculine figure. The combination of his deep, soft, lovable spirit, in which one felt all the tender parts of genius, with his immense, fair Russian physique, was one of the most attractive things conceivable. He had a frame which would have made it perfectly lawful, and even becoming, for him to be brutal; but there was not a grain of brutality in his composition. He had always been a passionate sportsman; to wander in the woods or the steppes, with his dog and gun, was the pleasure of his heart. Late in life he continued to shoot, and he had a friend in Cambridgeshire for the sake of whose partridges, which were famous, he used sometimes to cross the Channel. It would have been impossible to imagine a better representation of a Nimrod of the north. He was exceedingly tall, and broad and robust in proportion. His head was one of the finest, and though the line of his features was irregular, there was a great deal of beauty in his face. It was eminently of the Russian type—almost everything in it was wide. His expression had a singular sweetness, with a touch of Slav languor,

and his eye, the kindest of eyes, was deep and melancholy.
His hair, abundant and straight, was as white as silver, and
his beard, which he wore trimmed rather short, was of the
colour of his hair. In all his tall person, which was very striking wherever it appeared, there was an air of neglected
strength, as if it had been a part of his modesty never to remind himself that he was strong. He used sometimes to blush
like a boy of sixteen. He had very few forms and ceremonies,
and almost as little manner as was possible to a man of his
natural *prestance*. His noble appearance was in itself a manner; but whatever he did he did very simply, and he had not
the slightest pretension to not being subject to rectification. I
never saw any one receive it with less irritation. Friendly, candid, unaffectedly benignant, the impression that he produced
most strongly and most generally was, I think, simply that of
goodness.

When I made his acquaintance he had been living, since his
removal from Baden-Baden, which took place in consequence
of the Franco-Prussian war, in a large detached house on the
hill of Montmartre, with his friends of many years, Madame
Pauline Viardot and her husband, as his fellow-tenants. He
occupied the upper floor, and I like to recall, for the sake of
certain delightful talks, the aspect of his little green sitting-
room, which has, in memory, the consecration of irrecoverable hours. It was almost entirely green, and the walls were
not covered with paper, but draped in stuff. The *portières*
were green, and there was one of those immense divans, so
indispensable to Russians, which had apparently been fashioned for the great person of the master, so that smaller folk
had to lie upon it rather than sit. I remember the white light
of the Paris street, which came in through windows more or
less blinded in their lower part, like those of a studio. It
rested, during the first years that I went to see Turgénieff,
upon several choice pictures of the modern French school,
especially upon a very fine specimen of Théodore Rousseau,
which he valued exceedingly. He had a great love of painting,
and was an excellent critic of a picture. The last time I saw
him—it was at his house in the country—he showed me half
a dozen large copies of Italian works, made by a young Russian in whom he was interested, which he had, with charac-

teristic kindness, taken into his own apartments in order that he might bring them to the knowledge of his friends. He thought them, as copies, remarkable; and they were so, indeed, especially when one perceived that the original work of the artist had little value. Turgénieff warmed to the work of praising them, as he was very apt to do; like all men of imagination he had frequent and zealous admirations. As a matter of course there was almost always some young Russian in whom he was interested, and refugees and pilgrims of both sexes were his natural clients. I have heard it said by persons who had known him long and well that these enthusiasms sometimes led him into error, that he was apt to *se monter la tête* on behalf of his protégés. He was prone to believe that he had discovered the coming Russian genius; he talked about his discovery for a month, and then suddenly one heard no more of it. I remember his once telling me of a young woman who had come to see him on her return from America, where she had been studying obstetrics at some medical college, and who, without means and without friends, was in want of help and of work. He accidentally learned that she had written something, and asked her to let him see it. She sent it to him, and it proved to be a tale in which certain phases of rural life were described with striking truthfulness. He perceived in the young lady a great natural talent; he sent her story off to Russia to be printed, with the conviction that it would make a great impression, and he expressed the hope of being able to introduce her to French readers. When I mentioned this to an old friend of Turgénieff he smiled, and said that we should not hear of her again, that Ivan Serguéitch had already discovered a great many surprising talents, which, as a general thing, had not borne the test. There was apparently some truth in this, and Turgénieff's liability to be deceived was too generous a weakness for me to hesitate to allude to it, even after I have insisted on the usual certainty of his taste. He was deeply interested in his young Russians; they were what interested him most in the world. They were almost always unhappy, in want and in rebellion against an order of things which he himself detested. The study of the Russian character absorbed and fascinated him, as all readers of his stories know. Rich, unformed, undeveloped, with all

sorts of adumbrations, of qualities in a state of fusion, it
stretched itself out as a mysterious expanse in which it was
impossible as yet to perceive the relation between gifts and
weaknesses. Of its weaknesses he was keenly conscious, and I
once heard him express himself with an energy that did him
honour and a frankness that even surprised me (considering
that it was of his countrymen that he spoke), in regard to a
weakness which he deemed the greatest of all—a weakness
for which a man whose love of veracity was his strongest feeling would have least toleration. His young compatriots, seeking their fortune in foreign lands, touched his imagination
and his pity, and it is easy to conceive that under the circumstances the impression they often made upon him may have
had great intensity. The Parisian background, with its brilliant
sameness, its absence of surprises (for those who have known
it long), threw them into relief and made him see them as he
saw the figures in his tales, in relations, in situations which
brought them out. There passed before him in the course of
time many wonderful Russian types. He told me once of his
having been visited by a religious sect. The sect consisted of
but two persons, one of whom was the object of worship and
the other the worshipper. The divinity apparently was travelling about Europe in company with his prophet. They were
intensely serious but it was very handy, as the term is, for
each. The god had always his altar and the altar had (unlike
some altars) always its god.

    In his little green salon nothing was out of place; there
were none of the odds and ends of the usual man of letters,
which indeed Turgénieff was not; and the case was the same
in his library at Bougival, of which I shall presently speak.
Few books even were visible; it was as if everything had been
put away. The traces of work had been carefully removed. An
air of great comfort, an immeasurable divan and several valuable pictures—that was the effect of the place. I know not
exactly at what hours Turgénieff did his work; I think he had
no regular times and seasons, being in this respect as different
as possible from Anthony Trollope, whose autobiography,
with its candid revelation of intellectual economies, is so curious. It is my impression that in Paris Turgénieff wrote little;
his times of production being rather those weeks of the sum-

mer that he spent at Bougival, and the period of that visit to Russia which he supposed himself to make every year. I say "supposed himself," because it was impossible to see much of him without discovering that he was a man of delays. As on the part of some other Russians whom I have known, there was something Asiatic in his faculty of procrastination. But even if one suffered from it a little one thought of it with kindness, as a part of his general mildness and want of rigidity. He went to Russia, at any rate, at intervals not infrequent, and he spoke of these visits as his best time for production. He had an estate far in the interior, and here, amid the stillness of the country and the scenes and figures which give such a charm to the *Memoirs of a Sportsman*, he drove his pen without interruption.

It is not out of place to allude to the fact that he possessed considerable fortune; this is too important in the life of a man of letters. It had been of great value to Turgénieff, and I think that much of the fine quality of his work is owing to it. He could write according to his taste and his mood; he was never pressed nor checked (putting the Russian censorship aside) by considerations foreign to his plan, and never was in danger of becoming a hack. Indeed, taking into consideration the absence of a pecuniary spur and that complicated indolence from which he was not exempt, his industry is surprising, for his tales are a long list. In Paris, at all events, he was always open to proposals for the midday breakfast. He liked to breakfast *au cabaret*, and freely consented to an appointment. It is not unkind to add that, at first, he never kept it. I may mention without reserve this idiosyncrasy of Turgénieff's, because in the first place it was so inveterate as to be very amusing—it amused not only his friends but himself; and in the second, he was as sure to come in the end as he was sure not to come in the beginning. After the appointment had been made or the invitation accepted, when the occasion was at hand, there arrived a note or a telegram in which Ivan Serguéitch excused himself, and begged that the meeting might be deferred to another date, which he usually himself proposed. For this second date still another was sometimes substituted; but if I remember no appointment that he exactly kept, I remember none that he completely missed. His friends waited for him frequently, but they never lost him. He was very fond of that wonderful Parisian *déjeûner*—fond of it I mean as a feast of reason. He was extremely temperate, and often ate no breakfast at all; but he found it a good hour for talk, and little, on general grounds, as one might be prepared to agree with him, if he was at the table one was speedily convinced. I call it wonderful, the *déjeûner* of Paris, on account of the assurance with which it plants itself in the very middle of the morning. It divides the day between rising and dinner so unequally, and opposes such barriers of repletion to any prospect of ulterior labours, that the unacclimated stranger wonders when the fertile French people do their work. Not the least wonderful part of it is that the stranger himself likes it, at last, and manages to piece together his day with the shattered fragments that survive. It was not, at any rate, when one had the good fortune to breakfast at twelve o'clock with Turgénieff that one was struck with its being an inconvenient hour. Any hour was convenient for meeting a human being who conformed so completely to one's idea of the best that human nature is capable of. There are places in Paris which I can think of only in relation to some occasion on which he was present, and when I pass them the particular things I heard him say there come back to me. There is a café in the Avenue de l'Opéra—a new, sumptuous establishment, with very deep settees, on the right as you leave the Boulevard—where I once had a talk with him, over an order singularly moderate, which was prolonged far into the afternoon, and in the course of which he was extraordinarily suggestive and interesting, so that my memory now reverts affectionately to all the circumstances. It evokes the grey damp of a Parisian December, which made the dark interior of the café look more and more rich and hospitable, while the light faded, the lamps were lit, the habitués came in to drink absinthe and play their afternoon game of dominoes, and we still lingered over our morning meal. Turgénieff talked almost exclusively about Russia, the nihilists, the remarkable figures that came to light among them, the curious visits he received, the dark prospects of his native land. When he was in the vein, no man could speak more to the imagination of his auditor. For myself, at least, at such times, there was something extraordinarily vivifying and stimulating in his talk, and I always left him in a state of "intimate" excitement, with a feeling that all sorts of valuable things had been suggested to me; the condition in which a man swings his cane as he walks, leaps lightly over gutters, and then stops, for no reason at all, to look, with an air of being struck, into a shop window where he sees nothing. I remember another symposium, at a restaurant on one of the corners of the little *place* in front of the Opéra Comique, where we were four, including Ivan Serguéitch, and the two other guests were also Russian, one of them uniting to the charm of this nationality the merit of a sex that makes the combination irresistible. The establishment had been a discovery of Turgénieff's—a discovery, at least, as far as our particular needs were concerned—and I remember that we hardly congratulated him on it. The dinner, in a low entresol, was not what it had been intended to be, but the talk was better even than our expectations. It was not about nihilism but about some more agreeable features of life, and I have no recollection of Turgénieff in a mood more spontaneous and charming. One of our friends had, when he spoke French, a peculiar way of sounding the word *adorable*, which was frequently on his lips, and I remember well his expressive prolongation of the *a* when, in speaking of the occasion afterwards, he applied this term to Ivan Serguéitch. I scarcely know, however, why I should drop into the detail of such reminiscences, and my excuse is but the desire that we all have, when a human relationship is closed, to save a little of it from the past—to make a mark which may stand for some of the happy moments of it.

Nothing that Turgénieff had to say could be more interesting than his talk about his own work, his manner of writing. What I have heard him tell of these things was worthy of the beautiful results he produced; of the deep purpose, pervading them all, to show us life itself. The germ of a story, with him, was never an affair of plot—that was the last thing he thought of: it was the representation of certain persons. The first form in which a tale appeared to him was as the figure of an individual, or a combination of individuals, whom he wished to see in action, being sure that such people must do something very special and interesting. They stood before him definite, vivid, and he wished to know, and to show, as much as possible of their nature. The first thing was to make clear to himself what he did know, to begin with; and to this end, he wrote out a sort of biography of each of his characters, and everything that they had done and that had happened to them up to the opening of the story. He had their *dossier*, as the French say, and as the police has of that of every conspicuous criminal. With this material in his hand he was able to proceed; the story all lay in the question, What shall I make them do? He always made them do things that showed them completely; but, as he said, the defect of his manner and the reproach that was made him was his want of "architecture"—in other words, of composition. The great thing, of course, is to have architecture as well as precious material, as Walter Scott had them, as Balzac had them. If one reads Turgénieff's stories with the knowledge that they were composed—or rather that they came into being—in this way, one can trace the process in every line. Story, in the conventional sense of the word—a fable constructed, like Wordsworth's phantom, "to startle and waylay"—there is as little as possible. The thing consists of the motions of a group of selected creatures, which are not the result of a preconceived action, but a consequence of the qualities of the actors. Works of art are produced from every possible point of view, and stories, and very good ones, will continue to be written in which the evolution is that of a dance—a series of steps the more complicated and lively the better, of course, determined from without and forming a figure. This figure will always, probably, find favour with many readers, because it reminds them enough, without reminding them too much, of life. On this opposition many young talents in France are ready to rend each other, for there is a numerous school on either side. We have not yet in England and America arrived at the point of treating such questions with passion, for we have not yet arrived at the point of feeling them intensely, or indeed, for that matter, of understanding them very well. It is not open to us as yet to discuss whether a novel had better be an excision from life or a structure built up of picture-cards, for we have not made up our mind as to whether life in general may be described. There is evidence of a good deal of shyness on this point—a tendency rather to put up fences than to jump over them. Among us, therefore, even a certain ridicule attaches to the consideration of such alternatives. But individuals may feel their way, and perhaps even pass unchallenged, if they remark that for them the manner in which Turgénieff worked will always seem the most fruitful. It has the immense recommendation that in relation to any human occurrence it begins, as it were, further back. It lies in its power to tell us the most about men and women. Of course it will but slenderly satisfy those numerous readers among whom the answer to this would be, "Hang it, we don't care a straw about men and women: we want a good story!"

And yet, after all, *Elena* is a good story, and *Lisa* and *Virgin Soil* are good stories. Reading over lately several of Turgénieff's novels and tales, I was struck afresh with their combination of beauty and reality. One must never forget, in speaking of him, that he was both an observer and a poet. The poetic element was constant, and it had great strangeness and power. It inspired most of the short things that he wrote during the last few years of his life, since the publication of *Virgin Soil*, things that are in the highest degree fanciful and exotic. It pervades the frequent little reveries, visions, epigrams of the *Senilia*. It was no part of my intention, here, to criticise his writings, having said my say about them, so far as possible, some years ago. But I may mention that in re-reading them I find in them all that I formerly found of two other elements—their richness and their sadness. They give one the impression of life itself, and not of an arrangement, a réchauffé of life. I remember Turgénieff's once saying in regard to Homais, the little Norman country apothecary, with his pedantry of "enlightened opinions," in *Madame Bovary*, that the great strength of such a portrait consisted in its being at once an individual, of the most concrete sort, and a type. This is the great strength of his own representations of character; they are so strangely, fascinatingly particular, and yet they are so recognisably general. Such a remark as that about Homais makes me wonder why it was that Turgénieff should have rated Dickens so high, the weakness of Dickens being in regard to just that point. If Dickens fail to live long, it will be because his figures are particular without being general;

because they are individuals without being types; because we do not feel their continuity with the rest of humanity—see the matching of the pattern with the piece out of which all the creations of the novelist and the dramatist are cut. I often meant, but accidentally neglected, to put Turgénieff on the subject of Dickens again, and ask him to explain his opinion. I suspect that his opinion was in a large measure merely that Dickens diverted him, as well he might. That complexity of the pattern was in itself fascinating. I have mentioned Flaubert, and I will return to him simply to say that there was something very touching in the nature of the friendship that united these two men. It is much to the honour of Flaubert, to my sense, that he appreciated Ivan Turgénieff. There was a partial similarity between them. Both were large, massive men, though the Russian reached to a greater height than the Norman; both were completely honest and sincere, and both had the pessimistic element in their composition. Each had a tender regard for the other, and I think that I am neither incorrect nor indiscreet in saying that on Turgénieff's part this regard had in it a strain of compassion. There was something in Gustave Flaubert that appealed to such a feeling. He had failed, on the whole, more than he had succeeded, and the great machinery of erudition,—the great polishing process,—which he brought to bear upon his productions, was not accompanied with proportionate results. He had talent without having cleverness, and imagination without having fancy. His effort was heroic, but except in the case of *Madame Bovary*, a masterpiece, he imparted something to his works (it was as if he had covered them with metallic plates) which made them sink rather than sail. He had a passion for perfection of form and for a certain splendid suggestiveness of style. He wished to produce perfect phrases, perfectly interrelated, and as closely woven together as a suit of chain-mail. He looked at life altogether as an artist, and took his work with a seriousness that never belied itself. To write an admirable page—and his idea of what constituted an admirable page was transcendent—seemed to him something to live for. He tried it again and again, and he came very near it; more than once he touched it, for *Madame Bovary* surely will live. But there was something ungenerous in his genius. He was cold, and he would have given everything he had to be able to glow. There is nothing in his novels like the passion of Elena for Inssaroff, like the purity of Lisa, like the anguish of the parents of Bazaroff, like the hidden wound of Tatiana; and yet Flaubert yearned, with all the accumulations of his vocabulary, to touch the chord of pathos. There were some parts of his mind that did not "give," that did not render a sound. He had had too much of some sorts of experience and not enough of others. And yet this failure of an organ, as I may call it, inspired those who knew him with a kindness. If Flaubert was powerful and limited, there is something human, after all, and even rather august in a strong man who has not been able completely to express himself.

After the first year of my acquaintance with Turgénieff I saw him much less often. I was seldom in Paris, and sometimes when I was there he was absent. But I neglected no opportunity of seeing him, and fortune frequently assisted me. He came two or three times to London, for visits provokingly brief. He went to shoot in Cambridgeshire, and he passed through town in arriving and departing. He liked the English, but I am not sure that he liked London, where he had passed a lugubrious winter in 1870–71. I remember some of his impressions of that period, especially a visit that he had paid to a "bishopess" surrounded by her daughters, and a description of the cookery at the lodgings which he occupied. After 1876 I frequently saw him as an invalid. He was tormented by gout, and sometimes terribly besieged; but his account of what he suffered was as charming—I can apply no other word to it—as his description of everything else. He had so the habit of observation, that he perceived in excruciating sensations all sorts of curious images and analogies, and analysed them to an extraordinary fineness. Several times I found him at Bougival, above the Seine, in a very spacious and handsome chalet—a little unsunned, it is true—which he had built alongside of the villa occupied by the family to which, for years, his life had been devoted. The place is delightful; the two houses are midway up a long slope, which descends, with the softest inclination, to the river, and behind them the hill rises to a wooded crest. On the left, in the distance, high up and above an horizon of woods, stretches the romantic aqueduct of Marly. It is a very pretty domain. The last time I saw him, in November 1882, it was at Bougival. He had been very ill, with strange, intolerable symptoms, but he was better, and he had good hopes. They were not justified by the event. He got worse again, and the months that followed were cruel. His beautiful serene mind should not have been darkened and made acquainted with violence; it should have been able to the last to take part, as it had always done, in the decrees and mysteries of fate. At the moment I saw him, however, he was, as they say in London, in very good form, and my last impression of him was almost bright. He was to drive into Paris, not being able to bear the railway, and he gave me a seat in the carriage. For an hour and a half he constantly talked, and never better. When we got into the city I alighted on the boulevard extérieur, as we were to go in different directions. I bade him good-bye at the carriage window, and never saw him again. There was a kind of fair going on, near by, in the chill November air, beneath the denuded little trees of the Boulevard, and a Punch and Judy show, from which nasal sounds proceeded. I almost regret having accidentally to mix up so much of Paris with this perhaps too complacent enumeration of occasions, for the effect of it may be to suggest that Ivan Turgénieff had been Gallicised. But this was not the case; the French capital was an accident for him, not a necessity. It touched him at many points, but it let him alone at many others, and he had, with that great tradition of ventilation of the Russian mind, windows open into distances which stretched far beyond the *banlieue*. I have spoken of him from the limited point of view of my own acquaintance with him, and unfortunately left myself little space to allude to a matter which filled his existence a good deal more than the consideration of how a story should be written—his hopes and fears on behalf of his native land. He wrote fictions and dramas, but the great drama of his life was the struggle for a better state of things in Russia. In this drama he played a distinguished part, and the splendid obsequies that, simple and modest as he was, have unfolded themselves over his grave, sufficiently attest the recognition of it by his countrymen. His funeral, restricted and officialised, was none the less a magnificent "manifestation." I have read the accounts of it, however, with a kind of chill, a feeling in which assent to the honours paid him bore less part than it ought. All this pomp and ceremony seemed to lift him out of the range of familiar recollection, of valued reciprocity, into the majestic position of a national glory. And yet it is in the presence of this obstacle to social contact that those who knew and loved him must address their farewell to him now. After all, it is difficult to see how the obstacle can be removed. He was the most generous, the most tender, the most delightful, of men; his large nature overflowed with the love of justice: but he also was of the stuff of which glories are made.

Atlantic Monthly, January 1884
Reprinted in *Partial Portraits*, 1888

IVAN TURGENEFF (1818–1883)

THERE IS PERHAPS no novelist of alien race who more naturally than Ivan Turgeneff inherits a niche in a Library for English readers; and this not because of any advance or concession that in his peculiar artistic independence he ever made, or could dream of making, such readers, but because it was one of the effects of his peculiar genius to give him, even in his lifetime, a special place in the regard of foreign publics. His position is in this respect singular; for it is his Russian savor that as much as anything has helped generally to domesticate him.

Born in 1818, at Orel in the heart of Russia, and dying in 1883, at Bougival near Paris, he had spent in Germany and France the latter half of his life; and had incurred in his own country in some degree the reprobation that is apt to attach to the absent,—the penalty they pay for such extension or such beguilement as they may have happened to find over the border. He belonged to the class of large rural proprietors of land and of serfs; and with his ample patrimony, offered one of the few examples of literary labor achieved in high independence of the question of gain,—a character that he shares with his illustrious contemporary Tolstoy, who is of a type in other respects so different. It may give us an idea of his primary situation to imagine some large Virginian or Carolinian slaveholder, during the first half of the century, inclining to "Northern" views; and becoming (though not predominantly under pressure of these, but rather by the operation of an exquisite genius) the great American novelist—one of the great novelists of the world. Born under a social and political order sternly repressive, all Turgeneff's deep instincts, all his moral passion, placed him on the liberal side; with the consequence that early in life, after a period spent at a German university, he found himself, through the accident of a trifling public utterance, under such suspicion in high places as to be sentenced to a term of tempered exile,—confinement to his own estate. It was partly under these circumstances perhaps that he gathered material for the work from the appearance of which his reputation dates,—'A Sportsman's Sketches,' published in two volumes in 1852. This admirable collection of impressions of homely country life, as the old state of servitude had made it, is often spoken of as having borne to the great decree of Alexander II. the relation borne by Mrs. Beecher Stowe's famous novel to the emancipation of the Southern slaves. Incontestably, at any rate, Turgeneff's rustic studies sounded, like 'Uncle Tom's Cabin,' a particular hour: with the difference, however, of not having at the time produced an agitation,—of having rather presented the case with an art too insidious for instant recognition, an art that stirred the depths more than the surface.

The author was designated promptly enough, at any rate, for such influence as might best be exercised at a distance: he traveled, he lived abroad; early in the sixties he was settled in Germany; he acquired property at Baden-Baden, and spent there the last years of the prosperous period—in the history of the place—of which the Franco-Prussian War was to mark the violent term. He cast in his lot after that event mainly with the victims of the lost cause; setting up a fresh home in Paris,—near which city he had, on the Seine, a charming alternate residence,—and passing in it, and in the country, save for brief revisitations, the remainder of his days. His friendships, his attachments, in the world of art and of letters, were numerous and distinguished; he never married; he produced, as the years went on, without precipitation or frequency; and these were the years during which his reputation gradually established itself as, according to the phrase, European,—a phrase denoting in this case, perhaps, a public more alert in the United States even than elsewhere.

Tolstoy, his junior by ten years, had meanwhile come to fruition; though, as in fact happened, it was not till after Turgeneff's death that the greater fame of 'War and Peace' and of 'Anna Karénina' began to be blown about the world. One of the last acts of the elder writer, performed on his death-bed, was to address to the other (from whom for a considerable term he had been estranged by circumstances needless to reproduce) an appeal to return to the exercise of the genius that Tolstoy had already so lamentably, so monstrously forsworn. "I am on my death-bed; there is no possibility of my recovery. I write you expressly to tell you how happy I have been to be your contemporary, and to utter my last, my urgent prayer. Come back, my friend, to your literary labors. That gift came to you from the source from which all comes to us. Ah, how happy I should be could I think you would listen to my entreaty! My friend, great writer of our Russian land, respond to it, obey it!" These words, among the most touching surely ever addressed by one great spirit to another, throw an indirect light—perhaps I may even say a direct one—upon the nature and quality of Turgeneff's artistic temperament; so much so that I regret being without opportunity, in this place, to gather such aid for a portrait of him as might be supplied by following out the unlikeness between the pair. It would be too easy to say that Tolstoy was, from the Russian point of view, for home consumption, and Turgeneff for foreign: 'War and Peace' has probably had more readers in Europe and America than 'A House of Gentlefolk' or 'On the Eve' or 'Smoke,'—a circumstance less detrimental than it may appear to my claim of our having, in the Western world, supremely adopted the author of the latter works. Turgeneff is in a peculiar degree what I may call the novelists' novelist,—an artistic influence extraordinarily valuable and ineradicably established. The perusal of Tolstoy—a wonderful mass of life—is an immense event, a kind of splendid accident, for each of us: his name represents nevertheless no such eternal spell of method, no such quiet irresistibility of presentation, as shines, close to us and lighting our possible steps, in that of his precursor. Tolstoy is a reflector as vast as a natural lake; a monster harnessed to his great subject—all human life!—as an elephant might be harnessed, for purposes of traction, not to a carriage, but to a coach-house. His own case is prodigious, but his example for others dire: disciples not elephantine he can only mislead and betray.

One by one, for thirty years, with a firm, deliberate hand, with intervals and patiences and waits, Turgeneff pricked in his sharp outlines. His great external mark is probably his concision: an ideal he never threw over,—it shines most perhaps even when he is least brief,—and that he often applied with a rare felicity. He has masterpieces of a few pages; his perfect things are sometimes his least prolonged. He abounds in short tales, episodes clipped as by the scissors of Atropos; but for a direct translation of the whole we have still to wait,—depending meanwhile upon the French and German versions, which have been, instead of the original text (thanks to the paucity among us of readers of Russian), the source of several published in English. For the novels and 'A Sportsman's Sketches' we depend upon the nine volumes (1897) of Mrs. Garnett. We touch here upon the remarkable side, to our vision, of the writer's fortune,—the anomaly of his having constrained to intimacy even those who are shut out from the enjoyment of his medium, for whom that question is positively prevented from existing. Putting aside extrinsic intimations, it is impossible to read him without the conviction of his being, in the vividness of his own tongue, of the strong type of those made to bring home to us the happy truth of the unity, in a generous talent, of material and form,—of their being inevitable faces of the same medal; the type of those, in a word, whose example deals death to the perpetual clumsy assumption that subject and style are—æsthetically speaking, or in the living work—different and separable things. We are conscious, reading him in a language not his own, of not being reached by his personal tone, his individual accent.

It is a testimony therefore to the intensity of his presence, that so much of his particular charm does reach us; that the mask turned to us has, even without his expression, still so much beauty. It is the beauty (since we must try to formulate) of the finest presentation of the familiar. His vision is of the world of character and feeling, the world of the relations life throws up at every hour and on every spot; he deals little, on the whole, in the miracles of chance,—the hours and spots over the edge of time and space; his air is that of the great central region of passion and motive, of the usual, the inevitable, the intimate—the intimate for weal or woe. No theme that he ever chooses but strikes us as full; yet with all have we the sense that their animation comes from within, and is not pinned to their backs like the pricking objects used of old in the horse-races of the Roman carnival, to make the animals run. Without a patch of "plot" to draw blood, the story he mainly tells us, the situation he mainly gives, runs as if for dear life. His first book was practically full evidence of what, if we have to specify, is finest in him,—the effect, for the commonest truth, of an exquisite envelope of poetry. In this medium of feeling,—full, as it were, of all the echoes and shocks of the universal danger and need,—everything in him goes on; the sense of fate and folly and pity and wonder and beauty. The tenderness, the humor, the variety of 'A Sportsman's Sketches' revealed on the spot an observer with a rare imagination. These faculties had attached themselves, together, to small things and to great: to the misery, the simplicity, the piety, the patience, of the unemancipated peasant; to all the natural wonderful life of earth and air and winter and summer and field and forest; to queer apparitions of country neighbors, of strange local eccentrics; to old-world practices and superstitions; to secrets gathered and types disinterred and impressions absorbed in the long, close contacts with man and nature involved in the passionate pursuit of game. Magnificent in stature and original vigor, Turgeneff, with his love of the chase, or rather perhaps of the inspiration he found in it, would have been the model of the mighty hunter, had not such an image been a little at variance with his natural mildness, the softness that often accompanies the sense of an extraordinary reach of limb and play of muscle. He was in person the model rather of the strong man at rest: massive and towering, with the voice of innocence and the smile almost of childhood. What seemed still more of a contradiction to so much of him, however, was that his work was all delicacy and fancy, penetration and compression.

If I add, in their order of succession, 'Rudin,' 'Fathers and Children,' 'Spring Floods,' and 'Virgin Soil,' to the three novels I have (also in their relation of time) named above, I shall have indicated the larger blocks of the compact monument, with a base resting deep and interstices well filled, into which that work disposes itself. The list of his minor productions is too long to draw out: I can only mention, as a few of the most striking—'A Correspondence,' 'The Wayside Inn,' 'The Brigadier,' 'The Dog,' 'The Jew,' 'Visions,' 'Mumu,' 'Three Meetings,' 'A First Love,' 'The Forsaken,' 'Assia,' 'The Journal of a Superfluous Man,' 'The Story of Lieutenant Yergunov,' 'A King Lear of the Steppe.' The first place among his novels would be difficult to assign: general opinion probably hesitates between 'A House of Gentlefolk' and 'Fathers and Children.' My own predilection is great for the exquisite 'On the Eve'; though I admit that in such a company it draws no supremacy from being exquisite. What is less contestable is that 'Virgin Soil'—published shortly before his death, and the longest of his fictions—has, although full of beauty, a minor perfection.

Character, character expressed and exposed, is in all these things what we inveterately find. Turgeneff's sense of it was the great light that artistically guided him; the simplest account of him is to say that the mere play of it constitutes in every case his sufficient drama. No one has had a closer vision, or a hand at once more ironic and more tender, for the individual figure. He sees it with its minutest signs and tricks,—all its heredity of idiosyncrasies, all its particulars of weakness and strength, of ugliness and beauty, of oddity and charm; and yet it is of his essence that he sees it in the general flood of life, steeped in its relations and contacts, struggling or submerged, a hurried particle in the stream. This gives him, with his quiet method, his extraordinary breadth; dissociates his rare power to particularize from dryness or hardness, from any peril of caricature. He understands so much that we almost wonder he can express anything; and his expression is indeed wholly in absolute projection, in illustration, in giving of everything the unexplained and irresponsible specimen. He is of a spirit so human that we almost wonder at his control of his matter; of a pity so deep and so general that we almost wonder at his curiosity. The element of poetry in him is constant, and yet reality stares through it without the loss of a wrinkle. No one has more of that sign of the born novelist which resides in a respect unconditioned for the freedom and vitality, the absoluteness when summoned, of the creatures he invokes; or is more superior to the strange and second-rate policy of explaining or presenting them by reprobation or apology,—of taking the short cuts and anticipating the emotions and judgments about them that should be left, at the best, to the perhaps not most intelligent reader. And yet his system, as it may summarily be called, of the mere particularized report, has a lucidity beyond the virtue of the cruder moralist.

If character, as I say, is what he gives us at every turn, I should speedily add that he offers it not in the least as a synonym, in our Western sense, of resolution and prosperity. It wears the form of the almost helpless detachment of the short-sighted individual soul; and the perfection of his exhibition of it is in truth too often but the intensity of what, for success, it just does not produce. What works in him most is the question of the will; and the most constant induction he suggests, bears upon the sad figure that principle seems mainly to make among his countrymen. He had seen—he suggests to us—its collapse in a thousand quarters; and the most general tragedy, to his view, is that of its desperate adventures and disasters, its inevitable abdication and defeat. But if the men, for the most part, let it go, it takes refuge in the other sex; many of the representatives of which, in his pages, are supremely strong—in wonderful addition, in various cases, to being otherwise admirable. This is true of such a number—the younger women, the girls, the "heroines" in especial—that they form in themselves, on the ground of moral beauty, of the finest distinction of soul, one of the most striking groups the modern novel has given us. They are heroines to the letter, and of a heroism obscure and undecorated: it is almost they alone who have the energy to determine and to act. Elena, Lisa, Tatyana, Gemma, Marianna—we can write their names and call up their images, but I lack space to take them in turn. It is by a succession of the finest and tenderest touches that they live; and this, in all Turgeneff's work, is the process by which he persuades and succeeds.

It was his own view of his main danger that he sacrificed too much to detail; was wanting in composition, in the gift that conduces to unity of impression. But no novelist is closer and more cumulative; in none does distinction spring from a quality of truth more independent of everything but the subject, but the idea itself. This idea, this subject, moreover,—a spark kindled by the innermost friction of things,—is always as interesting as an unopened telegram. The genial freedom— with its exquisite delicacy—of his approach to this "innermost" world, the world of our finer consciousness, has in short a side that I can only describe and commemorate as nobly disinterested; a side that makes too many of his rivals appear to hold us in comparison by violent means, and introduce us in comparison to vulgar things.

Library of the World's Best Literature, ed. Charles Dudley Warner. New York: R. S. Peale and J. A. Hill, 1896

PREFACES
TO THE
NEW YORK EDITION

Contents

Roderick Hudson

R ODERICK HUDSON" was begun in Florence in the spring
of 1874, designed from the first for serial publication in
"The Atlantic Monthly," where it opened in January 1875 and
persisted through the year. I yield to the pleasure of placing
these circumstances on record, as I shall place others, and as
I have yielded to the need of renewing acquaintance with the
book after a quarter of a century. This revival of an all but
extinct relation with an early work may often produce for an
artist, I think, more kinds of interest and emotion than he
shall find it easy to express, and yet will light not a little, to
his eyes, that veiled face of his Muse which he is condemned
for ever and all anxiously to study. The art of representation
bristles with questions the very terms of which are difficult to
apply and to appreciate; but whatever makes it arduous makes
it, for our refreshment, infinite, causes the practice of it, with
experience, to spread around us in a widening, not in a narrowing circle. Therefore it is that experience has to organise,
for convenience and cheer, some system of observation—for
fear, in the admirable immensity, of losing its way. We see it
as pausing from time to time to consult its notes, to measure,
for guidance, as many aspects and distances as possible, as
many steps taken and obstacles mastered and fruits gathered
and beauties enjoyed. Everything counts, nothing is superfluous in such a survey; the explorer's note-book strikes me here
as endlessly receptive. This accordingly is what I mean by the
contributive value—or put it simply as, to one's own sense,
the beguiling charm—of the *accessory* facts in a given artistic
case. This is why, as one looks back, the private history of any
sincere work, however modest its pretensions, looms with its
own completeness in the rich, ambiguous æsthetic air, and
seems at once to borrow a dignity and to mark, so to say, a
station. This is why, reading over, for revision, correction and
republication, the volumes here in hand, I find myself, all attentively, in presence of some such recording scroll or engraved commemorative table—from which the "private"
character, moreover, quite insists on dropping out. These
notes represent, over a considerable course, the continuity of

an artist's endeavour, the growth of his whole operative consciousness and, best of all, perhaps, their own tendency to
multiply, with the implication, thereby, of a memory much
enriched. Addicted to "stories" and inclined to retrospect, he
fondly takes, under this backward view, his whole unfolding,
his process of production, for a thrilling tale, almost for a
wondrous adventure, only asking himself at what stage of
remembrance the mark of the relevant will begin to fail.
He frankly proposes to take this mark everywhere for
granted.

"Roderick Hudson" was my first attempt at a novel, a long
fiction with a "complicated" subject, and I recall again the
quite uplifted sense with which my idea, such as it was, permitted me at last to put quite out to sea. I had but hugged
the shore on sundry previous small occasions; bumping
about, to acquire skill, in the shallow waters and sandy coves
of the "short story" and master as yet of no vessel constructed
to carry a sail. The subject of "Roderick" figured to me vividly this employment of canvas, and I have not forgotten,
even after long years, how the blue southern sea seemed to
spread immediately before me and the breath of the spice-
islands to be already in the breeze. Yet it must even then have
begun for me too, the ache of fear, that was to become so
familiar, of being unduly tempted and led on by "developments"; which is but the desperate discipline of the question
involved in them. They are of the very essence of the novelist's process, and it is by their aid, fundamentally, that his
idea takes form and lives; but they impose on him, through
the principle of continuity that rides them, a proportionate
anxiety. They are the very condition of interest, which lan-
guishes and drops without them; the painter's subject consisting ever, obviously, of the related state, to each other, of
certain figures and things. To exhibit these relations, once
they have all been recognised, is to "treat" his idea, which
involves neglecting none of those that directly minister to interest; the degree of that directness remaining meanwhile a
matter of highly difficult appreciation, and one on which felicity of form and composition, as a part of the total effect,
mercilessly rests. Up to what point is such and such a development *indispensable* to the interest? What is the point

beyond which it ceases to be rigorously so? Where, for the complete expression of one's subject, does a particular relation stop—giving way to some other not concerned in that expression?

Really, universally, relations stop nowhere, and the exquisite problem of the artist is eternally but to draw, by a geometry of his own, the circle within which they shall happily *appear* to do so. He is in the perpetual predicament that the continuity of things is the whole matter, for him, of comedy and tragedy; that this continuity is never, by the space of an instant or an inch, broken, and that, to do anything at all, he has at once intensely to consult and intensely to ignore it. All of which will perhaps pass but for a supersubtle way of pointing the plain moral that a young embroiderer of the canvas of life soon began to work in terror, fairly, of the vast expanse of that surface, of the boundless number of its distinct perforations for the needle, and of the tendency inherent in his many-coloured flowers and figures to cover and consume as many as possible of the little holes. The development of the flower, of the figure, involved thus an immense counting of holes and a careful selection among them. That would have been, it seemed to him, a brave enough process, were it not the very nature of the holes so to invite, to solicit, to persuade, to practise positively a thousand lures and deceits. The prime effect of so sustained a system, so prepared a surface, is to lead on and on; while the fascination of following resides, by the same token, in the presumability *somewhere* of a convenient, of a visibly-appointed stopping-place. Art would be easy indeed if, by a fond power disposed to "patronise" it, such conveniences, such simplifications, had been provided. We have, as the case stands, to invent and establish them, to arrive at them by a difficult, dire process of selection and comparison, of surrender and sacrifice. The very meaning of expertness is acquired courage to brace one's self for the cruel crisis from the moment one sees it grimly loom.

"Roderick Hudson" was further, was earnestly pursued during a summer partly spent in the Black Forest and (as I had returned to America early in September) during three months passed near Boston. It is one of the silver threads of the recoverable texture of that embarrassed phase, however, that the book was not finished when it had to begin appearing in monthly fragments: a fact in the light of which I find myself live over again, and quite with wonderment and tenderness, so intimate an experience of difficulty and delay. To have "liked" so much writing it, to have worked out with such conviction the pale embroidery, and yet not, at the end of so many months, to have come through, was clearly still to have fallen short of any facility and any confidence: though the long-drawn process now most appeals to memory, I confess, by this very quality of shy and groping duration. One fact about it indeed outlives all others; the fact that, as the loved Italy was the scene of my fiction—so much more loved than one has ever been able, even after fifty efforts, to say!— and as having had to leave it persisted as an inward ache, so there was soreness in still contriving, after a fashion, to hang about it and in prolonging, from month to month, the illusion of the golden air. Little enough of that medium may the novel, read over to-day, seem to supply; yet half the actual interest lurks for me in the earnest, baffled intention of making it felt. A whole side of the old consciousness, under this mild pressure, flushes up and prevails again; a reminder, ever so penetrating, of the quantity of "evocation" involved in my plan, and of the quantity I must even have supposed myself to achieve. I take the lingering perception of all this, I may add—that is of the various admonitions of the whole reminiscence—for a signal instance of the way a work of art, however small, if but sufficiently sincere, may vivify and even dignify the accidents and incidents of its growth.

I must that winter (which I again like to put on record that I spent in New York) have brought up my last instalments in due time, for I recall no haunting anxiety: what I do recall perfectly is the felt pleasure, during those months—and in East Twenty-fifth Street!—of trying, on the other side of the world, still to surround with the appropriate local glow the characters that had combined, to my vision, the previous year in Florence. A benediction, a great advantage, as seemed to me, had so from the first rested on them, and to nurse them along was really to sit again in the high, charming, shabby old room which had originally overarched them and which, in the hot May and June, had looked out, through the slits of cooling shutters, at the rather dusty but ever-romantic glare of Piazza Santa Maria Novella. The house formed the corner (I delight to specify) of Via della Scala, and I fear that what the early chapters of the book most "render" to me to-day is not the umbrageous air of their New England town, but the view of the small cab-stand sleepily disposed—long before the days of strident electric cars—round the rococo obelisk of the Piazza, which is supported on its pedestal, if I remember rightly, by four delightful little elephants. (That, at any rate, is how the object in question, deprecating verification, comes back to me with the clatter of the horse-pails, the discussions, in the intervals of repose under well-drawn hoods, of the unbuttoned *cocchieri*, sons of the most garrulous of races, and the occasional stillness as of the noonday desert.)

Pathetic, as we say, on the other hand, no doubt, to re-perusal, the manner in which the evocation, so far as attempted, of the small New England town of my first two chapters, fails of intensity—if intensity, in such a connexion, had been indeed to be looked for. *Could* I verily, by the terms of my little plan, have "gone in" for it at the best, and even though one of these terms was the projection, for my fable, at the outset, of some more or less vivid antithesis to a state of civilisation providing for "art"? What I wanted, in essence, was the image of some perfectly humane community which was yet all incapable of providing for it, and I had to take what my scant experience furnished me. I remember feeling meanwhile no drawback in this scantness, but a complete, an exquisite little adequacy, so that the presentation arrived at would quite have served its purpose, I think, had I not misled myself into naming my place. To name a place, in fiction, is to pretend in some degree to represent it—and I speak here of course but of the use of existing names, the only ones that carry weight. I wanted one that carried weight—so at least I supposed; but obviously I was wrong, since my effect lay, so superficially, and could only lie, in the local *type*, as to which I had my handful of impressions. The particular local case was another matter, and I was to see again, after long years, the case into which, all recklessly, the opening passages of "Roderick Hudson" put their foot. I was to have nothing then, on the spot, to sustain me but the rather feeble plea that I had not *pretended* so very much to "do" Northampton Mass. The plea was charmingly allowed, but nothing could have been more to the point than the way in which, in such a situation, the whole question of the novelist's "doing," with its eternal wealth, or in other words its eternal torment of interest, once more came up. He embarks, rash adventurer, under the star of "representation," and is pledged thereby to remember that the art of interesting us in things—once these things are the right ones for his case—can *only* be the art of representing them. This relation to them, for invoked interest, involves his accordingly "doing"; and it is for him to settle with his intelligence what that variable process shall commit him to.

Its fortune rests primarily, beyond doubt, on somebody's having, under suggestion, a *sense* for it—even the reader will do, on occasion, when the writer, as so often happens, completely falls out. The way in which this sense has been, or has not been, applied constitutes, at all events, in respect to any fiction, the very ground of critical appreciation. Such appreciation takes account, primarily, of the thing, in the case, to have *been* done, and I now see what, for the first and second chapters of "Roderick," that was. It was a peaceful, rural New England community *quelconque*—it was not, it was under no necessity of being, Northampton Mass. But one nestled, technically, in those days, and with yearning, in the great shadow of Balzac; his august example, little as the secret might ever be guessed, towered for me over the scene; so that what was clearer than anything else was how, if it was a question of Saumur, of Limoges, of Guérande, he "did" Saumur, did Limoges, did Guérande. I remember how, in my feebler fashion, I yearned over the preliminary presentation of my small square patch of the American scene, and yet was not sufficiently on my guard to see how easily his high practice might be delusive for my case. Balzac talked of Nemours and Provins: therefore why should n't one, with fond fatuity, talk of almost the only small American *ville de province* of which one had happened to lay up, long before, a pleased vision? The reason was plain: one was not in the least, in one's prudence, emulating his systematic closeness. It did n't confuse the question either that he would verily, after all, addressed as he was to a due density in his material, have found little enough in

Northampton Mass to tackle. He tackled no group of appearances, no presented face of the social organism (conspicuity thus attending it), *but* to make something of it. To name it simply and not in some degree tackle it would have seemed to him an act reflecting on his general course the deepest dishonour. Therefore it was that, as the moral of these many remarks, I "named," under his contagion, when I was really most conscious of not being held to it; and therefore it was, above all, that for all the effect of representation I was to achieve, I might have let the occasion pass. A "fancy" indication would have served my turn—except that I should so have failed perhaps of a pretext for my present insistence.

Since I do insist, at all events, I find this ghostly interest perhaps even more reasserted for me by the questions begotten within the very covers of the book, those that wander and idle there as in some sweet old overtangled walled garden, a safe paradise of self-criticism. Here it is that if there be air for it to breathe at all, the critical question swarms, and here it is, in particular, that one of the happy hours of the painter's long day may strike. I speak of the painter in general and of his relation to the old picture, the work of his hand, that has been lost to sight and that, when found again, is put back on the easel for measure of what time and the weather may, in the interval, have done to it. Has it too fatally faded, has it blackened or "sunk," or otherwise abdicated, or has it only, blest thought, strengthened, for its allotted duration, and taken up, in its degree, poor dear brave thing, some shade of the all appreciable, yet all indescribable grace that we know as pictorial "tone"? The anxious artist has to wipe it over, in the first place, to see; he has to "clean it up," say, or to varnish it anew, or at the least to place it in a light, for any right judgement of its aspect or its worth. But the very uncertainties themselves yield a thrill, and if subject and treatment, working together, have had their felicity, the artist, the prime creator, may find a strange charm in this stage of the connexion. It helps him to live back into a forgotten state, into convictions, credulities too early spent perhaps, it breathes upon the dead reasons of things, buried as they are in the texture of the work, and makes them revive, so that the actual appearances and the old motives fall together once more, and a lesson and a moral and a consecrating final light are somehow disengaged.

All this, I mean of course, if the case will wonderfully take any such pressure, if the work does n't break down under even such mild overhauling. The author knows well enough how easily that may happen—which he in fact frequently enough sees it do. The old reasons then are too dead to revive; they were not, it is plain, good enough reasons to live. The only possible relation of the present mind to the thing is to dismiss it altogether. On the other hand, when it is not dismissed—as the only detachment is the detachment of aversion—the creative intimacy is reaffirmed, and appreciation, critical apprehension, insists on becoming as active as it can. Who shall say, granted this, where it shall not begin and where it shall consent to end? The painter who passes over his old sunk canvas the wet sponge that shows him what may still come out again makes his criticism essentially active. When having seen, while his momentary glaze remains, that the canvas *has* kept a few buried secrets, he proceeds to repeat the process with due care and with a bottle of varnish and a brush, he is "living back," as I say, to the top of his bent, is taking up the old relation, so workable apparently, yet, and there is nothing logically to stay him from following it all the way. I have felt myself then, on looking over past productions, the painter making use again and again of the tentative wet sponge. The sunk surface has here and there, beyond doubt, refused to respond: the buried secrets, the intentions, are buried too deep to rise again, and were indeed, it would appear, not much worth the burying. Not so, however, when the moistened canvas does obscurely flush and when resort to the varnish-bottle is thereby immediately indicated. The simplest figure for my revision of this present array of earlier, later, larger, smaller, canvases, is to say that I have achieved it by the very aid of the varnish-bottle. It is true of them throughout that, in words I have had occasion to use in another connexion (where too I had revised with a view to "possible amendment of form and enhancement of meaning"), I have "nowhere scrupled to re-write a sentence or a passage on judging it susceptible of a better turn."

To re-read "Roderick Hudson" was to find one remark so

promptly and so urgently prescribed that I could at once only take it as pointing almost too stern a moral. It stared me in the face that the time-scheme of the story is quite inadequate, and positively to that degree that the fault but just fails to wreck it. The thing escapes, I conceive, with its life: the effect sought is fortunately more achieved than missed, since the interest of the subject bears down, auspiciously dissimulates, this particular flaw in the treatment. Everything occurs, none the less, too punctually and moves too fast: Roderick's disintegration, a gradual process, and of which the exhibitional interest is exactly that it *is* gradual and occasional, and thereby traceable and watchable, swallows two years in a mouthful, proceeds quite *not* by years, but by weeks and months, and thus renders the whole view the disservice of appearing to present him as a morbidly special case. The very claim of the fable is naturally that he *is* special, that his great gift makes and keeps him highly exceptional; but that is not for a moment supposed to preclude his appearing typical (of the general type) as well; for the fictive hero successfully appeals to us only as an eminent instance, as eminent as we like, of our own conscious kind. My mistake on Roderick's behalf—and not in the least of conception, but of composition and expression—is that, at the rate at which he falls to pieces, he seems to place himself beyond our understanding and our sympathy. These are not our rates, we say; we ourselves certainly, under like pressure,—for what is it after all?—would make more of a fight. We conceive going to pieces—nothing is easier, since we see people do it, one way or another, all round us; but this young man must either have had less of the principle of development to have had so much of the principle of collapse, or less of the principle of collapse to have had so much of the principle of development. "On the basis of so great a weakness," one hears the reader say, "where was your idea of the interest? On the basis of so great an interest, where is the provision for so much weakness?" One feels indeed, in the light of this challenge, on how much too scantly projected and suggested a field poor Roderick and his large capacity for ruin are made to turn round. It has all begun too soon, as I say, and too simply, and the determinant function attributed to Christina Light, the character of well-nigh sole agent of his catastrophe that this unfortunate young woman has forced upon her, fails to commend itself to our sense of truth and proportion.

It was not, however, that I was at ease on this score even in the first fond good faith of composition; I felt too, all the while, how many more ups and downs, how many more adventures and complications my young man would have had to know, how much more experience it would have taken, in short, either to make him go under or to make him triumph. The greater complexity, the superior truth, was all more or less present to me; only the question was, too dreadfully, how make it present to the reader? How boil down so many facts in the alembic, so that the distilled result, the produced appearance, should have intensity, lucidity, brevity, beauty, all the merits required for my effect? How, when it was already so difficult, as I found, to proceed even as I *was* proceeding? It did n't help, alas, it only maddened, to remember that Balzac would have known how, and would have yet asked no additional credit for it. All the difficulty I could dodge still struck me, at any rate, as leaving more than enough; and yet I was already consciously in presence, here, of the most interesting question the artist has to consider. To give the image and the sense of certain things while still keeping them subordinate to his plan, keeping them in relation to matters more immediate and apparent, to give all the sense, in a word, without all the substance or all the surface, and so to summarise and foreshorten, so to make values both rich and sharp, that the mere procession of items and profiles is not only, for the occasion, superseded, but is, for essential quality, almost "compromised"—such a case of delicacy proposes itself at every turn to the painter of life who wishes both to treat his chosen subject and to confine his necessary picture. It is only by doing such things that art becomes exquisite, and it is only by positively becoming exquisite that it keeps clear of becoming vulgar, repudiates the coarse industries that masquerade in its name. This eternal time-question is accordingly, for the novelist, always there and always formidable; always insisting on the *effect* of the great lapse and passage, of the "dark backward and abysm," by the terms of truth, and on the effect of compression, of composition and form, by the terms of literary arrangement. It is really a business to terrify all but stout hearts into abject omission and mutilation, though the terror would indeed be more general were the general consciousness of the difficulty greater. It is not by consciousness of difficulty, in truth, that the story-teller is mostly ridden; so prodigious a number of stories would otherwise scarce get themselves (shall it be called?) "told." None was ever very well told, I think, under the law of mere elimination—inordinately as that device appears in many quarters to be depended on. I remember doing my best not to be reduced to it for "Roderick," at the same time that I did so helplessly and consciously beg a thousand questions. What I clung to as my principle of simplification was the precious truth that I was dealing, after all, essentially with an Action, and that no action, further, was ever made historically vivid without a certain factitious compactness; though this logic indeed opened up horizons and abysses of its own. But into these we must plunge on some other occasion.

It was at any rate under an admonition or two fished out of their depths that I must have tightened my hold of the remedy afforded, such as it was, for the absence of those more adequate illustrations of Roderick's character and history. Since one was dealing with an Action one might borrow a scrap of the Dramatist's all-in-all, his intensity—which the novelist so often ruefully envies him as a fortune in itself. The amount of illustration I could allow to the grounds of my young man's disaster was unquestionably meagre, but I might perhaps make it lively; I might produce illusion if I should be able to achieve intensity. It was for that I must have tried, I now see, with such art as I could command; but I make out in another quarter above all what really saved me. My subject, all blissfully, in face of difficulties, had defined itself—and this in spite of the title of the book—as not directly, in the least, my young sculptor's adventure. This it had been but indirectly, being all the while in essence and in final effect another man's, his friend's and patron's, view and experience of him. One's luck was to have felt one's subject right—whether instinct or calculation, in those dim days, most served; and the circumstance even amounts perhaps to a little lesson that when this has happily occurred faults may show, faults may disfigure, and yet not upset the work. It remains in equilibrium by having found its centre, the point of command of all the rest. From this centre the subject has been treated, from this centre the interest has spread, and so, whatever else it may do or may not do, the thing has acknowledged a principle of composition and contrives at least to hang together. We see in such a case why it should so hang; we escape that dreariest displeasure it is open to experiments in this general order to inflict, the sense of any hanging-together precluded as by the very terms of the case.

The centre of interest throughout "Roderick" is in Rowland Mallet's consciousness, and the drama is the very drama of that consciousness—which I had of course to make sufficiently acute in order to enable it, like a set and lighted scene, to hold the play. By making it acute, meanwhile, one made its own movement—or rather, strictly, its movement in the particular connexion—interesting; this movement really being quite the stuff of one's thesis. It had, naturally, Rowland's consciousness, not to be *too* acute—which would have disconnected it and made it superhuman: the beautiful little problem was to keep it connected, connected intimately, with the general human exposure, and thereby bedimmed and befooled and bewildered, anxious, restless, fallible, and yet to endow it with such intelligence that the appearances reflected in it, and constituting together there the situation and the "story," should become by that fact intelligible. Discernible from the first the joy of such a "job" as this making of his relation to everything involved a sufficiently limited, a sufficiently pathetic, tragic, comic, ironic, personal state to be thoroughly natural, and yet at the same time a sufficiently clear medium to represent a whole. This whole was to be the sum of what "happened" to him, or in other words his total adventure; but as what happened to him was above all to feel certain things happening to others, to Roderick, to Christina, to Mary Garland, to Mrs. Hudson, to the Cavaliere, to the Prince, so the beauty of the constructional game was to preserve in everything its especial value for *him*. The ironic effect of his having fallen in love with the girl who is herself in love with Roderick, though he is unwitting, at the time, of that secret—the conception of this last irony, I must add, has

remained happier than my execution of it; which should logically have involved the reader's being put into position to
take more closely home the impression made by Mary Garland. The ground has not been laid for it, and when that is
the case one builds all vainly in the air: one patches up one's
superstructure, one paints it in the prettiest colours, one
hangs fine old tapestry and rare brocade over its window-sills,
one flies emblazoned banners from its roof—the building
none the less totters and refuses to stand square.

It is not really *worked-in* that Roderick himself could have
pledged his faith in such a quarter, much more at such a crisis, before leaving America: and that weakness, clearly, produces a limp in the whole march of the fable. Just so, though
there was no reason on earth (unless I except one, presently
to be mentioned) why Rowland should *not*, at Northampton,
have conceived a passion, or as near an approach to one as he
was capable of, for a remarkable young woman there suddenly dawning on his sight, a particular fundamental care was
required for the vivification of that possibility. The care, unfortunately, has not been skilfully enough taken, in spite of
the later patching-up of the girl's figure. We fail to accept it,
on the actual showing, as that of a young person irresistible
at any moment, and above all irresistible at a moment of the
liveliest *other* preoccupation, as that of the weaver of (even
the highly conditioned) spell that the narrative imputes to
her. The spell of attraction is cast upon young men by young
women in all sorts of ways, and the novel has no more constant office than to remind us of that. But Mary Garland's
way does n't, indubitably, convince us; any more than we are
truly convinced, I think, that Rowland's destiny, or say his
nature, would have made him accessible at the same hour to
two quite distinct commotions, each a very deep one, of his
whole personal economy. Rigidly viewed, each of these upheavals of his sensibility must have been exclusive of other
upheavals, yet the reader is asked to accept them as working
together. They are different vibrations, but the whole sense
of the situation depicted is that they should each have been
of the strongest, too strong to walk hand in hand. Therefore
it is that when, on the ship, under the stars, Roderick suddenly takes his friend into the confidence of his engagement,

we instinctively disallow the friend's title to discomfiture. The whole picture presents him as for the time on the mounting wave, exposed highly enough, no doubt, to a hundred discomfitures, but least exposed to that one. The damage to verisimilitude is deep.

The difficulty had been from the first that I required my antithesis—my antithesis to Christina Light, one of the main terms of the subject. One is ridden by the law that antitheses, to be efficient, shall be both direct and complete. Directness seemed to fail unless Mary should be, so to speak, "plain," Christina being essentially so "coloured"; and completeness seemed to fail unless she too should have her potency. She could moreover, by which I mean the antithetic young woman could, perfectly have had it; only success would have been then in the narrator's art to attest it. Christina's own presence and action are, on the other hand, I think, all firm ground; the truth probably being that the ideal antithesis rarely does "come off," and that it has to content itself for the most part with a strong term and a weak term, and even then to feel itself lucky. If one of the terms *is* strong, that perhaps may pass, in the most difficult of the arts, for a triumph. I remember at all events feeling, toward the end of "Roderick," that the Princess Casamassima had been launched, that, wound-up with the right silver key, she would go on a certain time by the motion communicated; thanks to which I knew the pity, the real pang of losing sight of her. I desired as in no other such case I can recall to preserve, to recover the vision; and I have seemed to myself in re-reading the book quite to understand why. The multiplication of touches had produced even more life than the subject required, and that life, in other conditions, in some other prime relation, would still have somehow to be spent. Thus one would watch for her and waylay her at some turn of the road to come—all that was to be needed was to give her time. This I did in fact, meeting her again and taking her up later on.

The American

"THE AMERICAN," which I had begun in Paris early in the winter of 1875–76, made its first appearance in "The Atlantic Monthly" in June of the latter year and continued there, from month to month, till May of the next. It started on its course while much was still unwritten, and there again come back to me, with this remembrance, the frequent hauntings and alarms of that comparatively early time; the habit of wondering what would happen if anything *should* "happen," if one should break one's arm by an accident or make a long illness or suffer, in body, mind, fortune, any other visitation involving a loss of time. The habit of apprehension became of course in some degree the habit of confidence that one would pull through, that, with opportunity enough, grave interruption never yet *had* descended, and that a special Providence, in short, despite the sad warning of Thackeray's "Denis Duval" and of Mrs. Gaskell's "Wives and Daughters" (that of Stevenson's "Weir of Hermiston" was yet to come) watches over anxious novelists condemned to the economy of serialisation. I make myself out in memory as having at least for many months and in many places given my Providence much to do: so great a variety of scenes of labour, implying all so much renewal of application, glimmer out of the book as I now read it over. And yet as the faded interest of the whole episode becomes again mildly vivid what I seem most to recover is, in its pale spectrality, a degree of joy, an eagerness on behalf of my recital, that must recklessly enough have overridden anxieties of every sort, including any view of inherent difficulties.

I seem to recall no other like connexion in which the case was met, to my measure, by so fond a complacency, in which my subject can have appeared so apt to take care of itself. I see now that I might all the while have taken much better care of it; yet, as I had at the time no sense of neglecting it, neither acute nor rueful solicitude, I can but speculate all vainly to-day on the oddity of my composure. I ask myself indeed if, possibly, recognising after I was launched the danger of an inordinate leak—since the ship has truly a hole in its side more than sufficient to have sunk it—I may not have managed, as a counsel of mere despair, to stop my ears against the noise of waters and *pretend* to myself I was afloat; being indubitably, in any case, at sea, with no harbour of refuge till the end of my serial voyage. If I succeeded at all in that emulation (in another sphere) of the pursued ostrich I must have succeeded altogether; must have buried my head in the sand and there found beatitude. The explanation of my enjoyment of it, no doubt, is that I was more than commonly enamoured of my idea, and that I believed it, so trusted, so imaginatively fostered, not less capable of limping to its goal on three feet than on one. The lameness might be what it would: I clearly, for myself, felt the thing *go*—which is the most a dramatist can ever ask of his drama; and I shall here accordingly indulge myself in speaking first of how, superficially, it did so proceed; explaining then what I mean by its practical dependence on a miracle.

It had come to me, this happy, halting view of an interesting case, abruptly enough, some years before: I recall sharply the felicity of the first glimpse, though I forget the accident of thought that produced it. I recall that I was seated in an American "horse-car" when I found myself, of a sudden, considering with enthusiasm, as the theme of a "story," the situation, in another country and an aristocratic society, of some robust but insidiously beguiled and betrayed, some cruelly wronged, compatriot: the point being in especial that he should suffer at the hands of persons pretending to represent the highest possible civilisation and to be of an order in every way superior to his own. What would he "do" in that predicament, how would he right himself, or how, failing a remedy, would he conduct himself under his wrong? This would be the question involved, and I remember well how, having entered the horse-car without a dream of it, I was presently to leave that vehicle in full possession of my answer. He would behave in the most interesting manner—it would all depend on that: stricken, smarting, sore, he would arrive at his just vindication and then would fail of all triumphantly and all vulgarly enjoying it. He would hold his revenge and cherish it and feel its sweetness, and then in the very act of forcing it home would sacrifice it in disgust. He would let them go, in short, his haughty contemners, even while feeling them, with joy, in his power, and he would obey, in so doing, one of the large and easy impulses *generally* characteristic of his type. He wouldn't "forgive"—that would have, in the case, no application; he would simply turn, at the supreme moment, away, the bitterness of his personal loss yielding to the very force of his aversion. All he would have at the end would be therefore just the moral convenience, indeed the moral necessity, of his practical, but quite unappreciated, magnanimity; and one's last view of him would be that of a strong man indifferent to his strength and too wrapped in fine, too wrapped above all in *other* and intenser, reflexions for the assertion of his "rights." This last point was of the essence and constituted in fact the subject: there would be no subject at all, obviously,— or simply the commonest of the common,—if my gentleman should enjoy his advantage. I was charmed with my idea, which would take, however, much working out; and precisely because it had so much to give, I think, must I have dropped it for the time into the deep well of unconscious cerebration: not without the hope, doubtless, that it might eventually emerge from that reservoir, as one had already known the buried treasure to come to light, with a firm iridescent surface and a notable increase of weight.

This resurrection then took place in Paris, where I was at the moment living, and in December 1875; my good fortune being apparently that Paris had ever so promptly offered me, and with an immediate directness at which I now marvel (since I had come back there, after earlier visitations, but a few weeks before), everything that was needed to make my conception concrete. I seem again at this distant day to see it become so quickly and easily, quite as if filling itself with life in that air. The objectivity it had wanted it promptly put on, and if the questions had been, with the usual intensity, for my hero and his crisis—the whole formidable list, the who? the what? the where? the when? the why? the how?—they gathered their answers in the cold shadow of the Arc de Triomphe, for fine reasons, very much as if they had been plucking spring flowers for the weaving of a frolic garland. I saw from one day to another my particular cluster of circumstances, with the life of the splendid city playing up in it like

a flashing fountain in a marble basin. The very splendour
seemed somehow to witness and intervene; it was important
for the effect of my friend's discomfiture that it should take
place on a high and lighted stage, and that his original ambition, the project exposing him, should have sprung from
beautiful and noble suggestions—those that, at certain hours
and under certain impressions, we feel the many-tinted medium by the Seine irresistibly to communicate. It was all
charmingly simple, this conception, and the current must
have gushed, full and clear, to my imagination, from the moment Christopher Newman rose before me, on a perfect day
of the divine Paris spring, in the great gilded Salon Carré of
the Louvre. Under this strong contagion of the place he
would, by the happiest of hazards, meet his old comrade, now
initiated and domiciled; after which the rest would go of itself. If he was to be wronged he would be wronged with just
that conspicuity, with his felicity at just that pitch and with
the highest aggravation of the general effect of misery mocked
at. Great and gilded the whole trap set, in fine, for his wary
freshness and into which it would blunder upon its fate. I
have, I confess, no memory of a disturbing doubt; once the
man himself was imaged to me (and *that* germination is a
process almost always untraceable) he must have walked into
the situation as by taking a pass-key from his pocket.

But what then meanwhile would be the affront one would
see him as most feeling? The affront of course done him as a
lover; and yet not that done by his mistress herself, since injuries of this order are the stalest stuff of romance. I was not
to have him jilted, any more than I was to have him successfully vindictive: both his wrong and his right would have
been in these cases of too vulgar a type. I doubtless even then
felt that the conception of Paris as the consecrated scene of
rash infatuations and bold bad treacheries belongs, in the Anglo-Saxon imagination, to the infancy of art. The right renovation of any such theme as *that* would place it in Boston or
at Cleveland, at Hartford or at Utica—give it some local connexion in which we had not already had so much of it. No, I
should make my heroine herself, if heroine there was to be,
an equal victim—just as Romeo was not less the sport of fate
for not having been interestedly sacrificed by Juliet; and to

this end I had but to imagine "great people" again, imagine my hero confronted and involved with them, and impute to them, with a fine free hand, the arrogance and cruelty, the tortuous behaviour, in given conditions, of which great people have been historically so often capable. But as this was the light in which they were to show, so the essence of the matter would be that he should at the right moment find them in his power, and so the situation would reach its highest interest with the question of his utilisation of that knowledge. It would be here, in the possession and application of his power, that he would come out strong and would so deeply appeal to our sympathy. Here above all it really was, however, that my conception unfurled, with the best conscience in the world, the emblazoned flag of romance; which venerable ensign it had, though quite unwittingly, from the first and at every point sported in perfect good faith. I had been plotting arch-romance without knowing it, just as I began to write it that December day without recognising it and just as I all serenely and blissfully pursued the process from month to month and from place to place; just as I now, in short, reading the book over, find it yields me no interest and no reward comparable to the fond perception of this truth.

The thing is consistently, consummately—and I would fain really make bold to say charmingly—romantic; and all without intention, presumption, hesitation, contrition. The effect is equally undesigned and unabashed, and I lose myself, at this late hour, I am bound to add, in a certain sad envy of the free play of so much unchallenged instinct. One would like to woo back such hours of fine precipitation. They represent to the critical sense which the exercise of one's *whole* faculty has, with time, so inevitably and so thoroughly waked up, the happiest season of surrender to the invoked muse and the projected fable: the season of images so free and confident and ready that they brush questions aside and disport themselves, like the artless schoolboys of Gray's beautiful Ode, in all the ecstasy of the ignorance attending them. The time doubtless comes soon enough when questions, as I call them, rule the roost and when the little victim, to adjust Gray's term again to the creature of frolic fancy, does n't dare propose a gambol till they have all (like a board of trustees discussing a new outlay) sat on the possibly scandalous case. I somehow feel, accordingly, that it was lucky to have sacrificed on this particular altar while one still could; though it is perhaps droll—in a yet higher degree—to have done so not simply because one was guileless, but even quite under the conviction, in a general way, that, since no "rendering" of any object and no painting of any picture can take effect without some form of reference and control, so these guarantees could but reside in a high probity of observation. I must decidedly have supposed, all the while, that I was acutely observing—and with a blest absence of wonder at its being so easy. Let me certainly at present rejoice in that absence; for I ask myself how without it I could have written "The American."

Was it indeed meanwhile my excellent conscience that kept the charm as unbroken as it appears to me, in rich retrospect, to have remained?—or is it that I suffer the mere influence of remembered, of associated places and hours, all acute impressions, to palm itself off as the sign of a finer confidence than I could justly claim? It is a pleasure to perceive how again and again the shrunken depths of old work yet permit themselves to be sounded or—even if rather terrible the image— "dragged": the long pole of memory stirs and rummages the bottom, and we fish up such fragments and relics of the submerged life and the extinct consciousness as tempt us to piece them together. My windows looked into the Rue de Luxembourg—since then meagrely re-named Rue Cambon—and the particular light Parisian click of the small cab-horse on the clear asphalt, with its sharpness of detonation between the high houses, makes for the faded page to-day a sort of interlineation of sound. This sound rises to a martial clatter at the moment a troop of cuirassiers charges down the narrow street, each morning, to file, directly opposite my house, through the plain portal of the barracks occupying part of the vast domain attached in a rearward manner to one of the Ministères that front on the Place Vendôme; an expanse marked, along a considerable stretch of the street, by one of those high painted and administratively-placarded garden walls that form deep, vague, recurrent notes in the organic vastness of the city. I have but to re-read ten lines to recall my daily effort not to waste time in hanging over the window-bar for a sight of the cavalry the hard music of whose hoofs so directly and thrillingly appealed; an effort that inveterately failed—and a trivial circumstance now dignified, to my imagination, I may add, by the fact that the fruits of this weakness, the various items of the vivid picture, so constantly recaptured, must have been in themselves suggestive and inspiring, must have been rich strains, in their way, of the great Paris harmony. I have ever, in general, found it difficult to write of places under too immediate an impression—the impression that prevents standing off and allows neither space nor time for perspective. The image has had for the most part to be dim if the reflexion was to be, as is proper for a reflexion, both sharp and quiet: one has a horror, I think, artistically, of agitated reflexions.

Perhaps that is why the novel, after all, was to achieve, as it went on, no great—certainly no very direct—transfusion of the immense overhanging presence. It had to save as it could its own life, to keep tight hold of the tenuous silver thread, the one hope for which was that it should n't be tangled or clipped. This earnest grasp of the silver thread was doubtless an easier business in other places—though as I remount the stream of composition I see it faintly coloured again: with the bright protection of the Normandy coast (I worked away a few weeks at Etretat); with the stronger glow of southernmost France, breaking in during a stay at Bayonne; then with the fine historic and other "psychic" substance of Saint-Germain-en-Laye, a purple patch of terraced October before returning to Paris. There comes after that the memory of a last brief intense invocation of the enclosing scene, of the pious effort to unwind my tangle, with a firm hand, in the very light (that light of high, narrowish French windows in old rooms, the light somehow, as one always feels, of "style" itself) that had quickened my original vision. I was to pass over to London that autumn; which was a reason the more for considering the matter—the matter of Newman's final predicament—with due intensity: to let a loose end dangle over into alien air would so fix upon the whole, I strenuously felt, the dishonour of piecemeal composition. Therefore I strove to finish—first in a small dusky hotel of the Rive Gauche, where, though the windows again were high, the days were dim and the crepuscular court, domestic, intimate, "quaint," testified to ancient manners almost as if it had been that of Balzac's Maison Vauquer in "Le Père Goriot": and then once more in the Rue de Luxembourg, where a black-framed Empire portrait-medallion, suspended in the centre of each white panel of my almost noble old salon, made the coolest, discreetest, most measured decoration, and where, through casements open to the last mildness of the year, a belated Saint Martin's summer, the tale was taken up afresh by the charming light click and clatter, that sound as of the thin, quick, quite feminine surface-breathing of Paris, the shortest of rhythms for so huge an organism.

I shall not tell whether I did there bring my book to a close—and indeed I shrink, for myself, from putting the question to the test of memory. I follow it so far, the old urgent ingenious business, and then I lose sight of it: from which I infer—all exact recovery of the matter failing—that I did not in the event drag over the Channel a lengthening chain; which would have been detestable. I reduce to the absurd perhaps, however, by that small subjective issue, any undue measure of the interest of this insistent recovery of what I have called attendant facts. There always has been, for the valid work of art, a history—though mainly inviting, doubtless, but to the curious critic, for whom such things grow up and are formed very much in the manner of attaching young lives and characters, those conspicuous cases of happy development as to which evidence and anecdote are always in order. The development indeed must be certain to have been happy, the life sincere, the character fine: the work of art, to create or repay critical curiosity, must in short have been very "valid" indeed. Yet there is on the other hand no mathematical measure of that importance—it may be a matter of widely-varying appreciation; and I am willing to grant, assuredly, that this interest, in a given relation, will nowhere so effectually kindle as on the artist's own part. And I am afraid that after all even his best excuse for it must remain the highly personal plea—the joy of living over, as a chapter of experience, the particular intellectual adventure. Here lurks an immense homage to the general privilege of the artist, to that constructive, that creative passion—portentous words, but they are convenient—the exercise of which finds so many an occasion for appearing to him the highest of human fortunes, the rarest boon of the gods. He values it, all sublimely and perhaps a little fatuously, for itself—as the great extension, great beyond all others, of experience and of consciousness; with the toil and trouble a mere sun-cast shadow that falls, shifts and vanishes, the result of his living in so large a light. On the constant nameless felicity of this Robert Louis Stevenson has, in an admirable passage and as in so many other connexions, said the right word: that the partaker of the "life of art" who repines at the absence of the rewards, as they are called, of the pursuit might surely be better occupied. Much rather should he endlessly wonder at his not having to pay half his substance for his luxurious immersion. He enjoys it, so to speak, without a tax; the effort of labour involved, the torment of expression, of which we have heard in our time so much, being after all but the last refinement of his privilege. It may leave him weary and worn; but how, after his fashion, he will have lived! As if one were to expect at once freedom and ease! That silly safety is but the sign of bondage and forfeiture. Who can imagine free selection—which is the beautiful, terrible *whole* of art—without free difficulty? This is the very franchise of the city and high ambition of the citizen. The vision of the difficulty, as one looks back, bathes one's course in a golden glow by which the very objects along the road are transfigured and glorified; so that one exhibits them to other eyes with an elation possibly presumptuous.

Since I accuse myself at all events of these complacencies I take advantage of them to repeat that I value, in my retrospect, nothing so much as the lively light on the romantic property of my subject that I had not expected to encounter. If in "The American" I invoked the romantic association without malice prepense, yet with a production of the romantic effect that is for myself unmistakeable, the occasion is of the best perhaps for penetrating a little the obscurity of that principle. By what art or mystery, what craft of selection, omission or commission, does a given picture of life appear to us to surround its theme, its figures and images, with the air of romance while another picture close beside it may affect us as steeping the whole matter in the element of reality? It is a question, no doubt, on the painter's part, very much more of perceived effect, effect *after* the fact, than of conscious design—though indeed I have ever failed to see how a coherent picture of anything is producible save by a complex of fine measurements. The cause of the deflexion, in one pronounced sense or the other, must lie deep, however; so that for the most part we recognise the character of our interest only after the particular magic, as I say, has thoroughly operated—and then in truth but if we be a bit critically minded, if we find our pleasure, that is, in these intimate appreciations (for which, as I am well aware, ninety-nine readers in a hundred have no use whatever). The determining condition would at any rate seem so latent that one may well doubt if the full artistic consciousness ever reaches it; leaving the matter thus a case, ever, not of an author's plotting and planning and calculating, but just of his feeling and seeing, of his conceiving, in a word, and of his thereby inevitably expressing himself, under the influence of one value or the other. These values represent different sorts and degrees of the communicable thrill, and I doubt if any novelist, for instance, ever proposed to commit himself to one kind or the other with as little mitigation as we are sometimes able to find for him. The interest is greatest—the interest of his genius, I mean, and of his general wealth—when he commits himself in both directions; not quite at the same time or to the same effect, of course, but by some need of performing his whole possible revolution, by the law of some rich passion in him for extremes.

Of the men of largest responding imagination before the human scene, of Scott, of Balzac, even of the coarse, comprehensive, prodigious Zola, we feel, I think, that the deflexion toward either quarter has never taken place; that neither the nature of the man's faculty nor the nature of his experience has ever quite determined it. His current remains therefore extraordinarily rich and mixed, washing us successively with the warm wave of the near and familiar and the tonic shock, as may be, of the far and strange. (In making which opposition I suggest not that the strange and the far are at all necessarily romantic: they happen to be simply the unknown, which is quite a different matter. The real represents to my

perception the things we cannot possibly *not* know, sooner
or later, in one way or another; it being but one of the accidents of our hampered state, and one of the incidents of their
quantity and number, that particular instances have not yet
come our way. The romantic stands, on the other hand, for
the things that, with all the facilities in the world, all the
wealth and all the courage and all the wit and all the adventure, we never *can* directly know; the things that can reach us
only through the beautiful circuit and subterfuge of our
thought and our desire.) There have been, I gather, many
definitions of romance, as a matter indispensably of boats, or
of caravans, or of tigers, or of "historical characters," or of
ghosts, or of forgers, or of detectives, or of beautiful wicked
women, or of pistols and knives, but they appear for the most
part reducible to the idea of the facing of danger, the acceptance of great risks for the fascination, the very love, of their
uncertainty, the joy of success if possible and of battle in any
case. This would be a fine formula if it bore examination; but
it strikes me as weak and inadequate, as by no means covering
the true ground and yet as landing us in strange confusions.

The panting pursuit of danger is the pursuit of life itself, in
which danger awaits us possibly at every step and faces us at
every turn; so that the dream of an intenser experience easily
becomes rather some vision of a sublime security like that enjoyed on the flowery plains of heaven, where we may conceive
ourselves proceeding in ecstasy from one prodigious phase
and form of it to another. And if it be insisted that the measure of the type is then in the *appreciation* of danger—the
sign of our projection of the real being the smallness of its
dangers, and that of our projection of the romantic the hugeness, the mark of the distinction being in short, as they say of
collars and gloves and shoes, the size and "number" of the
danger—this discrimination again surely fails, since it makes
our difference not a difference of kind, which is what we
want, but a difference only of degree, and subject by that
condition to the indignity of a sliding scale and a shifting
measure. There are immense and flagrant dangers that are but
sordid and squalid ones, as we feel, tainting with their quality
the very defiances they provoke; while there are common and
covert ones, that "look like nothing" and that can be but in-

wardly and occultly dealt with, which involve the sharpest hazards to life and honour and the highest instant decisions and intrepidities of action. It is an arbitrary stamp that keeps these latter prosaic and makes the former heroic; and yet I should still less subscribe to a mere "subjective" division—I mean one that would place the difference wholly in the temper of the imperilled agent. It would be impossible to have a more romantic temper than Flaubert's Madame Bovary, and yet nothing less resembles a romance than the record of her adventures. To classify it by that aspect—the definition of the spirit that happens to animate her—is like settling the question (as I have seen it witlessly settled) by the presence or absence of "costume." Where again then does costume begin or end?—save with the "run" of one or another sort of play? We must reserve vague labels for artless mixtures.

The only *general* attribute of projected romance that I can see, the only one that fits all its cases, is the fact of the kind of experience with which it deals—experience liberated, so to speak; experience disengaged, disembroiled, disencumbered, exempt from the conditions that we usually know to attach to it and, if we wish so to put the matter, drag upon it, and operating in a medium which relieves it, in a particular interest, of the inconvenience of a *related*, a measurable state, a state subject to all our vulgar communities. The greatest intensity may so be arrived at evidently—when the sacrifice of community, of the "related" sides of situations, has not been too rash. It must to this end not flagrantly betray itself; we must even be kept if possible, for our illusion, from suspecting any sacrifice at all. The balloon of experience is in fact of course tied to the earth, and under that necessity we swing, thanks to a rope of remarkable length, in the more or less commodious car of the imagination; but it is by the rope we know where we are, and from the moment that cable is cut we are at large and unrelated: we only swing apart from the globe—though remaining as exhilarated, naturally, as we like, especially when all goes well. The art of the romancer is, "for the fun of it," insidiously to cut the cable, to cut it without our detecting him. What I have recognised then in "The American," much to my surprise and after long years, is that the experience here represented is the disconnected and uncontrolled experience—uncontrolled by our general sense of "the way things happen"—which romance alone more or less successfully palms off on us. It is a case of Newman's own intimate experience all, that being my subject, the thread of which, from beginning to end, is not once exchanged, however momentarily, for any other thread; and the experience of others concerning us, and concerning him, only so far as it touches him and as he recognises, feels or divines it. There is our general sense of the way things happen—it abides with us indefeasibly, as readers of fiction, from the moment we demand that our fiction shall be intelligible; and there is our particular sense of the way they don't happen, which is liable to wake up unless reflexion and criticism, in us, have been skilfully and successfully drugged. There are drugs enough, clearly—it is all a question of applying them with tact; in which case the way things don't happen may be artfully made to pass for the way things do.

Amusing and even touching to me, I profess, at this time of day, the ingenuity (worthy, with whatever lapses, of a better cause) with which, on behalf of Newman's adventure, this hocus-pocus is attempted: the value of the instance not being diminished either, surely, by its having been attempted in such evident good faith. Yes, all is romantic to my actual vision here, and not least so, I hasten to add, the fabulous felicity of my candour. The way things happen is frankly not the way in which they are represented as having happened, in Paris, to my hero: the situation I had conceived only saddled me with that for want of my invention of something better. The great house of Bellegarde, in a word, would, I now feel, given the circumstances, given the *whole* of the ground, have comported itself in a manner as different as possible from the manner to which my narrative commits it; of which truth, moreover, I am by no means sure that, in spite of what I have called my serenity, I had not all the while an uneasy suspicion. I had dug in my path, alas, a hole into which I was destined to fall. I was so possessed of my idea that Newman should be ill-used—which was the essence of my subject—that I attached too scant an importance to its fashion of coming about. Almost any fashion would serve, I appear to have assumed, that would give me my main chance for him; a matter depending not so much on the particular trick played him as on the interesting face presented by him to *any* damnable trick. So where I part company with *terra-firma* is in making that projected, that performed outrage so much more showy, dramatically speaking, than sound. Had I patched it up to a greater apparent soundness my own trick, artistically speaking, would have been played; I should have cut the cable without my reader's suspecting it. I doubtless at the time, I repeat, believed I had taken my precautions; but truly they should have been greater, to impart the air of truth to the attitude—that is first to the pomp and circumstance, and second to the queer falsity—of the Bellegardes.

They would positively have jumped then, the Bellegardes, at my rich and easy American, and not have "minded" in the least any drawback—especially as, after all, given the pleasant palette from which I have painted him, there were few drawbacks to mind. My subject imposed on me a group of closely-allied persons animated by immense pretensions—which was all very well, which might be full of the promise of interest: only of interest felt most of all in the light of comedy and of irony. This, better understood, would have dwelt in the idea not in the least of their not finding Newman good enough for their alliance and thence being ready to sacrifice him, but in that of their taking with alacrity everything he could give them, only asking for more and more, and then adjusting their pretensions and their pride to it with all the comfort in life. Such accommodation of the theory of a noble indifference to the practice of a deep avidity is the real note of policy in forlorn aristocracies—and I meant of course that the Bellegardes should be virtually forlorn. The perversion of truth is by no means, I think, in the displayed acuteness of their remembrance of " who" and " what" they are, or at any rate take themselves for; since it is the misfortune of all insistence on " worldly" advantages—and the situation of such people bristles at the best (by which I mean under whatever invocation of a superficial simplicity) with emphasis, accent, assumption—to produce at times an effect of grossness. The picture of their tergiversation, at all events, however it may originally have seemed to me to hang together, has taken on this rococo appearance precisely because their preferred course, a thousand times preferred, would have been to haul him and his fortune into their boat under cover of night perhaps, in any case as quietly and with as little bumping and splashing as possible, and there accommodate him with the very safest and most convenient seat. Given Newman, given the fact that the thing constitutes itself organically as *his* adventure, that too might very well be a situation and a subject: only it would n't have been the theme of "The American" as the book stands, the theme to which I was from so early pledged. Since I had wanted a "wrong" this other turn might even have been arranged to give me *that*, might even have been arranged to meet my requirement that somebody or something should be "in his power" so delightfully; and with the signal effect, after all, of "defining" everything. (It is as difficult, I said above, to trace the dividing-line between the real and the romantic as to plant a milestone between north and south; but I am not sure an infallible sign of the latter is not this rank vegetation of the "power" of bad people that good get into, or *vice versa*. It is so rarely, alas, into *our* power that any one gets!)

It is difficult for me to-day to believe that I had not, as my work went on, *some* shade of the rueful sense of my affront to verisimilitude; yet I catch the memory at least of no great sharpness, no true critical anguish, of remorse: an anomaly the reason of which in fact now glimmers interestingly out. My concern, as I saw it, was to make and to keep Newman consistent; the picture of his consistency was all my undertaking, and the memory of *that* infatuation perfectly abides with me. He was to be the lighted figure, the others—even doubtless to an excessive degree the woman who is made the agent of his discomfiture—were to be the obscured; by which I should largely get the very effect most to be invoked, that of a generous nature engaged with forces, with difficulties and dangers, that it but half understands. If Newman was attaching enough, I must have argued, his tangle would be sensible enough; for the interest of everything is all that it is *his* vision, *his* conception, *his* interpretation: at the window of his wide, quite sufficiently wide, consciousness we are seated, from that admirable position we "assist." He therefore supremely matters; all the rest matters only as he feels it, treats it, meets it. A beautiful infatuation this, always, I think, the intensity of the creative effort to get into the skin of the creature; the act of personal possession of one being by another at its completest—and with the high enhancement, ever, that it is, by the same stroke, the effort of the artist to preserve for his subject that unity, and for his use of it (in other words for the interest he desires to excite) that effect of a *centre*, which most economise its value. Its value is most discussable when that economy has most operated; the content and the "importance" of a work of art are in fine wholly dependent on its *being* one: outside of which all prate of its representative character, its meaning and its bearing, its morality and humanity, are an impudent thing. Strong in that character, which is the condition of its really bearing witness at all, it is strong every way. So much remains true then on behalf of my instinct of multiplying the fine touches by which Newman should live and communicate life; and yet I still ask myself, I confess, what I can have made of "life," in my picture, at such a juncture as the interval offered as elapsing between my hero's first accepted state and the nuptial rites that are to crown it. Nothing here is in truth "offered"—everything is evaded, and the effect of this, I recognise, is of the oddest. His relation to Madame de Cintré takes a great stride, but the author appears to view that but as a signal for letting it severely alone.

I have been stupefied, in so thoroughly revising the book, to find, on turning a page, that the light in which he is presented immediately after Madame de Bellegarde has conspicuously introduced him to all her circle as her daughter's husband-to-be is that of an evening at the opera quite alone; as if he would n't surely spend his leisure, and especially those hours of it, with his intended. Instinctively, from that moment, one would have seen them intimately and, for one's interest, beautifully together; with some illustration of the beauty incumbent on the author. The truth was that at this point the author, all gracelessly, could but hold his breath and pass; lingering was too difficult—he had made for himself a crushing complication. Since Madame de Cintré was after all to "back out" every touch in the picture of her apparent loyalty would add to her eventual shame. She had acted in clear good faith, but how could I give the *detail* of an attitude, on her part, of which the foundation was yet so weak? I preferred, as the minor evil, to shirk the attempt—at the cost evidently of a signal loss of "charm"; and with this lady, altogether, I recognise, a light plank, too light a plank, is laid for the reader over a dark "psychological" abyss. The delicate clue to her conduct is never definitely placed in his hand: I must have liked verily to think it *was* delicate and to flatter myself it was to be felt with finger-tips rather than heavily tugged at. Here then, at any rate, is the romantic *tout craché*—the fine flower of Newman's experience blooming in a medium "cut off" and shut up to itself. I don't for a moment pronounce any spell proceeding from it necessarily the less workable, to a rejoicing ingenuity, for that; beguile the reader's suspicion of *his* being shut up, transform it for *him* into a positive illusion of the largest liberty, and the success will ever be proportionate to the chance. Only all this gave me, I make out, a great deal to look to, and I was perhaps wrong in thinking that Newman by himself, and for any occasional extra inch or so I might smuggle into his measurements, would see me through my wood. Anything more liberated and disconnected, to repeat my terms, than his prompt general profession, before the Tristrams, of aspiring to a "great" marriage, for example, could surely not well be imagined. I had to take that over with the rest of him and fit it in—I had indeed to exclude the outer air. Still, I find on re-perusal that I have been able to breathe at least in my aching void; so that, clinging to my hero as to a tall, protective, good-natured elder brother in a rough place, I leave the record to stand or fall by his more or less convincing image.

The Portrait of a Lady

T HE PORTRAIT of a Lady" was, like "Roderick Hudson," begun in Florence, during three months spent there in the spring of 1879. Like "Roderick" and like "The American," it had been designed for publication in "The Atlantic Monthly," where it began to appear in 1880. It differed from its two predecessors, however, in finding a course also open to it, from month to month, in "Macmillan's Magazine"; which was to be for me one of the last occasions of simultaneous "serialisation" in the two countries that the changing conditions of literary intercourse between England and the United States had up to then left unaltered. It is a long novel, and I was long in writing it; I remember being again much occupied with it, the following year, during a stay of several weeks made in Venice. I had rooms on Riva Schiavoni, at the top of a house near the passage leading off to San Zaccaria; the waterside life, the wondrous lagoon spread before me, and the ceaseless human chatter of Venice came in at my windows, to which I seem to myself to have been constantly driven, in the fruitless fidget of composition, as if to see whether, out in the blue channel, the ship of some right suggestion, of some better phrase, of the next happy twist of my subject, the next true touch for my canvas, might n't come into sight. But I recall vividly enough that the response most elicited, in general, to these restless appeals was the rather grim admonition that romantic and historic sites, such as the land of Italy abounds in, offer the artist a questionable aid to concentration when they themselves are not to be the subject of it. They are too rich in their own life and too charged with their own meanings merely to help him out with a lame phrase; they draw him away from his small question to their own greater ones; so that, after a little, he feels, while thus yearning toward them in his difficulty, as if he were asking an army of glorious veterans to help him to arrest a peddler who has given him the wrong change.

There are pages of the book which, in the reading over, have seemed to make me see again the bristling curve of the wide Riva, the large colour-spots of the balconied houses and the repeated undulation of the little hunchbacked bridges, marked by the rise and drop again, with the wave, of foreshortened clicking pedestrians. The Venetian footfall and the Venetian cry—all talk there, wherever uttered, having the pitch of a call across the water—come in once more at the window, renewing one's old impression of the delighted senses and the divided, frustrated mind. How can places that speak *in general* so to the imagination not give it, at the moment, the particular thing it wants? I recollect again and again, in beautiful places, dropping into that wonderment. The real truth is, I think, that they express, under this appeal, only too much—more than, in the given case, one has use for; so that one finds one's self working less congruously, after all, so far as the surrounding picture is concerned, than in presence of the moderate and the neutral, to which we may lend something of the light of our vision. Such a place as Venice is too proud for such charities; Venice does n't borrow, she but all magnificently gives. We profit by that enormously, but to do so we must either be quite off duty or be on it in her service alone. Such, and so rueful, are these reminiscences; though on the whole, no doubt, one's book, and one's "literary effort" at large, were to be the better for them. Strangely fertilising, in the long run, does a wasted effort of attention often prove. It all depends on *how* the attention has been cheated, has been squandered. There are high-handed insolent frauds, and there are insidious sneaking ones. And there is, I fear, even on the most designing artist's part, always witless enough good faith, always anxious enough desire, to fail to guard him against their deceits.

Trying to recover here, for recognition, the germ of my idea, I see that it must have consisted not at all in any conceit of a "plot," nefarious name, in any flash, upon the fancy, of a set of relations, or in any one of those situations that, by a logic of their own, immediately fall, for the fabulist, into movement, into a march or a rush, a patter of quick steps; but altogether in the sense of a single character, the character and aspect of a particular engaging young woman, to which all the usual elements of a "subject," certainly of a setting, were to need to be superadded. Quite as interesting as the young woman herself, at her best, do I find, I must again repeat, this projection of memory upon the whole matter of the growth, in one's imagination, of some such apology for a motive. These are the fascinations of the fabulist's art, these lurking forces of expansion, these necessities of upspringing in the seed, these beautiful determinations, on the part of the idea entertained, to grow as tall as possible, to push into the light and the air and thickly flower there; and, quite as much, these fine possibilities of recovering, from some good stand-point on the ground gained, the intimate history of the business—of retracing and reconstructing its steps and stages. I have always fondly remembered a remark that I heard fall years ago from the lips of Ivan Turgenieff in regard to his own experience of the usual origin of the fictive picture. It began for him almost always with the vision of some person or persons, who hovered before him, soliciting him, as the active or passive figure, interesting him and appealing to him just as they were and by what they were. He saw them, in that fashion, as *disponibles*, saw them subject to the chances, the complications of existence, and saw them vividly, but then had to find for them the right relations, those that would most bring them out; to imagine, to invent and select and piece together the situations most useful and favourable to the sense of the creatures themselves, the complications they would be most likely to produce and to feel.

"To arrive at these things is to arrive at my 'story,' " he said, "and that's the way I look for it. The result is that I'm often accused of not having 'story' enough. I seem to myself to have as much as I need—to show my people, to exhibit their relations with each other; for that is all my measure. If I watch them long enough I see them come together, I see them *placed*, I see them engaged in this or that act and in this or that difficulty. How they look and move and speak and behave, always in the setting I have found for them, is my account of them—of which I dare say, alas, *que cela manque souvent d'architecture*. But I would rather, I think, have too little architecture than too much—when there's danger of its interfering with my measure of the truth. The French of course like more of it than I give—having by their own genius such a hand for it; and indeed one must give all one can. As for the origin of one's wind-blown germs themselves, who shall say, as you ask, where *they* come from? We have to go too far back, too far behind, to say. Is n't it all we can say that they come from every quarter of heaven, that they are *there* at almost any turn of the road? They accumulate, and we are always picking them over, selecting among them. They are the breath of life—by which I mean that life, in its own way, breathes them upon us. They are so, in a manner prescribed and imposed—floated into our minds by the current of life. That reduces to imbecility the vain critic's quarrel, so often, with one's subject, when he has n't the wit to accept it. Will he point out then which other it should properly have been?—his office being, essentially *to* point out. *Il en serait bien embarrassé.* Ah, when he points out what I 've done or failed to do with it, that 's another matter: there he 's on his ground. I give him up my 'architecture,' " my distinguished friend concluded, "as much as he will."

So this beautiful genius, and I recall with comfort the gratitude I drew from his reference to the intensity of suggestion that may reside in the stray figure, the unattached character, the image *en disponibilité*. It gave me higher warrant than I seemed then to have met for just that blest habit of one's own imagination, the trick of investing some conceived or encountered individual, some brace or group of individuals, with the germinal property and authority. I was myself so much more antecedently conscious of my figures than of their setting—a too preliminary, a preferential interest in which struck me as in general such a putting of the cart before the horse. I might envy, though I could n't emulate, the imaginative writer so constituted as to see his fable first and to make out its agents afterwards: I could think so little of any fable that did n't need its agents positively to launch it; I could think so little of any situation that did n't depend for its interest on the nature of the persons situated, and thereby on their way of taking it. There are methods of so-called presentation, I believe—among novelists who have appeared to flourish—that offer the situation as indifferent to that support; but I have not lost the sense of the value for me, at the time, of the admirable Russian's testimony to my not needing, all superstitiously, to try and perform any such gymnastic. Other echoes from the same source linger with me, I confess, as unfadingly—if it be not all indeed one much-embracing echo. It was impossible after that not to read, for one's uses, high lucidity into the tormented and disfigured and bemuddled question of the objective value, and even quite into that of the critical appreciation, of "subject" in the novel.

One had had from an early time, for that matter, the instinct of the right estimate of such values and of its reducing to the inane the dull dispute over the "immoral" subject and the moral. Recognising so promptly the one measure of the worth of a given subject, the question about it that, rightly answered, disposes of all others—is it valid, in a word, is it genuine, is it sincere, the result of some direct impression or perception of life?—I had found small edification, mostly, in a critical pretension that had neglected from the first all delimitation of ground and all definition of terms. The air of my earlier time shows, to memory, as darkened, all round, with that vanity—unless the difference to-day be just in one's own final impatience, the lapse of one's attention. There is, I think, no more nutritive or suggestive truth in this connexion than that of the perfect dependence of the "moral" sense of a work of art on the amount of felt life concerned in producing it. The question comes back thus, obviously, to the kind and the degree of the artist's prime sensibility, which is the soil out of which his subject springs. The quality and capacity of that soil, its ability to "grow" with due freshness and straightness any vision of life, represents, strongly or weakly, the projected morality. That element is but another name for the more or less close connexion of the subject with some mark made on the intelligence, with some sincere experience. By which, at the same time, of course, one is far from contending that this enveloping air of the artist's humanity—which gives the last touch to the worth of the work—is not a widely and wondrously varying element; being on one occasion a rich and magnificent medium and on another a comparatively poor and ungenerous one. Here we get exactly the high price of the novel as a literary form—its power not only, while preserving that form with closeness, to range through all the differences of the individual relation to its general subject-matter, all the varieties of outlook on life, of disposition to reflect and project, created by conditions that are never the same from man to man (or, so far as that goes, from man to woman), but positively to appear more true to its character in proportion as it strains, or tends to burst, with a latent extravagance, its mould.

The house of fiction has in short not one window, but a million—a number of possible windows not to be reckoned, rather; every one of which has been pierced, or is still pierceable, in its vast front, by the need of the individual vision and by the pressure of the individual will. These apertures, of dissimilar shape and size, hang so, all together, over the human scene that we might have expected of them a greater sameness of report than we find. They are but windows at the best, mere holes in a dead wall, disconnected, perched aloft; they are not hinged doors opening straight upon life. But they have this mark of their own that at each of them stands a figure with a pair of eyes, or at least with a field-glass, which forms, again and again, for observation, a unique instrument, insuring to the person making use of it an impression distinct from every other. He and his neighbours are watching the same show, but one seeing more where the other sees less, one seeing black where the other sees white, one seeing big where the other sees small, one seeing coarse where the other sees fine. And so on, and so on; there is fortunately no saying on what, for the particular pair of eyes, the window may *not* open; "fortunately" by reason, precisely, of this incalculability of range. The spreading field, the human scene, is the "choice of subject"; the pierced aperture, either broad or balconied or slit-like and low-browed, is the "literary form"; but they are, singly or together, as nothing without the posted presence of the watcher—without, in other words, the consciousness of the artist. Tell me what the artist is, and I will tell you of what he has *been* conscious. Thereby I shall express to you at once his boundless freedom and his "moral" reference.

All this is a long way round, however, for my word about my dim first move toward "The Portrait," which was exactly my grasp of a single character—an acquisition I had made, moreover, after a fashion not here to be retraced. Enough that I was, as seemed to me, in complete possession of it, that I had been so for a long time, that this had made it familiar and yet had not blurred its charm, and that, all urgently, all tormentingly, I saw it in motion and, so to speak, in transit. This amounts to saying that I saw it as bent upon its fate— some fate or other; *which*, among the possibilities, being precisely the question. Thus I had my vivid individual—vivid, so strangely, in spite of being still at large, not confined by the conditions, not engaged in the tangle, to which we look for much of the impress that constitutes an identity. If the apparition was still all to be placed how came it to be vivid?— since we puzzle such quantities out, mostly, just by the business of placing them. One could answer such a question beautifully, doubtless, if one could do so subtle, if not so monstrous, a thing as to write the history of the growth of one's imagination. One would describe then what, at a given time, had extraordinarily happened to it, and one would so, for instance, be in a position to tell, with an approach to clearness, how, under favour of occasion, it had been able to take over (take over straight from life) such and such a constituted, animated figure or form. The figure has to that extent, as you see, *been* placed—placed in the imagination that detains it, preserves, protects, enjoys it, conscious of its presence in the dusky, crowded, heterogeneous back-shop of the mind very much as a wary dealer in precious odds and ends, competent to make an "advance" on rare objects confided to him, is conscious of the rare little "piece" left in deposit by the reduced, mysterious lady of title or the speculative amateur, and which is already there to disclose its merit afresh as soon as a key shall have clicked in a cupboard-door.

That may be, I recognise, a somewhat superfine analogy for the particular "value" I here speak of, the image of the young feminine nature that I had had for so considerable a time all curiously at my disposal; but it appears to fond memory quite to fit the fact—with the recall, in addition, of my pious desire but to place my treasure right. I quite remind myself thus of the dealer resigned not to "realise," resigned to keeping the precious object locked up indefinitely rather than commit it, at no matter what price, to vulgar hands. For there *are* dealers in these forms and figures and treasures capable of that refinement. The point is, however, that this single small cornerstone, the conception of a certain young woman affronting her destiny, had begun with being all my outfit for the large building of "The Portrait of a Lady." It came to be a square and spacious house—or has at least seemed so to me in this going over it again; but, such as it is, it had to be put up round my young woman while she stood there in perfect isolation. That is to me, artistically speaking, the circumstance of interest; for I have lost myself once more, I confess, in the curiosity of analysing the structure. By what process of logical accretion was this slight "personality," the mere slim shade of an intelligent but presumptuous girl, to find itself endowed with the high attributes of a Subject?—and indeed by what thinness, at the best, would such a subject not be vitiated? Millions of presumptuous girls, intelligent or not intelligent, daily affront their destiny, and what is it open to their destiny to *be*, at the most, that we should make an ado about it? The novel is of its very nature an "ado," an ado about something, and the larger the form it takes the greater of course the ado. Therefore, consciously, that was what one was in for—for positively organising an ado about Isabel Archer.

One looked it well in the face, I seem to remember, this extravagance; and with the effect precisely of recognising the charm of the problem. Challenge any such problem with any intelligence, and you immediately see how full it is of substance; the wonder being, all the while, as we look at the world, how absolutely, how inordinately, the Isabel Archers, and even much smaller female fry, insist on mattering. George Eliot has admirably noted it—"In these frail vessels is borne onward through the ages the treasure of human affection." In "Romeo and Juliet" Juliet has to be important, just as, in "Adam Bede" and "The Mill on the Floss" and "Middlemarch" and "Daniel Deronda," Hetty Sorrel and Maggie Tulliver and Rosamond Vincy and Gwendolen Harleth have to be; with that much of firm ground, that much of bracing air, at the disposal all the while of their feet and their lungs. They are typical, none the less, of a class difficult, in the individual case, to make a centre of interest; so difficult in fact that many an expert painter, as for instance Dickens and Walter Scott, as for instance even, in the main, so subtle a hand as that of R. L. Stevenson, has preferred to leave the task unattempted. There are in fact writers as to whom we make out that their refuge from this is to assume it to be not worth their attempting; by which pusillanimity in truth their honour is scantly saved. It is never an attestation of a value, or even of our imperfect sense of one, it is never a tribute to any truth at all, that we shall represent that value badly. It never makes up, artistically, for an artist's dim feeling about a thing that he shall "do" the thing as ill as possible. There are better ways than that, the best of all of which is to begin with less stupidity.

It may be answered meanwhile, in regard to Shakespeare's and to George Eliot's testimony, that their concession to the "importance" of their Juliets and Cleopatras and Portias (even with Portia as the very type and model of the young person intelligent and presumptuous) and to that of their Hettys and Maggies and Rosamonds and Gwendolens, suffers the abatement that these slimnesses are, when figuring as the main props of the theme, never suffered to be sole ministers of its appeal, but have their inadequacy eked out with comic relief and underplots, as the playwrights say, when not with murders and battles and the great mutations of the world. If they are shown as "mattering" as much as they could possibly pretend to, the proof of it is in a hundred other persons, made of much stouter stuff, and each involved moreover in a hundred relations which matter to *them* concomitantly with that one. Cleopatra matters, beyond bounds, to Antony, but his colleagues, his antagonists, the state of Rome and the impending battle also prodigiously matter; Portia matters to Antonio, and to Shylock, and to the Prince of Morocco, to the fifty aspiring princes, but for these gentry there are other lively concerns; for Antonio, notably, there are Shylock and Bassanio and his lost ventures and the extremity of his predicament. This extremity indeed, by the same token, matters to Portia—though its doing so becomes of interest all by the fact that Portia matters to *us*. That she does so, at any rate, and that almost everything comes round to it again, supports my contention as to this fine example of the value recognised in the mere young thing. (I say "mere" young thing because I guess that even Shakespeare, preoccupied mainly though he may have been with the passions of princes, would scarce have pretended to found the best of his appeal for her on her high social position.) It is an example exactly of the deep difficulty braved—the difficulty of making George Eliot's "frail vessel," if not the all-in-all for our attention, at least the clearest of the call.

Now to see deep difficulty braved is at any time, for the really addicted artist, to feel almost even as a pang the beautiful incentive, and to feel it verily in such sort as to wish the danger intensified. The difficulty most worth tackling can only be for him, in these conditions, the greatest the case permits of. So I remember feeling here (in presence, always, that is, of the particular uncertainty of my ground), that there would be one way better than another—oh, ever so much better than any other!—of making it fight out its battle. The frail vessel, that charged with George Eliot's "treasure," and thereby of such importance to those who curiously approach it, has likewise possibilities of importance to itself, possibilities which permit of treatment and in fact peculiarly require it from the moment they are considered at all. There is always the escape from any close account of the weak agent of such spells by using as a bridge for evasion, for retreat and flight, the view of her relation to those surrounding her. Make it predominantly a view of *their* relation and the trick is played: you give the general sense of her effect, and you give it, so far as the raising on it of a superstructure goes, with the maximum of ease. Well, I recall perfectly how little, in my now quite established connexion, the maximum of ease appealed to me, and how I seemed to get rid of it by an honest transposition of the weights in the two scales. "Place the centre of the subject in the young woman's own consciousness," I said to myself, "and you get as interesting and as beautiful a difficulty as you could wish. Stick to *that*—for the centre; put the heaviest weight into *that* scale, which will be so largely the scale of her relation to herself. Make her only interested enough, at the same time, in the things that are not herself, and this relation need n't fear to be too limited. Place meanwhile in the other scale the lighter weight (which is usually the one that tips the balance of interest): press least hard, in short, on the consciousness of your heroine's satellites, especially the male; make it an interest contributive only to the greater one. See, at all events, what can be done in this way. What better field could there be for a due ingenuity? The girl hovers, inextinguishable, as a charming creature, and the job will be to translate her into the highest terms of that formula, and as nearly as possible moreover into *all* of them. To depend upon her and her little concerns wholly to see you through will necessitate, remember, your really 'doing' her."

So far I reasoned, and it took nothing less than that technical rigour, I now easily see, to inspire me with the right confidence for erecting on such a plot of ground the neat and careful and proportioned pile of bricks that arches over it and that was thus to form, constructionally speaking, a literary monument. Such is the aspect that to-day "The Portrait" wears for me: a structure reared with an "architectural" competence, as Turgenieff would have said, that makes it, to the author's own sense, the most proportioned of his productions after "The Ambassadors"—which was to follow it so many years later and which has, no doubt, a superior roundness. On one thing I was determined; that, though I should clearly have to pile brick upon brick for the creation of an interest, I would leave no pretext for saying that anything is out of line, scale or perspective. I would build large—in fine embossed vaults and painted arches, as who should say, and yet never let it appear that the chequered pavement, the ground under the reader's feet, fails to stretch at every point to the base of the walls. That precautionary spirit, on re-perusal of the book, is the old note that most touches me: it testifies so, for my own ear, to the anxiety of my provision for the reader's amusement. I felt, in view of the possible limitations of my subject, that no such provision could be excessive, and the development of the latter was simply the general form of that earnest quest. And I find indeed that this is the only account I can give myself of the evolution of the fable: it is all under the head thus named that I conceive the needful accretion as having taken place, the right complications as having started. It was naturally of the essence that the young woman should be herself complex; that was rudimentary—or was at any rate the light in which Isabel Archer had originally dawned. It went, however, but a certain way, and other lights, contending, conflicting lights, and of as many different colours, if possible, as the rockets, the Roman candles and Catherine-wheels of a "pyrotechnic display," would be employable to attest that she was. I had, no doubt, a groping instinct for the right complications, since I am quite unable to track the footsteps of those that constitute, as the case stands, the general situation exhibited. They are there, for what they are worth, and as numerous as might be; but my memory, I confess, is a blank as to how and whence they came.

I seem to myself to have waked up one morning in possession of them—of Ralph Touchett and his parents, of Madame Merle, of Gilbert Osmond and his daughter and his sister, of Lord Warburton, Caspar Goodwood and Miss Stackpole, the definite array of contributions to Isabel Archer's history. I recognised them, I knew them, they were the numbered pieces of my puzzle, the concrete terms of my "plot." It was as if they had simply, by an impulse of their own, floated into my ken, and all in response to my primary question: "Well, what will she *do*?" Their answer seemed to be that if I would trust them they would show me; on which, with an urgent appeal to them to make it at least as interesting as they could, I trusted them. They were like the group of attendants and entertainers who come down by train when people in the country give a party; they represented the contract for carrying the party on. That was an excellent relation with them—a possible one even with so broken a reed (from her slightness of cohesion) as Henrietta Stackpole. It is a familiar truth to the novelist, at the strenuous hour, that, as certain elements in any work are of the essence, so others are only of the form; that as this or that character, this or that disposition of the material, belongs to the subject directly, so to speak, so this or that other belongs to it but indirectly—belongs intimately to the treatment. This is a truth, however, of which he rarely gets the benefit—since it could be assured to him, really, but by criticism based upon perception, criticism which is too little of this world. He must not think of benefits, moreover, I freely recognise, for that way dishonour lies: he has, that is, but one to think of—the benefit, whatever it may be, involved in his having cast a spell upon the simpler, the very simplest, forms of attention. This is all he is entitled to; he is entitled to nothing, he is bound to admit, that can come to him, from the reader, as a result on the latter's part of any act of reflexion or discrimination. He may *enjoy* this finer tribute—that is another affair, but on condition only of taking it as a gratuity "thrown in," a mere miraculous windfall, the fruit of a tree he may not pretend to have shaken. Against reflexion, against discrimination, in his interest, all earth and air conspire; wherefore it is that, as I say, he must in many a case have schooled himself, from the first, to work but for a "living wage." The living wage is the reader's grant of the least possible quantity of attention required for consciousness of a "spell." The occasional charming "tip" is an act of his intelligence over and beyond this, a golden apple, for the writer's lap, straight from the wind-stirred tree. The artist may of course, in wanton moods, dream of some Paradise (for art) where the direct appeal to the intelligence might be legalised; for to such extravagances as these his yearning mind can scarce hope ever completely to close itself. The most he can do is to remember they *are* extravagances.

All of which is perhaps but a gracefully devious way of saying that Henrietta Stackpole was a good example, in "The Portrait," of the truth to which I just adverted—as good an example as I could name were it not that Maria Gostrey, in "The Ambassadors," then in the bosom of time, may be mentioned as a better. Each of these persons is but wheels to the coach; neither belongs to the body of that vehicle, or is for a moment accommodated with a seat inside. There the subject alone is ensconced, in the form of its "hero and heroine," and of the privileged high officials, say, who ride with the king and queen. There are reasons why one would have liked this to be felt, as in general one would like almost anything to be felt, in one's work, that one has one's self contributively felt. We have seen, however, how idle is that pretension, which I should be sorry to make too much of. Maria Gostrey and Miss Stackpole then are cases, each, of the light *ficelle*, not of the true agent; they may run beside the coach "for all they are worth," they may cling to it till they are out of breath (as poor Miss Stackpole all so visibly does), but neither, all the while, so much as gets her foot on the step, neither ceases for a moment to tread the dusty road. Put it even that they are like the fishwives who helped to bring back to Paris from Versailles, on that most ominous day of the first half of the French Revolution, the carriage of the royal family. The only thing is that I may well be asked, I acknowledge, why then, in the present fiction, I have suffered Henrietta (of whom we have indubitably too much) so officiously, so strangely, so almost inexplicably, to pervade. I will presently say what I can for that anomaly—and in the most conciliatory fashion.

A point I wish still more to make is that if my relation of confidence with the actors in my drama who *were*, unlike Miss Stackpole, true agents, was an excellent one to have arrived at, there still remained my relation with the reader, which was another affair altogether and as to which I felt no one to be trusted but myself. That solicitude was to be accordingly expressed in the artful patience with which, as I have said, I piled brick upon brick. The bricks, for the whole counting-over—putting for bricks little touches and inventions and enhancements by the way—affect me in truth as well-nigh innumerable and as ever so scrupulously fitted together and packed-in. It is an effect of detail, of the minutest; though, if one were in this connexion to say all, one would express the hope that the general, the ampler air of the modest monument still survives. I do at least seem to catch the key to a part of this abundance of small anxious, ingenious illustration as I recollect putting my finger, in my young woman's interest, on the most obvious of her predicates. "What will she 'do'? Why, the first thing she 'll do will be to come to Europe; which in fact will form, and all inevitably, no small part of her principal adventure. Coming to Europe is even for the 'frail vessels,' in this wonderful age, a mild adventure; but what is truer than that on one side—the side of their independence of flood and field, of the moving accident, of battle and murder and sudden death—her adventures are to be mild? Without her sense of them, her sense *for* them, as one may say, they are next to nothing at all; but is n't the beauty and the difficulty just in showing their mystic conversion by that sense, conversion into the stuff of drama or, even more delightful word still, of 'story'?" It was all as clear, my contention, as a silver bell. Two very good instances, I think, of this effect of conversion, two cases of the rare chemistry, are the pages in which Isabel, coming into the drawing-room at Gardencourt, coming in from a wet walk or whatever, that rainy afternoon, finds Madame Merle in possession of the place, Madame Merle seated, all absorbed but all serene, at the piano, and deeply recognises, in the striking of such an hour, in the presence there, among the gathering shades, of this personage, of whom a moment before she had never so much as heard, a turning-point in her life. It is dreadful to have too much, for any artistic demonstration, to dot one's i's and insist on one's intentions, and I am not eager to do it now; but the question here was that of producing the maximum of intensity with the minimum of strain.

The interest was to be raised to its pitch and yet the elements to be kept in their key; so that, should the whole thing duly impress, I might show what an "exciting" inward life may do for the person leading it even while it remains perfectly normal. And I cannot think of a more consistent application of that ideal unless it be in the long statement, just beyond the middle of the book, of my young woman's extraordinary meditative vigil on the occasion that was to become for her such a landmark. Reduced to its essence, it is but the vigil of searching criticism; but it throws the action further forward than twenty "incidents" might have done. It was designed to have all the vivacity of incident and all the economy of picture. She sits up, by her dying fire, far into the night, under the spell of recognitions on which she finds the last sharpness suddenly wait. It is a representation simply of her motionlessly *seeing*, and an attempt withal to make the mere still lucidity of her act as "interesting" as the surprise of a caravan or the identification of a pirate. It represents, for that matter, one of the identifications dear to the novelist, and even indispensable to him; but it all goes on without her being approached by another person and without her leaving her chair. It is obviously the best thing in the book, but it is only a supreme illustration of the general plan. As to Henrietta, my apology for whom I just left incomplete, she exemplifies, I fear, in her superabundance, not an element of my plan, but only an excess of my zeal. So early was to begin my tendency to *overtreat*, rather than undertreat (when there was choice or danger) my subject. (Many members of my craft, I gather, are far from agreeing with me, but I have always held overtreating the minor disservice.) "Treating" that of "The Portrait" amounted to never forgetting, by any lapse, that the thing was under a special obligation to be amusing. There was the danger of the noted "thinness"—which was to be averted, tooth and nail, by cultivation of the lively. That is at least how I see it to-day. Henrietta must have been at that time a part of my wonderful notion of the lively. And then there was another matter. I had, within the few preceding years, come to live in London, and the "international" light lay, in those days, to my sense, thick and rich upon the scene. It was the light in which so much of the picture hung. But that *is* another matter. There is really too much to say.

The Princess Casamassima

THE SIMPLEST ACCOUNT of the origin of "The Princess Casamassima" is, I think, that this fiction proceeded quite directly, during the first year of a long residence in London, from the habit and the interest of walking the streets. I walked a great deal—for exercise, for amusement, for acquisition, and above all I always walked home at the evening's end, when the evening had been spent elsewhere, as happened more often than not; and as to do this was to receive many impressions, so the impressions worked and sought an issue, so the book after a time was born. It is a fact that, as I look back, the attentive exploration of London, the assault directly made by the great city upon an imagination quick to react, fully explains a large part of it. There is a minor element that refers itself to another source, of which I shall presently speak; but the prime idea was unmistakeably the ripe round fruit of perambulation. One walked of course with one's eyes greatly open, and I hasten to declare that such a practice, carried on for a long time and over a considerable space, positively provokes, all round, a mystic solicitation, the urgent appeal, on the part of everything, to be interpreted and, so far as may be, reproduced. "Subjects" and situations, character and history, the tragedy and comedy of life, are things of which the common air, in such conditions, seems pungently to taste; and to a mind curious, before the human scene, of meanings and revelations the great grey Babylon easily becomes, on its face, a garden bristling with an immense illustrative flora. Possible stories, presentable figures, rise from the thick jungle as the observer moves, fluttering up like startled game, and before he knows it indeed he has fairly to guard himself against the brush of importunate wings. He goes on as with his head in a cloud of humming presences—especially during the younger, the initiatory time, the fresh, the sharply-apprehensive months or years, more or less numerous. We use our material up, we use up even the thick tribute of the London streets—if perception and attention but sufficiently light our steps. But I think of them as lasting, for myself, quite sufficiently long; I think of them as even still—dreadfully changed for the worse in respect to any romantic idea as I find them—breaking out on occasion into eloquence, throwing out deep notes from their vast vague murmur.

There was a moment at any rate when they offered me no image more vivid than that of some individual sensitive nature or fine mind, some small obscure intelligent creature whose education should have been almost wholly derived from them, capable of profiting by all the civilisation, all the accumulations to which they testify, yet condemned to see these things only from outside—in mere quickened consideration, mere wistfulness and envy and despair. It seemed to me I had only to imagine such a spirit intent enough and troubled enough, and to place it in presence of the comings and goings, the great gregarious company, of the more fortunate than himself—all on the scale on which London could show them—to get possession of an interesting theme. I arrived so at the history of little Hyacinth Robinson—he sprang up for me out of the London pavement. To find his possible adventure interesting I had only to conceive his watching the same public show, the same innumerable appearances, I had watched myself, and of his watching very much as I had watched; save indeed for one little difference. This difference would be that so far as all the swarming facts should speak of freedom and ease, knowledge and power, money, opportunity and satiety, he should be able to revolve round them but at the most respectful of distances and with every door of approach shut in his face. For one's self, all conveniently, there had been doors that opened—opened into light and warmth and cheer, into good and charming relations; and if the place as a whole lay heavy on one's consciousness there was yet always for relief this implication of one's own lucky share of the freedom and ease, lucky acquaintance with the number of lurking springs at light pressure of which particular vistas would begin to recede, great lighted, furnished, peopled galleries, sending forth gusts of agreeable sound.

That main happy sense of the picture was always there and that retreat from the general grimness never forbidden; whereby one's own relation to the mere formidable mass and weight of things was eased off and adjusted. One learned from an early period what it might be to know London in such a way as that—an immense and interesting discipline, an education on terms mostly convenient and delightful. But what would be the effect of the other way, of having so many precious things perpetually in one's eyes, yet of missing them all for any closer knowledge, and of the confinement of closer knowledge entirely to matters with which a connexion, however intimate, could n't possibly pass for a privilege? Truly, of course, there are London mysteries (dense categories of dark arcana) for every spectator, and it 's in a degree an exclusion and a state of weakness to be without experience of the meaner conditions, the lower manners and types, the general sordid struggle, the weight of the burden of labour, the ignorance, the misery and the vice. With such matters as those my tormented young man would have had contact—they would have formed, fundamentally, from the first, his natural and immediate London. But the reward of a romantic curiosity would be the question of what the total assault, that of the world of his work-a-day life and the world of his divination and his envy together, would have made of him, and what in especial he would have made of them. As tormented, I say, I thought of him, and that would be the point—if one could only see him feel enough to be interesting without his feeling so much as not to be natural.

This in fact I have ever found rather terribly the point— that the figures in any picture, the agents in any drama, are interesting only in proportion as they feel their respective situations; since the consciousness, on their part, of the complication exhibited forms for us their link of connexion with it. But there are degrees of feeling—the muffled, the faint, the just sufficient, the barely intelligent, as we may say; and the acute, the intense, the complete, in a word—the power to be finely aware and richly responsible. It is those moved in this latter fashion who "get most" out of all that happens to them and who in so doing enable us, as readers of their record, as participators by a fond attention, also to get most. Their being finely aware—as Hamlet and Lear, say, are finely aware—*makes* absolutely the intensity of their adventure, gives the maximum of sense to what befalls them. We care, our curiosity and our sympathy care, comparatively little for what happens to the stupid, the coarse and the blind; care for it, and for the effects of it, at the most as helping to precipitate what happens to the more deeply wondering, to the really sentient. Hamlet and Lear are surrounded, amid their complications, by the stupid and the blind, who minister in all sorts of ways to their recorded fate. Persons of markedly limited sense would, on such a principle as that, play a part in the career of my tormented youth; but he would n't be of markedly limited sense himself—he would note as many things and vibrate to as many occasions as I might venture to make him.

There would n't moreover simply be the question of his suffering—of which we might soon get enough; there would be the question of what, all beset and all perceptive, he should thus adventurously do, thus dream and hazard and attempt. The interest of the attitude and the act would be the actor's imagination and vision of them, together with the nature and degree of their felt return upon him. So the intelligent creature would be required and so some picture of his intelligence involved. The picture of an intelligence appears for the most part, it is true, a dead weight for the reader of the English novel to carry, this reader having so often the wondrous property of caring for the displayed tangle of human relations without caring for its intelligibility. The teller of a story is primarily, none the less, the listener to it, the reader of it, too; and, having needed thus to make it out, distinctly, on the crabbed page of life, to disengage it from the rude human character and the more or less gothic text in which it has been packed away, the very essence of his affair has been the *imputing* of intelligence. The basis of his attention has been that such and such an imbroglio has got started—on the page of life—because of something that some one has felt and more or less understood.

I recognise at the same time, and in planning "The Princess Casamassima" felt it highly important to recognise, the danger of filling too full any supposed and above all any obviously limited vessel of consciousness. If persons either tragically or comically embroiled with life allow us the comic or tragic value of their embroilment in proportion as their struggle is a measured and directed one, it is strangely true, none the less, that beyond a certain point they are spoiled for us by this carrying of a due light. They may carry too much of it for our credence, for our compassion, for our derision. They may be shown as knowing too much and feeling too much—not certainly for their remaining remarkable, but for their remaining "natural" and typical, for their having the needful communities with our own precious liability to fall into traps and be bewildered. It seems probable that if we were never bewildered there would never be a story to tell about us; we should partake of the superior nature of the all-knowing immortals whose annals are dreadfully dull so long as flurried humans are not, for the positive relief of bored Olympians, mixed up with them. Therefore it is that the wary reader for the most part warns the novelist against making his characters too *interpretative* of the muddle of fate, or in other words too divinely, too priggishly clever. "Give us plenty of bewilderment," this monitor seems to say, "so long as there is plenty of slashing out in the bewilderment too. But don't, we beseech you, give us too much intelligence; for intelligence—well, *endangers*; endangers not perhaps the slasher himself, but the very slashing, the subject-matter of any self-respecting story. It opens up too many considerations, possibilities, issues; it *may* lead the slasher into dreary realms where slashing somehow fails and falls to the ground."

That is well reasoned on the part of the reader, who can in spite of it never have an idea—or his earnest discriminations would come to him less easily—of the extreme difficulty, for the painter of the human mixture, of reproducing that mixture aright. "Give us in the persons represented, the subjects of the bewilderment (that bewilderment without which there would be no question of an issue or of the fact of suspense, prime implications in any story) as much experience as possible, but keep down the terms in which you report that experience, because we only understand the very simplest": such in effect are the words in which the novelist constantly hears himself addressed, such the plea made him by the would-be victims of his spell on behalf of that sovereign principle the economy of interest, a principle as to which their instinct is justly strong. He listens anxiously to the charge—nothing can exceed his own solicitude for an economy of interest; but feels himself all in presence of an abyss of ambiguities, the mutual accommodations in which the reader wholly leaves to him. Experience, as I see it, is our apprehension and our measure of what happens to us as social creatures—any intelligent report of which has to be based on that apprehension. The picture of the exposed and entangled state is what is required, and there are certainly always plenty of grounds for keeping down the complexities of a picture. A picture it still has to be, however, and by that condition has to deal effectually with its subject, so that the simple device of more and more keeping down may well not see us quite to our end or even quite to our middle. One suggested way of keeping down, for instance, is not to attribute feeling, or feelings, to persons who would n't in all probability have had any to speak of. The less space, within the frame of the picture, their feelings take up the more space is left for their doings—a fact that may at first seem to make for a refinement of economy.

All of which is charming—yet would be infinitely more so if here at once ambiguity did n't yawn; the unreality of the sharp distinction, where the interest of observation is at stake, between doing and feeling. In the immediate field of life, for action, for application, for getting through a job, nothing may so much matter perhaps as the descent of a suspended weight on this, that or the other spot, with all its subjective concomitants quite secondary and irrelevant. But the affair of the painter is not the immediate, it is the reflected field of life, the realm not of application, but of *appreciation*—a truth that makes our measure of effect altogether different. My report of people's experience—my report as a "story-teller"—is essentially my appreciation of it, and there is no "interest" for me in what my hero, my heroine or any one else does save through that admirable process. As soon as I begin to appreciate simplification is imperilled: the sharply distinguished parts of any adventure, any case of endurance and performance, melt together as an appeal. I then see their "doing," that of the persons just mentioned, as, immensely, their feeling, their feeling as their doing; since I can have none of the conveyed sense and taste of their situation without becoming intimate with them. I can't be intimate without that sense and taste, and I can't appreciate save by intimacy, any more than

I can report save by a projected light. Intimacy with a man's specific behaviour, with his given case, is desperately certain to make us see it as a whole—in which event arbitrary limitations of our vision lose whatever beauty they may on occasion have pretended to. What a man thinks and what he feels are the history and the character of what he does; on all of which things the logic of intensity rests. Without intensity where is vividness, and without vividness where is presentability? If I have called the most general state of one's most exposed and assaulted figures the state of bewilderment—the condition for instance on which Thackeray so much insists in the interest of *his* exhibited careers, the condition of a humble heart, a bowed head, a patient wonder, a suspended judgement, before the "awful will" and the mysterious decrees of Providence—so it is rather witless to talk of merely getting rid of that displayed mode of reaction, one of the oft-encountered, one of the highly recommended, categories of feeling.

The whole thing comes to depend thus on the *quality* of bewilderment characteristic of one's creature, the quality involved in the given case or supplied by one's data. There are doubtless many such qualities, ranging from vague and crepuscular to sharpest and most critical; and we have but to imagine one of these latter to see how easily—from the moment it gets its head at all—it may insist on playing a part. There we have then at once a case of feeling, of ever so many possible feelings, stretched across the scene like an attached thread on which the pearls of interest are strung. There are threads shorter and less tense, and I am far from implying that the minor, the coarser and less fruitful forms and degrees of moral reaction, as we may conveniently call it, may not yield lively results. They have their subordinate, comparative, illustrative human value—that appeal of the witless which is often so penetrating. Verily even, I think, no "story" is possible without its fools—as most of the fine painters of life, Shakespeare, Cervantes and Balzac, Fielding, Scott, Thackeray, Dickens, George Meredith, George Eliot, Jane Austen, have abundantly felt. At the same time I confess I never see the *leading* interest of any human hazard but in a consciousness (on the part of the moved and moving creature) subject to fine intensification and wide enlargement. It is as mirrored in that consciousness that the gross fools, the headlong fools, the fatal fools play their part for us—they have much less to show us in themselves. The troubled life mostly at the centre of our subject—whatever our subject, for the artistic hour, happens to be—embraces them and deals with them for its amusement and its anguish: they are apt largely indeed, on a near view, to be all the cause of its trouble. This means, exactly, that the person capable of feeling in the given case more than another of what is to be felt for it, and so serving in the highest degree to *record* it dramatically and objectively, is the only sort of person on whom we can count not to betray, to cheapen or, as we say, give away, the value and beauty of the thing. By so much as the affair matters *for* some such individual, by so much do we get the best there is of it, and by so much as it falls within the scope of a denser and duller, a more vulgar and more shallow capacity, do we get a picture dim and meagre.

The great chroniclers have clearly always been aware of this; they have at least always either placed a mind of some sort—in the sense of a reflecting and colouring medium—in possession of the general adventure (when the latter has not been purely epic, as with Scott, say, as with old Dumas and with Zola); or else paid signally, as to the interest created, for their failure to do so. We may note moreover in passing that this failure is in almost no case intentional or part of a plan, but has sprung from their limited curiosity, their short conception of the particular sensibility projected. Edgar of Ravenswood for instance, visited by the tragic tempest of "The Bride of Lammermoor," has a black cloak and hat and feathers more than he has a mind; just as Hamlet, while equally sabled and draped and plumed, while at least equally romantic, has yet a mind still more than he has a costume. The situation represented is that Ravenswood loves Lucy Ashton through dire difficulty and danger, and that she in the same way loves him; but the relation so created between them is by this neglect of the "feeling" question never shown us as primarily taking place. It is shown only in its secondary, its confused and disfigured aspects—where, however, luckily, it is presented with great romantic good faith. The thing has nevertheless paid for its deviation, as I say, by a sacrifice of

intensity; the centre of the subject is empty and the development pushed off, all round, toward the frame—which is, so
to speak, beautifully rich and curious. But I mention that relation to each other of the appearances in a particular work
only as a striking negative case; there are in the connexion I
have glanced at plenty of striking positive ones. It is very true
that Fielding's hero in "Tom Jones" is but as "finely," that is
but as intimately, bewildered as a young man of great health
and spirits may be when he has n't a grain of imagination:
the point to be made is, at all events, that his sense of bewilderment obtains altogether on the comic, never on the tragic
plane. He has so much "life" that it amounts, for the effect of
comedy and application of satire, almost to his having a mind,
that is to his having reactions and a full consciousness; besides
which his author— *he* handsomely possessed of a mind—has
such an amplitude of reflexion for him and round him that
we see him through the mellow air of Fielding's fine old mor-
alism, fine old humour and fine old style, which somehow
really enlarge, make every one and every thing important.

All of which furthers my remarking how much I have been
interested, on reading "The Princess Casamassima" over, to
recognise my sense, sharp from far back, that clearness and
concreteness constantly depend, for any pictorial whole, on
some *concentrated* individual notation of them. That notation
goes forward here in the mind of little Hyacinth, immensely
quickened by the fact of its so mattering to his very life what
he does make of things: which passion of intelligence is, as I
have already hinted, precisely his highest value for our curiosity and our sympathy. Yet if his highest it is not at all his
only one, since the truth for "a young man in a book" by no
means entirely resides in his being either exquisitely sensitive
or shiningly clever. It resides in some such measure of these
things as may consort with the fine measure of other things
too—with that of the other faces of his situation and character. If he 's too sensitive and too clever for *them*, if he knows
more than is likely or natural—for *him*—it 's as if he were
n't at all, as if he were false and impossible. Extreme and attaching always the difficulty of fixing at a hundred points the
place where one's impelled *bonhomme* may feel enough and
"know" enough—or be in the way of learning enough—for

his maximum dramatic value without feeling and knowing too much for his minimum verisimilitude, his proper fusion with the fable. This is the charming, the tormenting, the eternal little matter *to be made right*, in all the weaving of silver threads and tapping on golden nails; and I should take perhaps too fantastic a comfort—I mean were not the comforts of the artist just of the raw essence of fantasy—in any glimpse of such achieved rightnesses, whether in my own work or that of others. In no work whatever, doubtless, are they the felicities the most frequent; but they have so inherent a price that even the traceable attempt at them, wherever met, sheds, I think, a fine influence about.

I have for example a weakness of sympathy with that constant effort of George Eliot's which plays through Adam Bede and Felix Holt and Tito Melema, through Daniel Deronda and through Lydgate in "Middlemarch," through Maggie Tulliver, through Romola, through Dorothea Brooke and Gwendolen Harleth; the effort to show their adventures and their history—the author's subject-matter all—as determined by their feelings and the nature of their minds. Their emotions, their stirred intelligence, their moral consciousness, become thus, by sufficiently charmed perusal, our own very adventure. The creator of Deronda and of Romola is charged, I know, with having on occasion—as in dealing with those very celebrities themselves—left the figure, the concrete man and woman, too abstract by reason of the quantity of soul employed; but such mischances, where imagination and humour still keep them company, often have an interest that is wanting to agitations of the mere surface or to those that may be only taken for granted. I should even like to give myself the pleasure of retracing from one of my own productions to another the play of a like instinctive disposition, of catching in the fact, at one point after another, from "Roderick Hudson" to "The Golden Bowl," that provision for interest which consists in placing advantageously, placing right in the middle of the light, the most polished of possible mirrors of the subject. Rowland Mallet, in "Roderick Hudson," is exactly such a mirror, not a bit autobiographic or formally "first person" though he be, and I might exemplify the case through a long list, through the nature of such a "mind" even as the all-objective Newman in "The American," through the thickly-peopled imagination of Isabel Archer in "The Portrait of a Lady" (her imagination positively the deepest depth of her imbroglio) down to such unmistakeable examples as that of Merton Densher in "The Wings of the Dove," that of Lambert Strether in "The Ambassadors" (*he* a mirror verily of miraculous silver and quite pre-eminent, I think, for the connexion) and that of the Prince in the first half and that of the Princess in the second half of "The Golden Bowl." I should note the extent to which these persons are, so far as their other passions permit, intense *perceivers*, all, of their respective predicaments, and I should go on from them to fifty other examples; even to the divided Vanderbank of "The Awkward Age," the extreme pinch of whose romance is the vivacity in him, to his positive sorrow and loss, of the state of being aware; even to scanted Fleda Vetch in "The Spoils of Poynton," through whose own delicate vision of everything so little of the human value of her situation is wasted for us; even to the small recording governess confronted with the horrors of "The Turn of the Screw" and to the innocent child patching together all ineffectually those of "What Maisie Knew"; even in short, since I may name so few cases, to the disaffected guardian of an overgrown legend in "The Birthplace," to the luckless fine artist of "The Next Time," trying to despoil himself, for a "hit" and bread and butter, of his fatal fineness, to blunt the tips of his intellectual fingers, and to the hapless butler Brooksmith, ruined by good talk, disqualified for common domestic service by the beautiful growth of his habit of quiet attention, his faculty of appreciation. But though this demonstration of a rooted vice—since a vice it would appear mainly accounted—might yield amusement, the examples referred to must await their turn.

I had had for a long time well before me, at any rate, my small obscure but ardent observer of the "London world," saw him roam and wonder and yearn, saw all the unanswered questions and baffled passions that might ferment in him—once he should be made both sufficiently thoughtful and sufficiently "disinherited"; but this image, however interesting, was of course not by itself a progression, an action, did n't by itself make a drama. I got my action however—failing which one has nothing—under the prompt sense that the state of feeling I was concerned with might develop and beget another state, might return at a given moment, and with the greatest vivacity, on itself. To see this was really to feel one's subject swim into one's ken, especially after a certain other ingenious connexion had been made for it. I find myself again recalling, and with the possible "fun" of it reviving too, how I recognised, as revealed and prescribed, the particular complexion, profession and other conditions of my little presumptuous adventurer, with his combination of intrinsic fineness and fortuitous adversity, his small cluster of "dingy" London associations and the swelling spirit in him which was to be the field of his strange experience. Accessible through his imagination, as I have hinted, to a thousand provocations and intimations, he would become most acquainted with destiny in the form of a lively inward revolution. His being jealous of all the ease of life of which he tastes so little, and, bitten, under this exasperation, with an aggressive, vindictive, destructive social faith, his turning to "treasons, stratagems and spoils" might be as vivid a picture as one chose, but would move to pity and terror only by the aid of some deeper complication, some imposed and formidable issue.

The complication most interesting then would be that he should fall in love with the beauty of the world, actual order and all, at the moment of his most feeling and most hating the famous "iniquity of its social arrangements"; so that his position as an irreconcileable pledged enemy to it, thus rendered false by something more personal than his opinions and his vows, becomes the sharpest of his torments. To make it a torment that really matters, however, he must have got practically involved, specifically committed to the stand he has, under the pressure of more knowledge, found impossible; out of which has come for him the deep dilemma of the disillusioned and repentant conspirator. He has thrown himself into the more than "shady" underworld of militant socialism, he has undertaken to play a part—a part that with the drop of his exasperation and the growth, simply expressed, of his taste, is out of all tune with his passion, at any cost, for life itself, the life, whatever it be, that surrounds him. Dabbling deeply in revolutionary politics of a hole-and-corner sort, he would be "in" up to his neck, and with that precarious part of him particularly involved, so that his tergiversation is the climax of his adventure. What was essential with this was that he should have a social—not less than a socialist—connexion, find a door somehow open to him into the appeased and civilised state, into that warmer glow of things he is precisely to help to undermine. To look for this necessary connexion was for me to meet it suddenly in the form of that extremely *disponible* figure of Christina Light whom I had ten years before found left on my hands at the conclusion of "Roderick Hudson." She had for so long, in the vague limbo of those ghosts we have conjured but not exorcised, been looking for a situation, awaiting a niche and a function.

I shall not pretend to trace the steps and stages by which the imputability of a future to that young woman—which was like the act of clothing her chilled and patient nakedness—had for its prime effect to plant her in my little bookbinder's path. Nothing would doubtless beckon us on further, with a large leisure, than such a chance to study the obscure law under which certain of a novelist's characters, more or less honourably buried, revive for him by a force or a whim of their own and " walk" round his house of art like haunting ghosts, feeling for the old doors they knew, fumbling at stiff latches and pressing their pale faces, in the outer dark, to lighted windows. I mistrust them, I confess, in general; my sense of a really expressed character is that it shall have originally so tasted of the ordeal of service as to feel no disposition to yield again to the strain. Why should the Princess of the climax of "Roderick Hudson" still have made her desire felt, unless in fact to testify that she had not been—for what she was—completely recorded? To continue in evidence, that had struck me from far back as her natural passion; in evidence at any price, not consenting to be laid away with folded hands in the pasteboard tomb, the doll's box, to which we usually relegate the spent puppet after the fashion of a recumbent worthy on the slab of a sepulchral monument. I was to see this, after all, in the event, as the fruit of a restless vanity: Christina had felt herself, known herself, striking, in the earlier connexion, and could n't resign herself not to strike again. Her pressure then was not to be resisted—sharply as the question might come up of why she should pretend to strike, just *there*. I shall not attempt to answer it with reasons (one can never tell everything); it was enough that I could recognise her claim to have travelled far—far from where I had last left her: that, one felt, was in character—that was what she naturally *would* have done. Her prime note had been an aversion to the *banal*, and nothing could be of an effect less *banal*, I judged, than her intervention in the life of a dingy little London bookbinder whose sensibility, whose flow of opinions on "public questions" in especial, should have been poisoned at the source.

She would be world-weary—that was another of her notes; and the extravagance of her attitude in these new relations would have its root and its apparent logic in her need to feel freshly about something or other—it might scarce matter what. She can, or she believes she can, feel freshly about the "people" and their wrongs and their sorrows and their perpetual smothered ferment; for these things are furthest removed from those others among which she has hitherto tried to make her life. That was to a certainty where I was to have looked for her—quite *off* and away (once granted the wisdom of listening to her anew at all): therefore Hyacinth's encounter with her could pass for natural, and it was fortunately to be noted that she was to serve for his experience in quite another and a more "leading" sense than any in which he was to serve for hers. I confess I was not averse—such are the possible weaknesses of the artist in face of high difficulties—to feeling that if his appearance of consistency were obtained I might at least try to remain comparatively at my ease about hers. I may add moreover that the resuscitation of Christina (and, on the minor scale, of the Prince and of Madame Grandoni) put in a strong light for me the whole question, for the romancer, of "going on with a character": as Balzac first of all systematically went on, as Thackeray, as Trollope, as Zola all more or less ingeniously went on. I was to find no small savour in the reflexions so precipitated; though I may treat myself here only to this remark about them—that the revivalist impulse on the fond writer's part strikes me as one thing, a charmingly conceivable thing, but the effect of a free indulgence in it (effect, that is, on the nerves of the reader) as, for twenty rather ineffable reasons, quite another.

I remember at any rate feeling myself all in possession of little Hyacinth's consistency, as I have called it, down at Dover during certain weeks that were none too remotely precedent to the autumn of 1885 and the appearance, in the "Atlantic Monthly" again, of the first chapters of the story. There were certain sunny, breezy balconied rooms at the quieter end of the Esplanade of that cheerful castle-crested little town—now infinitely perturbed by gigantic "harbour works," but then only faded and over-soldiered and all pleasantly and humbly submissive to the law that snubs in due course the presumption of flourishing resorts—to which I had already more than once had recourse in hours of quickened industry and which, though much else has been swept away, still archaically exist. To have lately noted this again from the old benched and asphalted walk by the sea, the twinkling Channel beyond which on occasion the opposite coast of France used to gleam as an incident of the charming tendency of the whole prospect (immediate picture and fond design alike) amusingly to *shine*, was somehow to taste afresh, and with a certain surprise, the odd quality of that original confidence that the parts of my plan *would* somehow hang together. I may wonder at my confidence now—given the extreme, the very particular truth and "authority" required at so many points; but to wonder is to live back gratefully into the finer reasons of things, with all the detail of harsh application and friction (that there must have been) quite happily blurred and dim. The finest of reasons—I mean for the sublime confidence I speak of—was that I felt in full *personal* possession of my matter; this really seemed the fruit of direct experience. My scheme called for the suggested nearness (to all our apparently ordered life) of some sinister anarchic underworld, heaving in its pain, its power and its hate; a presentation not of sharp particulars, but of loose appearances, vague motions and sounds and symptoms, just perceptible presences and general looming possibilities. To have adopted the scheme was to have had to meet the question of one's "notes," over the whole ground, the question of what, in such directions, one had "gone into" and how far one had gone; and to have answered that question—to one's own satisfaction at least—was truly to see one's way.

My notes then, on the much-mixed world of my hero's both overt and covert consciousness, were exactly my gathered impressions and stirred perceptions, the deposit in my working imagination of all my visual and all my constructive sense of London. The very plan of my book had in fact directly confronted me with the rich principle of the Note, and was to do much to clear up, once for all, my practical view of it. If one was to undertake to tell tales and to report with truth on the human scene, it could be but because "notes" had been from the cradle the ineluctable consequence of one's greatest inward energy: to take them was as natural as to look, to think, to feel, to recognise, to remember, as to perform any act of understanding. The play of the energy had been continuous and could n't change; what changed was only the objects and situations pressing the spring of it. Notes had been in other words the things one could n't *not* take, and the prime result of all fresh experience was to remind one of that. I have endeavoured to characterise the peremptory fashion in which my fresh experience of London—the London of the habitual observer, the preoccupied painter, the pedestrian prowler—reminded me; an admonition that represented, I think, the sum of my investigations. I recall pulling no wires, knocking at no closed doors, applying for no "authentic" information; but I recall also on the other hand the practice of never missing an opportunity to add a drop, however small, to the bucket of my impressions or to renew my sense of being able to dip into it. To haunt the great city and by this habit to penetrate it, imaginatively, in as many places as possible—*that* was to be informed, *that* was to pull wires, *that* was to open doors, *that* positively was to groan at times under the weight of one's accumulations.

Face to face with the idea of Hyacinth's subterraneous politics and occult affiliations, I recollect perfectly feeling, in short, that I might well be ashamed if, with my advantages— and there was n't a street, a corner, an hour, of London that was not an advantage—I should n't be able to piece together a proper semblance of those things, as indeed a proper semblance of all the odd parts of his life. There was always of course the chance that the propriety might be challenged—challenged by readers of a knowledge greater than mine. Yet knowledge, after all, of what? My vision of the aspects I more or less fortunately rendered *was*, exactly, my knowledge. If I made my appearances live, what was this but the utmost one could do with them? Let me at the same time not deny that, in answer to probable ironic reflexions on the full licence for sketchiness and vagueness and dimness taken indeed by my picture, I had to bethink myself in advance of a defence of my "artistic position." Should n't I find it in the happy contention that the value I wished most to render and the effect I wished most to produce were precisely those of our not knowing, of society's not knowing, but only guessing and suspecting and trying to ignore, what "goes on" irreconcileably, subversively, beneath the vast smug surface? I could n't deal with that positive quantity for itself—my subject had another too exacting side; but I might perhaps show the social ear as on occasion applied to the ground, or catch some gust of the hot breath that I had at many an hour seemed to see escape and hover. What it all came back to was, no doubt, something like *this* wisdom—that if you have n't, for fiction, the root of the matter in you, have n't the sense of life and the penetrating imagination, you are a fool in the very presence of the revealed and assured; but that if you *are* so armed you are not really helpless, not without your resource, even before mysteries abysmal.

The Tragic Muse

I PROFESS a certain vagueness of remembrance in respect to the origin and growth of "The Tragic Muse," which appeared in the "Atlantic Monthly" again, beginning January 1889 and running on, inordinately, several months beyond its proper twelve. If it be ever of interest and profit to put one's finger on the productive germ of a work of art, and if in fact a lucid account of any such work involves that prime identification, I can but look on the present fiction as a poor fatherless and motherless, a sort of unregistered and unacknowledged birth. I fail to recover my precious first moment of consciousness of the idea to which it was to give form; to recognise in it—as I like to do in general—the effect of some particular sharp impression or concussion. I call such remembered glimmers always precious, because without them comes no clear vision of what one may have intended, and without that vision no straight measure of what one may have succeeded in doing. What I make out from furthest back is that I must have had from still further back, must in fact practically have always had, the happy thought of some dramatic picture of the "artist-life" and of the difficult terms on which it is at the best secured and enjoyed, the general question of its having to be not altogether easily paid for. To "do something about art"—art, that is, as a human complication and a social stumbling-block—must have been for me early a good deal of a nursed intention, the conflict between art and "the world" striking me thus betimes as one of the half-dozen great primary motives. I remember even having taken for granted with this fond inveteracy that no one of these pregnant themes was likely to prove under the test more full of matter. This being the case, meanwhile, what would all experience have done but enrich one's conviction?—since if on the one hand I had gained a more and more intimate view of the nature of art and the conditions therewith imposed, so the world was a conception that clearly required, and that would for ever continue to take, any amount of filling-in. The happy and fruitful truth, at all events, was that there was opposition—why there *should* be was another matter—and that the opposition would beget an infinity of situations. What had doubtless occurred in fact, moreover, was that just this question of the essence and the reasons of the opposition had shown itself to demand the light of experience; so that to the growth of experience, truly, the treatment of the subject had yielded. It had waited for that advantage.

Yet I continue to see experience giving me its jog mainly in the form of an invitation from the gentle editor of the "Atlantic," the late Thomas Bailey Aldrich, to contribute to his pages a serial that should run through the year. That friendly appeal becomes thus the most definite statement I can make of the "genesis" of the book; though from the moment of its reaching me everything else in the matter seems to live again. What lives not least, to be quite candid, is the fact that I was to see this production make a virtual end, for the time, as by its sinister effect—though for reasons still obscure to me—of the pleasant old custom of the "running" of the novel. Not for many years was I to feel the practice, for my benefit, confidingly revive. The influence of "The Tragic Muse" was thus exactly other than what I had all earnestly (if of course privately enough) invoked for it, and I remember well the particular chill, at last, of the sense of my having launched it in a great grey void from which no echo or message whatever would come back. None, in the event, ever came, and as I now read the book over I find the circumstances make, in its name, for a special tenderness of charity; even for that finer consideration hanging in the parental breast about the maimed or slighted, the disfigured or defeated, the unlucky or unlikely child—with this hapless small mortal thought of further as somehow "compromising." I am thus able to take the thing as having quite wittingly and undisturbedly existed for itself alone, and to liken it to some aromatic bag of gathered herbs of which the string has never been loosed; or, better still, to some jar of potpourri, shaped and overfigured and polished, but of which the lid, never lifted, has provided for the intense accumulation of the fragrance within. The consistent, the sustained, preserved *tone* of "The Tragic Muse," its constant and doubtless rather fine-drawn truth to its particular sought pitch and accent, are, critically speaking, its principal merit—the inner harmony that I perhaps pre-sumptuously permit myself to compare to an unevaporated scent.

After which indeed I may well be summoned to say what I mean, in such a business, by an appreciable "tone" and how I can justify my claim to it—a demonstration that will await us later. Suffice it just here that I find the latent historic clue in my hand again with the easy recall of my prompt grasp of such a chance to make a story about art. *There* was my subject this time—all mature with having long waited, and with the blest dignity that my original perception of its value was quite lost in the mists of youth. I must long have carried in my head the notion of a young man who should amid diffi-culty—the difficulties being the story—have abandoned "public life" for the zealous pursuit of some supposedly minor craft; just as, evidently, there had hovered before me some possible picture (but all comic and ironic) of one of the most salient London "social" passions, the unappeasable curiosity for the things of the theatre; for every one of them, that is, except the drama itself, and for the "personality" of the per-former (almost any performer quite sufficiently serving) in particular. This latter, verily, had struck me as an aspect ap-pealing mainly to satiric treatment; the only adequate or ef-fective treatment, I had again and again felt, for most of the distinctively social aspects of London: the general artlessly histrionised air of things caused so many examples to spring from behind any hedge. What came up, however, at once, for my own stretched canvas, was that it would have to be ample, give me really space to turn round, and that a single illustra-tive case might easily be meagre fare. The young man who should "chuck" admired politics, and of course some other admired object with them, would be all very well; but he would n't be enough—therefore what should one say to some other young man who would chuck something and somebody else, admired in their way too?

There need never, at the worst, be any difficulty about the things advantageously chuckable for art; the question is all but of choosing them in the heap. Yet were I to represent a struggle—an interesting one, indispensably—with the pas-sions of the theatre (as a profession, or at least as an absorp-

tion) I should have to place the theatre in another light than
the satiric. This, however, would by good luck be perfectly
possible too—without a sacrifice of truth; and I should
doubtless even be able to make my theatric case as important
as I might desire it. It seemed clear that I needed big cases—
small ones would practically give my central idea away; and I
make out now my still labouring under the illusion that the
case of the sacrifice for art *can* ever be, with truth, with taste,
with discretion involved, apparently and showily "big." I dare
say it glimmered upon me even then that the very sharpest
difficulty of the victim of the conflict I should seek to represent, and the very highest interest of his predicament, dwell
deep in the fact that his repudiation of the great obvious,
great moral or functional or useful character, shall just have
to consent to resemble a surrender for absolutely nothing.
Those characters are all large and expansive, seated and established and endowed; whereas the most charming truth about
the preference for art is that to parade abroad so thoroughly
inward and so naturally embarrassed a matter is to falsify and
vulgarise it; that as a preference attended with the honours of
publicity it is indeed nowhere; that in fact, under the rule of
its sincerity, its only honours are those of contraction, concentration and a seemingly deplorable indifference to everything but itself. Nothing can well figure as less "big," in an
honest thesis, than a marked instance of somebody's willing-
ness to pass mainly for an ass. Of these things I must, I say,
have been in strictness aware; what I perhaps failed of was to
note that if a certain romantic glamour (even that of mere
eccentricity or of a fine perversity) may be flung over the act
of exchange of a "career" for the æsthetic life in general, the
prose and the modesty of the matter yet come in with any
exhibition of the particular branch of æsthetics selected. Then
it is that the attitude of hero or heroine may look too much—
for the romantic effect—like a low crouching over proved
trifles. Art indeed has in our day taken on so many honours
and emoluments that the recognition of its importance is
more than a custom, has become on occasion almost a fury:
the line is drawn—especially in the English world—only at
the importance of heeding what it may mean.

The more I turn my pieces over, at any rate, the more I

now see I must have found in them, and I remember how, once well in presence of my three typical examples, my fear of too ample a canvas quite dropped. The only question was that if I had marked my political case, from so far back, for "a story by itself," and then marked my theatrical case for another, the joining together of these interests, originally seen as separate, might, all disgracefully, betray the seam, show for mechanical and superficial. A story was a story, a picture a picture, and I had a mortal horror of two stories, two pictures, in one. The reason of this was the clearest—my subject was immediately, under that disadvantage, so cheated of its indispensable centre as to become of no more use for expressing a main intention than a wheel without a hub is of use for moving a cart. It was a fact, apparently, that one *had* on occasion seen two pictures in one; were there not for instance certain sublime Tintorettos at Venice, a measureless Crucifixion in especial, which showed without loss of authority half a dozen actions separately taking place? Yes, that might be, but there had surely been nevertheless a mighty pictorial fusion, so that the virtue of composition had somehow thereby come all mysteriously to its own. Of course the affair would be simple enough if composition could be kept out of the question; yet by what art or process, what bars and bolts, what unmuzzled dogs and pointed guns, perform that feat? I had to know myself utterly inapt for any such valour and recognise that, to make it possible, sundry things should have begun for me much further back than I had felt them even in their dawn. A picture without composition slights its most precious chance for beauty, and is moreover not composed at all unless the painter knows *how* that principle of health and safety, working as an absolutely premeditated art, has prevailed. There may in its absence be life, incontestably, as "The Newcomes" has life, as "Les Trois Mousquetaires," as Tolstoi's "Peace and War," have it; but what do such large loose baggy monsters, with their queer elements of the accidental and the arbitrary, artistically *mean*? We have heard it maintained, we well remember, that such things are "superior to art"; but we understand least of all what *that* may mean, and we look in vain for the artist, the divine explanatory genius, who will come to our aid and tell us. There is life and life, and as waste is only life sacrificed and thereby prevented from "counting," I delight in a deep-breathing economy and an organic form. My business was accordingly to "go in" for complete pictorial fusion, some such common interest between my two first notions as would, in spite of their birth under quite different stars, do them no violence at all.

I recall with this confirmed infatuation of retrospect that through the mild perceptions I here glance at there struck for "The Tragic Muse" the first hour of a season of no small subjective felicity; lighted mainly, I seem to see, by a wide west window that, high aloft, looked over near and far London sunsets, a half-grey, half-flushed expanse of London life. The production of the thing, which yet took a good many months, lives for me again all contemporaneously in that full projection, upon my very table, of the good fog-filtered Kensington mornings; which had a way indeed of seeing the sunset in and which at the very last are merged to memory in a different and a sharper pressure, that of an hotel bedroom in Paris during the autumn of 1889, with the Exposition du Centenaire about to end—and my long story, through the usual difficulties, as well. The usual difficulties—and I fairly cherish the record as some adventurer in another line may hug the sense of his inveterate habit of just saving in time the neck he ever undiscourageably risks—were those bequeathed as a particular vice of the artistic spirit, against which vigilance had been destined from the first to exert itself in vain, and the effect of which was that again and again, perversely, incurably, the centre of my structure would insist on placing itself *not*, so to speak, in the middle. It mattered little that the reader with the idea or the suspicion of a structural centre is the rarest of friends and of critics—a bird, it would seem, as merely fabled as the phœnix: the terminational terror was none the less certain to break in and my work threaten to masquerade for me as an active figure condemned to the disgrace of legs too short, ever so much too short, for its body. I urge myself to the candid confession that in very few of my productions, to my eye, *has* the organic centre succeeded in getting into proper position.

Time after time, then, has the precious waistband or girdle, studded and buckled and placed for brave outward show,

practically worked itself, and in spite of desperate remonstrance, or in other words essential counterplotting, to a point
perilously near the knees—perilously I mean for the freedom
of these parts. In several of my compositions this displacement has so succeeded, at the crisis, in defying and resisting
me, has appeared so fraught with probable dishonour, that I
still turn upon them, in spite of the greater or less success of
final dissimulation, a rueful and wondering eye. These productions have in fact, if I may be so bold about it, specious
and spurious centres altogether, to make up for the failure of
the true. As to which in my list they are, however, that is
another business, not on any terms to be made known. Such
at least would seem my resolution so far as I have thus proceeded. Of any attention ever arrested by the pages forming
the object of this reference that rigour of discrimination has
wholly and consistently failed, I gather, to constitute a part.
In which fact there is perhaps after all a rough justice—since
the infirmity I speak of, for example, has been always but the
direct and immediate fruit of a positive excess of foresight,
the overdone desire to provide for future need and lay up
heavenly treasure against the demands of my climax. If the art
of the drama, as a great French master of it has said, is above
all the art of preparations, that is true only to a less extent of
the art of the novel, and true exactly in the degree in which
the art of the particular novel comes near that of the drama.
The first half of a fiction insists ever on figuring to me as the
stage or theatre for the second half, and I have in general
given so much space to making the theatre propitious that
my halves have too often proved strangely unequal. Thereby
has arisen with grim regularity the question of artfully, of
consummately masking the fault and conferring on the false
quantity the brave appearance of the true.

But I am far from pretending that these desperations of
ingenuity have not—as through seeming *most* of the very essence of the problem—their exasperated charm; so far from
it that my particular supreme predicament in the Paris hotel,
after an undue primary leakage of time, no doubt, over at the
great river-spanning museum of the Champ de Mars and the
Trocadero, fairly takes on to me now the tender grace of a
day that is dead. Re-reading the last chapters of "The Tragic

Muse" I catch again the very odour of Paris, which comes up
in the rich rumble of the Rue de la Paix—with which my
room itself, for that matter, seems impregnated—and which
hangs for reminiscence about the embarrassed effort to "finish," not ignobly, within my already exceeded limits; an effort
prolonged each day to those late afternoon hours during
which the tone of the terrible city seemed to deepen about
one to an effect strangely composed at once of the auspicious
and the fatal. The "plot" of Paris thickened at such hours
beyond any other plot in the world, I think; but there one sat
meanwhile with another, on one's hands, absolutely requiring
precedence. Not the least imperative of one's conditions was
thus that one should have really, should have finely and
(given one's scale) concisely treated one's subject, in spite of
there being so much of the confounded irreducible quantity
still to treat. If I spoke just now, however, of the "exasperated" charm of supreme difficulty, that is because the challenge of economic representation so easily becomes, in any of
the arts, intensely interesting to meet. To put all that is possible of one's idea into a form and compass that will contain
and express it only by delicate adjustments and an exquisite
chemistry, so that there will at the end be neither a drop of
one's liquor left nor a hair's breadth of the rim of one's glass
to spare—every artist will remember how often that sort of
necessity has carried with it its particular inspiration. Therein
lies the secret of the appeal, to his mind, of the successfully
foreshortened thing, where representation is arrived at, as I
have already elsewhere had occasion to urge, not by the addition of items (a light that has for its attendant shadow a
possible dryness) but by the art of figuring synthetically, a
compactness into which the imagination may cut thick, as
into the rich density of wedding-cake. The moral of all which
indeed, I fear, is, perhaps too trivially, but that the "thick,"
the false, the dissembling second half of the work before me,
associated throughout with the effort to weight my dramatic
values as heavily as might be, since they had to be so few,
presents that effort as at the very last a quite convulsive, yet
in its way highly agreeable, spasm. Of such mild prodigies is
the "history" of any specific creative effort composed!

But I have got too much out of the "old" Kensington light

of twenty years ago—a lingering oblique ray of which, to-day surely quite extinct, played for a benediction over my canvas. From the moment I made out, at my high-perched west window, my lucky title, that is from the moment Miriam Rooth herself had given it me, so this young woman had given me with it her own position in the book, and so that in turn had given me my precious unity, to which no more than Miriam was either Nick Dormer or Peter Sherringham to be sacrificed. Much of the interest of the matter was immediately therefore in working out the detail of that unity and—always entrancing range of questions—the order, the reason, the relation, of presented aspects. With three *general* aspects, that of Miriam's case, that of Nick's and that of Sherringham's, there was work in plenty cut out; since happy as it might be to say "My several actions beautifully become one," the point of the affair would be in *showing* them beautifully become so—without which showing foul failure hovered and pounced. Well, the pleasure of handling an action (or, otherwise expressed, of a "story") is at the worst, for a storyteller, immense, and the interest of such a question as for example keeping Nick Dormer's story his and yet making it also and all effectively in a large part Peter Sherringham's, of keeping Sherringham's his and yet making it in its high degree his kinsman's too, and Miriam Rooth's into the bargain; just as Miriam Rooth's is by the same token quite operatively his and Nick's, and just as that of each of the young men, by an equal logic, very contributively hers—the interest of such a question, I say, is ever so considerably the interest of the system on which the whole thing is done. I see to-day that it was but half a system to say: "Oh Miriam, a case herself, is the *link* between the two other cases"; that device was to ask for as much help as it gave and to require a good deal more application than it announced on the surface. The sense of a system saves the painter from the baseness of the *arbitrary* stroke, the touch without its reason, but as payment for that service the process insists on being kept impeccably the right one.

These are intimate truths indeed, of which the charm mainly comes out but on experiment and in practice; yet I like to have it well before me here that, after all, "The Tragic

Muse" makes it not easy to say which of the situations concerned in it predominates and rules. What has become in that
imperfect order, accordingly, of the famous centre of one's
subject? It is surely not in Nick's consciousness—since why,
if it be, are we treated to such an intolerable dose of Sherringham's? It can't be in Sherringham's—we have for that
altogether an excess of Nick's. How on the other hand can it
be in Miriam's, given that we have no direct exhibition of
hers whatever, that we get at it all inferentially and induc-
tively, seeing it only through a more or less bewildered interpretation of it by others. The emphasis is all on an absolutely
objective Miriam, and, this affirmed, how—with such an
amount of exposed subjectivity all round her—can so dense
a medium be a centre? Such questions as those go straight—
thanks to which they are, I profess, delightful; going straight
they are of the sort that makes answers possible. Miriam *is*
central then to analysis, in spite of being objective; central in
virtue of the fact that the whole thing has visibly, from the
first, to get itself done in dramatic, or at least in scenic conditions—though scenic conditions which are as near an approach to the dramatic as the novel may permit itself and
which have this in common with the latter, that they move in
the light of *alternation*. This imposes a consistency other than
that of the novel at its loosest, and, for one's subject, a different view and a different placing of the centre. The charm of
the scenic consistency, the consistency of the multiplication of
aspects, that of making them amusingly various, had haunted
the author of "The Tragic Muse" from far back, and he was
in due course to yield to it all luxuriously, too luxuriously
perhaps, in "The Awkward Age," as will doubtless with the
extension of these remarks be complacently shown.

To put himself at any rate as much as possible under the
protection of it had been ever his practice (he had notably
done so in "The Princess Casamassima," so frankly panoramic
and processional); and in what case could this protection have
had more price than in the one before us? No character in a
play (any play not a mere monologue) has, for the right
expression of the thing, a *usurping* consciousness; the consciousness of others is exhibited exactly in the same way as
that of the "hero"; the prodigious consciousness of Hamlet,

the most capacious and most crowded, the moral presence the most asserted, in the whole range of fiction, only takes its turn with that of the other agents of the story, no matter how occasional these may be. It is left in other words to answer for itself equally with theirs: wherefore (by a parity of reasoning if not of example) Miriam's might without inconsequence be placed on the same footing; and all in spite of the fact that the "moral presence" of each of the men most importantly concerned with her—or with the second of whom she at least is importantly concerned—*is* independently answered for. The idea of the book being, as I have said, a picture of some of the personal consequences of the art-appetite raised to intensity, swollen to voracity, the heavy emphasis falls where the symbol of some of the complications so begotten might be made (as I judged, heaven forgive me!) most "amusing": amusing I mean in the blest very modern sense. I never "go behind" Miriam; only poor Sherringham goes, a great deal, and Nick Dormer goes a little, and the author, while they so waste wonderment, goes behind *them*: but none the less she is as thoroughly symbolic, as functional, for illustration of the idea, as either of them, while her image had seemed susceptible of a livelier and "prettier" concretion. I had desired for her, I remember, all manageable vividness—so ineluctable had it long appeared to "do the actress," to touch the theatre, to meet that connexion somehow or other, in any free plunge of the speculative fork into the contemporary social salad.

The late R. L. Stevenson was to write to me, I recall—and precisely on the occasion of "The Tragic Muse"—that he was at a loss to conceive how one could find an interest in anything so vulgar or pretend to gather fruit in so scrubby an orchard; but the view of a creature of the stage, the view of the "histrionic temperament," as suggestive much less, verily, in respect to the poor stage *per se* than in respect to "art" at large, affected me in spite of that as justly tenable. An objection of a more pointed order was forced upon me by an acute friend later on and in another connexion: the challenge of one's right, in any pretended show of social realities, to attach to the image of a "public character," a supposed particular celebrity, a range of interest, of intrinsic distinction, greater than any such display of importance on the part of eminent members of the class as we see them about us. There *was* a nice point if one would—yet only nice enough, after all, to be easily amusing. We shall deal with it later on, however, in a more urgent connexion. What would have worried me much more had it dawned earlier is the light lately thrown by that admirable writer M. Anatole France on the question of any animated view of the histrionic temperament—a light that may well dazzle to distress any ingenuous worker in the same field. In those parts of his brief but inimitable *Histoire Comique* on which he is most to be congratulated—for there are some that prompt to reserves—he has "done the actress," as well as the actor, done above all the mountebank, the mummer and the *cabotin*, and mixed them up with the queer theatric air, in a manner that practically warns all other hands off the material for ever. At the same time I think I saw Miriam, and without a sacrifice of truth, that is of the particular glow of verisimilitude I wished her most to benefit by, in a complexity of relations finer than any that appear possible for the gentry of M. Anatole France.

Her relation to Nick Dormer, for instance, was intended as a superior interest—that of being (while perfectly sincere, sincere for *her*, and therefore perfectly consonant with her impulse perpetually to perform and with her success in performing) the result of a touched imagination, a touched pride for "art," as well as of the charm cast on other sensibilities still. Dormer's relation to herself is a different matter, of which more presently; but the sympathy she, poor young woman, very generously and intelligently offers him where most people have so stinted it, is disclosed largely at the cost of her egotism and her personal pretensions, even though in fact determined by her sense of their together, Nick and she, postponing the "world" to their conception of other and finer decencies. Nick can't on the whole see—for I have represented him as in his day quite sufficiently troubled and anxious—why he should condemn to ugly feebleness his most prized faculty (most prized, at least, by himself) even in order to keep his seat in Parliament, to inherit Mr. Carteret's blessing and money, to gratify his mother and carry out the mission of his father, to marry Julia Dallow in fine, a beautiful imperative woman with a great many thousands a year. It all

comes back in the last analysis to the individual vision of decency, the critical as well as the passionate judgement of it
under sharp stress; and Nick's vision and judgement, all on
the æsthetic ground, have beautifully coincided, to Miriam's
imagination, with a now fully marked, an inspired and impenitent, choice of her own: so that, other considerations powerfully aiding indeed, she is ready to see their interest all
splendidly as one. She is in the uplifted state to which sacrifices and submissions loom large, but loom so just because
they must write sympathy, write passion, large. Her measure
of what she would be capable of for him—capable, that is, of
not asking of him—will depend on what he shall ask of *her*,
but she has no fear of not being able to satisfy him, even to
the point of "chucking" for him, if need be, that artistic identity of her own which she has begun to build up. It will all
be to the glory therefore of their common infatuation with
"art": she will doubtless be no less willing to serve his than
she was eager to serve her own, purged now of the too great
shrillness.

This puts her quite on a different level from that of the
vivid monsters of M. France, whose artistic identity is the last
thing *they* wish to chuck—their only dismissal is of all material and social overdraping. Nick Dormer in point of fact asks
of Miriam nothing but that she shall remain "awfully interesting to paint"; but that is *his* relation, which, as I say, is quite
a matter by itself. He at any rate, luckily for both of them it
may be, does n't put her to the test: he is so busy with his
own case, busy with testing himself and feeling his reality. He
has seen himself as giving up precious things for an object,
and that object has somehow not been the young woman in
question, nor anything very nearly like her. She on the other
hand has asked everything of Peter Sherringham, who has
asked everything of *her*; and it is in so doing that she has
really most testified for art and invited him to testify. With
his professed interest in the theatre—one of those deep sub-
jections that, in men of "taste," the Comédie Française used
in old days to conspire for and some such odd and affecting
examples of which were to be noted—he yet offers her his
hand and an introduction to the very best society if she will
leave the stage. The power—and her having the sense of the

power—to "shine" in the world is his highest measure of her, the test applied by him to her beautiful human value; just as the manner in which she turns on him is the application of her own standard and touchstone. She is perfectly sure of her own; for—if there were nothing else, and there is much— she has tasted blood, so to speak, in the form of her so prompt and auspicious success with the public, leaving all probations behind (the whole of which, as the book gives it, is too rapid and sudden, though inevitably so: processes, periods, intervals, stages, degrees, connexions, may be easily enough and barely enough named, may be unconvincingly stated, in fiction, to the deep discredit of the writer, but it remains the very deuce to *represent* them, especially represent them under strong compression and in brief and subordinate terms; and this even though the novelist who does n't represent, and represent "all the time," is lost, exactly as much lost as the painter who, at his work and given his intention, does n't paint "all the time").

Turn upon her friend at any rate Miriam does; and one of my main points is missed if it fails to appear that she does so with absolute sincerity and with the cold passion of the high critic who knows, on sight of them together, the more or less dazzling false from the comparatively grey-coloured true. Sherringham's whole profession has been that he rejoices in her as she is, and that the theatre, the organised theatre, will be, as Matthew Arnold was in those very days pronouncing it, irresistible; and it is the promptness with which he sheds his pretended faith as soon as it feels in the air the breath of reality, as soon as it asks of him a proof or a sacrifice, it is this that excites her doubtless sufficiently arrogant scorn. Where is the virtue of his high interest if it has verily never *been* an interest to speak of and if all it has suddenly to suggest is that, in face of a serious call, it shall be unblushingly relinquished? If he and she together, and her great field and future, and the whole cause they had armed and declared for, have not been serious things they have been base make-believes and trivialities—which is what in fact the homage of society to art always turns out so soon as art presumes not to be vulgar and futile. It is immensely the fashion and immensely edifying to listen to, this homage, while it confines its attention to vanities and frauds; but it knows only terror, feels only horror, the moment that, instead of making all the concessions, art proceeds to ask for a few. Miriam is nothing if not strenuous, and evidently nothing if not "cheeky," where Sherringham is concerned at least: these, in the all-egotistical exhibition to which she is condemned, are the very elements of her figure and the very colours of her portrait. But she is mild and inconsequent for Nick Dormer (who demands of her so little); as if gravely and pityingly embracing the truth that *his* sacrifice, on the right side, is probably to have very little of her sort of recompense. I must have had it well before me that she was all aware of the small strain a great sacrifice to Nick would cost her—by reason of the strong effect on her of his own superior logic, in which the very intensity of concentration was so to find its account.

If the man, however, who holds her personally dear yet holds her extremely personal message to the world cheap, so the man capable of a consistency and, as she regards the matter, of an honesty so much higher than Sherringham's, virtually cares, "really" cares, no straw for his fellow struggler. If Nick Dormer attracts and all-indifferently holds her it is because, like herself and unlike Peter, he puts "art" first; but the most he thus does for her in the event is to let her see how she may enjoy, in intimacy, the rigour it has taught him and which he cultivates at her expense. This is the situation in which we leave her, though there would be more still to be said about the difference for her of the two relations— that to each of the men—could I fondly suppose as much of the interest of the book "left over" for the reader as for myself. Sherringham for instance offers Miriam marriage, ever so "handsomely"; but if nothing might lead me on further than the question of what it would have been open to us—us novelists, especially in the old days—to show, "serially," a young man in Nick Dormer's quite different position as offering or a young woman in Miriam's as taking, so for that very reason such an excursion is forbidden me. The trade of the stage-player, and above all of the actress, must have so many detestable sides for the person exercising it that we scarce imagine a full surrender to it without a full surrender, not less, to every immediate compensation, to every freedom and the largest ease within reach: which presentment of the possible case for Miriam would yet have been condemned—and on grounds both various and interesting to trace—to remain very imperfect.

I feel moreover that I might still, with space, abound in remarks about Nick's character and Nick's crisis suggested to my present more reflective vision. It strikes me, alas, that he is not quite so interesting as he was fondly intended to be, and this in spite of the multiplication, within the picture, of his pains and penalties; so that while I turn this slight anomaly over I come upon a reason that affects me as singularly charming and touching and at which indeed I have already glanced. Any presentation of the artist *in triumph* must be flat in proportion as it really sticks to its subject—it can only smuggle in relief and variety. For, to put the matter in an image, all we then—in his triumph—see of the charm-compeller is the back he turns to us as he bends over his work. "His" triumph, decently, is but the triumph of what he produces, and that is another affair. His romance is the romance he himself projects; he eats the cake of the very rarest privilege, the most luscious baked in the oven of the gods—therefore he may n't "have" it, in the form of the privilege of the hero, at the same time. The privilege of the hero—that is of the martyr or of the interesting and appealing and comparatively floundering *person*—places him in quite a different category, belongs to him only as to the artist deluded, diverted, frustrated or vanquished; when the "amateur" in him gains, for our admiration or compassion or whatever, all that the expert has to do without. Therefore I strove in vain, I feel, to embroil and adorn this young man on whom a hundred ingenious touches are thus lavished: he has insisted in the event on looking as simple and flat as some mere brass check or engraved number, the symbol and guarantee of a stored treasure. The better part of him is locked too much away from us, and the part we see has to pass for—well, what it passes for, so lamentedly, among his friends and relatives. No, accordingly, Nick Dormer is n't "the best thing in the book," as I judge I imagined he would be, and it contains nothing better, I make out, than that preserved and achieved unity and quality of tone, a value in itself, which I referred to at the beginning of these remarks. What I mean by this is that the interest created, and the expression of that interest, are things kept, as to kind, genuine and true to themselves. The appeal, the fidelity to the prime motive, is, with no little art, strained clear (even as silver is polished) in a degree answering—at least by intention—to the air of beauty. There is an awkwardness again in having thus belatedly to point such features out; but in that wrought appearance of animation and harmony, that effect of free movement and yet of recurrent and insistent reference, "The Tragic Muse" has struck me again as conscious of a bright advantage.

The Awkward Age

I RECALL with perfect ease the idea in which "The Awkward Age" had its origin, but re-perusal gives me pause in respect to naming it. This composition, as it stands, makes, to my vision—and will have made perhaps still more to that of its readers—so considerable a mass beside the germ sunk in it and still possibly distinguishable, that I am half-moved to leave my small secret undivulged. I shall encounter, I think, in the course of this copious commentary, no better example, and none on behalf of which I shall venture to invite more interest, of the quite incalculable tendency of a mere grain of subject-matter to expand and develop and cover the ground when conditions happen to favour it. I say all, surely, when I speak of the thing as planned, in perfect good faith, for brevity, for levity, for simplicity, for jocosity, in fine, and for an accommodating irony. I invoked, for my protection, the spirit of the lightest comedy, but "The Awkward Age" was to belong, in the event, to a group of productions, here re-introduced, which have in common, to their author's eyes, the endearing sign that they asserted in each case an unforeseen principle of growth. They were projected as small things, yet had finally to be provided for as comparative monsters. That is my own title for them, though I should perhaps resent it if applied by another critic—above all in the case of the piece before us, the careful measure of which I have just freshly taken. The result of this consideration has been in the first place to render sharp for me again the interest of the whole process thus illustrated, and in the second quite to place me on unexpectedly good terms with the work itself. As I scan my list I encounter none the "history" of which embodies a greater number of curious truths—or of truths at least by which I find contemplation more enlivened. The thing done and dismissed has ever, at the best, for the ambitious workman, a trick of looking dead, if not buried, so that he almost throbs with ecstasy when, on an anxious review, the flush of life reappears. It is verily on recognising that flush on a whole side of "The Awkward Age" that I brand it all, but ever so tenderly, as monstrous—which is but my way of noting the *quantity* of finish it stows away. Since I speak so undauntedly, when need is, of the value of composition, I shall not beat about the bush to claim for these pages the maximum of that advantage. If such a feat be possible in this field as really taking a lesson from one's own adventure I feel I have now not failed of it—to so much more demonstration of my profit than I can hope to carry through do I find myself urged. Thus it is that, still with a remnant of self-respect, or at least of sanity, one may turn to complacency, one may linger with pride. Let my pride provoke a frown till I justify it; which—though with more matters to be noted here than I have room for—I shall accordingly proceed to do.

Yet I must first make a brave face, no doubt, and present in its native humility my scant but quite ponderable germ. The seed sprouted in that vast nursery of sharp appeals and concrete images which calls itself, for blest convenience, London; it fell even into the order of the minor "social phenomena" with which, as fruit for the observer, that mightiest of the trees of suggestion bristles. It was not, no doubt, a fine purple peach, but it might pass for a round ripe plum, the note one had inevitably had to take of the difference made in certain friendly houses and for certain flourishing mothers by the sometimes dreaded, often delayed, but never fully arrested coming to the forefront of some vague slip of a daughter. For such mild revolutions as these not, to one's imagination, to remain mild one had had, I dare say, to be infinitely addicted to "noticing"; under the rule of that secret vice or that unfair advantage, at any rate, the "sitting downstairs," from a given date, of the merciless maiden previously perched aloft could easily be felt as a crisis. This crisis, and the sense for it in those whom it most concerns, has to confess itself courageously the prime propulsive force of "The Awkward Age." Such a matter might well make a scant show for a "thick book," and no thick book, but just a quite charmingly thin one, was in fact originally dreamt of. For its proposed scale the little idea seemed happy—happy, that is, above all in having come very straight; but its proposed scale was the limit of a small square canvas. One had been present again and again at the exhibition I refer to—which is what I mean by the "coming straight" of this particular London impression; yet one was (and through fallibilities that after all had their sweetness, so that one would on the whole rather have kept them than parted with them) still capable of so false a measurement. When I think indeed of those of my many false measurements that have resulted, after much anguish, in decent symmetries, I find the whole case, I profess, a theme for the philosopher. The little ideas one would n't have treated save for the design of keeping them small, the developed situations that one would never with malice prepense have undertaken, the long stories that had thoroughly meant to be short, the short subjects that had underhandedly plotted to be long, the hypocrisy of modest beginnings, the audacity of misplaced middles, the triumph of intentions never entertained—with these patches, as I look about, I see my experience paved: an experience to which nothing is wanting save, I confess, some grasp of its final lesson.

This lesson would, if operative, surely provide some law for the recognition, the determination in advance, of the just limits and the just extent of the situation, *any* situation, that appeals, and that yet, by the presumable, the helpful law of situations, must have its reserves as well as its promises. The storyteller considers it because it promises, and undertakes it, often, just because also making out, as he believes, where the promise conveniently drops. The promise, for instance, of the case I have just named, the case of the account to be taken, in a circle of free talk, of a new and innocent, a wholly unacclimatised presence, as to which such accommodations have never had to come up, might well have appeared as limited as it was lively; and if these pages were not before us to register my illusion I should never have made a braver claim for it. They themselves admonish me, however, in fifty interesting ways, and they especially emphasise that truth of the vanity of the *a priori* test of what an *idée-mère* may have to give. The truth is that what a happy thought has to give depends immensely on the general turn of the mind capable of it, and on the fact that its loyal entertainer, cultivating fondly its possible relations and extensions, the bright efflorescence latent in it, but having to take other things in their order too, is terribly at the mercy of his mind. That organ has only to exhale, in its degree, a fostering tropic air in order to produce complications almost beyond reckoning. The trap laid for his superficial convenience resides in the fact that, though the relations of a human figure or a social occurrence are what make such objects interesting, they also make them, to the same tune, difficult to isolate, to surround with the sharp black line, to frame in the square, the circle, the charming oval, that helps any arrangement of objects to become a picture. The storyteller has but to have been condemned by nature to a liberally amused and beguiled, a richly sophisticated, view of relations and a fine inquisitive speculative sense for them, to find himself at moments flounder in a deep warm jungle. These are the moments at which he recalls ruefully that the great merit of such and such a small case, the merit for his particular advised use, had been precisely in the smallness.

I may say at once that this had seemed to me, under the first flush of recognition, the good mark for the pretty notion of the "free circle" put about by having, of a sudden, an ingenuous mind and a pair of limpid searching eyes to count with. Half the attraction was in the current actuality of the thing: repeatedly, right and left, as I have said, one had seen such a drama constituted, and always to the effect of proposing to the interested view one of those questions that are of the essence of drama: what will happen, who suffer, who not suffer, what turn be determined, what crisis created, what issue found? There had of course to be, as a basis, the free circle, but this was material of that admirable order with which the good London never leaves its true lover and believer long unprovided. One could count them on one's fingers (an abundant allowance), the liberal firesides beyond the wide glow of which, in a comparative dimness, female adolescence hovered and waited. The wide glow was bright, was favourable to "real" talk, to play of mind, to an explicit interest in life, a due demonstration of the interest by persons qualified to feel it: all of which meant frankness and ease, the perfection, almost, as it were, of intercourse, and a tone as far as possible removed from that of the nursery and the schoolroom—as far as possible removed even, no doubt, in its appealing "modernity," from that of supposedly privileged scenes of conversation twenty years ago. The charm was, with

a hundred other things, in the freedom—the freedom menaced by the inevitable irruption of the ingenuous mind;
whereby, if the freedom should be sacrificed, what would
truly *become* of the charm? The charm might be figured as
dear to members of the circle consciously contributing to it,
but it was none the less true that some sacrifice in some
quarter would have to be made, and what meditator worth
his salt could fail to hold his breath while waiting on the
event? The ingenuous mind might, it was true, be suppressed
altogether, the general disconcertment averted either by some
master-stroke of diplomacy or some rude simplification; yet
these were ugly matters, and in the examples before one's eyes
nothing ugly, nothing harsh or crude, had flourished. A girl
might be married off the day after her irruption, or better still
the day before it, to remove her from the sphere of the play
of mind; but these were exactly not crudities, and even then,
at the worst, an interval had to be bridged. "The Awkward
Age" is precisely a study of one of these curtailed or extended
periods of tension and apprehension, an account of the manner in which the resented interference with ancient liberties
came to be in a particular instance dealt with.

I note once again that I had not escaped seeing it actually
and traceably dealt with—after (I admit) a good deal of
friendly suspense; also with the nature and degree of the "sacrifice" left very much to one's appreciation. In circles highly
civilised the great things, the real things, the hard, the cruel
and even the tender things, the true elements of any tension
and true facts of any crisis, have ever, for the outsider's, for
the critic's use, to be translated into terms—terms in the distinguished name of which, terms for the right employment of
which, more than one situation of the type I glance at had
struck me as all irresistibly appealing. There appeared in fact
at moments no end to the things they said, the suggestions
into which they flowered; one of these latter in especial arriving at the highest intensity. Putting vividly before one the
perfect system on which the awkward age is handled in most
other European societies, it threw again into relief the inveterate English trick of the so morally well-meant and so intellectually helpless compromise. We live notoriously, as I
suppose every age lives, in an "epoch of transition"; but it

may still be said of the French for instance, I assume, that their social scheme absolutely provides against awkwardness. That is it would be, by this scheme, so infinitely awkward, so awkward beyond any patching-up, for the hovering female young to be conceived as present at "good" talk, that their presence is, theoretically at least, not permitted till their youth has been promptly corrected by marriage—in which case they have ceased to be merely young. The better the talk prevailing in any circle, accordingly, the more organised, the more complete, the element of precaution and exclusion. Talk—giving the term a wide application—is one thing, and a proper inexperience another; and it has never occurred to a logical people that the interest of the greater, the general, need be sacrificed to that of the less, the particular. Such sacrifices strike them as gratuitous and barbarous, as cruel above all to the social intelligence; also as perfectly preventable by wise arrangement. Nothing comes home more, on the other hand, to the observer of English manners than the very moderate degree in which wise arrangement, in the French sense of a scientific economy, has ever been invoked; a fact indeed largely explaining the great interest of their incoherence, their heterogeneity, their wild abundance. The French, all analytically, have conceived of fifty different proprieties, meeting fifty different cases, whereas the English mind, less intensely at work, has never conceived but of one—the grand propriety, for every case, it should in fairness be said, of just being English. As practice, however, has always to be a looser thing than theory, so no application of that rigour has been possible in the London world without a thousand departures from the grim ideal.

The American theory, if I may "drag it in," would be, I think, that talk should never become "better" than the female young, either actually or constructively present, are minded to allow it. *That* system involves as little compromise as the French; it has been absolutely simple, and the beauty of its success shines out in every record of our conditions of intercourse—premising always our "basic" assumption that the female young read the newspapers. The English theory may be in itself almost as simple, but different and much more complex forces have ruled the application of it; so much does the goodness of talk depend on what there may be to talk about. There are more things in London, I think, than anywhere in the world; hence the charm of the dramatic struggle reflected in my book, the struggle somehow to fit propriety into a smooth general case which is really all the while bristling and crumbling into fierce particular ones. The circle surrounding Mrs. Brookenham, in my pages, is of course nothing if not a particular, even a "peculiar" one—and its rather vain effort (the vanity, the real inexpertness, being precisely part of my tale) is toward the courage of that condition. It has cropped up in a social order where individual appreciations of propriety have not been formally allowed for, in spite of their having very often quite rudely and violently and insolently, rather of course than insidiously, flourished; so that as the matter stands, rightly or wrongly, Nanda's retarded, but eventually none the less real, incorporation means virtually Nanda's exposure. It means this, that is, and many things beside— means them for Nanda herself and, with a various intensity, for the other participants in the action; but what it particularly means, surely, is the failure of successful arrangement and the very moral, sharply pointed, of the fruits of compromise. It is compromise that has suffered her to be in question at all, and that has condemned the freedom of the circle to be self-conscious, compunctious, on the whole much more timid than brave—the consequent muddle, if the term be not too gross, representing meanwhile a great inconvenience for life, but, as I found myself feeling, an immense promise, a much greater one than on the "foreign" showing, for the painted picture of life. Beyond which let me add that here immediately is a prime specimen of the way in which the obscurer, the lurking relations of a motive apparently simple, always in wait for their spring, may by seizing their chance for it send simplicity flying. Poor Nanda's little case, and her mother's, and Mr. Longdon's and Vanderbank's and Mitchy's, to say nothing of that of the others, has only to catch a reflected light from over the Channel in order to double at once its appeal to the imagination. (I am considering all these matters, I need scarce say, only as they are concerned with that faculty. With a relation *not* imaginative to his material the storyteller has nothing whatever to do.)

It exactly happened moreover that my own material here was to profit in a particular way by that extension of view. My idea was to be treated with light irony—it would be light and ironical or it would be nothing; so that I asked myself, naturally, what might be the least solemn form to give it, among recognised and familiar forms. The question thus at once arose: What form so familiar, so recognised among alert readers, as that in which the ingenious and inexhaustible, the charming philosophic "Gyp" casts most of her social studies? Gyp had long struck me as mistress, in her levity, of one of the happiest of forms—the only objection to my use of which was a certain extraordinary benightedness on the part of the Anglo-Saxon reader. One had noted this reader as perverse and inconsequent in respect to the absorption of "dialogue"—observed the "public for fiction" consume it, in certain connexions, on the scale and with the smack of lips that mark the consumption of bread-and-jam by a children's school-feast, consume it even at the theatre, so far as our theatre ever vouchsafes it, and yet as flagrantly reject it when served, so to speak, *au naturel*. One had seen good solid slices of fiction, well endued, one might surely have thought, with this easiest of lubrications, deplored by editor and publisher as positively not, for the general gullet as known to *them*, made adequately "slick." " 'Dialogue,' always 'dialogue'!" I had seemed from far back to hear them mostly cry: "We can't have too much of it, we can't have enough of it, and no excess of it, in the form of no matter what savourless dilution, or what boneless dispersion, ever began to injure a book so much as even the very scantest claim put in for form and substance." This wisdom had always been in one's ears; but it had at the same time been equally in one's eyes that really constructive dialogue, dialogue organic and dramatic, speaking for itself, representing and embodying substance and form, is among us an uncanny and abhorrent thing, not to be dealt with on any terms. A comedy or a tragedy may run for a thousand nights without prompting twenty persons in London or in New York to desire that view of its text which is so desired in Paris, as soon as a play begins to loom at all large, that the number of copies of the printed piece in circulation far exceeds at last the number of performances. But as with the printed piece our own public, infatuated as it may be with the theatre, refuses all commerce—though indeed this can't but be, without cynicism, very much through the infirmity the piece, *if* printed, would reveal—so the same horror seems to attach to any typographic hint of the proscribed playbook or any insidious plea for it. The immense oddity resides in the almost exclusively typographic order of the offence. An English, an American Gyp would typographically offend, and that would be the end of her. *There* gloomed at me my warning, as well as shone at me my provocation, in respect to the example of this delightful writer. I might emulate her, since I presumptuously would, but dishonour would await me if, proposing to treat the different faces of my subject in the most completely instituted colloquial form, I should evoke the figure and affirm the presence of participants by the repeated and prefixed name rather than by the recurrent and *af*fixed "said he" and "said she." All I have space to go into here—much as the funny fact I refer to might seem to invite us to dance hand in hand round it—is that I was at any rate duly admonished, that I took my measures accordingly, and that the manner in which I took them has lived again for me ever so arrestingly, so amusingly, on re-examination of the book.

But that I did, positively and seriously—ah so seriously!—emulate the levity of Gyp and, by the same token, of that hardiest of flowers fostered in her school, M. Henri Lavedan, is a contribution to the history of "The Awkward Age" that I shall obviously have had to brace myself in order to make. Vivid enough to me the expression of face of any kindest of critics, even, moved to declare that he would never in the least have suspected it. Let me say at once, in extenuation of the too respectful distance at which I may thus have appeared to follow my model, that my first care *had* to be the covering of my tracks—lest I truly should be caught in the act of arranging, of organising dialogue to "speak for itself." What I now see to have happened is that I organised and arranged but too well—too well, I mean, for any betrayal of the Gyp taint, however faded and feeble. The trouble appears to have been that while I on the one hand exorcised the baleful association, I succeeded in rousing on nobody's part a sense of any other association whatever, or of my having cast myself into any conceivable or calculable form. My private inspiration had been in the Gyp plan (artfully dissimulated, for dear life, and applied with the very subtlest consistency, but none the less kept in secret view); yet I was to fail to make out in the event that the book succeeded in producing the impression of *any* plan on any person. No hint of that sort of success, or of any critical perception at all in relation to the business, has ever come my way; in spite of which when I speak, as just above, of what was to "happen" under the law of my ingenious labour, I fairly lose myself in the vision of a hundred bright phenomena. Some of these incidents I must treat myself to naming, for they are among the best I shall have on any occasion to retail. But I must first give the measure of the degree in which they were mere matters of the study. This composition had originally appeared in "Harper's Weekly" during the autumn of 1898 and the first weeks of the winter, and the volume containing it was published that spring. I had meanwhile been absent from England, and it was not till my return, some time later, that I had from my publisher any news of our venture. But the news then met at a stroke all my curiosity: "I 'm sorry to say the book has done nothing to speak of; I 've never in all my experience seen one treated with more general and complete disrespect." There was thus to be nothing left me for fond subsequent reference—of which I doubtless give even now so adequate an illustration—save the rich reward of the singular interest attaching to the very intimacies of the effort.

It comes back to me, the whole "job," as wonderfully amusing and delightfully difficult from the first; since amusement deeply abides, I think, in any artistic attempt the basis and groundwork of which are conscious of a particular firmness. On that hard fine floor the element of execution feels it may more or less confidently *dance*; in which case puzzling questions, sharp obstacles, dangers of detail, may come up for it by the dozen without breaking its heart or shaking its nerve. It is the difficulty produced by the loose foundation or the vague scheme that breaks the heart—when a luckless fatuity has over-persuaded an author of the "saving" virtue of treatment. Being "treated" is never, in a workable idea, a mere

passive condition, and I hold no subject ever susceptible of
help that is n't, like the embarrassed man of our proverbial
wisdom, first of all able to help itself. I was thus to have here
an envious glimpse, in carrying my design through, of that
artistic rage and that artistic felicity which I have ever supposed to be intensest and highest, the confidence of the dramatist strong in the sense of his postulate. The dramatist has
verily to *build*, is committed to architecture, to construction
at any cost; to driving in deep his vertical supports and laying
across and firmly fixing his horizontal, his resting pieces—at
the risk of no matter what vibration from the tap of his mas-
ter-hammer. This makes the active value of his basis immense,
enabling him, with his flanks protected, to advance undis-
tractedly, even if not at all carelessly, into the comparative
fairy-land of the mere minor anxiety. In other words his
scheme *holds*, and as he feels this in spite of noted strains and
under repeated tests, so he keeps his face to the day. I rejoiced, by that same token, to feel *my* scheme hold, and even
a little ruefully watched it give me much more than I had
ventured to hope. For I promptly found my conceived arrangement of my material open the door wide to ingenuity. I
remember that in sketching my project for the conductors of
the periodical I have named I drew on a sheet of paper—and
possibly with an effect of the cabalistic, it now comes over
me, that even anxious amplification may have but vainly attenuated—the neat figure of a circle consisting of a number
of small rounds disposed at equal distance about a central object. The central object was my situation, my subject in itself,
to which the thing would owe its title, and the small rounds
represented so many distinct lamps, as I liked to call them,
the function of each of which would be to light with all due
intensity one of its aspects. I had divided it, did n't they see?
into aspects—uncanny as the little term might sound (though
not for a moment did I suggest we should use it for the public), and by that sign we would conquer.

They "saw," all genially and generously—for I must add
that I had made, to the best of my recollection, no morbid
scruple of not blabbing about Gyp and her strange incitement. I the more boldly held my tongue over this that the
more I, by my intelligence, lived in my arrangement and

moved about in it, the more I sank into satisfaction. It was clearly to work to a charm and, during this process—by calling at every step for an exquisite management—"to haunt, to startle and waylay." Each of my "lamps" would be the light of a single "social occasion" in the history and intercourse of the characters concerned, and would bring out to the full the latent colour of the scene in question and cause it to illustrate, to the last drop, its bearing on my theme. I revelled in this notion of the Occasion as a thing by itself, really and completely a scenic thing, and could scarce name it, while crouching amid the thick arcana of my plan, with a large enough O. The beauty of the conception was in this approximation of the respective divisions of my form to the successive Acts of a Play—as to which it was more than ever a case for charmed capitals. The divine distinction of the act of a play—and a greater than any other it easily succeeds in arriving at—was, I reasoned, in its special, its guarded objectivity. This objectivity, in turn, when achieving its ideal, came from the imposed absence of that "going behind," to compass explanations and amplifications, to drag out odds and ends from the "mere" storyteller's great property-shop of aids to illusion: a resource under denial of which it was equally perplexing and delightful, for a change, to proceed. Everything, for that matter, becomes interesting from the moment it has closely to consider, for full effect positively to bestride, the law of its kind. "Kinds" are the very life of literature, and truth and strength come from the complete recognition of them, from abounding to the utmost in their respective senses and sinking deep into their consistency. I myself have scarcely to plead the cause of "going behind," which is right and beautiful and fruitful in its place and order; but as the confusion of kinds is the inelegance of letters and the stultification of values, so to renounce that line utterly and do something quite different instead may become in another connexion the true course and the vehicle of effect. Something in the very nature, in the fine rigour, of this special sacrifice (which is capable of affecting the form-lover, I think, as really more of a projected form than any other) lends it moreover a coercive charm; a charm that grows in proportion as the appeal to it tests and stretches and strains it, puts it powerfully to the touch. To make the presented occasion tell all its story itself, remain shut up in its own presence and yet on that patch of staked-out ground become thoroughly interesting and remain thoroughly clear, is a process not remarkable, no doubt, so long as a very light weight is laid on it, but difficult enough to challenge and inspire great adroitness so soon as the elements to be dealt with begin at all to "size up."

The disdainers of the contemporary drama deny, obviously, with all promptness, that the matter to be expressed by its means—richly and successfully expressed that is— *can* loom with any largeness; since from the moment it does one of the conditions breaks down. The process simply collapses under pressure, they contend, proves its weakness as quickly as the office laid on it ceases to be simple. "Remember," they say to the dramatist, "that you have to be, supremely, three things: you have to be true to your form, you have to be interesting, you have to be clear. You have in other words to prove yourself adequate to taking a heavy weight. But we defy you really to conform to your conditions with any but a light one. Make the thing you have to convey, make the picture you have to paint, at all rich and complex, and you cease to be clear. Remain clear—and with the clearness required by the infantine intelligence of any public consenting to see a play—and what becomes of the 'importance' of your subject? If it 's important by any other critical measure than the little foot-rule the 'produced' piece has to conform to, it is predestined to be a muddle. When it has escaped being a muddle the note it has succeeded in striking at the furthest will be recognised as one of those that are called high but by the courtesy, by the intellectual provinciality, of theatrical criticism, which, as we can see for ourselves any morning, is—well, an abyss even deeper than the theatre itself. Don't attempt to crush us with Dumas and Ibsen, for such values are from any informed and enlightened point of view, that is measured by other high values, literary, critical, philosophic, of the most moderate order. Ibsen and Dumas are precisely cases of men, men in their degree, in their poor theatrical straight-jacket, speculative, who have *had* to renounce the finer thing for the coarser, the thick, in short, for the thin and the curious for the self-evident. What earthly intellectual distinction, what 'prestige' of achievement, would have attached to the substance of such things as 'Denise,' as 'Monsieur Alphonse,' as 'Francillon' (and we take the Dumas of the supposedly subtler period) in any other form? What virtues of the same order would have attached to 'The Pillars of Society,' to 'An Enemy of the People,' to 'Ghosts,' to 'Rosmersholm' (or taking also Ibsen's 'subtler period') to 'John Gabriel Borkmann,' to 'The Master-Builder'? Ibsen is in fact wonderfully a case in point, since from the moment he 's clear, from the moment he 's 'amusing,' it 's on the footing of a thesis as simple and superficial as that of 'A Doll's House'—while from the moment he 's by apparent intention comprehensive and searching it 's on the footing of an effect as confused and obscure as 'The Wild Duck.' From which you easily see *all* the conditions can't be met. The dramatist has to choose but those he 's most capable of, and by that choice he's known."

So the objector concludes, and never surely without great profit from his having been "drawn." His apparent triumph— if it be even apparent—still leaves, it will be noted, convenient cover for retort in the riddled face of the opposite stronghold. The last word in these cases is for nobody who can't pretend to an *absolute* test. The terms here used, obviously, are matters of appreciation, and there is no short cut to proof (luckily for us all round) either that "Monsieur Alphonse" develops itself on the highest plane of irony or that "Ghosts" simplifies almost to excruciation. If "John Gabriel Borkmann" is but a pennyworth of effect as to a character we can imagine much more amply presented, and if "Hedda Gabler" makes an appeal enfeebled by remarkable vagueness, there is by the nature of the case no catching the convinced, or call him the deluded, spectator or reader in the act of a mistake. He is to be caught at the worst in the act of attention, of the very greatest attention, and that is all, as a precious preliminary at least, that the playwright asks of him, besides being all the very divinest poet can get. I remember rejoicing as much to remark this, after getting launched in "The Awkward Age," as if I were in fact constructing a play; just as I may doubtless appear now not less anxious to keep the philosophy of the dramatist's course before me than if I belonged to his order. I felt, certainly, the support he feels, I participated in his technical amusement, I tasted to the full the bitter-sweetness of his draught—the beauty and the difficulty (to harp again on that string) of escaping poverty *even though* the references in one's action can only be, with intensity, to each other, to things exactly on the same plane of exhibition with themselves. Exhibition may mean in a "story" twenty different ways, fifty excursions, alternatives, excrescences, and the novel, as largely practised in English, is the perfect paradise of the loose end. The play consents to the logic of but one way, mathematically right, and with the loose end as gross an impertinence on its surface, and as grave a dishonour, as the dangle of a snippet of silk or wool on the right side of a tapestry. We are shut up wholly to cross-relations, relations all within the action itself; no part of which is related to anything but some other part—save of course by the relation of the total to life. And, after invoking the protection of Gyp, I saw the point of my game all in the problem of keeping these conditioned relations crystalline at the same time that I should, in emulation of life, consent to their being numerous and fine and characteristic of the London world (as the London world was in this quarter and that to be deciphered). All of which was to make in the event for complications.

I see now of course how far, with my complications, I got away from Gyp; but I see to-day so much else too that this particular deflexion from simplicity makes scarce a figure among the others; after having once served its purpose, I mean, of lighting my original imitative innocence. For I recognise in especial, with a waking vibration of that interest in which, as I say, the plan of the book is embalmed for me, that my subject was probably condemned in advance to appreciable, or more exactly perhaps to almost preposterously appreciative, over-treatment. It places itself for me thus in a group of small productions exhibiting this perversity, representations of conceived cases in which my process has been to pump the case gaspingly dry, dry not only of superfluous moisture, but absolutely (for I have encountered the charge) of breatheable air. I may note, in fine, that coming back to the pages before us with a strong impression of their record-

ing, to my shame, that disaster, even to the extent of its dis-
qualifying them for decent reappearance, I have found the
adventure taking, to my relief, quite another turn, and have
lost myself in the wonder of what "over-treatment" may, in
the detail of its desperate ingenuity, consist of. The revived
interest I speak of has been therefore that of following critically, from page to page, even as the red Indian tracks in the
forest the pale-face, the footsteps of the systematic loyalty I
was able to achieve. The amusement of this *constatation* is, as
I have hinted, in the detail of the matter, and the detail is so
dense, the texture of the figured and smoothed tapestry so
close, that the genius of Gyp herself, muse of general looseness, would certainly, once warned, have uttered the first disavowal of my homage. But what has occurred meanwhile is
that this high consistency has itself, so to speak, constituted
an exhibition, and that an important artistic truth has seemed
to me thereby lighted. We brushed against that truth just now
in our glance at the denial of expansibility to any idea the
mould of the "stage-play" may hope to express without cracking and bursting; and we bear in mind at the same time that
the picture of Nanda Brookenham's situation, though perhaps seeming to a careless eye so to wander and sprawl, yet
presents itself on absolutely scenic lines, and that each of these
scenes in itself, and each as related to each and to all of its
companions, abides without a moment's deflexion by the
principle of the stage-play.

   In doing this then it does more—it helps us ever so happily
to see the grave distinction between substance and form in a
really wrought work of art signally break down. I hold it impossible to say, before "The Awkward Age," where one of
these elements ends and the other begins: I have been unable
at least myself, on re-examination, to mark any such joint or
seam, to see the two *discharged* offices as separate. They are
separate before the fact, but the sacrament of execution indissolubly marries them, and the marriage, like any other marriage, has only to be a "true" one for the scandal of a breach
not to show. The thing "done," artistically, is a fusion, or it
has not *been* done—in which case of course the artist may be,
and all deservedly, pelted with any fragment of his botch the
critic shall choose to pick up. But his ground once conquered,

in this particular field, he knows nothing of fragments and may say in all security: "Detach one if you can. You can analyse in *your* way, oh yes—to relate, to report, to explain; but you can't disintegrate my synthesis; you can't resolve the elements of my whole into different responsible agents or find your way at all (for your own fell purpose). My mixture has only to be perfect literally to bewilder you—you are lost in the tangle of the forest. Prove this value, this effect, in the air of the whole result, to be of my subject, and that other value, other effect, to be of my treatment, prove that I have n't so shaken them together as the conjurer I profess to be *must* consummately shake, and I consent but to parade as before a booth at the fair." The exemplary closeness of "The Awkward Age" even affects me, on re-perusal, I confess, as treasure quite instinctively and foreseeingly laid up against my present opportunity for these remarks. I have been positively struck by the quantity of meaning and the number of intentions, the extent of *ground for interest*, as I may call it, that I have succeeded in working scenically, yet without loss of sharpness, clearness or "atmosphere," into each of my illuminating Occasions—where, at certain junctures, the due preservation of all these values took, in the familiar phrase, a good deal of doing.

I should have liked just here to re-examine with the reader some of the positively most artful passages I have in mind—such as the hour of Mr. Longdon's beautiful and, as it were, mystic attempt at a compact with Vanderbank, late at night, in the billiard-room of the country-house at which they are staying; such as the other nocturnal passage, under Mr. Longdon's roof, between Vanderbank and Mitchy, where the conduct of so much fine meaning, so many flares of the exhibitory torch through the labyrinth of mere immediate appearances, mere familiar allusions, is successfully and safely effected; such as the whole array of the terms of presentation that are made to serve, all systematically, yet without a gap anywhere, for the presentation, throughout, of a Mitchy "subtle" no less than concrete and concrete no less than deprived of that officious explanation which we know as "going behind"; such as, briefly, the general service of co-ordination and vivification rendered, on lines of ferocious, of really quite heroic compression, by the picture of the assembled group at Mrs. Grendon's, where the "cross-references" of the action are as thick as the green leaves of a garden, but none the less, as they have scenically to be, counted and disposed, weighted with responsibility. Were I minded to use in this connexion a "loud" word—and the critic in general hates loud words as a man of taste may hate loud colours—I should speak of the composition of the chapters entitled "Tishy Grendon," with all the pieces of the game on the table together and each unconfusedly and contributively placed, as triumphantly scientific. I must properly remind myself, rather, that the better lesson of my retrospect would seem to be really a supreme revision of the question of what it may be for a subject to suffer, to call it suffering, by over-treatment. Bowed down so long by the inference that its product had in this case proved such a betrayal, my artistic conscience meets the relief of having to recognise truly here no traces of suffering. The thing carries itself to my maturer and gratified sense as with every symptom of soundness, an insolence of health and joy. And from this precisely I deduce my moral; which is to the effect that, since our only way, in general, of knowing that we have had too much of anything is by *feeling* that too much: so, by the same token, when we don't feel the excess (and I am contending, mind, that in "The Awkward Age" the multiplicity yields to the order) how do we know that the measure not recorded, the notch not reached, does represent adequacy or satiety? The mere feeling helps us for certain degrees of congestion, but for exact science, that is for the criticism of "fine" art, we want the notation. The notation, however, is what we lack, and the verdict of the mere feeling is liable to fluctuate. In other words an imputed defect is never, at the worst, disengageable, or other than matter for appreciation—to come back to my claim for that felicity of the dramatist's case that his synthetic "whole" *is* his form, the only one we have to do with. I like to profit in his company by the fact that if our art has certainly, for the impression it produces, to defer to the rise and fall, in the critical temperature, of the telltale mercury, it still has n't to reckon with the engraved thermometer-face.

The Spoils of Poynton, A London Life, The Chaperon

IT WAS YEARS AGO, I remember, one Christmas Eve when I was dining with friends: a lady beside me made in the course of talk one of those allusions that I have always found myself recognising on the spot as "germs." The germ, wherever gathered, has ever been for me the germ of a "story," and most of the stories straining to shape under my hand have sprung from a single small seed, a seed as minute and wind-blown as that casual hint for "The Spoils of Poynton" dropped unwitting by my neighbour, a mere floating particle in the stream of talk. What above all comes back to me with this reminiscence is the sense of the inveterate minuteness, on such happy occasions, of the precious particle—reduced, that is, to its mere fruitful essence. Such is the interesting truth about the stray suggestion, the wandering word, the vague echo, at touch of which the novelist's imagination winces as at the prick of some sharp point: its virtue is all in its needle-like quality, the power to penetrate as finely as possible. This fineness it is that communicates the virus of suggestion, anything more than the minimum of which spoils the operation. If one is given a hint at all designedly one is sure to be given too much; one's subject is in the merest grain, the speck of truth, of beauty, of reality, scarce visible to the common eye—since, I firmly hold, a good eye for a subject is anything but usual. Strange and attaching, certainly, the consistency with which the first thing to be done for the communicated and seized idea is to reduce almost to nought the form, the air as of a mere disjoined and lacerated lump of life, in which we may have happened to meet it. Life being all inclusion and confusion, and art being all discrimination and selection, the latter, in search of the hard latent *value* with which alone it is concerned, sniffs round the mass as instinctively and unerringly as a dog suspicious of some buried bone. The difference here, however, is that, while the dog desires his bone but to destroy it, the artist finds in *his* tiny nugget, washed free of awkward accretions and hammered into a sacred hardness, the very stuff for a clear affirmation, the happiest chance for the indestructible. It at the same time amuses him again and again to note how, beyond the first step of the actual case, the case that constitutes for him his germ, his vital particle, his grain of gold, life persistently blunders and deviates, loses herself in the sand. The reason is of course that life has no direct sense whatever for the subject and is capable, luckily for us, of nothing but splendid waste. Hence the opportunity for the sublime economy of art, which rescues, which saves, and hoards and "banks," investing and reinvesting these fruits of toil in wondrous useful " works" and thus making up for us, desperate spendthrifts that we all naturally are, the most princely of incomes. It is the subtle secrets of that system, however, that are meanwhile the charming study, with an endless attraction, above all, in the question—endlessly baffling indeed—of the method at the heart of the madness; the madness, I mean, of a zeal, among the reflective sort, so disinterested. If life, presenting us the germ, and left merely to herself in such a business, gives the case away, almost always, before we can stop her, what are the signs for our guidance, what the primary laws for a saving selection, how do we know when and where to intervene, where do we place the beginnings of the wrong or the right deviation? Such would be the elements of an enquiry upon which, I hasten to say, it is quite forbidden me here to embark: I but glance at them in evidence of the rich pasture that at every turn surrounds the ruminant critic. The answer may be after all that mysteries here elude us, that general considerations fail or mislead, and that even the fondest of artists need ask no wider range than the logic of the particular case. The particular case, or in other words his relation to a given subject, once the relation is established, forms in itself a little world of exercise and agitation. Let him hold himself perhaps supremely fortunate if he can meet half the questions with which that air alone may swarm.

So it was, at any rate, that when my amiable friend, on the Christmas Eve, before the table that glowed safe and fair through the brown London night, spoke of such an odd matter as that a good lady in the north, always well looked on, was at daggers drawn with her only son, ever hitherto exemplary, over the ownership of the valuable furniture of a fine old house just accruing to the young man by his father's death, I instantly became aware, with my "sense for the subject," of the prick of inoculation; the *whole* of the virus, as I have called it, being infused by that single touch. There had been but ten words, yet I had recognised in them, as in a flash, all the possibilities of the little drama of my "Spoils," which glimmered then and there into life; so that when in the next breath I began to hear of action taken, on the beautiful ground, by our engaged adversaries, tipped each, from that instant, with the light of the highest distinction, I saw clumsy Life again at her stupid work. For the action taken, and on which my friend, as I knew she would, had already begun all complacently and benightedly further to report, I had absolutely, and could have, no scrap of use; one had been so perfectly qualified to say in advance: "It 's the perfect little workable thing, but she 'll strangle it in the cradle, even while she pretends, all so cheeringly, to rock it; wherefore I 'll stay her hand while yet there 's time." I did n't, of course, stay her hand—there never *is* in such cases "time"; and I had once more the full demonstration of the fatal futility of Fact. The turn taken by the excellent situation—excellent, for development, if arrested in the right place, that is in the germ—had the full measure of the classic ineptitude; to which with the full measure of the artistic irony one could once more, and for the thousandth time, but take off one's hat. It was not, however, that this in the least mattered, once the seed had been transplanted to richer soil; and I dwell on that almost inveterate redundancy of the wrong, as opposed to the ideal right, in any free flowering of the actual, by reason only of its approach to calculable regularity.

If there was nothing regular meanwhile, nothing more so than the habit of vigilance, in my quickly feeling where interest would really lie, so I could none the less acknowledge afresh that these small private cheers of recognition made the spirit easy and the temper bland for the confused whole. I "took" in fine, on the spot, to the rich bare little fact of the two related figures, embroiled perhaps all so sordidly; and for reasons of which I could most probably have given at the moment no decent account. Had I been asked why they were, in that stark nudity, to say nothing of that ugliness of attitude, "interesting," I fear I could have said nothing more to the point, even to my own questioning spirit, than "Well, you 'll see!" By which of course I should have meant "Well, *I* shall see"—confident meanwhile (as against the appearance or the imputation of poor taste) that interest would spring as soon as one should begin really to see *anything*. That points, I think, to a large part of the very source of interest for the artist: it resides in the strong consciousness of his seeing all for himself. He has to borrow his motive, which is certainly half the battle; and this motive is his ground, his site and his foundation. But after that he only lends and gives, only builds and piles high, lays together the blocks quarried in the deeps of his imagination and on his personal premises. He thus remains all the while in intimate commerce with his motive, and can say to himself—what really more than anything else inflames and sustains him—that he alone has the *secret* of the particular case, he alone can measure the truth of the direction to be taken by his developed data. There can be for him, evidently, only one logic for these things; there can be for him only one truth and one direction—the quarter in which his subject most completely expresses itself. The careful ascertainment of how it shall do so, and the art of guiding it with consequent authority—since this sense of "authority" is for the master-builder the treasure of treasures, or at least the joy of joys—renews in the modern alchemist something like the old dream of the secret of life.

Extravagant as the mere statement sounds, one seemed accordingly to handle the secret of life in drawing the positive right truth out of the so easy muddle of wrong truths in which the interesting possibilities of that "row," so to call it, between mother and son over their household gods might have been stifled. I find it odd to consider, as I thus revert, that I could have had none but the most general warrant for "seeing anything in it," as the phrase would have been; that I could n't in the least, on the spot, as I have already hinted, have justified my faith. One thing was "in it," in the sordid situation, on the first blush, and one thing only—though this, in its limited way, no doubt, a curious enough value: the sharp light it might project on that most modern of our current passions, the fierce appetite for the upholsterer's and joiner's and brazier's work, the chairs and tables, the cabinets and presses, the material odds and ends, of the more labouring ages. A lively mark of our manners indeed the diffusion of this curiosity and this avidity, and full of suggestion, clearly, as to their possible influence on other passions and other relations. On the face of it the "things" themselves would form the very centre of such a crisis; these grouped objects, all conscious of their eminence and their price, would enjoy, in any picture of a conflict, the heroic importance. They would have to be presented, they would have to be painted—arduous and desperate thought; something would have to be done for them not too ignobly unlike the great array in which Balzac, say, would have marshalled them: *that* amount of workable interest at least would evidently be "in it."

It would be wrapped in the silver tissue of some such conviction, at any rate, that I must have laid away my prime impression for a rest not disturbed till long afterwards, till the year 1896, I make out, when there arose a question of my contributing three "short stories" to "The Atlantic Monthly"; or supplying rather perhaps a third to complete a trio two members of which had appeared. The echo of the situation mentioned to me at our Christmas Eve dinner awoke again, I recall, at that touch—I recall, no doubt, with true humility, in view of my renewed mismeasurement of my charge. Painfully associated for me had "The Spoils of Poynton" remained, until recent re-perusal, with the awkward consequence of that fond error. The subject had emerged from cool reclusion all suffused with a flush of meaning; thanks to which irresistible air, as I could but plead in the event, I found myself—as against a mere commercial austerity—beguiled and led on. The thing had "come," the flower of conception had bloomed—all in the happy dusk of indifference and neglect; yet, strongly and frankly as it might now appeal, my idea would n't surely overstrain a *natural* brevity. A story that could n't possibly be long would have inevitably to be "short," and out of the depths of that delusion it accordingly began to struggle. To my own view, after the "first number," this composition (which in the magazine bore another title) conformed but to its nature, which was not to transcend a modest amplitude; but, dispatched in instalments, it felt itself eyed, from month to month, I seem to remember, with an editorial ruefulness excellently well founded—from the moment such differences of sense could exist, that is, as to the short and the long. The sole impression it made, I woefully gathered, was that of length, and it has till lately, as I say, been present to me but as the poor little "long" thing.

It began to appear in April 1896, and, as is apt blessedly to occur for me throughout this process of revision, the old, the shrunken concomitants muster again as I turn the pages. They lurk between the lines; these serve for them as the barred sera-glio-windows behind which, to the outsider in the glare of the Eastern street, forms indistinguishable seem to move and peer; "association" in fine bears upon them with its infinite magic. Peering through the lattice from without inward I re-capture a cottage on a cliff-side, to which, at the earliest ap-proach of the summer-time, redoubtable in London through the luxuriance of still other than "natural" forces, I had be-taken myself to finish a book in quiet and to begin another in fear. The cottage was, in its kind, perfection; mainly by rea-son of a small paved terrace which, curving forward from the cliff-edge like the prow of a ship, overhung a view as level, as purple, as full of rich change, as the expanse of the sea. The horizon was in fact a band of sea; a small red-roofed town, of great antiquity, perched on its sea-rock, clustered within the picture off to the right; while above one's head rustled a dense summer shade, that of a trained and arching ash, rising from the middle of the terrace, brushing the parapet with a heavy fringe and covering the place like a vast umbrella. Be-neath this umbrella and really under exquisite protection "The Spoils of Poynton" managed more or less symmetrically to grow.

I recall that I was committed to begin, the day I finished it, short of dire penalties, "The Other House"; with which work, however, of whatever high profit the considerations springing from it might be too, we have nothing to do here—and to the felt jealousy of which, as that of a grudging neighbour, I allude only for sweet recovery of the fact, mainly interesting to myself I admit, that the rhythm of the earlier book shows no flurry of hand. I "liked" it—the earlier book:

I venture now, after years, to welcome the sense of that amenity as well; so immensely refreshing is it to be moved, in any case, toward these retrospective simplicities. Painters and writers, I gather, are, when easily accessible to such appeals, frequently questioned as to those of their productions they may most have delighted in; but the profession of delight has always struck me as the last to consort, for the artist, with any candid account of his troubled effort—ever the sum, for the most part, of so many lapses and compromises, simplifications and surrenders. Which is the work in which he has n't surrendered, under dire difficulty, the best thing he meant to have kept? In which indeed, before the dreadful *done*, does n't he ask himself what has become of the thing all for the sweet sake of which it was to proceed to that extremity? Preference and complacency, on these terms, riot in general as they best may; not disputing, however, a grain of which weighty truth, I still make out, between my reconsidered lines, as it were, that I must—my opera-box of a terrace and my great green umbrella indeed aiding—have assisted at the growth and predominance of Fleda Vetch.

For something like Fleda Vetch had surely been latent in one's first apprehension of the theme; it wanted, for treatment, a centre, and, the most obvious centre being "barred," this image, while I still wondered, had, with all the assurance in the world, sprung up in its place. The real centre, as I say, the citadel of the interest, with the fight waged round it, would have been the felt beauty and value of the prize of battle, the Things, always the splendid Things, placed in the middle light, figured and constituted, with each identity made vivid, each character discriminated, and their common consciousness of their great dramatic part established. The rendered tribute of these honours, however, no vigilant editor, as I have intimated, could be conceived as allowing room for; since, by so much as the general glittering presence should spread, by so much as it should suggest the gleam of brazen idols and precious metals and inserted gems in the tempered light of some arching place of worship, by just so much would the muse of "dialogue," most usurping influence of all the romancingly invoked, be routed without ceremony, to lay her grievance at the feet of her gods. The spoils of Poynton were not directly articulate, and though they might have, and constantly did have, wondrous things to say, their message fostered about them a certain hush of cheaper sound—as a consequence of which, in fine, they would have been costly to keep up. In this manner Fleda Vetch, maintainable at less expense—though even she, I make out, less expert in spreading chatter thin than the readers of romance mainly like their heroines to-day—marked her place in my foreground at one ingratiating stroke. She planted herself centrally, and the stroke, as I call it, the demonstration after which she could n't be gainsaid, was the simple act of letting it be seen she had character.

For somehow—that was the way interest broke out, once the germ had been transferred to the sunny south window-sill of one's fonder attention—character, the question of what my agitated friends should individually, and all intimately and at the core, show themselves, would unmistakeably be the key to my modest drama, and would indeed alone make a drama of any sort possible. Yes, it is a story of cabinets and chairs and tables; they formed the bone of contention, but what would merely "become" of them, magnificently passive, seemed to represent a comparatively vulgar issue. The passions, the faculties, the forces their beauty would, like that of antique Helen of Troy, set in motion, was what, as a painter, one had really wanted of them, was the power in them that one had from the first appreciated. Emphatically, by that truth, there would have to be moral developments—dreadful as such a prospect might loom for a poor interpreter committed to brevity. A character is interesting as it comes out, and by the process and duration of that emergence; just as a procession is effective by the way it unrolls, turning to a mere mob if all of it passes at once. My little procession, I foresaw then from an early stage, would refuse to pass at once; though I could keep it more or less down, of course, by reducing it to three or four persons. Practically, in "The Spoils," the reduction is to four, though indeed—and I clung to that as to my plea for simplicity—the main agents, with the others all dependent, are Mrs. Gereth and Fleda. Fleda's ingratiating stroke, for importance, on the threshold, had been that she would understand; and positively, from that

moment, the progress and march of my tale became and remained that of her understanding.

Absolutely, with this, I committed myself to making the
affirmation and the penetration of it my action and my
"story"; once more, too, with the re-entertained perception
that a subject so lighted, a subject residing in somebody's excited and concentrated feeling about something—both the
something and the somebody being of course as important as
possible—has more beauty to give out than under any other
style of pressure. One is confronted obviously thus with the
question of the importances; with that in particular, no
doubt, of the weight of intelligent consciousness, consciousness of the whole, or of something ominously like it, that one
may decently permit a represented figure to appear to throw.
Some plea for this cause, that of the intelligence of the moved
mannikin, I have already had occasion to make, and can scarce
hope too often to evade it. This intelligence, an honourable
amount of it, on the part of the person to whom one most
invites attention, has but to play with sufficient freedom and
ease, or call it with the right grace, to guarantee us that quantum of the impression of beauty which is the most fixed of
the possible advantages of our producible effect. It may fail,
as a positive presence, on other sides and in other connexions;
but more or less of the treasure is stored safe from the moment such a quality of inward life is distilled, or in other
words from the moment so fine an interpretation and criticism as that of Fleda Vetch's—to cite the present case—is
applied without waste to the surrounding tangle.

It is easy to object of course "Why the deuce then Fleda
Vetch, why a mere little flurried bundle of petticoats, why not
Hamlet or Milton's Satan at once, if you 're going in for a
superior display of 'mind'?" To which I fear I can only reply
that in pedestrian prose, and in the "short story," one is, for
the best reasons, no less on one's guard than on the stretch;
and also that I have ever recognised, even in the midst of the
curiosity that such displays may quicken, the rule of an exquisite economy. The thing is to lodge somewhere at the
heart of one's complexity an irrepressible *appreciation*, but
where a light lamp will carry all the flame I incline to look
askance at a heavy. From beginning to end, in "The Spoils of

Poynton," appreciation, even to that of the very whole, lives in Fleda; which is precisely why, as a consequence rather grandly imposed, every one else shows for comparatively stupid; the tangle, the drama, the tragedy and comedy of those who appreciate consisting so much of their relation with those who don't. From the presented reflexion of this truth my story draws, I think, a certain assured appearance of roundness and felicity. The "things" are radiant, shedding afar, with a merciless monotony, all their light, exerting their ravage without remorse; and Fleda almost demonically both sees and feels, while the others but feel without seeing. Thus we get perhaps a vivid enough little example, in the concrete, of the general truth, for the spectator of life, that the fixed constituents of almost any reproducible action are the fools who minister, at a particular crisis, to the intensity of the free spirit engaged with them. The fools are interesting by contrast, by the salience they acquire, and by a hundred other of their advantages; and the free spirit, always much tormented, and by no means always triumphant, is heroic, ironic, pathetic or whatever, and, as exemplified in the record of Fleda Vetch, for instance, "successful," only through having remained free.

I recognise that the novelist with a weakness for that ground of appeal is foredoomed to a well-nigh extravagant insistence on the free spirit, seeing the possibility of one in every bush; I may perhaps speak of it as noteworthy that this very volume happens to exhibit in two other cases my disposition to let the interest stand or fall by the tried spontaneity and vivacity of the freedom. It is in fact for that respectable reason that I enclose "A London Life" and "The Chaperon" between these covers; my purpose having been here to class my reprintable productions as far as possible according to their kinds. The two tales I have just named are of the same "kind" as "The Spoils," to the extent of their each dealing with a human predicament in the light, for the charm of the thing, of the amount of "appreciation" to be plausibly imputed to the subject of it. They are each—and truly there are more of such to come—"stories about women," very young women, who, affected with a certain high lucidity, thereby become characters; in consequence of which their doings, their sufferings or whatever, take on, I assume, an importance. Laura Wing, in "A London Life," has, like Fleda Vetch, acuteness and intensity, reflexion and passion, has above all a contributive and participant view of her situation; just as Rose Tramore, in "The Chaperon," rejoices, almost to insolence, very much in the same cluster of attributes and advantages. They are thus of a family—which shall have also for us, we seem forewarned, more members, and of each sex.

As to our young woman of "The Spoils," meanwhile, I briefly come back to my claim for a certain definiteness of beauty in the special effect wrought by her aid. My problem had decently to be met—that of establishing for the other persons the vividness of their appearance of comparative stupidity, that of exposing them to the full thick wash of the penumbra surrounding the central light, and yet keeping their motions, within it, distinct, coherent and "amusing." But these are exactly of course the most "amusing" things to do; nothing, for example, being of a higher reward artistically than the shade of success aimed at in such a figure as Mrs. Gereth. A character she too, absolutely, yet the very reverse of a free spirit. I have found myself so pleased with Mrs. Gereth, I confess, on resuming acquaintance with her, that, complete and all in equilibrium as she seems to me to stand and move there, I shrink from breathing upon her any breath of qualification; without which, however, I fail of my point that, thanks to the "value" represented by Fleda, and to the position to which the elder woman is confined by that irradiation, the latter is at the best a "false" character, floundering as she does in the dusk of disproportionate passion. She is a *figure*, oh definitely—which is a very different matter; for you may be a figure with all the blinding, with all the hampering passion in life, and may have the grand air in what shall yet prove to the finer view (which Fleda again, *e. g.*, could at any time strike off) but a perfect rage of awkwardness. Mrs. Gereth was, obviously, with her pride and her pluck, of an admirable fine paste; but she was not intelligent, was only clever, and therefore would have been no use to us at all as centre of our subject—compared with Fleda, who was only intelligent, not distinctively able. The little drama confirms at all events excellently, I think, the contention of the old wisdom that the question of the personal will has more than all else to say to the verisimilitude of these exhibitions. The will that rides the crisis quite most triumphantly is that of the awful Mona Brigstock, who is *all* will, without the smallest leak of force into taste or tenderness or vision, into any sense of shades or relations or proportions. She loses no minute in that perception of incongruities in which half Fleda's passion is wasted and misled, and into which Mrs. Gereth, to her practical loss, that is by the fatal grace of a sense of comedy, occasionally and disinterestedly strays. Every one, every thing, in the story is accordingly sterile *but* the so thriftily constructed Mona, able at any moment to bear the whole of her dead weight at once on any given inch of a resisting surface. Fleda, obliged to neglect inches, sees and feels but in acres and expanses and blue perspectives; Mrs. Gereth too, in comparison, while her imagination broods, drops half the stitches of the web she seeks to weave.

If I speak of classifying I hasten to recognise that there are other marks for the purpose still and that, failing other considerations, "A London Life" would properly consort, in this series, with a dozen of the tales by which I at one period sought to illustrate and enliven the supposed "international" conflict of manners; a general theme dealing for the most part with the bewilderment of the good American, of either sex and of almost any age, in presence of the "European" order. This group of data might possibly have shown, for the reverse of its medal, the more or less desperate contortions of the European under American social pressure. Three or four tried glances in that direction seemed to suggest, however, no great harvest to be gathered; so that the pictorial value of the general opposition was practically confined to one phase. More reasons are here involved than I can begin to go into—as indeed I confess that the reflexions set in motion by the international fallacy at large, as I am now moved to regard it, quite crowd upon me; I simply note therefore, on one corner of the ground, the scant results, above all for interesting detail, promised by confronting the fruits of a constituted order with the fruits of no order at all. We may strike lights by opposing order to order, one sort to another sort; for in that case we get the correspondences and equivalents that make differences mean something; we get the interest and the tension of disparity where a certain parity may have been in question. Where it may *not* have been in question, where the dramatic encounter is but the poor concussion of positives on one side with negatives on the other, we get little beyond a consideration of the differences between fishes and fowls.

By which I don't mean to say that the appeal of the fallacy, as I call it, was not at one time quite inevitably irresistible; had it nothing else to recommend it to the imagination it would always have had the advantage of its showy surface, of suggesting situations as to which assurance seemed easy, founded, as it felt itself, on constant observation. The attraction was thus not a little, I judge, the attraction of facility; the international was easy to do, because, as one's wayside bloomed with it, one had but to put forth one's hand and pluck the frequent flower. Add to this that the flower *was*, so often, quite positively a flower—that of the young American innocence transplanted to European air. The general subject had, in fine, a charm while it lasted; but I shall have much more to say about it on another occasion. What here concerns us is that "A London Life" breaks down altogether, I have had to recognise, as a contribution to my comprehensive picture of bewildered Americanism. I fail to make out to-day why I need have conceived my three principal persons as sharers in that particular bewilderment. There was enough of the general human and social sort for them without it; poor young Wendover in especial, I think, fails on any such ground to attest himself—I need n't, surely, have been at costs to bring him all the way from New York. Laura Wing, touching creature as she was designed to appear, strikes me as a rare little person who would have been a rare little person anywhere, and who, in that character, must have felt and judged and suffered and acted as she did, whatever her producing clime.

The great anomaly, however, is Mrs. Lionel; a study of a type quite sufficiently to be accounted for on the very scene of her development, and with her signs and marks easily mistakeable, in London, for the notes of a native luxuriance. I recall the emphasis, quite the derision, with which a remarkably wise old friend, not American, a trenchant judge who had observed manners in many countries and had done me

the honour to read my tale, put to me: "What on earth possessed you to make of your Selina an American, or to make
one of your two or three Americans a Selina?—resembling so
to the life something quite else, something which hereabouts
one need n't go far to seek, but failing of any felicity for a
creature engendered *là-bas*." And I think my friend conveyed,
or desired to convey, that the wicked woman of my story was
falsified above all, as an imported product, by something distinctly other than so engendered in the superficial "form" of
her perversity, a high stiff-backed angular action which is, or
was then, beyond any American "faking." The truth is, no
doubt, that, though Mrs. Lionel, on my page, does n't in the
least achieve character, she yet passes before us as a sufficiently vivid image, which was to be the effect designed for
her—an image the hard rustle of whose long steps and the
sinister tinkle of whose multiplied trinkets belie the association invoked for them and positively operate for another. Not
perhaps, moreover, as I am moved to subjoin, that the point
greatly matters. What matters, for one's appreciation of a
work of art, however modest, is that the prime intention shall
have been justified—for any judgment of which we must be
clear as to what it was. It was n't after all of the prime,
the very most prime, intention of the tale in question that the
persons concerned in them should have had this, that or the
other land of birth; but that the central situation should really
be rendered—that of a charming and decent young thing,
from wheresoever proceeding, who has her decision and her
action to take, horribly and unexpectedly, in face of a squalid
"scandal" the main agent of which is her nearest relative, and
who, at the dreadful crisis, to guard against personal bespat-
tering, is moved, with a miserable want of effect, to a wild
vague frantic gesture, an appeal for protection that virtually
proves a precipitation of her disgrace.

Nobody concerned need, as I say, have come from New
York for that; though, as I have likewise intimated, I must
have seen the creation of my heroine, in 1888, and the representation of the differences I wished to establish between her
own known world and the world from which she finds herself
recoiling, facilitated in a high degree by assured reference to
the simpler social order across the sea. I had my vision (as I

recover the happy spell) of her having "come over" to find, to her dismay, what "London" had made of the person in the world hitherto most akin to her; in addition to which I was during those years infinitely interested in almost any demonstration of the effect of London. This was a form of response to the incessant appeal of the great city, one's grateful, one's devoted recognition of which fairly broke out from day to day. It was material ever to one's hand; and the impression was always there that no one so much as the candid outsider, caught up and involved in the sweep of the machine, could measure the values revealed. Laura Wing must have figured for me thus as the necessary candid outsider—from the moment some received impression of the elements about me was to be projected and embodied. In fact as I remount the stream it is the particular freshness of that enjoyed relation I seem to taste again; the positive fond belief that I had my right oppositions. They seemed to ensure somehow the perfect march of my tolerably simple action; the straightness, the artful economy of which—save that of a particular point where my ingenuity shows to so small advantage that, to anticipate opprobrium, I can but hold it up to derision—has n't ceased to be appreciable. The thing made its first appearance in "Scribner's Magazine" during the summer of 1888, and I remember being not long before at work upon it, remember in fact beginning it, in one of the wonderful faded back rooms of an old Venetian palace, a room with a pompous Tiepolo ceiling and walls of ancient pale-green damask, slightly shredded and patched, which, on the warm mornings, looked into the shade of a court where a high outer staircase, strikingly bold, yet strikingly relaxed, held together one scarce knew how; where Gothic windows broke out, on discoloured blanks of wall, at quite arbitrary levels, and where above all the strong Venetian voice, full of history and humanity and waking perpetual echoes, seemed to say more in ten warm words, of whatever tone, than any twenty pages of one's cold pale prose.

In spite of all of which, I may add, I do penance here only for the awkwardness of that departure from the adopted form of my recital which resides in the picture of the interview with young Wendover contrived by Lady Davenant in the interest of some better provision for their poor young friend. Here indeed is a lapse from artistic dignity, a confession of want of resource, which I may not pretend to explain to-day, and on behalf of which I have nothing to urge save a consciousness of my dereliction presumably too vague at the time. I had seen my elements presented in a certain way, settled the little law under which my story was to be told, and with this consistency, as any reader of the tale may easily make out for himself, interviews to which my central figure was not a party, scenes revolving on an improvised pivot of their own, had nothing to do with the affair. I might of course have adopted another plan—the artist is free, surely, to adopt any he fancies, provided it *be* a plan and he adopt it intelligently; and to that scheme of composition the independent picture of a passage between Lady Davenant and young Wendover might perfectly have conformed. As the case stands it conforms to nothing; whereas the beauty of a thing of this order really done as a whole is ever, certainly, that its parts are in abject dependence, and that even any great charm they may individually and capriciously put forth is infirm so far as it does n't measurably contribute to a harmony. My momentary helplessness sprang, no doubt, from my failure to devise in time some way of giving the value of Lady Davenant's appeal to the young man, of making it play its part in my heroine's history and consciousness, without so awkwardly thrusting the lump sum on the reader.

Circumventions of difficulty of this degree are precisely the finest privilege of the craftsman, who, to be worth his salt, and master of *any* contrived harmony, must take no tough technical problem for insoluble. These technical subterfuges and subtleties, these indirectly-expressed values, kept indirect in a higher interest, made subordinate to some general beauty, some artistic intention that can give an account of itself, what are they after all but one of the nobler parts of our amusement? Superficially, in "A London Life," it might well have seemed that the only way to picture the intervention on Laura Wing's behalf of the couple just named was to break the chain of the girl's own consciousness and report the matter quite straight and quite shamelessly; this course had indeed every merit but that of its playing the particular game to which I had addressed myself. My prime loyalty was to the interest of the game, and the honour to be won the more desirable by that fact. Any muddle-headed designer can beg the question of perspective, but science is required for making it rule the scene. If it be asked how then we were to have assisted at the copious passage I thus incriminate without our privilege of presence, I can only say that my discovery of the right way should—and would—have been the very flower of the performance. The real "fun" of the thing would have been exactly to sacrifice my comparative platitude of statement—a deplorable depth at any time, I have attempted elsewhere to signify, for any pretending master of representation to sink to—without sacrificing a grain of what was to be conveyed. The real fun, in other words, would have been in not, by an exceptional collapse of other ingenuity, making my attack on the spectator's consciousness a call as immediate as a post-man's knock. This attack, at every other point, reaches that objective only through the medium of the interesting girl's own vision, own experience, with which all the facts are richly charged and coloured. That saturates our sense of them with the savour of Laura's sense—thanks to which enhancement we get intensity. But from the chapter to which I have called attention, so that it may serve perhaps as a lesson, intensity ruefully drops. I can't say worse for it—and have been the more concerned to say what I do that without this flaw the execution might have appeared from beginning to end close and exemplary.

It is with all that better confidence, I think, that the last of my three tales here carries itself. I recapture perfectly again, in respect to "The Chaperon," both the first jog of my imag-ination and the particular local influence that presided at its birth—the latter a ramshackle inn on the Irish coast, where the table at which I wrote was of an equilibrium so vague that I wonder to-day how any object constructed on it should stand so firm. The strange sad charm of the tearful Irish light hangs about the memory of the labour of which this small fiction—first published in two numbers of "The Atlantic Monthly" of 1891—was one of the fruits; but the subject had glimmered upon me, two or three years before, in an air of comedy comparatively free from sharp under-tastes. Once more, as in the case of its companions here, the single spoken word, in London, had said all—after the manner of that clear ring of the electric bell that the barest touch of the button may produce. The talk being of a certain lady who, in consequence of early passages, had lived for years apart from her husband and in no affluence of good company, it was mentioned of her that her situation had improved, and the desert around her been more or less brought under cultivation, by the fact of her having at last made acquaintance with her young unmarried daughter, a charming girl just introduced to the world and thereby qualified for "taking her out," floating her in spite of whatever past damage. Here in truth, it seemed to me, *was* a morsel of queer comedy to play with, and my tale embodies the neat experiment. Fortunately in this case the principle of composition adopted is loyally observed; the values gathered are, without exception, gathered by the light of the intense little personal consciousness, invoked from the first, that shines over my field and the predominance of which is usurped by none other. That is the main note to be made about "The Chaperon"; except this further, which I must reserve, however—as I shall find excellent occasion— for an ampler development. A short story, to my sense and as the term is used in magazines, has to choose between being either an anecdote or a picture and can but play its part strictly according to its kind. I rejoice in the anecdote, but I revel in the picture; though having doubtless at times to note that a given attempt may place itself near the dividing-line. This is in some degree the case with "The Chaperon," in which, none the less, on the whole, picture ingeniously prevails; picture aiming at those richly summarised and foreshortened effects—the opposite pole again from expansion inorganic and thin—that refer their terms of production, for which the magician has ever to don his best cap and gown, to the inner compartment of our box of tricks. From *them* comes the true grave close consistency in which parts hang together even as the interweavings of a tapestry. "The Chaperon" has perhaps, so far as it goes, something of that texture. Yet I shall be able, I think, to cite examples with still more.

What Maisie Knew, The Pupil, In the Cage

I RECOGNISE AGAIN, for the first of these three Tales, another instance of the growth of the "great oak" from the little acorn; since "What Maisie Knew" is at least a tree that spreads beyond any provision its small germ might on a first handling have appeared likely to make for it. The accidental mention had been made to me of the manner in which the situation of some luckless child of a divorced couple was affected, under my informant's eyes, by the re-marriage of one of its parents—I forget which; so that, thanks to the limited desire for its company expressed by the step-parent, the law of its little life, its being entertained in rotation by its father and its mother, would n't easily prevail. Whereas each of these persons had at first vindictively desired to keep it from the other, so at present the re-married relative sought now rather to be rid of it—that is to leave it as much as possible, and beyond the appointed times and seasons, on the hands of the adversary; which malpractice, resented by the latter as bad faith, would of course be repaid and avenged by an equal treachery. The wretched infant was thus to find itself practically disowned, rebounding from racquet to racquet like a tennis-ball or a shuttlecock. This figure could but touch the fancy to the quick and strike one as the beginning of a story—a story commanding a great choice of developments. I recollect, however, promptly thinking that for a proper symmetry the second parent should marry too—which in the case named to me indeed would probably soon occur, and was in any case what the ideal of the situation required. The second step-parent would have but to be correspondingly incommoded by obligations to the offspring of a hated predecessor for the misfortune of the little victim to become altogether exemplary. The business would accordingly be sad enough, yet I am not sure its possibility of interest would so much have appealed to me had I not soon felt that the ugly facts, so stated or conceived, by no means constituted the whole appeal.

The light of an imagination touched by them could n't help therefore projecting a further ray, thanks to which it became rather quaintly clear that, not less than the chance of misery and of a degraded state, the chance of happiness and of an improved state might be here involved for the child, round about whom the complexity of life would thus turn to fineness, to richness—and indeed would have but so to turn for the small creature to be steeped in security and ease. Sketchily clustered even, these elements gave out that vague pictorial glow which forms the first appeal of a living "subject" to the painter's consciousness; but the glimmer became intense as I proceeded to a further analysis. The further analysis is for that matter almost always the torch of rapture and victory, as the artist's firm hand grasps and plays it—I mean, naturally, of the smothered rapture and the obscure victory, enjoyed and celebrated not in the street but before some innermost shrine; the odds being a hundred to one, in almost any connexion, that it does n't arrive by any easy first process at the *best* residuum of truth. That was the charm, sensibly, of the picture thus at first confusedly showing; the elements so could n't but flush, to their very surface, with some deeper depth of irony than the mere obvious. It lurked in the crude postulate like a buried scent; the more the attention hovered the more aware it became of the fragrance. To which I may add that the more I scratched the surface and penetrated, the more potent, to the intellectual nostril, became this virtue. At last, accordingly, the residuum, as I have called it, reached, I was in presence of the red dramatic spark that glowed at the core of my vision and that, as I gently blew upon it, burned higher and clearer. This precious particle was the *full* ironic truth—the most interesting item to be read into the child's situation. For satisfaction of the mind, in other words, the small expanding consciousness would have to be saved, have to become presentable as a register of impressions; and saved by the experience of certain advantages, by some enjoyed profit and some achieved confidence, rather than coarsened, blurred, sterilised, by ignorance and pain. This better state, in the young life, would reside in the exercise of a function other than that of disconcerting the selfishness of its parents—which was all that had on the face of the matter seemed reserved to it in the way of criticism applied to their rupture. The early relation would be exchanged for a later; instead of simply submitting to the inherited tie and the imposed complication, of suffering from them, our little wonder-working agent would create, without design, quite fresh elements of this order—contribute, that is, to the formation of a fresh tie, from which it would then (and for all the world as if through a small demonic foresight) proceed to derive great profit.

This is but to say that the light in which the vision so readily grew to a wholeness was that of a second marriage on both sides; the father having, in the freedom of divorce, but to take another wife, as well as the mother, under a like licence, another husband, for the case to begin, at least, to stand beautifully on its feet. There would be thus a perfect logic for what might come—come even with the mere attribution of a certain sensibility (if but a mere relative fineness) to either of the new parties. Say the prime cause making for the ultimate attempt to shirk on one side or the other, and better still if on both, a due share of the decreed burden should have been, after all, in each progenitor, a constitutional inaptitude for *any* burden, and a base intolerance of it: we should thus get a motive not requiring, but happily dispensing with, too particular a perversity in the step-parents. The child seen as creating by the fact of its forlornness a relation between its step-parents, the more intimate the better, dramatically speaking; the child, by the mere appeal of neglectedness and the mere consciousness of relief, weaving about, with the best faith in the world, the close web of sophistication; the child becoming a centre and pretext for a fresh system of misbehaviour, a system moreover of a nature to spread and ramify: *there* would be the "full" irony, there the promising theme into which the hint I had originally picked up would logically flower. No themes are so human as those that reflect for us, out of the confusion of life, the close connexion of bliss and bale, of the things that help with the things that hurt, so dangling before us for ever that bright hard medal, of so strange an alloy, one face of which is somebody's right and ease and the other somebody's pain and wrong. To live with all intensity and perplexity and felicity in its terribly mixed little world would thus be the part of my interesting small mortal; bringing people together who would be at least more correctly separate; keeping people separate who would be at least more correctly together; flourishing, to a degree, at the cost of many conventions and proprieties, even decencies; really keeping the torch of virtue alive in an air tending infinitely to smother it; really in short making confusion worse confounded by drawing some stray fragrance of an ideal across the scent of selfishness, by sowing on barren strands, through the mere fact of presence, the seed of the moral life.

All this would be to say, I at once recognised, that my light vessel of consciousness, swaying in such a draught, could n't be with verisimilitude a rude little boy; since, beyond the fact that little boys are never so "present," the sensibility of the female young is indubitably, for early youth, the greater, and my plan would call, on the part of my protagonist, for "no end" of sensibility. I might impute that amount of it without extravagance to a slip of a girl whose faculties should have been well shaken up; but I should have so to depend on its action to keep my story clear that I must be able to show it in all assurance as naturally intense. To this end I should have of course to suppose for my heroine dispositions originally promising, but above all I should have to invest her with perceptions easily and almost infinitely quickened. So handsomely fitted out, yet not in a manner too grossly to affront probability, she might well see me through the whole course of my design; which design, more and more attractive as I turned it over, and dignified by the most delightful difficulty, would be to make and to keep her so limited consciousness the very field of my picture while at the same time guarding with care the integrity of the objects represented. With the charm of this possibility, therefore, the project for "Maisie" rounded itself and loomed large—any subject looming large, for that matter, I am bound to add, from the moment one is ridden by the law of entire expression. I have already elsewhere noted, I think, that the memory of my own work preserves for me no theme that, at some moment or other of its development, and always only waiting for the right connexion or chance, has n't signally refused to remain humble, even (or perhaps all the more resentfully) when fondly selected for its conscious and hopeless humility. Once "out," like a housedog of a temper above confinement, it defies the mere whistle, it roams, it hunts, it seeks out and "sees" life; it can be brought back but by hand and then only to take its futile thrashing. It was n't at any rate for an idea seen in the light I here glance at not to have due warrant of its value—how could the value of a scheme so finely workable *not* be great? The one presented register of the whole complexity would be the play of the child's confused and obscure notation of it, and yet the whole, as I say, should be unmistakeably, should be honourably there, seen through the faint intelligence, or at the least attested by the imponderable presence, and still advertising its sense.

I recall that my first view of this neat possibility was as the attaching problem of the picture restricted (while yet achieving, as I say, completeness and coherency) to what the child might be conceived to have *understood*—to have been able to interpret and appreciate. Further reflexion and experiment showed me my subject strangled in that extreme of rigour. The infant mind would at the best leave great gaps and voids; so that with a systematic surface possibly beyond reproach we should nevertheless fail of clearness of sense. I should have to stretch the matter to what my wondering witness materially and inevitably *saw*; a great deal of which quantity she either would n't understand at all or would quite misunderstand—and on those lines, only on those, my task would be prettily cut out. To that then I settled—to the question of giving it *all*, the whole situation surrounding her, but of giving it only through the occasions and connexions of her proximity and her attention; only as it might pass before her and appeal to her, as it might touch her and affect her, for better or worse, for perceptive gain or perceptive loss: so that we fellow witnesses, we not more invited but only more expert critics, should feel in strong possession of it. This would be, to begin with, a plan of absolutely definite and measurable application—that in itself always a mark of beauty; and I have been interested to find on re-perusal of the work that some such controlling grace successfully rules it. Nothing could be more "done," I think, in the light of its happiest intention; and this in spite of an appearance that at moments obscures my consistency. Small children have many more perceptions than they have terms to translate them; their vision is at any moment much richer, their apprehension even constantly stronger, than their prompt, their at all producible, vocabulary. Amusing therefore as it might at the first blush have seemed to restrict myself in this case to the terms as well as to the experience, it became at once plain that such an attempt would fail. Maisie's terms accordingly play their part—since her simpler conclusions quite depend on them; but our own commentary constantly attends and amplifies. This it is that on occasion, doubtless, seems to represent us as going so "behind" the facts of her spectacle as to exaggerate the activity of her relation to them. The difference here is but of a shade: it is her relation, her activity of spirit, that determines all our own concern—we simply take advantage of these things better than she herself. Only, even though it is her interest that mainly makes matters interesting for us, we inevitably note this in figures that are not yet at her command and that are nevertheless required whenever those aspects about her and those parts of her experience that she understands darken off into others that she rather tormentedly misses. All of which gave me a high firm logic to observe; supplied the force for which the straightener of almost any tangle is grateful while he labours, the sense of pulling at threads intrinsically worth it—strong enough and fine enough and entire enough.

Of course, beyond this, was another and well-nigh equal charm—equal in spite of its being almost independent of the acute constructional, the endless expressional question. This was the quite different question of the particular kind of truth of resistance I might be able to impute to my central figure—*some* intensity, some continuity of resistance being naturally of the essence of the subject. Successfully to resist (to resist, that is, the strain of observation and the assault of experience) what would that be, on the part of so young a person, but to remain fresh, and still fresh, and to have even a freshness to communicate?—the case being with Maisie to the end that she treats her friends to the rich little spectacle of objects embalmed in her wonder. She wonders, in other words, to the end, to the death—the death of her childhood, properly speaking; after which (with the inevitable shift, sooner or later, of her point of view) her situation will change and become another affair, subject to other measurements and with a new centre altogether. The particular reaction that will have led her to that point, and that it has been of an exquisite interest to study in her, will have spent itself; there will be another scale, another perspective, another horizon. Our business meanwhile therefore is to extract from her current reaction whatever it may be worth; and for that matter we recognise in it the highest exhibitional virtue. Truly, I reflect, if the theme had had no other beauty it would still have had this rare and distinguished one of its so expressing the variety of the child's values. She is not only the extraordinary "ironic centre" I have already noted; she has the wonderful importance of shedding a light far beyond any reach of her comprehension; of lending to poorer persons and things, by the mere fact of their being involved with her and by the special scale she creates for them, a precious element of dignity. I lose myself, truly, in appreciation of my theme on noting what she does by her "freshness" for appearances in themselves vulgar and empty enough. They become, as she deals with them, the stuff of poetry and tragedy and art; she has simply to wonder, as I say, about them, and they begin to have meanings, aspects, solidities, connexions—connexions with the "universal!"—that they could scarce have hoped for. Ida Farange alone, so to speak, or Beale alone, that is either of them otherwise connected—what intensity, what "objectivity" (the most developed degree of *being* anyhow thinkable for them) would they have? How would they repay at all the favour of our attention?

Maisie makes them portentous all by the play of her good faith, makes her mother above all, to my vision—unless I have wholly failed to render it—concrete, immense and awful; so that we get, for our profit, and get by an economy of process interesting in itself, the thoroughly pictured creature, the striking figured symbol. At two points in particular, I seem to recognise, we enjoy at its maximum this effect of associational magic. The passage in which her father's terms of intercourse with the insinuating but so strange and unattractive lady whom he has had the detestable levity to whisk her off to see late at night, is a signal example of the all but incalculable way in which interest may be constituted. The facts involved are that Beale Farange is ignoble, that the friend to whom he introduces his daughter is deplorable, and that from the commerce of the two, *as* the two merely, we would fain avert our heads. Yet the thing has but to become a part of the child's bewilderment for these small sterilities to drop from it and for the *scene* to emerge and prevail—vivid, special, wrought hard, to the hardness of the unforgettable; the scene that is exactly what Beale and Ida and Mrs. Cuddon, and even Sir Claude and Mrs. Beale, would never for a moment have succeeded in making their scant unredeemed importances—namely *appreciable*. I find another instance in the episode of Maisie's unprepared encounter, while walking in the Park with Sir Claude, of her mother and that beguiled attendant of her mother, the encouraging, the appealing "Captain," to whom this lady contrives to commit her for twenty minutes while she herself deals with the second husband. The human substance here would have seemed in advance well-nigh too poor for conversion, the three "mature" figures of too short a radiation, too stupid (*so* stupid it was for Sir Claude to have married Ida!) too vain, too thin, for any clear application; but promptly, immediately, the child's own importance, spreading and contagiously acting, has determined the *total* value otherwise. Nothing of course, meanwhile, is an older story to the observer of manners and the painter of life than the grotesque finality with which such terms as "painful," "unpleasant" and "disgusting" are often applied to his results; to that degree, in truth, that the free use of them as weightily conclusive again and again re-enforces his estimate of the critical sense of circles in which they artlessly flourish. Of course under that superstition I was punctually to have had read to me the lesson that the "mixing-up" of a child with anything unpleasant confessed itself an aggravation of the unpleasantness, and that nothing could well be more disgusting than to attribute to Maisie so intimate an "acquaintance" with the gross immoralities surrounding her.

The only thing to say of such lucidities is that, however one may have "discounted" in advance, and as once for all, their general radiance, one is disappointed if the hour for them, in the particular connexion, does n't strike—they so keep before us elements with which even the most sedate philosopher must always reckon. The painter of life has indeed work cut out for him when a considerable part of life offers itself in the guise of that sapience. The effort really to see and really to represent is no idle business in face of the *constant* force that makes for muddlement. The great thing is indeed that the muddled state too is one of the very sharpest of the realities, that it also has colour and form and character, has often in fact a broad and rich comicality, many of the signs and values of the appreciable. Thus it was to be, for example, I might gather, that the very principle of Maisie's appeal, her unde-stroyed freshness, in other words that vivacity of intelligence by which she indeed does vibrate in the infected air, indeed does flourish in her immoral world, may pass for a barren and senseless thing, or at best a negligible one. For nobody to whom life at large is *easily* interesting do the finer, the shyer, the more anxious small vibrations, fine and shy and anxious with the passion that precedes knowledge, succeed in being negligible: which is doubtless one of many reasons why the passage between the child and the kindly, friendly, ugly gen-tleman who, seated with her in Kensington Gardens under a spreading tree, positively answers to her for her mother as no one has ever answered, and so stirs her, filially and morally, as she has never been stirred, throws into highest relief, to my sense at least, the side on which the subject is strong, and becomes the type-passage—other advantages certainly aiding, as I may say—for the expression of its beauty. The active, contributive close-circling wonder, as I have called it, in which the child's identity is guarded and preserved, and which makes her case remarkable exactly by the weight of the tax on it, provides distinction for her, provides vitality and variety, through the operation of the tax—which would have done comparatively little for us had n't it been monstrous. A pity for us surely to have been deprived of this just reflexion. "Maisie" is of 1907.

I pass by, for the moment, the second of these composi-tions, finding in the third, which again deals with the experi-ence of a very young person, a connexion more immediate; and this even at the risk of seeming to undermine my remark of a few pages back as to the comparative sensibility of the sexes. My urchin of "The Pupil" (1891) has sensibility in abun-dance, it would seem—and yet preserves in spite of it, I judge, his strong little male quality. But there are fifty things to say here; which indeed rush upon me within my present close limits in such a cloud as to demand much clearance. This is perhaps indeed but the aftersense of the assault made on my mind, as I perfectly recall, by every aspect of the original vision, which struck me as abounding in aspects. It lives again for me, this vision, as it first alighted; though the inimitable prime flutter, the air as of an ineffable sign made by the immediate beat of the wings of the poised figure of fancy that has just settled, is one of those guarantees of value that can never be re-captured. The sign has been made to the seer only—it is *his* queer affair; of which any report to others, not as yet involved, has but the same effect of flatness as attends, amid a group gathered under the canopy of night, any stray allusion to a shooting star. The miracle, since miracle it seems, is all for the candid exclaimer. The miracle for the author of "The Pupil," at any rate, was when, years ago, one summer day, in a very hot Italian railway-carriage, which stopped and dawdled everywhere, favouring conversation, a friend with whom I shared it, a doctor of medicine who had come from a far country to settle in Florence, happened to speak to me of a wonderful American family, an odd adventurous, extravagant band, of high but rather unauthenticated pretensions, the most interesting member of which was a small boy, acute and precocious, afflicted with a heart of weak action, but beautifully intelligent, who saw their prowling precarious life exactly as it was, and measured and judged it, and measured and judged *them*, all round, ever so quaintly; presenting himself in short as an extraordinary little person. Here was more than enough for a summer's day even in old Italy—here was a thumping windfall. No process and no steps intervened: I *saw*, on the spot, little Morgan Moreen, I saw all the rest of the Moreens; I felt, to the last delicacy, the nature of my young friend's relation with them (he had become at once my young friend) and, by the same stroke, to its uttermost fine throb, the subjection to *him* of the beguiled, bewildered, defrauded, unremunerated, yet after all richly repaid youth who would to a certainty, under stress of compassion, embark with the tribe on tutorship, and whose edifying connexion with it would be my leading document.

This must serve as my account of the origin of "The Pu-pil": it will commend itself, I feel, to all imaginative and pro-jective persons who have had—and what imaginative and projective person has n't?—any like experience of the sud-denly-determined *absolute* of perception. The whole cluster of items forming the image is on these occasions born at once; the parts are not pieced together, they conspire and interde-pend; but what it really comes to, no doubt, is that at a sim-ple touch an old latent and dormant impression, a buried germ, implanted by experience and then forgotten, flashes to the surface as a fish, with a single "squirm," rises to the baited hook, and there meets instantly the vivifying ray. I remember at all events having no doubt of anything or anyone here; the vision kept to the end its ease and its charm; it worked itself out with confidence. These are minor matters when the ques-tion is of minor results; yet almost any assured and downright imaginative act is—granted the sort of record in which I here indulge—worth fondly commemorating. One cherishes, after the fact, any proved case of the independent life of the imag-ination; above all if by that faculty one has been appointed mainly to live. We are then *never* detached from the question of what it may out of simple charity do for us. Besides which, in relation to the poor Moreens, innumerable notes, as I have intimated, all equally urging their relevance, press here to the front. The general adventure of the little composition itself— for singular things were to happen to it, though among such importunities not the most worth noting now—would be, occasion favouring, a thing to live over; moving as one did, roundabout it, in I scarce know what thick and coloured air of slightly tarnished anecdote, of dim association, of casual confused romance; a compound defying analysis, but truly, for the social chronicler, any student in especial of the copious "cosmopolite" legend, a boundless and tangled, but highly ex-plorable, garden. Why, somehow—these were the intensify-ing questions—did one see the Moreens, whom I place at Nice, at Venice, in Paris, as of the special essence of the little old miscellaneous cosmopolite Florence, the Florence of other, of irrecoverable years, the restless yet withal so conve-nient scene of a society that has passed away for ever with all its faded ghosts and fragile relics; immaterial presences that have quite ceased to revisit (trust an old romancer's, an old pious observer's fine sense to have made sure of it!) walks and prospects once sacred and shaded, but now laid bare, gaping wide, despoiled of their past and unfriendly to any appreciation of it?—through which the unconscious Barbarians troop with the regularity and passivity of "supplies," or other promiscuous goods, prepaid and forwarded.

They had nothing to do, the dear Moreens, with this dreadful period, any more than I, as occupied and charmed with them, was humiliatingly subject to it; we were, all together, of a better romantic age and faith; we referred ourselves, with our highest complacency, to the classic years of the great Americano-European legend; the years of limited communication, of monstrous and unattenuated contrast, of prodigious and unrecorded adventure. The comparatively brief but infinitely rich "cycle" of romance embedded in the earlier, the very early American reactions and returns (mediæval in the sense of being, at most, of the mid-century), what does it resemble to-day but a gold-mine overgrown and smothered, dislocated, and no longer workable?—all for want of the right indications for sounding, the right implements for digging, doubtless even of the right workmen, those with the right tradition and "feeling," for the job. The most extraordinary things appear to have happened, during that golden age, in the "old" countries—in Asia and Africa as well as in Europe—to the candid children of the West, things admirably incongruous and incredible; but no story of all the list was to find its just interpreter, and nothing is now more probable than that every key to interpretation has been lost. The modern reporter's big brushes, attached to broom-handles that match the height of his sky-scrapers, would sadly besmear the fine parchment of our missing record. We were to lose, clearly, at any rate, a vast body of precious anecdote, a long gallery of wonderful portraits, an array of the oddest possible figures in the oddest possible attitudes. The Moreens were of the family then of the great unstudied precursors— poor and shabby members, no doubt; dim and superseded types. I must add indeed that, such as they were, or as they may at present incoherently appear, I don't pretend really to have "done" them; all I have given in "The Pupil" is little

Morgan's troubled vision of them as reflected in the vision, also troubled enough, of his devoted friend. The manner of the thing may thus illustrate the author's incorrigible taste for gradations and superpositions of effect; his love, when it is a question of a picture, of anything that makes for proportion and perspective, that contributes to a view of *all* the dimensions. Addicted to seeing "through"—one thing through another, accordingly, and still other things through *that*—he takes, too greedily perhaps, on any errand, as many things as possible by the way. It is after this fashion that he incurs the stigma of labouring uncannily for a certain fulness of truth— truth diffused, distributed and, as it were, atmospheric.

The second in order of these fictions speaks for itself, I think, so frankly as scarce to suffer further expatiation. Its origin is written upon it large, and the idea it puts into play so abides in one of the commonest and most taken-for-granted of London impressions that some such experimentally-figured situation as that of "In the Cage" must again and again have flowered (granted the grain of observation) in generous minds. It had become for me, at any rate, an old story by the time (1898) I cast it into this particular form. The postal-telegraph office in general, and above all the small local office of one's immediate neighbourhood, scene of the transaction of so much of one's daily business, haunt of one's needs and one's duties, of one's labours and one's patiences, almost of one's rewards and one's disappointments, one's joys and one's sorrows, had ever had, to my sense, so much of London to give out, so much of its huge perpetual story to tell, that any momentary wait there seemed to take place in a strong social draught, the stiffest possible breeze of the human comedy. One had of course in these connexions one's especial resort, the office nearest one's own door, where one had come to enjoy in a manner the fruits of frequentation and the amenities of intercourse. So had grown up, for speculation—prone as one's mind had ever been to that form of waste—the question of what it might "mean," wherever the admirable service was installed, for confined and cramped and yet considerably tutored young officials of either sex to be made so free, intellectually, of a range of experience otherwise quite closed to them. This wonderment, once the spark was kindled, became an amusement, or an obsession, like another; though falling indeed, at the best, no doubt, but into that deepest abyss of all the wonderments that break out for the student of great cities. From the moment that he *is* a student, this most beset of critics, his danger is inevitably of imputing to too many others, right and left, the critical impulse and the acuter vision—so very long may it take him to learn that the mass of mankind are banded, probably by the sanest of instincts, to defend themselves to the death against any such vitiation of their simplicity. To criticise is to appreciate, to appropriate, to take intellectual possession, to establish in fine a relation with the criticised thing and make it one's own. The large intellectual appetite projects itself thus on many things, while the small—not better advised, but unconscious of need for advice—projects itself on few.

Admirable thus its economic instinct; it is curious of nothing that it has n't vital use for. You may starve in London, it is clear, without discovering a use for any theory of the more equal division of victuals—which is moreover exactly what it would appear that thousands of the non-speculative annually do. Their example is much to the point, in the light of all the barren trouble they are saved; but somehow, after all, it gives no pause to the "artist," to the morbid, imagination. That rash, that idle faculty continues to abound in questions, and to supply answers to as many of them as possible; all of which makes a great occupation for idleness. To the fantastic scale on which this last-named state may, in favoring conditions, organise itself, to the activities it may practise when the favouring conditions happen to crop up in Mayfair or in Kensington, our portrayal of the caged telegraphist may well appear a proper little monument. The composition before us tells in fact clearly enough, it seems to me, the story of its growth; and relevance will probably be found in any moral it may pluck—by which I mean any moral the impulse to have framed it may pluck—from the vice of reading rank subtleties into simple souls and reckless expenditure into thrifty ones. The matter comes back again, I fear, but to the author's irrepressible and insatiable, his extravagant and immoral, interest in personal character and in the "nature" of a mind, of almost any mind the heaving little sea of his subject may cast

up—as to which these remarks have already, in other connexions, recorded his apology: all without prejudice to such
shrines and stations of penance as still shall enliven our way.
The range of wonderment attributed in our tale to the young
woman employed at Cocker's differs little in essence from the
speculative thread on which the pearls of Maisie's experience,
in this same volume—pearls of so strange an iridescence—
are mostly strung. She wonders, putting it simply, very much
as Morgan Moreen wonders; and they all wonder, for that
matter, very much after the fashion of our portentous little
Hyacinth of "The Princess Casamassima," tainted to the core,
as we have seen him, with the trick of mental reaction on the
things about him and fairly staggering under the appropriations, as I have called them, that he owes to the critical spirit.
He collapses, poor Hyacinth, like a thief at night, overcharged with treasures of reflexion and spoils of passion of
which he can give, in his poverty and obscurity, no honest
account.

It is much in this manner, we see on analysis, that Morgan
Moreen breaks down—his burden indeed not so heavy, but
his strength so much less formed. The two little spirits of
maidens, in the group, bear up, oddly enough, beyond those
of their brothers; but the just remark for each of these small
exhibited lives is of course that, in the longer or the shorter
piece, they are actively, are luxuriously, lived. The luxury is
that of the number of their moral vibrations, well-nigh unrestricted—not that of an account at the grocer's: whatever it
be, at any rate, it makes them, as examples and "cases," rare.
My brooding telegraphist may be in fact, on her ground of
ingenuity, scarcely more thinkable than desirable; yet if I have
made her but a libel, up and down the city, on an estimable
class, I feel it still something to have admonished that class,
even though obscurely enough, of neglected interests and un-
divined occasions. My central spirit, in the anecdote, is, for
verisimilitude, I grant, too ardent a focus of divination; but
without this excess the phenomena detailed would have
lacked their principle of cohesion. The action of the drama is
simply the girl's "subjective" adventure—that of her quite definitely winged intelligence; just as the catastrophe, just as the

solution, depends on her winged wit. Why, however, should
I explain further—for a case that, modestly as it would seem
to present itself, has yet already whirled us so far? A course
of incident complicated by the intervention of winged wit—
which is here, as I say, confessed to—would be generally expected, I judge, to commit me to the explanation of everything. But from that undertaking I shrink, and take refuge
instead, for an instant, in a much looser privilege.

If I speak, as just above, of the *action* embodied, each time,
in these so "quiet" recitals, it is under renewed recognition of
the inveterate instinct with which they keep conforming to
the "scenic" law. They demean themselves for all the world—
they quite insist on it, that is, whenever they have a chance—
as little constituted dramas, little exhibitions founded on the
logic of the "scene," the unit of the scene, the general scenic
consistency, and knowing little more than that. To read them
over has been to find them on this ground never at fault. The
process repeats and renews itself, moving in the light it has
once for all adopted. These finer idiosyncrasies of a literary
form seem to be regarded as outside the scope of criticism—
small reference to them do I remember ever to have met; such
surprises of re-perusal, such recoveries of old fundamental intention, such moments of almost ruefully independent discrimination, would doubtless in that case not have waylaid
my steps. Going over the pages here placed together has been
for me, at all events, quite to watch the scenic system at play.
The treatment by "scene," regularly, quite rhythmically recurs; the intervals between, the massing of the elements to a
different effect and by a quite other law, remain, in this fashion, all preparative, just as the scenic occasions in themselves
become, at a given moment, illustrative, each of the agents,
true to its function, taking up the theme from the other very
much as the fiddles, in an orchestra, may take it up from the
cornets and flutes, or the wind-instruments take it up from
the violins. The point, however, is that the scenic passages are
wholly and logically scenic, having for their rule of beauty the
principles of the "conduct," the organic development, of a
scene—the entire succession of values that flower and bear
fruit on ground solidly laid for them. The great advantage for

the total effect is that we feel, with the definite alternation, how the theme *is* being treated. That is we feel it when, in such tangled connexions, we happen to care. I should n't really go on as if this were the case with many readers.

The Aspern Papers, The Turn of the Screw, The Liar, The Two Faces

I NOT ONLY RECOVER with ease, but I delight to recall, the first impulse given to the idea of "The Aspern Papers." It is at the same time true that my present mention of it may perhaps too effectually dispose of any complacent claim to my having "found" the situation. Not that I quite know indeed what situations the seeking fabulist does "find"; he seeks them enough assuredly, but his discoveries are, like those of the navigator, the chemist, the biologist, scarce more than alert recognitions. He *comes upon* the interesting thing as Columbus came upon the isle of San Salvador, because he had moved in the right direction for it—also because he knew, with the encounter, what "making land" then and there represented. Nature had so placed it, to profit—if as profit we may measure the matter!—by his fine unrest, just as history, "literary history" we in this connexion call it, had in an out-of-the-way corner of the great garden of life thrown off a curious flower that I was to feel worth gathering as soon as I saw it. I got wind of my positive fact, I followed the scent. It was in Florence years ago; which is precisely, of the whole matter, what I like most to remember. The air of the old-time Italy invests it, a mixture that on the faintest invitation I rejoice again to inhale—and this in spite of the mere cold renewal, ever, of the infirm side of that felicity, the sense, in the whole element, of things too numerous, too deep, too obscure, too strange, or even simply too beautiful, for any ease of intellectual relation. One must pay one's self largely with words, I think, one must induce almost any "Italian subject" to *make believe* it gives up its secret, in order to keep at all on working—or call them perhaps rather playing—terms with the general impression. We entertain it thus, the impression, by the aid of a merciful convention which resembles the fashion of our intercourse with Iberians or Orientals whose form of courtesy places everything they have at our disposal. We thank them and call upon them, but without acting on their professions. The offer has been too large and our assurance is too small; we peep at most into two or three of the chambers of their hospitality, with the rest of the case stretching beyond our ken and escaping our penetration. The pious fiction suffices; we have entered, we have seen, we are charmed. So, right and left, in Italy—before the great historic complexity at least—penetration fails; we scratch at the extensive surface, we meet the perfunctory smile, we hang about in the golden air. But we exaggerate our gathered values only if we are eminently witless. It is fortunately the exhibition in all the world before which, as admirers, we can most remain superficial without feeling silly.

All of which I note, however, perhaps with too scant relevance to the inexhaustible charm of Roman and Florentine memories. Off the ground, at a distance, our fond indifference to being "silly" grows fonder still; the working convention, as I have called it—the convention of the real revelations and surrenders on one side and the real immersions and appreciations on the other—has not only nothing to keep it down, but every glimpse of contrast, every pang of exile and every nostalgic twinge to keep it up. These latter haunting presences in fact, let me note, almost reduce at first to a mere blurred, sad, scarcely consolable vision this present revisiting, re-appropriating impulse. There are parts of one's past, evidently, that bask consentingly and serenely enough in the light of other days—which is but the intensity of thought; and there are other parts that take it as with agitation and pain, a troubled consciousness that heaves as with the disorder of drinking it deeply in. So it is at any rate, fairly in too thick and rich a retrospect, that I see my old Venice of "The Aspern Papers," that I see the still earlier one of Jeffrey Aspern himself, and that I see even the comparatively recent Florence that was to drop into my ear the solicitation of these things. I would fain "lay it on" thick for the very love of them—that at least I may profess; and, with the ground of this desire frankly admitted, something that somehow makes, in the whole story, for a romantic harmony. I have had occasion in the course of these remarks to define my sense of the romantic, and I am glad to encounter again here an instance of that virtue as I understand it. I shall presently say why this small case so ranges itself, but must first refer more exactly to the thrill of appreciation it was immediately to excite in me. I saw it somehow at the very first blush as romantic—for the use, of course I mean, I should certainly have had to make of it—that Jane Clairmont, the half-sister of Mary Godwin, Shelley's second wife and for a while the intimate friend of Byron and the mother of his daughter Allegra, should have been living on in Florence, where she had long lived, up to our own day, and that in fact, had I happened to hear of her but a little sooner, I might have seen her in the flesh. The question of whether I should have wished to do so was another matter—the question of whether I should n't have preferred to keep her preciously unseen, to run no risk, in other words, by too rude a choice, of depreciating that romance-value which, as I say, it was instantly inevitable to attach (through association above all, with another signal circumstance) to her long survival.

I had luckily not had to deal with the difficult option; difficult in such a case by reason of that odd law which somehow always makes the minimum of valid suggestion serve the man of imagination better than the maximum. The historian, essentially, wants more documents than he can really use; the dramatist only wants more liberties than he can really take. Nothing, fortunately, however, had, as the case stood, depended on my delicacy; I might have "looked up" Miss Clairmont in previous years had I been earlier informed—the silence about her seemed full of the "irony of fate"; but I felt myself more concerned with the mere strong fact of her having testified for the reality and the closeness of our relation to the past than with any question of the particular sort of person I might have flattered myself I "found." I had certainly at the very least been saved the undue simplicity of pretending to read meanings into things absolutely sealed and beyond test or proof—to tap a fount of waters that could n't possibly not have run dry. The thrill of learning that she had "overlapped," and by so much, and the wonder of my having doubtless at several earlier seasons passed again and again, all unknowing, the door of her house, where she sat above, within call and in her habit as she lived, these things gave me all I wanted; I seem to remember in fact that my more or less immediately recognising that I positively ought n't—"for anything to come of it"—to have wanted more. I saw, quickly, how something might come of it *thus*; whereas a fine instinct told me that the effect of a nearer view of the case (the case of the overlapping) would probably have had to be quite differently calculable. It was really with another item of knowledge, however, that I measured the mistake I should have made in waking up sooner to the question of opportunity. That item consisted of the action taken on the premises by a person who *had* waked up in time, and the legend of whose consequent adventure, as a few spoken words put it before me, at once kindled a flame. This gentleman, an American of long ago, an ardent Shelleyite, a singularly marked figure and himself in the highest degree a subject for a free sketch—I had known him a little, but there is not a reflected glint of him in "The Aspern Papers"—was named to me as having made interest with Miss Clairmont to be accepted as a lodger on the calculation that she would have Shelley documents for which, in the possibly not remote event of her death, he would thus enjoy priority of chance to treat with her representatives. He had at any rate, according to the legend, become, on earnest Shelley grounds, her yearning, though also her highly diplomatic, *pensionnaire*—but without gathering, as was to befall, the fruit of his design.

Legend here dropped to another key; it remained in a manner interesting, but became to my ear a trifle coarse, or at least rather vague and obscure. It mentioned a younger female relative of the ancient woman as a person who, for a queer climax, had had to be dealt with; it flickered so for a moment and then, as a light, to my great relief, quite went out. It had flickered indeed but at the best—yet had flickered enough to give me my "facts," bare facts of intimation; which, scant handful though they were, were more distinct and more numerous than I mostly *like* facts: like them, that is, as we say of an etcher's progressive subject, in an early "state." Nine tenths of the artist's interest in them is that of what he shall add to them and how he shall turn them. Mine, however, in the connexion I speak of, had fortunately got away from me, and quite of their own movement, in time not to crush me. So it was, at all events, that my imagination preserved power to react under the mere essential charm—that, I mean, of a final scene of the rich dim Shelley drama played out in the very theatre of our own "modernity." This was the beauty that appealed to me; there had been, so to speak, a forward continuity, from the actual man, the divine poet, on; and the curious, the ingenious, the admirable thing would be to throw it backward again, to compress—squeezing it hard!—the connexion that had drawn itself out, and convert so the stretched relation into a value of nearness on our own part. In short I saw my chance as admirable, and one reason, when the direction is right, may serve as well as fifty; but if I "took over," as I say, everything that was of the essence, I stayed my hand for the rest. The Italian side of the legend closely clung; if only because the so possible terms of my Juliana's life in the Italy of other days could make conceivable for her the fortunate privacy, the long uninvaded and uninterviewed state on which I represent her situation as founded. Yes, a surviving unexploited unparagraphed Juliana was up to a quarter of a century since still supposeable—as much so as any such buried treasure, any such grave unprofaned, would defy probability now. And then the case had the air of the past just in the degree in which that air, I confess, most appeals to me—when the region over which it hangs is far enough away without being too far.

I delight in a palpable imaginable *visitable* past—in the nearer distances and the clearer mysteries, the marks and signs of a world we may reach over to as by making a long arm we grasp an object at the other end of our own table. The table is the one, the common expanse, and where we lean, so stretching, we find it firm and continuous. That, to my imagination, is the past fragrant of all, or of almost all, the poetry of the thing outlived and lost and gone, and yet in which the precious element of closeness, telling so of connexions but tasting so of differences, remains appreciable. With more moves back the element of the appreciable shrinks—just as the charm of looking over a garden-wall into another garden breaks down when successions of walls appear. The other gardens, those still beyond, may be there, but even by use of our longest ladder we are baffled and bewildered—the view is mainly a view of barriers. The one partition makes the place we have wondered about *other*, both richly and recogniseably so; but who shall pretend to impute an effect of composition to the twenty? We are divided of course between liking to feel the past strange and liking to feel it familiar; the difficulty is, for intensity, to catch it at the moment when the scales of the balance hang with the right evenness. I say for intensity, for we may profit by them in other aspects enough if we are content to measure or to feel loosely. It would take me too far, however, to tell why the particular afternoon light that I thus call intense rests clearer to my sense on the Byronic age, as I conveniently name it, than on periods more protected by the "dignity" of history. With the times beyond, intrinsically more "strange," the tender grace, for the backward vision, has faded, the afternoon darkened; for any time nearer to us the special effect has n't begun. So there, to put the matter crudely, is the appeal I fondly recognise, an appeal residing doubtless more in the "special effect," in some deep associational force, than in a virtue more intrinsic. I am afraid I must add, since I allow myself so much to fantasticate, that the impulse had more than once taken me to project the Byronic age and the afternoon light across the great sea, to see in short whether association would carry so far and what the young century might pass for on that side of the modern world where it was not only itself so irremediably youngest, but was bound up with youth in everything else. There was a refinement of curiosity in this imputation of a golden strangeness to American social facts—though I cannot pretend, I fear, that there was any greater wisdom.

Since what it had come to then was, harmlessly enough, cultivating a sense of the past under that close protection, it was natural, it was fond and filial, to wonder if a few of the distilled drops might n't be gathered from some vision of, say, "old" New York. Would that human congeries, to aid obligingly in the production of a fable, be conceivable as "taking" the afternoon light with the right happy slant?—or could a recogniseable reflexion of the Byronic age, in other words, be picked up on the banks of the Hudson? (Only just there, beyond the great sea, if anywhere: in no other connexion would the question so much as raise its head. I admit that Jeffrey Aspern is n't even feebly localised, but I *thought* New York as I projected him.) It was "amusing," in any case, always, to try experiments; and the experiment for the right *transposition* of my Juliana would be to fit her out with an immortalising poet as transposed as herself. Delicacy had demanded, I felt, that my appropriation of the Florentine legend should purge it, first of all, of references too obvious; so that, to begin with, I shifted the scene of the adventure. Juliana, as I saw her, was thinkable only in Byronic and more or less immediately post-Byronic Italy; but there were conditions in which she was ideally arrangeable, as happened, especially in respect to the later time and the long undetected survival; there being absolutely no refinement of the mouldy rococo, in human or whatever other form, that you may not disembark at the dislocated water-steps of almost any decayed monument of Venetian greatness in auspicious quest of. It was a question, in fine, of covering one's tracks—though with no great elaboration I am bound to admit; and I felt I could n't cover mine more than in postulating a comparative American Byron to match an American Miss Clairmont—she as absolute as she would. I scarce know whether best to say for this device to-day that it cost me little or that it cost me much; it was "cheap" or expensive according to the degree of verisimilitude artfully obtained. If that degree appears *nil* the "art," such as it was, is wasted, and my remembrance of the contention, on the part of a highly critical friend who at that time and later on often had my ear, that it had been simply foredoomed to be wasted, puts before me the passage in the private history of "The Aspern Papers" that I now find, I confess, most interesting. I comfort myself for the needful brevity of a present glance at it by the sense that the general question involved, under criticism, can't but come up for us again at higher pressure.

My friend's argument bore then—at the time and afterward—on my vicious practice, as he maintained, of postulating for the purpose of my fable celebrities who not only *had n't* existed in the conditions I imputed to them, but who for the most part (and in no case more markedly than in that of Jeffrey Aspern) could n't possibly have done so. The stricture was to apply itself to a whole group of short fictions in which I had, with whatever ingenuity, assigned to several so-called eminent figures positions absolutely unthinkable in our actual encompassing air, an air definitely unfavourable to certain

forms of eminence. It was vicious, my critic contended, to
flourish forth on one's page "great people," public persons,
who should n't more or less square with our quite definite
and calculable array of such notabilities; and by this rule I was
heavily incriminated. The rule demanded that the "public person" portrayed should be at least of the tradition, of the general complexion, of the face-value, exactly, of some past or
present producible counterfoil. Mere private figures, under
one's hand, might correspond with nobody, it being of their
essence to be but narrowly known; the represented state of
being conspicuous, on the other hand, involved before anything else a recognition—and none of my eminent folk were
recogniseable. It was all very well for instance to have put
one's self at such pains for Miriam Rooth in "The Tragic
Muse"; but *there* was misapplied zeal, there a case of pitiful
waste, crying aloud to be denounced. Miriam is offered not
as a young person passing unnoticed by her age—like the
Biddy Dormers and Julia Dallows, say, of the same book, but
as a high rarity, a time-figure of the scope inevitably attended
by other commemorations. Where on earth would be then
Miriam's inscribed "counterfoil," and in what conditions of
the contemporary English theatre, in what conditions of criticism, of appreciation, under what conceivable Anglo-Saxon
star, might we take an artistic value of this order either for
produced or for recognised? We are, as a "public," chalk-
marked by nothing, more unmistakeably, than by the truth
that we know nothing of such values—any more than, as my
friend was to impress on me, we are susceptible of consciousness of such others (these in the sphere of literary eminence)
as my Neil Paraday in "The Death of the Lion," as my Hugh
Vereker in "The Figure in the Carpet," as my Ralph Limbert,
above all, in "The Next Time," as sundry unprecedented and
unmatched heroes and martyrs of the artistic ideal, in short,
elsewhere exemplified in my pages. We shall come to these
objects of animadversion in another hour, when I shall have
no difficulty in producing the defence I found for them—
since, obviously, I had n't cast them into the world *all* naked
and ashamed; and I deal for the moment but with the stigma
in general as Jeffrey Aspern carries it.

The charge being that I foist upon our early American

annals a distinguished presence for which they yield me absolutely no warrant—"Where, within them, gracious heaven, were we to look for so much as an approach to the social elements of habitat and climate of birds of that note and plumage?"—I find his link with reality then just in the tone of the picture wrought round him. What was that tone but exactly, but exquisitely, calculated, the harmless hocus-pocus under cover of which we might suppose him to have existed? This tone is the tone, artistically speaking, of "amusement," the current floating that precious influence home quite as one of those high tides watched by the smugglers of old might, in case of their boat's being boarded, be trusted to wash far up the strand the cask of foreign liquor expertly committed to it. If through our lean prime Western period no dim and charming ghost of an adventurous lyric genius might by a stretch of fancy flit, if the time was really too hard to "take," in the light form proposed, the elegant reflexion, then so much the worse for the time—it was all one could say! The retort to that of course was that such a plea represented no "link" with reality—which was what was under discussion— but only a link, and flimsy enough too, with the deepest depths of the artificial: the restrictive truth exactly contended for, which may embody my critic's last word rather of course than my own. My own, so far as I shall pretend in that especial connexion to report it, was that one's warrant, in such a case, hangs essentially on the question of whether or no the false element imputed would have borne that test of further development which so exposes the wrong and so consecrates the right. My last word was, heaven forgive me, that, occasion favouring, I could have perfectly "worked out" Jeffrey Aspern. The boast remains indeed to be verified when we shall arrive at the other challenged cases.

That particular challenge at least "The Turn of the Screw" does n't incur; and this perfectly independent and irresponsible little fiction rejoices, beyond any rival on a like ground, in a conscious provision of prompt retort to the sharpest question that may be addressed to it. For it has the small strength—if I should n't say rather the unattackable ease—of a perfect homogeneity, of being, to the very last grain of its virtue, all of a kind; the very kind, as happens, least apt to be baited by earnest criticism, the only sort of criticism of which account need be taken. To have handled again this so full-blown flower of high fancy is to be led back by it to easy and happy recognitions. Let the first of these be that of the starting-point itself—the sense, all charming again, of the circle, one winter afternoon, round the hall-fire of a grave old country-house where (for all the world as if to resolve itself promptly and obligingly into convertible, into "literary" stuff) the talk turned, on I forget what homely pretext, to apparitions and night-fears, to the marked and sad drop in the general supply, and still more in the general quality, of such commodities. The good, the really effective and heart-shaking ghost-stories (roughly so to term them) appeared all to have been told, and neither new crop nor new type in any quarter awaited us. The new type indeed, the mere modern "psychical" case, washed clean of all queerness as by exposure to a flowing laboratory tap, and equipped with credentials vouching for this—the new type clearly promised little, for the more it was respectably certified the less it seemed of a nature to rouse the dear old sacred terror. Thus it was, I remember, that amid our lament for a beautiful lost form, our distinguished host expressed the wish that he might but have recovered for us one of the scantest of fragments of this form at its best. He had never forgotten the impression made on him as a young man by the withheld glimpse, as it were, of a dreadful matter that had been reported years before, and with as few particulars, to a lady with whom he had youthfully talked. The story would have been thrilling could she but have found herself in better possession of it, dealing as it did with a couple of small children in an out-of-the-way place, to whom the spirits of certain "bad" servants, dead in the employ of the house, were believed to have appeared with the design of "getting hold" of them. This was all, but there had been more, which my friend's old converser had lost the thread of: she could only assure him of the wonder of the allegations as she had anciently heard them made. He himself could give us but this shadow of a shadow—my own appreciation of which, I need scarcely say, was exactly wrapped up in that thinness. On the surface there was n't much, but another grain, none the less, would have spoiled the precious pinch addressed to its end as neatly as some modicum extracted from an old silver snuff-box and held between finger and thumb. I was to remember the haunted children and the prowling servile spirits as a "value," of the disquieting sort, in all conscience sufficient; so that when, after an interval, I was asked for something seasonable by the promoters of a periodical dealing in the time-honoured Christmas-tide toy, I bethought myself at once of the vividest little note for sinister romance that I had ever jotted down.

Such was the private source of "The Turn of the Screw"; and I wondered, I confess, why so fine a germ, gleaming there in the wayside dust of life, had never been deftly picked up. The thing had for me the immense merit of allowing the imagination absolute freedom of hand, of inviting it to act on a perfectly clear field, with no "outside" control involved, no pattern of the usual or the true or the terrible "pleasant" (save always of course the high pleasantry of one's very form) to consort with. This makes in fact the charm of my second reference, that I find here a perfect example of an exercise of the imagination unassisted, unassociated—playing the game, making the score, in the phrase of our sporting day, off its own bat. To what degree the game was worth playing I need n't attempt to say: the exercise I have noted strikes me now, I confess, as the interesting thing, the imaginative faculty acting with the *whole* of the case on its hands. The exhibition involved is in other words a fairy-tale pure and simple—save indeed as to its springing not from an artless and measureless, but from a conscious and cultivated credulity. Yet the fairy-tale belongs mainly to either of two classes, the short and sharp and single, charged more or less with the compactness of anecdote (as to which let the familiars of our childhood, Cinderella and Blue-Beard and Hop o' my Thumb and Little Red Riding Hood and many of the gems of the Brothers Grimm directly testify), or else the long and loose, the copious, the various, the endless, where, dramatically speaking, roundness is quite sacrificed—sacrificed to fulness, sacrificed to exuberance, if one will: witness at hazard almost any one of the Arabian Nights. The charm of all these things for the distracted modern mind is in the clear field of experience, as I call it, over which we are thus led to roam; an annexed but

independent world in which nothing is right save as we
rightly imagine it. We have to do *that*, and we do it happily
for the short spurt and in the smaller piece, achieving so perhaps beauty and lucidity; we flounder, we lose breath, on the
other hand—that is we fail, not of continuity, but of an
agreeable unity, of the "roundness" in which beauty and lucidity largely reside—when we go in, as they say, for great
lengths and breadths. And this, oddly enough, not because
"keeping it up" is n't abundantly within the compass of the
imagination appealed to in certain conditions, but because the
finer interest depends just on *how* it is kept up.

Nothing is so easy as improvisation, the running on and on
of invention; it is sadly compromised, however, from the moment its stream breaks bounds and gets into flood. Then the
waters may spread indeed, gathering houses and herds and
crops and cities into their arms and wrenching off, for our
amusement, the whole face of the land—only violating by the
same stroke our sense of the course and the channel, which is
our sense of the uses of a stream and the virtue of a story.
Improvisation, as in the Arabian Nights, may keep on terms
with encountered objects by sweeping them in and floating
them on its breast; but the great effect it so loses—that of
keeping on terms with itself. This is ever, I intimate, the hard
thing for the fairy-tale; but by just so much as it struck me as
hard did it in "The Turn of the Screw" affect me as irresistibly prescribed. To improvise with extreme freedom and yet at
the same time without the possibility of ravage, without the
hint of a flood; to keep the stream, in a word, on something
like ideal terms with itself: that was here my definite business.
The thing was to aim at absolute singleness, clearness and
roundness, and yet to depend on an imagination working
freely, working (call it) with extravagance; by which law it
would n't be thinkable except as free and would n't be amusing except as controlled. The merit of the tale, as it stands, is
accordingly, I judge, that it has struggled successfully with its
dangers. It is an excursion into chaos while remaining, like
Blue-Beard and Cinderella, but an anecdote—though an anecdote amplified and highly emphasised and returning upon
itself; as, for that matter, Cinderella and Blue-Beard return. I
need scarcely add after this that it is a piece of ingenuity pure

and simple, of cold artistic calculation, an *amusette* to catch those not easily caught (the "fun" of the capture of the merely witless being ever but small), the jaded, the disillusioned, the fastidious. Otherwise expressed, the study is of a conceived "tone," the tone of suspected and felt trouble, of an inordinate and incalculable sort—the tone of tragic, yet of exquisite, mystification. To knead the subject of my young friend's, the supposititious narrator's, mystification thick, and yet strain the expression of it so clear and fine that beauty would result: no side of the matter so revives for me as that endeavour. Indeed if the artistic value of such an experiment be measured by the intellectual echoes it may again, long after, set in motion, the case would make in favour of this little firm fantasy—which I seem to see draw behind it to-day a train of associations. I ought doubtless to blush for thus confessing them so numerous that I can but pick among them for reference. I recall for instance a reproach made me by a reader capable evidently, for the time, of some attention, but not quite capable of enough, who complained that I had n't sufficiently "characterised" my young woman engaged in her labyrinth; had n't endowed her with signs and marks, features and humours, had n't in a word invited her to deal with her own mystery as well as with that of Peter Quint, Miss Jessel and the hapless children. I remember well, whatever the absurdity of its now coming back to me, my reply to that criticism—under which one's artistic, one's ironic heart shook for the instant almost to breaking. "You indulge in that stricture at your ease, and I don't mind confiding to you that—strange as it may appear!—one has to choose ever so delicately among one's difficulties, attaching one's self to the greatest, bearing hard on those and intelligently neglecting the others. If one attempts to tackle them all one is certain to deal completely with none; whereas the effectual dealing with a few casts a blest golden haze under cover of which, like wanton mocking goddesses in clouds, the others find prudent to retire. It was 'déjà très-joli,' in 'The Turn of the Screw,' please believe, the general proposition of our young woman's keeping crystalline her record of so many intense anomalies and obscurities—by which I don't of course mean her explanation of them, a different matter; and I saw no way, I feebly grant (fighting, at the best too, periodically, for every grudged inch of my space) to exhibit her in relations other than those; one of which, precisely, would have been her relation to her own nature. We have surely as much of her own nature as we can swallow in watching it reflect her anxieties and inductions. It constitutes no little of a character indeed, in such conditions, for a young person, as she says, 'privately bred,' that she is able to make her particular credible statement of such strange matters. She has 'authority,' which is a good deal to have given her, and I could n't have arrived at so much had I clumsily tried for more."

For which truth I claim part of the charm latent on occasion in the extracted reasons of beautiful things—putting for the beautiful always, in a work of art, the close, the curious, the deep. Let me place above all, however, under the protection of that presence the side by which this fiction appeals most to consideration: its choice of its way of meeting its gravest difficulty. There were difficulties not so grave: I had for instance simply to renounce all attempt to keep the kind and degree of impression I wished to produce on terms with the to-day so copious psychical record of cases of apparitions. Different signs and circumstances, in the reports, mark these cases; different things are done—though on the whole very little appears to be—by the persons appearing; the point is, however, that some things are never done at all: this negative quantity is large—certain reserves and proprieties and immobilities consistently impose themselves. Recorded and attested "ghosts" are in other words as little expressive, as little dramatic, above all as little continuous and conscious and responsive, as is consistent with their taking the trouble—and an immense trouble they find it, we gather—to appear at all. Wonderful and interesting therefore at a given moment, they are inconceivable figures in an *action*—and "The Turn of the Screw" was an action, desperately, or it was nothing. I had to decide in fine between having my apparitions correct and having my story "good"—that is producing my impression of the dreadful, my designed horror. Good ghosts, speaking by book, make poor subjects, and it was clear that from the first my hovering prowling blighting presences, my pair of abnormal agents, would have to depart altogether from the rules. They would be agents in fact; there would be laid on them the dire duty of causing the situation to reek with the air of Evil. Their desire and their ability to do so, visibly measuring meanwhile their effect, together with their observed and described success—this was exactly my central idea; so that, briefly, I cast my lot with pure romance, the appearances conforming to the true type being so little romantic.

This is to say, I recognise again, that Peter Quint and Miss Jessel are not "ghosts" at all, as we now know the ghost, but goblins, elves, imps, demons as loosely constructed as those of the old trials for witchcraft; if not, more pleasingly, fairies of the legendary order, wooing their victims forth to see them dance under the moon. Not indeed that I suggest their reducibility to any form of the pleasing pure and simple; they please at the best but through having helped me to express my subject all directly and intensely. Here it was—in the use made of them—that I felt a high degree of art really required; and here it is that, on reading the tale over, I find my precautions justified. The essence of the matter was the villainy of motive in the evoked predatory creatures; so that the result would be ignoble—by which I mean would be trivial—were this element of evil but feebly or inanely suggested. Thus arose on behalf of my idea the lively interest of a possible suggestion and process of *adumbration*; the question of how best to convey that sense of the depths of the sinister without which my fable would so woefully limp. Portentous evil— how was I to save that, as an intention on the part of my demon-spirits, from the drop, the comparative vulgarity, inevitably attending, throughout the whole range of possible brief illustration, the offered example, the imputed vice, the cited act, the limited deplorable presentable instance? To bring the bad dead back to life for a second round of badness is to warrant them as indeed prodigious, and to become hence as shy of specifications as of a waiting anti-climax. One had seen, in fiction, some grand form of wrong-doing, or better still of wrong-being, imputed, seen it promised and announced as by the hot breath of the Pit—and then, all lamentably, shrink to the compass of some particular brutality, some particular immorality, some particular infamy portrayed: with the result, alas, of the demonstration's falling sadly short. If *my* bad things, for "The Turn of the Screw," I felt, should succumb to this danger, if they should n't seem sufficiently bad, there would be nothing for me but to hang my artistic head lower than I had ever known occasion to do.

The view of that discomfort and the fear of that dishonour, it accordingly must have been, that struck the proper light for my right, though by no means easy, short cut. What, in the last analysis, had I to give the sense of? Of their being, the haunting pair, capable, as the phrase is, of everything—that is of exerting, in respect to the children, the very worst action small victims so conditioned might be conceived as subject to. What would *be* then, on reflexion, this utmost conceivability?—a question to which the answer all admirably came. There is for such a case no eligible *absolute* of the wrong; it remains relative to fifty other elements, a matter of appreciation, speculation, imagination—these things moreover quite exactly in the light of the spectator's, the critic's, the reader's experience. Only make the reader's general vision of evil intense enough, I said to myself—and that already is a charming job—and his own experience, his own imagination, his own sympathy (with the children) and horror (of their false friends) will supply him quite sufficiently with all the particulars. Make him *think* the evil, make him think it for himself, and you are released from weak specifications. This ingenuity I took pains—as indeed great pains were required—to apply; and with a success apparently beyond my liveliest hope. Droll enough at the same time, I must add, some of the evidence—even when most convincing—of this success. How can I feel my calculation to have failed, my wrought suggestion not to have worked, that is, on my being assailed, as has befallen me, with the charge of a monstrous emphasis, the charge of all indecently expatiating? There is not only from beginning to end of the matter not an inch of expatiation, but my values are positively all blanks save so far as an excited horror, a promoted pity, a created expertness—on which punctual effects of strong causes no writer can ever fail to plume himself—proceed to read into them more or less fantastic figures. Of high interest to the author meanwhile—and by the same stroke a theme for the moralist—the artless resentful reaction of the entertained person who has abounded in the sense of the situation. He visits his abundance, morally, on the artist—who has but clung to an ideal of faultlessness. Such indeed, for this latter, are some of the observations by which the prolonged strain of that clinging may be enlivened!

I arrive with "The Liar" (1888) and "The Two Faces" (1900) at the first members of the considerable group of shorter, of shortest tales here republished; though I should perhaps place quite in the forefront "The Chaperon" and "The Pupil," at which we have already glanced. I am conscious of much to say of these numerous small productions as a family—a family indeed quite organised as such, with its proper representatives, its "heads," its subdivisions and its branches, its poor relations perhaps not least: its unmistakeable train of poor relations in fact, the very poorer, the poorest of whom I am, in family parlance, for this formal appearance in society, "cutting" without a scruple. These repudiated members, some of them, for that matter, well-nourished and substantial presences enough, with their compromising rustiness plausibly, almost touchingly dissimulated, I fondly figure as standing wistful but excluded, after the fashion of the outer fringe of the connected whom there are not carriages enough to convey from the church—whether (for we have our choice of similes) to the wedding-feast or to the interment! Great for me from far back had been the interest of the whole "question of the short story," roundabout which our age has, for lamentable reasons, heard so vain a babble; but I foresee occasions yet to come when it will abundantly waylay me. Then it will insist on presenting itself but in too many lights. Little else perhaps meanwhile is more relevant as to "The Liar" than the small fact of its having, when its hour came, quite especially conformed to that custom of shooting straight from the planted seed, of responding at once to the touched spring, of which my fond appeal here to "origins" and evolutions so depicts the sway. When it shall come to fitting, historically, anything like *all* my small children of fancy with their pair of progenitors, and all my reproductive unions with their inevitable fruit, I shall seem to offer my backward consciousness in the image of a shell charged and recharged by the Fates with some patent and infallible explosive. Never would

there seem to have been a pretence to such economy of am-
munition!

However this may be, I come back, for "The Liar," as for
so many of its fellows, to holding my personal experience,
poor thing though it may have been, immediately accountable. For by what else in the world but by fatal design had I
been placed at dinner one autumn evening of old London
days face to face with a gentleman, met for the first time,
though favourably known to me by name and fame, in whom
I recognised the most unbridled colloquial romancer the "joy
of life" had ever found occasion to envy? Under what other
conceivable coercion had I been invited to reckon, through
the evening, with the type, with the character, with the countenance, of this magnificent master's wife, who, veracious, serene and charming, yet not once meeting straight the eyes of
one of us, did her duty by each, and by her husband most of
all, without so much as, in the vulgar phrase, turning a hair?
It was long ago, but I have never, to this hour, forgotten the
evening itself—embalmed for me now in an old-time sweetness beyond any aspect of my reproduction. I made but a fifth
person, the other couple our host and hostess; between
whom and one of the company, while we listened to the
woven wonders of a summer holiday, the exploits of a sala-
mander, among Mediterranean isles, were exchanged, dimly
and discreetly, ever so guardedly, but all expressively, imperceptible lingering looks. It was exquisite, it *could* but become,
inevitably, some "short story" or other, which it clearly pre-
fitted as the hand the glove. I must reserve "The Two Faces"
till I come to speak of the thrilling question of the poor painter's tormented acceptance, in advance, of the scanted canvas;
of the writer's rueful hopeful assent to the conditions known
to him as "too little room to turn round." Of the liveliest
interest then—or so at least I could luckily always project the
case—to see how he may nevertheless, in the event, effectively manœuvre. The value of "The Two Faces"—by reason
of which I have not hesitated to gather it in—is thus peculiarly an economic one. It may conceal rather than exhale its
intense little principle of calculation; but the neat evolution,
as I call it, the example of the turn of the *whole* coach and
pair in the contracted court, without the "spill" of a single

passenger or the derangement of a single parcel, is only in three or four cases (where the coach is fuller still) more appreciable.

The Reverberator, Madame de Mauves, A Passionate Pilgrim, The Madonna of the Future, Louisa Pallant

I HAVE GATHERED into this volume some early brevities, the third in order of which dates from further back than any tale comprised in the Edition. The first in order appeared considerably later, but I have given it precedence in this group by reason of its greatest length. It is the most recent in the list, but, as having originally (in the good old days, though they are as yet none so remote, of "pleasant" publication) enjoyed the honour of two pretty little volumes "all to itself," it falls into the category of Shorter Novels—under an indulgence not extended to several of its compeers. "The Reverberator," which figured at birth (1888) in half a dozen numbers of "Macmillan's Magazine" may be described, I suppose, beyond any fiction here reproduced, as a *jeu d'esprit*: I can think at least of none other on the brow of which I may presume to place that laurel. And yet as I cast about me for the nameable grounds of the hospitality I thus give it I find myself think of it in other rich lights as well; quite in the light of an exemplary anecdote, and at the same time quite in that of a little rounded drama. This is to press hard, it might seem, on so slight a composition; but I brave the extravagance under the interest of recognising again how the weight of expatiation is ever met in such cases—that of the slender production equally with that of the stout—by a surface really much larger than the mere offered face of the work. The face of the work may be small in itself, and yet the surface, the whole thing, the associational margin and connexion, may spread, beneath the fond remembering eye, like nothing more noble than an insidious grease-spot. It is of the essence of the anecdote to get itself told as it can—which truth represented clearly the best chance of life for the matter involved in "The Reverberator"; but also it is of the essence of the drama to conform to logic, and the pages I here treat of may appear at moments not quite predominantly sure either of their luck or of their law. This, however, I think, but to a cursory glance, for I perhaps do them a wrong in emphasising their anecdotic cast. Might I not, certainly, have invoked for them in some degree the anecdotic grace I would n't have undertaken them at all; but I now see how they were still to have been provided for if this had failed them.

The anecdote consists, ever, of something that has oddly happened to some one, and the first of its duties is to point directly to the person whom it so distinguishes. He may be you or I or any one else, but a condition of our interest— perhaps the principal one—is that the anecdote shall know him, and shall accordingly speak of him, as its subject. Who is it then that by this rule the specimen before us adopts and sticks to? Something happens, and to a certain person, or, better, to a certain group of persons, in "The Reverberator," but of whom, when it comes to the point, is the fable narrated? The anecdote has always a question to answer—of whom necessarily is it told? Is it told here of the Proberts or of the Dossons? To whom in the instance before us does the principal thing, the thing worth the telling, happen? To the fatal Mr. Flack, to Francie Dosson and her father and sister, lumping them, on the ground of their "racial consciousness," all together?—or to the cluster of scandalised Parisians in general, if not to the girl's distracted young lover in particular? It is easy, alas, to defy a clear statement on this head to be made ("No, I can't say whom or what or *which* I 'm about: I seem so sometimes to be about one set and sometimes about another!" the little story is free to plead) whereby anecdotic grace does break down. Fortunately there remains another string, a second, to my bow. I should have been nowhere, in the event of a challenge, had I not concomitantly felt my subject, for all its slightness, as a small straight *action*, and so placed it in that blest drama-light which, really making for intelligibility as nothing else does, orders and regulates, even when but faintly turned on; squares things and keeps them in happy relation to each other. What "happens," by that felicity, happens thus to every one concerned, exactly as in much more prodigious recitals: it 's a case—just as we have seen it before, in more portentous connexions and with the support of mightier comparisons—of the planned rotation of aspects and of that "scenic" determination of them about which I fear I may already have been a bore.

After which perhaps too vertiginous explanatory flight I feel that I drop indeed to the very concrete and comparatively trivial origin of my story—short, that is, of some competent critical attribution of triviality all round. I am afraid, at any rate, that with this reminiscence I but watch my grease-spot (for I cling to the homely metaphor) engagingly extend its bounds. Who shall say thus—and I have put the vain question but too often before!—where the associational nimbus of the all but lost, of the miraculously recovered, chapter of experience shall absolutely fade and stop? That would be possible only were experience a chessboard of sharp black-and-white squares. Taking one of these for a convenient plot, I have but to see my particle of suggestion lurk in its breast, and then but to repeat in this connexion the act of picking it up, for the whole of the *rest* of the connexion straightway to loom into life, its parts all clinging together and pleading with a collective friendly voice that I can't pretend to resist: "Oh but we too, you know; what were *we* but of the experience?" Which comes to scarce more than saying indeed, no doubt, that nothing more complicates and overloads the act of retrospect than to let one's imagination itself work backward as part of the business. Some art of preventing this by keeping that interference out would be here of a useful application; and would include the question of providing conveniently for the officious faculty in the absence of its natural caretakers, the judgement, the memory, the conscience, occupied, as it were, elsewhere. These truants, the other faculties of the mind without exception, I surmise, would then be free to remount the stream of time (as an earnest and enquiring band) with the flower of the flock, the hope of the family, left at home or "boarded out," say, for the time of the excursion. I have been unable, I confess, to make such an arrangement; the consequence of which failure is that everything I "find," as I look back, lives for me again in the light of *all* the parts, such as they are, of my intelligence. Or to express the phenomenon otherwise, and perhaps with still more complacency for it, the effort to reconstitute the medium and the season that favoured the first stir of life, the first perceived gleam of the vital spark, in the trifle before us, fairly makes everything in the picture revive, fairly even extends the influence to matters remote and strange. The musing artist's imagination—thus *not* excluded and confined—supplies the link that is missing and makes the whole occasion (the occasion of the glorious birth to him of still another infant motive) comprehensively and richly *one*. And this if that addition to his flock—his effusive parental welcome to which seems immediately to cause so splendid and furnished and fitted a world to arch over it—happens to be even of so modest a promise as the tiny principle of "The Reverberator."

It was in a grand old city of the south of Europe (though neither in Rome nor yet in Florence) long years ago, and during a winter spent there in the seeing of many people on the pleasantest terms in the world, as they now seem to me to have been, as well as in the hearing of infinite talk, talk mainly, inexhaustibly, about persons and the "personal equation" and the personal mystery. This somehow *had* to be in an odd, easy, friendly, a miscellaneous, many-coloured little cosmopolis, where the casual exotic society was a thing of heterogeneous vivid patches, but with a fine old native basis, the basis that held stoutly enough together while the patches dangled and fluttered, stitched on as with thread of silver, pinned on as with pearls, lasting their time above all and brightening the scene. To allude to the scene, alas! seems half an undertaking to reproduce it, any humoursome indulgence in which would lead us much too far. Nor am I strictly—as if I cultivated an ideal of strictness!—concerned with any fact but that of the appearance among us, that winter, of a charming free young person, superlatively introduced and infinitely admired, who, taken to twenty social bosoms, figured "success" in a form, that of the acclaimed and confident pretty girl of our prosaic and temperate climes, for which the old-world salon, with its windows of iridescent view and its different conception of the range of charm, had never much provided. The old-world salon, in our community, still, when all was said, more or less imposed the type and prescribed the tone; yet to the charming stranger even these penetralia had not been closed, and, over them, to be brief, she had shed her influence, just as among them, not less, she had gathered her harvest. She had come, in fine, she had seen and had conquered; after which she had withdrawn with her spoil. Her spoil, to put it plainly, had been a treasure of impressions; her harvest, as I have said, a wealth of revelations. I made an absence of several weeks, I went to Florence and to Rome, but I came back in the spring—and all to encounter the live-liest chatter of surprise that had perhaps ever spent itself under the elegant massive ceilings for which the old-world salons were famous. The ingenious stranger—it was awfully coming to light—had *written* about them, about these still consciously critical retreats, many of them temples harbouring the very altar of the exclusive; she had made free with them, pen in hand, with the best conscience in the world, no doubt, but to a high effect of confidence betrayed, and to the amaze-ment and consternation of every one involved, though most of all, naturally, to the dismay of her primary backers.

The young lady, frankly, a graceful amateur journalist, had made use of her gathered material; she had addressed to a newspaper in her native city (which no power on earth would induce me to designate, so that as to this and to the larger issue, not less, of the glamour of its big State-name, I defy all guesses) a letter as long, as confidential, as "chatty," as full of headlong history and limping legend, of aberration and con-fusion, as she might have indited to the most trusted of friends. The friend trusted had been, as happened, simply the biggest "reading public" in the world, and the performance, typographically bristling, had winged its way back to its dis-honoured nest like some monstrous black bird or beetle, an embodiment of popping eyes, a whirl of brandished feathers and claws. Strange, it struck me, to tell the truth, the fact itself of "anybody's knowing," and still more of anybody's caring—the fact itself, that is, of such prompt repercussion and recognition: one would so little, in advance, have sup-posed the reverberation of the bomb, its heeded reverbera-tion, conceivable. No such consequence, clearly, had been allowed for by its innocent maker, for whose imagination, one felt sure, the explosion had not been designed to be world-shaking. The recording, slobbering sheet, as an object thinkable or visible in a medium so non-conducting, made of actual recognition, made even of the barest allusion, the fals-est of false notes. The scandal reigned, however, and the com-motion lasted, a nine days' wonder; the ingenuous stranger's name became anathema, and all to the high profit of an incorrigible collector of "cases." Him in his depth of perversity, I profess, the flurry of resentment could only, after a little, affect as scarce more charged with wisdom than the poor young lady's miscalculated overflow itself; so completely beside the question of the finer *comparative* interest remained that of the force of the libel and that of the degree of the injury. The finer interest was in the facts that made the incident a case, and the true note of that, I promptly made sure, was just in the extraordinary amount of native innocence that positively *had* to be read into the perpetrated act. The couple of columns in the vulgar newspaper constituted no document whatever on the manners and morals of the company of persons "betrayed," but on the other hand, in its indirect way, flooded "American society" with light, became on *that* side in the highest degree documentary. So it was, I soon saw, that though the perpetrated act was in itself and immediately no "situation," it nevertheless pointed to one, and was for that value to be stored up.

It remained for a long time thus a mere sketched finger-post: the perpetrated act had, unmistakeably, *meant* something—one could n't make out at first exactly what; till at last, after several years of oblivion, its connexions, its illustrative worth, came quite naturally into view. It fell in short into the wider perspective, the very largest fund of impressions and appearances, perhaps, that the particular observer's and designer's mind was to have felt itself for so long queerly weighted with. I have already had occasion to say that the "international" light lay thick, from period to period, on the general scene of my observation—a truth the reasons and bearings of which will require in due course to be intelligibly stated; everything that possibly could, at any rate, managed at that time (as it had done before and was undiscourageably to continue to do) to *be* international for me: which was an immense resource and a happy circumstance from many points of view. Therefore I may say at once that if no particular element or feature of the view had struck me from far back as receiving so much of the illumination as the comparative *state of innocence* of the spirit of my countryfolk, by that same token everything had a price, was of immediate application and found itself closely interwoven, that could tend to emphasise or vivify the innocence. I had indeed early to recognise that I was in a manner shut up to the contemplation of it—really to the point, it has often seemed to me these pages must testify, of appearing to wander, as under some uncanny spell, amid the level sands and across the pathless desert of a single and of a not especially rich or fruitful aspect. Here, for that matter, comes in one of the oddest and most interesting of facts—as I measure it; which again will take much stating, but to which I may provisionally give *this* importance, that, sketchily speaking, if I had n't had, on behalf of the American character, the negative aspects to deal with, I should practically, and given the limits of my range, have had no aspects at all. I shall on a near pretext, as I say, develop the sense of this; but let it now stand for the obvious truth that the negative sides were always *at* me, for illustration, for interpretation, and that though I looked yearningly, from time to time, over their collective head, though, after an experimental baffled sniff, I was apt to find myself languish for sharper air than any they exhaled, they constantly gave me enough, and more than enough, to "tackle," so that I might even well ask myself what more miscellaneous justice I should have been able to render.

Given, after this fashion, my condition of knowledge, the most general appearance of the American (of those days) in Europe, that of being almost incredibly *unaware of life*—as the European order expressed life—had to represent for me the *whole* exhibitional range; the particular initiation on my own part that would have helped me to other apprehensions being absolutely bolted and barred to me. What this alternative would have stood for we shall immediately see; but meanwhile—and nothing could have been at once more inevitable, more logical and more ridiculous—I was reduced to studying my New Yorkers and my Bostonians, since there were enough of these alone and to spare, under the queer rubric of their more or less stranded helplessness. If asked why I describe in such terms the appearances that most appealed to me, I can only wonder how the bewildered state of the persons principally figuring in the Americano-European prospect could have been otherwise expressed. They come

back to me, in the lurid light of contrast, as irresistibly destitute of those elements of preparedness that my pages show
even the most limited European adventure to call into play.
This at least was, by my retrospect, the inveterate case for the
men—it differed only for certain of the women, the younger,
the youngest, those of whom least might at the best have
been expected, and in the interest of whose "success" their
share of the characteristic blankness underwent what one
might call a sea-change. Conscious of so few things in the
world, these unprecedented creatures—since that is what it
came to for them—were least of all conscious of deficiencies
and dangers; so that, the grace of youth and innocence and
freshness aiding, their negatives were converted and became
in certain relations lively positives and values. I might give a
considerable list of those of my fictions, longer and shorter,
in which this curious conversion is noted. Suffice it, at all
events, in respect to the show at large, that, even as testifying
but to a suffered and suffering state, and working beauty and
comedy and pathos but into that compass, my procession of
figures—which kept passing, and indeed kept pausing, by no
act of my own—left me with all I could manage on my
hands.

This will have seemed doubtless a roundabout approach to
my saying that I seized the right connexion for our roaring
young lioness of the old-world salons from the moment I
qualified her as, in spite of the stimulating commerce enjoyed
with them, signally "unaware of life." What had she lacked
for interest? what had her case lacked for application? what in
the world but just that perceived reference to something
larger, something more widely significant? What was so large,
what so widely significant in its general sphere, as that, "otherwise" so well endowed and appointed, as that, altogether so
well constituted and introduced, she *could* have kept up to
the end (the end of our concern with her) the state of unawareness? Immense at any rate the service she so rendered
the brooding critic capable of taking a hint from her, for she
became on the spot an inimitable link with the question of
what it might distinguishably be in their own flourishing
Order that could *keep* them, the passionless pilgrims, so unaware? This was the point—one had caught them in the act

of it; of a disposition, which had perhaps even most a comic side, to treat "Europe," collectively, as a vast painted and gilded holiday toy, serving its purpose on the spot and for the time, but to be relinquished, sacrificed, broken and cast away, at the dawn of any other convenience. It seemed to figure thus not only as a gorgeous dressed doll, the most expensive plaything, no doubt, in the world, but as a *living* doll, precisely, who would speak and act and perform, all for a "charge"—which was the reason both of the amusement and of the cost. Only there was no more *responsibility* to a living doll than to a dead—so that, in fine, what seemed most absent from the frolic intercourse was the note of anything like reciprocity: unless indeed the so prompt and frequent newspaperisation of any quaint confidence extracted by pressure on the poor doll's stomach, of any droll sight of powers set in motion by twitch of whatever string, might serve for a rendering of that ideal. It had reached one's ear again and again from beyond the sea, this inveteracy, as one might almost call it, of the artless ventilation, and mainly in the public prints, of European matter originally gathered in under the supposed law of privilege enjoyed on the one hand and security enjoyed on the other. A hundred good instances confirmed this tradition that nothing in the new world was held accountable to anything in the old, that the hemispheres would have been as dissociated as different planets had n't one of them, by a happy miracle, come in for the comparatively antique right of free fishing in the other.

It was the so oft-attested American sense of the matter that was meanwhile the oddity—the sense on the part of remote adventurous islanders that no custom of give-and-take between their bustling archipelago and the far, the massed continent was thinkable. Strangely enough, none the less, the continent was anecdotically interesting to the islands— though as soon as these were reached all difference between the fruit of the private and the fruit of the public garden naturally dropped. More than all was it striking that the "naturalness" was all of American making—in spite, as had ever seemed to me, of the American tradition to the contrary; the tradition that Europe, much rather, had originally made social commerce unequal. Europe had had quite other matters on her hands; Europe had, into the bargain, on what might n't be newspaperised or otherwise ventilated, quite her own religion and her own practice. This superstition held true of the fruits of curiosity *wherever* socially gathered, whether in bustling archipelagos or in neighbouring kingdoms. It did n't, one felt, immensely signify, all the while; small harm was done, and it was surely rare that any was intended; for supreme, more and more, is the blest truth—sole safety, as it mostly seems, of our distracting age—that a given thing has but to be newspaperised *enough* (which it may, at our present rate of perfection, in a few hours) to return, as a quick consequence, to the common, the abysmal air and become without form and void. This life of scant seconds, as it were, by the sky-scraping clock, is as good for our sense and measure of the vulgar thing, for keeping apprehension down and keeping immunity up, as no life at all; since in the midst of such preposterous pretensions to recorded or reflected existence what particular vulgarity, what individual blatancy, can prevail? Still over and above all of which, too, we are made aware of a large new direct convenience or resource—the beautiful facility thus rendered the individual mind for what it shall denominate henceforth ignoring in the lump: than which nothing is more likely to work better, I suggest, toward a finer economy of consciousness. For the new beauty is that the lump, the vast concretion of the negligible, is, thanks to prodigious expensive machinery working all *ad hoc*, carefully wrought and prepared for our so dealing with it; to the great saving of our labour of selection, our own not always too beguiled or too sweetened picking-over of the heap.

Our ingenious young friend of the shocked saloons—to finish *her* history—had just simply acted in the tradition; she had figured herself one of the islanders, irresponsible in their very degree, and with a mind as closed to the "coming back" of her disseminated prattle as if it would have had in fact to be wafted from another planet. Thus, as I say, the friendliest initiations offered her among ancient seats had still failed to make her what I have called "aware." Here it was that she became documentary, and that in the flash of some new and accessory light, the continued procession of figures equally fallible, yet as little criminal, her bedimmed precedent shone

out for me once more; so that when I got my right and true
reference, as I say, for the instance commemorated in "The
Reverberator," and which dangled loosely from the peg supplied by the earlier case, this reference was much more directly to the pathetic than to anything else. The Dosson
family, here before us, are sunk in their innocence, sunk in
their irremediable unawareness almost beyond fishing out.
This constituted for handling them, I quite felt, a serious difficulty; they could be too abandoned and pathetic, as the
phrase is, to live, and yet be perfectly true; but on the other
hand they could be perfectly true and yet too abandoned for
vivification, too consentingly feeble to be worth saving. Even
this, still, would n't materially limit in them the force of the
characteristic—it was exactly in such formless terms that they
would speak best for the majority of their congeners; and, in
fine, moreover, there was *this* that I absolutely had to save for
the love of my subject-matter at large—the special appeal attached to the mild figure of Francina. I need scarcely point
out that "round" Francie Dosson the tale is systematically
constructed; with which fact was involved for me the clear
sense that if I did n't see the Francie Dossons (by whom I
mean the general quaint sisterhood, perfectly distinguishable
then, but displaced, disfeatured, "discounted" to-day, for all I
know) as always and at any cost—at whatever cost of repetition, that is—worth saving, I might as well shut up my international department. For practically—as I have said already
more than enough to convey—they were what the American
branch of that equation constantly threw me back upon; by
reason indeed of a brace of conditions only one of which
strictly inhered in the show itself.

In the heavy light of "Europe" thirty or forty years ago,
there were more of the Francie Dossons and the Daisy Millers
and the Bessie Aldens and the Pandora Days than of all the
other attested American objects put together—more of them,
of course I mean, from the moment the weird harvester was
at all preoccupied with charm, or at all committed to "having
to have" it. But quite apart from that truth was always the
stiff fact, against which I might have dashed myself in vain,
that I had n't the *data* for a right approach to the minor
quantities, such as they might have been made out to be. The

minor quantities appeared, consistently, but in a single light—that of promiscuous obscure attendance on the Daisies and Bessies and Francies; a generalised crepuscular state at best, even though yielding little by little a view of dim forms and vague differences. These adumbrations, sufficient tests once applied, claimed identities as fathers, mothers, even sometimes as satellites more directly "engaged"; but there was always, for the author of this record, a prompt and urgent remark to be made about them—which placed him, when all was said, quite at his ease. The men, the non-European, in these queer clusters, the fathers, brothers, playmates, male appendages of whatever presumption, were visible and thinkable only as the American "business-man"; and before the American business-man, as I have been prompt to declare, I was absolutely and irredeemably helpless, with no fibre of my intelligence responding to his mystery. No approach I could make to him on his "business side" really got near it. That is where I was fatally incompetent, and this in turn—the case goes into a nutshell—is so obviously why, for any decent documentation, I was simply shut up to what was left me. It takes but a glance to see how the matter was in such a fashion simplified. With the men wiped out, at a stroke, so far as any grasp of the principle of their activity was concerned (what in the name of goodness did I, or could I, know, to call know, about the very alphabet of their activity?), it was n't the *elder* woman I could take, on any reckoning, as compensatory: her inveterate blankness of surface had a manner all its own of defying the imagination to hover or to hope. There was really, as a rule, nothing whatever to be done with the elder woman; not only were reason and fancy alike forewarned not to waste their time, but any attempt upon her, one somehow felt, would have been indecorous and almost monstrous. She was n't so much as in question; since if one could work it out for the men that the depreciated state with which *they* vaguely and, as it were, somnolently struggled, was perhaps but casual and temporary, might be regarded in fact as the mere state of the medal with its right face accidentally turned down, this redemption never glimmered for the wife and mother, in whom nothing was in eclipse, but everything rather (everything there was at all) straight in evidence, and to whom therefore any round and complete embodiment had simply been denied.

"A Passionate Pilgrim," written in the year 1870, the earliest date to which anything in the whole present series refers itself, strikes me to-day, and by the same token indescribably touches me, with the two compositions that follow it, as sops instinctively thrown to the international Cerberus formidably posted where I doubtless then did n't quite make him out, yet from whose capacity to loom larger and larger with the years there must already have sprung some chilling portent. Cerberus would have been, thus, to one's younger artistic conscience, the keeper of the international "books"; the hovering disembodied critical spirit with a disengaged eye upon sneaking attempts to substitute the American romantic for the American real. To that comparatively artless category the fiction I have just named, together with "Madame de Mauves" and "The Madonna of the Future," belong. As American as possible, and even to the pitch of fondly coaxing it, I then desired my ground-stuff to remain; so that such situations as are thus offered must have represented my prime view of the telling effect with which the business-man would be dodged. He *is* dodged, here, doubtless, to a charm—he is made to wait as in the furthest and coldest of an infinite perspective of more or less quaint antechambers; where my ingenuous theory of the matter must have been that, artfully trifled with from room to room and from pretext to pretext, he might be kept indefinitely at bay. Thus if a sufficient amount of golden dust were kicked up in the foreground—and I began to kick it, under all these other possible pretexts, as hard as I knew how, he would probably never be able, to my confusion, to break through at all. I had in the spring of 1869, and again in that of 1870, spent several weeks in England, renewing and extending, with infinite zest, an acquaintance with the country that had previously been but an uneffaced little chapter of boyish, or—putting it again far enough back for the dimmest dawn of sensibility—of infantine experience; and had, perceptively and æsthetically speaking, taken the adventure of my twenty-sixth year "hard," as "A Passionate Pilgrim" quite sufficiently attests.

A part of that adventure had been the never-to-be-forgotten thrill of a first sight of Italy, from late in the summer of 1869 on; so that a return to America at the beginning of the following year was to drag with it, as a lengthening chain, the torment of losses and regrets. The repatriated victim of that unrest was, beyond doubt, acutely conscious of his case: the fifteen months just spent in Europe had absolutely determined his situation. The nostalgic poison had been distilled for him, the future presented to him but as a single intense question: was he to spend it in brooding exile, or might he somehow come into his "own"?—as I liked betimes to put it for a romantic analogy with the state of dispossessed princes and wandering heirs. The question was to answer itself promptly enough—yet after a delay sufficient to give me the measure of a whole previous relation to it. I had from as far back as I could remember carried in my side, buried and unextracted, the head of one of those well-directed shafts from the European quiver to which, of old, tender American flesh was more helplessly and bleedingly exposed, I think, than to-day: the nostalgic cup had been applied to my lips even before I was conscious of it—I had been hurried off to London and to Paris immediately after my birth, and then and there, I was ever afterwards strangely to feel, that poison had entered my veins. This was so much the case that when again, in my thirteenth year, re-exposure was decreed, and was made effective and prolonged, my inward sense of it was, in the oddest way, not of my finding myself in the vague and the uncharted, but much rather restored to air already breathed and to a harmony already disclosed. The unnatural precocity with which I had in fine "taken" to Europe was to be revealed to me later on and during another quite languishing American interval; an interval during which I supposed my young life to have been made bitter, under whatever appearances of smug accommodation, by too prompt a mouthful—recklessly administered to one's helplessness by responsible hands—of the fruit of the tree of knowledge. Why otherwise so queer a taste, always, in so juvenile, so *generally* gaping, a mouth? Well, the queer taste doubtless had been there, but the point of my anecdote, with my brace of infatuated "short stories" for its occasion, is in the infinitely greater queerness it was to take on between the summer of '70 and that of '72, when it set me again in motion.

As I read over "A Passionate Pilgrim" and "The Madonna of the Future" they become in the highest degree documentary for myself—from all measure of such interest as they may possibly have at this time of day for others I stand off; though I disengage from them but one thing, their betrayal of their consolatory use. The deep beguilement of the lost vision recovered, in comparative indigence, by a certain inexpert intensity of art—the service rendered by them at need, with whatever awkwardness and difficulty—sticks out of them for me to the exclusion of everything else and consecrates them, I freely admit, to memory. "Madame de Mauves" and "Louisa Pallant" are another matter; the latter, in especial, belongs to recent years. The former is of the small group of my productions yielding to present research no dimmest responsive ghost of a traceable origin. These remarks have constituted to excess perhaps the record of what may have put this, that and the other treated idea into my head; but I am quite unable to say what, in the summer of 1873, may have put "Madame de Mauves." Save for a single pleasant image, and for the fact that, dispatched to New York, the tale appeared, early in the following year, in "The Galaxy," a periodical to which I find, with this, twenty other remembrances gratefully attached, not a glimmer of attendant reference survives. I recall the tolerably wide court of an old inn at Bad-Homburg in the Taunus hills—a dejected and forlorn little place (its *seconde jeunesse* not yet in sight) during the years immediately following the Franco-Prussian war, which had overturned, with that of Baden-Baden, its altar, the well-appointed worship of the great goddess Chance—a homely enclosure on the ground-level of which I occupied a dampish, dusky, unsunned room, cool, however, to the relief of the fevered muse, during some very hot weather. The place was so dark that I could see my way to and from my inkstand, I remember, but by keeping the door to the court open—thanks to which also the muse, witness of many mild domestic incidents, was distracted and beguiled. In this retreat I was visited by the gentle Euphemia; I sat in crepuscular comfort pouring forth again, and, no doubt, artfully editing, the confidences with which she honoured me. She again, after her fashion, was what I might have called experimentally international; she muffled her charming head in the lightest, finest, vaguest tissue of romance and put twenty questions by. "Louisa Pallant," with still subtler art, I find, completely covers her tracks—her repudiation of every ray of legend being the more marked by the later date (1888) of her appearance. Charitably affected to her and thus disposed, if the term be not arrogant, to hand her down, I yet win from her no shadow of an intelligible account of herself. I had taken possession, at Florence, during the previous year, of a couple of sunny rooms on the Arno just at the point where the Borg' Ognissanti begins to bore duskily westward; and in those cheerful chambers (where the pitch of brightness differed so from that of the others just commemorated) I seem to have found my subject seated in extreme assurance. I did my best for it one February while the light and the colour and the sound of old Italy played in again through my open windows and about my patient table after the bold loud fashion that I had had, from so much before, to teach myself to think directly auspicious when it might be, and indirectly when it might n't.

Lady Barbarina, The Siege of London, An International Episode, The Pension Beaurepas, A Bundle of Letters, The Point of View

I HAVE GATHERED into this volume several short fictions of the type I have already found it convenient to refer to as "international"—though I freely recognise, before the array of my productions, of whatever length and whatever brevity, the general applicability of that term. On the interest of *contrasted* things any painter of life and manners inevitably much depends, and contrast, fortunately for him, is easy to seek and to recognise; the only difficulty is in presenting it again with effect, in extracting from it its sense and its lesson. The reader of these volumes will certainly see it offered in no form so frequent or so salient as that of the opposition of aspects from country to country. Their author, I am quite aware, would seem struck with no possibility of contrast in the human lot so great as that encountered as we turn back and forth between the distinctively American and the distinctively European outlook. He might even perhaps on such a showing be represented as scarce aware, before the human scene, of any other sharp antithesis at all. He is far from denying that this one has always been vivid for him; yet there are cases in which, however obvious and however contributive, its office for the particular demonstration, has been quite secondary, and in which the work is by no means merely addressed to the illustration of it. These things have had in the latter case their proper subject: as, for instance, the subject of "The Wings of the Dove," or that of "The Golden Bowl," has not been the exhibited behaviour of certain Americans as Americans, of certain English persons as English, of certain Romans as Romans. Americans, Englishmen, Romans are, in the whole matter, agents or victims; but this is in virtue of an association nowadays so developed, so easily to be taken for granted, as to have created a new scale of relations altogether, a state of things from which *emphasised* internationalism has either quite dropped or is well on its way to drop. The dramatic side of human situations subsists of course on contrast; and when we come to the two novels I have just named we shall see, for example, just how they positively provide themselves with that source of interest. We shall see nevertheless at the same time that the subject could in each case have been perfectly expressed had *all* the persons concerned been only American or only English or only Roman or whatever.

If it be asked then, in this light, why they deviate from that natural harmony, why the author resorts to the greater extravagance when the less would serve, the answer is simply that the course taken has been, on reflexion, the course of the greater amusement. That is an explanation adequate, I admit, only when itself a little explained—but I shall have due occasion to explain it. Let me for the moment merely note that the very condition I here glance at—that of the achieved social fusion, say, without the sense and experience of which neither "The Wings of the Dove," nor "The Golden Bowl," nor "The Portrait of a Lady," nor even, after all, I think, "The Ambassadors," would have been written—represents a series of facts of the highest interest and one that, at this time of day, the late-coming observer and painter, the novelist sometimes depressed by all the drawbacks of a literary form overworked and relaxed, can only rejoice to meet in his path and to measure more and more as a portent and an opportunity. In proportion as he intelligently meets it, and more especially in proportion as he may happen to have "assisted" from far back at so many of the odd and fresh phenomena involved, must he see a vast new province, infinitely peopled and infinitely elastic—by which I mean with incalculable power to grow—annexed to the kingdom of the dramatist. On this point, however, much more is to be said than I can touch on by the way—so that I return to my minor contention; which is that in a whole group of tales I here collect the principle of illustration has on the other hand quite definitely been that the idea could *not* have expressed itself without the narrower application of international terms. The contrast in "Lady Barbarina" depends altogether on the immitigable Anglicism of this young woman and that equally marked projection of New York elements and objects which, surrounding and framing her figure, throws it into eminent relief. She has her personal qualities, but the very interest, the very curiosity of the matter is that her imbroglio is able to attest itself with scarce so much as a reference to them. It plays itself out quite consistently on the plane of her general, her instinctive, her exasperatedly conscious ones. The others, the more intimate, the subtler, the finer—so far as there may have been such—virtually become, while the story is enacted, not relevant, though their relevancy might have come up on some other basis.

But that this is true, always in its degree, of each of the other contributions to the class before us, we shall sufficiently make out, I think, as we take them in their order. I am only struck, I may indeed parenthesise, with the inveteracy of the general ground (not to say of the extension I give it) over which my present remarks play. It does thus in truth come home to me that, combining and comparing in whatever proportions and by whatever lights, my "America" and its products would doubtless, as a theme, have betrayed gaps and infirmities enough without such a kicking-up of the dramatic dust (mainly in the foreground) as I could set my "Europe" in motion for; just as my Europe would probably have limped across our stage to no great effect of processional state without an ingenuous young America (constantly seen as ingenuous and young) to hold up its legendary train. At the same time I pretend not at all to regret my having had from the very first to see my workable world all and only as an unnatural mixture. No mixture, for that matter, is quite unnatural unless quite sterile, and the particular range of associations that betimes, to my eyes, blocked out everything else, blocked out aspects and combinations more simply conditioned, was at least not open to the reproach of not giving me results. These were but what they could be, of course; but such as they were, at all events, here am I at this time of day quite earnestly grouping, distinguishing, discussing them. The great truth in the whole connexion, however, is, I think, that one never really chooses one's general range of vision—the experience from which ideas and themes and suggestions spring: this proves ever what it has *had* to be, this is one with the very turn one's life has taken; so that whatever it "gives," whatever it makes us feel and think of, we regard very much as imposed and inevitable. The subject thus pressed upon the artist is the necessity of his case and the fruit of his consciousness; which truth makes and has ever made of any quarrel with his subject, any stupid attempt to go behind *that*, the true stultification of criticism. The author of these remarks has in any case felt it, from far back, quite his least stupid course to meet halfway, as it were, the turn taken and the perceptions engendered by the tenor of his days. Here it is that he has never pretended to "go behind"—which would have been for him a deplorable waste of time. The thing of profit is to *have* your experience—to recognise and understand it, and for this almost any will do; there being surely no absolute ideal about it beyond getting from it all it has to give. The artist—for it is of this strange brood we speak—has but to have his honest sense of life to find it fed at every pore even as the birds of the air are fed; with more and more to give, in turn, as a consequence, and, quite by the same law that governs the responsive affection of a kindly-used animal, in proportion as more and more is confidently asked.

All of which, however, doubtless wanders a little far from my mild argument—that of my so grateful and above all so well-advised primary acceptance of a *determined* array of appearances. What I was clearly to be treated to by fate—with the early-taken ply I have already elsewhere glanced at—was (should I have the intelligence to embrace it) some considerable occasion to appreciate the mixture of manners. So, as I say, there would be a decent economy in cultivating the intelligence; through the sincerity of which process I have plucked, I hold, every little flower of a "subject" pressed between the leaves of these volumes. I am tempted indeed to make for my original lucidity the claim of something more than bare prudence—almost that of a happy instinctive foresight. This is what I mean by having been "well-advised." It was as if I had, vulgarly speaking, received quite at first the "straight tip"—to back the right horse or buy the right shares. The mixture of manners was to become in other words not a less but a very much more appreciable and interesting subject of study. The mixture of manners was in fine to loom large and constantly larger all round; it was to be a matter, plainly, about which the future would have much to say. Nothing appeals to me more, I confess, as a "critic of life" in any sense worthy of the name, than the finer—if indeed thereby the less easily formulated—group of the conquests of civilisation, the multiplied symptoms among educated people, from wherever drawn, of a common intelligence and a social fusion tending to abridge old rigours of separation. This too, I must admit, in spite of the many-coloured sanctity of such rigours in general, which have hitherto made countries smaller but kept the globe larger, and by which immediate strangeness, immediate beauty, immediate curiosity were so much fostered. Half our instincts work for the maintained differences; without them, for instance, what would have been the point of the history of poor Lady Barbarina? I have but to put that question, I must add, to feel it beautifully large; for there looms before me at its touch the vision of a Lady Barbarina reconciled, domesticated, developed, of possibly greater vividness than the quite other vision expressed in these pages. It is a question, however, of the tendency, perceptive as well as reflective too, of the braver imagination—which faculty, in our future, strikes me as likely to be appealed to much less by the fact, by the pity and the misery and the greater or less grotesqueness, of the courageous, or even of the timid, missing their lives beyond certain stiff barriers, than by the picture of their more and more steadily making out their opportunities and their possible communications. Behind all the small comedies and tragedies of the international, in a word, has exquisitely lurked for me the idea of some eventual sublime consensus of the educated; the exquisite conceivabilities of which, intellectual, moral, emotional, sensual, social, political—all, I mean, in the face of felt difficulty and danger—constitute stuff for such "situations" as may easily make many of those of a more familiar type turn pale. *There*, if one will—in the dauntless fusions to come—is the personal drama of the future.

We are far from it certainly—as I have delayed much too long to remark—in the chronicle of Lady Barb. I have placed this composition (1888) at the top of my list, in the present cluster, despite the earlier date of some of its companions; consistently giving it precedence by reason of its greatest length. The idea at the root of it scarcely brooks indication, so inevitable had it surely become, in all the conditions, that a young Englishwoman in some such predicament should figure as the happy pictorial thought. The whole thing rests, I need scarce point out, on the most primitive logic. The international relation had begun to present itself "socially," after the liveliest fashion, a quarter of a century ago and earlier, as a relation of intermarrying; but nothing was meanwhile so striking as that these manifestations took always the same turn. The European of "position" married the young American woman, or the young American woman married the European of position—one scarce knew how best to express the regularity of it; but the social field was scanned in vain for a different pairing. No American citizen appeared to offer his hand to the "European" girl, or if he did so offered it in vain. The bridal migrations were eastward without exception—as rigidly as if settled by statute. Custom clearly had acquired the force of law; a fact remarkable, significant, interesting and even amusing. And yet, withal, it seemed scarce to demand explanations. So far as they appeared indeed they were confident on the American side. The representatives of that interest had no call in life to go "outside" for their wives—having obviously close at hand the largest and choicest assortment of such conveniences; as was sufficiently proved by the European "run" on the market. What American run on any foreign market had been noted?—save indeed always on the part of the women! It all redounded to the honour and glory of the young woman grown in American conditions—to cast discredit on whose general peerlessness by attested preference for other types could but strike the domestic aspirant as an act of disloyalty or treachery. It was just the observed rarity of the case therefore that prompted me to put it to the imaginative test. Any case so unlikely to happen—taking it for at all conceivable—could only be worth attention when it *should*, once in a blue moon, occur. There was nothing meanwhile, in truth, to "go by"; we had seen the American girl "of position" absorbed again and again into the European social system, but we had only seen young foreign candidates for places as cooks and house-maids absorbed into the American. The more one viewed the possible instance, accordingly, the more it appealed to speculative study; so that, failing all valid testimony, one had studiously, as it were, to forge the very documents.

I have only to add that I found mine, once I had produced them, thoroughly convincing: the most one could do, in the conditions, was to make one's picture appear to hang together, and I should have broken down, no doubt, had my own, after a superficial question or two, not struck me as decently hanging. The essential, at the threshold, I seem to recall, was to get my young man right—I somehow quite took for granted the getting of my young woman. Was this because, for the portrait of Lady Barb, I felt appealed to so little in the name of *shades*? Shades would be decidedly neither of her general world nor of her particular consciousness: the image I had in view was a maiden nature that, after a fashion all its own, should show as fine and complete, show as neither coarse nor poor, show above all as a resultant of many causes, quite without them. I felt in short sure of Lady Barb, and I think there is no question about her, or about the depth of root she might strike in American soil, that I should n't have been ready on the spot to answer. Such is the luck of the conception that imposes itself *en bloc*—or such at least the artist's luck in face of it; such certainly, to begin with and "subjectively" speaking, is the great advantage of a character all of a piece: immediacy of representation, the best omens for felicity, then so honourably await it. It was Jackson Lemon and *his* shades, comparatively, and his comparative sense for shades, that, in the tale, most interested me. The one thing fine-drawn in his wife was that she had been able to care for him as he was: to almost every one and every thing else equally American, to almost every one and every thing else so sensibly stamped, toned and warranted, she was to find herself quite otherwise affected. With her husband the law was reversed—he had, much rather, imputed authority and dignity, imputed weight and charm, to the antecedents of which she was so fine and so direct a consequence; his estimate, his appreciation of her being founded thus on a vision of innumerable close correspondences. It is that vision in him that is racked, and at so many fine points, when he finds their experiment come so near failure; all of which—at least as I seem to see it again so late in the day—lights his inward drama as with the never-quenched lamp of a sacred place. His wife's, on the other hand, goes on in comparatively close darkness.

It is indeed late in the day that I thus project the ray of *my* critical lantern, however; for it comes over me even as I write that the general air in which most of these particular flowers of fancy bloom is an air we have pretty well ceased to breathe. "Lady Barbarina" is, as I have said, scarce a quarter of a century old; but so many of the perceived conditions in which it took birth have changed that the account of them embodied in that tale and its associates will already pass for ancient history. "Civilisation" and education move fast, after all, and too many things have happened; too many *sorts* of things, above all, seem more and more likely to happen. This multiplication of kinds of occurrences, I make no doubt, will promote the inspiration of observers and poets to come; but it may meanwhile well make for an effect of superannuation in any record of the leaner years. Jackson Lemon's has become a more frequent adventure, and Lady Barbarina is to-day as much at her ease in New York, in Washington, at Newport, as in London or in Rome. If this is her case, moreover, it is still more that of little Mrs. Headway, of "The Siege of London" (1883), who suffers, I feel, by the sad circumstance that her type of complication, or, more exactly speaking perhaps, that of the gentlemen concerned with her, is no longer eminent, or at least salient. Both she and her friends have had too many companions and successors; so that to reinvest them with historic importance, with individual dignity, I have to think of them rather as brave precursors, as adventurous skirmishers and *éclaireurs*. This does n't diminish, I recognise, any interest that may reside in the form either of "The Siege" aforesaid or of its congeners "An International Episode," "A Bundle of Letters" and "The Pension Beaurepas." Or rather indeed perhaps I should distinguish among these things and, if presuming to claim for several some hint of the distinction we may see exemplified in any first-class art-museum, the distinction of the archaic subject treated by a "primitive" master of high finish, yet notice duly that others are no more "quaint" than need be. What has really happened, I think, is that the *great* international cases, those that bristle with fifty sorts of social reference and overflow, and, by the same token, with a hundred illustrations of social incoherence, are now equally taken for granted on all sides of the sea, have simply become incidents and examples of the mixture of manners, as I call it, and the thicker fusion: which may mean nothing more, in truth, but that social incoherence (with the sense for its opposite practically extinct among the nations) has at last got itself accepted, right and left, as normal.

So much, as I put it, for the great cases; but a certain freshness, I make out, still hangs strangely enough about the smaller and the more numerous; those to which we owe it that such anecdotes—in my general array—as "Pandora," as "Fordham Castle," as "Flickerbridge," as "Miss Gunton of Poughkeepsie," are by no means false even to present appearances. "The Pension Beaurepas" is not alone, thanks to some of its associations, in glowing for me with the tender grace of a day that is dead; and yet, though the accidents and accessories, in such a picture, may have been marked for change, why shall not the essence of the matter, the situation of Mr. and Mrs. Ruck and their daughter at old Geneva—for there is of course a new, a newer Geneva—freely recur? I am careful to put it as a question, and all for a particular reason— the reason that, to be frank, I find myself, before the vast diluvian occidental presence in Europe, with its remorseless rising tide and its positive expression of almost nothing but quantity and number, deprived, on definite and ample grounds, of the precious faculty of confidence. This confidence was of old all instinctive, in face of the "common run" of appearances, the even then multitudinous, miscellaneous minor international phenomena, those of which the "short story," as contemporaneously practised, could effect a fairly prompt and easy notation; but it is now unmistakeable that to come forth, from whatever privacy, to almost any one of the great European highways, and more particularly perhaps to approach the ports of traffic for the lately-developed and so flourishing "southern route" from New York and Boston, is to encounter one of those big general questions that sturdily brush away the multiplication of small answers. "Who are they, what are they, whence and whither and why," the "critic of life," international or other, still, or more and more, asks himself, as he of course always asked, but with the actual difference that the reply that used to come so conveniently straight, "Why, they're just the American vague variety of the dear old Anglo-Saxon race," not only hangs fire and leaves him to wait and wonder, but really affects him as having for this act of deference (as to which he can't choose, I admit) little more than a conscious mocking, baffling, in fact a just all but sinister, grimace. "Don't you wish you knew, or even *could* know?" the inscrutable grin seems to convey; and with resources of cynicism behind it not in the least to be disturbed by any such cheap retort as "Don't you wish that, on your side, *you* could say—or even, for your own convenience, so much as guess?"

For there is no communicating to the diluvian presence, on such a scale, any suspicion that convenience shall anywhere fail it: all its consciousness, on that general head, is that of itself representing and actively *being* the biggest convenience of the world. Little need to insist on the guarantee of subjective ease involved in such an attitude—the immense noted growth of which casts its chill, as I intimate, on the enquirer proceeding from settled premises. He was aware formerly, when it came to an analysis, of all his presumptions; he had but to glance for an immemorial assurance at a dozen of the myriad "registers" disposed in the vestibules of bankers, the reading-rooms of hotels and "exchanges," open on the most conspicuous table of visited palace and castle, to see them bristle with names of a more or less conceivable tradition. Queer enough often, whether in isolation or in association, were these gages of identity: but their queerness, not independent of some more or less traceable weird law, was exactly, after all, their most familiar note. They had their way of not breaking, through it all, the old sweet Anglo-Saxon spell; they had their way of not failing, when all was said, to suggest more communities and comprehensions than conundrums and "stunts." He would be brave, however, who should say that any such ghost of a quiet conformity presides in the fullness of time over the interminable passenger-lists that proclaim the prosperity of the great conveying companies. If little books have their fates, little names—and long ones still more—have their eloquence; the emphasis of nominal reference in the general roll-call falls so strongly upon alien syllables and sounds, representative signs that fit into our "English" legend (as we were mainly conscious up to a few years since of having inherited that boon) scarcely more than if borrowed from the stony slabs of Nineveh. I may not here attempt to weigh the question of what these exotic symbols positively represent—a prodigious question, I cannot but think; I content myself with noting the difference made for fond fancy by the so rapidly established change, by the so considerable drop of old associations. The point is of one's having the heart to assume that the Ninevites, as I may momentarily call them for convenience, are to be constantly taken as feeling in the same way about fifty associational matters as we used, in all satisfaction, to observe our earlier generations feel. One can but speak for one's self, and my imagination, on the great highways, I find, does n't rise to such people, who are obviously beyond my divination. They strike one, above all, as giving no account of themselves in any terms already consecrated by human use; to this inarticulate state they probably form, collectively, the most unprecedented of monuments; abysmal the mystery of what they think, what they feel, what they want, what they suppose themselves to be saying. There would appear to be to-day no slim scrap even of a Daisy Miller to bridge the chasm; no light-footed Francie Dosson or Pandora Day to dance before one across the wavering plank.

I plead a blank of memory as to the origin of "The Siege of London"; I get no nearer to the birth of the idea than by recalling a certain agitation of the spirit, a lively irritation of the temper, under which, one evening early in the autumn of 1877, that is more than thirty years ago, I walked away from the close of a performance at the Théâtre Français. The play had been "Le Demi-Monde" of the younger Dumas, a masterpiece which I had not heard for the first time, but a particular feature of which on this occasion more than ever yet filled up the measure of my impatience. I could less than ever swallow it, Olivier de Jalin's denunciation of Madame d'Ange; the play, from the beginning, marches toward it—it is the main hinge of the action; but the very perfection with which the part was rendered in those years by Delaunay (just as

Croizette was pure perfection as Suzanne) seemed to have made me present at something inhuman and odious. It was the old story—that from the positive, the prodigious *morality* of such a painter of the sophisticated life as Dumas, not from anything else or less edifying, one must pray to be delivered. There are doubtless many possible views of such a dilemma as Olivier's, the conflict of propriety for him between the man he likes and esteems and the woman he has loved but has n't esteemed and does n't, and as to whom he sees his friend blind, and, as he thinks, befooled; in consequence of which I am not re-judging his case. But I recover with a pensive pleasure that is almost all a pang the intensity with which I could then feel it; to the extent of wondering whether the general situation of the three persons concerned, or something like it, might n't be shown as taking quite another turn. Was there not conceivable an Olivier of our race, a different Olivier altogether, moved to ask himself how at such a juncture a "real gentleman," distressed and perplexed, would yet most naturally act? The question would be interesting, it was easy to judge, if only by the light it might throw on some of the other, the antecedent and concomitant, phases of a real gentleman's connexion "at all at all" with such a business and such a world. It remained with me, at all events, and was to prove in time the germ of "The Siege of London"; of the conception of which the state of mind so reflected strikes me as making, I confess, very ancient history.

Far away and unspeakably regretted the days, alas, or, more exactly, the nights, on which one could walk away from the Français under the spell of such fond convictions and such deep and agitating problems. The emphasis of the international proposition has indeed had time, as I say, to place itself elsewhere—if, for that matter, there be any emphasis or any proposition left at all—since the age when that particular pleasure seemed the keenest in life. A few months ago, one evening, I found myself withdrawing from the very temple and the supposedly sacred rites before these latter were a third over: beneath that haunted dome itself they seemed to have become at last so accessible, cynically making their bargain with them, to the profanations long kept at bay. Only, with that evolution of taste possible on the part of the old worshipper in question, what world-convulsions might n't, in general, well have taken place? Let me continue to speak of the rest of the matter here before us as therefore of almost pre-historic reference. I was to make, in due course, at any rate, my limited application of that glimmering image of a M. de Jalin with whom we might have more fellow-feeling, and I sent "The Siege of London" accordingly to my admirable friend the late Leslie Stephen, then editor of *The Cornhill Magazine*, where it appeared during the two first months of 1883. That is all I remember about it save always the particular London light in which at that period I invoked the muse and drove the pen and with which the compositions resulting strike my fancy to-day as so closely interfused that in reading over those of them I here preserve every aspect and element of my scene of application lives again for me. This scene consisted of small chambers in a small street that opened, at a very near corner, into Piccadilly and a view of the Green Park; I had dropped into them almost instantaneously, under the accepted heavy pressure of the autumnal London of 1876, and was to sit scribbling in them for nearly ten years. The big human rumble of Piccadilly (all human and equine then and long after) was close at hand; I liked to think that Thackeray's Curzon Street, in which Becky Sharp, or rather Mrs. Rawdon Crawley, had lived, was not much further off: I thought of it preponderantly, in my comings and goings, as Becky's and her creator's; just as I was to find fifty other London neighbourhoods speak to me almost only with the voice, the thousand voices, of Dickens.

A "great house," forming the southwest corner of Piccadilly and with its long and practically featureless side, continued by the high wall of its ample court, opposite my open-eyed windows, gloomed, in dusky brick, as the extent of my view, but with a vast convenient neutrality which I found, soon enough, protective and not inquisitive, so that whatever there was of my sedentary life and regular habits took a sort of local wealth of colour from the special greyish-brown tone of the surface always before me. This surface hung there like the most voluminous of curtains—it masked the very stage of the great theatre of the town. To sit for certain hours at one's desk before it was somehow to occupy in the most suitable way in the world the proportionately ample interacts of the mightiest of dramas. When I went out it was as if the curtain rose; so that, to repeat, I think of my tolerably copious artistry of that time as all the fruit of the interacts, with the curtain more or less quietly down and with the tuning of fiddles and only the vague rumble of shifted scenery playing round it and through it. There were absences of course: "A Bundle of Letters," here reproduced took birth (1879) during certain autumn weeks spent in Paris, where a friend of those years, a young London journalist, the late Theodore Child (of Merton College Oxford, who was to die, prematurely and lamentedly, during a gallant professional tour of exploration in Persia) was fondly carrying on, under difficulties, an Anglo-American periodical called *The Parisian*. He invited me to contribute to its pages, and, again, a small sharply-resonant street off the Rue de la Paix, where all existence somehow went on as a repercussion from well-brushed asphalt, lives for me as the scene of my response. A snowstorm of a violence rare in Paris raged, I recollect, for many hours, for the greater part of a couple of days; muffling me noiselessly into the small, shiny, shabby salon of an *hôtel garni* with a droll combinational, almost cosmic sign, and promoting (it comes back to me) a deep concentration, an unusual straightness of labour. "A Bundle of Letters" was written in a single long session and, the temperature apart, at a "heat." Its companion-piece, "The Point of View," marks not less for memory, I find, an excursion associated with diligence. I have no heart to "go into" these mere ingenious and more or less effective pleasantries to any tune beyond this of glancing at the *other*, the extinct, actualities they hold up the glimmering taper to. They are still faintly scented, doubtless, with something of that authenticity, and a living work of art, however limited, pretends always, as for part of its grace, to some good faith of community, however indirect, with its period and place.

To read over "The Point of View" has opened up for me, I confess, no contentious vista whatever, nothing but the faded iridescence of a far-away Washington spring. This, in 1881, had been my first glimpse of that interesting city, where I then spent a few weeks, a visit repeated the following year; and I remember beginning on the first occasion a short imag-

inary correspondence after the pattern of the then already
published "Bundle of Letters." After an absence from America of some five years I inevitably, on the spot again, had
impressions; and not less inevitably and promptly, I remember, recognised the truth that if one really was subject to such,
and to a good many, and they were at all worth entertaining
or imparting, one was likely to bristle with a quite proportionately smaller number of neat and complacent conclusions.
Impressions could mutually conflict—which was exactly the
interest of them; whereas in ninety-nine connexions out of a
hundred, conclusions could but raise the wind for large
groups of persons incapable, to all appearance, of intelligently
opening their eyes, though much occupied, to make up for it,
with opening, and all vociferously, their mouths. "The Point
of View," in fine, I fear, was but to commemorate, punctually
enough, its author's perverse and incurable disposition to interest himself less in his own (always so quickly stale) experience, under certain sorts of pressure, than in that of
conceivable fellow mortals, which might be mysteriously and
refreshingly different. The thing indeed may also serve, in its
degree, as a punctual small monument to a recognition that
was never to fail; that of the nature of the burden bequeathed
by such rash multiplications of the candid consciousness.
They are splendid for experience, the multiplications, each in
its way an intensifier; but expression, liking things above all
to be made comfortable and easy for it, views them askance.
The case remains, none the less—alas for this faculty!—that
no representation of life worth speaking of can go forward
without them. All of which will perhaps be judged to have
but a strained relevance, however, to the fact that, though the
design of the short imaginary correspondence I speak of was
interrupted during those first weeks in Washington, a second
visit, the following spring, served it better; I had kept the
thread (through a return to London and a return again
thence) and, if I remember rightly, I brought my small
scheme to a climax on the spot. The finished thing appeared
in *The Century Magazine* of December 1882. I recently had
the chance to "look up," for old sake's sake, that momentary
seat of the good-humoured satiric muse—the seats of the
muses, even when the merest flutter of one of their robes has

been involved, losing no scrap of sanctity for me, I profess, by the accident of my having myself had the honour to offer the visitant the chair. The chair I had anciently been able to push forward in Washington had not, I found, survived the ravage of nearly thirty years; its place knew it no more, infirm and precarious dependence as it had struck me even at the time as being. So, quite exquisitely, as whenever that lapse occurs, the lost presence, the obliterated scene, translated itself for me at last into terms of almost more than earthly beauty and poetry. Fifty intimate figures and objects flushed with life in the other time had passed away since then; a great chapter of history had made itself, tremendous things had happened; the ghosts of old cherished names, of old tragedies, of old comedies, even of old mere mystifications, had marshalled their array. Only the little rounded composition remained; which glowed, ever so strangely, like a swinging, playing lantern, with a light that brought out the past. The past had been most concretely that vanished and slightly sordid tenement of the current housing of the muse. I had had "rooms" in it, and I could remember how the rooms, how the whole place, a nest of rickety tables and chairs, lame and disqualified utensils of every sort, and of smiling, shuffling, procrastinating persons of colour, had exhaled for me, to pungency, the domestic spirit of the "old South." I had nursed the unmistakeable scent; I had read history by its aid; I had learned more than I could say of what had anciently been the matter under the reign of the great problem of persons of colour —so badly the matter, by my vision, that a deluge of blood and fire and tears had been needed to correct it. These complacencies of perception swarmed for me again—while yet no brick of the little old temple of the revelation stood on another.

I could scarcely have said where the bricks *had* stood; the other, the superseded Washington of the exquisite springtime, of the earlier initiation, of the hovering plaintive ghosts, reduced itself to a great vague blur of warmth and colour and fragrance. It kept flushing through the present—very much as if I had had my small secret for making it. I could turn on my finger the magic ring—it was strange how slight a thing, a mere handful of pages of light persistent prose, could act as that talisman. So, at all events, I like to date, and essentially to synchronise, these sincere little studies in general. Nothing perhaps can vouch better for their having applied to conditions that superficially at least have changed than the fact that to fond memory—I speak of my own—there hangs about the last item on this list, the picture of "The Pension Beaurepas," the unearthly poetry, as I call it, of the Paquis, and that I should yet have to plunge into gulfs of explanation as to where and what the Paquis may have been. An old-world nook of one's youth was so named, a scrap of the lakeside fringe of ancient Geneva, now practically quite reformed and improved away. The Pension Beaurepas, across the years, looks to me prodigiously archaic and incredibly quaint; I ask myself why, at the time, I so wasted the precious treasure of a sense that absolutely primitive pre-revolutionary "Europe" had never really been swept out of its cupboards, shaken out of its curtains, thumped out of its mattresses. The echoes of the eighteenth century, to go no further back, must have been thick on its rather greasy stone staircase, up and down which, unconscious of the character of the fine old wrought-iron *rampe*, as of most other things in the world besides, Mr. and Mrs. and Miss Ruck, to speak only of them, used mournfully to straggle. But I must n't really so *much* as speak only, as even speak, of them. They would carry me too far back— which possibly outlived verisimilitude in them is what I wish to acknowledge.

The Lesson of the Master, The Death of the Lion, The Next Time, The Figure in the Carpet, The Coxon Fund

M<small>Y CLEAREST REMEMBRANCE</small> of any provoking cause connected with the matter of the present volume applies, not to the composition at the head of my list—which owes that precedence to its greatest length and earliest date—but to the next in order, an effort embalmed, to fond memory, in a delightful association. I make the most of this passage of literary history—I like so, as I find, to recall it. It lives there for me in old Kensington days; which, though I look back at them over no such great gulf of years—"The Death of the Lion" first appeared but in 1894—have already faded for me to the complexion of ever so long ago. It was of a Sunday afternoon early in the spring of that year: a young friend, a Kensington neighbour and an ardent man of letters, called on me to introduce a young friend of his own and to bespeak my interest for a periodical about to take birth, in his hands, on the most original "lines" and with the happiest omens. What omen could be happier for instance than that this infant *recueil*, joyously christened even before reaching the cradle, should take the name of *The Yellow Book?*—which so certainly would command for it the liveliest attention. What, further, should one rejoice more to hear than that this venture was, for all its constitutional gaiety, to brave the quarterly form, a thing hitherto of austere, of awful tradition, and was indeed in still other ways to sound the note of bright young defiance? The project, modestly and a little vaguely but all communicatively set forth, amused me, charmed me, on the spot—or at least the touchingly convinced and inflamed projector did. It was the happy fortune of the late Henry Harland to charge everything he touched, whether in life or in literature, with that influence—an effect by which he was always himself the first to profit. If he came to me, about *The Yellow Book*, amused, he pursued the enterprise under the same hilarious star; its difficulties no less than its felicities excited, in the event, his mirth; and he was never more amused (nor, I may certainly add, more amusing) than when, after no very prolonged career, it encountered suddenly and all distressfully its term. The thing had then been to him, for the few years, a humorous uneasy care, a business attended both with other troubles and other pleasures; yet when, before the too prompt harshness of his final frustration, I reflect that he had adventurously lived, wrought and enjoyed, the small square lemon-coloured quarterly, "failure" and all, figures to me perhaps his most beguiling dream and most rewarding hours.

The bravest of the portents that Sunday afternoon—the intrinsic, of course I mean; the only ones to-day worth speaking of—I have yet to mention; for I recall my rather embarrassed inability to measure as yet the contributory value of Mr. Aubrey Beardsley, by whom my friend was accompanied and who, as his prime illustrator, his perhaps even quite independent picture-maker, was to be in charge of the "art department." This young man, slender, pale, delicate, unmistakeably intelligent, somehow invested the whole proposition with a detached, a slightly ironic and melancholy grace. I had met him before, on a single occasion, and had seen an example or two of his so curious and so disconcerting talent—my appreciation of which seems to me, however, as I look back, to have stopped quite short. The young *recueil* was to have pictures, yes, and they were to be as often as possible from Beardsley's hand; but they were to wear this unprecedented distinction, and were to scatter it all about them, that they should have nothing to do with the text—which put the whole matter on an ideal basis. To those who remember the short string of numbers of *The Yellow Book* the spasmodic independence of these contributions will still be present. They were, as illustrations, related surely to nothing else in the same pages—save once or twice, as I imperfectly recall, to some literary effort of Beardsley's own that matched them in perversity; and I might well be at peace as to any disposition on the part of the strange young artist ever to emulate *my* comparatively so incurious text. There would be more to say about him, but he must not draw me off from a greater relevance—my point being simply that he had associated himself with Harland that brave day to dangle before me the sweetest aid to inspiration ever snatched by a poor scribbler from editorial lips. I should sooner have come to this turn of the affair, which at once bathed the whole prospect in the rosiest glow.

I was invited, and all urgently, to contribute to the first number, and was regaled with the golden truth that my composition might absolutely assume, might shamelessly parade in, its own organic form. It was disclosed to me, wonderfully, that—so golden the air pervading the enterprise—any projected contribution might conform, not only unchallenged but by this circumstance itself the more esteemed, to its true intelligible nature. For any idea I might wish to express I might have space, in other words, elegantly to express it—an offered licence that, on the spot, opened up the millennium to the "short story." One had so often known this product to struggle, in one's hands, under the rude prescription of brevity at any cost, with the opposition so offered to its really becoming a story, that my friend's emphasised indifference to the arbitrary limit of length struck me, I remember, as the fruit of the finest artistic intelligence. We had been at one— that we already knew—on the truth that the forms of wrought things, in this order, *were*, all exquisitely and effectively, the things; so that, for the delight of mankind, form might compete with form and might correspond to fitness; might, that is, in the given case, have an inevitability, a marked felicity. Among forms, moreover, we had had, on the dimensional ground—for length and breadth—our ideal, the beautiful and blest *nouvelle*; the generous, the enlightened hour for which appeared thus at last to shine. It was under the star of the *nouvelle* that, in other languages, a hundred interesting and charming results, such studies on the minor scale as the best of Turgenieff's, of Balzac's, of Maupassant's, of Bourget's, and just lately, in our own tongue, of Kipling's, had been, all economically, arrived at—thanks to their authors', as "contributors," having been able to count, right and left, on a wise and liberal support. It had taken the blank misery of our Anglo-Saxon sense of such matters to organise, as might be said, the general indifference to this fine type of composition. In that dull view a "short story" was a "short story," and that was the end of it. Shades and differences, varieties and styles, the value above all of the idea happily *developed*, languished, to extinction, under the hard-and-fast rule of the "from six to eight thousand words"—when, for one's benefit, the rigour was a little relaxed. For myself, I delighted in the shapely *nouvelle*—as, for that matter, I had from time to time and here and there been almost encouraged to show.

However, these are facts quite of the smaller significance and at which I glance only because I seem still to recognise in those of my three bantlings held by Harland at the baptismal font—"The Death of the Lion" (1894), "The Coxon Fund" (1894), "The Next Time" (1895), *plus* a paper not here to be reproduced—something of the less troubled confidence with which they entered on their first state of being. These pieces have this in common that they deal all with the literary life, gathering their motive, in each case, from some noted adventure, some felt embarrassment, some extreme predicament, of the artist enamoured of perfection, ridden by his idea or paying for his sincerity. They testify indeed, as they thus stand together, to no general intention—they minister only, I think, to an emphasised effect. The particular case, in respect to each situation depicted, appealed to me but on its merits; though I was to note with interest, as my sense more and more opened itself, that situations of the order I speak of might again and again be conceived. They rose before me, in fine, as numerous, and thus, here, even with everything not included, they have added themselves up. I must further mention that if they enjoy in common their reference to the troubled artistic consciousness, they make together, by the same stroke, this other rather blank profession, that few of them recall to me, however dimly, any scant pre-natal phase.

In putting them sundry such critical questions so much after the fact I find it interesting to make out—critically interesting of course, which is all our interest here pretends to be—that whereas any anecdote about life pure and simple, as it were, proceeds almost as a matter of course from some good jog of fond fancy's elbow, some pencilled note on somebody else's case, so the material for any picture of personal states so specifically complicated as those of my hapless friends in the present volume will have been drawn preponderantly from the depths of the designer's own mind. This,

amusingly enough, is what, on the evidence before us, I seem
critically, as I say, to gather—that the states represented, the
embarrassments and predicaments studied, the tragedies and
comedies recorded, can be intelligibly fathered but on his
own intimate experience. I have already mentioned the particular rebuke once addressed me on all this ground, the question of where on earth, where roundabout us at this hour, I
had "found" my Neil Paradays, my Ralph Limberts, my
Hugh Verekers and other such supersubtle fry. I was reminded then, as I have said, that these represented eminent
cases fell to the ground, as by their foolish weight, unless I
could give chapter and verse for the eminence. I was reduced
to confessing I could n't, and yet must repeat again here how
little I was so abashed. On going over these things I see, to
our critical edification, exactly why—which was because I
was able to plead that my postulates, my animating presences,
were all, to their great enrichment, their intensification of
value, ironic; the strength of applied irony being surely in the
sincerities, the lucidities, the utilities that stand behind it.
When it 's not a campaign, of a sort, on behalf of the something better (better than the obnoxious, the provoking object) that blessedly, as is assumed, *might* be, it 's not worth
speaking of. But this is exactly what we mean by operative
irony. It implies and projects the possible other case, the case
rich and edifying where the actuality is pretentious and vain.
So it plays its lamp; so, essentially, it carries that smokeless
flame, which makes clear, with all the rest, the good cause
that guides it. My application of which remarks is that the
studies here collected have their justification in the ironic
spirit, the spirit expressed by my being able to reply promptly
enough to my friend: "If the life about us for the last thirty
years refuses warrant for these examples, then so much the
worse for that life. The *constatation* would be so deplorable
that instead of making it we must dodge it: there are decencies that in the name of the general self-respect we must take
for granted, there 's a kind of rudimentary intellectual honour
to which we must, in the interest of civilisation, at least pretend." But I must really reproduce the whole passion of my
retort.

"What does your contention of non-existent conscious

exposures, in the midst of all the stupidity and vulgarity and hypocrisy, imply but that we have been, nationally, so to speak, graced with no instance of recorded sensibility fine enough to react against these things?—an admission too distressing. What one would accordingly fain do is to baffle any such calamity, to *create* the record, in default of any other enjoyment of it; to imagine, in a word, the honourable, the producible case. What better example than this of the high and helpful public and, as it were, civic use of the imagination? —a faculty for the possible fine employments of which in the interest of morality my esteem grows every hour I live. How can one consent to make a picture of the preponderant futilities and vulgarities and miseries of life without the impulse to exhibit as well from time to time, in its place, some fine example of the reaction, the opposition or the escape? One does, thank heaven, encounter here and there symptoms of immunity from the general infection; one recognises with rapture, on occasion, signs of a protest against the rule of the cheap and easy; and one sees thus that the tradition of a high æsthetic temper need n't, after all, helplessly and ignobly perish. These reassurances are one's warrant, accordingly, for so many recognitions of the apparent doom and the exasperated temper—whether with the spirit and the career fatally bruised and finally broken in the fray, or privileged but to gain from it a finer and more militant edge. I have had, I admit, to project *signal* specimens—have had, naturally, to make and to keep my cases interesting; the only way to achieve which was to suppose and represent them eminent. In other words I was inevitably committed, always, to the superior case; so that if this is what you reprehensively mean, that I have been thus beguiled into citing celebrities without analogues and painting portraits without models, I plead guilty to the critical charge. Only what I myself mean is that I carry my guilt lightly and have really in face of each perpetrated licence scarce patience to defend myself." So I made my point and so I continued.

"I can't tell you, no, who it is I 'aimed at' in the story of Henry St. George; and it would n't indeed do for me to name his exemplar publicly even were I able. But I none the less maintain his situation to have been in *essence* an observed reality—though I should be utterly ashamed, I equally declare, if I had n't done quite my best for it. It was the fault of this notable truth, and not my own, that it too obscurely lurked —dim and disengaged; but where is the work of the intelligent painter of life if not precisely in some such aid given to true meanings to be born? He must bear up as he can if it be in consequence laid to him that the flat grows salient and the tangled clear, the common—worst of all!—even amusingly rare, by passing through his hands. Just so when you ask who in the world I had in mind for a victim, and what in the world for a treasure, so sacrificed to the advertisement not even of their own merits but of all sorts of independent, of really indifferent, exhibitory egotism, as the practically harried and hunted Neil Paraday and his borrowed, brandished and then fatally mislaid manuscript, I 'm equally confident of having again and again closely noted in the social air all the elements of such a drama. I 've put these elements together— that was my business, and in doing this wished of course to give them their maximum sense, which depended, for irony, for comedy, for tragedy, in other words for beauty, on the 'importance' of the poor foredoomed monarch of the jungle. And then, I 'm not ashamed to allow, it was *amusing* to make these people 'great,' so far as one could do so without making them intrinsically false. (Yes—for the mere accidental and relative falsity I don't care.) It was amusing because it was more difficult—from the moment, of course I mean, that one worked out at all their greatness; from the moment one did n't simply give it to be taken on trust. Working out economically almost anything is the very life of the art of representation; just as the request to take on trust, tinged with the least extravagance, is the very death of the same. (There may be such a state of mind brought about on the reader's part, I think, as a positive desire to take on trust; but that is only the final fruit of insidious proceedings, operative to a sublime end, on the author's side; and is at any rate a different matter.) As for the all-ingenious 'Figure in the Carpet,' let me perhaps a little pusillanimously conclude, nothing would induce me to come into close quarters with you on the correspondences of this anecdote. Here exactly is a good example for you of the virtue of your taking on trust—when I have artfully begotten in you a disposition. All I can at this point say is that if ever I was aware of ground and matter for a significant fable, I was aware of them in that connexion."

My plea for "correspondences" will perhaps, however, after all, but bring my reader back to my having, at the outset of these remarks, owned to full unconsciousness of seed dropped here by that quick hand of occasion that had elsewhere generally operated; which comes to saying, no doubt, that in the world of letters things don't at this time of day very strikingly happen. Suggestive and illuminating incident is indeed scarce frequent enough to be referred to as administering the shake that starts up afresh the stopped watch of attention. I should n't therefore probably have accumulated these illustrations without the sense of something interchangeable, or perhaps even almost indistinguishable, between my own general adventure and the more or less lively illustration into which I was to find this experiment so repeatedly flower. Let it pass that if I am so oddly unable to say here, at any point, " what gave me my idea," I must just a trifle freely have helped myself to it from hidden stores. But, burdened thus with the imputation of that irregularity, I shall give a poor account of my homogeneous group without the charity of a glance, however brief, at its successive components. However I might have been introduced in fact to Henry St. George, of "The Lesson of the Master," or however I might have been deprived of him, my complete possession of him, my active sympathy with him as a known and understood and admired and pitied, in fine as a fully measured, quantity, hangs about the pages still as a vague scent hangs about thick orchard trees. The great sign of a grasped warrant—for identification, arrest or whatever—is, after all, in the confidence that dissipates vagueness; and the logic of such developed situations as those of the pair commemorated at the head of my list imposed itself all triumphantly. Had n't one again and again caught "society" in the very fact of not caring in the least what might become of the subject, however essentially fine and fragile, of a patronage reflecting such credit on all concerned, so long as the social game might be played a little more intensely, and if possible more irrelevantly, by this unfortunate's aid? Given the Lion, his "death" was but too conceivably the issue of the cruel exposure thus involved for him; and if it be claimed by what I can but feel rather a pedantic view that so precious an animal exactly *could n't*, in our conditions, have been "given," I must reply that I yet had met him—though in a preserve not perhaps known in all its extent to geographers.

Of such a fantasy as "The Next Time" the principle would surely soon turn up among the consulted notes of any sincere man of letters—taking literature, that is, on the side of the money to be earned by it. There are beautiful talents the exercise of which yet is n't lucrative, and there are pressing needs the satisfaction of which may well appear difficult under stress of that failure of felicity. Just so there are other talents that leave any fine appreciation mystified and gaping, and the active play of which may yet be observed to become on occasion a source of vast pecuniary profit. Nothing then is at moments more attaching, in the light of "comparative" science, than the study of just where and when, just how and why recognition denies itself to the appeal at all artfully, and responds largely to the appeal coarsely enough, commingled. The critical spirit—with leisure indeed to spare—may well, in its restlessness, seek to fix a bit exactly the point at which a beautiful talent, as I have called it, ceases, when imperilled by an empty pocket, to be a "worldly" advantage. The case in which impunity, for the *malheureux* ridden by that questionable boon, insists on breaking down would seem thus to become susceptible of much fine measurement. I don't know, I confess, that it proveably is; but the critical spirit at all afraid of so slight a misadventure as a waste of curiosity is of course deplorably false to its nature. The difficulty here, in truth, is that, from the moment a straight dependence on the broad-backed public is a part of the issue, the explicative quantity to be sought is precisely the mood of that monster—which, consistently and consummately unable to give the smallest account of itself, naturally renders no grain of help to enquiry. Such a study as that of Ray Limbert's so prolonged, so intensified, but so vain continuance in hope (hope of successfully growing in his temperate garden some specimen of the rank exotic whose leaves are rustling cheques) is in essence a "story about the public," only wearing a little the reduced face by reason of the too huge scale, for direct portrayal, of the monstrous countenance itself. Herein resides, as I have hinted, the anxious and easy interest of almost any sincere man of letters in the mere vicinage, even if that be all, of such strained situations as Ray Limbert's. They speak of the public, such situations, to whoever it may concern. They at all events had from far back insidiously beset the imagination of the author of "The Next Time," who can scarce remember the day when he was n't all sympathetically, all tenderly occupied with some presumed literary watcher—and quite of a sublime constitution—for that postponed redress. Therefore in however developed a state the image in question was at last to hover before him, some form of it had at least never been far to seek.

I to *this* extent recover the acute impression that may have given birth to "The Figure in the Carpet," that no truce, in English-speaking air, had ever seemed to me really struck, or even approximately strikeable, with our so marked collective mistrust of anything like close or analytic appreciation—appreciation, to *be* appreciation, implying of course some such rudimentary zeal; and this though that fine process be the Beautiful Gate itself of enjoyment. To have become consistently aware of this odd numbness of the general sensibility, which seemed ever to condemn it, in presence of a work of art, to a view scarce of half the intentions embodied, and moreover but to the scantest measure of these, was to have been directed from an early day to some of the possible implications of the matter, and so to have been led on by seductive steps, albeit perhaps by devious ways, to such a congruous and, as I would fain call it, fascinating case as that of Hugh Vereker and his undiscovered, not to say undiscoverable, secret. That strikes me, when all is said, as an ample indication of the starting-point of this particular portrayal. There may be links missing between the chronic consciousness I have glanced at—that of Hugh Vereker's own analytic projector, speaking through the mouth of the anonymous scribe—and the poor man's attributive dependence, for the sense of being understood and enjoyed, on some responsive reach of critical perception that he is destined never to waylay with success; but even so they scarce signify, and I may not here attempt to catch them. This too in spite of the amusement almost always yielded by such recoveries and reminiscences, or to be gathered from the manipulation of any string of evolutionary pearls. What I most remember of my proper process is the lively impulse, at the root of it, to reinstate analytic appreciation, by some ironic or fantastic stroke, so far as possible, in its virtually forfeited rights and dignities. Importunate to this end had I long found the charming idea of some artist whose most characteristic intention, or cluster of intentions, should have taken all vainly for granted the public, or at the worst the not unthinkable private, exercise of penetration. I could n't, I confess, be indifferent to those rare and beautiful, or at all events odd and attaching, elements that might be imagined to grow in the shade of so much spent intensity and so much baffled calculation. The mere quality and play of an ironic consciousness in the designer left wholly alone, amid a chattering unperceiving world, with the thing he has most wanted to do, with the design more or less realised—some effectual glimpse of that might by itself, for instance, reward one's experiment. I came to Hugh Vereker, in fine, by this travelled road of a generalisation; the habit of having noted for many years how strangely and helplessly, among us all, what we call criticism—its curiosity never emerging from the limp state—is apt to stand off from the intended sense of things, from such finely-attested matters, on the artist's part, as a spirit and a form, a bias and a logic, of his own. From my definite preliminary it was no far cry to the conception of an intent worker who should find himself to the very end in presence but of the limp curiosity. Vereker's drama indeed—or I should perhaps rather say that of the aspiring young analyst whose report we read and to whom, I ruefully grant, I have ventured to impute a developed wit— is that at a given moment the limpness begins vaguely to throb and heave, to become conscious of a comparative tension. As an effect of this mild convulsion acuteness, at several points, struggles to enter the field, and the question that accordingly comes up, the issue of the affair, can be but whether the very secret of perception has n't been lost. That is the situation, and "The Figure in the Carpet" exhibits a small group of well-meaning persons engaged in a test. The reader is, on the evidence, left to conclude.

The subject of "The Coxon Fund," published in *The Yellow Book* in 1894, had long been with me, but was, beyond doubt, to have found its interest clinched by my perusal, shortly before the above date, of Mr. J. Dyke Campbell's admirable monograph on S. T. Coleridge. The wondrous figure of that genius had long haunted me, and circumstances into which I need n't here enter had within a few years contributed much to making it vivid. Yet it 's none the less true that the Frank Saltram of "The Coxon Fund" pretends to be of his great suggester no more than a dim reflexion and above all a free rearrangement. More interesting still than the man—for the dramatist at any rate—is the S. T. Coleridge *type*; so what I was to do was merely to recognise the type, to borrow it, to re-embody and freshly place it; an ideal under the law of which I could but cultivate a free hand. I proceeded to do so; I reconstructed the scene and the figures—I had my own idea, which required, to express itself, a new set of relations—though, when all this is said, it had assuredly taken the recorded, transmitted person, the image embalmed in literary history, to fertilise my fancy. What I should, for that matter, like most to go into here, space serving, is the so interesting question—for the most part, it strikes me, too confusedly treated—of the story-teller's "real person" or actual contemporary transplanted and exhibited. But this pursuit would take us far, such radical revision do the common laxities of the case, as generally handled, seem to call for. No such process is *effectively* possible, we must hold, as the imputed act of transplanting; an act essentially not mechanical, but thinkable rather—so far as thinkable at all—in chemical, almost in mystical terms. We can surely account for nothing in the novelist's work that has n't passed through the crucible of his imagination, has n't, in that perpetually simmering cauldron his intellectual *pot-au-feu*, been reduced to savoury fusion. We here figure the morsel, of course, not as boiled to nothing, but as exposed, in return for the taste it gives out, to a new and richer saturation. In this state it is in due course picked out and served, and a meagre esteem will await, a poor importance attend it, if it does n't speak most of its late genial medium, the good, the wonderful company it has, as I hint, æsthetically kept. It has entered, in fine, into new relations, it emerges for new ones. Its final savour has been constituted, but its prime identity destroyed—which is what was to be demonstrated. Thus it has become a different and, thanks to a rare alchemy, a better thing. Therefore let us have here as little as possible about its "being" Mr. This or Mrs. That. If it adjusts itself with the least truth to its new life it can't possibly be either. If it gracelessly refers itself to either, if it persists as the impression not artistically dealt with, it shames the honour offered it and can only be spoken of as having ceased to be a thing of fact and yet not become a thing of truth. I am tempted to add that this recommemorative strain might easily woo me to another light step or two roundabout "The Coxon Fund." For I find myself look at it most interestedly to-day, after all, in the light of a significance quite other than that just noted. A marked example of the possible scope, at once, and the possible neatness of the *nouvelle*, it takes its place for me in a series of which the main merit and sign is the effort to do the complicated thing with a strong brevity and lucidity—to arrive, on behalf of the multiplicity, at a certain science of control. Infinitely attractive—though I risk here again doubtless an effect of reiteration—the question of how to exert this control in accepted conditions and how yet to sacrifice no real value; problem ever dearest to any economic soul desirous to keep renewing, and with a frugal splendour, its ideal of economy. Sacred altogether to memory, in short, such labours and such lights. Thus "The Coxon Fund" is such a complicated thing that if it still seems to carry itself—by which I mean if its clearness still rules here, or still serves—some pursued question of how the trick was played would probably not be thankless.

*The Author of Beltraffio, The Middle Years, Greville
Fane, Broken Wings, The Tree of Knowledge, The
Abasement of the Northmores, The Great Good Place,
Four Meetings, Paste, Europe, Miss Gunton of
Poughkeepsie, Fordham Castle*

WHAT I HAD lately and most particularly to say of "The
Coxon Fund" is no less true of "The Middle Years,"
first published in *Scribner's Magazine* (1893)—that recollection
mainly and most promptly associates with it the number of
times I had to do it over to make sure of it. To get it right
was to squeeze my subject into the five or six thousand words
I had been invited to make it consist of—it consists, in fact,
should the curious care to know, of some 5550—and I scarce
perhaps recall another case, with the exception I shall presently name, in which my struggle to keep compression rich,
if not, better still, to keep accretions compressed, betrayed for
me such community with the anxious effort of some warden
of the insane engaged at a critical moment in making fast a
victim's straitjacket. The form of "The Middle Years" is not
that of the *nouvelle*, but that of the concise anecdote; whereas
the subject treated would perhaps seem one comparatively demanding "developments"—if indeed, amid these mysteries,
distinctions were so absolute. (There is of course neither close
nor fixed measure of the reach of a development, which in
some connexions seems almost superfluous and then in others
to represent the whole sense of the matter; and we should
doubtless speak more thoroughly by book had we some secret
for exactly tracing deflexions and returns.) However this may
be, it was as an anecdote, an anecdote only, that I was determined my little situation here should figure; to which end my
effort was of course to follow it as much as possible from its
outer edge in, rather than from its centre outward. That fond
formula, I had alas already discovered, may set as many traps
in the garden as its opposite may set in the wood; so that
after boilings and reboilings of the contents of my small
cauldron, after added pounds of salutary sugar, as numerous
as those prescribed in the choicest recipe for the thickest jam,
I well remember finding the whole process and act (which, to

the exclusion of everything else, dragged itself out for a month) one of the most expensive of its sort in which I had ever engaged.

But I recall, by good luck, no less vividly how much finer a sweetness than any mere spooned-out saccharine dwelt in the fascination of the questions involved. Treating a theme that "gave" much in a form that, at the best, would give little, might indeed represent a peck of troubles; yet who, none the less, beforehand, was to pronounce with authority such and such an idea anecdotic and such and such another developmental? One had, for the vanity of *a priori* wisdom here, only to be so constituted that to see any form of beauty, for a particular application, proscribed or even questioned, was forthwith to covet that form more than any other and to desire the benefit of it exactly there. One had only to be reminded that for the effect of quick roundness the small smooth situation, though as intense as one will, is prudently indicated, and that for a fine complicated entangled air nothing will serve that does n't naturally swell and bristle—one had only, I say, to be so warned off or warned on, to see forthwith no beauty for the simple thing that should n't, and even to perversity, enrich it, and none for the other, the comparatively intricate, that should n't press it out as a mosaic. After which fashion the careful craftsman would have prepared himself the special inviting treat of scarce being able to say, at his highest infatuation, before any series, which might be the light thing weighted and which the dense thing clarified. The very attempt so to discriminate leaves him in fact at moments even a little ashamed; whereby let him shirk here frankly certain of the issues presented by the remainder of our company—there being, independently of these mystic matters, other remarks to make. Blankness overtakes me, I confess, in connexion with the brief but concentrated "Greville Fane"—*that* emerges, how concentrated I tried to make it— which must have appeared in a London weekly journal at the beginning of the "nineties"; but as to which I further retain only a dim warm pleasantness as of old Kensington summer hours. I re-read, ever so kindly, to the promotion of a mild aftertaste—that of a certain feverish pressure, in a cool north room resorted to in heavy London Augusts, with stray, rare echoes of the town, beyond near roofs and chimneys, making harmless detonations, and with the perception, over my page, as I felt poor Greville grow, that her scant record, to be anything at all, would have to be a minor miracle of foreshortening. For here is exactly an illustrative case: the subject, in this little composition, is "developmental" enough, while the form has to make the anecdotic concession; and yet who shall say that for the right effect of a small harmony the fusion has failed? We desire doubtless a more detailed notation of the behaviour of the son and daughter, and yet had I believed the right effect missed "Greville Fane" would n't have figured here.

Nothing, by the same stroke, could well have been condemned to struggle more for that harmony than "The Abasement of the Northmores" and "The Tree of Knowledge": the idea in these examples (1900) being developmental with a vengeance and the need of an apparent ease and a general congruity having to enforce none the less—as on behalf of some victim of the income-tax who would minimise his "return"—an almost heroic dissimulation of capital. These things, especially the former, are novels intensely compressed, and with that character in them yet keeping at bay, under stress of their failing else to be good short stories, any air of mutilation. They had had to be good short stories in order to earn, however precariously, their possible wage and "appear"—so certain was it that there would be no appearance, and consequently no wage, for them as frank and brave *nouvelles*. They could but conceal the fact that they *were* "nouvelles"; they could but masquerade as little anecdotes. I include them here by reason of that successful, that achieved and consummate—as it strikes me—duplicity: which, however, I may add, was in the event to avail them little—since they were to find nowhere, the unfortunates, hospitality and the reward of their effort. It is to "The Tree of Knowledge" I referred just above, I may further mention, as the production that had cost me, for keeping it "down," even a greater number of full revolutions of the merciless screw than "The Middle Years." On behalf also of this member of the group, as well as for "The Author of Beltraffio," I recover exceptionally the sense of the grain of suggestion, the tiny air-blown particle. In presence of a small interesting example of a young artist long dead, and whom I had yet briefly seen and was to remember with kindness, a friend had made, thanks to a still greater personal knowledge of him and of his quasi-conspicuous father, likewise an artist, one of those brief remarks that the dramatist feels as fertilising. "And then," the lady I quote had said in allusion to certain troubled first steps of the young man's career, to complications of consciousness that had made his early death perhaps less strange and less lamentable, even though superficially more tragic; "and then he had found his father out, artistically: having grown up in so happy a personal relation with him only to feel, at last, quite awfully, that he did n't and could n't believe in him." That fell on one's ear of course only to prompt the inward cry: "How can there possibly *not* be all sorts of good things in it?" Just so for "The Author of Beltraffio"—long before this and some time before the first appearance of the tale in *The English Illustrated Magazine* (1884): it had been said to me of an eminent author, these several years dead and on some of the embarrassments of whose life and character a common friend was enlarging: "Add to them all, moreover, that his wife objects intensely to what he writes. She can't bear it (as you can for that matter rather easily conceive) and that naturally creates a tension—!" *There* had come the air-blown grain which, lodged in a handful of kindly earth, was to produce the story of Mark Ambient.

Elliptic, I allow, and much of a skipping of stages, so bare an account of such performances; yet with the constitutive process for each idea quite sufficiently noted by my having had, always, only to say to myself sharply enough: "Dramatise it, dramatise it!" That answered, in the connexion, always, all my questions—that provided for all my "fun." The two tales I have named but represent therefore their respective grains of seed dramatically handled. In the case of "Broken Wings" (1900), however, I but see to-day the produced result—I fail to disinter again the buried germ. Little matters it, no doubt, that I recall as operative here the brush of no winged word; for when had I been, as a fellow scribbler, closed to the general admonition of such adventures as poor Mrs. Harvey's, the elegant representative of literature at Mundham?—to such predicaments as Stuart Straith's, gallant victim of the same hospitality and with the same confirmed ache beneath his white waistcoat? The appeal of mature purveyors obliged, in the very interest of their presumed, their marketable, freshness, to dissimulate the grim realities of shrunken "custom," the felt chill of a lower professional temperature—any old note-book would show *that* laid away as a tragic "value" not much less tenderly than some small plucked flower of association left between the leaves for pressing. What had happened here, visibly, was that the value had had to wait long to become active. "Dramatise, dramatise, dramatise!" had been just there more of an easy admonition than of a ready feat; the case for dramatisation was somehow not whole. Under some forgotten touch, however, at its right hour, it was to round itself. What the single situation lacked the *pair* of situations would supply—there was drama enough, with economy, from the moment sad companions, looking each other, with their identities of pluck and despair, a little hard in the face, should confess each to the other, relievingly, what they kept from every one else. With the right encounter and the right surprise, that is with the right persons, postulated, the relief, if in the right degree exquisite, might be the drama— and the right persons, in fine, to make it exquisite, were Stuart Straith and Mrs. Harvey. There remains "The Great Good Place" (1900)—to the spirit of which, however, it strikes me, any gloss or comment would be a tactless challenge. It embodies a calculated effect, and to plunge into it, I find, even for a beguiled glance—a course I indeed recommend—is to have left all else outside. There then my indications must wait.

The origin of "Paste" is rather more expressible, since it was to consist but of the ingenious thought of transposing the terms of one of Guy de Maupassant's admirable *contes*. In "La Parure" a poor young woman, under "social" stress, the need of making an appearance on an important occasion, borrows from an old school friend, now much richer than herself, a pearl necklace which she has the appalling misfortune to lose by some mischance never afterwards cleared up. Her life and her pride, as well as her husband's with them, become subject, from the hour of the awful accident, to the redemption of their debt; which, effort by effort, sacrifice by sacrifice, franc by franc, with specious pretexts, excuses, a rage of desperate explanation of their failure to restore the missing object, they finally obliterate—all to find that their whole consciousness and life have been convulsed and deformed in vain, that the pearls were but highly artful "imitation" and that their passionate penance has ruined them for nothing. It seemed harmless sport simply to turn that situation round—to shift, in other words, the ground of the horrid mistake, making this a matter not of a false treasure supposed to be true and precious, but of a real treasure supposed to be false and hollow: though a new little "drama," a new setting for *my* pearls— and as different as possible from the other—had of course withal to be found.

"Europe," which is of 1899, when it appeared in *Scribner's Magazine*, conspicuously fails, on the other hand, to disown its parentage; so distinct has its "genesis" remained to me. I had preserved for long years an impression of an early time, a visit, in a sedate American city—for there *were* such cities then—to an ancient lady whose talk, whose allusions and relics and spoils and mementoes and credentials, so to call them, bore upon a triumphant sojourn in Europe, long years before, in the hey-day of the high scholarly reputation of her husband, a dim displaced superseded celebrity at the time of my own observation. They had been "much made of," he and she, at various foreign centres of polite learning, and above all in the England of early Victorian days; and my hostess had lived ever since on the name and fame of it; a treasure of legend and anecdote laid up against the comparatively lean half-century, or whatever, that was to follow. For myself even, after this, a good slice of such a period had elapsed; yet with my continuing to believe that fond memory would still somehow be justified of this scrap too, along with so many others: the unextinguished sense of the temperature of the January morning on which the little Sunday breakfast-party, at half-past nine across the snow, had met to the music of a chilly ghostly kindly tinkle; that of the roomful of cherished echoes and of framed and glazed, presented and autographed and thumb-marked mementoes—the wealth of which was somehow explained (this was part of the legend) by the ancient, the at last almost prehistoric, glory of like matutinal hours, type and model of the emulous shrunken actual.

The justification I awaited, however, only came much later, on my catching some tender mention of certain admirable ladies, sisters and spinsters under the maternal roof, for whom the century was ebbing without remedy brought to their eminent misfortune (such a ground of sympathy always in the "good old" American days when the touching case was still possible) of not having "been to Europe." Exceptionally prepared by culture for going, they yet could n't leave their immemorial mother, the headspring, precisely, of that grace in them, who on the occasion of each proposed start announced her approaching end—only to postpone it again after the plan was dished and the flight relinquished. So the century ebbed, and so Europe altered—for the worse—and so perhaps even a little did the sisters who sat in bondage; only so did n't at all the immemorial, the inextinguishable, the eternal mother. Striking to the last degree, I thought, that obscure, or at least that muffled, tragedy, which had the further interest of giving me on the spot a setting for my own so long uninserted gem and of enabling me to bring out with maximum confidence my inveterate "Dramatise!" "Make this *one* with such projection as you are free to permit yourself of the brooding parent in the other case," I duly remarked, "and the whole thing falls together; the paradise the good sisters are apparently never to attain becoming by this conversion just the social cake on which they have always been fed and that has so notoriously opened their appetite." Or something of that sort. I recognise that I so but express here the "plot" of my tale as it stands; except for so far as my formula, "something of that sort," was to make the case bristle with as many vivid values, with as thick and yet as clear a little complexity of interest, as possible. The merit of the thing is in the feat, once more, of the transfusion; the receptacle (of form) being so exiguous, the brevity imposed so great. I undertook the brevity, so often undertaken on a like scale before, and again arrived at it by the innumerable repeated chemical reductions and condensations that tend to make of the very short story, as I risk again noting, one of the costliest, even if, like the hard, shining sonnet, one of the most indestructible, forms of composition in general use. I accepted the rigour of its having, all sternly, in this case, to treat so many of its most appealing values as waste; and I now seek my comfort perforce in the mere exhibited result, the union of whatever fulness with whatever clearness.

The Altar of the Dead, The Beast in the Jungle,
The Birthplace, The Private Life, Owen Wingrave,
The Friends of the Friends, Sir Edmund Orme,
The Real Right Thing, The Jolly Corner, Julia Bride

"THE ALTAR OF THE DEAD" forms part of a volume bearing the title of "Terminations," which appeared in 1895. Figuring last in that collection of short pieces, it here stands at the head of my list, not as prevailing over its companions by length, but as being ample enough and of an earlier date than several. I have to add that with this fact of its temporal order, and the fact that, as I remember, it had vainly been "hawked about," knocking, in the world of magazines, at half a dozen editorial doors impenetrably closed to it, I shall have exhausted my fund of allusion to the influences attending its birth. I consult memory further to no effect; so that if I should seem to have lost every trace of "how I came to think" of such a motive, did n't I, by a longer reach of reflexion, help myself back to the state of not having *had* to think of it? The idea embodied in this composition must in other words never have been so absent from my view as to call for an organised search. It was "there" — it had always, or from ever so far back, been there, not interfering with other conceits, yet at the same time not interfered with; and it naturally found expression at the first hour something more urgently undertaken happened not to stop the way. The way here, I recognise, would ever have been easy to stop, for the general patience, the inherent waiting faculty, of the principle of interest involved, was conscious of no strain, and above all of no loss, in amusedly biding its time. Other conceits might indeed come and go, born of light impressions and passing hours, for what sort of free intelligence would it be that, addressed to the human scene, should propose to itself, all vulgarly, never to be waylaid or arrested, never effectively inspired, by some imaged appeal of the lost Dead? The subject of my story is obviously, and quite as usual, the exhibition of a case; the case being that of an accepted, a cultivated habit (the cultivation is really the point) of regularly taking thought for them. Frankly, I can but gather, the desire, at last of the acutest, to give an example and represent an instance of some such practised communion, was a foredoomed consequence of life, year after year, amid the densest and most materialised aggregation of men upon earth, the society most wedded by all its conditions to the immediate and the finite. More exactly speaking, it was impossible for any critic or "creator" at all worth his wage not, as a matter of course, again and again to ask himself what may not become of individual sensibility, of the faculty and the fibre itself, when everything makes against the indulgence of it save as a conscious, and indeed highly emphasised, dead loss.

The impression went back for its full intensity, no doubt, neither to a definite moment nor to a particular shock; but the author of the tale before us was long to cherish the memory of a pair of illuminating incidents that, happily for him— by which I mean happily for the generalisation he here makes—placed themselves, at no great distance apart, so late in a sustained experience of London as to find him profitably prepared for them, and yet early enough to let confirmatory matter gather in abundance round. Not to this day, in fine, has he forgotten the hard, handsome, gentlemanly face, as it was expressionally affected in a particular conjunction, of a personage occasionally met in other years at one of the friend-liest, the most liberal of "entertaining" houses and then lost to sight till after a long interval. The end of all mortal things had, during this period, and in the fulness of time, overtaken our delightful hosts and the scene of their long hospitality, a scene of constant welcome to my personage, as I have called him (a police-magistrate then seated, by reason of his office, well in the eye of London, but as conspicuous for his private urbanity as for his high magisterial and penal mask). He too has now passed away, but what could exactly better attest the power of prized survival in personal signs than my even yet felt chill as I saw the old penal glare rekindled in him by the form of my aid to his memory. "We used sometimes to meet, in the old days, at the dear So-and-So's, you may recall." "The So-and-So's?" said the awful gentleman, who appeared to recognise the name, across the table, only to be shocked at the allusion. "Why, they 're Dead, sir—dead these many years." "Indeed they are, sir, alas," I could but reply with spirit; "and it's precisely why I like so to speak of them!—Il ne manquerait plus que cela, that because they're dead I should n't!" is what I came within an ace of adding; or rather *might* have come had n't I felt my indecency too utterly put in its place. I was left with it in fact on my hands—where however I was quite everlastingly, as you see, to cherish it. My anecdote is mild and its companion perhaps milder; but impressions come as they can and stay as they will.

A distinguished old friend, a very eminent lady and highly marked character, though technically, as it were, a private person, unencompassed by literary luggage or other monumental matter, had dropped from the rank at a great age and, as I was to note after a sufficient interval, to my surprise, with a singularly uncommemorated and unchronicled effect: given, I mean, her social and historical value. One blushed, as the days passed, for the want of manners in it—there being twenty reasons in the case why manners should have been remembered. A friend of the interesting woman, thereupon, seeing his opportunity, asked leave of an acquaintance of his own, the conductor of a "high class" periodical, to intervene on behalf of her memory in the pages under the latter's control. The amiable editor so far yielded to a first good impulse as to welcome the proposal; but the proposer was disconcerted to receive on the morrow a colder retractation. "I really don't see why I should publish an article about Mrs. X *because—* and because *only*, so far as I can make out—she's dead." Again I felt the inhibition, as the psychologists say, that I had felt in the other case; the vanity, *in the conditions*, of any yearning plea that this was the most beautiful of reasons. Clearly the conditions were against its being for an effective moment felt as such; and the article in question never appeared—nor, to the best of my knowledge, anything else of the sort: which fact was to take its place among other grim values. These pointed, as they all too largely accumulated, to the general black truth that London was a terrible place to die in; doubtless not so much moreover by conscious cruelty or perversity as under the awful doom of general dishumanisation. It takes space to feel, it takes time to know, and great organisms as well as small have to pause, more or less, to possess themselves and to be aware. Monstrous masses are, by this truth, so impervious to vibration that the sharpest forces of feeling, locally applied, no more penetrate than a pin or a paper-cutter penetrates an elephant's hide. Thus the very tradition of sensibility would perish if left only to their care. It has here and there to be rescued, to be saved by independent, intelligent zeal; which type of effort however, to avail, has to fly in the face of the conditions.

These are easily, one is obliged to add, too many for it; nothing being more visible for instance than that the life of inordinately numerous companies is hostile to friendship and intimacy—unless indeed it be the impropriety of such names applied to the actual terms of intercourse. The sense of the state of the dead is but part of the sense of the state of the living; and, congruously with that, life is cheated to almost the same degree of the finest homage (precisely this our possible friendships and intimacies) that we fain would render it. We clutch indeed at some shadow of these things, we stay our yearning with snatches and stop-gaps; but our struggle yields to the other arrayed things that defeat the *cultivation*, in such an air, of the finer flowers—creatures of cultivation as the finer flowers essentially are. We perforce fall back, for the application of that process, on the coarser—which form together the rank and showy bloom of "success," of multiplied contact and multiplied motion; the bloom of a myriad many-coloured "relations"—amid which the precious plant that is rare at the best becomes rare indeed. "The Altar of the Dead" then commemorates a case of what I have called the individual independent effort to keep it none the less tended and watered, to cultivate it, as I say, with an exasperated piety. I am not however here reconstituting my more or less vivid fable, but simply glancing at the natural growth of its prime idea, that of an invoked, a restorative reaction against certain general brutalities. Brutal, more and more, to wondering eyes, the great fact that the poor dead, all about one, were nowhere so dead as there; where to be caught in any rueful glance at them was to be branded at once as "morbid." "Mourir, à Londres, c'est être bien mort!"—I have not forgotten the ironic emphasis of a distinguished foreign friend, for some years officially resident in England, as we happened once to watch together a funeral-train, on its way to Kensal

Green or wherever, bound merrily by. That truth, to any man of memories, was too repeatedly and intolerably driven home, and the situation of my depicted George Stransom is that of the poor gentleman who simply at last could n't "stand" it.

To desire, amid these collocations, to place, so far as possible, like with like, was to invite "The Beast in the Jungle" to stand here next in order. As to the accidental determinant of which composition, once more—of comparatively recent date and destined, like its predecessor, first to see the light in a volume of miscellanies ("The Better Sort," 1903)—I remount the stream of time, all enquiringly, but to come back empty-handed. The subject of this elaborated fantasy—which, I must add, I hold a successful thing only as its motive may seem to the reader to stand out sharp—can't quite have belonged to the immemorial company of such solicitations; though in spite of this I meet it, in ten lines of an old note-book, but as a recorded conceit and an accomplished fact. Another poor sensitive gentleman, fit indeed to mate with Stransom of "The Altar"—my attested predilection for poor sensitive gentlemen almost embarrasses me as I march!—was to have been, after a strange fashion and from the threshold of his career, condemned to keep counting with the unreasoned prevision of some extraordinary fate; the conviction, lodged in his brain, part and parcel of his imagination from far back, that experience would be marked for him, and whether for good or for ill, by some rare distinction, some incalculable violence or unprecedented stroke. So I seemed to see him start in life—under the so mixed star of the extreme of apprehension and the extreme of confidence; all to the logical, the quite inevitable effect of the complication aforesaid: his having to wait and wait for the right recognition; none of the mere usual and normal human adventures, whether delights or disconcertments, appearing to conform to the great type of his fortune. So it is that he 's depicted. No gathering appearance, no descried or interpreted promise or portent, affects his superstitious soul either as a damnation deep enough (if damnation be in question) for his appointed *quality* of consciousness, or as a translation into bliss sublime enough (on *that* hypothesis) to fill, in vulgar parlance, the bill. Therefore as each item of experience comes, with its possibilities, into view, he can but dismiss it under this sterilising habit of the failure to find it good enough and thence to appropriate it.

His one desire remains of course to meet his fate, or at least to divine it, to see it as intelligible, to learn it, in a word; but none of its harbingers, pretended or supposed, speak his ear in the true voice; they wait their moment at his door only to pass on unheeded, and the years ebb while he holds his breath and stays his hand and—from the dread not less of imputed pride than of imputed pusillanimity—stifles his distinguished secret. He perforce lets everything go—leaving all the while his general presumption disguised and his general abstention unexplained; since he 's ridden by the idea of what things may lead to, since they mostly always lead to human communities, wider or intenser, of experience, and since, above all, in his uncertainty, he must n't compromise others. Like the blinded seeker in the old-fashioned game he "burns," on occasion, as with the sense of the hidden thing near—only to deviate again however into the chill; the chill that indeed settles on him as the striking of his hour is deferred. His career thus resolves itself into a great negative adventure, my report of which presents, for its centre, the fine case that has caused him most tormentedly to "burn," and then most unprofitably to stray. He is afraid to recognise what he incidentally misses, since what his high belief amounts to is not that he shall have felt and vibrated less than any one else, but that he shall have felt and vibrated more; which no acknowledgement of the minor loss must conflict with. Such a course of existence naturally involves a climax—the final flash of the light under which he reads his lifelong riddle and sees his conviction proved. He has indeed been marked and indeed suffered his fortune—which is precisely to have been the man in the world to whom nothing whatever was to happen. My picture leaves him overwhelmed—at last he has understood; though in thus disengaging my treated theme for the reader's benefit I seem to acknowledge that this more detached witness may not successfully have done so. I certainly grant that any felt merit in the thing must all depend on the clearness and charm with which the subject just noted expresses itself.

If "The Birthplace" deals with another poor gentleman—

of interest as being yet again too fine for his rough fate—
here at least I can claim to have gone by book, here once
more I lay my hand, for my warrant, on the clue of actuality.
It was one of the cases in which I was to say at the first brush
of the hint: "How can there possibly *not* be innumerable
things in it?" "It" was the mentioned adventure of a good
intelligent man rather recently appointed to the care of a great
place of pilgrimage, a shrine sacred to the piety and curiosity
of the whole English-speaking race, and haunted by other
persons as well; who, coming to his office with infinite zest,
had after a while desperately thrown it up—as a climax to his
struggle, some time prolonged, with "the awful nonsense he
found himself expected and paid, and thence quite obliged,
to talk." It was in these simple terms his predicament was
named to me—not that I would have had a word more, not
indeed that I had n't at once to turn my back for very joy of
the suppressed details: so unmistakeably, on the spot, was a
splendid case all there, so complete, in fine, as it stood, was
the appeal to fond fancy; an appeal the more direct, I may
add, by reason, as happened, of an acquaintance, lately much
confirmed, on my own part, with the particular temple of our
poor gentleman's priesthood. It struck me, at any rate, that
here, if ever, was the perfect theme of a *nouvelle*—and to
some such composition I addressed myself with a confidence
unchilled by the certainty that it would nowhere, at the best
(a prevision not falsified) find "acceptance." For the rest I
must but leave "The Birthplace" to plead its own cause; only
adding that here afresh and in the highest degree were the
conditions reproduced for that mystic, that "chemical" change
wrought in the impression of life by its dedication to an
æsthetic use, that I lately spoke of in connexion with "The
Coxon Fund." Beautiful on all this ground exactly, to the
projector's mind, the process by which the small cluster of
actualities latent in the fact reported to him was to be
reconstituted and, so far as they might need, altered; the felt
fermentation, ever interesting, but flagrantly so in the example before us, that enables the sense originally communicated
to make fresh and possibly quite different terms for the new
employment there awaiting it. It has been liberated (to repeat,
I believe, my figure) after the fashion of some sound young

draught-horse who may, in the great meadow, have to be re-captured and re-broken for the saddle.

I proceed almost eagerly, in any case, to "The Private Life"—and at the cost of reaching for a moment over "The Jolly Corner": I find myself so fondly return to ground on which the history even of small experiments may be more or less written. This mild documentation fairly thickens for me, I confess, the air of the first-mentioned of these tales; the scraps of records flit through that medium, to memory, as with the incalculable brush of wings of the imprisoned bat at eventide. This piece of ingenuity rests for me on such a hand-ful of acute impressions as I may not here tell over at once; so that, to be brief, I select two of the sharpest. Neither of these was, in old London days, I make out, to be resisted even under its single pressure; so that the hour struck with a vengeance for "Dramatise it, dramatise it!" (dramatise, that is, the combination) from the first glimpse of a good way to work together two cases that happened to have been given me. They were those—as distinct as possible save for belong-ing alike to the "world," the London world of a time when Discrimination still a little lifted its head—of a highly distin-guished man, constantly to be encountered, whose fortune and whose peculiarity it was to bear out personally as little as possible (at least to *my* wondering sense) the high denote-ments, the rich implications and rare associations, of the ge-nius to which he owed his position and his renown. One may go, naturally, in such a connexion, but by one's own applied measure; and I have never ceased to ask myself, in this partic-ular loud, sound, normal, hearty presence, all so assertive and so whole, all bristling with prompt responses and expected opinions and usual views, radiating all a broad daylight equal-ity of emphasis and impartiality of address (for most rela-tions)—I never ceased, I say, to ask myself what lodgement, on such premises, the rich proud genius one adored could ever have contrived, what domestic commerce the subtlety that was its prime ornament and the world's wonder have enjoyed, under what shelter the obscurity that was its luckless drawback and the world's despair have flourished. The whole aspect and *allure* of the fresh sane man, illustrious and undistinguished—no "sensitive poor gentleman" he!—was mystifying; they made the question of who then had written the immortal things such a puzzle.

So at least one could but take the case—though one's need for relief depended, no doubt, on what one (so to speak) suffered. The writer of these lines, at any rate, suffered so much—I mean of course but by the unanswered question—that light *had* at last to break under pressure of the whimsical theory of two distinct and alternate presences, the assertion of either of which on any occasion directly involved the entire extinction of the other. This explained to the imagination the mystery: our delightful inconceivable celebrity was *double*, constructed in two quite distinct and " water-tight" compartments—one of these figured by the gentleman who sat at a table all alone, silent and unseen, and wrote admirably deep and brave and intricate things; while the gentleman who regularly came forth to sit at a quite different table and substantially and promiscuously and multitudinously dine stood for its companion. They had nothing to do, the so dissimilar twins, with each other; the diner could exist but by the cessation of the writer, whose emergence, on his side, depended on his—and our!—ignoring the diner. Thus it was amusing to think of the real great man as a presence known, in the late London days, all and only to himself—unseen of other human eye and converted into his perfectly positive, but quite secondary, *alter ego* by any approach to a social contact. To the same tune was the social personage known all and only to society, was he conceivable but as "cut dead," on the return home and the threshold of the closed study, by the waiting spirit who would flash at that signal into form and possession. Once I had so seen the case I could n't see it otherwise; and so to see it moreover was inevitably to feel in it a situation and a motive. The ever-importunate murmur, "Dramatise it, dramatise it!" haunted, as I say, one's perception; yet without giving the idea much support till, by the happiest turn, the whole possibility was made to glow.

For did n't there immensely flourish in those very days and exactly in that society the apparition the most qualified to balance with the odd character I have referred to and to supply to "drama," if "drama" there was to be, the precious element of contrast and antithesis?—that most accomplished of artists and most dazzling of men of the world whose effect on the mind repeatedly invited to appraise him was to beget in it an image of representation and figuration so exclusive of any possible inner self that, so far from there being here a question of an *alter ego*, a double personality, there seemed scarce a question of a real and single one, scarce foothold or margin for any private and domestic *ego* at all. Immense in this case too, for any analytic witness, the solicitation of wonder—which struggled all the while, not less amusingly than in the other example, toward the explanatory secret; a clear view of the perpetual, essential performer, consummate, infallible, impeccable, and with his high shining elegance, his intensity of presence, on these lines, involving to the imagination an absolutely blank reverse or starved residuum, no *other* power of presence whatever. One said it under one's breath, one really yearned to know: was he, such an embodiment of skill and taste and tone and composition, of every public gloss and grace, thinkable even as occasionally single?—since to be truly single is to be able, under stress, to be separate, to be *solus*, to know at need the interlunar swoon of *some* independent consciousness. Yes, *had* our dazzling friend any such alternative, could he so unattestedly exist, and was the withdrawn, the sequestered, the unobserved and unhonoured condition so much as imputable to him? Was n't his potentiality of existence public, in fine, to the last squeeze of the golden orange, and when he passed from our admiring sight into the chamber of mystery what, the next minute, was on the other side of the door? It was irresistible to believe at last that there was at such junctures inveterately nothing; and the more so, once I had begun to dramatise, as this supplied the most natural opposition in the world to my fond companion-view—the other side of the door *only* cognisant of the true Robert Browning. One's harmless formula for the poetic employment of this pair of conceits could n't go much further than "Play them against each other"—the ingenuity of which small game "The Private Life" reflects as it can.

I fear I can defend such doings but under the plea of my amusement in them—an amusement I of course hoped others might succeed in sharing. But so comes in exactly the principle under the wide strong wing of which several such matters are here harvested; things of a type that might move me, had I space, to a pleading eloquence. Such compositions as "The Jolly Corner," printed here not for the first time, but printed elsewhere only as I write and after my quite ceasing to expect it; "The Friends of the Friends," to which I here change the colourless title of "The Way It Came" (1896), "Owen Wingrave" (1893), "Sir Edmund Orme" (1891), "The Real Right Thing" (1900), would obviously never have existed but for that love of "a story as a story" which had from far back beset and beguiled their author. To this passion, the vital flame at the heart of any sincere attempt to lay a scene and launch a drama, he flatters himself he has never been false; and he will indeed have done his duty but little by it if he has failed to let it, whether robustly or quite insidiously, fire his fancy and rule his scheme. He has consistently felt it (the appeal to wonder and terror and curiosity and pity and to the delight of fine recognitions, as well as to the joy, perhaps sharper still, of the mystified state) the very source of wise counsel and the very law of charming effect. He has revelled in the creation of alarm and suspense and surprise and relief, in all the arts that practise, with a scruple for nothing but any lapse of application, on the credulous soul of the candid or, immeasurably better, on the seasoned spirit of the cunning, reader. He has built, rejoicingly, on that blest faculty of wonder just named, in the latent eagerness of which the novelist so finds, throughout, his best warrant that he can but pin his faith and attach his car to it, rest in fine his monstrous weight and his queer case on it, as on a strange passion planted in the heart of man for his benefit, a mysterious provision made for him in the scheme of nature. He has seen this particular sensibility, the need and the love of wondering and the quick response to any pretext for it, as the beginning and the end of his affair—thanks to the innumerable ways in which that chord may vibrate. His prime care has been to master those most congruous with his own faculty, to make it vibrate as finely as possible—or in other words to the production of the interest appealing most (by its kind) to himself. This last is of course the particular clear light by which the genius of representation ever best proceeds—with its beauty of adjustment to any strain of attention whatever. Essentially, meanwhile, excited wonder must have a subject, must face in a direction, must be, increasingly, *about* something. Here comes in then the artist's bias and his range—determined, these things, by his own fond inclination. About what, good man, does he himself most wonder?—for upon that, whatever it may be, he will naturally most abound. Under that star will he gather in what he shall most seek to represent; so that if you follow thus his range of representation you will know how, you will see where, again, good man, he for himself most aptly vibrates.

All of which makes a desired point for the little group of compositions here placed together; the point that, since the question has ever been for me but of wondering and, with all achievable adroitness, of causing to wonder, so the whole fairy-tale side of life has used, for its tug at my sensibility, a cord all its own. When we want to wonder there 's no such good ground for it as the wonderful—premising indeed always, by an induction as prompt, that this element can but be at best, to fit its different cases, a thing of appreciation. What is wonderful in one set of conditions may quite fail of its spell in another set; and, for that matter, the peril of the unmeasured strange, in fiction, being the silly, just as its strength, when it saves itself, is the charming, the wind of interest blows where it lists, the surrender of attention persists where it can. The ideal, obviously, on these lines, is the straight fairy-tale, the case that has purged in the crucible all its *bêtises* while keeping all its grace. It may seem odd, in a search for the amusing, to try to steer wide of the silly by hugging close the "supernatural"; but one man's amusement is at the best (we have surely long had to recognise) another's desolation; and I am prepared with the confession that the "ghost-story," as we for convenience call it, has ever been for me the most possible form of the fairy-tale. It enjoys, to my eyes, this honour by being so much the neatest—neat with that neatness without which *representation*, and therewith beauty, drops. One's working of the spell is of course—decently and effectively—but by the represented thing, and the grace of the more or less closely represented state is the measure of any success; a truth by the general smug neglect of which it 's difficult not to be struck. To begin to wonder, over a case, I must begin to believe—to begin to give out (that is to attend) I must begin to take in, and to enjoy *that* profit I must begin to see and hear and feel. This would n't seem, I allow, the general requirement—as appears from the fact that so many persons profess delight in the picture of marvels and prodigies which by any, even the easiest, critical measure *is* no picture; in the recital of wonderful horrific or beatific things that are neither represented nor, so far as one makes out, seen as representable: a weakness not invalidating, round about us, the most resounding appeals to curiosity. The main condition of interest—that of some appreciable rendering of sought effects—is absent from them; so that when, as often happens, one is asked how one "likes" such and such a "story" one can but point responsively to the lack of material for a judgement.

The apprehension at work, we thus see, would be of certain projected conditions, and its first need therefore is that these appearances be constituted in some other and more colourable fashion than by the author's answering for them on his more or less gentlemanly honour. This is n't enough; *give* me your elements, *treat* me your subject, one has to say—I must wait till then to tell you how I like them. I might "rave" about them all were they given and treated; but there is no basis of opinion in such matters without a basis of vision, and no ground for that, in turn, without some communicated closeness of truth. There are portentous situations, there are prodigies and marvels and miracles as to which this communication, whether by necessity or by chance, works comparatively straight—works, by our measure, to some convincing consequence; there are others as to which the report, the picture, the plea, answers no tithe of the questions we would put. Those questions *may* perhaps then, by the very nature of the case, be unanswerable—though often again, no doubt, the felt vice is but in the quality of the provision made for them: on any showing, my own instinct, even in the service of great adventures, is all for the best *terms* of things; all for ground on which touches and tricks may be multiplied, the greatest number of questions answered, the greatest appearance of truth conveyed. With the preference I have noted for the "neat" evocation—the image, of any sort, with fewest attendant vaguenesses and cheapnesses, fewest loose ends dangling and fewest features missing, the image kept in fine the most susceptible of intensity—with this predilection, I say, the safest arena for the play of moving accidents and mighty mutations and strange encounters, or whatever odd matters, is the field, as I may call it, rather of their second than of their first exhibition. By which, to avoid obscurity, I mean nothing more cryptic than I feel myself show them best by showing almost exclusively the way they are felt, by recognising as their main interest some impression strongly made by them and intensely received. We but too probably break down, I have ever reasoned, when we attempt the prodigy, the appeal to mystification, in itself; with its "objective" side too emphasised the report (it is ten to one) will practically run thin. We want it clear, goodness knows, but we also want it thick, and we get the thickness in the human consciousness that entertains and records, that amplifies and interprets it. That indeed, when the question is (to repeat) of the "supernatural," constitutes the only thickness we do get; here prodigies, when they come straight, come with an effect imperiled; they keep all their character, on the other hand, by looming through some other history—the indispensable history of somebody's *normal* relation to something. It 's in such connexions as these that they most interest, for what we are then mainly concerned with is their imputed and borrowed dignity. Intrinsic values they have none—as we feel for instance in such a matter as the would-be portentous climax of Edgar Poe's "Arthur Gordon Pym," where the indispensable history is absent, where the phenomena evoked, the moving accidents, coming straight, as I say, are immediate and flat, and the attempt is all at the horrific in itself. The result is that, to my sense, the climax fails—fails because it stops short, and stops short for want of connexions. There *are* no connexions; not only, I mean, in the sense of further statement, but of our own further relation to the elements, which hang in the void: whereby we see the effect lost, the imaginative effort wasted.

I dare say, to conclude, that whenever, in quest, as I have noted, of the amusing, I have invoked the horrific, I have invoked it, in such air as that of "The Turn of the Screw," that of "The Jolly Corner," that of "The Friends of the

Friends," that of "Sir Edmund Orme," that of "The Real
Right Thing," in earnest aversion to waste and from the sense
that in art economy is always beauty. The apparitions of Peter
Quint and Miss Jessel, in the first of the tales just named, the
elusive presence nightly "stalked" through the New York
house by the poor gentleman in the second, are matters as to
which in themselves, really, the critical challenge (essentially
nothing ever but the spirit of fine attention) may take a
hundred forms—and a hundred felt or possibly proved infirmities is too great a number. Our friends' respective minds
about them, on the other hand, are a different matter—challengeable, and repeatedly, if you like, but never challengeable
without some consequent further stiffening of the whole texture. Which proposition involves, I think, a moral. The moving accident, the rare conjunction, whatever it be, does n't
make the story—in the sense that the story is our excitement,
our amusement, our thrill and our suspense; the human emotion and the human attestation, the clustering human conditions we expect presented, only make it. The extraordinary is
most extraordinary in that it happens to you and me, and
it 's of value (of value for others) but so far as visibly brought
home to us. At any rate, odd though it may sound to pretend
that one feels on safer ground in tracing such an adventure as
that of the hero of "The Jolly Corner" than in pursuing a
bright career among pirates or detectives, I allow that composition to pass as the measure or limit, on my own part, of
any achievable comfort in the "adventure-story"; and this not
because I may "render"—well, what my poor gentleman attempted and suffered in the New York house—better than I
may render detectives or pirates or other splendid despera-
does, though even here too there would be something to say;
but because the spirit engaged with the forces of violence interests me most when I can think of it as engaged most
deeply, most finely and most "subtly" (precious term!). For
then it is that, as with the longest and firmest prongs of consciousness, I grasp and hold the throbbing subject; *there* it is
above all that I find the steady light of the picture.

After which attempted demonstration I drop with scant
grace perhaps to the admission here of a general vagueness on
the article of my different little origins. I have spoken of these

in three or four connexions, but ask myself to no purpose, I fear, what put such a matter as "Owen Wingrave" or as "The Friends of the Friends," such a fantasy as "Sir Edmund Orme," into my head. The habitual teller of tales finds these things in old note-books—which however but shifts the burden a step; since how, and under what inspiration, did they first wake up in these rude cradles? One's notes, as all writers remember, sometimes explicitly mention, sometimes indirectly reveal, and sometimes wholly dissimulate, such clues and such obligations. The search for these last indeed, through faded or pencilled pages, is perhaps one of the sweetest of our more pensive pleasures. Then we chance on some idea we *have* afterwards treated; then, greeting it with tenderness, we wonder at the first form of a motive that was to lead us so far and to show, no doubt, to eyes not our own, for so other; then we heave the deep sigh of relief over all that is never, thank goodness, to be done again. Would we have embarked on *that* stream had we known?—and what might n't we have made of this one *had n't* we known! How, in a proportion of cases, could we have dreamed "there might be something"?—and why, in another proportion, did n't we *try* what there might be, since there are sorts of trials (ah indeed more than one sort!) for which the day will soon have passed? Most of all, of a certainty, is brought back, before these promiscuities, the old burden of the much life and the little art, and of the portentous dose of the one it takes to make any show of the other. It is n't however that one "minds" not recovering lost hints; the special pride of any tinted flower of fable, however small, is to be able to opine with the celebrated Topsy that it can only have "growed." Does n't the fabulist himself indeed recall even as one of his best joys the particular pang (both quickening and, in a manner, profaning possession) of parting with some conceit of which he can give no account but that his sense—of beauty or truth or whatever—has been for ever so long saturated with it? Not, I hasten to add, that measurements of time may n't here be agreeably fallacious, and that the "ever so long" of saturation shan't often have consisted but of ten minutes of perception. It comes back to me of "Owen Wingrave," for example, simply that one summer afternoon many years ago, on a penny chair and under a great tree in Kensington Gardens, I must at the end of a few such visionary moments have been able to equip him even with details not involved or not mentioned in the story. Would that adequate intensity *all* have sprung from the fact that while I sat there in the immense mild summer rustle and the ever so softened London hum a young man should have taken his place on another chair within my limit of contemplation, a tall quiet slim studious young man, of admirable type, and have settled to a book with immediate gravity? Did the young man then, on the spot, just *become* Owen Wingrave, establishing by the mere magic of type the situation, creating at a stroke all the implications and filling out all the picture? That he would have been capable of it is all I can say—unless it be, otherwise put, that I should have been capable of letting him; though there hovers the happy alternative that Owen Wingrave, nebulous and fluid, may only, at the touch, have found *himself* in this gentleman; found, that is, a figure and a habit, a form, a face, a fate, the interesting aspect presented and the dreadful doom recorded; together with the required and multiplied connexions, not least that presence of some self-conscious dangerous girl of lockets and amulets offered by the full-blown idea to my very first glance. These questions are as answerless as they are, luckily, the reverse of pressing—since my poor point is only that at the beginning of my session in the penny chair the seedless fable had n't a claim to make or an excuse to give, and that, the very next thing, the penny-worth still partly unconsumed, it was fairly bristling with pretexts. "Dramatise it, dramatise it!" would seem to have rung with sudden intensity in my ears. But dramatise what? The young man in the chair? Him perhaps indeed—however disproportionately to his mere inoffensive stillness; though no imaginative response *can* be disproportionate, after all, I think, to any right, any really penetrating, appeal. Only, where and whence and why and how sneaked in, during so few seconds, so much penetration, so very much rightness? However, these mysteries are really irrecoverable; besides being doubtless of interest, in general, at the best, but to the infatuated author.

Moved to say that of "Sir Edmund Orme" I remember

absolutely nothing, I yet pull myself up ruefully to retrace the presumption that this morsel must first have appeared, with a large picture, in a weekly newspaper and, as then struck me, in the very smallest of all possible print—at sight of which I felt sure that, in spite of the picture (a thing, in its way, to be thankful for) no one would ever read it. I was never to hear in fact that any one had done so—and I therefore surround it here with every advantage and give it without compunction a new chance. For as I meditate I do a little live it over, do a little remember in connexion with it the felt challenge of some experiment or two in one of the finer shades, the finest (*that* was the point) of the gruesome. The gruesome gross and obvious might be charmless enough; but why should n't one, with ingenuity, almost infinitely refine upon it?—as one was prone at any time to refine almost on anything? The study of certain of the situations that keep, as we say, the heart in the mouth might renew itself under this star; and in the recital in question, as in "The Friends of the Friends," "The Jolly Corner" and "The Real Right Thing," the pursuit of such verily leads us into rarefied air. Two sources of effect must have seemed to me happy for "Sir Edmund Orme"; one of these the bright thought of a state of *unconscious* obsession or, in romantic parlance, hauntedness, on the part of a given person; the consciousness of it on the part of some other, in anguish lest a wrong turn or forced betrayal shall determine a break in the blest ignorance, becoming thus the subject of portrayal, with plenty of suspense for the occurrence or non-occurrence of the feared mischance. Not to be liable herself to a dark visitation, but to see such a danger play about her child as incessantly as forked lightning may play unheeded about the blind, this is the penalty suffered by the mother, in "Sir Edmund Orme," for some hardness or baseness of her own youth. There I must doubtless have found my escape from the obvious; there I avoided a low directness and achieved one of those redoubled twists or sportive—by which I don't at all mean wanton—gambols dear to the fastidious, the creative fancy and that make for the higher interest. The higher interest—and this is the second of the two flowers of evidence that I pluck from the faded cluster—must further have dwelt, to my appraisement, in my placing my

scene at Brighton, the old, the mid-Victorian, the Thacker-
ayan Brighton; where the twinkling sea and the breezy air,
the great friendly, fluttered, animated, many-coloured "front,"
would emphasise the note I wanted; that of the strange and
sinister embroidered on the very type of the normal and easy.

This was to be again, after years, the idea entertained for
"The Jolly Corner," about the composition of which there
would be more to say than my space allows; almost more in
fact than categorical clearness might see its way to. A very
limited thing being on this occasion in question, I was moved
to adopt as my motive an analysis of some one of the conceivably rarest and intensest grounds for an "unnatural" anxiety, a *malaise* so incongruous and discordant, in the given
prosaic prosperous conditions, as almost to be compromising.
Spencer Brydon's adventure however is one of those finished
fantasies that, achieving success or not, speak best even to the
critical sense for themselves—which I leave it to do, while I
apply the remark as well to "The Friends of the Friends" (and
all the more that this last piece allows probably for no other
comment).

I have placed "Julia Bride," for material reasons, at the end
of this Volume, quite out of her congruous company, though
not very much out of her temporal order; and mainly with
this drawback alone that any play of criticism she may seem
formed to provoke rather misses its link with the reflexions I
have here been making. That link is with others to come, and
I must leave it to suggest itself on the occasion of these others; when I shall be inevitably saying, for instance, that if
there are voluminous, gross and obvious ways of seeking that
effect of the distinctively rich presentation for which it has
been my possibly rather thankless fate to strive, so doubtless
the application of patches and the multiplication of parts
make up a system with a train of votaries; but that the
achieved iridescence from within works, I feel sure, more
kinds of magic; and our interest, our decency and our dignity
can of course only be to work as many kinds as possible. Such
value as may dwell in "Julia Bride," for example, seems to me,
on re-perusal, to consist to a high degree in the strength of
the flushing through on the part of the subject-matter, and in

the mantle of iridescence naturally and logically so produced. Julia is "foreshortened," I admit, to within an inch of her life; but I judge her life still saved and yet at the same time the equal desideratum, its depicted full fusion with other lives that remain undepicted, not lost. The other lives, the rest of the quantity of life, press in, squeeze forward, to the best of their ability; but, restricted as the whole thing is to implications and involutions only, they prevail at best by indirectness; and the bid for amusement, the effect presumably sought, is by making us conceive and respond to them, making us feel, taste, smell and enjoy them, without our really knowing why or how. Full-fed statement here, to repeat my expression—the imaged résumé of as many of the vivifying elements as may be coherently packed into an image at once—is the predominant artifice; thanks to which we catch by the very small reflector, which is of absolutely minimum size for its task, a quite "unlikely" amount, I surmise, of the movement of life. But, again and again, it would take me long to retail the refinements of ingenuity I felt poor re-invoked Julia all anxiously, all intelligently invite me to place, for this belated, for this positively final appearance, at her disposal. "Here we are again!" she seemed, with a chalked grimace, to call out to me, even as the clown at the circus launches the familiar greeting; and it was quite as if, while she understood all I asked of her, I confessed to her the oddity of my predicament. This was but a way, no doubt, of confessing it to myself—except indeed that she might be able to bear it. Her plea was—well, anything she would; but mine, in return, was that I really did n't take her for particularly important in herself, and would in fact have had no heart for her without the note, attaching to her as not in the least to poor little dim and archaic Daisy Miller, say; the note, so to call it, of multitudinous reference. I had had, for any confidence, to make it out to myself that my little frisking haunter, under private stress, of the New York public scene, was related with a certain intensity to the world about her; so that her case might lose itself promptly enough in a complexus of larger and stranger cases—even in the very air, by what seemed to promise, of the largest possibilities of comedy. What if she were the silver key, tiny in itself, that would unlock a treasure?—the treasure of a whole view of manners and morals, a whole range of American social aspects?

To put that question was to see one's subject swell at its mere touch; but to do this, by the same stroke, was to ask one's self, alas, how such a majestic mass could be made to turn round in a *nouvelle*. For, all tainted with the up-town debility though it still might be—and this too, after all, comparative—did n't it yet strain the minor key, to re-employ my expression, almost to breaking? How had the prime idea come to me, in the first place, but as possibly and perhaps even minutely illustrating, in respect of consequences and remoter bearings, that freedom repeatedly to contract for the fond preliminaries of marriage which has been immemorially cherished by the American female young? The freedoms of American life are, together with some of its queer restrictions and timidities, the suggestive matter for painter, poet or satirist; and who should say that one of the greatest of all such birthrights, the large juvenile licence as to getting "engaged," disengaged and re-engaged, had received half the attention the charmed dramatist or moralist would appear consistently to owe it? Presumably of the greatest its bearing on the social tone at large, on the manners, habits and ideals of communities clinging to it—of generations wedded, that is, to the young *speculative* exchange of intimate vows—as to the palladium of their liberties. What had struck me nevertheless was that, in common with a hundred other native traditions and practices, it had suffered from the attitude of poets and statisticians banded alike to display it as quite devoid of attendant signs or appreciable effects. From far back a more perverse student, doubtless, of the human scene in general had ventured to suspect in it some at least of the properties of presentable truth: so hard it appeared to believe that the number of a young lady's accepted lovers would n't in some degree determine the mixture of the elements in the young lady's consciousness and have much to "say," in one way and another, to the young lady's general case. *What* it might have to say (of most interest to poet and moralist) was certainly meanwhile no matter for *a priori* judgement—it might have to say but the most charming, the most thrilling things in the world; this, however, was exactly the field for dramatic analysis, no such fine quantities being ever determinable till they have with due intelligence been "gone into." "Dramatise, dramatise!" one had, in fine, before the so signal appearance, said to one's self: then, and not sooner, would one see.

By the same token and the same process would one arrive at a similar profit on the score of that other almost equally prized social provision—which has indeed received more critical attention—the unrestricted freedom of re-marriage in the lifetime of the parties, the unhampered ease of rupture and repudiation for each. On this ground, as I say, the fond interpreter of life has had, wherever we observe him, the acute appeal apparently enough in his ears; and it was to reach me in the present connexion but as a source of sound re-enforcement to my possibly too exiguous other example. "Superadd some view of the so enjoyed and so typical freedoms of the mother to the element, however presented, of the daughter's inimitable career of licence; work in, as who should say, a tablespoonful of the due display of responsible consciousness, of roused and reflective taste, of delicacy spreading a tentative wing; season and stir according to judgement and then set the whole to simmer, to stew, or whatever, serving hot and with extreme neatness"; such, briefly stated, had been my careful formula or recipe—by which I of course had to abide in spite of suspecting the process to promise, from an early stage, a much stronger broth, smoking in a much bigger bowl, than I had engaged to prepare. The fumes exhaled by the mixture were the gage, somehow, of twenty more ingredients than I had consciously put in; and this means in short that, even with the actual liquid drained off, I make out a residuum of admirable rich "stock," which—in common deference to professional and technical thrift—must again certainly serve. Such are both the penalties and the profits of that obsession by the sense of an ampler comedy in human things—latent and a little lost, but all responsive to the interested squeeze, to the roused passion of pursuit—than even quite expert and anxious preliminaries of artistic relation to any theme may always be trusted to give the measure of. So what does this truth amount to, after all, but a sort of consecration of what I have called, for "Julia Bride," my predicament?—the consciousness, in that connexion, but of finding myself, after so many years astride the silver-shod, sober-paced, short-stepping, but oh so hugely nosing, so tenderly and yearningly and ruefully sniffing, grey mule of the "few thousand words," ridiculously back where I had started. I clutch at the claim in question indeed, since I feel that without it the shadow I may have cast might n't bear comparison even with that of limping Don Quixote assisted through his castle-gate and showing but thankless bruises for laurels—might in fact resign itself rather to recalling Moses Primrose welcomed home from the Fair.

Daisy Miller, Pandora, The Patagonia, The Marriages, The Real Thing, Brooksmith, The Beldonald Holbein, The Story In It, Flickerbridge, Mrs. Medwin

IT WAS IN ROME during the autumn of 1877; a friend then living there but settled now in a South less weighted with appeals and memories happened to mention—which she might perfectly not have done—some simple and uninformed American lady of the previous winter, whose young daughter, a child of nature and of freedom, accompanying her from hotel to hotel, had "picked up" by the wayside, with the best conscience in the world, a good-looking Roman, of vague identity, astonished at his luck, yet (so far as might be, by the pair) all innocently, all serenely exhibited and introduced: this at least till the occurrence of some small social check, some interrupting incident, of no great gravity or dignity, and which I forget. I had never heard, save on this showing, of the amiable but not otherwise eminent ladies, who were n't in fact named, I think, and whose case had merely served to point a familiar moral; and it must have been just their want of salience that left a margin for the small pencil-mark inveterately signifying, in such connexions, "Dramatise, dramatise!" The result of my recognising a few months later the sense of my pencil-mark was the short chronicle of "Daisy Miller," which I indited in London the following spring and then addressed, with no conditions attached, as I remember, to the editor of a magazine that had its seat of publication at Philadelphia and had lately appeared to appreciate my contributions. That gentleman however (an historian of some repute) promptly returned me my missive, and with an absence of comment that struck me at the time as rather grim—as, given the circumstances, requiring indeed some explanation: till a friend to whom I appealed for light, giving him the thing to read, declared it could only have passed with the Philadelphian critic for "an outrage on American girlhood." This was verily a light, and of bewildering intensity; though I was presently to read into the matter a further helpful inference. To the fault of being outrageous this little composition added that of being essentially and pre-eminently a *nouvelle*; a signal example in fact of that type, foredoomed at the best, in more cases than not, to editorial disfavour. If accordingly I was afterwards to be cradled, almost blissfully, in the conception that "Daisy" at least, among my productions, might approach "success," such success for example, on her eventual appearance, as the state of being promptly pirated in Boston—a sweet tribute I had n't yet received and was never again to know—the irony of things yet claimed its rights, I could n't but long continue to feel, in the circumstance that quite a special reprobation had waited on the first appearance in the world of the ultimately most prosperous child of my invention. So doubly discredited, at all events, this bantling met indulgence, with no great delay, in the eyes of my admirable friend the late Leslie Stephen and was published in two numbers of *The Cornhill Magazine* (1878).

It qualified itself in that publication and afterwards as "a Study"; for reasons which I confess I fail to recapture unless they may have taken account simply of a certain flatness in my poor little heroine's literal denomination. Flatness indeed, one must have felt, was the very sum of her story; so that perhaps after all the attached epithet was meant but as a deprecation, addressed to the reader, of any great critical hope of stirring scenes. It provided for mere concentration, and on an object scant and superficially vulgar—from which, however, a sufficiently brooding tenderness might eventually extract a shy incongruous charm. I suppress at all events here the appended qualification—in view of the simple truth, which ought from the first to have been apparent to me, that my little exhibition is made to no degree whatever in critical but, quite inordinately and extravagantly, in poetical terms. It comes back to me that I was at a certain hour long afterwards to have reflected, in this connexion, on the characteristic free play of the whirligig of time. It was in Italy again—in Venice and in the prized society of an interesting friend, now dead, with whom I happened to wait, on the Grand Canal, at the animated water-steps of one of the hotels. The considerable little terrace there was so disposed as to make a salient stage for certain demonstrations on the part of two young girls, children *they*, if ever, of nature and of freedom, whose use of those resources, in the general public eye, and under our own as we sat in the gondola, drew from the lips of a second companion, sociably afloat with us, the remark that there before us, with no sign absent, were a couple of attesting Daisy Millers. Then it was that, in my charming hostess's prompt protest, the whirligig, as I have called it, at once betrayed itself. "How can you liken *those* creatures to a figure of which the only fault is touchingly to have transmuted so sorry a type and to have, by a poetic artifice, not only led our judgement of it astray, but made *any* judgement quite impossible?" With which this gentle lady and admirable critic turned on the author himself. "You *know* you quite falsified, by the turn you gave it, the thing you had begun with having in mind, the thing you had had, to satiety, the chance of 'observing': your pretty perversion of it, or your unprincipled mystification of our sense of it, does it really too much honour—in spite of which, none the less, as anything charming or touching always to that extent justifies itself, we after a fashion forgive and understand you. But why *waste* your romance? There are cases, too many, in which you 've done it again; in which, provoked by a spirit of observation at first no doubt sufficiently sincere, and with the measured and felt truth fairly twitching your sleeve, you have yielded to your incurable prejudice in favour of grace—to whatever it is in you that makes so inordinately for form and prettiness and pathos; not to say sometimes for misplaced drolling. Is it that you 've after all too much imagination? Those awful young women capering at the hotel-door, *they* are the real little Daisy Millers that were; whereas yours in the tale is such a one, more 's the pity, as—for pitch of the ingenuous, for quality of the artless—could n't possibly have been at all." My answer to all which bristled of course with more professions than I can or need report here; the chief of them inevitably to the effect that my supposedly typical little figure was of course pure poetry, and had never been anything else; since this is what helpful imagination, in however slight a dose, ever directly makes for. As for the original grossness of readers, I dare say I added, that was another matter—but one which at any rate had then quite ceased to signify.

A good deal of the same element has doubtless sneaked

into "Pandora," which I also reprint here for congruity's sake, and even while the circumstances attending the birth of this anecdote, given to the light in a New York newspaper (1884), pretty well lose themselves for me in the mists of time. I do nevertheless connect "Pandora" with one of the scantest of memoranda, twenty words jotted down in New York during a few weeks spent there a year or two before. I had put a question to a friend about a young lady present at a certain pleasure-party, but present in rather perceptibly unsupported and unguaranteed fashion, as without other connexions, without more operative "backers," than a proposer possibly half-hearted and a slightly sceptical seconder; and had been answered to the effect that she was an interesting representative of a new social and local variety, the "self-made," or at least self-making, girl, whose sign was that—given some measurably amusing appeal in her to more or less ironic curiosity or to a certain complacency of patronage—she was anywhere made welcome enough if she only came, like one of the dismembered charges of Little Bo-Peep, leaving her "tail" behind her. Docked of all natural appendages and having enjoyed, as was supposed, no natural advantages; with the "line drawn," that is, at her father and her mother, her sisters and her brothers, at everything that was hers, and with the presumption crushing as against these adjuncts, she was yet held free to prove her case and sail her boat herself; even quite quaintly or quite touchingly free, as might be—working out thus on her own lines her social salvation. This was but five-and-twenty years ago; yet what to-day most strikes me in the connexion, and quite with surprise, is that at a period so recent there should have been novelty for me in a situation so little formed by more contemporary lights to startle or waylay. The evolution of varieties moves fast; the Pandora Days can no longer, I fear, pass for quaint or fresh or for exclusively native to any one tract of Anglo-Saxon soil. Little Bo-Peep's charges may, as manners have developed, leave their tails behind them for the season, but quite knowing what they have done with them and where they shall find them again—as is proved for the most part by the promptest disavowal of any apparent ground for ruefulness. To "dramatise" the hint thus gathered was of course, rudimentarily, to see the self-made girl apply her very first independent measure to the renovation of her house, founding its fortunes, introducing her parents, placing her brothers, marrying her sisters (this care on her own behalf being—a high note of superiority—quite secondary), in fine floating the heavy mass on the flood she had learned to breast. Something of that sort must have proposed itself to me at that time as the latent "drama" of the case; very little of which, however, I am obliged to recognise, was to struggle to the surface. What is more to the point is the moral I at present find myself drawing from the fact that, then turning over my American impressions, those proceeding from a brief but profusely peopled stay in New York, I should have fished up that none so very precious particle as one of the pearls of the collection. Such a circumstance comes back, for me, to that fact of my insuperably restricted experience and my various missing American clues—or rather at least to my felt lack of the most important of them all—on which the current of these remarks has already led me to dilate. There had been indubitably and multitudinously, for me, in my native city, the world "down-town"—since how otherwise should the sense of "going" down, the sense of hovering at the narrow gates and skirting the so violently overscored outer face of the monstrous labyrinth that stretches from Canal Street to the Battery, have taken on, to me, the intensity of a worrying, a tormenting impression? Yet it was an impression any attempt at the active cultivation of which, one had been almost violently admonished, could but find one in the last degree unprepared and uneducated. It was essentially New York, and New York was, for force and accent, nothing else worth speaking of; but without the special lights it remained impenetrable and inconceivable; so that one but mooned about superficially, circumferentially, taking in, through the pores of whatever wistfulness, no good material at all. I had had to retire, accordingly, with my yearning presumptions all unverified—presumptions, I mean, as to the privilege of the imaginative initiation, as to the hived stuff of drama, at the service there of the literary adventurer really informed enough and bold enough; and with my one drop of comfort the observation already made—that at least I descried, for my own early humiliation and exposure, no semblance of such a competitor slipping in at any door or perched, for raking the scene, on any coign of vantage. *That* invidious attestation of my own appointed and incurable deafness to the major key I frankly surmise I could scarce have borne. For there it was; not only that the major key was "down-town" but that down-town was, all itself, the major key—absolutely, exclusively; with the inevitable consequence that if the minor was "up-town," and (by a parity of reasoning) up-town the minor, so the field was meagre and the inspiration thin for any unfortunate practically banished from the true pasture. Such an unfortunate, even at the time I speak of, had still to confess to the memory of a not inconsiderably earlier season when, seated for several months at the very moderate altitude of Twenty-Fifth Street, he felt himself day by day alone in that scale of the balance; alone, I mean, with the music-masters and French pastry-cooks, the ladies and children—immensely present and immensely numerous these, but testifying with a collective voice to the extraordinary absence (save as pieced together through a thousand gaps and indirectnesses) of a serious male interest. One had heard and seen novels and plays appraised as lacking, detrimentally, a serious female; but the higher walks in that community might at the period I speak of have formed a picture bright and animated, no doubt, but marked with the very opposite defect.

Here it was accordingly that loomed into view more than ever the anomaly, in various ways dissimulated to a first impression, rendering one of the biggest and loudest of cities one of the very least of Capitals; together with the immediate reminder, on the scene, that an adequate muster of Capital characteristics would have remedied half my complaint. To have lived in capitals, even in some of the smaller, was to be sure of that and to know why—and all the more was this a consequence of having happened to live in some of the greater. Neither scale of the balance, in these, had ever struck one as so monstrously heaped-up at the expense of the other; there had been manners and customs enough, so to speak, there had been features and functions, elements, appearances, social material, enough to go round. The question was to have appeared, however, and the question was to remain, this interrogated mystery of what American town-life had left to

entertain the observer withal when nineteen twentieths of it,
or in other words the huge organised mystery of the consummately, the supremely applied money-passion, were inexorably closed to him. My own practical answer figures here
perforce in the terms, and in them only, of such propositions
as are constituted by the four or five longest tales comprised
in this series. What it came to was that up-town would do for
me simply what up-town could—and seemed in a manner
apologetically conscious that this might n't be described as
much. The kind of appeal to interest embodied in these por-
trayals and in several of their like companions was the measure of the whole minor exhibition, which affected me as
virtually saying: "Yes I 'm either *that*—that range and order
of things, or I 'm nothing at all; therefore make the most of
me!" Whether "Daisy Miller," "Pandora," "The Patagonia,"
"Miss Gunton," "Julia Bride" and *tutti quanti* do in fact conform to any such admonition would be an issue by itself and
which must n't overcome my shyness; all the more that the
point of interest is really but this—that I was on the basis of
the loved *nouvelle* form, with the best will in the world and
the best conscience, almost helplessly cornered. To ride the
nouvelle down-town, to prance and curvet and caracole with
it there—that would have been the true ecstasy. But a single
"spill"—such as I so easily might have had in Wall Street or
wherever—would have forbidden me, for very shame, in the
eyes of the expert and the knowing, ever to mount again; so
that in short it was n't to be risked on any terms.

There were meanwhile the alternatives of course—that I
might renounce the *nouvelle*, or else might abjure that "American life" the characteristic towniness of which was lighted for
me, even though so imperfectly, by New York and Boston—
by those centres only. Such extremities, however, I simply
could n't afford—artistically, sentimentally, financially, or by
any other sacrifice—to face; and if the fact nevertheless remains that an adjustment, under both the heads in question,
had eventually to take place, every inch of my doubtless
meagre ground was yet first contested, every turn and twist
of my scant material economically used. Add to this that if
the other constituents of the volume, the intermediate ones,
serve to specify what I was then thrown back on, I need n't

perhaps even at the worst have found within my limits a thinness of interest to resent: seeing that still after years the common appeal remained sharp enough to flower again into such
a composition as "Julia Bride" (which independently of its
appearance here has seen the light but in *Harper's Magazine*,
1908). As I wind up with this companion-study to "Daisy
Miller" the considerable assortment of my shorter tales I seem
to see it symbolise my sense of my having waited with something of a subtle patience, my having still hoped as against
hope that the so ebbing and obliging seasons would somehow strike for me some small flash of what I have called the
major light—would suffer, I mean, to glimmer out, through
however odd a crevice or however vouchsafed a contact, just
enough of a wandering air from the down-town penetralia as
might embolden, as might inform, as might, straining a
point, even conceivably inspire (always where the *nouvelle*,
and the *nouvelle* only, should be concerned); all to the advantage of my extension of view and my variation of theme. A
whole passage of intellectual history, if the term be not too
pompous, occupies in fact, to my present sense, the waiting,
the so fondly speculative interval: in which I seem to see myself rather a high and dry, yet irrepressibly hopeful artistic
Micawber, cocking an ostensibly confident hat and practising
an almost passionate system of "bluff"; insisting, in fine, that
something (out of the just-named penetralia) *would* turn up
if only the right imaginative hanging-about on the chance, if
only the true intelligent attention, were piously persisted in.

I forget exactly what Micawber, who had hung about so
on the chance, I forget exactly what *he*, at the climax of his
exquisite consciousness, found himself in fact reverting to;
but I feel that my analogy loses nothing from the circumstance that so recently as on the publication of "Fordham
Castle" (1904), for which I refer my reader to Volume XVI,
the miracle, after all, alas, had n't happened, the stray emitted
gleam had n't fallen across my page, the particular supreme
"something" those who live by their wits finally and *most*
yearningly look for had n't, in fine, turned up. What better
proof of this than that, with the call of the "four or five thousand words" of "Fordham Castle" for instance to meet, or
even with the easier allowance of space for its successor to

rise to, I was but to feel myself fumble again in the old limp pocket of the minor exhibition, was but to know myself reduced to finger once more, not a little ruefully, a chord perhaps now at last too warped and rusty for complicated music at short order? I trace myself, for that matter, in "Fordham Castle" positively "squirming" with the ingenuity of my effort to create for my scrap of an up-town subject—*such* a scrap as I at the same time felt myself admonished to keep it down to!—a certain larger connexion; I may also add that of the exceedingly close complexus of intentions represented by the packed density of those few pages it would take some ampler glance here to give an account. My point is that my pair of little up-town identities, the respectively typical objects of parental and conjugal interest, the more or less mitigated, more or less embellished or disfigured, intensified or modernised Daisy Millers, Pandora Days, Julia Brides, Miss Guntons or whatever, of the anxious pair, the ignored husband and relegated mother, brought together in the Swiss lakeside pension—my point is that these irrepressible agents yet betrayed the conscious need of tricking-out their time-honoured case. To this we owe it that the elder couple bear the brunt of immediate appearance and are charged with the function of adorning at least the foreground of the general scene; they convey, by implication, the moral of the tale, at least its æsthetic one, if there be such a thing: they fairly hint, and from the very centre of the familiar field, at positive deprecation (should an imagined critic care not to neglect such a shade) of too unbroken an eternity of mere international young ladies. It 's as if the international young ladies, felt by me as once more, as verily once too much, my appointed thematic doom, had inspired me with the fond thought of attacking them at an angle and from a quarter by which the peril and discredit of their rash inveteracy might be a bit conjured away.

These in fact are the saving sanities of the dramatic poet's always rather mad undertaking—the rigour of his artistic need to cultivate almost at any price variety of appearance and experiment, to dissimulate likenesses, samenesses, stalenesses, by the infinite play of a form pretending to a life of its own. There are not so many quite distinct things in his field, I

think, as there are sides by which the main masses may be
approached; and he is after all but a nimble besieger or nocturnal sneaking adventurer who perpetually plans, watches,
circles for penetrable places. I offer "Fordham Castle," positively for a rare little memento of that truth: once I had to
be, for the light wind of it in my sails, "internationally"
American, what amount of truth my subject might n't aspire
to was urgently enough indicated—which condition straightway placed it in the time-honoured category; but the range
of choice as to treatment, by which I mean as to my pressing
the clear liquor of amusement and refreshment from the
golden apple of composition, *that* blest freedom, with its infinite power of renewal, was still my resource, and I felt myself invoke it not in vain. There was always the difficulty—I
have in the course of these so numerous preliminary observations repeatedly referred to it, but the point is so interesting
that it can scarce be made too often—that the simplest truth
about a human entity, a situation, a relation, an aspect of life,
however small, on behalf of which the claim to charmed attention is made, strains ever, under one's hand, more intensely, *most* intensely, to justify that claim; strains ever, as it
were, toward the uttermost end or aim of one's meaning or
of its own numerous connexions; struggles at each step, and
in defiance of one's raised admonitory finger, fully and completely to express itself. Any real art of representation is, I
make out, a controlled and guarded acceptance, in fact a perfect economic mastery, of that conflict: the general sense of
the expansive, the explosive principle in one's material thoroughly noted, adroitly allowed to flush and colour and animate the disputed value, but with its other appetites and
treacheries, its characteristic space-hunger and space-cunning,
kept down. The fair flower of this artful compromise is to my
sense the secret of "foreshortening"—the particular economic
device for which one must have a name and which has in its
single blessedness and its determined pitch, I think, a higher
price than twenty other clustered loosenesses; and just because full-fed statement, just because the picture of as many
of the conditions as possible made and kept proportionate,
just because the surface iridescent, even in the short piece,
by what is beneath it and what throbs and gleams through,

are things all conducive to the only compactness that has a charm, to the only spareness that has a force, to the only simplicity that has a grace—those, in each order, that produce the *rich* effect.

Let me say, however, that such reflexions had never helped to close my eyes, at any moment, to all that had come and gone, over the rest of the field, in the fictive world of adventure more complacently so called—the American world, I particularly mean, that might have put me so completely out of countenance by having drawn its inspiration, that of thousands of celebrated works, neither from up-town nor from down-town nor from my lady's chamber, but from the vast wild garden of "unconventional" life in no matter what part of our country. I grant in fact that this demonstration of how consummately my own meagerly-conceived sources were to be dispensed with by the more initiated minds would but for a single circumstance, grasped at in recovery of self-respect, have thrown me back in absolute dejection on the poverty of my own categories. Why had n't so quickened a vision of the great neglected native quarry *at large* more troubled my dreams, instead of leaving my imagination on the whole so resigned? Well, with many reasons I could count over, there was one that all exhaustively covered the ground and all completely answered the question: the reflexion, namely, that the common sign of the productions "unconventionally" prompted (and this positively without exception) was nothing less than the birthmark of Dialect, general or special—dialect with the literary rein loose on its agitated back and with its shambling power of traction, not to say, more analytically, of *at*traction, trusted for all such a magic might be worth. Distinctly that was the odd case: the key to the *whole* of the treasure of romance independently garnered was the riot of the vulgar tongue. One might state it more freely still and the truth would be as evident: the plural number, the vulgar tongues, each with its intensest note, but pointed the moral more luridly. Grand generalised continental riot or particular pedantic, particular discriminated and "sectional" and self-conscious riot—to feel the thick breath, to catch the ugly snarl, of all or of either, was to be reminded afresh of the only conditions that guard the grace, the only origins that save the honour, or even the life, of dialect: those precedent to the invasion, to the sophistication, of schools and unconscious of the smartness of echoes and the taint of slang. The thousands of celebrated productions raised their monument but to the bastard vernacular of communities disinherited of the felt difference between the speech of the soil and the speech of the newspaper, and capable thereby, accordingly, of taking slang for simplicity, the composite for the quaint and the vulgar for the natural. These were unutterable depths, and, as they yawned about one, *what* appreciable coherent sound did they seem most to give out? Well, to my ear surely, at the worst, none that determined even a tardy compunction. The monument was there, if one would, but was one to regret one's own failure to have contributed a stone? Perish, and all ignobly, the thought!

Each of the other pieces of which this volume is composed would have its small history; but they have above all in common that they mark my escape from the predicament, as I have called it, just glanced at; my at least partial way out of the dilemma formed by the respective discouragements of down-town, of up-town and of the great dialectic tracts. Various up-town figures flit, I allow, across these pages; but they too, as it were, have for the time dodged the dilemma; I meet them, I exhibit them, in an air of different and, I think, more numerous alternatives. Such is the case with the young American subject in "Flickerbridge" (1902) and with the old American subject, as my signally mature heroine may here be pronounced, in "The Beldonald Holbein" (1901). In these two cases the idea is but a stray spark of the old "international" flame; of course, however, it was quite internationally that I from far back sought my salvation. Let such matters as those I have named represent accordingly so many renewed, and perhaps at moments even rather desperate, clutches of that useful torch. We may put it in this way that the scale of variety had, by the facts of one's situation, been rather oddly predetermined—with Europe so constantly in requisition as the more salient American stage or more effective *repoussoir*, and yet with any particular *action* on this great lighted and decorated scene depending for half its sense on one of my outland importations. Comparatively few those of my productions in which I appear to have felt, and with confidence, that source of credit freely negligible; "The Princess Casamassima," "The Tragic Muse," "The Spoils of Poynton," "The Other House," "What Maisie Knew," "The Sacred Fount," practically, among the more or less sustained things, exhausting the list—in which moreover I have set down two compositions not included in the present series. Against these longer and shorter novels stand many of the other category; though when it comes to the array of mere brevities—as in "The Marriages" (1891) and four of its companions here—the balance is more evenly struck: a proof, doubtless, that confidence in what he may call the *indirect* initiation, in the comparatively hampered saturation, may even after long years often fail an earnest worker in these fields. Conclusive that, in turn, as to the innumerable parts of the huge machine, a thing of a myriad parts, about which the intending painter of even a few aspects of the life of a great old complex society must either be right or be ridiculous. He has to be, for authority—and on all such ground authority is everything—but continuously and confidently right; to which end, in many a case, if he happens to be but a civil alien, he had best be simply born again—I mean born differently.

Only then, as he 's quite liable to say to himself, what would perhaps become, under the dead collective weight of those knowledges that he may, as the case stands for him, often separately miss, what would become of the free intensity of the perceptions which serve him in their stead, in which he never hesitates to rejoice, and to which, in a hundred connexions, he just impudently trusts? The question is too beguiling, alas, now to be gone into; though the mere putting of it fairly *describes* the racked consciousness of the unfortunate who has incurred the dread heritage of easy comparisons. His wealth, in this possession, is supposed to be his freedom of choice, but there are too many days when he asks himself if the artist may n't easily know an excess of that freedom. Those of the smaller sort never use all the freedom they have—which is the sign, exactly, by which we know them; but those of the greater have never had too much immediately to use—which is the sovereign mark of their felicity. From which range of speculation let me narrow down none the less a little ruefully; since I confess to no great provision of "history" on behalf of "The Marriages." The embodied notion, for this matter, sufficiently tells its story; one has never to go far afield to speculate on the possible pangs of filial piety in face of the successor, in the given instance, to either lost parent, but perhaps more particularly to the lost mother, often inflicted on it by the parent surviving. As in the classic case of Mrs. Glasse's receipt, it 's but a question of "first catching" the example of piety intense enough. Granted that, the drama is all there—all in the consciousness, the fond imagination, the possibly poisoned and inflamed judgement, of the suffering subject; where, exactly, "The Marriages" was to find it.

As to the "The Real Thing" (1890) and "Brooksmith" (1891) my recollection is sharp; the subject of each of these tales was suggested to me by a briefly-reported case. To begin with the second-named of them, the appreciative daughter of a friend some time dead had mentioned to me a visit received by her from a servant of the late distinguished lady, a devoted maid whom I remembered well to have repeatedly seen at the latter's side and who had come to discharge herself so far as she might of a sorry burden. She had lived in her mistress's delightful society and in that of the many so interesting friends of the house; she had been formed by nature, as unluckily happened, to enjoy this privilege to the utmost, and the deprivation of everything was now bitterness in her cup. She had had her choice, and had made her trial, of common situations or of a return to her own people, and had found these ordeals alike too cruel. She had in her years of service tasted of conversation and been spoiled for life; she had, in recall of Stendhal's inveterate motto, caught a glimpse, all untimely, of "la beauté parfaite," and should never find again what she had lost—so that nothing was left her but to languish to her end. *There* was a touched spring, of course, to make "Dramatise, dramatise!" ring out; only my little derived drama, in the event, seemed to require, to be ample enough, a hero rather than a heroine. I desired for my poor lost spirit the measured maximum of the fatal experience: the thing became, in a word, to my imagination, the obscure tragedy of the "intelligent" butler present at rare table-talk, rather than that of the more effaced tirewoman; with which of course was involved a corresponding change from mistress to master.

In like manner my much-loved friend George du Maurier had spoken to me of a call from a strange and striking couple desirous to propose themselves as artist's models for his weekly "social" illustrations to *Punch*, and the acceptance of whose services would have entailed the dismissal of an undistinguished but highly expert pair, also husband and wife, who had come to him from far back on the irregular day and whom, thanks to a happy, and to that extent lucrative, appearance of "type" on the part of each, he had reproduced, to the best effect, in a thousand drawing-room attitudes and combinations. Exceedingly modest members of society, they earned their bread by looking and, with the aid of supplied toggery, dressing, greater favourites of fortune to the life; or, otherwise expressed, by skilfully feigning a virtue not in the least native to them. Here meanwhile were their so handsome proposed, so anxious, so almost haggard competitors, originally, by every sign, of the best condition and estate, but overtaken by reverses even while conforming impeccably to the standard of superficial "smartness" and pleading with well-bred ease and the right light tone, not to say with feverish gaiety, that (as in the interest of art itself) *they* at least should n't have to "make believe." The question thus thrown up by the two friendly critics of the rather lurid little passage was of whether their not having to make believe *would* in fact serve them, and above all serve their interpreter as well as the borrowed graces of the comparatively sordid professionals who had had, for dear life, to *know how* (which was to have learnt how) to do something. The question, I recall, struck me as exquisite, and out of a momentary fond consideration of it "The Real Thing" sprang at a bound.

"Flickerbridge" indeed I verily give up: so thoroughly does this highly-finished little anecdote cover its tracks; looking at me, over the few years and out of its bland neatness, with the fine inscrutability, in fact the positive coquetry, of the refusal to answer free-and-easy questions, the mere cold smile for their impertinence, characteristic of any complete artistic thing. "Dramatise, dramatise!"—there had of course been that preliminary, there could n't not have been; but how represent here clearly enough the small succession of steps by which such a case as the admonition is applied to in my picture of Frank Granger's visit to Miss Wenham came to issue from the whole thick-looming cloud of the noted appearances, the dark and dismal consequences, involved more and more to-day in our celebration, our commemoration, our unguardedly-uttered appreciation, of any charming impression? Living as we do under permanent visitation of the deadly epidemic of publicity, any rash word, any light thought that chances to escape us, may instantly, by that accident, find itself propagated and perverted, multiplied and diffused, after a fashion poisonous, practically, and speedily fatal, to its subject—that is to our idea, our sentiment, our figured interest, our too foolishly blabbed secret. Fine old leisure, in George Eliot's phrase, was long ago extinct, but rarity, precious rarity, its twin-sister, lingered on a while only to begin, in like manner, to perish by inches—to learn, in other words, that to be so much as breathed about is to be handed over to the big drum and the brazen blare, with all the effects of the vulgarised, trampled, desecrated state after the cyclone of sound and fury has spent itself. To have observed that, in turn, is to learn to dread reverberation, mere mechanical ventilation, more than the Black Death; which lesson the hero of my little apologue is represented as, all by himself and with anguish at his heart, spelling out the rudiments of. Of course it was a far cry, over intervals of thought, artistically speaking, from the dire truth I here glance at to my small projected example, looking so all unconscious of any such portentous burden of sense; but through that wilderness I shall not attempt to guide my reader. Let the accomplishment of the march figure for him, on the author's part, the arduous sport, in such a waste, of "dramatising."

Intervals of thought and a desolation of missing links strike me, not less, as marking the approach to any simple expression of my "original hint" for "The Story In It." What I definitely recall of the history of this tolerably recent production is that, even after I had exerted a ferocious and far from fruitless ingenuity to keep it from becoming a *nouvelle*—for it is in fact one of the briefest of my compositions—it still haunted, a graceless beggar, for a couple of years, the cold avenues of publicity; till finally an old acquaintance, about to "start a magazine," begged it in turn of me and published it (1903) at no cost to himself but the cost of his confidence, in that first number which was in the event, if I mistake not, to prove only one of a pair. I like perhaps "morbidly" to think that the Story in it may have been more than the magazine could carry. There at any rate—*for* the "story," that is for the pure pearl of my idea—I had to take, in the name of the particular instance, no less deep and straight a dive into the deep sea of a certain general truth than I had taken in quest of "Flickerbridge." The general truth had been positively phrased for me by a distinguished friend, a novelist not to *our* manner either born or bred, on the occasion of his having made such answer as he could to an interlocutor (he, oh distinctly, indigenous and glib!) bent on learning from him why the adventures he imputed to his heroines were so perversely and persistently but of a type impossible to ladies respecting themselves. My friend's reply had been, not unnaturally, and above all not incongruously, that ladies who respected themselves took particular care never to *have* adventures; not the least little adventure that would be worth (worth any self-respecting novelist's) speaking of. There were certainly, it was to be hoped, ladies who practised that reserve—which, however beneficial to themselves, was yet fatally detrimental to literature, in the sense of promptly making any artistic harmony pitched in the same low key trivial and empty. A picture of life founded on the mere reserves and omissions and suppressions of life, what sort of a performance—for beauty, for interest, for tone—could *that* hope to be? The enquiry was n't answered in any hearing of mine, and of course indeed, on all such ground, discussion, to be really luminous, would have to rest on some such perfect definition of terms as is not of this muddled world. It is, not surprisingly, one of the rudiments of criticism that a human, a personal "adventure" is no *a priori*, no positive and absolute and inelastic thing, but just a matter of relation and appreciation—a name we conveniently give, after the fact, to any passage, to any situation, that has added the sharp taste of uncertainty to a quickened sense of life. Therefore the thing is, all beautifully, a matter of interpretation and of the particular conditions;

without a view of which latter some of the most prodigious adventures, as one has often had occasion to say, may vulgarly show for nothing. However that may be, I hasten to add, the mere stir of the air round the question reflected in the brief but earnest interchange I have just reported was to cause a "subject," to my sense, immediately to bloom there. So it suddenly, on its small scale, seemed to stand erect—or at least quite intelligently to lift its head; just *a* subject, clearly, though I could n't immediately tell which or what. To find out I had to get a little closer to it, and "The Story In It" precisely represents that undertaking.

As for "The Beldonald Holbein," about which I have said nothing, *that* story—by which I mean the story *of* it—would take us much too far. "Mrs. Medwin," published in *Punch* (1902) and in "The Better Sort" (1903), I have also accommodated here for convenience. There is a note or two I would fain add to this; but I check myself with the sense of having, as it is, to all probability, vindicated with a due zeal, not to say a due extravagance, the most general truth of many a story-teller's case: the truth, already more than once elsewhere glanced at, that what longest lives to his backward vision, in the whole business, is not the variable question of the "success," but the inveterate romance of the labour.

THE WINGS OF THE DOVE," published in 1902, represents to my memory a very old—if I should n't perhaps rather say a very young—motive; I can scarce remember the time when the situation on which this long-drawn fiction mainly rests was not vividly present to me. The idea, reduced to its essence, is that a of young person conscious of a great capacity for life, but early stricken and doomed, condemned to die under short respite, while also enamoured of the world; aware moreover of the condemnation and passionately desiring to "put in" before extinction as many of the finer vibrations as possible, and so achieve, however briefly and brokenly, the sense of having lived. Long had I turned it over, standing off from it, yet coming back to it; convinced of what might be done with it, yet seeing the theme as formidable. The image so figured would be, at best, but half the matter; the rest would be all the picture of the struggle involved, the adventure brought about, the gain recorded or the loss incurred, the precious experience somehow compassed. These things, I had from the first felt, would require much working-out; that indeed was the case with most things worth working at all; yet there are subjects and subjects, and this one seemed particularly to bristle. It was formed, I judged, to make the wary adventurer walk round and round it—it had in fact a charm that invited and mystified alike that attention; not being somehow what one thought of as a "frank" subject, after the fashion of some, with its elements well in view and its whole character in its face. It stood there with secrets and compartments, with possible treacheries and traps; it might have a great deal to give, but would probably ask for equal services in return, and would collect this debt to the last shilling. It involved, to begin with, the placing in the strongest light a person infirm and ill—a case sure to prove difficult and to require much handling; though giving perhaps, with other matters, one of those chances for good taste, possibly even for the play of the very best in the world, that are not only always to be invoked and cultivated, but that are absolutely to be jumped at from the moment they make a sign.

Yes then, the case prescribed for its central figure a sick young woman, at the whole course of whose disintegration and the whole ordeal of whose consciousness one would have quite honestly to assist. The expression of her state and that of one's intimate relation to it might therefore well need to be discreet and ingenious; a reflexion that fortunately grew and grew, however, in proportion as I focussed my image— roundabout which, as it persisted, I repeat, the interesting possibilities and the attaching wonderments, not to say the insoluble mysteries, thickened apace. Why had one to look so straight in the face and so closely to cross-question that idea of making one's protagonist "sick"?—as if to be menaced with death or danger had n't been from time immemorial, for heroine or hero, the very shortest of all cuts to the interesting state. Why should a figure be disqualified for a central position by the particular circumstance that might most quicken, that might crown with a fine intensity, its liability to many accidents, its consciousness of all relations? This circumstance, true enough, might disqualify it for many activities—even though we should have imputed to it the unsurpassable activity of passionate, of inspired resistance. This last fact was the real issue, for the way grew straight from the moment one recognised that the poet essentially *can't* be concerned with the act of dying. Let him deal with the sickest of the sick, it is still by the act of living that they appeal to him, and appeal the more as the conditions plot against them and prescribe the battle. The process of life gives way fighting, and often may so shine out on the lost ground as in no other connexion. One had had moreover, as a various chronicler, one's secondary physical weaklings and failures, one's accessory invalids—introduced with a complacency that made light of criticism. To Ralph Touchett in "The Portrait of a Lady," for instance, his deplorable state of health was not only no drawback; I had clearly been right in counting it, for any happy effect he should produce, a positive good mark, a direct aid to pleasantness and vividness. The reason of this moreover could never in the world have been his fact of sex; since men, among the mortally afflicted, suffer on the whole more overtly and more grossly than women, and resist with a ruder, an inferior strategy. I had thus to take *that* anomaly for what it was worth, and I give it here but as one of the ambiguities amid which my subject ended by making itself at home and seating itself quite in confidence.

With the clearness I have just noted, accordingly, the last thing in the world it proposed to itself was to be the record predominantly of a collapse. I don't mean to say that my offered victim was not present to my imagination, constantly, as dragged by a greater force than any she herself could exert; she had been given me from far back as contesting every inch of the road, as catching at every object the grasp of which might make for delay, as clutching these things to the last moment of her strength. Such an attitude and such movements, the passion they expressed and the success they in fact represented, what were they in truth but the soul of drama?— which is the portrayal, as we know, of a catastrophe determined in spite of oppositions. My young woman would *herself* be the opposition—to the catastrophe announced by the associated Fates, powers conspiring to a sinister end and, with their command of means, finally achieving it, yet in such straits really to *stifle* the sacred spark that, obviously, a creature so animated, an adversary so subtle, could n't but be felt worthy, under whatever weaknesses, of the foreground and the limelight. She would meanwhile wish, moreover, all along, to live for particular things, she would found her struggle on particular human interests, which would inevitably determine, in respect to her, the attitude of other persons, persons affected in such a manner as to make them part of the action. If her impulse to wrest from her shrinking hour still as much of the fruit of life as possible, if this longing can take effect only by the aid of others, their participation (appealed to, entangled and coerced as they find themselves) becomes their drama too—that of their promoting her illusion, under her importunity, for reasons, for interests and advantages, from motives and points of view, of their own. Some of these promptings, evidently, would be of the highest order—others doubtless might n't; but they would make up together, for her, contributively, her sum of experience, represent to her somehow, in good faith or in bad, what she should have *known*. Somehow, too, at such a rate, one would see the persons subject to them drawn in as by some pool of a Lorelei—see them terrified and tempted and charmed; bribed away, it may even be, from more prescribed and natural orbits, inheriting from their connexion with her strange difficulties and still stranger opportunities, confronted with rare questions and called upon for new discriminations. Thus the scheme of her situation would, in a comprehensive way, see itself constituted; the rest of the interest would be in the number and nature of the particulars. Strong among these, naturally, the need that life should, apart from her infirmity, present itself to our young woman as quite dazzlingly liveable, and that if the great pang for her is in what she must give up we shall appreciate it the more from the sight of all she has.

One would see her then as possessed of all things, all but the single most precious assurance; freedom and money and a mobile mind and personal charm, the power to interest and attach; attributes, each one, enhancing the value of a future. From the moment his imagination began to deal with her at close quarters, in fact, nothing could more engage her designer than to work out the detail of her perfect rightness for her part; nothing above all more solicit him than to recognise fifty reasons for her national and social status. She should be the last fine flower—blooming alone, for the fullest attestation of her freedom—of an "old" New York stem; the happy congruities thus preserved for her being matters, however, that I may not now go into, and this even though the fine association that shall yet elsewhere await me is of a sort, at the best, rather to defy than to encourage exact expression. There goes with it, for the heroine of "The Wings of the Dove," a strong and special implication of liberty, liberty of action, of choice, of appreciation, of contact—proceeding from sources that provide better for large independence, I think, than any other conditions in the world—and this would be in particular what we should feel ourselves deeply concerned with. I had from far back mentally projected a certain sort of young American as more the "heir of all the ages" than any other young person whatever (and precisely on those grounds I have just glanced at but to pass them by for the moment); so that here was a chance to confer on some such figure a supremely touching value. To be the heir of all the ages only to know yourself, as that consciousness should deepen, balked of your inheritance, would be to play the part, it struck me, or at least to arrive at the type, in the light on the whole the most becoming. Otherwise, truly, what a perilous part to play *out*—what a suspicion of "swagger" in positively attempting it! So at least I could reason—so I even think I *had* to—to keep my subject to a decent compactness. For already, from an early stage, it had begun richly to people itself: the difficulty was to see whom the situation I had primarily projected might, by this, that or the other turn, *not* draw in. My business was to watch its turns as the fond parent watches a child perched, for its first riding-lesson, in the saddle; yet its interest, I had all the while to recall, was just in its making, on such a scale, for developments.

What one had discerned, at all events, from an early stage, was that a young person so devoted and exposed, a creature with her security hanging so by a hair, could n't but fall somehow into some abysmal trap—this being, dramatically speaking, what such a situation most naturally implied and imposed. Did n't the truth and a great part of the interest also reside in the appearance that she would constitute for others (given her passionate yearning to live while she might) a complication as great as any they might constitute for herself?— which is what I mean when I speak of such matters as "natural." They would be as natural, these tragic, pathetic, ironic, these indeed for the most part sinister, liabilities, to her living associates, as they could be to herself as prime subject. If her story was to consist, as it could so little help doing, of her being let in, as we say, for this, that and the other irreducible anxiety, how could she not have put a premium on the acquisition, by any close sharer of her life, of a consciousness similarly embarrassed? I have named the Rhine-maiden, but our young friend's existence would create rather, all round her, very much that whirlpool movement of the waters produced by the sinking of a big vessel or the failure of a great business; when we figure to ourselves the strong narrowing eddies, the immense force of suction, the general engulfment that, for any neighbouring object, makes immersion inevitable. I need scarce say, however, that in spite of these communities of doom I saw the main dramatic complication much more prepared *for* my vessel of sensibility than by her—the work of other hands (though with her own imbrued too, after all, in the measure of their never not being, in some direction, generous and extravagant, and thereby provoking).

The great point was, at all events, that if in a predicament she was to be, accordingly, it would be of the essence to create the predicament promptly and build it up solidly, so that it should have for us as much as possible its ominous air of awaiting her. That reflexion I found, betimes, not less inspiring than urgent; one begins so, in such a business, by looking about for one's compositional key, unable as one can only be to move till one has found it. To start without it is to pretend to enter the train and, still more, to remain in one's seat, without a ticket. Well—in the steady light and for the continued charm of these verifications—I had secured my ticket over the tolerably long line laid down for "The Wings of the Dove" from the moment I had noted that there could be no full presentation of Milly Theale as *engaged* with elements amid which she was to draw her breath in such pain, should not the elements have been, with all solicitude, duly prefigured. If one had seen that her stricken state was but half her case, the correlative half being the state of others as affected by her (they too should have a "case," bless them, quite as much as she!) then I was free to choose, as it were, the half with which I should begin. If, as I had fondly noted, the little world determined for her was to "bristle"—I delighted in the term!—with meanings, so, by the same token, could I but make my medal hang free, its obverse and its reverse, its face and its back, would beautifully become optional for the spectator. I somehow wanted them correspondingly embossed, wanted them inscribed and figured with an equal salience; yet it was none the less visibly my "key," as I have said, that though my regenerate young New Yorker, and what might depend on her, should form my centre, my circumference was every whit as treatable. Therefore I must trust myself to know when to proceed from the one and when from the other. Preparatively and, as it were, yearningly—given the whole ground—one began, in the event, with the outer ring, approaching the centre thus by narrowing circumvallations. There, full-blown, accordingly, from one hour to the other, rose one's process—for which there remained all the while so many amusing formulae.

The medal *did* hang free—I felt this perfectly, I remember, from the moment I had comfortably laid the ground provided in my first Book, ground from which Milly is superficially so absent. I scarce remember perhaps a case—I like even with this public grossness to insist on it—in which the curiosity of "beginning far back," as far back as possible, and even of going, to the same tune, far "behind," that is behind the face of the subject, was to assert itself with less scruple. The free hand, in this connexion, was above all agreeable—the hand the freedom of which I owed to the fact that the work had ignominiously failed, in advance, of all power to see itself "serialised." This failure had repeatedly waited, for me, upon shorter fictions; but the considerable production we here discuss was (as "The Golden Bowl" was to be, two or three years later) born, not otherwise than a little bewilderedly, into a world of periodicals and editors, of roaring "successes" in fine, amid which it was well-nigh unnotedly to lose itself. There is fortunately something bracing, ever, in the alpine chill, that of some high icy *arête*, shed by the cold editorial shoulder; sour grapes may at moments fairly intoxicate and the story-teller worth his salt rejoice to feel again how many accommodations he can practise. Those addressed to "conditions of publication" have in a degree their interesting, or at least their provoking, side; but their charm is qualified by the fact that the prescriptions here spring from a soil often wholly alien to the ground of the work itself. They are almost always the fruit of another air altogether and conceived in a light liable to represent *within* the circle of the work itself little else than darkness. Still, when not too blighting, they often operate as a tax on ingenuity—that ingenuity of the expert craftsman which likes to be taxed very much to the same tune to which a well-bred horse likes to be saddled. The best and finest ingenuities, nevertheless, with all respect to that truth, are apt to be, not one's compromises, but one's fullest conformities, and I well remember, in the case before us, the pleasure of feeling my divisions, my proportions and general rhythm, rest all on permanent rather than in any degree on momentary proprieties. It was enough for my alternations, thus, that they were good in themselves; it was in fact so much for them that I really think any further account of the constitution of the book reduces itself to a just notation of the law they followed.

There was the "fun," to begin with, of establishing one's successive centres—of fixing them so exactly that the portions of the subject commanded by them as by happy points of view, and accordingly treated from them, would constitute, so to speak, sufficiently solid *blocks* of wrought material, squared to the sharp edge, as to have weight and mass and carrying power; to make for construction, that is, to conduce to effect and to provide for beauty. Such a block, obviously, is the whole preliminary presentation of Kate Croy, which, from the first, I recall, absolutely declined to enact itself save in terms of amplitude. Terms of amplitude, terms of atmosphere, those terms, and those terms only, in which images assert their fulness and roundness, their power to revolve, so that they have sides and backs, parts in the shade as true as parts in the sun—these were plainly to be my conditions, right and left, and I was so far from overrating the amount of expression the whole thing, as I saw and felt it, would require, that to retrace the way at present is, alas, more than anything else, but to mark the gaps and the lapses, to miss, one by one, the intentions that, with the best will in the world, were not to fructify. I have just said that the process of the general attempt is described from the moment the "blocks" are numbered, and that would be a true enough picture of my plan. Yet one's plan, alas, is one thing and one's result another; so that I am perhaps nearer the point in saying that this last strikes me at present as most characterised by the happy features that *were*, under my first and most blest illusion, to have contributed to it. I meet them all, as I renew acquaintance, I mourn for them all as I remount the stream, the absent values, the palpable voids, the missing links, the mocking shadows, that reflect, taken together, the early bloom of one's good faith. Such cases are of course far from abnormal—so far from it that some acute mind ought surely to have worked out by this time the "law" of the degree in which the artist's energy fairly depends on his fallibility. How much and how often, and in what connexions and with what almost infinite variety, must he be a dupe, that of his prime object, to be at all measurably a master, that of his actual substitute for it—or in other words at all appreciably to exist? He places, after an earnest survey, the piers of his bridge— he has at least sounded deep enough, heaven knows, for their brave position; yet the bridge spans the stream, after the fact, in apparently complete independence of these properties, the principal grace of the original design. *They* were an illusion, for their necessary hour; but the span itself, whether of a single arch or of many, seems by the oddest chance in the world to be a reality; since, actually, the rueful builder, passing under it, sees figures and hears sounds above: he makes out, with his heart in his throat, that it bears and is positively being "used."

The building-up of Kate Croy's consciousness to the capacity for the load little by little to be laid on it was, by way of example, to have been a matter of as many hundred close-packed bricks as there are actually poor dozens. The image of her so compromised and compromising father was all effectively to have pervaded her life, was in a certain particular way to have tampered with her spring; by which I mean that the shame and the irritation and the depression, the general poisonous influence of him, were to have been *shown*, with a truth beyond the compass even of one's most emphasised "word of honour" for it, to do these things. But where do we find him, at this time of day, save in a beggarly scene or two which scarce arrives at the dignity of functional reference? He but "looks in," poor beautiful dazzling, damning apparition that he was to have been; he sees his place so taken, his company so little missed, that, cocking again that fine form of hat which has yielded him for so long his one effective cover, he turns away with a whistle of indifference that nobly misrepresents the deepest disappointment of his life. One's poor word of honour has *had* to pass muster for the show. Every one, in short, was to have enjoyed so much better a chance that, like stars of the theatre condescending to oblige, they have had to take small parts, to content them-

selves with minor identities, in order to come on at all. I
have n't the heart now, I confess, to adduce the detail of so
many lapsed importances; the explanation of most of which,
after all, I take to have been in the crudity of a truth beating
full upon me through these reconsiderations, the odd inveteracy with which picture, at almost any turn, is jealous of
drama, and drama (though on the whole with a greater patience, I think) suspicious of picture. Between them, no
doubt, they do much for the theme; yet each baffles insidiously the other's ideal and eats round the edges of its position; each is too ready to say "I can take the thing for 'done'
only when done in *my* way." The residuum of comfort for
the witness of these broils is of course meanwhile in the convenient reflexion, invented for him in the twilight of time and
the infancy of art by the Angel, not to say by the Demon, of
Compromise, that nothing is so easy to "do" as not to be
thankful for almost any stray help in its getting done. It was
n't, after this fashion, by making good one's dream of Lionel
Croy that my structure was to stand on its feet—any more
than it was by letting him go that I was to be left irretrievably
lamenting. The who and the what, the how and the why, the
whence and the whither of Merton Densher, these, no less,
were quantities and attributes that should have danced about
him with the antique grace of nymphs and fauns circling
round a bland Hermes and crowning him with flowers. One's
main anxiety, for each one's agents, is that the air of each shall
be *given*; but what does the whole thing become, after all, as
one goes, but a series of sad places at which the hand of generosity has been cautioned and stayed? The young man's situation, personal, professional, social, was to have been so
decanted for us that we should get all the taste; we were to
have been penetrated with Mrs. Lowder, by the same token,
saturated with her presence, her "personality," and felt all her
weight in the scale. We were to have revelled in Mrs.
Stringham, my heroine's attendant friend, her fairly choral
Bostonian, a subject for innumerable touches, and in an extended and above all an *animated* reflexion of Milly Theale's
experience of English society; just as the strength and sense
of the situation in Venice, for our gathered friends, was to
have come to us in a deeper draught out of a larger cup, and

just as the pattern of Densher's final position and fullest consciousness there was to have been marked in fine stitches, all
silk and gold, all pink and silver, that have had to remain,
alas, but entwined upon the reel.

It is n't, no doubt, however—to recover, after all, our critical balance—that the pattern did n't, for each compartment,
get itself somehow wrought, and that we might n't thus,
piece by piece, opportunity offering, trace it over and study
it. The thing has doubtless, as a whole, the advantage that
each piece is true to its pattern, and that while it pretends to
make no simple statement it yet never lets go its scheme of
clearness. Applications of this scheme are continuous and exemplary enough, though I scarce leave myself room to glance
at them. The clearness is obtained in Book First—or otherwise, as I have said, in the first "piece," each Book having its
subordinate and contributive pattern—through the associated consciousness of my two prime young persons, for
whom I early recognised that I should have to consent, under
stress, to a practical *fusion* of consciousness. It is into the
young woman's "ken" that Merton Densher is represented as
swimming; but her mind is not here, rigorously, the one reflector. There are occasions when it plays this part, just as
there are others when his plays it, and an intelligible plan
consists naturally not a little in fixing such occasions and making them, on one side and the other, sufficient to themselves.
Do I sometimes in fact forfeit the advantage of that distinctness? Do I ever abandon one centre for another after the former has been postulated? From the moment we proceed by
"centres"—and I have never, I confess, embraced the logic of
any superior process—they must *be*, each, as a basis, selected
and fixed; after which it is that, in the high interest of economy of treatment, they determine and rule. There is no economy of treatment without an adopted, a related point of view,
and though I understand, under certain degrees of pressure,
a represented community of vision between several parties to
the action when it makes for concentration, I understand no
breaking-up of the register, no sacrifice of the recording consistency, that does n't rather scatter and weaken. In this truth
resides the secret of the discriminated occasion—that aspect
of the subject which we have our noted choice of treating

either as picture or scenically, but which is apt, I think, to
show its fullest worth in the Scene. Beautiful exceedingly, for
that matter, those occasions or parts of an occasion when the
boundary line between picture and scene bears a little the
weight of the double pressure.

Such would be the case, I can't but surmise, for the long
passage that forms here before us the opening of Book
Fourth, where all the offered life centres, to intensity, in the
disclosure of Milly's single throbbing consciousness, but
where, for a due rendering, everything has to be brought to
a head. This passage, the view of her introduction to Mrs.
Lowder's circle, has its mate, for illustration, later on in the
book and at a crisis for which the occasion submits to another
rule. My registers or "reflectors," as I so conveniently name
them (burnished indeed as they generally are by the intelligence, the curiosity, the passion, the force of the moment,
whatever it be, directing them), work, as we have seen, in
arranged alternation; so that in the second connexion I here
glance at it is Kate Croy who is, "for all she is worth," turned
on. She is turned on largely at Venice, where the appearances,
rich and obscure and portentous (another word I rejoice in)
as they have by that time become and altogether exquisite as
they remain, are treated almost wholly through her vision of
them and Densher's (as to the lucid interplay of which conspiring and conflicting agents there would be a great deal to
say). It is in Kate's consciousness that at the stage in question
the drama is brought to a head, and the occasion on which,
in the splendid saloon of poor Milly's hired palace, she takes
the measure of her friend's festal evening, squares itself to the
same synthetic firmness as the compact constructional block
inserted by the scene at Lancaster Gate. Milly's situation
ceases at a given moment to be "renderable" in terms closer
than those supplied by Kate's intelligence, or, in a richer degree, by Densher's, or, for one fond hour, by poor Mrs.
Stringham's (since to that sole brief futility is this last participant, crowned by my original plan with the quaintest functions, in fact reduced); just as Kate's relation with Densher
and Densher's with Kate have ceased previously, and are then
to cease again, to be projected for us, so far as Milly is concerned with them, on any more responsible plate than that of

the latter's admirable anxiety. It is as if, for these aspects, the impersonal plate—in other words the poor author's comparatively cold affirmation or thin guarantee—had felt itself a figure of attestation at once too gross and too bloodless, likely to affect us as an abuse of privilege when not as an abuse of knowledge.

Heaven forbid, we say to ourselves during almost the whole Venetian climax, heaven forbid we should "know" anything more of our ravaged sister than what Densher darkly pieces together, or than what Kate Croy pays, heroically, it must be owned, at the hour of her visit alone to Densher's lodging, for her superior handling and her dire profanation of. For we have time, while this passage lasts, to turn round critically; we have time to recognise intentions and proprieties; we have time to catch glimpses of an economy of composition, as I put it, interesting in itself: all in spite of the author's scarce more than half-dissimulated despair at the inveterate displacement of his general centre. "The Wings of the Dove" happens to offer perhaps the most striking example I may cite (though with public penance for it already performed) of my regular failure to keep the appointed halves of my whole equal. Here the makeshift middle—for which the best I can say is that it 's always rueful and never impudent—reigns with even more than its customary contrition, though passing itself off perhaps too with more than its usual craft. Nowhere, I seem to recall, had the need of dissimulation been felt so as anguish; nowhere had I condemned a luckless theme to complete its revolution, burdened with the accumulation of its difficulties, the difficulties that grow with a theme's development, in quarters so cramped. Of course, as every novelist knows, it is difficulty that inspires; only, for that perfection of charm, it must have been difficulty inherent and congenital, and not difficulty "caught" by the wrong frequentations. The latter half, that is the false and deformed half, of "The Wings" would verily, I think, form a signal object-lesson for a literary critic bent on improving his occasion to the profit of the budding artist. This whole corner of the picture bristles with "dodges"—such as he should feel himself all committed to recognise and denounce—for disguising the reduced scale of the exhibition, for foreshortening at any cost, for imparting to patches the value of presences, for dressing objects in an *air* as of the dimensions they can't possibly have. Thus he would have his free hand for pointing out what a tangled web we weave when—well, when, through our mis-laying or otherwise trifling with our blest pair of compasses, we have to produce the illusion of mass without the illusion of extent. *There* is a job quite to the measure of most of our monitors—and with the interest for them well enhanced by the preliminary cunning quest for the spot where deformity has begun.

I recognise meanwhile, throughout the long earlier reach of the book, not only no deformities but, I think, a positively close and felicitous application of method, the preserved con-sistencies of which, often illusive, but never really lapsing, it would be of a certain diversion, and might be of some profit, to follow. The author's accepted task at the outset has been to suggest with force the nature of the tie formed between the two young persons first introduced—to give the full impression of its peculiar worried and baffled, yet clinging and confident, ardour. The picture constituted, so far as may be, is that of a pair of natures well-nigh consumed by a sense of their intimate affinity and congruity, the reciprocity of their desire, and thus passionately impatient of barriers and delays, yet with qualities of intelligence and character that they are meanwhile extraordinarily able to draw upon for the enrichment of their relation, the extension of their prospect and the support of their "game." They are far from a common couple, Merton Densher and Kate Croy, as befits the remark-able fashion in which fortune was to waylay and opportunity was to distinguish them—the whole strange truth of their response to which opening involves also, in its order, no vul-gar art of exhibition; but what they have most to tell us is that, all unconsciously and with the best faith in the world, all by mere force of the terms of their superior passion com-bined with their superior diplomacy, they are laying a trap for the great innocence to come. If I like, as I have confessed, the "portentous" look, I was perhaps never to set so high a value on it as for all this prompt provision of forces unwittingly waiting to close round my eager heroine (to the eventual deep chill of her eagerness) as the result of her mere lifting of a latch. Infinitely interesting to have built up the relation of the others to the point at which its aching restlessness, its need to affirm itself otherwise than by an exasperated patience, meets as with instinctive relief and recognition the possibilities shining out of Milly Theale. Infinitely interesting to have prepared and organised, correspondingly, that young woman's precipitations and liabilities, to have constructed, for Drama essentially to take possession, the whole bright house of her exposure.

These references, however, reflect too little of the detail of the treatment imposed; such a detail as I for instance get hold of in the fact of Densher's interview with Mrs. Lowder before he goes to America. It forms, in this preliminary picture, the one patch not strictly seen over Kate Croy's shoulder; though it 's notable that immediately after, at the first possible moment, we surrender again to our major convenience, as it happens to be at the time, that of our drawing breath through the young woman's lungs. Once more, in other words, before we know it, Densher's direct vision of the scene at Lancaster Gate is replaced by her apprehension, her contributive assimilation, of his experience: it melts back into that accumulation, which we have been, as it were, saving up. Does my apparent deviation here count accordingly as a muddle?—one of the muddles ever blooming so thick in any soil that fails to grow reasons and determinants. No, distinctly not; for I had definitely opened the door, as attention of perusal of the first two Books will show, to the subjective community of my young pair. (Attention of perusal, I thus confess by the way, is what I at every point, as well as here, absolutely invoke and take for granted; a truth I avail myself of this occasion to note once for all—in the interest of that variety of ideal reigning, I gather, in the connexion. The enjoyment of a work of art, the acceptance of an irresistible illusion, constituting, to my sense, our highest experience of "luxury," the luxury is not greatest, by my consequent measure, when the work asks for as little attention as possible. It is greatest, it is delightfully, divinely great, when we feel the surface, like the thick ice of the skater's pond, bear without cracking the strongest pressure we throw on it. The sound of the crack one may recognise, but never surely to call it a luxury.) That I had scarce availed myself of the privilege of seeing with Densher's eyes is another matter; the point is that I had intelligently marked my possible, my occasional need of it. So, at all events, the constructional "block" of the first two Books compactly forms itself. A new block, all of the squarest and not a little of the smoothest, begins with the Third—by which I mean of course a new mass of interest governed from a new centre. Here again I make prudent *provision*—to be sure to keep my centre strong. It dwells mainly, we at once see, in the depths of Milly Theale's "case," where, close beside it, however, we meet a supplementary reflector, that of the lucid even though so quivering spirit of her dedicated friend.

The more or less associated consciousness of the two women deals thus, unequally, with the next presented face of the subject—deals with it to the exclusion of the dealing of others; and if, for a highly particular moment, I allot to Mrs. Stringham the responsibility of the direct appeal to us, it is again, charming to relate, on behalf of that play of the portentous which I cherish so as a "value" and am accordingly for ever setting in motion. There is an hour of evening, on the alpine height, at which it becomes of the last importance that our young woman should testify eminently in this direction. But as I was to find it long since of a blest wisdom that no expense should be incurred or met, in any corner of picture of mine, without some concrete image of the account kept of it, that is of its being organically re-economised, so under that dispensation Mrs. Stringham has to register the transaction. Book Fifth is a new block mainly in its provision of a new set of occasions, which readopt, for their order, the previous centre, Milly's now almost full-blown consciousness. At my game, with renewed zest, of driving portents home, I have by this time all the choice of those that are to brush that surface with a dark wing. They are used, to our profit, on an elastic but a definite system; by which I mean that having to sound here and there a little deep, as a test, for my basis of method, I find it everywhere obstinately present. It draws the "occasion" into tune and keeps it so, to repeat my tiresome term; my nearest approach to muddlement is to have sometimes—but not too often—to break my occasions small. Some of them succeed in remaining ample and in really aspiring then to the higher, the sustained lucidity. The whole actual centre of the work, resting on a misplaced pivot and lodged in Book Fifth, pretends to a long reach, or at any rate to the larger foreshortening—though bringing home to me, on re-perusal, what I find striking, charming and curious, the author's instinct everywhere for the *indirect* presentation of his main image. I note how, again and again, I go but a little way with the direct—that is with the straight exhibition of Milly; it resorts for relief, this process, whenever it can, to some kinder, some merciful indirection: all as if to approach her circuitously, deal with her at second hand, as an unspotted princess is ever dealt with; the pressure all round her kept easy for her, the sounds, the movements regulated, the forms and ambiguities made charming. All of which proceeds, obviously, from her painter's tenderness of imagination about her, which reduces him to watching her, as it were, through the successive windows of other people's interest in her. So, if we talk of princesses, do the balconies opposite the palace gates, do the coigns of vantage and respect enjoyed for a fee, rake from afar the mystic figure in the gilded coach as it comes forth into the great *place*. But my use of windows and balconies is doubtless at best an extravagance by itself, and as to what there may be to note, of this and other supersubtleties, other arch-refinements, of tact and taste, of design and instinct, in "The Wings of the Dove," I become conscious of overstepping my space without having brought the full quantity to light. The failure leaves me with a burden of residuary comment of which I yet boldly hope elsewhere to discharge myself.

The Ambassadors

NOTHING IS MORE easy than to state the subject of "The Ambassadors," which first appeared in twelve numbers of *The North American Review* (1903) and was published as a whole the same year. The situation involved is gathered up betimes, that is in the second chapter of Book Fifth, for the reader's benefit, into as few words as possible—planted or "sunk," stiffly and saliently, in the centre of the current, almost perhaps to the obstruction of traffic. Never can a composition of this sort have sprung straighter from a dropped grain of suggestion, and never can that grain, developed, overgrown and smothered, have yet lurked more in the mass as an independent particle. The whole case, in fine, is in Lambert Strether's irrepressible outbreak to little Bilham on the Sunday afternoon in Gloriani's garden, the candour with which he yields, for his young friend's enlightenment, to the charming admonition of that crisis. The idea of the tale resides indeed in the very fact that an hour of such unprecedented ease should have been felt by him *as* a crisis, and he is at pains to express it for us as neatly as we could desire. The remarks to which he thus gives utterance contain the essence of "The Ambassadors," his fingers close, before he has done, round the stem of the full-blown flower; which, after that fashion, he continues officiously to present to us. "Live all you can; it 's a mistake not to. It does n't so much matter what you do in particular so long as you have your life. If you have n't had that what *have* you had? I 'm too old—too old at any rate for what I see. What one loses one loses; make no mistake about that. Still, we have the illusion of freedom; therefore don't, like me to-day, be without the memory of that illusion. I was either, at the right time, too stupid or too intelligent to have it, and now I 'm a case of reaction against the mistake. Do what you like so long as you don't make it. For it *was* a mistake. Live, live!" Such is the gist of Strether's appeal to the impressed youth, whom he likes and whom he desires to befriend; the word "mistake" occurs several times, it will be seen, in the course of his remarks—which gives the measure of the signal warning he feels attached to his case.

He has accordingly missed too much, though perhaps after all constitutionally qualified for a better part, and he wakes up to it in conditions that press the spring of a terrible question. *Would* there yet perhaps be time for reparation?—reparation, that is, for the injury done his character; for the affront, he is quite ready to say, so stupidly put upon it and in which he has even himself had so clumsy a hand? The answer to which is that he now at all events *sees*; so that the business of my tale and the march of my action, not to say the precious moral of everything, is just my demonstration of this process of vision.

Nothing can exceed the closeness with which the whole fits again into its germ. That had been given me bodily, as usual, by the spoken word, for I was to take the image over exactly as I happened to have met it. A friend had repeated to me, with great appreciation, a thing or two said to him by a man of distinction, much his senior, and to which a sense akin to that of Strether's melancholy eloquence might be imputed— said as chance would have, and so easily might, in Paris, and in a charming old garden attached to a house of art, and on a Sunday afternoon of summer, many persons of great interest being present. The observation there listened to and gathered up had contained part of the "note" that I was to recognise on the spot as to my purpose—had contained in fact the greater part; the rest was in the place and the time and the scene they sketched: these constituents clustered and combined to give me further support, to give me what I may call the note absolute. There it stands, accordingly, full in the tideway; driven in, with hard taps, like some strong stake for the noose of a cable, the swirl of the current roundabout it. What amplified the hint to more than the bulk of hints in general was the gift with it of the old Paris garden, for in that token were sealed up values infinitely precious. There was of course the seal to break and each item of the packet to count over and handle and estimate; but somehow, in the light of the hint, all the elements of a situation of the sort most to my taste were there. I could even remember no occasion on which, so confronted, I had found it of a livelier interest to take stock, in this fashion, of suggested wealth. For I think, verily, that there are degrees of merit in subjects—in spite of the fact that to treat even one of the most ambiguous with due decency we must for the time, for the feverish and prejudiced hour, at least figure its merit and its dignity as *possibly* absolute. What it comes to, doubtless, is that even among the supremely good—since with such alone is it one's theory of one's honour to be concerned—there is an ideal *beauty* of goodness the invoked action of which is to raise the artistic faith to its maximum. Then truly, I hold, one's theme may be said to shine, and that of "The Ambassadors," I confess, wore this glow for me from beginning to end. Fortunately thus I am able to estimate this as, frankly, quite the best, "all round," of all my productions; any failure of that justification would have made such an extreme of complacency publicly fatuous.

I recall then in this connexion no moment of subjective intermittence, never one of those alarms as for a suspected hollow beneath one's feet, a felt ingratitude in the scheme adopted, under which confidence fails and opportunity seems but to mock. If the motive of "The Wings of the Dove," as I have noted, was to worry me at moments by a sealing-up of its face—though without prejudice to its again, of a sudden, fairly grimacing with expression—so in this other business I had absolute conviction and constant clearness to deal with; it had been a frank proposition, the whole bunch of data, installed on my premises like a monotony of fine weather. (The order of composition, in these things, I may mention, was reversed by the order of publication; the earlier written of the two books having appeared as the later.) Even under the weight of my hero's years I could feel my postulate firm; even under the strain of the difference between those of Madame de Vionnet and those of Chad Newsome, a difference liable to be denounced as shocking, I could still feel it serene. Nothing resisted, nothing betrayed, I seem to make out, in this full and sound sense of the matter; it shed from any side I could turn it to the same golden glow. I rejoiced in the promise of a hero so mature, who would give me thereby the more to bite into—since it 's only into thickened motive and accumulated character, I think, that the painter of life bites more than a little. My poor friend should have accumulated character, certainly; or rather would be quite naturally and handsomely possessed of it, in the sense that he would have, and would always have felt he had, imagination galore, and that this yet would n't have wrecked him. It was immeasurable, the opportunity to "do" a man of imagination, for if *there* might n't be a chance to "bite," where in the world might it be? This personage of course, so enriched, would n't give me, for his type, imagination in *predominance* or as his prime faculty, nor should I, in view of other matters, have found that convenient. So particular a luxury—some occasion, that is, for study of the high gift in *supreme* command of a case or of a career—would still doubtless come on the day I should be ready to pay for it; and till then might, as from far back, remain hung up well in view and just out of reach. The comparative case meanwhile would serve—it was only on the minor scale that I had treated myself even to comparative cases.

I was to hasten to add however that, happy stopgaps as the minor scale had thus yielded, the instance in hand should enjoy the advantage of the full range of the major; since most immediately to the point was the question of that *supplement* of situation logically involved in our gentleman's impulse to deliver himself in the Paris garden on the Sunday afternoon— or if not involved by strict logic then all ideally and enchantingly implied in it. (I say "ideally," because I need scarce mention that for development, for expression of its maximum, my glimmering story was, at the earliest stage, to have nipped the thread of connexion with the possibilities of the actual reported speaker. *He* remains but the happiest of accidents; his actualities, all too definite, precluded any range of possibilities; it had only been his charming office to project upon that wide field of the artist's vision—which hangs there ever in place like the white sheet suspended for the figures of a child's magic-lantern—a more fantastic and more moveable shadow.) No privilege of the teller of tales and the handler of puppets is more delightful, or has more of the suspense and the thrill of a game of difficulty breathlessly played, than just this business of looking for the unseen and the occult, in a scheme half-grasped, by the light or, so to speak, by the clinging scent, of the gage already in hand. No dreadful old pursuit of the hidden slave with bloodhounds and the rag of association can ever, for "excitement," I judge, have bettered it at its best. For the dramatist always, by the very law of his genius, believes not only in a possible right issue from the rightly-conceived tight place; he does much more than this—he believes, irresistibly, in the necessary, the precious "tightness" of the place (whatever the issue) on the strength of any respectable hint. It being thus the respectable hint that I had with such avidity picked up, what would be the story to which it would most inevitably form the centre? It is part of the charm attendant on such questions that the "story," with the omens true, as I say, puts on from this stage the authenticity of concrete existence. It then *is*, essentially—it begins to be, though it may more or less obscurely lurk; so that the point is not in the least what to make of it, but only, very delightfully and very damnably, where to put one's hand on it.

In which truth resides surely much of the interest of that admirable mixture for salutary application which we know as art. Art deals with what we see, it must first contribute full-handed that ingredient; it plucks its material, otherwise expressed, in the garden of life—which material elsewhere grown is stale and uneatable. But it has no sooner done this than it has to take account of a *process*—from which only when it 's the basest of the servants of man, incurring ignominious dismissal with no "character," does it, and whether under some muddled pretext of morality or on any other, pusillanimously edge away. The process, that of the expression, the literal squeezing-out, of value is another affair—with which the happy luck of mere finding has little to do. The joys of finding, at this stage, are pretty well over; that quest of the subject as a whole by "matching," as the ladies say at the shops, the big piece with the snippet, having ended, we assume, with a capture. The subject is found, and if the problem is then transferred to the ground of what to do with it the field opens out for any amount of doing. This is precisely the infusion that, as I submit, completes the strong mixture. It is on the other hand the part of the business that can least be likened to the chase with horn and hound. It 's all a sedentary part—involves as much ciphering, of sorts, as would merit the highest salary paid to a chief accountant.

Not, however, that the chief accountant has n't *his* gleams of bliss; for the felicity, or at least the equilibrium, of the artist's state dwells less, surely, in the further delightful complications he can smuggle in than in those he succeeds in keeping out. He sows his seed at the risk of too thick a crop; wherefore yet again, like the gentlemen who audit ledgers, he must keep his head at any price. In consequence of all which, for the interest of the matter, I might seem here to have my choice of narrating my "hunt" for Lambert Strether, of describing the capture of the shadow projected by my friend's anecdote, or of reporting on the occurrences subsequent to that triumph. But I had probably best attempt a little to glance in each direction; since it comes to me again and again, over this licentious record, that one's bag of adventures, conceived or conceivable, has been only half-emptied by the mere telling of one's story. It depends so on what one means by that equivocal quantity. There is the story of one's hero, and then, thanks to the intimate connexion of things, the story of one's story itself. I blush to confess it, but if one 's a dramatist one 's a dramatist, and the latter imbroglio is liable on occasion to strike me as really the more objective of the two.

The philosophy imputed to him in that beautiful outbreak, the hour there, amid such happy provision, striking for him, would have been then, on behalf of my man of imagination, to be logically and, as the artless craft of comedy has it, "led up" to; the probable course to such a goal, the goal of so conscious a predicament, would have in short to be finely calculated. Where has he come from and why has he come, what is he doing (as we Anglo-Saxons, and we only, say, in our foredoomed clutch of exotic aids to expression) in that *galère*? To answer these questions plausibly, to answer them as under cross-examination in the witness-box by counsel for the prosecution, in other words satisfactorily to account for Strether and for his "peculiar tone," was to possess myself of the entire fabric. At the same time the clue to its whereabouts would lie in a certain *principle* of probability: he would n't have indulged in his peculiar tone without a reason; it would take a felt predicament or a false position to give him so ironic an accent. One had n't been noting "tones" all one's life without recognising when one heard it the voice of the false position.

1310 PREFACES TO THE NEW YORK EDITION

The dear man in the Paris garden was then admirably and unmistakeably *in* one—which was no small point gained; what next accordingly concerned us was the determination of *this* identity. One could only go by probabilities, but there was the advantage that the most general of the probabilities were virtual certainties. Possessed of our friend's nationality, to start with, there was a general probability in his narrower localism; which, for that matter, one had really but to keep under the lens for an hour to see it give up its secrets. He would have issued, our rueful worthy, from the very heart of New England—at the heels of which matter of course a perfect train of secrets tumbled for me into the light. They had to be sifted and sorted, and I shall not reproduce the detail of that process; but unmistakeably they were all there, and it was but a question, auspiciously, of picking among them. What the "position" would infallibly be, and why, on his hands, it had turned "false"—these inductive steps could only be as rapid as they were distinct. I accounted for everything—and "everything" had by this time become the most promising quantity—by the view that he had come to Paris in some state of mind which was literally undergoing, as a result of new and unexpected assaults and infusions, a change almost from hour to hour. He had come with a view that might have been figured by a clear green liquid, say, in a neat glass phial; and the liquid, once poured into the open cup of *application*, once exposed to the action of another air, had begun to turn from green to red, or whatever, and might, for all he knew, be on its way to purple, to black, to yellow. At the still wilder extremes represented perhaps, for all he could say to the contrary, by a variability so violent, he would at first, naturally, but have gazed in surprise and alarm; whereby the *situation* clearly would spring from the play of wildness and the development of extremes. I saw in a moment that, should this development proceed both with force and logic, my "story" would leave nothing to be desired. There is always, of course, for the story-teller, the irresistible determinant and the incalculable advantage of his interest in the story *as such*; it is ever, obviously, overwhelmingly, the prime and precious thing (as other than this I have never been able to see it); as to which what makes for it, with whatever headlong energy, may be said to pale before the energy with which it simply makes for itself. It rejoices, none the less, at its best, to seem to offer itself in a light, to seem to know, and with the very last knowledge, what it 's about—liable as it yet is at moments to be caught by us with its tongue in its cheek and absolutely no warrant but its splendid impudence. Let us grant then that the impudence is always there—there, so to speak, for grace and effect and *allure*; there, above all, because the Story is just the spoiled child of art, and because, as we are always disappointed when the pampered don't "play up," we like it, to that extent, to look all its character. It probably does so, in truth, even when we most flatter ourselves that we negotiate with it by treaty.

All of which, again, is but to say that the *steps*, for my fable, placed themselves with a prompt and, as it were, functional assurance—an air quite as of readiness to have dispensed with logic had I been in fact too stupid for my clue. Never, positively, none the less, as the links multiplied, had I felt less stupid than for the determination of poor Strether's errand and for the apprehension of his issue. These things continued to fall together, as by the neat action of their own weight and form, even while their commentator scratched his head about them; he easily sees now that they were always well in advance of him. As the case completed itself he had in fact, from a good way behind, to catch up with them, breathless and a little flurried, as he best could. *The* false position, for our belated man of the world—belated because he had endeavoured so long to escape being one, and now at last had really to face his doom—the false position for him, I say, was obviously to have presented himself at the gate of that boundless menagerie primed with a moral scheme of the most approved pattern which was yet framed to break down on any approach to vivid facts; that is to any at all liberal appreciation of them. There would have been of course the case of the Strether prepared, wherever presenting himself, only to judge and to feel meanly; but *he* would have moved for me, I confess, enveloped in no legend whatever. The actual man's note, from the first of our seeing it struck, is the note of discrimination, just as his drama is to become, under stress, the drama of discrimination. It would have been his blest imagination, we have seen, that had already helped him to discriminate; the element that was for so much of the pleasure of my cutting thick, as I have intimated, into his intellectual, into his moral substance. Yet here it was, at the same time, just here, that a shade for a moment fell across the scene.

There was the dreadful little old tradition, one of the platitudes of the human comedy, that people's moral scheme *does* break down in Paris; that nothing is more frequently observed; that hundreds of thousands of more or less hypocritical or more or less cynical persons annually visit the place for the sake of the probable catastrophe, and that I came late in the day to work myself up about it. There was in fine the *trivial* association, one of the vulgarest in the world; but which gave me pause no longer, I think, simply because its vulgarity is so advertised. The revolution performed by Strether under the influence of the most interesting of great cities was to have nothing to do with any *bêtise* of the imputably "tempted" state; he was to be thrown forward, rather, thrown quite with violence, upon his lifelong trick of intense reflexion: which friendly test indeed was to bring him out, through winding passages, through alternations of darkness and light, very much *in* Paris, but with the surrounding scene itself a minor matter, a mere symbol for more things than had been dreamt of in the philosophy of Woollett. Another surrounding scene would have done as well for our show could it have represented a place in which Strether's errand was likely to lie and his crisis to await him. The *likely* place had the great merit of sparing me preparations; there would have been too many involved—not at all impossibilities, only rather worrying and delaying difficulties—in positing elsewhere Chad Newsome's interesting relation, his so interesting complexity of relations. Strether's appointed stage, in fine, could be but Chad's most luckily selected one. The young man had gone in, as they say, for circumjacent charm; and where he would have found it, by the turn of his mind, most "authentic," was where his earnest friend's analysis would most find *him*; as well as where, for that matter, the former's whole analytic faculty would be led such a wonderful dance.

"The Ambassadors" had been, all conveniently, "arranged for"; its first appearance was from month to month, in the

North American Review during 1903, and I had been open
from far back to any pleasant provocation for ingenuity that
might reside in one's actively adopting—so as to make it, in
its way, a small compositional law—recurrent breaks and re-
sumptions. I had made up my mind here regularly to exploit
and enjoy these often rather rude jolts—having found, as I
believed, an admirable way to it; yet every question of form
and pressure, I easily remember, paled in the light of the major propriety, recognised as soon as really weighed; that of
employing but one centre and keeping it all within my hero's
compass. The thing was to be so much this worthy's intimate
adventure that even the projection of his consciousness upon
it from beginning to end without intermission or deviation
would probably still leave a part of its value for him, and *a
fortiori* for ourselves, unexpressed. I might, however, express
every grain of it that there would be room for—on condition
of contriving a splendid particular economy. Other persons in
no small number were to people the scene, and each with his
or her axe to grind, his or her situation to treat, his or her
coherency not to fail of, his or her relation to my leading
motive, in a word, to establish and carry on. But Strether's
sense of these things, and Strether's only, should avail me for
showing them; I should know them but through his more or
less groping knowledge of them, since his very gropings
would figure among his most interesting motions, and a full
observance of the rich rigour I speak of would give me more
of the effect I should be most "after" than all other possible
observances together. It would give me a large unity, and that
in turn would crown me with the grace to which the enlightened story-teller will at any time, for his interest, sacrifice if
need be all other graces whatever. I refer of course to the
grace of intensity, which there are ways of signally achieving
and ways of signally missing—as we see it, all round us, helplessly and woefully missed. Not that it is n't, on the other
hand, a virtue eminently subject to appreciation—there being
no strict, no absolute measure of it; so that one may hear it
acclaimed where it has quite escaped one's perception, and see
it unnoticed where one has gratefully hailed it. After all of
which I am not sure, either, that the immense amusement of
the whole cluster of difficulties so arrayed may not operate,

for the fond fabulist, when judicious not less than fond, as his best of determinants. That charming principle is always there, at all events, to keep interest fresh: it is a principle, we remember, essentially ravenous, without scruple and without mercy, appeased with no cheap nor easy nourishment. It enjoys the costly sacrifice and rejoices thereby in the very odour of difficulty—even as ogres, with their "Fee-faw-fum!" rejoice in the smell of the blood of Englishmen.

Thus it was, at all events, that the ultimate, though after all so speedy, definition of my gentleman's job—his coming out, all solemnly appointed and deputed, to "save" Chad, and his then finding the young man so disobligingly and, at first, so bewilderingly not lost that a new issue altogether, in the connexion, prodigiously faces them, which has to be dealt with in a light—promised as many calls on ingenuity and on the higher branches of the compositional art as one could possibly desire. Again and yet again, as, from book to book, I proceed with my survey, I find no source of interest equal to this verification after the fact, as I may call it, and the more in detail the better, of the scheme of consistency "gone in" for. As always—since the charm never fails—the retracing of the process from point to point brings back the old illusion. The old intentions bloom again and flower—in spite of all the blossoms they were to have dropped by the way. This is the charm, as I say, of adventure *transposed*—the thrilling ups and downs, the intricate ins and outs of the compositional problem, made after such a fashion admirably objective, becoming the question at issue and keeping the author's heart in his mouth. Such an element, for instance, as his intention that Mrs. Newsome, away off with her finger on the pulse of Massachusetts, should yet be no less intensely than circuitously present through the whole thing, should be no less felt as to be reckoned with than the most direct exhibition, the finest portrayal at first hand could make her, such a sign of artistic good faith, I say, once it 's unmistakeably there, takes on again an actuality not too much impaired by the comparative dimness of the particular success. Cherished intention too inevitably acts and operates, in the book, about fifty times as little as I had fondly dreamt it might; but that scarce spoils for me the pleasure of recognising the fifty ways in which I had sought to provide for it. The mere charm of seeing such an idea constituent, in its degree; the fineness of the measures taken—a real extension, if successful, of the very terms and possibilities of representation and figuration—such things alone were, after this fashion, inspiring, such things alone were a gage of the probable success of that dissimulated calculation with which the whole effort was to square. But oh the cares begotten, none the less, of that same "judicious" sacrifice to a particular form of interest! One's work should have composition, because composition alone is positive beauty; but all the while—apart from one's inevitable consciousness too of the dire paucity of readers ever recognising or ever missing positive beauty—how, as to the cheap and easy, at every turn, how, as to immediacy and facility, and even as to the commoner vivacity, positive beauty might have to be sweated for and paid for! Once achieved and installed it may always be trusted to make the poor seeker feel he would have blushed to the roots of his hair for failing of it; yet, how, as its virtue can be essentially but the virtue of the whole, the wayside traps set in the interest of muddlement and pleading but the cause of the moment, of the particular bit in itself, have to be kicked out of the path! All the sophistications in life, for example, might have appeared to muster on behalf of the menace—the menace to a bright variety—involved in Strether's having all the subjective "say," as it were, to himself.

Had I, meanwhile, made him at once hero and historian, endowed him with the romantic privilege of the "first person"—the darkest abyss of romance this, inveterately, when enjoyed on the grand scale—variety, and many other queer matters as well, might have been smuggled in by a back door. Suffice it, to be brief, that the first person, in the long piece, is a form foredoomed to looseness, and that looseness, never much my affair, had never been so little so as on this particular occasion. All of which reflexions flocked to the standard from the moment—a very early one—the question of how to keep my form amusing while sticking so close to my central figure and constantly taking its pattern from him had to be faced. He arrives (arrives at Chester) as for the dreadful purpose of giving his creator "no end" to tell about him—

before which rigorous mission the serenest of creators might well have quailed. I was far from the serenest; I was more than agitated enough to reflect that, grimly deprived of one alternative or one substitute for "telling," I must address myself tooth and nail to another. I could n't, save by implication, make other persons tell *each other* about him—blest resource, blest necessity, of the drama, which reaches its effects of unity, all remarkably, by paths absolutely opposite to the paths of the novel: with other persons, save as they were primarily *his* persons (not he primarily but one of theirs), I had simply nothing to do. I had relations for him none the less, by the mercy of Providence, quite as much as if my exhibition *was* to be a muddle; if I could only by implication and a show of consequence make other persons tell each other about him, I could at least make him tell *them* whatever in the world he must; and could so, by the same token—which was a further luxury thrown in—see straight into the deep differences between what that could do for me, or at all events for *him*, and the large ease of "autobiography." It may be asked why, if one so keeps to one's hero, one should n't make a single mouthful of "method," should n't throw the reins on his neck and, letting them flap there as free as in "Gil Blas" or in "David Copperfield," equip him with the double privilege of subject and object—a course that has at least the merit of brushing away questions at a sweep. The answer to which is, I think, that one makes that surrender only if one is prepared *not* to make certain precious discriminations.

The "first person" then, so employed, is addressed by the author directly to ourselves, his possible readers, whom he has to reckon with, at the best, by our English tradition, so loosely and vaguely after all, so little respectfully, on so scant a presumption of exposure to criticism. Strether, on the other hand, encaged and provided for as "The Ambassadors" encages and provides, has to keep in view proprieties much stiffer and more salutary than any our straight and credulous gape are likely to bring home to him, has exhibitional conditions to meet, in a word, that forbid the terrible *fluidity* of self-revelation. I may seem not to better the case for my discrimination if I say that, for my first care, I had thus inevitably to set him up a confidant or two, to wave away with energy the custom of the seated mass of explanation after the fact, the inserted block of merely referential narrative, which flourishes so, to the shame of the modern impatience, on the serried page of Balzac, but which seems simply to appal our actual, our general weaker, digestion. "Harking back to make up" took at any rate more doing, as the phrase is, not only than the reader of to-day demands, but than he will tolerate at any price any call upon him either to understand or remotely to measure; and for the beauty of the thing when done the current editorial mind in particular appears wholly without sense. It is not, however, primarily for either of these reasons, whatever their weight, that Strether's friend Waymarsh is so keenly clutched at, on the threshold of the book, or that no less a pounce is made on Maria Gostrey—without even the pretext, either, of *her* being, in essence, Strether's friend. She is the reader's friend much rather—in consequence of dispositions that make him so eminently require one; and she acts in that capacity, and *really* in that capacity alone, with exemplary devotion, from beginning to end of the book. She is an enrolled, a direct, aid to lucidity; she is in fine, to tear off her mask, the most unmitigated and abandoned of *ficelles*. Half the dramatist's art, as we well know— since if we don't it 's not the fault of the proofs that lie scattered about us—is in the use of *ficelles*; by which I mean in a deep dissimulation of his dependence on them. Waymarsh only to a slighter degree belongs, in the whole business, less to my subject than to my treatment of it; the interesting proof, in these connexions, being that one has but to take one's subject for the stuff of drama to interweave with enthusiasm as many Gostreys as need be.

The material of "The Ambassadors," conforming in this respect exactly to that of "The Wings of the Dove," published just before it, is taken absolutely for the stuff of drama; so that, availing myself of the opportunity given me by this edition for some prefatory remarks on the latter work, I had mainly to make on its behalf the point of its scenic consistency. It disguises that virtue, in the oddest way in the world, by just *looking*, as we turn its pages, as little scenic as possible; but it sharply divides itself, just as the composition before us does, into the parts that prepare, that tend in fact to over-prepare, for scenes, and the parts, or otherwise into the scenes, that justify and crown the preparation. It may definitely be said, I think, that everything in it that is not scene (not, I of course mean, complete and functional scene, treating *all* the submitted matter, as by logical start, logical turn, and logical finish) is discriminated preparation, is the fusion and synthesis of picture. These alternations propose themselves all recogniseably, I think, from an early stage, as the very form and figure of "The Ambassadors"; so that, to repeat, such an agent as Miss Gostrey, pre-engaged at a high salary, but waits in the draughty wing with her shawl and her smelling-salts. Her function speaks at once for itself, and by the time she has dined with Strether in London and gone to a play with him her intervention as a *ficelle* is, I hold, expertly justified. Thanks to it we have treated scenically, and scenically alone, the whole lumpish question of Strether's "past," which has seen us more happily on the way than anything else could have done; we have strained to a high lucidity and vivacity (or at least we hope we have) certain indispensable facts; we have seen our two or three immediate friends all conveniently and profitably in "action"; to say nothing of our beginning to descry others, of a remoter intensity, getting into motion, even if a bit vaguely as yet, for our further enrichment. Let my first point be here that the scene in question, that in which the whole situation at Woollett and the complex forces that have propelled my hero to where this lively extractor of his value and distiller of his essence awaits him, is normal and entire, is really an excellent *standard* scene; copious, comprehensive, and accordingly never short, but with its office as definite as that of the hammer on the gong of the clock, the office of expressing *all that is in* the hour.

The "*ficelle*" character of the subordinate party is as artfully dissimulated, throughout, as may be, and to that extent that, with the seams or joints of Maria Gostrey's ostensible connectedness taken particular care of, duly smoothed over, that is, and anxiously kept from showing as "pieced on," this figure doubtless achieves, after a fashion, something of the dignity of a prime idea: which circumstance but shows us afresh how many quite incalculable but none the less clear sources of enjoyment for the infatuated artist, how many copious springs of our never-to-be-slighted "fun" for the reader and critic susceptible of contagion, may sound their incidental plash as soon as an artistic process begins to enjoy free development. Exquisite—in illustration of this—the mere interest and amusement of such at once "creative" and critical questions as how and where and why to make Miss Gostrey's false connexion carry itself, under a due high polish, as a real one. Nowhere is it more of an artful expedient for mere consistency of form, to mention a case, than in the last "scene" of the book, where its function is to give or to add nothing whatever, but only to express as vividly as possible certain things quite other than itself and that are of the already fixed and appointed measure. Since, however, all art is *expression*, and is thereby vividness, one was to find the door open here to any amount of delightful dissimulation. These verily are the refinements and ecstasies of method—amid which, or certainly under the influence of any exhilarated demonstration of which, one must keep one's head and not lose one's way. To cultivate an adequate intelligence for them and to make that sense operative is positively to find a charm in any produced ambiguity of appearance that is not by the same stroke, and all helplessly, an ambiguity of sense. To project imaginatively, for my hero, a relation that has nothing to do with the matter (the matter of my subject) but has everything to do with the manner (the manner of my presentation of the same) and yet to treat it, at close quarters and for fully economic expression's possible sake, as if it were important and essential—to do that sort of thing and yet muddle nothing may easily become, as one goes, a signally attaching proposition; even though it all remains but part and parcel, I hasten to recognise, of the merely general and related question of expressional curiosity and expressional decency.

I am moved to add after so much insistence on the scenic side of my labour that I have found the steps of re-perusal almost as much waylaid here by quite another style of effort in the same signal interest—or have in other words not failed to note how, even so associated and so discriminated, the finest proprieties and charms of the non-scenic may, under the right hand for them, still keep their intelligibility and assert their office. Infinitely suggestive such an observation as this last on the whole delightful head, where representation is concerned, of possible variety, of effective expressional change and contrast. One would like, at such an hour as this, for critical licence, to go into the matter of the noted inevitable deviation (from too fond an original vision) that the exquisite treachery even of the straightest execution may ever be trusted to inflict even on the most mature plan—the case being that, though one's last reconsidered production always seems to bristle with that particular evidence, "The Ambassadors" would place a flood of such light at my service. I must attach to my final remark here a different import; noting in the other connexion I just glanced at that such passages as that of my hero's first encounter with Chad Newsome, absolute attestations of the non-scenic form though they be, yet lay the firmest hand too—so far at least as intention goes—on representational effect. To report at all closely and completely of what "passes" on a given occasion is inevitably to become more or less scenic; and yet in the instance I allude to, *with* the conveyance, expressional curiosity and expressional decency are sought and arrived at under quite another law. The true inwardness of this may be at bottom but that one of the suffered treacheries has consisted precisely, for Chad's whole figure and presence, of a direct presentability diminished and compromised—despoiled, that is, of its *proportional* advantage; so that, in a word, the whole economy of his author's relation to him has at important points to be redetermined. The book, however, critically viewed, is touchingly full of these disguised and repaired losses, these insidious recoveries, these intensely redemptive consistencies. The pages in which Mamie Pocock gives her appointed and, I can't but think, duly felt lift to the whole action by the so inscrutably-applied side-stroke or short-cut of our just watching, and as quite at an angle of vision as yet untried, her single hour of suspense in the hotel salon, in our partaking of her concentrated study of the sense of matters bearing on her own case, all the bright warm Paris afternoon, from the balcony that overlooks the Tuileries garden—these are as marked an example of the representational virtue that insists here and there on being, for the charm of opposition and renewal, other than the scenic.

It would n't take much to make me further argue that from an equal play of such oppositions the book gathers an intensity that fairly adds to the dramatic—though the latter is supposed to be the sum of all intensities; or that has at any rate nothing to fear from juxtaposition with it. I consciously fail to shrink in fact from that extravagance—I risk it, rather, for the sake of the moral involved; which is not that the particular production before us exhausts the interesting questions it raises, but that the Novel remains still, under the right persuasion, the most independent, most elastic, most prodigious of literary forms.

The Golden Bowl

AMONG MANY MATTERS thrown into relief by a refreshed acquaintance with "The Golden Bowl" what perhaps most stands out for me is the still marked inveteracy of a certain indirect and oblique view of my presented action; unless indeed I make up my mind to call this mode of treatment, on the contrary, any superficial appearance notwithstanding, the very straightest and closest possible. I have already betrayed, as an accepted habit, and even to extravagance commented on, my preference for dealing with my subject-matter, for "seeing my story," through the opportunity and the sensibility of some more or less detached, some not strictly involved, though thoroughly interested and intelligent, witness or reporter, some person who contributes to the case mainly a certain amount of criticism and interpretation of it. Again and again, on review, the shorter things in especial that I have gathered into this Series have ranged themselves not as my own impersonal account of the affair in hand, but as my account of somebody's impression of it—the terms of this person's access to it and estimate of it contributing thus by some fine little law to intensification of interest. The somebody is often, among my shorter tales I recognise, but an unnamed, unintroduced and (save by right of intrinsic wit) unwarranted participant, the impersonal author's concrete deputy or delegate, a convenient substitute or apologist for the creative power otherwise so veiled and disembodied. My instinct appears repeatedly to have been that to arrive at the facts retailed and the figures introduced by the given help of some other conscious and confessed agent is essentially to find the whole business—that is, as I say, its effective interest—enriched *by the way*. I have in other words constantly inclined to the idea of the particular attaching case *plus* some near individual view of it; that nearness quite having thus to become an imagined observer's, a projected, charmed painter's or poet's—however avowed the "minor" quality in the latter—close and sensitive contact with it. Anything, in short, I now reflect, must always have seemed to me better—better for the process and the effect of representation, my irrepressible ideal—than the mere muffled majesty of irresponsible "authorship." Beset constantly with the sense that the painter of the picture or the chanter of the ballad (whatever we may call him) can never be responsible *enough*, and for every inch of his surface and note of his song, I track my uncontrollable footsteps, right and left, after the fact, while they take their quick turn, even on stealthiest tiptoe, toward the point of view that, within the compass, will give me most instead of least to answer for.

I am aware of having glanced a good deal already in the direction of this embarrassed truth—which I give for what it is worth; but I feel it come home to me afresh on recognising that the manner in which it betrays itself may be one of the liveliest sources of amusement in "The Golden Bowl." It 's not that the muffled majesty of authorship does n't here *ostensibly* reign; but I catch myself again shaking it off and disavowing the pretence of it while I get down into the arena and do my best to live and breathe and rub shoulders and converse with the persons engaged in the struggle that provides for the others in the circling tiers the entertainment of the great game. There is no other participant, of course, than each of the real, the deeply involved and immersed and more or less bleeding participants; but I nevertheless affect myself as having held my system fast and fondly, with one hand at least, by the manner in which the whole thing remains subject to the register, ever so closely kept, of the consciousness of but two of the characters. The Prince, in the first half of the book, virtually sees and knows and makes out, virtually represents to himself everything that concerns us—very nearly (though he does n't speak in the first person) after the fashion of other reporters and critics of other situations. Having a consciousness highly susceptible of registration, he thus makes us see the things that may most interest us reflected in it as in the clean glass held up to so many of the "short stories" of our long list; and yet after all never a whit to the prejudice of his being just as consistently a foredoomed, entangled, embarrassed agent in the general imbroglio, actor in the offered play. The function of the Princess, in the remainder, matches exactly with his; the register of *her* consciousness is as closely kept—as closely, say, not only as his own, but as that (to cite examples) either of the intelligent but quite unindividualised witness of the destruction of "The Aspern Papers," or of the all-noting heroine of "The Spoils of Poynton," highly individualised *though* highly intelligent; the Princess, in fine, in addition to feeling everything she has to, and to playing her part just in that proportion, duplicates, as it were, her value and becomes a compositional resource, and of the finest order, as well as a value intrinsic. So it is that the admirably-endowed pair, between them, as I retrace their fortune and my own method, point again for me the moral of the endless interest, endless worth for "delight," of the compositional contribution. Their chronicle strikes me as quite of the stuff to keep us from forgetting that absolutely *no* refinement of ingenuity or of precaution need be dreamed of as wasted in that most exquisite of all good causes the appeal to variety, the appeal to incalculability, the appeal to a high refinement and a handsome wholeness of effect.

There are other things I might remark here, despite its perhaps seeming a general connexion that I have elsewhere sufficiently shown as suggestive; but I have other matter in hand and I take a moment only to meet a possible objection— should any reader be so far solicitous or even attentive—to what I have just said. It may be noted, that is, that the Prince, in the volume over which he nominally presides, is represented as in comprehensive cognition only of those aspects as to which Mrs. Assingham does n't functionally—perhaps all too officiously, as the reader may sometimes feel it— supersede him. This disparity in my plan is, however, but superficial; the thing abides rigidly by its law of showing Maggie Verver at first through her suitor's and her husband's exhibitory vision of her, and of then showing the Prince, with at least an equal intensity, through his wife's; the advantage thus being that these attributions of experience display the sentient subjects themselves at the same time and by the same stroke with the nearest possible approach to a desirable vividness. It is the Prince who opens the door to half our light upon Maggie, just as it is she who opens it to half our light upon himself; the rest of our impression, in either case, coming straight from the very motion with which that act is performed. We see Charlotte also at first, and we see Adam

Verver, let alone our seeing Mrs. Assingham, and every one
and every thing else, but as they are visible in the Prince's
interest, so to speak—by which I mean of course in the interest of his being himself handed over to us. With a like
consistency we see the same persons and things again but as
Maggie's interest, *her* exhibitional charm, determines the
view. In making which remark, with its apparently so limited
enumeration of my elements, I naturally am brought up
against the fact of the fundamental fewness of these latter—
of the fact that my large demand is made for a group of
agents who may be counted on the fingers of one hand. We
see very few persons in "The Golden Bowl," but the scheme
of the book, to make up for that, is that we shall really see
about as much of them as a coherent literary form permits.
That was my problem, so to speak, and my *gageure*—to play
the small handful of values really for all they were worth—
and to work my system, my particular propriety of appeal,
particular degree of pressure on the spring of interest, for all
that this specific ingenuity itself might be. To have a scheme
and a view of its dignity is of course congruously to work it
out, and the "amusement" of the chronicle in question—by
which, once more, I always mean the gathered cluster of all
the *kinds* of interest—was exactly to see what a consummate
application of such sincerities would give.

So much for some only of the suggestions of re-perusal
here—since, all the while, I feel myself awaited by a pair of
appeals really more pressing than either of those just met; a
minor and a major appeal, as I may call them: the former of
which I take first. I have so thoroughly "gone into" things, in
an expository way, on the ground covered by this collection
of my writings, that I should still judge it superficial to have
spoken no word for so salient a feature of our Edition as the
couple of dozen decorative "illustrations." This series of frontispieces contribute less to ornament, I recognise, than if Mr.
Alvin Langdon Coburn's beautiful photographs, which they
reproduce, had had to suffer less reduction; but of those that
have suffered least the beauty, to my sense, remains great, and
I indulge at any rate in this glance at our general intention
for the sake of the small page of history thereby added to my
already voluminous, yet on the whole so unabashed, memo-

randa. I should in fact be tempted here, but for lack of space, by the very question itself at large—that question of the general acceptability of illustration coming up sooner or later, in these days, for the author of any text putting forward illustrative claims (that is producing an effect of illustration) by its own intrinsic virtue and so finding itself elbowed, on that ground, by another and a competitive process. The essence of any representational work is of course to bristle with immediate images; and I, for one, should have looked much askance at the proposal, on the part of my associates in the whole business, to graft or "grow," at whatever point, a picture by another hand on my own picture—this being always, to my sense, a lawless incident. Which remark reflects heavily, of course, on the "picture-book" quality that contemporary English and American prose appears more and more destined, by the conditions of publication, to consent, however grudgingly, to see imputed to it. But a moment's thought points the moral of the danger.

Anything that relieves responsible prose of the duty of being, while placed before us, good enough, interesting enough and, if the question be of picture, pictorial enough, above all *in itself*, does it the worst of services, and may well inspire in the lover of literature certain lively questions as to the future of that institution. That one should, as an author, reduce one's reader, "artistically" inclined, to such a state of hallucination by the images one has evoked as does n't permit him to rest till he has noted or recorded them, set up some semblance of them in his own other medium, by his own other art—nothing could better consort than *that*, I naturally allow, with the desire or the pretension to cast a literary spell. Charming, that is, for the projector and creator of figures and scenes that are as nought from the moment they fail to become more or less visible appearances, charming for this manipulator of aspects to see such power as he may possess approved and registered by the springing of such fruit from his seed. His own garden, however, remains one thing, and the garden he has prompted the cultivation of at other hands becomes quite another; which means that the frame of one's own work no more provides place for such a plot than we expect flesh and fish to be served on the same platter. One welcomes illustration, in other words, with pride and joy; but also with the emphatic view that, might one's "literary jealousy" be duly deferred to, it would quite stand off and on its own feet and thus, as a separate and independent subject of publication, carrying its text in its spirit, just as that text correspondingly carries the plastic possibility, become a still more glorious tribute. So far my invidious distinction between the writer's "frame" and the draughtsman's; and if in spite of it I could still make place for the idea of a contribution of value by Mr. A. L. Coburn to each of these volumes—and a contribution in as different a "medium" as possible—this was just because the proposed photographic studies were to seek the way, which they have happily found, I think, not to keep, or to pretend to keep, anything like dramatic step with their suggestive matter. This would quite have disqualified them, to my rigour; but they were "all right," in the so analytic modern critical phrase, through their discreetly disavowing emulation. Nothing in fact could more have amused the author than the opportunity of a hunt for a series of reproducible subjects—such moreover as might best consort with photography—the reference of which to Novel or Tale should exactly be *not* competitive and obvious, should on the contrary plead its case with some shyness, that of images always confessing themselves mere optical symbols or echoes, expressions of no particular thing in the text, but only of the type or idea of this or that thing. They were to remain at the most small pictures of our "set" stage with the actors left out; and what was above all interesting was that they were first to be constituted.

This involved an amusing search which I would fain more fully commemorate; since it took, to a great degree, and rather unexpectedly and incalculably, the vastly, though but incidentally, instructive form of an enquiry into the street-scenery of London; a field yielding a ripe harvest of treasure from the moment I held up to it, in my fellow artist's company, the light of our fond idea—the idea, that is, of the aspect of things or the combination of objects that might, by a latent virtue in it, speak for its connexion with something in the book, and yet at the same time speak enough for its odd or interesting self. It will be noticed that our series of

frontispieces, while doing all justice to our need, largely consists in a "rendering" of certain inanimate characteristics of
London streets; the ability of which to suffice to this furnishing forth of my Volumes ministered alike to surprise and convenience. Even at the cost of inconsistency of attitude in the
matter of the "grafted" image, I should have been tempted, I
confess, by the mere pleasure of exploration, abounding as
the business at once began to do in those prizes of curiosity
for which the London-lover is at any time ready to "back" the
prodigious city. It was n't always that I straightway found,
with my fellow searcher, what we were looking for, but that
the looking itself so often flooded with light the question of
what a "subject," what "character," what a saving sense in
things, is and is n't; and that when our quest was rewarded,
it was, I make bold to say, rewarded in perfection. On the
question, for instance, of the proper preliminary compliment
to the first volume of "The Golden Bowl" we easily felt that
nothing would so serve as a view of the small shop in which
the Bowl is first encountered.

The problem thus was thrilling, for though the small shop
was but a shop of the mind, of the author's projected world,
in which objects are primarily related to each other, and
therefore not "taken from" a particular establishment anywhere, only an image distilled and intensified, as it were, from
a drop of the essence of such establishments in general, our
need (since the picture was, as I have said, also completely to
speak for itself) prescribed a concrete, independent, vivid instance, the instance that should oblige us by the marvel of an
accidental rightness. It might so easily be wrong—by the act
of being at all. It would have to be in the first place what
London and chance and an extreme improbability should
have made it, and then it would have to let us truthfully read
into it the Prince's and Charlotte's and the Princess's visits. It
of course on these terms long evaded us, but all the while
really without prejudice to our fond confidence that, as London ends by giving one absolutely everything one asks, so it
awaited us somewhere. It awaited us in fact—but I check
myself; nothing, I find now, would induce me to say where.
Just so, to conclude, it was equally obvious that for the second volume of the same fiction nothing would so nobly serve

as some generalised vision of Portland Place. Both our limit and the very extent of our occasion, however, lay in the fact that, unlike wanton designers, we had, not to "create" but simply to recognise—recognise, that is, with the last fineness. The thing was to induce the vision of Portland Place *to* generalise itself. This is precisely, however, the fashion after which the prodigious city, as I have called it, does on occasion meet halfway those forms of intelligence of it that *it* recognises. All of which meant that at a given moment the great featureless Philistine vista would itself perform a miracle, would become interesting, for a splendid atmospheric hour, as only London knows how; and that our business would be then to understand. But my record of that lesson takes me too far.

So much for some only of the suggestions of re-perusal, and some of those of re-representation here, since, all the while, I feel myself awaited by an occasion more urgent than any of these. To re-read in their order my final things, all of comparatively recent date, has been to become aware of my putting the process through, for the latter end of my series (as well as, throughout, for most of its later constituents) quite in the same terms as the apparent and actual, the contemporary terms; to become aware in other words that the march of my present attention coincides sufficiently with the march of my original expression; that my apprehension fits, more concretely stated, without an effort or a struggle, certainly without bewilderment or anguish, into the innumerable places prepared for it. As the historian of the matter sees and speaks, so my intelligence of it, as a reader, meets him halfway, passive, receptive, appreciative, often even grateful; unconscious, quite blissfully, of any bar to intercourse, any disparity of sense between us. Into his very footprints the responsive, the imaginative steps of the docile reader that I consentingly become for him all comfortably sink; his vision, superimposed on my own as an image in cut paper is applied to a sharp shadow on a wall, matches, at every point, without excess or deficiency. This truth throws into relief for me the very different dance that the taking in hand of my earlier productions was to lead me; the quite other kind of consciousness proceeding from *that* return. Nothing in my whole renewal of attention to these things, to almost any instance of my work previous to some dozen years ago, was more evident than that no such active, appreciative process could take place on the mere palpable lines of expression—thanks to the so frequent lapse of harmony between my present mode of motion and that to which the existing footprints were due. It was, all sensibly, as if the clear matter being still there, even as a shining expanse of snow spread over a plain, my exploring tread, for application to it, had quite unlearned the old pace and found itself naturally falling into another, which might sometimes indeed more or less agree with the original tracks, but might most often, or very nearly, break the surface in other places. What was thus predominantly interesting to note, at all events, was the high spontaneity of these deviations and differences, which became thus things not of choice, but of immediate and perfect necessity: necessity to the end of dealing with the quantities in question at all.

No march, accordingly, I was soon enough aware, could possibly be more confident and free than this infinitely interesting and amusing *act* of re-appropriation; shaking off all shackles of theory, unattended, as was speedily to appear, with humiliating uncertainties, and almost as enlivening, or at least as momentous, as, to a philosophic mind, a sudden large apprehension of the Absolute. What indeed could be more delightful than to enjoy a sense of the absolute in such easy conditions? The deviations and differences might of course not have broken out at all, but from the moment they began so naturally to multiply they became, as I say, my very terms of cognition. The question of the "revision" of existing work had loomed large for me, had seemed even at moments to bristle with difficulties; but that phase of anxiety, I was rejoicingly to learn, belonged all but to the state of postponed experience or to that of a prolonged and fatalistic indifference. Since to get and to keep finished and dismissed work well behind one, and to have as little to say to it and about it as possible, had been for years one's only law, so, during that flat interregnum, involving, as who should say, the very cultivation of unacquaintedness, creeping superstitions as to what it might really have been had time to grow up and flourish. Not least among these rioted doubtless the fond fear that any tidying-up of the uncanny brood, any removal of accumulated dust, any washing of wizened faces, or straightening of grizzled locks, or twitching, to a better effect, of superannuated garments, might let one in, as the phrase is, for expensive renovations. I make use here of the figure of age and infirmity, but in point of fact I had rather viewed the reappearance of the first-born of my progeny—a reappearance unimaginable save to some inheritance of brighter and more congruous material form, of stored-up braveries of type and margin and ample page, of general dignity and attitude, than had mostly waited on their respective casual cradles—as a descent of awkward infants from the nursery to the drawing-room under the kind appeal of enquiring, of possibly interested, visitors. I had accordingly taken for granted the common decencies of such a case—the responsible glance of some power above from one nursling to another, the rapid flash of an anxious needle, the not imperceptible effect of a certain audible splash of soap-and-water; all in consideration of the searching radiance of drawing-room lamps as compared with nursery candles. But it had been all the while present to me that from the moment a stitch should be taken or a hair-brush applied the *principle* of my making my brood more presentable under the nobler illumination would be accepted and established, and it was there complications might await me. I am afraid I had at stray moments wasted time in wondering what discrimination against the freedom of the needle and the sponge would be able to describe itself as not arbitrary. For it to confess to that taint would be of course to write itself detestable.

"Hands off altogether on the nurse's part!" was, as a merely barbarous injunction, strictly conceivable; but only in the light of the truth that it had never taken effect in any fair and stately, in any not vulgarly irresponsible re-issue of anything. Therefore it was easy to see that any such apologetic suppression as that of the "altogether," any such admission as that of a single dab of the soap, left the door very much ajar. Any request that an indulgent objector to drawing-room discipline, to the purification, in other words, of innocent childhood, should kindly measure out then the appropriate amount of ablutional fluid for the whole case, would, on twenty grounds, indubitably leave that invoked judge gaping. I had none the less, I repeat, at muddled moments, seemed to see myself confusedly invoke him; thanks to my but too naturally not being able to forecast the perfect grace with which an answer to all my questions was meanwhile awaiting me. To expose the case frankly to a test—in other words to begin to re-read—was at once to get nearer all its elements and so, as by the next felicity, feel it purged of every doubt. It was the nervous postponement of that respectful approach that I spoke of just now as, in the connexion, my waste of time. This felt awkwardness sprang, as I was at a given moment to perceive, from my too abject acceptance of the grand air with which the term Revision had somehow, to my imagination, carried itself—and from my frivolous failure to analyse the content of the word. To revise is to see, or to look over, again—which means in the case of a written thing neither more nor less than to re-read it. I had attached to it, in a brooding spirit, the idea of re-writing—with which it was to have in the event, for my *conscious* play of mind, almost nothing in common. I had thought of re-writing as so difficult, and even so absurd, as to be impossible—having also indeed, for that matter, thought of re-reading in the same light. But the felicity under the test was that where I had thus ruefully prefigured two efforts there proved to be but one— and this an effort but at the first blush. What re-writing might be was to remain—it has remained for me to this hour—a mystery. On the other hand the act of revision, the act of seeing it again, caused whatever I looked at on any page to flower before me as into the only terms that honourably expressed it; and the "revised" element in the present Edition is accordingly these terms, these rigid conditions of re-perusal, registered; so many close notes, as who should say, on the particular vision of the matter itself that experience had at last made the only possible one.

What it would be really interesting, and I dare say admirably difficult, to go into would be the very history of this effect of experience; the history, in other words, of the growth of the immense array of terms, perceptional and expressional, that, after the fashion I have indicated, in sentence, passage and page, simply looked over the heads of the standing terms—or perhaps rather, like alert winged creatures, perched on those diminished summits and aspired to a clearer air. What it comes back to, for the maturer mind—granting of course, to begin with, a mind accessible to questions of such an order—is this attaching speculative interest of the matter, or in vulgar parlance the inordinate intellectual "sport" of it: the how and the whence and the why these intenser lights of experience come into being and insist on shining. The interest of the question is attaching, as I say, because really half the artist's life seems involved in it—or doubtless, to speak more justly, the whole of his life intellectual. The "old" matter is there, re-accepted, re-tasted, exquisitely re-assimilated and re-enjoyed—believed in, to be brief, with the same "old" grateful faith (since wherever the faith, in a particular case, has become aware of a twinge of doubt I have simply concluded against the matter itself and left it out); yet for due testimony, for re-assertion of value, perforating as by some strange and fine, some latent and gathered force, a myriad more adequate channels. It is over the fact of such a phenomenon and its so possibly rich little history that I am moved just fondly to linger—and for the reason I glanced at above, that to do so is in a manner to retrace the whole growth of one's "taste," as our fathers used to say: a blessed comprehensive name for many of the things deepest in us. The "taste" of the poet is, at bottom and so far as the poet in him prevails over everything else, his active sense of life: in accordance with which truth to keep one's hand on it is to hold the silver clue to the whole labyrinth of his consciousness. He feels this himself, good man—he recognises an attached importance—whenever he feels that consciousness bristle with the notes, as I have called them, of consenting re-perusal; as has again and again publicly befallen him, to our no small edification, on occasions within recent view. It has befallen him most frequently, I recognise, when the supersessive terms of his expression have happened to be verse; but that does n't in the least isolate his case, since it is clear to the most limited intelligence that the title we give him is the only title of *general* application and convenience for those who passionately cultivate the image of life and the art, on the whole so beneficial, of projecting it. The seer and speaker under the descent of the god is the "poet," whatever his form, and he ceases to be one only when his form, whatever else it may nominally or superficially or vulgarly be, is unworthy of the god: in which event, we promptly submit, he is n't worth talking of at all. He becomes so worth it, and the god so adopts him, and so confirms his charming office and name, in the degree in which his impulse and passion are general and comprehensive—a definitional provision for them that makes but a mouthful of so minor a distinction, in the fields of light, as that between verse and prose.

The circumstance that the poets then, and the more charming ones, *have* in a number of instances, with existing matter in hand, "registered" their renewals of vision, attests quite enough the attraction deeply working whenever the mind is, as I have said, accessible—accessible, that is, to the finer appeal of accumulated "good stuff" and to the interest of taking it in hand at all. For myself, I am prompted to note, the "taking" has been to my consciousness, through the whole procession of this re-issue, the least part of the affair: under the first touch of the spring my hands were to feel themselves full; so much more did it become a question, on the part of the accumulated good stuff, of seeming insistently to give and give. I have alluded indeed to certain lapses of that munificence—or at least to certain connexions in which I found myself declining to receive again on *any* terms; but for the rest the sense of receiving has borne me company without a break; a luxury making for its sole condition that I should intelligently attend. The blest good stuff, sitting up, in its myriad forms, so touchingly responsive to new care of any sort whatever, seemed to pass with me a delightful bargain, and in the fewest possible words. "Actively believe in us and then you 'll see!"—it was n't more complicated than that, and yet was to become as thrilling as if conditioned on depth within depth. I saw therefore what I saw, and what these numerous pages record, I trust, with clearness; though one element of fascination tended all the while to rule the business—a fascination, at each stage of my journey, on the noted score of that so shifting and uneven character of the tracks of my original passage. This by itself introduced the charm of suspense: what would the operative terms, in the given case,

prove, under criticism, to have been—a series of waiting satisfactions or an array of waiting misfits? The misfits had but
to be positive and concordant, in the special intenser light, to
represent together (as the two sides of a coin show different
legends) just so many effective felicities and substitutes. But I
could n't at all, in general, forecast these chances and changes
and proportions; they could but show for what they were as
I went; criticism after the fact was to find in them arrests and
surprises, emotions alike of disappointment and of elation: all
of which means, obviously, that the whole thing was a *living*
affair.

The rate at which new readings, new conductors of sense
interposed, to make any total sense at all right, became, to
this wonderful tune, the very record and mirror of the general
adventure of one's intelligence; so that one at all times quite
marvelled at the fair reach, the very length of arm, of such a
developed difference of measure as to what might and what
might n't constitute, all round, a due decency of "rendering."
What I have been most aware of asking myself, however, is
how writers, on such occasions of "revision," arrive at that
successful resistance to the confident assault of the new reading which appears in the great majority of examples to have
marked their course. The term that superlatively, that finally
"renders," is a flower that blooms by a beautiful law of its
own (the fiftieth part of a second often so sufficing it) in the
very heart of the gathered sheaf; it is *there* already, at any
moment, almost before one can either miss or suspect it—so
that in short we shall never guess, I think, the working secret
of the revisionist for whom its colour and scent stir the air
but as immediately to be assimilated. Failing our divination,
too, we shall apparently not otherwise learn, for the simple
reason that no revisionist I can recall has ever been communicative. "People don't do such things," we remember to have
heard it, in this connexion, declared; in other words they
don't really re-read—no, not *really*; at least they do so to the
effect either of seeing the buried, the latent life of a past composition vibrate, at renewal of touch, into no activity and
break through its settled and "sunk" surface at no point whatever—on which conclusion, I hasten to add, the situation remains simple and their responsibility may lie down beside

their work even as the lion beside the lamb; or else they have in advance and on system stopped their ears, their eyes and even their very noses. This latter heroic policy I find myself glancing at, however, to wonder in what particular cases— failing, as I say, all the really confessed—it can have been applied. The actual non-revisionists (on any terms) are of course numerous enough, and with plenty to say for them- selves; their faith, clearly, is great, their lot serene and their peace, above all, equally protected and undisturbed. But the tantalising image of the revisionist who is n't one, the partial, the piecemeal revisionist, inconsequent and insincere, this obscure and decidedly *louche* personage hovers before me mainly, I think, but to challenge my belief. Where have we met him, when it comes to that, in the walks of interesting prose literature, and why assume that we *have* to believe in him before we are absolutely forced?

If I turn for relief and contrast to some image of his op- posite I at once encounter it, and with a completeness that leaves nothing to be desired, on any "old" ground, in pres- ence of any "old" life, in the vast example of Balzac. He (and these things, as we know, grew behind him at an extraordi- nary rate) re-assaulted by supersessive terms, re-penetrated by finer channels, never had on the one hand seen or said all or had on the other ceased to press forward. His case has equal mass and authority—and beneath its protecting shade, at any rate, I move for the brief remainder of these remarks. We owe to the never-extinct operation of his sensibility, we have but meanwhile to recall, our greatest exhibition of felt finalities, our richest and hugest inheritance of imaginative prose. That by itself might intensify for me the interest of this general question of the reviving and reacting vision—did n't my very own lucky experience, all so publicly incurred, give me, as my reader may easily make out, quite enough to think of. I al- most lose myself, it may perhaps seem to him, in that obscure quantity; obscure doubtless because of its consisting of the manifold delicate things, the shy and illusive, the inscrutable, the indefinable, that minister to deep and quite confident pro- cesses of change. It is enough, in any event, to be both be- guiled and mystified by evolutions so near home, without sounding strange and probably even more abysmal waters.

Since, however, an agreeable flurry and an imperfect presence of mind might, on the former ground, still be such a source of refreshment, so the constant refrain humming through the agitation, "If only one *could* re-write, if only one *could* do better justice to the patches of crude surface, the poor morsels of consciously-decent matter that catch one's eye with their rueful reproach for old stupidities of touch!"—so that yearning reflexion, I say, was to have its superlative as well as its positive moments. It was to reach its maximum, no doubt, over many of the sorry businesses of "The American," for instance, where, given the elements and the essence, the long-stored grievance of the subject bristling with a sense of over-prolonged exposure in a garment misfitted, a garment cheaply embroidered and unworthy of it, thereby most proportion-ately sounded their plaint. This sharpness of appeal, the claim for exemplary damages, or at least for poetic justice, was re-duced to nothing, on the other hand, in presence of the al-together better literary manners of "The Ambassadors" and "The Golden Bowl"—a list I might much extend by the men-tion of several shorter pieces.

Inevitably, in such a case as that of "The American," and scarce less indeed in those of "The Portrait of a Lady" and "The Princess Casamassima," each of these efforts so redolent of good intentions baffled by a treacherous vehicle, an expert-ness too retarded, I could but dream the whole thing over as I went—as I read; and, bathing it, so to speak, in that me-dium, hope that, some still newer and shrewder critic's intel-ligence subtly operating, I should n't have breathed upon the old catastrophes and accidents, the old wounds and mutila-tions and disfigurements, wholly in vain. The same is true of the possible effect of this process of re-dreaming on many of these gathered compositions, shorter and longer; I have prayed that the finer air of the better form may sufficiently seem to hang about them and gild them over—at least for readers, however few, at all *curious* of questions of air and form. Nothing even at this point, and in these quite final re-marks, I confess, could strike me as more pertinent than— with a great wealth of margin—to attempt to scatter here a few gleams of the light in which some of my visions have all sturdily and complacently repeated and others have, according to their kind and law, all joyously and blushingly renewed themselves. These have doubtless both been ways of remaining unshamed; though, for myself, on the whole, as I seem to make out, the interest of the watched renewal has been livelier than that of the accepted repetition. What has the affair been at the worst, I am most moved to ask, but an earnest invitation to the reader to dream again in my company and in the interest of his own larger absorption of my sense? The prime consequence on one's own part of re-perusal is a sense for ever so many more of the shining silver fish afloat in the deep sea of one's endeavour than the net of widest casting could pretend to gather in; an author's common courtesy dictating thus the best general course for making that sense contagious—so beautifully tangled a web, when not so glorious a crown, does he weave by having at heart, and by cherishing there, the confidence he has invited or imagined. There is then absolutely no release to his pledged honour on the question of repaying that confidence.

The ideally handsome way is for him to multiply in any given connexion all the possible sources of entertainment— or, more grossly expressing it again, to intensify his whole chance of pleasure. (It all comes back to that, to my and your "fun"—if we but allow the term its full extension; to the production of which no humblest question involved, even to that of the shade of a cadence or the position of a comma, is not richly pertinent.) We have but to think a moment of such a matter as the play of *representational* values, those that make it a part, and an important part, of our taking offered things in that we should take them as aspects and visibilities—take them to the utmost as appearances, images, figures, objects, so many important, so many contributive items of the furniture of the world—in order to feel immediately the effect of such a condition at every turn of our adventure and every point of the representative surface. One has but to open the door to any forces of exhibition at all worthy of the name in order to see the imaging and qualifying agency called at once into play and put on its mettle. We may traverse acres of pretended exhibitory prose from which the touch that directly evokes and finely presents, the touch that operates for closeness and for charm, for conviction and illusion, for communication, in a word, is unsurpassably absent. All of which but means of course that the reader is, in the common phrase, "sold"—even when, poor passive spirit, systematically bewildered and bamboozled on the article of his dues, he may be but dimly aware of it. He has by the same token and for the most part, I fear, a scarce quicker sensibility on other heads, least of all perhaps on such a matter as his really quite swindled state when the pledge given for his true beguilement fails to ensure him that fullest experience of his pleasure which waits but on a direct reading *out* of the addressed appeal. It is scarce necessary to note that the highest test of any literary form conceived in the light of "poetry"—to apply that term in its largest literary sense—hangs back unpardonably from its office when it fails to lend itself to *vivâ-voce* treatment. We talk here, naturally, not of non-poetic forms, but of those whose highest bid is addressed to the imagination, to the spiritual and the æsthetic vision, the mind led captive by a charm and a spell, an incalculable art. The essential property of such a form as that is to give out its finest and most numerous secrets, and to give them out most gratefully, under the closest pressure—which is of course the pressure of the attention articulately *sounded*. Let it reward as much as it will and can the soundless, the "quiet" reading, it still deplorably "muffs" its chance and its success, still trifles with the roused appetite to which it can never honestly be indifferent, by not having so arranged itself as to owe the flower of its effect to the act and process of apprehension that so beautifully asks most from it. It then infallibly, and not less beautifully, most responds; for I have nowhere found vindicated the queer thesis that the right values of interesting prose depend all on withheld tests—that is on its being, for very pity and shame, but skimmed and scanted, shuffled and mumbled. Gustave Flaubert has somewhere in this connexion an excellent word—to the effect that any imaged prose that fails to be richly rewarding in return for a competent utterance ranks itself as wrong through not being "in the conditions of life." The more we remain in *them*, all round, the more pleasure we dispense; the moral of which is—and there would be fifty other pertinent things to say about this—that I have found revision intensify at every step my impulse intimately to answer, by my light, to those conditions.

All of which amounts doubtless but to saying that as the whole conduct of life consists of things done, which do other things in their turn, just so our behaviour and its fruits are essentially one and continuous and persistent and unquenchable, so the act has its way of abiding and showing and testifying, and so, among our innumerable acts, are no arbitrary, no senseless separations. The more we are capable of acting the less gropingly we plead such differences; whereby, with any capability, we recognise betimes that to "put" things is very exactly and responsibly and interminably to do them. Our expression of them, and the terms on which we understand that, belong as nearly to our conduct and our life as every other feature of our freedom; these things yield in fact some of its most exquisite material to the religion of doing. More than that, our literary deeds enjoy this marked advantage over many of our acts, that, though they go forth into the world and stray even in the desert, they don't to the same extent lose themselves; their attachment and reference to us, however strained, need n't necessarily lapse—while of the tie that binds us to *them* we may make almost anything we like. We are condemned, in other words, whether we will or no, to abandon and outlive, to forget and disown and hand over to desolation, many vital or social performances—if only because the traces, records, connexions, the very memorials we would fain preserve, are practically impossible to rescue for that purpose from the general mixture. We give them up even when we would n't—it is not a question of choice. Not so on the other hand our really "done" things of this superior and more appreciable order—which leave us indeed all licence of disconnexion and disavowal, but positively impose on us no such necessity. Our relation to them is essentially traceable, and in that fact abides, we feel, the incomparable luxury of the artist. It rests altogether with himself not to break with his values, not to "give away" his importances. Not to *be* disconnected, for the tradition of behaviour, he has but to feel that he is not; by his lightest touch the whole chain of relation and responsibility is reconstituted. Thus if he is always doing he can scarce, by his own measure, ever have done. All of which means for him conduct with a vengeance, since it is conduct minutely and publicly attested. Our noted behaviour at large may show for ragged, because it perpetually escapes our control; we have again and again to consent to its appearing in undress—that is in no state to brook criticism. But on all the ground to which the pretension of performance by a series of exquisite laws may apply there reigns one sovereign truth—which decrees that, as art is nothing if not exemplary, care nothing if not active, finish nothing if not consistent, the proved error is the base apologetic deed, the helpless regret is the barren commentary, and "connexions" are employable for finer purposes than mere gaping contrition.

Chronology

1843   Born April 15 at 21 Washington Place, New York City, the second child (after William, born January 11, 1842, N.Y.) of Henry James of Albany and Mary Robertson Walsh of New York. Father lives on inheritance of $10,000 a year, his share of litigated $3,000,000 fortune of his Albany father William James, an Irish immigrant who came to the U.S. immediately after the Revolution.

1843–45   Accompanied by mother's sister, Catharine Walsh, and servants, the James parents take infant children to England and later to France. Reside at Windsor, where father has nervous collapse ("vastation") and experiences spiritual illumination. He becomes a Swedenborgian (May 1844), devoting his time to lecturing and religious-philosophical writings. James later claimed his earliest memory was a glimpse, during his second year, of the Place Vendôme in Paris with its Napoleonic column.

1845–47   Family returns to New York. Garth Wilkinson James (Wilky) born July 21, 1845. Family moves to Albany at 50 N. Pearl St., a few doors from grandmother Catharine Barber James. Robertson James (Bob or Rob) born August 29, 1846.

1847–55   Family moves to a large house at 58 W. 14th St., New York. Alice James born August 7, 1848. Relatives and father's friends and acquaintances—Horace Greeley, George Ripley, Charles Anderson Dana, William Cullen Bryant, Bronson Alcott, and Ralph Waldo Emerson ("I knew he was great, greater than any of our friends")—are frequent visitors. Thackeray calls during his lecture tour on the English humorists. Summers at New Brighton on Staten Island and Fort Hamilton on Long Island's south shore. On steamboat to Fort Hamilton August 1850, hears Washington Irving tell his father of Margaret Fuller's drowning in shipwreck off Fire Island. Frequently visits Barnum's American Museum on free days. Taken to art shows and theaters; writes and draws stage scenes. Described by father as "a devourer of libraries." Taught in assorted private schools and by tutors in lower Broadway and Greenwich Village. But father claims in 1848 that American schooling fails to provide "sensuous education" for his children and plans to take them to Europe.

1855–58   Family (with Aunt Kate) sails for Liverpool, June 27. James is intermittently sick with malarial fever as they travel to Paris, Lyon, and Geneva. After Swiss summer, leaves for London where Robert Thomson (later Robert Louis Stevenson's tutor) is engaged. Early summer 1856, family moves to Paris. Another tutor engaged and children attend experimental Fourierist school. Acquires fluency in French. Family goes to Boulogne-sur-mer in summer, where James contracts typhoid. Spends late October in Paris, but American crash of 1857 returns family to Boulogne where they can live more cheaply. Attends public school (fellow classmate is Coquelin, the future French actor).

1858–59   Family returns to America and settles in Newport, Rhode Island. Goes boating, fishing, and riding. Attends Reverend W. C. Leverett's Berkeley Institute, and forms friendship with classmate Thomas Sergeant Perry. Takes long walks and sketches with the painter John La Farge.

1859–60   Father, still dissatisfied with American education, returns family to Geneva in October. James attends a pre-engineering school, Institution Rochette, because parents, with "a flattering misconception of my aptitudes," feel he might benefit from less reading and more mathematics. After a few months withdraws from all classes except French, German, and Latin, and joins William as a special student at the Academy (later the University of Geneva) where he attends lectures on literary subjects. Studies German in Bonn during summer 1860.

1860–62   Family returns to Newport in September where William studies with William Morris Hunt, and James sits in on his classes. La Farge introduces him to works of Balzac, Merimée, Musset, and Browning. Wilky and Bob attend Frank Sanborn's experimental school in Concord with children of Hawthorne and Emerson and John Brown's daughter. Early in 1861, orphaned Temple cousins come to live in Newport. Develops close friendship with cousin

Mary (Minnie) Temple. Goes on a week's walking tour in July in New Hampshire with Perry. William abandons art in autumn 1861 and enters Lawrence Scientific School at Harvard. James suffers back injury in a stable fire while serving as a volunteer fireman. Reads Hawthorne ("an American could be an artist, one of the finest").

1862–63 Enters Harvard Law School (Dane Hall). Wilky enlists in the Massachusetts 44th Regiment, and later in Colonel Robert Gould Shaw's 54th, the first black regiment. Summer 1863, Bob joins the Massachusetts 55th, another black regiment, under Colonel Hollowell. James withdraws from law studies to try writing. Sends unsigned stories to magazines. Wilky is badly wounded and brought home to Newport in August.

1864 Family moves from Newport to 13 Ashburton Place, Boston. First tale, "A Tragedy of Error" (unsigned), published in *Continental Monthly* (Feb. 1864). Stays in Northampton, Massachusetts, early August–November. Begins writing book reviews for *North American Review* and forms friendship with its editor, Charles Eliot Norton, and his family, including his sister Grace (with whom he maintains a long-lasting correspondence). Wilky returns to his regiment.

1865 First signed tale, "The Story of a Year," published in *Atlantic Monthly* (March 1865). Begins to write reviews for the newly founded *Nation* and publishes anonymously in it during next fifteen years. William sails on a scientific expedition with Louis Agassiz to the Amazon. During summer James vacations in the White Mountains with Minnie Temple and her family; joined by Oliver Wendell Holmes Jr. and John Chipman Gray, both recently demobilized. Father subsidizes plantation for Wilky and Bob in Florida with black hired workers. The idealistic but impractical venture fails in 1870.

1866–68 Continues to publish reviews and tales in Boston and New York journals. William returns from Brazil and resumes medical education. James has recurrence of back ailment and spends summer in Swampscott, Massachusetts. Begins friendship with William Dean Howells. Family moves to 20 Quincy St., Cambridge. William, suffering from nervous ailments, goes to Germany in spring 1867. "Poor Richard," James's longest story to date, published in *Atlantic Monthly* (June–Aug. 1867). William begins intermittent criticism of Henry's story-telling and style (which will continue throughout their careers). Momentary meeting with Charles Dickens at Norton's house. Vacations in Jefferson, New Hampshire, summer 1868. William returns from Europe.

1869–70   Sails in February for European tour. Visits English towns and cathedrals. Through Nortons meets Leslie Stephen, William Morris, Dante Gabriel Rossetti, Edward Burne-Jones, John Ruskin, Charles Darwin, and George Eliot (the "one marvel" of his stay in London). Goes to Paris in May, then travels in Switzerland in summer and hikes into Italy in autumn, where he stays in Milan, Venice (Sept.), Florence, and Rome (Oct. 30–Dec. 28). Returns to England to drink the waters at Malvern health spa in Worcestershire because of digestive troubles. Stays in Paris en route and has first experience of Comédie Française. Learns that his beloved cousin, Minnie Temple, has died of tuberculosis.

1870–72   Returns to Cambridge in May. Travels to Rhode Island, Vermont, and New York to write travel sketches for *The Nation*. Spends a few days with Emerson in Concord. Meets Bret Harte at Howells' home April 1871. *Watch and Ward*, his first novel, published in *Atlantic Monthly* (Aug.–Dec. 1871). Serves as occasional art reviewer for the *Atlantic* January–March 1872.

1872–74   Accompanies Aunt Kate and sister Alice on tour of England, France, Switzerland, Italy, Austria, and Germany from May through October. Writes travel sketches for *The Nation*. Spends autumn in Paris, becoming friends with James Russell Lowell. Escorts Emerson through the Louvre. (Later, on Emerson's return from Egypt, will show him the Vatican.) Goes to Florence in December and from there to Rome, where he becomes friends with actress Fanny Kemble, her daughter Sarah Butler Wister, and William Wetmore Story and his family. In Italy sees old family friend Francis Boott and his daughter Elizabeth (Lizzie), expatriates who have lived for many years in Florentine villa on Bellosguardo. Takes up horseback riding on the Campagna. Encounters Matthew Arnold in April 1873 at Story's. Moves from Rome hotel to rooms of his own. Continues writing and now earns enough to support himself. Leaves Rome in June, spends summer in Bad Homburg. In October goes to Florence, where William joins him. They also visit Rome, William returning to America in March. In Baden-Baden June–August and returns to America September 4, with *Roderick Hudson* all but finished.

1875   *Roderick Hudson* serialized in *Atlantic Monthly* from January (published by Osgood at the end of the year). First book, *A Passionate Pilgrim and Other Tales*, published January 31. Tries living and writing in New York, in rooms at 111 E. 25th Street. Earns $200 a month from novel installments and continued reviewing, but finds New York too expensive. *Transatlantic Sketches*, published in April, sells almost 1,000 copies in three months. In Cambridge in July decides to return to Europe; arranges with John Hay, assistant to the publisher, to write Paris letters for the New York *Tribune*.

1875–76   Arriving in Paris in November, he takes rooms at 29 Rue de Luxembourg (since renamed Cambon). Becomes friend of Ivan Turgenev and is introduced by him to Gustave Flaubert's Sunday parties. Meets Edmond de Goncourt, Émile Zola, G. Charpentier (the publisher), Catulle Mendès, Alphonse Daudet, Guy de Maupassant, Ernest Renan, Gustave Doré. Makes friends with Charles Sanders Peirce, who is in Paris. Reviews (unfavorably) the early Impressionists at the Durand-Ruel gallery. By midsummer has received $400 for *Tribune* pieces, but editor asks for more Parisian gossip and James resigns. Travels in France during July, visiting Normandy and the Midi, and in September crosses to San Sebastian, Spain, to see a bullfight ("I thought the bull, in any case, a finer fellow than any of his tormentors"). Moves to London in December, taking rooms at 3 Bolton Street, Piccadilly, where he will live for the next decade.

1877   *The American* published. Meets Robert Browning and George du Maurier. Leaves London in midsummer for visit to Paris and then goes to Italy. In Rome rides again in Campagna and hears of an episode that inspires "Daisy

Miller." Back in England, spends Christmas at Stratford with Fanny Kemble.

1878   Publishes first book in England, *French Poets and Novelists* (by Macmillan). Appearance of "Daisy Miller" in *Cornhill Magazine*, edited by Leslie Stephen, is international success, but by publishing it abroad loses American copyright and story is pirated in U.S. *Cornhill* also prints "An International Episode." *The Europeans* is serialized in *Atlantic*. Now a celebrity, he dines out often, visits country houses, gains weight, takes long walks, fences, and does weight-lifting to reduce. Elected to Reform Club. Meets Tennyson, George Meredith, and James McNeill Whistler. William marries Alice Howe Gibbens.

1879   Immersed in London society (". . . dined out during the past winter 107 times!"). Meets Edmund Gosse and Robert Louis Stevenson, who will later become his close friends. Sees much of Henry Adams and his wife, Marian (Clover), in London and later in Paris. Takes rooms in Paris, September–December. *Confidence* is serialized in *Scribner's* and published by Chatto & Windus. *Hawthorne* appears in Macmillan's "English Men of Letters" series.

1880–81   Stays in Florence March–May to work on *The Portrait of a Lady*. Meets Constance Fenimore Woolson, American novelist and grandniece of James Fenimore Cooper. Returns to Bolton Street in June, where William visits him. *Washington Square* serialized in *Cornhill Magazine* and published in U.S. by Harper & Brothers (Dec. 1880). *The Portrait of a Lady* serialized in *Macmillan's Magazine* (Oct. 1880–Nov. 1881) and *Atlantic Monthly*; published by Macmillan and Houghton, Mifflin (Nov. 1881). Publication both in United States and in England yields him the then-large income of $500 a month, though book sales are disappointing. Leaves London in February for Paris, the south of France, the Italian Riviera, and Venice, and returns home in July. Sister Alice comes to London with her friend Katharine Loring. James goes to Scotland in September.

1881–83   In November revisits America after absence of six years. Lionized in New York. Returns to Quincy Street for Christmas and sees ailing brother Wilky for the first time in ten years. In January visits Washington and the Henry Adamses and meets President Chester A. Arthur. Summoned to Cambridge by mother's death January 29 ("the sweetest, gentlest, most beneficent human being I have ever known"). All four brothers are together for the first time in fifteen years at her funeral. Alice and father move from Cambridge to Boston. Prepares a stage version of "Daisy Miller" and returns to England in May. William, now a Harvard professor, comes to Europe in September. Proposed by Leslie Stephen, James becomes member, without the usual red tape, of the Atheneum Club. Travels in France in October to write *A Little Tour in France* (published 1884) and has last visit with Turgenev, who is dying. Returns to England in December and learns of father's illness. Sails for America but Henry James Sr. dies December 18, 1882, before his arrival. Made executor of father's will. Visits brothers Wilky and Bob in Milwaukee in January. Quarrels with William over division of property—James wants to restore Wilky's share. Macmillan publishes a collected pocket edition of James's novels and tales in fourteen volumes. *Siege of London* and *Portraits of Places* published. Returns to Bolton Street in September. Wilky dies in November. Constance Fenimore Woolson comes to London for the winter.

1884–86   Goes to Paris in February and visits Daudet, Zola, and Goncourt. Again impressed with their intense concern with "art, form, manner" but calls them "mandarins." Misses Turgenev, who had died a few months before. Meets John Singer Sargent and persuades him to settle in London. Returns to Bolton Street. Sargent introduces him to young Paul Bourget. During country visits encounters many British political and social figures, including W. E. Gladstone, John Bright, Charles Dilke, and others. Alice, suffering from nervous ailment, arrives in England for visit in November but is too ill to travel and settles near her brother. *Tales of Three Cities* ("The Impressions of a Cousin," "Lady Barbarina," "A New England Winter") and "The Art of Fiction" published 1884. Alice goes to Bournemouth in late January. James joins her in May and becomes an intimate of Robert Louis Stevenson, who resides nearby. Spends August at Dover and is visited by Paul Bourget. Stays in Paris for the next two months. Moves into a flat at 34 De Vere Gardens in Kensington early in March 1886. Alice takes rooms in London. *The Bostonians* serialized in *Century* (Feb. 1885–Feb. 1886; published 1886), *Princess Casamassima* serialized in *Atlantic Monthly* (Sept. 1885–Oct. 1886; published 1886).

1886–87   Leaves for Italy in December for extended stay, mainly in Florence and Venice. Sees much of Constance Fenimore Woolson and stays in her villa. Writes "The Aspern Papers" and other tales. Returns to De Vere Gardens in July and begins work on *The Tragic Muse*. Pays several country visits. Dines out less often ("I know it all—all that one sees by 'going out'—today, as if I had made it. But if I had, I would have made it better!").

1888   *The Reverberator*, *The Aspern Papers*, *Louisa Pallant*, *The Modern Warning*, and *Partial Portraits* published. Elizabeth Boott Duveneck dies. Robert Louis Stevenson leaves for the South Seas. Engages fencing teacher to combat "symptoms of a portentous corpulence." Goes abroad in October to Geneva (where he visits Miss Woolson), Genoa, Monte Carlo, and Paris.

1889–90   Catharine Walsh (Aunt Kate) dies March 1889. William comes to England to visit Alice in August. James goes to Dover in September and then to Paris for five weeks. Writes account of Robert Browning's funeral in Westminster Abbey. Dramatizes *The American* for the Compton Comedy Company. Meets and becomes close friends with American journalist William Morton Fullerton and young American publisher Wolcott Balestier. Goes to Italy for the summer, staying in Venice and Florence, and takes a brief walking tour in Tuscany with W. W. Baldwin, an American physician practicing in Florence. Miss Woolson moves to Cheltenham, England, to be near James. *Atlantic Monthly* rejects his story "The Pupil," but it appears in England. Writes series of drawing-room comedies for theater. Meets Rudyard Kipling. *The Tragic Muse* serialized in *Atlantic Monthly* (Jan. 1889–May 1890; published 1890). *A London Life* (including "The Patagonia," "The Liar," "Mrs. Temperly") published 1889.

1891   *The American* produced at Southport has a success during road tour. After residence in Leamington, Alice returns to London, cared for by Katharine Loring. Doctors discover she has breast cancer. James circulates comedies (*Mrs. Vibert*, later called *Tenants*, and *Mrs. Jasper*, later named *Disengaged*) among theater managers who are cool to his work. Unimpressed at first by Ibsen, writes an appreciative review after seeing a performance of *Hedda Gabler* with Elizabeth Robins, a young Kentucky actress; persuades her to take the part of Mme. de Cintré in the London production of *The American*. Recuperates from flu in Ireland. James Russell Lowell dies. *The American* opens in London, September 26, and runs for seventy nights. Wolcott Balestier dies, and James attends his funeral in Dresden in December.

1892   Alice James dies March 6. James travels to Siena to be near the Paul Bourgets, and Venice, June–July, to visit the Daniel Curtises, then to Lausanne to meet William and his family, who have come abroad for sabbatical. Attends funeral of Tennyson at Westminster Abbey. Augustin Daly agrees to produce *Mrs. Jasper*. *The American* continues to be performed on the road by the Compton Company. *The Lesson of the Master* (with a collection of stories including "The Marriages," "The Pupil," "Brooksmith," "The Solution," and "Sir Edmund Orme") published.

1893   Fanny Kemble dies in January. Continues to write unproduced plays. In March goes to Paris for two months. Sends Edward Compton first act and scenario for *Guy Domville*. Meets William and family in Lucerne and stays a month, returning to London in June. Spends July completing *Guy Domville* in Ramsgate. George Alexander, actor-manager, agrees to produce the play. Daly stages first reading of *Mrs. Jasper*, and James withdraws it, calling the rehearsal a mockery. *The Real Thing and Other Tales* (including "The Wheel of Time," "Lord Beaupré," "The Visit") published.

1894   Constance Fenimore Woolson dies in Venice, January. Shocked and upset, James prepares to attend funeral in Rome but changes his mind on learning she is a suicide. Goes to Venice in April to help her family settle her affairs. Receives one of four copies, privately printed by Miss Loring, of Alice's diary. Finds it impressive but is concerned that so much gossip he told Alice in private has been included (later burns his copy). Robert Louis Stevenson dies in the South Pacific. *Guy Domville* goes into rehearsal. *Theatricals: Two Comedies* and *Theatricals: Second Series* published.

1895   *Guy Domville* opens January 5 at St. James's Theatre. At play's end James is greeted by a fifteen-minute roar of boos, catcalls, and applause. Horrified and depressed, abandons the theater. Play earns him $1,300 after five-week run. Feels he can salvage something useful from playwriting for his fiction ("a key that, working in the same *general* way fits the complicated chambers of *both* the dramatic and the narrative lock"). Writes scenario for *The Spoils of Poynton*. Visits Lord Wolseley and Lord Houghton in Ireland. In the summer goes to Torquay in Devonshire and stays until November while electricity is being installed in De Vere Gardens flat. Friendship with W. E. Norris, who resides at Torquay. Writes a one-act play ("Mrs. Gracedew") at request of Ellen Terry. *Terminations* (containing "The Death of the Lion," "The Coxon Fund," "The Middle Years," "The Altar of the Dead") published.

1896–97   Finishes *The Spoils of Poynton* (serialized in *Atlantic Monthly* April–Oct. 1896 as *The Old Things;* published 1897). *Embarrassments* ("The Figure in the Carpet," "Glasses," "The Next Time," "The Way It Came") published. Takes a house on Point Hill, Playden, opposite the old town of Rye, Sussex, August–September. Ford Madox Hueffer (later Ford Madox Ford) visits him. Converts play *The Other House* into novel and works on *What Maisie Knew* (published Sept. 1897). George du Maurier dies early in October. Because of increasing pain in wrist, hires stenographer William MacAlpine in February and then purchases a typewriter; soon begins direct dictation to MacAlpine at the machine. Invites Joseph Conrad to lunch at De Vere Gardens and begins their friendship. Goes to Bournemouth in July. Serves on jury in London before going to Dunwich, Suffolk, to spend time with Temple-Emmet cousins. In late September 1897 signs a twenty-one-year lease for Lamb House in Rye for £70 a year ($350). Takes on extra work to pay for setting up his house—the life of William Wetmore Story ($1,250 advance) and will furnish an "American Letter" for new magazine *Literature* (precursor of *Times Literary Supplement*) for $200 a month. Howells visits.

1898   "The Turn of the Screw" (serialized in *Collier's* Jan.–April;
        published with "Covering End" under the title *The Two
        Magics*) proves his most popular work since "Daisy
        Miller." Sleeps in Lamb House for first time June 28. Soon
        after is visited by William's son, Henry James Jr. (Harry),
        followed by a stream of visitors: future Justice Oliver
        Wendell Holmes, Mrs. J. T. Fields, Sarah Orne Jewett, the
        Paul Bourgets, the Edward Warrens, the Daniel Curtises,
        the Edmund Gosses, and Howard Sturgis. His witty
        friend Jonathan Sturges, a young crippled New Yorker,
        stays for two months during autumn. *In the Cage* pub-
        lished. Meets neighbors Stephen Crane and H. G. Wells.

1899   Finishes *The Awkward Age* and plans trip to the Conti-
        nent. Fire in Lamb House delays departure. To Paris in
        March and then visits the Paul Bourgets at Hyères. Stays
        with the Curtises in their Venice palazzo, where he meets
        and becomes friends with Jessie Allen. In Rome meets
        young American-Norwegian sculptor Hendrik C. Ander-
        sen; buys one of his busts. Returns to England in July and
        Andersen comes for three days in August. William, his
        wife, Alice, and daughter, Peggy, arrive at Lamb House
        in October. First meeting of brothers in six years. William
        now has confirmed heart condition. James B. Pinker be-
        comes literary agent and for first time James's professional
        relations are systematically organized; he reviews copy-
        rights, finds new publishers, and obtains better prices for
        work ("the germ of a new career"). Purchases Lamb
        House for $10,000 with an easy mortgage.

1900   Unhappy at whiteness of beard which he has worn since
        the Civil War, he shaves if off. Alternates between Rye
        and London. Works on *The Sacred Fount* and begins *The
        Ambassadors*. *The Soft Side*, a collection of twelve tales,
        published. Niece Peggy comes to Lamb House for Christ-
        mas.

1901   Obtains permanent room at the Reform Club for London
        visits and spends eight weeks in town. Sees funeral of
        Queen Victoria. Decides to employ a woman typist, Mary
        Weld, to replace the more expensive shorthand stenogra-
        pher, MacAlpine. Completes *The Ambassadors* and begins
        The Wings of the Dove. *The Sacred Fount* published. Has
        meeting with George Gissing. William James, much im-

proved, returns home after two years in Europe. Young
Cambridge admirer, Percy Lubbock visits. Discharges his
alcoholic servants of sixteen years (the Smiths). Mrs. Pad-
dington is new housekeeper.

1902   In London for the winter but gout and stomach disorder
           force him home earlier. Finishes *The Wings of the Dove*
           (published in August). William James Jr. (Billy) visits in
           October and becomes a favorite nephew. Writes "The
           Beast in the Jungle" and "The Birthplace."

1903   *The Ambassadors, The Better Sort* (a collection of twelve
           tales), and *William Wetmore Story and His Friends* pub-
           lished. After another spell in town, returns to Lamb
           House in May and begins work on *The Golden Bowl*.
           Meets and establishes close friendship with Dudley Joce-
           lyn Persse, a nephew of Lady Gregory. First meeting with
           Edith Wharton in December.

1904–05   Completes *The Golden Bowl* (published Nov. 1904). Rents
           Lamb House for six months, and sails in August for
           America after twenty years absence. Sees new Manhattan
           skyline from New Jersey on arrival and stays with Colonel
           George Harvey, president of Harper's, in Jersey shore
           house with Mark Twain as fellow guest. Goes to Wil-
           liam's country house at Chocorua in the White Moun-
           tains, New Hampshire. Re-explores Cambridge, Boston,
           Salem, Newport, and Concord, where he visits brother
           Bob. In October stays with Edith Wharton in the Berk-
           shires and motors with her through Massachusetts and
           New York. Later visits New York, Philadelphia (where he
           delivers lecture "The Lesson of Balzac"), and then Wash-
           ington, D.C., as a guest in Henry Adams' house. Meets
           (and is critical of) President Theodore Roosevelt. Returns
           to Philadelphia to lecture at Bryn Mawr. Travels to Rich-
           mond, Charleston, Jacksonville, Palm Beach, and St. Au-
           gustine. Then lectures in St. Louis, Chicago, South Bend,
           Indianapolis, Los Angeles (with a short vacation at Co-
           ronado Beach near San Diego), San Francisco, Portland,
           and Seattle. Returns to explore New York City ("the ter-
           rible town"), May–June. Lectures on "The Question of
           Our Speech" at Bryn Mawr commencement. Elected to
           newly founded American Academy of Arts and Letters
           (William declines). Returns to England in July; lectures

had more than covered expenses of his trip. Begins revision of novels for the New York Edition.

1906–08   Writes "The Jolly Corner" and *The American Scene* (published 1907). Writes 18 prefaces for the New York Edition (twenty-four volumes published 1907–09). Visits Paris and Edith Wharton in spring 1907 and motors with her in Midi. Travels to Italy for the last time, visiting Hendrik Andersen in Rome, and goes on to Florence and Venice. Engages Theodora Bosanquet as his typist in autumn. Again visits Mrs. Wharton in Paris, spring 1908. William comes to England to give a series of lectures at Oxford and receives an honorary Doctor of Science degree. James goes to Edinburgh in March to see a tryout by the Forbes-Robertsons of his play, *The High Bid*, a rewrite in three acts of the one-act play originally written for Ellen Terry (revised earlier as the story "Covering End"). Play gets only five special matinees in London. Shocked by slim royalties from sales of the New York Edition.

1909   Growing acquaintance with young writers and artists of Bloomsbury, including Virginia and Vanessa Stephen and others. Meets and befriends young Hugh Walpole in February. Goes to Cambridge in June as guest of admiring dons and undergraduates and meets John Maynard Keynes. Feels unwell and sees doctors about what he believes may be heart trouble. They reassure him. Late in year burns forty years of his letters and papers at Rye. Suffers severe attacks of gout. *Italian Hours* published.

1910   Very ill in January ("food-loathing") and spends much time in bed. Nephew Harry comes to be with him in February. In March is examined by Sir William Osler, who finds nothing physically wrong. James begins to realize that he has had "a sort of nervous breakdown." William, in spite of now severe heart trouble, and his wife, Alice, come to England to give him support. Brothers and Alice go to Bad Nauheim for cure, then travel to Zurich, Lucerne, and Geneva, where they learn Robertson (Bob) James has died in America of heart attack. James's health begins to improve but William is failing. Sails with William and Alice for America in August. William dies at Chocorua soon after arrival, and James remains with the family for the winter. *The Finer Grain* and *The Outcry* published.

1911   Honorary degree from Harvard in spring. Visits with
        Howells and Grace Norton. Sails for England July 30. On
        return to Lamb House, decides he will be too lonely there
        and starts search for a London flat. Theodora Bosanquet
        obtains two work rooms adjoining her flat in Chelsea and
        he begins autobiography, *A Small Boy and Others*. Contin-
        ues to reside at the Reform Club.

1912   Delivers "The Novel in *The Ring and the Book*," on the
        100th anniversary of Browning's birth, to the Royal Soci-
        ety of Literature. Honorary Doctor of Letters from Ox-
        ford University June 26. Spends summer at Lamb House.
        Sees much of Edith Wharton ("the Firebird"), who
        spends summer in England. (She secretly arranges to have
        Scribner's put $8,000 into James's account.) Takes 21 Car-
        lyle Mansions, in Cheyne Walk, Chelsea, as London quar-
        ters. Writes a long admiring letter for William Dean
        Howells' seventy-fifth birthday. Meets André Gide. Con-
        tracts bad case of shingles and is ill four months, much of
        the time not able to leave bed.

1913   Moves into Cheyne Walk flat. Two hundred and seventy
        friends and admirers subscribe for seventieth birthday por-
        trait by Sargent and present also a silver-gilt Charles II
        porringer and dish ("Golden Bowl"). Sargent turns over
        his payment to young sculptor Derwent Wood, who does
        a bust of James. Autobiography *A Small Boy and Others*
        published. Goes with niece Peggy to Lamb House for the
        summer.

1914   *Notes of a Son and Brother* published. Works on "The Ivory
        Tower." Returns to Lamb House in July. Niece Peggy
        joins him. Horrified by the war ("this crash of our civili-
        sation," "a nightmare from which there is no waking"). In
        London in September participates in Belgian Relief, visits
        wounded in St. Bartholomew's and other hospitals; feels
        less "finished and useless and doddering" and recalls Walt
        Whitman and his Civil War hospital visits. Accepts chair-
        manship of American Volunteer Motor Ambulance Corps
        in France. *Notes on Novelists* (essays on Balzac, Flaubert,
        Zola) published.

1915–16 Continues work with the wounded and war relief. Has
        occasional lunches with Prime Minister Asquith and fam-

ily, and meets Winston Churchill and other war leaders. Discovers that he is considered an alien and has to report to police before going to coastal Rye. Decides to become a British national and asks Asquith to be one of his sponsors. Is granted citizenship on July 28. H. G. Wells satirizes him in *Boon* ("leviathan retrieving pebbles") and James, in the correspondence that follows, writes: "Art *makes* life, makes interest, makes importance." Burns more papers and photographs at Lamb House in autumn. Has a stroke December 2 in his flat, followed by another two days later. Develops pneumonia and during delirium gives his last confused dictation (dealing with the Napoleonic legend) to Theodora Bosanquet, who types it on the familiar typewriter. Mrs. William James arrives December 13 to care for him. On New Year's Day, George V confers the Order of Merit. Dies February 28. Funeral services held at the Chelsea Old Church. The body is cremated and the ashes are buried in Cambridge Cemetery family plot.

Note on the Texts

Between 1864, when Henry James reviewed a volume dealing with the art of the novel, and 1916, when his last essay was published, he produced more than 300 literary essays, prefaces, notes, and commentaries. These, distinct from his essays on drama and art and his travel writings, are published in two volumes; this contains French writers, other European writers, and the prefaces to the New York Edition, and the second contains essays on literature, American writers, and English writers. Many of the periodical articles appeared unsigned, but scholars have established James's authorship for a large number of these pieces by drawing their evidence from such sources as the account books of magazines, which show the records of payment to authors, and the letters James wrote at the time. The novelist himself reprinted forty-eight of these items, revising them for his four volumes of literary appreciation and criticism—*French Poets and Novelists* (1878), *Partial Portraits* (1888), *Essays in London and Elsewhere* (1893), and *Notes on Novelists* (1914). James also wrote a book on Nathaniel Hawthorne, contributed a few essays to literary encyclopedias and collections, and wrote prefaces to a number of works. These have all been included so that the two volumes in the Library of America present the complete literary-critical non-fictional writings of the novelist. About one third of the pieces included here have never before been published in book form.

Any edition of James's criticism must rely on the published texts, for only eight manuscripts of his literary reviews are known to survive (six for reviews that were printed during his life and two manuscripts that have been discovered and printed more recently in scholarly journals). James asked to see proof of an article whenever possible, and it can be assumed that most of his writings for American magazines while he lived in Cambridge and New York, and those for English magazines while he lived in England, had the benefit of his corrections. However, pieces written in Europe for American magazines, as so many of these were, could not be

proofread in time for publication, and errors resulting from
the difficulty of reading his handwriting could easily occur.
James began to use public stenographers in the late 1880s and
he acquired a typist in the late 1890s.

When James reprinted articles in book form, he often made
minor revisions, and in some cases fairly substantial ones. His
essay "The Journal of the Brothers de Goncourt," for instance, first published in *Fortnightly Review*, October 1888, and
then in *Essays in London and Elsewhere* in 1893, was very much
revised between publications. The following are a few typical
examples of the revisions James made throughout the essay.
The first is from the periodical version.

. . . has become more so—has become so much so indeed that I
am oppressively conscious of the difficulty of treating it. It was, I
think, never an easy one; for persons interested in questions of literature, of art, of form, in the general question of the observation of
life for an artistic purpose, the appeal and solicitation of Edmond
and Jules de Goncourt were not simple and soothing; their manner,
their temper, their elaborate effort and conscious system suggested a
quick solution of the problems that seemed to hum in our ears as
we read, almost as little as their curious, uncomfortable style, with
its multiplied touches and pictorial verbosity, evoked as a general
thing an immediate vision of the objects to which it made such sacrifices of the synthetic and the rythmic.

James revised the passage to read:

. . . has become more so, has become so absorbing that I am oppressively conscious of the difficulty of treating it. It was never, I
think, an easy one; inasmuch as for persons interested in questions
of literature, of art, of form, in the general question of the observation of life for an artistic purpose, the appeal and the solicitation of
Edmond and Jules de Goncourt were essentially not simple and
soothing. The manner of this extraordinary pair, their temper, their
strenuous effort and conscious system, suggested anything but a
quick solution of the problems that seemed to hum in our ears as
we read; suggested it almost as little indeed as their curious, uncomfortable style, with its multiplied touches and pictorial verbosity, was
apt to evoke an immediate vision of the objects to which it made
such sacrifices of the synthetic and the rhythmic. (405.3–17)

In the second paragraph "he has transformed his position
with a thoroughness" is changed to "he has shifted his posi-

tion with a carelessness of consequences" (406.3–4). The first lines of the third paragraph are deleted. Some change has been made in every paragraph, both in wording and punctuation. One last example occurs in the final paragraph, which is both shortened and slightly revised. This passage in the periodical version:

It is a poor reward for our philosophy that providence should appoint MM. de Goncourt to turn the proposition the other end up and insist upon it during three substantial volumes. However, that is no reason why we should be peevish in return; inasmuch as certainly on the whole the cause is left about where it was: it is not an exceptionally great spirit that we have seen exposed. People of the profession will continue to read MM. de Goncourt, but if people of the profession will regret most the disagreeable things they have put into their apology it will not be they who will miss least the fine elements they have omitted from their novels.

becomes in *Essays in London and Elsewhere*:

It is a poor reward for our philosophy that Providence should appoint MM. de Goncourt to insist upon the converse of the proposition during three substantial volumes. (428.18–21)

Because James engaged in such revision, the text used here for each piece is the last version which James himself corrected. Thus his four collections of criticism provide the texts for the pieces he reprinted. For the other pieces, the original periodical or book publication has been used. Because the letters Henry James wrote for the *New York Tribune* were not only on literary topics, they are not reprinted in full here. Instead, the portions on literature have been placed under the individual writer discussed.

The New York Edition (1907–09) of his works provides the text used here for the eighteen prefaces, since they were not reprinted by James. No manuscripts survive. These were probably burned with a great portion of his papers in the years before 1910. In proposing the prefaces to his publisher, James said they would be "freely colloquial . . . representing, in a manner, the history of the work . . . a frank critical talk about its subject, its origin, its place in the whole artistic chain, and embodying, in short, whatever of interest there may be to be said about it." Thus, this volume of James's criticism ends with the critical appraisal of his own works.

The following is a list of the articles with their page numbers in this volume arranged in chronological order according to date of first publication. If the article was later revised and republished by James, the later text is listed immediately below the first.

Chronological List of Sources

Taine, *Notes on Paris*, p. 848 — *Nation*, XX (May 6, 1875), 318–19

Cherbuliez, *Miss Rovel*, p. 193 — *Nation*, XX (June 3, 1875), 381

Gautier, *Constantinople*, p. 387 — *Nation*, XXI (July 15, 1875), 45

Daudet, *Fromont Jeune et Risler Ainé*; Bornier, *La Fille de Roland*; Wallon, *Jeanne d'Arc*, p. 205 — *Galaxy*, XX (Aug. 1875), 276–80

Sabran, *Correspondance Inédite*, p. 646 — *Galaxy*, XX (Oct. 1875), 536–46
Reprinted as "Madame de Sabran" in *French Poets and Novelists* (1878)

The Two Ampères, p. 9 — *Galaxy*, XX (Nov. 1875), 662–74
Reprinted in *French Poets and Novelists* (1878)

Honoré de Balzac, p. 31 — *Galaxy*, XX (Dec. 1875), 814–36
Reprinted in *French Poets and Novelists* (1878)

Mazade, "La Littérature et nos Désastres," p. 555 — *Nation*, XXI (Dec. 30, 1875), 419

Ernest Renan at Ischia, p. 628 — *Nation*, XXI (Dec. 30, 1875), 419

"Versailles as It Is" (Taine), p. 851 — *New York Tribune*, January 8, 1876, 2:1–2

Mérimée, *Lettres*, p. 572 — *Nation*, XXII (Jan. 27, 1876), 67–68

The Minor French Novelists (Bernard and Flaubert), p. 159 — *Galaxy*, XXI (Feb. 1876), 219–33

"Paris in Election Time" (Girardin), p. 395 — *New York Tribune*, March 4, 1876, 3:4–5

Rodenberg, *England, Literary and Social*, p. 950 — *Nation*, XXII (Mar. 16, 1876), 182

Geoffrin, *Correspondance*, p. 390 — *Galaxy*, XXI (Apr. 1876), 548–50

Parisian Topics (Lemoinne, p. 478; Tissot, p. 857) — *New York Tribune*, April 1, 1876, 3:1–2

Schérer, *Études Critiques de Littérature*, p. 807 — *Nation*, XXII (Apr. 6, 1876), 233

"Arts and Letters in Paris" (Ernest Renan), p. 629 — *New York Tribune*, April 22, 1876, 3:1–2

Charles Baudelaire, p. 152

Nation, XXII (Apr. 27, 1876), 279–81

Reprinted in *French Poets and Novelists* (1878)

Parisian Festivity (Sainte-Beuve, p. 678; Zola, p. 861)

New York Tribune, May 13, 1876, 2:1–2

Parisian Topics (Renan), p. 630

New York Tribune, June 17, 1876, 3:1–2

Parisian Topics (Doudan, p. 258; Sand, p. 701)

New York Tribune, July 1, 1876, 3:1–2

Fromentin, *Maîtres d'Autrefois*, p. 347

Nation, XXIII (July 13, 1876), 29–30

George Sand, p. 702

New York Tribune, July 22, 1876, 3:1–2

M. Taine's Letter on George Sand, p. 854

Nation, XXIII (July 27, 1876), 61

Turgenev, Translation of a Short Poem, p. 999

Nation, XXIII (Oct. 5, 1876), 213

Gobineau, *Nouvelles Asiatiques*, p. 397

Nation, XXIII (Dec. 7, 1876), 344–45

Correspondance de H. de Balzac, p. 68

Galaxy, XXIII (Feb. 1877), 183–95

Reprinted as "Balzac's Letters" in *French Poets and Novelists* (1878)

Molinari, *Lettres sur les États-Unis et le Canada*, p. 582

Nation, XXIV (Feb. 22, 1877), 119–20

Lagardie, "French Novels and French Life," p. 466

Nation, XXIV (Mar. 29, 1877), 194–95

Turgenev, *Terres Vierges*, p. 1000

Nation, XXIV (Apr. 26, 1877), 252–53

Hugo, *Légende des Siècles*, p. 460

Nation, XXIV (May 3, 1877), 266

Goncourt, *La Fille Elisa*, p. 403

Nation, XXIV (May 10, 1877), 280

Tissot, *Voyage aux Pays Annexés*, p. 857

Nation, XXIV (May 17, 1877), 297

P. Musset, *Biographie de Alfred de Musset*, p. 596

Galaxy, XXIII (June 1877), 790–802

Reprinted as "Alfred de Musset" in *French Poets and Novelists* (1878)

	Reprinted in *Partial Portraits* (1888)
Pierre Loti, p. 482	*Fortnightly Review*, XLIX (May 1888), 647–64
	Reprinted in *Essays in London and Elsewhere* (1893)
The Journal of the Brothers de Goncourt, p. 404	*Fortnightly Review*, L (Oct. 1888), 501–20
	Reprinted in *Essays in London and Elsewhere* (1893)
Guy de Maupassant, p. 549	*Harper's Weekly*, XXXIII (Oct. 19, 1889), 834–35
Daudet, *Port Tarascon*, p. 249	*Harper's New Monthly Magazine*, LXXXI (June 1890), 3–25
	Reprinted in Alphonse Daudet, *Port Tarascon*, trans. Henry James (New York: Harper & Brothers, 1891)
Flaubert, *Correspondance*, p. 295	*Macmillan's Magazine*, LXVII (Mar. 1893), 332–43
	Reprinted in *Essays in London and Elsewhere* (1893)
Ivan Turgénieff (1818–1883), p. 1027	Charles Dudley Warner, ed., *Library of the World's Best Literature, Ancient and Modern* (New York: R. S. Peale and J. A. Hill, 1896), vol. XXV, pp. 15057–62
She and He: Recent Documents, p. 736	*The Yellow Book*, XII (Jan. 1897), 15–38
	Reprinted as "George Sand, 1897" in *Notes on Novelists* (1914)
Alphonse Daudet, p. 253	*Literature*, I (Dec. 25, 1897), 306–07
Pierre Loti, p. 505	Pierre Loti, *Impressions*, introduction by Henry James (Westminster: Archibald Constable and Co., 1898) pp. 1–21
Prosper Mérimée, p. 575	*Literature*, III (July 23, 1898), 66–68

Matilde Serao, p. 953 · *North American Review*, CLXXII (Mar. 1901), 367–80

Reprinted in *Notes on Novelists* (1914)

Honoré de Balzac, 1902, p. 90 · Honoré de Balzac, *The Two Young Brides*, trans. Mary Loyd, introduction by Henry James (London: William Heinemann, 1902; New York: D. Appleton, 1902), pp. v–xliii

Reprinted as "Honoré de Balzac, 1902" in *Notes on Novelists* (1914)

Gustave Flaubert, p. 314 · Gustave Flaubert, *Madame Bovary*, trans. W. G. Blaydes, introduction by Henry James (New York: D. Appleton & Co., 1902; London: William Heinemann, 1902), pp. v–xliii

Reprinted in *Notes on Novelists* (1914)

George Sand: The New Life, p. 755 · *North American Review*, CLXXIV (Apr. 1902), 536–54

Reprinted as "George Sand, 1899" in *Notes on Novelists* (1914)

Gabriele D'Annunzio, p. 907 · *Quarterly Review*, CXCIX (Apr. 1904), 383–419

Reprinted in *Notes on Novelists* (1914)

The Lesson of Balzac, p. 115 · *Atlantic Monthly*, XCVI (Aug. 1905), 166–80

Reprinted in *The Question of Our Speech. The Lesson of Balzac. Two Lectures* (1905)

Faguet, *Balzac*, p. 139 · *The Times Literary Supplement*, No. 597 (June 19, 1913), 261–63

Living Age, CCLXXVIII (Aug. 9, 1913), 364–72

Reprinted as "Honoré de Balzac, 1913" in *Notes on Novelists* (1914)

Karénine, *George Sand: Sa Vie et*   *Quarterly Review*, CCXX (Apr.
Ses Œuvres, p. 775   1914), 315–38
                                Living Age, CCLXXXI (June 13,
                                1914), 643–57
                                Reprinted as "George Sand,
                                1914" in *Notes on Novelists*
                                (1914)

The standards for American English continue to fluctuate, and in some ways are conspicuously different now from what they were in earlier periods. In nineteenth-century writings, for example, a word might be spelled in more than one way, even in the same work, and such variations might be carried into print. Commas were sometimes used expressively to suggest the movement of voice, and capitals were sometimes meant to give significances to a word beyond those it might have in its uncapitalized form. Since modernization would remove such effects, this volume preserves the spelling, punctuation, capitalization, and the wording of the texts reprinted here. This volume represents the *texts* of these editions; it does not attempt to reproduce the headings or the features of typographic design—such as display capitalization. Typographical errors have been corrected; the following is a list of those errors by page and line number: 14.32, Jean-Jacques; 24.32, sway; 25.8, future?; 28.16, on; 30.6, Collége; 37.4, consiousness; 38.1, many; 40.6, Blazac's; 49.32, *scéne*; 54.12, skill; 62.24, vemon; 79.38–39, another; 84.8, Austrain; 86.29, acclammation; 87.31, Verzschovnia; 89.5, hullucination; 98.37, largest; 141.5, than; 145.38, through; 156.33, *d'étre*; 167.9, Hausmann; 167.34, Mme.; 174.34, *sur le nife*; 199.20, reputatation; 210.10, *flâuerie*; 211.11, Compèigne; 260.3–4, or own; 260.31, M; 271.21, *Autou*[ ]; 278.40, Sharpe; 281.7, translalation; 283.33, Camor's; 288.21, humilitated; 353.30, Titan's; 355.23, Siége; 362.15, "effects,'; 362.18, imitati on; 365.29, Siége; 387.33, liége; 397.5, 'Pléiades"; 452.14, sucker."; 474.23–24, nobility.; 478.18, 19, Cavillier-Fleury; 478.36, faultfinder.; 500.2, Tahitans; 507.3, I.; 514.33, missles; 517.36–37, n otheodhsa ronnee; 518.21, leaxes; 535.39, *Tellier*; 564.7, 'Venus d'Ile'; 576.32, *Columba*; 604.21, say; 610.19, readers; 610.20, was was; 611.34, magazine she;

612.24, (passion).; 614.29, n éteint; 618.22, *them*); 630.16, Bois du; 676.11, Châteaubriand; 705.27, said:; 711.25, Couvent; 713.35, outline; 719.36, prefumed; 787.1, language; 815.37, indutrious; 852.5, arrangment; 852.26, miuntest; 857.5, Tissot' ssecond; 857.8, au; 857.14, execeedingly; 868.23, is has; 912.22, to; 951.19, Shakspere's; 966.5, is be; 969.3, discriptive; 974.27, Spring Torrents; 978.32, Correspondence,; 987.15, sweatmeats; 1104.26, circumstance; 1182.30, out-of-the way; 1231.36, "Figure in the Carpet,"; 1260.34, term!).

Notes

In the notes below, the reference numbers denote page and line of the present volume (the line count includes chapter headings). No note is made for material included in a standard desk-reference book.

FRENCH WRITERS

10.16   Hébert] Ernest Hébert (1817–1908), French genre and portrait painter who won the Prix de Rome at the age of twenty-two and studied in Rome.

11.39   Madame L——] Louise Cheuvreux, whose parents later took care of Ampère during his final illness.

14.20–21   'Lettres Provinciales.'] Pascal's *Lettres Provinciales* (1656–57) consists of eighteen letters dealing with divine grace and the ethical code of the Jesuits.

14.32   André] Both *Galaxy* and *French Poets and Novelists* texts read "Jean-Jacques," but the reference clearly is to André.

17.38   'Adèle,'] Nicolas Restif de la Bretonne's *Adèle de Comm***, *ou Lettres d'une fille à son père* (1772).

31.38   flimsy gossip] Gozlan (1806–66) wrote two "gossipy" books on Balzac: *Balzac en pantoufles* (1856) and *Balzac chez lui* (1862), later collected in one volume under the title *Balzac intime* (1886).

65.28–29   The caste . . . repose.] The second stanza of Tennyson's "Lady Clara Vere de Vere" (1833) contains the lines: "Her manners had not that repose / Which stamps the caste of Vere-de-Vere."

104.23   study] Taine's "Balzac" appears in his *Nouvelles essais de critique et d'histoire* (1865).

143.22–23   monograph] Ferdinand Brunetière, *Honoré de Balzac, 1799–1850* (Paris, n.d.).

205.28   American tales] A French translation of James's own "The Last of the Valerii" would appear in the November 15 issue of the *Revue des Deux Mondes* a few months later.

223.11   a great little novelist] James subsequently explained that he used this phrase "with levity" and intended it as "a term of endearment"; see p. 228.23–27.

235.13   François Bravais] François Bravais (1760–1853), noted physician.

236.38   *Les Aventures . . . Tarascon*]   Six years later James translated Daudet's final Tartarin novel, *Port Tarascon: The Last Adventures of the Illustrious Tartarin*. James's preface is included here on pp. 249–53.

260.31   M. de Langsdorf]   Baron Georges-Henri de Langsdorff (1774–1852), physician, naturalist, and world traveler who wrote about his travels in Brazil and elsewhere.

263.4   blindly . . . policy]   In return for supporting Marshal MacMahon for the presidency of the French Republic in 1873, the Duc de Broglie had been asked to form a cabinet in which he himself served successively as minister of foreign affairs and minister of the interior. His minister of public instruction, Oscar de Bardi de Fourtou, carried out aggressively conservative policies by dismissing certain liberal professors and re-establishing censorship. In May of 1877, in an attempt to strengthen the conservative wing at the expense of both leftist and extreme rightist elements, the Duc de Broglie dissolved the Chambre des Députés and staged new elections. However, his conservative candidates did not win a majority of seats, and he resigned his office in November of that year.

263.18   Fourtou]   See preceding note.

263.37   the 'Country Parson.']   George Jones Bevan's anonymously published series of "pastoral sermons": *A Country Parson's First Offering to His Mother Church* (1821), *A Country Parson's Second Offering to His Mother Church* (1822), *A Country Parson's Third Offering to His Mother Church* (1823).

268.9–14   When . . . up,]   James is referring to the recent bloody suppression of *la Commune*, the council set up by the insurrectionists who gained control of Paris in March 1871. The *communards* were besieged and, by the end of May, overcome by government forces.

303.30–31   Mr. Besant's . . . Society]   In late 1883, Walter Besant (1836–1901), whose essay "The Art of Fiction" (1884) elicited a response from James in his well-known essay of the same title, helped found the Incorporated Society of Authors, the threefold purpose of which was to define and protect literary property, to consolidate and amend domestic copyright laws, and to promote an international copyright. Tennyson was the society's first president; in addition to Besant, charter members included Matthew Arnold, Thomas Henry Huxley, James Anthony Froude, Wilkie Collins, and Charles Reade.

311.23–24   he would . . . Vatel]   François Vatel (d. 1671), steward to the Grand Condé (captain in the wars of Louis XIV), committed suicide because he feared that the fish ordered would not arrive in time for a Friday's meal he was to prepare for Louis XIV.

313.3   M. Louis Enault]   Pseudonym of Louis de Vernon (1824–1900), literary and art critic who also published novels and travel books based on his journeys throughout Europe and the Near East.

320.27–29   poem . . . recover it]   References to this scene in James's
journal and in a letter written to his father a few days after the visit with
Flaubert identify the Gautier poem in question as "Pastel."

351.11   Terburg]   Fromentin's French spelling of ter Borch (Gerard ter
Borch, 17th-century Dutch portrait painter).

358.33–34   it might . . . Merton]   The Rev. Mr. Barlow is the fictional
tutor of the poor but virtuous Harry Sandford and the spoiled and selfish
Tommy Merton in *The History of Sandford and Merton* (1783–89), a moralistic
work in three volumes by Thomas Day (1748–89).

371.29   the delightful . . . Regnault]   James reviewed Regnault's *Correspondance* for the *Nation*; see pp. 619–27.

380.21   Le 4 Septembre]   Flaubert is referring to the *Révolution du 4 Sep-
tembre 1870*, the bloodless revolution that ended the Second Empire and inaugurated the Third Republic. Three days after the surrender of Napoleon
III to the Prussians at Sedan (September 1, 1870), republican leaders Léon
Gambetta and Jules Favre led a Parisian crowd to the Hôtel de Ville and
proclaimed the Third Republic.

381.29   Dévéria]   Eugène Dévéria (1805–65), French painter and lithogra-
pher, friend of Victor Hugo.

381.30   Madame Dorval]   Marie Dorval (Marie Thomas Delaunay, 1798–
1849), actress at the Comédie-Française.

386.15   Burns's "chiel"]   Robert Burns's "On the Late Captain Grose's
Peregrinations Thro' Scotland" (1793) contains the lines:

> If there's a hole in a' your coats,
> I rede you tent it;
> A chield's amang you takin' notes,
> And faith he'll prent it.

396.21   M. Georges Lachaud]   Lachaud (1846–96) was a Bonapartist who
defended the Empire in works such as *Essai sur la Dictature* (1875) and *L'Empire* (1877).

416.17   Madame de Païva]   Usually known simply as La Païva, the Marquise de Païva (1819–?) was a Russian Jew (Thérèse Lachmann) who had
married a Portuguese marquis, whose name she kept after leaving him to live
with a wealthy Prussian in Paris. There she entertained a circle of writers,
artists, and musicians before being forced by charges of political intrigue to
leave the French capital in the wake of the Franco-Prussian War.

419.1   the Dîner Magny]   The Dîners Magny were fortnightly gatherings
of writers and artists at the restaurant Magny in the Latin Quarter of Paris.
Regular participants from 1862 through about 1875 included the Goncourts,
Flaubert, Gautier, Renan, Sainte-Beuve, Taine, and Turgenev.

466.7   a clever lady]   Comtesse Caroline (Bertin) de Peyronnet.

482.6–7   a celebrated actress]   Sarah Bernhardt.

507.14   Tom Cringle]   Pseudonym under which William Walker of Bombay wrote a series of letters to Bombay newspapers that were collected as *Tom Cringle's Letters on Practical Subjects, Suggested by Experiences in Bombay* (1863).

544.12   "Bradshaw"]   *Bradshaw's Railway Guide*, monthly railway timetables first published in 1839 by George Bradshaw (1801–53), a printer and engraver.

555.2   "LA LITTÉRATURE ET NOS DÉSASTRES"]   James takes his title from the running head of the article, but the actual title is "La Littérature et les Malheurs de la France."

556.16   'Rocambole']   *Les Exploits de Rocambole* (1859), a popular adventure by Pierre-Alexis de Ponson du Terrail (1829–71).

566.22–23   a lady]   In 1831 Jeanne-Françoise (Jenny) Dacquin (1811–95), daughter of a Boulogne lawyer, wrote to Mérimée in English to ask for an autograph, signing her first letter "Lady Algernon Seymour." Mérimée's reply began a correspondence that continued until his death in 1870, by which time he had long since met his correspondent and learned her actual identity.

572.26   another "unknown"]   Comtesse Lise (Lachmann) Przezdziecka, who is said to have used the royalties from *Lettres à une autre Inconnue* to pay for masses for the soul of the agnostic Mérimée.

580.17   Mme. de Montijo]   Maria Kirkpatrick y Grevigné, Comtesse de Montijo (1794–1879), whose younger daughter married Napoleon III (1853) and became the Empress Eugénie.

601.36–37   Bassompierre and Lauzun]   Both François de Bassompierre (1579–1646) and Armand-Louis de Gontaut-Biron, Duc de Lauzun (1747–93), left lively memoirs detailing their exploits in numerous boudoirs as well as on the battlefield.

608.29–30   "Il . . . l'Amour,"]   The title is *On ne badine pas avec l'Amour*.

628.9–10   just published . . . *Mondes*]   This issue of the *Revue des Deux Mondes* also contained a French translation of James's story "The Last of the Valerii."

670.13   one . . . executors]   Jules Troubat (1836–1914), who had served as Sainte-Beuve's secretary.

676.12–13   Gustave Planche]   Planche (1808–57) was literary and art critic for the *Revue des Deux Mondes* and a contributor to the *Journal des Débats* and other journals. Collections of his articles include many on English literature.

688.1   Littré by Dupanloup]   When philologist and lexicographer Émile Littré was elected to the Académie Française in 1873, Monseigneur Félix-Antoine Dupanloup resigned from the Académie in protest. Littré, who espoused the positivist philosophy of Comte, was identified with atheism and materialism.

693.32   Frédéric Soulié]   Soulié (1800–47) produced dozens of sensational popular novels and collaborated with Dumas *père* on a number of melodramas.

695.3–4   volume . . . M. Graindorge]   James reviewed the English translation of Taine's *Notes on Paris: The Life and Opinions of M. Frederic-Thomas Graindorge* (1875) for the *Nation*; see pp. 848–51.

732.21–22   distinguished men]   Chopin and Alfred de Musset, respectively.

741.23   Dr. Toulouse]   In 1896 Dr. Édouard Toulouse published *Enquête médico-psychologique sur les rapports de la supériorité intellectuelle avec la névropathie, Émile Zola.*

746.37   Alfred Tattet]   Tattet, the son of a wealthy Parisian banker, was a playboy friend of Alfred de Musset. During Musset's stay in Venice with George Sand, Tattet came there with his mistress and occasionally escorted George Sand during Musset's illness. It was Tattet who later in Paris informed his friend Musset of George Sand's affair with Pagello in Venice, thus leading to Musset's final break with his mistress.

755.35   GEORGE . . . LIFE]   The title here is from the first printing in *North American Review.*

776.7–8   Russian . . . pseudonym]   Varvara Dmitrïevna (Stasova) Komarova (1862–1942).

812.2   *Stendahl*]   This spelling of Stendhal appears throughout this essay.

839.14   the author . . . World."]   Susan B. Warner (1819–85), popular and prolific American novelist who published under the pseudonym Elizabeth Wetherell. Her sentimental novel *The Wide, Wide World* (1850) was a bestseller in both England and America.

839.34   Johnston]   Alexander Johnston (1815–91), Scots genre painter known for melancholy subjects.

857.3–4   this brave burlesque]   *Chevaliers de la Patrie*, a play by Albert Delpit that James had just been discussing.

857.18   a gentleman . . . sympathies]   This was probably Baron Holstein, secretary of the German embassy, with whom James often dined during his stay in Paris.

861.11–12   who Clorinda . . . is]   It was widely assumed that Clorinda

Balbi was inspired by the Comtesse de Castiglione, notorious during the Second Empire for her combined political and amatory intrigues.

872.7–8   the most . . . quarrels]   The Dreyfus Affair, on which Zola spoke out in *J'Accuse* (1898).

872.9   his last-finished novel]   *Verité* (1903).

881.14   the most . . . number]   Gustave Flaubert.

OTHER EUROPEAN WRITERS

943.31   1902]   This is one of several instances of misdating in *Notes on Novelists*.

968.2   Iwan Turgéniew]   The *North American Review* text uses the Germanic "Iwan Turgéniew," but in revising the piece for *French Poets and Novelists* James adopted the French spelling. The spelling of Turgenev went through many variations during the time James wrote about him, and all of these are reprinted here as they appeared in the print of the time.

PREFACES TO THE NEW YORK EDITION

1040.11   first attempt]   *Roderick Hudson* was in reality James's second novel. He had, after achieving fame, disowned *Watch and Ward*, his first attempt at a novel, serialized in the *Atlantic Monthly* August–December 1871, but he extensively revised it and published it in 1878 in book form to forestall piratical publication.

1046.38–39   "nowhere . . . turn."]   James is quoting from his introductory note to *English Hours* (1905), a gathering of various of his travel papers dealing with England.

1053.17–18   "Denis Duval" . . . to come)]   Thackeray left *Denis Duval* unfinished at the time of his death in 1863, and two years later Mrs. Gaskell's *Wives and Daughters* was also cut short by the death of its author. Stevenson was working on *Weir of Hermiston* when he died in 1894.

1070.4   spring of 1879]   James's notebooks indicate that he began the novel in Florence in the spring of 1880 and completed it in the following summer, months after its installments had begun to appear in both *Macmillan's Magazine* (Oct. 1880–Nov. 1881) and the *Atlantic Monthly* (Nov. 1880–Dec. 1881).

1070.15   in Venice]   In a long passage in his notebook, November 25, 1881, James has given an earlier account of his stay in Venice when he was writing *The Portrait of a Lady*.

1086.4   the first year]   James had moved from Paris to London in December 1876.

1103.2   vagueness of remembrance]   One of James's sources for *The Tragic Muse* was a novel about an actress by Mrs. Humphry Ward, *Mrs. Bretherton*, published in 1884; see *Notebooks*, June 19, 1884, and James's letter to Mrs. Ward on reading the novel in *Letters*, II, December 9, 1884.

1103.5   several months]   The work, James's longest serial, ran to seventeen installments in the *Atlantic Monthly* January 1889 through May 1890.

1108.15–16   Kensington]   James had moved in 1886 from his rooms in Bolton Street, Piccadilly, to a large flat at 34 De Vere Gardens W.

1115.36   Comédie Française]   James visited the Green Room of the Théâtre Française during the writing of *The Tragic Muse* and talked with some of the actors. See *Notebooks*, February 2, 1889.

1120.8   secret undivulged]   The origin of *The Awkward Age* is recorded in James's notebooks, February 27 and March 4, 1895.

1127.9   "Gyp"]   This was the pen name of the French Countess Martel de Janville, who wrote dialogue novels widely read in the 1880s and 1890s. James had a number of them in his library.

1138.3   YEARS AGO]   James's notebook entry recording the "germ" for *The Spoils of Poynton* is dated December 24, 1893.

1142.18–19   the year 1896]   The notebook entry recording Horace Scudder's request for three stories for the *Atlantic Monthly* and James's decision to develop the "germ" that was to become *The Spoils of Poynton* is actually dated May 13, 1895, though the work did not appear in the *Atlantic* until the following year (Apr.–Oct. 1896).

1142.39–40   another title]   The title of the serialized version was *The Old Things*; James's original title had been *The House Beautiful*.

1143.16   a cottage]   James had rented a cottage at Playden from the eminent Victorian architect Reginald Blomfield. It was on Point Hill, which commanded a view of the valley across which James could see the ancient town of Rye and its church-crowned hilltop.

1152.26   Venetian palace]   The Palazzo Barbaro, where James was guest of Daniel and Ariana Curtis from the end of May until early July 1887.

1156.6–7   accidental mention]   A notebook entry of November 12, 1892, attributes this "accidental mention" to a Mrs. Ashton at a recent dinner party given by her sister and brother-in-law, the James Bryces. James did not begin to work on the story in earnest until the end of 1895.

1156.10   I forget which]   James's notebook entry states that both parents remarried.

1165.19–20   a friend] Dr. William Wilberforce Baldwin, an eminent American physician, who had established a practice in Florence and with whom James made a short tour of Tuscany during the summer of 1890.

1176.10   This gentleman] James's notebook identifies the gentleman as Captain Silsbee, "the Boston art-critic and Shelley-worshipper."

1182.21–22   our distinguished host] James recorded in his notebook on January 12, 1895, the anecdote told him by the Archbishop of Canterbury, whom he had visited at Addington, the archiepiscopal residence outside London.

1183.6–7   a periodical] *Collier's Weekly*, where "The Turn of the Screw" appeared January 27–April 16, 1898.

1190.8   a gentleman] A notebook entry in 1884 indicates that Daudet's *Numa Roumestan*, which James praised in an 1883 essay on the French author, was at least as significant an inspiration for his tale.

1192.5   further back] "A Passionate Pilgrim" first appeared in the *Atlantic Monthly*, March–April 1871, and became the title piece in James's first book four years later.

1195.10   grand old city] The city is Venice, where James had visited Mrs. Arthur Bronson in her Grand Canal house, the Casa Alvisi, during March of 1887.

1195.28   free young person] May Marcy McClellan, daughter of Civil War general George Brinton McClellan, who was touring Europe with her widowed mother.

1196.17   her native city] New York, where Miss McClellan's letter appeared in the *New York World* of November 14, 1886.

1197.23   years of oblivion] The incident had occurred the year before. The date of James's notebook entry of November 17, 1887, suggests that he started writing his story a few weeks after recording the idea for *The Reverberator*.

1208.1   *Lady Barbarina*] Though James uses this spelling throughout the preface and in the text of the New York Edition, his original spelling, both in his notebook plan for the story and in earlier printings, was "Barberina."

1212.35   (1888)] "Lady Barbarina" was first published in *Century Magazine*, May–July 1884, and was collected in *Tales of Three Cities* later that same year.

1218.40–1219.1   Delaunay . . . Croizette] Louise Arsène Delaunay (1826–1903), for four decades one of the principals at the Théâtre Française; Sophie Alexandrine Croizette (1847–1901), member of the Comédie Française from 1873 to her retirement in 1882.

1220.29   "great house"]   This was the palatial residence of Lord Ashburton.

1228.11–12   a paper . . . reproduced]   "She and He: Recent Documents," a piece occasioned by the publication of George Sand's letters to Alfred de Musset, appeared in the *Yellow Book* in January 1897.

1239.35   London weekly journal]   "Greville Fane" first appeared in the *Illustrated London News*, September 17 and 24, 1892.

1241.1–2   a young artist]   Gordon Greenough, son of the Boston-born sculptor Horatio Greenough (1805–52).

1241.18   an eminent author]   John Addington Symonds, historian of the Italian renaissance, whose homosexuality was known to his intimate friends.

1241.20   a common friend]   Edmund Gosse. See *Letters*, III, February 15, 1885, to William James and January 7, 1893, to Gosse.

1243.20   an ancient lady]   Mrs. John Gorham Palfrey, widow of the Boston cleric and historian.

1248.9   distinguished old friend]   This was probably Mrs. Duncan Stewart, a figure in London society of whom James was fond. See *Letters*, II, July 6, 1879, and October 31, 1880, to his mother.

1249.38   foreign friend]   Probably J. J. Jusserand of the French legation in London and later ambassador to the United States.

1252.8   a shrine]   In the anecdote that served as germ for "The Birthplace," told to James by Lady Trevelyan, the shrine in question was the Shakespeare house in Stratford on Avon.

1254.40   that . . . artists]   At the end of this paragraph James identifies the writer described in the previous paragraph as Robert Browning; his notebooks give the initials of the artist here referred to as Browning's foil, "F. L." This was Frederick Lord Leighton, the Victorian classical painter, whose career James followed with deep interest.

1256.4   as I write]   James's original version of this preface, stating that "The Jolly Corner" had never been published before, was already in proof when he received a request to publish the story, and thus he had to alter his reference. The story was first published in the *English Review*, December 1908.

1256.8   (1900)]   "The Real Right Thing" appeared in *Collier's Weekly* of December 16, 1899, and was reprinted in *The Soft Side* the following year.

1261.39   "Owen Wingrave"]   The "young man" here described may have become James's hero in this tale of a pacifist in a military family, but the notebooks (March 26, 1892) show that the original idea for "Owen Wingrave" occurred to James while he was reading the three volumes of General Marcelin Marbot's Napoleonic memoirs.

1264.21   for material reasons]   James had not intended in his grouping of
related stories to include "Julia Bride" in this volume. The "material reasons"
were his having to rearrange the contents of the short-story volumes to cut
publishing costs. He wrote to Scribner's December 14, 1908: "I see no redis-
tribution possible *but* the mere mechanical ones. . . . My groupings had
been, of course, exceedingly considered, so each volume should offer, as to
contents, a certain harmonious physiognomy; and now that felicity is perforce—I abundantly recognize!—disturbed." James added: "The mechanical
can now be our only law." "Julia Bride" was removed from the "Daisy
Miller" volume. These changes necessitated revision of the relevant prefaces
and rearrangement of plans for the Coburn frontispieces. Occasionally unre-
vised references in the prefaces reflect the original plan.

1269.5   a friend]   The idea for James's celebrated tale was suggested in an
anecdote told him by Alice Bartlett, one of James's riding companions in the
Roman Campagna during 1873–74. The novelist had met her again in Rome
during his 1877 trip. After her repatriation, she married a man named Warren
and lived in Aiken, South Carolina.

1269.27–28   a magazine . . . Philadelphia]   *Lippincott's Magazine.*

1272.3   New York newspaper]   The *New York Sun.*

1272.8   a friend]   This was probably Mrs. Henry (Clover) Adams; she and
her husband figured as the Bonnycastles in the tale "Pandora."

1281.6–7   two compositions . . . series.]   *The Other House* (1896) and *The
Sacred Fount* (1901) are among the novels James did not include in his choices
for the New York Edition.

1282.14   (1890)]   "The Real Thing" was actually published two years
later, first appearing in *Black and White* April 16, 1892.

1282.19   late distinguished lady]   This may have been Frances Anne Kemble, whose daughters, Mrs. Leigh and Mrs. Wister, were friends of James's.

1283.33–34   "Flickerbridge" . . . its tracks;]   A notebook entry of February 19, 1899, outlines James's original plan for "Flickerbridge" and credits a
passage from Sarah Orne Jewett's "A Lost Lover," which James had just read,
with providing his inspiration.

1285.3   (1903)]   "The Story In It" was actually published a year earlier
than James recalls, first appearing in the *Anglo-American Magazine*, January
1902; it was reprinted the following year in *The Better Sort.*

1285.12   distinguished friend]   Probably Paul Bourget.

1286.12–14   As for . . . too far.]   A notebook entry made in Rome on
May 16, 1899, indicates that the germ for "The Beldonald Holbein" was
Maude Howe Elliot's account of the *succès de beauté* enjoyed by her elderly
mother, Julia Ward Howe, the previous winter: ". . . her coming out (*après*)

at the end of her long, arduous life and having a wonderful unexpected final moment—at 78!—of being thought *the* most picturesque, striking, lovely old (wrinkled and *marked*) 'Holbein,' etc., that ever was."

1286.15   (1902)]   "Mrs. Medwin" actually appeared in *Punch* the previous year, August 28–September 18, 1901.

1287.4–6   I can . . . to me.]   The situation had been "present to" James since 1870, the year in which his beloved cousin Minny Temple died of tuberculosis at twenty-four. He gives her initials as well as her dilemma to the heroine Milly Theale. William Wilberforce Baldwin (see note 1165.19–20) is probably the original for the physican, Sir Luke Strett.

1305.15–17   A friend . . . distinction,]   The friend referred to was Jonathan Sturges of New York, and the "man of distinction" was William Dean Howells. In 1895 Sturges told James of a conversation he had had with Howells some eighteen months earlier in the garden of James McNeill Whistler in Paris. On that occasion Howells gave the advice Lambert Strether gives to Little Bilham in *The Ambassadors*: "Live all you can; it's a mistake not to. . . . If you haven't had that what *have* you had?" (*Notebooks*, October 31, 1895)

1328.38   nothing, . . . say where.]   Following James's lead, Coburn himself always refused to reveal the location of the actual shop he had photographed, though he did note that he and the novelist had found it in almost the same spot where it was located in the novel.

1330.8   expanse of snow]   James here adapts a phrase remembered from a conversation with Daudet, who talked about Turgenev: "How I used to envy the calm serenity of Turgenev, working in a field and in a language the white snow of which had so few footprints."

Index

LIBRARY OF CONGRESS CATALOGING IN PUBLICATION DATA

James, Henry, 1843–1916
   Literary criticism.

   (The Library of America; 23)
   Contents: v. I. Essays on literature. American writers.
English writers—v. II. French writers. Other European writers.
The prefaces to the New York edition.
   1. Literature—Addresses, essays, lectures. I. Title.
II. Series.
PN37.J26 1984   809'.034   84–11241
ISBN 0–940450–23–2 (v. II)

This book is set in 10 point Linotron Galliard, a face designed for photocomposition by Matthew Carter and based on the sixteenth-century face Granjon. The paper is Olin Nyalite and conforms to guidelines adopted by the Committee on Book Longevity of the Council on Library Resources. The binding material is Brillianta, a 100% rayon cloth made by Van Heek-Scholco Textielfabrieken, Holland. Composition by Haddon Craftsmen, Inc. and The Clarinda Company. Printing and binding by R. R. Donnelley & Sons Company. Designed by Bruce Campbell.